D1359150

F.H. BUCKLEY
Professor
George Mason University School of Law

MARK GILLEN
Associate Professor
Faculty of Law
University of Victoria

ROBERT YALDEN
Osler, Hoskin & Harcourt
and of the Bars of Ontario
and Quebec

Corporations

Principles and Policies

Third Edition

1995
EMOND MONTGOMERY PUBLICATIONS LIMITED
TORONTO, CANADA

Copyright © 1995 Emond Montgomery Publications Limited. All rights reserved. No part of this publication may be reproduced, stored in a retrieval system, or transmitted, in any form or by any means, photocopying, electronic, mechanical, recording, or otherwise, without the prior written permission of the copyright holder.

Printed in Canada

Produced by WordsWorth Communications of Toronto, Canada.

Canadian Cataloguing in Publication Data

Buckley, F. H. (Francis H.), 1948–
    Corporations : principles and policies

3rd ed.
First ed. published under title: Corporations :
cases, texts, and materials.
Includes index.
ISBN 0-920722-73-3

1. Corporation law – Canada – cases. I. Yalden,
Robert. II. Gillen, Mark R., 1957–
III. Title.

KE1369.B8 1995   346.71'066   C95-931991-3
KF1415.ZA2B8 1995

Preface to Third Edition

Gone are the days when it was possible to provide a complete picture of the law governing Canadian corporations solely through a study of business corporations statutes and the common law surrounding those statues. Whether by accident or design, Canadian securities law is now inexorably intertwined with Canadian corporate law. In preparing this, the third edition of *Corporations*, it has become even more evident than in previous editions that in order to appreciate the legal context that helps to shape corporations, it is necessary to explore both corporate and securities law.

At the same time, we have been sensitive to the fact that this evolution in Canadian business law has not given rise to the happiest of marriages. Corporate and securities law do not always come at a given problem in the same way and each body of law embodies distinct objectives and priorities. As if this were not enough, corporate law is experiencing its own growing pains: renewed interest in stakeholder theory and 20 years of living with the oppression remedy have given rise to law whose theoretical basis is not always clear. Although these developments inevitably mean that it is frequently difficult to provide a crisp snapshot of the principles and policies that underlie particular aspects of Canadian business law, we have nonetheless endeavoured to provide an accurate picture of the law and to combine this with an analysis of underlying tensions.

In pursuit of these objectives we have revised a number of chapters: for example, Chapter Five contains a restructured and updated treatment of securities law; Chapter Four includes new material on the nature of a share; and the material on take-over bids in Chapter Eleven has been revised to capture recent developments in an area that rarely sits still. References to the Canada Business Corporations Act and to relevant provincial corporate and securities legislation have been updated and expanded. At the same time, we have had to reorganize portions of the book in order to highlight emerging issues. Recent events have made clear that it is no longer possible to segregate the oppression remedy within a chapter devoted solely to closely held corporations: the way in which the remedy is being used simply raises too many questions for the broader picture governing liability strategies under the corporate law and their interaction with securities law. Hence the decision to fold the oppression remedy into Chapter Seven and to incorporate the analysis of closely held corporations within the discussion of governance structures in Chapter Six. We have also noted a number of important developments whose impact is still being felt, not the least of which is the advent of an expanded OSC Policy 9.1.

To these changes we have added questions and discussion concerning the ramifications of these developments for the principles and policies underlying Canadian business law. We have therefore made extensive reference to a fast moving and extremely stimulating body of academic literature. The book continues to link substantive business problems with theoretical issues, frequently from finance economics. Additional emphasis is given in this edition to the literature on public choice theory. Attention is also paid to recent developments concerning such matters as proxy regulation, the mandatory/enabling debate in corporate law, the corporate chartering competition debate, the role of institutional investors as monitors of corporate management and the stakeholder debate.

This edition is therefore very much a reflection of Canadian business law as a work in progress: not quite the same beast that it was when the first edition was published and no doubt different from how it will look 10 to 20 years from now. Rough edges abound within Canada's corporate and securities law. The challenge is to determine how best to smooth them out: a process that is far from free of frustration, but that has the virtue of providing much food for thought.

We wish to thank Paul Emond of Emond Montgomery. We also wish to thank Paula Pike and Jim Lyons of WordsWorth Communications for their superb editorial assistance throughout the entire process of producing this edition. In addition, each of us has a particular group of people and institutions that we would like to thank. Frank Buckley wishes to acknowledge the generous support of the George Mason University School of Law and wishes to thank Jane Barton. Mark Gillen wishes to thank his research assistant Shannon Craig for her assistance in updating the law and academic literature, and his secretary Rosemary Garton for her patient assistance in formatting and cleaning typos from drafts. Robert Yalden wishes to thank both the Faculty of Law at McGill University, notably Deans Morissette and Toope, for providing a vibrant setting in which to explore issues that have found their way into this edition and Verita Karkouti for her assistance with the preparation of the manuscript.

July 1995   F.H.B.
                                                                                             M.RG.
                                                                                             R.M.Y.

Acknowledgments

This book, like others of this nature, contains extracts from published materials. We have attempted to request permission from and to acknowledge in the text all sources of such material. We wish to make specific reference here to the authors, publishers, journals, and institutions that have been generous in giving their permission to reproduce works in this text. If we have inadvertently overlooked any acknowledgment, we offer our sincere apologies and undertake to rectify the omission in any further editions.

American Bar Association (Section of Corporation, Banking and Business Law), The Business Lawyer. Kripke, *The Myth of the Informed Layman*, 28 Bus. Law. 631 (1973).

American Enterprise Institute for Public Policy Research. R. Romano, *The Genius of American Corporate Law* (1993). Reprinted with the permission of the American Enterprise Institute for Public Policy Research, Washington, D.C.

Butterworths Canada Ltd. D. Johnston, *Canadian Securities Regulation* (1977).

California Law Review. Hills, *Convertible Securities—Legal Aspects and Draftsmanship*, 19 Calif. L. Rev. 1 (1930).

Canada Law Book Ltd. Case extracts from the Dominion Law Reports.

Carswell Co. Ltd. Case extracts from the Western Weekly Reports and the Business Law Reports.

Leon Getz. Getz, *The Alberta Proxy Legislation: Borrowed Variations on an Eighteenth Century Theme*, 8 Alta. L. Rev. 18 (1970).

Harvard Law Review Association. Andrews, *The Stockholder's Right to Equal Opportunity in the Sale of Shares*, 78 Harv. L. Rev. 505 (1965).

Richard D. Irwin Co. P. Hunt, C. Williams & G. Donaldson, *Basic Business Finance* (5th ed. 1974).

Journal of Law and Economics. Katz, *Responsibility and the Modern Corporation*, 3 J.L. & Econ. 75 (1960).

Law Society of Upper Canada. Cameron, *The Form and Organization of the Business Entity*, in *Advising the Small Businessman* (1977).

Law Society of Upper Canada. Case extracts from the Ontario Reports.

Prentice Hall of Canada, Ltd. J. Van Horne, C. Dipchand & J.R. Hanrahan, *Financial Management and Policy* (Canadian 9th ed. 1992).

Queen's Printer for Ontario. Report on Mergers, Amalgamations and Certain Related Matters (Ontario Select Committee on Company Law 1973).

Queen's Printer for Ontario. 1967 Interim Report of the Select Committee on Company Law (1967).

Securities and Exchange Commission. Report of the Advisory Committee on Corporate Disclosure to the SEC, 95th Cong., 1st Sess. 618 (House Comm. Print 95-29 1977).

Stanford Law Review. Carlton & Fischel, *The Regulation of Insider Trading*, 35 Stan. L. Rev. 857 (1983). Copyright 1983 by the Board of Trustees of the Leland Stanford Junior University.

University of Chicago Law Review. Easterbrook & Fischel, *Limited Liability in the Corporation*, 52 U. Chi. L. Rev. 89 (1985).

University of Chicago Law Review. Javaras, *Equal Opportunity in the Sale of Controlling Shares: A Reply to Professor Andrews*, 32 U. Chi. L. Rev. 420 (1965).

University of Toronto Law Journal. Gold, *Fixed and Circulating Capital in the English Law of Dividends*, 6 U. of Toronto L.J. 14 (1945).

West Publishing Company. Case extracts from the Atlantic Reporter, California Reporter, Federal Reporter, Federal Supplement, New York Supplement, North Eastern Reporter, and North Western Reporter.

Wisconsin Law Review. Bratton, *The Economics and Jurisprudence of Convertible Bonds*, 1984 Wisc. L. Rev. 667.

John Wiley & Sons, Inc. Dewing, *The Financial Policy of Corporations* (5th ed. 1953).

Yale Law Journal. Brudney & Chirelstein, *A Restatement of Corporate Freezeouts*, 87 Yale L.J. 1354 (1978).

Yale Law Journal. Williamson, *Corporate Governance*, 93 Yale L.J. (1984).

Summary of Contents

CHAPTER TEN DISTRIBUTIONS TO SHAREHOLDERS

CHAPTER ELEVEN   MERGERS AND ACQUISITIONS

Detailed Table of Contents

CHAPTER FIVE   DISTRIBUTION OF SECURITIES

CHAPTER SIX   GOVERNANCE STRUCTURES

CHAPTER EIGHT   INSIDER TRADING

Table of Cases

A page number in bold face type indicates that the text of the case or a portion thereof is reproduced. A page number in light face type indicates that the case is merely quoted briefly, referred to, or mentioned.

Table of Abbreviations

ABCA	Business Corporations Act, R.S.A., c. B-15 (Alberta)
BCCA	Company Act, R.S.B.C., c. 59 (British Columbia)
CBCA	Canada Business Corporations Act, S.C. 1974-75-76, c. 33 as am.
Del.	Delaware General Corporation Law
LPA	Limited Partnership Act, R.S.O. 1980, c. 241 (Ontario)
MBCA	Model Business Corporations Act (as approved June 1984)
OBCA	Business Corporations Act, 1982, S.O. 1982, c. 4 (Ontario)
OSA	Securities Act, R.S.O. 1980, c. 466 (Ontario) as am.
PA	Partnerships Act, R.S.O. 1980, c. 370 (Ontario)
Clark	R. Clark, *Corporate Law* (1986)
Dickerson Report	1 *Proposals for a New Business Corporations Law for Canada* (1971)
Easterbrook & Fischel	F.H. Easterbrook & D.R. Fischel, *The Economic Structure of Corporate Law* (Cambridge, Mass.: Harvard University Press, 1991)
Gillen	M.R. Gillen, *Securities Regulation in Canada* (Toronto: Carswell, 1992)
Gower	L. Gower, J. Cronin, A. Easson & Lord Wedderburn, *Gower's Principles of Modern Company Law* (4th ed. 1979)
Lawrence Report	*1967 Interim Report of the Select Committee on Company Law* (Ontario) (1967)
Posner & Scott	*Economics of Corporation Law and Securities Regulation* (R. Posner & K. Scott eds. 1980)

Romano   R. Romano, *Foundations of Corporate Law* (New York: Oxford
                University Press, 1993)

Wegenast   F. Wegenast, *The Law of Canadian Companies* (1931)

1 Ziegel   1 *Studies in Canadian Company Law* (J. Ziegel ed. 1967)

2 Ziegel   2 *Studies in Canadian Company Law* (J. Ziegel ed. 1973)

Note: Abbreviations are used only for statutes in force at the time of writing.
         Predecessor versions no longer in force are written out or otherwise indicated.
         American authorities are cited in accordance with *A Uniform System of Citation*
         (14th ed. 1986).

CHAPTER ONE

Enterprise Organization

A. VALUATION THEORY

PROBLEM ONE

Since her graduation five years ago with an M.B.A., Carol Gray, 30 and divorced, has sought an opportunity to become the part-owner of a business with a large potential for growth. After graduation, Gray worked in the marketing departments of two large corporations. The first of these was a national retail store and the second, where Gray is now happily employed, is a stereo component manufacturer. Her present annual salary is $55,000, and she has accumulated $5,000 in savings.

Recently Gray learned from a friend of a brilliant new program for a home computer. In addition to the usual video games, the program is particularly adapted to solving a wide range of household problems. Its main virtue is the simplicity of its language, which makes it accessible to a broad range of people. It was designed by Don Smith, 28 and married with one child. Smith is an assistant professor of computer science at a university, and developed the program at home in his spare time. Smith's salary is $44,000 a year, and he has $3,000 in savings. He would like to produce his design in the highly competitive home computer market, but is acutely conscious of his lack of funds. The product also requires a certain amount of refinement before it can be sold commercially, and Smith expects he will have to tinker with it a bit.

A meeting between Smith and Gray is arranged. Gray believes that Smith's project has excellent potential, and Smith is in turn impressed with Gray's plans for marketing the program. Beyond that, Smith does not feel at home in business and thinks that it would be useful to have someone with Gray's general business acumen working with him.

Smith has heard of a small computer manufacturer whose owner, Michel Gagnon, is interested in retiring. Gagnon is 62 and married with no children. His assets consist of the computer business and a retirement fund of $150,000, mostly invested in low-return government bonds. Gagnon thinks that $150,000 is not enough to retire on, and would be extremely reluctant to invest any of that money in a speculative enterprise. The most recent financial statements of the business are provided below.

Gagnon Computer Business
Balance Sheet
(January 31, 199X)

		Liabilities and Proprietorship	
Assets			
Cash	$ 2,000	Accounts Payable	$25,000
Accounts Receivable (net)	35,000	Expenses Payable	17,000
Inventory and Work in Progress	37,000	Proprietorship	43,000
Fixed Assets			
Machinery and			
Equipment	$12,000		
Furniture	4,000		
	$16,000		
Less: Depreciation	5,000 11,000	Total Liabilities and	
Total Assets	$85,000	Proprietorship	$85,000

Gagnon Computer Business
Statement of Income
(For the year ended January 31, 199X)

Sales Revenues	$128,000
Cost of Sales	44,000
Gross Profit	$ 84,000
Administrative Expenses	
Employees' Wages	47,000
Rent	17,000
Depreciation	2,000
Travel	2,000
Office and General	4,000
	$ 72,000
Net Operating Income	$ 12,000

The firm leases the property on which it carries on business, and employs two people: Gagnon, who earns $31,000 a year, and a secretary who earns $19,000.

Gagnon founded his business six years ago, after retiring from the telecommunications branch of the Canadian Armed Forces. He had noted that law firms wanted to computerize their billings and internal memoranda, but that existing programs could not accommodate them easily. He developed the business software to meet this need, and sold it to law firms for $5,000 each.

Since then Gagnon has sold an average of 80 software packages a year. However, costs are high, and the business's earnings have remained constant at $20,000 a year, except for the last year, when they declined to $12,000. Gagnon feels that his business will probably never earn more than $20,000 a year. It is probably only a matter of time before he loses most of his market. The business really needs a new software package if it is to stay afloat. However, Gagnon had a heart attack last year and does not want to work particularly hard or spend more than a few more years at the business.

Gagnon has made several attempts to sell his business but to no avail. He has made a rough estimate that he would obtain at most $17,000 on a piecemeal sale of the assets, after paying off creditors.

When approached by Gray and Smith, Gagnon is interested in the new venture's prospects. He would like to retire from active management of the business, but still participate in the growth of the new venture.

The three parties decide to work together. Gagnon's business can be adapted without undue difficulty to Smith's software. Start-up costs during the transition period would likely amount to a minimum of $20,000 in the first year. At least initially, only Gagnon will be employed by the business. The question now is how profits in the new business should be divided amongst the three participants.

1. A Thumbnail Accounting Primer

It is impossible to make sense of much of corporate law without some knowledge of accounting. Fortunately, for the purposes of this casebook, a relatively little accounting will go a long way.

Financial Statements. The firm's *balance sheet* indicates an accountant's valuation of the business at a particular date. The assets are listed on the left hand side of the page and liabilities and proprietorship on the right.

The stated value of the assets in the balance sheet may bear little relation to their true value, as measured by how much they would fetch in an arm's length transaction. This is because, under cost accounting, fixed assets are valued at their cost of acquisition, which may have occurred many years previously. Fixed assets other than land are depreciated; that is, a specified amount is deducted each year from their value. But the amount depreciated is derived from an abstract formula and not from the unrealized decline in resale value of the goods. For example, if the "declining balance" method of depreciation is used, then a fixed percentage of the asset's original acquisition cost less accumulated depreciation will be depreciated or deducted from the asset each year. With 10% depreciation on an asset that cost $100, $10 will then be deducted in the first year and $9 in the second. There is a movement today toward current value accounting, which reflects the effect of inflation and changes in technology on a balance sheet. But this is still experimental and is restricted to large corporations.

Cash on hand, inventory and accounts receivable are described as current assets. Apart from cash, such assets are not necessarily worth their book values, and may be worth substantially less if the inventory is obsolete or if an insufficient deduction is made for bad debts.

Liabilities represent how much the firm owes. In purchasing a business, some attention should be given to whether all of the firm's present or contingent liabilities are in fact recorded in the balance sheet. For example, has sufficient account been taken of claims in litigation against the firm? At a minimum, searches will be made for bills of sale, judgment liens and security interests of secured creditors. Beyond that, in an asset purchase agreement the vendor (and its owner) will ordinarily be required to give warranties with respect to the assets, liabilities and financial statements.

The proprietorship or *equity* indicates the residual value of the enterprise, or its value to Gagnon. The "book value" of the firm is the equity figure. While students sometimes assume that the worth of a firm is measured by its assets, this ignores the fact that a deduction must be made for liabilities. A firm is worth what it has less what it owes. This is its equity, which is always the mathematical product of assets less liabilities (even if this turns out to be a negative figure). The value of the equity is therefore a derived figure, and not an independent variable, as are assets and liabilities. The relationship between assets, liabilities and equity is expressed in the following equation:

$$Assets = Liabilities + Equity$$

The left and right sides of the equation are equal by definition. For example, in the case of the Gagnon Computer Business, both sides of the balance sheet equation equal $85,000. Any further transaction may change this figure so long as, in accounting for the change, the balance sheet equation continues to hold. If the firm buys equipment for $2,000 on credit, for example, both assets and liabilities will increase by that amount, while equity remains constant. Equity will, however, change when changes in assets and liabilities are unequal. If the firm sold inventory that had cost it $1,000 for $2,000 cash, the following changes would be recorded on the balance sheet:

	Assets		*Liabilities*
Cash	(+$2,000)		(no change)
Inventory	(−$1,000)		
			Equity
			(+$1,000)

Note that the $1,000 increase in equity is required if the balance sheet equation is to continue to hold. In the same way, a decline in firm liabilities without a change in assets, as where one of its creditors forgives a debt, would increase the equity.

Students are sometimes puzzled about why debt and equity claims are both listed on the right hand side of the balance sheet. Debt claims represent a legal obligation of the firm, which can be sued by creditors on default. By contrast, the firm is ordinarily not under an obligation to repay equity holders their contribution to it. Yet both types of interests are claims against firm value, and both are therefore found on the same side of the balance sheet. While liabilities represent the interests of creditors in the firm, equity measures the interests of the proprietors (or shareholders).

The balance sheet lacks at time frame, with all values given as at a particular day. For example, liabilities are carried at their face amount, whether owed today or next year. In addition, assets are carried on an accrual and not a cash basis. In other words, a billing is represented when made as an account receivable, and not merely when paid as cash. In an effort to add a time perspective, accountants may compare certain kinds of assets and liabilities, with the various ratios of assets and liabilities providing a measure of the firm's short-run ability to stay solvent. Examples of this include the current ratio (current assets : current liabilities) and the quick (acid-test) ratio (cash and accounts receivable : current liabilities). This is referred to as *ratio analysis*, and may be a useful tool in predicting financial disaster. One of the best known ratios is the debt : equity ratio, comparing the total amount of a firm's liabilities (or debts) and its equity. A "high" debt : equity ratio then suggests instability, since the firm may have difficulty meeting the interest payment on the debt.

While the balance sheet represents an accountant's valuation of a firm at a particular moment, the *income statement* shows business activity over a period of time (usually one year). The net income indicates the change in value in the firm over the fiscal period, and, after drawings by the proprietors (or dividends to a corporation's shareholders) are deducted, is added to the proprietorship account on the balance sheet. A large equity figure in a going concern may therefore suggest sustained retained earnings over the years.

2. Methods of Valuation

The decision by the parties to pool their efforts in a firm can be seen as a sale by each to the firm of their separate contributions, in return for claims or interests in the firm. The parties must then decide how such claims are to be distributed amongst them. One solution would be to divide them according to each party's separate contribution. Valuing Gagnon's contribution would then require a valuation of the Gagnon Computer Business. There are three different methods commonly used to value a business: (1) market value, (2) asset value, and (3) capitalized earnings (or going concern) value.

Market Value. A corporation listed on a stock exchange can be valued through the quoted price for each share, with equity value equal to the value of all issued shares of all classes. If the demand for the firm's securities is competitive, with a large number of potential purchasers in the investment community, the resulting market price will provide a reliable measure of firm value according to an important financial theory called the *efficient capital market hypothesis* ("ECMH"). The ECMH is variously stated, but in its most widely accepted form holds that, when a competitive market exists for firm securities, all public information about prospects for the firm will be fully and virtually instantaneously reflected in the market price of the securities. Under the ECMH, the market's determination of value cannot ordinarily be second-guessed except by (1) institutional investors willing to absorb costs of acquiring newly revealed information, or (2) those with access to non-public, material (or inside) information about the firm. Only the latter are likely to be able to predict future stock movements for most widely traded shares beyond an extremely brief period, since virtually all public information (including forward looking information) will almost immediately be fully impacted in share prices. Future movements in share prices are then unrelated to past history and are entirely random, such that the ECMH is also known as the "random walk" theory. It follows that no amount of study of past business trends will enable one to make a prediction of future price movements for any firm. What this means is that lay investors may generally trust market prices for widely traded firms, while distrusting the analyst who claims he can "pick" stocks on any basis other than inside information.

Under the ECMH, what drives market efficiency is the competition among informed investors for stock price bargains. This assumes that a cadre of market professionals or insiders sift through the market for mispriced stocks. It does not assume that all stocks will be heavily traded each day. Neither does it assume that lay investors must search out price discrepancies. Instead the lay investor might free ride on prices set in an efficient market. Where mispricings are arbitraged or competed away by the competition for bargains by market professionals, the optimal amount of money that lay investors will spend on the production of information concerning mispriced stock is zero dollars.

The ECMH can be tested by observing how quickly stock price reacts to new information. For example, a finding that one could make money through a program of purchasing stock on which a dividend increase had been announced a month before would be inconsistent with the theory. So too would be any finding that future price movements could be predicted on the basis of historical information concerning the firm or the economy. In general, the proposition that stock prices of widely traded firms digest new information very quickly is as widely accepted as any theory in finance economists. For a review of Canadian evidence of stock market efficiency, see Daniels & MacIntosh, *Toward a Distinctive Canadian Corporate Law Regime*, 29 Osgoode Hall L.J. 863, 872-74 (1991).

The ECMH is of great interest to lawyers, because it suggests a method of testing the efficiency of legal rules or corporate decisions. Suppose that a province announces plans to pass a law for the stated purpose of benefitting shareholders. Suppose further that this news was unanticipated, and that the announcement is taken as a reliable signal that the law will in fact be passed. Now, if the market reacts almost at once to news concerning a particular firm, we would also expect it to react quickly to news affecting a group of firms, such as all firms incorporated in a particular province or state. This prediction may be tested through an *event study*, which examines whether, in the days after the announcement, the stock price of the affected firms is significantly different from that of similar firms not affected by the news. Where a rule, passed ostensibly for the benefit of shareholders, is greeted with a significant stock price decline, we might reasonably suppose it to be inefficient, whatever politicians or academic lawyers might say in its favor. For example, a study of state anti-takeover laws passed in the mid-1980s reported significant negative returns in the two-day window after announcement. See Karpoff & Malatesta, *The Wealth Effects of Second-Generation State Takeover Legislation*, 25 J. Fin. Econ. 291 (1989). Whoever was helped by such legislation, it was not the shareholders. Other studies suggest that corporate transactions commonly regarded as suspect are in fact benign. See, e.g., Buckley, *The Divestiture Decision*, 16 J. Corp. L. 805 (1991) (reviewing evidence that sell-offs and spin-offs of corporate divisions are associated with abnormal stock price increases).

To test the significance of an announcement, one needs to be able to estimate what a firm's stock price would be on the assumption that it is unaffected by the announcement. This is the null hypothesis, and may be tested through regression analysis. Where the actual returns are different from the predicted price, on standard tests of statistical significance, we may reject the null hypothesis and conclude that the announcement does indeed affect shareholder wealth. For a discussion of event study methodology, see

Schwert, *Using Financial Data to Measure Effects of Financial Regulation*, 24 J. Law Econ. 121 (1981).

To perform an event study, then, one requires a stock price model. The most common such model is CAPM, the *Capital Asset Pricing Model*. Under CAPM, the rate of return on investing in a firm is a function of (1) the riskiness of the firm's earnings, based on historical data, (2) the expected return of the market as a whole, and (3) the risk-free rate of return from the most secure investments. Other factors are irrelevant. All that investors care about are the firm's earnings and the risk associated with them. CAPM thus predicts that the return for firm *I* may be estimated according to the following equation:

$$R_i = \alpha + \beta_i R_m + \varepsilon_i$$

where R_i is the expected return for firm *I*, α is the risk-free rate of return, β_i (or beta) is the measure of historic idiosyncratic risk for firm *I*,* R_m is the rate of return on a market portfolio of securities above the risk-free rate, and ε_i is a firm *I* error term. This is equivalent to saying that total firm returns are composed of a normal or predicted return $(\alpha + \beta_i R_m)$ and an abnormal return ε_i, which represents deviations from predicted returns. When one knows the risk-free rate and the market return, then, one can predict the return for every firm simply through its beta. This is equivalent to saying that all difference in expected firm returns or firm prices are attributable solely to differences in beta.

Early tests of CAPM found that it had considerable predictive power, with beta fairly accurately predicting firm returns. See Fama & MacBeth, *Risk, Return and Equilibrium: Empirical Tests*, 81 J. Pol. Econ. 607 (1973). However, more recent studies report that beta's predictive power was much weaker during the 1970s and 1980s. See Fama & French, *The Cross-Section of Expected Stock Returns*, 47 J. Fin. 427 (1992). As well, findings that firms with small market values have abnormally high returns at the beginning of January are inconsistent with CAPM, as are findings of abnormally negative returns on Mondays. Other studies report that beta is unstable over time, such that historical measures of firm riskiness must be flawed. See, e.g., B. Malkiel, *A Random Walk Down Wall Street* (5th ed. 1990), at Romano 29, 42-43. As a consequence, finance economists have sought to refine CAPM to capture other elements of risk, such as changes in monetary policy. A more general objection to all such theories is that they offer predictions about *expected*, not actual, returns. There is no way of measuring expected returns, and subsequent actual returns might differ from expected returns because of unexpected changes in a firm's business opportunities. Thus all such models rest on an assumption that investor expectations are rational, in the sense that assets are priced correctly based on the information available at that time.

Doubts about CAPM might infect tests of the ECMH based on CAPM groupings of equivalent risk firms. For example, where several firms are placed in the same risk category, based on historical data about the variance of earnings, a test of how their

---

* Beta is defined in terms of a standardized measure of the contribution of the riskiness of the firm to the riskiness of the market portfolio. More formally, for those with a knowledge of econometrics, $\beta = \text{cov}(R_i, R_m)/\sigma^2 R_m$.

stock prices react to new information is simultaneously a test of CAPM and the ECMH. Nevertheless, finance economists generally accept the evidence provided by event studies of the efficiency consequences of legal rules or corporate transactions. This is because evidence of a sharp price change over a two or three day period, using data with hundreds of observations, is likely robust whatever the model used to predict stock prices. See generally Fama, *Efficient Capital Markets: II*, 46 J. Fin. 1575 (1991).

The ECMH is subject to an important qualification. The market's estimate of a firm's value will reflect the identity of its participants, including most crucially its managers. If they are perceived as inefficient, firm value will be discounted accordingly. Market value might then be rationally second-guessed by possible acquiring firms, which intend to replace existing management. See Leebron, *Games Corporations Play: A Theory of Tender Offers*, 61 N.Y.U.L. Rev. 153, 171-74 (1986). The techniques by which existing managers can be displaced are discussed in Chapters Six (proxy battles) and Eleven (take-over bids).

Though the market's judgment of the relative value of a widely traded firm may generally not be impeached under the ECMH, recent studies have investigated inefficiencies that characterize the stock market as a whole. Under the ECMH, information is reflected almost immediately after its release in the price of widely traded shares. Thus, as between any two firms, market price is shown to be "correct," in the sense that the market has adjusted to the information and eliminated the possibility of trading gains made by using the information. However, prices may be relatively (or "speculatively") efficient in this sense and still incorrect for *all* firms. One example of this might be stock market "bubbles," where prices quickly reach very high levels, only to fall precipitously. See Blanchard & Watson, *Bubbles, Rational Expectations, and Financial Markets*, in *Crises in Economic and Financial Structures* 295 (P. Wachtel ed. 1982) (possibility of gains on speculation may create "rational" bubbles). Similarly, "chaos" theorists seek to model extraordinary and unexpected price changes in markets as a whole when apparently innocuous individual trading decisions are aggregated. Following the 1987 stock market crash, in which all listed firms on average saw a 25% decline in their market price, these theories became a hot academic topic. However, they have not yet been persuasively applied to discussions of the contours of corporate law.

For prescient (i.e., pre-crash) analyses of these issues, see Gordon & Kornhauser, *Efficient Markets, Costly Information, and Securities Research*, 60 N.Y.U. L. Rev. 761 (1985) (distinguishing between "speculative" and "allocational" efficiency); Kraakman, *Taking Discounts Seriously: The Implications of "Discounted" Share Prices as an Acquisition Motive*, 88 Colum. L. Rev. 549 (1988) (market price "discounts" from asset value seen as an incentive for take-over bids).

Book Value. The present enterprise organization problem deals with a business whose shares are not traded on an efficient market. If the business is to be valued, then, it must be on some other basis.

For example, an accountant's *book value* is his measure of equity value or proprietorship. An obvious objection to book value is that assets may not be carried on the books at their true present value, but only at the historical cost of acquisition less any depreciation. The firm may therefore value its assets according to *replacement value*. This normally involves adjusting book value upward to account for increases in prices of machinery and equipment. *Liquidation value* is the amount that would be realized on a piecemeal sale of the assets on a liquidation. This assumes the withdrawal of the firm's productive capacity and will be of diminished importance if the firm is likely to continue in operation. However, liquidation value will at least establish a minimum asking price for the firm.

Capitalized Earnings Value. Asset value is often misleading because it lacks an adequate time frame, with long-term debts ranked on the same basis as obligations due tomorrow. The primary objection to asset value is, however, that it ignores the true source of value of a going concern—its ability to generate earnings in the future. The resale value of the firm's assets is not of great relevance if it does not propose to sell them. If the firm is profitable, it will instead retain its assets to carry on business. The assets will then be valuable only to the extent that they can be used to earn profits, and valuing a going concern will require a valuation of the anticipated future earnings stream.

The present value of $100 received one year from now must be less than $100 received today. This is because the $100 available today can be invested to produce more than $100 a year from now. For example, the investor might purchase treasury bills (T-bills) that offer a higher future payoff. Money received in the future must then be *discounted* if its present value is to be given. This is done by applying a *discount factor* to the amount (A) to be received.

$$\text{Present value } (PV) = \text{discount factor} \times A \tag{1}$$

An investor will thus require compensation for delayed payment of A. Suppose that for the particular period of time during which the receipt of A is deferred, investors demand a rate of return r. What this means is that they will be indifferent as between $PV(1 + r)$ and A. For example, at a 10% rate of return, the investor is indifferent as between $100(1.1)$ and $110. Since $PV(1 + r) = A$, the discount factor of equation (1) is $1/1 + r$, which can be rewritten as:

$$PV = \frac{A}{1+r} \tag{2}$$

It can then be shown that the present value of an amount received two periods hence is:

$$PV = \frac{A}{(1+r)^2} \tag{3}$$

Extending this, the present value of an annuity to be received at the end of each of the following n periods of time is:

$$PV = \frac{A}{(1+r)} + \frac{A}{(1+r)^2} + ,\dots, + \frac{A}{(1+r)^n} \tag{4}$$

A shorthand version of equation (4) is provided by introducing the Σ sign, which means the sum of the series:

$$PV = \sum \frac{A}{(1+r)^n} \tag{5}$$

At present interest rates, most of the present value of a long-term annuity is derived from amounts received over the first 15-20 years. For example, at a 20% discount factor, the present value of a $100 annuity received over the first 5 years is $299; over the first 10 years—$419; over the first 15 years—$468; over the first 20 years—$487; over the first 25 years—$495; and in perpetuity—$500. In other words, the present value of the income stream from year 25 to infinity is only ($500 − $495 = $5). (These figures are available in the present value tables of many finance texts.) Because a constant earnings stream may be much more valuable in earlier than in later years, valuers frequently assume that the earnings will extend to infinity even when they are only reasonably foreseen for a 10 year period of time.

The above equations can be simplified when it is assumed that the annuity will extend to infinity. In that case, equation (5) is equivalent to:

$$PV = \frac{A}{r} \tag{6}$$

If the earnings stream is expected to continue in perpetuity, the discount factor is usually referred to as a *capitalization factor*, and equation (6) is said to provide the capitalized value of the earnings.

When firms are valued by the capitalization of earnings method, the same formulae are applied. If earnings are expected to be constant in amount for a period of time approximately equivalent to infinity under present value tables, equation (6) may be rewritten as:

$$PV = \frac{E}{k} \tag{7}$$

where

PV = the firm's present value;
E = the firm's anticipated earnings each year; and
k = the capitalization rate

Equation (7) may also be given as:

$$PV = ME$$

where

$$M = 1/k$$

M is called a *multiplier*, and is the reciprocal of k: when multiplied together, their product is 1. For example, a multiplier of 5 is derived from a capitalization rate of 20%. Multipliers are easier to work with than capitalization rates if one finds multiplication easier than division. When two firms have the same anticipated earnings streams, the more highly valued one will have a higher multiplier and a lower capitalization rate.*

---

*   These figures are provided by market prices when the firm's securities are widely traded. For example, the present value of shares listed on a stock exchange may be obtained through the financial pages of a newspaper. Taking the firm's earnings per share as reported in its financial statements as E and market value as PV then permits the market capitalization rate to be determined.

Applying the valuation procedure to a firm is then a two-step procedure. The first step is to estimate what the firm is expected to earn each year. This normally involves looking at the firm's earnings over a representative period in the past, such as the previous five years. Adjustments may have to be made to these figures to eliminate non-recurring items, write-offs of bad debts or inventory, or excessive salaries. Making the heroic assumption that the future will resemble the past, one or an average figure is selected as the firm's expected future earnings per year. In some cases, the firm will be expected to carry on business for a few years and then dissolve, so that it is valued with the use of equation (4) rather than equation (7).

Having determined what the firm's anticipated earnings are, the second step involves valuing these earnings, using the present value equations. The firm's discount or capitalization rate will depend on (1) the current rate of interest for risk-free investments and (2) the risk attributes of the firm. As to the first question, a discount factor would have to be applied even with a 100% certainty of the firm's making the anticipated earnings each year, because of the risk-free returns available through other investment opportunities. These other earnings (e.g., interest on T-bills) represent an *opportunity cost*, in the sense that turning down such an investment for an equivalent one promising a lower reward is equivalent to absorbing a loss. The opportunity cost of a risk-free investment is referred to as the *time value of money*.

In the capitalization of earnings method of valuation, the risk-free capitalization rate is adjusted upward to account for the presence of risk in the firm's expected earnings. Other things being equal, the greater the downside risk, the less valuable the investment; the higher k is, the lower PV will be.* If asked to choose between an investment promising a $100 return with certainty, and one with an 80% probability of $100 and a 20% probability of nothing, an investor will prefer the former, whatever his attitude to risk. One way of reflecting this is to note that the weighted average or *expected monetary value (EMV)* of the second investment is only $80.

Table 1.1   Expected Monetary Value

Probability	Outcome		
80%	$100	=	$80
20%	0	=	0
	EMV	=	$80

The *EMV* of $80 might then be taken as the value of the annuity A, with a discount figure applied to it. Alternatively, A might be taken as $100, with a greater discount figure applied. (More impressionistically, the presence of risk might influence both the annuity and the discount figure.) Suppose then that the second method of reflecting risk is adopted, and that an investor is asked to choose between investing $1 in a bank at a certain 10%

---

*   Risk here is taken as synonymous with probability of loss. However, a more technical explanation of risk is adopted in finance economics. There risk is defined in terms of a dispersion of possible outcomes: where two investment projects have the same weighted average (or expected monetary value), the riskier one has the broader dispersion of (mean-preserving) values.

rate of return, and $1 in the Gagnon Computer Business, with its attendant risks of default. What anticipated return would he require from the Gagnon Computer Business before he is indifferent between the two investments? 25%? 50%? Note that, in answering this question, he will have selected a capitalization rate of the Gagnon Computer Business.

It is impossible to establish an appropriate capitalization rate with any degree of precision. Two valuers may differ substantially on how the risk should be assessed, and even a slight difference of opinion on the capitalization rate may result in enormous variances in the valuation of the firm. For example, if the business is expected to earn $100,000 a year, a capitalization rate of 20% will produce a valuation of $500,000, while a capitalization rate of 25% will result in a figure of only $400,000. Any two valuers, using the capitalized earnings method, may then arrive at widely different estimates of the worth of an enterprise. For a discussion of some of the sources of uncertainty, see J. Bonbright, *The Valuation of Property* 259-64 (1937).

This lack of precision explains why going concern values are not reflected on the balance sheet of the firm. Accountants seek certain standards and this produces a conservative bias. Asset valuation may not measure the right thing, but at least it measures it fairly objectively. On the other hand, when a measure of firm value is sought, this may be one of those areas where it is better to be approximately right than certainly wrong. The capitalized earnings value is generally considered to produce the best estimate of the worth of the business in the absence of a reliable market value.

Some writers have sought greater precision in the capitalized earnings method of valuation, most notably Arthur Dewing in his classic treatise *The Financial Policy of Corporations* (5th ed. 1953). Dewing categorized varieties of firms according to their risk features, with a particular capitalization rate associated with each category. For example, with the much lower interest rates (or time-values of money) of his day, he would have capitalized personal service businesses at 100%, or a value equal to approximately the earnings of a single year. Such businesses were described as follows:

They require no capital, or at the most a desk, some envelopes and a few sheets of paper. The manager must have a special skill coupled with an intensive and thorough knowledge of his subjects. The earnings of the enterprise are the objective reflection of his skill; and he is not likely to be able to create "an organization" which can successfully "carry on" after he is gone. He can sell the business, including the reputation and the "plan of business," but he cannot sell himself, the only truly valuable part of the enterprise ... [*Id.* at 391]

Dewing's efforts at standardization are undoubtedly of assistance, but it may be objected that they merely push back the uncertainty one level, and that the identification of a firm as belonging to one category or another still depends on subjective judgments.

See further R. Brealey & S. Myers, *Principles of Corporate Finance* 12-15 (4th ed. 1991); W. Klein & J. Coffee, *Business Organization and Finance: Legal and Economic Principles*, ch. 5 (3d ed. 1988).

We began our discussion of valuation theory by suggesting that claims in the combined firm be distributed in proportion to the parties' separate contributions. Before leaving this section, how feasible is such a procedure, given the difficulty of valuing each party's contribution? Even if valuation uncertainties could be overcome, are such standards likely to be met once strategic considerations are taken into account? See H.

Raiffa, *The Art and Science of Negotiation* 44-58 (1982). (Clue: What is each party's best alternative to joining the firm? What happens if this is known to the other party?) Can a principled distinction be made between these strategic factors and the valuation of the contributions?

B. THE ECONOMIC ANALYSIS OF CORPORATE LAW

Problem One concerns a bargain about enterprise organization, with three parties seeking to arrive at a mutually advantageous transaction. In negotiating the agreement that creates the firm, its terms will have been dictated by a variety of business and economic considerations. An understanding of these background issues therefore assists the lawyer in preparing such a contract. In addition, economic principles offer an insight into rules and institutions of corporations and partnership law. Legal structures have frequently been observed to serve economic purposes, and economics may therefore seek to provide a *positive* theory of corporate law, describing rules that cannot easily be understood in other ways. Were the economic analysis of law able to do this in a coherent way, it would of course be of the greatest use to corporate lawyers. But economics might also inform *normative* theories of law by indicating what corporate institutions ought to look like. This casebook generally eschews prescriptive language, but it should not be concluded from this that those inclined to take the moral high road may safely ignore insights offered by economics on any issue of public policy.

1. Paretian Standards

From an economic point of view, transactions and institutions are judged in terms of their efficiency. To understand how efficiency standards may apply to a bargain, consider first the simplest possible case, that of a two party contract entered into freely by parties of full capacity.* We imagine a world with only two individuals, Ben and Jerry, for whom only two kinds of goods exist: vanilla (V) and chocolate (C) ice cream. Since there is no one else around with whom to trade, the parties face each other in a *bilateral monopoly*.

Each party is assumed to have certain *tastes* with respect to the commodities, which may be measured with the assistance of the following two symbols: "~," which means "is indifferent to," and ">," which means "is preferred to." Ben and Jerry's preferences with respect to V and C are then measured in the following preference table.

Table 1.2   Preference Table of Ben and Jerry

Ben	Jerry
$1V \sim 1C$	$1V \sim 2C$
$2V \sim 2C$	$2V \sim 4C$
$3V \sim 3C$	$3V \sim 6C$
$4V \sim 4C$	

---

*   The following discussion of efficiency criteria is designed to provide a non-rigorous sketch of bargaining games, but students who wish to pursue these themes might consult J. Hirshleiffer, *Price Theory and Applications* 57-78 (3d ed. 1984).

The table indicates that Ben is indifferent as between $1V$ and $1C$; given the choice, he would not prefer one over the other. Note that it does not follow from this that he is indifferent as between $2V$ and $2C$. He might instead get tired of V more quickly than of C, though we assume not at least up to a quantity of 4. Jerry, on the other hand, is a V lover up to a quantity of $3V$, and can be made better off more easily with V than C.*

In the trades that follow, we assume that the parties are restricted to trades of discrete quantities of up to $4V$ or $4C$, and therefore assume away the possibility of a trade where preferences cannot be ranked. This assumption is called one of *completeness*, and can be defined more technically as meaning that there are no incomparable pairs of commodities. That is, there is no set of Vs and Cs, up to the indicated quantities, for which either party will be unable to express either preference or indifference. As a result, for any two collections of Vs and Cs, denoted as x and y, either $x > y$, $y > x$ or $x \sim y$.

Our second assumption is one of *non-satiation*, sometimes described under the tag "more is better." In other words, if a party has three items of a quantity, he will always be better off with a fourth: there is no point at which the individual will be indifferent as between a quantity of n and a quantity of $n + 1$ items of the commodity.† A marginal increase in quantity will, however, be more appreciated when the individual is endowed with fewer items of the commodity. In other words, getting one more quantity will ordinarily give him more pleasure when he moves from 0 to 1 scoop of ice cream than from 3 to 4 scoops. But even at 3 scoops, the individual will still be better off with 4.

The last assumption to be discussed in our simplified view of bargaining games is *transitivity*. This can be defined as a relation R under which, if $x R y$ and $y R z$, then $x R z$, for all x, y and z in the domain of alternatives. For example, if $x > y$ and $y > z$, then $x > z$. With the assumption of transitivity, we exclude the possibility of circular preference systems, as where $3V > 2V$ and $2V > 1V$, but $1V > 3V$. This kind of intransitivity is taken by economists to signify irrationality, for what an individual would choose would depend on the order in which choices were offered to him. (Do you see why?) When informed of any intransitive preferences he may have, it is then assumed that the individual could be persuaded to revert to transitive preference systems. For an example of the kinds of arguments that might be brought to bear to lead one to transitivity, see H. Raiffa, *Decision Analysis* 80-86 (1970).

We are now able to consider the trades that Ben and Jerry might work out between themselves. We begin by providing for their *endowments* of commodities, with Ben

---

*   The figures are chosen arbitrarily, and it does not matter much for the purpose of our example what the quantities are. One V might be a scoop, a brick or a gallon, so long as the same kind of quantities are compared throughout.

†   Students sometimes object that, while non-satiation is the general way of the world, yet there must at times be such a thing as too much. Indeed, nothing exceeds like excess, but this does not constitute a critique of economics but only of our model. At a more theoretical level than is worthwhile at this point, it can be shown that the assumption of satiation can be dispensed with. At the point of excess, what had been a *good* will have turned into a *bad*. For our purposes, it suffices that non-satiation obtains within the limited choices that are available to the parties.

having $2V$ and Jerry having $4C$. Each person's endowments are quite separate from his tastes, in that individuals with the same endowments may have very different preferences. On the other hand, a change in one person's endowments may affect his tastes: for example, with more wealth, more luxuries are desired. It is therefore more accurate to imagine our parties being provided with their tastes and their preferences at the same time.

Trade between the parties is now possible. Of course, any particular trade may be made, but we shall be interested in investigating only those trades that can be described as *rational*. Rationality may then be judged in accordance with either procedural or substantive norms. *Procedural rationality* concerns the deliberative quality of a choice, as where it seems thoughtful and informed. What matters here is how a bargain is arrived at, with agreements that pass such scrutiny deemed reasonable whatever their substantive outcome. *Substantive rationality* standards, on the other hand, qualify a choice in terms of the transformation that results. For example, if one's lot improves (or at least if one is no worse off), the choice may be said to be rational.

The criteria of economic rationality are formally those of substantive rationality. The best known economic standard is called *Pareto superiority*,* which is defined as a transformation in which at least one party is made better off and no one is made worse off. For example, consider a trade in which Ben gives $1V$ to Jerry in exchange for $1C$. After the trade, Ben is neither better off nor worse off. On the other hand, Jerry is made better off, since he is indifferent as between $5C$ and his post-bargain holdings ($1V$ and $3C$), and from the non-satiation assumption it follows that he prefers $5C$ to $4C$, his pre-bargain assets.

With this trade, the parties will not have exhausted all possible Pareto superior transformations. If Ben exchanges his remaining V for either $1C$ or $2C$, one party will have been made better off with no one worse off. Thereafter, no further Pareto superior transformations are possible, which is the definition of *Pareto optimality*. At this point, no one can be made better off without making someone worse off. It should, however, be noted that a transformation to a Pareto optimal state need not be Pareto superior. For example, if from the initial set of endowments all commodities were transferred to Jerry, the result would be Pareto optimal, but the transformation would certainly not have been Pareto superior. Similarly, our first trade demonstrated that a Pareto superior transformation need not lead to Pareto optimality.

Normative Theories of Bargaining. Pareto superior transformations may be morally desirable under either deontological or consequentialist theories. On a deontological theory, moral judgments rest on concepts of rights, which are to be respected without regard to end-state consequences. As applied to contract theory, a promise ought then to be performed because it represents a person's choice. Insofar as they focus on the quality of the choice, rights theories of contracting are procedural, with the quality of the transformation of importance only insofar as it provides a badge of the deliberative

---

*   Vilfredo Pareto (1848-1923), Italian economist.

quality of the choice. Were full information as to procedural rationality available, a contract's moral force would be undiminished even if it were Pareto inferior.

A second moral theory of promising is consequentialist, and focuses upon end-state results. If rights theories of promising are fundamentally concerned with procedural issues, consequentialist explanations of contractual institutions would defend them for their substantive outcomes. Amongst the outputs of bargaining, the most plausible desideratum is Pareto-superiority, so that consequentialist theories of bargaining generally endow efficiency criteria with a moral status. In particular, there may be a broad overlap between wealth maximization considered as an ethical norm and some versions of utilitarianism, the best-known variant of consequentialism.

While theoretical differences between rights and consequentialist theories are fundamental and important, they may overlap to a significant extent in a defence of promising. In real world conditions, substantive outcomes are largely obscured, and visible only with the aid of procedural criteria. That a transformation is Pareto superior cannot be observed without knowledge of the pre-bargaining preference maps of the parties. These, however, are generally imperfectly understood by everyone except perhaps the individual himself, so that the conclusion that consensual bargains effect Pareto superior transformations rests on assumptions of economic rationality, such as that of transitivity.

2. Restrictions on Bargaining

An analysis of bargain theory is incomplete without an examination of the circumstances where promises do not give rise to an obligation and where contracts are not binding. In what follows, three different reasons for refusing to enforce a contract, or for varying its terms, will be considered. These are:

- where the bargain imposes external costs on third parties;
- where the intervention is thought to be justified on grounds of distributive justice; and
- where the contract is impeached on standards of procedural rationality.

(a) External Costs

When the effects of a consensual agreement are felt only by parties to the contract, the assumption of Pareto superiority might seem uncontroversial, for no one will reasonably consent to a transaction that leaves him worse off. But it cannot be presumed that no one is harmed by a contract whose effects are felt by third parties, since they will not have consented to it. These third party effects are called *externalities*. In some cases externalities are benign, with the spillover effect considered desirable by the third party, and here one speaks of external goods. On the other hand, external goods must be distinguished from external bads, such as those that arise through pollution. When an agreement gives rise to *external costs* in this way, arguments for per se enforceability must be modified, and most of the cases where bargains are not enforced in contract law under the doctrine of illegality may indeed be explained on the basis of their external costs.

Two criteria as to when a contract should be held illegal because of externalities may be suggested. On the first, no bargain would be upheld if it gives rise to any external costs. However, this strategy would undoubtedly be extreme, and likely suffers from an impoverished view of external effects. Almost anything can give rise to a third party effect, like the case of the well-dressed person who provides pleasure to those who see her walking down the street. See Arneson, *The Principle of Fairness and Free Rider Problems*, 92 Ethics 616, 621 (1982). In the case of a firm, virtually every business decision may have an effect on the price that the firm charges for its commodities and, beyond the firm and its consumers, on the price that a competitor may charge. A more modest criterion for refusing to enforce a bargain would then seem indicated, and here it might be suggested that contracts be upheld so long as net gains to the contractors exceed all third party external costs. This is called the *Kaldor-Hicks* criterion of efficiency, with transformations qualified as Kaldor-Hicks efficient if gains to winners exceed losses to losers.* On this standard of enforceability, a contract would be upheld even if not Pareto superior because of its external costs provided that it *could* be made Pareto superior if the winners chose to compensate the losers. In the Kaldor-Hicks definition of efficiency, however, there is no requirement that the winners actually do compensate the losers, so the test is sometimes described as "potential Pareto superiority."

The Claimholders' Bargain. The Haldor-Hicks criterion offers a basis for analyzing transactions and institutions that give rise to externalities. In corporate law, not every party with an interest in a firm will have entered into a contractual relationship with it. For example, tort claimants are non-consensual creditors to the extent that they may assert damages claims against the firm. Externalities suffered by non-consensual claimants will not, however, suffice to impeach firm transactions on the Kaldor-Hicks standard of efficiency unless net losses exceed net gains. As a method of testing whether this will happen, the case may be taken of a hypothetical bargain or implicit contract amongst all parties with an interest or claim, whether consensual or non-consensual, in the firm. In such a *claimholders' bargain* the transaction will not be agreed to unless it is Kaldor-Hicks efficient.

A claimholders' bargain model may also inform the content of legal rules and institutions. In the same way that Kaldor-Hicks standards can be applied to transactions, legal structures may be thought of as the output of a hypothetical contract amongst every person affected by it. This contractarian analysis of law was first clearly developed by Richard Coase, who began a revolution in legal theory by posing the simplest of questions: why do legal rules matter? If a rule is Kaldor-Hicks inefficient, third parties may always form a coalition to bargain the parties to efficient rules. The affected third parties will then pay the contracting parties to give up the contract, in effect bargaining for a private doctrine of illegality. Were no transactions costs to arise, all hypothetical Kaldor-Hicks bargain opportunities would be exploited, with final outcomes dependent upon initial endowments but not otherwise upon legal rules. In this way, liability rules would not affect the ultimate allocation of resources under conditions of perfect bargaining. This irrelevance proposition is called the "Coase theorem" after its author, who suggested it in *The Problem of Social Cost*, 3 L.J. & Econ. 1 (1960). However, Coase did not claim that "legal rules do not matter," since perfect bargaining conditions will often

---

* For a particularly accessible analysis of efficiency criteria, including Kaldor-Hicks, see Coleman, *Efficiency, Utility, and Wealth Maximization*, 8 Hofstra L. Rev. 509 (1980).

not obtain. For example, third parties may be so dispersed that they cannot easily form a coalition to contract with one voice. Even if these hurdles could be overcome, there are further negotiation barriers, including the opportunity costs of forgone alternatives and lawyers' fees.* In addition, not every Pareto superior bargain will be struck as a consequence of tactical considerations, such as opportunism or hard bargaining. All of these barriers are described as *transaction costs*, and because of them, legal rules may in fact have an effect on the ultimate allocation of resources.

Normative Theories. It may then be suggested that, where legal rules do matter, their content should be the same as that for which all affected parties would have bargained were transaction costs erased, with Kaldor-Hicks efficiency standards raised to the status of a moral principle. An ethical basis for legal rules that "mimic the market" in this way might be sought in the same norms that underlie private bargains. If private contracts are defended on the basis of deontological or consequentialist theories, hypothetical bargains may be thought justified in similar ways. For example, Richard Posner has sought to provide a deontological basis for a hypothetical bargain view of the law, assimilating hypothetical consent to the real consent of an actual bargain (R. Posner, *The Economics of Justice* 88-89 (1981)). However, critics of this extension of deontological theories have insisted that there is a fundamental difference between the two kinds of consent. If a consent to a Kaldor-Hicks transformation is presumed because the end result is desirable, then the normative basis for the transformation may be sought in the desirability of the outcome, dispensing entirely with consent. See M. Sandel, *Liberalism and the Limits of Justice* 127 (1984). Hypothetical bargain models of law would therefore appear to rest on consequentialist ethical theories.

The consequentialist defence of Kaldor-Hicks principles is not quite so easy, it must be noted, as that of Pareto superiority. The impulse to compensate is strong, and Kaldor-Hicks standards do not require compensation. Compensation to losers may even serve efficiency goals in some cases, for without it doubts may arise about whether the transformation is in fact Kaldor-Hicks efficient. See R. Epstein, *Takings: Private Property and the Power of Eminent Domain* 104 (1985). And yet legal rules often leave losses uncompensated. This may be defended on the basis that even losers might consent to Kaldor-Hicks legal institutions, knowing that, in transformations effected by other efficient legal institutions, they will emerge as winners. See R. Posner, *The Economics of Justice* 94-97 (1981). Apart from this, mandating compensation to losers on every Kaldor-Hicks transformation would give rise to substantial information production costs in weighing claims and awarding damages.

A hypothetical bargain model of legal structures may strike one as inappropriate in some areas of law, where concerns for human dignity might seem shortchanged. These criticisms may, however, be less troubling in commercial law. For example, the leading theory of bankruptcy law today is one based on the model of a hypothetical creditors'

---

*   At the same time, a study of what business lawyers *really* do suggests that the value of employing a
     lawyer in a business transaction is that he may economize on transaction costs, for example, by reduc-
     ing uncertainty about the nature of the agreement. Gilson, *Value Creation by Business Lawyers: Legal
     Skills and Asset Pricing*, 94 Yale L.J. 239 (1984).

agreement. See T. Jackson, *The Logic and Limits of Bankruptcy Law* (1986). In this casebook, corporate law structures will frequently be examined from the perspective of a hypothetical claimholders' agreement, with legal principles justified on the basis that they would have been agreed to in a bargain amongst every party with a consensual or non-consensual interest in the firm.

This is not to say that reasonable men who subscribe to these standards must always agree on corporate law rules. The efficiency consequences of a rule are not always clear, even for a single constituency such as shareholders. When account is taken of other constituencies, such as creditors, employees and consumers, efficiency effects are more elusive still. These other constituencies are sometimes referred to as *stakeholders*. On stakeholder theories, then, corporate law rules that seek only to maximize shareholder wealth might inefficiently impose costs on these other groups. This need not be a critique of the law and economics view of corporate law. If the common goal is to maximize the wealth of all corporate constituencies, then the only dispute is the factual one about the costs of external effects and the efficiency consequences of rules meant to reduce such externalities. For even if corporate decisions do affect non-shareholder constituencies (as surely they must), it does not follow that such constituencies should have greater corporate law governance rights or remedies. While employees are affected by corporate layoff decisions, for example, it does not follow that an more efficient legal regime would permit them to veto all such decisions.

These issues will be taken up at various places in the book, including Chapter Two, Section B on veil-piercing, Chapter Six on corporate governance policies, Chapter Seven on management liability rules, and Chapter Eleven on take-over bids. As well, Chapter Nine deals with the rights of lenders, who (after shareholders and managers) are the most important corporate constituency. By way of introduction to these issues, the interested student might turn to Daniels, *Shareholders and Takeovers: Can Contractarianism Be Compassionate?* 43 U. of Toronto L.J. 315 (1993).

(b) *Distributive Justice*

Hypothetical bargain models of the law are also consistent with the Aristotelian concept of corrective justice, if wrongful behaviour is identified with inefficiency. See Posner, *The Concept of Corrective Justice in Recent Theories of Tort Law*, 10 J. Legal Stud. 187 (1981). However, efficiency considerations must be distinguished from principles of distributive justice, which examine how goods are distributed in society. For example, in our bargaining game we looked at how trades between Ben and Jerry were possible after the initial distribution of ice cream without asking whether the initial distribution was just, even though that endowment determined which trades were Pareto superior. The difference between efficiency (or allocational) and *distributional* issues is the difference between the creation of wealth (in the form of Kaldor-Hicks bargains) and its transfer, and is one more example of the distinction between the size of the pie and how it is sliced.

Restructuring legal rules on the basis of theories of distributive justice might be rejected as inconsistent with libertarian values, with the "taking" from one party to give to another regarded as an unjust interference with the former's rights. It might also be argued that such takings are self-defeating, with greater distributive justice thought to result in a society that bases legal institutions solely upon Kaldor-Hicks norms. Finally, one might seek to confine wealth transfer legislation to the tax and entitlements law of what used to be called the modern welfare state, leaving private law rules of contract, tort and corporate law to be resolved on efficiency norms. On the other hand, Anthony Kronman has argued that there is no reason in principle why private law regimes cannot in part be shaped by distributional considerations. See Kronman, *Contract Law and Distributive Justice*, 89 Yale L.J. 472 (1980). In corporate law, these issues sometimes surface in the debate concerning "corporate social responsibility," as discussed in Chapter Six. Even there, however, it is not always easy to distinguish distributional from efficiency issues. For example, an argument that employees should be offered a position on the board of directors of a corporation might possibly be based either on efficiency concerns or on theories of distributive justice.

A further distributional problem concerns the division of the benefits of an agreement. In monetary terms, a Pareto superior transaction is *non-zero sum*, since new wealth is created. But within the core of the bargaining game a *zero sum* dispute arises over the division of the "surplus" or "synergy." For example, a variety of Pareto superior transformations were possible in the bargain between Ben and Jerry. In some Ben was the "winner" and Jerry's lot was not improved, while in others the positions were reversed. Of course, the parties might themselves reject a judicial enquiry into such fairness issues, since the threat of unenforceability may mean an absolute loss for both. Critics of "divide the synergy" arguments may also point to the lack of success that game theorists have had in devising ethically attractive "solutions" to bargaining games, and to the virtually intractable problems in measuring synergy. These issues will be considered in the context of transactions between parent corporations and their partially owned subsidiary corporations in Chapters Seven and Eleven.

(c) *Procedural Concerns*

The last critique of bargain models of corporate law is addressed to its assumptions of rational consent. This is not in fact an attack upon hypothetical bargains, where consent is idealized and where concerns as to procedural fairness are absent. However, the decision of a party in an actual contract might be impeached if judicial errors are anticipated. The moral value of substantive outputs of a bargain may then be rendered doubtful by the difficulty in providing a clear demonstration of procedural fairness: given the wrong kind of inputs, the moral output does not take.

In defence of assumptions of rationality, it must be remembered that the quality of a choice is determined *ex ante* when the bargain is made, not *ex post* when outcomes are revealed. For example, an investment with a 0.5 probability of $200 and 0.5 probability of 0 has an *EMV* of $100, and will be preferred to a sure thing of $95 by risk neutral parties. If the outcome turns out to be 0, this will not retroactively impugn the choice.

Even then, however, observed choices are not always in one's best interests. Adults of full capacity often seemingly choose by instinct, and intransitive preferences may result from judgment biases. Yet when procedural requirements are levered up above common law antifraud standards, the revised theory of promising may seem uncomfortably paternalistic. If an individual's choice does not deserve respect when no question or duress arises, then his capacity to choose is impeached.

On the other hand, the interference with individual choice, so far from conflicting with hypothetical bargain principles, may perhaps be justified on the basis that the individual himself would have consented to the restriction on it *ex ante*. For example, bargaining gives rise to a cost when an individual must calculate whether the transformation will leave him better off. This decision will not always be easy, for in complicated, probabilistic choices, alternatives must be weighed to see if any one is ruled out of order by some other of one's preferences if transitivity is to obtain. If these information processing costs might exceed the benefit anticipated from the bargain, the individual will react either by avoiding such choices or by making them on the basis of imperfect information. Either decision carries with it the possibility of error. To minimize these error costs, the individual might have preferred a regime in which some categories of choices are withdrawn from him under theories of illegality, with other choices made mandatory. Arguments for and against paternalistic rules as a response to judgment biases are considered in Feinberg, *Legal Paternalism*, 1 Cdn. J. Phil. 106 (1971), reprinted in *Paternalism* 3 (R. Sartorius ed. 1983); Grether, Schwartz & Wilde, *The Irrelevance of Information Overload: An Analysis of Search and Disclosure*, 59 S. Cal. L. Rev. 277 (1986); Jackson, *The Fresh-Start Policy in Bankruptcy Law*, 98 Harv. L. Rev. 1393 (1985); Scott, *Error and Rationality in Individual Decisionmaking: An Essay on the Relationship Between Cognitive Illusions and the Management of Choice*, 59 S. Cal. L. Rev. 329 (1986); Sunstein, *Legal Interference with Private Preferences*, 53 U. Chi. L. Rev. 1129 (1986).

Judgment biases do not by themselves suffice to justify regimes of paternalism, since even if choice may at times be flawed, in general it provides better information of individual preferences than legal rules. What is needed, then, is a persuasive argument that, in a particular category of choices, the individual is made better off by binding legal rules. For example, one kind of case in which judgment biases are observed is one with an extremely small probability of a major loss. When tested against such choices, individuals frequently reveal intransitive preferences, applying a discount rate to the possibility of such events which appears irrational when compared with their choices in ordinary circumstances. These results might then perhaps justify mandatory insurance for catastrophic medical illness, though not for dental care. Applied to corporate law, such considerations might suggest the need for a greater readiness to second-guess bargains as to low probability events. In addition, information barriers may suggest that some choices be viewed through at least a veil of strong presumptive rules. See Brudney, *Corporate Governance, Agency Costs, and the Rhetoric of Contract*, 85 Colum. L. Rev. 1403, 1411-20 (1985) (information costs prevent investors from freely and knowingly choosing management duties). On the other hand, when parties negotiate firm structures, as on the Gagnon reorganization, most writers would incline strongly against mandatory rules. The bias against paternalism is stronger still when the negotiations are carried out through legal or investment intermediaries, as where share conditions are crafted by an issuer and an underwriter and their counsel on a public issue of shares. In addition, if the justification for the imposition of mandatory rules is utilitarian, it must be shown that individuals are made better off when choices are removed from them. What counts are not the paternalist's preferences but rather those of his subjects.

3. Economic Theories of the Firm

Problem One assumed that the contribution of the three parties were worth more when united in a single firm than when held apart. As such, the organization of the firm created new wealth. But this does not explain why it was efficient to form a firm, since the parties might instead have sought to provide for the management of the enterprise through separate contracts. Were no costs associated with the production of information, the promoters of a firm might then have written a *complete contingent contract*, in which all future investment decisions were specified *ex ante* at the time of organization. In a classic article, Ronald Coase discussed how a demand for firm structures arises because the information required to write such a contract is in fact costly. Coase, *The Nature of the Firm*, 4 Economica (N.S.) 386 (1937), reprinted in Posner & Scott 3.

Optimal Firm Size. The problem identified by Coase was how to determine the optimal size of the firm, as against the alternative of organizing production through separate contracts with claimants of the firm. For example, in what circumstances should a firm expand through *vertical integration*, merging with suppliers of inputs or customers of outputs? Coase contended that the demand to organize production through a firm rather than by contracts is a function of two kinds of costs. First, if the firm is the sole supplier to itself of inputs that are shifted out of the market and into the firm, fewer transactions will have to be entered into. This will save the firm the transaction costs associated with negotiating each contract separately. Second, the grant of agency to a hierarchy of managers to make investment decisions on behalf of the firm economizes on the costs of producing information which would arise were all such future decisions to be made on the firm's formation in a complete contingent contract.

Production through a firm will also economize on a third kind of cost, which economists call *opportunism*. In a contractual relationship, not every performance standard can be enforced by a court. Some terms must be left to the good faith of the parties, without a legal sanction for bad faith performance. For example, a party's strict enforcement of termination rights might constitute a form of post-contractual opportunism, when the parties had understood that such rights would be waived in the particular circumstances of the case. Nor might the parties wish to remedy such problems by giving a court the prerogative to imply a thick set of good faith legal norms, so that the entire bargain might be rewritten. Because of the risk of premature termination, then, the parties will lack adequate incentives to invest in the production of assets (called *transaction-specific assets*) that are worthless when the contract is at an end. For example, the parties might underinvest in skills of use only in production under the contract. These problems dissipate when production is undertaken by a firm, for the hierarchical structures of firm governance may police misbehavior of this kind more effectively than a court. For a further discussion of these issues, see O. Williamson, *Markets and Hierarchies: Analysis and Antitrust Implications* (1975); Klein, Crawford & Alchian, *Vertical Integration, Appropriable Rents, and the Competitive Contracting Hypothesis*, 21 J. L. & Econ. 297 (1978); Goetz & Scott, *Principles of Relational Contracts*, 67 Va. L. Rev. 1089 (1981); Williamson, *Assessing Contract*, 1 J. L. Econ. & Org. 177 (1985).

On the other hand, firm structures give rise to countervailing costs; otherwise they would have entirely replaced markets (and Russia would not have lost the Cold War).

These costs include information costs, for production through contracts generates information about the prices of commodities. We have already seen one application of this in the ECMH. Lay investors may observe the market valuation of a firm by reading the financial pages of a newspaper, where stock quotes are given. In this way, the lay investor may free ride on the information produced by market intermediaries, without having to value the firm himself. Such free riding usefully economizes on information costs.

Production through a firm imposes a second kind of cost, which economists call *agency costs*. The term agency here refers to the authority to manage a firm which passive investors (as principals) delegate to firm managers (as agents) of publicly held firms. The term agency is here used broadly, and extends beyond the legal definition of principal and agent, as discussed in the next section, to embrace all cases where one party in a firm can make decisions affecting another party. The grant of authority is made because it is more efficient to delegate in this way than to eliminate the principal-agent relationship. Even so, this will give rise to costs insofar as the agent's incentives are to maximize his own rather than firm interests. The problem of strategic behaviour by agents is the subject of several chapters of this book, particularly Chapter Seven on management duties.

A Nexus of Contracts. It would be highly misleading to suggest that firms exist in hierarchial worlds without contracts. The modern theory of the firm in fact views it as a legal fiction that serves as a nexus for contracts among all individuals with a consensual claim against it. Such parties include not merely shareholders and managers, but also such stakeholders as creditors (whether long or short term), employees, customers and suppliers. On a "nexus of contracts" view of the firm, it makes little sense to try to distinguish who is "inside" from who is "outside" the firm, or to ask who its "owner" is. It is instead more fruitful to analyze the terms by which each class contributes to joint production in order to determine how the wealth of all participants may be maximized. From this perspective, the distinction between hierarchical firm structures and contracts in markets is blurred. Indeed, the market for firm inputs might be competitive as well as markets for its outputs. For example, the market for the supply of equity capital to large firms is highly competitive, and there is also competition in the market for the provision of managerial services to large firms. The information generated by markets is a public good, and in the case of the market for managerial services, may usefully inform standards as to executive compensation. See Chapter Seven.

The seminal statements of the nexus of contracts approach to corporate structures are Alchian & Demsetz, *Production, Information Costs, and Economic Organization*, 62 Am. Econ. Rev. 777 (1972), reprinted in part in Posner & Scott 12; Jensen & Meckling, *Theory of the Firm: Managerial Behaviour, Agency Costs and Ownership Structure*, 3 J. Fin. Econ. 305 (1976), reprinted in part in Posner & Scott 39 and Ramano 7.

C. PARTNERSHIPS

In the materials that follow, you are asked to consider what form of enterprise is most suitable for Gagnon, Gray and Smith. Various alternatives will be examined. Should

Gagnon become a general partner? A creditor? A limited partner? A shareholder of a corporation? In examining these options, you must decide how the participants will share in the profits and perhaps in the management of the enterprise, while taking into account the risk of financial loss.

The subject of this section is not partnership law in general, nor even business partnerships in particular. Instead, the section merely reviews the advantages of the partnership form of organization for the Gagnon business. Basic concepts of partnership and agency will, however, be discussed. Some of these principles will also be seen within a corporate setting, and it will be observed that the problems faced by the promoters of the new business will require a similar solution, whatever form of enterprise organization is adopted. For example, the parties will likely wish to restrict the transferability of shares whether they form a partnership or incorporate.

Enterprise organization requires a knowledge of more than partnership and corporate law. A decision to incorporate is often made for tax reasons, which are beyond the scope of this casebook. However, it should be noted that corporations, unlike partnerships, are separate entities for the purpose of federal and provincial taxation statutes. An individual taxpayer in a high income bracket may therefore prefer to shelter firm income behind a corporation.

1. Partnership Organization

Cameron, The Form and Organization of the Business Entity
Advising the Small Businessman 11-16
(Law Society of Upper Canada 1977)

Sole Proprietor

Organization

An individual, or corporation with objects and powers sufficiently broad to encompass such an activity, may commence carrying on a business in Ontario subject only to certain registration requirements.

The person carrying on the business is directly responsible for the performance of all contracts and for all liabilities of the business. All of his personal assets are available to satisfy his business obligations and all of the business income is his income.

Registration

The Partnerships Registration Act requires that every person engaged in business for trading, manufacturing or mining purposes who is not associated in partnership with any other person but uses as his business style a name or designation other than his own name or his own name with the addition of the expression "and company" or some other expression indicating a plurality of members in the firm, shall sign a declaration in the prescribed form. The declaration must be filed with the Registrar of Partnerships ... within sixty days of the time when the name or designation is first used. Registration must be renewed every 5 years. A similar declaration should similarly be filed whenever any change takes place in the ownership of the business or in the name. No person who

restricting generally the transfer of shares

has failed so to file a declaration is capable of maintaining any action or other proceeding in any court in Ontario in respect of which a declaration is required to be filed. In addition, a penalty is provided on summary conviction for non-compliance with any provisions of this Act.

An individual, partnership or association may notify the Minister of the name under which his or its business is carried on and the Minister shall make a note of it in his records. (Ontario Business Corporations Act, s. 12.) This would protect the name from use of a similar name by some other person on a subsequent incorporation.

A corporation carrying on business by a name other than its corporate name must register the name with the Minister under section 2 of The Corporations Information Act and renew the registration every five years and in such event need not file under The Partnerships Registration Act.

• • •

Partnership

• • •

Existence and Nature

Partnership is the relation that subsists between persons, including corporations, carrying on business in common with a view to profit but does not include the relationship between the shareholders of a corporation (s. 2). "Business" includes every trade, occupation and profession (s. 1). Joint ventures and syndicates are often partnerships entered into for specific purposes. (A joint venture will not be a partnership if it is so structured to be merely two business entities working side by side on the same project or one party has a guaranteed return and the other takes all the risk and standards to make all the profit over the guaranteed return.)

A partnership is not a legal entity separate from its partners and its partners cannot sue it. A corporation is a legal entity separate and distinct from its shareholders who can contract with and sue the corporation.

The true intention and effect of the contract between the parties is the determining factor in whether or not a partnership exists, not merely the fact that they call themselves partners. The parties must agree to participate in business with a view to profit. Participation in losses is not an essential element.

The Act provides certain rules which must be considered in determining whether a partnership exists (s. 3). Joint ownership of property and sharing of gross returns do not of themselves create a partnership. Receipt of a share of profits of a business is *prima facie* evidence that a person is a partner but receipt of such a share or payment varying with the profits of business does not itself make him a partner. However, money loaned at a rate of interest payable to the lender varying with profits or on terms entitling the lender to a share of profits could well make the lender liable as a partner of the borrower unless the loan contract is in writing signed by all the parties thereto. However, the lender under such an agreement or a purchaser of the goodwill of a business in exchange for a share of the profits will rank as deferred creditors of the partnership (s. 4). Such a lender is not deprived of any security taken for the loan nor the right to foreclose on it.

Nor does the lender rank as a deferred creditor if the money is loaned on terms that provide that a third person shall receive a share of the profits.

Relationship to Outsiders

With respect to outsiders dealing with the firm, The Partnerships Act provides for the liabilities of the firm and the partners. The essence of a partnership is that each partner is an agent of the firm and his other partners for the purpose of the business of the partnership (s. 6). Each partner in a firm is liable jointly (i.e. judgment against or release to one bars action against others) with the other partners to the full extent of his personal assets for all debts and obligations of the firm incurred while he is a partner, and after his death his estate is also severally liable in the due course of administration for such debts and obligations so far as they remain unsatisfied, but subject to the prior payment of his separate debts (s. 10). The firm is liable, and each partner is jointly and severally liable, for any penalty or loss or injury caused to a non-partner by the wrongful act or omission of a partner acting in the ordinary course of business of the firm or with the authority of his partners to the same extent as the wrongdoing partner (s. 11). If a partner acting within the scope of his apparent authority receives money of a third person and misapplies it or a partner misapplies money of a third person received by the firm in the course of its business, the firm is liable, and each partner is jointly and severally liable, to make good the loss (s. 12). In comparison, a shareholder has no liability for the obligations of the corporation beyond the amount paid to the company for fully paid shares held by him.

• • •

Agreements

No agreement can provide the good faith that must exist between partners but it can provide for foreseeable events which will cause disputes and undermine that good faith if there is no provision for such a contingency in the agreement.

It is apparent that most partners will desire terms of partnership differing from those presumed by the Act. Such provisions together with such additional terms necessary to a harmonious relationship should be evidenced by a written agreement. Certain mandatory provisions of The Partnerships Act might also be reiterated in the agreement for the information of the partners.

Partnerships Act
R.S.O. 1990, c. P.5

Nature of Partnership

2. Partnership is the relation that subsists between persons carrying on a business in common with a view to profit, but the relation between the members of a company or association that is incorporated by or under the authority of any special or general Act in force in Ontario or elsewhere, or registered as a corporation under any such Act, is not a partnership within the meaning of this Act.

3. In determining whether a partnership does or does not exist, regard shall be had to the following rules:

1. Joint tenancy, tenancy in common, joint property, common property, or part ownership does not of itself create a partnership as to anything so held or owned, whether the tenants or owners do or do not share any profits made by the use thereof.

2. The sharing of gross returns does not of itself create a partnership, whether the persons sharing such returns have or have not a joint or common right or interest in any property from which or from the use of which the returns are derived.

3. The receipt by a person of a share of the profits of a business is proof, in the absence of evidence to the contrary, that the person is a partner in the business, but the receipt of such a share or payment, contingent on or varying with the profits of a business, does not of itself make him or her a partner in the business, and in particular,

(a) the receipt by a person of a debt or other liquidated amount by instalments or otherwise out of the accruing profits of a business does not of itself make him or her a partner in the business or liable as such;

(b) a contract for the remuneration of a servant or agent or a person engaged in a business by a share of the profits of the business does not of itself make the servant or agent a partner in the business or liable as such;

(c) a person who,

(i) was married to a deceased partner immediately before the deceased partner died,

(ii) was living with a deceased partner of the opposite sex in a conjugal relationship outside marriage immediately before the deceased partner died, or

(iii) is a child of a deceased partner,

and who receives by way of annuity a portion of the profits made in the business in which the deceased partner was a partner is not by reason only of such receipt a partner in the business or liable as such;

(d) the advance of money by way of loan to a person engaged or about to engage in a business on a contract with that person that the lender is to receive a rate of interest varying with the profits, or is to receive a share of the profits arising from carrying on the business, does not of itself make the lender a partner with the person or persons carrying on the business or liable as such, provided that the contract is in writing and signed by or on behalf of all parties thereto;

(e) a person receiving by way of annuity or otherwise a portion of the profits of a business in consideration of the sale by him or her of the goodwill of the business, is not by reason only of such receipt a partner in the business or liable as such.

4. In the event of a person to whom money has been advanced by way of loan upon such a contract as is mentioned in section 3, or of a buyer of the goodwill in consideration of a share of the profits of the business, becoming insolvent or entering into an arrangement to pay his or her creditors less than 100 cents on the dollar or dying in

insolvent circumstances, the lender of the loan is not entitled to recover anything in respect of the loan, and the seller of the goodwill is not entitled to recover anything in respect of the share of profits contracted for, until the claims of the other creditors of the borrower or buyer, for valuable consideration in money or money's worth, are satisfied.

5. Persons who have entered into partnership with one another are, for the purposes of this Act, called collectively a firm, and the name under which their business is carried on is called the firm name.

Relation of Partners to Persons Dealing with Them

6. Every partner is an agent of the firm and of the other partners for the purpose of the business of the partnership, and the acts of every partner who does any act for carrying on in the usual way business of the kind carried on by the firm of which he or she is a member, bind the firm and the other partners unless the partner so acting has in fact no authority to act for the firm in the particular matter and the person with whom the partner is dealing either knows that the partner has no authority, or does not know or believe him or her to be a partner.

7. An act or instrument relating to the business of the firm and done or executed in the firm name, or in any other manner showing an intention to bind the firm by a person thereto authorized, whether a partner or not, is binding on the firm and all the partners, but this section does not affect any general rule of law relating to the execution of deeds or negotiable instruments.

8. Where one partner pledges the credit of the firm for a purpose apparently not connected with the firm's ordinary course of business, the firm is not bound, unless he or she is in fact specially authorized by the other partners, but this section does not affect any personal liability incurred by an individual partner.

9. If it is agreed between the partners to restrict the power of any one or more of them to bind the firm, no act done in contravention of the agreement is binding on the firm with respect to persons having notice of the agreement.

10. Every partner in a firm is liable jointly with the other partners for all debts and obligations of the firm incurred while the person is a partner, and after the partner's death the partner's estate is also severally liable in a due course of administration for such debts and obligations so far as they remain unsatisfied, but subject to the prior payment of his or her separate debts.

11. Where by any wrongful act or omission of a partner acting in the ordinary course of the business of the firm, or with the authority of the co-partners, loss or injury is caused to a person not being a partner of the firm, or any penalty is incurred, the firm is liable therefor to the same extent as the partner so acting or omitting to act.

12. In the following cases, namely,

(a) where one partner, acting within the scope of the partner's apparent authority, receives the money or property of a third person and misapplies it; and

(b) where a firm in the course of its business receives money or property of a third person, and the money or property so received is misapplied by one or more of the partners while it is in the custody of the firm,

the firm is liable to make good the loss.

13. Every partner is liable jointly with the co-partners and also severally for everything for which the firm, while the person is a partner therein, becomes liable under section 11 or 12.

• • •

15.(1) Every person, who by words spoken or written or by conduct represents himself or herself or who knowingly suffers himself or herself to be represented as a partner in a particular firm, is liable as a partner to any person who has on the faith of any such representation given credit to the firm, whether the representation has or has not been made or communicated to the persons so giving credit by or with the knowledge of the apparent partner making the representation or suffering it to be made.

(2) Where after a partner's death the partnership business is continued in the old firm name, the continued use of that name or of the deceased partner's name as part thereof does not of itself make his or her executor's or administrator's estate or effects liable for any partnership debts contracted after his or her death.

• • •

18.(1) A person who is admitted as a partner into an existing firm does not thereby become liable to the creditors of the firm for anything done before the person became a partner.

(2) A partner who retires from a firm does not thereby cease to be liable for partnership debts or obligations incurred before the partner's retirement.

(3) A retiring partner may be discharged from any existing liabilities by an agreement to that effect between the partner and the members of the firm as newly constituted and the creditors, and this agreement may be either express or inferred as a fact from the course of dealing between the creditors and the firm as newly constituted.

• • •

Relation of Partners to One Another

20. The mutual rights and duties of partners, whether ascertained by agreement or defined by this Act, may be varied by the consent of all the partners, and such consent may be either expressed or inferred from a course of dealing.

21.(1) All property and rights and interests in property originally brought into the partnership stock or acquired, whether by purchase or otherwise, on account of the firm, or for the purposes and in the course of the partnership business, are called in this Act "partnership property," and must be held and applied by the partners exclusively for the purposes of the partnership and in accordance with the partnership agreement.

• • •

24. The interests of partners in the partnership property and their rights and duties in relation to the partnership shall be determined, subject to any agreement express or implied between the partners, by the following rules:

1. All the partners are entitled to share equally in the capital and profits of the business, and must contribute equally towards the losses, whether of capital or otherwise, sustained by the firm.

2. The firm must indemnify every partner in respect of payments made and personal liabilities incurred by him or her,

(a) in the ordinary and proper conduct of the business of the firm; or

(b) in or about anything necessarily done for the preservation of the business or property of the firm.

3. A partner making, for the purpose of the partnership, any actual payment or advance beyond the amount of capital that he or she has agreed to subscribe is entitled to interest at the rate of 5 per cent per annum from the date of the payment or advance.

4. A partner is not entitled, before the ascertainment of profits, to interest on the capital subscribed by the partner.

5. Every partner may take part in the management of the partnership business.

6. No partner is entitled to remuneration for acting in the partnership business.

7. No person may be introduced as a partner without the consent of all existing partners.

8. Any difference arising as to ordinary matters connected with the partnership business may be decided by a majority of the partners, but no change may be made in the nature of the partnership business without the consent of all existing partners.

9. The partnership books are to be kept at the place of business of the partnership, or the principal place, if there is more than one, and every partner may, when he or she thinks fit, have access to and inspect and copy any of them.

25. No majority of the partners can expel any partner unless a power to do so has been conferred by express agreement between the partners.

26.(1) Where no fixed term is agreed upon for the duration of the partnership, any partner may determine the partnership at any time on giving notice of his or her intention to do so to all the other partners.

• • •

28. Partners are bound to render true accounts and full information of all things affecting the partnership to any partner or the partner's legal representatives.

29.(1) Every partner must account to the firm for any benefit derived by the partner without the consent of the other partners from any transaction concerning the partnership or from any use by the partner of the partnership property, name or business connection.

• • •

30. If a partner, without the consent of the other partners, carries on a business of the same nature as and competing with that of the firm, the partner must account for and pay over to the firm all profits made by the partner in that business.

31.(1) An assignment by a partner of the partner's share in the partnership, either absolute or by way of mortgage or redeemable charge, does not, as against the other partners, entitle the assignee, during the continuance of the partnership, to interfere in the management or administration of the partnership business or affairs, or to require any accounts of the partnership transactions, or to inspect the partnership books, but entitles the assignee only to receive the share of profits to which the assigning partner would otherwise be entitled, and the assignee must accept the account of profits agreed to by the partners.

(2) In the case of a dissolution of the partnership, whether as respects all the partners or as respects the assigning partner, the assignee is entitled to receive the share of the partnership assets to which the assigning partner is entitled as between the assigning partner and the other partners, and, for the purpose of ascertaining that share, to an account as from the date of the dissolution.

Dissolution of Partnership

32. Subject to any agreement between the partners, a partnership is dissolved,

(a) if entered into for a fixed term, by the expiration of that term;

(b) if entered into for a single adventure or undertaking, by the termination of that adventure or undertaking; or

(c) if entered into for an undefined time, by a partner giving notice to the other or others of his or her intention to disolve the partnership, in which case the partnership is dissolved as from the date mentioned in the notice as the date of dissolution, or, if no date is so mentioned, as from the date of the communication of the notice.

33.(1) Subject to any agreement between the partners, every partnership is dissolved as regards all the partners by the death or insolvency of a partner.

• • •

35. On application by a partner, the court may order a dissolution of the partnership,

(a) when a partner is found mentally incompetent by inquisition or is shown to the satisfaction of the court to be of permanently unsound mind, in either of which cases the application may be made as well on behalf of that partner by his or her committee or litigation guardian or person having title to intervene as by any other partner;

(b) when a partner, other than the partner suing, becomes in any other way permanently incapable of performing the partner's part of the partnership contract;

(c) when a partner, other than the partner suing, has been guilty of such conduct as, in the opinion of the court, regard being had to the nature of the business, is calculated to prejudicially affect the carrying on of the business;

(d) when a partner, other than the partner suing, wilfully or persistently commits a breach of the partnership agreement, or otherwise so conducts himself or herself in matters relating to the partnership business that it is not reasonably practicable for the other partner or partners to carry on the business in partnership with the partner;

(e) when the business of the partnership can only be carried on at a loss; or

(f) when in any case circumstances have arisen that in the opinion of the court render it just and equitable that the partnership be dissolved.

36.(1) Where a person deals with a firm after a change in its constitution, the person is entitled to treat all apparent members of the old firm as still being members of the firm until the person has notice of the change.

(2) An advertisement in *The Ontario Gazette* shall be notice as to persons who had not dealings with the firm before the dissolution or change so advertised.

(3) The estate of a partner who dies, or who becomes insolvent, or of a partner who, not having been known to the person dealing with the firm to be a partner, retires from the firm, is not liable for partnership debts contracted after the date of the death, insolvency, or retirement.

37. On the dissolution of a partnership or retirement of a partner, any partner may publicly give notice of the same, and may require the other partner or partners to concur for that purpose in all necessary or proper acts, if any, that cannot be done without his, her or their concurrence.

38. After the dissolution of a partnership, the authority of each partner to bind the firm and the other rights and obligations of the partners continue despite the dissolution so far as is necessary to wind up the affairs of the partnership and to complete transactions begun but unfinished at the time of the dissolution, but not otherwise; provided that the firm is in no case bound by the acts of a partner who has become insolvent; but this proviso does not affect the liability of a person who has, after the insolvency, represented himself or herself or knowingly suffered himself or herself to be represented as a partner of the insolvent.

39. On the dissolution of a partnership every partner is entitled, as against the other partners in the firm and all persons claiming through them in respect of their interests as partners, to have the property of the partnership applied in payment of the debts and liabilities of the firm and to have the surplus assets after such payment applied in payment of what may be due to the partners respectively after deducting what may be due from them as partners to the firm, and for that purpose any partner or the partner's representative may, on the termination of the partnership, apply to the court to wind up the business and affairs of the firm.

40. Where one partner paid a premium to another on entering into a partnership for a fixed term and the partnership is dissolved before the expiration of that term otherwise than by the death of a partner, the court may order the repayment of the premium, or of such part thereof as it thinks just, having regard to the terms of the partnership contract and to the length of time during which the partnership has continued, unless,

(a) the dissolution is, in the judgment of the court, wholly or chiefly due to the misconduct of the partner who paid the premium; or

(b) the partnership has been dissolved by an agreement containing no provision for a return of a part of the premium.

41. Where a partnership contract is rescinded on the ground of the fraud or misrepresentation of one of the parties thereto, the party entitled to rescind is, without prejudice to any other right, entitled,

(a) to a lien on, or right of retention of, the surplus of the partnership assets, after satisfying the partnership liabilities, for any sum of money paid by the party for the purchase of a share in the partnership and for any capital contributed by him or her; and

(b) to stand in the place of the creditors of the firm for any payments made by the party in respect of the partnership liabilities; and

(c) to be indemnified by the person guilty of the fraud or making the representation against all the debts and liabilities of the firm.

42.(1) Where any member of a firm dies or otherwise ceases to be a partner and the surviving or continuing partners carry on the business of the firm with its capital or assets without any final settlement of accounts as between the firm and the outgoing partner or his or her estate, then, in the absence of an agreement to the contrary, the outgoing partner or his or her estate is entitled, at the option of the outgoing partner or his or her representatives, to such share of the profits made since the dissolution as the court finds to be attributable to the use of the outgoing partner's share of the partnership assets, or to interest at the rate of 5 per cent per annum on the amount of his or her share of the partnership assets.

(2) Where by the partnership contract an option is given to surviving or continuing partners to purchase the interest of a deceased or outgoing partner and that option is duly exercised, the estate of the deceased partner, or the outgoing partner or his or her estate, as the case may be, is not entitled to any further or other share of profits, but if any partner, assuming to act in exercise of the option, does not in all material respects comply with the terms thereof, he or she is liable to account under the foregoing provisions of this section.

43. Subject to any agreement between the partners, the amount due from surviving or continuing partners to an outgoing partner or the representatives of a deceased partner in respect of the outgoing or deceased partner's share, is a debt accruing at the date of the dissolution or death.

44. In settling accounts between the partners after a dissolution of partnership, the following rules shall, subject to any agreement, be observed:

1. Losses, including losses and deficiencies of capital, are to be paid first out of profits, next out of capital, and lastly, if necessary, by the partners individually in the proportion in which they were entitled to share profits.

2. The assets of the firm, including the sums, if any, contributed by the partners to make up losses or deficiencies of capital, are to be applied in the following manner and order,

(a) in paying the debts and liabilities of the firm to persons who are not partners therein;

(b) in paying to each partner rateably what is due from the firm to him or her for advances as distinguished from capital;

(c) in paying to each partner rateably what is due from the firm to him or her in respect of capital.

3. After making the payments required by paragraph 2, the ultimate residue, if any, is to be divided among the partners in the proportion in which profits are divisible.

---

2. An Overview of Agency Law

Sections 6-13 of the Ontario Partnerships Act (OPA) are based on agency principles, which govern when an agent may bind his principal in contract or tort to a third party. A knowledge of agency concepts is also necessary in corporate law, for a corporation can act only through agents.

In a business context, the agency relationship usually arises through a consensual relationship between agent and principal in which the former agrees to act for the latter in such a way as to create a binding contract between the principal and a third party. Disputes about such obligations are most likely to be litigated when the existence of the contractual bond between principal and third party is denied by one of them. Such problems are resolved by determining whether an agency relationship existed and what the scope of the agent's authority was.

If the agency relationship is normally said to be consensual, it need not be contractual. No consideration is required to support it. Moreover, it may generally be constituted without formalities. One exception to this exists in land law, since an agent to execute a deed must be appointed under deed.

Actual and Apparent Authority. There are two major ways in which an agent can bind his principal to a third party. The first of these arises by agreement between principal and agent, whereby the former clothes the latter with *actual authority* to act on his behalf. The scope of the authority depends solely on the terms of the agency agreement and may exceed that normally given to agents of that kind. The authority need not relate to the principal's ordinary course of business. See OPA s. 8. Nor does it matter that the third party thinks he is contracting with the agent and is not aware of the principal's existence. Such an *undisclosed principal* may take the benefits and is subject to the burdens of such a contract. For example, in a four-person firm, all partners may be liable even if the third party only knew of three of them.

The agreement may be either express or implied. Express authority will arise when the scope of an officer's duties is defined in the employment contract or firm charter. Implied authority simply fills in the gaps left by the parties in their express agreement, and is also a species of actual authority. Thus, appointing a person to a particular senior position in a firm may amount to a grant of authority, if that position normally carries with it certain responsibilities that are not negatived in the express terms of the agreement. For example, a general manager might ordinarily have authority to enter into a wide variety of contracts on behalf of the firm in the ordinary course of its business. However, when the general manager's actual authority is restricted by an express term, contracts that contravene the restriction cannot be upheld by reference to the agent's actual authority.

The second major way by which an agent can bind his principal is by means of *ostensible authority*. This is sometimes referred to as apparent authority or agency by estoppel. It arises not by agreement between principal and agent but through the relationship between principal and third party. The principal holds out the agent as possessing the actual authority to bind the principal, and the third party contracts with the agent in reliance on this representation. Thereafter the principal is estopped from denying the agent's authority.

In some cases, the ostensible authority may fairly be described as consensual, insofar as the principal has consented to a representation to the third party that the agent is clothed with authority. But the principal's behaviour may often seem less consensual than negligent, except in the technical sense that he is estopped from denying that he agreed to the grant of authority. Ostensible authority should probably not even be described as authority, since the principal does not authorize the agent to act on his behalf. Nevertheless, the agent has the power to bind the principal because the latter has created an appearance of actual authority.

The distinction between actual and apparent authority is not always clear. If an agent contracts for his firm in the normal course of his duties, the firm may be liable under either implied actual authority or ostensible authority. But if the agent's authority is restricted by express agreement to something less than that usually associated with his position so that implied authority is negatived, the firm may still be liable under ostensible authority. It will then be necessary for the firm to communicate the restriction to third parties if it wishes not to be bound. See OPA ss. 6, 9 and 36.

Efficiency Explanations. A justification for doctrines of ostensible authority may be sought on efficiency grounds. Contracts entered into by an agent without actual authority represent a possible harm to one or other of the parties, and may be thought of as the tort of "wrongful contracting." In a hypothetical bargain between principal and third party, the parties would seek to minimize the level of wrongful contracting, so long as the marginal cost of harm avoidance is less than the marginal cost of wrongful contracting. That is to say, the parties will continue to invest in harm prevention (the taking of care) until $1 spent on harm prevention no longer generates a $1 gain in reduced harm. Further investments in harm prevention will be inefficient, in the sense that more money will have been spent to prevent harm than is saved in harm forgone. If one party has unique harm reduction skills, both parties will then seek to assign the harm prevention role to him, with his promise to take care made more creditable by his assumption of liability on default. In this way, the imposition of liability on the party best able to prevent the loss (the *least cost risk avoider*) is Kaldor-Hicks efficient.

Efficiency theories also explain why the principal should bear the risk of wrongful contracting when the contract is in the agent's usual course of the authority, and there is nothing to alert the third party of the possibility of wrongful contracting. While the third party may undoubtedly do a variety of things to verify the grant of authority, it is likely that the principal can prevent the harm at lower cost through his hiring and training procedures as well as through such devices as standard form documents. When the transaction is an extraordinary one, on the other hand, it may be cheaper for the third party to confirm the authority by speaking to the principal or to a superior agent, and here the doctrine of ostensible authority would ordinarily not bind the principal.

The analysis thus far suggests that the principle of ostensible authority in OPA s. 6 serves efficiency purposes. However, a further justification is required for the mandatory nature of the provision. In this respect, it may be instructive to compare s. 6 with OPA s. 24, which details the governance structures of the firm. While s. 6 is mandatory, s. 24 is merely presumptive. OPA s. 20 explicitly permits partners in a partnership agreement to change the governance structures that otherwise would be implied by s. 24, but this privilege does not extend to the liability rules of ss. 6-18.

The presumptive governance rules of OPA s. 24 serve efficiency purposes insofar as they provide the parties with approximately the same management structure for which they would otherwise have bargained. This will reduce the transaction costs that the parties would have incurred in drafting their partnership agreement absent the statute. So long as the costs of bargaining over governance structures are positive, the implication in s. 24 of the same terms that the parties would have bargained for will permit them to prepare an express partnership agreement with greater economy. Legislative *gap-filling* then reduces the costs of bargaining.

Though gap-filling theories supply a justification for a presumptive legal rule, it would clearly be inconvenient to prevent partners from bargaining around s. 24. While the governance structure proposed by the provision may be preferred in many firms, it is not to be presumed that one size fits all. For example, review the method in which management responsibilities are allocated by s. 24 and ask yourself whether Gagnon, Gray and Smith would wish to adopt all such rules in the firm they are organizing. What about the presumptive right of any one partner to terminate the partnership under OPA ss. 26(1) and 32(c)? If the justification for a presumptive rule is that it would have been desired by the parties, a contrary provision in an express agreement must be taken as better evidence of their wishes.

Unlike OPA s. 24, the ostensible ownership principle in OPA s. 6 is mandatory, and cannot be varied in an express partnership agreement. Ostensible ownership appears to serve efficiency goals, but something more than this is required to justify a mandatory regime. However, mandatory rules might economize on information production costs when (1) it prescribes efficient behaviour, and (2) transaction costs or other barriers would prevent the parties from devising optimal rules in a non-mandatory regime. In the context of OPA s. 6, a hypothetical claimholder's bargain would require partners of the firm to agree to a rule of ostensible authority, such that the first part of this test would be met. In addition, the second step would also seem satisfied as a consequence of the information costs that would arise if the rule were merely presumptive. Were partners permitted to bargain around s. 6 in their partnership agreement, outside creditors would have to examine the agreement to determine whether or not they had done so. This investigation would impose its own screening (information production) costs, and indeed it was these very barriers that suggested the efficiency of s. 6. Mandatory rules such as s. 6 then provide a simple solution to the problem. This explanation of mandatory rules also suggests why the governance structures of OPA s. 24 should not be made mandatory. Since the parties affected by the rule are only the partners themselves, their screening costs in reading the partnership agreement are presumably slight in most cases.

Freeman & Lockyer v. Buckhurst Park Properties (Mangal) Ltd.
English Court of Appeal
[1964] 2 Q.B. 480, [1964] 2 W.L.R. 618

[The following recitation of facts has been excerpted from the opinion of Willmer L.J.]

The plaintiffs, who carry on business as architects and surveyors, bring this action to recover fees alleged to be due to them in respect of work done during the autumn of 1959 in relation to Buckhurst Park Estate at Sunninghill, the property of the defendant company. The plaintiffs received their instructions in August, 1959, from the second defendant, Shiv Kumar Kapoor, who was at all material times a director of the defendant company. The plaintiffs admittedly executed the work which they were employed to do, and there is no dispute as to the quantum of the fees earned by them, namely, £291 6s. The question is whether the liability in respect of those fees is that of the defendant company or that of the second defendant, Kapoor. By an amendment Kapoor was added as second defendant, but at all material times up to the date of trial his whereabouts were unknown, and he was never served with the proceedings. The action accordingly proceeded against the defendant company alone. The trial took place before Judge Herbert at Westminster County Court on three days during March and April, 1963, and by a reserved judgment which he delivered on May 2, 1963, he found in favour of the plaintiffs. The defendant company now appeals to this court, contending that the liability is not theirs but that of Kapoor.

In September, 1958, Kapoor entered into a contract to purchase Buckhurst Park Estate for a sum of £75,000. Unfortunately for him he had not sufficient cash resources to enable him to complete the purchase. In these circumstances he sought and obtained assistance from Nimarjit Singh Hoon, who was willing to advance a sum of approximately £40,000. On October 11, 1958, the two men entered into a written agreement (a copy of which is before us) whereby they agreed to form a private limited company with a nominal capital of £70,000 which they were to subscribe in equal shares. The directors of the company were to be Kapoor and Hoon and a nominee of each. The object of the company was as soon as practicable to complete the purchase of the Buckhurst Park Estate.

In due course the defendant company was formed, and it was provided by article 12 of the articles of association that the directors were to be Kapoor and Hoon, together with Cohen (described in the memorandum of association as a company director, but in fact a managing clerk employed by Kapoor's solicitors) who was Kapoor's nominee, and Hubbard (a managing clerk employed by Hoon's solicitors) who was Hoon's nominee. Article 14 of the articles of association made provision for alternate directors to act in the place of any director who might be unable to be present at a meeting. By article 19 it was provided that the quorum necessary for the transaction of the business of the directors should be four.

The property was duly conveyed to the company, and the minutes of the first meeting of the board held on December 11, 1958, record that it was resolved that the company's seal should be affixed to the conveyance. It had been agreed between Kapoor and Hoon that, pending resale of the property, the running expenses of maintaining it were to be defrayed by Kapoor personally, and that he was to be reimbursed out of the profit of the resale. This agreement appears to have been accepted by the board, although I cannot find that it was ever the subject of any resolution at a board meeting. A board meeting was held on April 3, 1959, by which time it is clear from the minutes that any prospect of a quick resale of the property had already disappeared. It is to be observed that none of the resolutions purported to be carried at this board meeting could be of any legal effect since only three members of the board were present thereat. The minutes of the meeting, however, are of considerable evidential value as showing what was taking place at the time and what was in the minds of the respective parties. The minutes show (1) that Kapoor (through another of his companies called Gurjveer Ltd.) was in fact paying the expenses of upkeep of Buckhurst Park and thereby discharging his obligation to maintain the property, and (2) that consideration was being given to the obtaining of planning permission for the development of the property. There was in fact a purported resolution authorising payment on account of £100 to agents who had been employed.

In the summer of 1959 Kapoor instructed an architect, one Hayler, to make application for planning permission for certain development in respect of Buckhurst Park Estate. This Hayler proceeded to do, and an application for planning permission was submitted by him dated July 8, 1959. It is noteworthy that this application was expressed to be made on behalf of Kapoor personally as owner. The application was in fact refused by a notice of refusal dated August 10, 1959. In the meantime, however, on August 4 or 5 Kapoor instructed the plaintiffs to act for him because, as he said, he wanted a local firm to act on his behalf. The plaintiffs duly submitted a fresh application for planning permission dated September 1, 1959, which was again expressed to be made on behalf of Kapoor as owner. A little later they also entered an appeal on behalf of Kapoor against the refusal of the original application for planning permission. During the ensuing months the plaintiffs did other work for Kapoor, not only in respect of Buckhurst Park Estate, but also on behalf of several of his other companies. The fees due to them in respect of work done for the other companies have all been paid, but those relating to work in respect of the Buckhurst Park Estate remain outstanding, and form the subject of the present action. The work done by the plaintiffs in respect of the Buckhurst Park Estate falls under three heads, namely, (a) submitting application of planning permission and preparing appeal against the refusal of the application made by Hayler; (b) preparing plans of each floor of the main house and ancillary buildings; and (c) defining the boundaries of the estate and preparing plans. So far as concerned the work done in respect of the Buckhurst Park Estate, David Peter Freeman of the plaintiff firm gave evidence, which was corroborated by Mackay, that he was instructed by Kapoor on behalf of the defendant company. This evidence was specifically accepted by the judge.

The plaintiffs contended (1) that on the true inference from all the facts Kapoor had actual authority to engage the plaintiffs on behalf of the defendant company; alternatively (2) that Kapoor was held out by the defendant company as having ostensible authority, so that the latter is estopped from denying responsibility for his acts. The submissions on behalf of the defendant company are conveniently summarised in paragraphs 2 and 3 of the defence as follows: "2. ... The said Kapoor was at all material times a director of the defendants, but the defendants deny that he was authorised expressly or impliedly to enter into the alleged or any agreement with the plaintiffs for and on behalf of the defendants. 3. Further, or in the alternative, the said Kapoor at all material times acted without the knowledge and/or the approval of the defendants, and/ or outside the scope of his authority as a director of the defendant company." The judge found that Kapoor, although never appointed as managing director, had throughout been acting as such in employing agents and taking other steps to find a purchaser, and that this was well known to the board. In the light of this finding he gave judgment in favour of the plaintiffs, basing himself upon the principles stated by Lopes L.J. in *Biggerstaff v. Rowatt's Wharf Ltd.* [[1896] 2 Ch. 93, 104, C.A.]. I take this to be a finding, not that Kapoor had actual authority to employ the plaintiffs, but that in doing so he was acting within the scope of his ostensible authority.

DIPLOCK L.J.: The county court judge made the following findings of fact: (1) that the plaintiffs intended to contract with Kapoor as agent for the company, and not on his own account; (2) that the board of the company intended that Kapoor should do what he could to obtain the best possible price for the estate; (3) that Kapoor, although never appointed as managing director, had throughout been acting as such in employing agents and taking other steps to find a purchaser; (4) that Kapoor was so acting was well known to the board. The only findings which have been challenged on appeal are (3) and (4), but for the reasons given by Willmer L.J. I think that the challenge failed.

The county court judge did not hold (although he might have done) that actual authority had been conferred upon Kapoor by the board to employ agents. He proceeded on the basis of apparent authority, that is, that the defendant company had so acted as to be estopped from denying Kapoor's authority. This rendered it unnecessary for the judge to inquire whether actual authority to employ agents had been conferred upon Kapoor by the board to whom the management of the company's business was confided by the articles of association.

•   •   •

It is necessary at the outset to distinguish between an "actual" authority of an agent on the one hand, and an "apparent" or "ostensible" authority on the other. Actual authority and apparent authority are quite independent of one another. Generally they co-exist and coincide, but either may exist without the other and their respective scopes may be different. As I shall endeavour to show, it is upon the apparent authority of the agent that the contractor normally relies in the ordinary course of business when entering into contracts.

An "actual" authority is a legal relationship between principal and agent created by a consensual agreement to which they alone are parties. Its scope is to be ascertained by applying ordinary principles of construction of contracts, including any proper implications from the express words used, the usages of the trade, or the course of business between the parties. To this agreement the contractor is a stranger; he may be totally ignorant of the existence of any authority on the part of the agent. Nevertheless, if the agent does enter into a contract pursuant to the "actual" authority, it does create contractual rights and liabilities between the principal and the contractor. It may be that this rule relating to "undisclosed principals," which is peculiar to English law, can be rationalized as avoiding circuity of action, for the principal could in equity compel the agent to lend his name in an action to enforce the contract against the contractor, and would at common law be liable to indemnify the agent in respect of the performance of the obligations assumed by the agent under the contract.

An "apparent" or "ostensible" authority, on the other hand, is a legal relationship between the principal and the contractor created by a representation, made by the principal to the contractor, intended to be and in fact acted upon by the contractor, that the agent has authority to enter on behalf of the principal into a contract of a kind within the scope of the "apparent" authority, so as to render the principal liable to perform any obligations imposed upon him by such contract. To the relationship so created the agent is a stranger. He need not be (although he generally is) aware of the existence of the representation but he must not purport to make the agreement as principal himself. The representation, when acted upon by the contractor by entering into a contract with the agent, operates as an estoppel, preventing the principal from asserting that he is not bound by the contract. It is irrelevant whether the agent had actual authority to enter into the contract.

In ordinary business dealings the contractor at the time of entering into the contract can in the nature of things hardly ever rely on the "actual" authority of the agent. His information as to the authority must be derived either from the principal or from the agent or from both, for they alone know what the agent's actual authority is. All that the contractor can know is what they tell him, which may or may not be true. In the ultimate analysis he relies either upon the representation of the principal, that is, apparent authority, or upon the representation of the agent, that is, warranty of authority.

The representation which creates "apparent" authority may take a variety of forms of which the commonest is representation by conduct, that is, by permitting the agent to act in some way in the conduct of the principal's business with other persons. By so doing the principal represents to anyone who becomes aware that the agent is so acting that the agent has authority to enter on behalf of the principal into contracts with other persons of the kind which an agent so acting in the conduct of his principal's business has usually "actual" authority to enter into.

In applying the law as I have endeavoured to summarise it to the case where the principal is not a natural person, but a fictitious person, namely, a corporation, two further factors arising from the legal characteristics of a corporation have to be borne in mind. The first is that the capacity of a corporation is limited by its constitution, that is, in the case of a company incorporated under the Companies Act, by its memorandum and articles of association; the second is that a corporation cannot do any act, and that includes making a representation, except through its agent.

Under the doctrine of ultra vires the limitation of the capacity of a corporation by its constitution to do any acts is absolute. This affects the rules as to the "apparent" authority of an agent of a corporation in two ways. First, no representation can operate to estop the corporation from denying the authority of the agent to do on behalf of the corporation an act which the corporation is not permitted by its constitution to do itself. Secondly, since the conferring of actual authority upon an agent is itself an act of the corporation, the capacity to do which is regulated by its constitution, the corporation cannot be estopped from denying that it has conferred upon a particular agent authority to do acts which by its constitution, it is incapable of delegating to that particular agent.

To recognise that these are direct consequences of the doctrine of ultra vires is, I think, preferable to saying that a contractor who enters into a contract with a corporation has constructive notice of its constitution, for the expression "constructive notice" tends to disguise that constructive notice is not a positive, but a negative doctrine, like that of estoppel of which it forms a part. It appears to prevent the contractor from saying that he did not know that the constitution of the corporation rendered a particular act or a particular delegation of authority ultra vires the corporation. It does not entitle him to say that he relied upon some unusual provision in the constitution of the corporation if he did not in fact so rely.

The second characteristic of a corporation, namely, that unlike a natural person it can only make a representation through an agent, has the consequence that in order to create an estoppel between the corporation and the contractor, the representation as to the authority of the agent which creates his "apparent" authority must be made by some person or persons who have "actual" authority from the corporation to make the representation. Such "actual" authority may be conferred by the constitution of the corporation itself, as, for example, in the case of a company, upon the board of directors, or it may be conferred by those who under its constitution have the powers of management upon some other person to whom the constitution permits them to delegate authority to make representations of this kind. It follows that where the agent upon whose "apparent" authority the contractor relies has no "actual" authority from the corporation to enter into a particular kind of contract with the contractor on behalf of the corporation, the contractor cannot rely upon the agent's own representation as to his actual authority. He can rely only upon a representation by a person or persons who have actual authority to manage or conduct that part of the business of the corporation to which the contract relates.

The commonest form of representation by a principal creating an "apparent" authority of an agent is by conduct, namely, by permitting the agent to act in the management or conduct of the principal's business. Thus, if in the case of a company the board of directors who have "actual" authority under the memorandum and articles of association to manage the company's business permit the agent to act in the management or conduct of the company's business, they thereby represent to all persons dealing with such agent that he has authority to enter on behalf of the corporation into contracts of a kind which an agent authorised to do acts of the kind which he is in fact permitted to do usually enters into in the ordinary course of such business. The making of such a representation is itself an act of management of the company's business. Prima facie it falls within the "actual" authority of the board of directors, and unless the memorandum or articles of the company either make such a contract ultra vires the company or prohibit the delegation of such authority to the agent, the company is estopped from denying to anyone who has entered into a contract with the agent in reliance upon such "apparent" authority that the agent had authority to contract on behalf of the company.

If the foregoing analysis of the relevant law is correct, it can be summarised by stating four conditions which must be fulfilled to entitle a contractor to enforce against a company a contract entered into on behalf of the company by an agent who had no actual authority to do so. It must be shown:

(1) that a representation that the agent had authority to enter on behalf of the company into a contract of the kind sought to be enforced was made to the contractor;
(2) that such representation was made by a person or persons who had "actual" authority to manage the business of the company either generally or in respect of those matters to which the contract relates;
(3) that he (the contractor) was induced by such representation to enter into the contract, that is, that he in fact relied upon it; and
(4) that under its memorandum or articles of association the company was not deprived of the capacity either to enter into a contract of the kind sought to be enforced or to delegate authority to enter into a contract of that kind to the agent.

The confusion which, I venture to think, has sometimes crept into the cases is in my view due to a failure to distinguish between these four separate conditions, and in particular to keep steadfastly in mind (a) that the only "actual" authority which is relevant is that of the persons making the representation relied upon, and (b) that the memorandum and articles of association of the company are always relevant (whether they are in fact known to the contractor or not) to the questions (i) whether condition (2) is fulfilled, and (ii) whether condition (4) is fulfilled, and (but only if they are in fact known to the contractor) may be relevant (iii) as part of the representation on which the contractor relied.

• • •

In the present case the findings of fact by the county court judge are sufficient to satisfy the four conditions, and thus to establish that Kapoor had "apparent" authority to enter into contracts on behalf of the company for their services in connection with the sale of the company's property, including the obtaining of development permission with respect to its use. The judge found that the board knew that Kapoor had throughout been acting as managing director in employing agents and taking other steps to find a purchaser. They permitted him to do so, and by such conduct represented that he had authority to enter into contracts of a kind which a managing director or an executive director responsible for finding a purchaser would in the normal course be authorised to enter into on behalf of the company. Condition (1) was thus fulfilled. The articles of association conferred full powers of management on the board. Condition (2) was thus fulfilled. The plaintiffs, finding Kapoor acting in relation to the company's property as he was authorised by the board to act, were induced to believe that he was authorised by the company to enter into contracts on behalf of the company for their services in connection with the sale of the company's property, including the obtaining of development permission with respect to its use. Condition (3) was thus fulfilled. The articles of association, which contained powers for the board to delegate any of the functions of management to a managing director or to a single director, did not deprive the company of capacity to delegate authority to Kapoor, a director, to enter into contracts of that kind on behalf of the company. Condition (4) was thus fulfilled.

I think the judgment was right, and would dismiss the appeal.

Appeal dismissed with costs.
Leave to appeal refused.

Ratification. If an agent, without actual or apparent authority, purports to act on behalf of a principal when dealing with the third party, the principal may subsequently ratify the contract. The contract between principal and third party will then be as valid as if it had been originally made with actual authority.

Ratification is not permitted where it would unfairly prejudice a third party, as when a long time has elapsed. *Metropolitan Asylums Board Managers v. Kingham &*

Sons (1890), 6 T.L.R. 217. But no consideration by the third party to the principal is required to support a ratification. And a contract may be ratified notwithstanding that the third party has given notice that he wishes to withdraw from it. *Bolton Partners v. Lambert* (1889), 41 Ch. D. 295. On the other hand, if the principal decides to ratify the contract, he cannot afterwards unilaterally set it aside.

As between principal and third party, the doctrine of ratification operates uniquely for the benefit of the former: if the bargain turns out to have been a good one for him, he can ratify; if it is bad, he can walk away. If this might seem anomalous, the doctrine of ratification may be defended as efficient, and therefore as replicating a provision in a hypothetical bargain. To see this, note how ratification is symmetrical with the doctrine of ostensible authority. That doctrine places upon the third party the risk that a contract not in the usual course of the agent's actual authority (or one for which the agent has not been held out to the third party as authorized) will not bind the principal, on the theory that the third party is in the best position to verify the agent's actual authority. Now, if the third party is the person best able to determine that non-ordinary course contracts are unauthorized, he would also seem in the best position to determine whether the principal will adopt them. In both cases, it comes down to the third party communicating directly with the principal. As a result, the principal will normally bear all risk of wrongful contracting by agents acting in the usual course of their authority, and the third party will normally take the risks in all other cases. This may explain some of the otherwise puzzling features of the doctrine of ratification, such as the inability of the third party to withdraw from the contract prior to the act of ratification. If ratification is justified on the basis of what the third party might have done when negotiating with the agent, a subsequent withdrawal ought not to be effective.

Some other features of the ratification doctrine deserve attention. While the ratifying act often takes the form of an express resolution of the principal, formal approval may not be necessary. Unless the Statute of Frauds requires a writing, ratification might be implied from the principal's action, as where he is seen by his conduct to adopt the contract. Where the principal has formally ratified the contract, however, it is unnecessary to show that either party has changed his position in reliance on the contract. Ratification need not work an estoppel.

Duties of Agents. Agents owe fiduciary duties (duties of loyalty) to their principals. Partners, as agents of the firm and of each other under s. 6, must therefore account to the firm for benefits derived from any transaction concerning the firm or from any use of firm property, unless the firm after full disclosure consents to such transactions or use. OPA s. 29. See also ss. 28 and 30. In addition, the right to a winding-up on just and equitable grounds under s. 35(f), while an extreme remedy, has been justified on the basis that the parties would not have wished the firm to continue when mutual expectations of loyalty have disappeared because of the bad faith of one partner. The "just and equitable" winding-up of a corporation is discussed in Chapter Seven.

The general rule is that an agent is not liable to third parties on contracts entered into on behalf of the principal. In some cases, however, an agent is personally liable on the contract. For example, the third party might have insisted on the agent's personal liability if there was a serious risk of the principal's default. Or the agent may have been acting for an undisclosed principal. Apart from this, the agent may be liable for breach of warranty of authority if his acts were unauthorized and the principal does not ratify. Agents are presumed to warrant that they have the authority to bind their principals when entering into agreements with third parties. *Yonge v. Toynbee*, [1910] 1 K.B. 215 (C.A.). Agent liability in these circumstances will serve efficiency goals if it is feared that, without a warranty of authority, the agent may negotiate an excessive number of unauthorized contracts. Warranty of authority therefore implicates a tripartite liability strategy in the reduction of wrongful contracting costs. The warranty, it should be noted, is simply that the principal authorizes the act; there is no warranty that he will perform the contract. Damages for breach of warranty of authority will ordinarily be nominal if the principal turns out to have been insolvent.

The above is merely a skeletal outline of agency principles, some of which will be observed more closely in the following materials on corporate law. There are, however, many excellent texts on agency that one may profitably consult. See F. Reynolds & B. Davenport, *Bowstead on Agency* (14th ed. 1976); W. Seavey, *Handbook of the Law of Agency* (1964). The leading text on partnership law is E. Scamell & R. Banks, *Lindley on the Law of Partnership* (15th ed. 1984).

NOTES

1) Assume that Gagnon, Gray and Smith decide to work together to produce Smith's program at Gagon's plant. Do the parties become partners at that point?

2) Assuming that the parties are partners, what are the terms of their partnership under the OPA? How are profits to be divided? How are management decisions to be taken? Can one of the parties terminate the partnership unilaterally? How many of these terms, imposed by statute in the absence of contrary intention, will the parties wish to vary? Is it possible to do so in an oral agreement? Even then, as a matter of prudence, would you prefer a written partnership agreement?

3) Suppose that, in the firm of Gagnon, Gray and Smith, Gagnon is charged by the other two parties with the responsibility for making ordinary business decisions, with the proviso that purchases of components at a cost exceeding $1,000 are to be cleared with the other two partners. Nevertheless, Gagnon agrees to buy computer components from Brown for $1,500 without obtaining such approval. Is the firm bound by this agreement? Is Gray liable for the debt?

4) Assume that, by virtue of Smith's negligence, a computer program custom made by the firm for a law firm proves defective, erasing all records of the law firm's accounts receivable. A claim for damages of $500,000 is brought by the law firm. Is the firm of Gagnon, Gray and Smith liable for this breach? Could the law firm sue Gagnon for the entire amount of the loss, on the basis that he has the deepest pockets?

5) On dissolution, what scheme of distribution is provided in OPA ss. 4 and 44 as between trade creditors, ordinary partners and partners who have lent the firm money in the manner provided by OPA s. 3.3(d)?

3. Choice of Enterprise Organization

Cameron, The Form and Organization of the Business Entity
Advising the Small Businessman 1-5
(Law Society of Upper Canada 1977)

Alternative Forms of Business Entity

The alternative forms of business entity by or through which a person may carry on business in Ontario are:

(1) Sole Proprietorship;
(2) Partnership (including Joint Ventures and Syndicates);
(3) Limited Partnership; and
(4) Corporation with Share Capital.

Criteria for Selection

The reasons for selecting one form in preference to the others will normally be determined by some of the following considerations applied to the circumstances.

Limited Liability and Nature of Business

A corporation is an entity separate and distinct from its shareholders. The corporation owns and operates the business and incurs the liabilities. Each partner is a co-owner of the partnership assets.

A sole proprietor is liable and partners are jointly and severally liable to the full extent of their personal assets for liabilities of their businesses. A shareholder's liability to the creditors of the corporation is limited to the amount of his investment.

However, the directors, officers and major shareholders of a corporation have specific statutory liabilities to the shareholders and creditors of the corporation in such areas as issuance of shares for improper consideration, wages, filing of tax and annual returns, directors' conflicting interests in contracts with the company, improper declaration of dividends, improper loans to shareholders, etc. ...

If a substantial uninsurable risk is possible, a limited partnership or corporation is preferable to limit the proprietor's liability to the amount of capital he has invested and isolate his personal assets from execution to satisfy liabilities of the business.

There are certain tax considerations which depend on the nature of the business mentioned below.

Desirability of Perpetual Existence

A corporation can have a perpetual existence and will not dissolve on the death of a shareholder or director. If the venture is for a limited time only, partnership may be preferable.

Unless there are provisions to the contrary in the partnership agreement, death or a minor difference of opinion provoking a notice to dissolve could result in a dissolution and it would be necessary to renegotiate major contracts, file notices of dissolution and a new declaration of partnership, enter a new agreement, provide for new banking signing authorities. A partnership might have to dissolve to pay a deceased partner's estate or retiring partner's interest unless there is buy-sell provision in the agreement. The dislocation of the business on the death of a sole proprietor is even more serious.

A corporation continues notwithstanding the death or withdrawal of a shareholder or a director and the remaining directors carry on the business. In a corporation, the shares would be more readily marketable on distribution than interests in a partnership and there would not necessarily be any loss of cash to the corporation on the death of a shareholder.

Dissolution of a corporation is a more complex procedure than dissolution of a partnership.

Number and Relationship of Proposed Proprietors

If there is a large number or if the public are to be offered any securities, incorporation is preferable because of the absence of any duty of good faith to other shareholders and its established and accepted rules for control, procedures, investors' rights, limited liability and flexibility of financing. In addition, it is much simpler to transfer shares in a corporation than to either execute new partnership agreements or amend subsisting agreements on admission of new partners or to assign separately the business assets belonging to a sole proprietorship.

All partners in a general partnership are entitled to participate in the business, subject to contrary agreement. One partner can bind the partnership. A shareholder alone is not entitled to participate in the corporation's business and cannot subject the corporation to obligations.

A shareholder can contract with or sue the corporation but a partner cannot contract with or sue the firm. A partner must contract with and sue the partners individually.

Degree of Participation and Assumption of Financial Risks by Each Proprietor

If some proprietors want to limit the risk or have greater security for their investment than others, or if there are to be several degrees of control and of risk taking, some bordering on the status of lenders, incorporation and the varying classes of shares and conditions available will be preferable.

Minority shareholders are subject to the will of the majority and their shares are not very marketable in the absence of a compulsory buy-sell agreement on retirement of a shareholder. In a partnership, if they want out and the majority will not buy them out, they can normally dissolve the partnership and require liquidation of the assets.

Borrowing Requirements, Available Terms and Relationship of Proposed Lenders

The liabilities of a corporation or a limited partnership are limited to its assets. Many lenders will require guarantees by principal shareholders or limited partners which will nullify for them the advantages of limited liability offered by limited partnerships or incorporation.

If securities are to be issued to arm's-length lenders or the public, incorporation will make them more marketable, enable flexibility and financing will thus be easier.

Some lenders may insist on an equity position or a right to it which will indicate incorporation since it could be easier to issue new shares than admit a new partner.

If borrowings are to be from a non-arm's length foreigner, interest on borrowings in excess of three times the equity of a corporation is not a deductible expense for income tax purposes; such "thin capitalization" rules can be avoided if the borrower is not a corporation.

Availability of Government Grants

Some grants and loans are available only to corporations.

•   •   •

Estate Planning

(a) Freezing of taxable value of a father's interest on death at present value and permitting growth of business to enure to his son free of capital gains or succession duties on the father's death can be done by giving the son one common share for a nominal value and the father taking back a note or preferred shares with a par value in exchange for the assets of his business transferred to the corporation (there are hazards which should be considered carefully before embarking on such a plan);

(b) Passing on an interest in the business to one or more legatees who will not take part in the operation of the business is best done by shares in a corporation;

(c) In the event of the death of a shareholder, only the shares and not the assets are frozen pending succession duty releases. The directors of the corporation can sell the assets when they wish in order to minimize losses which might accrue if the assets are frozen.

•   •   •

Proprietor's Other Income

Partnership profits are payable regularly to the partners but a poor shareholder who relies on his dividends could be subject to the decision of wealthy directors to [forgo] dividends and reinvest profits in the business. This factor should be weighed against the tax advantage to take a minimal salary and the balance of profit by way of dividend.

Number and Location of Offices and Establishments

A partnership must register under The Partnerships Registration Act, R.S.O. 1970, c. 340. A corporation which is a partner must register under that Act or The Corporations Information Act, 1976, S.O. 1976, c. 66, s. 2 and possibly both. If operating in another province, that province's partnership laws and registration provisions will apply to the partnership in that province. A corporation may have to register as an extra-provincial company.

Employees' Share

In order to give employees a share in growth and profits without the management rights of a partner, incorporation is indicated.

Expenses and Changes

Preparation of or changes to a carefully drawn partnership agreement can cost as much or more in legal fees as incorporation or major corporate amendments but fees payable to government are less. A partnership agreement can be changed by agreement or as provided in the agreement and capital can be easily withdrawn. Major corporate changes require approvals by directors and shareholders and filing of amending documents.

The Corporations Tax Act (Ontario) imposes not only a tax on income but also a tax of 3/10 of 1% on the taxable paid up capital of the corporation which includes paid up capital, surplus, loans from corporations (excluding a bank) and all secured debt. (Minimum of $50 for paid up capital of up to $50,000; flat $100 if paid up capital between $50,000 and $100,000.)

Corporations must also keep records, comply with certain formalities respecting maintenance of records and procedures to withdraw capital, qualify to carry on business in other jurisdictions which are continuing and additional costs not required by law of proprietorships or partnerships.

Prestige

Is the intangible *prestige* of incorporation desirable? Is it too sophisticated?

Corporate Partnership—Flexibility

A corporation may have in its articles of incorporation any provision that could be contained in a by-law (... C.B.C.A., s. 6(2)). In addition, under the C.B.C.A., a "unanimous shareholders agreement" is permitted (C.B.C.A., s. 146). Effective use of these provisions permits the flexibility and controls available under a partnership agreement.

---

4. Limitations on Liability

Martin v. Peyton
New York Court of Appeals
158 N.E. 77 (1927)

[The investment firm of Knauth, Nachod & Kuhne found itself in financial difficulties in 1921. One of the partners, Hall, was a friend of one Peyton, who loaned the firm $500,000 in bonds to use as collateral to secure bank advances. But this was not enough to rescue the firm. Hall therefore approached Peyton and two other parties, Perkins and Freeman, with a suggestion that they become partners in Knauth, Nachod & Kuhne. They refused, but agreed to lend the firm $2,500,00 in liquid securities. The agreement provided:

the parties of the first part [Peyton, Perkins and Freeman] shall not be interested in "profits" as such. Their interest in profits shall be construed merely as a measure of compensation for loaning said active securities to said firm and granting permission to the firm to hypothecate the same, and for the services to be rendered by the Trustees. The parties of the first part shall not be responsible for any losses that may be made by said firm. The parties of the first part shall not in any way be deemed or treated or held as partners in said firm. No one of the parties of the first part shall be under any partnership liability or obligation. ... [219 N.Y. App. Div. 297, 302]

When the firm failed, its creditors sought to recover from Peyton, Perkins and Freeman as partners.]

ANDREWS J.: ... Partnership results from contract, express or implied. If denied, it may be proved by the production of some written instrument, by testimony as to some conversation, by circumstantial evidence. If nothing else appears, the receipt by the defendant of a share of the profits of the business is enough. ...

Assuming some written contract between the parties, the question may arise whether it creates a partnership. If it be complete, if it expresses in good faith the full understanding and obligation of the parties, then it is for the court to say whether a partnership exists. It may, however, be a mere sham intended to hide the real relationship. Then other results follow. In passing upon it, effect is to be given to each provision. Mere words will not blind us to realities. Statements that no partnership is intended are not conclusive. If as a whole a contract contemplates an association of two or more persons to carry on as co-owners a business for profit, a partnership there is. Section 10. On the other hand, if it be less than this, no partnership exists. Passing on the contract as a whole, an arrangement for sharing profits is to be considered. It is to be given its due weight. But it is to be weighed in connection with all the rest. It is not decisive. It may be merely the method adopted to pay a debt or wages, as interest on a loan or for other reasons.

• • •

Remitted then, as we are, to the documents themselves, we refer to circumstances surrounding their execution only so far as is necessary to make them intelligible. And we are to remember that although the intention of the parties to avoid liability as partners is clear, although in language precise and definite they deny any design to then join the firm of K. N. & K.; although they say their interests in profits should be construed merely as a measure of compensation for loans, not an interest in profits as such; although they provide that they shall not be liable for any losses or treated as partners, the question still remains whether in fact they agree to so associate themselves with the firm as to "carry on as co-owners a business for profit."

• • •

The respondents were to loan K. N. & K. $2,500,000 worth of liquid securities, which were to be returned to them on or before April 15, 1923. The firm might hypothecate them to secure loans totalling $2,000,000, using the proceeds as its business necessities required. To insure respondents against loss K. N. & K. were to turn over to them a large number of their own securities which may have been valuable, but which were of so speculative a nature that they could not be used as collateral for bank loans. In compensation for the loan the respondents were to receive 40 per cent of the profits of the firm until the return was made, not exceeding, however, $500,000, and not less than $100,000. Merely because the transaction involved the transfer of securities and not of cash does not prevent its being a loan, within the meaning of section 11. The respondents also were given an option to join the firm if they, or any of them, expressed a desire to do so before June 4, 1923.

• • •

As representing the lenders, Mr. Peyton and Mr. Freeman are called "trustees." The loaned securities when used as collateral are not to be mingled with other securities of K. N. & K., and the trustees at all times are to be kept informed of all transactions affecting them. To them shall be paid all dividends and income accruing therefrom. They may also substitute for any of the securities loaned securities of equal value. With their consent the firm may sell any of its securities held by the respondents, the proceeds to go, however, to the trustees. In other similar ways the trustees may deal with these same securities, but the securities loaned shall always be sufficient in value to permit of their hypothecation for $2,000,000. If they rise in price, the excess may be withdrawn by the defendants. If they fall, they shall make good the deficiency.

So far, there is no hint that the transaction is not a loan of securities with a provision for compensation. Later a somewhat closer connection with the firm appears. Until the securities are returned, the directing management of the firm is to be in the hands of John R. Hall, and his life is to be insured for $1,000,000, and the policies are to be assigned as further collateral security to the trustees. These requirements are not unnatural. Hall was the one known and trusted by the defendants. Their acquaintance with the other members of the firm was of the slightest. These others had brought an old and established business to the verge of bankruptcy. As the respondents knew, they also had engaged in unsafe speculation. The respondents were about to loan $2,500,000 of good securities. As collateral they were to receive others of problematical value. What they required seems but ordinary caution. Nor does it imply an association in the business.

The trustees are to be kept advised as to the conduct of the business and consulted as to important matters. They may inspect the firm books and are entitled to any information they think important. Finally, they may veto any business they think highly speculative or injurious. Again we hold this but a proper precaution to safeguard the loan. The trustees may not initiate any transaction as a partner may do. They may not bind the firm by any action of their own. Under the circumstances the safety of the loan depended upon the business success of K. N. & K. This success was likely to be compromised by the inclination of its members to engage in speculation. No longer, if the respondents were to be protected, should it be allowed. The trustees therefore might prohibit it, and that their prohibition might be effective, information was to be furnished them. Not dissimilar agreements have been held proper to guard the interests of the lender.

As further security each member of K. N. & K. is to assign to the trustees their interest in the firm. No loan by the firm to any member is permitted and the amount each may draw is fixed. No other distribution of profits is to be made. So that realized profits may be calculated the existing capital is stated to be $700,000, and profits are to be realized as promptly as good business practice will permit. In case the trustees think this is not done, the question is left to them and to Mr. Hall, and if they differ then to an arbitrator. There is no obligation that the firm shall continue the business. It may dissolve at any time. Again we conclude there is nothing here not properly adapted to secure the interest of the respondents as lenders. If their compensation is dependent on a percentage of the profits, still provision must be made to define what these profits shall be.

The "indenture" is substantially a mortgage of the collateral delivered by K. N. & K. to the trustees to secure the performance of the "agreement." It certainly does not strengthen the claim that the respondents were partners.

Finally we have the "option." It permits the respondents, or any of them, or their assignees or nominees to enter the firm at a later date if they desire to do so by buying 50 per cent or less of the interests therein of all or any of the members at a stated price. Or a corporation may, if the respondents and the members agree, be formed in place of the firm. Meanwhile, apparently with the design of protecting the firm business against improper or ill-judged action which might render the option valueless, each member of the firm is to place his resignation in the hands of Mr. Hall. If at any time he and the trustees agree that such resignation should be accepted, that member shall then retire, receiving the value of his interest calculated as of the date of such retirement.

This last provision is somewhat unusual, yet it is not enough in itself to show that on June 4, 1921, a present partnership was created, nor taking these various papers as a whole do we reach such a result. It is quite true that even if one or two or three like provisions contained in such a contract do not require this conclusion, yet it is also true that when taken together a point may come where stipulations immaterial separately cover so wide a field that we should hold a partnership exists. As in other branches of the law, a question of degree is often the determining factor. Here that point has not been reached. *Cox v. Hickman* (1860), 8 H.L. Cas. 268. ...

[CARDOZO C.J. and POUND, CRANE, LEHMAN, KELLOGG and O'BRIEN JJ. concur.]

NOTE

Martin v. Peyton suggests an alternative to the partnership form of organization. The creditors stipulated for a share of the firm's profits while securing a degree of control over its business. They had therefore many of the advantages of membership in a firm without being visited with the unlimited liability of general partners.

Would such an agreement be upheld in Canada? There are few Canadian cases on the distinction between creditors and partners, but the question arose in several English cases. An argument that partnership liability should be imposed on creditors failed in *Cox v. Hickman* (1860), 8 H.L.C. 268, 11 E.R. 431. The firm of B. Smith and Son operated the Stanton Iron Works, which encountered financial difficulties in 1849. At a meeting of creditors, five of them, including Cox and Wheatcroft, were chosen as "trustees." The firm's assets were assigned to the trustees, who were given the power to manage the business for the benefit of the creditors. The trustees' discretion could be fettered by a decision of the creditors at general meetings. The Smiths had no vote in determining how the business was to be managed. Profits were to go first to repay the creditors, with the residue, if any remained, to the Smiths. The business failed a second time, and intervening creditors sought to hold Cox and Wheatcroft liable for firm debts. Cox had never acted as a trustee and Wheatcroft had resigned six weeks after his appointment. The House of Lords held that they were not partners. Lord Cranworth stated that:

It is often said that the test, or one of the tests, whether a person not ostensibly a partner, is nevertheless, in contemplation of law, a partner, is, whether he is entitled to participate in the profits. This, no doubt, is, in general, a sufficiently accurate test; for a right to participate in profits affords cogent, often conclusive evidence, that the trade in which the profits have been made, was carried on in part for or on behalf of the person setting up such a claim. But the real ground of the liability is, that the trade has been carried on by persons acting on his behalf. When that is the case, he is liable to the trade obligations, and entitled to its profits or to a share of them.

· · ·

Taking this to be the ground of liability as a partner, it seems to me to follow that the mere concurrence of creditors in an arrangement under which they permit their debtor, or trustees for their debtor, to continue his trade, applying the profits in discharge of their demands, does not make them partners with their debtor, or the trustees. The debtor is still the person solely interested in the profits, save only that he has mortgaged them to his creditors. He receives the benefit of the profits as they accrue, though he has precluded himself from applying them to any other purpose than the discharge of his debts. The trade is not carried on by or on account of the creditors; though their consent is necessary in such a case, for without it all the property might be seized by them in execution. But the trade still remains the trade of the debtor or his trustees; the debtor or the trustees are the persons by or on behalf of whom it is carried on.

I have hitherto considered the case as it would have stood if the creditors had been merely passively assenting parties to the carrying on of the trade, on the terms that the profits should be applied in liquidation of their demands. But I am aware that in this deed special powers are given to the creditors, which, it was said, showed that they had become partners, even if that had not been the consequence of their concurrence in the previous trust. The powers may be described briefly as, first, a power of determining by a majority in value of their body, that the trade should be discontinued, or, if not discontinued, then, secondly, a power of making rules and orders as to its conduct and management.

These powers do not appear to me to alter the case. The creditors might, by process of law, have obtained possession of the whole of the property. By the earlier provisions of the deed, they consented to abandon that right, and to allow the trade to be carried on by the trustees. The effect of these powers is only to qualify their consent. They stipulate for a right to withdraw it altogether; or, if not, then to impose terms as to the mode in which the trusts to which they had agreed should be executed.

· · ·

I have, on these grounds, come to the conclusion that the creditors did not, by executing this deed, make themselves partners in the Stanton Iron Company, and I must add that a contrary decision would be much to be deprecated. Deeds of arrangement, like that now before us, are, I believe, of frequent occurrence; and it is impossible to imagine that creditors who execute them, have any notion that by so doing they are making themselves liable as partners.

. . .

The deed now before us was executed by above a hundred joint creditors; and a mere glance at their names is sufficient to show that there was no intention on their part of doing anything which should involve them in the obligations of a partnership. I do not rely on this; but, at least, it shows the general opinion of the mercantile world on the subject. I may remark that one of the creditors I see is the Midland Railway Company, which is a creditor for a sum only of £39, and to suppose that the directors could imagine that they were making themselves partners in absurd. [8 H.L.C. at 446-48]

However, partnership liability was imposed on a would-be creditor in *Ex p. Delhasse* (1878), 7 Ch. D. 511 (C.A.). Delhasse was a partner of Megevand, Schlapffer and Notz until June 30, 1869, when the firm was dissolved. Its assets were sold to Megevand and Schoeppi, who continued to carry on the business under the old firm name. Delhasse agreed to lend the new firm £10,000 on June 11, 1869. The agreement stated that the money was advanced by way of loan and would not render Delhasse liable as a partner. He was to receive 25% of the profits and had a right to examine the firm's books at any time. He could elect to dissolve the firm on the death of a partner or when the £10,000 was reduced by losses to £5,000. After the firm's liquidation in 1876, Delhasse sought to prove as a creditor. The English Court of Appeal held that he could not do so because he was really a partner. James L.J. stated that:

If ever there was a case of partnership this is it. There is every element of partnership in it. There is the right to control the property, the right to receive profits, and the liability to share in losses. The loan is a mere pretence, the object being to enable the so-called lender to be, not only a dormant partner, but the real and substantial owner of the business, for whom and on whose behalf it is to be carried on, and yet to provide that he shall not be liable for the loss, in case loss shall be incurred. In my view, it is the same thing as if *B.* were to set up a business to be carried on by *A.*, he being nothing but a manager, *B.* being the real principal, although *A.* was buying and selling everything, and then, when the public found out who the principal was, when the thing came to an end, he could say, *A.* is the man you trusted. I was the real principal, but I am not liable to you, although the whole thing was mine from beginning to end. The law of *England* does not allow this to be done, and it appears to me that it equally does not allow a man to escape liability, who, though he is not the entire owner, yet is the substantial owner of a business, but takes in two persons as nominal partners to carry on the business, while in truth it is his business during the whole time. In my opinion this business was really *Delhasse*'s business. [7 Ch. D. at 526-27]

Reviewing a similar contract, Jessel M.R. held that a financer's attempt to avoid personal liability failed in *Pooley v. Driver* (1876), 5 Ch. D. 458. The financer argued that Bovill's Act absolved him from liability (see now OPA s. 3.3(d)), but the learned Master of the Rolls held that the provision was inapplicable.

The Act is this, that the advance must be "by way of loan." Now what does that mean? It is not the "advance of money," but "the advance of money by way of loan." I take it to mean this, that the person advancing must be a real lender ... [T]he Act does not decide that for you. You must decide that without the Act. [*Id.* at 485]

Jessel M.R. went on to hold that in substance the financer was a partner and not a lender. Do you see a problem with holding that the issue of partnership liability had to be decided before considering the statutory presumption as to partnership liability?

BIA s. 139, modeled upon the same section of Bovill's Act as OPA s. 3.3(d), provides that "where a lender advances money to a borrower engaged or about to engage in a trade or business under a contract with the borrower that the lender shall receive a rate of interest varying with the profits or shall receive a share of the profits arising from carrying on the trade or business, and the borrower subsequently becomes bankrupt, the lender of the money is not entitled to recover anything in respect of the loan until the claims of all other creditors of the borrower have been satisfied."

Capital Structure Irrelevance Proposition. Delhasse's attempt to limit his liability by changing his status from partner to creditor was roundly rejected by the English court. Yet, on reflection, it is not immediately apparent why a partner should not be free to do just that. Certainly, the restrictions which Peyton and his associates bargained for were comparable to those in *Delhasse*. What then is the reason for the barriers in the firm's capital structure or financing decision?

One fear that might appear to underly restrictions on the firm's financing decision is that of distributional consequences—that systematic wealth transfers from unsophisticated outside claimants to the firm might result. Such transfers would arise on issuance of outside claims for an overvalue by the firm. For example, if creditors purchase debt claims in a limited liability regime under the mistaken impression that they may sue equity owners on firm default, they will overpay for their claims. If this is likely to happen, the firm can be expected to adopt limited liability in order to maximize firm value. But these wealth transfer effects will arise only if claimants are unable to react to the firm's capital structure decision. Since the harm would arise through a misrepresentation, it assumes claimant reliance. If all claimants are informed that liability is limited and bargain on that basis when purchasing claims, then the choice by the firm of a limited liability regime would not give rise to distributional effects.

The proposition that limited liability will not give rise to distributional effects if all parties are informed about the firm's capital structure decision is related to a broader theory, associated with Franco Modigliani and Merton Miller. Modigliani and Miller (M-M) demonstrated that, assuming perfect market conditions,* the market value of any firm is independent of its capital structure, and is dependent only on its earnings payout and risk features. On these assumptions, financing decisions have neither distributional nor efficiency consequences. In other words, the special features of the debt and equity claims issued by a firm will not transfer wealth from one class of claimholders to another, nor will they increase firm value. What gives value to the firm is its anticipated earnings, and not how those earnings are to be distributed among claimholders. The firm's invest-

---

*   The components of this assumption are variously listed, but usually include the following: (1) all traders have equal and costless access to information concerning firm and claim value; (2) traders have the same expectations as to firm and claim value, and the same preferences as to risk; (3) capital markets are competitive and there are no (4) transaction costs, (5) agency costs or (6) corporate taxes.

ment decision, in which opportunities are taken up, is then wholly independent of its financing decision, in which the opportunities are paid for by an issue of claims.

The M-M capital structure irrelevance theory is itself an instance of a more general law of conservation of value: an asset's value is independent of the kinds of claims issued against it. However it is sliced, the size of the pie is constant. Under this theory, which M-M called Proposition I, the firm cannot affect its value through a creative capital structure decision unless a net bias for one financing strategy arises when the assumption of perfect capital markets is relaxed. See Modigliani & Miller, *The Cost of Capital, Corporation Finance and the Theory of Investment*, 48 Am. Econ. Rev. 261 (1958), reprinted in Posner & Scott 237. Nor did they think that an optimum capital structure would arise under real world conditions. M-M issued a correction to their article a few years later, suggesting that firms might have a preference for debt securities once U.S. corporate taxes are taken into account by virtue of the tax subsidy of debt financing. The American tax subsidy arises because the firm may deduct interest but not dividend payments. See Modigliani & Miller, *Corporate Income Taxes and the Cost of Capital: A Correction*, 53 Am. Econ. Rev. 433 (1963). When corporate taxes are aggregated with personal taxes, and the firm adopts a low dividend policy, the tax subsidy to debt financing lessens, and Merton Miller has argued that it disappears entirely. See Miller, *Debt and Taxes*, 32 J. Fin. 261 (1977). But the shareholder will incur tax liability when he sells his shares, and a summary of the debate concludes that there is a moderate tax subsidy to debt financing, at least for firms that are likely to generate sufficient earnings to use the tax shield. See Richard A. Brealey & Stewart C. Myers, *Principles of Corporate Finance* 431-33 (4th ed. 1991).

Part of the mystery surrounding capital structure decisions may be dispelled with a better understanding of the relation between debt and equity claims. When trying to raise money, a firm might issue either kind of claim without affecting firm value, according to M-M Proposition I. To see this, note that Diagram 1.1 plots firm value on the horizontal axis and the value of claims against the firm on the vertical axis.

In the simplest case, that of a firm with only equity interests, OA indicates the function of payoffs to equity holders for any particular firm value. Since the firm has no debt claims of any kind, it has not even the liabilities to trade creditors of the Gagnon Computer Business as represented in its balance sheet by the items of Accounts and Expenses Payable. Because the value of claims against the firm equals firm value, OA is a straight line equidistant at all points from both axes. The line ends at a point when firm value = X because it is assumed that, for our particular firm, there is no possibility that firm value > X.

In Diagram 1.2, the formerly all-equity firm issues debt claims with a total face value of $L to creditors. Because the face value of the creditors' claim does not vary with share price, LL* is a straight line parallel to the horizontal axis at all points. Maximum firm value is still X, since firm value is independent of capital structure according to M-M Proposition I. The value of the equity claim is represented by BAL*, while the debt claim is indicated by OBL*X. The debt claim is composed of the area CBL*X, which represents a payoff to debt holders of $L when firm value > L, as well as the triangle OBC, where firm value < L. OBC therefore indicates the rights of debt holders on default by the firm. Under limited liability, OBL represents the possible loss

Diagram 1.1   Claims Against Unleveraged Firm

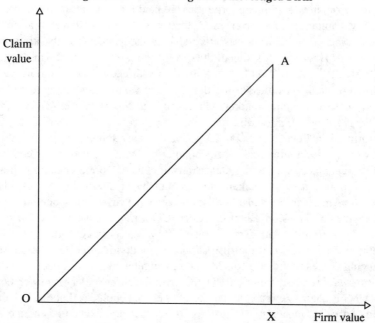

Diagram 1.2   Claims Against Leveraged Firm

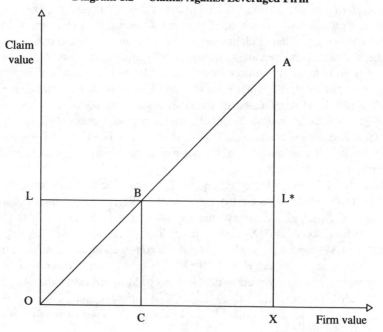

by debt holders on the firm's bankruptcy, and the benefit to equity holders of their forgone liability. If liability is unlimited and the personal assets of equity holders exceed OLB, an issue of debt claims amounts to a sale of OLB to debt holders, and equity claims will be worth BAL* − OLB. Now, it is not to be expected that OLB will be sold for free, and creditors can be expected to pay for unlimited liability through a lower interest rate than would be offered them under limited liability. Distributional effects would then be eliminated. Whether there may be other reasons for a firm to adopt a limited liability regime, based on efficiency and not distributional concerns, will be considered in the next chapter.

Canada Deposit Insurance Corp. v. Canadian Commercial Bank
Supreme Court of Canada
(1992), 97 D.L.R. (4th) 385

[This case arose out of the failed 1985 $255 million bailout of a western Canadian bank. The bailout took the form of a sale by the bank of its bad debts to the "Participants," who included the Canadian and Alberta governments and other participating lenders whose loans under the agreement were guaranteed by the federal government. In return, the bank promised the Participants an indemnity equal to the price paid for the assigned debts should they turn out to be bad debts, with the Participants to be repaid on these loans in priority to the bank. Each Participant would receive from the bank, on a proportionate basis, warrants to purchase common shares of the bank at a price of $0.25 per share. If all warrants were exercised, the Participants would have 75% of the bank's equity. In addition to proceeds from the assigned debts, the Participants were entitled to receive proportionately from the bank, on a quarterly basis, an amount equal to 50% of the bank's pre-tax income. The bank's obligation to make such payments would terminate after each Participant was paid in full. If the bank failed by October 31, 1985, to obtain the shareholder and regulatory approval necessary for it to increase its authorized capital to the extent required for it to issue shares under the warrant agreement, then the bank was required to pay to the Participants 100% of C.C.B.'s pre-tax income. This obligation would continue until the Participants were paid in full, with interest at prime rate. This was the only circumstance under which C.C.B. was to pay interest to the Participants.

In announcing the bailout, the federal Minister of State said that she had "full confidence" that this program "involving Canada's largest chartered banks and the two Governments will permit the Canadian Commercial Bank to continue its active and important role in the growing economy of Western Canada." A winding-up order was made within six months thereafter, and the Participants sought to rank equally with the other unsecured creditors.]

IACOBUCCI J. (per curiam): [T]he fact that the transaction contains both debt and equity features does not, in itself, pose an insurmountable obstacle to characterizing the advance of $255 million. Instead of trying to pigeon-hole the entire agreement between the Participants and C.C.B. in one of two categories, I see nothing wrong in recognizing the arrangement for what it is, namely, one of a hybrid nature, combining elements of both debt and equity but which, in substance, reflects a debtor-creditor relationship. Financial and capital markets have been most creative in the variety of investments and securities that have been fashioned to meet the needs and interests of those who participate in those markets. It is not because an agreement has certain equity features that a court must either ignore these features as if they did not exist or characterize the transaction on the whole as an investment. There is an alternative. It is permissible, and often required, or desirable, for debt and equity to coexist in a given financial transaction without altering the substance of the agreement. Furthermore, it does not follow that each and every aspect of such an agreement must be given the exact same weight when addressing a characterization issue. Again, it is not because there are equity features that it is necessarily an investment in capital. This is particularly true when, as here, the equity features are nothing more than supplementary to and not definitive of the essence of the transaction. When a court is searching for the substance of a particular transaction, it should not too easily be distracted by aspects which are, in reality, only incidental or secondary in nature to the main thrust of the agreement. ...

I agree with the Court of Appeal that the true effectiveness of the [options agreement] was highly contingent and that the learned chambers judge erred in not considering the warrants for what they really were, namely, so-called "sweeteners" or "kickers" with respect to the advance of $255 million which were simply additional features to the underlying loan arrangement between the parties. ...

Wachowich J. also erred in concluding that the Participants would be "sharing in the profits" of C.C.B. under the support agreements. ... While full repayment from the [assigned debts] alone was unlikely, the fact remains that the amount of money to be paid to the Participants from both sources was fixed at the amount advanced by each for their participation certificate. Regardless of where the repayments were coming from, they remained mere repayments for moneys advanced. Of course, the Participants would benefit from the success of C.C.B.'s business; however, this benefit would be capped by the amount of the advance.

[In rejecting the argument that the participating lenders were subordinated by OPA s. 4, Mr. Justice Iacobucci stated that:]

Alberta argues, persuasively in my view, that a lender does not receive a "share of the profits" within the meaning of ss. 3, para. 3, cl. (d) and 4 of the Ontario Partnerships Act unless he or she is entitled to be paid amounts referable to profits other than in repayment of the principal amount of the loan. It is submitted that a lender does not share in profits merely by having a contingent right to acquire or possibly even by having the right to acquire or by owning shares of the borrower. In the case at bar, Alberta submits that all amounts which the Participants were entitled to be paid were to be applied only in repayment of the principal amount due and hence they were not entitled to and did not share in C.C.B.'s profits.

In order to determine the applicability of s. 4 of the Partnerships Act to the facts of this case, a provision which may apply regardless of whether a partnership exists, the general question to be answered is whether this loan was made "upon such a contract as is mentioned in section 3" of the Act. If so, then, subject to any constitutional arguments not made herein, the respondents would not be entitled to recover anything in respect of the loan until the claims of the other ordinary creditors of C.C.B. are satisfied.

The only provisions in s. 3 of the Partnerships Act which make specific reference to a "contract" are s. 3, para. 3, cls. (b) and (d). Section 3, para. 3, cl. (b) is clearly irrelevant to this appeal. Thus, at least at first glance, the contracts in the case at bar must fall within the ambit of s. 3, para. 3, cl. (d) of the Partnerships Act in order to trigger the application of s. 4. The specific question then becomes whether or not the support agreements provided that the Participants were to receive a "rate of interest varying with the profits" of C.C.B., or a "share of the profits arising from carrying on the business" of C.C.B.

While the Legal Representative [representing the bank's ordinary creditors] originally structured his s. 4 argument exclusively around the wording in s. 3, para. 3, cl. (d) of the Partnerships Act, he expanded this argument during oral submissions to include s. 3, para. 3, cl. (a). He submitted that, even if the transaction does not fall within the ambit of the former subsection, it clearly falls within the latter. Accordingly, another specific question to be considered is whether s. 4 of the Partnerships Act can be triggered by "the receipt by a person of a debt or other liquidated amount by instalments or otherwise out of the accruing profits of a business" which does not involve a contract of the sort described in s. 3, para. 3, cl. (d). I will deal with both of these questions in turn.

Sections 3, para. 3, cl. (d) and 4 of the Partnerships Act originate from the now repealed 1865 Act to Amend the Law of Partnership (U.K.), c. 86 ("Bovill's Act"). The intent of what is now s. 3 of the Partnerships Act was evidently to mitigate the harshness of the old common law rule, which was that any person who shared in the profits of the partnership was deemed to be a partner, and so liable for any debts of the partnership on insolvency: *Grace v. Smith* (1775), 2 Black W. 997, at p. 1001, 96 E.R. 587 at p. 588, per De Grey C.J.: "[E]very man who has a share of the profits of a trade ought also to bear his share of the loss"; and *Waugh v. Carver* (1793), 2 H. Bl. 235, 126 E.R. 525.

The old common law rule was first modified by the decision in *Cox v. Hickman* (1860), 8 H.L.C. 268, 11 E.R. 431, which in some respects was very similar on the facts to the present case. The company of Smith and Son fell into financial difficulties and was unable to pay its creditors. The Smiths entered into an arrangement with five of its creditors assigning the company to them (as trustees for all of the creditors), for a term of 21 years. During that period, the trustees were to carry on the business of the company "and to pay the net income, after answering all expenses; which net income was always to be deemed the property of the two Smiths, among [all] the creditors of the Smiths" (at p. 269). In other words, the creditors "were to be paid their debts out of the profits of their debtors' business": Nathaniel Lindley, *Lindley on the Law of Partnership*, 15th ed., by Ernest H. Scamell and R.C. L'Anson Banks (London: Sweet & Maxwell, 1984), at p. 104. The most significant fact for our purposes is that the repayment was to be only to the extent of the debts; when all the debts had been paid, the trustees were to hold the estate in trust for the Smiths. Financial troubles continued under the new management, and the company once again became unable to pay its debts.

Since at that time the law was thought to be that a person who shared in the profits was liable as a partner, the question in *Cox v. Hickman*, supra, was not, as here, whether those creditors who were being paid out of profits were to be ranked equally with subsequent creditors, but whether the former group were to be themselves liable as partners to subsequent creditors. In deciding that they were not so liable, the House of Lords is considered to have established, amongst other things, that receipt of a share of the profits is not conclusive proof of a partnership as was previously thought (*Lindley on the Law of Partnership*, supra, at p. 104). However, it is interesting to note one excerpt of the opinion of Wightman J. (one of the judges who came to advise the House of Lords in *Cox v. Hickman*) who, instead of modifying the old common rule, would simply have not applied it to the facts of the case (at p. 296 H.L.C., p. 443 E.R.):

It is said that a person who shares in net profits is a partner; that may be so in some cases, but not in all; and it may be material to consider in what sense the words, "sharing in the profits" are used. In the present case, I greatly doubt whether the creditor, who merely obtains payment of a debt incurred in the business by being paid the exact amount of his debt, and no more, out of the profits of the business, can be said to share the profits. If in the present case, the property of the Smiths had been assigned to the trustees to carry on the business, and divide the net profits, not amongst those creditors who signed the deed, but amongst all the creditors, until their debts were paid, would a creditor, by receiving from time to time a rateable proportion out of the net profits, become a partner? I should think not.

In my view, the undesirability of the result foreseen by Wightman J. is equally compelling in the context of ss. 3, para. 3, cl. (d) and 4 of the Partnerships Act.

Historically, s. 3, para. 3, cl. (d) of the Partnerships Act appears to refer to loans similar to those involved in *Sukloff v. Rushforth*, [1964] S.C.R. 459, namely, loans in which the creditor advances money to the debtor on the terms that it shall be repaid with interest, and in addition the creditor is to receive a share of the profits over and above any payments on principal until the amount is paid off, as opposed to loans such as those in the present case where the share of the profits is used solely to repay the principal. In other words, s. 3, para. 3, cl. (d) applied to loans which had no cap or limit on the amount to be paid to the creditor from the profits of the debtor's business or which had a cap unrelated to the principal owing on the debt.

It is not entirely clear in *Sukloff v. Rushforth*, whether the lender actually received any of the profits of the company via the arrangement for 50% of the profits. However, in many older cases it is clear that the lender did receive interest and the stated share of the profits for a period, and then claimed for the entire amount of the principal on bankruptcy of the debtor. In these cases ss. 2(3)(d) and 3 of the Partnership Act, 1890 (U.K.), c. 39 (similar to ss. 3, para. 3, cl. (d) and 4 of the Partnerships Act), were applied to subordinate the claims: see *Ex p. Taylor; Re Grason* (1879), 12 Ch. D. 366 (C.A.); *Re Stone* (1886), 33 Ch. D. 541; *Re Hildesheim*, [1893] 2 Q.B. 357; *Re Mason*, [1899] 1 Q.B. 810; and *Re Fort; Ex p. Schofield*, [1897] 2 Q.B. 495 (C.A.). These sections of the Partnership Act, 1890 essentially repeated Bovill's Act so it seems reasonable that this was the specific situation envisaged by the Act.

Contrary to the oral submission of the Legal Representative, *Re Young; Ex p. Jones*, [1896] 2 Q.B. 484, is not inconsistent with the distinction I am drawing. There, Mr. Jones lent money to Mr. Young which was to be used to pay the expenses of Mr. Young's business. The terms of the agreement provided that, in return for the use of this sum, Jones was to be paid a fixed weekly sum out of the profits of the business. When Young became insolvent, Jones claimed for the entire amount of principal, without making allowance for the amounts received by virtue of the weekly payments. In other words, the weekly sum received by Jones out of profits was not for the purpose of repaying the principal sum on the debt. Thus, *Re Young* is clearly distinguishable from the facts of this case and should not be seen as foreclosing the interpretation of s. 3, para. 3, cl. (d) that I am advancing.

In addition, s. 3, para. 3, cl. (a) of the Partnerships Act provides strong support for the distinction between profits as the source of repayment, and a share in the profits, with any repayment of a fixed debt falling into the former category. Indeed, it provides that:

(a) the receipt by a person of a debt or other liquidated amount by instalments or otherwise out of the accruing profits of a business does not of itself make him or her a partner in the business or liable as such.

This seems to preclude any reading of s. 3, para. 3, cl. (d) which would catch debts which are to be repaid "out of profits." In this respect, it is interesting to note that the authors of *Lindley on the Law of Partnership* are of the view that the equivalent of s. 3, para. 3, cl. (a), not s. 3, para. 3, cl. (d), applies to cases such as *Cox v. Hickman*, where, as we have seen, an arrangement similar to the one at bar was involved (at p. 108).

For the foregoing reasons, I would conclude that any fixed debt to be repaid out of profits does not in itself constitute a "share of the profits" within the meaning of s. 3, para. 3, cl. (d) of the Partnerships Act. As argued by Alberta, a lender does not receive a "share of the profits" under this provision unless he or she is entitled to be paid amounts referable to profits other than in repayment of the principal amount of the loan.

Having said this, the question of whether the support agreements provided that the Participants were to receive a "rate of interest varying with the profits" of C.C.B., or a "share of the profits arising from carrying on the business" of C.C.B., as to trigger s. 4 of the Partnerships Act, may be readily answered. Clearly, the Participants were not to receive in return for the advance of $255 million a rate of interest varying with C.C.B.'s profits. The rate of interest to be paid was fixed according to the prime rate and was contingent on whether or not the Equity Agreement could be carried out. As for C.C.B.'s profits, they merely represented the source from which the Participants were to be repaid their advance. In this respect, I entirely agree with the following excerpt taken from the reasons of Harradence J.A. in the case at bar:

It is important to recognize that while repayment was to be made from pre-tax income of C.C.B., there was no direct link between the success of the C.C.B. and the overall quantum of the amount due to or payable to the support group participants. I have been referred to no authority which supports the proposition that a repayment, the instalments of which are referable to the quantum of the income of the debtor, is a situation of "joint benefit." Since sums to be received by the participants were limited to repayment of moneys advanced, with a contingent right to interest, the source of the repayment moneys is not relevant and, with respect, the learned chambers judge erred in concluding the participants were "sharing the profits" in this respect.

The Participants had a fixed debt which would be repaid in part by the moneys received from the [collection of the assigned debts] and in part by C.C.B.'s pre-tax income. With the exception of the contingent interest at prime rate, under no circumstance were the payments from the pre-tax income to be applied to anything but the repayment of the loan. All amounts that the Participants were entitled to be paid were to be applied only in repayment of the principal amount of the loan. Once the loan was fully repaid, all payments from C.C.B.'s pre-tax income were to stop. Accordingly, I find that the Participants were not to receive a "share of the profits" of C.C.B. within the meaning of s. 3, para. 3, cl. (d) of the Partnerships Act by virtue of the repayment scheme for the $255 million advance. I also do not accept that the contemplated granting of warrants under the highly contingent circumstances of this case alters this conclusion.

The question then is whether s. 4 of the Partnerships Act can be triggered by an arrangement falling under s. 3, para. 3, cl. (a). Indeed, as previously noted, the Legal Representative takes the alternative position that, even if s. 3, para. 3, cl. (d) does not apply, the transaction in this case is surely one contemplating "the receipt by a person of a debt or other liquidated amount by instalments or otherwise out of the accruing profits of a business." While one cannot seriously dispute this proposition, the fact remains that s. 4 cannot apply unless "money has been advanced by way of loan upon such a contract as is mentioned in section 3."

The first point to note is that s. 3, para. 3, cl. (a) of the Partnerships Act makes no reference whatsoever to a "contract" and thus appears to be beyond the realm of s. 4. Clearly, the legislature could have chosen a more general term than "contract" in s. 4 had it wished this postponement provision to apply to every transaction described in s. 3. The same could also be said about the absence of the word "loan" in s. 3, para. 3, cl. (a). It is not without significance that we were not presented with any jurisprudence in which a person who had a fixed debt to be paid out of profits (i.e., who would fall under s. 3, para. 3, cl. (a) and not s. 3, para. 3, cl. (d)) was subordinated under the Act.

Further, if the policy on which s. 4 of the Partnerships Act is based is that a person who reaps the rewards of profits must share some risk, then this would not apply to a creditor with a fixed debt, notwithstanding that the fund or source of repayment is profits, because his or her total return will not vary with the profitability of the company.

From the above, I conclude that s. 4 of the Partnerships Act cannot be triggered by what is described in s. 3, para. 3, cl. (a) as "the receipt by a person of a debt or other liquidated amount by instalments or otherwise out of the accruing profits of a business," which does not involve a contract of the sort described in s. 3, para. 3, cl. (d). The present case may very well fall within s. 3, para. 3, cl. (a) of the Act. However, that section only deals with a guideline for determining whether or not a partnership has been created, an issue which is not raised in this appeal. Contrary to s. 3, para. 3, cl. (d) of the Partnerships Act, s. 3, para. 3, cl. (a) does not have the added function of triggering the postponement provision of the Act. As the Participants were not to receive a "rate of interest varying with the profits" of C.C.B. or a "share of the profits arising from carrying on the business" of C.C.B., their claims for the return of the moneys advanced cannot be postponed under s. 4.

Accordingly, I would dismiss this ground of appeal. The Court of Appeal did not err in declining to postpone the respondents' claims under s. 4 of the Partnerships Act.

Equitable subordination

In the further alternative, the Legal Representative submits that even if the transaction in question is a loan and the Partnerships Act does not apply, the Participants' claims should be subordinated on equitable grounds based on the United States doctrine of "equitable subordination."

More specifically, it is argued that the equitable jurisdiction of superior courts gives them authority in insolvency matters to subordinate claims that, while valid as against the insolvent's estate, arise from or are connected with conduct prejudicial to the interests of other creditors. While the Legal Representative does not assert that the conduct of the Participants was fraudulent or worthy of censure, he argues that the Participants acted to the detriment of the ordinary creditors of C.C.B. in ways (which I shall outline below) that should invoke this equitable jurisdiction. Both the Bank Group and Alberta challenge the proposition that equitable subordination is available under Canadian law in insolvency matters. In addition, the respondents argue that the facts of this case do not call for the application of equitable principles.

This issue does not appear to have been raised before Wachowich J. or the Court of Appeal and consequently this court does not have the benefit of any findings of fact as to the actual or potential prejudice suffered by C.C.B.'s depositors and other creditors as a result of the conduct of the Participants. ...

This court also does not have the benefit of the insight of the courts below as to whether or not, in the first place, the doctrine of equitable subordination should become part of Canadian insolvency law. As I see the matter, however, it is not necessary in the circumstances of this case to answer the question of whether a comparable equitable doctrine should exist in Canadian law and I expressly refrain from doing so. Assuming, for the sake of argument only, that Canadian courts have the power in insolvency matters to subordinate otherwise valid claims to those of other creditors on equitable grounds relating to the conduct of these creditors inter se, this court has been presented with insufficient grounds to justify the exercise of such a power in the case at bar. Briefly put, the reasons and limited evidence advanced by the Legal Representative before this court disclose neither inequitable conduct on the part of the Participants nor injury to the ordinary creditors of C.C.B. as a result of the alleged misconduct.

As I understand it, in the United States there are three requirements for a successful claim of equitable subordination: (1) the claimant must have engaged in some type of inequitable conduct; (2) the misconduct must have resulted in injury to the creditors of the bankrupt or conferred an unfair advantage on the claimant; and (3) equitable subordination of the claim must not be inconsistent with the provisions of the bankruptcy statute: see *Re Mobile Steel Co.*, 563 F.2d 692 (5th Cir., 1977) at p. 700; *Re Multiponics Inc.*, 622 F.2d 709 (5th Cir., 1980); A. DeNatale and P.B. Abram, "The Doctrine of Equitable Subordination as Applied to Nonmanagement Creditors" (1985), 40 Bus. Law. 417 at p. 423; and L.J. Crozier, "Equitable Subordination of Claims in Canadian Bankruptcy Law" (1992), 7 C.B.R. (3d) 40 at pp. 41-2. Even if this court were to accept that a comparable doctrine to equitable subordination should exist in Canadian law, I do not view the facts of this case as giving rise to the "inequitable conduct" and ensuing "detriment" necessary to trigger its application.

In this regard, the actions cited by the Legal Representative as being detrimental to the ordinary creditors of C.C.B., thereby giving rise to equitable subordination, come down to two elements: (1) the press release of March 25, 1985, issued by the Department of Finance announcing to the general public that the support program would leave

C.C.B. "in a strong position of solvency" and that sufficient funds were being advanced "to ensure solvency"; and (2) the flaws in the support program outlined in the Estey Report and described by the Legal Representative as: (a) the inadequacy of the support program to ensure C.C.B.'s solvency; (b) the accounting treatment disguised the fact that the Participation Agreement required the entire amount advanced to be repaid; (c) the accounting treatment used by the Bank Group gave rise to tax benefits not available to ordinary depositors; (d) the Participation Agreement allegedly obliged C.C.B. to apply all amounts received on the [assigned debts] to the Participants; (e) the warrants would have the effect of prohibiting C.C.B. from raising funds in the equity market since they would enable the Participants to acquire 75% of the common shares of C.C.B. up to 10 years after the advances had been paid in full; and (f) after making their advances and receiving their participation certificates, the Bank Group ceased dealing with C.C.B. in the normal manner.

At the outset, I note that many of the actions relied on by the Legal Representative cannot be attributable to the Participants. For example, the press release was not issued by the respondents and the accounting treatment given by C.C.B. to the advance of $255 million simply followed the instructions given by the Office of the Inspector General of Banks. Thus, even if some inequitable connotation could be given to these actions, they would not represent misconduct on the part of the respondents to whom the ordinary creditors of C.C.B. are now attempting to rank in priority.

Another difficulty with the Legal Representative's submission, however, is that I fail to see anything remotely inequitable in the conduct complained of. With respect to the press release, the evidence does not show that the Participants were necessarily of a different opinion from that set out in the press release. Certainly, they advanced the funds on the condition that the Inspector General of Banks provide them with an opinion letter confirming the solvency of C.C.B. on the infusion of the proposed funds. As for the flaws in the support program, there is nothing to show that the Participants' plans were other than well-intentioned. As stated at the beginning of these reasons, it is beyond the scope of this appeal to engage in a detailed review of the reasons which led to the failure of the support program. Suffice it to say that the assertions of the Legal Representative in substance do not show wrongdoing or unfairness on the part of the Participants, but merely show that the support program did not work, and perhaps with hindsight, offer some explanations as to why.

In any event, it does not appear to have been suggested at any time in the courts below nor was any evidence led to suggest that any creditor of C.C.B. was misled by any of the above actions or that the press release, accounting treatment or any flaw in the support program operated to cause any creditor to act to its detriment. Thus, even if this court were to find that the Participants acted in an inequitable manner in their dealings with C.C.B. and its depositors and other creditors, we do not have a shred of evidence upon which to conclude that the improper conduct resulted in actual harm to the ordinary creditors of C.C.B. now before this court. One can only speculate that depositors and other creditors relied on the press release or accounting treatment and thereby suffered damages. We have been offered no United States' decision in which mere speculation of harm to other creditors has been found sufficient to meet the second requirement of the doctrine of equitable subordination. Of course, the ordinary creditors of C.C.B. who appear before this court have, to a varying extent, suffered from the winding-up of C.C.B., just as any creditor (including the Participants) suffer following an insolvency or bankruptcy. The Legal Representative has not shown, however, that these ordinary creditors have suffered identifiable prejudice attributable specifically to the alleged misconduct of the Participants.

Accordingly, I would reject this alternative ground of appeal. Even if equitable subordination is available under Canadian law, a question which I leave open for another day, the facts of this case do not call for an intervention with the pari passu ranking of the respondents in the name of equity.

Disposition

For the foregoing reasons, I would dismiss the appeal with costs here and in the courts below. As found by the learned chambers judge and upheld by the Court of Appeal, the Participants are entitled to their proportionate share of the moneys recovered from the [assigned debts]. Moreover, as found by the Court of Appeal, the respondents are entitled to rank pari passu with the ordinary creditors of C.C.B. for all moneys advanced pursuant to the Participation Agreement and not repaid by moneys recovered from the [assigned debts].

Appeal dismissed.

NOTES

1) Do you think that the warrant rights were aptly characterized as a "kicker"? Could the rights of the participants under the loan agreements be valued simply as debt contracts, with the equity rights seen simply as the icing on the cake? Put another way, could you hazard a guess as to the likelihood that the warrants would have been exercised had the bailout succeeded? Or was Mr. Justice Iacobucci saying that all non-governmental participants expected that the bailout would fail, and that their real debtor was the federal government, which had guaranteed their claims?

2) Had the bailout succeeded, the ordinary creditors of the bank would have been paid off in due course. Presumably, they had little standing to complain about it. What about future creditors, who might have argued that they were gulled by the Minister's statement into thinking that the bank was on a surer foundation than it really was? Do you think that such arguments should have grounded a claim in fraud or in equitable subordination? In noting that the Court did not have "a shred of evidence upon which to conclude that the improper conduct resulted in actual harm to the ordinary creditors," was Mr. Justice Iacobucci saying that no reasonable creditor would have thought that this was anything other than a politically motivated bailout?

3) While the facts in this case are exceptional, the Supreme Court also refused to subordinate a business lender in similar circumstances in *Sukloff v. A.H. Rushforth & Co.*, [1964] S.C.R. 459. The lender had bargained for a 50% share of the debtor's equity, but later agreed to surrender this on being paid in full.

4) Equitable subordination principles are discussed further in Chapter Two, Section B.

Limited Partnerships Act
R.S.O. 1990, c. L.16

2.(1) A limited partnership may, subject to this Act, be formed to carry on any business that a partnership without limited partners may carry on.

(2) A limited partnership shall consist of one or more persons who are general partners and one or more persons who are limited partners.

•   •   •

4.(1) The general partners of every limited partnership other than an extra-provincial limited partnership shall maintain a current record of the limited partners stating, for each limited partner, the prescribed information.

(2) The record of limited partners shall be kept at the limited partnership's principal place of business in Ontario.

(3) Any person may inspect the record of limited partners during the normal business hours of the limited partnership and may make copies of and take extracts from it.

(4) The Registrar may at any time by written notice require any general partner to provide to the Registrar or any other person a copy of the record of limited partners.

(5) Upon receipt of the Registrar's notice, the general partner to whom it is directed shall, within the time specified in the notice, provide a copy of the record of limited partners to the Registrar or any other person specified in the notice.

5.(1) A person may be a general partner and a limited partner at the same time in the same limited partnership.

(2) A person who is at the same time a general partner and a limited partner in the same limited partnership has the rights and powers and is subject to the restrictions and liabilities of a general partner except that in respect of the person's contribution as a limited partner the person has the same rights against the other partners as a limited partner.

6.(1) The surname or a distinctive part of the corporate name of a limited partner shall not appear in the firm name of the limited partnership unless it is also the surname or a distinctive part of the corporate name of one of the general partners.

(2) Where the surname or a distinctive part of the corporate name of a limited partner appears in the firm name contrary to subsection (1), the limited partner is liable as a general partner to any creditor of the limited partnership who has extended credit without actual knowledge that the limited partner is not a general partner.

(3) Despite any Act, the word "Limited" may be used in the firm name but only in the expression "Limited Partnership."

7.(1) A limited partner may contribute money and other property to the limited partnership, but not services.

(2) A limited partner's interest in the limited partnership is personal property.

8. A general partner in a limited partnership has all the rights and powers and is subject to all the restrictions and liabilities of a partner in a partnership without limited partners except that, without the written consent to or ratification of the specific act by all the limited partners, a general partner has no authority to,

(a) do any act in contravention of the partnership agreement;

(b) do any act which makes it impossible to carry on the ordinary business of the limited partnership;

(c) consent to a judgment against the limited partnership;

(d) possess limited partnership property, or assign any rights in specific partnership property, for other than a partnership purpose;

(e) admit a person as a general partner;

(f) admit a person as a limited partner, unless the right to do so is given in the partnership agreement; or

(g) continue the business of the limited partnership on the death, retirement or mental incompetence of a general partner or dissolution of a corporate general partner, unless the right to do so is given in the partnership agreement.

9. Subject to this Act, a limited partner is not liable for the obligations of the limited partnership except in respect of the value of money and other property the limited partner contributes or agrees to contribute to the limited partnership, as stated in the record of limited partners.

10. A limited partner has the same right as a general partner,

(a) to inspect and make copies of or take extracts from the limited partnership books at all times;

(b) to be given, on demand, true and full information concerning all matters affecting the limited partnership, and to be given a complete and formal account of the partnership affairs; and

(c) to obtain dissolution of the limited partnership by court order.

11.(1) A limited partner has, subject to this Act, the right,

(a) to a share of the profits or other compensation by way of income; and

(b) to have the limited partner's contribution to the limited partnership returned.

(2) No payment of a share of the profits or other compensation by way of income shall be made to a limited partner from the assets of the limited partnership or of a general partner if the payment would reduce the assets of the limited partnership to an amount insufficient to discharge the liabilities of the limited partnership to persons who are not general or limited partners.

12.(1) A limited partner may loan money to and transact other business with the limited partnership and, unless the limited partner is also a general partner, may receive on account of resulting claims against the limited partnership with general creditors a prorated share of the assets, but no limited partner shall, in respect of any such claim,

(a) receive or hold as collateral security any of the limited partnership property; or

(b) receive from a general partner or the limited partnership any payment, conveyance or release from liability if at the time the assets of the partnership are not sufficient to discharge partnership liabilities to persons who are not general or limited partners.

(2) A limited partner may from time to time,

(a) examine into the state and progress of the limited partnership business and may advise as to its management;

(b) act as a contractor for or an agent or employee of the limited partnership or of a general partner; or

(c) act as a surety for the limited partnership.

13.(1) A limited partner is not liable as a general partner unless, in addition to exercising rights and powers as a limited partner, the limited partner takes part in the control of the business.

(2) For the purposes of subsection (1), a limited partner shall not be presumed to be taking part in the control of the business by reason only that the limited partner exercises rights and powers in addition to the rights and powers conferred upon the limited partner by this Act.

14.(1) Subject to subsection (2), limited partners, in relation to one another, share in the limited partnership assets,

(a) for the return of contributions; and

(b) for profits or other compensation by way of income on account of their contributions,

in proportion to the respective amounts of money and other property actually contributed by the limited partners to the limited partnership.

(2) Where there are several limited partners, the partners may agree that one or more of the limited partners is to have priority over other limited partners,

(a) as to the return of contributions;

(b) as to profits or other compensation by way of income; or

(c) as to any other matter,

but the terms of this agreement shall be set out in the partnership agreement.

(3) Where the partnership agreement does not contain an agreement referred to in subsection (2), the shares of the limited partners in the partnership assets shall be determined in accordance with subsection (1).

15.(1) A limited partner has the right to demand and receive the return of the limited partner's contribution,

(a) upon the dissolution of the limited partnership;

(b) when the time specified in the partnership agreement for the return of the contribution occurs;

(c) after the limited partner has given six months notice in writing to all other partners, if no time is specified in the partnership agreement for the return of the contribution or for the dissolution of the limited partnership; or

(d) when all the partners consent to the return of the contribution.

(2) Despite subsection (1), a limited partner is not entitled to receive any part of the limited partner's contribution out of the limited partnership assets or from a general partner until,

(a) all liabilities of the limited partnership, except liabilities to general partners and to limited partners on account of their contributions, have been paid or there remains sufficient limited partnership assets to pay them; and

(b) the partnership agreement is terminated or so amended, if necessary, to set forth the withdrawal or reduction of the contribution.

(3) A limited partner has, irrespective of the nature of the limited partner's contribution, only the right to demand and receive money in return therefor, unless,

(a) the partnership agreement provides otherwise; or

(b) all the partners consent to some other manner of returning the contribution.

(4) A limited partner is entitled to have the limited partnership dissolved and its affairs wound up where,

    (a) the limited partner is entitled to the return of the limited partner's contribution but, upon demand, the contribution is not returned to the limited partner; or

    (b) the other liabilities of the limited partnership have not been paid or the limited partnership assets are insufficient for their payment as required by clause (2)(a) and the limited partner seeking dissolution would otherwise be entitled to the return of the limited partner's contribution.

16.(1) A limited partner is liable to the limited partnership for the difference, if any, between the value of money or other property actually contributed by the limited partner to the limited partnership and the value of money or other property stated in the record of limited partners as being contributed or to be contributed by the limited partner to the limited partnership.

• • •

18.(1) A limited partner's interest is assignable.

(2) A substituted limited partner is a person admitted to all the rights and powers of a limited partner who has died or who has assigned the limited partner's interest in the limited partnership.

(3) An assignee who is not a substituted limited partner has no right,

    (a) to inspect the limited partnership books;

    (b) to be given any information about matters affecting the limited partnership or to be given an account of the partnership affairs,

but is entitled only to receive the share of the profits or other compensation by way of income or the return of the contribution to which the assignor would otherwise be entitled.

(4) An assignee may become a substituted limited partner,

    (a) if all the partners, except the assignor, consent in writing thereto; or

    (b) if the assignor, being so authorized by the partnership agreement, constitutes the assignee a substituted limited partner.

(5) An assignee, who is otherwise entitled to become a substituted limited partner, becomes a substituted limited partner when the record of limited partners is amended.

(6) A substituted limited partner has all the rights and powers and is subject to all the restrictions and liabilities of the limited partner's assignor, except any liability of which the limited partner did not have notice at the time the limited partner became a limited partner and which could not be ascertained from the partnership agreement, the declaration or the record of limited partners.

(7) The substitution of an assignee as a limited partner does not release the assignor from liability under section 16 or 30.

• • •

21. The retirement, death or mental incompetence of a general partner or dissolution of a corporate general partner dissolves a limited partnership unless the business is continued by the remaining general partners,

    (a) pursuant to a right to do so contained in the partnership agreement; and

    (b) with the consent of all the remaining partners.

• • •

24. In settling accounts after the dissolution of a limited partnership, the liabilities of the limited partnership to creditors, except to limited partners on account of their contributions and to general partners, shall be paid first, and then, unless the partnership agreement or a subsequent agreement provides otherwise, shall be paid in the following order:

1. To limited partners in respect of their share of the profits and other compensation by way of income on account of their contributions.
2. To limited partners in respect of their contributions.
3. To general partners other than for capital and profits.
4. To general partners in respect of profits.
5. To general partners in respect of capital.

• • •

31. A person who contributes to the capital of a business carried on by a person or partnership erroneously believing that the person has become a limited partner in a limited partnership,

(a) is not, by reason only of exercising the rights of a limited partner, a general partner with the person or in the partnership carrying on the business; and

(b) is not bound by the obligations of the person or partnership carrying on the business,

if, upon ascertaining the fact that the person is not a limited partner, promptly,

(c) renounces the person's interest in the profits or other compensation by way of income from the business; or

(d) takes steps to cause the record of limited partners to be amended to show the person to be a limited partner.

Limited Partnerships. Limited partnerships are frequently encountered in the Canadian resource industry because of tax considerations. The firm is not a taxable entity under federal or provincial legislation and is not required to file a return. Instead, the limited partners will do so. They will first compute the firm's income on an accrual basis without deducting depletion allowances. The limited partners, in computing their income for that year, will then include their share of the firm's income, whether or not distributed to them, deducting the depletion allowance themselves. These deductions make limited partnership an attractive investment vehicle for taxpayers in high income brackets.

The purpose of the Limited Partnerships Act (OLPA) is to give contributors of capital limited liability so long as they do not take an active part in managing the firm. At least one member of the firm must be a general partner who is personally liable for firm debts. OLPA s. 2(2).

A limited partnership is formed by filing a declaration signed by all the partners and stating their contribution to the firm and the general nature of its business. A written partnership agreement is not required but, as in the case of a general partnership, is highly advisable.

A limited partner is liable for his capital contribution or the value of the assets he agrees to transfer to the firm in return for his interest in it. OLPA s. 16. Limited liability does not mean the absence of liability since, on joining the firm, the limited partner must contribute the value of his equity interest. But beyond that he is not liable for firm debts. OLPA s. 9. On distribution, ordinary trade creditors rank ahead of limited partners. OLPA s. 24. A limited partner cannot attain a better priority position by taking a security interest in firm assets. OLPA s. 12(1)(a). General partners rank after limited partners. OLPA s. 24.

Management of a limited partnership is vested in the hands of the general partners, subject to the restrictions in s. 8, where the consent of all the limited partners is required. Limited partners do have special rights to access or disclosure of information about the firm under ss. 10 and 12(2). However, should they venture beyond investigating the firm to taking part in the control of its business, they become subject to the unlimited liability of general partners under s. 13.

Can this problem be avoided by incorporating a corporation to serve as the sole general partner and appointing the limited partners as the directors and officers of the corporation? When this was done in *Delaney v. Fidelity Lease Ltd.*, 526 S.W. 2d 543 (1975), the Texas Supreme Court held that the limited partners had incurred unlimited liability because of their control of the firm. The Court further suggested that it is improper to appoint a corporation as general partner if the corporation is "inadequately capitalized" (organized with a relatively small injection of equity).* The *Delaney* case was distinguished in *Frigidaire Sales Corp. v. Union Properties*, 562 P.2d 244 (Wash. 1977), where the Court refused to impose general liability on the limited partners, who were officers, directors and shareholders of the incorporated general partner. The Court stated that corporations that are adequately capitalized may serve as general partners, and noted that the petitioning creditor was aware that a corporation had been so appointed.

[B]ecause respondents scrupulously separated their actions on behalf of the corporation from their personal actions, petitioner never mistakenly assumed that respondents were general partners with general liability. ... Petitioner knew [the corporation] was the sole general partner and did not rely on respondents' control by assuming that they were also general partners. If petitioner had not wished to rely on the solvency of [the corporation] as the only general partner, it could have insisted that respondents personally guarantee contractual performance. [*Id.* at 247]

The British Columbia Court of Appeal also refused to impose unlimited liability on limited partners who ran the firm as directors and officers of the incorporated general partner in *Nordile Holdings Ltd. v. Breckenridge* (1992), 66 B.C.L.R. (2d) 183 (C.A.). See also Basile, *Limited Liability for Limited Partners: An Argument for the Abolition of the Control Rule*, 38 Vand. L. Rev. 1199 (1985); Flannigan, *The Control Test of Investor Liability in Limited Partnerships*, 21 Alta. L. Rev. 303 (1983).

Under *Delhasse* and OLPA s. 13 limited liability is purchased at the cost of relinquishing rights of control. But why are investors put to this election? Is there an implicit representation that those ostensibly in control of a partnership are general partners, so that credit is lent on the assumption that their assets are available to auditors on the firm's bankruptcy? If liability is based on a misrepresentation, however, there is no

---

* Thin capitalization is discussed in Chapter Two, Section B.

reason to impose unlimited liability when the limited partner's control is exercised covertly. Was there any real reliance on the unlimited liability of the controlling creditors in *Martin v. Peyton* or *Cox v. Hickman*? Was there a greater risk of such reliance in *Delhasse*?

Adverse Incentive Costs. Even with full disclosure to outside claimants, it may be inefficient to assign rights of control solely to debt holders. When the firm issues only one kind of claim, the claimholders' incentives are the same as those of the firm. But with separate classes of claims, each claimholder will seek to maximize not firm value but the value of claims of his class. When a limited liability firm has issued both debt and equity interests, the value of the debt claim D is min (L, FV), or the lower value of the face value of debt L and firm value FV. Equity claims are worth max $(FV - L, 0)$, the higher of $FV - L$ and 0. (How would you write this formula under unlimited liability?) Debt and equity holders will then look at investment opportunities differently. When managed by equity or by groups allied to equity, "[a] corporation will be indifferent between enormous liability and lesser liability if *both* would bankrupt it." Note, *The Inapplicability of Traditional Tort Analysis to Environmental Risks: The Example of Toxic Waste Pollution Victim Compensation*, 35 Stan. L. Rev. 575, 602 (1983). Similarly, debt holders will be indifferent to expected returns exceeding L if the probability of default is not reduced.

The different incentives of debt and equity holders give rise to *adverse incentive costs* that reflect the decline in firm value because of the possibility that it will forgo valuable investment opportunities. These costs, which are a species of agency costs, arise whenever the right to make investment decisions is assigned to a class of claimholders whose interests may diverge from those of the firm. To see this, assume that the firm must choose between the following two investment opportunities, which have the same take-up cost.

Table 1.3   Investment Opportunities

		Investment I	
State	Outcome R	Probability p	Value
1	10,000	1.0	10,000
			$E(R) = 10,000$

		Investment II	
State	Outcome R	Probability p	Value
1	80,000	.1	8,000
2	0	.9	0
			$E(R) = 8,000$

A firm that has not issued debt claims will take up the more valuable Investment I. But it is otherwise if the firm has issued debt claims with a face value of 10,000, and share value, not firm value, is maximized. Share value is 0 under Investment I, with all earnings given to the creditors. If Investment II is taken up, however, and State 1 obtains, there is 70,000 left over for shareholders after paying off creditors. Since there is a 10%

probability of State 1, the expected value of equity claims is 7,000, while the expected value of debt claims is 1,000. In other words, the move to the less valuable second investment opportunity effects a wealth transfer of 9,000 from creditors. Of this, 7,000 ends up in the pockets of equity holders, while 2,000 represents a deadweight efficiency loss.

The wealth transfer from debt to equity holders disappears when all parties are aware of the incentive problem when they bargain for their claims against the firm. Creditors will exact a higher interest rate *ex ante* on issuance when they expect a wealth transfer *ex post* on the choice of investment policies. Shareholders will then have to pay for the expropriation option, and since it represents an efficiency loss, will seek to commit to efficient investment policies. The problem, however, is that a promise of efficient investment policies is largely unenforceable. How could a court find that a manager has breached such policies, when Investment I might have been offered to the manager in passing in an elevator, and rejected as quickly?

Nor can the misincentive problem be solved by assigning investment policies to creditors. To see this, suppose that the firm faces a choice between Investment I above and the following investment opportunity.

Investment III

State	Outcome R	Probability p	Value
1	80,000	.5	40,000
2	8,000	.5	4,000
			$E(R) = 44,000$

When the choice of investments is left to shareholders, they will take up the more valuable Investment III. Shareholders receive nothing under Investment I, while they have a 50% chance of 70,000 under Investment III. However, debt claims are worth only 9,000 in Investment III (can you explain why?), while they are worth 10,000 in Investment I. In other words, the choice of investment policies is now more efficiently delegated to shareholders.

What these examples show is that the adverse incentive problem cannot be eliminated by assigning responsibility for investment policies uniquely to one constituency. Instead, management responsibilities are efficiently assigned to shareholders when the firm is solvent, with creditors given the right to displace shareholder-appointed managers when the firm slides toward insolvency. At that point, the investment choices more closely resemble those between Investments I and II, and firm shareholders will be gambling with other people's money. (It might help to imagine this as the way you would gamble in Las Vegas if you got the winnings but your banker bore the losses.) In assigning management rights, therefore, the firm will seek to minimize total misincentive costs. Typically, it will do so by permitting creditors to displace shareholder-appointed managers at an *optimal termination time*, which minimizes the costs of equity and debt holder misbehavior.

Does the possibility of creditor misbehavior explain the OLPA's barriers to the exercise of management rights by limited partners? Does it suggest that *Martin v. Peyton* was wrongly decided, and that *Delhasse* was rightly decided? But then why do the parties need help in specifying efficient management policies? If all management rights are efficiently assigned to the creditors on insolvency, does it follow that no management powers can be efficiently reserved to them while the firm is solvent? See further Galai & Masulis, *The Option Pricing Model and the Risk Factors of Stock*, 3 J. Fin. Econ. 53 (1976); Buckley, *The Termination Decision*, 61 U.M.K.C. L. Rev. 243 (1992); Buckley, *A Corporate Governance Theory of Repossessory Rights*, 23 C.B.L.J. 96 (1994).

Fraudulent Conveyances. Adverse incentive costs also explain the prohibition of certain eve-of-bankruptcy transactions that prejudice creditors. On insolvency, $FV < L$, and ownership of residual firm value passes to the creditors. But this does not mean that the firm will cease operations, which only happens if liquidation value exceeds going concern value. If, instead, going concern value exceeds liquidation value, the firm will maximize its value by continuing as a going concern. It will then reorganize its capital structure, typically with old debt claims traded off for new equity interests in the reorganized firm. Under M-M Proposition I, the reorganization decision is a financing one, and is entirely independent of the (dis)investment decision to sell off assets in a liquidation or to continue in business. In other words, the decision to redistribute claims in the firm through a reorganization should have no effect on firm wealth under perfect market assumptions.

M-M Proposition I may not, however, hold as a consequence of agency costs, which constitute a market failure that would not arise in perfect market conditions. Because greater incentive costs may be anticipated when insolvent firms are managed by equity claimants, firm value may increase when bankruptcy proceedings are commenced, and for the same reason pre-bankruptcy transactions may be impeached. Since bankruptcy need not mean the withdrawal of the firm from production, the trustee will decide to operate it as a going concern if its assets are worth more when held by the firm than if sold off piecemeal. (The assets are then said to be *firm specific*.) Unless the trustee steps in, firm specific assets might be sold off by equity-appointed managers immediately prior to bankruptcy in order to stave off default. The grant of investment responsibility to management may therefore be impeached in eve-of-bankruptcy asset transfers (fraudulent conveyances), as may payments of one creditor in priority to the others (fraudulent preferences) immediately prior to default. If such transactions were permitted, bankruptcy priority rights might be worth little to creditors, who would therefore pay little for them *ex ante* when the claims are issued.

Prohibitions of these transactions may be thought of as "me-first" rules, in which the integrity of firm claims is protected by covenants aimed at preventing their destruction. Without such rules, the market for these claims by investors might disappear. Me-first rules are discussed in E. Fama & M. Miller, *The Theory of Finance* 151-52 (1972). For a further discussion of fraudulent transaction prohibitions, see T. Jackson, *The Logic and Limits of Bankruptcy Law* 122-38 (1986).

CHAPTER TWO

The Corporate Form of Organization

This chapter examines the doctrine of limited liability in corporate law. Section A reviews the doctrine and how it might be justified on efficiency grounds. Section B deals with veil-piercing, where a court disregards the separate legal existence of a corporation to impose liability or to confer benefits on shareholders. Finally, Section C reviews the liability of promoters for contracts entered into by them on behalf of a firm before it is incorporated.

A. THE CORPORATE ENTITY

Salomon v. A. Salomon & Co.
House of Lords
[1897] A.C. 22

[The following statement of facts is taken from the judgment of Lord Watson.]

The appellant, Aron Salomon, for many years carried on business, on his own account, as a leather merchant and wholesale boot manufacturer. With the design of transferring his business to a joint stock company, which was to consist exclusively of himself and members of his own family, he, on July 20, 1892, entered into a preliminary agreement with one Adolph Anholt, as trustee for the future company, settling the terms upon which the transfer was to be made by him, one of its conditions being that part payment might be made to him in debentures of the company. A memorandum of association was then executed by the appellant, his wife, a daughter, and four sons, each of them sub-scribing for one share, in which the leading object for which the company was formed was stated to be the adoption and carrying into effect, with such modifications (if any) as might be agreed on, of the provisional agreement of July 20. The memorandum was registered on July 28, 1892; and the effect of registration, if otherwise valid, was to incorporate the company, under the name of "Aron Salomon and Company, Limited," with liability limited by shares, and having a nominal capital of £40,000, divided into 40,000 shares of £1 each. The company adopted the agreement of July 20, subject to certain modifications which are not material; and an agreement to that effect was executed between them and the appellant on August 2, 1892. Within a month or two after that date the whole stipulations of the agreement were fulfilled by both parties. In terms thereof, 100 debentures, for £100 each, were issued to the appellant, who, upon the security of these documents, obtained an advance of £5,000 from Edmund Broderip. In February 1893 the original debentures were returned to the company and cancelled; and in lieu thereof, with the consent of the appellant as beneficial owner, fresh debentures to the same amount were issued to Mr. Broderip, in order to secure the repayment of his loan, with interest at 8 per cent.

In September 1892 the appellant applied for and obtained an allotment of 20,000 shares; and from that date until an order was made for its compulsory liquidation, the share register of the company remained unaltered, 20,001 shares being held by the appellant, and six shares by his wife and family. It was all along the intention of these persons to retain the business in their own hands, and not to permit any outsider to acquire an interest in it.

Default having been made in the payment of interest upon his debentures, Mr. Broderip, in September 1893, instituted an action in order to enforce his security against the assets of the company. Thereafter a liquidation order was made, and a liquidator appointed, at the instance of unsecured creditors of the company. It has now been ascertained that, if the amount realised from the assets of the company were, in the first place, applied in extinction of Mr. Broderip's debt and interest, there would remain a balance of about £1,055, which is claimed by the appellant as beneficial owner of the debentures. In the event of his claim being sustained there will be no funds left for payment of the unsecured creditors, whose debts amount to £7,733 8s. 3d.

The liquidator lodged a defence, in name of the company, to the debenture suit, in which he counter-claimed against the appellant (who was made a party to the counter-claim), (1.) to have the agreements of July 20 and August 2, 1892 rescinded, (2.) to have the debentures already mentioned delivered up and cancelled, (3.) judgment against the appellant for all sums paid by the company to the appellant under these agreements, and (4.) a lien for these sums upon the business and assets. The averments made in support of these claims were to the effect that the price paid by the company exceeded the real value of the business and assets by upwards of £8,200; that the arrangements made by the appellant for the formation of the company were a fraud upon the creditors of the company; that no board of directors of the company was ever appointed, and that in any case such board consisted entirely of the appellant, and there never was an independent board. The action came on for trial on the counter-claim before Vaughan Williams J., when the liquidator was examined as a witness on behalf of the company, whilst evidence was given for the appellant by himself, and by his son, Emanuel Salomon, one of the members of the company, who had been employed in the business for nearly twenty years.

The evidence shews that, before its transfer to the new company, the business had been prosperous, and had yielded to the appellant annual profits sufficient to maintain himself and his family, and to add to his capital. It also shews that at the date of transfer the business was perfectly solvent. The liquidator, whose testimony was chiefly directed toward proving that the price paid by the company was excessive, admitted on cross-examination that the business, when transferred to the company, was in a sound condition, and that there was a substantial surplus. No evidence was led tending to support the allegation that no board of directors was ever appointed, or that the board consisted entirely of the appellant. The non-success and ultimate insolvency of the business, after it came into the hands of the company, was attributed by the witness Emanuel Salomon to a succession of strikes in the boot trade, and there is not a tittle of evidence tending to modify or contradict his statement. It also appears from the evidence that all the members of the company were fully cognisant of the terms of the agreements of July 20 and August 2, 1892, and that they were willing to accept and did accept these terms. ...

[Vaughan Williams J. held at [1895] 2 Ch. 323, sub nom. *Broderip v. Salomon*, that Mr. Salomon was personally liable to the company's unsecured creditors. The company was Salomon's agent, and his taking a security interest in it in the form of a debenture amounted to a fraudulent conveyance. Vaughan Williams J. also stated that the purchase price was exorbitant.

The Court of Appeal affirmed this decision. Lindley L.J. stated that "one-man companies" were contrary to the spirit of the 1862 English Companies Act, which required seven shareholders. However, he added that:

[Mr. Salomon's] liability does not arise simply from the fact that he holds nearly all the shares in the company. ... [It] rests on the purpose for which he formed the company, on the way he formed it, and on the use which he made of it. There are many small companies which will be quite unaffected by this decision. But there may possibly be some which, like this, are mere devices to enable a man to carry on trade with limited liability, to incur debts in the name of a registered company, and to sweep off the company's assets by means of [secured] debentures which he has caused to be issued to himself in order to defeat the claims of those who have been incautious enough to trade with the company without perceiving the trap which he has laid for them. [[1895] 2 Ch. at 338-39]

The learned judge held that the sale of the business to the company was a mere sham to defraud creditors.

Mr. Salomon appealed to the House of Lords.* Broderip, having been paid off, was not a party to the appeal.]

LORD HALSBURY L.C.: ... My Lords, the important question in this case, I am not certain it is the only question, is whether the respondent company was a company at all—whether in truth that artificial creation of the Legislature had been validly constituted in this instance; and in order to determine that question it is necessary to look at what the statute itself has determined in that respect. I have no right to add to the requirements of the statute, nor to take from the requirements thus enacted. The sole guide must be the statute itself.

Now, that there were seven actual living persons who held shares in the company has not been doubted. As to the proportionate amounts held by each I will deal

---

* Though solvent, he appealed *in forma pauperis*. However, his counsel included four eminent lawyers, three of whom were Queen's Counsel. One of them, the future Lord Wrenbury, was perhaps the leading company lawyer of his day. His treatise on Company Law is now in its fourteenth edition.

presently; but it is important to observe that this first condition of the statute is satisfied, and it follows as a consequence that it would not be competent to any one—and certainly not to these persons themselves—to deny that they were shareholders.

I must pause here to point out that the statute enacts nothing as to the extent or degree of interest which may be held by each of the seven, or as to the proportion of interest or influence possessed by one or the majority of the shareholders over the others. One share is enough. Still less is it possible to contend that the motive of becoming shareholders or of making them shareholders is a field of inquiry which the statute itself recognises as legitimate. If they are shareholders, they are shareholders for all purposes; and even if the statute was silent as to the recognition of trusts, I should be prepared to hold that if six of them were the cestuis que trust of the seventh, whatever might be their rights inter se, the statute would have made them shareholders to all intents and purposes with their respective rights and liabilities, and, dealing with them in their relation to the company, the only relations which I believe the law would sanction would be that they were corporators of the corporate body.

I am simply here dealing with the provisions of the statute, and it seems to me to be essential to the artificial creation that the law should recognise only that artificial existence—quite apart from the motives or conduct of individual corporators. In saying this, I do not at all mean to suggest that if it could be established that this provision of the statute to which I am adverting had not been complied with, you could not go behind the certificate of incorporation to shew that a fraud had been committed upon the officer entrusted with the duty of giving the certificate, and that by some proceeding in the nature of scire facias you could not prove the fact that the company had no real legal existence. But short of such proof it seems to me impossible to dispute that once the company is legally incorporated it must be treated like any other independent person with its rights and liabilities appropriate to itself, and that the motives of those who took part in the promotion of the company are absolutely irrelevant in discussing what those rights and liabilities are.

I will for the sake of argument assume the proposition that the Court of Appeal lays down—that the formation of the company was a mere scheme to enable Aron Salomon to carry on business in the name of the company. I am wholly unable to follow the proposition that this was contrary to the true intent and meaning of the Companies Act. I can only find the true intent and meaning of the Act from the Act itself; and the Act appears to me to give a company a legal existence with, as I have said, rights and liabilities of its own, whatever may have been the ideas or schemes of those who brought it into existence.

I observe that the learned judge (Vaughan Williams J.) held that the business was Mr. Salomon's business, and no one else's, and that he chose to employ as agent a limited company; and he proceeded to argue that he was employing that limited company as agent, and that he was bound to indemnify that agent (the company). I confess it seems to me that that very learned judge becomes involved by this argument in a very singular contradiction. Either the limited company was a legal entity or it was not. If it was, the business belonged to it and not to Mr. Salomon. If it was not, there was no person and no thing to be an agent at all; and it is impossible to say at the same time that there is a company and there is not.

Lindley L.J., on the other hand, affirms that there were seven members of the company; but he says it is manifest that six of them were members simply in order to enable the seventh himself to carry on business with limited liability. The object of the whole arrangement is to do the very thing which the Legislature intended not to be done.

It is obvious to inquire where is that intention of the Legislature manifested in the statute. Even if we were at liberty to insert words to manifest that intention, I should have great difficulty in ascertaining what the exact intention thus imputed to the Legislature is, or was. In this particular case it is the members of one family that represent all the shares; but if the supposed intention is not limited to so narrow a proposition as this, that the seven shareholders must not be members of one family, to what extent may influence or authority or intentional purchase of a majority among the shareholders be carried so as to bring it within the supposed prohibition? It is, of course, easy to say that it was contrary to the intention of the Legislature—a proposition which, by reason of its generality, it is difficult to bring to the test; but when one seeks to put as an affirmative proposition what the thing is which the Legislature has prohibited, there is, as it appears to me, an insuperable difficulty in the way of those who seek to insert by construction such a prohibition into the statute.

As one mode of testing the proposition, it would be pertinent to ask whether two or three, or indeed all seven, may constitute the whole of the shareholders? Whether they must be all independent of each other in the sense of each having an independent beneficial interest? And this is a question that cannot be answered by the reply that it is a matter of degree. If the Legislature intended to prohibit something, you ought to know what that something is. All it has said is that one share is sufficient to constitute a shareholder, though the shares may be 100,000 in number. Where am I to get from the statute itself a limitation of that provision that that shareholder must be an independent and beneficially interested person?

My Lords, I find all through the judgment of the Court of Appeal a repetition of the same proposition to which I have already adverted—that the business was the business of Aron Salomon, and that the company is variously described as a myth and a fiction. Lopes L.J. says: "The Act contemplated the incorporation of seven independent bona fide members, who had a mind and a will of their own, and were not the mere puppets of an individual who, adopting the machinery of the Act, carried on his old business in the same way as before, when he was a sole trader." The words "seven independent bona fide members with a mind and will of their own, and not the puppets of an individual," are by construction to be read into the Act. Lopes L.J. also said tht the company was a mere nominis umbra. Kay L.J. says: "The statutes were intended to allow seven or more persons, bona fide associated for the purpose of trade, to limit their liability under certain conditions and to become a corporation. But they were not intended to legalise a pretended association for the purpose of enabling an individual to carry on his own business with limited liability in the name of a joint stock company."

My Lords, the learned judges appear to me not to have been absolutely certain in their own minds whether to treat the company as a real thing or not. If it was a real thing; if it had a legal existence, and if consequently the law attributed to it certain rights and liabilities in its constitution as a company, it appears to me to follow as a consequence that it is impossible to deny the validity of the transactions into which it has entered.

Vaughan Williams J. appears to me to have disposed of the argument that the company (which for this purpose he assumed to be a legal entity) was defrauded into the purchase of Aron Salomon's business because, assuming that the price paid for the business was an exorbitant one, as to which I am myself not satisfied, but assuming that it was, the learned judge most cogently observes that when all the shareholders are perfectly cognisant of the conditions under which the company is formed and the conditions of the purchase, it is impossible to contend that the company is being defrauded.

The proposition laid down in *Erlanger v. New Sombrero Phosphate Co.* [3 App. Cas. 1218] (I quote the head-note), is that "Persons who purchase property and then create a company to purchase from them the property they possess, stand in a fiduciary position towards that company, and must faithfully state to the company the facts which apply to the property, and would influence the company in deciding on the reasonableness of acquiring it." But if every member of the company—every shareholder—knows exactly what is the true state of the facts (which for this purpose must be assumed to be the case here), Vaughan Williams J.'s conclusion seems to me to be inevitable that no case of fraud upon the company could here be established. If there was no fraud and no agency, and if the company was a real one and not a fiction or a myth, every one of the grounds upon which it is sought to support the judgment is disposed of.

My Lords, the truth is that the learned judges have never allowed in their own minds the proposition that the company has a real existence. They have been struck by what they have considered the inexpediency of permitting one man to be in influence and authority the whole company; and, assuming that such a thing could not have been intended by the Legislature, they have sought various grounds upon which they might insert into the Act some prohibition of such a result. Whether such a result be right or wrong, politic or impolitic, I say, with the utmost deference to the learned judges, that we have nothing to do with that question if this company has been duly constituted by law; and, whatever may be the motives of those who constitute it, I must decline to insert into that Act of Parliament limitations which are not to be found there.

I have dealt with this matter upon the narrow hypothesis propounded by the learned judges below; but it is, I think, only justice to the appellant to say that I see nothing whatever to justify the imputations which are implied in some of the observations made by more than one of the learned judges. The appellant, in my opinion, is not shewn to have done or to have intended to do anything dishonest or unworthy, but to have suffered a great misfortune without any fault of his own.

The result is that I move your Lordships that the judgment appealed from be reversed. ...

LORD WATSON: ... The memorandum of association gave notice that the main object for which the company was formed was to adopt and carry into effect, with or without modifications, the agreement of July, 1892, in terms of which the debentures for £10,000 were subsequently given to the appellant in part payment of the price. By the articles of association (art. 62(e)) the directors were empowered to issue mortgage or other debentures or bonds for any debts due, or to become due, from the company; and it is not alleged or proved that there was any failure to comply with s. 43 or the other clauses (Part III. of the Act) which relate to the protection of creditors. The unpaid creditors of the company, whose unfortunate position has been attributed to the fraud of the appellant, if they had thought fit to avail themselves of the means of protecting their interests which the Act provides, could have informed themselves of the terms of purchase by the company, of the issue of debentures to the appellant, and of the amount of shares held by each member. In my opinion, the statute casts upon them the duty of making inquiry in regard to these matters. Whatever may be the moral duty of a limited company and its shareholders, when the trade of the company is not thriving, the law does not lay any obligation upon them to warn those members of the public who deal with them on credit that they run the risk of not being paid. One of the learned judges asserts, and I see no reason to question the accuracy of his statement, that creditors never think of examining the register of debentures. But the apathy of a creditor cannot justify an imputation of fraud against a limited company or its members, who have provided all the means of information which the Act of 1862 requires; and, in my opinion, a creditor who will not take the trouble to use the means which the statute provides for enabling him to protect himself must bear the consequences of his own negligence. ...

LORD MACNAGHTEN: My Lords, I cannot help thinking that the appellant, Aron Salomon, has been dealt with somewhat hardly in this case.

Mr. Salomon, who is now suing as a pauper, was a wealthy man in July, 1892. He was a boot and shoe manufacturer trading on his own sole account under the firm of "A. Salomon & Co.," in High Street, Whitechapel, where he had extensive warehouses and a large establishment. He had been in the trade over thirty years. He had lived in the same neighbourhood all along, and for many years past he had occupied the same premises. So far things had gone very well with him. Beginning with little or no capital, he had gradually built up a thriving business, and he was undoubtedly in good credit and repute.

It is impossible to say exactly what the value of the business was. But there was a substantial surplus of assets over liabilities. And it seems to me to be pretty clear that if Mr. Salomon had been minded to dispose of his business in the market as a going concern he might fairly have counted upon retiring with at least £10,000 in his pocket.

* * *

The company was intended from the first to be a private company; it remained a private company to the end. No prospectus was issued; no invitation to take shares was ever addressed to the public.

The subscribers to the memorandum were Mr. Salomon, his wife, and five of his children who were grown up. The subscribers met and appointed Mr. Salomon and his two elder sons directors. The directors then proceeded to carry out the proposed transfer. By an agreement dated August 2, 1892, the company adopted the preliminary contract, and in accordance with it the business was taken over by the company as from June 1, 1892. The price fixed by the contract was duly paid. The price on paper was extravagant. It amounted to over £39,000—a sum which represented the sanguine expectations of a fond owner rather than anything that can be called a businesslike or reasonable estimate of value. That, no doubt, is a circumstance which at first sight calls for observation; but when the facts of the case and the position of the parties are considered, it is difficult to see what bearing it has on the question before your Lordships. The purchase-money was paid in this way: as money came in, sums amounting in all to £30,000 were paid to Mr. Salomon, and then immediately returned to the company in exchange for fully-paid shares. The sum of £10,000 was paid in debentures for the like amount. The balance, with the exception of about £1,000 which Mr. Salomon seems to have received and retained, went in discharge of the debts and liabilities of the business at the time of the transfer, which were thus entirely wiped off. In the result, therefore, Mr. Salomon received for his business about £1,000 in cash, £10,000 in debentures, and half the nominal capital of the company in fully paid shares for what they were worth. No other shares were issued except the seven shares taken by the subscribers to the memorandum, who, of course, knew all the circumstances, and had therefore no ground for complaint on the score of overvaluation.

The company had a brief career: it fell upon evil days. Shortly after it was started there seems to have come a period of great depression in the boot and shoe trade. There were strikes of workmen too; and in view of that danger contracts with public bodies, which were the principal source of Mr. Salomon's profit, were split up and divided between different firms. The attempts made to push the business on behalf of the new company crammed its warehouses with unsaleable stock. Mr. Salomon seems to have done what he could: both he and his wife lent the company money; and then he got his debentures cancelled and reissued to a Mr. Broderip, who advanced him £5,000, which he immediately handed over to the company on loan. The temporary relief only hastened ruin. Mr. Broderip's interest was not paid when it became due. He took proceedings at once and got a receiver appointed. Then, of course, came liquidation and a forced sale of the company's assets. They realized enough to pay Mr. Broderip, but not enough to pay the debentures in full; and the unsecured creditors were consequently left out in the cold.

• • •

When the memorandum is duly signed and registered, though there be only seven shares taken, the subscribers are a body corporate "capable forthwith," to use the words of the enactment, "of exercising all the functions of an incorporated company." Those are strong words. The company attains maturity on its birth. There is no period of minority—no interval of incapacity. I cannot understand how a body corporate thus made "capable" by statute can lose its individuality by issuing the bulk of its capital to one person, whether he be a subscriber to the memorandum or not. The company is at law a different person altogether from the subscribers to the memorandum; and, though it may be that after incorporation the business is precisely the same as it was before, and the same persons are managers, and the same hands receive the profits, the company is not in law the agent of the subscribers or trustee for them. Nor are the subscribers as members liable, in any shape or form, except to the extent and in the manner provided by the Act. That is, I think, the declared intention of the enactment. If the view of the learned judge were sound, it would follow that no common law partnership could register as a company limited by shares without remaining subject to unlimited liability.

• • •

Among the principal reasons which induce persons to form private companies, as is stated very clearly by Mr. Palmer in his treatise on the subject, are the desire to avoid the risk of bankruptcy, and the increased facility afforded for borrowing money. By means of a private company, as Mr. Palmer observes, a trade can be carried on with limited liability, and without exposing the persons interested in it in the event of failure to the harsh provisions of the bankruptcy law. A company, too, can raise money on debentures, which an ordinary trader cannot do. Any member of a company, acting in good faith, is as much entitled to take and hold the company's debentures as any outside creditor. Every creditor is entitled to get and to hold the best security the law allows him to take.

If, however, the declaration of the Court of Appeal means that Mr. Salomon acted fraudulently or dishonestly, I must say I can find nothing in the evidence to support such an imputation. The purpose for which Mr. Salomon and the other subscribers to the memorandum were associated was "lawful." The fact that Mr. Salomon raised £5,000 for the company on debentures that belonged to him seems to me strong evidence of his good faith and of his confidence in the company. The unsecured creditors of A. Salomon and Company, Limited, may be entitled to sympathy, but they have only themselves to blame for their misfortunes. They trusted the company, I suppose, because they had long dealt with Mr. Salomon, and he had always paid his way; but they had full notice that they were no longer dealing with an individual, and they must be taken to have been cognisant of the memorandum and of the articles of association. For such a catastrophe as has occurred in this case some would blame the law that allows the creation of a floating charge. But a floating charge is too convenient a form of security to be lightly abolished. I have long thought, and I believe some of your Lordships also think, that the ordinary trade creditors of a trading company ought to have a preferential claim on the assets in liquidation in respect of debts incurred within a certain limited time before the winding-up. But that is not the law at present. Everybody knows that when there is a winding-up debenture-holders generally step in and sweep off everything; and a great scandal it is. ...

I am of opinion that the appeal ought to be allowed. ...

[The concurring judgments of Lords HERSCHELL, MORRIS and DAVEY are omitted.]

Order of the Court of Appeal reversed.

NOTES

1) Separate legal existence is not accorded to partnerships, and general partners are personally liable for firm debts. But a corporation is an entity separate from its shareholders, who are not ordinarily liable to corporate creditors. See CBCA s. 45(1). Statutory corporations not incorporated under general business corporations legislation such as the CBCA are also presumed to have been accorded limited liability. Cf. Interpretation Act, R.S.C. 1985, c. I-21, s. 21(1)(d).

2) What book value was attributed to the Salomon business prior to incorporation? Was it £39,000 or £31,000? What were the liabilities and equity on the completion of all the transactions described in the case?

3) On incorporation, was the business overvalued? If it was, was anyone thereby injured? How were any existing creditors of the business prejudiced if all of them were

paid off at incorporation? Would subsequent creditors be injured unless they had had access to the balance sheet of the corporation?

4) Part of the consideration received by Salomon on incorporation was an issue of £10,000 in debentures. A debenture is an evidence of indebtedness like a promissory note. Debentures are often, as in *Salomon*, secured with an interest in the collateral of the debtor corporation. There the debentures were pledged with Broderip as security for an advance of £5,000, such that they were still valuable to Salomon to the extent that the business in bankruptcy was worth more than that amount. Suppose that on incorporation the corporation had issued to Salomon shares with a stated value of £1,000 and a debenture for £29,000. Would this have prejudiced creditors? In what way?

5) What was the rationale for the requirement of seven shareholders in the English Companies Act? The trend in modern corporations statutes is to less formality on incorporation. Canadian corporations statutes, for example, uniformly permit "one-man" companies. As a device to prevent small firms from incorporating, a seven shareholder requirement was never a very reliable tool after *Salomon*.

Shareholder Liability. In general, shareholders are not liable for corporate debts under CBCA s. 45(1). Because of this, a corporation lacks the power to impose an annual assessment on its shareholders for the purpose of providing operating revenue, even if the firm is a non-profit one. *Case v. Edmonton Country Club* (1972), 30 D.L.R. (3d) 211 (Alta. App. Div.). The parties may bargain around this, and in small firms often do so. For example, the principals of a small firm will often find themselves providing its bank with personal guarantees, replicating a regime of unlimited liability for that creditor. In the same way, a partner can bargain out of unlimited liability under the OPA by private agreement with each of his creditors. Absent transaction costs, therefore, the choice of limited or unlimited liability regime is trivial. Shareholders who seek limited liability could either incorporate or carry on business as a partnership with costless agreements with all of their creditors. That said, the costs of negotiating such contracts will not be trivial in a world with positive transaction costs. Because of this, all parties may be better off where shareholders and partners are given the choice of limited liability regime, through a menu with both partnerships and corporate statutes upon it.

The CBCA imposes personal liability on shareholders in certain cases where the shareholders have participated in management wrongdoing. Under CBCA s. 45(1), shareholders are liable in three cases:

- a reduction of stated capital under s. 38 when the corporation is thereby rendered insolvent;
- a breach of duties imposed on shareholders under s. 146(5) when they assume management powers under a unanimous shareholders' agreement; and
- a claim by judgment creditors under s. 226(5) with respect to actions continued against a corporation after dissolution.

CBCA s. 118(5) also permits a court, if satisfied that it is equitable to do so, to order shareholders to repay money or property improperly distributed to them to the corporation. Such orders may be made when:

- payments are made when the corporation is insolvent or would be insolvent after a payment is made upon a share repurchase (s. 34), a redemption of preferred shares (s. 36), a dividend payment (s. 42), a loan (s. 44) and a repurchase under the appraisal remedy (s. 190) or the oppression remedy (s. 241); or
- an excessive commission is paid on an issue or sale of shares (s. 41).

These provisions find a parallel in Canadian bankruptcy and provincial fraudulent conveyance legislation. It is also possible that shareholders may be held liable when an insufficient consideration is paid on an issue of shares. Such liability, similar to that imposed under OLPA s. 16 (Chapter One, Section C), is discussed further in Chapter Four, Section B. Finally, in the circumstances described in the next section, separate corporate personality may be disregarded to subordinate shareholder claims or even impose personal liability.

Minimum Stated Capital. While the authority of the *Salomon* case is undisputed, the decision has generally been unpopular with academic commentators. Professor Kahn-Freund described it as "calamitous" and said "that the courts have failed to give that protection to the business creditors which should be the corollary of the privilege of limited liability." *Some Reflections on Company Law Reform*, 7 Mod. L. Rev. 54, 54, 55 (1944). As one remedy for this, the author suggested a minimum stated capital requirement. In other words, on incorporation the corporation would be required to receive at least a stipulated amount as consideration for the issue of shares. The only Canadian jurisdiction that adopted such a provision was New Brunswick, whose Companies Act prescribed an initial contribution of at least $500. R.S.N.B. 1973, c. C-13, s. 13(8). The $500 did not, of course, have to be set aside in a fund for the creditors, but could have been spent and lost in the course of business provided that it was not distributed to shareholders. Did this offer much protection to creditors? If not, would you prefer a minimum stated capital for all corporations of $10,000? of $100,000? How much benefit does this provide to a creditor who lends the firm money years later? A minimum stated capital requirement at one time was found in the American Model Business Corporations Act, but has long since been deleted. The provision has also been removed from the New Brunswick Business Corporations Act, S.N.B. 1981, c. B-9.1, which replaced the old Companies Act of that province.

How serious is the likelihood of distributional effects being visited upon consensual claimants which appears to underlie the demand for minimum stated capital requirements? Lord Macnaghten observed in *Salomon* that "Everybody knows that when there is a winding-up debenture-holders generally step in and sweep off everything. ..." If so, how are consensual creditors harmed? The problem might instead have been, *pace* Lord Macnaghten, that creditors were unaware of the special bankruptcy rights accorded Mr. Salomon, since "floating charges" over current assets of the kind he took were still in their infancy. A shift in legal regimes, such as occurs when a novel kind of claim is enforced, may indeed produce transitional wealth transfer effects. But can much be left of these effects today, when the existence of secured lending (and of limited liability) is well known to businessmen?

It is in any event possible to overemphasize the benefits to creditors of their debtors' unlimited liability; similarly, the dangers of limited liability may be exaggerated.

First, the fact that unlimited liability provides access to the personal assets of partners (or guarantors of the firm's debts) will not be equivalent to payment in full when those persons are insufficiently wealthy to cover the shortfall in the firm's assets. This is, in fact, the usual situation. Second, businessmen have developed techniques to avoid debilitating losses from the insolvency of debtors with limited liability. For example, with limited liability regimes trade creditors may diversify away much of the risk of serious prejudice to their business on an individual debtor's default when they conduct a volume business with many debtors. A reserve will be established for bad debts, which will simply be treated as a cost of doing business. If further insurance is required, the creditor can sell his accounts receivable to a factor, who takes on the risk of non-payment in exchange for a discount off the face value of the accounts. Finally, bad debt losses are split with taxing authorities through bad debt deductibility. See further B. Manning, *Legal Capital* 91-101 (3d ed. 1990).

Theories of Limited Liability. If a firm's capital structure decision does not give rise to distributional effects, there would seem to be little need for legal barriers to limited liability regimes. But if liability regimes are distributionally neutral, an efficiency explanation is required for the popularity of limited liability. When incorporation does not shift wealth from claimants to firms (or equity claimants), the transaction costs of incorporating (approximately $1,000) will chill the organization of corporations unless new wealth is created. Some of the advantages of incorporation that do not relate to liability regimes were discussed by Cameron in Chapter One; is there, however, a further advantage associated with limited liability?

At first glance, the most apparent benefit of limited liability is that it permits those promoters most averse to risk (e.g., Gagnon) to shift the burden of default to the shoulders of creditors. To understand what *risk aversion* means, it is necessary to recall how we defined expected monetary value in Chapter One, Section A. One who is *risk neutral* will always choose the investment opportunity with the highest *EMV*. For example, a risk neutral investor will prefer an opportunity with a 0.5 probability of $200 and a 0.5 probability of 0 to a 100% certainty of $95. But a risk averse investor may prefer the sure thing, in effect paying a $5 insurance premium to pass up the first opportunity. Individuals are ordinarily presumed to be risk averse, particularly if nearing retirement age like Gagnon. On the other hand, large businesses (which is what most creditors are) are frequently presumed risk neutral, since the risk of a default on a single account may be dissipated (or diversified away) when the creditor holds accounts with many debtors. The creditor might then consider itself effectively insured against the risk of default by one debtor due to risks idiosyncratic to that debtor. Offering limited liability to Gagnon would then be efficient if it replicates the insurance features of the contract the parties would have negotiated in a hypothetical agreement. The claimholder's contract on incorporation would resemble an insurance contract, in which risk averse equity holders insure with creditors who are more tolerant of risk.

A differential risk aversion argument for limited liability might not seem convincing, since it assumes that shareholders fear risk more than creditors. At first glance, one might have presumed just the opposite, since equity claims are more volatile than debt ones. The paradox is more apparent than real, however, for the shareholder of a small enterprise will generally have far more to lose on the firm's default than its creditors. For creditors, default typically means that a small portion of their accounts receivable have gone bad. For the shareholder, however, the consequences of default are far more severe, even under limited liability. Default will often mean the loss of his job as well as of a significant portion of his current assets. Because of this, the shareholder may indeed be more risk averse than the creditors.

The following article discusses other possible efficiencies of limited liability in the case of public firms, where equity interests are widely distributed in the hands of outside shareholders who do not take part in firm management. The directors and officers of a corporation who supervise and manage such firms are to be distinguished from outside equity interests, unlike small businesses where ownership and control are in the same hands. This separation of ownership and control in widely held corporations introduces an agency cost problem, since firm managers (as agents) have imperfect incentives to maximize the interest of all claimholders (as principals). In competitive markets for firm claims, such agency costs (which include the adverse incentive costs discussed above) are ultimately borne by the firm, which will therefore seek to minimize them. One strategy that it may rely on is claimholder monitoring, in which firm managers are supervised for misbehaviour by claimholders. Since these monitoring costs are also incurred by the firm, it will seek to minimize the sum of monitoring and of residual agency costs. One device it may use for this purpose, according to Easterbrook and Fischel, is the selection of a limited liability regime.

Easterbrook & Fischel, Limited Liability in the Corporation
52 U. Chi. L. Rev. 89, 93-101 (1985)

A. Limited Liability and the Theory of the Firm

People can conduct economic activity in many forms. Those who perceive entrepreneurial opportunities must decide whether to organize a sole proprietorship, general or limited partnership, business trust, close or publicly held corporation. Debt investors in all of these ventures possess limited liability. Equity investors in publicly held corporations, limited partnerships, and business trusts do too. Limited liability for equity investors has long been explained as a benefit bestowed on investors by the state. It is much more accurately analyzed as a logical consequence of the differences among the forms for conducting economic activity.

Publicly held corporations typically dominate other organizational forms when the technology of production requires firms to combine both the specialized skills of multiple agents and large amounts of capital.[6] The publicly held corporation facilitates the division of labor. The distinct functions of managerial skills and the provision of capital (and the bearing of risk) may be separated and assigned to different people—workers who lack capital, and owners of funds who lack specialized production skills. Those

---

6   For a fuller analysis, see Fama, *Agency Problems and the Theory of the Firm*, 88 J. Pol. Econ. 288 (1980) ...; Fama & Jensen, *Separation of Ownership and Control*, 26 J.L. & Econ. 301 (1983).

who invest capital can bear additional risk, because each investor is free to participate in many ventures. The holder of a diversified portfolio of investments is more willing to bear the risk that a small fraction of his investments will not pan out.

Of course this separation of functions is not costless. The separation of investment and management requires firms to create devices by which these participants monitor each other and guarantee their own performance. Neither group will be perfectly trustworthy. Moreover, managers who do not obtain the full benefits of their own performance do not have the best incentives to work efficiently. The costs of the separation of investment and management (agency costs) may be substantial. Nonetheless, we know from the survival of large corporations that the costs generated by agency relations are outweighed by the gains from separation and specialization of function. Limited liability reduces the costs of this separation and specialization.[7]

First, limited liability decreases the need to monitor. All investors risk losing wealth because of the actions of agents. They could monitor these agents more closely. The more risk they bear, the more they will monitor. But beyond a point more monitoring is not worth the cost. Moreover, specialized risk bearing implies that many investors will have diversified holdings. Only a small portion of their wealth will be invested in any one firm. These diversified investors have neither the expertise nor the incentive to monitor the actions of specialized agents. Limited liability makes diversification and passivity a more rational strategy and so potentially reduces the cost of operating the corporation.

Of course, rational shareholders understand the risk that the managers' acts will cause them loss. They do not meekly accept it. The price they are willing to pay for shares will reflect the risk. Managers therefore find ways to offer assurances to investors without the need for direct monitoring; those who do this best will attract the most capital from investors. Managers who do not implement effective controls increase the discount. As it grows, so does the investors' incentive to incur costs to reduce the divergence of interest between specialized managers and risk bearers.[8] Limited liability reduces these costs. Because investors' potential losses are "limited" to the amount of their investment as opposed to their entire wealth, they spend less to protect their positions.

Second, limited liability reduces the costs of monitoring other shareholders. Under a rule exposing equity investors to additional liability, the greater the wealth of other shareholders, the lower the probability that any one shareholder's assets will be needed to pay a judgment. Thus existing shareholders would have incentives to engage in costly monitoring of other shareholders to ensure that they do not transfer assets to others or sell to others with less wealth. Limited liability makes the identity of other shareholders irrelevant and thus avoids these costs.

---

7   Firms develop a large number of other devices that reduce the costs of the agency relation. See generally Agency: The Structure of Business (J. Pratt & R. Zeckhauser eds. forthcoming); Easterbrook, *Manager's Discretion and Investors' Welfare: Theories and Evidence*, Del. J. Corp. L. (forthcoming).

8   See Jensen & Meckling, *Theory of the Firm: Managerial Behavior, Agency Costs and Ownership Structure*, 3 J. Fin. Econ. 305, 313 (1976).

Third, by promoting free transfer of shares, limited liability gives managers incentives to act efficiently. We have emphasized that individual shareholders lack the expertise and incentive to monitor the actions of specialized agents. Investors individually respond to excessive agency costs by disinvesting. Of course, the price at which shareholders are able to sell reflects the value of the firm as affected by decisions of specialized agents. But the ability of individual investors to sell creates new opportunities for investors as a group and thus constrains agents' actions. So long as shares are tied to votes, poorly run firms will attract new investors who can assemble large blocs at a discount and install new managerial teams.[10] This potential for displacement gives existing managers incentives to operate efficiently in order to keep share prices high.

Although this effect of the takeover mechanism is well known, the relation between takeovers and limited liability is not. Limited liability reduces the costs of purchasing shares. Under a rule of limited liability, the value of shares is determined by the present value of the income stream generated by a firm's assets. The identity and wealth of other investors is irrelevant. Shares are fungible; they trade at one price in liquid markets. Under a rule of unlimited liability, as Halpern, Trebilcock, and Turnbull emphasized, shares would not be fungible. Their value would be a function of the present value of future cash flows *and* of the wealth of shareholders. The lack of fungibility would impede their acquisition. An acquiror who wanted to purchase a control bloc of shares under a rule of unlimited liability might have to negotiate separately with individual shareholders, paying different prices to each. Worse, the acquiror in corporate control transactions typically is much wealthier than the investors from which it acquires the shares. The anticipated cost of additional capital contributions would be higher to the new holder than the old ones. This may be quite important to a buyer considering the acquisition of a firm in financial trouble, for there would be a decent chance of being required to contribute to satisfy debts if the plan for revitalization of the firm should go awry. Limited liability allows a person to buy a large bloc without taking any risk of being surcharged, and thus it facilitates beneficial control transactions. A rule that facilitates transfers of control also induces managers to work more effectively to stave off such transfers, and so it reduces the costs of specialization whether or not a firm is acquired.

Fourth, limited liability makes it possible for market prices to impound additional information about the value of firms. With unlimited liability, shares would not be homogeneous commodities, so they would no longer have one market price. Investors would therefore be required to expend greater resources analyzing the prospects of the firm in order to know whether "the price is right." When all can trade on the same terms, though, investors trade until the price of shares reflects the available information about a firm's prospects. Most investors need not expend resources on search; they can accept the market price as given and purchase at a "fair" price.[11]

---

10   See ... Easterbrook & Fischel, *Corporate Control Transactions*, 91 Yale L.J. 698 (1982); Manne, *Mergers and the Market for Corporate Control*, 73 J. Pol. Econ. 110 (1965).

11   See J. Lorie & M. Hamilton, *The Stock Market: Theories and Evidence* (1973); Fischel, *Use of Modern Finance Theory in Securities Fraud Cases Involving Actively Traded Securities*, 38 Bus. Law 1 (1982); Gilson & Kraakman, *The Mechanisms of Market Efficiency*, 70 Va. L. Rev. 549 (1984).

Fifth, as Henry Manne emphasized, limited liability allows more efficient diversification. Investors can minimize risk by owning a diversified portfolio of assets. Firms can raise capital at lower costs because investors need not bear the special risk associated with nondiversified holdings. This is true, though, only under a rule of limited liability or some good substitute. Diversification would increase rather than reduce risk under a rule of unlimited liability. If any one firm went bankrupt, an investor could lose his entire wealth. The rational strategy under unlimited liability, therefore, would be to minimize the number of securities held. As a result, investors would be forced to bear risk that could have been avoided by diversification, and the cost to firms of raising capital would rise.

Sixth, limited liability facilitates optimal investment decisions. When investors hold diversified portfolios, managers maximize investors' welfare by investing in any project with a positive net present value. They can accept high-variance ventures (such as the development of new products) without exposing the investors to ruin. Each investor can hedge against the failure of one project by holding stock in other firms. In a world of unlimited liability, though, managers would behave differently. They would reject as "too risky" some projects with positive net present values. Investors would want them to do this because it would be the best way to reduce risks.[12] By definition this would be a social loss, because projects with a positive net present value are beneficial uses of capital.

Both those who want to raise capital for entrepreneurial ventures, and society as a whole, receive benefits from limited liability. The equity investors will do about as well under one rule of liability as another. Every investor must choose between riskless T-bills and riskier investments. The more risk comes with an equity investment, the less the investor will pay. Investors bid down the price of equity until, at the margin, the risk-adjusted returns of stock and T-bills are the same. So long as the rule of liability is known, investors will price shares accordingly.[13] The choice of an inefficient rule, however, will shrink the pool of funds available for investment in projects that would subject investors to risk. The increased availability of funds for projects with positive net values is the real benefit of limited liability.

B. Limited Liability and Firms' Costs of Capital

Limited liability does not eliminate the risk of business failure. Someone must bear that loss. Limited liability is an arrangement under which the loss largely lies where it falls. Loss is swallowed rather than shifted. Each investor has a guaranteed maximum on the loss he will bear. In a firm with debt, that guaranteed maximum is combined with a preference for the debtholder. The shareholder is wiped out first. To this extent risk is "shifted" from debt investor to equity investor. In a regime of unlimited liability still more risk would be shifted.

---

12   In the jargon of portfolio theory, when investors are or can be diversified, managers should consider only systematic risk in making decisions. When investors cannot diversify their holdings, managers should consider both systematic and unsystematic risk. The consideration of unsystematic risk may lead them to forgo profitable investments.

13   This is an implication of the Coase Theorem. Coase, *The Problem of Social Cost,* 3 J.L. & Econ. 1 (1960).

Because someone must bear the entire risk of business failure under any rule, some have argued that the importance of limited liability has been exaggerated.[14] The benefit to stockholders from limited liability, the argument runs, is exactly offset by the detriment to creditors. Stockholders are more secure and so demand a lower rate of return under limited liability, but creditors demand a higher rate; the opposite is true under unlimited liability. The firm's cost of capital, the argument continues, is the same under either rule. ...

The validity of this argument depends on whether the risk that the value of the firm will be less than the value of the creditors' claims can be borne equally well by creditors and stockholders. Several factors are pertinent to this question: the extent of common interests, relative monitoring costs, relative information and coordination costs, and attitudes toward risk.

1. *The Extent of Common Interests.* The argument that firms' cost of capital does not vary with the liability rule depends on the assumption that the benefit to stockholders from limited liability is exactly offset by the detriment to creditors. This assumption is false, for the reasons developed in Part [A].

Consider the relation between limited liability and takeover bids. Takeovers are beneficial for shareholders—takeovers are a mechanism for transferring assets to higher-valued uses, and even the threat of takeover provides managers with an incentive to operate efficiently and keep share prices high. The effect of takeovers on creditors is less clear. Managers who pursue an overly conservative investment strategy that benefits creditors but does not maximize the value of the firm, for example, may be ousted in a takeover. Thus some takeovers may cause creditors to be worse off ex post. But so long as takeovers increase the probability that the value of firms' assets will be maximized, shareholders and creditors, joint claimants on a bigger pie, will be better off. Thus a regime including takeovers benefits creditors as well as shareholders.[15] The other effects are straightforward, too. The capital market is more likely to be efficient under a rule of limited liability. An efficient capital market generates price signals that are useful to all investors in a firm, including creditors. Limited liability decreases the cost of searching for good investments for creditors as well as stockholders.

2. *Relative Monitoring Costs.* Shareholders have less reason to incur costs in monitoring managers and other shareholders under limited than under unlimited liability. The decreased incentive to monitor managers is arguably offset by the increased incentive of creditors to monitor managers' actions. But this will not happen because of the preference among the investors. Because equity investors lose their investments first, they will have a greater interest in monitoring the firm. Indeed, this intra-investor preference is an important ingredient in a system of optimal monitoring. Concentrating the entire marginal gain and loss on one group of investors induces them to make the appropriate expenditures on monitoring (or to sell to someone who will), while enabling the more

---

14   Ekelund & Tollison, *Mercantilist Origins of the Corporation*, 11 Bell J. Econ. 715 (1980); Meiners, Mofsky & Tollison, *Piercing the Veil of Limited Liability*, 4 Del. J. Corp. L. 351 (1979).

15   The available evidence suggests that shareholders gain and creditors do not lose in control transactions. Asquith & Kim, *The Impact of Merger Bids on the Participating Firms' Security Holders*, 37 J. Fin. 1209 (1982).

secure investors to avoid making redundant expenditures. The secured creditor has the safest claim of all and may elect to monitor only the state of its security rather than the state of the whole firm. Secured debt thus may be a way of reducing monitoring costs still further.[16]

So debt claimants do not increase their monitoring of managers to offset shareholders' reductions exactly. Moreover, debt investors do not incur costs that offset the reduction of intra-shareholder monitoring under limited liability. The wealth of other creditors is irrelevant whether or not shareholders possess limited liability, because creditors possess limited liability under either rule. The monitoring costs are lower when both shareholders and creditors possess limited liability than when only creditors do.

3. *Relative Information and Coordination Costs.* Another reason why shareholders pay creditors to assume more of the risk of business failure might be that the creditors possess a comparative advantage in monitoring particular managerial actions. As we have stressed, individual shareholders, specialized suppliers of capital, do not actively monitor managers' actions. They rely on third parties (such as large institutional holders or prospective contestants for control) to do so and buy shares at appropriate moments. Though the debt investors do not have the residual claim, and thus do not have optimal incentives to monitor day-to-day activities, they may be especially well suited to watch certain kinds of conduct.

Banks and other institutional investors tend to have specialized knowledge about particular industries and may be good monitors of major decisions such as building new plants. The lender may provide financing to several firms in an industry and thus augment its knowledge. These debt investors commonly negotiate detailed contracts giving them the right to disapprove managers' decisions that are important enough to create significant new risk for the firm, though perhaps not important enough to spark a contest for control.

An investor's possession of particular information does not, however, explain why an investment takes the form of debt rather than equity. Lower coordination costs might explain debt financing. Compare the situation of a sophisticated shareholder with a sophisticated creditor (or the indenture trustee for a group of creditors). Even if the sophisticated shareholder has the ability to monitor, he has little incentive to do so. He bears all the costs, but the benefits accrue to all other shareholders according to the size of their holdings. The creditor, by contrast, captures more of the benefits of his monitoring activity, because there are fewer other members of the same class of investor. When there are many creditors of the same class, the indenture trustee is the response to the freerider problem. Because the costs of monitoring by the trustee are shared by all the bondholders of a particular class, the trustee is not plagued by the same coordination problems facing any individual investor.[17] When creditors have lower coordination and

---

16   This argument avoids the critique Alan Schwartz offers of previous efforts to explain secured debt. Compare Schwartz, *The Continuing Puzzle of Secured Debt*, 37 Vand. L. Rev. 1051, 1055-59 (1984), with Levmore, *Monitors and Freeriders in Commercial and Corporate Settings*, 92 Yale L.J. 49, 55, 59 (1982).

17   For a discussion of the role of secured creditors and indentures trustees in overcoming the free-rider problem, see Levmore, supra note 16, at 68-73. The introduction of multiple classes of investors creates problems of its own, but we do not address them here. See Jackson, *Bankruptcy, Non-Bankruptcy Entitlements, and the Creditors' Bargain*, 91 Yale L.J. 857 (1982).

information costs than shareholders, limited liability has a clear advantage. Because creditors bear more of the risk of business failure under a rule of limited liability, they have more incentive to employ their knowledge.

4. *Attitudes Toward Risk.* Both equity and debt investors can diversify their holdings, thus minimizing the risk of investing in any one firm. Economy-wide (systematic) risk, however, cannot be eliminated by diversification. Where two parties are risk averse, the optimal contractual arrangement is one in which each bears some risk.[18] Limited liability is such a risk-sharing arrangement. Under limited liability, both shareholders and creditors risk the loss of their investments; under unlimited liability, shareholders would bear almost all risk. Risk sharing therefore might be a good explanation of limited liability.

Limited Liability. Easterbrook and Fischel argue that limited liability economizes on costs associated with information production and risk aversion, both kinds of costs being borne by the firm in efficient capital markets. As such, limited liability permits a firm to lower its cost of capital, enabling it to raise more money when it issues claims against itself than it would under unlimited liability.

In Arguments One, Two and Four, Easterbrook and Fischel assert that limited liability reduces information costs. The first argument posits monitoring efficiencies, and assumes (1) that information about management misbehaviour may be produced through the monitoring of managers by claimants, and (2) that there are economies of scale in the production of such information. Monitoring costs may then be reduced if monitoring responsibilities are assigned in a hypothetical claimholders' bargain to those with the largest stakes in the firm, with investors with a small interest in the firm free riding on the monitoring performed by major claimants. Given economies of scale, a major investor can produce more information about the firm than could many small investors who together absorb the same total amount of costs in the production of information. Limited liability thus facilitates a broadly based equity market, characterized by investors with relatively small stakes in the firm. Easterbrook and Fischel's fourth argument of limited liability is then that, with such markets for equity claims, better information about equity and firm value will result. The information produced by a market for stock will exceed that which any single mind could produce, even if it were in possession of all of the facts. Moreover, when the facts about the value of various firms are dispersed among many people, market prices may coordinate all of their search activities, with individual investors trading without any one of them knowing all of the information disclosed to the market. The now classic statement of this theory may be found in Hayek, *The Use of Knowledge in Society*, 35 Am. Econ. Rev. 519 (1945). In addition, under limited liability

---

18   For applications of this point, see Marcus, *Risk Sharing and the Theory of the Firm*, 13 Bell J. Econ. 369 (1982); Polinsky, *Risk Sharing through Breach of Contract Remedies*, 12 J. Legal Stud. 427, 433 (1983); Shavell, *Risk Sharing and Incentives in the Principal-Agent Relationship*, 10 Bell J. Econ. 55, 65 (1979).

shareholders would not be required to monitor the wealth of other shareholders, which is available as a common fund on the firm's default under unlimited liability.

In their third argument, Easterbrook and Fischel note that limited liability may reduce agency costs. Under a theory first propounded by Henry Manne (and discussed below in Chapters Six and Eleven), the possibility of a take-over is an incentive to managerial efficiency: share prices of inefficiently run firms trade at a discount, and therefore represent a bargain investment for acquiring firms which believe that they can operate them more efficiently. Since management of the acquired firm can expect to be displaced on a successful take-over bid, it will seek to manage the firm efficiently in order to remove the threat of a take-over. The market for corporate control would, however, be made more expensive by unlimited liability, since the acquiring firm would have to bear the special costs associated with the non-fungibility of the stock.

Easterbrook and Fischel's fifth and sixth arguments refer to the ways in which limited liability dissipates the effects of risk aversion. Investors can diversify away risk specific to any one firm by investing in a variety of firms in different industries. Where investors are risk averse, such a diversification strategy amounts to a cheap form of insurance against risks idiosyncratic to any firm. In addition, when investors have spread their investment portfolio around several different firms in this way, they can be presumed to want each firm to invest in a risk neutral fashion. That is to say, they will not wish the firms to choose low return-low risk investments where investments with a higher *EMV* are available. This will in turn increase firm value. Both of these advantages may, however, be lost with unlimited liability since investor risk aversion will then be heightened.

Limited liability theories are also discussed in Halpern, Trebilcock & Turnbull, *An Economic Analysis of Limited Liability in Corporation Law*, 30 U. of Toronto L.J. 117 (1980); Posner, *The Rights of Creditors of Affiliated Corporations*, 43 U. Chi. L. Rev. 499 (1976).

B. DISREGARDING THE CORPORATE ENTITY

The House of Lords decided in *Salomon* that a "one-man" corporation formed to limit its promoter's liability was not a sham, but there are other circumstances where the incorporation decision might reasonably be impeached, with courts disregarding the corporate entity by "piercing the corporate veil." Limited liability or separate corporate status may at times be inefficient, with net claimant wealth maximized when the veil is pierced. An argument for disregarding the corporate entity may then be made when (1) the assertion of separate corporate status amounts to the breach of an implicit contractual provision or statutory policy; (2) the firm has in effect represented that liability is unlimited; and (3) unlimited liability can be justified as a response to incentive costs which may arise when some firm claimants are non-consensual. Such efficiency arguments for disregarding the corporate entity may overlap with lingering distributional concerns, since not all claimants are as able to react to a liability regime as are trade creditors. If creditors assume that liability is unlimited, then, incorporation will transfer wealth from them to the firm.

1. Gap-Filling

Saskatchewan Economic Development Corp. v. Patterson-Boyd Mfg. Corp.
Saskatchewan Court of Appeal
[1981] 2 W.W.R. 40, 6 Sask. R. 325

HALL J.A. (by whom the judgment of the Court was delivered; Woods and Bayda JJ.A. concurring): This is an appeal from Halvorson J., who held that a debenture in favour of the respondent P-B Fabricators Ltd. took priority over one in favour of the appellant as a charge on some of the assets of the respondent Patterson-Boyd Manufacturing Corporation ([1980] 5 W.W.R. 381).

Patterson-Boyd Manufacturing Corporation was incorporated on 4th April 1978. It was in the business of marketing pumps and of custom manufacturing. The directors and principal shareholders were C. Robert Patterson, Hugh J.C. Boyd and Leo Hoffman.

On 28th April 1978 pursuant to an agreement in writing the appellant loaned to the respondent Patterson-Boyd Manufacturing Corporation the sum of $131,175. As security the respondent Patterson-Boyd Manufacturing Corporation executed a debenture which provided a fixed and specific charge on certain of its chattels and a first floating charge on all of its other assets. This debenture was registered under the provisions of the Corporation Securities Registration Act, R.S.S. 1978, c. C-39, on 1st May 1978.

Patterson, Boyd and Hoffman, who executed the loan agreement as officers of the respondent Patterson Boyd Manufacturing Corporation, were also parties to the agreement in their personal capacities. They agreed to personally guarantee the performance by Patterson Boyd Manufacturing Corporation of its obligations under the agreement.

Among the terms of the loan agreement are the following:

Article III
Special Covenants by the Borrower

2. That the Borrower will not, during the term of this Agreement and while any moneys owing hereunder remain unpaid, without the consent in writing of the Corporation being first had and obtained ...

(b) change or alter its capital structure, create any subsidiary company, amalgamate, consolidate or merge with any other company or sell or otherwise dispose of its business or assets or any redeemable shares or securities; ...

(e) pay principal or interest on any loan heretofore made or hereafter to be made to it by any shareholder, and/or associated company; ...

(h) make any sales to or purchases from any company, organization or person, in which the Borrower or any of its directors, officers or known major shareholders are interested, directly or indirectly, except at prevailing market prices, with credit terms consistent with granted other nonrelated customers: the intention of this provision being that all its dealings with any company or organization in which such directors, officers or shareholders may be interested shall be on an arm's length basis.

Patterson, Boyd and Hoffman also executed a document entitled "Assignment and Postponement of Claim" whereby they agreed to postpone all debts and liabilities, present and future, of the respondent Patterson Boyd Manufacturing Corporation to them in favour of the appellant.

There is nothing in the evidence to support the finding by the learned trial judge that at the time the appellant took its debenture the respondent Patterson Boyd Manufacturing Corporation was in the pump business only. Indeed, the evidence of Patterson indicated otherwise.

• • •

However, by January 1979 Patterson-Boyd Manufacturing Corporation was experiencing financial difficulty. It defaulted in the payment due to the appellant on 1st January 1979 and continued in default until the appellant appointed a receiver-manager under the terms of its debenture on 4th April 1979.

About the time that the appellant made its loan to Patterson-Boyd Manufacturing Corporation the company's bank agreed to extend its line of credit from $100,000 to $200,000. In January 1979 the balance owing to the bank was approximately $170,000. In January the bank called the amount over $100,000. For the company to continue in business it was necessary to pay the bank approximately $70,000 and also to raise funds to meet the payroll.

Patterson and Boyd, on or about 11th January 1979, started a bank account in the name of "P-B Fabricators." The initial balance of $116,000 was made up by the following contributions:

Patterson and family	$99,000
Boyd	15,000
Ron Proctor	2,000

On 11th January 1979 Patterson issued a cheque on this account in favour of Patterson-Boyd Manufacturing Corporation for $113,900.

On 16th January 1979 the respondent P-B Fabricators Ltd. was incorporated. Patterson and Boyd were the directors and principal shareholders. On 19th January 1979 Patterson-Boyd Manufacturing Corporation executed a debenture in favour of P-B Fabricators Ltd. to secure the amount of $200,000. This debenture was registered on 25th January 1979. It purported to give P-B Fabricators Ltd. "a first and paramount encumbrance upon the Borrower's inventory and the proceeds thereof."

The inventory referred to was defined as follows:

goods held for sale or being processed for sale in the Borrower's business as now or hereafter conducted, including all raw materials, supplies, and other materials used or consumed in the Borrower's business, goods in process, finished goods and all other items customarily classified as inventory, but shall exclude all pumps, pump parts, work in progress in respect of pumps and inventory commonly held or sold in connection with the Borrower's pump business.

The money which P-B Fabricators Ltd. advanced to Patterson-Boyd Manufacturing Corporation had been loaned to it by its shareholders, who were also the principal shareholders and directors of Patterson-Boyd Manufacturing Corporation. When examined for discovery, Patterson testified:

Q. 45. And was the purpose of the loan? A. Patterson-Boyd Manufacturing Corporation wished to expand its custom manufacturing phase of its business. There was a willingness on the part of Patterson-Boyd shareholders and of various other investors to invest in the custom manufacturing because it promised to generate substantial profit, but none of the parties were prepared to invest directly in Patterson-Boyd because of other difficulties which it had experienced. ...

Q. 48. Okay, sorry, go ahead. A. The moneys were loaned through this vehicle in order to provide protection to the investors in support of that custom manufacturing operation. ...

Q. 71. Why did you and the other investors simply not loan the money directly to Patterson-Boyd Manufacturing Corporation? A. As I mentioned before, the other aspect of Patterson-Boyd appeared to be threatened and we wished to provide ourselves maximum protection in this regard. There was an excellent investment opportunity in the custom manufacturing.

The shareholders were clearly using P-B Fabricators Ltd. as an intermediary in the hope of escaping the provision in the loan agreement that the repayment of advances by them would be postponed in favour of the appellant.

P-B Fabricators Ltd. was also placed between Patterson-Boyd Manufacturing Corporation and its only two customers. It received the proceeds of the Patterson-Boyd Manufacturing Corporation products which had been manufactured and sold to the customers. Patterson intended that P-B Fabricators Ltd. would eventually take over entirely the manufacturing arm of Patterson-Boyd Manufacturing Corporation. The relationship between the two companies was described by Patterson as:

Q. Well, I think perhaps we don't need to go beyond that. But in any event, the bank, at this point, indicated that they wanted the loan back down to a hundred thousand, is that correct? A. That's correct.

Q. They indicated that to you— A. Yes.

Q. —so that's the trigger I think we're really concerned about. Now, then your problem was that you had to find quite a bit of money to give to the bank and some money to continue with your manufacturing—is that what you've indicated? A. That is correct.

Q. Okay now, can you tell me what you did about that? A. We had reason to believe that Mar-Kee would be making a very large payment in January, and additional payments on a monthly basis from then on. The—as I said in the examination for discovery, there was a great deal of interest in investing in the aspect of Patterson-Boyd—the custom manufacturing aspect of Patterson-Boyd, however, not directly. There was a great deal of concern regarding the serious issues between Patterson-Boyd and SEDCO, so that in order for funds to be raised, it was appropriate to establish a separate company, which would in turn loan to Patterson-Boyd on the basis of what we understood was a very secure debenture.

Q. Okay, now, what was the intention with respect to this company, was it just to loan money, or did it have other functions? A. It was intended that, in due course, it would probably take over the custom manufacturing business.

Q. Well, did it order goods? A. No, it did not,—it didn't progress to that point.

Q. It didn't? A. It ordered—it purchased materials—

Q. I'm not referring to materials, I'm referring to finished goods—did it order finished goods? A. Oh, Yes, it ordered finished goods—it purchased all the finished goods of Patterson-Boyd as soon as they were finished, both the goods to be sold to Westshop and the goods to be sold for Mar-kee. It then in turn received the orders from the two customers and supplied to them. So it became the sales agent for the equipment, in order to provide a maximum cash flow in Patterson-Boyd without creating interest expense to Patterson-Boyd.

Q. Well, was it a sales agent, or was it, in fact, a principal, ordering goods from Patterson-Boyd Manufacturing Corporation. A. Oh, it was a—it was a totally independent company ordering goods from Patterson-Boyd.

Q. And— A. Receiving orders from Mat-Kee and Westshop.

When cross-examined, Patterson testified:

Q. So, up until P-B Fabricators was incorporated in January 1979 the sales to Westshop and to Mar-Kee Enterprises, which you mentioned, had been made by Patterson-Boyd Manufacturing Corporation—is that correct? A. That's correct.

Q. And after P-B Fabricators Limited was incorporated, what it did was simply step in and take them from Patterson-Boyd Manufacturing Corporation and sell them again to those same customers, Mar-Kee Enterprises and Westshops—is that right? A. That is correct, yes.

                                    • • •

Westshop Equipment Limited, referred to by Patterson as one of the two customers for the manufactured goods, was established in April 1978. In November 1978 55 per cent of the issued shares of Westshop Equipment Limited were acquired by the wives of Patterson, Boyd and Hoffman. In May 1979 the remainder of the outstanding shares were acquired by Mrs. Patterson, Mrs. Boyd and Patterson himself.

On 5th February 1979 P-B Fabricators Ltd. purported to issue a purchase order to Patterson-Boyd Manufacturing Company for the 50 hoists which had been ordered by Mar-Kee on 28th November 1978. Patterson-Boyd Manufacturing Company then invoiced P-B Fabricators Ltd. for them, also on 5th February.

Patterson claimed that the total amount advanced by P-B Fabricators Ltd. under its debenture amounted to $163,000. A statement of receipts and disbursements of P-B Fabricators Ltd. for the period 11th January 1979 to 30th March 1979 was entered as an exhibit by the respondents. It discloses that P-B Fabricators Ltd. collected $16,000 from Mar-Kee in February 1979 and $31,555.89 from Westshop in March 1979. The total claimed to be advanced by P-B Fabricators Ltd. to Patterson-Boyd Manufacturing Corporation includes a payment of $16,000 in February and one of $30,000 in March. It is manifest from that statement and the testimony of Patterson that these were the proceeds of payments for goods to which Patterson-Boyd Manufacturing Corporation was entitled in any event. The evidence does not disclose whether the balance of the proceeds of the $50,000 order from Mar-Kee was ever paid to Patterson-Boyd Manufacturing Corporation.

It is not necessary to determine whether the loan reportedly made by P-B Fabricators Ltd. could be called borrowing from bankers or others in the ordinary course of the business of Patterson-Boyd Manufacturing Corporation to bring the transaction within the proviso of the appellant's debenture relied upon by the respondents. It does not matter that the appellant's security on the assets in question did not crystallize before the registration of the respondents' debenture. In my opinion, the entire dealing between P-B Fabricators Ltd. and Patterson-Boyd Manufacturing Corporation was a breach of those terms of the loan agreement which have been above set out.

Article III 2(e) covers loans made to the company by any shareholder and/or associated company. This must mean the company with which the shareholders are associated and certainly refers to P-B Fabricators Ltd. On this ground, the appellant is entitled to priority.

If it could be said that P-B Fabricators Ltd. was not an associated company within the provisions of art. III 2(e), the appellant would still be entitled to priority. While a corporation is a legal entity separate and distinct from its shareholders, there are occasions when the court can and will look through the corporate structure in a process which has been described as "lifting the corporate veil."

The principles involved in this process were dealt with by this court in *Nedco Ltd. v. Clark*, [1973] 6 W.W.R. 425, 43 D.L.R. (3d) 714. In that case, Culliton C.J.S. said, at p. 430:

Notwithstanding that, since the judgment of the House of Lords in *Salomon v. Salomon & Co. Ltd.*, [1897] A.C. 22, the autonomous and independent existence of the corporate entity has generally been accepted as a fundamental feature of both English and Canadian law, there have been occasions when the courts have found it both possible and necessary to pierce the corporate veil.

Culliton C.J.S. also quoted the following passage from the judgment of Ormerod L.J. in *Tunstall v. Steigman*, [1962] 2 Q.B. 593, [1962] 2 All E.R. 417 [p. 432]:

If there has been any departure from a strict observance of the principle of *Salomon v. Salomon & Co. Ltd.* [supra], it has only been made to deal with special circumstances where a limited company might well be a facade concealing the real facts.

After reviewing a number of authorities, Culliton C.J.S. came to the conclusion which he stated at p. 433 as:

After reviewing the foregoing, and many other cases, the only conclusion I can reach is this: while the principle laid down in *Salomon v. Salomon & Co. Ltd.*, supra, is and continues to be a fundamental feature of Canadian law, there are instances in which the court can and should lift the corporate veil, but whether it does so depends upon the facts in each particular case. Moreover, the fact that the court does lift the corporate veil for a specific purpose in no way destroys the recognition of the corporation as an independent and autonomous entity for all other purposes.

An occasion on which the corporate veil will be lifted is when individuals create a corporation in order to do so something they cannot do in their individual capacity. In the instant case, the shareholders of Patterson-Boyd Manufacturing Corporation were using the corporate front of P-B Fabricators Ltd. to do those things which they had contracted not to do under the terms of their agreement with the appellant. The loan covered by the respondents' debenture was in reality a loan by the shareholders to Patterson-Boyd Manufacturing Corporation.

A similar situation was encountered in *Gilford Motor Co. v. Horne*, [1933] Ch. 935, where the Court of Appeal held that a person could not incorporate a company as a cloak or sham to enable him to breach the terms of his individual agreement. At p. 969, Romer L.J. stated:

In my opinion Farwell J. was right in the conclusion to which he came as to the effect of the oral agreement come to between the parties in the month of November, 1931, and was right in coming to the conclusion, as I think he did conclude, that this defendant company was formed and was carrying on business merely as cloak or sham for the purpose of enabling the defendant Horne to commit the breach of the covenant that he entered into deliberately with the plaintiffs on the occasion of and as consideration for his employment as managing director.

Gilford Motor Co. v. Horne was followed in *Jones v. Lipman*, [1962] 1 W.L.R. 832, [1962] 1 All E.R. 443.

In the instant case, in addition to using the corporate front of P-B Fabricators Ltd. to make the loan to Patterson-Boyd Manufacturing, the directors sought to take over the manufacturing end of the Patterson-Boyd Manufacturing Corporation business which was in contravention of cl. 2(b) of art. III. The insertion of P-B Fabricators Ltd. between Patterson-Boyd Manufacturing Company and its customers was a breach of cl. 2(h) of art. III.

P-B Fabricators Limited was merely a facade to conceal the real facts, namely, that its actions were those of Patterson-Boyd and Hoffman. Under these circumstances the corporate veil should be lifted, and the transactions treated as being personally those of the directors.

The appeal is therefore allowed with costs. The appellant is entitled to rank in priority to the respondent P-B Fabricators Ltd. in its claim upon the assets of Patterson-Boyd Manufacturing Company Limited.

Appeal allowed.

Implied Contractual Terms. SEDCO sought to protect itself against self-dealing by Patterson-Boyd through the restrictive covenants of Article III of the loan agreement. Was the attempt by P.B. to assert priority rights over SEDCO on Patterson-Boyd's default expressly prohibited by Article III (in particular the restrictions on payment of intercorporate debt in s. 2(e))? As a matter of interpretation, would you construe such provisions narrowly against the lender, for whose protection they are meant? In that case, loan agreements would doubtless become lengthier, with every kind of possible self-dealing specifically referred to. While this might be thought to reduce error costs arising through mistaken judicial interpretation, it would clearly impose its own transaction costs. It would then be efficient for courts to fill in the gaps of an express agreement by implying the terms to which the parties would very likely have agreed. Optimal gap-filling policies would seek to minimize the sum of error costs of implied terms and transaction costs of express ones.

When separate corporate status is asserted, gap-filling policies may suggest a need for "recognizing" an implied term that prohibits end runs around express contractual requirements. Promoters of a firm might then be prevented from incorporating a corporation solely to avoid express personal obligations. For example, in *Gilford Motor Co. v. Horn*, [1933] Ch. 935 (C.A.), Horne had been Gilford Motors' managing director until he resigned in 1931. A clause in his employment contract had prohibited him from competing directly or indirectly with the corporation within three miles of Gilford's premises for five years after the employment ended. Shortly after resigning, Horne began to carry on a competing business within the proscribed radius. However, he became worried about breaching the employment contract and his solicitor requested a copy of it. The solicitor received it on March 30, and on April 8 the J. M. Horne Co. was incorporated. The corporation's shares were issued in equal numbers to Horne's wife and to an employee, and it carried on the business Horne had begun. The English Court of Appeal held that J. M. Horne Co. was a sham designed to avoid Horne's duties under the employment contract. An injunction against both Horne and the company was therefore granted. See also *Fern Brand Waxes Ltd. v. Pearl*, [1972] 3 O.R. 829 (C.A.).

Affiliated Corporations. Courts seem more willing to pierce the corporate veil between affiliated corporations, particularly when this is done not to impose liability but to benefit the group. This would seem desirable on gap-filling theories, since group managers can be presumed to have wished to have maximized the total value of the group. A policy that disregards corporate entities for the benefit of the firm therefore economizes on corporate planning. One example of this is the "three in one" case of *DHN Food Distributors Ltd. v. London Borough of Tower Hamlets*, [1976] 3 All E.R. 462 (C.A.). A group of corporations carried on a grocery wholesale and retail business, where the land was owned by Bronze Investments Ltd. and a fleet of trucks by DHN Food Transport Ltd. DHN Food Distributors Ltd. (DHN) carried on the business and held all the shares of the other two corporations. The land was expropriated in 1970 and the Borough offered compensation for its value to Bronze. It did not, however, offer to pay full compensation for the loss the business suffered, since it was carried on not by Bronze but by DHN.* The English Court of Appeal held that the corporations as a group were entitled to compensation for the disturbance to the business as well as for the loss of the land. Lord Denning M.R. stated that:

We all know that in many respects a group of companies are treated together for the purpose of general accounts, balance sheet and profit and loss account. They are treated as one concern. Professor Gower in his book on company law says: "there is evidence of a general tendency to ignore the separate legal entities of various companies within a group, and to look instead at the economic entity of the whole group." This is especially the case when a parent company owns all the shares of the subsidiaries, so much so that it can control every movement of the subsidiaries. These subsidiaries are bound hand and foot to the parent company and must do just what the parent company says. [*Id.* at 467]

---

*   "Sometimes ... 'corporate entity' works like a boomerang and hits the man who is trying to use it." Kahn-Freund, *Some Reflections on Company Law Reform*, 7 Mod. L. Rev. 54, 56 (1944). A spectacular example of how the corporate veil may work a hardship on shareholders formerly arose when sole shareholders took out insurance on corporate assets. Under insurance law, only parties with an "insurable interest" in assets may legitimately insure them. This doctrine, aimed at prohibiting wagering contracts, was applied in *Macaura v. Northern Assurance Co.*, [1925] A.C. 619, by the House of Lords to prevent a sole shareholder who had insured in his own name his corporation's assets from recovering upon the policy. However, this restrictive interpretation of insurable interest was rejected in *Constitution Insurance Co. v. Kosmopoulos*, [1987] 1 S.C.R. 2.

Golf L.J. would also have pierced the corporate veil, though on narrower grounds:

I would not at this juncture accept that in every case where one has a group of companies one is entitled to pierce the veil, but in this case the two subsidiaries were both wholly owned; further, they had no separate business operations whatsoever; thirdly, in my judgment, the nature of the question involved is highly relevant, namely whether the owners of this business have been disturbed in their possession and enjoyment of it. [*Id.* at 468]

See also *Smith, Stone and Knight Ltd. v. Birmingham Corp.*, [1939] 4 All E.R. 116.

Corporations Formed to Avoid Statutory Requirements. Promoters may also incorporate in an attempt to avoid the burden of statutory or regulatory duties. Whether the veil is pierced in such cases will depend on the legislative purpose behind the requirement, for the need to insure compliance is greater in some cases than in others. When a statutory provision does not expressly refer to an affiliated corporation, the courts might simply construe the statute narrowly, leaving it to be cured by legislative amendment if need be. The question is therefore whether courts should fill in legislative gaps in order to serve drafting efficiencies. Once again, these economies must be balanced against the error costs of judicial intervention.

Courts are particularly willing to disregard separate corporate entities in tax cases. With the extraordinary length and complexity of the Income Tax Act, judicial gap-filling may seem particularly desirable here. Of course, minimizing tax liability is often a primary reason for incorporating. A taxpayer in a high personal bracket can shelter his business income behind a corporation, which is liable for taxes at the corporate rate. When the corporation eventually pays dividends to him, the promoter must add such amounts to his personal income for tax purposes, such that a double taxation problem arises. This is alleviated by gross-up and credit provisions designed to integrate in part corporate and individual income, but a net incentive to incorporate for tax reasons may still remain.

While the separate existence of a corporation would undoubtedly be upheld in such cases, tax courts have frequently pierced the veil for other purposes. For example, a real estate developer may attempt to pay capital gains tax rather than a higher income tax by selling shares in a subsidiary corporation whose sole asset is land rather than the land itself. In such cases, the profits will likely be held to be income, with the transaction treated as one in the ordinary course of a combined enterprise. In effect, the separate corporate existence of affiliated firms is ignored. See *De Salaberry Realties Ltd. v. The Queen* (1976), 70 D.L.R. (3d) 706 (Fed. C.A.). See further Durnford, *The Corporate Veil in Tax Law*, 27 C.T.J. 282 (1979).

The Saskatchewan Court of Appeal has looked to the economic entity behind affiliated corporations to permit "secondary picketing." *Nedco Ltd. v. Clark* (1973), 43 D.L.R. (3d) 714, [1973] 6 W.W.R. 425. Such picketing occurs when workers extend their picketing from their employer to other corporations, such as consumers or suppliers of the employer. The workers in *Nedco* were on a lawful strike against Northern Electric Co., and began to picket Nedco. Nedco was a wholly owned subsidiary of Northern Electric, formed when the sales division was cleaved off from the parent. The two corporations occupied the same building in Regina, but Nedco had separate offices in Saskatoon. At trial, an injunction was granted prohibiting picketing against Nedco. This was reversed on appeal. Culliton C.J.S. stated that:

As such wholly-owned subsidiary, it is controlled, directed and dominated by Northern Electric Company Limited. Thus, viewing it from a realistic standpoint, rather than its legal form, I am of the opinion that it constitutes an integral component of Northern Electric Company Limited in the carrying on of its business. That being so, I can see no grounds upon which lawful picketing of Nedco Ltd. ... should be restrained. [43 D.L.R. (3d) at 722]

However, he noted that "the fact that the Court does lift the corporate veil for a specific purpose in no way destroys the recognition of the corporation as an independent and autonomous entity for all other purposes" (43 D.L.R. (3d) at 721).

The corporate veil is often pierced when corporations are formed to avoid substantive requirements in securities legislation, which, like tax law, has achieved a remarkable degree of complexity. One such case was *In the Matter of A.E. Ames & Co.*, [1972] O.S.C.B. 98. In that case, Kaiser Resources Ltd. issued a prospectus in Ontario, filing it with the Ontario Securities Commission (O.S.C.). Because the prospectus was not filed with the American Securities and Exchange Commission, it stated that no shares would be sold to residents of the United States. However, to permit American executives of Kaiser to subscribe for its shares, another company called KRL Investments Ltd. was formed. Kaiser's shares were allotted to KRL, whose shares were beneficially held by the American executives. Though any prejudice to Ontario residents was conspicuously absent, the O.S.C. disregarded the separate existence of KRL to find a misrepresentation in the prospectus inasmuch as Kaiser's shares were in substance sold to American residents.

[I]t is ... true that the corporate veil will be lifted and the real parties in interest identified, and the assets held to be the property of the shareholders when the corporation is used to perpetrate a fraud, or it is used as an agent by the shareholders, or the corporate entity is ignored by the shareholders themselves. The manner of its operation indicates that KRL was operated merely as an agent—a Canadian agent—of the U.S. resident shareholders to allow them to purchase the Kaiser shares. When any one of the 36 U.S. resident shareholders of KRL wished to sell all or part of his holdings in Kaiser he instructed KRL to sell a certain number of Kaiser shares. The funds from that sale were remitted to the KRL shareholders and a purported reduction in capital by cancellation of an equivalent number of KRL shares was gone through. As was noted above, this reduction of capital did not appear to be in accord with the law as set down in the Canada Corporations Act, and even if the dictates of that Act had been followed the position would not, in our opinion, have been different.

The purpose of The Securities Act is to protect the investing public and when the argument is made that the corporate veil may not be pierced the question must be asked in what circumstances and for what purposes it is being contended that the corporation should be identified with its shareholders? If the purpose is the furtherance of the objective of investor protection and the prevention of misleading or inaccurate disclosure through a prospectus then there is a good case to be made for lifting the corporate veil.

Again, we do not want to be understood to be laying down any general rule, or to be understood to be saying that we will ignore the corporate entity in all cases. But we think, in the circumstances of this case, that it is perfectly appropriate that we do so. In ignoring the corporate entity in this case, we do no more than the shareholders of KRL themselves did. [*Id.* at 114-15]

See also *Bay Street West Securities (1983) Inc. v. Alta. Securities Comm'n.* (1984), 56 A.R. 19 (C.A.).

In other cases, parent corporations have been found to be subject to regulatory regimes established for industries in which their subsidiaries operate. See *Atco Ltd. v. Calgary Power Ltd.*, [1982] 2 S.C.R. 557 (owner of 58% of shares of subsidiary that owned a public utility was itself deemed to be an "owner of a public utility" under the Alberta Public Utilities Act). Sometimes the veil is pierced from the other direction, with subsidiaries bound by statutory requirements that apply directly to the parent. See *Daimler Co. v. Continental Tyre & Rubber Co.*, [1916] 2 A.C. 307 (English-incorporated subsidiary held bound by U.K. Trading with the Enemy Proclamation when parent corporation was German).

2. Representations of Unlimited Liability

Veil piercing on a misrepresentation theory assumes that the decision to incorporate may have distributional effects. In other words, it is feared that wealth will be transferred to the firm from outside claimholders who overpay for their interests in the firm. This in turn assumes that the claimholders mistakenly rely on the unlimited liability of the firm's shareholders on its default. Absent creditor reliance, the limited liability decision would not be troubling on a distributional perspective.

It is unlikely that many business creditors today rely on the unlimited liability of firm promoters. If, however, a firm were to represent that its liability is unlimited, a subsequent assertion of limited liability would be a straightforward case of fraud, and the denial of separate corporate status would be unexceptional. Beyond this, a plausible case may be made for veil piercing where the representation, though real, is only tacit. Moreover, there may be special concerns for distributional effects with respect to consensual claimholders, such as customers and employees of the firm, who may seem less sophisticated than trade creditors. But though such claimholders may lack the business sophistication of trade creditors, substantial wealth transfer effects are still unlikely if they presume that a limited liability regime is in place.

Apart from distributional justifications for veil piercing, a sanction of unlimited liability may be thought efficient where third parties reasonably believe that liability is not limited, and their error can be cured at least cost by the firm's promoters. On a hypothetical bargain, a duty to disclose the limitation on liability would then be imposed on the promoters. On this explanation of veil piercing, outside claimholders would not be skilled at distinguishing between limited and unlimited liability regimes, and a presumption of unlimited liability would reduce their screening (or information production) costs. This argument for disregarding the corporate entity would, however, be unpersuasive if outside claimholders routinely expected that the firm is incorporated, and that their bankruptcy claim is valueless.

This section also considers two related veil piercing theories. First, the firm's failure to observe corporate formalities in the preparation of documents is sometimes said to justify disregarding its separate existence. Though these arguments are often made in cases where an outside claimant alleges a representation of unlimited liability, the two issues are formally quite distinct, and it is difficult to see why sloppiness should merit a veil piercing sanction. Second, this section concludes with an examination of "thin capitalization" prohibitions, which amount to a judicially imposed minimum stated capital requirement. Thin capitalization prohibitions may resemble misrepresentation theories of veil piercing if it is assumed that outside claimholders rely on a large stated capital. (Would you expect that they in fact do so?)

In order to minimize the possibility of misrepresentations, corporations statutes require the firm name to include a word or abbreviation such as "Limited," "Corp." or "Inc." See CBCA s. 10(1). The name must be set out in all contracts, invoices, negotiable instruments and orders for goods and services, so as to let firm claimants know that they are not dealing with the partnership. CBCA s. 10(5). Not surprisingly, many of the cases that impose unlimited liability focus on non-compliance with these provisions.

One of the strongest cases for veil piercing on a misrepresentation theory arises when a firm has recently incorporated without so informing the old creditors of the partnership. If they continue to extend credit to the firm, it may well be in reliance on the personal liability of the former partners. You will recall that an apparent partner is required to notify firm creditors of his retirement in order to avoid being held liable for firm debts. OPA s. 36. Similarly, proprietors and partners remain liable for post-incorporation debts until they notify the creditors of the change. *Corkum v. Lohnes* (1981), 81 A.P.R. 477, 486 per Cooper J.A. (N.S. App. Div.); *Gelhorn Motors Ltd. v. Yee* (1969), 71 W.W.R. 526, 529 per Smith C.J.M. (Man. C.A.). Where the creditor should be aware of the fact of incorporation by virtue of long-standing business ties, the shareholder will be found to have discharged his burden even if he did not expressly inform the creditor of the change. *William A. Flemming Ltd. v. Fisher* (1978), 45 A.P.R. 338 (N.S.). But see *Thompson & Sutherland Ltd. v. Redden* (1978), 59 A.P.R. 91 (N.S.).

Less plausibly, personal liability is sometimes imposed on shareholders when the creditors have not had prior dealings with the corporation in its former guise as an unincorporated partnership or sole proprietorship. Where there is any uncertainty about who the creditor is contracting with, a presumption of personal liability may arise. For example, in *Chaing v. Heppner* (1978), 85 D.L.R. (3d) 487 (B.C.), the plaintiff's watch was damaged in a fire at the defendant's jewellery shop, and the plaintiff sued the defendant personally. In rejecting the defendant's argument that the contract was with the incorporated business, the Court stated:

It is clear that Mr. Heppner held himself out to be a sole proprietor and his claim ticket ..., showing the name "Heppner Credit Jewellers," gives no indication of the limited company. There is no evidence that the plaintiff could in any way have been aware of the organization, Heppner Jewellers Ltd. All the plaintiff's dealings were with Heppner on a personal basis. Accordingly, I hold that Heppner has personal responsibility to the plaintiff. [*Id.* at 493-94 per McMorran Co. Ct. J.]

In a review of 1,600 American veil-piercing cases, Robert Thompson reported that courts were more likely to disregard the corporate entity where there was a representation of unlimited liability. See Thompson, *Piercing the Corporate Veil: An Empirical Study*, 76 Cornell L. Rev. 1036 (1991).

Wolfe v. Moir
Alberta Supreme Court
(1969), 69 W.W.R. 70

SINCLAIR J.: The plaintiff Barry Alan Wolfe was injured while roller skating at "Fort Whoop-Up" in Lethbridge on December 4, 1964. He was then 14.

Three issues are involved: (1) Liability; (2) Damages; (3) Is the defendant Moir personally liable?

[After determining that the operator of the rink was liable and assessing damages, Sinclair J. continued.]

The defendants are described in the statement of claim as "Gordon L. Moir, carrying on business in the firm name and style of Fort Whoop-Up Playland."

Mr. Brennan made it plain that he was representing only Mr. Moir. He took the position that the roller-skating rink was being operated by a limited company called Chinook Sport Shop Ltd., and that a Mr. Neil McKinnon was the manager of the rink on the occasion in question. Accordingly, it is claimed, the wrong party has been sued. A detailed examination of the evidence on this vital point is required.

Moir had been a recreation director for the city of Lethbridge and his name was well and favourably known in the city for that reason.

On the outskirts of Lethbridge there was a fun centre known as Fort Whoop-Up. It is not clear from the evidence how long Moir or the company Chinook Sport Shop Ltd. (the "company") had been associated with Fort Whoop-Up. Moir says the operation at Fort Whoop-Up was run by the company as soon as he became involved with it, and that the company was formed to run Fort Whoop-Up. The evidence is clear, however, that Moir was involved with Fort Whoop-Up at least by June, 1964.

It is also clear that the recreational facilities at Fort Whoop-Up had been in operation by at least one other person before Moir or the company took over. The roller-skating facilities, at least, had been in operation at that location as far back as eight years before the accident took place. The name "Fort Whoop-Up" was worked into the tiles on the roof and were presumably visible for some distance.

Moir says that in the beginning he was the actual manager at Fort Whoop-Up, but that on the day in question, particularly because of the time of the year, he was manager of Glendale Bowl, and spent most of his time there.

He had, however, come out to the rink that evening "to see what was going on." He arrived at the roller-skating rink at approximately the time the accident happened.

A copy of the type of ticket issued to Barry is shown on Ex. 2. The name appearing at the bottom is "Fort Whoop-Up." The name of the company does not appear on the ticket.

Ex. 1 consists of a copy made by the plaintiff of advertisements that appeared in the *Lethbridge Herald* on June 2, 4, 9 and 11, 1964, and which read as follows:

Roller Skating
Tonight
8:00 to 10:30 p.m.
Moir's Sport Land
(Fort Whoop-Up)
Special Group Rates.

Jim Donaldson, a friend of Barry Wolfe's in 1964, testified that he knew the premises as "Moir's Sport Land." He knew Mr. Moir to see him. He says there was quite a lot of advertising—a few ads in the paper, and quite a bit on radio. The advertising said, in effect, "come to Moir's Sport Land."

In cross-examination, Mrs. Moir who says she was president of the company, was asked the following questions:

Q. As far as advertising, the area, or the roller skating rink, would be referred to in advertising as Moir's Sport Land? A. Yes—but the *Herald* billed all things to Chinook Sport Shop Ltd.

Q. I see. They billed Chinook Sports but they put the ads in this way without anything about Chinook Sport Shop Ltd.? A. We paid our bills under Chinook Sport Shop.

Q. I see. But this is the way the ads went out to the public? A. Yes.

Q. And I imagine there would be radio advertising in the same manner? A. I don't believe we did too much radio advertising.

In his cross-examination, Mr. Moir was questioned about the use of the name "Moir" in the advertising placed in the *Lethbridge Herald*:

Q. And that would be used because of the fact that it was at Fort Whoop-Up, you had been a former recreation director in the City, and were known as such, and that's why your name was used in respect to it? A. That is correct.

It may be significant to note that when Moir was asked, in direct examination, as to the capacity in which Neil McKinnon was running the skating rink, he referred to McKinnon as "*my*" manager. (Italicizing supplied.)

Again, just after he testified that the company had been running Fort Whoop-Up since its inception, Moir said "Before *I* went out there it was called Fort Whoop-Up." (Italicizing supplied.)

While the court was not told, I will assume that Chinook Sport Shop Ltd. was, or is, an Alberta company. Evidence was given that Mrs. Moir was president, and Mr. Moir secretary of the company. No other evidence was given with respect to the corporate affairs of the company. I do not know, for instance, if shares were ever issued or directors appointed.

Counsel for the plaintiffs pointed out that there is no evidence to the effect that the names "Fort Whoop-Up" or "Moir's Sportland" used in the ads, had been registered by the company or by Moir under sec. 72 of The Partnership Act, RSA, 1955, ch. 230. Briefly put, that section provides that every person (which by sec. 21 [1][t] of The Interpretation Act, 1958, 1958, ch. 32, includes a corporation) who is engaged in business for trading, manufacturing, contracting or mining purposes, not in partnership, and who uses as his business name some name or designation other than his own, must sign and cause to be filed a declaration in writing of the fact.

I do not think the somewhat archaic words "trading, manufacturing, contracting or mining purposes" used in the section and its predecessors since 1908 apply to the type of operation conducted at Fort Whoop-Up. And even if they did, I am not sure that non-registration under The Partnership Act would be relevant.

But what I do think are relevant and important are the provisions contained in sec. 82(1)(c) of The Companies Act, RSA, 1955, ch. 53, which read as follows:

82.(1) Every company

...

(c) shall have its name set forth in legible characters in all notices, advertisements, and other official publications of the company, and in all bills of exchange, promissory notes, endorsements, cheques, and orders for money or goods purporting to be signed by or on behalf of the company, and in all bills or parcels, invoices, receipts, and letters of credit of the company.

The evidence is that, in breach of this section, no mention was made of the company name either in the newspaper advertisements, or in the ticket (which I think could fairly be said to be one of the "official publications" of this particular company).

The defence, baldly put, is that the business was operated by a body corporate and not by Mr. Moir. That amounts, it seems to me, to a complete reliance upon the classic words of Lord Halsbury, L.C. in *Salomon v. Salomon & Co.*, [1897] A.C. 22, 66 L.J. Ch. 35, where he said at p. 31:

Either the limited company was a legal entity or it was not. If it was, the business belonged to it and not to Mr. Salomon. If it was not, there was no person and no thing to be an agent at all; and it is impossible to say at the same time that there is a company and there is not.

It must be remembered, however, as a careful reading of the judgments in the *Salomon* case will show, that it proceeded on the basis that all the requirements of the Companies Act, 1862, had been complied with. This is clear, for instance, in the following passage from Lord Macnaghten's judgment at p. 48:

All the usual formalities were gone through; all the requirements of the Companies Act, 1862, were duly observed.

In the present case, as I have already pointed out, other than for the evidence of Mr. and Mrs. Moir that the business was operated by Chinook Sport Shop Ltd. of which they were, respectively, secretary and president, there was nothing to indicate that the usual corporate formalities were gone through. It seems to me that for a person to successfully rely upon what is, after all, the extraordinary protection from personal liability granted to an individual by The Companies Act, it is incumbent upon him to establish that at least the formalities prescribed by the statute have been complied with. This he has failed completely to do.

Further, in my view, the effect of sec. 82(1)(b) of The Companies Act is that if a person chooses to advertise and to hold himself out to the public without identifying the name of a company with which he is associated, he runs the risk of being held personally liable. There are many cases in which an individual has been held personally responsible for an obligation because he did not make it clear when the obligation was incurred that he was acting on behalf of a company.

In principle, I can see no difference between that type of situation and the present one.

I therefore hold that the defendant, Gordon L. Moir, is liable for damages to the plaintiff. ...

Corporate Formalities. *Wolfe* may be thought a case of prosaic justice: when firm managers themselves ignore the formalities of separate corporate existence, why should they be permitted to insist upon it in their dealings with third parties? Such considerations were thought important by Adolf Berle in his enterprise entity theory, under which one member of a group of affiliated firms might be held subject to the duties of another member of the group:

If it be shown that the enterprise is not reflected and comprehended by the corporate papers, books and operation, the court may reconstruct the actual enterprise, giving entity to it, based on the economic facts. Thus one corporation may be shown to be in fact only an "instrumentality" of a larger enterprise, or to be so intermingled with the operations of such larger enterprise as to have lost its own identity. On such reconstruction of the true entity, the court may assign the liabilities of the paper fragment to the economic whole; or may (as in the *Deep Rock* case) assign priority or subordination to its liabilities or securities stock, so as to attain, as nearly as possible, a financial result corresponding to the reasonable expectations of the creditors and security holders.

Berle, *The Theory of Enterprise Entity*, 47 Colum. L. Rev. 343, 354 (1947). But if the harm is explained as resting upon a misrepresentation, what is the relevance of the corporation's non-compliance with corporate formalities that do not come to the attention of outsiders? How could this have misled the 14-year-old plaintiff in *Wolfe*, or any outside creditor? If observance of such formalities, with well-tended minutes of meetings and regularly filed information returns is in fact of some utility for the firm, does sloppiness merit a sanction (in particular, the loss of limited liability)? When the offence comes down to a failure to retain a lawyer, does the legal profession systematically overpenalize the offender? If, instead, the penalty is a covert tool aimed at fostering a higher norm than neatness, just what is that higher norm?

Some courts have indeed focused more attention on the relationship between the defendant shareholder and the corporation than on the representation to the plaintiff creditor. For example, in *Frankel Structural Steel Ltd. v. Goden Holdings Ltd.*, [1971] S.C.R. 250, Gotfrid & Dennis, a firm of solicitors, formed Goden Holdings Ltd. as an investment company to make commercial loans to its clients. Joseph Burnett was a solicitor in the firm and a shareholder of the corporation. Goden agreed to lend $300,000 to Hyacinthe Properties Ltd. to erect a building, the loan being secured by a mortgage. In September 1964, Hyacinthe asked Frankel to supply it with $69,000 worth of steel. Frankel refused to do so without a direction from Hyacinthe to Goden under which Goden was directed to advance loan moneys directly to Frankel, by-passing Hyacinthe. Frankel was dissatisfied with the form of the direction and telephoned Burnett, who agreed that Frankel would in fact be paid by Goden out of advances on the loan as the work progressed. Burnett repeated this assurance several times thereafter. However, in breach of the direction and the assurances, Goden made advances on the loan directly to Hyacinthe. On Hyacinthe's bankruptcy, Frankel sought to impose liability on both Goden and Gotfrid & Dennis. In the Ontario Court of Appeal, Laskin J.A. held that the partners were not personally bound: "In no sense could it be said that [they] were personally involved in the transactions of Frankel, Hyacinthe and Goden; they were solicitors for a party, and not themselves parties." [1969] 2 O.R. at 227. The Supreme Court reversed this decision. In holding the law firm liable, the Court stated:

Goden was a very unusual company. Its officers and shareholders were three in number, Mr. Gotfrid, Mr. Dennis and Mr. Burnett, three solicitors associated in practice. Burnett was the one in charge of the transactions with which we are concerned. The company had no separate bank account. It kept no books or records. It was used as a means of making interim building loans on behalf of clients of the law firm. The money contributed by these clients appeared in the trust account of the law firm under the name of Goden Holdings Limited. The legal position appears to be that the clients were creditors of Goden and the law firm was the trustee of these funds. Goden could not act in any way without the solicitors willing it.

How can these solicitors say that their undertaking was given through Burnett on behalf of Goden; that they neglected or refused to carry out their undertaking on behalf of Goden; that this neglect or refusal on behalf of Goden involves Goden in responsibility but not them? They were Goden to the extent that they were the only shareholders and officers and that they had management and control. Goden had no independent volition.

Frankel in its conversations with Burnett was asking for and received the assurance in the only capacity in which it knew Burnett, that is, as a solicitor in a firm who was in charge of the transaction. It was not talking to Burnett in his capacity as solicitor for Goden, which might or might not carry out his undertaking. It asked for and received the personal assurance of an individual that he would see to it that the client paid. He had full control over the disbursements made by the client. For some reason these disbursements were made on the decision of the firm through Burnett in disregard of the undertaking. My opinion is that this involves liability on the firm of solicitors. There is no question that Burnett committed the firm.

The evidence of the head of the firm is that "since advances were being made out of the firm's trust account, he would be making them as a member of the firm." He also said that the advances would have been authorized by Goden and to the extent that they were so authorized he may have been acting as an officer of Goden, but I have already pointed out that Goden had no independent volition. [[1971] S.C.R. at 255-56 per Judson J.]

Separate corporate existence has even been disregarded when the creditor has clearly not relied on a shareholder's personal liability. One such case was *Tato Enterprises Ltd. v. Rode* (1979), 17 A.R. 432, where a creditor entered into a contract with "Scott Bradley Ltd." when no such company existed. There was a Scott Bradley Marketing Ltd., but nothing was ever done in its name. Still, the creditor must have assumed that he was dealing with a corporation with limited liability. The Court nevertheless imposed personal liability on the shareholder:

In this case ... the corporate formalities have clearly been offended and, in fact, there has been a wide and broad failure of compliance with corporate formalities. The failure of the defendant Rode to take the time and trouble to determine the correct name of the corporation and to conduct his business in that name is simply a further evidence of his failure to comply with those requirements of The Companies Act which are necessary if a person purporting to be an agent of a corporation is to avoid personal liability. Accordingly, the limited liability otherwise available to a director or officer of a body corporate as the agent of that corporation, is not available to the defendant Rode and it is my view that the contracting parties in the matters before me are the plaintiff and the defendant Rode personally. [*Id.* at 438 per Dea D.C.J.]

Similarly, in *Roydent Products Inc. v. Inter-dent Int'l Dental Supply Co.*, 1993 Ont. C.J. LEXIS 426, the plaintiff Roydent did business with the defendant Inter-Dent without any investigation as to who Inter-Dent was or what individuals or corporations were carrying on business as Inter-Dent. All dealings with Inter-Dent were done with one Holland. In fact, Inter-Dent was an unincorporated division of Steven Holland and Sales Ltd. The Court held that Holland was personally liable. "Since he failed to register as required in order to shield himself from personal liability, he is caught by the well established principle of law that 'one seeking the law's ordinary protection from personal liability must comply with the formalities prescribed by the legislation.' See *Aron Salomon (Pauper) v. A. Salomon and Company, Limited ... .*" In the United States, by contrast, promoters may be absolved from liability on an honest but ineffective attempt to incorporate when third parties did not rely on the promoters' personal liability. For an econometric analysis of the American defective incorporation doctrine, see McChesney, *Doctrinal Analysis and Statistical Modeling in Law: The Case of Defective Incorporation*, 71 Wash. U.L. Rev. 493 (1993). Does the American doctrine inefficiently shield the party who could have cured the problem at least cost? For example, wasn't Rode in the *Tato* case in the best position to cure the error? On the other hand, in a major business transaction, third party contractors normally seek certificates of incorporation and opinion letters to assure themselves as to the corporate status of the party with which they are dealing. In such cases, veil-piercing is less likely to promote information efficiencies.

The liability of promoters on contracts entered into before the corporation was incorporated, or where it was never incorporated, is dealt with in the next Section.

Where corporate formalities have been observed, Canadian courts will not permit a third party that has contracted with one member of a group of affiliated corporations to pick and choose which member of the group it will sue. Thus an outside creditor was not permitted to assert a claim against an affiliated firm of whose separate existence the creditor was unaware in *Scotsburn Co-operative Services Ltd. v. W. T. Goodwin Ltd.*, [1985] 1 S.C.R. 54. A supermarket incorporated under the name G changed its name in 1965 to S, and in 1969 its principals incorporated a new firm under the name G to carry on a real estate business. In 1972, S sold all of its assets to D. The three firms had the same owners and managers. No notice of the new corporations was given to the super-market's creditors, but when they addressed their invoices to G they were paid in the name of S. The supermarket went into receivership and a creditor sued G on the basis that it had dealt with a firm bearing that name. The creditor's claim was denied because it had not relied on G's credit. The creditor's whole claim depended on the fact that G used S's former name, and this was not enough to hold it liable for S's debts.

Customers and Employees. Customers and employees can be seen as firm claim-holders. While they might not have a present claim against the firm, customers are potential future creditors to the extent that there is a positive probability that they will be able to assert future warranty claims. As well, the firm's default might mean the loss of spare parts and repair facilities.

Employees might have present claims against the firm with respect to back pay and accumulated holiday time, as well as unfunded pension liabilities. In addition, employees will suffer human capital losses on the firm's default. These losses are of two kinds. First, the employee's expected future earnings will often be reduced unless he can quickly find a better job thereafter. Second, the job loss will mean the destruction of *firm-specific* human capital. Employees are usually asked to acquire fresh skills for their jobs. Some of these skills are not idiosyncratic to their employer, and can be transferred to a new employer. For example, the immigrant from Norway will find it useful to learn English or French both for his present job and for any future job he might seek in this country. But other skills are firm-specific, in that they are of use to the employee only in his present job. The loss of his job will then mean the destruction of the employee's firm-specific human capital. Human capital theories are most closely associated with the work of Nobel laureate Gary Becker. See G. Becker, *Human Capital* (1975).

Is any of this a reason to waive limited liability? Bankruptcy effects a net wealth transfer from customers and employees (as well as creditors generally) when they have overpaid for their claims (or as employees overinvested in firm-specific human capital), thinking that they will participate in a bankruptcy distribution when in fact their claims will be valueless. Wealth transfer effects will therefore unwind when customers and employees assume on the initial bargain that their bankruptcy claims are valueless. See Buckley, *The Bankruptcy Priority Puzzle*, 72 Va. L. Rev. 1393 (1986). Similarly, limited liability does not effect a wealth transfer from customers or creditors when they bargain on the basis that their only recourse is against the firm. *Wolfe* and *Tato* might thus be explained on the basis that (1) customers believed that unlimited liability regimes were in place, and (2) the firm was the party that could have cured this misapprehension at least cost.

On this analysis, veil-piercing is justified on gap-filling theories. In their contracts of sale and of employment, customers and employees assumed that they would be able to sue the promoters or shareholders on the firm's default. A court that permits them to do so would then supply an implied term for which they would have bargained had they turned their minds to it. But would the firm have consented to such an implied term, sacrificing the efficiency gains of limited liability? And is it plausible to assume that customers and employees generally believe that unlimited liability regimes are in place? More than 100 years ago, corporations began to append the word "Limited" or "Incorporated" at the end of their names to signal to claimholders that a limited liability regime was in place. Should you think, for whatever reason, that the signal misfired, would you be satisfied with a clear and prominent clause in the contract of sale or of employment that liability is limited?

Alternatively, a justification for unlimited liability might be sought in distributional rather than gap-filling theories. On distributional theories, mandatory unlimited liability policies amount to a business tax for the benefit of the protected classes. Whether it is right to levy such a tax is more properly a question of politics rather than law, and we should therefore expect that it is more properly consigned to legislatures rather than to common law judges in the application of veil-piercing rules. Moreover, to the extent that unlimited liability regimes would inefficiently effect a substantial wealth transfer to employees, we would expect promoters to react by exporting jobs and factories to jurisdictions less protective of employees. We might also expect promoters to reduce employment by investing more heavily in labour-saving capital equipment.

In any event, employers are unlikely to skip a pay day. Under CBCA s. 119(1), unpaid employees can recover up to six months' back wages from the employer's directors. This includes bonuses and vacation pay, though not severance payments or damages for wrongful dismissal. See *Barrette v. Crabtree* (1993), 101 D.L.R. (4th) 66 (S.C.C.); *Mills-Hughes v. Raynor* (1988), 47 D.L.R. (4th) 381; 63 O.R. (2d) 343 (C.A.). Even without s. 119, employers who are struggling to stay alive in a financial crisis are unlikely to skip a pay-day when the loss of disgruntled employees will put it out of business.

Human capital theories are sometimes thought to provide a justification for barriers to take-over bids. See, e.g., Shleifer & Summers, *Breach of Trust in Hostile Takeovers*, in *Corporate Takeovers: Causes and Consequences* 33 (A. Auerbach ed. 1988). Because of the possibility of job loss on a take-over, employees might underinvest in firm-specific human capital. Job tenure protection, in the form of barriers to job-threatening take-overs, might thus in theory be justified on efficiency grounds. However, it is difficult to see how this might supply a justification for relaxing shareholder limited liability. Permitting the employee to pierce the corporate veil will effect an *ex post* wealth transfer to him, but will not affect incentives to invest in firm-specific human capital. Whether or not the employee makes an efficient human capital investment, he will still lose his job on the employer's demise, and be permitted to sue the shareholders under unlimited liability. Marginal incentives to invest in human capital are thus unaffected.

Costello v. Fazio
United States Court of Appeals, Ninth Circuit
256 F.2d 903 (1958)

[A partnership known as "Leonard Plumbing and Heating Supply Co." was organized in October 1948 by Fazio, Ambrose and Leonard. For the year ended September 30, 1951 the partnership earned $41,000 on sales of $665,000. For the year ended September 30, 1952, it lost $22,000 on sales of $389,000. At that point the partners' capital contributions stood at: Fazio—$43,000; Ambrose—$6,000; and Leonard—$2,000. In September 1952 Fazio and Ambrose each withdrew all but $2,000 of their respective capital, receiving the balance as non-interest bearing demand promissory notes of the partnership. Immediately thereafter, the partners incorporated the business.

The partnership's closing balance sheet showed current assets of $161,000 and current liabilities of $162,000. Accounts receivable of $42,000 had been assigned to a creditor. The new corporation issued promissory notes to Fazio and Ambrose in lieu of the notes of the partnership, and issued 200 $10 par value shares apiece to the three owners. The corporation went into bankruptcy in June 1954. Fazio and Ambrose sought to prove as creditors, but the trustee in bankruptcy moved for an order subordinating them to the claims of general unsecured creditors. The referee in bankruptcy denied the motion, and his action was sustained by the District Court. The trustee appealed.]

HAMLEY C.J.: ... Clifford V. Heimbucher, a certified public accountant and management consultant, called by the trustee, expressed the view that, at the time of incorporation, capitalization was inadequate. He further stated that, in incorporating a business already in existence, where the approximate amount of permanent capital needed has been established by experience, normal procedure called for continuing such capital in the form of common or preferred stock.

Stating that only additional capital needed temporarily is normally set up as loans, Heimbucher testified that "… the amount of capital employed in the business was at all times substantially more than the $6,000 employed in the opening of the corporation." He also expressed the opinion that, at the time of incorporation, there was "very little hope [of financial success] in view of the fact that for the year immediately preceding the opening of the corporation, losses were running a little less than $2,000 a month. …"

William B. Logan, a business analyst and consultant called by the trustee, expressed the view that $6,000 was inadequate capitalization for this company. John S. Curran, a business analyst, also called by the trustee, expressed the view that the corporation needed at least as much capital as the partnership required prior to the reduction of capital.

Robert H. Laborde, Jr., a certified public accountant, had handled the accounting problems of the partnership and corporation. He was called by the trustee as an adverse witness. … Laborde readily conceded that the transaction whereby Fazio and Ambrose obtained promissory notes from the partnership was for the purpose of transferring a capital account into a loan or debt account. He stated that this was done in contemplation of the formation of the corporation, and with knowledge that the partnership was losing money.

The prime reason for incorporating the business, according to Laborde, was to protect the personal interest of Fazio, who had made the greatest capital contribution to the business. In this connection, it was pointed out that the "liabilities on the business as a partnership were pretty heavy." There was apparently also a tax angle. Laborde testified that it was contemplated that the notes would be paid out of the profits of the business. He agreed that, if promissory notes had not been issued, the profits would have been distributed only as dividends, and that as such they would have been taxable. …

Laborde did express the opinion that the corporation had adequate working capital at the time of incorporation. This was disputed by Heimbucher and Curran. They called attention to the fact that the corporate books showed that current liabilities exceeded current assets at that time, and that there was thus a minus working capital on the opening day of business of the corporation.

In any event, when we speak of inadequacy of capital in regard to whether loans to shareholders shall be subordinated to claims of general creditors, we are not referring to working capital. We are referring to the amount of the investment of the shareholders in the corporation. This capital is usually referred to as legal capital, or stated capital in reference to restrictions on the declaration of dividends to stockholders. As before stated, Laborde expressed no opinion as to the adequacy of proprietary capital put at the risk of the business. On the other hand, the corporate accounts and the undisputed testimony of three accounting experts demonstrate that stated capital was wholly inadequate.

On the evidence produced at this hearing, as summarized above, the referee found that the paid-in stated capital of the corporation at the time of its incorporation was adequate for the continued operation of the business. He found that while Fazio and Ambrose controlled and dominated the corporation and its affairs they did not mismanage the business. He further found that claimants did not practice any fraud or deception, and did not act for their own personal or private benefit and to the detriment of the corporation or its stockholders and creditors. The referee also found that the transaction which had been described was not a part of any scheme or plan to place the claimants in the same class as unsecured creditors of the partnership.

On the basis of these findings, the referee concluded that, in procuring the promissory notes, the claimants acted in all respects in good faith and took no unfair advantage of the corporation, or of its stockholders or creditors.

Pursuant to §39 sub. c of the Bankruptcy Act, 11 U.S.C.A. §67 sub. c, the trustee filed a petition for review of the referee's order. The district court, after examining the record certified to it by the referee, entered an order affirming the order of the referee.

On this appeal, the trustee advances two grounds for reversal of the district court order. The first of these is that claims of controlling shareholders will be deferred or subordinated to outside creditors where a corporation in bankruptcy has not been adequately or honestly capitalized, or has been managed to the prejudice of creditors, or where to do otherwise would be unfair to creditors.

As a basis for applying this asserted rule in the case before us, the trustee challenges most of the findings of fact noted above.

• • •

It does not require the confirmatory opinion of experts to determine from this data that the corporation was grossly undercapitalized. In the year immediately preceding incorporation, net sales aggregated $390,000. In order to handle such a turnover, the partners apparently found that capital in excess of $50,000 was necessary. They actually had $51,620.78 in the business at that time. Even then, the business was only "two jumps ahead of the wolf." A net loss of $22,000 was sustained in that year; there was only $66.66 in the bank; and there was an overdraft of $3,422.78.

Yet, despite this precarious financial condition, Fazio and Ambrose withdrew $45,620.78 of the partnership capital—more than eighty-eight per cent of the total capital. The $6,000 capital left in the business was only one-sixty-fifth of the last annual net sales. All this is revealed by the books of the company.

But if there is need to confirm this conclusion that the corporation was grossly undercapitalized, such confirmation is provided by three of the four experts who testified. The fourth expert, called by appellees, did not express an opinion to the contrary.

We therefore hold that the factual conclusion of the referee, that the corporation was adequately capitalized at the time of its organization, is clearly erroneous.

The factual conclusion of the trial court, that the claimants, in withdrawing capital from the partnership in contemplation of incorporation, did not act for their own personal or private benefit and to the detriment of the corporation or of its stockholders and creditors, is based upon the same accounting data and expert testimony.

Laborde, testifying for the claimants, made it perfectly clear that the depletion of the capital account in favor of a debt account was for the purpose of equalizing the capital investments of the partners and to reduce tax liability when there were profits to distribute. It is therefore certain, contrary to the finding just noted, that, in withdrawing this capital, Fazio and Ambrose did act for their own personal and private benefit.

It is equally certain, from the undisputed facts, that in so doing they acted to the detriment of the corporation and its creditors. The best evidence of this is what happened to the business after incorporation, and what will happen to its creditors if the reduction in capital is allowed to stand. The likelihood that business failure would result from such undercapitalization should have been apparent to anyone who knew the company's financial and business history and who had access to its balance sheet and profit and loss statements. Three expert witnesses confirmed this view, and none expressed a contrary opinion.

Accordingly, we hold that the factual conclusion, that the claimants, in withdrawing capital, did not act for their own personal or private benefit and to the detriment of the corporation and creditors, is clearly erroneous.

Recasting the facts in the light of what is said above, the question which appellant presents is this:

Where, in connection with the incorporation of a partnership, and for their own personal and private benefit, two partners who are to become officers, directors, and controlling stockholders of the corporation, convert the bulk of their capital contributions into loans, taking promissory notes, thereby leaving the partnership and succeeding corporation grossly undercapitalized, to the detriment of the corporation and its creditors, should their claims against the estate of the subsequently bankrupted corporation be subordinated to the claims of the general unsecured creditors?

The question almost answers itself.

In allowing and disallowing claims, courts of bankruptcy apply the rules and principles of equity jurisprudence. *Pepper v. Litton*, 308 U.S. 295, 304, 60 S. Ct. 238, 84 L. Ed. 281. Where the claim is found to be inequitable, it may be set aside (*Pepper v. Litton*, supra), or subordinated to the claims of other creditors. As stated in *Taylor v. Standard Gas Co.*, supra, 306 U.S. at page 315, 59 S. Ct. at page 547, the question to be determined when the plan or transaction which gives rise to a claim is challenged as inequitable is "whether, within the bounds of reason and fairness, such a plan can be justified."

Where, as here, the claims are filed by persons standing in a fiduciary relationship to the corporation, another test which equity will apply is "whether or not under all the circumstances the transaction carries the earmarks of an arm's length bargain." *Pepper v. Litton*, supra, 308 U.S. at page 306, 60 S. Ct. at page 245.

Under either of these tests, the transaction here in question stands condemned.

Appellees argue that more must be shown than mere undercapitalization if the claims are to be subordinated. Much more than mere undercapitalization was shown here. Persons serving in a fiduciary relationship to the corporation actually withdrew capital already committed to the business, in the face of recent adverse financial experience. They stripped the business of eighty-eight per cent of its stated capital at a time when it had a minus working capital and had suffered substantial business losses. This was done for personal gain, under circumstances which charge them with knowledge that the corporation and its creditors would be endangered. Taking advantage of their fiduciary position, they thus sought to gain equality of treatment with general creditors.

In *Taylor v. Standard Gas & Electric Co.*, 306 U.S. 308, 59 S. Ct. 543, 83 L. Ed. 669, and some other cases, there was fraud and mismanagement present in addition to undercapitalization. Appellees argue from this that fraud and mismanagement must always be present if claims are to be subordinated in a situation involving undercapitalization.

This is not the rule. The test to be applied, as announced in the Taylor case and quoted above, is whether the transaction can be justified "within the bounds of reason and fairness." In the more recent *Heiser* case, supra, 327 U.S. pages 732-733, 66 S. Ct. at page 856, the Supreme Court made clear, in these words, that fraud is not an essential ingredient:

"... In appropriate cases, acting upon equitable principles, it [bankruptcy court] may also subordinate the claim of one creditor to those of others in order to prevent the consummation of a course of conduct by the claimant, which, as to them, would be fraudulent *or otherwise inequitable. ...*" (Emphasis supplied.)

The fact that the withdrawal of capital occurred prior to incorporation is immaterial. This transaction occurred in contemplation of incorporation. The participants then occupied a fiduciary relationship to the partnership; and expected to become controlling stockholders, directors, and officers of the corporation. This plan was effectuated, and they were serving in those fiduciary capacities when the corporation assumed the liabilities of the partnership, including the notes here in question.

Nor is the fact that the business, after being stripped of necessary capital, was able to survive long enough to have a turnover of creditors a mitigating circumstance. The inequitable conduct of appellees consisted not in acting to the detriment of creditors then known, but in acting to the detriment of present or future creditors, whoever they may be.

In our opinion, it was error to affirm the order of the referee denying the motion to subordinate the claims in question. We do not reach appellant's other major contention, that the notes are not provable in bankruptcy because they were to be paid only out of profits, and there were no profits.

Reversed and remanded for further proceedings not inconsistent with this opinion.

Equitable Subordination. Equitable subordination reflects a compromise between limited and unlimited liability regimes. The owners of a corporation are not personally liable for its debts as they would be in the case of a partnership, but cannot prove as creditors either. The compromise is similar to the treatment accorded to lenders under OPA s. 4.

What is the rationale for the prohibition of "undercapitalization"? In *Costello*, no interest appears to have been paid upon the notes. How then can it be said that the transfer of the partners' interests from equity to debt contributed to the business failure?

Even if the notes in *Costello* had been interest bearing, the distributional argument for equitable subordination would be troubling. Thin capitalization does not prejudice creditors who react to the firm's stated capital when extending credit. Moreover, since the firm's stated capital is as apparent to creditors as any item in the firm's financial statements, the possibility of a mistaken reliance on a "thick" capitalization would seem slight. In addition, a corporation's stated capital is usually of very little utility as a predictor of bankruptcy. A corporation's solvency is determined by its ability to generate earnings, not by its stated capital—the amount for which the shares were issued, possibly years before. Would a stated capital of $51,000 in *Costello* have retarded bankruptcy by one day?

For small firms, the threat of thin capitalization prohibitions might impose severe adverse incentive costs. As we have noted, shareholders in small firms often have a substantial portion of their wealth, in the form of current assets and expected earnings, tied up in the firm. Because of this, they might pass up valuable but risky investment opportunities in favour of less valuable but more secure investments. The loss of the more valuable opportunity would then amount to an incentive cost. Requiring the manager to hold a large equity interest in the firm through thin capitalization prohibitions would increase the incentive costs. With a greater stake in the firm, managers could be expected to be more cautious still.

This assumes that the firm is solvent. Does anything change when the firm verges on insolvency? As we have seen, the shareholder may then have a strong incentive to take value-decreasing risks. He will then be too risk-loving, and not too cautious. He will have an incentive to pass up more valuable but smaller-risk opportunities for more risky but less valuable opportunities. This is because only the latter offers him a chance to participate in firm earnings. Thin capitalization prohibitions, which were value-reducing when the firm was solvent, might here reduce his adverse incentives. With a greater personal investment in the firm, he is less likely to be gambling with other people's money, more likely to be investing efficiently with his own.

Permitting the shareholder to hold a security interest in his firm might usefully reduce incentive costs for both solvent and insolvent firms. For solvent firms, the manager would have less to fear from default, and would be less likely to pass up high risk, high return opportunities. Shareholders of insolvent firms might also have weaker misincentives, since they will not be gambling so much with other people's money. As a consequence, equitable subordination rules, which impeach the grant of security on a loan by a shareholder, might impose incentive costs.

There is one further difficulty with thin capitalization and equitable subordination requirements. Both are mandatory rules, imposed on the parties in the face of their private bargains. By contrast, the parties may bargain for thin capitalization and equitable subordination in their private agreements where such rules are not imposed on them. For example, a bank may bargain for private subordination rights or might require the shareholder to guarantee the loan in its entirety or to a stipulated amount. Do banks require mandatory rules, like thin capitalization and equitable subordination rules, to protect them? Do other creditors, who are adequately protected if they bargain on the basis that they will receive nothing on default? Are such rules more likely to benefit the firm's established business competitors, to the extent that they impose additional costs upon entrepreneurs starting new businesses?

See further Easterbrook & Fischel 52-62.

Was Leonard Plumbing insolvent at the moment of incorporation? If so, should *Costello* have been decided on the basis that the issue of notese was a fraudulent preference as against existing creditors? Robert Clark has noted that nearly all of the leading subordination cases arose where existing creditors had been prejudiced. See Clark, *The Duties of the Corporate Debtor to Its Creditors*, 90 Harv. L. Rev. 505, 526 (1977).

Fraudulent transactions may be set aside under BIA s. 91 ff., or under provincial fraudulent conveyances statutes. In general, however, Canadian courts will not set aside transactions on a corporation's formation as fraudulent unless the corporation is actually insolvent. In *Rielle v. Reid* (1897), 28 O.R. 497, Reid carried on a speculative unincorporated business in serious financial difficulties. For four years it had not earned enough to pay interest on debt and taxes, and no improvement was in sight. The business was then incorporated with a stated capital of $50,000 and operated as a going concern for two more years, during which time the firm's old creditors were all paid off. Falconbridge J. set aside the transfer of assets on incorporation as a fraudulent conveyance. The Ontario Court of Appeal reversed at 26 O.A.R. 54. Osler J.A., who delivered the judgment of the Court, stated that the evidence fell short of fraud since Reid was merely in financial difficulties and had not been expressly found to be insolvent.

The equitable subordination rule has more frequently been applied in the United States when the corporation's shares are held by another corporation than when they are held by individuals. The claims of the holding corporation (or parent) are then deferred to those of the other creditors of the issuing corporation (or subsidiary). The principle of subordination in such cases is referred to as the Deep Rock doctrine, after the subsidiary in the leading case of *Taylor v. Standard Gas & Electric Co.*, 306 U.S. 307 (1939). However, problems of fairness are more vexed when both corporations carry on business and the subsidiary is not wholly owned by the parent. The courts might then have to sort out a large number of allegedly unfair business dealings between the corporations, with a view to protecting the subsidiary's minority shareholders as well as its creditors.

On equitable subordination, see further Israels, *The Implications and Limitations of the "Deep Rock" Doctrine*, 42 Colum. L. Rev. 376 (1942); Landers, *A Unified Approach to Parent, Subsidiary and Affiliate Questions in Bankruptcy*, 42 U. Chi. L. Rev. 589 (1975); Landers, *Another Word on Parents, Subsidiaries and Affiliates in Bankruptcy*, 42 U. Chi. L. Rev. 527 (1976); Posner, *The Rights of Creditors of Affiliated Corporations*, 43 U. Chi. L. Rev. 499 (1976).

3. Non-Consensual Claimants and Incentive Costs

Walkovszky v. Carlton
New York Court of Appeals
276 N.Y.S. 2d 585, 223 N.E. 2d 6 (1966)

FULD J.: This case involves what appears to be a rather common practice in the taxicab industry of vesting the ownership of a taxi fleet in many corporations, each owning only one or two cabs.

The complaint alleges that the plaintiff was severely injured four years ago in New York City when he was run down by a taxicab owned by the defendant Seon Cab Corporation and negligently operated at the time by the defendant Marchese. The individual defendant, Carlton, is claimed to be a stockholder of 10 corporations, including Seon, each of which has but two cabs registered in its name, and it is implied that only the minimum automobile liability insurance required by law (in the amount of $10,000) is carried on any one cab. Although seemingly independent of one another, these corporations are alleged to be "operated ... as a single entity, unit and enterprise" with regard to financing, supplies, repairs, employees and garaging, and all are named as defendants.

The plaintiff asserts that he is also entitled to hold their stockholders personally liable for damages sought because the multiple corporate structure constitutes an unlawful attempt "to defraud members of the general public" who might be injured by the cabs.

The defendant Carlton has moved, pursuant to CPLR 3211(a)7, to dismiss the complaint on the ground that as to him it "fails to state a cause of action." The court at Special Term granted the motion but the Appellate Division, by a divided vote, reversed, holding that a valid cause of action was sufficiently stated. The defendant Carlton appeals to us, from the nonfinal order, by leave of the Appellate Division on a certified question.

The law permits the incorporation of a business for the very purpose of enabling its proprietors to escape personal liability (see, e.g., *Bartle v. Home Owners Co-op*, 309 N.Y. 103, 106, 127 N.E. 2d 832, 833) but, manifestly, the privilege is not without its limits. Broadly speaking, the courts will disregard the corporate form, or, to use accepted terminology, "pierce the corporate veil," whenever necessary "to prevent fraud or to achieve equity." (*International Aircraft Trading Co. v. Manufacturers Trust Co.*, 297 N.Y. 285, 292, 79 N.E. 2d 249, 252.) In determining whether liability should be extended to reach assets beyond those belonging to the corporation, we are guided, as Judge Cardozo noted, by "general rules of agency." (*Berkey v. Third Ave. Ry. Co.*, 244 N.Y. 84, 95, 155 N.E. 58, 61, 50 A.L.R. 599.) In other words, whenever anyone uses control of the corporation to further his own rather than the corporation's business, he will be liable for the corporation's acts "upon the principle of *respondeat superior* applicable even where the agent is a natural person." (*Rapid Tr. Subway Constr. Co. v. City of New York*, 259 N.Y. 472, 488, 182 N.E. 145, 150.) Such liability, moreover, extends not only to the corporation's commercial dealings ... but to its negligent acts as well. ...

In the *Mangen* case (247 App. Div. 853, 286 N.Y.S. 666, mot, for Iv. to app. den. 272 N.Y. 676, 286 N.Y.S. 666, supra), the plaintiff was injured as a result of the negligent operation of a cab owned and operated by one of four corporations affiliated with the defendant Terminal. Although the defendant was not a stockholder of any of the operating companies, both the defendant and the operating companies were owned, for the most part, by the same parties. The defendant's name (Terminal) was conspicuously displayed on the sides of all of the taxis used in the enterprise and, in point of fact, the defendant actually serviced, inspected, repaired and dispatched them. These facts were deemed to provide sufficient cause for piercing the corporate veil of the operating company—the nominal owner of the cab which injured the plaintiff—and holding the defendant liable. The operating companies were simply instrumentalities for carrying on the business of the defendant without imposing upon it financial and other liabilities incident to the actual ownership and operation of the cabs. ...

In the case before us, the plaintiff has explicitly alleged that none of the corporations "had a separate existence of their own" and, as indicated above, all are named as defendants. However, it is one thing to assert that a corporation is a fragment of a larger corporate combine which actually conducts the business. (See Berle, *The Theory of Enterprise Entity*, 47 Col. L. Rev. 343, 348-350.) It is quite another to claim that the corporation is a "dummy" for its individual stockholders who are in reality carrying on the business in their personal capacities for purely personal rather than corporate ends. (See *African Metals Corp. v. Bullowa*, 288 N.Y. 78, 85, 41 N.E. 2d 366, 469.) Either circumstance would justify treating the corporation as an agent and piercing the corporate veil to reach the principal but a different result would follow in each case. In the first, only a larger *corporate* entity would be held financially responsible ... while, in the other, the stockholder would be personally liable. ... Either the stockholder is conducting the business in his individual capacity or he is not. If he is, he will be liable; if he is not, then it does not matter—insofar as his personal liability is concerned—that the enterprise is actually being carried on by a larger "enterprise entity." (See Berle, *The Theory of Enterprise Entity*, 47 Col. L. Rev. 343.)

At this stage in the present litigation, we are concerned only with the pleadings and, since CPLR 3014 permits causes of action to be stated "alternatively or hypothetically," it is possible for the plaintiff to allege both theories as the basis for his demand for judgment. In ascertaining whether he has done so, we must consider the entire pleading, educing therefrom " 'whatever can be imputed from its statements by fair and reasonable intendment.' " ... Reading the complaint in this case most favorably and liberally, we do not believe that there can be gathered from its averments the allegations required to spell out a valid cause of action against the defendant Carlton.

The individual defendant is charged with having "organized, managed, dominated and controlled" a fragmented corporate entity but there are no allegations that he was conducting business in his individual capacity. Had the taxicab fleet been owned by a single corporation, it would be readily apparent that the plaintiff would face formidable barriers in attempting to establish personal liability on the part of the corporation's stockholders. The fact that the fleet ownership has been deliberately split up among many corporations does not ease the plaintiff's burden in that respect. The corporate form may not be disregarded merely because the assets of the corporation, together with the mandatory insurance coverage of the vehicle which struck the plaintiff, are insufficient to assure him the recovery sought. If Carlton were to be held individually liable on those facts alone, the decision would apply equally to the thousands of cabs which are owned by their individual drivers who conduct their businesses through corporations organized pursuant to section 401 of the Business Corporation Law, Consol. Laws, c. 4 and carry the minimum insurance required by [section 370 of the Vehicle and Traffic Law]. These taxi owner-operators are entitled to form such corporations (cf. *Elenkrieg v. Siebrecht*, 238 N.Y. 254, 144 N.E. 519, 34 A.L.R. 592), and we agree with the court at Special Term that, if the insurance coverage required by statute "is inadequate for the protection of the public, the remedy lies not with the courts but with the Legislature." It may very well be sound policy to require that certain corporations must take out liability insurance which will afford adequate compensation to their potential tort victims. However, the responsibility for imposing conditions in the privilege of incorporation has been committed by the Constitution to the Legislature ... and it may not be fairly implied, from any statute, that the Legislature intended, without the slightest discussion or debate, to require of taxi corporations that they carry automobile liability insurance over and above that mandated by the Vehicle and Traffic Law.

This is not to say that it is impossible for the plaintiff to state a valid cause of action against the defendant Carlton. However, the simple fact is that the plaintiff has just not done so here. While the complaint alleges that the separate corporations were undercapitalized and that their assets have been intermingled, it is barren of any "sufficiently particular[ized] statements" ... that the defendant Carlton and his associates are actually doing business in their individual capacities, shuttling their personal funds in and out of the corporations "without regard to formality and to suit their immediate convenience." (*Weisser v. Mursam Shoe Corp.*, 2 Cir., 127 F.2d 344, 345, 145 A.L.R. 467, supra.) Such a "perversion of the privilege to do business in a corporate form" (*Berkey v. Third Ave. Ry. Co.*, 244 N.Y. 84, 95, 155 N.E. 58, 61, 50 A.L.R. 599, supra) would justify imposing personal liability on the individual stockholders. (See *African Metals Corp. v. Bullowa*, 288 N.Y. 78, 41 N.E. 2d 466, supra.) Nothing of the sort has in fact been charged, and it cannot reasonably or logically be inferred from the happenstance that the business of Seon Cab Corporation may actually be carried on by a larger corporate entity composed of many corporations which, under general principles of agency, would be liable to each other's creditors in contract and in tort.[3]

In point of fact, the principle relied upon in the complaint to sustain the imposition of personal liability is not agency but fraud. Such a cause of action cannot withstand analysis. If it is not fraudulent for the owner-operator of a single cab corporation to take out only the minimum required liability insurance, the enterprise does not become either illicit or fraudulent merely because it consists of many such corporations. The plaintiff's injuries are the same regardless of whether the cab which strikes him is owned by a single corporation or part of a fleet with ownership fragmented among many corporations. Whatever rights he may be able to assert against parties other than the registered owner of the vehicle come into being not because he has been defrauded but because, under the principle of *respondeat superior*, he is entitled to hold the whole enterprise responsible for the acts of its agents.

In sum, then, the complaint falls short of adequately stating a cause of action against the defendant Carlton in his individual capacity. ...

KEATING J. (dissenting): The defendant Carlton, the shareholder here sought to be held for the negligence of the driver of a taxicab, was a principal shareholder and organizer of the defendant corporation which owned the taxicab. The corporation was one of 10 organized by the defendant, each containing two cabs and each cab having the "minimum liability" insurance coverage mandated by section 370 of the Vehicle and Traffic Law. The sole assets of these operating corporations are the vehicles themselves and they are apparently subject to the mortgages.

From their inception these corporations were intentionally undercapitalized for the purpose of avoiding responsibility for acts which were bound to arise as a result of the operation of a large taxi fleet having cars out on the street 24 hours a day and engaged in public transportation. And during the course of the corporations' existence all income was continually drained out of the corporations for the same purpose.

---

3   In his affidavit in opposition to the motion to dismiss, the plaintiff's counsel claimed that corporate assets had been "milked out" of, and "siphoned off" from the enterprise. Quite apart from the fact that these allegations are far too vague and conclusory, the charge is premature. If the plaintiff succeeds in his action and becomes a judgment creditor of the corporation, he may then sue and attempt to hold the individual defendants accountable for any dividends and property that were wrongfully distributed (Business Corporation Law, §§510, 719, 720).

The issue presented by this action is whether the policy of this State, which affords those desiring to engage in a business enterprise the privilege of limited liability through the use of the corporate device, is so strong that it will permit that privilege to continue no matter how much it is abused, no matter how irresponsibly the corporation is operated, no matter what the cost to the public. I do not believe that it is.

Under the circumstances of this case the shareholders should all be held individually liable to this plaintiff for the injuries he suffered. (See *Mull v. Colt Co., D.C.*, 31 F.R.D. 154, 156; *Teller v. Clear Serv. Co.*, 9 Misc. 2d 495, 173 N.Y.S. 2d 183.) At least, the matter should not be disposed of on the pleadings by dismissal of the complaint. "If a corporation is organized and carries on business without substantial capital in such a way that the corporation is likely to have no sufficient assets available to meet its debts, it is inequitable that shareholders should set up such a flimsy organization to escape personal liability. The attempt to do corporate business without providing any sufficient basis of financial responsibility to creditors is an abuse of the separate entity and will be ineffectual to exempt the shareholders from corporate debts. It is coming to be recognized as the policy of law that shareholders should in good faith put at the risk of the business unincumbered capital reasonably adequate for its prospective liabilities. If capital is illusory or trifling compared with the business to be done and the risks of loss, this is a ground for denying the separate entity privilege." (Ballantine, *Corporations* [rev. ed., 1946], §129, pp. 302-303.)

In *Minton v. Cavaney*, 56 Cal. 2d 576, 15 Cal. Rptr. 641, 364 P.2d 473, the Supreme Court of California had occasion to discuss this problem in a negligence case. The corporation of which the defendant was an organizer, director and officer operated a public swimming pool. One afternoon the plaintiff's daughter drowned in the pool as a result of the alleged negligence of the corporation.

Justice Roger Traynor, speaking for the court, outlined the applicable law in this area. "The figurative terminology 'alter ego' and 'disregard of the corporate entity,'" he wrote, "is generally used to refer to the various situations that are an abuse of the corporate privilege. ... The equitable owners of a corporation, for example, are personally liable when they treat the assets of the corporation as their own and add or withdraw capital from the corporation at will ...; when they hold themselves out as being personally liable for the debts of the corporation ...; *or when they provide inadequate capitalization and actively participate in the conduct of corporate affairs.*" (56 Cal. 2d, p. 579, 15 Cal. Rptr., p. 643, 364 P.2d p. 475; italics supplied.)

Examining the facts of the case in light of the legal principles just enumerated, he found that "[it was] undisputed that there was no attempt to provide adequate capitalization. [The corporation] never had any substantial assets. It leased the pool that it operated, and the lease was forfeited for failure to pay the rent. Its capital was 'trifling compared with the business to be done and the risks of loss.'" (56 Cal. 2d, p. 580, 15 Cal. Rptr., p. 643, 364 P.2d, p. 475.)

It seems obvious that one of "the risks of loss" referred to was the possibility of drownings due to the negligence of the corporation. And the defendant's failure to provide such assets or any fund for recovery resulted in his being held personally liable.

In *Anderson v. Abbott*, 321 U.S. 349, 64 S. Ct. 531, 88 L. Ed. 793, the defendant shareholders had organized a holding company and transferred to that company shares which they held in various national banks in return for shares in the holding company. The holding company did not have sufficient assets to meet the double liability requirements of the governing Federal statutes which provided that the owners of shares in national banks were personally liable for corporate obligations "to the extent of the amount of their stock therein, at the par value thereof, in addition to the amount invested in such shares" (U.S. code, tit. 12, former 63).

The court had found that these transfers were made in good faith, that other defendant shareholders who had purchased shares in the holding company had done so in good faith and that the organization of such a holding company was entirely legal. Despite this finding, the Supreme Court, speaking through Mr. Justice Douglas, pierced the corporate veil of the holding company, and held all the shareholders, even those who had no part in the organization of the corporation, individually responsible for the corporate obligations as mandated by the statute.

"Limited liability," he wrote, "is the rule, not the exception; and on that assumption large undertakings are rested, vast enterprises are launched, and huge sums of capital attracted. But there are occasions when the limited liability sought to be obtained through the corporation will be qualified or denied. Mr. Chief Judge Cardozo stated that a surrender of that principle of limited liability would be made 'when the sacrifice is so essential to the end that some accepted public policy may be defended or upheld.' ... The cases of fraud make up part of that exception. ... But they do not exhaust it. *An obvious inadequacy of capital, measured by the nature and magnitude of the corporate undertaking, has frequently been an important factor in cases denying stockholders their defense of limited liability. ... That rule has been invoked even in absence of a legislative policy which undercapitalization would defeat.* It becomes more important in a situation such as the present one where the statutory policy of double liability will be defeated if impecunious bankstock holding companies are allowed to be interposed as non-conductors of liability. *It has often been held that the interposition of a corporation will not be allowed to defeat a legislative policy, whether that was the aim or only the result of the arrangement. ...* 'The courts will not permit themselves to be blinded or deceived by mere forms of law' but will deal 'with the substance of the transaction involved as if the corporate agency did not exist and as the justice of the case may require.' " (321 U.S., pp. 362-363, 64 S. Ct., p. 537; emphasis added.)

The policy of this State has always been to provide and facilitate recovery for those injured through the negligence of others. The automobile, by its very nature, is capable of causing severe and costly injuries when not operated in a proper manner. The great increase in the number of automobile accidents combined with the frequent financial irresponsibility of the individual driving the car led to the adoption of section 388 of the Vehicle and Traffic Law which had the effect of imposing upon the owner of the vehicle the responsibility for its negligent operation. It is upon this very statute that the cause of action against both the corporation and the individual defendant is predicated.

In addition the Legislature, still concerned with the financial irresponsibility of those who owned and operated motor vehicles, enacted a statute requiring minimum liability coverage for all owners of automobiles. The important public policy represented by both these statutes is outlined in section 310 of the Vehicle and Traffic Law. That section provides that: "The legislature is concerned over the rising toll of motor vehicle accidents and the suffering and loss thereby inflicted. The legislature determines that it is a matter of grave concern that motorists shall be financially able to respond in damages for their negligent acts, so that innocent victims of motor vehicle accidents may be recompensed for the injury and financial loss inflicted upon them."

The defendant Carlton claims that, because the minimum amount of insurance required by the statute was obtained, the corporate veil cannot and should not be pierced despite the fact that the assets of the corporation which owned the cab were "trifling compared with the business to be done and the risks of loss" which were certain to be encountered. I do not agree.

The Legislature in requiring minimum liability insurance of $10,000, no doubt, intended to provide at least some small fund for recovery against those individuals and corporations who just did not have and were not able to raise or accumulate assets sufficient to satisfy the claims of those who were injured as a result of their negligence. It certainly could not have intended to shield those individuals who organized corporations, with the specific intent of avoiding responsibility to the public, where the operation of the corporate enterprise yielded profits sufficient to purchase the additional insurance. Moreover, it is reasonable to assume that the Legislature believed that those individuals and corporations having substantial assets would take out insurance far in excess of the minimum in order to protect those assets from depletion. Given the costs of hospital care and treatment and the nature of injuries sustained in auto collisions, it would be unreasonable to assume that the Legislature believed that the minimum provided in the statute would in and of itself be sufficient to recompense "innocent victims of motor vehicle accidents ... for the injury and financial loss inflicted upon them."

The defendant, however, argues that the failure of the Legislature to increase the minimum insurance requirements indicates legislative acquiescence in this scheme to avoid liability and responsibility to the public. In the absence of a clear legislative statement, approval of a scheme having such serious consequences is not to be so lightly inferred.

The defendant contends that the court will be encroaching upon the legislative domain by ignoring the corporate veil and holding the individual shareholder. This argument was answered by Mr. Justice Douglas in *Anderson v. Abbott,* supra, pp. 366-367, 64 S. Ct. p. 540, where he wrote that: "In the field in which we are presently concerned, judicial power hardly oversteps the bounds when it refuses to lend its aid to a promotional project which would circumvent or undermine a legislative policy. To deny it that function would be to make it impotent in situations where historically it has made some of its most notable contributions. If the judicial power is helpless to protect a legislative program from schemes for easy avoidance, then indeed it has become a handy implement of high finance. *Judicial interference to cripple or defeat a legislative policy is one thing; judicial interference with the plans of those whose corporate or other devices would circumvent that policy is quite another.* Once the purpose or effect of the scheme is clear, once the legislative policy is plain, we would indeed forsake a great tradition to say we were helpless to fashion the instruments for appropriate relief." (Emphasis added.)

The defendant contends that a decision holding him personally liable would discourage people from engaging in corporate enterprise.

What I would merely hold is that a participating shareholder of a corporation vested with a public interest, organized with capital insufficient to meet liabilities which are certain to arise in the ordinary course of the corporation's business, may be held personally responsible for such liabilities. Where corporate income is not sufficient to cover the cost of insurance premiums above the statutory minimum or where initially adequate finances dwindle under the pressure of competition, bad times or extraordinary and unexpected liability, obviously the shareholder will not be held liable (Henn, *Corporations*, p. 208, n. 7).

The only types of corporate enterprises that will be discouraged as a result of a decision allowing the individual shareholder to be sued will be those such as the one in question, designed solely to abuse the corporate privilege at the expense of the public interest.

For the reasons I would vote to affirm the order of the Appellate Division.

[DESMOND C.J. and VAN VOORHIS, BURKE and SCILEPPI JJ. concurred with FULD J. and BERGAN J. concurred with KEATING J.]

Non-Consensual Claimants. If "thin capitalization" does not offer an adequate justification for veil-piercing for the benefit of consensual creditors, can a stronger argument be made for disregarding the corporate entity when a firm has non-consensual claimants? A consensual creditor may avoid wealth transfer effects by bargaining on the basis that liability is limited. But these defensive strategies are not available to non-consensual creditors, such as those tort claimants who do not bargain with the firm.

Tort claims in bankruptcy are now much more significant in the United States than in the past, in part as a consequence of expanded liability for compensatory and punitive damages. See, e.g., *Sindell v. Abbott Laboratories*, 607 P.2d 924 (Cal.), cert. denied, 449 U.S. 912 (1980) (apportionment of damages throughout an industry on the basis of market share). As a result, tort liabilities may be enormous, when to existing claims are added claims with an epidemiological probability of being asserted in the future. In the most highly publicized case, the Manville Corporation filed for reorganization in bankruptcy at a time when the firm had a book value of $1.2 billion but faced estimated liability of $1.9 billion in present and future asbestos-related tort claims. Moreover, inventive strategies have been devised to permit the interests of future tort claimants to be recognized in bankruptcy. See Roe, *Bankruptcy and Mass Tort*, 84 Colum. L. Rev. 846-92 (1984). For example, the Manville reorganization plan requires the corporation to assign equity interests in the firm worth $2.5 billion to a trust fund for the benefit of present and future tort claimants. See *In re Johns-Manville Corp.*, 801 F.2d 60 (2d Cir. 1986).

Even then, distributional concerns about the choice of limited liability by a firm with anticipated tort claimants are likely highly muted, particularly in Canada. Many tort claimants are not entirely "non-consensual": because of the expansion of tort liability, tort claims now frequently arise from consumer purchases or employment contracts. Such claimants are not affected by wealth transfer effects when they bargain on the basis of limited liability. In addition, legal barriers under Canadian tort and bankruptcy law will largely minimize the burden of future tort claimants. *Sindell* liability is untested in Canada, and would do violence to traditional doctrines of causation. Finally, even if such barriers were removed, it is unlikely that a future tort claimant could prove in a Canadian bankruptcy.

Where tort claimants are foreseen, however, the incorporation decision will clearly have efficiency and wealth transfer consequences. Nowhere is this more evident than in *Walkovszky*, where there was no economic advantage to incorporating 10 separate corporations except insofar as they served to set a cap on liability. Indeed, since incorporation is costly the liability rule resulted in an excessive level of incorporations.

Apart from increased costs associated with the incorporation process, further inefficiencies may arise from a reduced incentive to take care. Suppose that a firm has n taxis, each worth \$4,000, and that each taxi has a probability p of injuring a pedestrian. Let the average cost of injury to a given pedestrian be d, and the total harm cost be HC. Then

$$HC = pnd$$

If $n = 20$, $p = 10\%$ and $d = \$50,000$,

$$HC = \$100,000$$

Assuming that the total value of the firm is only \$80,000 (20 taxis times \$4,000 each), the firm would not commence operations if it bore all harm costs as damages. But now suppose that the firm may costlessly incorporate 20 corporations, each of which will own and operate one taxi. Two taxis will be expected to strike pedestrians, and two of the corporations, with a total firm value of \$8,000, will then go bankrupt. Separate incorporations may therefore permit the entire business to continue in operation, having an expected value not of 0 but of \$72,000.

A more general analysis of the adverse incentive program would compare the firm's due care decision under limited and unlimited liability regimes. Assume that HC can be reduced when the firm bears prevention costs (PC) associated with taking care. Absent transaction costs, the firm would then take such care as to minimize the total of $PC + HC$.

$$min \ (PC + HC)$$

In other words, if harm costs of \$10 could be reduced to 0 by an \$8 investment in PC, the firm would eliminate the harm by investing in harm prevention, whether or not it was liable in damages for the harm. If it did bear such liability, the likelihood of the damages award would in itself lead the firm to take care. But even without tort liability, the firm would still eliminate the harm, in a Coasean world of costless bargains. Here the victims would bribe the firm to take an efficient level of care, since they would be willing to pay at least \$8 to reduce the harm costs of \$10 which they would otherwise bear.

Liability rules will, however, matter where positive transaction costs make it unlikely that a coalition of victims could bargain the firm to take care. In particular, where tort victims are dispersed, with each one bearing only a small percentage of total harm, the transaction costs barriers to the formation of a coalition of victims may be substantial. In addition, even if such a coalition could be costlessly formed, each individual victim might be tempted to refrain from making his proportionate contribution to the coalition's *PC* fund in the hope that other tort victims would pay his share. The defecting tort victim would thus seek to free ride on the other victims. If other tort victims act in the same way, the coalition may unwind through free riding.

Given positive transactions costs, then, the firm would be more likely to take care if tort liability was imposed upon it. Suppose therefore that damages D_N based on a negligence standard will be levied against the firm unless it takes a "reasonable" amount of care, defined as prevention costs equal to PC'. D_N can then be defined as follows:

$$D_N = \begin{cases} 0 \text{ if } PC \geq PC' \\ nd \text{ if } PC < PC' \end{cases}$$

In other words, the firm will not bear any liability in damages if it absorbs *PC* equal to or greater than the optimal level of care PC', but will otherwise bear damages equal to *nd*. Provided that the reasonable care level PC' is defined as the level of care that minimizes $PC + HC$, the firm will then be led to take an efficient amount of care, or a level of care that minimizes total costs of harm prevention borne by the firm and of anticipated third party losses.* The firm would decide upon how much care to take by seeking to minimize the total of *PC* plus the expected monetary value of the anticipated damages award (the probability of a damages award times the anticipated damages award). The resulting minimization formula of $min \ (PC + pD)$ would lead it to make the same harm prevention decision as it would under the social minimization formula of $min \ (PC + HC)$. Note that the firm would not be led to eliminate all harm to third parties under this standard. Thus, if an investment in harm prevention would cost more than the benefits associated with an anticipated decrease in *HC*, this would amount to "excessive" care from an economic perspective.

Where the tort regime accurately assesses damages, it can now be shown that a possibility of bankruptcy may lead a firm to underinvest in harm prevention. Where the firm, at some levels of care, faces damages claims that exceed firm value *W*, it may be led to adopt an inefficient standard of care. In considering cost minimization, the firm will have regard not to D_N, but rather $\overline{D}_N$, defined as follows:

$$\overline{D}_N = \begin{cases} D_N \text{ if } D_N < W \\ W \text{ if } D_N \geq W \end{cases}$$

The firm's cost minimization formula is then $min \ (PC + p\overline{D}_N)$, and this may result in a level of care that is different from that which the firm would select under $min \ (PC + pD_N)$. In particular, the probability of adverse incentive costs (and of inadequate investments in harm prevention) is greatest where *W* is small in comparison with anticipated damages, and *PC* is relatively large in amount.

---

*   Note that the $min \ (PC + HC)$ standard would be adopted in a hypothetical claimholders' bargain to which anticipated tort victims were parties. For a demonstration that the firm would be led to take the same level of care where damages are assessed on the basis of strict liability, assuming that the optimal level of care and the amount of damages can be unambiguously determined, see C. Goetz, *Cases and Materials on Law and Economics* 293-99 (1984).

This adverse incentive problem may lead to increased harm costs in two different ways. First, because of limited liability, firms may be led to take less care than they otherwise would, leading directly to an increase in the number of accidents. In addition, a greater *level* of harm may arise where firms in the industry are more profitable than they would be if they and their shareholders bore all harm costs. The industry will then be larger than it would be under unlimited liability, and with increased levels of production there will also be increased levels of harm.

Piercing the corporate veil in these circumstances would then result in higher, more efficient levels of harm prevention. In the jargon of economists, the firm would "internalize" the external costs it imposes on tort plaintiffs. However, a general denial of limited liability to shareholders would sacrifice the efficiency gains described by Easterbrook and Fischel in Section A of this chapter. This suggests that veil-piercing be restricted in scope to non-consensual claimholders. Distinguishing between consensual and non-consensual claimholders will not always be easy. Is the customer who brings a product liability action asserting a non-consensual claim? What if the gravity of the harm is hidden, as in the asbestos or Dalkon shield cases? What is the relevance of privity of contract? And against which shareholders could the tort plaintiffs recover? Those who were shareholders at the time the product was manufactured? At the time it was sold? At the time of the injury? At the time the injury was discovered? At the time the action was brought? See Hansmann & Kraakman, *Toward Unlimited Liability for Corporate Torts*, 100 Yale L.J. 1879 (1991) (discussing how such difficulties might be addressed). As well, Joseph Grundfest suggests that under an unlimited tort liability regime domestic shareholders would simply sell off their shares to judgment-proof foreign shareholders. Grundfest, *The Limited Future of Unlimited Liability: A Capital Markets Perspective*, 102 Yale L.J. 387 (1992). Finally, could unlimited tort liability result in excessive care, particularly for small businesses, given shareholder risk aversion?

These problems, and the prospect of sacrificing the efficiency gains described by Easterbrook and Fischel, suggest that veil-piercing should not be adopted if the incentive problem can be addressed in less intrusive ways. One possible solution is a regulatory one, in which potential tortfeasors are required to seek insurance for tort claims in bankruptcy. This solution would have dealt with the *Walkovszky* problem, if taxi owners had been required to maintain adequate coverage for each cab. Veil-piercing might be a superior solution, if the firm would prefer to self-insure as a consequence of informational asymmetries between the firm and the insurer with respect to the size of the expected damages. Alternatively, monitoring responsibilities might be passed on to the firm's secured lenders, by subordinating them to tort claimants in bankruptcy. See Buckley, *The Bankruptcy Priority Puzzle*, 72 Va. L. Rev. 1393, 1415-19 (1986); Note, *Tort Creditor Priority in the Secured Credit System: Asbestos Times, The Worst of Times*, 36 Stan. L. Rev. 1045 (1984).

This discussion has assumed that limited liability law subverts efficient tort law principles. In the United States, however, the explosion in American tort liability law is arguably perverse, and bankruptcy restrictions on recovery might be no bad thing. For arguments that American tort law excessively benefits trial lawyers and fraudulent and self-pitying plaintiffs, see Walter K. Olsen, *The Litigation Explosion* (1991); Buckley, *After Virtue, Law*, in *This Will Hurt a Bit* (Digby Anderson ed. forthcoming 1995).

Berger v. Willowdale A.M.C.
Ontario Court of Appeal
(1983), 41 O.R. (2d) 89, 145 D.L.R. (3d) 247,
leave to appeal refused, 41 O.R. (2d) 89 n.

CORY J.A.: On December 20, 1975, the plaintiff Beryl Berger was injured when she slipped and fell on the icy, snow-covered sidewalk leading from the building where she worked as a telephone operator-receptionist. The trial judge found that the defendant Hans. J. Falkenberg, who was the president of the company employing Mrs. Berger, was personally liable for the injuries. Mr. Falkenberger is appealing that decision.

Factual background

Mrs. Berger was employed by Falken Automobiles Inc., which carried on business as an automobile dealership and repair shop at 7200 Yonge St. in Thornhill. Hans Falkenberg was the president and sole shareholder of the company.

The weather conditions that existed for a few days before and on the day of the accident bear significantly on this case. On December 15th it had been raining. The temperature then dropped and there was a considerable amount of freezing. The temperatures stayed below the freezing mark until some days after the accident. On December 16th, 2.6 in. of snow fell, on the 17th, 1.1 in., on the 18th, 4 in., on the 19th, .8 in. and on the day of the accident, the 20th, 3.2 in. of snow fell.

The company premises resemble many automobile dealerships. The focal point was the show-room on the east side of the building with large plate glass windows facing toward Yonge St. The west side of the building contained a large service garage. On the south side of the building there was the usual large garage door which provided access for vehicles to the company service and repair shop. There was a pedestrian door adjacent to the garage door.

The usual means of entrance to and exit from the automobile show-room and offices was through a door at the south-east corner of the building. A sidewalk led from this door to a ramp for automobiles. It was in this location that the accident occurred.

Falken Automobiles Inc. employed 25 to 35 people. The accident occurred on a Saturday when the service department and thus the garage was closed. There were some ten employees on the premises that day.

On the day of the accident, Mrs. Berger arrived at work around 9:00 a.m. She walked up the sidewalk and entered by the door located at the south-east corner of the building. She saw salesmen and customers using that door throughout the day.

It snowed all that day, to the extent that between 6:30 a.m. until 6:00 p.m., 2.5 in. fell. Mr. Falkenberg had issued standing instructions to clear ice and snow from the company premises. There was equipment available to remove the snow, including snow-shovels, salt, a salt spreader, a snow-plough and choppers. Ordinarily, the service manager was responsible for the clearing of snow and ice. On Saturdays, the sales manager assumed this responsibility, to be carried out with the assistance of a "car jockey."

The situation on December 20th then was that there were employees on the premises who could have removed the snow, there was equipment available for its removal and Mr. Falkenberg was present throughout the day. Mr. Falkenberg agreed that he was in control and was "the boss" of the business. He acknowledged that he could have asked someone to remove the ice and snow and that if he gave those instructions he would expect them to be carried out. The front sidewalk and ramp were clearly visible from almost any position in the show-room. Mr. Falkenberg agreed that it was important to have snow and ice removed from the sidewalk and ramp because the ice could be dangerous if it had snow on top. He confirmed that people might fall if the area were not cleared of ice and snow as this was the very location and means by which people would enter and leave the show-room.

The trial judge found that at the time of the accident there was ice on the sidewalk covered by several inches of old and fresh snow. He determined that it must have been obvious to Mr. Falkenberg for several days that his instructions as to snow removal were not being carried out. As a result, a dangerous condition had been created that Mr. Falkenberg could easily have remedied.

When she was told that she could leave early, Mrs. Berger telephoned her husband to pick her up. At about 5:00 p.m. she walked down the sidewalk to the ramp where her husband was waiting. Her son got out of the car and opened the door for her. Mrs. Berger walked carefully down the sidewalk and, upon raising her leg to get into the car, slipped and fell and broke her ankle. The trial judge found quite properly that there was no contributory negligence on the part of Mrs. Berger.

The order of the Workmen's Compensation Board

By s. 15 of the Workmen's Compensation Act, R.S.O. 1970, c. 505 (now R.S.O. 1980, c. 539), the Workmen's Compensation Board is given the exclusive right on the application of a party to an action to determine whether a right of action has been taken away by the Workmen's Compensation Act.

By an order dated February 13, 1979, the board ruled that Mrs. Berger's right of action against Falken Automobiles Inc. and the remaining corporate defendants had been excluded by the provisions of the Act but that her right of action against Hans Falkenberg and the other individual defendants had not. The action was then discontinued against all the individual defendants except Mr. Falkenberg.

Conclusions of the trial judge

On the basis of his factual findings the trial judge concluded that Mr. Falkenberg owed a duty of care to Mrs. Berger and that he was in breach of that duty. He found that the plaintiff was not prevented from recovery by reason of voluntary assumption of the risk, by contributory negligence or by the doctrine of common employment. He then assessed the damages flowing from the negligence of Mr. Falkenberg in an amount which is not in dispute.

Appellant's position

It is the position of the appellant that no duty of care was owed by Hans Falkenberg to Mrs. Berger. It is argued that it was only the employer of Mrs. Berger, Falken Automobiles Inc., which owed a duty to her to keep the premises in which she worked in a reasonably safe condition. The fact that the corporation was directed by Hans Falkenberg did not render him personally liable or responsible for the company's tortious acts. The sole exception to that rule, it is submitted, arises in circumstances where the individual executive officer expressly directs the plaintiff to perform a dangerous act, which is not the situation in this case. Rather, it was the company that was responsible for the acts or omissions of those employees responsible for clearing snow and ice from the company premises and, in the circumstances of this case, the company's liability did not attach to Hans Falkenberg personally.

In support of this position the appellant contends that to find Hans Falkenberg personally liable would contravene the policy and intent of the Workmen's Compensation Act. Under that statute, compensation is paid to employees for injuries suffered as a result of accidents arising out of and in the course of employment regardless of the negligence of the employee, the assumption of risk or common employment. The compensation is achieved by the contributions made by employers to a common fund. Therefore, if a remedy is made available against a corporate officer who is the directing mind of the corporate employer, the very intent of the Workmen's Compensation Act is circumvented.

Alternatively, it is submitted that the plaintiff should have been barred from recovery by reason of her voluntary assumption of the risk, her contributory negligence or because the doctrine of common employment is applicable in this case and stands as a bar to her recovery.

Can Hans Falkenberg be found personally liable for the damages suffered by Mrs. Berger?

(1) *The Workmen's Compensation Act*

Both the plaintiff and her employer, Falken Automobiles Inc., come within the first schedule of the Workmen's Compensation Act. As a result, the plaintiff cannot bring an action for damages against her employer or her fellow employees for injuries which she may have suffered during the course of her employment. Pursuant to the Act an injured employee in such circumstances has an absolute right to compensation by the statute without any diminution of that compensation as a result of either contributory negligence or voluntary assumption of the risks inherent in the employment. However, in my view, it is most significant and critical to the determination of this case to note that an executive officer of a corporation is specifically excluded from the definition of an "employee" contained in s. 1(1)(j) of the Act of 1980 and from the comparable definition of "workman" set out in s. 1(1)(x) of the 1970 version of the Act.

Further, pursuant to s. 15, the Workmen's Compensation Board held that the plaintiff was not barred by the provisions of the Act from bringing an action against Hans Falkenberg.

The Workmen's Compensation Act is thus not a bar to these proceedings.

(2) *Status at common law of an action by an employee against an executive officer of the employer based upon negligence*

Was Hans Falkenberg negligent?

In order to succeed, Mrs. Berger must first establish that it was the negligence of Mr. Falkenberg that caused her injuries. In considering this issue, it may be of assistance to set forth some elementary concepts of negligence.

It has been said that negligence is conduct which involves an unreasonably great risk of causing damage. Alderson B. in *Blyth v. Company of Proprietors of Birmingham Waterworks* (1856), 11 Ex. 781 at p. 784, 156 E.R. 1047, stated:

Negligence is the omission to do something which a reasonable man, guided upon those considerations which ordinarily regulate the conduct of human affairs, would do, or doing something which a prudent and reasonable man would not do.

It is apparent that for more than 125 years acts of omission have fallen within the definition of "negligence" as readily as acts of commission.

A plaintiff, to succeed, must demonstrate that there was a duty of care owed to him by the defendant, that the defendant was in breach of that duty and that damages were occasioned as a result of the breach of that duty. The problem remained for the courts to determine when a duty of care exists. Guide-lines to assist the court in deciding this issue were set out in *M'Alister (or Donoghue) v. Stevenson*, [1932] A.C. 562, by Lord Atkin at p. 580, where he stated his famous proposition:

You must take reasonable care to avoid acts or omissions which you can reasonably foresee would be likely to injure your neighbour. Who, then, in law is my neighbour? The answer seems to be—persons who are so closely and directly affected by my act that I ought reasonably to have them in contemplation as being so affected when I am directing my mind to the acts or omissions which are called in question.

In passing, it is to be noted that there is no distinction drawn between an act or omission in the determination of negligence.

The acts of omission of Hans Falkenberg fall within the definitions of negligence referred to above. He failed to have the snow and ice removed, when it was or ought to have been obvious to him that it was present, and that it created a dangerous situation. He was or ought to have been aware of the problem for several days prior to the accident. He was in total control of the situation at the place of work. He was in a unique position to remedy the dangerous situation and the means of alleviating the risk were readily available to him in the form of both manpower and equipment.

The plaintiff was a "neighbour" of Mr. Falkenberg whom he ought reasonably to have had in contemplation when he failed to remove the snow and ice. Mrs. Berger had to follow the icy and snowy route to her car when she left the premises. The risk of injury to her was readily foreseeable.

There was in my opinion a duty of care that rested upon Falkenberg as the person in control of the situation to render the premises reasonably safe for Mrs. Berger. He was in breach of that duty of care when he failed to rectify the dangerous situation which he saw or ought to have seen and which could be readily alleviated.

It still must be seen whether an employee can maintain an action for the negligence of an executive officer of the employer corporation.

Are there any bars by reason of policy, statute or common law which prevent an employee from bringing an action based on negligence against an executive officer of his employer?

It has been noted that the Workmen's Compensation Act of this province does not bar such an action. As well, there is strong authority for the proposition that the president of a company may be personally liable for his negligent acts leading to the injury of an employee.

In *Lewis v. Boutilier* (1919), 52 D.L.R. 383 (S.C.C.), the president of the company employing the injured worker was successfully sued for damages. He placed a young boy in a dangerous position which he knew or ought to have known lacked adequate safeguards. The jury found the president of the company personally responsible for the boy's injuries. Idington J., speaking for the majority of the Supreme Court of Canada, held that an employee could bring an action against a fellow employee in a supervisory position. He pointed out that it has always been open to a workman to maintain an action against a fellow workman who had been negligent if that fellow workman were worth suing. He concluded that in light of the president's knowledge of the youth and inexperience of the boy, his duty was either to remedy the dangerous situation or to refrain from putting the young boy into the position of danger. His conclusions are set out at p. 386:

Indeed Mr. Paton seemed to suggest that no case could be found holding the superintending fellow servant liable. He may be right in fact but I have not the time to search for such a case as the principle of law applicable seems abundantly clear.

I would refer the curious to Beven on Negligence (3rd ed.) vol. 1, book 4, ch. 5, page 685, under the caption of "Liability of Servants" and especially the authorities cited in the footnote to page 686.

The common sense and characteristics answer of Bramwell, L.J., to the Committee of the House of Commons considering an employer's liability is worth quoting.

It is as follows (p. 686):—

"A workman would undoubtedly be able to maintain an action against the fellow workman who had done the mischief if he were worth suing."

The peculiar offence of appellant is contained in his knowledge of the sort of person he was dealing with and of the actual situation. If he honestly could not have remedied that situation (which I gravely doubt if he tried) his duty was to refrain from putting a child who could not, and evidently did not, apprehend the risk he was running, in such a position of improper danger.

The sooner presidents of companies realize that they have duties, the better for themselves and their fellow men.

The appellant argued that the *Lewis* case should be distinguished from the case at bar for there the president of the company personally placed the youngster in a situation of danger. It was said that the scope of this case should not be extended to acts of omission.

I cannot accept this contention. Acts of omission have long been included in the definition of negligence. If there is a duty of care owed, then negligence by omission may, depending on the facts of the case, constitute a breach of that duty. Acts of omission can be every bit as dangerous as acts of commission.

American authorities

There are American authorities which support the principle that an employee may, in appropriate circumstances, bring an action against an executive officer of the company by which he is employed. The American cases indicate that the employee may be successful in such an action if he demonstrates (1) the executive officer owed a duty of care to him, and (2) that duty was breached by the executive officer through his own personal fault by malfeasance or non-feasance. Liability cannot be imposed on such an officer simply because he has an administrative responsibility. Rather, he must owe a personal duty to the employee. The officer may delegate the duty to a subordinate and thereby escape liability but only if (a) he is not personally at fault in creating the unsafe condition, or (b) he can show he did not personally know or should not be charged with constructive knowledge of the fact that the delegated duty is not being carried out: see *Canter et al. v. Koehring Co. et al.* (1973), 283 So. 2d 716; *McDonald v. Frontier Lanes Inc. et al.* (1971), 272 N.E. 2d 369; *Galloway v. Employers Mutual of Wausau et al.* (1973), 286 So. 2d 676.

Mrs. Berger has established the criteria for a successful action set forth in these American authorities.

On the facts of this case, there is no reason why the plaintiff cannot maintain this action against Mr. Falkenberg, the president of her employer, for his negligent omission to rectify a dangerous situation.

Should policy considerations deny the plaintiff's right of action?

It has been said that for policy reasons there must be some limits to actions based on negligence. Lord Atkins' doctrine should not be extended to impose liability in cases where it would be unjust to do so. The appellant argues that this is just such a situation. There are two bases for this submission. It is said that the employer corporation is responsible for the provision of a safe place of employment and, as a result, Mr. Falkenberg should not be made personally liable for the employer's failure to provide a safe working place. It is further argued that Mr. Falkenberg, through the employer corporation, contributes to the fund established by the Workmen's Compensation Act to compensate injured employees. To make him personally responsible for employees' injuries is to place him in double jeopardy and contravenes the intent and purpose of the Act.

These submissions should not be sustained. It is true that an employer owes a duty to its employee of providing and maintaining a safe working place including the means of reaching that working place: see *Hurley v. J. Sanders & Co., Ltd. et al.*, [1955] 1 All E.R. 833. There is no reason why this duty of care cannot co-exist in both the employer and Hans Falkenberg. Mr. Falkenberg had personal knowledge of the dangerous situation, he had control over and had the means available for readily rectifying the situation. This very situation was contemplated by Idington J. in *Lewis v. Boutilier*, supra, where the recovery by the employee against the president of the employer was upheld. The fact that the duty co-exists in the employer and the executive officer should not and does not constitute a bar to the plaintiff's action.

The argument that to maintain this action contravenes the intent of the Workmen's Compensation Act is defeated by the provision in that Act which specifically excludes executive officers from the definition of "employees." At common law, an employee could sue a fellow employee for his negligence. It is true that such a right of action has, to a large extent, been curtailed by the provisions of the Workmen's Compensation Act. The exclusion of the executive officers of corporations from the definition of "employee" in that Act maintains the right of an employee against such officers. Perhaps this definition of "employee" was deliberately enacted to permit an employee to bring an action in a situation such as that in *Lewis v. Boutilier*, supra.

The definition section constitutes a guide-post as to policy. There is a natural desire on the part of an employee to please persons in authority in the employer corporation. This is particularly true with respect to the president of a small corporation. To the employee the president is the symbol of job security and the source of possible promotion.

From a practical point of view, it is extremely difficult for an employee to refuse to follow the directions of an executive officer although to do so may place him in a dangerous situation. It is equally difficult for an employee to bring a dangerous situation to the attention of such an officer who must be aware of it but appears to ignore it.

The president of a corporation has great power over his employees. He should exercise that power responsibly with due regard for their safety. He cannot ignore a dangerous condition of which he is aware or should be. This is true particularly if he is in control of the situation and has available the means to rectify it.

I can find no basis for deciding that this action should be denied for reasons of policy. On the contrary, the Workmen's Compensation Act contemplates that such an action may be brought. Undoubtedly the legislators thought that such a provision would encourage executive officers to consider the safety of their employees and to avoid the creation or maintenance of dangerous situations. The court should be reluctant to interfere with such a legislative policy.

It was said that to reach this conclusion would "open the floodgates of litigation." This *in terrorem* argument is without foundation. The liability of an executive officer of a corporation will, of course, be dependent upon the facts of the individual case. The factors in determining liability will include the size of the company, particularly the number of employees and the nature of the business; whether or not the danger or risk was or should have been readily apparent to the executive officer; the length of time the dangerous situation was or should have been apparent to the executive officer; whether that officer had the authority and ability to control the situation and whether he had ready access to the means to rectify the danger.

Conclusions

From the foregoing review, I believe that the following conclusions can be drawn.

A plaintiff may bring an action based on negligence against an executive officer of his employer.

Such an action is not barred either by any reason of policy by common law or by the Workmen's Compensation Act. Rather, the Act appears to contemplate that just such an action may be brought.

On the facts of this case Hans Falkenberg was negligent. He owed a duty of care to Mrs. Berger and he was in breach of that duty. ...

WEATHERSTON J.A. (dissenting): ... Falkenberg, by his indifference when he ought not to have been indifferent, impliedly authorized the neglect of their duties by those other employees who were charged with the responsibility of snow removal. Those employees were in a sufficiently close relationship to Mrs. Berger as to owe her a duty to take care not to expose her to danger by neglect of their duties. They would be liable at common law to Mrs. Berger for the injuries she sustained by reason of their neglect. Falkenberg would be equally liable for having authorized this tort.

But the Legislature has said that neither the company, as employer, nor the neglectful employees, are guilty of a tort. The remedies under the Workmen's Compensation Act have been substituted for rights at common law. If they are not liable to Mrs. Berger, I do not see how Falkenberg can be liable as a party to their careless conduct. If a company were given statutory authority to execute a work that necessarily resulted in injury to its neighbour, it could not be seriously argued that the managing director of the company was liable in nuisance to the neighbour. In the present case the primary duty of care at common law lay with the company and the employees, and the removal of that duty of care insulates Falkenberg from secondary liability.

But then, it is said that he is liable for an independent tort, quite apart from his position as managing director for the company. R. E. Holland J. has quoted the famous passage from Lord Atkin's speech in *M'Alister (or Donoghue) v. Stevenson*, [1932] A.C. 562 at p. 580 (H.L.). Lord Reid said in *Home Office v. Dorset Yacht Co. Ltd.*, [1970] A.C. 1004 at p. 1027, that that passage should "be regarded as a statement of principle. It is not to be treated as if it were a statutory definition. It will require qualification in new circumstances. But I think that the time has come when we can and should say that it ought to apply unless there is some justification or valid explanation for its exclusion." And later on the same page, giving examples of cases where the application of the principle is excluded, he said:

And when a person has done nothing to put himself in any relationship with another person in distress or with his property mere accidental propinquity does not require him to go to that person's assistance. There may be a moral duty to do so, but it is not practicable to make it a legal duty.

I think the latter part of this passage shows that, despite what Willmer L.J. said in *The "Radiant,"* supra, in deciding whether a duty of care exists, it may matter a great deal whether the blameworthy act is an act of commission or omission.

If Falkenberg had been guilty of an actual act of commission, for instance, if he had accidentally knocked Mrs. Berger to the ground, there would be no question that he was in breach of a duty of care. But the complaint here is that he did nothing. If he had been a mere visitor to the premises, it could not be seriously argued that he owed a duty to Mrs. Berger, either to shovel the snow himself, or to bully someone else into doing it. It is only by reason of his position as president and general manager of the company that employed her that he can, arguably, be her "neighbour." I do not think you can couple his duty to his company with his physical propinquity to say that he owed a duty to Mrs. Berger to see to it that other servants of the company did the work that they had been instructed to do. He did not do anything that directly resulted in her injuries, or that required him to come to her "rescue." I think that loyalty to the principle enunciated in *Salomon v. A. Salomon & Co. Ltd.*, [1897] A.C. 22 (H.L.), as explained in *Rainham*, requires it to be held that he was not in breach of any duty to her.

Mrs. Berger has a remedy under the Workmen's Compensation Act, and it is to the Act that she must look. She has no cause of action against Falkenberg.

BROOKE J.A. concurred with CORY J.A.

Appeal dismissed.

Management Liability. Mrs. Berger had lost her right of action against Falken Automobiles Inc. as a consequence of the Ontario Workmen's Compensation Act, which provides employees with statutory insurance coverage for workplace accidents but forecloses tort actions against employers and fellow employees. Since tort recovery often greatly exceeds the amounts paid under workmen's compensation legislation, employers are perhaps the statute's chief beneficiaries. A perception that amounts paid under the statute are insufficient may perhaps assist in explaining Hans Falkenberg's personal liability.

These problems will not arise when the tort plaintiff is not an employee. In such cases, a corporation will ordinarily be vicariously liable for wrongs committed by its agents in the course of their employment. This may suffice to lead the firm to take adequate care, policing breaches of care standards by individual employees or managers, through monitoring strategies or compensation policies. A separate justification is therefore required for *dual liability* regimes, in which both managers and the firm may be sued. Even if managers are personally at fault, there would be no need to subject them to liability if the plaintiff is adequately compensated by a damages claim against the firm, and this possibility gives the firm an adequate incentive to take care. Dual liability will therefore make most sense in circumstances where the firm is nearly insolvent, or the damages claim would render it so. The plaintiff may then receive something less than full compensatory treatment in an action against the firm. Moreover, a *Walkovszky* deterrence gap may arise where liability to non-consensual claimants is foreseen and the firm bears a non-trivial probability of default. The imposition of dual liability might then alleviate this adverse incentive problem, with managers responding to possible personal liability by requiring the firm to divest from certain hazardous lines of business and to curtail its operations in others.

On the other hand, it is incorrect to assume that an optimal liability standard can be devised merely by levering up sanctions against managers. Firm managers may reasonably be thought risk averse, and may therefore react to the threat of personal liability by rejecting high risk-high return investments with a net positive *EMV*. In its harm prevention decisions, they might then require the firm to take excessive care, where *PC* exceeds the anticipated reduction in *HC*. As a consequence, the benefits of dual liability, in terms of the firm's stronger incentives to take care, must be balanced against reduced incentives by managers to maximize firm value.

These concerns, however, dissipate where managers can shift the liability back to the firm, for example, by securing routine indemnification from the firm or by purchasing insurance either in their own names or on behalf of the corporation. In such cases, the risk of a possible damages award will be borne by the firm or by the insurance company rather than by the manager. Where liability is "shiftable" in this way, managers can be expected to transfer the risk of loss back to the firm. "The iron law of tort and criminal liability for corporate delicts is this: Liability risks, if left unchannelled, ordinarily attach to the legal entity (the corporation) rather than to its officers, employees, or agents." Kraakman, *Corporate Liability Strategies and the Costs of Legal Controls*, 93 Yale L.J. 857, 858 (1954).

As will be seen in Chapter Seven, indemnification and insurance for firm managers may sometimes be troubling, since their incentives to adhere to legal norms will be weakened if they are held harmless on breach. However, dual liability may also overdeter managers, leading them to abandon profitable opportunities that bear a risk of possible enormous personal liability. This excessive caution would constitute an agency cost that would be eliminated in a claimholders' bargain among all of the parties (including tort victims). One device they may choose for this purpose is shiftable management liability, or the combination of personal manager liability plus insurance or indemnification. Though this would ordinarily reduce incentives to take care, Kraakman argues that indemnification and insurance for managers are appropriate where the reason for imposing personal liability on management in the first place is because of a concern for adverse incentives arising through liability to non-consensual creditors, as in *Walkovszky*. When managers require their firm to purchase director and officer insurance policies, the firm will bear all anticipated harm costs, in the form of insurance premiums, such that the external costs associated with tort liability will be internalized within the firm. For example, where the anticipated harm to tort victims is great, the insurance company will pass the expected cost back to the firm as the price of the insurance. An adequate level of deterrence will then be imposed on the firm. At the same time, because they are insured, firm managers will not be overdeterred as a consequence of the threat of personal liability.

Can you formulate the standard that the Ontario Court of Appeal would have adopted to *deny* recovery against corporate managers? Should Mr. Falkenberg have known of the problem because the ice was visible from the showroom? If not, should he have known about it because his salesmen should have reported it to him? See also *Henry Electric Ltd. v. Farwell* (1986), 29 D.L.R. (4th) 481 (B.C. C.A.) (sole manager/shareholder liable for firm's breach of trust). But see *Mentmore Mfg. Co. v. Nat'l Merchandising Mfg. Co.* (1978), 89 D.L.R. (3d) 195 (Fed. C.A.) (principal shareholder and president of corporation not personally liable for patent infringement by corporation since his participation in the infringement lacked "a knowing, deliberate, wilful quality"); *Schouls v. Canadian Meat Processing Corp.* (1983), 41 O.R. (2d) 600 (president and majority shareholder not personally liable for wrongful dismissal of comptroller who was aware that he had been hired by the corporation and not by the individual manager).

Another attack on dual liability regimes focuses upon the tort claim against the firm. If the fault is ultimately that of an individual employee, why should the firm bear vicarious liability? For a defense of vicarious liability, see Sykes, *The Economics of Vicarious Liability*, 93 Yale L.J. 1231 (1984). Sykes notes, for example, that the *Walkovszky* deterrence gap problem might be even more pronounced were the firm not liable, since an individual's probability of bankruptcy will be far higher than that of the much wealthier corporation that employs him.

The question of when a corporation or its managers might bear criminal liability, which gives rise to similar incentive problems, is left for criminal law courses. Criminal law issues involve very different problems of proof and sanctions, and assigning them to a criminal course mirrors the division of practice between corporate and criminal lawyers.

C. PRE-INCORPORATION CONTRACTS

PROBLEM TWO

Several weeks have passed since the parties decided to join forces in a new enterprise. They wish to incorporate the business, but have not yet made up their minds whether this should be done under the CBCA or the provincial corporations statute. They have agreed on the allocation of shares in the proposed corporation, and have tentatively selected its name, "Gator Computers Inc."

Gagnon now telephones to tell you that he agreed to purchase $4,000 of computer components last week from General Computers Ltd. Gagnon had not dealt with General Computers before, and told its representative that he was buying for Gator Computers Inc. Gagnon signed the contract as follows:

> Gator Computers Inc.
> Michel Gagnon
> General Manager.

The computers are to be delivered in about a month. The purchase price is very attractive, and since General Computers wanted an immediate decision, Gagnon agreed to buy components without seeking the consent of Gray and Smith. While no clear decision has been made on who will occupy which office in Gator, Gagnon understood that he would be general manager and Gray president.

General Computers has now discovered that Gator is not incorporated, and a General Computers employee telephones Gagnon to express his unease about this. What Gagnon wants to know from you is whether he has incurred any personal liability in the transaction. He also does not want to lose the contract, since its terms are still attractive. He therefore asks whether either he or Gator (after incorporation) may enforce it.

Varieties of Pre-Incorporation Contracts. A corporation comes into existence only after certain statutory formalities are observed. This may take as little as a few days, though it may take much longer if the parties do not act promptly. Before computerized name searches became standard, the process often took a full month. As a final step in the procedure, a certificate of incorporation is issued. Before that time, the corporation is not considered a separate legal entity. CBCA s. 9.

Pre-incorporation contracts are made before the corporation comes into existence and take a variety of forms. The first of these is contracts entered into on behalf of the proposed corporation, and this forms the subject of this section. Such contracts are made by proposed managers and shareholders of the corporation, here called promoters, with themselves or with outside third parties. The second kind is pre-incorporation subscriptions, contracts by proposed shareholders for the issue of shares by the corporation. While really a species of the first, this second kind of pre-incorporation contract has been dealt with somewhat differently in Canada, and is discussed in Chapter Four, Section A. The third kind is shareholder agreements, which may be entered into prior to incorporation to allocate rights and responsibilities for the operation of the new corporation among the promoters. It is usually desirable to make the proposed or new corporation a party to the shareholder agreement, but this is not necessary. Such contracts deal primarily with the rights of the promoters among themselves and are dealt with in Chapter Six. Finally, the corporate charter itself is, in some jurisdictions, a contract binding incorporators and even subsequent shareholders. See BCCA s. 13 and Chapter Three, Section A.

Kelner v. Baxter
English Court of Common Pleas
(1866), L.R. 2 C.P. 174

[Kelner owned a hotel in Gravesend, and agreed in August 1865 with several other promoters to form a company called The Gravesend Royal Alexandra Hotel Co. Kelner was to be a director and president of the company. It was agreed that Kelner would sell his hotel to Baxter on behalf of the company for £5,000, of which £3,000 was to be paid in cash and the balance in shares of the company.

On January 9, 1866, Kelner, Baxter and other promoters executed a memorandum of association for the proposed company. Kelner subsequently agreed to sell an inventory of wine on the following terms.

January 27, 1866.

To John Dacier Baxter, Nathan Jacob Calisher, and John Dales, on behalf of the proposed Gravesend Royal Alexandra Hotel Company, Limited.

Gentlemen,—I hereby propose to sell the extra stock now at the Assembly Rooms, Gravesend, as per schedule hereto, for the sum of £900, payable on the 28th of February, 1866.

(Signed) John Kelner.

At the bottom of the schedule was written the following:

To Mr. John Kelner,

Sir,—We have received your offer to sell the extra stock as above, and hereby agree to and accept the terms proposed.

(Signed) J. D. Baxter,
N. J. Calisher,
J. Dales,
On behalf of the Gravesend Royal Alexandra
Hotel Company, Limited.

Under this agreement the wine was provided to the hotel and consumed in its business. On February 1, 1866, the directors of the proposed company passed the following resolution:

That the arrangement entered into by Messrs. Calisher, Dales, and Baxter, on behalf of the company, for the purchase of the additional stock on the premises, as per list taken by Mr. Bright, the secretary, and pointed out by Mr. Kelner, amounting to £900, be, and the same is hereby ratified.

A certificate of incorporation for the company was issued on February 20, 1866. On April 11, the company again purported to ratify the contract of January 27.

On the failure of this company, Kelner sought to enforce the January 27 agreement against Baxter and the other signatories of the agreement. Oral evidence that it was never intended that the defendants should be personally liable was rejected by the Court.

The plaintiff argued that, there being no company in existence at the time of the agreement, the parties thereto had rendered themselves personally liable; and that there could be no ratification of the contract by a subsequently created company.

The Court held that the defendants were personally liable, and they appealed.]

ERLE C.J.: I am of opinion that this rule should be discharged. The action is for the price of goods sold and delivered: and the question is whether the goods were delivered to the defendants under a contract of sale. The alleged contract is in writing, and commences with a proposal addressed to the defendants, in these words:—"I hereby propose to sell the extra stock now at the Assembly Rooms, Gravesend, as per schedule hereto, for the sum of £900, payable on the 28th of February, 1866." Nothing can be more distinct than this as a vendor proposing to sell. It is signed by the plaintiff, and is followed by a schedule of the stock to be purchased. Then comes the other part of the agreement, signed by the defendants, in these words,—"Sir, We have received your offer to sell the extra stock as above, and hereby agree to and accept the terms proposed." If it had rested there, no one could doubt that there was a distinct proposal by the vendor to sell, accepted by the purchasers. A difficulty has arisen because the plaintiff has at the head of the paper addressed it to the plaintiffs, "on behalf of the proposed Gravesend Royal Alexandra Hotel Company, Limited," and the defendants have repeated those words after their signatures to the document; and the question is, whether this constitutes any ambiguity on the face of the agreement, or prevents the defendants from being bound by it. I agree that if the Gravesend Royal Alexandra Hotel Company had been an existing company at this time, the persons who signed the agreement would have signed as agents of the company. But, as there was no company in existence at the time, the agreement would be wholly inoperative unless it were held to be binding on the defendants personally. The cases referred to in the course of the argument fully bear out the proposition that, where a contract is signed by one who professes to be signing "as agent," but who has no principal existing at the time, and the contract would be altogether inoperative unless binding upon the person who signed it, he is bound thereby: and a stranger cannot by a subsequent ratification relieve him from that responsibility. When the company came afterwards into existence it was a totally new creature, having rights and obligations from that time, but no rights or obligations by reason of anything which might have been done before. It was once, indeed, thought that an inchoate liability might be incurred on behalf of a proposed company, which would become binding on it when subsequently formed: but that notion was manifestly contrary to the principles upon which the law of contract is founded. There must be two parties to a contract; and the rights and obligations which it creates cannot be transferred by one of them to a third person who was not in a condition to be bound by it at the time it was made. The history of this company makes this construction to my mind perfectly clear. It was no doubt the notion of all parties that success was certain: but the plaintiff parted with his stock upon the faith of the defendants' engagement that the price agreed on should be paid on the day named. It cannot be supposed that he for a moment contemplated that the payment was to be contingent on the formation of the company by the 28th of February. The paper expresses in terms a contract to buy. And it is a cardinal rule that no oral evidence should be admitted to shew an intention different from that which appears on the face of the writing. I come, therefore, to the conclusion that the defendants, having no principal who was bound originally, or who could become so by a subsequent ratification, were themselves bound, and that the oral evidence offered is not admissible to contradict the written contract.

WILLES J.: I am of the same opinion. Evidence was clearly inadmissible to shew that the parties contemplated that the liability on this contract should rest upon the company and not upon the persons contracting on behalf of the proposed company. The utmost it could amount to is, that both parties were satisfied at the time that all would go smoothly, and consequently that no liability would ensue to the defendants. The contract is, in substance, this,—"I, the plaintiff, agree to sell to you, the defendants, on behalf of the Gravesend Royal Alexandra Hotel Company, my stock of wines"; and, "We, the defendants, have received your offer, and agree to and accept the terms proposed; and you shall be paid on the 28th day of February next." Who is to pay? The company, if it should be formed. But, if the company should not be formed, who is to pay? That is tested by the fact of the immediate delivery of the subject of sale. If payment was not made by the company, it must, if by anybody, be by the defendants. That brings one to consider whether the company could be legally liable. I apprehend the company could only become liable upon a new contract. It would require the assent of the plaintiff to discharge the defendants. Could the company become liable by a mere ratification? Clearly not. Ratification can only be by a person ascertained at the time of the act done,—by a person in existence either actually or in contemplation of law. ... Putting in the words "on behalf of the Gravesend Royal Alexandra Hotel Company," would operate no more than if a person should contract for a quantity of corn "on behalf of my horses." ...

[The concurring judgments of BYLES and KEATING JJ. are omitted.]

Rule discharged.

Black v. Smallwood
High Court of Australia
(1966), 117 C.L.R. 52, 39 A.L.J.R. 405

BARWICK C.J., KITTO, TAYLOR and OWEN JJ.: On 22nd December 1959 the appellants purported to enter into a contract for the sale of certain land at Ingleburn to Western Suburbs Holdings Pty. Limited. The contract incorporated the conditions of sale approved by the Real Estate Institute of New South Wales and was executed by the appellants as vendors and it bore the following subscription as the signature of the purchaser:

> Western Suburbs Holdings Pty. Ltd.
> Robert Smallwood ⎫
>   ⎬ Directors.
>   J. Cooper ⎭

It was subsequently found that Western Suburbs Holdings Pty. Limited had not at that time been incorporated but it is common ground that both the appellants and the respondents, Smallwood and Cooper, who subscribed the name Western Suburbs Holdings Pty. Limited to the form of contract and added their own signatures as directors, believed that it had been and that the latter were directors of the company. Thereafter the appellants instituted a suit for specific performance against the respondents alleging that by a written contract made between the appellants as vendors and the respondents who "described themselves therein as 'Western Suburbs Holdings Pty. Limited' " agreed to purchase the subject land from the appellants. No attempt was made at the trial to make this allegation good but, without amendment, the case proceeded as one in which the appellants sought to impose a liability in accordance with the terms of the contract upon the respondents as agents contracting on behalf of a principal not yet in existence.

Upon the trial the appellants were successful in obtaining a decree for specific performance but on appeal to the Full Court the decree was set aside and the suit dismissed. All members of the Full Court thought the case was covered precisely by the decision of the Court of Appeal in *Newborne v. Sensolid (Great Britain) Ltd.* [[1954] 1 Q.B. 45], and although one of their number was, perhaps, more than disposed to doubt the correctness of that decision, the Court as a whole decided that it should be followed. It is from this decision that this appeal is brought. At the outset of the case we should say that the decision in *Newborne's Case* is directly in point but we propose to deal briefly with the arguments that were presented to us and which, if they were accepted, would establish that decision to be wrong.

The argument of the appellants was put in two ways. First of all it was said that the contract was, in fact, one entered into by the respondents on behalf of a company to be formed and that this involved them in a personal obligation to fulfil the terms of the contract upon the principle of *Kelner v. Baxter* [(1866), L.R. 2 C.P. 174 (Eng.)]. Alternatively, it was asserted that it was a principle of the common law prior to the cases of *Jenkins v. Hutchinson* ((1849), 13 Q.B. 744, 116 E.R. 1448) and *Lewis v. Nicholson* ((1852), 18 Q.B. 503, 118 E.R. 190) that when a person purported, without authority, to enter into a contract as agent with another person he was personally liable on the contract. It was acknowledged that this rule, if, indeed, any such rule ever existed, had been displaced by the two cases referred to but it was asserted that it was displaced only in cases where a person had purported to act on behalf of another existing person whose authority he lacked and that the rule has never been displaced in cases where an agent purports to act for a non-existent principal. If this latter contention be correct the case of *Kelner v. Baxter* might simply have been decided in conformity with it. But, as will appear, it was not and an examination of the contention may be left until consideration has been given to the decision in that case.

Kelner v. Baxter was cited as an authority for the proposition that there is a rule of law to the effect that where a person contracts on behalf on a non-existent principal he is himself liable on the contract. But we find it impossible to extract any such proposition from the decision. In that case it appeared from the contract itself that the defendants had no principal; they had purported to enter into a contract on behalf of the "proposed Gravesend Royal Alexandra Hotel Company," and the fact that they had no principal was obvious to both parties. But it was not by reason of this fact alone that the defendants were held to be liable; the Court proceeded to examine the written instrument in order to see if, in these circumstances, an intention should be imputed to the defendants to bind themselves personally, or, perhaps, to put it in another way, whether, the intention being sufficiently clear that a binding contract was intended, there was anything in the writing inconsistent with the conclusion that the defendants should be bound personally. The decision was that, in the circumstances, the writing disclosed an intention that the defendants should be bound. ... Where A, purporting to act as agent for a non-existent principal, purports to make a binding contract with B, and the circumstances are such that B would suppose that a binding contract had been made, there must be a strong presumption that A has meant to bind himself personally. Where, as in *Kelner v. Baxter*, the consideration on B's part has been fully executed in reliance on the existence of a contract binding on somebody, the presumption could, I should imagine, only be rebutted in very exceptional circumstances. But the fundamental question in every case must be what the parties intended or must be fairly understood to have intended. ...

WINDEYER J.: I agree that this appeal must be dismissed. I have to come to that conclusion without hesitation but with regret. The law requires it, but I do not think that it accords well with a belief that bargains should be kept.

If before the document sued upon was signed the registration of Western Suburbs Holdings Pty. Limited had been completed and it had emerged from the Registrar-General's office as a new-born entity in the law, no difficulty could have arisen. It could not then have been said that Smallwood and Cooper had contracted as agents on its behalf. It must have been said that it, not they, had made the contract. It, not they, would have been the purchaser entitled to a conveyance. Their putting the company's name to the document would have been purely in execution of its corporate act and their added signatures would have no more bound them personally to perform the contract than would the signatures of the directors or secretary of a company authenticating the affixing of its seal. There is a difference between a man's own acts and acts done for him by another man. The difficulty of the distinction in the case of a corporation is that a corporation must manifest its acts and intentions by the actions and declarations of human beings: and ambiguities and limitations of language make it difficult sometimes to express the distinction between acts done by a person as executant of the will of a corporation and acts done by a person as agent for a corporation, his principal. That the word "agent" is in each case apt to describe the actor helps to disguise their different legal characters.

I appreciate the force of what Walsh J. said in the Supreme Court concerning the narrow differences in language upon which the decision in *Newborne v. Sensolid (Great Britain) Ltd.* turned. But the distinction that differences in language reflect, sometimes not very clearly, is the distinction between the act of a man himself and acts done by another on his behalf. If in the case of a company the distinction is difficult to preserve, and may seem unreal, or merely verbal not conceptual, that is because the legal personality and capacity of the corporation are artifically created by law. Sometimes the result may be to allow a man to escape from an unprofitable bargain by a pure technicality, as has been said of *Newborne's Case*: Treitel, *Law of Contract* (1962). In many cases courts have had to decide whether an agent had, in the particular case, incurred a personal liability on a contract in writing made by him on behalf of a principal. And these decisions have sometimes turned upon narrow differences in wording, which seem to be the progeny by miscegenation of early technical rules relating to the form of the execution of deeds to which Doctor Stoljar has referred in his work, *The Law of Agency* (1961), pp. 251-255. But here that question does not really arise, for the document which the respondents signed does not purport to be a contract made by them as agents for the supposed company. They thought that the company existed and that they were in fact directors. It is therefore impossible to regard them as having used the name of the company as a mere pseudonym or firm name or as having intended to incur a personal liability. ...

Appeal dismissed.

Promoter Liability. Is *Kelner* a rule of construction or of law? In *Newborne v. Sensolid (Great Britain), Ltd.*, [1953] 1 All E.R. 708 (C.A.), the plaintiff formed "Leopold Newborne (London), Ltd." to deal in tinned ham. He was not advised by a lawyer and began to sell ham before the company was incorporated. One sale was to the defendant under a contract form that carried the name of the Newborne company. The form stated that Newborne was a director, and was signed "Leopold Newborne (London), Ltd.," with Mr. Newborne's personal signature underneath. The defendant was not aware that the company was not incorporated, but later resisted performance of the contract on that basis, the market price of tinned ham having fallen in the interim. Since the Newborne company could not recover, Mr. Newborne sought to do so personally on the authority of *Kelner v. Baxter*. The English Court held that the only contract that had been made was with the Newborne company, not with Mr. Newborne. Since the company was not in existence when the contract was signed, there never was a contract. Would the case have been decided differently if Newborne had signed the contract on behalf of the corporation? What if Sensolid had known that the corporation was not in existence?

Kelner v. Baxter was also interpreted as stating a rule of construction in *Dairy Supplies Ltd. v. Fuchs* (1959), 18 D.L.R. (2d) 408, 28 W.W.R. 1 (Sask. C.A.). The plaintiff entered into a contract with "Snowland Dairy Ltd.," a company not yet incorporated. Fuchs signed the contract for Snowland. However, the parties agreed that if the company was organized forthwith the plaintiff would look only to it for payment. The Court held that this agreement rebutted the presumption that a promoter is liable on a pre-incorporation contract. See also *Wickberg v. Shatsky* (1969), 4 D.L.R. (3d) 540 (B.C.); *Major v. Landsman* (1978), 19 Cah. de Dr. 821; *General Motors Acceptance Corp. v. Weisman* (1979), 23 O.R. (2d) 479, 96 D.L.R. (3d) 159; *Delta Construction Co. v. Lidstone* (1979), 96 D.L.R. (3d) 457 (Nfld.).

Can you think of a plausible reason why, as a matter of law, promoters and third parties should not be permitted to assume or waive liability as they see fit? If the issue is then one of construction, whether promoter liability will be presumed when both parties know that the firm has not been incorporated (as in *Kelner*) is a question of judicial gap-filling. Thus, in the absence of express provisions as to liability, the promoter was presumed personally bound in *Kelner*. A similar presumption is applied in CBCA s. 14(1), which has codified the law with respect to written pre-incorporation contracts. If the promoter seeks to avoid liability, he must specifically so provide under s. 14(4). The presumption might be justified on the basis that, without it, the parties would likely adopt a similar liability rule as an express term of the contract. The presumption would then reduce transaction costs by eliminating the need for an express term in the pre-incorporation contract.

It is, however, harder to explain the imposition of promoter liability where both parties honestly believe that the firm is incorporated, since everyone will then expect that the only contract is with the firm. For this reason, the promoters were not personally liable in *Black* and *Newborne*. Does s. 14(1) reverse the presumption in *Black* and *Newborne* by imposing liability whether or not the promoters are aware of the firm's corporate statutes? It was held not in *Westcom Radio Group Ltd. v. MacIsaac* (1989), 63 D.L.R. (4th) 433 (Ont. Div. Ct.), where the promoter was absolved from liability under the Ontario Business Corporations Act version of CBCA s. 14(1) when both parties believed that the corporation was in existence and that the only contract was with it. Austin J. held that statutory remedy is inapplicable where the plaintiff intended to contract with the non-existent company exclusively. The purported "contract" is then a nullity. Are you persuaded by this reasoning? As the learned judge noted:

In these cases, both parties are "innocent," but the party in the better position to control or know about incorporation is the defendant. In these cases, as in the present case, the plaintiff has performed its side of the bargain and the "agent" has had the benefit of that performance. Is it just in such circumstances that the "agent" should escape responsibility and the performing party go unpaid? Because the "agent" is in the better position to know the facts about incorporation and because he or she has usually had the benefit of performance, as a matter of policy, he or she should be found responsible.

Thus it may be argued that the promoter should be presumed to warrant the existence of the firm and his authority to represent it since, even if he acts in good faith, he is still the least cost risk avoider. If the promoter is not bound, a risk that the contract will be of no effect is introduced, which risk imposes costs on both parties. They may take steps to cure the problem, with the third party instructing his lawyer to conduct corporate searches with government registration officers. But the promoter is likely the party who can avoid the risk at least cost. Imposing liability on him might then reduce the level of errors and economize on the screening costs of outsiders. If so, a rule of promoter liability would be bargained for in a hypothetical agreement.

The statute of frauds restriction in s. 14(1) to written contracts should be noted. Because of it, the pre-CBCA law might survive for oral pre-incorporation agreements unless s. 14 is found to be an exclusive statement of the law.

Even under pre-CBCA law, the promoter might have incurred personal liability for breach of warranty of authority. As noted in Chapter One, Section C, an agent is presumed to represent that he possesses the authority to bind his principal. Since this is a separate obligation, a promoter who bargains on behalf of a non-existent firm can be liable for the breach of warranty of authority even when not a party to the contract under *Kelner*. Once again, however, the promoter may exempt himself from liability by expressly disclosing that the corporation has not been formed, for then no representation of authority can be said to have been made.

It is not entirely clear whether the remedy for breach of warranty of authority sounds in contract or in tort, though the better opinion inclines to the view that it is contractual. Cf. F. Reynolds & B. Davenport, *Bowstead on Agency* 379-80, 386-87 (14th ed. 1976). Certainly, liability is strict and it is unnecessary to aver negligence or fraud. Moreover, the measure of damages is contractual and not tortious, and places the plaintiff in the position he would have been in had the contract been performed rather than restoring him to his pre-contractual status. This measure of damages may at times be distinctly disadvantageous to the plaintiff. Had the contract been performed, he would have contracted with the corporation. But if the corporation is without assets, he has not really lost anything. *Wickberg v. Shatsky* (1969), 4 D.L.R. (3d) 540 (B.C.); *Delta Construction Co. v. Lidstone* (1979), 96 D.L.R. (3d) 457 (Nfld.). In the latter case, the plaintiff sought to recover $17,800 for work done by it prior to the incorporation of Algo Enterprises Ltd. Noel J. found the promoter, Lidstone, in breach of the warranty of authority but awarded only nominal damages:

At most, Lidstone represented that an existing company, Algo Enterprises Limited, required work to be done by the plaintiff. The plaintiff was, clearly, expected to extend credit to the company but Lidstone did not warrant that the company had any assets, that it was solvent, or that the plaintiff's account would be paid. The decision to extend credit was made by the plaintiff. Since the project foundered, it is reasonable to suppose that if the plaintiff were successful in this suit for the balance of its account, assuming the defendants to be solvent, it would be in a better position than it would have been in had the company been in existence as the parties believed. In short, the non-existence of the company would be a windfall to the plaintiff. If the defendants are obliged to pay the plaintiff's account, in effect, they would be guarantors of the account which neither they nor the plaintiff intended should be the case. [*Id.* at 462]

Under CBCA s. 14, the promoter is deemed to be the least cost risk avoider with respect to the subsequent incorporation of the firm and its ratification of the contract. Does it follow that the promoter is also the least cost risk avoider with respect to whether the firm will be solvent when the time for payment under the contract arises? The screening costs that the promoter would incur in determining whether the corporation has in fact been incorporated, or in predicting a subsequent ratification, may be slight. By contrast, predictions as to the firm's future solvency may give rise to substantial screening costs. Moreover, many promoters are inefficient risk bearers as compared with outside creditors, for whom the loss may be less catastrophic. What this means is that the burden of the risk of the firm's default may be felt more by risk averse individual promoters than by risk neutral corporate creditors. Promoter immunity under *Lidstone* would then appear to replicate an implicit term in the parties' bargain, and can be defended on gap-filling theories. Were promoters held to guarantee the firm's solvency in these circumstances, they would respond by expressly bargaining out of the warranty or by forswearing some pre-incorporation promises, and this would give rise to its own inefficiencies.

Liability of the Corporation. In what circumstances ought a corporation to be liable on pre-incorporation contracts? The *Kelner* rule against ratification was not followed in most American jurisdictions. There the corporation could become a party to the contract on a variety of theories. The agreement was, for example, considered a continuing offer by the third party which the corporation could later accept if it had not been revoked in the interim. The offer could even be irrevocable if the promoter undertook to use his best efforts to cause the corporation to accept the contract. The corporation might also have rights as a beneficiary of a trust, a third party beneficiary or an assignee of the contract. Alternatively, the corporation might be held liable under restitutionary principles or might be estopped from denying that it was a party to the contract. A continuing course of dealings after incorporation could give rise to an inference that a binding second contract had been formed. Finally, some states simply permitted ratification. See H. Henn, *Handbook of the Law of Corporations* 181-88 (2d ed. 1970).

While Canadian courts might have found the corporation bound under several of the above theories, they were quite reluctant to do so. Restitutionary claims did not succeed because the corporation had not requested the enrichment. Cf. *Re Crown Mutual Hail Insurance Co.* (1908), 8 W.L.R. 580, 18 Man. R. 51. Ratification was rejected in *Kelner v. Baxter* itself, and this was generally followed in Canada on the theory that ratification is not effective when the ratifying party was not in existence at the time the transaction was purportedly ratified. *Clergue v. Humphrey* (1900), 31 S.C.R. 66; *Crane v. Lavoie* (1912), 4 D.L.R. 175 (Man. C.A.); *Coit v. Dowling* (1901), 4 Terr. L.R. 464. A few cases held out the promise that a corporation could adopt pre-incorporation contracts by accepting benefits and burdens under them. *Re Red Deer Milling and Elevator Co.* (1907), 7 W.L.R. 284, 1 A.L.R. 237; *Van Hummell v. International Guarantee Co.* (1913), 10 D.L.R. 306, 310 (Man.); but see *Repetti Ltd. v. Oliver-Lee Ltd.* (1922), 52 O.L.R. 315 (App. Div.). The British Columbia Supreme Court stated that a continuing offer could not be made prior to incorporation since offerees must be in existence. However, it effectively validated such an offer by holding that it had been made to the promoters as agents of the offeror to relay it to the company after incorporation. *Associated Growers of B.C. Ltd. v. B.C. Fruit Land*

Ltd., [1925] 1 D.L.R. 871, [1925] 1 W.W.R. 505. In addition, the Ontario Court of Appeal, which refused to permit the adoption of a pre-incorporation contract in *Repetti Ltd. v. Oliver-Lee Ltd.* (1922), 52 O.L.R. 315, upheld a "tentative contract" six years later in *Hudson-Mattagami Exploration Mining Co. v. Wettlaufer Bros. Ltd.* (1928), 62 O.L.R. 387, [1928] 3 D.L.R. 661. In the latter case, the contract was formed when the company was incorporated and paid the price. Riddell J.A. stated that:

> [I]t is elementary law that, the company being non-existent when [the promoter] was negotiating with the defendants, he could not be its agent; and it is equally clear law that the company could not take advantage of any contract he entered into, purporting to act as its agent, whether by attempted ratification or otherwise. ... But there is no possible objection to a provisional contract not to become binding, i.e., not to be a contract at all, unless and until the company becomes entitled to commence business. ... [62 O.L.R. at 397]

Notwithstanding this limited recognition of pre-incorporation contracts, it was still hard to say when they would be enforced. See Getz, *Pre-Incorporation Contracts: Some Proposals*, [1967] U.B.C.L. Rev.-Cah. de Dr. 381.

In time, corporate lawyers developed devices to ensure that the corporation and not the promoters would be liable. Resort could be had, for example, to an already incorporated "shelf" corporation. Such corporations, with standard form charters but no assets, were sometimes formed with numerical names by law firms for just such purposes. After a meeting to turn the corporation over to its new shareholders and directors, it could immediately enter into binding contracts in its own name. Shelf corporations are of course seldom necessary in jurisdictions where the process of incorporation takes only a few days.

Law reformers considered making companies bound by all pre-incorporation contracts, but rejected this because of the impossibility of deciding which promoter would have the authority to bind the corporation. *Lawrence Report* 11-12. "Many people participate in the formation of a company, from one or a group of initiating principals to their agents, employees, associates and even friends." Nugan, *Pre-Incorporation Contracts*, in 1 Ziegel 197, 201.

However, there would seem no compelling reason why a firm should not be bound by contracts it ratifies after incorporation, and for this reason CBCA s. 14(2)(a) permits a corporation to adopt written pre-incorporation contracts. In ordinary circumstances promoters are liable before them under s. 14(1), while the corporation's ratification of the contract will absolve them under s. 14(2)(b). "Pursuant to these rules it would follow that promoters would bear the risk of non-adoption of pre-incorporation contracts—a risk that is properly inherent in the role of promoter." *Lawrence Report* 12. Does this section apply if the corporation never comes into existence? If it does, would this give rise to constitutional problems? See Chapter Three, Section A.

What sort of conduct will be held to constitute the adoption of a contract? Would a voluntary receipt of benefits under a contract amount to "action or conduct signifying its intention to be bound?" Cf. *Framingham Savings Bank v. Szabo*, 617 F.2d 897 (1st Cir. 1980); *DeCarlo v. Gerryco, Inc.*, 264 S.E.2d 370 (N.C. Ct. App. 1980). Would an application under s. 14(3) result in full liability being imposed, or would the corporation merely be required to give up the benefit on restitutionary principles?

While the interplay between promoter and corporate liability in s. 14 may in general seem appropriate, at times it is troubling. These are the circumstances in which a s. 14(3) application may be approved. First, a s. 14(3) action might seek to impose liability on a firm notwithstanding non-ratification. Suppose, for example, that the promoters quarrel and the corporation does not adopt the contract even though the parties had agreed that it would. Second, promoters might perhaps be held liable even with ratification. Assume that a promoter enters into a bad bargain on behalf of a corporation to be incorporated. Seeking to avoid liability under the contract, he forms the corporation and has it adopt the contract. However, the corporation is never endowed with assets and dissolves shortly afterwards. Should the promoter then take the risk of non-performance by the firm as well as of its non-ratification? If not, how creditable is the promoter's promise on transactions in volatile markets, where the possible loss to the promoter may exceed the expense of incorporation? What if the third party did not make any enquiry about the proposed corporation's solvency? Cf. *Bank of Nova Scotia v. Williams* (1976), 12 O.R. (2d) 709; *H. F. Philipsborn & Co. v. Suson*, 322 N.E.2d 45 (Ill. 1974).

Plaintiff agreed to sell property to Bon Street Developments Ltd. for $4,220,000. The sale was to close on September 25, 1985, but on September 5, 1985 the purchaser repudiated the agreement and offered $3,000,000. Later it offered $3,300,000. When the real estate agent pointed out that the purchaser would be liable on the agreement, a Bon Street director and shareholder replied that they could "walk away from the deal because their lawyer had some angle." The "angle" was that the firm with which the original discussions were held was a different company than the Bon Street Developments Ltd. that entered into the contract. The new Bon Street Developments Ltd. was a shell company. It had no assets. The company with whom they had originally dealt had changed its name to Bon Street Holdings Ltd. Result? See *B.G. Preeco I (Pacific Coast) Ltd. v. Bon Street Holdings Ltd.* (1989), 60 D.L.R. (4th) 30 (B.C.C.A.).

Imposing personal liability on promoters who secure ratification by a shell corporation resembles the device of holding shareholder/managers liable for inducing a breach of contract when they deprive a corporation of its assets for the purpose of rendering it incapable of contractual performance. In *Einhorn v. Westmount Investments Ltd.* (1969), 6 D.L.R. (3d) 71 (Sask.), the defendant corporation was stripped of its assets by three members of the Belzberg family, who were in control of it, such that it was unable to perform its contractual undertakings with the plaintiff. Disberry J. held the Belzbergs liable for the tort of inducing the corporation to breach the contract:

Ordinarily an agent is subject to the control of another person, his principal. A company perforce is only able to act through its agents and servants. Consequently, while company directors are referred to as "agents," the cold fact is that they control the company. As the directors pull the strings so the company must of necessity jump. Particularly is this true where, as here, the individual defendants were in "complete control" of the company. This Court in the exercise of its common law jurisdiction in the field of tort considers the realities of the situations which come before it for decision, and the court is not restricted in so doing because individuals carry out intentional tortious acts through the medium of a puppet corporation whose every action they control. Individuals guilty of intentional tortious acts do not escape personal liability by this device of clothing themselves in a corporate veil of their own spinning. [*Id.* at 75]

153-156
75-86
163-69.

neichel v. Lane (1982), 28 Sask. R. 311,
provincial cabinet ministers (among them,
a breach of an employment contract. The
vernment employees who were associated
nocratic Party.
rse of action whose effect is to jeopardize
ill management incur personal liability in
_ _ _ _ *v. ouri*, 395 N.E.2d 921 (Ill. 1979), unless
management was malicious or lacked a proper business purpose for its actions. In other
cases, the Court stated that it would not impeach management's business judgment.

For further discussions of pre-incorporation contracts, see F. Iacobucci, M.
Pilkington & J. Prichard, *Canadian Business Corporations* 53-59 (1977); Kessler, *Promoter's Contracts: A Statutory Solution*, 15 Rut. L. Rev. 566 (1961); Maloney,
Pre-Incorporation Transactions: A Statutory Solution? 10 C.B.L.J. 409 (1985).

Dissolution. Problems that arise on a corporation's death are not unlike those that
precede its birth. It is quite possible for a corporation to be dissolved without the
knowledge of its shareholders and managers. Thus a corporation may be dissolved under
s. 212 if in default for one year of any of the fee or notice requirements under the
CBCA. Directors must be given 120 days' notice in such cases, but when little attention
is given to formalities such warnings may be forgotten.

What rights do third parties have on post-dissolution contracts? On dissolution,
undistributed assets of the corporation vest in the Crown. CBCA s. 228. However, a
creditor may apply under s. 209 for an order to revive the corporation. Non-cash assets
revest in the corporation on revival under s. 228(2), and it is liable for obligations it
would have incurred had it not been dissolved under s. 209(4).

Can a creditor recover from a manager of the business instead of applying for a
revival order? If *Kelner v. Baxter* is applicable, one might argue that the manager must
have been bound when the contract was made. Cf. *Brennan v. Berwick Fruit Co.*, [1928]
1 D.L.R. 548 (N.S.). However, two British Columbia decisions have refused to impose
personal liability when the creditor believed he was dealing with a corporation, and did
not wish to revive it because it was insolvent. *Shaw v. Hyde* (1921), 61 D.L.R. 666;
Olympia & York Developers Ltd. v. Price, [1976] 5 W.W.R. 347. In *Shaw*, the defendant
had not taken an active part in the business at any time. The defendant in *Price* had been
a director, officer and principal shareholder of the defunct corporation, but had not
personally guaranteed the obligations. As was noted in *Shaw v. Hyde*, a revival order
gives a third party:

all the legal rights which he originally bargained for; which he believed in very truth he had, that
is his right to look to the company, and only the company, with whom he dealt for payment of his
debt. Why should he now get more? [61 D.L.R. at 670]

CHAPTER THREE

Historical and Constitutional Aspects and the Process of Incorporation

A. THE DEVELOPMENT OF CANADIAN CORPORATIONS STATUTES

1. Early Corporate Statutes

The modern corporation in England and North America grew out of the English "joint stock company," which was in reality a partnership with potentially many partners. Prior to 1844 in England, the creation through incorporation of a commercial entity with a legal personality independent of that of its owners or "members" could be obtained only by a royal charter or by a special Act of Parliament. The first general corporations statute was the Joint Stock Companies Act of 1844, 7-8 Vict., c. 110, under which promoters could file with the Registrar a "deed of settlement" containing the corporation's charter. The Registrar would then issue a certificate granting to the corporation the powers and privileges detailed in the deed of settlement.

Limited liability for shareholders was introduced in 1855 by the Limited Liability Act, 18-19 Vict., c. 133. If a corporation's assets proved insufficient to repay a debt, executions could be filed against individual shareholders, but only to the extent of the amount unpaid on their shares. The Companies Act, 1862, 25-26 Vict., c. 89, consolidated and revised the previous enactments. If the organizers of the corporation wished the doctrine of limited liability to apply, they would file a "memorandum of association," which recited the amount of the corporation's capital and the manner in which shares were to be divided. The memorandum was to be accompanied by the "articles of association," otherwise known as by-laws, which contained the internal regulations of the corporation. Both the memorandum and the articles were, and under English practice continue to be, public documents.

By the mid-nineteenth century, it was recognised in Canada, as in England, that the requirement of a special Act of the legislature for the incorporation of every company was highly inconvenient. In 1850, the Parliament of the United Province of Canada passed a general incorporation Act for joint stock companies with "Manufacturing, Mining, Mechanical or Chemical Purposes." 13-14 Vict., c. 28. Under the Act, five or more persons could apply to incorporate a business, with disclosure of the objects, capital structure and shareholders in the application. Incorporation followed automatically on filing the application, but was limited to a 50-year term. The Act generally afforded limited liability to the shareholders and was in this respect in advance of English developments.

In 1864, a new general incorporation statute was passed in the United Province of Canada, 27-28 Vict., c. 23, for corporations engaged in manufacturing and mining. Under this Act, the incorporators would apply for letters patent under the seal of the Governor in Council. The letters patent format of incorporation had antecedents in both American statutes and in certain specialized types of incorporation in England. Unlike the 1850 Act, the issuance of letters patent was discretionary. There was also no requirement that the by-laws be filed, unlike memorandum jurisdictions where articles of association are public documents.

After Confederation, the letters patent method became part of the new Dominion and Ontario Acts. Eventually Manitoba, Ontario, Quebec, New Brunswick, Prince Edward Island and Canada became "letters patent" jurisdictions, while British Columbia, Alberta, Saskatchewan, Nova Scotia and Newfoundland became "memorandum of association" or "registration" jurisdictions, following the English form. These differences remained until the latest round of statutory reform, which began with the Ontario Business Corporations Act in 1970.

In memorandum jurisdictions, the memorandum and the articles are deemed to be a contract among the incorporators *inter se* and also between them and the corporation, to which other persons as they become shareholders become parties. The basic allocation of power as between the directors and the shareholders is determined in accordance with the incorporating documents, and there is complete freedom to include in such documents any condition, term or provision not in conflict with the statute. In practice, however, very many corporations in the memorandum jurisdictions adopt the model articles set out in Table A following the incorporating statute. As a result, the constituting documents of the average memorandum corporation look rather like those of the average letters patent corporation. A second characteristic of memorandum jurisdictions is that on an application for incorporation the registrar has little discretion to reject the incorporating documents. If the statutory criteria are met, particularly if the stated objects of the corporation are not illegal and if its proposed name is not already spoken for, the registrar must accept the documents and issue a certificate of incorporation.

In theory at least, letters patent jurisdictions differ in both these respects. The corporation in a letters patent jurisdiction derives its existence from the sovereign executive act of issuance of the letters patent. *Bonanza Creek Gold Mining Co. v. The King*, [1916] 1 A.C. 566, 584, 26 D.L.R. 273 (P.C.). The allocation of power between the directors and the company in general meeting flows from the statute, and there is less freedom of contract in designing the corporate structure than in memorandum jurisdictions. The Minister in a letters patent jurisdiction has an absolute discretion in granting the letters patent or not and he may impose conditions.

2. Modern Corporate Statutes

In 1967, the Lawrence Report in Ontario criticized the letters patent system on two principal grounds: first, that the granting of corporate status should not be regarded as a privilege, and second, that the paperwork involved created undue delay. The Lawrence

Report recommended adoption of the current American system under which articles of incorporation, which roughly correspond to the memorandum in registration jurisdictions, are filed. If the articles conform to the Act, the Minister must issue a certificate granting incorporation. Under this method, the by-laws (which are similar to the articles of association in memorandum jurisdictions) are not publicly filed. In 1970, Ontario adopted the articles of incorporation system with its Business Corporations Act. In the following year, the Dickerson Report recommended broadly similar legislation for Canada, and this was enacted in 1975 as the CBCA.

The CBCA is modeled much more closely on the American Model Business Corporations Act (MBCA) than on any English precedent.* This fact is noteworthy in the light of the general Canadian judicial tendency to accept English case precedents uncritically while showing a marked reluctance to adopt American decisions. This tendency has of course greatly diminished in recent years. One reason for this in corporate law is that many of the CBCA and OSA provisions derive from American precedents and have no parallels in English legislation. However, there is less substantive difference among the corporations laws of the three jurisdictions than might appear superficially. In corporate litigation, it seems probable today that, given the same set of facts, a judge in England, the United States or Canada would reach the same result, although perhaps employing different verbal formulations to do so.

Though one might have thought that nineteenth century corporations legislation would offer greater freedom to incorporators, in fact modern corporations statutes are considerably more facilitative. The history of modern corporations law is one of reduction of management restrictions and shareholder rights in matters of investment and financial policy, including the term of the corporation's existence, the businesses it might take up, self-dealing standards, share issuances and repurchases, dividend policy and charter amendment. Corporate law barriers to business decisions have never been lower than under modern "enabling" corporate statutes such as the CBCA.†

On the development of Canadian corporate law, see Wegenast 17-47, 56-70; LaBrie & Palmer, *The Pre-Confederation History of Corporations in Canada*, in 1 Ziegel 33; Newman, *Letters Patent and Memorandum of Association Companies*, in 1 Ziegel 61; Risk, *The Nineteenth Century Foundations of the Business Corporation in Ontario*, 23 U. of Toronto L.J. 270 (1973).

3. The CBCA as a Uniform Canadian Act

Legislation modeled closely on the CBCA has been enacted in Manitoba (1976 and 1979), Saskatchewan (1978 and 1979), Alberta (1981), New Brunswick (1981), Ontario (1982) and Newfoundland (1986). It has also heavily influenced amendments made in

---

* The MBCA, a project of the American Bar Association, was first published in 1950 and has been amended many times since. As of 1993, it had been adopted virtually in its entirety in more than a dozen American states and had been influential in legislative developments in more than 25 other states.

† The removal of such barriers has, however, been accompanied by an expansion of shareholder remedies to litigate on alleged management self-dealing, a subject taken up in Chapters Seven to Nine.

1981 to the Quebec Companies Act. Among the CBCA-type jurisdictions, probably Ontario's new Act contains the most departures from the model: perhaps half a dozen substantive changes plus numerous "clean-up" changes. Conversely, Alberta has adopted the CBCA almost verbatim. Nova Scotia and British Columbia remain memorandum of association jurisdictions. Their statutes are based heavily on English ones, particularly, in the case of the Nova Scotia, the Act of 1862. British Columbia's situation is unique; of the many influences on its statute, the English Companies Act of 1948, 11-12 Geo. 6, c. 38, predominates. Only Prince Edward Island remains a letters patent jurisdiction.

Uniformity is frequently espoused as a desirable goal in provincial or state legislation within a federal system. The advantage of uniformity is that of greater standardization, which may economize on information production in two ways. First, claimholders in national capital markets will find it easier to gauge their rights, and firms will find it easier to comply with their requirements, when a single standard is imposed. Second, the quality of the law will improve, with legal uncertainties resolved more quickly as courts of one jurisdiction make use of the judgments of other jurisdictions.

On the other hand, uniformity may forestall the experimentation with new rules through which improvements develop. As Albert Breton has suggested, the competition between provinces or jurisdictions in the supply of public goods may be beneficial insofar as better quality goods may come to be provided. 3 *Royal Commission on the Economic Union and Development Prospects for Canada Report* (MacDonald Commission Report) 486 (1985) (supplementary statement by Albert Breton). If legal rules can be considered as a product, the competition principle can be extended to them, with diversity of provincial legal systems seen as resulting in better quality legal rules through increased experimentation. See also Rose-Ackerman, *Does Federalism Matter? Political Choice in a Federal Republic*, 85 J. Pol. Econ. 152 (1981) (discussing the importance of diversity in legislation of states in a federal system). Thus the freedom that parties have under private international law to choose an offshore jurisdiction's law as the one governing a contract is an example of the competitive provision of public goods. So too is facilitative corporate legislation, which permits incorporation in a jurisdiction even if the principal business is located elsewhere. The potential that this creates for competition between different jurisdictions in providing corporate laws is discussed in Chapter Six.

B. CONSTITUTIONAL CONSIDERATIONS AND EXTRA-PROVINCIAL LICENSING

1. Federal and Provincial Powers of Incorporation

Provincial Powers. Under the Constitution Act, 1867, the incorporation power is given to both provincial and the federal governments. Section 92(11) of the Constitution Act allocates to provincial legislatures "The Incorporation of Companies with Provincial Objects." Although the law on this matter has yet to be authoritatively declared, "with Provincial Objects" appears to impose a territorial rather than a functional limitation upon the provincial competence to incorporate companies. The phrase means "to carry out its activities within the province of incorporation." It does not restrict the activities of provincially incorporated corporations to substantive areas reserved to provincial legislative competence. Such corporations can engage in activities within the federal legislative sphere, but they would have to do so, of course, in compliance with applicable federal legislation. See *Alberta Government Telephones v. CRTC*, [1989] 2 S.C.R. 225, [1989] 5 W.W.R. 385; *The Queen (Ont.) v. Board of Transport Commissioners*, [1968] S.C.R. 118, 65 D.L.R. (2d) 425; and see the discussion in P. Hogg, *Constitutional Law of Canada* ch. 23 at section 23.1 (1992 looseleaf).

The restriction to "provincial objects" might be thought to impose a substantial territorial limitation, thus preventing Ontario corporations, for example, from doing business in Alberta or the Yukon. However, this interpretation was rejected in *Bonanza Creek Gold Mining Co. v. The King*, [1916] 1 A.C. 566, 583-84 (P.C.), which held that while a provincial legislature is not competent to bestow upon its corporate creation the *right* to engage in business outside the home province, it may grant it the *capacity* to engage in business in any other province that is willing to allow it to do business there. That such a capacity has been bestowed will be presumed in the absence of provisions in the letters patent excluding it. *Honsberger v. Weyburn Townsite Co.* (1919), 59 S.C.R. 281. As a result, by virtue of liberal provisions (discussed in the next sub-section) for the recognition of extra-provincial corporations, provincially incorporated companies commonly do business throughout Canada.

Federal Powers. There is also a broad and well-established federal incorporation power, although it is conferred explicitly in the Constitution Act only in respect of banks. Constitution Act, 1867, s. 91(15). Because s. 91 reserves to the federal government the right to make laws in respect of all matters not specifically assigned to the provinces, it follows that the Act assigns to exclusive federal competence the incorporation of corporations not "with Provincial Objects" or, more plainly, having objects to be carried out in more than one province. *Citizens Ins. Co. of Canada v. Parsons* (1881), 7 App. Cas. 96 (P.C.); *John Deere Plow Co. v. Wharton*, [1915] A.C. 330 (P.C.). It is not necessary for the validity of a federal incorporation that the company in fact be carrying on business in more than one province. *Colonial Bldg. and Investment Ass'n. v. A.G. Quebec* (1883), 9 App. Cas. 157 (P.C.). The federal powers of incorporation are also not limited to corporations having objects confined to the enumerated powers of the federal government. See *Canadian Pioneer Management v. Labour Relations Board of Saskatchewan*, [1980] 1 S.C.R. 433, [1980] 3 W.W.R. 214, 107 D.L.R. (3d) 1; and *Life Underwriters Association of Canada v. Provincial Association of Quebec Life Underwriters*, [1992] 1 S.C.R. 449, 133 N.R. 223. Beyond the power simply to incorporate corporations with objects to be carried out in more than one province, the federal Parliament is apparently competent to enact a full range of "corporate law" legislation for such corporations. Various specific types of federal corporations law legislation have withstood constitutional attack:

- legislation making directors of federal corporations personally liable for the improper payments of dividends. *Reference re Section 100 of The Dominion Companies Act*, [1934] S.C.R. 653;
- legislation regulating the method of making take-over bids for federal corporations. *Esso Standard (Inter-America) Inc. v. J.W. Enterprises Inc.*, [1963] S.C.R. 144;

- legislation governing insider trading in the securities of federal corporations, including the provision of civil remedies. *Multiple Access Ltd. v. McCutcheon*, [1982] 2 S.C.R. 161.

In addition, the Quebec Court of Appeal has sustained the constitutional validity of the oppression remedy in the CBCA. *Montel v. Groupe de Consultants P.G.L. Inc.* (1982), 20 B.L.R. 159.

Conflicts Between Federal and Provincial Laws Relating to Corporations. While provincial corporate legislation could not validly apply to federal corporations, some corporate law matters concern securities trading, which has traditionally been regarded as within provincial competence. *Intra vires* federal corporate legislation would be paramount to *intra vires* provincial securities legislation in its application to federal corporations to the extent of any conflict between the federal corporate legislation and the provincial securities legislation. If there were no federal law in the area, then the provincial legislation could validly be applied to the federal corporation. If there were federal legislation, the provincial legislation would still be upheld if not in conflict with the federal legislation. However, it is increasingly unlikely that a court would find that such a conflict exists. See *Multiple Access Ltd. v. McCutcheon*, [1982] 2 S.C.R. 161 (application of insider trading prohibition in Ontario Securities Act to federal corporations upheld notwithstanding virtually identical provision in federal corporations Act).

Constraints on the Application of Provincial Laws to Federal Corporations. The provinces have, of course, a broad legislative authority. Of special relevance for present purposes are their power of direct taxation (Constitution Act, 1867, s. 92(2)) and their power over property and civil rights in the province (s. 92(13)). In general, federal corporations are obligated to comply with provincial legislation in the same way as natural persons or provincial corporations. It has repeatedly been held, however, that what the provinces may not do with respect to federal corporations is to "sterilize their capacities and powers." *John Deere Plow Co. v. Wharton*, [1915] A.C. 330 (P.C.); *Great West Saddlery Co. v. The King*, [1921] 2 A.C. 91 (P.C.); *A.G. Manitoba v. A.G. Canada*, [1929] A.C. 260 (P.C.); *Re Constitution Act, 1867, ss. 91 and 92* (1991), 80 D.L.R. (4th) 431; [1991] 4 W.W.R. 193 (Man. C.A.). The first two cases held that a province may not condition the right of a federal corporation to do business within a province, or to bring suit in the courts of a province, upon compliance with licensing requirements for extra-provincial corporations. Yet a province may apparently impose monetary penalties upon a federal corporation that fails to pay a licence fee to qualify as an extra-provincial corporation. *Re Royalite Oil Co.*, [1931] 1 W.W.R. 484 (Alta. App. Div.).

Securities legislation in Canada is a provincial matter, even if share issuances seem near the heart of a federal corporation's status and corporate capacity. Such legislation has not passed without challenge. In *A.G. Manitoba v. A.G. Canada*, [1929] A.C. 260 (P.C.), the Manitoba Sale of Shares Act, which prohibited corporations from raising capital unless they received permission to do so from an official who might demand alterations in an applicant's capital structure, was held to deprive federal corporations of their essential capacities and powers. However, three years later an Alberta statute that prohibited the sale of securities except through a licensed broker was upheld in its application to federal corporations. *Lymburn v. Mayland*, [1932] A.C. 318 (P.C). Though these cases suggest that provincial securities legislation should focus on investment intermediaries, provisions similar to the impugned Manitoba statute are a feature in all of the leading provincial securities Acts. The application of these statutes to federal corporations has generally been assumed and not been tested.

Federal incorporation is not a licence to ignore provincial law. Even in the cases in which provincial legislation was held *ultra vires* in its application to federal corporations because it would sterilize their powers or essential capacities, the Privy Council was careful to observe that federal incorporation does not confer a general immunity from provincial regulatory laws. Indeed, provincial legislation of truly devastating impact upon the business of a federal corporation has been upheld in the British Columbia "Autoplan" case. *Canadian Indemnity Co. v. A.G. British Columbia*, [1977] 2 S.C.R. 504. In that case, the province's compulsory auto insurance scheme was to be administered by a provincial Crown corporation, which foreclosed the auto insurance market from the plaintiff federal corporations, but the legislation was still upheld. In *Great West Saddlery Co. Ltd. v. The King*, [1921] 2 A.C. 91 (P.C.), Viscount Haldane stated that a federal company incorporated for the purpose of holding land would be unable successfully to attack provincial legislation that prohibited corporations, wherever incorporated, from owning land. It is obvious that the test for whether provincial legislation sterilizes the federal corporation is not the seriousness of the legislation's effect on the firm's business. Perhaps a more fruitful attempt at characterization would classify as *ultra vires* provincial legislation that prevents a federal corporation from carrying on any business within the province, and as *intra vires* provincial legislation that restricts a particular line of business in non-discriminatory fashion for all corporations.

Federal Versus Provincial Incorporation. The result is that there is in general no constitutional reason why a federal incorporation is more desirable than a provincial one. As a practical matter, either type of corporation can engage in business throughout Canada. Some firms will, however, find minor advantages in a federal incorporation. Federal corporations enjoy a limited immunity from provincial extra-provincial licensing. Given the decision in *John Deere Plow Co. v. Wharton*, [1915] A.C. 330 (P.C.), incorporation under the CBCA may be of some assistance in preserving the corporate name for use throughout Canada (although it does not protect the corporation against an action for passing off). In addition, those who anticipate doing significant business abroad might choose to incorporate under the CBCA in the expectation that a federal corporation would attract more prestige than a provincial one.

See further P. Hogg, *Constitutional Law of Canada* ch. 23 (1992); Anisman & Hogg, *Constitutional Aspects of Federal Securities Law*, in 3 *Proposals for a Federal Securities Market Law for Canada* 135 (1979).

2. Corporations Under the Charter

Expressions Used in the Charter: Applicability to Corporations. One of the most interesting questions in Canadian constitutional law in recent years has been the scope of the protection afforded corporations under the Canadian Charter of Rights and

Freedoms. The Charter employs several distinct terms in delimiting the categories of persons who enjoy the rights established under it. Some rights are accorded to "everyone" (s. 2 on fundamental freedoms; ss. 7-10, 12 on legal rights), while others are restricted to "citizens of Canada" (s. 3 on voting rights; s. 6 on mobility rights, s. 23 on language of instruction), "any member of the public" (s. 20), "a witness" (s. 13), a "party or witness" (s. 14) or to "individuals" (s. 15 on equality rights). "Any person charged with an offence" has certain rights in connection with proceedings in criminal or penal matters, and "anyone" whose Charter rights are infringed may apply to Court for redress (s. 24).

The terms are not uniform in their application to corporations. It is beyond dispute that "any person" includes corporations, and it is probable that the terms "everyone" and "anyone" also refer to corporations. See Hogg, *Constitutional Law of Canada* (looseleaf 1992) section 34.1(b) and the cases cited in note 2. On the other hand, it is unlikely that corporations can be "citizens of Canada," and corporations are almost certainly not "individuals."

Approach of the Courts to the Protection of Corporations Under the Charter. In determining whether a corporation is itself entitled to a right courts have begun to focus on whether a corporation can exercise a right given the nature of the corporate entity. For instance, in *R. v. Amway*, [1989] 1 S.C.R. 21, it was held that since a corporation can not testify it is not entitled to protection against being compelled to be a witness against itself under s. 11(c) of the Charter. It has also been held that a corporation is not entitled to protection under s. 7 of the Charter since "life, liberty and security of the person" are attributes of natural persons but not of corporations. See *Irwin Toy v. Quebec (Procureur General)*, [1989] 1 S.C.R. 927, 1004; *Dywidag Systems v. Zutphen Bros.*, [1990] 1 S.C.R. 705, 709; *R. v. Wholesale Travel Group*, [1991] 3 S.C.R. 154.

However, a corporation may invoke a Charter right if it can show that it has an interest that falls within the scope or purpose of the right. In *R. v. CIP Inc.*, [1992] 1 S.C.R. 843, 135 N.R. 90, the court held that a corporation had a right to be tried within a reasonable time pursuant to s. 11(b) of the Charter if it could show that the availability of witnesses and the reliability of testimony would have a significant negative impact on the ability of the corporation to establish a defence.

Standing of Corporations to Challenge Laws Under the Charter. Even where a Charter right can not be invoked on behalf of a corporation the validity of a law under the Charter may still be challenged by a corporation that is a defendant in a criminal proceeding. In *R. v. Big M Drug Mart*, [1985] 1 S.C.R. 295, a corporation appealed a conviction under the Alberta Lord's Day Act, claiming that the Act offended s. 2(a) of the Charter (freedom of conscience and religion). The Crown contended that the section did not apply to corporations because a corporation cannot have a conscience or religious beliefs. However, the Supreme Court held that anyone may claim relief from the provisions of a law that violates a Charter right or freedom even if they are not among those explicitly protected by the infringed right. Any law that contravenes the Charter is void, and anyone may impugn a law as void. See also *Hunter v. Southam Inc.*, [1984] 2 S.C.R. 145 (corporation successfully claimed protection of s. 11 with respect to proceedings in criminal and penal matters). In *R. v. Wholesale Travel Group Inc.*, [1991] 3 S.C.R. 154; 84 D.L.R. (4th) 161, the court held that while the protection of "life, liberty and security of the person" could only apply to an individual, a corporation could challenge an absolute liability offence as contrary to the s. 7 protection of liberty on the basis that it violated the constitutional rights of individuals. However, the court left open the possibility that an absolute liability offence that applied only to a corporation could not be challenged under the charter and this approach was followed by the Court of Appeal of Prince Edward Island in *R. v. McGowan Motors Ltd.*, [1994] P.E.I.J. No. 8 Action No. AD-0471.

3. Extra-Provincial Licensing

As we have seen, outside of its province of incorporation a provincially incorporated company may exercise such powers as the host province allows it to exercise. Each of the provinces has enacted legislation requiring a corporation incorporated outside of the province to register with an official in order to carry on business in the province. A CBCA corporation will therefore have to file at least one extra-provincial registration and possibly more depending on where it is doing business. The official may, in his or her discretion, issue a licence to the extra-provincial corporation allowing it to carry on business in the province. Certain of the provinces have reciprocal arrangements so that a company incorporated in either of the provinces may carry on business in the other without a licence. For example, Ontario and Quebec have such an arrangement.

The term "extra-provincial corporation" as used in the statutes includes not just corporations organized under the laws of other provinces or the federal government but corporations organized outside of Canada. Section 219 of the Income Tax Act, however, generally makes it inexpedient for non-Canadian corporations to do business here without incorporating a Canadian subsidiary.

The Meaning of Carrying On Business. What constitutes "carrying on business" within a province? Or, to put the question in its practical perspective, what kinds of commercial transactions can a corporation have within a province before it is carrying on business there? In general, a corporation is not carrying on business within a province merely because goods manufactured by it are sold within that province—so long, at least, as the selling is done by contractors independent of the corporation who are not its agents. *Firestone Tire & Rubber Co. of Canada Ltd. v. C.I.T.*, [1942] S.C.R. 476, [1942] 4 D.L.R. 433; *Lainière de Roubaix, SA v. Craftsmen Distributors Inc.* (1991), 55 B.C.L.R. (2d) 103, [1991] 5 W.W.R. 217 (C.A.). It is better for the corporation that does not wish to register in a particular province if, in addition, the contracts for the sale of its goods to independent resellers are made outside of that province. See, e.g., *Re Geigy (Canada) Ltd.* (1969), 1 D.L.R. (3d) 354 in which it was said that "[i]n the absence of other evidence that a corporation is carrying on business in British Columbia, the evidence as to place where its contracts are made is decisive."

Several provincial statutes contain provisions that qualify the meaning of "carrying on business" in the province. For instance, the Ontario Extra-Provincial Corporations Act, R.S.O. 1990, c. E-27, s. 1(3) provides that:

An extra-provincial corporation does not carry on business in Ontario by reason only that,

(a) it takes orders for or buys or sells goods, wares or merchandise; or

(b) offers or sells services of any type,

by use of travelers or though advertising or correspondence

Subsection 1(2) provides that:

... an extra-provincial corporation carries on its business in Ontario if,

(a) it has a resident agent, representative, warehouse, office or place where it carries on business in Ontario;

(b) it holds an interest, otherwise than by way of security, in real property situate in Ontario; or

(c) it otherwise carries on business in Ontario.

ABCA s. 264 provides that a corporation carries on business within Alberta if it does any of the following (or "otherwise carries on business in Alberta"):

(i) lists its name in an Alberta telephone directory;

(ii) gives an Alberta address in an advertisement;

(iii) solicits business in Alberta;

(iv) owns land in Alberta or holds a license from Alberta to engage in a regulated business.

It would appear that by including "soliciting business" in the province as carrying on business there, Alberta is more restrictive of the activities that may be carried on without a licence than is Ontario (see, e.g., *Kroetsch v. Domnik (H.W.) Industries Ltd.* (1985), 60 A.R. 69). See also BCCA s. 1(8).

Requirements. In general, registration by an extra-provincial corporation entails paying a fee, making public filings of certain rudimentary corporate documents and, most importantly, appointing a local agent (who may be the provincial director of corporations) for service of process. The most common ground upon which registration is denied is confusion of corporate names between the applicant and a corporation already qualified to do business within the province.

Sanctions for Failure to Register. An extra-provincial corporation that fails to register but carries on business in the province is typically not capable of maintaining a legal action in the province and may also not be capable of owning land, or an interest in land, in the province. In addition, a daily fine against the corporation may be provided for, as in BCCA s. 337(2). By way of further sanctions for non-registration, it is typically provided that it is an offence for "any person" to contravene the provisions. "Person" in this context would include both the corporation itself and the natural persons who purport to carry on its business within the province. Section 338 of the BCCA further provides that a person who acts as an "agent or representative or in any other capacity for an [unregistered] extra-provincial company ... is personally liable for the debts and obligations incurred by him as agent."

Application to Federal Corporations. The provincial statutes usually specify that there is no discretion to deny registration to an applicant that is federally incorporated.

See, e.g., BCCA s. 18(5). To deny registration to such an applicant would presumably be unconstitutional since an unregistered extra-provincial corporation typically is disabled from doing business within the province. While the provincial extra-provincial licensing provisions all subject CBCA corporations to a duty to register, it would still appear that to provide as a sanction for non-registration a prohibition against doing business or suing in the province, as Alberta does, would be unconstitutional as applied to federal corporations.

C. THE INCORPORATION PROCESS

Once the jurisdiction of incorporation has been selected, it remains to incorporate the company and organize it within the requirements of the incorporating statute. This normally begins with one or more lawyers, students or clerks within a law firm acting as incorporators and is referred to as an "office incorporation." Many of the documents to be prepared may be conveniently carried on a word processor with relatively few blanks to be filled in. The procedure of incorporation has been simplified under new corporate statutes such as the CBCA, but it is still important to understand what steps are required in order to ensure that the company has been properly incorporated. At the end of the process, the new corporation is turned over to its promoters, who may commence carrying on business through it.

1. Steps in the Incorporation Process

Under the CBCA one or more individuals or corporations may form a corporation [CBCA s. 5; ABCA s. 5; OBCA s. 4]. Under the CBCA the corporation is formed by (i) filing articles of incorporation; (ii) filing a notice of the registered office of the corporation; (iii) filing a notice of directors; and (iv) paying the prescribed fee [CBCA ss. 7, 19 and 106; see also ABCA ss. 7, 12(3), 19 and 101]. As discussed below, where the name is other than a numbered name, a computer-based name search must also be submitted [CBCA Reg. s. 15; ABCA Reg. s. 7.81; OBCA Reg. s. 18(1)].

Under the BCCA a company can be incorporated by one or more natural persons by (i) subscribing to and filing a memorandum; (ii) filing articles signed by the subscribers to the memorandum; (iii) filing a notice of the registered office; and (iv) paying the prescribed fee [BCCA ss. 5-8].

2. Articles of Incorporation

The articles must set out all of the information referred to in CBCA s. 6(1) [ABCA s. 6(1); OBCA s. 5(1)], namely, the name of the corporation, the place in Canada where the registered office is to be situated, the classes of shares and, where there is more than one class of shares, the rights and restrictions on the shares, a statement of any restriction on the transfer of shares, the number of directors (or the minimum and maximum number of directors), and any restrictions on the business that the corporation may carry on. The articles may also include any provisions that may be found in the by-laws [CBCA s. 6(2); ABCA s. 6(2); OBCA s. 5(3)]. Should the incorporators so desire, the articles may then become a very lengthy document, since there is little restriction on the scope of by-laws under CBCA s. 103(1) [ABCA s. 98(1); OBCA s. 116(1)]. However, in practice one normally wishes to keep the provisions in the articles to a minimum. This simplifies the process of incorporation and also eliminates the need to amend the articles under s. 173 [ABCA s. 167; OBCA s. 168] if it is desired to change the provisions.

Under the BCCA the memorandum is normally a short document that sets out the name of the company, any businesses that the company is restricted from carrying on, any powers that the company is restricted from exercising, the authorized capital of the company [on authorized capital see Chapter Four] and the names, addresses and occupations of the subscribers to the memorandum and the number of shares to be taken by each subscriber. The articles under the BCCA deal in part with matters that are covered in the articles of incorporation under the CBCA and in part with matters dealt with in the by-laws under the CBCA. For instance, under the BCCA it would be the articles that deal with such matters as the number of directors and any restrictions on the transfer of shares. Otherwise the articles would normally deal with such matters as procedures for shareholders meetings, the election of directors, the appointment of officers, borrowing powers of directors and so on.

Various aspects of the articles of incorporation under the CBCA are discussed below with corresponding notes for the memorandum and articles under the BCCA.

Name. The articles of incorporation must set out the name of the corporation under s. 6(1)(a) [ABCA s. 6(1)(a); OBCA s. 5(1)(a)]. Unless one wishes a numbered name, one will make a name search prior to incorporation, using the computer facilities of a private name search company (using the "Newly Updated Automated Name Search" [or "NUANS" system]) [CBCA Reg. s. 15; ABCA Reg. s. 7.81; OBCA Reg. s. 18(1)]. The computer print-out will indicate any similarity between the proposed and existing names and is sent to the Director appointed under the CBCA together with the articles of incorporation.

If the proposed name is either prohibited or confusing with respect to existing trade marks or names under Part II of the Canada Business Corporations Regulations, the Director may direct the corporation to change its name after incorporation under s. 12(2)(a) [see also ABCA s. 12.1(1); OBCA s. 12(1)]. An example of a prohibited name is one that is too general or is merely descriptive of the business carried on by the corporation, such as "Computers Inc."

A corporation's name is an important asset of its business, and its officers will wish to request the Director to direct another corporation to change its name if the two names are likely to be confused. If the Director refuses to do so, the first corporation may appeal the decision under s. 246(b) [ABCA s. 239(b); see also OBCA s. 252]. If the corporation proposes to carry on business in Quebec, it will wish to set out its name in both a French and an English form in order to comply with the Charter of the French Language in that province. Incorporation statutes in Canada typically facilitate this by allowing the corporation to set out its name in an English form, a French form, an English form and a French form or a combined English and French form [see CBCA s. 10(3); ABCA s. 10(6); OBCA s. 10(2)].

Similar requirements with respect to company names apply under the BCCA. Under the BCCA the company name must be set out in the memorandum. The Registrar has the discretion to refuse to register a company having a name that is confusingly similar to the name of a company that has already been incorporated and the Registrar has the power to order the company to change its name (BCCA ss. 17, 18). A company may also set out its name in an English form, a French form, an English form and a French form or a combined English and French form (BCCA s. 16(4)).

The name of the corporation must include a suffix such as "Ltd.," "Inc." or "Corp." This suffix is provided to bring the limited liability aspect of the corporation to the attention of persons dealing with it. The corporate name with its accompanying suffix must be included in all contracts, invoices, negotiable instruments and orders for goods or services issued or made by or on behalf of the corporation (CBCA s. 10(5); ABCA s. 10(8); OBCA s. 10(5); BCCA s. 130).

Registered Office. A corporation must maintain a registered office at which it can be served with legal documents and at which it may be required to maintain corporate records. The location of the registered office must be provided in the articles under ss. 6(1)(b) and 19(1) [cf. ABCA s. 19 (must file a notice of the registered office); OBCA ss. 5(1)(b), 14]. Under the CBCA, one must state the municipality but not the street address of the registered office. The street address need only be given in the notice of registered office, to be filed with the articles of incorporation under CBCA s. 19(2). The street address may then be changed without amending the articles (CBCA ss. 19(3), (4); ABCA s. 19(3); OBCA s. 14(2)). The corporate records referred to in s. 20 are usually kept at the registered office.

Under the BCCA one must send a notice of the registered office (s. 8). The registered office may be changed by a resolution of the directors (s. 40). The company may maintain a separate office for the records the company is required to keep or it may have its registered office and records office in the same place (s. 39).

Classes and Maximum Number of Shares. The requirement in CBCA s. 6(1)(c) [ABCA s. 6(1)(b); BCCA Form 1; OBCA s. 5(1)(c)] regarding classes and maximum number of shares is discussed further in Chapter Four. Unless tax or business considerations dictate otherwise, small issuers are most often incorporated with common shares, to which no special rights or preferences are attached.

Additional Provisions. Substantial advantages may be available to "private companies" under Canadian securities legislation. Private companies are typically defined in Canadian securities legislation as corporations whose articles or constating documents (i) restrict the right to transfer its shares; (ii) limit the number of its shareholders to 50; and (iii) prohibit any invitation to the public to subscribe for its securities. See, e.g., the Ontario Securities Act ("OSA") s. 1(1). The articles may restrict the businesses that the corporation may carry on under CBCA s. 6(1)(f) [ABCA s. 6(1)(e); OBCA s. 5(1)(f); see also BCCA s. 5(2)(f) and Form 1 allowing a restriction on the businesses to be carried on to be set out in the memorandum]. Corporate objects clauses are discussed in the next section. The articles may set out further provisions under CBCA s. 6(2) [ABCA

s. 6(2); OBCA s. 5(3)]. Apart from restrictions applicable to private companies, the articles will sometimes deal with the following matters:

- Pre-emptive rights (discussed further in Chapter Four, Section C) [cf. CBCA s. 28(1); ABCA s. 28; BCCA s. 41; OBCA s. 26].
- Restrictions on share repurchases (discussed further in Chapter Eleven, Section B) [cf. CBCA s. 32(1); ABCA s. 32(1); BCCA s. 259(b); OBCA s. 30(1)].
- Cumulative voting (discussed further in Chapter Six, Section C) [cf. CBCA s. 107; ABCA s. 102; OBCA s. 120].
- Special majorities for directors' or shareholders' actions [cf. CBCA s. 6(3); ABCA s. 6(3); OBCA s. 5(4)].
- Provision for filling vacancies among directors [cf. CBCA s. 111(4); ABCA s. 106(4); OBCA s. 124(5)].
- Quorum of directors at less than a majority [cf. CBCA s. 114(2); ABCA s. 109(2); OBCA s. 126(3)].

Existence of the Corporation. When the Director receives the articles of incorporation, he is required by CBCA s. 8 [ABCA s. 8; BCCA ss. 8, 9; OBCA s. 6] to issue a certificate of incorporation. Under CBCA s. 9 [ABCA s. 9(1); BCCA s. 12; OBCA s. 7], the corporation comes into existence on that date.

The date of incorporation may give rise to legal problems, as the promoters discovered in *C.P.W. Valve & Instrument Ltd. v. Scott* (1978), 84 D.L.R. (3d) 673 (Alta. App. Div.). Scott had agreed to buy 5,000 industrial gauges prior to June 16, 1971 from C.P.W. Valve, either in Scott's name or through a corporation he would form. After purchasing 1,640 units in his own name, a further 3,360 units were ordered on June 15, 1971 in the name of "S. & V. Fluid Gauge Ltd." This was the corporation Scott had incorporated to carry on his business, and its certificate of incorporation from the Alberta Registrar of Companies was indeed dated June 15, 1971. However, C.P.W. Valve sought to introduce evidence that the Registrar had actually signed and sealed the certificate of incorporation on June 16, and had back-dated it to the day when he had actually received the articles from the incorporators. See CBCA s. 262(3); ABCA s. 255(3); OBCA s. 273(2). Scott relied on the following two sections of the Alberta Companies Act to establish that the purchase order was valid.

27. A certificate of incorporation given by the Registrar in respect of a company is conclusive proof that all the requirements of this Act in respect of registration and of matters precedent and incidental to incorporation have been complied with, and that the company is a company authorized to be registered and duly registered under this Act.

28. From the date of incorporation mentioned in the certificate of incorporation the subscribers, together with such other persons as may from time to time become members of the company, are a body corporate by the name contained in the memorandum, capable of exercising all the functions of an incorporated company, and having perpetual succession and a common seal, with power to hold lands, but with such liability on the part of the members to contribute to the assets of the company in the event of its being wound up as is mentioned in this Act.

Scott's argument was, however, rejected by the Alberta Court of Appeal, which held that these provisions could not retroactively cure a breach that had in fact arisen on June 15.

Would this case have been decided differently under CBCA s. 9? See also *Prim Invest-ments Ltd. v. Madison Development Corp.*, [1983] 1 W.W.R. 697, 709-10 (Alta.). The issue in such cases is of course simply one of construction: did the parties bargain for a purchase order from a corporation incorporated *on* or *as of* a certain date?

3. By-Laws

While the directors of the corporation need not be listed in the articles of incorporation, their names and addresses must be given in the notice of directors under CBCA s. 106(1) [ABCA s. 101(1); OBCA s. 5(1)(e) (requires identification of first directors in the articles) and the Ontario Corporations Information Act, R.S.O. 1990, c. C-39, s. 2(1) and Reg. 1a requires an initial report that must identify the directors while s. 4(1) of the Act requires a notice of any change in the directors]. In a CBCA incorporation, the directors will generally be the promoters. After the corporation comes into existence, the directors will pass organizational resolutions under CBCA s. 104(1) [ABCA s. 99(1); OBCA s. 117(1)], including one approving the corporation's general by-law.

By-laws may deal broadly with the business or affairs of the corporation under CBCA s. 103(1) [ABCA s. 98(1); OBCA s. 116(1)]. They should be distinguished from the articles of the corporation, which are more difficult to amend under CBCA s. 173 [ABCA s. 167; OBCA s. 168] than the by-laws under CBCA s. 103. By-laws may be made, amended or repealed by the directors. While subject to shareholder approval, the by-laws are effective from the date of the directors' resolution. They become invalid only if not confirmed by the shareholders at their next meeting. By contrast, an amend-ment to the articles does not come into effect until the date of the certificate of amend-ment granted by the Director [CBCA s. 179; ABCA s. 173; OBCA ss. 172, 273]. Given this difference between articles and by-laws, the latter will provide much greater detail than the former on how the affairs of the corporation are to be conducted.

By-laws are also to be distinguished from resolutions of directors or shareholders, which are usually more restricted in scope. A resolution may, for example, authorize a particular major transaction to be entered into by the corporation. Routine transactions will usually not require any formal authorization, whether by way of by-laws or resolutions.

The by-laws are usually a fairly lengthy document, since many of their sections merely repeat provisions in the CBCA. If these were eliminated, the document would be only several pages in length. Can you think of a worthwhile reason why the by-laws should include CBCA provisions?

On or shortly after incorporation, the corporation will also pass banking by-laws and resolutions. The text of these documents is provided by the bank, which requests that executed forms be returned to it.

Under the BCCA the first directors are the subscribers to the memorandum (s. 134) and notice of any change in the directors must be given (s. 137). Under the BCCA it is the articles that deal broadly with the business or affairs of the corporation. Amendments to either the memorandum or the articles require a special resolution of the shareholders (three-quarters of the shareholders who vote). See BCCA s. 1(1) "special resolution" and ss. 241, 243. However, the memorandum is usually limited to just the items specifi-cally required by the Act to be set out in the memorandum. The reason for this is that the memorandum can only be amended as permitted by the Act and the Act only provides for amendment of the memorandum with respect to the matters specifically required by the Act to be set out in the memorandum (ss. 241, 245, 247, 248). Putting provisions in the articles allows them to be amended.

4. Further Organizational Matters

Before the new corporation can commence doing business, a variety of organizational resolutions must be passed. Under the CBCA the first of these are the by-laws, referred to above. Beyond that, the directors will deal with the other matters listed in CBCA s. 104 [ABCA s. 99; OBCA s. 117]. With a small board of directors, these resolutions may be passed by unanimous written consent under CBCA s. 117(1) [ABCA s. 112(1); BCCA s. 149(3); OBCA s. 129(1)]. The resolutions may be signed at different times, and it is not necessary to convene a meeting with all the directors in attendance. In the same way, shareholder resolutions may be passed by the unanimous consent of share-holders under CBCA s. 142(1) [ABCA s. 136(1); BCCA s. 164; OBCA s. 104(1)] in-stead of holding a shareholders' meeting.

At this point in its organization a CBCA corporation will have directors but no shareholders. The directors will therefore allot shares in return for the agreed-upon con-sideration. The corporation need not issue share certificates to its new shareholders unless they request them under CBCA s. 49(1) [ABCA s. 45; OBCA s. 54]. However, the direc-tors will approve a form of share certificate against that possibility. The directors may also appoint an auditor to hold office until the next meeting of shareholders. But if the corporation is not large, it may seek to dispense with an auditor under CBCA s. 163 [ABCA s. 157; BCCA s. 203; OBCA s. 148]. In addition, the directors will appoint officers and order and approve a corporate seal. The corporate seal is normally affixed to major corporate contracts, even though the necessity for it has been dispensed with both by virtue of CBCA s. 23 [ABCA s. 23(2); BCCA s. 35; OBCA s. 13] and at common law. *J.H. McKnight Construction Co. v. Vansickler* (1915), 51 S.C.R. 374, 24 D.L.R. 298; *Canadian Market Place Ltd. v. Fallowfield* (1976), 13 O.R. (2d) 456, 71 D.L.R. (3d) 341.

The organizational process is similar under the BCCA. The corporation's first direc-tors are the subscribers to the memorandum. Unlike the CBCA the company will have shareholders upon its incorporation. The shareholders are the subscribers to the memo-randum. The organizational steps taken by directors involve the approval of share cer-tificates (under BCCA s. 49 a certificate must be prepared), the approval of the issuance of shares to subscribers (and possibly also the approval of an allotment and issuance of any additional shares), the appointment of officers, the adoption of a fiscal year end, the adoption of a banking resolution, and, unless waived by the shareholders, the appoint-ment of auditors.

5. Shareholders' Agreements

The promoters may often be advised to enter into a shareholders' agreement modifying their rights under the CBCA. For example, they may wish to agree at the outset on who will be elected to the board of directors, without leaving this to be decided solely by the holders of 50.1% of the shares at an annual shareholders' meeting. Other matters the promoters may wish to provide for on organizing the corporation include the election of officers, salaries for chief employees and the payment of dividends. Such agreements are expressly validated by CBCA s. 146 [ABCA s. 140; OBCA s. 108]. Shareholder agreements are also possible under the BCCA and are commonly used. It is, however, premature to consider them now, and they are dealt with in more detail in Chapter Six.

D. RESTRICTIONS ON MANAGEMENT AUTHORITY

The management structure of the corporation and the authority of managers to enter into binding legal arrangements on behalf of the corporation is another issue that must be addressed in the formation of the corporation. Under the partnership form of organization, the presumptive rule is for every partner to take part in management, with disputes resolved by a majority vote. Ontario Partnership Act ("OPA") s. 27. The majoritarian principle is, however, considerably undercut by the presumptive termination rights of individual partners, whose ability to dissolve the firm may give them significant leverage on any business decision. OPA ss. 29(1) and 35(c). Under the CBCA, shareholder presumptive rights are considerably narrower, since minority shareholders may not terminate the company unilaterally, and management authority rests in the holders of a majority of shares, who can elect the board of directors.

Not every firm will find that one or the other management structure is entirely appropriate, and both may be altered by private agreement. In a small corporation, for example, the parties might provide in a unanimous shareholder agreement for veto rights on certain "fundamental" business decisions, or for restrictions on an individual manager's authority to bind the firm. These devices may reduce agency costs (see Chapter One) by limiting the scope of the authority of managers to conduct the business.

1. The Ultra Vires Doctrine

Care must be taken to distinguish the rights of firm insiders to enforce restrictions on management authority from the effects of breach on outside contractors. Restrictions on management authority may be categorized according to the manner in which they may be enacted or waived. Some restrictions constrain only the agent and not the firm. Such restrictions may be waived by a senior executive, the board of directors, or, in some cases, upon shareholder approval. The firm and its agents may also be bound by restrictions found in relational contracts, such as those with major creditors. Another type of restriction is that which is found in the corporation's articles. When a manager acts in disregard of such a restriction, his action is said to be *ultra vires* the corporation, signifying that he went not only beyond the scope of his own authority, but beyond the powers of the corporation as well. A common type of this sort of restriction is one that constrains the types of business the corporation can engage in. This was often done by setting out the "objects" of the corporation (i.e. the purposes for which the corporation was incorporated).

Courts developed a doctrine of *ultra vires* under which a corporation was held not to be bound by acts of the corporation's agents that were beyond the powers of the corporation. This may have served to protect shareholders from changes in the risk associated with their investment in the corporation. This may have been a useful method of avoiding changes in investment risk where the shareholder could not readily control the risk by selling the shares of corporations that significantly increased the risk to which the shareholder was exposed. However, declaring a contract void on the basis that the contract is beyond the powers of the company can impose the risk of the corporation's agents acting beyond the powers of the corporation on outsiders who have contracted with the corporation. As between shareholders and outsiders, the shareholders are normally in a better position to control for such a risk. The party best able to monitor management of a small firm will ordinarily be the shareholders. The least cost risk avoider is unlikely to be a trade creditor, especially when the manager has acted in a way that appears to be consistent with his position.

Because it was in the joint interests of shareholders to put the risk of acts beyond the powers of the corporation on the shareholders who bear the risk at least cost, techniques were developed to avoid the effects of the *ultra vires* doctrine. Courts also developed techniques to facilitate the avoidance of the *ultra vires* doctrine.

Development of the Ultra Vires Doctrine. The case below was a leading case in the development of the *ultra vires* doctrine. The case is followed by a discussion of the techniques that were developed to avoid the application of the *ultra vires* doctrine and by a discussion of the legislative abolition of the *ultra vires* doctrine.

Ashbury Ry. Carriage & Iron Co. v. Riche
House of Lords
(1875), L.R. 7 H.L. 653

[The defendant was incorporated in 1862 under a memorandum of association which stated that its objects were:

to make and sell, or lend on hire, railway-carriages and wagons, and all kinds of railway plant, fittings, machinery, and rolling-stock; to carry on the business of mechanical engineers and general contractors; to purchase and sell, as merchants, timber, coal, metals, or other materials; and to buy and sell any such materials on commission, or as agents.

In 1865, the corporation's directors met with several Belgian businessmen, including Riche, to discuss constructing a railway from Antwerp to Tournai. It was agreed that the corporation would purchase the concession to build the line and contract out the construction work to Riche. The defendant corporation's shareholders did not regard the project as a desirable investment, and the corporation repudiated the contract with Riche as *ultra vires*.

Lord Cairns concluded that the contract to construct a railway did not fall within the objects of the corporation, reading the words "general contractors" to be confined by the other types of business set out in the objects of the corporation and thus not permitting the entering into of a contract for the construction of a railway.

LORD CAIRNS continued as follows:]

... [A] contract of this kind was not within the words of the memorandum of association. In point of fact it was not a contract in which, as the memorandum of association implies, the limited company were to be the employed, they were the employers. They purchased the concession of a railway—an object not at all within the memorandum of association; and having purchased that, they employed, or they contracted to pay, as persons employing, the Plaintiffs in the present action, as the persons who were to construct it. That was reversing entirely the whole hypothesis of the memorandum of association, and was the making of a contract not included within, but foreign to, the words of the memorandum of association.

Those being the results of the documents to which I have referred, I will ask your Lordships now to consider the effect of the Act of Parliament—the Joint Stock Companies Act of 1862—on this state of things. ... Your Lordships are well aware that this is the Act which put upon its present permanent footing the regulation of joint stock companies, and more especially of those joint stock companies which were to be authorized to trade with a limit to their liability.

The provisions under which that system of limiting liability was inaugurated, were provisions not merely, perhaps I might say not mainly, for the benefit of the shareholders for the time being in the company, but were enactments intended also to provide for the interests of two other very important bodies; in the first place, those who might become shareholders in succession to the persons who were shareholders for the time being; and secondly, the outside public, and more particularly those who might be creditors of companies of this kind. And I will ask your Lordships to observe, as I refer to some of the clauses, the marked and entire difference there is between the two documents which form the title deeds of companies of this description—I mean the Memorandum of Association on the one hand, and the Articles of Association on the other hand. With regard to the memorandum of association, your Lordships will find, as has often already been pointed out, although it appears somewhat to have been overlooked in the present case, that that is, as it were, the charter, and defines the limitation of the powers of a company to be established under the Act. With regard to the articles of association, those articles play a part subsidiary to the memorandum of association. They accept the memorandum of association as the charter of incorporation of the company, and so accepting it, the articles proceed to define the duties, the rights and the powers of the governing body as between themselves and the company at large, and the mode and form in which the business of the company is to be carried on, and the mode and form in which changes in the internal regulations of the company may from time to time be made. With regard, therefore, to the memorandum of association, if you find anything which goes beyond that memorandum, or is not warranted by it, the question will arise whether that which is so done is *ultra vires*, not only of the directors of the company, but of the company itself. With regard to the articles of association, if you find anything which, still keeping within the memorandum of association, is a violation of the articles of association, or in excess of them, the question will arise whether that is anything more than an act *extra vires* the directors, but *intra vires* the company.

The clauses of the statute to which it is necessary to refer are four: in the first place, the sixth clause. That provides that "Any seven or more persons associated for any lawful purpose may, by subscribing their names to a memorandum of association, and otherwise complying with the requisitions of this Act in respect of registration, form an incorporated company, with or without limited liability." My Lords, this is the first section which speaks of the incorporation of the company; but your Lordships will observe that it does not speak of that incorporation as the creation of a corporation with inherent common law rights, such rights as are by common law possessed by every corporation, and without any other limit than would by common law be assigned to them, but it speaks of the company being incorporated with reference to a memorandum of association; and you are referred thereby to the provisions which subsequently are to be found upon the subject of that memorandum of association.

The next clause which is material is the eighth: "Where a company is formed on the principle of having the liability of its members limited to the amount unpaid on their shares, hereinafter referred to as a company limited by shares, the Memorandum of Association shall contain the following things" (I pass over the first and second, and I come to the third item which is to be specified): "The objects for which the proposed company is to be established." That is, therefore, the memorandum which the persons are to sign as a preliminary to the incorporation of the company. They are to state "the objects for which the proposed company is to be established;" and the existence, the coming into existence, of the company is to be an existence and to be a coming into existence for those objects and for those objects alone.

Then, my Lords, the 11th section provides: "The memorandum of association shall bear the same stamp as if it were a deed, and shall be signed by each subscriber in the presence of, and be attested by, one witness at the least, and that attestation shall be a sufficient attestation in *Scotland*, as well as in *England* and *Ireland*. It shall, when registered, bind the company and the members thereof to the same extent as if each member had subscribed his name and affixed his seal thereto, and there were in the memorandum contained, on the part of himself, his heirs, executors, and administrators, a covenant to observe all the conditions of such memorandum, subject to the provisions of this Act." Your Lordships will observe, therefore, that it is to be a covenant in which every member of the company is to covenant that he will observe the conditions of the memorandum, one of which is that the objects for which the company is established are the objects mentioned in the memorandum, and that he not only will observe that, but will observe it subject to the provisions of this Act. Well, but the very next provision of the Act contained in the 12th section is this: "Any company limited by shares may so far modify the conditions contained in its memorandum of association, if authorized to do so by its regulations as originally framed, or as altered by special resolution in manner hereinafter mentioned, as to increase its capital by the issue of new shares of such amount as it thinks expedient, or to consolidate and divide its capital into shares of larger amount than its existing shares, or to convert its paid-up shares into stock, but, save as aforesaid, and save as is hereinafter provided in the case of a change of name, no alteration shall be made by any company in the conditions contained in its memorandum of association." The covenant, therefore, is not merely that every member will observe the conditions upon which the company is established, but that no change shall be made in those conditions; and if there is a covenant that no change shall be made in the objects for which the company is established, I apprehend that that includes within it the engagement that no object shall be pursued by the company, or attempted to be attained by the company in practice, except an object which is mentioned in the memorandum of association.

Now, my Lords, if that is so—if that is the condition upon which the corporation is established—if that is the purpose for which the corporation is established—it is a mode of incorporation which contains in it both that which is affirmative and that which is negative. It states affirmatively the ambit and extent of vitality and power which by law are given to the corporation, and it states, if it is necessary so to state, negatively, that nothing shall be done beyond that ambit, and that no attempt shall be made to use the corporate life for any other reason than that which is so specified.

Now, my Lords, with regard to the articles of association, observe how completely different the character of the legislation is. ... Of the internal regulations of the company the members of it are absolute masters, and, provided they pursue the course marked out in the Act, that is to say, holding a general meeting and obtaining the consent of the shareholders, they may alter those regulations from time to time; but all must be done in the way of alteration subject to the conditions contained in the memorandum of association. That is to override and overrule any provisions of the articles which may be at variance with it. The memorandum of association is, as it were, the area beyond which the action of the company cannot go; inside that area the shareholders may make such regulations for their own government as they think fit.

... It appears that there has come into the articles of association of this company one which is in these words: "An extension of the company's business beyond or for other than the objects or purposes expressed or implied in the memorandum of association shall take place only in pursuance of a special resolution." In point of fact, no resolution for the extension of the business of the company was in this case come to; but even if it had been come to, it would have been entirely inept and inefficacious. There was, in this 4th article, an attempt to do the very thing which, by the Act of Parliament, was prohibited to be done—to claim and arrogate to the company a power under the guise of internal regulation to go beyond the objects or purposes expressed or implied in the memorandum.

... I assume the contract in itself to be perfectly legal. ... The question is not as to the legality of the contract; the question is as to the competency and power of the company to make the contract. Now, I am clearly of opinion that this contract was entirely, as I have said, beyond the objects in the memorandum of association. If so, it was thereby placed beyond the powers of the company to make the contract. If so, my Lords, it is not a question whether the contract ever was ratified or was not ratified. If it was a contract void at its beginning, it was void because the company could not make the contract. If every shareholder of the company had been in the room, and every shareholder of the company had said, "That is a contract which we desire to make, which we authorize the directors to make, to which we sanction the placing the seal of the company," the case would not have stood in any different position from that in which it stands now. The shareholders would thereby, by unanimous consent, have been attempting to do the very thing which, by the Act of Parliament, they were prohibited from doing.

But, my Lords, if the shareholders of this company could not *ab ante* have authorized a contract of this kind to be made, how could they subsequently sanction the contract after it had, in point of fact, been made. I endeavoured to follow as accurately as I could the very able argument of Mr. *Benjamin* at your Lordships' Bar on this point; but it appeared to me that this was a difficulty with which he was entirely unable to grapple. He endeavoured to contend that when the shareholders had found that something had been done by the directors which ought not to have been done, they might be authorized to make the best they could of a difficulty into which they had thus been thrown, and therefrom might be deemed to possess power to sanction the contract being proceeded with. My Lords, I am unable to adopt that suggestion. It appears to me that it would be perfectly fatal to the whole scheme of legislation to which I have referred, if you were to hold that, in the first place, directors might do that which even the whole company could not do, and that then, the shareholders finding out what had been done, could sanction, subsequently, what they could not antecedently have authorized.

My Lords, if this be the proper view of the Act of Parliament, it reconciles, as it appears to me, the opinion of all the Judges of the Court of Exchequer Chamber; because I find Mr. Justice *Blackburn*, whose judgment was concurred in by two other judges who took the same view, expressing himself thus: "I do not entertain any doubt that if, on the true construction of a statute creating a corporation it appears to be the intention of the Legislature, expressed or implied, that the corporation shall not enter into a particular contract, every Court, whether of law or equity, is bound to treat a contract entered into contrary to the enactment as illegal, and therefore wholly void, and to hold that a contract wholly void cannot be ratified." My Lords, that sums up and exhausts the whole case. In my opinion, beyond all doubt, on the true construction of the statute of 1862, creating this corporation, it appears that it was the intention of the Legislature, not implied, but actually expressed, that the corporation should not enter, having regard to its memorandum of association, into a contract of this description. If so, according to the words of Mr. Justice *Blackburn*, every Court, whether of law or of equity, is bound to treat that contract, entered into contrary to the enactment, I will not say as illegal, but as *extra vires*, and wholly null and void, and to hold also that a contract wholly void cannot be ratified.

My Lords, that relieves me, and, if your Lordships agree with me, relieves your Lordships from any question with regard to ratification. I am bound to say that if ratification had to be considered I have found in this case no evidence which to my mind is at all sufficient to prove ratification; but I desire to say that I do not wish to found my opinion on any question of ratification. This contract, in my judgment, could not have been ratified by the unanimous assent of the whole corporation.

[Lords CHELMSFORD, HATHERLY, O'HAGEN and SELBORNE delivered concurring opinions.]

Avoidance Techniques. The lower courts in *Ashbury Ry. Carriage* had held that, though the Belgian contract was in fact unauthorized, it might be upheld since it had been approved by the shareholders over a period of time. This argument was rejected by the House of Lords, and Lord Cairns said that even had the shareholders unanimously desired to ratify the contract, they would have been unable to do so. If the *ultra vires* doctrine was meant for the protection of shareholders, there might seem little point to mandating observance of an objects clause in such a case. The remarkable rigour of the doctrine is all the more striking when it is realized that 100 years ago, when the doctrine was taking shape, it was not feasible, as it is today, to amend the corporation's constating document so as to change its objects.

Courts in the nineteenth century often enforced restrictions upon corporations with little regard to the interests of the parties the restrictions were intended to protect. It is paradoxical that modern corporations statutes are considerably more facilitative than those of 100 years ago, a period popularly identified with free market ideology. The differences in corporations law find an expression in the nineteenth century "concession" theory of incorporation, under which the right to do business under a corporate form was a privilege granted by the state, which might curb it in any way it saw fit. Thus it was argued that, if incorporators were to be accorded limited liability, they would have to conform strictly with the spirit of mandatory corporations legislation. This did not in itself provide a justification for restrictive statutory provisions, but an explanation for them was suggested by Brandeis J. in *Lewis K. Liggett Co. v. Lee*, 288 U.S. 517 (1933):

The prevalence of the corporation in America had led men of this generation to act, at times, as if the privilege of doing business in corporate form were inherent in the citizen; and has led them to accept the evils attendant upon the free and unrestricted use of the corporate mechanism as if these evils were the inescapable price of civilized life and, hence, to be borne with resignation. Throughout the greater part of our history a different view prevailed. Although the value of this instrumentality in commerce and industry was fully recognized, incorporation for business was commonly denied long after it had been freely granted for religious, educational and charitable purposes. It was denied because of fear. Fear of encroachment upon the liberties and opportunities of the individual. Fear of the subjection of labor to capital. Fear of monopoly. Fear that the absorption of capital by corporations, and their perpetual life, might bring evils similar to those which attended mortmain.

There was a sense of some insidious menace inherent in large aggregations of capital, particularly when held by corporations. So, at first, the corporate privilege was granted sparingly; and only when the grant seemed necessary in order to procure for the community some specific benefit otherwise unattainable. The later enactment of general incorporation laws does not signify that the apprehension of corporate domination had been overcome. The desire for business expansion created an irresistible demand for more charters; and it was believed that under general laws embodying safeguards of universal application the scandals and favoritism incident to special incorporation could be avoided. The general laws, which long embodied severe restrictions upon size and upon the scope of corporate activity, were, in part, an expression of the desire for equality of opportunity. [*Id.* at 548-49]

Few today would seek to limit the expansion of business in this way. The development of the *ultra vires* doctrine after *Ashbury Ry. Carriage* is in fact an instructive example of the collapse of the restrictive policies described by Brandeis J. Fairly early on it was discovered that a corporation might avoid the strictures of the principle through the proper drafting of an objects clause. Corporate lawyers first devised the technique of drafting objects clauses with a great number of heads so as to catch a wide variety of businesses which the corporation might at a future date decide to carry on. Here, however, the corporation ran the risk that the court might find that the listed purposes were merely *powers*, relating only to a business ancillary to one of the main objects or purposes. It will be recalled that this is what Lord Cairns thought that general contracting amounted to in *Ashbury Ry. Carriage.* But if the corporate draftsmen appended to a lengthy list of objects a clause stating that the *ejusdem generis* canon of interpretation should not apply, then the court would likely hold that each object was in fact independent. See *Cotman v. Brougham*, [1918] A.C. 514 (H.L.). A further technique for avoiding the *ultra vires* rule was provided in *Bell Houses Ltd. v. City Wall Properties Ltd.*, [1966] 2 Q.B. 656 (C.A.). In that case, the court upheld an extension to a new line of business on the basis of an objects clause that permitted the corporation "to carry on any other trade or business whatsoever which can, in the opinion of the board of directors, be advantageously carried on by the company in connection with or as ancillary to ... the general business of the company." See also *H. & H. Logging Co. v. Random Services Corp.* (1967), 63 D.L.R. (2d) 6 (B.C.C.A.).

In addition, a Privy Council decision had been interpreted as holding that the *ultra vires* doctrine does not apply to letters patent corporations so as to enable such corporations to avoid their contracts. *Bonanza Creek Gold Mining Co. v. The King*, [1916] 1 A.C. 566 (P.C.). The holding in *Bonanza Creek* would appear to be that a corporation incorporated in a letters patent jurisdiction has all of the powers of a natural person *unless* such powers are excluded by the particular letters patent or by the incorporating statute. In the only remaining Canadian letters patent jurisdiction, Prince Edward Island, the relevant corporate statute contains a long list of specific corporate powers, which perhaps does not amount in words or by application to "the powers of a natural person." If so, the *ultra vires* doctrine continues to apply in Prince Edward Island. It would clearly apply in Nova Scotia and Newfoundland, which are memorandum jurisdictions. In addition, corporations incorporated by a special Act and not by general business corporations legislation will continue to be limited to the businesses specified by the incorporating statute. See *Alta. Mortgage & Housing Corp. v. Ciereszko*, [1986] 2 W.W.R. 57 (Alta.).

In spite of the fact that under pre-CBCA law a corporation might largely avoid the *ultra vires* rule, outside creditors still ran the risk that their debtor's objects were restricted. An example of how this might impose a cost upon them is provided by *Re Introductions Ltd.*, [1970] Ch. 199 (C.A.). The corporation was formed with an objects clause that in essence established as within the permissible scope of its business all aspects of the tourist trade in Great Britain. After the corporation had been inactive for some years, it re-emerged as a breeder of pigs, a business of limited appeal to tourists. To finance this latter business, the corporation borrowed from a bank in return for debentures secured by its assets. The pig breeding business was a failure, and in bankruptcy proceedings the corporation's liquidator disputed the validity of the debenture on the grounds of *ultra vires*. The bank pointed to one of the clauses in the corporation's list of objects, which was "to borrow money ... by the issue of debentures." The memorandum of association stated that each clause of the objects was to be construed independently and without reference to any of the others. Even so, the trial court held the debenture unenforceable, and the Court of Appeal affirmed. Harman L.J. held that no matter what the objects clauses said, a power could not be elevated into an object simply by calling it such. A power to borrow money had to be exercised in furtherance of some other corporate object. While conceding that, if the bank did not know what the purpose of the borrowing was it was under no duty to inquire, Harman L.J. held against the bank because it had actual knowledge that the purpose of the loan was to finance the pig breeding business.

The possibility that their contracts would not be enforced placed a greater burden of screening or information production upon creditors. Since they took the risk of non-compliance with an objects clause, they might have responded by verifying that the contract was in fact covered by the purposes clause. What this sometimes meant was a request for the following:

(1) a copy of the corporation's articles, certified by its secretary;
(2) a certified copy of its by-laws;
(3) a certified copy of the board (and if need be, shareholders) resolutions authorizing the transaction; and
(4) an opinion letter from counsel for the corporation.

While this reduced the risk of unenforceability, it also increased the cost of doing business, and if shareholders could monitor for non-compliance with an objects clause at less cost than creditors, a deadweight efficiency loss resulted. This loss was particularly evident in the case of large public corporations that carried on business in a wide variety of industries, for they could be expected to wish to avoid the doctrine. Even here, however, creditors would omit to screen for compliance at their peril.

Legislative Abolition. Because of these considerations, the *ultra vires* doctrine has been substantially abolished in Canada outside of the Maritime Provinces. The first step in legislative abolition is the *prima facie* conferral of the broadest possible capacity upon corporations. For example, CBCA s. 15 provides that "[a] corporation has the capacity and, subject to this Act, the rights, powers and privileges of a natural person." See also ABCA s. 15; BCCA s. 21; OBCA s. 15. However, shareholders in small corporations might sometimes want to restrict the authority of the majority of the board of directors, and for this reason CBCA s. 16(2) provides that "[a] corporation shall not carry on any business or exercise any power that it is restricted by its articles from carrying on or exercising." See also ABCA s. 16(2); BCCA ss. 22(1), (2); OBCA s. 17(3). But here the burden of monitoring for default is placed upon the shareholders, with CBCA s. 16(3) stating that "[n]o act of a corporation ... is invalid by reason only that the act ... is contrary to its articles or this Act." See also ABCA s. 16(3); BCCA s. 22(3); OBCA s. 17(2). While CBCA s. 16(3) appears to prevent the corporation and persons with whom it contracts from raising an *ultra vires* defence in a breach of contract action, nonetheless a shareholder, a creditor, the Director and other interested parties may sue to restrain the corporation and its officers and directors from engaging in activities beyond the scope of its articles (CBCA s. 247; ABCA s. 240; OBCA s. 253; see also BCCA s. 25).

While the Dickerson Report sought to abolish the *ultra vires* doctrine as a defence to contractual claims, the CBCA has not entirely achieved that end. CBCA s. 18, which appears to be directed principally to the problem of management authority discussed in the next subsection, provides that a corporation may not assert the non-compliance of its articles or by-laws against the person dealing with it "except where the person has or ought to have by virtue of his position with or relationship to the corporation knowledge to the contrary" (see also ABCA s. 18; OBCA s. 19; and see BCCA s. 141(2)). Suppose then that a corporation contracts with a third party to engage in a lawful activity but one prohibited by the corporation's articles. The third party, say the corporation's solicitor, ought to but does not in fact know that the activity is not one in which the corporation may engage. The third party performs; the corporation does not; the third party sues. May the corporation argue in defence that the contract is invalid, not "by reason only that the [contract] is contrary to its articles," but for the additional reason that such fact ought to have been known to the plaintiff? Suppose that the third party has actually been told of the restriction. Does s. 16(3) entitle him to ignore that warning? Does CBCA s. 16(3) add anything to the abolition of constructive notice in CBCA s. 17 [ABCA s. 17; BCCA s. 26; OBCA s. 18]?

Current legal practice in major business transactions is to ignore CBCA s. 15, and to require a clear demonstration that the corporation with which one deals is in fact authorized to carry out the transaction. In practice, this results in the same demand for certified copies of corporate documents and opinion letters as occurred prior to the CBCA. Of course, it was just to avoid such formalities that CBCA s. 15 was enacted, but it does not follow that the proviso to s. 18 is inefficient. In major business transactions third party monitoring for compliance with the articles may in fact be efficient, since the monitoring costs will amount to a very small fraction of the consideration. In addition, monitoring costs may be trivial, since the objects need no longer be stated in the articles. Instead, if restrictions are desired the firm is to provide them, with the presumption of full capacity in s. 15 replacing the former presumption of incapacity absent express authorization. It is then an easy matter to verify that the *ultra vires* trap does not arise when the restriction clause has simply been left blank.

Where it is desired to restrict the objects of a small corporation, amending the articles to take on a new line of business would require two-thirds shareholder ratification in the form of a s. 173 amendment to the articles by "special resolution." See CBCA s. 2(1); ABCA s. 1(1); OBCA s. 1(1); and under the BCCA a resolution in the memorandum altering restrictions on the business is possible per s. 245, which requires a three-quarters shareholder ratification per s. 1(1) "special resolution." It is now possible to achieve the same result (with the requirement of unanimity, if that is desired) by enshrining the restriction not in the articles but in a unanimous shareholder agreement. See Chapter Six. This would also avoid the need to pay the statutory fee on amending the articles.

2. Authority of Agents to Contract for the Corporation

Assuming that it is within the powers of the corporation to embark upon a given transaction, questions arise as to: (1) who within the corporation has the capacity to contract for it, and (2) whether any necessary pre-conditions, such as the securing of shareholder approval for a particular transaction, have been fulfilled. The first item (who can bind) is a matter of agency law as applied to corporations. As discussed in Chapter One, Section C, agency may be created either by the actual conferral of authority upon the agent by the principal (actual authority) or by representations made by the principal to a third party that give rise to a reasonable belief in the third party, upon which the third party acts, that another is the agent of the principal, so that it would be inequitable to allow the principal to deny the agency (agency by estoppel or "ostensible" authority). Corporate transactions always give rise to agency questions since a corporation can act only through human agents.

Actual Authority. The actual authority of an officer of a corporation may be determined by his contract of employment or by a formal board resolution. Apart from this, merely appointing a person to serve as an officer will clothe him with the actual authority to make the business decisions that a person in his position usually makes, unless that authority is expressly restricted in some way by the corporation. For example, the secretary of the corporation will be presumed to have the authority to certify corporate documents as being the documents of the corporation, while the treasurer or chief financial officer will ordinarily have the authority to sign certificates with respect to the financial affairs of the corporation. Neither of these officers nor a director will ordinarily have actual authority to make business decisions, though the president or chief executive officer will generally be deemed to be authorized to make a broad range of investment decisions in the ordinary course of the corporation's business.

The authority of a "managing director," as the corporation's chief executive officer was formerly called, was the subject of a decision of the Supreme Court of Canada in *Mid-West Collieries Ltd. v. McEwen*, [1925] S.C.R. 326. This was an action for wrongful dismissal brought by the corporation's former managing director. The corporation asserted that the dismissal was justified because the plaintiff had exceeded his authority by executing a mortgage of the corporation's assets in favour of a bank that had been threatening to close the corporation down unless the mortgage was granted. In deciding for the plaintiff, Rinfret J. stated:

What is to be determined is whether the directors in fact purported to clothe the respondent with the authority which he exercised. ...

Now there was no formal resolution defining the extent of the powers of the respondent. It was moved at a directors' meeting ... "that T.M. McEwen be appointed managing director."

... [T]he authority of a managing director may be implied from the power to delegate vested in the body by which he was appointed. By the 68th article of Table A of The Companies Ordinance, which was embodied in the appellant's articles of association, the directors could delegate any of their powers to "committees consisting of such member or members of their body" as they thought fit.

It would appear that by appointing McEwen as they did, the directors intended thereby to delegate their powers to him under this article, subject of course to such direction and control as it was their duty to exercise. ... Now, generally speaking, unless otherwise provided by the Act under which the company was incorporated, by the articles of association or by the by-laws and regulations, the directors possess authority to exercise all the powers of the company; and Art. 55 of Table A says so in explicit terms. Strong J., later Chief Justice, delivering the judgment of this court in *Bickford v. Grand Junction Railway Co.*, [1877] 1 Can. S.C.R. 696, said at p. 730: "No enabling power is requisite to confer the authority to mortgage, but *prima facie* every corporation must be taken to possess it;" and he cites abundant authority in support of his proposition.

This power is not limited to the object of securing a loan, in which case "the sanction of a resolution of the company must be previously given in general meeting" (Companies' Ordinance, c. 20, Ords. of N.W.T. 1901, s. 98); but it may be exercised for other purposes, such as securing a debt which is an outstanding valid liability of the company, and for that the confirmatory vote of the shareholders is not required.

· · ·

It follows that the directors could have executed the chattel mortgage here in question without the sanction of the shareholders. After the board had vested the respondent with full authority and control, the least that can be said is that the company cannot urge as a valid ground of dismissal the fact that he has executed this chattel mortgage securing a past due indebtedness to the bank. [*Id.* at 329-31]

Actual authority will also be found to exist where an officer, without formal permission, exceeds the authority that usually attaches to his position, but does so with the knowledge and acquiescence of the corporation. For example, in *Hely-Hutchison v. Brayhead Ltd.*, [1968] 1 Q.B. 549 (C.A.), the chairman of the board of directors of the defendant corporation entered into an agreement on its behalf to guarantee a debt by a related corporation. The chairman of the board is usually not the chief executive officer, but the defendant was nevertheless held bound to the contract, since the chairman had been in the habit of committing the corporation to contracts without the knowledge of its board, to which he would afterwards report the matter. The board had acquiesced over time in the chairman's mode of conducting himself as the chief executive officer who made the final decision on any matter concerning finance. Since the board was on notice of the chairman's "wrongful contracting," it was clearly the least cost risk avoider.

Defective Appointments. Where a properly appointed officer or director would have authority to bind the corporation in a particular matter, that authority remains intact even if there has been some irregularity in the appointment or election of the particular person (CBCA s.116; ABCA s. 111(1); BCCA s. 148; OBCA s. 128). This amounts to a deemed actual authority to bind the corporation in dealings with third parties. The validity of corporate acts will not be open to wholesale retroactive attack where it later turns out, for example, that the board of directors has been invalidly elected because insufficient notice was given of the shareholders meeting at which they were elected. See *Oliver v. Elliot* (1960), 23 D.L.R. (2d) 486 (Alta.).

Section 116 is not without limits. Factions within a corporation have sometimes fallen out, with two different boards, each claiming to be *the* validly elected board, acting on behalf of the corporation. Presumably in such a case s. 116 would not validate the actions of both boards. In addition, there are limits to the extent to which s. 116 can be used by one faction to usurp power from a second. In *Morris v. Kanssen*, [1946] A.C. 459, a corporation incorporated in 1939 started off with two equal shareholders, C and

K, who were also its directors. They had a quarrel and C determined to get rid of K. To this end, C enlisted the aid of S, who was appointed a director by virtue of a fictitious minute entered in the corporation's books. C and S acted as directors throughout 1940. No meeting of the corporation's shareholders was held in 1941 and, as a result, the directorships automatically became vacant by the terms of the corporation's articles at the end of that year (even assuming that S's appointment had been valid). Nonetheless, C and S continued to act as directors, and they purported in March 1945 to appoint M as an additional director. The "directors," C, S and M, then caused shares to be issued to M. At this point K sued for a declaration that neither S nor M were directors and that all share issuances after the first one to himself and C were invalid. The plaintiff prevailed. The allotment to M was held a nullity because in 1942 the corporation had no directors. Lord Simonds stated:

There is, as it appears to me, a vital distinction between (a) an appointment in which there is a defect ... and (b) no appointment at all. In the first case it is implied that some act is done which purports to be an appointment but is by reason of some defect inadequate for the purpose; in the second case there is no defect, there is no act at all. The section does not say that the acts of a person acting as a director shall be valid notwithstanding that it is afterwards discovered that he was not appointed a director. Even if it did, it might well be contended that at least a purported appointment was postulated. But it does not do so, and it would, I think, be doing violence to plain language to construe the section as covering a case in which there has been no genuine attempt to appoint at all. These observations apply equally where the term of office of a director has expired, but he nevertheless continues to act as a director, and where the office has been from the outset usurped without the colour of authority. [*Id.* at 471]

Ostensible Authority: The Indoor Management Rule. Where a defectively appointed director's actions are not validated by s. 116, they may yet bind the corporation under principles of ostensible authority. How a partnership may come to be bound through ostensible authority has already been noted in OPA ss. 6-9. See Chapter One, Section C. The leading case on ostensible authority incorporate law is *Royal British Bank v. Turquand* (1856), 6 E. & B. 327, 119 E.R. 886 (Excheq. Ct.), where the plaintiff bank sued to collect on a demand note executed under seal by the defendant corporation and signed by two of its directors. The defence was that the company's deed of settlement (memorandum of association) allowed the directors to borrow on behalf of the company "such sums as should from time to time be authorized by general resolution of the Company," and that there had been in fact no such general resolution authorizing the borrowing in question. The defence was rejected, the Court observing:

We may now take for granted that the dealings with these companies are not like dealings with other partnerships, and that the parties dealing with them are bound to read the statute and the deed of settlement. But they are not bound to do more. And the party here, on reading the deed of settlement, would find, not a prohibition from borrowing, but a permission to do so on certain conditions. Finding that the authority might be made complete by a resolution, he would have the right to infer the fact of a resolution authorizing that which on the face of the document appeared to be legitimately done. [119 E.R. at 888]

The holding in *Turquand* has come to be known as "the indoor management rule." While all corporate lawyers know about the existence of the rule, there is no unanimity on how to formulate it. A suggested version is as follows:

Where an outsider dealing with a corporation satisfies himself that the transaction is valid on its face to bind the corporation, he need not inquire as to whether all of the preconditions to validity that the corporation's internal law might call for have in fact been satisfied.*

The indoor management rule has been both codified and expanded in an important respect in the CBCA. Section 18 (ABCA s. 18; OBCA s. 19) provides that a corporation may not assert as against a person dealing with it that:

(a) the articles, by-laws and any unanimous shareholder agreement have not been complied with,

. . .

(d) a person held out by a corporation as a director, an officer or an agent ... has not been duly appointed or has no authority to exercise the powers ... that are customary in the business of the corporation or usual for such director, officer or agent, [or]

(e) a document issued by any director, officer or agent ... with actual or usual authority to issue the document is not valid or genuine ...except where the person has or ought to have by virtue of his position with or relationship to the corporation knowledge to the contrary.†

It will be recalled that in *Turquand* the third party was affixed with constructive notice of the statute and the corporation's deed of settlement. While it likely remains the case that third parties will be held to know the provisions of the incorporating statute since "every man is presumed to know the law," they are no longer obliged to read the corporation's articles or by-laws. CBCA s. 17 provides that no person is deemed "to have notice or knowledge of the contents of a corporate document by reason only that the document has been filed" publicly (see also ABCA s. 17; BCCA s. 26; OBCA s. 18). (Furthermore, the by-laws, as opposed to the articles of incorporation, are not publicly filed under the CBCA.) Therefore, an outsider dealing with a corporation through an officer need not be concerned with unusual restrictions on the officer's authority.

The efficiency goals served by the indoor management rule are described by Estey J. in the following passage from *Canadian Laboratories Supplies Ltd. v. Englehard Indus. of Canada Ltd.*, [19791 2 S.C.R. 787:

Modern commerce at practically all levels and sectors operates through the corporate vehicle. That vehicle itself, by conglomerate grouping and divisionalization, has become increasingly complex. Persons, including corporate persons, dealing with a corporation must for practical reasons be able to deal in the ordinary course of trade with personnel of that corporation secure in the knowledge that the law will match these practicalities with binding consequences. The law

---

*   See *Sheppard v. Bonanza Nickel Mining Co. of Sudbury* (1894), 25 O.R. 305, 310; Prentice, *The Indoor Management Rule*, in 1 Ziegel 309.

†   The phrase "to the contrary" is undoubtedly a drafting error and should read "to that effect."

has long so provided. Both corporate sides to a contractual transaction must be able to make secure arrangements at the lowest level at which adequate business controls can operate. It is in the interest of both corporate and natural persons engaged in business that this be so. One alternative would be to retain corporate trading authority in the inner core of management; another would be to conduct the daily business of the undertaking on a committee basis. Neither law nor commerce has apparently found a practical alternative to the delegation of the corporate authority to agents, its employees. In undertakings of all but the smallest proportions, division of authority according to function is as necessary as it is commonplace. The day of the proprietor and the one man operation has, for better or for worse, long departed from the main stage of business, and the corporate vehicle with attendant business structures has taken over much of the commerce of the country. The law has altered old rules and developed new ones to facilitate the conduct of trade on this larger scale. Obviously some employee must be placed in charge of buying, another of selling, another of financing, and another in charge of accounting, and so on, and each must have the authority necessary to deal responsibly with his counterpart in other trading and governmental organizations. [*Id.* at 817]

The indoor management rule as expanded and codified remains, however, one to protect outsiders. It will not avail a person who knows or who "ought by virtue of his position with or relationship to the corporation" to know either that the corporation's documents restrict the authority of a particular officer or that a necessary internal procedure has not been carried out. CBCA s. 18. Thus in *Anderson Lumber Co. v. Canadian Conifer Ltd.* (1977), 77 D.L.R. (3d) 126 (Alta. App. Div.), the plaintiff Anderson Lumber sued to collect on a debenture issued to it by the defendant Conifer. Conifer's articles of association empowered its board of directors to borrow for corporate purposes. Directors were to be given seven days' notice of board meetings, but the notice requirement could be waived upon the written consent of all of the directors. No notice was given for the meeting at which the decision to borrow from Anderson Lumber was taken, and the written consent of at least one of the Conifer directors was missing. The debenture was therefore invalid, and the plaintiff was held not to be entitled to rely on the indoor management rule because Mr. Anderson, its president, director and controlling shareholder, was also a Conifer director and had attended the Conifer board meeting that voted to issue the debenture. The knowledge of Mr. Anderson that the Conifer meeting had been improperly constituted was attributed to the corporate plaintiff.

Shareholder Ratification. Certain corporate transactions require ratification by the shareholders as a condition of their validity. These extraordinary transactions may be undertaken only with the approval of the shareholders by special resolution, meaning approval by two-thirds of the votes cast (three-quarters under the BCCA), rather than by ordinary resolution, meaning a majority of the votes cast. (One is tempted to use the expressions "two-thirds of the shareholders" and "majority of the shareholders," but this would be seriously inaccurate. Do you see why?) These transactions include: amendments to the articles (CBCA s. 173; ABCA s. 167; BCCA s. 243; OBCA s. 168), amalgamations (CBCA s. 183; ABCA s. 177; BCCA s. 272; OBCA s. 176) and sales of substantially all of the assets (CBCA s. 189(5); ABCA s. 183(5); BCCA s. 150;

OBCA s. 184(5)). In addition, amendments to the by-laws require shareholder approval by ordinary resolution, though changes to the by-laws proposed by the directors continue in effect until confirmed, amended or rejected by the shareholders (CBCA s. 103; ABCA s. 98; OBCA s. 116; provisions corresponding to the by-laws in the CBCA are in the articles under the BCCA and changes thus require a special resolution of shareholders).

CHAPTER FOUR

Capitalization of the Corporation

A. THE NATURE OF A SHARE

The previous chapter considered issues concerning the formation of the corporation. This chapter will examine questions concerning a corporation's capital structure. The capital structure that is most appropriate for a corporation depends on a wide range of factors, including the stage of a corporation's development, the sector in which it competes, its profitability and the extent to which it is dependent on the capital markets for ongoing financing. Inevitably, the corporation's capital structure will include shares. One of the more challenging questions that courts have had to confront is how best to characterize the relationship between the purchaser of a share and the corporation whose share he or she now owns.

In North America, a shareholder is frequently said to be an owner of the corporation. Indeed, a sizeable body of literature has emerged over the course of the twentieth century that is devoted to exploring changes to the nature of the relationship between the corporation and its "owners." Much of this literature focuses on a thesis that A.A. Berle, Jr. and G.C. Means advanced in *The Modern Corporation and Private Property* (1932). Berle and Means claimed that at the same time that corporations were emerging as the dominant form of business organization, shares were becoming more and more widely dispersed among an ever expanding pool of shareholders. They concluded that as a result these owners of the corporation were slowly but surely surrendering control of the corporation to its professional managers. The Berle and Means thesis has frequently been the focal point for discussion about the history and structure of corporate finance in North America, and will be considered further in Chapter Six.

In many ways, however, the debate that has grown up around the Berle and Means thesis begs a critical question: has it ever made sense to think of shareholders as the "owners" of the corporation? Any answer to this question depends in part on an understanding of the legal relationship that results from purchasing a share. The outcome of an analysis of this relationship will in turn have a significant impact on how one conceives of the corporation's relationship with other constituencies, constituencies that might also be thought to have an interest in the way in which the corporation is run.

Sparling v. Caisse de dépôt et placement
[1988] 2 S.C.R. 1015

[The judgment of the Court was delivered by:]

LA FOREST J.: The sole issue in this appeal is whether the Caisse de dépôt et place-ment du Québec, as an agent of the Crown in right of the Province of Québec, may invoke Crown immunity as provided in s. 16 of the Interpretation Act, R.S.C. 1970, c. I-23, and put itself outside the purview of the provisions of the Canada Business Corporations Act, S.C. 1974-75-76, c. 33, as amended, relating to the rights and obliga-tions of shareholders, and in particular of ss. 121 to 125 of that Act, the insider trading provisions.

Facts

The appellant is a corporation created by An Act respecting the Caisse de dépôt et placement du Québec, R.S.Q. 1977, c. C-2. Section 4 of that Act provides in part:

4. The Fund [the Caisse] shall be an agent of the Crown in right of Québec.
The moveable and immovable property belonging to the Fund shall be the property of the Crown in right of Québec.

The Caisse de dépôt et placement du Québec was created for the purpose of manag-ing and investing funds received by the government under various statutory programs such as the Quebec Pension Plan. It accordingly handles very substantial sums of public money.
At the time the present motion was brought, the Caisse and the Société générale de financement du Québec jointly owned or controlled 44.3 per cent of the outstanding shares of Domtar Inc. The Caisse itself owned or controlled over 22.7 per cent of the issued common shares of Domtar, a publicly traded company governed by and continued under the Canada Business Corporations Act.
Subsections 122(2) and (4) of the Canada Business Corporations Act provide:

122 ...
(2) A person who becomes an insider shall, within ten days after the end of the month in which he becomes an insider, send to the Director an insider report in the prescribed form.

. . .

(4) An insider whose interest in securities of a distributing corporation changes from that shown or required to be shown in the last insider report sent or required to be sent by him shall, within ten days after the end of the month in which such change takes place, send to the Director an insider report in the prescribed form.

It is common ground that the Caisse by virtue of its ownership of more than 10 per cent of the shares of Domtar became an insider of that corporation for the purposes of ss. 121 and 122 of the Canada Business Corporations Act. Nevertheless, the Caisse refused to submit to the Director an insider report in the prescribed form. The Caisse contends that by virtue of Crown immunity as provided in s. 16 of the Interpretation Act it is exempt from the application of subss. 122(2) and (4) of the Canada Business Corporations Act. Section 16 of the Interpretation Act reads as follows:

16. No enactment is binding on Her Majesty or affects Her Majesty or Her Majesty's rights or prerogatives in any manner, except only as therein mentioned or referred to.

In response to the refusal by the Caisse to file the insider report, the respondent Director filed a motion for declaratory judgment declaring that the appellant is bound by the provisions of the Canada Business Corporations Act relating to the rights and obligations of shareholders and that the appellant is required to produce the insider report according to the terms of the Canada Business Corporations Act.

• • •

Analysis

I am in agreement with Tyndale J.A. that the benefit/burden exception to Crown immunity exists and that it applies in this case to render the insider reporting provisions of the Canada Business Corporations Act applicable to the Caisse.

There can be no disputing the existence of the benefit/burden exception (sometimes referred to as the "waiver" exception) to Crown immunity. It is of ancient vintage; see *Crooke's Case* (1691), 1 Show, K.B. 208, at pp. 210-11, 89 E.R. 540, at p. 42, where it is said:

If they have any right, the King can only have it by this Act of Parliament, and then they must have it as this Act of Parliament gives it.

The exception has been applied by this Court as recently as *The Queen v. Board of Transport Commissioners*, [1968] S.C.R. 118, and *The Queen v. Murray*, supra; see also *Toronto Transportation Commission v. The King*, [1949] S.C.R. 510.

• • •

The only question to be decided here, then, is whether the exception extends to this case.

• • •

Counsel for the appellant appears to admit the existence of the benefit/burden exception, but argues that by purchasing shares in Domtar, the Caisse did not invoke a benefit provided by the statute, but rather did nothing more than exercise a right conferred upon it by its charter. The Caisse, it is contended, could have purchased the shares in the absence of the Canada Business Corporations Act. As a consequence, no statutory benefit was acquired to which the burdens imposed by the Canada Business Corporations Act correspond. Only by taking particular advantage of a specific provision of the Act could the Crown subject itself to burdens attendant upon that provision. Counsel did not further elaborate on this claim.

A question which immediately comes to mind is whether by taking advantage of one right conferred by the Act (e.g. voting the shares) the Crown would subject itself to all or only some of the other provisions of the Act. If only some, it is difficult to conceive how it could be determined which provisions would apply—indeed it is hard to see how most provisions, including those relating to insider reports, would ever apply to the Crown. If, on the other hand, all of the Act would apply upon the Crown taking affirmative advantage of one provision, then it is difficult to see why this result should not follow from the purchase of the shares alone. Upon purchasing the shares certain rights, e.g., the right to vote the shares and the right to receive dividends, accrue immediately to the purchaser. As will be discussed, the aggregate of these rights and their attendant obligations are indeed definitive of the notion of a share. With respect, I cannot see why some affirmative act with regard to one right acquired by the purchaser of a share changes the situation in any relevant way.

Counsel for the Attorney General of Alberta put the same point somewhat differently, contending that there is not a sufficient "nexus" between the right claimed and the burden assumed. It is quite correct to conclude that whenever the question of the application of the benefit/burden exception arises, the issue is not whether the benefit and burden arise under the same statute, but whether there exists a sufficient nexus between the benefit and burden. As McNairn, op. cit., at p. 11, puts it:

It is not essential ... that the benefit and the restriction upon it occur in one and the same statute for the notion of crown submission to operate. Rather, the crucial question is whether the two elements are sufficiently related so that the benefit must have been intended to be conditional upon compliance with the restriction.

It is also true that the Caisse, as agent for the Crown in right of the Province, is not seeking affirmatively to take advantage of a provision of a statute or of the common law. It simply purchased shares in a corporation which happened to be governed by a statute, the Canada Business Corporations Act. It brought no action at law and sought no other advantage.

To conclude from this, however, that the Crown is not bound by the obligations attendant upon the rights conferred by the statute requires that one presuppose a rather simplistic view of the nature of a share and its purchase. A share is not an isolated piece of property. It is rather, in the well-known phrase, a "bundle" of interrelated rights and liabilities. A share is not an entity independent of the statutory provisions that govern its possession and exchange. Those provisions make up its constituent elements. They define the very rights and liabilities that constitute the share's existence. The Canada Business Corporations Act defines and governs the rights to vote at shareholders' meetings, to receive dividends, to inspect the books and records of the company, and to receive a portion of the corporation's capital upon a winding up of the company, among many others. A "share" and thus a "shareholder" are concepts inseparable from the comprehensive bundle of rights and liabilities created by the Act. Nothing in the statute, common sense or the common law indicates that this bundle can be parcelled out piecemeal at the whim of the Crown. It cannot pick and choose between the provisions it likes and those it does not. To do so would be to permit it to define an entity which is the creature of federal legislation. What the Caisse obtained was an integral whole.

The very act of purchasing a share, then, is an implicit acceptance of the benefits of this statutory regime. These benefits are indissolubly intertwined with the restrictions attendant upon them.

Absent the statutory regime, the idea of a share as an object of commerce is meaningless. The relationship between benefit and restriction is sufficiently close that the Crown must be determined to have taken the law as it found it. The relationship between the benefits of share ownership and the obligations of insiders is particularly close. As Dickson J. (as he then was) stated in another context in *Multiple Access Ltd. v. McCutcheon*, [1982] 2 S.C.R. 161, at p. 179:

The proper relationship between a company and its insiders is central to the law of companies and, from the inception of companies, that relationship has been regulated by the legislation sanctioning the company's incorporation.

Hannan J. in the court of first instance distinguished this Court's decision in *Murray*, supra, on the ground that the Court there held, at p. 268, that "... this is not a case in which a provincial legislature has sought to "bind" the federal Crown, in the sense of imposing a liability upon it or of derogating from existing Crown prerogatives, privileges or rights." Hannan J. concluded that this quotation:

... clearly implies that had the provincial legislation been intended to "bind" the Crown, it might well have been inapplicable. In the present case, the application by analogy of the words of Martland J., would dictate that, as the [*Canada Business Corporations Act*] seeks to bind the agent of the Crown in right of Quebec, it is inapplicable to such agent.

With respect, in my view the analogy between *Murray* and this case works to the benefit of the respondent. The Canada Business Corporations Act like the Exchequer Court Act which was the subject of *Murray*, merely "established a relationship from which certain results might flow," to use the words of Martland J. in *Murray*. Just as in *Murray* the Crown was not bound by the prejudicial provisions of the law until it chose to take advantage of its beneficial aspects, here no right or prerogative of the Crown is affected by the Canada Business Corporations Act standing alone. It was only by seeking the benefits of the statute by purchasing shares that the Caisse chose to bring itself within the purview of the law relating to shareholders. In the words of Professor Hogg, op. cit., at p. 183, "when the Crown claims a statutory right the Crown must take it as the statute gives it, that is, subject to any restrictions upon it." Otherwise, the Crown would receive a "larger right than the statute actually conferred" (p. 183).

Application of the benefit/burden exception does not result in subsuming the Crown under any and every regulatory scheme that happens to govern a particular state of affairs. Although some earlier authorities (see, e.g., *Bank of Montreal v. Bay Bus Terminal (North Bay), Ltd.* (1971), 24 D.L.R. (3d) 13 (Ont. H.C.), at p. 20, aff'd (1972), 30 D.L.R. (3d) 24 (Ont. C.A.)) had been thought by some to support the view that the Crown was bound by any regulatory scheme of sufficient scope, this approach was rejected by Laskin C.J. in the *P.W.A.* case (p. 69). The exception is not of such broad reach. Its application depends not upon the existence or breadth of a statutory scheme regulating an area of commerce or other activity, but, as noted earlier, upon the relationship or nexus between the benefit sought to be taken from a statutory or regulatory provision and the burdens attendant upon that benefit. The focus is not on the source of the rights and obligations but on their content, their interrelationship. As McNairn, op. cit., puts it at pp. 11-12:

Reliance upon a statute may ... be for such a limited purpose that the crown ought not, as a result, to be taken to have assumed the attendant burdens. Such is the case when a statute is resorted to for a purely defensive reason, for example to give notice under a registration scheme of the existence of a crown claim. The use of a statute in this way may be distinguished from active reliance to secure positive rights, the assumption of the burdens of a statute being a possible consequence only of the latter circumstance.

Here, the interrelationship between the rights and obligations acquired by the purchaser of a share is so close both conceptually and historically that there can be no question of the application of the benefit/burden exception. Indeed, as earlier mentioned, a share is an integral whole. Thus, the Crown, when it purchases a share of a company to which the Act applies, is bound by the entirety of the Canada Business Corporations Act in so far as it defines and regulates the rights and obligations of shareholders.

Disposition

I would accordingly dismiss the appeal.

NOTES

At no point does the CBCA state that in purchasing a share a shareholder is acquiring a right of ownership with respect to the corporation. The CBCA simply tells us that a shareholder may be entitled to certain rights relating to such things as voting for directors, the receipt of dividends and the receipt of a portion of the corporation's capital if and when that corporation is wound up: see s. 24(3). Why then would Berle and Means suggest that when a person has purchased a share, that person becomes an owner of the corporation? Does La Forest J. suggest that the bundle of rights and obligations that is a share gives rise to a relationship that can be characterized as "ownership"? For different perspectives on whether it is appropriate to view shareholders as owners, see L. De Alessi, *Private Property and Dispersion of Ownership in Large Corporations*, 28 J. Fin. 839-51 (1973) and E.F. Fama, *Agency Problems and the Theory of the Firm*, 88 J. Pol. Econ. 288-306 (1980).

The thesis that La Forest J. advances regarding the nature of a share is not new. There are many cases in England and Canada that have analyzed the nature of a share. These cases have usually involved disputes concerning different classes of shares and their relative rights. The rights that have typically been at the heart of these disputes are the very ones that La Forest J. identifies as part of the bundle of rights that is a share: the right to dividends (*Oakbank Oil Company v. Crum*, [1883] 8 A.C. 65 (H.L.)), the right to a portion of the company's assets on a winding up of that company (*Birch v. Cropper*, [1889] 14 A.C. 525 (H.L.), *Scottish Insurance v. Wilsons*, [1949] A.C. 462 (H.L.) and *Re Canada Trust Company*, [1950] O.R. 245 (Ont. Weekly Ct.)), and the right to vote (*Re Bowater Canada Ltd.* (1987), 62 O.R. (2d) 752 (Ont. C.A.), reproduced below). These cases have also stressed that in order to determine the rights that make up a share, it is necessary to look to a company's articles since it is there that one will see the rights of a given class of shares spelt out. More recent case-law, such as the *Sparling* decision, has gone on to make clear that these rights are also addressed in applicable business corporations acts. As a result, in ascertaining a shareholder's rights it is essential to examine the interaction between the corporation's articles and the corporate finance sections of the applicable corporations statute.

Re Bowater Canada Ltd.
Ontario Court of Appeal
(1987), 62 O.R. (2d) 752

[The judgment of the court was delivered orally by]

HOULDEN J.A.: The appellant Bowater Canadian Limited ("Bowater") filed an application in weekly court before McRae J. challenging the voting provisions contained in the respondent R.L. Crain Inc.'s ("Crain") articles of incorporation. McRae J. held that the voting provisions offended the Canada Business Corporations Act, 1974-75-76 (Can.) c. 33 ("CBCA"), as amended, to the extent that the special common shares held by the respondent Craisec Ltd. ("Craisec") carry ten votes per share in the hands of Craisec, but only one vote per share in the hands of a potential transferee. However, having regard to the knowledge and intentions of the parties and in light of the general principles of contract, and corporate law, he held that the "step-down" provision of the special common shares was severable with the result that the special common shares carry ten votes irrespective of whether they are held by Craisec or by a transferee.

The following are the provisions of the articles of amalgamation dealing with the capital of Crain:

The Corporation is authorized to issue two million four hundred thousand (2,400,000) common shares and four hundred and seventy-one thousand (471,000) special common shares.

The special common shares carry and are subject to the following terms, conditions and restrictions:—

(1) The said special common shares shall carry and the holder thereof shall be entitled to ten (10) votes per share at all meetings of the shareholders of the Corporation so long as such special common shares shall be held by the person or corporation to whom such shares were issued originally by the Corporation. In the event any such special common shares cease to be held by the corporation to whom such shares were issued originally by the Corporation, then such special common shares shall carry and the holder thereof shall be entitled to one (1) vote only per share at all meetings of the shareholders of the Corporation.

(2) Such special common shares may at any time be converted, either in whole or in part, into common shares of the Corporation on the basis of one (1) common share for each special common share held. Following any such conversion as aforesaid, the special common shares so converted shall be cancelled and shall not be released. In the event any such special common shares are presented for conversion as aforesaid the Corporation shall take all such steps as may be necessary, including, if necessary, the obtaining of Articles of Amendment, to effect such conversion.

(3) In the event of the liquidation, dissolution or winding-up of the Corporation, whether voluntary or involuntary, or in the event of any other distribution of assets among the Sharehold-

ers for the purpose of winding-up its affairs, the holders of the common shares and the special common shares shall be equally entitled, share for share, to receive the remaining property of the Corporation.

It will be noted that on liquidation, dissolution or winding-up of the Corporation the holder of the special common shares share equally with the other shareholders. Furthermore, we were informed by counsel for Crain that all shareholders, regardless of class, share equally in the distribution of dividends.

On the argument of this appeal all counsel were agreed that although the step-down provision was created at a time when the Companies Act, R.S.C. 1952, c. 53, was in force, the appeal could be decided on the basis of the CBCA, this being the procedure followed by McRae J.

There is no doubt, as McRae J. pointed out, that Bowater was not misled by the voting provisions of the Crain shares. Mr. Thomson conceded that Bowater, when it purchased its shares, was fully cognizant of the restrictions and conditions attaching to the two classes of shares.

In his reasons for judgment, McRae J. held that although there was no express prohibition in the CBCA against a step-down provision, s. 24(4) of the Act should be interpreted in accordance with the general principles of corporation law with the result that the rights which are attached to a class of shares must be provided equally to all shares of that class, this interpretation being founded on the principle that rights, including votes, attach to the share and not to the shareholder. Subsections (8) and (4) of s. 24 of the CBCA, as amended by 1978-79 (Can.), c. 9, s. 9, provide:

24(3) Where a corporation has only one class of shares, the rights of the holders thereof are equal in all respects and include the rights
    (a) to vote at any meeting of shareholders of the corporation;
    (b) to receive any dividend declared by the corporation; and
    (c) to receive the remaining property of the corporation on dissolution.
(4) The articles may provide for more than one class of shares and, if they so provide,
    (a) the rights, privileges, restrictions and conditions attaching to the shares of each
class shall be set out therein; and
    (b) the rights set out in subsection (3) shall be attached to at least one class of shares
but all such rights are not required to be attached to one class.

Counsel for the appellant did not, of course, challenge McRae J.'s interpretation of s. 24(4). It was, however, challenged by counsel for the respondents; but, notwithstanding the able arguments that have been addressed to us, we are not persuaded that it is wrong. In our opinion if there was not equality of rights within a class of shareholders, there would be great opportunity for fraud, even though that is not a problem in this case. Section 24(5) of the Alberta Business Corporations Act, 1981 (Alta.), c. B-15, reflects what we take to be the applicable principle of corporate law, it provides:

24(5) Subject to section 27, if a corporation has more than one class of shares, the rights of the holders of the shares of any class are equal in all respects.

Mr. Garrow contended that even if the step-down provision violates the provision of the CBCA, it was saved by s. 181(7) of the Act which reads:

181(7) Subject to subsection 45(8), a share of a body corporate issued before the body corporate was continued under this Act is deemed to have been issued in compliance with this Act and with the provisions of the Articles of continuance irrespective of whether the share is fully paid and irrespective of any designation, rights, privileges, restrictions or conditions set out on or referred to in the certificate representing the share; and continuance under this section does not deprive a holder of any right or privilege that he claims under, or relieve him of any liability in respect of, an issued share.

With respect, we do not agree with Mr. Garrow's submission. We do not think that the subsection was intended to protect "rights, privileges, restrictions or conditions" that are unlawful. Having held that the step-down provision of the special common shares was invalid, McRae J. turned his attention to the issue of severability. After a careful review of the submissions of counsel, he concluded that the step-down provision was severable, with the result, as we have stated, that special common shares now carry ten votes each regardless of whether they are held by Craisec or a transferee. Again, we agree with this ruling. In this connection, we are particularly impressed with the minutes of a meeting of shareholders of Crain held January 19, 1959. This is the meeting which authorized the creation of the special common shares. The portion of the minutes dealing with the special common shares reads as follows:

On motion duly made by Mr. MacTavish and seconded by Mr. Plummer, it was resolved that the shareholders sanction, ratify and confirm By-law number 80 being a By-law sub-dividing the present 100,000 Common Shares into 400,000 Common shares, creating an additional 400,000 Common shares ranking pari passu in all respects with the existing Common shares as subdivided and creating 167,000 Special Common Shares which shall carry the right to ten votes per share, and authorizing an application to the Secretary of State of Canada for Supplementary Letters Patent confirming such changes.

It will be noted that no mention is made of the step-down provision, only that each special common share is to carry the right to ten votes per share.

When the special common shares were created, Crain was making a very advantageous purchase of a majority interest in a company known as Business Systems Limited ("BSL"). Under the purchase agreement the vendors were to receive either four common shares of Crain or $40 cash. At the time of the purchase Craisec had effective control of Crain. Craisec agreed to exchange 41,750 common shares of Crain for BSL common and Class "C" preferred shares in consideration for which it received 167,000 special common shares of Crain enabling it to maintain control of Crain.

The provisions for ten votes per share have now been in force for almost 30 years and, prior to this application, have not been questioned by shareholders, although the share capital of Crain has been rearranged on several occasions, the last being August, 1986.

Mr. Thomson contended that because the step-down provision was invalid, the whole of cl. 1 of the articles of amalgamation was also invalid so that the special common shares and the subordinate voting shares would all carry only one vote. We do not agree. Rather, as we have said, we agree with McRae J. that the step-down provision can be severed without affecting the validity of the provision for ten votes for each special common share. We believe that this accords with the intention of the parties at the time that the shares were created.

In the result, the appeal is dismissed with costs. The cross-appeals are also dismissed but in the circumstances without costs.

The decision in *Bowater* has been the source of some debate concerning the nature of the equality principles that apply to shareholders and/or to shares. In particular, the debate centres on whether *Bowater* stands for the broad proposition that all shareholders of a class must be treated equally or simply for the proposition that the rights that are constitutive of shares of a given class must be the same for all shares of that class. Is it possible to reach a definitive conclusion based on the decision in *Bowater*? Does La Forest J.'s analysis in *Sparling* assist in resolving the debate?

At first sight, the debate appears rather arcane. But in practice it has important implications for such matters as the law concerning mergers and acquisitions. If the correct proposition is the narrower one relating to the nature of a share, then a corporation may be able to effect changes to its capital structure in ways that discriminate between shareholders, provided that there is no discrimination between the rights that are constitutive of shares of a class. If, on the other hand, the correct proposition is the broader one relating to shareholders, then it will be that much harder for a corporation to treat its shareholders differently when pursuing a given objective. For an example of the implications of this debate, see the different views expressed in MacIntosh, *Poison Pills in Canada: A Reply to Dey and Yalden*, (1992) 17 Can. Bus. L.J. 323, 345; Yalden, *Controlling the Use and Abuse of Poison Pills in Canada: 347883 Alberta Ltd. v. Producers Pipelines Inc.*, 37 McGill L.J. 887, 897-903 (1992).

Regardless of the interpretation of *Bowater* that one favours, one's views on the broader question whether shareholders may be said to be owners of the corporation is likely to have some effect on the equality principle that one believes *should* govern relations between the corporation and its shareholders. If one thinks that shareholders are owners, then one may well feel that in addition to the bundle of rights that are constitutive of a share, shareholders are entitled to additional rights such as the right to equal treatment. If one is not inclined to view shareholders as owners, then one may be more open to the suggestion that in certain circumstances it may be necessary for a corporation to discriminate between its shareholders.

Atco v. Calgary Power Ltd.
[1982] 2 S.C.R. 557

[Atco and Calgary Power owned 58.1 per cent and 41 per cent, respectively, of the shares of Canadian Utilities, which in turn owned virtually all the shares of three Alberta public utilities, including Alberta Power. Atco offered to buy 50.1 per cent of the outstanding stock of Calgary Power. In an attempt to prevent the takeover bid, Calgary Power successfully applied to the Public Utilities Board of Alberta for an interim order restraining Atco from proceeding. Section 98 of The Public Utilities Board Act provided that where an owner of a public utility proposed to unite with the owner of any other public utility, the union was subject to the Board's consent. The Board, in making its interim order, found Atco to be an "owner of a public utility" for the purposes of the Act and therefore subject to its jurisdiction. The Court of Appeal upheld the Board's finding. In its appeal to the Supreme Court of Canada, Atco maintained that it was not an "owner of a public utility" and so not subject to the Board's jurisdiction.]

WILSON J. (dissenting): My colleague, Mr. Justice Estey, has set out in his reasons for judgment the context in which the issue before the Court on this appeal has arisen and it is not necessary to deal with it further. The issue is a very narrow one: does a parent company own the public utility of its subsidiary for purposes of The Public Utilities Board Act of Alberta?

[Section 2(i) of The Public Utilities Act reads as follows:

2(i) "owner of a public utility" means
a person owning, operating managing or controlling a public utility and whose business and operations are subject to the legislative authority of the Province, and the lessees, trustees, liquidators thereof or any receivers thereof appointed by any court, ...]

• • •

I agree with my colleague that the public utility as defined is the physical plant and associated service. I differ from him in my analysis of the definition of "owner of a public utility."

I do not believe that a parent company as a matter of law "owns" or "operates" or "manages" or "controls" the physical plant of its subsidiary. To so hold would be to completely ignore a well-settled and, I believe, quite fundamental principle of corporate law, namely, that shareholders have no proprietary interest in the assets of the company in which they hold shares. Their proprietary interest is in their shares only. It is submitted, however, on behalf of Calgary Power Ltd. (and the submission was successful before both the Public Utilities Board and the Alberta Court of Appeal) that a parent may "control" the assets of its subsidiary in fact if not in law and that *de facto* control of such assets brings the parent within the meaning of "owner of a public utility" as defined.

I think that in considering the merits of that submission it is necessary to distinguish between the word "control" as a term of art in a corporate law context and the word "control" in its ordinary dictionary meaning. As I understand the word "control" as a term of art in a corporate law context, it is not directed to control of the physical assets of the underlying company but to control of the company itself. This is the kind of *de facto* control Atco may have over the public utility company if its offer is accepted. *De facto* control in this sense may obviously be obtained in a number of ways. It may be obtained by a majority holding of shares but it may be obtained by considerably less than a majority holding if the shares are widely held. It may be obtained through voting rights not commensurate with shareholding at all or through the right to appoint and remove directors. But it seems to me that when we are talking about this kind of *de facto* control we are always talking of control over the company and not over its assets. The company itself continues to own, operate, manage and control its assets regardless of who owns or controls it. This, as I understand it, is the essence of the separate legal personality of the incorporated company recognized by the House of Lords in the celebrated case of *Salomon v. Salomon and Co.* [1897] A.C. 22. Since the *Salomon* case the complete separation of the company and its members has never been doubted. It is true that there are instances in which the legislature and the courts have allowed the corporate veil to be lifted but when the legislature has done this it has done it by express statutory provision, for example, by expressly providing that the members of a company may become personally liable for the company's debts if the company continues to do business at a time when the number of its members has fallen below a prescribed minimum. The courts have permitted the veil to be lifted if the corporate personality was being used as a cloak for fraud or improper conduct. The courts, however, have only construed statutes as permitting the corporate veil to be lifted if compelled to do so by the clear language of the legislation.

The question, it seems to me, boils down to this. Even supposing that the acceptance of the appellant's offer gives it *de facto* control over the public utility companies whose shares are the subject of the offer, does this give it control over the assets of those companies within the meaning of s. 2(1) of the Act? I do not think it does. I think the word "control" here is used in its ordinary dictionary meaning and means the person having the day to day control of the physical plant and its operations. This, in my view, means the public utility companies themselves. I am confirmed in this view by three things. The first is that the definition of owner includes lessees, trustees, liquidators and receivers and it seems to me that those are persons into whose hands the physical plant and its operation might fall. The second is that the obligations imposed on "owners" under the various sections of the statute are more appropriately discharged by persons having the day to day control of the physical plant and its operations, e.g. the filing of the required rates and schedules. But perhaps most important of all, I find it hard to believe that the legislature intended by inserting the word "controlling" in s. 2(1) to extend the definition of owner to shareholders and others controlling the company which owns the public utility plant and operation. I am persuaded that it is not necessary to give that meaning to the word "controlling" because its ordinary dictionary meaning is fully in accord with the other language of the section, particularly "operating" and "managing." I think the common denominator of the persons identified as owners within the definition is that they are in charge of the plant. They either operate it, manage or control it. They are, in other words, in the corporate context the operating companies or public utility companies themselves.

• • •

I may say that I do not view the task of the Court on this appeal as being to decide whether to give a narrow or a broad interpretation to the word "controlling" in s. 2(1), the narrow being allegedly the one which would exclude the appellant from being an owner and the broad being the one which would include it. In my opinion, the issue is whether the concept of control as a term of art should be injected into a definition which makes very good sense in its ordinary dictionary meaning. In other words, the question is whether the Court should find that the legislature intended, when it spoke of a person controlling the assets of a public utility company, to look through the public utility company itself to its shareholders and find that they controlled the assets. We are concerned with the intention of the legislature in using the word "controlling" in the context of the definition section. Does it simply mean "controlling" in an analogous sense to "operating" or "managing," i.e. exercising physical control over the plant or does it have this more sophisticated meaning of control through share ownership? That, it seems to me, is the issue before us and I think that in resolving it the Court must have regard to well-settled principles of corporate law. I would respectfully adopt the reasons of Mr. Justice Spence in *Her Majesty in Right of Alberta v. Canadian Transport Commission*, [1978] 1 S.C.R. 61, where he said at p. 82:

To give the interpretation to regulation 19 sought by the respondent would have very far reaching effect in corporate shareholding and dealing in corporate shares. PWA is a public company. Its shares, therefore, may be traded freely on the market whether or not its stock is listed. The shares in a very large number of air carriers are similarly traded. It would be impossible to determine whether any particular sale and purchase of shares in an air carrier would affect the control of that air carrier let alone the commercial air service which it operates. It is often said that one may control a company with very much less than a majority of the issued stock and a shareholder who held X thousand shares of a particular air carrier could not possibly determine whether he would control the company were he to purchase an additional thousand shares or even an additional one share. It surely was not intended by this regulation that every transfer of shares in a public company which was an air carrier should be subject to the submission to the respondent of an application for approval before the share transaction should be consummated.

After quoting the above passage from the judgment of Spence J., Mr. Justice Clement, in giving the unanimous judgment of the Alberta Court of Appeal, said this:

With respect, I do not think it useful to draw a distinction as to the means by which shareholder control of a public utility is gained. We start with the premise that a person (whether a company or not) has in fact gained shareholder control or is on a proclaimed course that, upon completion, will have that end result.

In my view, this comment discloses that the Court of Appeal failed to distinguish between *de facto* control of the company and *de facto* control of the company's assets, the latter being the real concern on the appeal before it, and on this appeal. The appellant may well on the acceptance of its offer obtain *de facto* control of the public utility companies. Indeed, this was the finding of fact made by the Board. It said:

For the purpose of this Decision, the Board finds as a fact that Atco is "managing and controlling" CUI and its subsidiaries and therefore is an owner of a public/gas utility.

The Board may be perfectly correct in its finding that the share transaction if consummated will give Atco *de facto* control of Canadian Utilities and its subsidiaries but, with respect, its conclusion does not follow and its conclusion is the issue before us. Will Atco by acquiring *de facto* control of Canadian Utilities and its subsidiaries acquire *de facto* control of the assets of Canadian Utilities and its subsidiaries?

It seems to me that if the legislature had intended to cover control through share ownership, voting rights or powers to appoint and remove directors, it would not have done it in such an enigmatic fashion. I prefer to assume rather than the legislature was well aware of the basic principle of corporate law referred to earlier in these reasons, namely, that shareholders do not own or control the assets of the companies in which they hold shares. If this is a proper assumption and legislature had intended to extend the reach of the Act to dealings in the shares of public utility companies, then I believe it would have done so in explicit terms. It would have been very easy for the legislature to prohibit dealings in the shares of company-owned public utilities without the prior approval of the Board. Indeed, it has expressly done so in the case of Alberta companies in s. 88 of the Act which in itself strongly suggests a "hands off" approach to companies incorporated elsewhere. Section 88 would, of course, be quite superfluous if all parent companies were caught through the combined effect of the definition section and s. 98.

In view of the conclusion I have reached that the appellants are not owners within the meaning of the definition section, it is unnecessary for me to consider whether the proposed transaction would result in a "union" within the meaning of s. 98.

NOTES

Wilson J. suggests that one can meaningfully talk about a corporation owning its assets. She is clearly a good deal less convinced that it makes sense to talk about the shareholders of that corporation owning the corporation's assets. While Wilson J. dissented in *Atco*, the majority did not disagree with her objection to the notion that a holding company can be said to own its subsidiary's assets (the majority finding instead that Atco could be said to control those assets). If the shareholders do not own the corporation's assets, can they nonetheless be said to own the corporation? Does Wilson J. provide us with a clear answer?

The question whether shareholders may be said to own the corporation is important. As noted in connection with the *Bowater* case, if one concludes that ownership is a concept with a role to play in describing the relationship between shareholder and corporation, then one is more likely to think that some of the entitlements that we typically associate with ownership are also relevant to understanding this relationship. If, on the other hand, shareholders cannot be said to own the corporation, one may be inclined to distinguish between the rights and obligations that are constitutive of a share and any other rights that are typically said to belong to owners.

The debate is also important in assessing the relative rights and entitlements that belong to shareholders and to other constituencies that might be thought to have some interest in the way in which the corporation is managed.

Dickerson Committee, Proposals for a New Business Corporations Law for Canada, Vol. I
(1971)

Creditors, employees and others as directors

31. Suggestions have been made from time to time that corporation law focuses too narrowly on shareholders and ignores the reality that others, especially the corporation's

employees and creditors, are affected by and concerned with what corporations do. It follows from this, so the argument goes, that these groups should have some voice in the choice of corporate directors. Moreover, it is said, there is a broad public interest in corporations, and this interest should also be represented in corporate boardrooms.

32. We are not disposed to quarrel here with the validity of the premise on which this argument is based, but we do not see any practical way, in the context of a corporations act, in which it can be implemented. The problem is one of establishing the electorate. How does one provide the machinery for giving notice of meetings to those who do not have a crystallized and identifiable interest in the corporation? How can votes be allocated fairly amongst those who do not have the kind of precise rights given by a share, and how could such voting rights be equitably balanced with those of the shareholders?

33. The Draft Act does not prohibit a corporation from making arrangements with its creditors, employees or others under which directors representing those groups could be elected. The influence of such outside groups would have to be brought upon the shareholders, however, for it is only the shareholders who can cast the necessary votes. It is inconceivable, for example, that if a major creditor demanded representation on a corporation's board of directors, he would not be accommodated, because, presumably, he would not extend credit unless the shareholders did accede to his wishes. In fact, such representation by creditors is not uncommon today. Management has no difficulty making the point known to the shareholders; in practice, of course, management usually controls sufficient proxies to guarantee the election of the creditor's representative anyway. There is no requirement in the Draft Act that directors hold qualifying shares, therefore this cannot be a barrier.

34. Similarly, with employees, representation on the board could be bargained for in the collective agreement if the employees thought the matter important. In fact, trade unions have not shown much interest in having representation on the boards of corporations, but this could change. It is extremely unlikely that such a provision in a collective agreement would not be honoured when the shareholders' votes were cast as, otherwise, the collective agreement would be broken.

35. The public interest must be reflected through government. It is highly unlikely that governments would ever be interested in having representation on the boards of more than a few highly important or significant corporations. If government policy develops in this direction there should be little practical difficulty in implementing it, but through special legislation, not in a general corporations Act.

NOTES

Which of the arguments, if any, set out in paragraphs 32 to 35 of the Dickerson Committee's Report provide convincing reasons for treating constituencies other than shareholders differently from shareholders? Should the rights of groups like creditors or employees be seen as qualitatively different from the rights that business corporations acts provide to shareholders? Bearing in mind that in some countries (e.g. Germany) the law requires worker representation on many companies' boards of directors and provides a mechanism whereby workers may elect those representatives, how convincing is the Dickerson Committee's suggestion that it is too complicated to require that constituencies of this kind be represented on the board of directors?

The extent to which one finds the Dickerson Committee's analysis convincing is likely to depend in part on where one stands on the ownership debate discussed earlier in this section. If one views shareholders as owners and other constituencies as having a qualitatively different relationship with the corporation, then there may be a convincing case to be made for the Dickerson Committee's analysis. If one is not convinced that the rights that shareholders have are qualitatively different from those of other constituencies that have relationships with the corporation, then one may be more inclined to criticize the merits of the Dickerson Committee's analysis. The question concerning the proper characterization of the relationship between the holder of a share and the corporation is therefore central to the broader debate concerning stakeholder theory discussed in Chapters One and Six. As you review the rest of this chapter, consider how you would characterize the relationship between shareholder and corporation.

B. FORMALITIES OF CAPITALIZATION

1. Authorized and Issued Capital

On the organization of a corporation, several decisions must be made about its capital structure. How many shares will be issued, and for what consideration? Will the corporation have only one kind of shares, or will different classes with different rights and preferences be created? Lastly, should management of the corporation be restricted in the number of shares it may issue?

The last question was answered prior to the CBCA by determining what the corporation's "authorized" capital would be. The authorized capital, which had to be stated in the corporation's articles, memorandum or letters patent (as is still the case under corporations statutes not based on the CBCA), indicated how many shares the corporation was authorized to issue. By contrast, the "issued" or "outstanding" capital referred to the shares actually issued. Decisions on when and how many shares would be issued were made by the directors under provisions similar to CBCA s. 25(1). They could therefore issue shares to the ceiling provided by the authorized capital without seeking the approval of the shareholders. But beyond that they could not issue shares without amending the corporation's constitution to increase the authorized capital. This required a special resolution approved by two-thirds of the votes at a shareholders' meeting.

The principal function of authorized capital was therefore to restrict the directors' discretion to issue shares. While it is not necessary to place an upward limit on the number of shares that the directors of a CBCA corporation can issue, it is still possible to enshrine such restrictions in the articles under s. 6(1)(c). Of course, in some cases it makes little sense to limit that discretion. Thus the authorized capital of many publicly held corporations was often far higher than the number of shares the directors would be likely to want to issue for a long time to come. Under CBCA s. 6(1)(c), the articles of such corporations would simply omit to list any maximum number of shares that the corporation is authorized to issue. However, a substantial minority shareholder in a widely held corporation may desire such a restriction to ensure that his interest in the corporation is not diluted by a further public issue of shares. For this reason, many financial institutions prefer such restrictions in the articles of corporations in which they invest. In small issuers, minority shareholders may also be unwilling to leave decisions on issuing shares solely to the directors, and may insist on restrictions on issued capital. By itself, this may be a relatively inefficient method of preventing abuses and shareholders in small issuers might well be advised to seek further protection through pre-emptive rights or a shareholders' agreement, topics discussed below in Section C and Chapter Six, respectively.

2. Common and Preferred Shares

On incorporation, a decision must also be made as to how many classes of shares may be issued, since such classes must be stated in the articles. See CBCA s. 6(1)(c). Frequently, small issuers have only one class of shares, although further classes may be created for tax-inspired or other motives. If two or more classes of shares are created, one class is often designated as "common shares," while the other classes are described as "preferred shares." Preferred shares bear special rights or restrictions with respect to such matters as voting rights, dividends and distributions on liquidation. By contrast, common shares are generally free of all preferences or conditions. Some corporations statutes formerly required at least one class of common shares. However, there are no such restrictions in the CBCA, where the capital may consist solely of "Class A Common" and "Class B Common" shares, both with special rights.

Preferred shares are often referred to as senior securities, and the special rights of holders of such securities are discussed in Chapter Nine, Section C. Such preferences may include a right to be paid dividends before the common shares. Preferred shares may also be made redeemable by the corporation, which can then require the shareholders to surrender them back to the corporation for a particular price. The preferred shares may also be made retractable, in which case the decision to return them to the corporation for cash is made by the shareholder.

Preferred shares do not always put their holders in a preferred position. Thus non-voting shares may be referred to as preferred shares since they are subject to special conditions, unlike common shares.

The rights attached to preferred shares must be stated in the articles under CBCA s. 6(1)(c)(i). If the directors wish thereafter to issue a class of shares not provided for in the articles, they must cause the articles to be amended. However, directors may determine the special rights attaching to preferred shares if the shares may be issued in series under s. 6(1)(c)(ii). The rights and restrictions may then be left unspecified until the shares are issued, when the needs of the corporation and the investors may more easily be determined. When the directors fix the special rights and issue the shares, articles of amendment must be prepared under CBCA s. 27(4). Note that s. 27(3) prohibits the issue of any such series of shares with rights to a payment of dividends or a return of capital that are prior to the rights of any other outstanding shares of the same class.

One must be careful not to suggest that the various needs of participants in a small issuer may easily be met by an artful juggling of preferences attached to shares. If the shareholders will also be officers and employees of the corporation, they will be equally interested in their remuneration and the security of their tenure. Indeed, so far as they are concerned, it matters little whether the corporation returns money to them as wages or as dividends, except insofar as this affects tax liability. The question of employment remuneration and tenure will frequently be dealt with in a shareholders' agreement.

3. Subscriptions for Shares

A subscription agreement is a contract in which a corporation undertakes to issue shares to subscribers. Subscription agreements were at one time a rich source of litigation, but today such cases are rare. One reason for this is the abolition of partly paid shares in modern corporations statutes. Prior to provisions such as CBCA s. 25(3), shares could be issued on credit with only part of the purchase price paid. The balance was due on a "call" by the corporation. On bankruptcy, the trustee would require subscribers to pay the unpaid purchase price for the benefit of creditors. This raised the question of whether a binding subscription agreement had been created through the corporation's acceptance of the subscription offer.

These difficulties were particularly acute in pre-incorporation subscriptions. Where the articles, memoranda or letters patent required the incorporators to subscribe for shares, they could not withdraw thereafter. *Buff Pressed Brick Co. v. Ford* (1915), 33 O.L.R. 264, 23 D.L.R. 718 (App. Div.). Apart from this, subscriptions prior to incorporation suffered from the same defects as pre-incorporation contracts generally. See Chapter Two, Section C. When the corporation was formed, it was not bound by prior contracts and could decide not to issue the shares to subscribers. For their part, the subscribers were entitled to withdraw prior to acceptance by the issuer. *Re Canadian Tractor Co. (Clarke's case)* (1914), 7 W.W.R. 562 (Sask. S.C.). Indeed, under *Kelner v. Baxter* a corporation could not ratify a pre-incorporation subscription. However, Canadian courts resisted the orthodox view of pre-incorporation contracts in these cases when the issuer was in bankruptcy and where the subscriber had held himself out as a shareholder after incorporation. Subscribers were then held liable for the unpaid purchase price to their shares on three separate theories. First, the pre-incorporation subscription was interpreted as a continuing offer that the corporation could accept after incorporation. Second, the subscriber's conduct after incorporation was found to constitute a new offer that the corporation might accept. Finally, the subscriber was held to be estopped by his conduct from denying his liability on the call by the trustee in bankruptcy.

All three theories were discussed in *Re Canadian Tractor Co. (Svaigher's case)* (1914), 7 W.W.R. 562 (Sask. S.C.). Svaigher had signed a subscription list on October 1, 1912, but the company was only incorporated two days later. The company's liquidator sought to add Svaigher's name to the list of contributories. Park M. stated that:

The subscriber in his examination for discovery, admits his signature to the subscription list, admits having received from time to time notices of shareholder's meetings, and admits paying the first call on his stock, amounting to $250, being 25% of his subscription for ten shares. He also admits in his examination that he understood all along that he was a shareholder in the company. Under these circumstances, I do not see how the subscriber can now set up that there was no binding contract between himself and the company. It makes, in my opinion, no difference that the company undertook to allot stock at the meeting on October 1st, before its incorporation. The fact remains that it was incorporated on October 3, 1912, that the subscriber never repudiated or withdrew his offer before that time, and subsequently paid money on account of his stock. It is true that if he had repudiated the offer at any time prior to the legal acceptance of the same on the part of the company, there would be no binding contract. In *Re London Speaker Printing Co., Pearce's case,* 16 O.A.R. 508, at p. 512, an offer made to a company not in existence is, it is true, "merely waste paper," as between the subscriber and the company (per Osler J. at p. 517). But the same learned judge goes on to say on the same page:

> I have said that the alleged agreement cannot by itself and without more constitute an application for I have no doubt that an application for shares may be prepared and signed previous to the formation of a company and entrusted to a promoter or broker or other persons interested in the company to be made use of or acted upon afterwards.

That, I think, is what happened in this case. The subscribers in question signed the form and handed the same to the promoters for no other purpose, it seems to me, but to be used as applications for shares after the formation of the company. Moreover, I think, the payment of the money on account of the stock by the subscriber after the formation of the company constitutes a renewal of the offer to purchase shares, and the acceptance of the money by the company constituted an acceptance of the application on its part. Test the matter in this way: If the company had turned out to be prosperous, could the applicant have insisted upon being registered as a shareholder and upon delivery of the stock to him? To my mind, there is no doubt about the matter. ... This subscriber should therefore be added to the list of contributories. [*Id.* at 564-65]

A pre-incorporation subscription will now be governed by CBCA s. 14, and the corporation will be able to ratify the contract. Until then, the subscriber will undoubtedly not be held to be under any duty to the corporation. Would he however be liable to the other signatories to the agreement under s. 14?

C. CONSIDERATION ON AN ISSUE OF SHARES

1. The Need for Consideration

CBCA s. 25(1) states that "shares may be issued ... for such consideration as the directors may determine," and similar provisions may be found in all other corporations statutes in Canada. "Bonus stock," or shares issued for no consideration whatever, is not expressly prohibited, but these provisions have been interpreted to require a consideration.

Few promoters were so bold as to issue shares without any stated consideration. Instead, problems of bonus stock arose when the consideration was entirely fictitious. In such cases, the allotments were uniformly set aside. *Re Eddystone Marine Insurance Co.,* [1893] 3 Ch. 9 (C.A.); *Re McGill Chair Co.* (1912), 26 O.L.R. 254; *Re Dorenwends Ltd.* (1924), 55 O.L.R. 413, 418-19 per Fisher J. (App. Div.); *Compagnie d'Immeubles v. St-Amour* (1920), 59 C.S. 391.

2. Discount Stock

Ooregum Gold Mining Co. v. Roper
House of Lords
[1892] A.C. 125

[The following statement of facts is taken from judgment of Lord Herschell.]

The Ooregum Gold Mining Company, Limited, was incorporated in October 1880 under the Joint Stock Companies Acts 1862 to 1880. The statement contained in the memorandum of association with reference to the capital of the company was as follows: "The capital of the company is £125,000 divided into 125,000 shares of £1 each, and the shares of which the original or increased capital may consist may be divided into different classes and issued with such preference, privilege, guarantee, or condition as the company may direct." Forty thousand of the shares were allotted to the vendors to the company, the residue were issued to the public, and the full amount paid thereon. The operations of the company were not, in the first instance, successful, and a winding-up order was obtained. An application was subsequently made to the Court for an order to stay the winding-up, with a view to the introduction of fresh capital and a resumption of mining operations, and an order was made accordingly. In pursuance of this policy an extraordinary general meeting of the company was summoned in 1885, at which it was resolved that the capital should be increased by the issue of 120,000 preference shares of £1 each, to be credited in the capital and books of the company as having the sum of 15s. per share paid thereon, such preference shares carrying the right to a non-cumulative preference dividend up to 10 per cent on the nominal amount of such preference capital out of the profits of the undertaking each year, and to equal participation (share per share) with the ordinary shares in such further profits as should remain for distribution each year after the payment of the above 10 per cent preference dividend. The special resolution so passed was duly confirmed. At this time the market value of the ordinary shares was only 2s. 6d. per share.

Upwards of 100,000 of these preference shares were allotted, with 15s. credited as paid thereon. Prior to the actual allotment an agreement was entered into between the company, of the one part, and an agent or trustee for the several persons whose names were entered in the schedule thereto, of the other part, whereby, after reciting the agreement to issue the shares at a discount of 15s. per share, and that 1s. had been paid on allotment, it was agreed that the shares to be allotted should be held as shares on which 16s. per share had been paid, and should be subject and liable to further payment of 4s. per share, and no more, and the company thereby undertook to cause the agreement to be registered at the Joint Stock Registration Office, pursuant to the Companies Act 1867, before the issue of the shares. The agreement was duly filed accordingly. The capital raised by means of the issue of the preference shares sufficed to discharge the obligations of the company, to extricate it from its difficulties, and to give it a new start. Gold to a considerable amount was shortly afterwards raised from the mines, and the company has since been prosperous, the market value of the ordinary shares having risen to about 40s.

In February 1889 the Respondent, George Roper, purchased on the Stock Exchange and paid for ten fully paid-up ordinary shares in the company. On the 15th of July following on behalf of himself and the other ordinary shareholders Roper brought this action against the company and Wallroth (as an original allottee of the preference shares and as representing the other original allottees) to have it declared that the issue by the company of the 120,000 preferred shares, at a discount of 15s. per share, was ultra vires, and to have the register rectified accordingly and other consequent relief granted. The statement of claim contained the allegation that the company had in 1889 issued debentures to the amount of £20,000, which were charged on all the property of the company, and which were then outstanding. It further alleged as follows: "The defendant company had no power to issue the said preferred shares at a discount, and the entry of the preferred shares in the register book as fully paid-up should be rectified. The said preferred shares are now quoted on the Stock Exchange at a premium, and if the said entry is rectified the ordinary shares will benefit thereby, and the 15s. unpaid on the preferred shares will be available for paying off the said debentures as and when they fall due."

North J. upon the authority of *In re Almada and Tirito Company* [38 Ch. D. 415] without argument made an order declaring that the issue of the preferred shares of £1 each at a discount of 15s. per share was beyond the powers of the company, and that the said shares so far as the same were held by Wallroth or by original allottees represented by him were held subject to the liability of the holders to pay to the company in cash so much of the £1 per share as had not been paid on the same; and ordering that the company do rectify the register in accordance with the above declaration. This order was affirmed by the Court of Appeal without argument. Against these orders appeals were brought by the company and by Wallroth.

[Counsel for the company and for Wallroth argued that:

These consolidated appeals raise the same question, viz. whether a limited company registered under the Companies Acts of 1862 and 1867 can issue shares as fully paid up upon which a less sum than the nominal value has been paid. ... There is no question in the present case as to the bona fides of the transaction, and the issue was sanctioned both by the memorandum of association and the articles. ... The only dispute is as to the issue being prohibited by the Companies Acts. This company was in difficulties: money was wanted; unless a large sum could be raised the undertaking must fail and the company be wound up. No other means of raising money were available except the issue of shares at a discount so as to place the new holders on the same footing as the old. A commercial company may do in the furtherance of its legitimate objects anything which is not prohibited, and there is no intrinsic impropriety in such a transaction as the present, either under the general law of partnership or under Companies Acts. ...]

LORD HALSBURY L.C.: My Lords, the question in this case has been more or less in debate since 1883, when Chitty J. decided that a company limited by shares was not prohibited by law from issuing its shares at a discount. That decision was overruled, though in a different case, by the Court of Appeal in 1888, and it has now come to your Lordships for final determination.

My Lords, the whole structure of a limited company owes its existence to the Act of Parliament, and it is to the Act of Parliament one must refer to see what are its powers, and within what limits it is free to act. Now, confining myself for the moment to the Act of 1862, it makes one of the conditions of the limitation of liability that the memorandum of association shall contain the amount of capital with which the company proposes to be registered, divided into shares of a *certain fixed amount*. It seems to me that the system thus created by which the shareholder's liability is to be limited by the amount unpaid upon his shares, renders it impossible for the company to depart from that requirement, and by any expedient to arrange with their shareholders that they shall not be liable for the amount unpaid on the shares, although the amount of those shares has been, in accordance with the Act of Parliament, fixed at a certain sum of money. It is manifest that if the company could do so the provision in question would operate nothing.

I observe in the argument it has been sought to draw a distinction between the nominal capital and the capital which is assumed to be the real capital. I can find no authority for such a distinction. The capital is fixed and certain, and every creditor of the company is entitled to look to that capital as his security.

It may be that such limitations on the power of a company to manage its own affairs may occasionally be inconvenient, and prevent its obtaining money for the purposes of its trading on terms so favourable as it could do if it were more free to act. But, speaking for myself, I recognise the wisdom of enforcing on a company the disclosure of what its real capital is, and not permitting a statement of its affairs to be such as may mislead and deceive those who are either about to become its shareholders or about to give it credit.

I think, with Fry L.J. in the *Almada and Tirito Company's Case* [38 Ch. D. 415], that the question which your Lordships have to solve is one which may be answered by reference to an inquiry: What is the nature of an agreement to take a share in a limited company? and that that question may be answered by saying, that it is an agreement to become liable to pay to the company the amount for which the share has been created. That agreement is one which the company itself has no authority to alter or qualify, and I am therefore of opinion that, treating the question as unaffected by the Act of 1867, the company were prohibited by law, upon the principle laid down in *Ashbury Company v. Riche* [L.R. 7 H.L. 653], from doing that which is compendiously described as issuing shares at a discount.

[The concurring judgments of Lords WATSON, HERSCHELL, MACNAGHTEN and MORRIS are omitted.]

Appeal dismissed with costs.

Discount Stock. When *Ooregum* was decided, corporate statutes in England and North America required that a par value be given to each share. The articles, memoranda or letters patent provided for authorized shares of a stated amount or par value. This was an arbitrary figure and shares could be issued for more than par. The issuer would then add the par value of each allotted share to the stated capital account on the equity side of the balance sheet. The premium over par was added to a separate contributed surplus account, under equity. Thus a $5 par value share could be issued for $15, with $5 added to stated capital and $10 to contributed surplus. However, shares could not be issued for a consideration less than par, at a discount below par.

The judicial hostility to discount stock was nowhere so evident as in *North-West Electric Co. v. Walsh* (1898), 29 S.C.R. 33, rev'g., 11 Man. L.R. 629 (Q.B.). The plaintiff corporation had issued 160 $100 par shares for $20 each to the wife of one of its promoters, who was also its managing-director. However, the corporation was seemingly near insolvency and the shares were apparently worth no more than their issue price. The Manitoba Court distinguished the *Ooregum* decision in two ways. First, the Manitoba statute was a letters patent one and it was not clear that the *ultra vires* rule applied in the same way to such companies, if it applied at all. Moreover, the Manitoba Joint Stock Companies Act, R.S.M. 1891, c. 25 appeared expressly to permit discount stock. Section 30(b) stated that directors could not issue shares at a greater discount or less premium than that authorized by the shareholders. The Supreme Court held the issue of shares to be *ultra vires* and illegal, though the interpretation given to s. 30(b) is not easy to explain.

Corporations like the Ooregum Gold Mining Co., whose shares traded at less than par, found the prohibition of discount stock inconvenient when they sought to issue new shares. They could of course have amended the articles to create a new class of low par shares. Thus, instead of issuing at a 75% discount £1 shares with a 10% dividend (2s.), the Ooregum company might have issued at face value 5s. shares with a 40% dividend (2s.), or £1 shares promising 8s.

In the United States, a corporation was permitted in these circumstances to issue discount stock. In *Handley v. Stutz*, 139 U.S. 417 (1891), the Clifton Coal Co. required money to expand. The corporation's initial attempt to issue bonds failed and shares were therefore added as a "sweetener." Eventually, the corporation received $45,000 for an issue of $45,000 of bonds and an equal face value of shares. The Supreme Court upheld the allotment. The transaction was fair and the parties were in good faith. The Court stated that "[t]o say that a corporation may not, under the circumstances above indicated, put its stock upon the market and sell it to the highest bidder, is practically to declare that a corporation can never increase its capital by a sale of shares, if the original stock has fallen below par" (139 U.S. at 43).

Is there any reason why an issue of shares deserves closer scrutiny than other transactions a corporation may enter into, such as an issue of debt securities? In *Mosely v. Koffyfontein Mines Ltd.*, [1904] 2 Ch. 108, the defendant company sought an injection of capital at a time when its shares were trading at three-eighths to half of their par value. The company issued new debentures at a 20% discount, convertible immediately at their face amount to par value shares of a like amount, and it was argued that this was in effect an issue of discount stock. Buckley J. upheld the allotment. Even if the debentures were converted immediately, the shares would be issued not for cash but for property. The prohibition against discount stock would not apply in such cases and the transaction would not be impeached whatever the true value of the property. The Court of Appeal reversed this decision, holding that the issue of debentures was invalid since it might result in shares being issued at a discount. Because the debentures were convertible immediately into shares, there was "an obvious money measure" between the consideration received and the par value of the shares. In such circumstances, it was not sufficient that the bargain was made in good faith and that the shares were not in fact worth their par value. It appears that, without the conversion privilege, the issue of debentures would not have been set aside. Why is it illegal to issue discount stock, but not discount debt?

If the prohibition of discount stock was meant primarily to protect creditors, as Lord Halsbury suggested, just how would they be prejudiced by it? A creditor's claim is made more valuable by anything that increases the firm's solvency, its value on default or the creditor's share of firm value on default. A further injection of equity, so long as *any* consideration is received, will increase solvency and firm value on default without creating new claims that rank equal to or ahead of the creditors. Existing creditors are then made better off by an issue of discount stock. This leaves open the possibility of a prejudice to existing shareholders or future creditors or shareholders. This is discussed in the next sub-section, but, before we leave it, did not *Ooregum* result in a windfall to those future shareholders who, like Roper, purchased their shares after the corporation had (literally) struck gold?

3. Watered Stock

One of the reasons why a rule prohibiting discount stock developed was perhaps the ease with which it could be applied. When, as in *Mosley v. Koffyfontein Mines Ltd.*, "an obvious money measure" existed, it was a simple matter to see whether the consideration was adequate at law. Discount stock would then be impeached even if the transaction had not prejudiced anyone, since a determination of the fairness of the exchange required a valuation of the shares from a financial point of view, a task that courts were loath to perform. A prohibition of discount stock would thus give the appearance of offering protection to creditors and shareholders without the hard, financial analysis required to see if anyone was really harmed.

It soon became apparent that corporations that sought to avoid the prohibition of discount stock could do so in any one of three ways:

- The corporation might simply issue shares with a low par value and a high premium. Instead of issuing a $100 par share for $100, it might issue a $10 par share for the same amount, with that figure added to the issued capital account and the $90 premium added to the contributed surplus account. If the market price for the shares falls, new shares issued for any price exceeding $10 will not be discount stock.
- Since 1924, Canadian corporations statutes have permitted the creation of no par value shares which, unlike par value shares, do not bear a monetary figure on their face. The movement to no par value shares, which began with a New York statute in 1912, offered three reasons for detaching the dollar sign from the share certificate. First, it would avoid cases like *Ooregum* where an issue of discount stock is set aside even if the transaction is fair. Indeed, discount stock cases are, strictly speaking, restricted to issues of par value share, though there are other prohibitions against an issue of no par value shares for an inadequate consideration. Second, it

would emphasize that the true value of the share is a function of its right to participate in the earnings of a going concern, and is quite independent of par value. Retaining par value might even seem like a misrepresentation, if a gullible investor imagines that a $100 par value share in a worthless corporation must be worth something, and is likely a bargain at $20. Finally, all the consideration received by the corporation on an issue of no par value shares is normally added to stated capital, with artificial contributed surplus accounts eliminated. See CBCA s. 26(1). For these reasons, par value shares are prohibited by CBCA s. 24(1). However, no par value shares also do away with the "obvious money measure," and early reactions to them suggested that they facilitated an issue of shares for an inadequate consideration. Jackson, *Some Random Reflections on No-Par Share Legislation*, 7 Can. Bar Rev. 373, 374-75 (1929); Fraser, *No Par Shares*, 7 Can. Bar Rev. 84, 88 (1929); Bruneau, *Dominion Companies and No-Par Shares*, 13 Can. Bar Rev. 290, 297-98 (1935).

• Corporations statutes have always permitted an issue of shares for a non-monetary consideration. The consideration might still be inadequate, but without an "obvious money measure" it was more difficult to impeach the issue. Such shares are called *watered stock*, a term derived from the efforts of ranchers to increase the weight of their cattle before a sale. Watered stock will arise whenever no par value shares are issued for an inadequate consideration, whether in a monetary or non-monetary form.

Valuation of Property or Services. Anglo-Canadian decisions in the past, particularly in the nineteenth century, exhibited a great reluctance to impeach the directors' valuation of property or services received on an issue of shares. Thus Lord Watson said in *Ooregum Gold Mining Co. v. Roper*, [1892] A.C. 125, 137 that "so long as the company honestly regards the consideration given as fairly representing the nominal value of the shares in cash, its estimate ought not to be critically examined." The high water mark of this approach may be found in *Re Hess Mfg. Co.* (1894), 23 S.C.R. 644. There a corporation had issued shares to a promoter for a consideration, in the form of a factory together with the land upon which it was built, which the Master found to be inadequate. Strong C.J., delivering the judgment of the Supreme Court, stated that:

The only principle upon which the master could have acted in making the order he did was in assuming that no consideration whatever had been given for the shares. If any consideration was given it was beyond the master's competence to enquire into the adequacy of it.

. . .

So that unless a case of fraud was made and proved which could only be done in a formal action to rescind it must be held that there was a valuable consideration given *bona fide* for the 126 shares in question. [*Id.* at 653-54]

See also *Page v. Austin* (1882), 10 S.C.R. 132, 152-53 and *Re Wragg Ltd.*, [1897] 1 Ch. 796 (C.A.).

Theories of Liability. The above cases come very close to holding that no liability arises on an issue of watered stock. On the other hand, CBCA s. 118(1) creates an express remedy against the directors in such cases. Since s. 118(1) represents a fundamental shift in the treatment of watered stock, it may be well at this point to reflect on theories of liability that developed in such cases in England and the United States.

Obviously, an issue of shares for an inadequate consideration can prejudice existing shareholders by diluting their interest. This problem, and the judicial response to it, are discussed in the next section as an aspect of pre-emptive rights, although existing shareholders might also apply to set aside an issue of watered stock as prohibited by CBCA s. 25(3). Without legal barriers to a dilution of their interest, it is not even clear that a market for equity securities would develop. Watered stock prohibitions then constitute a me-first rule that the parties would expressly adopt in a claimholders' bargain. In addition, future claimholders might assert that watered stock harmed them on three theories of liability, all of which may be found in Lord Halsbury's judgment in *Ooregum*.

The first theory is one of statutory liability. In *Ooregum*, Lord Halsbury noted that the English Companies Act required the par value of a corporation's shares to be stated in its memorandum of association, and from this he implied a prohibition against discount stock. Statutory liability theories also arose in the United States. This basis of liability was not particularly satisfactory, since the corporations statutes did not expressly prohibit discount stock. In addition, the theory lacked a rationale, and never made clear whom it was protecting or why it was doing so.

The second theory was that the capital constituted a trust fund for the benefit of creditors. In *Ooregum*, Lord Halsbury stated that "[t]he capital is fixed and certain, and every creditor of the company is entitled to look to that capital as his security." So too, in *Trevor v. Whitworth* (1887), 12 App. Cas. 409, 414, Lord Herschell found that it was illegal for a company to reduce its stated capital by repurchasing its own shares. "The creditors of the company ... have a right to look to the paid-up capital as the fund out of which their debts are to be discharged." See also *North-West Electric Co. v. Walsh* (1898), 29 S.C.R. 33, 46 per Sedgewick J. But see *Page v. Austin* (1882), 10 S.C.R. 132, 152-53. The theory that stated capital constitutes a "trust fund" for the benefit of creditors also emerged in the United States in the last century. However, the stated capital is not a fund of any kind, but only an entry on the right hand side of the balance sheet, equal in value to the consideration received on the issue of shares. In addition, this consideration, carried under Assets on the left hand side of the balance sheet, is not to be kept aside and preserved, like the property held by trustees, but will instead be invested in the operations of the business. If they are successful, as in *Ooregum*, all well and good; and if they are not, the creditors must be deemed to have taken the risk of business failure. From the perspective of creditors, what is important is the possibility of default, and here the relevance of the amount of stated capital is severely limited. How will knowing the amount of stated capital, which might represent an allotment made 10 years previously, assist in measuring firm value?

The third theory of watered stock liability is that it amounts to a misrepresentation to future creditors and shareholders if they are led to overvalue the firm. Misrepresentation theories were never entirely absent from English cases on discount or watered stock, and Lord Halsbury stated in *Ooregum* that "I recognize the wisdom of enforcing on a company the disclosure of what its real capital is, and not permitting a statement of its affairs to be such as may mislead and deceive those who are either about to become its shareholders or about to give it credit." [1892] A.C. at 134.

The seminal American case on the misrepresentation theory is *Hospes v. Northwestern Mfg. & Car Co.*, 50 N.W. 1117 (Minn. 1892), where Mitchell J. stated that:

It is well settled that an equity in favor of a creditor does not arise absolutely and in every case to have the holder of "bonus" stock pay for it contrary to his actual contract with the corporation. Thus no such equity exists in favor of one whose debt was contracted prior to the issue, since he could not have trusted the company upon the faith of such stock. ... It does not exist in favor of a subsequent creditor who has dealt with the corporation with full knowledge of the arrangement by which the "bonus" stock was issued, for a man cannot be defrauded by that which he knows when he acts. *First Nat. Bank v. Gustin M.C. Min. Co.*, supra. It has also been held not to exist where stock has been issued and turned out at its full market value to pay corporate debts. *Clark v. Bever*, supra. The same has been held to be the case where an active corporation, whose original capital has been impaired, for the purpose of recuperating itself issues new stock, and sells it on the market for the best price obtainable, but for less than par (*Handley v. Stutz*, supra), although it is difficult to perceive, in the absence of a statute authorizing such a thing (of which every one dealing with the corporations is bound to take notice), any difference between the original stock of a new corporation and additional stock issued by a "going concern." It is difficult, if not impossible, to explain or reconcile these cases upon the "trust-fund" doctrine, or, in the light of them, to predicate the liability of the stockholder upon that doctrine. But by putting it upon the ground of fraud, and applying the old and familiar rules of law on that subject to the peculiar nature of a corporation and the relation which its stockholders bear to it and to the public, we have at once rational and logical ground on which to stand. The capital of a corporation is the basis of its credit. It is a substitute for the individual liability of those who own its stock. People deal with it and give it credit on the faith of it. They have a right to assume that it has paid in capital to the amount which it represents itself as having; and if they give it credit on the faith of that representation, and if the representation is false, it is a fraud upon them; and, in case the corporation becomes insolvent, the law, upon the plainest principles of common justice, says to the delinquent stockholder, "Make that representation good by paying for your stock." It certainly cannot require the invention of any new doctrine in order to enforce so familiar a rule of equity. It is the misrepresentation of fact in stating the amount of capital to be greater than it really is that is the true basis of the liability of the stockholder in such cases; and it follows that it is only those creditors who have relied, or who can fairly be presumed to have relied, upon the professed amount of capital, in whose favor the law will recognize and enforce an equity against the holders of "bonus" stock. This furnishes a rational and uniform rule, to which familiar principles are easily applied, and which frees the subject from many of the difficulties and apparent inconsistencies into which the "trust-fund" doctrine has involved it. [*Id.* at 1120-21]

Re Dorenwends Ltd.
Ontario Supreme Court, Appellate Division
(1924), 55 O.L.R. 413

ORDE J.A. (by whom the judgment of the Court was delivered): The circumstances under which the 160 shares were issued on the 12th January, 1911, to the late Hildebert Dorenwend are set forth in the judgment appealed from. But the question as to whether or not, upon the bankruptcy of the company, the shares are to be regarded as unpaid shares has been treated by the learned Judge in Bankruptcy in the light of an absolute gift by the company to Dorenwend, that gift taking the form of an issue of its own shares in return for services theretofore rendered the company in respect of which the company was under no legal obligation to him whatever.

In dealing with a transaction of this character it is important to get at its substance first and then see what technical rules are necessarily applicable.

In January, 1911, out of its authorised capital of $10,000, the company had already issued 40 shares of $50 each or $2,000 in all. It was then under no obligation to issue any further shares, and as long as it had assets sufficient in value to meet its liabilities to creditors and to keep that $2,000 of capital unimpaired it could treat its surplus assets as profits, and, having due regard to the rights of its shareholders *inter se*, could deal with that surplus as it pleased.

The majority of the 40 shares belonged to Hildebert Dorenwend, who was the president and general manager of the company. The company had been exceedingly prosperous, and at the end of 1910 its surplus of assets over all its liabilities, including the $2,000 of issued capital, was many thousands of dollars in excess of $8,000, and it was within the power of the company to distribute that surplus by way of dividend among its shareholders if it saw fit to do so. The difficulties in the present case have really arisen from the failure of the shareholders to use appropriate language to carry out a perfectly legitimate object. It is because the resolution of the 12th January, 1911, declares that the remaining 160 shares are to be issued (the resolution uses the inapt words "assigned and transferred") to Hildebert Dorenwend "in consideration of his valuable services to the company" that the present difficulty has arisen.

Now the underlying principle upon which a transaction of this kind is not permitted to stand as against the creditors of the company is, that the effect is to create, or give the appearance of creating, capital which does not in fact exist. The company is attempting to carry on business with a mere shadow, instead of the substance upon which those who deal with it are entitled to rely. As the company is not really indebted to the person to whom the shares are issued, it becomes necessary to add the fictitious indebtedness to the existing liabilities and to treat the fictitious services as an additional asset of the company. When the fictitious liability is wiped out by the issue of the stock against it, the completed transaction finds the company with a corresponding increase in its book assets for which there is no real value; the issue of the shares in such a case is really without consideration and the shares cannot be regarded as paid-up.

But that is not what really happened in the present case. It is rather unfortunate that the earlier books and balance-sheets have disappeared or been destroyed since the bankruptcy proceedings commenced, but it is stated in the evidence, and the fact was not attempted to be controverted upon the argument before us, that when the 160 shares were issued the amount standing at the credit of the surplus account, or the profit and loss account (it is really immaterial by what name it is styled), which exceeded the liabilities of the company by a sum far greater than $8,000, was immediately reduced by that amount, by the debiting against it of the $8,000 in respect of the issue of the 160 shares.

Now what did this mean in substance? Here was a surplus available for distribution by way of dividend among the shareholders. While it might be beyond the power of a majority, against the will of the minority, to vote it away to one shareholder, or to devote it to any other purpose outside the objects of the company except by a *pro rata* distribution among the shareholders by way of dividend, it was open to the shareholders, if unanimous, to deal with the surplus as they might see fit. No creditor could object, and every shareholder would necessarily be estopped by his own conduct. The action of the shareholders, instead of being one to which creditors either present or future could object, was in reality for their benefit, because by it there was added to the fixed capital of the company available to creditors the sum of $8,000, which otherwise might have been distributed by way of dividend. The assets of the company immediately available for creditors were not disturbed in the slightest degree, but the shareholders, by transferring the sum of $8,000 from their profits to the company's fixed capital, forever thereafter tied their own hands as to that portion of the company's assets, and thereby increased the security of present and future creditors.

Whatever the wording of the resolution may be, it is the substance of the transaction which is of importance. What the shareholders really did was in effect to declare a dividend or distribution of profits to the extent of $8,000, and, waiving their individual rights to a *pro rata* distribution, to hand the whole sum over to Dorenwend to enable him to pay for the 160 shares in full. Or the transaction may be treated as the unanimous agreement of the shareholders to pay Dorenwend the sum of $8,000, out of accumulated profits, for his past services to the company, a resolution which was clearly within their power if no shareholder objected.

It is not suggested by counsel for the trustee that the transaction could not have been lawfully carried out by the shareholders if they had passed the customary resolutions. All that was necessary was to declare a dividend of 400 per cent upon the $2,000 of issued capital, to allot 160 shares to Dorenwend, and then for each of the other shareholders to hand Dorenwend his dividend. But there is no magic in the word "dividend," and no special form of words is necessary when declaring one. Any language used to authorize a proper disposal of the company's profits would suffice. The Court will not ordinarily allow mere adherence to technical procedure to stand in the way of setting aside a dishonest transaction, and it ought not, by a too rigid adherence to mere formalities, to upset an honest one.

The judgment of the Judicial Committee in *Swan Brewery Co. Ltd. v. The King*, [1914] A.C. 231, is in point here. That was a case involving the taxation of dividends, but the reasoning is applicable to the present case. The company had passed resolutions that its capital be increased by £101,450, that the sum of £101,450 should be transferred from its accumulated profits to the credit of capital account, and that the new shares be allotted, as fully paid-up, among the shareholders *pro rata*. The transaction was in reality what is usually called a stock-dividend, but it does not appear that the company acted under any authority to declare a stock-dividend as such. Presumably the transaction had the approval of all the shareholders. The Crown claimed to be entitled to certain duties upon the ground that the transaction was in substance a dividend. The Supreme Court of Australia held that it was, and their judgment was affirmed by the Judicial Committee. At pp. 235, 236, in dealing with the question as to what the real transaction was, the Committee says:

The new shares were credited as fully paid, and, what is more, they were fully paid, for after the allotment the company held £101,450 as capital produced by the issue of those shares and for that consideration, and no longer as an undivided part of its accumulated reserve fund. True, that in a sense it was all one transaction, but that is an ambiguous expression. In business, as in contemplation of law, there were two transactions, the creation and issue of new shares on the company's part, and on the allotees' part the satisfaction of the liability to pay for them by acquiescing in such a transfer from reserve to share-capital as put an end to any participation in the sum of £101,450 in right of the old shares, and created instead a right of general participation in the company's profits and assets in right of the new shares, without any further liability to make a cash contribution in respect of them. In the words of Parker C.J., "Had the company distributed the £101,450 among the shareholders and had the shareholders repaid such sums to the company as the price of the 81,160 new shares, the duty on the £101,450 would clearly have been payable. Is not this virtually the effect of what was actually done? I think it is."

This reasoning is peculiarly applicable to the present case, and I think is sufficient, without any further references, to uphold the transaction.

I do not think any useful purpose will be served by entering into an elaborate discussion of the authorities cited on the argument. Many of them involve the power of a majority as against a dissenting minority. No such question arises here. The sole question is whether what the shareholders, acting unanimously, had a clear right to do, was done in such a way as to injure the rights of creditors, either present or future. In my judgment, it was not.

The appeal will be allowed with costs both here and in the proceedings before the learned Judge in Bankruptcy. Such costs to be paid personally by the trustee, with the right to indemnify himself out of the estate.

Appeal allowed.

NOTES

1) As Orde J.A. stated, there were two possible ways to account for the issue of 160 shares to Dorenwend. Why was the allotment upheld? Why would it have been set aside on the alternative method of accounting for the transaction?

2) If fraud is necessary to impeach an issue of watered stock, can it be found in balance sheet misrepresentation?

3) If the basis for liability is balance sheet misrepresentation, is there any justification for a distinction between par and no par value shares when it is argued that the consideration is inadequate?

4) If balance sheet misrepresentation does in fact prejudice creditors, why is it not made illegal *per se*? Assets may be stated at an artificially high value in ways other than an issue of shares, as where they are simply revalued. Does the absence of a perceived need for such prohibitions suggest that the problem is more theoretical than real?

Israels, Problems of Par and No-Par Shares: A Reappraisal*
47 Colum. L. Rev. 1279, 1279-98 (1947)

There would appear to be some widespread misconceptions as to the relation between no-par shares and the law of stock watering; in particular an impression that the impact of that law can be entirely avoided by employment of the no-par device.

• • •

An analysis of the material now available refutes to a substantial extent the conception that the use of no-par shares in and of itself affords protection against liability for stock watering or balance sheet inflation. At the same time, it reveals the ease with which the skilled practitioner can minimize, if not completely avoid, such liabilities in almost any situation.

• • •

[M]odern accounting convention calls for the balance sheet to show the amount of the consideration for outstanding no-par shares intended to constitute statutory "capital" allocable to them. That figure is the aggregate "stated" or "assigned" value and use of the term is not limited today to shares issued under a statute requiring a minimum dollar figure of capital per share to be specified in the certificate of incorporation.

The figure is usually (but not invariably) expressed on a per share basis, thus:

> 10,000 shares, no par value
> (stated value $10 per share) $100,000

The absence of a per share figure probably (but not necessarily) indicates that all of the issue was not sold in a single transaction or at a single price, so that no single figure would represent the capital allocable to each of the shares. When a per share stated or assigned value is shown, the analogy to the par figure is obvious. Even where the stated value is shown merely in the aggregate the accounting history of the enterprise would be available to determine the amount of stated capital a particular subscriber was supposed to have contributed.

Berle argued in 1925 that the subscriber should be held to the same liability regardless of the type of shares to which he subscribes.

• • •

Berle's main argument follows clearly from the logic of the par value cases and the modern necessity for a balance sheet, and thus for a capital account no matter how insignificant in size in relation to the total assets. ...

Present Day Practice: Minimizing the Risk

No case has been found which speaks in terms of stock watering liability either upon a subscriber or a director because of a deficiency in the value of the property or services

---

*   Copyright 1947 by the Directors of the Columbia Law Review Association Inc. This article is now in the public domain.

received by the corporation for either type of shares where the overvaluation appears on the balance sheet as surplus rather than as capital. In reliance on this much modern practice has been built up.

• • •

Counsel who has doubts about his clients' ability to defend the "value" of the consideration they desire to accept may today advise the use of either type, so far as the decided cases are concerned, provided only that the total par value of the issued shares, or the proportion of the consideration for no-par shares which is allocated to capital, is kept well below a conservative valuation of the property or services. Suppose that property "valued" at $10,000 is to be transferred to a Delaware corporation for 1,000 shares—all that are to be issued. The transferor acquired the property for $5,000 and could easily resell it at that figure. If one's clients are willing to run the risk of possible liability for balance sheet inflation they can be assured that under the decided cases either par value or no-par value shares will be equally "fully paid and non-assessable" in the subscribers' hands, if they set up the balance sheet like this:

Assets		*Liabilities*	
Property	$10,000	Capital Stock (1,000 shares $5 par value)	$ 5,000
		Paid-in Surplus	5,000
	$10,000		$10,000

or like this:

Assets		*Liabilities*	
Property	$10,000	Capital Stock (1,000 shares no-par value)	$ 5,000
		Paid-in Surplus	5,000
	$10,000		$10,000

The inflation is avoidable on either balance sheet by reducing the carrying value of the property to $5,000 and eliminating the surplus item. Nor would the fact that another subscriber proposes to pay $10,000 cash for another thousand shares, all of the purchase price of which is to be capital make the inflation necessary. All that is needed is to separate the two transactions and sell the two lots of a thousand shares each, at different prices. Market conditions often require this practise in large enterprises. The close corporation or any enterprise in the promotional stage has even greater freedom. The subscriber who pays the higher price and has knowledge of or consents (either by his vote as a shareholder, or as a director, or by separate instrument or even oral agreement) to the sale of shares of the same class to another at a price lower than he paid obviously is estopped to claim the benefit of the rule of equitable contribution.

If par value shares are used the initial balance sheet would look like this:

Assets		*Liabilities*	
Cash	$10,000	Capital Stock (2,000 shares $5 par value)	$10,000
Property	5,000	Paid-in Surplus	5,000
	$15,000		$15,000

The directors then transfer the paid-in surplus to capital and the balance sheet then looks like this:

Assets		Liabilities	
Cash	$10,000	Capital Stock (2,000 shares $5 par value)	$10,000
Property	5,000	Paid-in Surplus transferred to capital	5,000
	$15,000		$15,000

No stock watering case had upheld the right of either a creditor or a shareholder to complain of sales of par value shares at *more* than par. ...

There is less flexibility in the case of no-par shares only where the statute requires that the entire consideration for shares without par value be shown as capital. There under the present statutory scheme greater care must be taken with respect to valuation than in any other case, and counsel should advise his clients to issue low par value shares rather than no-par shares under such a statute.

• • •

The Problem of Balance Sheet Inflation

The stock watering cases have been justifiably criticized for their fiction of "reliance" by creditors on stated capital. Realistically, if creditors rely at all they rely upon the carrying values of the assets. What harm is done a creditor, if the balance sheet shows $1,000 of assets, by how the balancing figure is apportioned between capital and surplus except in so far as the applicable dividend statute permits the payment of a dividend from paid-in surplus? If, however, the property carried at $1,000 is only worth $500 and insolvency ensues, with or without a dividend in the interim the creditor has suffered.

• • •

The pattern is varied and incomplete but, in the writer's view, it is nonetheless clear that the use of no-par rather than par value shares will not protect the director or officer against liability to creditors under statute or at common law for overvaluation of property or services received as consideration for the shares, and that the likelihood of liability being imposed, at least where the balance sheet was published to anyone, increases as lawyers and the courts become increasingly aware of financial realities. To extend the rule of equitable contribution and hold the director liable to existing shareholders for breach of fiduciary duty in selling a new issue at less than it should bring would not be startling, but would merely round out the picture.

Subscribers' liability also is today largely statutory. As stated above, no case has yet arisen where such liability was sought to be imposed for inflation reflected in surplus rather than in stated capital. This is understandable in light of the origins of the law of stock watering in the trust fund theory. However the logic of the fraud or holding out theory, particularly where actual reliance on balance sheet carrying values could be shown, would seem easily to permit of extension to such a case, subject perhaps to an exception where the subscriber can show an arm's length transaction, not conducted in terms of dollars, and thus complete lack of connection with the directors' valuation.

Modern Statutory Liability. One can no longer argue under modern corporations statutes in Canada that the use of no par value shares will insulate an issuer from liability. CBCA s. 24(1) prohibits par value shares and s. 25(3) requires that a consideration in property or services be "not less in value than the fair equivalent of the money that the corporation would have received if the share had been issued for money." Moreover, s. 118(1) imposes liability on directors who vote for an issue of shares that contravenes s. 25(3). Do these sections require a judicial determination of the true value of the non-cash consideration when the transaction is impeached? When the directors determine by resolution the respective values of the shares and the consideration received on their issue, as they are required to do by OBCA s. 23(4), how ready will a court be to second-guess such valuations? Note the due diligence and reliance defences provided directors with respect to s. 118(1) under ss. 118(6) and 123(4). Should the corporation retain outside professional valuers in such cases if the allotment is significant and the transaction is non-arm's length? In addition, the s. 118(1) liability is subject to a two-year limitation period under s. 118(7).

As Israels notes, watered stock liability may be better hidden by an issue of low par than no par value shares. This was undoubtedly one reason for the abolition of share premiums in CBCA s. 26(2). However, s. 26(3) creates an exception for shares issued in arrangements, amalgamations or in certain non-arm's length transactions, as when a promoter deals with his corporation. The corporation may then add "the whole or any part of the amount of the consideration" to the stated capital account. Presumably, this permits the corporation to allocate the balance of this amount to contributed surplus. For tax-inspired reasons, s. 26(3) was added to the CBCA in 1979.

Does CBCA s. 25(3) prohibit balance sheet misrepresentation? Suppose that a shell corporation issues shares with a stated capital of $1,000,000 for a property consideration worth far less than that. Since the shares of the corporation would not fetch much if issued for cash, is it possible that s. 25(3) has not been breached?

4. Unacceptable Consideration

Some kinds of consideration on a share issuance are flatly prohibited by Canadian corporations statutes. For example, CBCA s. 25(3) requires a consideration of money, property or past services. Other forms for consideration are not permitted even if they are not inadequate and the bargain is otherwise fair. Such consideration is "unacceptable," whatever its real worth. Under the CBCA, three kinds of consideration are unacceptable: (1) promissory notes or promises to pay; (2) non-"property" assets; and (3) future services.

The unacceptability of promissory notes or promises to pay under s. 25(5) supplements the prohibition of partly paid shares in s. 25(3). On the other hand, an issuing corporation might circumvent the prohibition of partly paid shares by lending the investor the money to make the purchase, so long as the solvency standards of CBCA ss. 44(1)(c)-(d) are met. But for the solvency barrier, the entire firm value could be transferred to equity holders when bankruptcy looms, such that the market for bankruptcy priority rights in the hands of creditors might disappear. Solvent firms may then finance the purchase of their shares even if the effect of the transaction is identical to an issue of partly paid shares. Is there, however, any reason why the loan should be impeached without clear evidence of self-dealing? Suppose that an employee of the firm seeks to borrow money from it to purchase a car. Should this be permitted, but not a loan to purchase shares? Might X Corp. lend its employees money to purchase shares of Y Corp. but not of X Corp.? The barriers to partly paid shares may also be thought to protect the purchasers of such shares themselves, on the theory that they might otherwise subscribe for too many securities from a credit-granting issuer. That was at least one justification preferred for restrictions in the American Securities Exchange Act of 1934 on credit granted by investment brokers and dealers for share purchases by their clients. Congress established high margin ratios to prevent investors from agreeing to purchase shares with little down and the balance advanced by the investment intermediary. These paternalistic restrictions may now seem hard to justify, and in any event they ignore the fungeability of credit, with other lenders (such as banks) able to lend money to potential investors on any margin ratio the parties see fit. Margin requirements are discussed in *A Review and Evaluation of Federal Margin Regulations* (Board of Governors, Federal Reserve System 1985), Fed. Sec. L. Rep. (CCH) para. 83,728 [1984-85 Transfer Binder].

The CBCA also prohibits non-"property" payments for a share issuance. What does "property" mean here? Can shares be issued in exchange for intangibles like accounts receivable, ideas, inventions and patents?

See v. Heppenheimer
New Jersey Court of Chancery
61 A. 843 (1905)

[The Columbia Straw Paper Co. was incorporated in 1892 to acquire a monopoly over the manufacture of wrapping paper. Columbia's promoters purchased 39 paper mills for $2,250,000, which they sold to Columbia for securities with a value of $5,000,000, of which $1,000,000 was in bonds and the balance in shares. The corporation failed in 1895 and its creditors sought to recover from its shareholders.]

PITNEY V.C.: ... The clients of Messrs. Lindabury and Marshall, as I interpret their argument, ... contend that the valuation of $5,000,000 was arrived at after a careful calculation of the quantity of the paper, viz., 90,000 tons, which the 39 mills were able to produce per year, and the greatly increased price which would be realized from its sale by the suppression of the competition theretofore practiced between the several mill owners. They say that the cost of producing the paper was less than $20 per ton, and that its selling price had been reduced by competition to a trifle over $20 per ton, but that by a concentration of the ownership of the mills they found and believed that the price could be easily maintained, and the whole product of 90,000 tons a year could be marketed, at about $28 per ton, which would pay interest on the bonded debt, with 1 per cent per year for a sinking fund, and a dividend at 8 per cent per year on the preferred stock of $1,000,000, and leave a very large dividend, at least 15 per cent each year, for the common stock of the amount mentioned, $3,000,000. In short, they estimated the value of the property upon a capitalization of the profits expected to be made out of its use by control of the price of its product. So that, taking the aspect of the case most favorable to the defendants, the question which arises out of its ultimate analysis is whether, under our statute above cited, it is competent and lawful to make up the valuation of the visible property to be purchased for stock issued, by adding to the actual market value, or cost of its reproduction, a sum of money ascertained by the capitalization of the annual profits expected to be realized from a favorable marketing of the product of the company by a suppression of competition; or, as I believe I asked counsel in argument, can prospective profits, however promising, be considered as property, as that word is used in the statute above quoted? I repeat its language: "The directors of any company incorporated under this act may purchase mines, manufactories or other property necessary for their business ... and issue stock to the amount of the value thereof in payment therefor." There the word "property" must evidently be construed by its context, which refers to something visible and tangible and necessary for the business, and the amount of stock to be issued therefor is limited to the value thereof; that is, to the value of that property. If the question above put be the true one, it seems to me that it answers itself, and adversely to the contention of counsel of defendants.

• • •

With regard to the defense based on the item of good will, advanced by the defendants, complainant replies that it is an entire misapplication of the term, and all the law growing out of it, to use it in that connection, and they point out that the conveyances and the contract preceding them, made by the original owners of the 39 mills, included by express terms the good will of the mills, which was included in the original valuation of the mills at $2,250,000, and, besides, that the original contracts were in each case accompanied by an undertaking on the part of the vendor not to engage in business for five years, and that the preliminary contract with Stein also included the good will. I shall deal with this element of good will at once. Lord Eldon, in *Cruttwell v. Lye* (1810) 17 Vesey, 335, at page 346, said: "The good will which has been the subject of sale is nothing more than the probability that the old customers will resort to the old place." This definition, though often criticised, seems to me to contain the germ of all the more modern and complete definitions. I am willing to adopt, for present purposes, that written by Judge Lacombe, of the United States Circuit Court, and reported in *Washburn v. National Wall Paper Co.*, 81 Fed. 17, 20, 26 C.C.A. 312, 315, and cited in extenso in defendants' printed argument: "Good will has been denied as 'all that good disposition which customers entertain towards the house of business identified by the particular name or firm, and which may induce them to continue giving their custom to it.' There is nothing marvellous or mysterious about it. When an individual, or a firm, or a corporation, has gone on for an unbroken series of years, conducting a particular business, and has been so scrupulous in fulfilling every obligation, so careful of maintaining the standard of the goods dealt in, so absolutely honest and fair in all business dealings, that customers of the concern have become convinced that their experience in the future will be as satisfactory as it has been in the past, while such customers' good report of their own experience tends continually to bring new customers to the same concern, there has been produced an element of value quite as important as—in some cases, perhaps, far more important than—the plant or machinery with which the business is carried on. That it is property is abundantly settled by authority, and, indeed, is not disputed. That in some cases it may be very valuable property is manifest. The individual who has created it by years of hard work and fair business dealing usually experiences no difficulty in finding men willing to pay him for it, if he be willing to sell it to them." This language was used in a case where the capital stock was issued, as here, for the value of several manufacturing establishments in which the individual good will of each separate factory was added to the value of its visible property (precisely as would have been the case here, if the stock had been issued for the amount of the sum of the valuations of the several mills with their good will added, to wit, $2,200,000), and the bill was filed by stockholders who received their stock in payment for a mill which they owned and conveyed to the corporation, and they sought by their bill to enjoin the payment of dividends on the stock so issued. It was held that they were estopped from setting up that the property had been overvalued and, further, that the evidence was insufficient to show such a depreciation in value as would warrant the relief prayed for.

Turning to the present case we find, as before remarked, that the individual good will of the different properties was included in the individual valuations thereof and conveyed for the consideration above mentioned to the corporation. Further, the inference is irresistible that the corporation itself could not possibly, at the time of its organization, have acquired any good will in the proper sense of that word, or, indeed, in any sense of that word. It had made no business friends, nor any business reputation. Moreover, an examination in detail of the plan of business laid out and adopted by the promoters of the enterprise, from which they expected to reap such great profits, contemplated a complete destruction of the old good will of the individual establishments. Mr. Stein had, in fact, no good will to convey with the mills, except what he had acquired from the individual owners: hence the increase in price cannot be justified on that basis. It follows that we are driven back to the question first stated, whether prospective and contingent profits of any business, depending, as they always must and do, upon good management and the general course of business of the country, including always the element of competition, can be treated as property in the sense in which that word is used in the statute above cited.

• • •

The present case is a painful illustration of the utter impossibility of giving the word "property" the construction claimed for it. The rose-coloured future, presently to be stated at length, for this enterprise, created with so much confidence by its promoters, failed entirely in the face of actual experience. In the first place the combination did not include all the mills which it was intended to include. There is some dispute and some indefiniteness in the evidence on this subject. The complainant contends that there were, in fact, 73 mills engaged in the manufacture of straw paper, and that the original plan and appraisement included all of them. The defendants admit 41, 2 of which they were unable to purchase, except at prohibitory prices. The proof is clear that there were several more, but just how many is in doubt. It appears from defendants' printed argument, sustained by the proofs, that the failure of the enterprise was due to four causes:

first, the financial depression of 1893; second, the starting up of old mills, and the building of new mills as soon as the corporation put up the price of paper; third, bad management of its affairs; and, fourth, the introduction of wood pulp as the basic material of wrapping paper such as was manufactured out of straw.

• • •

It will be observed that the consolidation of the ownership of these 39 mills did not increase in the least degree the producing capacity of each, nor did it increase the range of the farming country in the neighbourhood of each from which they were to derive their raw material. They were, in the main, widely separated from each other, so that the case is in marked contrast with those which occur where several properties lying contiguous to each other may be applied to a purpose for which they could not be used, except under a combined ownership. Instances of this readily occur to the mind and are found in the books. Several small city lots, covered, if you will, with moderate dwellings, may be worth a great deal more for the purpose of erecting a large hotel or other building requiring considerable ground space than the aggregate of the separate value of each for individual dwelling house purposes. So several contiguous lots of unimproved land, under which a large vein of valuable minerals is known to exist, may be more valuable by reason of combined ownership, which enables the minerals to be sought for and brought to the surface much cheaper and to a better advantage than under separate ownerships.

• • •

But the defendants say: The practice of so valuing property under our statute has been indulged in frequently before, and numerous corporations have been organized and have existed upon such a basis, so that, (they argue) the practice has become well-nigh crystallized and sanctioned by long usage. I am sorry to feel constrained to admit that this practice has been frequently indulged in, and, further, that it has brought obloquy upon our state and its legislation. But I am happy to be able to assert with confidence that such practice is entirely unwarranted by anything either in our statute or in the decisions of our courts, and whenever it has been indulged in it has involved a clear infringement of, if not a fraud upon, the plain letter and spirit of our legislation.

• • •

But, say the defendants: "We acted in perfectly good faith. We really believed this property was worth the amount at which it was appraised, and we were guilty of no fraud in that behalf. And to show our good faith we invested therein several hundred thousand dollars ($467,000) in cash, besides $50,000 in services and expenses of the law firm of Guggenheimer & Untermeyer and their correspondents in Chicago, and have lost it all." And a powerful appeal was made to the court not to subject the defendants to further loss by saddling these enormous debts upon them. Let us consider the affair from the standpoint of the defendants, and inquire just how and for what they invested their money. The real estate and good will of the 39 mills footed up in value, for purposes of sale to the corporation, to nearly $2,200,000, and, after allowing for the overvaluation which we all know that the individual owners of these industrial properties about to be united usually manage to maintain for that purpose, and of which there is some proof in this case, we may reasonably suppose to be worth $1,500,000, and thus to furnish reasonably good security for $1,000,000 of bonds. Hence it was reasonably safe to invest at par in the bonds to the extent of $1,000,000, secured by a mortgage upon the property. There was little reason to anticipate the completeness of the final catastrophe. The cause of that completeness I have already stated. Now, that investment at par in 6 per cent bonds secured by a mortgage on property worth at least 1¹/₂ times the amount of the sum secured is all that any of the defendants risked. Not one dollar was invested by any of them beyond the par value of the mortgage bonds of the company. For every $1,000 paid into the company they received a mortgage bond for that amount, and, besides, a bonus of two shares of preferred and four shares of common stock. It is thus made clear that, when the faith of these investors in the value of the property purchased was put to the actual test, it went no further than to invest at par in first mortgage 6 per cent bonds, secured by property estimated to be worth about twice the amount of the mortgage, to which bonds was added as a bonus 60 per cent of stock representing the value of the property above the mortgage. This transaction is known in the language employed in these financial transactions as "getting in on the ground floor," and was so understood by each of the investors. Mr. Heppenheimer, in fact, uses this very language in his evidence. In answer to a question put by me as to whether he "did not think Mr. Untermeyer was making you a big present," he replied: "No; he was not making me any present, but letting me in on the ground floor. That is the way all these corporations have been formed in the state of New Jersey." No doubt each of these investors really, and therefore in good faith, hoped and expected that the enterprise would prove what they called a success; that is, that the bonds were entirely safe, and so, probably, was the preferred stock. And in like manner it was hoped and expected that the common stock would receive periodical dividends for a period of time long enough at least to enable some, if not all, of it to be marketed, or, to use the apt phrase which has been applied to such transactions, "to be distributed to" and later to be "digested by the public."

I am unable to find that the defendants' belief and faith went beyond this. But I am unwilling to adopt the notion that this sort of good faith is that which is required in order to legalize transactions like this under consideration. And here we find the real motive and reason which gives rise to these inflated values and "watering" of capital stock. It is the desire and intention to sell shares in a property owned by the corporation, for that is what capital stock represents, for more than they are really worth. And therein lies the intrinsically fraudulent character of these transactions. I feel justified in so characterizing them, since the overvaluation of the property does not at all or in any manner increase its intrinsic or practical value, or in the least degree promote the real prosperity of the enterprise. A single paper mill will turn out just as much product capitalized at $100,000 as $200,000, and its rental value will be practically the same. The earnings and profit due to good management and skillful handling of the product will be the same, and these last do not depend at all upon the producing capacity of the mill. Finally, the division of the profits, if any there be, among the stockholders will be on the same basis, and the amount received by each stockholder will be the same, the only difference being in the percentage of the division, and the market values of the shares will finally settle down to the gauge of the dividends earned and declared. But this straightforward mode of doing business does not satisfy the present-day promoter, whose object in making an overvaluation is twofold: First, to sell shares at more than their real value, and thereby secure a profit immediately in hand ("profit" is the word used by Mr. Samuel Untermeyer in his evidence); second, to obtain mercantile credit based on a large capital.

· · ·

The distinction between the contemplated issue of corporate stock for property and its issue for money lies, not in the rule for valuation, but in the fact that different estimates may be formed of the value of property. When such differences are brought before judicial tribunals, the judgment of those who are by law intrusted with the power of issuing stock [to the amount of the value of the property], and on whom, therefore, is placed the first duty of valuing the property, must be accorded considerable weight; but it cannot be deemed conclusive, when duly subjected to judicial scrutiny. Nor is it necessary that conscious overvaluation or any other form of fraudulent conduct on the part of these primary valuers should be shown to justify judicial interposition. Their honest judgment, if reached without due examination into the elements of value, or if based in part upon an estimate of matters which really are not property, or if plainly warped by self-interest, may lead to a violation of the statutory rule as surely as would corrupt motive.

· · ·

The intention of the Legislature, expressed in these sections in question, in my judgment manifestly was that the capital stock of all corporations should at the start represent the same value, whether paid for in property or money. That result can only be obtained by supposing that the property is to be appraised at its actual cash value, precisely as if a board of directors, with the whole capital stock actually paid in cash, is dealing at actual arm's length as real purchasers with the owner of property proposed to be purchased as a real vendor, without any interest in the directors to overvalue the property, or other interests inconsistent with the real interest of the stockholders as such. I say "at the start," because we all know that property purchased in good faith for cash is liable afterwards to depreciate in value, owing to circumstances not foreseen at the time of its purchase. After all, it seems to me that the true test, under this statute, as applied to the case here in hand, is this: If the company actually had to its credit in bank the sum of $5,000,000, would it have been willing to have paid that price in cash for the property in question for the uses and purposes to which it proposed to devote it? Would the property be worth that sum in cash to the company? Any less severe test will, it seems to me, fail to satisfy the letter and spirit of the two sections of the act before recited, which seem to me clearly to require that the shares of capital stock of any company organized under the act in force when this company was organized should be of equal value, whether paid for in cash or property purchased.

· · ·

NOTE

Does this case decide that upon incorporation a business cannot be valued by a capitalization of future earnings? A subsequent New Jersey case permitted a valuation on a going concern basis when the promoter derived his estimate of future earnings from the business's past earnings record. *Railway Review v. Groff Drill & Machine Tool Co.*, 91 A. 1021 (Ch. 1914), aff'd. sub nom. *Sloan v. Paul*, 96 A. 1103. Other cases have not followed the *See* decision on such non-tangible property as patent rights or goodwill. See, for example, *Re R.P. Clark & Co.*, [1938] 3 W.W.R. 233 (B.C.) (goodwill). Would a court be likely to follow Pitney V.C.'s definition of "property" today?

An agreement to provide future services to an issuer is clearly a thing of value for which an employee may be rewarded by prepayments of his salary. But he may not be issued shares for future services. This may create problems for small businesses which, on incorporation, issue shares to a promoter in recognition of his expertise.

5. Remedies

Who May Sue? An action for breach of CBCA s. 25(3) or 118(1) may perhaps be brought by one or all of the following parties.

(1) The corporation itself is expressly permitted to recover from the directors under s. 118(1). Prior to modern corporations statutes the liquidator of an insolvent corporation was permitted to bring an action against the shareholders on an issue of discount stock for the amount of the discount. This suggests that an issuer may recover from subscribers of watered stock in addition to the directors who authorized the allotment.

(2) Shareholders might be permitted to sue under a variety of theories.

    (a) They might first apply to bring a derivative action under CBCA s. 239 on behalf of the issuer, asserting a breach of duties owed to it by the directors. Derivative actions, in which individual shareholders sue on behalf of the corporation, are discussed further in Chapter Seven, Part I, Section F.

    (b) Alternatively, a shareholder who subscribed for shares after an issue of watered stock might argue that he had suffered direct personal loss by balance sheet misrepresentation, paying more for his shares than he would have had he known all the facts concerning the initial allotment.

    (c) Those holding shares at the time of an issue of watered stock might, so long as they did not consent to the allotment, argue that their interests were thereby diluted.

    (d) Creditors might also be permitted to bring an action, although it is difficult to see how they are prejudiced by watered stock unless they can claim reliance on the attendant balance sheet misrepresentation.

Apart from s. 118(1), causes of action for breach of CBCA s. 25(3) are still hypothetical. Nearly all actions for discount stock were brought by liquidators, and it is not clear to what extent creditors or even shareholders would have standing to complain of watered stock. As seen in Chapter Seven, real prejudice to a shareholder does not guarantee that he will have standing to complain. For that matter, an absence of prejudice may not ensure that he will not be able to sue.

Reliance on the Balance Sheet. The difficulty with the misrepresentation theory is that any prejudice under it presumes reliance. How is a creditor who has not examined the balance sheet injured by a prior issue of watered stock? But if reliance is a necessary element of liability, creditors often do not examine the debtor's balance sheet in deciding whether to extend credit. Moreover, the stated capital figure is not related in any way to the issuer's ability to pay its debts as they fall due. Even if the misrepresentation is on the left hand side of the balance sheet, under Assets, the figures may have little to do with either the current value of the assets or the value of the issuer as a going concern. Credit managers will also be more interested in the debtor's short-term ability to pay its bills on time than in its long-term earnings prospects. In this, creditors will be assisted by professional credit agencies, such as Dun & Bradstreet. Creditors will realize that some debtors will default, and a reserve for doubtful accounts will be set up to account for this, deducting such reserves against taxable income. See generally B. Manning, *A Concise Textbook on Legal Capital* 84-108 (2d ed. 1981), for a ringing indictment of stated capital requirements.

Bing Crosby Minute Maid Corp. v. Eaton
Supreme Court of California
297 P.2d 5 (1956)

SHENK J.: The plaintiff appeals from an order granting a new trial after judgment in its favor. The defendant appeals from the judgment.

As a judgment creditor of a corporation the plaintiff brought this action against a shareholder of the corporation to recover the difference between the par value of stock issued to him and the fair value of the consideration he paid for the stock. At the conclusion of the trial, the court, sitting without a jury, made findings of fact and conclusions of law and entered judgment for the plaintiff. In support of his motion for a new trial the defendant assigned certain alleged defects in the findings as errors of law.

The defendant formed a corporation to acquire his frozen foods business. The Commissioner of Corporations issued a permit authorizing the corporation to sell and issue not more than 4,500 shares of $10 par value stock to the defendant and other named individuals in consideration of the transfer of the business. The permit provided that 1,022 shares be deposited in escrow and not be transferred without the written consent of the Commissioner, and that the escrowed shares not be sold or issued until the prospective shareholders named in the permit waived certain rights to dividends and to participation in any distribution of assets.

The defendant transferred his business to the corporation. The corporation placed 1,022 shares in escrow in his name pursuant to the provisions of the permit. The remaining 3,478 shares were issued outright to the defendant and after three years were transferred to the other persons named in the permit. Although the 1,022 shares were listed on the corporate records as held by the defendant (accompanied by the notation "escrowed"), they were never released from escrow. The corporation had financial difficulties and executed an assignment of its assets for the benefit of creditors to a credit association. The plaintiff recovered a judgment against the corporation for $21,246.42. A writ of execution on the judgment was returned unsatisfied.

The trial court found that the value to the corporation of the consideration from the defendant was $34,780.83; that 4,500 shares of stock having a par value of $10 each were issued to the defendant and he became the owner of those shares; that subsequent to the issue of the shares the corporation purchased merchandise from the plaintiff and has not yet paid for all of it; that some $15,000 of the judgment the plaintiff recovered from the corporation remains unsatisfied, and that the corporation is insolvent.

The judgment for the plaintiff was for $10,219.17—approximately the par value of the 1,022 shares of stock placed in escrow. The judgment was based on the trial court's conclusion that the defendant was liable for the difference between the par value of the 4,500 shares and the value of the consideration the defendant paid for them.

The plaintiff contends that the trial court's findings of fact were supported by the evidence and required a judgment in its favor, and therefore that it was in error to grant a new trial. The defendant contends that the order granting a new trial was proper because (1) the finding that he was the owner of 4,500 shares was unsupported by the evidence, and (2) the trial court failed to make a finding on a material issue raised by his answer.

In this state a shareholder is ordinarily not personally liable for the debts of the corporation; he undertakes only the risk that his shares may become worthless. ... There are, however, certain exceptions to this rule of limited liability. For example, a subscriber to shares who pays in only part of what he agreed to pay is liable to creditors for the balance. Corp. Code, §§ 1300, 1306. Although the trial court in the present case found that the defendant had agreed to pay par value for the 4,500 shares registered in his name, the record on appeal discloses no evidence supporting this finding. Therefore, the defendant's liability cannot be predicated upon the theory that a subscribing shareholder is liable for the full consideration agreed to be paid for the shares.

The plaintiff seeks to base its recovery on the only other exception to the limited liability rule that the record could support, namely, liability for holding watered stock, which is stock issued in return for properties or services worth less than its par value. Accordingly, this case calls for an analysis of the rights of a creditor of an insolvent corporation against a holder of watered stock. Holders of watered stock are generally held liable to the corporation's creditors for the difference between the par value of the stock and the amount paid in.

[Despite the fact that the defendant held the shares in escrow, it was held that he had sufficient title in them for the plaintiff to proceed against him for their par value.]

The defendant's second contention is that the trial court failed to make a finding on a material issue raised by his answer.

The liability of a holder of watered stock has been based on one of two theories: the misrepresentation theory or the statutory obligation theory. The misrepresentation theory is the one accepted in most jurisdictions. The courts view the issue of watered stock as a misrepresentation of the corporation's capital. Creditors who rely on this misrepresentation are entitled to recover the "water" from the holders of the watered shares.

• • •

Statutes expressly prohibiting watered stock are commonplace today. See statutes collected in 11 Fletcher, Cyclopedia of the Law of Private Corporations, rev. and perm. ed. 1932, sec. 5209. In some jurisdictions where they have been enacted, the statutory obligation theory has been applied. ... Under that theory the holder of watered stock is held responsible to creditors whether or not they have relied on an overvaluation of corporate capital.

In his answer the defendant alleged that in extending credit to the corporation the plaintiff did not rely on the par value of the shares issued, but only on independent investigation and reports as to the corporation's current cash position, its physical assets and its business experience. At the trial the plaintiff's district manager admitted that during the period when the plaintiff extended credit to the corporation, (1) the district manager believed that the original capital of the corporation amounted to only $25,000, and (2) the only financial statement of the corporation that the plaintiff ever saw showed a capital stock account of less than $33,000. These admissions would be sufficient to support a finding that the plaintiff did not rely on any misrepresentation arising out of the issuance of watered stock. The court made no finding on the issue of reliance. If the misrepresentation theory prevails in California, that issue was material and the defendant was entitled to a finding thereon. Code Civ. Proc. § 632; see *Edgar v. Hitch*, ... 294 P.2d 3. If the statutory obligation theory prevails, the fact that the plaintiff did not rely on any misrepresentation arising out of the issuance of watered stock is irrelevant and accordingly a finding on the issue of reliance would be surplusage.

It is therefore necessary to determine which theory prevails in this state. The plaintiff concedes that before the enactment of section 1110 of the Corporations Code (originally Civ. Code, § 299) in 1931, the misrepresentation theory was the only one available to creditors seeking to recover from holders of watered stock. ... However, he contends that the enactment of that section reflected a legislative intent to impose on the holders of watered stock a statutory obligation to creditors to make good the "water." Section 1110 provides that "The value of the consideration to be received by a corporation for the issue of shares having par value shall be at least equal to the par value thereof, except that: (a) A corporation may issue par value shares, as fully paid up, at less than par, if the board of directors determines that such shares cannot be sold at par. ..." The statute does not expressly impose an obligation to creditors. Most jurisdictions having similar statutes have applied the misrepresentation theory obviously on the ground that creditors are sufficiently protected against stock watering schemes under that theory. ... In view of the cases in this state prior to 1931 adopting the misrepresentation theory, it is reasonable to assume that the Legislature would have used clear language expressing an intent to broaden the basis of liability of holders of watered stock had it entertained such an intention. In this state the liability of a holder of watered stock may only be based on the misrepresentation theory.

The plaintiff contends that even under the misrepresentation theory a creditor's reliance on the misrepresentation arising out of the issuance of watered stock should be conclusively presumed. This contention is without substantial merit. If it should prevail, the misrepresentation theory and the statutory obligation theory would be essentially identical. This court has held that under the misrepresentation theory a person who extended credit to a corporation (1) before the watered stock was issued, *Clark v. Tomkins,* supra, 205 Cal. 373, 270 P. 946, or (2) with full knowledge that watered stock was outstanding ... cannot recover from the holders of the watered stock. These decisions indicate that under the misrepresentation theory reliance by the creditor is a prerequisite to the liability of a holder of watered stock. The trial court was therefore justified in ordering a new trial because of the absence of a finding on that issue. It is unnecessary to further consider the defendant's appeal from the judgment.

The order granting the new trial is affirmed. The appeal from the judgment is dismissed:

GIBSON C.J. and CARTER, TRAYNOR, SCHAUER, SPENCE and McCOMB JJ. concur.

NOTES

Who has the onus of proof of reliance? An intermediate position was adopted in *Hospes v. Northwestern Mfg. & Car Co.,* 50 N.W. 1117 (Minn. 1892):

Inasmuch as the capital of a corporation is the basis of its credit, its financial standing and reputation in the community has its source in, and is founded upon, the amount of its professed and supposed capital, and every one who deals with it does so upon the faith of that standing and reputation, although, as a matter of fact, he may have no personal knowledge of the amount of its professed capital, and in a majority of cases knows nothing about the shares of stock held by any particular stockholder, or, if so, what was paid for them. Hence, in a suit by such creditor against the holders of "bonus" stock, he could not truthfully allege, and could not affirmatively prove, that he believed that the defendants' stock had been paid for, and that he gave the corporation credit on the faith of it, although, as a matter of fact, he actually gave the credit on the faith of the financial standing of the corporation, which was based upon its apparent and professed amount of capital. The misrepresentation as to the amount of capital would operate as a fraud on such a creditor as fully and effectually as if he had personal knowledge of the existence of the defendants' stock, and believed it to have been paid for when he gave the credit. For this reason, among others, we think that all that it is necessary to allege or prove in that regard is that the plaintiff is a subsequent creditor; and that, if the fact was that he dealt with the corporation with knowledge of the arrangement by which the "bonus" stock was issued, this is a matter of defense. [*Id.* at 1121]

How close does this come to the statutory liability theory? Is a prophylactic remedy, which does not depend on proof of harm to the claimant, needed on an issue of watered stock?

Which theory of liability will be applied on a breach of CBCA s. 25(3)?

What Remedies Are Available? Most discount stock cases involved insolvent issuers. Indeed, on the misrepresentation theory, it is difficult to see how creditors are harmed except in such cases. On bankruptcy, liquidators often sought to add the shareholders as contributories to the extent of the discount. This was done on the basis of a continuing obligation to pay the full amount of the required consideration. The liquidator would not have wished to have the issue set aside altogether, for the shareholder would then be not a contributory but a competing creditor to the extent that he did pay something on allotment.

An issue of bonus stock was held void in *Re Dunham (No. 1)* (1978), 20 O.R. (2d) 3. The applicant, as a shareholder, sought an order to wind up a corporation. However, he admitted not having paid any consideration on the issue of his shares. The Court concluded that the allotment was a nullity and that the applicant lacked standing as a shareholder to bring the application. Leave was nevertheless granted to him to pay $1 for an incorporator's share so that the application could proceed. Would this decision be extended to shareholders of an insolvent issuer? On the other hand, when the issuer is a profitable going concern, complainants might seek to set aside the transaction and hold recipients of watered stock liable to account for dividends received on the shares. Any claim for rescission or damages arising from the purchase of a security of a debtor will now be subordinated in the United States to the claims of ordinary creditors on the debtor's bankruptcy. 11 U.S.C. s. 510(b) (1978). See Davis, *The Status of Defrauded Securityholders in Corporate Bankruptcy*, [1983] Duke L.J. 1. See also *Re Richmond Hill Hotel Co. (Pellatt's case)* (1867), L.R. 2 Ch.App. 527.

The corporation has a remedy against the directors under CBCA s. 118(1). Are rights of recovery against shareholders restricted to the circumstances referred to in s. 118(4), such that shareholders cannot be sued on an issue of watered stock for a property consideration?

Transfers of Watered Stock. Does liability for watered stock extend to good faith purchasers without notice of the inadequate consideration to whom the initial allotees sell the shares? A related problem arose in the past when liquidators sought to hold transferees of partly paid shares liable for calls. If the shares were purchased on the assumption that they were fully paid, liability for calls could have led to transferees paying the purchase price twice. They were therefore held immune from calls when the issuer could be held estopped from asserting liability. Such an estoppel might arise either by a direct communication to the transferee or by a legend on the share certificate that the shares were fully paid. *Burkinshaw v. Nicolls* (1878), 3 App. Cas. 1004 (H.L.); *McCracken v. McIntyre* (1877), 1 S.C.R. 479; *Page v. Austin* (1882), 10 S.C.R. 132, 154 per Strong J.*

Can these decisions be extended to the duty to pay the full consideration under CBCA s. 25(3)? From the transferee's point of view, there may be nothing to suggest that the initial allotment was improper, and liability might once again amount to requiring him to pay the purchase price twice. A transferee might, however, find it more

---

*   A transferee of discount stock was, however, held liable to contribute to other shareholders in *Welton v. Saffery*, [1897] A.C. 299 (H.L.), where the *Burkinshaw* decision was not cited.

difficult to raise an estoppel against the issuer here. Watered stock is flatly prohibited by statute, while partly paid shares were not in the above cases. The distinction is important, since estoppel may not ordinarily be raised to avoid statutory duties. *Maritime Electric Co. v. General Dairies Ltd.,* [1937] A.C. 610 (P.C.). But see *Dorsch v. Freeholders Oil Co.,* [1965] S.C.R. 670 (right to set aside an issue of shares for failure to provide a prospectus lost through waiver). It would, however, be inefficient to permit a widely held corporation to sue a transferee for breach of s. 25(3), since secondary markets for the securities (such as the Toronto Stock Exchange) would then disappear. For this reason, claims against transferees for watered stock liability are likely extinguished by CBCA s. 55(2): "A security is valid in the hands of a purchaser for value without notice of any defect going to its validity." This provision, adopted from Article 8-301(2) of the 1962 draft of the Uniform Commercial Code, is intended to endow share certificates with negotiability. In the United States, subsequent holders under Article 8 will apparently take the security free and clear of any claims based on stock watering. See Folk, *Article Eight: Investment Securities,* 44 N.C.L. Rev. 654, 668-69 (1966).

Can the transferor be exonerated from liability in such cases? In *Tremblay v. Vermette,* [1959] S.C.R. 690, shares were issued for property without complying with the registration requirements of the Quebec Companies Act. While the purpose of the requirement was to restrict issues of watered stock, there was no evidence that the consideration was inadequate, and the trustee in bankruptcy's claim to add the transferor as a contributory rested solely on his non-compliance with the Quebec statute. The Supreme Court held that the shareholder could not be added as a contributory after the transfer in these circumstances. An attempt to add a transferor of bonus stock as a contributory in *Re Wiarton Beet Sugar Co.* (1906), 12 O.L.R. 149, was also rejected on the theory that the issuer's registration of the transfer constituted a release of its claim against him.

D. PRE-EMPTIVE RIGHTS

The discussion in the previous section deals primarily with how subsequent creditors or shareholders are prejudiced on an issue of watered stock. The focus now shifts to the present shareholders of the issuer. A new issue of watered stock will dilute their financial interest in the corporation, and may radically affect control positions even if the consideration is adequate. Present shareholders may seek relief in either of these cases by an action to have the issue set aside. Alternatively, they may argue for a rule of equal opportunity, with the right to have a proportionate number of shares issued to them on the same terms. These options to purchase shares are called pre-emptive rights.

As compared with an action to void an issue of watered stock under s. 25(3), an assertion of pre-emptive rights may be an expensive remedy since the shareholder might have to purchase a large number of shares to prevent a dilution of his interest. Of course, he will end up with an equal portion of a more valuable venture, to the extent that it has been enriched by the contributions received on the new share allotments. However, the shareholder will have been required to transfer a portion of his assets to the firm when he might prefer to diversify his investments. But even if costly, absolute pre-emptive rights may at times be the shareholder's preferred remedy, since they do not require a demonstration of stock watering, as would a claim under s. 25(3).

Absolute pre-emptive rights, whose exercise is not conditioned on a prior issuance of watered stock, may also be costly for a firm. Suppose that it has found a new investor willing to provide needed capital for a particular percentage of firm equity. Pre-emptive rights may frustrate the transaction by introducing a risk that the new investor will not obtain the percentage of shares he requires.

Stokes v. Continental Trust Co.
New York Court of Appeals
78 N.E. 1090 (1906)

[Stokes was a shareholder in the defendant banking corporation, and sought to compel it to issue to him a proportionate number of additional common shares. Alternatively, he asked for damages.

On January 2, 1902, another bank, Blair & Co., offered to acquire a majority of the defendant's shares through a subscription for 5,000 shares at $450 each. At this time, the book value of the shares was $310 and their par value was $100. Their market value increased from $450 in September 1901 to $550 in January 1902.

The issue of shares to Blair & Co. was approved on January 29, 1902 at a meeting of the defendant's shareholders by a vote of 3,596 to 241. Stokes owned 221 of the shares held by the dissenters. The new shares were issued to Blair & Co. on January 30, 1902.

The trial Court found that the plaintiff had the right to subscribe for his *pro rata* share of the number of shares issued to Blair & Co., and that he was entitled to $99,450, the difference between the market value of 221 shares on January 30, 1902 and their par value, together with interest. This judgment was reversed by the Appellate Division, and the plaintiff appealed.]

VANN J.: ... [T]he question presented for decision is whether according to the facts found the plaintiff had the legal right to subscribe for and take the same number of shares of the new stock that he held of the old? The subject is not regulated by statute, and the question presented has never been directly passed upon by this court, and only to a limited extent has it been considered by courts in this state. ... The leading authority is *Gray v. Portland Bank*, decided in 1807 and reported in 3 Mass. 364, 3 Am. Dec. 156. In that case a verdict was found for the plaintiff, subject, by the agreement of the parties, to the opinion of the court upon the evidence in the case whether the plaintiff was entitled to recover, and, if so, as to the measure of damages. The court held that stockholders who held old stock have a right to subscribe for and take new stock in proportion to their respective shares. As the corporation refused this right to the plaintiff he was permitted to recover the excess of the market value above the par value, with interest. ... This decision has stood unquestioned for nearly a hundred years and has been followed generally by courts of the highest standing. It is the foundation of the rule upon the subject that prevails, almost without exception, throughout the entire country.

• • •

If the right claimed by the plaintiff was a right of property belonging to him as a stockholder, he could not be deprived of it by the joint action of the other stockholders, and of all the directors and officers of the corporation. What is the nature of the right acquired by a stockholder through the ownership of shares of stock? What rights can he assert against the will of a majority of the stockholders, and all the officers and directors? While he does not own and cannot dispose of any specific property of the corporation, yet he and his associates own the corporation itself, its charter, franchises, and all rights conferred thereby, including the right to increase the stock. He has an inherent right to his proportionate share of any dividend declared, or of any surplus arising upon dissolution, and he can prevent waste or misappropriation of the property of the corporation by those in control. Finally, he has the right to vote for directors and upon all propositions subject by law to the control of the stockholders, and this is his supreme right and main protection. Stockholders have no direct voice in transacting the corporate business, but through their right to vote they can select those to whom the law intrusts the power of management and control. A corporation is somewhat like a partnership, if one were possible, conducted wholly by agents where the copartners have power to appoint the agents, but are not responsible for their acts. The power to manage its affairs resides in the directors, who are its agents, but the power to elect directors resides in the stockholders. This right to vote for directors, and upon propositions to increase the stock or mortgage the assets, is about all the power the stockholder has. So long as the management is honest, within the corporate powers, and involves no waste, the stockholders cannot interfere, even if the administration is feeble and unsatisfactory, but must correct such evils through their power to elect other directors. Hence, the power of the individual stockholder to vote in proportion to the number of his shares is vital, and cannot be cut off or curtailed by the action of all the other stockholders, even with the co-operation of the directors and officers.

In the case before us the new stock came into existence through the exercise of a right belonging wholly to the stockholders. As the right to increase the stock belonged to them, the stock when increased belonged to them also, as it was issued for money and not for property or for some purpose other than the sale thereof for money. By the increase of stock the voting power of the plaintiff was reduced one-half, and while he consented to the increase he did not consent to the disposition of the new stock by a sale thereof to Blair & Co. at less than its market value, nor by sale to any person in any way except by an allotment to the stockholders. The increase and sale involved the transfer of rights belonging to the stockholders as part of their investment. The issue of new stock and the sale thereof to Blair & Co. was not only a transfer to them of one-half the voting power of the old stockholders, but also of an equitable right to one-half the surplus which belonged to them. In other words, it was a partial division of the property of the old stockholders. The right to increase stock is not an asset of the corporation any more than the original stock when it was issued pursuant to subscription. The ownership of stock is in the nature of an inherent but indirect power to control the corporation. The stock when issued ready for delivery does not belong to the corporation in the way that it holds its real and personal property, with power to sell the same, but is held by it with no power of alienation in trust for the stockholders, who are the beneficial owners, and become the legal owners upon paying therefor. The corporation has no rights hostile to those of the stockholders, but is the trustee for all including the minority. The new stock issued by the defendant under the permission of the statute did not belong to it, but was held by it the same as the original stock when first issued was held in trust for the stockholders. It has the same voting power as the old, share for share. The stockholders decided to enlarge their holdings, not by increasing the amount of each share, but by increasing the number of shares. The new stock belonged to the stockholders as an inherent right by virtue of their being stockholders, to be shared in proportion upon paying its par value or the value per share fixed by vote of a majority of the stockholders, or ascertained by a sale at public auction. While the corporation could not compel the plaintiff to take new shares at any price, since they were issued for money and not for property, it could not lawfully dispose of those shares without giving him a chance to get his proportion at the same price that outsiders got theirs. He had an inchoate right to one share of the new stock for each share owned by him of the old stock, provided he was ready to pay the price fixed by the stockholders. If so situated that he could not take it himself, he was entitled to sell the right to one who could, as is frequently done. Even this gives an advantage to capital, but capital necessarily has some advantage. Of course, there is a distinction when the new stock is issued in payment for property, but that is not this case. The stock in question was issued to be sold for money and was sold for money only. A majority of the stockholders, as part of their power to increase the stock, may attach reasonable conditions to the disposition thereof, such as the requirement that every old stockholder electing to take new stock shall pay a fixed price therefor, not less than par, however, owing to the limitation of the statute. They may also provide for a sale in parcels or bulk at public auction, when every stockholder can bid the same as strangers. They cannot, however, dispose of it to strangers against the protest of any stockholder who insists that he has a right to his proportion. Otherwise the majority could deprive the minority of their proportionate power in the election of directors and their proportionate right to share in the surplus, each of which is an inherent, pre-emptive, and vested right of property. It is inviolable, and can neither be taken away nor lessened without consent, or a waiver implying consent. The plaintiff had power, before the increase of stock, to vote on 221 shares of stock, out of a total of 5,000, at any meeting held by the stockholders for any purpose. By the action of the majority, taken against his will and protest, he now has only one-half the voting power that he had before, because the number of shares has been doubled while he still owns but 221. This touches him as a stockholder in such a way as to deprive him of a right of property. Blair & Co. acquired virtual control, while he and the other stockholders lost it. We are not discussing equities, but legal rights, for this is an action at law, and the plaintiff was deprived of a strictly legal right. If the result gives him an advantage over other stockholders, it is because he stood upon his legal rights, while they did not. The question is what were his legal rights, not what his profit may be under the sale to Blair & Co., but what it might have been if the new stock had been issued to him in proportion to his holding of the old. The other stockholders could give their property to Blair & Co., but they could not give his. A share of stock is a share in the power to increase the stock, and belongs to the stockholders the same as the stock itself. When that power is exercised, the new stock belongs to the old stockholders in proportion to their holding of old stock, subject to compliance with the lawful terms upon which it is issued.

• • •

We are thus led to lay down the rule that a stockholder has an inherent right to a proportionate share of new stock issued for money only and not to purchase property for the purposes of the corporation or to effect a consolidation, and while he can waive that right, he cannot be deprived of it without his consent except when the stock is issued at a fixed price not less than par, and he is given the right to take at that price in proportion to his holding, or in some other equitable way that will enable him to protect his interest by acting on his own judgment and using his own resources. This rule is just to all and tends to prevent the tyranny of majorities which needs restraint, as well as virtual attempts to blackmail by small minorities which should be prevented.

The remaining question is whether the plaintiff waived his rights by failing to do what he ought to have done, or by doing something he ought not to have done. He demanded his share of the new stock at par, instead of at the price fixed by the stockholders, for the authorization to sell at $450 a share was virtually fixing the price of the stock. He did more than this, however, for he not only voted against the proposition to sell to Blair & Co. at $450, but, as the court expressly found, he "protested against the proposed sale of his proportionate share of the stock, and again demanded the right to subscribe and pay for the same which demands were again refused," and "the resolution was carried notwithstanding such protest and demands." Thus he protested against the sale of his share before the price was fixed, for the same resolution fixed the price, and directed the sale, which was promptly carried into effect. If he had not attended the meeting, called upon due notice to do precisely what was done, perhaps he would have waived his rights, but he attended the meeting and, before the price was fixed, demanded the right to subscribe for 221 shares at par, and offered to pay for the same immediately. It is true that after the price was fixed he did not offer to take his share at that price, but he did not acquiesce in the sale of his proportion to Blair & Co., and unless he acquiesced the sale as to him was without right. He was under no obligation to put the corporation in default by making a demand. The ordinary doctrine of demand, tender, and refusal has no application to this case. The plaintiff had made no contract. He had not promised to do anything. No duty of performance rested upon him. He had an absolute right to the new stock in proportion to his holding of the old, and he gave notice that he wanted it. It was his property, and could not be disposed of without his consent. He did not consent. He protested in due time, and the sale was made in defiance of his protest. While in connection with his protest he demanded the right to subscribe at par, that demand was entirely proper when made, because the price had not then been fixed. After the price was fixed it was the duty of the defendant to offer him his proportion at that price, for it had notice that he had not acquiesced to the proposed sale of his share, but wanted it himself. The directors were under the legal obligation to give him an opportunity to purchase at the price fixed before they could sell his property to a third party, even with the approval of a large majority of the stockholders. If he had remained silent, and had made no request or protest he would have waived his rights, but after he had given notice that he wanted his part and had protested against the sale thereof, and defendant was bound to offer it to him at the price fixed by the stockholders. By selling to strangers without thus offering to sell to him, the defendant wrongfully deprived him of his property, and is liable for such damages as he actually sustained.

The learned trial court, however, did not measure the damages according to law. The plaintiff was not entitled to the difference between the par value of the new stock and the market value thereof, for the stockholders had the right to fix the price at which the stock should be sold. They fixed the price at $450 a share, and for the failure of the defendant to offer the plaintiff his share at that price we hold it liable in damages. His actual loss, therefore, is $100 per share, or the difference between $450, the price that he would have been obliged to pay had he been permitted to purchase, and the market value on the day of sale, which was $550. This conclusion requires a reversal of the judgment rendered by the Appellate Division and a modification of that rendered by the trial court.

• • •

HAIGHT J. (dissenting): I agree that the rule that we should adopt is that a stockholder in a corporation has an inherent right to purchase a proportionate share of new stock issued for money only, and not to purchase property necessary for the purposes of the corporation or to effect a consolidation. While he can waive that right he cannot be deprived of it without his consent, except by sale at a fixed price at or above par, in which he may buy at that price in proportion to his holding or in some other equitable way that will enable him to protect his interest by acting on his own judgment and using his own resources. I, however, differ with Judge Vann as to his conclusions as to the rights of the plaintiff herein. Under the findings of the trial court the plaintiff demanded that his share of the new stock should be issued to him at par, or $100 per share, instead of $450 per share, the price offered by Blair & Co. and the price fixed at the stockholders' meeting at which the new stock was authorized to be sold. This demand was made after the passage of the resolution authorizing the increase of the capital stock of the defendant company and before the passage of the resolution authorizing a sale of the new stock to Blair & Co. at the price specified. After the passage of the second resolution he objected to the sale of his proportionate share of the new stock to Blair & Co., and again demanded that it be issued to him, and the following day he made a legal tender for the amount of his portion of the new stock at $100 per share. There is no finding of fact or evidence in the record showing that he was ever ready or willing to pay $450 per share for the stock. He knew that Blair & Co. represented Marshall Field and others at Chicago, great dry goods merchants, and that they had made a written offer to purchase the new stock of the company provided the stockholders would authorize an increase of its capital stock from $500,000 to $1,000,000. He knew that the trustees of the company had called a special meeting of the stockholders for the purpose of considering the offer so made by Blair & Co. He knew that the increased capitalization proposed was for the purpose of enlarging the business of the company and bringing into its management the gentlemen referred to. There is no pretense that any of the stockholders would have voted for an increase of the capital stock otherwise than for the purpose of accepting the offer of Blair & Co. All were evidently desirous of interesting the gentlemen referred to in the company, and by securing their business and deposits increase the earnings of the company. This the trustees carefully considered, and in their notice, calling the special meeting of the stockholders, distinctly recommended the acceptance of the offer. What, then, was the legal effect of the plaintiff's demand and tender? To my mind it was simply an attempt to make something out of his associates, to get for $100 per share the stock which Blair & Co. had offered to purchase for $450 per share; and that it was the equivalent of a refusal to pay $450 per share, and its effect is to waive his right to procure the stock by paying that amount. An acceptance of his offer would have been most unjust to the remaining stockholders. It would not only have deprived them of the additional sum of $350 per share, which has been offered for the stock, but it would have defeated the object and purpose for which the meeting was called, for it was well understood that Blair & Co. would not accept less than the whole issue of the new stock. But this is not all. It appears that prior to the offer of Blair & Co. the stock of the company had never been sold above $450 per share; that thereafter the stock rapidly advanced until the day of the completion of the sale on the 30th of January, when its market value was $550 per share; but this, under the stipulation of facts, was caused by the rumor and subsequent announcement and consummation of the proposition for the increase of the stock and the sale of such increase to Blair & Co. and their associates. It is now proposed to give the plaintiff as damages such increase in the market value of the stock, even though such value was based upon the understanding that Blair & Co. were to become stockholders in the corporation, which the acceptance of plaintiff's offer would have prevented. This, to my mind, should not be done. I, therefore, favor an affirmance.

CULLEN C.J. and WERNER and HISCOCK JJ. concur with VANN J.; WILLARD BARTLETT J. concurs with HAIGHT J.; and O'BRIEN J. is absent.

The Movement to Fault-Based Rights. Pre-emptive rights developed in a very different way in American than in Anglo-Canadian law. In England and Canada, such rights were merely a matter of contract, with a presumption that they did not arise unless specifically bargained for. This policy is continued in CBCA s. 28, which is merely permissive in nature. By contrast, early American decisions held that shareholders had a vested pre-emptive right.

Given La Forest J.'s analysis of the nature of a share in *Sparling v. Caisse de dépot et placement* (seen in Section A of this chapter), how much sense would it have made in Canada to speak of a shareholder having an "inherent right" to a proportionate share of an issuance of new stock? Is the language of "inherent rights" that is seen in the *Stokes* decision linked to ideas about shareholders as "owners" of the corporation?

While the Dickerson Committee recommended that the CBCA be drafted so as to provide that a pre-emptive right be one of the rights associated with owning a share, the Legislature chose not to follow this recommendation. In part, the Legislature was no doubt concerned to leave the corporation flexibility with respect to the way in which it raises capital and, accordingly, did not wish to put in place statutory guarantees respecting the size of a shareholder's holdings relative to that of other shareholders. What are the implications of this decision for the debate (seen in Section A of this chapter) concerning the nature of the equality principle that is applicable to shareholders and/or shares?

As the American economy expanded, absolute pre-emptive rights began to be seen as inconvenient relics of a less industrialized past. Large corporations required unfettered access to capital markets and pre-emptive rights were cumbersome to the extent that they inhibited capital formation and expansion. Shareholders with a small stake in a widely held corporation would not need such rights, and a strict insistence on vested rights might even result in a windfall to the shareholders, as Haight J. suggested occurred in *Stokes*.

Exceptions to pre-emptive rights therefore developed. One of these, referred to in *Stokes*, involves the issue of shares for a non-cash consideration. Cf. CBCA s. 28(2)(a). Pre-emptive rights were also excluded on an issue of part of the initial authorized capital. If these exemptions made little sense in themselves, they at least provided a covert tool to avoid the result in cases like *Stokes*.

More recent American cases have concentrated on whether the initial issue of shares involved a breach of fiduciary duties. So too, Canadian courts, unencumbered by American doctrines of vested rights, have found that pre-emptive rights may be asserted as a remedy against oppressive conduct by management. See Blais, *Shareholder's Protection from Share Watering Caused by the Additional Issue of Shares: Pre-emptive Rights*, 19 U. of Toronto Fac. L. Rev. 43 (1961). The preemptive rights doctrines in Canada and the United States, which began in very different ways, have therefore largely merged in recent years, with a likelihood that the same case would be decided in the same way in the two countries. To suggest that doctrines of pre-emptive rights are now assimilated to fiduciary principles does not, however, supply a content to such rights. Consider why it is desirable to grant a remedy in circumstances like those of the following case.

Beauchamp v. Contenants sanitaires C.S. Inc.
Quebec Superior Court
[1979] C.S. 414, 7 B.L.R. 200

BEAUDOIN J.: Le requérant demande l'émission d'une ordonnance d'injonction interlocutoire ordonnant à l'intimée, Les Contenants sanitaires C.S. Inc., et aux intimés de s'abstenir de procéder dorénavant à toute émission de capital-actions de l'intimée autrement qu'à la valeur marchande des actions et après avoir offert au requérant de souscrire proportionnellement à son interêt.

Il est à noter qu'à cette requête en injonction interlocutoire est jointe une déclaration sur action en injonction permanente et en annulation de souscriptions d'actions faites par les intimés auprès de la compagnie intimée après le 30 novembre 1977, action qui inclut aussi une réclamation en dommages-intérêts contre les intimés.

La preuve révèle que:

Le 20 août 1974, des lettres patentes étaient émises constituant en corporation sous le nom de les Contenants sanitaires C.S. Inc. le réquerant et l'intimé Denis Gamache ainsi que Marc Vaillancourt, qui en étaient les administrateurs provisoires, et le capital-actions autorisé de la compagnie était fixé à $40,000, divisé en deux cents actions privilégiées de $100 chacune et deux mille actions ordinaires de $10 chacune, tel qu'il appert auxdites lettres patentes produites sous la cote P-1.

À la suite de cette incorporation, l'intimé Denis Gamache détenait 51% des actions ordinaires, le requérant 40% et Marc Vaillancourt 9%.

Ladite compagnie avait pour objets principaux de manufacturer, louer, acheter, vendre et généralement faire le commerce de produits sanitaires, contenants de toutes sortes et de nettoyeurs industriels.

Un ou deux mois après l'incorporation de la compagnie, Marc Vaillancourt s'en retira et fut remplacé par un nommé Pellerin qui, à son tour, vendit 7% de ses actions a dame Irène Gamache, mère de l'intimé Denis Gamache, et 2% au requérant.

En fèvrier 1978, à la suite d'une mésentente avec l'intimé Denis Gamache, le requérant quitta la compagnie tant en sa qualité de représentant des ventes qu'en sa qualité d'administrateur alors que l'intimé Denis Gamache détenait cinq cent quatre-vingt-dix actions, dame Irène Gamache cent vingt et le requérant quatre cent quatre-vingt-treize, soit 42%, qu'il conserva, dit-il, et n'offrit pas de vendre a l'intimé Denis Gamache qui lui avait toutefois laissé entendre qu'il voulait les acheter, mais ne lui fit pas d'offre formelle.

Or, le 16 juin 1978, l'intimé Denis Gamache avisait le requérant que, sur réception de sa part d'une offre écrite de lui vendre la totalité des actions qu'il détenait dans le capital-actions de la compagnie intimée, il était disposé a prendre cette offre en considération afin de régler définitivement cette affaire, le tout tel qu'il appert à la lettre déposée comme pièce D-2, et la preuve ne révèle pas que le requérant ait donné suite à cette offre de l'intimé Denis Gamache.

À la suite du départ du requérant, l'épouse de l'intimé Denis Gamache, Hélène, qui détenait à ce moment-là une action la qualifiant, fut nommée administrateur de la compagnie intimée.

Il est à noter qu'avant le départ du requérant, soit le 15 juillet 1977, en vertu d'un règlement d'emprunt de la compagnie intimée, celle-ci avait fait un emprunt auprès de la compagnie de financement Roy-Nat ainsi qu'auprès de la Banque royale où elle avait une marge de crédit de $35,000.

Or, à la suite de son départ de la compagnie intimée, le requérant, le 15 mars 1978, écrivait à la Banque royale demandant d'être libéré des engagements et endossements qu'il avait pris auprès de cette banque vu qu'il ne faisait plus partie du conseil d'administration de la compagnie intimée malgré, mentionne-t-il, qu'il détenait toujours 40% des actions. Il ajoutait:

M. Denis Gamache, le président, n'a pas semble-t-il l'argent nécessaire pour racheter mes actions à la valeur réelle comptable aux livres.

et qu'il serait donc très normal que la personne désignée pour le remplacer comme administrateur endosse personnellement auprès de la banque, le tout tel qu'il appert à ladite lettre versée sous la cote D-5.

En outre, le 22 mars 1978, le requérant adressait à Roy-Nat une lettre dans le même sens que celle envoyée à la Banque royale le 15 mars 1978 (D-5), à savoir qu'il voulait être dégagé des endossements qu'il avait faits pour des emprunts contractés par la compagnie intimée, tel qu'il appert à la pièce D-4.

Or, il appert du témoignage de l'intimé Denis Gamache que le requérant n'a pas été libéré de ses endossements auprès de la Banque royale et de Roy-Nat et qu'actuellement, la compagnie intimée doit $24,000 à la Banque royale et $100,000 à Roy-Nat, précisant que la compagnie intimée n'a pas emprunté à la Banque provinciale du Canada, malgré la production de la pièce D-6.

Denis Gamache ajoute qu'à la suite des lettres écrites par le requérant à Roy-Nat et à la Banque royale, celle-ci, comme la plupart des créanciers, prit panique du fait qu'il y avait zizanie entre les actionnaires et qu'il y avait urgence de convoquer le conseil d'administration pour être seul autorisé à signer les chèques; que, dans ce but, il fallait qu'il détienne les deux tiers des actions *votantes* et que c'est pourquoi il y eut une nouvelle émission d'actions faite à l'intérieur du capital-actions autorisé par les lettres patentes, précisant qu'il detient maintenant huit cent quatre-vingt-dix actions, le réquerant quatre cent quatre-vingt-treize, sa mère, l'intimée Irène Gamache, deux cent soixante-dix et son épouse, l'intimée Hélène Gamache, deux cent cinquante et une.

Denis Gamache produit sous la cote D-3 un extrait du livre des minutes, soit l'article 4 qui est un règlement qui était en vigueur, dit-il, lors du départ du requérant et intitulé *Pouvoir de répartir les actions et d'accorder des options* et qui prévoit plus spécialement que:

Les parts de la Compagnie devront, en tout temps, demeurer sous le contrôle des directeurs qui pourront, par résolution, de temps à autre, accepter des soumissions, répartir, émettre ou accorder des options à cet effet, ou autrement disposer de la totalité ou d'une partie des parts non émises de la Compagnie ...

article qui fut adopté le 6 septembre 1974.

Or, pour avoir une marge de crédit additionnelle de $15,000 auprès de la Banque royale, une mise de fonds supplémentaire était requise et l'intimé Denis Gamache déclare qu'il voulait détenir 75% des actions afin de pouvoir administrer la compagnie intimée sans avoir à consulter les actionnaires et, en outre, pour éviter la prise du contrôle de la compagnie intimée par une compagnie compétitrice, comme celle qu'exploite le requérant, ajoutant qu'il était du devoir des administrateurs de protéger la compagnie et que, de plus, il ne voulait rien demander au requérant qui était leur compétiteur.

À ce sujet, le requérant répond que le commerce qu'il exploite depuis qu'il a quitté la compagnie intimée est compétitif et complémentaire de celle-ci.

Gamache invoque comme autre motif le fait qu'à la suite de l'augmentation des opérations de la compagnie intimée qui était devenue manufacturière, ce qui exigeait une marge de crédit supplémentaire, les banques lui demandèrent de faire des mises de fonds supplémentaires et de trouver d'autres investissements et qu'ayant eu de la difficulté avec un actionnaire (le requérant?), il n'était pas intéressé à aller en chercher d'autres et décida d'investir le plus qu'il pouvait pour donner en garantie à la banque une *équité* suffisamment élevée pour justifier une marge de crédit adéquate pour les opérations de la compagnie, soit $50,000 au total.

Dans sa requête pour l'émission d'une injonction interlocutoire appuyée de sa déclaration sous serment, le requérant allègue qu'au moment où les intimés se firent émettre de nouvelles actions, la valeur marchande desdites actions de la compagnie intimée était *largement* supérieure à leur valeur nominale de $10 que les intimés ont payée; qu'elles peuvent être évaluées actuellement à $75 chacune et qu'en aucun moment avant cette émission, les intimés ne lui ont offert la possibilité de souscrire à l'achat de nouvelles actions en vue de conserver sa *position relative* dans la compagnie.

Le requérant ajoute que le fait d'émettre ces actions à leur valeur nominale a eu pour effet évident de diminuer la valeur de son capital dans cette compagnie, qui n'avait aucun besoin de procéder à une emission d'actions, et que ceci n'a été fait que dans le but de la frauder; que si la compagnie avait eu besoin de capital et que d'autres moyens de financement étaient impossibles, elle était obligée de lui offrir de souscrire personnellement (proportionnellement?) à la nouvelle émission de capital-actions en vue de lui permettre de conserver sa *position relative* dans la compagnie; que le seul fait de l'émission de ces actions à leur valeur nominale, sans prime pour en faire correspondre le prix à leur valeur réelle, aurait constitué une fraude manifeste à son égard, meme s'il avait refusé de souscrire du nouveau capital-actions.

En outre, le requérant soumet dans sa requête que la compagnie intimée étant contrôlée par l'intimé Denis Gamache et sa famille, il a toutes les raisons de croire que sa position financière dans cette compagnie sera encore mise en péril sans l'intervention des Tribunaux et qu'il est impératif qu'une ordonnance d'injonction interlocutoire soit émise "dans cette compagnie pour empêcher de nouvelles émissions d'actions contraires à ses droits."

Or, il appert au bilan de la compagnie intimée daté du 30 novembre 1977 et produit comme pièce P-2 que douze cent trois actions ordinaires à $10 chacune ont été émises, formant un total de $12,030, alors que les bénéfices non répartis s'élèvent à $21,330, soit un total de $33,360, ce qui, selon le requérant, établit la valeur de chaque action à $27.70 avant son départ comme administrateur de la compagnie en février 1978.

Par ailleurs, le 28 novembre 1978, le requérant recevait une lettre de l'intimé Denis Gamache l'avisant que les actions maintenant émises et détenues par les administrateurs, qui les avaient payées $10 chacune, étaient réparties comme suit:

Denis Gamache	890
Marc Beauchamp	493
Irène Gamache	270
Hélène G. Gamache	251
	1904

tel qu'il appert à ladite lettre déposée sous la cote P-3.

Le requérant souligne que les intimés ne lui ont pas offert d'acheter des actions lors de cette dernière émission dont il fut informé par son comptable et par la lettre P-3 et qu'il n'a recu le bilan daté du 30 novembre 1978, produit comme pièce P-4 qu'au début d'avril 1979.

Or, à l'état numéro 1 de ce bilan P-4, au titre *Avoir des actionnaires,* le capital-actions s'élève à $19,040 et les bénéfices non répartis à $16,339, formant un total de $35,379 qui, selon le requérant, divisé en mille neuf cent trois actions, fixe la valeur de chaque action à $18.90, bilan qui indique qu'en 1977, les bénéfices non répartis se chiffraient à $19,939 au lieu de $21,330 apparaissant au bilan de 1977 (P-2), soit une diminution de $3,600 en 1978.

En outre, le requérant note que le bilan indique une dépréciation de 100% sur les moules servant à la fabrication des équipements par la compagnie intimée alors que, selon lui, ces moules ont une durée de cinq à dix ans et que cette dépréciation fait disparaître des actifs d'une valeur de $6,530, ajoutant par ailleurs que des contenants pour un montant de $93,644 ont été achetés, tel qu'il appert à l'état numéro 4 de la pièce P-4 au titre *Utilisation des fonds*.

Le requérant affirme que, sur l'émission des sept cent une nouvelles actions qui ont été achetées pour le montant de $10 chacune par les intimés, il en aurait acheté dans la proportion de 42%, des actions qu'il détenait dans la compagnie, preuve que le Tribunal permet bien qu'une objection y ait été faite, car au prix que les actions étaient offertes, l'on peut conclure que le requérant pouvait être intéressé à les acheter.

Or, selon les dispositions de l'article 88 de la Loi des compagnies de Québec,

Les administrateurs de la compagnie peuvent en administrer les affaires et ... faire des règlements non contraires à la loi et aux lettres patentes pour régler les objets suivants: a) La répartition des actions ...

Toutefois, les Tribunaux sont intervenus lorsque les administrateurs ont commis des abus de pouvoir dans leur administration, alors qu'au lieu d'agir dans l'intérêt de la compagnie ils ont agi dans leur intérêt personnel ou celui de leurs amis au préjudice des actionnaires minoritaires.

F.W. Wegenast [*The Law of Canadian Companies,* Toronto, Burroughs, 1931, pp. 322 et 323] fait l'exposé sommaire suivant de certains arrêts des Tribunaux:

If the company's stock is increased the minority shareholders must be given an equal opportunity with the majority to acquire their due proportion of the new stock, and if the directors take over at less than its market value any more than their proportion of a new issue, they must account to the company for the profits.

(...) the fact that directors had received stock on more favourable terms than the other shareholders was held sufficient to invalidate subscriptions for stock which had been given on the assumption that all were being treated equally.

(...)

This principle, requiring an equality of treatment amongst the shareholders in the distribution of property represented in the company's assets, will be found to cover the cases in which the transaction complained of has been described by the terms "fraudulent" or "oppressive" or "harsh" or "unfair" which, as we have seen, have been applied in different cases where there has been an attempt on the part of one set of shareholders to benefit themselves at the expense of the rest, or to use a majority power for purposes other than the benefit of the company as a whole.

Et le même auteur, sous le titre *Allotment of Stock*:

It is open to the directors, if they choose to do so, to allot the shares to the existing shareholders at par though they may be worth more. But the directors cannot allot to themselves at par shares worth more than par, at all events not without offering to let the minority have their due proportion, and any improper or fraudulent motive on the part of the directors in manipulating a stock issue will furnish ground for the interference of the Court [p. 485].

Le Tribunal se réfère aussi aux arrêts suivants:

A proceeding may be taken by the directors in violation of the good faith they owe to the company and to the shareholders because the purpose of the proceeding is to benefit themselves personally or some individual shareholder or some group of shareholders at the expense or to the detriment of the shareholders as a whole. [*In re Crédit canadien Inc.: Sun Trust Co. c. Bégin*, [1937] R.C.S. 305, 309].

Held, the company being in no need of additional funds at the time, the increase of capital was unnecessary and fictitious, the real purpose being to secure control of the company and keep the existing directors in office, against the will of the majority of the shareholders. The issue, and all transactions following upon it, were therefore set aside. [*Perreault c. Milot*, (1886), 14 R.L. 417].

En outre, dans la cause *In re Sabex internationale Ltée: Lavigne c. Sagebec Inc.*, monsieur le juge Gonthier a interdit la souscription et l'émission d'actions ordinaires en faveur des actionnaires actuels au prorata des actions ordinaires qu'ils détenaient parce que cette émission avait pour effet de diluer le capital-actions émis.

Marc Giguère [*Les devoirs des dirigeants de société par actions*, Québec, P.U.L., 1967, pp. 32 et 33] écrit, dans une étude, au titre *Nouvelle émission de titres*:

(...) une société (...) peut emprunter ou procéder à une nouvelle émission de titres. Dans ce dernier cas, les effets secondaires de l'opération peuvent être très importants. Tel ou tel conseil d'administration pourra y voir une occasion propice de renforcer ses positions ou celles de ses amis au sein de l'assemblée générale. Peut-être sera-ce là même le seul objectif de l'opération (...)

Bien aménagée, une nouvelle émission de titres pourrait faciliter ces desseins. La loi (et sa présence se manifeste ici plutôt par l'intermédiaire du contrôle des tribunaux) n'a pas voulu qu'on utilise ainsi à son propre profit des pouvoirs qu'on a voulu affectés à l'intérêt exclusif de la société. On trouve en droit anglais et canadien d'importantes applications de ce souhait *(Fraser v. Walley* (1864), 2, H. & M., 10).

Dans cet arrêt, le conseil d'administration d'une société de chemin de fer s'était autorisé d'une vieille résolution permettant une émission de titres pour certaines fins particulières et s'était, sous le couvert de cette résolution, gratifié de nouveaux titres qui lui permettaient ou permettaient à ses amis de se maintenir en fonction. Le Tribunal cassa l'opération.

L'auteur Giguère cite aussi les arrêts *Punt c. Symons Co.* [[1903] 2 Ch. D. 506] et *Martin c. Gibson* [[1908] 15 O.L.R. 623], où il fut décidé qu'on ne peut procéder à une nouvelle émission de titres afin d'empêcher que n'accède à la direction un important actionnaire que l'on estimait peu désirable et, plus particulièrement, que lorsqu'une société n'a pas besoin de nouveaux capitaux, il n'est pas permis aux administrateurs de procéder à de nouvelles émissions de titres dans le simple but de se perpétuer dans l'exercice de leur pouvoir en maintenant leur contrôle ou celui de leurs amis au sein de l'assemblée générale.

• • •

Or, en vertu de l'article 752 du Code de procédure civile, outre l'injonction qu'une partie peut demander par action, elle peut, au début ou au cours d'une instance, obtenir une injonction interlocutoire qui peut être accordée lorsque celui qui la demande paraît y avoir droit et qu'elle est jugée nécessaire pour empêcher que ne lui soit causé un préjudice sérieux ou irréparable ou que ne soit crée un état de fait ou de droit de nature à rendre le jugement final inefficace.

Comme on l'a vu, dans la présente cause, outre une requête en injonction interlocutoire demandée par le requérant, celui-ci requiert aussi que lui soit accordée une injonction permanente ordonnant aux intimés de s'abstenir de procéder dorénavant à toute émission de capital-actions de la compagnie intimée autrement qu'à la valeur marchande des actions et après avoir offert au requérant de souscrire proportionnellement à son intérêt.

De la preuve faite, le Tribunal, sans préjuger du fond, est d'opinion que le requérant a établi un droit *prima facie* apparent et suffisamment clair à l'émission d'une injonction interlocutoire, d'autant plus que c'est le requérant, et non les intimés, qui assumera le poids des inconvénients pouvant en résulter si la présente requête n'est pas accueillie.

Par ailleurs, même si le poids des inconvénients s'équilibre pour le requérant et les intimés à ce stade des procédures, il suffit, pour accorder l'ordonnance, qu'il apparaisse au juge que celui qui en fait la demande a un droit sérieux et valable à faire valoir sans tenir compte du poids des inconvénients, si ce problème ne se présente pas avec assez d'acuité pour faire pencher la balance d'un côté ou de l'autre.

Par ces motifs, le Tribunal accueille la requête du requérant pour l'émission d'une injonction interlocutoire qui restera en vigueur pendant l'instance jusqu'au jugement final; ordonne aux intimés de s'abstenir de procéder dorénavant à toute émission de capital-actions de la compagnie intimée autrement qu'à la valeur marchande des actions et après avoir offert au requérant de souscrire proportionnellement à son intérêt.

An Exclusive Remedy? When watered stock is issued to some but not all shareholders, those left out are clearly prejudiced. But how are they harmed if all shareholders are issued rights to purchase shares at a price that is lower than current value? Suppose that a firm has issued one share each to 10 shareholders. Each share is worth $10 for a total firm value of $100. The firm then issues one right to each shareholder, with each right giving its holder the privilege of subscribing for one new share at an *exercise price* of $5. After all rights are exercised, the firm will have issued 20 shares worth $150/20 = $7.50 each. The old $10 shares with their rights attached are called *rights-on* shares, and the new $7.50 shares after exercise are referred to as *ex-rights* shares. The value of the right prior to exercise is then the rights-on price less the ex-rights price, or $2.50. (Another way of looking at the value of the right is to note that it permits its holder to purchase a $7.50 share for $5.) The firm has in other words diluted share value by the value of the rights. Since the rights holder's gain equals the shareholder's loss, the rights issue appears distributionally neutral.

On the other hand, a rights offering may not guarantee the fairness of an issue of watered stock. Where the rights themselves do not trade, the shareholder must exercise them or suffer dilution. If the outside shareholder will have difficulty subscribing, either because of a short exercise period or simply through impecuniosity, the transaction might then be impeached. For example, in *Browning v. C & C Plywood Corp.*, 434 P.2d 339 (Or. 1967), an issue of shares that reduced the plaintiff's interest from 32% to 1%

was set aside. The issued share capital was increased from 1,000 to 500,000 shares and the plaintiff was given 30 days to take up 152,000 shares at $1 each. Management knew that the plaintiff could not afford this, and the sole purpose of the increase of stock was found to be to eliminate Browning's interest. See further W. Cary & M. Eisenberg, *Cases and Materials on Corporations*, 1097-1101 (5th ed. 1980). However, in *Hyman v. Velsicol Corp.*, 97 N.E.2d 122 (Ill. Ct. App. 1951), securities in the defendant corporation were offered on a proportionate basis as part of a plan of reorganization. They were issued at less than their true value, but the plaintiff would have had to raise $136,000 within 10 days to take them up. He had formed a corporation to compete with Velsicol and testified that he might not have taken up the shares even if he had had the money. The Court upheld the allotment.

In *Re Sabex Internationale Ltée* (1979), 6 B.L.R. 65 (Que.), the applicants, holding 44% of Sabex's common shares, sought an order under CBCA s. 234 (now s. 241) to prohibit a rights offering that would have enabled existing shareholders to subscribe for further shares on a *pro rata* basis. The corporation had 800,000 outstanding common shares, and the rights issue would have permitted the issue of 3,000,000 additional common shares at 5¢ each. This offering came after the corporation's bankers required a further $100,000 be invested in the business. The applicants had lost a struggle for control of Sabex, and had been fired from their positions in it. They formed a competing corporation and could not afford to take up the shares offered to them. They sought a variety of remedies, all of which failed save for the order prohibiting the rights offering. Management of the corporation argued that the transaction was not unfair because its bankers demanded a further issue of shares and because the offering was on a *pro rata* basis. For these reasons, the Quebec Securities Commission did not object to the offering. However, the Court held it oppressive under CBCA s. 234 (now s. 241). Since the issue was at an undervalue, minority shareholders were obliged to subscribe if their holdings were not to be severely diluted.

Do these concerns arise when an active market for the rights exists? Instead of exercising the right, a shareholder could simply sell it, which would eliminate the unfairness in cases like *Browning*. Without a market for the rights, however, the price of non-dilution is subscription for new shares. By way of shareholder protection, Ontario Securities Commission Policy s. 6.2(VI) states that the Commission will object to rights offerings with an exercise price equal to or above market price. This will of course raise issues of non-compliance within s. 25(3). In addition, would shareholders be better protected if the exercise price equalled market price? They would then not be called on to subscribe at the risk of dilution.

A corporation that finances through a rights issue might then be thought to transfer wealth from non-exercising minority shareholders. These concerns may, however, be dissipated for three reasons. First, share values have not been shown to decline on a rights issue, as they would if rights issues had distributional effects. See R. Brealey & S. Myers, *Principles of Corporate Finance* 313-15 (2d ed. 1984). Second, there are important reasons, apart from distributional motives, why a firm may wish to raise capital through a rights issue rather than a cash offer. Chief among these is that rights offerings are considerably less costly to a firm than cash offerings. Smith, *Alternative Methods for Raising Capital: Rights Versus Underwritten Offerings*, 5 J. Fin. Econ. 273 (1977).

Finally, the possibility of litigation by minority shareholders under CBCA s. 241 may deter managers from overt self-dealing on a rights issue.

To ensure that all the shares available under the offering will be subscribed for, a controlling shareholder will often underwrite the offering through a *stand-by agreement* in which he undertakes to take up any shares not subscribed for by the minority share-holders. Unless minority shareholders are also given a right to take up unsubscribed securities, the controlling shareholder will be enabled to increase his holding relative to the minority shareholders. If the exercise price is below market price, this would be very much to the controlling shareholder's advantage. Because of this, the O.S.C. requires that minority shareholders be given a second stage right to take up unsubscribed securities on a *pro rata* basis. See OSC Policies s. 6.2(VI). This is sometimes accomplished by breaking down the issue of shares into three stages. In the first stage, the controlling shareholder will exercise his rights to subscribe for shares together with any other minority shareholders who desire to do so. In the second stage, shares that were not taken up in the first stage may be subscribed for by the shareholders in proportion to their holdings. The controlling shareholder will elect not to take up such shares at this point, but instead in the third stage will purchase all of the shares remaining after the first two stages. In this way, minority shareholders may participate both in the rights offering and in the underwriting.

E. PROMOTERS' DUTIES

Before there were securities regulations, there were promoters' duties. The problem arose in the following way. A Victorian businessman of dubious antecedents acquired a rubber plantation in Brazil or a copper mine in Canada. He then formed a corporation and resold the property to it for a much higher stated price in return for an issue of shares. The corporation subsequently made a distribution of securities to the public. On these facts, it was asserted that the promoter was liable to account to the corporation for profits made in the transaction. Alternatively, the sale of assets could be set aside for misrepresentation by the corporation, so long as the right of rescission had not been lost by the lapse of time or the difficulties in making restitution. However stated, the duties were owed to the corporation and not to the defrauded shareholders.

Whether a promoter's liability in such cases turned on misrepresentation or over-compensation exacted by him from the corporation was never wholly clear. Dicta in several cases suggested that, even with full disclosure of all profits, a promoter might still be liable to account if under a duty on the first purchase to act for the proposed corporation. Thus it was stated that a promoter might be held to have acquired the property in trust for the proposed corporation. He would then be under a duty to convey it to the corporation at its cost price even if full disclosure was made. See *Re Hess Mfg. Co.* (1894), 23 S.C.R. 644, 655-58 per Strong C.J. But no case appears to have held that, full disclosure being made, the property was acquired in trust. Instead, promoters were held to have acquired it for themselves and, if they chose, might have refused to convey it to the corporation. If they did sell to the corporation, their duties were generally said to end at full disclosure.

Behind the uncertainty about the nature of the duty is an unresolved economic problem: how are promoters' services to be measured? No automobile patent bears the name of Henry Ford. Instead, he merely realized the benefits available if the techniques of mass production were applied to a novel invention. In recent years, there has been an enormous growth in inexpensive home computers. What reward is the first successful promoter of such a manufacturer entitled to? The difficulty is that what the promoter contributes to a new business is not simply the property he transfers to it but the idea and creation of the business itself. His entrepreneurial services are of a different order than the assets a capitalist places at risk or the services contributed by an employee. Economists have not been able to provide guidance on how such services should be measured. Cf. Dewing, *The Financial Policy of Corporations* 402-17 (5th ed. 1953).

There are other reasons why the problem is better seen as one of misrepresentation rather than overcompensation. If the promotion is wrongful, its victims are the shareholders who later subscribe on the faith of an inflated valuation of the enterprise. Where no further issue of shares to the public is contemplated, as in *Salomon v. A. Salomon & Co.*, promoters' duties do not arise. And if shareholders do subsequently subscribe, it is difficult to see how they are hurt if full disclosure of promoters' profits is made to them. In competitive markets for equity claims, these profits will be taken into account when share prices are established. It would then be perverse, in the name of distributional neutrality, to endow shareholders with claims for which they have not bargained. Promoters' profits are also unrelated to the anticipated payoffs and risk characteristics of a security, which alone give it value in competitive markets. In other words, one would expect to see two kinds of securities with identical risk/return features trading at the same price even if promoters' profits could be observed in one but not the other case. It would of course be otherwise if the legal regime forced promoters to account for any identifiable profits, but as an argument for a duty to account this is circular. Finally, promoters' profits will be made on any initial issue of securities by a firm newly organized through the efforts of an entrepreneur. A prohibition of promoters' profits must then have an enormous chilling effect on the capital formation of new businesses.

Were one able to establish that a promoter is overcompensated on an issue of shares, watered stock liability would also arise. How much latitude is provided by CBCA s. 25(4), which provides that, in issuing shares, "directors may take into account reasonable charges and expenses of organization"? Do you think that the supply of entrepreneurship should be regulated through judicial price controls?

Gluckstein v. Barnes
House of Lords
[1900] A.C. 240

[In 1893, the National Agricultural Hall Co., which operated a theatre called "Olympia," was being wound up. A syndicate of four people, including Gluckstein, was formed to acquire the theatre and promote a new company. The syndicate first began to purchase at a discount debentures and a mortgage of the bankrupt company. It then acquired the theatre for £140,000.

The second stage of the promotion involved the incorporation by the promoters of Olympia Ltd., and the sale by the syndicate of the theatre to the new company for £180,000. Of this amount, the agreement provided that £171,000 was in cash and the balance in shares. Clause 7 of the agreement provided that:

The validity of this agreement shall not be impeached on the ground that the vendors parties hereto as promoters or otherwise stand in a fiduciary relation to the company, nor shall the vendors ... be required to account for any profit made or to be made by them by the purchase of any debentures or of any other charge upon any of the property of the National Agricultural Hall Company, Limited, which are to be satisfied wholly or in part of the fund paid or to be paid into court.

With the £140,000 paid for the theatre, the trustee of the bankrupt company was able to pay off the debentures and mortgage. In this way, the syndicate made a profit of £20,734 on its purchase of the bankrupt company's senior debts.

The third step in the promotion was a distribution to the public of securities in Olympia Ltd. The prospectus disclosed that the syndicate had purchased the theatre for £140,000 and resold it to the company for £180,000. It did not however disclose the profit of £20,734 made by the syndicate in its purchase of the debentures and mortgage. More than £112,000 of securities of Olympia Ltd. were issued on this distribution.

Olympia Ltd. became bankrupt in 1895. Barnes, its liquidator, sought to recover £6,341 from Gluckstein for profits made in trading in the debt obligations of the National Hall Agricultural Co.

Wright J. held at 78 L.T. 159 that the defendant was not a promoter at the time the syndicate bought the debt obligations and accordingly dismissed the action. The Court of Appeal at [1898] 2 Ch. 153 allowed the appeal. Gluckstein was held to be a promoter and liability was imposed for a non-disclosure of the profits. Gluckstein appealed to the House of Lords.]

LORD MACNAGHTEN: ... For my part, I cannot see any ingenuity or any novelty in the trick which Mr. Gluckstein and his associates practised on the persons whom they invited to take shares in Olympia, Limited. It is the old story. It has been done over and over again.

These gentlemen set about forming a company to pay them a handsome sum for taking off their hands a property which they had contracted to buy with that end in view. They bring the company into existence by means of the usual machinery. They appoint themselves sole guardians and protectors of this creature of theirs, half-fledged and just struggling into life, bound hand and foot while yet unborn by contracts tending to their private advantage, and so fashioned by its makers that it could only act by their hands and only see through their eyes. They issue a prospectus representing that they had agreed to purchase the property for a sum largely in excess of the amount which they had, in fact, to pay. On the faith of this prospectus they collect subscriptions from a confiding and credulous public. And then comes the last act. Secretly, and therefore dishonestly, they put into their own pockets the difference between the real and the pretended price. After a brief career the company is ordered to be wound up. In the course of the liquidation the trick is discovered. Mr. Gluckstein is called upon to make good a portion of the sum which he and his associates had misappropriated. Why Mr.

Gluckstein alone was selected for attack I do not know any more than I know why he was only asked to pay back a fraction of the money improperly withdrawn from the coffers of the company.

However that may be, Mr. Gluckstein defends his conduct, or, rather I should say, resists the demand, on four grounds, which have been gravely argued at the bar. In the first place, he says that he was not in a fiduciary position towards Olympia, Limited, before the company was formed. Well, for some purposes he was not. For others he was. A good deal might be said on the point. But to my mind the point is immaterial, for it is not necessary to go back beyond the formation of the company.

In the second place, he says, that if he was in a fiduciary position he did in fact make a proper disclosure. With all deference to the learned counsel for the appellant, that seems to me to be absurd. "Disclosure" is not the most appropriate word to use when a person who plays many parts announces to himself in one character what he has done and is doing in another. To talk of disclosure to the thing called the company, when as yet there were no shareholders, is a mere farce. To the intended shareholders there was no disclosure at all. On them was practised an elaborate system of deception.

The third ground of defence was that the only remedy was rescission. That defence, in the circumstances of the present case, seems to me to be as contrary to common sense as it is to authority. The point was settled more than sixty years ago by the decision in *Hichens v. Congreve* [(1831), 4 Sim. 420], and, so far as I know, that case has never been questioned.

The last defence of all was that, however much the shareholders may have been wronged, they have bound themselves by a special bargain, sacred under the provisions of the Companies Act, 1862, to bear their wrongs in silence. In other words, Mr. Gluckstein boldly asserts that he is entitled to use the provisions of an Act of Parliament, which are directed to a very different purpose, as a shield and shelter against the just consequences of his fraud.

My Lords, I am afraid I must call your Lordships' attention for a moment to the prospectus of Olympia, Limited. In my opinion it is the cardinal point of the case, and I do not think full justice has been done to it. The prospectus, I am sorry to find, was prepared in the office of a well-known solicitor. I wish I could say that it displays the simplicity and candour which some persons perhaps might expect from such an origin. Now this is what the self-constituted guardians of Olympia, Limited, and its sharehold-ers tell those whom they invite to join with them in their enterprise:

The promoters of this company, hereinafter called the vendors, who constitute the entire board of the company which lately produced "Venice in London," recently entered into a contract on be-half of a syndicate of which they themselves are members, for the purchase of the entire Olympia property. The vendors effected this purchase on the 8th February, 1893, at competition before the chief clerk of Mr. Justice North in the Chancery Division of the High Court of Justice for the sum of £140,000 payable in cash, and they will, acting on behalf of such syndicate, be the vendors of that property to this company. ... Any other profits made by the syndicate from interim invest-ments are excluded from the sale to the company. A printed form of the memorandum of agree-ment which was signed by each member of that syndicate may be inspected by intending applicants for shares or debentures at the offices of the solicitors of the company. The vendors have agreed to resell to the company the whole of the property purchased by them on the 8th February, 1893, for the sum of £180,000 (being nearly £18,000 less than the amount of Messrs. Driver & Co.'s valuation) payable as to £155,000 in cash, and the balance in cash or shares of the company. ... Out of the profit to be made by the vendors on behalf of the syndicate the vendors have agreed to pay interest at the rate of 5 per cent per annum upon the amount for the time being paid up on the shares and debentures until the opening of the first entertainment. They will also provide all the preliminary expenses of the formation and bringing out of the company, and the issue of its capital up to and including allotment, and all costs including stamp duty in connection with the completion of the purchase of the property and the mortgage to secure debentures. The conveyance will be made direct to the company by direction of the vendors.

My Lords, it is a trite observation that every document as against its author must be read in the sense which it was intended to convey. And everybody knows that sometimes half a truth is no better than a downright falsehood. Is the statement in the prospectus which I have just read as to the price which the vendors had to pay for the property true or false? In the letter it is true. The vendors had bid £140,000 for the property, and had formally agreed to pay that sum for it. But for all that, the sum of £140,000 was not the sum they were going to pay, and they knew that well enough. They had provided themselves with counters, obtained at little cost, which in reckoning the price would be taken, as they knew, at their face value, so that the price of the property to them would be only about £120,000. Is that what Mr. Gluckstein and his associates meant the public to understand? Surely ordinary persons reading the prospectus, and attracted by the hopes of profit held out by it, would say to themselves, "Here is a scheme which promises well. The gentlemen who are putting the property on the market know something about it, for they were the sole directors and managers of 'Venice in London,' which was a very profitable speculation. They have had the whole property valued by well-known auctioneers, who say that it is worth more than is asked for it. True, they secure a profit of £40,000 for themselves, but then they disclose it frankly, and it is not all clear profit. There is interest to be paid, and all the expense of forming the company. And they have actually agreed to pay £140,000 down. That sum, they tell us, is 'payable in cash.'" You will observe those last words, "payable in cash." Their introduction is almost a stroke of genius. That slight touch seems to give an air of reality and bona fides to the story. Would anybody after that suppose that the directors were only going to pay £120,000 for the property, and pocket the difference without saying anything to the shareholders? "But then," says Mr. Gluckstein, "there is something in the prospectus about 'interim investments,' and if you had only distrusted us properly and read the prospectus with the caution with which all prospectuses ought to be read, and sifted the matter to the bottom, you might have found a clue to our meaning. You might have discovered that what we call 'interim investments' was really the abatement in price effected by purchasing charges on the property at a discount." My Lords, I decline altogether to take any notice of such an argument. I think the statement in the prospectus as to the price of the property was deliberately intended to mislead the shareholders and to conceal the truth from them.

• • •

There are two things in this case which puzzle me much, and I do not suppose that I shall ever understand them. I mention them merely because I should be very sorry if it were thought that in those two matters the House unanimously approved of what has been done. I do not understand why Mr. Gluckstein and his associates were not called upon to refund the whole of the money which they misappropriated. What they did with it, whether they put it in their own pockets or distributed it among their confederates, or spent it in charity, seems to me absolutely immaterial. In the next place, I do not understand why Mr. Gluckstein was only charged with interest at the rate of 3 per cent. I should have thought it was a case for penal interest.

In these two matters Mr. Gluckstein has been in my opinion extremely fortunate. But he complains that he may have a difficulty in recovering from his co-directors their share of the spoil, and he asks that the official liquidator may proceed against his associates before calling upon him to make good the whole amount with which he has been charged. My Lords, there may be occasions in which that would be a proper course to take. But I cannot think that this is a case in which any indulgence ought to be shewn to Mr. Gluckstein. He may or may not be able to recover a contribution from those who joined with him in defrauding the company. He can bring an action at law if he likes. If he hesitates to take that course or takes it and fails, then his only remedy lies in an appeal to that sense of honour which is popularly supposed to exist among robbers of a humbler type.

[The concurring judgments of LORD HALSBURY L.C. and LORD ROBERTSON are omitted.]

Appeal dismissed with costs.

NOTES

If full disclosure may cure distributional problems, it does not follow that silence must give rise to them. Did the purchasers of shares in this case rely on the *absence* of profits by promoters in their dealings in debt securities? But then the antipathy to financial intermediaries or to entrepreneurs is not always well-focused. Was Lord Macnaghten's genteel aversion to those such as Mr. Gluckstein rooted solely in legal considerations?

Profits made prior to the commencement of a promotion may be retained by a promoter. In *Cavendish Bentinck v. Fenn* (1887), 12 App. Cas. 652 (H.L.), Fenn joined a syndicate that purchased coal mines in Nova Scotia in 1871 for a price of £5,500. The syndicate formed a corporation called the Coal Area Association Ltd. in 1872, and sold the coal mines to it. In the following year, the corporation sold the mines to the Cape Breton Coal Co. for £42,000. Of this amount, £12,000 was paid in cash and the balance in shares of the new corporation. Fenn was a director of the Cape Breton Coal Co. at the time of sale. It was alleged, but not proven, that he had not fully disclosed his interest at the time of the sale. The Cape Breton Coal Co. later reaffirmed the contract, apparently with full knowledge of the defendant's interest, and then sold the property. The Cape Breton Coal Co. was wound up in 1875. The plaintiff, as a shareholder, brought an action against Fenn for breach of his duties as a director of the Cape Breton Coal Co. on its purchase of the mines in 1873. The action failed because there was no clear proof of non-disclosure. In addition, Lord Herschell found that the promotion had not begun in 1871. "[I]t is beyond question that at the time when the purchase was made Mr. Fenn and his co-adventurers were none of them in any sort of fiduciary relation to the company, the existence of which was at the time not even contemplated." *Id.* at 658. Finally, Lord FitzGerald stated that the fact that £5,500 was paid for the mines in 1871 did not establish that they were not worth £42,000 in 1873.

Old Dominion Copper Mining and Smelting Co. v. Lewisohn
United States Supreme Court
210 U.S. 206, 28 S. Ct. 634, 52 L.Ed. 1025 (1907)

MR. JUSTICE HOLMES delivered the opinion of the court: ... The facts alleged are as follows: The property embraced in the plan was the mining property of the old Dominion Copper Company of Baltimore, and also the mining rights and land now in question, the latter being held by one Keyser, for the benefit of himself and of the executors of one Simpson, who with Keyser owned the stock of the Baltimore company. Bigelow and Lewisohn, in May and June, 1895, obtained options from Simpson's executors and Keyser for the purchase of the stock and the property now in question. They also formed a syndicate to carry out their plan, with the agreement that the money subscribed by the members should be used for the purchase and the sale to a new corporation, at a large advance, and that the members, in the proportion of their subscriptions, should receive in cash or in stock of the new corporation the profit made by the sale. On May 28, 1895, Bigelow paid Simpson's executors for their stock on behalf of the syndicate, in cash and notes of himself and Lewisohn, and in June Keyser was paid in the same way.

On July 8, 1895, Bigelow and Lewisohn started the plaintiff corporation, the seven members being their nominees and tools. The next day the stock of the company was increased to 150,000 shares of twenty-five dollars each, officers were elected, and the corporation became duly organized. On July 11, pursuant to instructions, some of the officers resigned, and Bigelow and Lewisohn and three other absent members of the syndicate came in. Thereupon an offer was received from the Baltimore company, the stock of which had been bought, as stated, by Bigelow and Lewisohn, to sell substantially all its property for 100,000 shares of the plaintiff company. The offer was accepted, and then Lewisohn offered to sell the real estate now in question, obtained from Keyser, for 30,000 shares, to be issued to Bigelow and himself. This also was accepted and possession of all the mining property was delivered the next day. The sales "were consummated" by delivery of deeds, and afterwards, on July 18, to raise working capital, it was voted to offer the remaining 20,000 shares to the public at par, and they were taken by subscribers who did not know of the profit made by Bigelow and Lewisohn and the syndicate. On September 18, the 100,000 and 30,000 shares were issued, and it was voted to issue the 20,000 when paid for. The bill alleges that the property of the Baltimore company was not worth more than $1,000,000, the sum paid for its stock, and the property here concerned not over $5,000, as Bigelow and Lewisohn knew. The market value of the petitioner's stock was less than par, so that the price paid was $2,500,000, it is said, for the Baltimore company's property and $750,000 for that here concerned. Whether this view of the price paid is correct, it is unnecessary to decide.

· · ·

The argument for the petitioner is that all would admit that the promoters (assuming the English phrase to be well applied) stood in a fiduciary relation to it, if, when the transaction took place, there were members who were not informed of the profits made and who did not acquiesce, and that the same obligation of good faith extends down to the time of the later subscriptions, which it was the promoters' plan to obtain. ... The difficulty that meets the petitioner at the outset is that it has assented to the transaction with the full knowledge of the facts. ... The contract had been made and the property delivered on July 11 and 12, when Bigelow, Lewisohn and some other members of the syndicate held all the outstanding stock, and it is alleged in terms that the sales were consummated before the vote of July 18 to offer the stock to the public had been passed.

At the time of the sale to the plaintiff, then, there was no wrong done to any one. Bigelow, Lewisohn and their syndicate were on both sides of the bargain, and they might issue to themselves as much stock in their corporation as they liked in exchange for their conveyance of their land. *Salomon v. Salomon & Co.* [1897], A.C. 22; *Blum v. Whitney*, 185 N.Y. 232; *Tompkins v. Sperry*, 96 Maryland, 560. If there was a wrong it was when the innocent public subscribed. But what one would expect to find, if a wrong happened then, would not be that the sale became a breach of duty to the corporation *nunc pro tunc,* but that the invitation to the public without disclosure, when acted upon, became a fraud upon the subscribers from an equitable point of view, accompanied by what they might treat as damage. For it is only by virtue of the innocent subscribers' position and the promoter's invitation that the corporation has any pretense for a standing in court. If the promoters after starting their scheme had sold their stock before any subscriptions were taken, and then the purchasers of their stock with notice had invited the public to come in and it did, we do not see how the company could maintain this suit. If it could not then, we do not see how it can now.

But it is said from a business point of view the agreement was not made merely to bind the corporation as it then was, with only forty shares issued, but to bind the corporation when it should have a capital of $3,750,000; and the implication is that practically this was a new and different corporation. Of course, legally speaking, a corporation does not change its identity by adding a cubit to its stature. The nominal capital of the corporation was the same when the contract was made and after the public had subscribed. Therefore what must be meant is, as we have said, that the corporation got a new right from the fact that new men who did not know what it had done had put in their money and had become members. It is assumed in argument that the new members had no ground for a suit in their own names, but it is assumed also that their position changed that of the corporation, and thus that the indirect effect of their acts was greater than the direct; that facts that gave them no claim gave one to the corporation because of them, notwithstanding its assent.

· · ·

But if we are to leave technical law on one side and approach the case from what is supposed to be a business point of view, there are new matters to be taken into account. If the corporation recovers, all the stockholders, guilty as well as innocent, get the benefit.

• • •

To sum up: In our opinion, on the one hand, the plaintiff cannot recover without departing from the fundamental conception embodied in the law that created it; the conception that a corporation remains unchanged and unaffected in its identity by changes in its members. *Donnell v. Herring-Hall-Marvin Safe Co.*, 208 U.S. 267, 273; *Salomon v. Salomon & Co.* [1897], A.C. 22, 30. On the other hand, if we should undertake to look through fiction to facts, it appears to us that substantial justice would not be accomplished, but rather a great injustice done, if the corporation were allowed to disregard its previous assent in order to charge a single member with the whole results of a transaction to which thirteen-fifteenths of its stock were parties, for the benefit of the guilty, if there was guilt in any one, and the innocent alike. ...

Corporate Recovery. Notwithstanding this decision, most state courts preferred to follow the Massachusetts rule in *Old Dominion Copper Mining & Smelting Co. v. Bigelow*, 89 N.E. 193 (Mass. 1909), where liability was imposed on the same facts. Rugg J. stated at p. 206 that:

It would be a vain thing for the law to say that the promoter is a trustee subject to all the stringent liabilities which inhere in that character and at the same time say that, at any period during his trusteeship and long before an essential part of it was executed or his general duty as such ended, he could, by changing for a moment the cloak of the promoter for that of director or stockholder, by his own act alone, absolve himself from all past, present or future liability in his capacity as promoter. The plaintiff was fully organized and authorized to do business on July 8 and 11, 1895, when only $1,000 in capital stock had been paid in. It would be an idle ceremony indeed to establish for promoters the obligations of trustees, and at the same time hold that by their tool and with only $1,000 paid in, and that as a mere form (for it was soon after repaid to one of them) they could vote to themselves a wholly unwarranted profit of $1,250,000, kept secret from other initial shareholders, because at that moment they were the only stockholders. By such a course the law would be holding out apples of Sodom to the wronged corporation. ... It is answered that the plaintiff has assented to the transaction with full knowledge of the facts. But it has not assented when it stood where it could act independently. The assent to the wrongful act of the promoters was given at the behest and by vote of the promoters themselves, while still occupying the position of protectors to their own creature, while it was bound hand and foot by them and prevented from taking any action except through them as a step in its further exploitation, and while their trust was uncompleted. The corporation although by law fully organized was still in its swaddling clothes, so far as the plans of the promoters were concerned.

He continued at p. 208:

It is also urged that the maintenance of this suit works an injustice to the defendant in requiring a repayment to the corporation, which will result in a benefit to the 13/15 of the capital stock taken by the defendant and Lewisohn (who condoned the wrong) as well as to the 2/15 subscribed for by the innocent public. The size of the repayment which may be required of the defendant is due to the enormous profit at the outset. ... The true answer, however, is given by Jessel M.R., in *New Som. P. Co. v. Erlanger*, 5 Ch. D., at page 114: " ... If the argument were once allowed to prevail, it would only be necessary to corrupt one single shareholder in order to prevent a company from ever setting the contract aside ... ."

The Supreme Court itself subsequently cast doubt upon the *Lewisohn* decision in *Davis v. Las Ovas Co.*, 227 U.S. 80 (1913) and *McCandless v. Furland*, 296 U.S. 140 (1935).

Promoters were held to owe fiduciary duties to their corporation under Anglo-Canadian and American law. Recovery for breaches of such duties was therefore at the instance of the corporation rather than the defrauded shareholder. A shareholder would of course share *pari passu* in any corporate recovery, but unless he was the sole shareholder this would not make him whole. Moreover, corporate recovery might over-compensate other shareholders. Suppose that an initial public subscriber sold his shares after the promoter's misrepresentations came to light. Such a shareholder would not share in any corporate recovery thereafter. His purchaser, however, would, even though the price of the shares had been discounted when he purchased them.

A Vestigial Problem. Nineteenth century cases on promoters' duties would today be mostly decided under provincial securities legislation. These Acts require full, true and plain disclosure of all material facts in a prospectus on a distribution of shares. See OSA s. 56(1). Moreover, the issuer's promoters must sign a certificate under s. 58(1) stating that full disclosure has been made. More specific disclosure of sales of property to the corporation by a promoter is mandated in the regulations to the statute. See, for example, Form 12, Item 15. Promoters will thereafter be liable to subscribers for misrepresentations in the prospectus under OSA s. 130(1)(e).

Given the personal remedy in s. 130, the corporate cause of action for promoters' secret profits is of greatly diminished importance. However, promoters' duties to the corporation have not entirely gone the way of the passenger pigeon. Where securities are issued under an exemption from the prospectus requirements, as often happen in the case of small issuers, promoters' duties are still with us.

CHAPTER FIVE

Distribution of Securities

Businesses raise capital to purchase assets used to produce goods and services. A sole proprietor contributes some of her own funds to the business (equity capital) in addition to borrowing funds in, for instance, the form of a bank loan. Partners in a partnership also typically contribute their own funds (equity capital) in addition to borrowing funds (usually in the form of a bank loan). Limited partnerships sell units in the limited partnership to raise capital. Corporations sell shares to raise equity capital. The shares sold can have any of a wide variety of rights but the most typical types of shares are common shares (discussed in Chapter Four) and preferred shares (discussed in Chapter Nine). Corporations also borrow funds. Borrowed funds often come in the form of a bank loan but may also come from selling bonds or debentures (which are discussed in Chapter Nine). Shares, bonds, debentures and units in a limited partnership are, in more general terms, referred to as "securities." Securities are "distributed" to investors to raise the capital necessary to carry on business. Securities may be distributed at the inception of a business or subsequently to take advantage of business opportunities where the funds available from the earnings of the business are insufficient.

This chapter addresses legal requirements with respect to the distribution of securities. Section A deals with how securities are normally distributed. Section B briefly notes the development and nature of Canadian securities regulation. Sections C and D address the mandatory disclosure requirements on the distribution of securities, namely, the prospectus requirement (Section C) coupled with continuous disclosure requirements (Section D). Section E notes exemptions from the prospectus requirement and Section F discusses the closed system. Sections G and H provide a reassessment of the policy of mandatory disclosure and note some emerging interest group explanations of securities regulation. Section I deals with the requirement to be registered for trading.

A. DISTRIBUTION OF AND TRADING IN SECURITIES

Before addressing the legal issues associated with a distribution of securities it is useful to begin with an understanding of how public firms distribute their securities. It is also useful, by way of background, to note a few things about trading in securities.

1. The Distribution of Securities

The following excerpt notes the most common methods of distributing securities.

D. Johnston, Canadian Securities Regulation
135-39 (1977)

There is no typical example of distribution of a security to the public. One example is provided by the small family-owned company with a stable earnings history over the past few years, a proven product and capable management, which is anxious to expand and requires substantial increments of capital. It decides to raise this capital by selling some of its shares to the public through an underwriter. If the company's growth and need for capital continue, it may effect a number of subsequent distributions of the same sort so that eventually its securities become widely held, with many institutions and individuals looking to their investments in these securities for a profitable return. And if capital needs of the enterprise over that period have been both substantial and complex, it may have outstanding several categories of debt obligation—bonds, debentures and notes; these may be further subdivided into classes and series with different maturities and interest rates. The firm's equity capital structure may also be variegated, with several classes of preferred shares resting on a common share base.

• • •

[B]efore examining the mechanics of prospectus obligations and exemptions, it may be helpful to examine briefly the characteristics of the different types of distribution which occur in practice. There are three main functional categories: the direct issue, the offer to sell, and the best efforts "underwriting."

(1) Direct Issue

The direct issue is the simplest distribution to understand. It is the most difficult to effect if the issue is large and the issuer relatively unknown. In a direct issue the company or person proposing to sell its securities, called the "issuer," does so by making direct contact with potential purchasers of its securities, without the services of an investment dealer or broker. This procedure will be most successful where a small group of purchasers who have intimate knowledge of the company's affairs can absorb the entire issue. A frequent example is a rights issue by a company to its shareholders. The company offers existing shareholders an opportunity to purchase newly issued shares, usually on a basis which enables each shareholder to maintain his proportionate holding in the company.

Another method of direct issue is the private placement of securities with one or more institutional purchasers. In order to arrange the transaction, the issuer negotiates with the investor either directly or through an investment dealer who participates on a purely agency basis. ... Formerly this method was employed almost exclusively in the case of debt securities held by the purchaser to maturity, but more recently substantial blocks of shares have been issued in this manner.

(2) Offer to Sell [or "Bought Deal" or "Firm Offer"]

In the offer to sell ["firm offer" or "bought deal"], the issuer negotiates a firm underwriting agreement with an investment dealer. The latter agrees to purchase all of the securities of the issuer for resale to purchasers whom he locates through his own business resources. The dealer's profit results from his purchasing the securities from the issuer at a discount from the price at which he will offer them for sale to his purchasers; the difference is referred to as the underwriter's "spread." The phrase "firm underwriting" requires explanation. The transaction is firm in the sense that the investment dealer is committed to purchase the securities from the issuer, subject [to] any escape or "market out" clauses included in the underwriting agreement, and the issuer is thus assured of receiving the amount agreed to between it and the underwriter. By contrast underwriting in the literal or classic sense is based on an insurance principle whereby the underwriter only becomes obliged to purchase securities from the issuer if members of the public do not purchase the entire issue, and even then only that part of the issue not taken up by the public. Derived from this classical type of underwriting is the modern device of a stand-by underwriting. Here an investment dealer agrees to step in and purchase the unsold balance (or some fixed amount) if the selling efforts of the issuer, or the dealer, or other brokers do not result in the distribution of the entire issue. Stand-by underwriting is very often coupled with a rights issue of the sort discussed earlier as a form of direct issue.

The techniques used in firm underwritings have become very sophisticated and complex with a view to minimizing the risk of an unsuccessful issue. In the case of a very large offering the underwriter may join as his associates one or several other investment dealers who will contract directly with the issuer to buy the securities. The liability of this "purchase group" may be joint and several or, alternatively, several only with each member of the purchase group being obliged to take no more than a fixed percentage. Normally one underwriter (the "lead" or "managing" underwriter) will act on behalf of the purchase group in dealing with the issuer; he will do the negotiating, sign the underwriting agreement and prepare the necessary documentation.

Whether or not the lead underwriter chooses to form a purchase group, he will invariably, in an issue of any significant size, assemble a number of other investment dealers to join what is known as a banking group. Under this arrangement the underwriter (or the purchase group if the lead underwriter has formed such) will contract with other investment dealers, each of whom agrees to take some fixed percentage of the issue from the lead or managing underwriter. Places in the banking group are taken according to a very competitive pecking order.

The purchasing underwriter, or the purchasing group if one is used, realizes its profit on the difference between the price it pays to the issuer for the securities and that for which it sells them. Thus it may pay the issuer $96 for a share which is sold to the public at $100. Where the share is sold to another member of the banking group, the lead underwriter will realize as profit the difference between what is paid for the share and what it receives for it from the banking group member. The remaining members of the banking group realize their profit on the basis of a slightly lower discount. They might, for example, purchase the same share from the lead underwriter or purchase group at $97 and sell to their public clients at $100. Since their risk is somewhat less than that of the purchase group, their profit is less.

Finally the lead underwriter and the banking group may choose to form a "selling group," to ensure a wide-spread distribution of the issue to public clients. Such a group, when formed, could include all members of the Investment Dealers' Association (IDA).

In the previous example the selling group members might buy a designated amount of the securities from the banking group at $98 and thus be liable as principals to pay for that amount. Selling group members would then resell them to the public at $100, thus realizing a $2 gross profit.

Occasionally the underwriting agreement results from competitive bidding for the issue by various dealers, or in response to public tender by the issuer. More commonly, however, the issuer simply negotiates directly with the dealer who has traditionally served as its fiscal agent. Some critics of practices in the Canadian industry have suggested more frequent competitive bidding or at least negotiations with several underwriters by a potential issuer would be desirable.

The "tombstone advertisement" on the next page illustrates some of these points. It announces the distribution of $90,000,000 in securities of a trust and a related corporation. The two underwriters who constitute the purchase group, Dominion Securities Corporation Limited and A.E. Ames & Co. Limited, appear as the first names in the banking group, distinctly separated from the other members of the group. Dominion's name appears first, since it is the lead underwriter.

The names of those in the banking group are usually arranged in a distinct order. The higher the place in the list, the greater the amount of the issue which the particular member has agreed to "bank" or be liable for to the purchase group. The names of the selling group members do not appear here. In fact, on this issue every member of the IDA was included.

(3) Best Efforts Underwriting

In a best efforts underwriting a dealer contracts with the issuer to give his best efforts to sell the issue. The dealer expects to distribute the entire offering successfully, but does not agree to purchase the securities as principal; he therefore incurs no loss in the event of failure. His incentive is a commission from the issuer over and above the amount which he will receive from his purchasing clients for acting as broker on each sale. The best efforts type of underwriting has many variants. For example, an issue may be underwritten partially on a firm basis and partially on a best efforts basis. Or it may be an "all or nothing" arrangement under which the entire issue must be sold within a specified time before any commission is paid. On a rights issue by an issuer to its shareholders, a dealer may in the absence of a stand-by underwriting contract for an extra commission from the issuer for using his best efforts to encourage the sale of rights to shareholders or to other members of the public who are not shareholders.

---

2. The Role of the Underwriter

As the excerpt from Johnston suggests, underwriters may provide a variety of functions. When the distribution is effected through a best efforts underwriting the underwriter's function is to provide services in marketing the securities. When the arrangement is an "offer to sell" (which is also referred to as a "firm offer" or "bought deal") the underwriter provides a form of insurance against fluctuations in the market price of the

This advertisement is not to be construed as a public offering in any Province of Canada unless a prospectus relating thereto has been accepted for filing by a securities commission or similar authority in such province. The offering is made by the prospectus only and copies thereof may be obtained from such of the undersigned and other dealers as may lawfully offer these securities in such province.

New Issues

$90,000,000

consisting of

$40,000,000

BM-RT Realty Investments

(A trust created under the laws of the Province of Ontario)

4,000,000 Trust Units

Price: $10.00 per Trust Unit

Applications have been made to list the Trust Units on the Montreal, Toronto and Vancouver Stock Exchanges. Acceptance of the listings will be subject to the filing of required documents and evidence of satisfactory distribution, both within 90 days.

$50,000,000

BM-RT Ltd.

(Incorporated under the laws of the Province of Quebec)

6¼% Debentures
And Trust Unit Purchase Warrants

To be dated March 28, 1973   To mature April 1, 1978

Price: 100 and accrued interest, if any

Trust Unit Purchase Warrants in bearer form will be mailed to the holders of Debentures of record at the close of business on June 29, 1973, entitling the bearers to purchase Trust Units at the price of $12.50 per Trust Unit on or prior to April 1, 1978, on the basis of 20 Trust Units for each $1,000 principal amount of Debentures. Further particulars of the Warrants are set out in the prospectus.

Dominion Securities Corporation Limited   A.E. Ames & Co. Limited

Wood Gundy Limited
Greenshields Incorporated
Midland-Osler Securities Limited
Pitfield, Mackay, Ross & Company Limited
Burns Bros. and Denton Limited
Walwyn, Stodgell & Co. Limited
Mead & Co. Limited
Graham Armstrong Securities Ltd.
MacDougall, MacDougall & MacTier Ltd.

Richardson Securities of Canada
Fry Mills Spence Limited
Cochran Murray Limited
Lévesque, Beaubien Inc.
Harris & Partners Limited
R.A. Daly & Company Limited
Casgrain & Company Limited
C.J. Hodgson Securities Ltd.
Odlum Brown & T.B. Read Ltd.
Scotia Bond Company Limited   Tassé & Associés, Ltée

McLeod, Young, Weir & Company Limited
Nesbitt Thomson Securities Limited
Merrill Lynch, Royal Securities Limited
Bell, Gouinlock & Company Limited
Gairdner & Company Limited
Crang & Ostiguy Inc.
Cliche et Associés, Ltée
Houston, Willoughby and Company Limited
Pemberton Securities Limited

securities. With the firm offer the issuer can have some assurance of the amount of funds the issue of the securities will raise and can then better plan its investment objectives.

The underwriter performs another, perhaps less obvious service, namely, providing some assurance to market that the information with respect to the issuer is credible. It may be difficult for the issuer to convince investors that the information it provides with respect to itself and the securities it is offering is accurate. The issuer will have some incentive to be honest if it anticipates going to the market for further financing at some future date. However, the market will often have limited experience with the issuer and there is always the risk that the issuer is attempting to perpetrate a fraud. An underwriter, on the other hand, will have a much greater incentive to protect its reputation. It will be involved in many issues of securities and the market will thus have more experience with the credibility of the underwriter. If the underwriter is repeatedly involved in issues of securities where information about the issuer and the securities is deceptive or fraudulent, investors will begin to discount the price of securities offered through that underwriter. Consequently, the underwriter has an incentive to investigate the issuer to provide some assurance that the disclosures of information by the issuer are accurate. Thus engaging an underwriter assists the issuer in signaling to the market that its disclosures of information relating to the value of the securities can be relied upon.

3. Primary and Secondary Markets

The market in which securities distributed by the issuer to investors is referred to as the "primary market." Once the securities have been distributed to investors, the investors can normally trade the securities among themselves. These trades are referred to as trades in the "secondary market." The issuer of the securities is not itself involved in these trades.

Secondary market trades of shares are often effected through a stock exchange such as the Toronto Stock Exchange, the Vancouver Stock Exchange or the Montreal Exchange. However, shares do not have to be listed on a stock exchange and consequently trades in some shares are not effected through a stock exchange. Trades in unlisted shares are referred to as "over-the-counter" trades.

Investors in the primary and secondary markets for securities include both institutions and individuals. The institutions involved in the trading of securities in Canadian securities markets include banks, trust companies, life insurance companies, pension funds, investment companies and mutual funds. Institutions are by far the major players in Canadian capital markets.

B. CANADIAN SECURITIES REGULATION

1. Securities Legislation in Canada

Canadian securities legislation began with the Manitoba Sale of Shares Act of 1912, only one year after the first North American securities Act in Kansas. In the United States such Acts were called "blue sky" statutes, since they sought to prevent eastern security dealers from selling to western farmers a fee simple in the heavens above. Since then, state legislation in the United States has been dwarfed by federal securities law, beginning with the Securities Act of 1933 and the Securities Exchange Act of 1934. The Canadian federal government has refrained from enacting general securities legislation. Proposals for a securities market law for Canada were prepared for the federal Department of Consumer and Corporate Affairs in 1979. See P. Anisman, *Proposals for a Securities Market Law for Canada* (1979). The proposals contained a draft of a Canadian Securities Market Law, which incorporates the themes of the 1933 and 1934 American statutes. However, in the face of provincial opposition, the federal government has yet to enact national securities legislation. A more recent proposal for increased federal involvement in securities regulation has been developed in consultation with the provinces in response to the First Ministers' Meeting in December 1993. The proposal is for a national securities commission, which would replace provincial securities commissions. The proposed national securities commission would take over the administration of securities laws which would remain a matter of provincial jurisdiction.

Prior to amendments to the Ontario Securities Act in 1978 the securities acts in Ontario and all of the western provinces were closely modeled on the 1966 Ontario statute, R.S.O. 1970, c. 426. However, several provinces have since revised their securities acts on the basis of the 1978 Ontario Securities Act. The 1978 Ontario Securities Act has since been followed, with a few notable variations, in Alberta, British Columbia, Saskatchewan, Nova Scotia and Newfoundland. The influence of the OSA can also be seen in the Quebec Securities Act.

In the absence of a competing federal statute, Ontario securities legislation has assumed an importance that extends far beyond its borders. Not only are many large issuers located in Toronto, but so too are a majority of the dealers, underwriters and other financial intermediaries. Decisions by the Ontario Securities Commission have a national importance. One reason for this prominence is the readiness of the O.S.C. to enforce the Ontario statute when Ontario investors may be affected. The scope that the O.S.C. may give to its jurisdiction is potentially quite broad. See, e.g., *Re Asbestos Corp. Ltd.*, [1988] O.S.C.B. 3419 aff'd (1991), 1 O.R. (3d) 723 (Div. Ct.), aff'd (sub nom. *Quebec (Sa Majeste du Chef) v. Ontario Securities Commission*) (1993), 10 O.R. (3d) 577 (C.A.), leave to appeal to the S.C.C. refused May 27, 1993.

Notwithstanding the differences in these statutes, all are broadly similar requiring the registration of persons involved in the securities business, prospectus disclosure on the distribution of securities, continuous disclosure of information after the distribution of securities, insider trading regulation and take-over bid regulation. This chapter deals primarily with prospectus disclosure, continuous disclosure and registration of persons involved in the securities business.

2. Policy Statements and Orders

Policy Statements. In addition to the securities acts and regulations, other important sources of securities regulation are policy statements and orders made by securities administrators. The securities acts and regulations call for decisions by securities administrators and typically allow securities administrators broad discretionary powers. Securities administrators indicate how they intend to exercise their discretion by publishing policy statements. The securities administrators of each provincial jurisdiction publish their own policy statements, which are generally referred to as "local policy statements."

Over the past 35 years securities administrators have met with increasing regularity to develop policy jointly. Collectively the securities administrators from the various jurisdictions in Canada are known as the "Canadian Securities Administrators." Ontario and the western provinces developed a series of "Uniform Policy Statements" on the basis of the 1966 Ontario Act that was adopted in the western provinces. These Uniform Policy Statements have largely been replaced by National Policy Statements, which are applied by securities administrators throughout Canada. National Policy Statements attempt to coordinate securities regulation policy throughout Canada and make the securities regulations of the different jurisdictions more compatible.

Policy statements not only indicate the policy directions of securities administrators but also often contain quite detailed requirements. The detailed requirements in the policy statements can take on the appearance of legislation or regulations. Indeed, the requirements in the policy statements often appear much more detailed than the securities act or regulations. However, the policy statements are promulgated by securities administrators and not by elected politicians. Consequently the authority of securities administrators to pass policy statements that are tantamount to legislation has been challenged. See *Ainsley Financial Corporation v. Ontario Securities Commission* (1995), 18 O.S.C.B. 43 (C.A.), aff'g [1993] O.S.C.B. 4077, 14 O.R. (3d) 280, 106 D.L.R. (4th) 507. The decision in *Ainsley* put the validity of many of the requirements in the policy statements of securities administrators in doubt. In response to the *Ainsley* case a Task Force on securities regulation was created in Ontario [*Responsibility and Responsiveness: Final Report of the Ontario Task Force on Securities Regulation* (1994)]. The recommendations of the Task Force led to the enactment of An Act to Amend the Securities Act, S.O. 1994, c. 33. The Act amends the Ontario Securities Act to set out the purposes of the Securities Act and the principles that the O.S.C. should consider in pursuing the purposes of the Securities Act. The Act also amends the Ontario Securities Act by granting the O.S.C. broad powers to make rules for the regulation of securities markets in Ontario. Section 143 of the Ontario Securities Act now sets out a list (consisting of 46 items) of matters that the O.S.C. may make rules on.

Orders and Blanket Orders. In the exercise of their discretion securities administrators issue orders. The orders may, for instance, exempt a particular person or company from the requirements of the securities act or regulations or may enforce the Act or regulations based on the enforcement powers of securities administrators. The situations giving rise to exemption orders often repeat themselves and to avoid excessive repetitive work securities administrators often issue blanket orders under which a person is entitled to an exemption if the person meets the particular circumstances set out in the order. Orders and blanket orders indicate how securities administrators will exercise their discretion and are thus an important source of securities regulation that lawyers practising in the securities law area need to keep abreast of.

C. PROSPECTUS DISCLOSURE

When securities are distributed to the investing public, the issuer must provide a document called a "prospectus." In addition, the persons involved in trading in the security in the process of the distribution must be registered for trading. This part of the chapter looks at the prospectus requirement. It examines the nature of a prospectus, when it is required, the process of distributing securities under a prospectus and the sanctions associated with non-compliance with the prospectus requirements and misrepresentations in a prospectus. The requirement to be registered for trading is considered at the end of the chapter.

1. The Prospectus

The prospectus provides information about the security being sold and about the issuer of the security for the purpose of assisting investors in valuing the security. Regulations passed pursuant to securities acts in Canada typically set out forms for prospectuses of different types of issuers, such as industrial issuers, finance companies, natural resource companies and mutual funds. These forms contain lists of items that must be disclosed in the prospectus. For instance, the prospectus usually must provide information on such matters as the attributes of the security being offered for sale, factors that may make the purchase of the security risky or speculative, the estimated proceeds of the issue, what the proceeds will be used for, the method of distributing the securities (including the underwriting arrangements) and information on the issuer, such as a description of the issuer's business, the development of the business over the past five years, the loan and share capital of the business, the occupations of the directors and officers of the issuer over the previous five years, their backgrounds and executive compensation. In addition to the specific items of disclosure the issuer must provide "full, true and plain disclosure" of all "material facts." A "material fact" is a fact that significantly affects, or would reasonably be expected to have a significant effect on, the market price or value of the securities.

Estimates of future earnings were formerly prohibited in prospectuses in Canada. While there was no question that such information was relevant, Canadian securities administrators feared that unsophisticated investors might be too easily misled by such "soft information." However, Canadian securities laws now permit the use of earnings forecasts subject to constraints intended to protect the investor against being misled. The prospectus need not include future oriented financial information, but a securities administrator may allow future oriented financial information to be included in a prospectus. The future oriented financial information must be accompanied by an accountant's written comments based on a review of the future oriented financial information. See, e.g., ASA Reg. s. 112; BCSA Reg. s. 109 and B.C. Local Policy 3-02, Part 5; OSA Reg. s. 60; and National Policy No. 48. National Policy No. 48 also requires that the forecast be reviewed and compared with actual results each time the issuer is required to file financial statements based on historical data. The issuer must identify and address material differences between the forecast and the actual results.

2. When a Prospectus Is Required

Subject to exemptions, which are discussed below, securities legislation throughout Canada requires prospectus disclosure when securities are distributed. Under most provincial securities acts the requirement is expressed as follows:

No person or company shall trade in a security on his, her or its own account or on behalf of any other person or company where such trade would be a distribution of such security, unless a preliminary prospectus and a prospectus have been filed and receipts therefor obtained from the Director. [OSA s. 53; see also ASA s. 81; BCSA s. 42]

Thus a preliminary prospectus and a prospectus are required when one "distributes a security." A "distribution" is typically defined as involving a "trade in a security." "Trade" and "security" are defined terms under most provincial securities acts. Thus whenever someone is raising capital a prospectus will be required when it involves: (1) a "trade," (2) in a "security" that (3) constitutes a "distribution."

The Definition of "Security." Since the definition of "trade" involves the use of the term "security" it is helpful to begin working one's way through the definitions by beginning with the definition of "security."

The term is defined in most Canadian securities acts by setting out several items that fall within the ambit of the term. These include specific items that cover the most frequently used types of securities such as shares, bonds and debentures. For instance, the OSA provides that a "security" includes:

... a bond, debenture, note or other evidence of indebtedness, share, stock, unit certificate, participation certificate, certificate of share or interest, preorganization certificate or subscription ... [OSA s. 1(1) "security" (e); see also ASA s. 1(v)(v); and BCSA s. 1(1) "security" (d)]

The definition of "security" also includes:

... any document constituting evidence of an option, subscription or other interest in or to a security ... [ASA s. 1(v)(iv); BCSA s. 1(1) "security" (c); OSA s. 1(1) "security" (d)]

Given that other sets of rights that may be sold to investors could come to be a common type of security, Canadian securities acts also generally provide that "security" includes anything that is "commonly known as a security." See, e.g., ASA s. 1(1)(v)(i); BCSA s. 1(1) "security" (a); OSA s. 1(1) "security" (a).

The definition of "security" also sets out a number of other specific but less common types of securities that have been sold from time to time. For instance, the definition includes:

... a certificate of interest in an oil, natural gas or mining lease, claim or royalty voting trust certificate [ASA s. 1(v)(x); BCSA s. 1(1) "security" (h); OSA s. 1(1) "security" (j)]

... a document evidencing an interest in a scholarship or educational plan or trust [ASA s. 1(1)(v)(xv); BCSA s. 1(1) "security" (m); OSA s. 1(1) "security" (o)]

The definition also contains several potentially broad terms under which a virtually infinite variety of novel financing techniques may also be subject to securities laws. For instance, the term "security" includes "an interest in property," "a profit sharing agreement" and "an investment contract." See ASA ss. 1(1)(v)(ii), (ix), (xiv); BCSA s. 1(1) "security" (b), (g), (l); OSA s. 1(1) "security" (b), (i), (n). In addition to these potentially broad terms the definition of "security" under most Canadian securities acts begins by saying that the term "includes" each of the items set out. Thus the definition could be extended to cover items not set out in the definition itself.

By far the most widely used of the broad terms in the definition of "security" is the expression "an investment contract." In discussing the meaning of this term the Ontario Securities Commission has generally referred to U.S. cases that have interpreted the term under a very similar definition of "security" in U.S. securities laws. In particular, it has adopted the tests for "investment contract" set out in *S.E.C. v. W.J. Howey Co.*, 328 U.S. 293 (1946) and *State of Hawaii v. Hawaii Market Center Inc.*, 485 P.2d 105 (Hawaii 1971). See, e.g., *Re Shelter Corporation of Canada Ltd.*, [1977] O.S.C.B. 6; and *Re George Albino*, [1991] 14 O.S.C.B. 365. The Supreme Court of Canada has also sanctioned the use of U.S. cases and adopted the *Howey* and *Hawaii* tests. See *Pacific Coast Coin Exchange v. O.S.C.*, [1978] 2 S.C.R. 112, 2 B.L.R. 212, 80 D.L.R. (3d) 529.

Securities & Exchange Comm'n v. W.J. Howey Co.
United States Supreme Court
382 U.S. 293, 66 S.Ct. 1100, 90 L.Ed. 1244 (1946)

MR. JUSTICE MURPHY delivered the opinion of the Court: This case involves the application of § 2(1) of the Securities Act of [May 27] 1933 to an offering of units of a citrus grove development coupled with a contract for cultivating, marketing and remitting the net proceeds to the investor.

The Securities and Exchange Commission instituted this action to restrain the respondents from using the mails and instrumentalities of interstate commerce in the offer and sale of unregistered and non-exempt securities in violation of § 5(a) of the Act, 15 USCA § 77e, 4 FCA title 15, § 77e. The District Court denied the injunction, 60 F. Supp. 440, and the Fifth Circuit Court of Appeals affirmed the judgment. 151 F.2d 714. We granted certiorari on a petition alleging that the ruling of the Circuit Court of Appeals conflicted with other federal and state decisions and that it introduced a novel and unwarranted test under the statute which the Commission regarded as administratively impractical.

Most of the facts are stipulated. The respondents, W.J. Howey Company and Howey-in-the-Hills Service, Inc., are Florida corporations under direct common control and management. The Howey Company owns large tracts of citrus acreage in Lake County, Florida. During the past several years it has planted about 500 acres annually, keeping half of the groves itself and offering the other half to the public "to help us finance additional development." Howey-in-the-Hills Service, Inc., is a service company engaged in cultivating and developing many of these groves, including the harvesting and marketing of the crops.

Each prospective customer is offered both a land sales contract and a service contract, after having been told that it is not feasible to invest in a grove unless service arrangements are made. While the purchaser is free to make arrangements with other service companies, the superiority of Howey-in-the-Hills Service, Inc., is stressed. Indeed, 85% of the acreage sold during the 3-year period ending May 31, 1943, was covered by service contracts with Howey-in-the-Hills Service, Inc.

The land sales contract with the Howey Company provides for a uniform purchase price per acre or fraction thereof, varying in amount only in accordance with the number of years the particular plot has been planted with citrus trees. Upon full payment of the purchase price the land is conveyed to the purchaser by warranty deed. Purchases are usually made in narrow strips of land arranged so that an acre consists of a row of 48 trees. During the period between February 1, 1941, and May 31, 1943, 31 of the 42 persons making purchases bought less than 5 acres each. The average holding of these 31 persons was 1.33 acres and sales of as little as 0.65, 0.7 and 0.73 of an acre were made. These tracts are not separately fenced and the sole indication of several ownership is found in small land marks intelligible only through a plot book record.

The service contract, generally of a 10-year duration without option of cancellation, gives Howey-in-the-Hills Service, Inc., a leasehold interest and "full and complete" possession of the acreage. For a specified fee plus the cost of labor and materials, the company is given full discretion and authority over the cultivation of the groves and the harvest and marketing of the crops. The company is well established in the citrus business and maintains a large force of skilled personnel and a great deal of equipment, including 75 tractors, sprayer wagons, fertilizer trucks and the like. Without the consent of the company, the land owner or purchaser has no right of entry to market the crop.* Thus there is ordinarily no right to specific fruit. The company is accountable only for an allocation of the net profits based upon a check made at the time of picking. All the produce is pooled by the respondent companies, which do business under their own names.

The purchasers for the most part are non-residents of Florida. They are predominantly business and professional people who lack the knowledge, skill and equipment necessary for the care and cultivation of citrus trees. They are attracted by the expectation of substantial profits. It was represented, for example, that profits during the 1943-1944 season amounted to 20% and that even greater profits might be expected during the 1944-1945 season, although only a 10% annual return was to be expected over a 10-year period. Many of these purchasers are patrons of a resort hotel owned and operated by the Howey Company in a scenic section adjacent to the groves. The hotel's advertising mentions the fine groves in the vicinity and the attention of the patrons is drawn to the groves as they are being escorted about the surrounding countryside. They are told that the groves are for sale; if they indicate an interest in the matter they are then given a sales talk.

It is admitted that the mails and instrumentalities of interstate commerce are used in the sale of the land and service contracts and that no registration statement or letter of notification has ever been filed with the Commission in accordance with the Securities Act of 1933 and the rules and regulations thereunder.

---

*   Some investors visited their particular plots annually, making suggestions as to care and cultivation, but
      without any legal rights in the matters.

Section 2(1) of the Act defines the term "security" to include the commonly known documents traded for speculation or investment.* This definition also includes "securities" of a more variable character, designated by such descriptive terms as "certificate of interest of participation in any profit-sharing agreement," "investment contract" and "in general, any interest or instrument commonly known as a 'security.'" The legal issue in this case turns upon a determination of whether, under the circumstances, the land sales contract, the warranty deed and the service contract together constitute an "investment contract" within the meaning of § 2(1). An affirmative answer brings into operation the registration requirements of § 5(a), unless the security is granted an exemption under § 3(b), 15 USCA § 77c, 4 FCA title 15, § 77c. The lower courts, in reaching a negative answer to this problem, treated the contracts and deeds as separate transactions involving no more than an ordinary real estate sale and an agreement by the seller to manage the property for the buyer.

The term "investment contract" is undefined by the Securities Act or by relevant legislative reports. But the term was common in many state "blue sky" laws in existence prior to the adoption of the federal statute and, although the term was also undefined by the state laws, it had been broadly construed by state courts as to afford the investing public a full measure of protection. Form was disregarded for substance and emphasis was placed upon economic reality. An investment contract thus came to mean a contract or scheme for "the placing of capital or laying out of money in a way intended to secure income or profit from its employment." *State v. Gopher Tire & Rubber Co.* 146 Minn 52, 56 177 NW 937, 938. This definition was uniformly applied by state courts to a variety of situations where individuals were led to invest money in a common enterprise with the expectation that they would earn a profit solely through the efforts of the promoter or of someone other than themselves.

By including an investment contract within the scope of § 2(1) of the Securities Act, Congress was using a term the meaning of which had been crystallized by this prior judicial interpretation. It is therefore reasonable to attach that meaning to the term as used by Congress, especially since such a definition is consistent with the statutory aims. In other words, an investment contract for purposes of the Securities Act means a contract, transaction or scheme whereby a person invests his money in a common enterprise and is led to expect profits solely from the efforts of the promoter or a third party, it being immaterial whether the shares in the enterprise are evidenced by formal certificates or by nominal interests in the physical assets employed in the enterprise. Such a definition necessarily underlies this Court's decision in *Securities & Exch. Commission v. C.M. Joiner Leasing Corp.* 320 US 344, 88 L Ed 88, 64 S Ct 120, and has been enunciated and applied many times by lower federal courts. It permits the

---

* "The term 'security' means any note, stock, treasury stock, bond, debenture, evidence of indebtedness, certificate of interest or participation in any profit-sharing agreement, collateral-trust certificate, pre-organization certificate or subscription, transferable share, investment contract, voting-trust certificate, certificate or deposit for a security, fractional undivided interest in oil, gas, or other mineral rights, or in general, any interest or instrument commonly known as a 'security,' or any certificate of interest or participation in, temporary or interim certificate for, receipt for, guarantee of, or warrant or right to subscribe to or purchase, any of the foregoing."

fulfillment of the statutory purpose of compelling full and fair disclosure relative to the issuance of "the many types of instruments that in our commercial world fall within the ordinary concept of a security," H. Rep No. 85, 73d Cong. 1st Sess. p. 11. It embodies a flexible rather than a static principle, one that is capable of adaptation to meet the countless and variable schemes devised by those who seek the use of the money of others on the promise of profits.

The transactions in this case clearly involve investment contracts as so defined. The respondent companies are offering something more than fee simple interests in land, something different from a farm or orchard coupled with management services. They are offering an opportunity to contribute money and to share in the profits of a large citrus fruit enterprise managed and partly owned by respondents. They are offering this opportunity to persons who reside in distant localities and who lack the equipment and experience requisite to the cultivation, harvesting and marketing of the citrus products. Such persons have no desire to occupy the land or to develop it themselves; they are attracted solely by the prospects of a return on their investment. Indeed, individual development of the plots of land that are offered and sold would seldom be economically feasible due to their small size. Such tracts gain utility as citrus groves only when cultivated and developed as component parts of a larger area. A common enterprise managed by respondents or third parties with adequate personnel and equipment is therefore essential if the investors are to achieve their paramount aim of a return on their investments. Their respective shares in this enterprise are evidenced by land sales contracts and warranty deeds, which serve as a convenient method of determining the investors' allocable shares of the profits. The resulting transfer of rights in land is purely incidental.

Thus all the elements of a profit-seeking business venture are present here. The investors provide the capital and share in the earnings and profits; the promoters manage, control and operate the enterprise. It follows that the arrangements whereby the investors' interests are made manifest involve investment contracts, regardless of the legal terminology in which such contracts are clothed. The investment contracts in this instance take the form of land sales contracts, warranty deeds and service contracts which respondents offer to prospective investors. And respondents' failure to abide by the statutory and administrative rules in making such offerings, even though the failure result from a bona fide mistake as to the law, cannot be sanctioned under the Act.

This conclusion is unaffected by the fact that some purchasers choose not to accept the full offer of an investment contract by declining to enter into a service contract with the respondents. The Securities Act prohibits the offer as well as the sale of unregistered, non-exempt securities. Hence it is enough that the respondents merely offer the essential ingredients of an investment contract.

We reject the suggestion of the Circuit Court of Appeals, 151 F.2d at 717, that an investment contract is necessarily missing where the enterprise is not speculative or promotional in character and where the tangible interest which is sold has intrinsic value independent of the success of the enterprise as a whole. The test is whether the scheme involves an investment of money in a common enterprise with profits to come solely from the efforts of others. If that test be satisfied, it is immaterial whether the enterprise is speculative or non-speculative or whether there is a sale of property with or without intrinsic value. See *Securities & Exch. Commission v. C.M. Joiner Leasing Corp.*, supra

(320 US 352, 88 L Ed 93, 64 S Ct 120). The statutory policy of affording broad protection to investors is not to be thwarted by unrealistic and irrelevant formulae.

Reserved.

[The dissenting opinion of Justice FRANKFURTER is omitted.]

The test set out in the Howey case is known as the "common enterprise test." In *Pacific Coast Coin Exchange v. O.S.C.*, [1978] 2 S.C.R. 112, 2 B.L.R. 212, 80 D.L.R. (3d) 529 it was held that "there is no need for the enterprise to be common to the investors between themselves." According to *Pacific Coast* a common enterprise exists where "[t]he key to success of the venture" was "the efforts of the promoter alone, for a benefit that [would] accrue to both the investor and the promoter" (*Id.* at [1978] 2 S.C.R. 129-30). With respect to the requirement that the profits accrue "solely" from the efforts of a promoter or third party, the *Pacific Coast* case held that it is not necessary that profits accrue "solely" from the efforts of a third party as long as the efforts of the third party are "undeniably significant" for the success of the enterprise (*Id.* at [1978] 2 S.C.R. 129).

A different test for the existence of an investment contract was applied in *State of Hawaii v. Hawaii Market Center Inc.*, 485 P.2d 105 (Hawaii 1971). In the *Hawaii* case a pyramid scheme used by the Hawaii Market Center was found to involve a security. Capital for the store was raised by selling memberships in the store. A membership could be acquired by either buying merchandise worth $70 for $320, or buying a different set of merchandise worth $140 for $820. Members could then earn returns by selling other memberships. When these other members sold memberships the initial member would earn commissions. The members returns thus did not come "solely" from the efforts of third parties.

The Hawaii Securities Commission granted an injunction against sales of the memberships on the basis that the memberships constituted investment contracts.

The test applied in the *Hawaii* case is known as the "risk capital test." According to the risk capital test an investment contract is created whenever:

(1) An offeree furnishes initial value to an offeror, and
(2) a portion of this initial value is subjected to the risks of the enterprise, and
(3) the furnishing of the initial value is induced by the offeror's promises or representations, which give rise to a reasonable understanding that a valuable benefit of some kind, over and above the initial value, will accrue to the offeree as a result of the operation of the enterprise, and
(4) the offeree does not receive the right to exercise practical and actual control over the managerial decisions of the enterprise.

See 485 P.2d 109.

If the transaction involved does not fit within the broad terms set out in the definition of "security" the transaction can still be brought within the definition of "security" because the definition provides that a security "includes" the specified items in the definition. Thus the definition of "security" can be extended beyond the listed items where the transaction does not fit within the listed items but is of a type that securities regulators or the courts are of the opinion should be covered by securities regulation. For an example of such a use of the word "includes" in the definition of "security" see *Re George Albino*, [1991] O.S.C.B. 365.

3. The Definition of Trade

As noted above, under most Canadian securities acts the requirement to produce a prospectus depends on whether there is a "trade" in a "security" that constitutes a "distribution." The definition of "trade" is also important with respect to the registration requirement for persons involved in the securities business. There are two aspects of the definition of "trade" that are of most significance in the context of the prospectus requirement. First, under most Canadian securities acts a "trade" is defined to include "any sale or disposition of a security for valuable consideration." See, e.g., ASA s. 1(x)(i); BCSA s.1(1) "trade" (a); OSA s.1(1) "trade" (a). Second, pre-sale activities with respect to a distribution of securities are included in the definition of "trade" since a "trade" is typically defined to include "any act, advertisement, solicitation, conduct or negotiation directly or indirectly in furtherance of" any sale or disposition of a security for valuable consideration. See ASA s. 1(x)(v); BCSA s. 1(1) "trade" (e); OSA s. 1(1) "trade" (e). Consequently, almost any attempt to distribute securities to the public will involve a "trade" in the security.

4. The Definition of "Distribution"

The definition of "distribution" under most Canadian securities acts is cast in very wide terms. Prior securities acts used the expression "distribution to the public." However, uncertainty associated with the meaning of "the public" led to the adoption of the so-called closed system (discussed in Section F below) under which the expression "to the public" has been dropped in favour of capturing virtually all distributions of securities under the term "distribution." Specific exemptions are then provided from the prospectus requirement where it is deemed appropriate.

Most distributions of securities will be subject to the prospectus requirement by virtue of the branch of the definition of "distribution" that refers to "a trade in a security of an issuer that has not been previously issued." See, e.g., ASA s. 1(f)(i); BCSA s. 1(1) "distribution" (a); OSA s. 1(1) "distribution" (a). If the issuer buys back its securities, or has its securities returned to it, an attempt to resell the securities will be covered by the branch of the definition of "distribution" that refers to "a trade by or on behalf of an issuer in previously issued securities of that issuer that have been redeemed or purchased by or donated to that issuer." See, e.g., ASA s. 1(f)(ii); BCSA s. 1(1) "distribution" (b); OSA s. 1(1) "distribution" (b).

Prospectus disclosure is also required where there is a sale of securities by persons having a controlling interest in the securities of an issuer. The prospectus is required by virtue of the branch of the definition of "distribution" that refers to "a trade in a previously issued security of an issuer from the holdings of a control person." See ASA

s. 1(f)(iii); BCSA s. 1(1) "distribution" (c); OSA s. 1(1) "distribution" (c). A "control person" is defined as a person (or a group of persons acting together) holding a sufficient number of the voting rights attached to all outstanding voting securities of an issuer to materially affect the control of the issuer. A person (or a group of persons acting together) holding more than 20% of the voting rights attached to all outstanding voting securities of an issuer is deemed, in the absence of evidence to the contrary, to hold sufficient voting rights to materially affect the control of the issuer. See ASA s. 1(c.2); BCSA s. 1(1) "control person"; OSA s. 1(1) "distribution" (c).

The sale of securities by persons having a controlling interest in an issuer is considered to have potentially important ramifications. For instance, it is argued that (1) the fact that the control person may be departing the corporation may be material to the corporation's affairs; (2) if a large block of shares is to be disposed of, that fact is material to the market for the issuer's shares; (3) the control person may be choosing to trade precisely when he is in possession of undisclosed material information concerning the issuer; and (4) the control person may be a conduit for a distribution of securities to members of the public who would not qualify for an exemption from the prospectus requirement. Of these, the last reason is likely the strongest. However, sales by a control person are a distribution even where there is no possibility that he is acting as an underwriter on a primary distribution. For example, a sale by a control person requires a prospectus even where he acquired the securities in secondary markets.

While a presumption arises that a 20% interest in voting securities will give its holder control of the issuing corporation, no corresponding presumption seems to arise that a smaller holding does not make one a control person. In *In the Matter of Deer Horn Mines Ltd.*, [1968] O.S.C.B. 12, the O.S.C. held that a 14.5% interest sufficed when the shareholder nominated the board of directors. The O.S.C. held that it was "of the opinion that the question of whether or not a block of shares materially affects control is not one capable of arithmetic measurement alone" ([1968] O.S.C.B. at 13).

5. The Prospectus Distribution Process

Vetting and Clearance of the Prospectus. Under most Canadian securities acts the process of distributing securities under a prospectus involves filing a preliminary prospectus followed by a final version of the prospectus. The securities administrator gives a receipt for the preliminary prospectus when it has been filed with the required supporting documents. The securities administrator's staff then vets the prospectus looking for deficiencies in terms of its compliance with the requirements of the Act and regulations and in terms of any apparent gaps in disclosure. The vetting process is not considered a passing on the merits of the securities offered nor is it a representation that the prospectus contains full disclosure. See, e.g., ASA Reg. s. 100; BCSA Reg. s. 91(1); OSA Reg. s. 51.

When the vetting process is complete the securities administrator issues a "comment letter" or "deficiency letter," which informs the issuer of any problems the securities administrator has with the preliminary prospectus. The issuer will then have to respond to or clear up the deficiencies identified by the securities administrator. Once the deficiencies are cleared to the satisfaction of the securities administrator the issuer can file the final prospectus together with supporting documents and obtain a receipt for the prospectus. When the receipt is given for the final prospectus the issuer can begin to distribute the securities.

National (or Multi-Province) Distributions. Because distributions of securities are the subject of provincial regulation, this process for the vetting of a prospectus can become particularly tedious and time consuming where a distribution of securities is being effected in more than one province. It is further complicated by the potential for deficiency letters with conflicting concerns and suggestions. Canadian securities administrators have responded to this problem by agreeing, in National Policy No. 1, to a system that simplifies the vetting process where securities are being distributed in more than one province.

Under National Policy No. 1 the issuer files the preliminary prospectus and the supporting materials contemporaneously in each jurisdiction where the securities are to be distributed. When it does so the issuer selects a principal jurisdiction for the vetting of the prospectus. The principal jurisdiction then issues a receipt for the preliminary prospectus and proceeds to prepare a first comment letter. The comment letter is then circulated to the other jurisdictions who provide any additional comments and forward them to the principal jurisdiction. The principal jurisdiction then prepares a second comment letter on the basis of the additional comments provided by other jurisdictions. The second comment letter is sent to the issuer. When the issuer has responded to the deficiencies the principal jurisdiction will send a notice indicating it is ready to accept the final prospectus and supporting documents. The issuer can then contemporaneously file the final prospectus and supporting documents in each of the jurisdictions in which the securities are to be distributed.

Simultaneous Distributions in Canada and the United States. Agreements between securities administrators in Canada and the United States allow for distributions in Canada on the basis of compliance with U.S. securities laws and distributions in the United States in compliance with Canadian securities laws. National Policy No. 45 permits an offering of securities in Canada based on compliance with U.S. securities laws. The issuer must prepare a preliminary prospectus and prospectus for the Canadian offering based on the S.E.C. requirements in the United States supplemented with additional information required by National Policy No. 45. The issuer can either prepare a separate preliminary prospectus and prospectus for use in Canada or use the prospectus prepared for the distribution in the United States together with a "wrap-around" document that provides the additional information required for the distribution in Canada.

Not all issuers are eligible to use the multi-jurisdictional disclosure system described in National Policy No 45. There are different eligibility criteria for different types of securities offerings. In general terms, the eligibility criteria are directed to assuring a sufficient base of information and market following with respect to the issuer to allow the market to adjust for any differences in the standard of disclosure. Thus the criteria focus on the issuer having provided a base of disclosure through continuous disclosure requirements (discussed in Section D below) and evidence of market following based on such criteria as listing on a stock exchange or having a substantial outstanding public float of equity (i.e. a substantial dollar volume of equity securities available for trading).

Similar rules of the S.E.C. allow Canadian issuers to offer certain types of securities in the United States on the basis of Canadian disclosure requirements supplemented with additional information to make the Canadian disclosure comparable to disclosure in the United States.

"Blue Sky" or Merit Discretion. Early securities laws in several states in the United States regulated the distribution of securities by retaining a discretion to assess the merits of the securities being distributed. This discretion was referred to as "blue sky" discretion because it was said to be intended to protect investors from "eastern industrialists selling everything including the blue sky." See T.L. Hazen, *Treatise on the Law of Securities Regulation* 368 (2d ed. 1990). Some scope for a merit review is also provided for under most Canadian securities acts. Several Canadian securities acts set out several bases on which securities administrators can refuse to issue a receipt for a prospectus on the basis of the merit of the particular distribution. For instance, among other grounds, securities administrators may refuse to issue a receipt for a prospectus where: (1) an unconscionable consideration has been, or will be, paid or given for services, promotional purposes or the acquisition of property; (2) any escrow or pooling agreement the administrator considers necessary has not been entered into; (3) the proceeds of the issue and the resources of the issuer are insufficient to accomplish the purpose of the issue; (4) the issuer cannot reasonably be expected to be financially responsible in the conduct of its business because of the financial condition of the issuer or of its officers, directors, promoters or control persons; (5) the interests of the issuer can not be expected to be conducted with integrity in the best interests of security holders because of the past conduct of its officers, directors, promoters or control persons; or (6) a person who has prepared or certified any part of the prospectus or who is named as having prepared a report or valuation used in or with the prospectus is not acceptable. See, e.g., ASA s. 96(2); BCSA Reg. s. 115(2); OSA s. 61(2).

Restrictions During the "Waiting Period." The time between the filing of the preliminary prospectus and the final prospectus is known as the "waiting period." Securities cannot be sold during the waiting period and selling activities during the waiting period are restricted. Selling activities are restricted with a view to assuring that the representations on which investors base their decisions are those contained in the prospectus and thus subject to statutory civil liability for misrepresentations (discussed below). During the waiting period one can only identify the security and its price (if it has been determined), give out a copy of the preliminary prospectus, solicit expressions of interest in the security and indicate where it can be bought. See, e.g., ASA s. 99; BCSA s. 61(2); OSA s. 65(2). Advertisements can only identify the security, its price, where it can be purchased and otherwise solicit expressions of interest. See Uniform Act Policy 2-13 and see also National Policies 21 and 42.

Delivery of Prospectus and Cooling-Off Period. Once the receipts have been given for the final prospectus, the securities can be sold. A dealer receiving an order or subscription for a security offered under the prospectus must deliver a copy of the prospectus to the prospective investor within two business days of entering into a written confirmation of the sale of the security. See ASA s. 105; BCSA s. 66(1); OSA s. 71(1). The purchaser is then entitled to a two day cooling-off period. The purchaser has two business days from the receipt of the prospectus to withdraw from the obligation to buy the securities. See ASA s. 106; BCSA s. 66(3); OSA s. 71(2).

6. Sanctions for Non-Compliance

A failure to deliver a prospectus or to obtain a receipt for a prospectus where one is required can lead to penal sanctions, administrative sanctions or civil sanctions. The consequences may be extremely serious. Moreover, such breaches may arise not through fraud but through an honest though mistaken belief that an exemption from the prospectus requirement exists.

Failure to Deliver a Prospectus. Failure to deliver a prospectus can lead to a penal sanction of fine or imprisonment. See ASA s. 161(1)(e); BCSA s. 138(1)(a.1); OSA s. 122(1)(c). Under the OSA this can lead to a fine of up to $1,000,000, or, for an individual, a fine of up to $1,000,000 and up to two years imprisonment. A range of administrative orders may also be available. For instance, failure to deliver the prospectus could result in an order directing compliance, an order that trading in the securities of any person or by any person cease, a denial of exemptions from the requirements of the securities act and regulations, or, in the case of a registered dealer, a reprimand or suspension, cancellation or restriction of registration for trading in securities. See, e.g., ASA s. 56, 164, 165 166; BCSA s. 144(1); and OSA s. 127.

There is also a statutory civil sanction for failure to deliver a prospectus. If the prospectus has not been delivered the purchaser of the security has a right of action for rescission or damages. See ASA s. 170(a); BCSA s. 118(a); OSA s. 133. Under the securities acts in most jurisdictions in Canada the right of rescission must be exercised within 180 days of the date of the transaction that gave rise to the cause of action. An action for damages must be brought within the earlier of 180 days after the purchaser first had knowledge of the facts giving rise to the action and, under the OSA and the BCSA, within three years of the purchase (one year under the ASA). See ASA s. 175; BCSA s. 124; OSA s. 138.

Failure to File. Failure to obtain a receipt for a prospectus where it is required can lead to a fine or imprisonment. See ASA s. 161(1)(e); BCSA s. 138(1)(c); OSA s. 122(1)(c). It can also lead to administrative orders such as an order that trading in the security cease until the prospectus is filed and a receipt is obtained, or a denial of exemptions under the securities act or regulations. ASA s. 164, 165; 166; BCSA s. 144, 146; OSA s. 127.

There is no specific statutory civil sanction for a failure to file a prospectus. It might be thought that the statutory civil sanction for a failure to deliver a would apply where no prospectus has been filed. However, the provisions requiring the delivery of a prospectus typically require the delivery of "the latest prospectus filed respecting the security" (see, e.g., ASA s. 105; BCSA s. 66(1); OSA s. 71(1)) and it has been held that the effect of this is that the statutory civil sanction for a failure to deliver a prospectus does not apply to a failure to file a prospectus. See *Jones v. F.H. Deacon Hodgson Inc.* (1986), 56 O.R. (2d) 540, 31 D.L.R. (4th) 455 (set out below).

While there may be no statutory civil sanction for a failure to file a prospectus there may still be a common law action for rescission. The case of *Jones v. F.H. Deacon Hodgson Inc.*, set out below, addresses this issue.

Jones v. F.H. Deacon Hodgson Inc.
Ontario High Court
(1986), 31 D.L.R. (4th) 455

HENRY J.: The issue on this motion is whether a sale of shares in contravention of s. 52 of the Securities Act, R.S.O. 1980, c. 466, is void for failure to file a prospectus with the Ontario Securities Commission. That section provides in part:

52(1) No person or company shall trade in a security on his own account or on behalf of any other person or company,

(a) before the 15th day of March, 1981, where such trade would be a distribution to the public of such security;

(b) on and after the 15th day of March, 1981, where such trade would be a distribution of such security,

unless a preliminary prospectus and a prospectus have been filed and receipts therefor obtained from the Director.

The facts as pleaded by the plaintiff in the action are as follows and are not disputed for the purposes of this motion.

The defendant F.H. Deacon Hodgson Inc. (Deacon), is an investment dealer. In December, 1980, Deacon caused a private company Bacova Investments Limited to be incorporated for the purpose of investing in Lumax Oil and Gas Limited, an oil exploration company whose shares are traded over the counter. In January, 1982, Deacon offered for sale shares in Bacova and solicited subscribers. It is common ground that this constituted a distribution of shares to the public within the meaning of s. 52(1) of the Securities Act; it is also common ground that Bacova did not file a prospectus with the Ontario Securities Commission as required by s. 52(1)(a).

The plaintiff purchased shares in Bacova through the defendant Deacon in January, 1982. The plaintiff's action, commenced in February, 1986, is for a declaration that the contract of purchase and sale of the shares is void; he also claims return of $24,000, the price paid by him to Deacon for the shares together with interest. The defendant now brings this motion to dismiss the action on the ground that it is statute-barred. The rationale of this position is as follows:

(1) Section 70(1) of the Securities Act creates an obligation for a dealer to deliver a prospectus to a purchaser of securities and states as follows:

70(1) A dealer not acting as agent of the purchaser who receives an order or subscription for a security offered in a distribution to which subsection 52(1) or section 61 is applicable shall, unless he has previously done so, send by prepaid mail or deliver to the purchaser the latest prospectus and any amendment to the prospectus filed either before entering into an agreement of purchase and sale resulting from the order or subscription or not later than midnight on the second day, exclusive of Saturdays, Sundays, and holidays after entering into such agreement.

(2) Section 130 of the Securities Act creates civil liability for a dealer or offeror who fails to deliver a prospectus to a purchaser of securities. That section provides:

130. A purchaser of a security to whom a prospectus was required to be sent or delivered but was not sent or delivered in compliance with subsection 70(1) or an offeree to whom a take-over bid circular or issuer bid circular was required to be communicated but was not communicated in compliance with section 92 has a right of action for rescission or damages against the dealer or offeror who failed to comply with the applicable requirement.

(3) Section 135 of the Securities Act provides a maximum three-year limitation period in the following language:

135. Unless otherwise provided in this Act, no action shall be commenced to enforce a right created by this Part more than,

    (a) in the case of an action for rescission, 180 days after the date of the transaction that gave rise to the cause of action; or

    (b) in the case of any action, other than an action for rescission, the earlier of,

        (i) 180 days after the plaintiff first had knowledge of the facts giving rise to the cause of action, or

        (ii) three years after the date of the transaction that gave rise to the cause of action.

To this the plaintiff simply replies that he is not relying on s. 130 which creates a civil remedy for breach of s. 70(1); he relies solely on the breach of s. 52(1) which he submits gives rise to a common-law right of action for its breach; it is not a right of action created by Part XXII of the Act and the limitation provision in s. 135 does not apply to it.

The defendant counters by saying that by enacting s. 52(1) the Legislature did not intend to provide a civil remedy for its breach but has provided a criminal penalty only. The only civil remedy available to the plaintiff is s. 70 which is "triggered" by the breach of s. 52(1) and s. 130; hence the action, being commenced more than three years after the shares were purchased and sold, is statute-barred.

I have reached the conclusion on the basis of the full and able submissions of counsel, that the plaintiff's cause of action properly lies for breach of s. 52(1) and that the limitation period prescribed by s. 135 does not apply to it.

The starting point in the resolution of this issue is the decision of the Supreme Court of Canada in *Re Northwestern Trust Co., McAskill's Case*, [1926] 3 D.L.R. 612, [1926] S.C.R. 412, 7 C.B.R. 440. That decision applied the general principle that a contract expressly or impliedly prohibited by statute is void. McAskill subscribed for shares of Northwestern Trust and was allotted shares which were not fully paid. Subsequently, one and a half years later, the company was ordered to be wound up by the court and the liquidator called on McAskill for the balance of his contribution. It transpired that the company had failed to obtain the permission and authority of Public Utilities Commission of Manitoba to sell its shares as required by the Manitoba Sale of Shares Act, R.S.M. 1913, c. 175. It had failed to file documents disclosing the financial and other affairs of the company (analogous to a prospectus) and had not obtained for itself or its agents a certificate and a licence of the commission to sell its shares. Unknown to McAskill at the time, the sale to McAskill thereby contravened the Manitoba Sale of

Shares Act. The court held the sale to be void so that the liquidator was precluded from getting in the balance of his contribution for the shares. As Mignault J. put it at p. 627 D.L.R., pp. 430-1 S.C.R.:

Taking into consideration the character of the statute, its language and also the purpose for which it was enacted—which was to protect the general public against schemes or campaigns to sell shares or securities of doubtful value to unwary investors through agents, and with the aid of advertisements, circulars or other methods of publicity—the conclusion seems inevitable that the Sale of Shares Act deals with a matter of public policy and that anything done in contravention of its prohibitions is void and not merely voidable. It is true that *per se* every sale of its shares by a company is not made unlawful (1913-14 (Man.), c. 105, s. 5). It is the sale effected "in the course of continued and successive acts," as defined, which falls under the prohibitions of the statute. A sale so made, and all steps taken to carry it out, such as an allotment of shares, are void.

This general principle again came before the Supreme Court of Canada in relation to sale of shares in *Meyers v. Freeholders Oil Co. Ltd.* (1960), 25 D.L.R. (2d) 81, [1960] S.C.R. 761, 33 W.W.R. 193. The Security Frauds Prevention Act, R.S.S. 1940, c. 287 (later the Securities Act, 1954, c. 49), was invoked to nullify trading in the shares of a mining lease. The salesman's qualification to sell the shares was not in issue as the company itself was licensed as a broker; but the Act prohibited salesmen calling at a private residence to trade in securities with the public. The court, per Martland J., reiterated the principle in *Re Northwestern Trust Co., McAskill's Case*, but said that where the statute provided a penalty for the offence the court must then look to the Act as a whole to determine if that is the sole remedy intended by the Legislature. The court concluded that the prohibition against salesman calling at investors' homes to sell securities was not part of the fundamental scheme of protecting the public against unauthorized trading; the penalty prescribed was the only remedy and the sale was not void.

The analysis of Martland J. is instructive as to the proper approach that the courts should take (pp. 92-3):

The determination of the effect of the breach of a statutory provision upon a contract is often a difficult one and must, of course, depend upon the terms and the intent of the provision under consideration. In some cases the statute clearly forbids the making of a certain kind of contract. In such a case the contract cannot be valid if it is in breach of the provision. An example of this kind is found in the provisions of the Manitoba Sale of Shares Act, R.S.M. 1913, c. 175, which was considered by this Court in *Re Northwestern Trust Co., McAskill's Case*, [1926] 3 D.L.R. 612, S.C.R. 412, 7 C.B.R. 440. Section 4 of that Act provided:

It shall hereafter be unlawful for any person or persons, corporation or company, or any agent acting on his, their or its behalf, to sell or offer to sell, or to directly or indirectly attempt to sell, in the Province of Manitoba, any shares, stocks, bonds or other securities of any corporation or company, syndicate or association of persons, incorporated or unincorporated, other than the securities hereinafter excepted, without first obtaining from the Public Utility Commissioner, hereinafter styled the commissioner, a certificate to the effect hereinafter set forth and a license to such agent in the manner hereinafter provided for.

Section 6, in part, read:

It shall not be lawful for any person or any such company, either as principal or agent, to transact any business, in form or character similar to that set forth in section 4, until such person or such company shall have filed the papers and documents hereinafter provided for.

The Court held in that case that a sale of shares made by a company which had failed to comply with the statutory provisions was void and not voidable.

Section 16 of the Security Frauds Prevention Act, itself, contains an express provision whereby, in the circumstances therein defined, a contract by a customer of a broker shall be void, at the option of such customer.

On the other hand, some statutes have been construed as only imposing a penalty, where the Act provides for one, although that is not necessarily the result of a penalty being incorporated in the Act. Lord Esher posed the question which must be determined in *Melliss v. Shirley Local Board* (1885), 16 Q.B.D. 446 at pp. 451-2, as follows:

> Although a statute contains no express words making void a contract which it prohibits, yet, when it inflicts a penalty for the breach of the prohibition, you must consider the whole Act as well as the particular enactment in question, and come to a decision, either from the context or the subject matter, whether the penalty is imposed with intent merely to deter persons from entering into the contract, or for the purposes of revenue, or whether it is intended that the contract shall not be entered into as to be valid at law.

In the present case I have come to the conclusion that it was not the intention of s. 17a of the Security Frauds Prevention Act to render completely void a trade in securities because it is made at a residence. The general intent of the statute is to afford protection to the public against trades in securities by persons seeking to trade who have not satisfied the Registrar as to their proper qualification so to do. For that reason the registration provisions of s. 3 are incorporated in the Act. But s. 17a is not a part of this general pattern, because it applies to registered brokers and salesmen as well as to those who are not registered. As I see it, its purpose is not to prevent trading of an unauthorized kind, but is intended to prevent persons in their own residences from being sought out there by stock salesmen. It is the place at which the negotiations occur which is important in this section and not the character of the negotiations themselves. It seeks to deter salesmen from attempting to make contracts, which otherwise may be quite proper, at a particular place. This being so, it is my opinion that a breach of s. 17a, in relation to a transaction otherwise lawful, results, not in preventing the contract from being valid, but in the incurring of a penalty by the person who is in breach of it.

I do not think, therefore, that the breach of s. 17a resulted in the agreement in question here being rendered void.

In my opinion the appeal should be dismissed with costs.

This, in my opinion, is the proper approach which ought to be followed by this court in determining whether the Ontario Securities Act by the clear and unambiguous prohibition in s. 52(1) leaves unimpaired the common law principle that a breach of its injunction results in a sale of shares that is void as was the case in *Re Northwestern Trust*. I add that the British Columbia Court of Appeal in *Ames et al. v. Investo-Plan Ltd. et al.* (1973), 35 D.L.R. (3d) 613, [1973] 5 W.W.R. 451, which appears to be the last word on a statute *in pari materia* reached the conclusion that breach of a provision similar to s. 52(1) in the British Columbia Securities Act did not result in a contract that was void or voidable. I shall return to this decision which, with respect, I consider should not be applied to the Ontario Act before me.

Section 52(1) of the Ontario Securities Act in clear terms prohibits any person from trading shares of a company unless a prospectus has been filed with the Ontario Securities Commission and a receipt therefor obtained from the director. By s. 60(1) the director shall issue a receipt for a prospectus filed unless it appears to him that it is not in the public interest to do so; the remainder of the section sets out the grounds on which the director shall not issue the receipt and for a hearing before the commission where he intends to refuse to issue it. In short, not only must the prospectus be filed but the commission and the director must be satisfied that the prospectus does not contain any element that is contrary to the public interest. Absent the receipt, no person may trade in the shares of the issuing company.

There can be no question but that the filing of a prospectus and its acceptance by the commission is fundamental to the protection of the investing public who are contemplating purchase of the shares. The effect of s. 60 is, by the issue of the receipt, to authorize the sale of the company's shares; the effect of s. 52 is to prohibit outright trading in the shares by way of distribution to the public unless the distribution is authorized by the commission. In the language of Mignault J. in *Re Northwestern Trust*, the purpose of the statute "is to protect the general public against schemes or campaigns to sell shares or securities of doubtful value to unwary investors." That, as the court said, "deals with a matter of public policy and that anything done in contravention of its prohibitions is void and not merely voidable." The principle as applied to the fundamental as opposed to non-fundamental provisions in my opinion, is not in any way impaired by the court's subsequent decision in *Meyers*: see per Martland J. at p. 93 set out above.

Breach of that provision without more, gives rise to a common law right in the purchaser (the plaintiff in this case) to have the sale declared a nullity. There are, however, three factors that must also be considered:

(a) The Act by s. 118 in Part XXI entitled "Enforcement" provides that any person who contravenes the Act is guilty of an offence and on summary conviction is liable to a fine or in the case of an individual to a fine and imprisonment or both; the penal provisions are applied by the courts in accordance with the procedure for offences punishable on summary conviction with the consent and under the direction of the Minister (s. 119). Part XXI also provides authority to the commission, where a person or company has failed to comply with a provision of the Act or regulations, to apply to a High Court judge for an order directing compliance or restraining further violation (s. 122). The commission may, where in its opinion it is in the public interest to do so, order that trading shall cease in the securities affected (s. 123). Proceedings under this Part are subject to periods of limitation in s. 125. No doubt in the case at Bar, it would have been open to the Minister to institute a prosecution for the breach of s. 52(1) or to the commission to have taken the regulatory action authorized by ss. 122 and 123 had the breach been drawn to the attention of the commission in the first place; but none of the provisions in Part XXI appears to me to assist a purchaser of securities who is already committed to an unlawful transaction such as that before me. Part XXI merely permits the barn door to be locked after the horse has bolted.

(b) The Act by Part XXII prescribes civil remedies by creating causes of action for breach of specific provisions of the Act. There is no reference to a civil remedy for breach of s. 52(1). The cause of action is provided only in the case of a purchaser of shares who is not provided with a prospectus as required by s. 70 which does not apply here.

(c) There is no provision in the Act that expressly deprives a person of his common law remedy for breach of s. 52(1).

Counsel have not been able to discover any judicial decisions on the effect of s. 52 of the Ontario Securities Act. (The decision of the British Columbia Court of Appeal in *Ames*, however, relates to the corresponding provision in the British Columbia Securities Act, but I pass it over for the present.)

The combined effect of the Supreme Court of Canada's decisions in *Re Northwestern Trust* and *Meyers* is that a sale of securities that is prohibited by the statute is void; but that where a penalty is provided the court must determine whether that penalty is intended merely to deter persons from entering into the contract or is also intended to invalidate the contract of purchase and sale in law. The court held in *Meyers* that the prohibition of sales at a residence, i.e., at a particular place, was not part of the "general pattern" of protecting the public against trading in securities by persons who have not satisfied the regulatory authority of their proper qualifications to do so; its purpose was not to prevent trading of an unauthorized kind but it was to prevent trading at a specified place. The penalty was held to be merely a deterrent and the contract of sale was not invalidated by the breach. That is not the case here; the breach is of a fundamental element of the statutory scheme to protect the public against unauthorized trading.

The statutory scheme in the Ontario Securities Act as it relates to this subject is this: first the seller may not trade in the shares unless the company has filed a prospectus and it has been accepted by the commission. The prohibition is absolute (s. 52(1)) and the provision is fundamental.

Second, part XXII creates several civil remedies. Section 70(1) makes a special provision respecting a purchaser who places an order to purchase shares to which s. 52(1) applies; the dealer is required to deliver to the purchaser the latest prospectus and amendments *filed with the commission*. He must do so either before entering into the agreement of purchase and sale or within two days after making the agreement. By s. 70(2) the purchaser may reject the sale within two days after receiving the prospectus. It is therefore open to the purchaser to abort the transaction after receiving the prospectus.

It is important to recognize that the prospectus that s. 70(1) requires to be delivered to the purchaser is the most recent prospectus and amendments thereto filed with the commission in accordance with s. 52(1). The investing public is protected first by the requirement that the prospectus be filed and accepted and second by ensuring that the purchaser is provided with a copy of it before he is finally committed to the contract of purchase and sale.

It is also noteworthy that s.70(1) does not make the resulting sale unlawful or prohibited as does s. 52(1). By contrast the contract is one that can be aborted or rescinded at the option of the purchaser; he may avoid being bound once he receives the prospectus or if he does not receive it he may if so advised proceed by way of an action for rescission or damages against the dealer who failed to comply with s. 70(1). That cause of action is created by s. 130, in Part XXII; it is one of several created by Part

XXII of the Act; others in that part relate to liability for misrepresentation in a prospectus or circular (ss. 126 and 127), liability for failure to make a follow-up of or take up securities under s. 91 (s. 129) and liability of a person or company in a special relationship with a reporting issuer for failure to disclose a material fact or change or an insider who improperly uses his knowledge or information (s. 131). By s. 135 no action shall be commenced to enforce the right created by Part XXII after the expiry of the limitation period therein prescribed.

In ss. 126 and 127, which create special liability for misrepresentation in a prospectus it is also provided that the right of action for rescission or damages thereby conferred is in addition to and not in derogation of any other right the purchaser may have at law, thereby preserving any common law action he may have for fraud or misrepresentation.

Third, none of the remedies created by Part XXII applies to a breach of s. 52(1) by failure to file any prospectus at all. In such a case s. 70 does not avail the purchaser because it assists him only when the dealer fails to provide him with a prospectus filed with the commission; if none is filed there is no breach as no such prospectus exists. There is a lacuna; the Act neither provides a cause of action for breach of s. 52(1) nor does it expressly or by necessary intendment abolish the purchaser's remedy in common law or equity to have the prohibited transaction declared null and void as in *Re Northwestern Trust*.

It is therefore not correct to say, as Mr. Steep submits, that breach of s. 52(1) "triggers" the cause of action created by s. 70 so that the purchaser has a remedy created by Part XXII albeit one that is limited by s. 135. Section 70 applies only where a prospectus has been filed; the Act does not contemplate a sale where no prospectus that is required by s. 52(1) has been filed with the commission. Where none is filed the purchaser is left to such remedy as he may otherwise have in law or equity. (I add that s. 52(1) does not apply to certain distributions of securities which are exempted by Part XVI from prospectus requirements; those provisions are not relevant here.)

The rule as applied in *Re Northwestern Trust* is founded on public policy for the protection of the investing public. The requirement in s. 52(1) is equally to protect the public and it is one of the fundamental components of the scheme of the Securities Act. The prohibition is clearly expressed; the result of its breach is that the sale of shares to the plaintiff is void. Having regard to the scheme of the Act and the central place in that scheme of the requirement to file a prospectus, that result in law is not to be taken to be abrogated by the Legislature unless it is abrogated in clear terms or by necessary intendment. The creation of specific causes of action in Part XXII, even on the *expressio unius* rule, does not achieve that result; nor is that result achieved by mere failure to deal with the effect of a breach. The transaction is illegal and void and there is no contract of purchase and sale of the shares. That is the effect in law and I cannot find any ground for holding that the Legislature has altered it.

I do not overlook the decision of the British Columbia Court of Appeal in *Ames v. Investo-Plan* which I have mentioned earlier. The court considered [at p. 615], *inter alia*, s. 37 of the Securities Act, 1967 (B.C.), c. 45, which provided:

37. No person or company shall trade in any security issued by a ... mutual fund company ... where the trade would be in the course of primary distribution to the public of the secu-

rity until there has been filed with and accepted by the Commission a prospectus in respect of the offering of the security and a receipt therefor in writing has been obtained from the Commission.

The mutual fund company whose shares were sold to the plaintiff had submitted a prospectus to the Alberta Securities Commission. It had been cleared by the Quebec commission and is said to have conformed to the requirements of the Securities Acts of Nova Scotia and Newfoundland. The British Columbia commission had not, however, accepted it. Anderson J. held that the contract of purchase and sale was void *ab initio* as being prohibited by s. 37, relying on *Re Northwestern Trust*. The Court of Appeal distinguished that case on the ground that the provisions of the British Columbia Securities Act were "substantially different" from the Manitoba Sale of Shares Act which was at the root of the decision in *Re Northwestern Trust*. It is not clear to me from the judgment what the differences were; the Court of Appeal firstly said that in the case of the Manitoba statute the language used was "it shall hereafter be unlawful" and "it shall not be lawful" to sell securities in the circumstances of that case. I can see no difference in substance between that language and s. 37 of the British Columbia Securities Act.

The Court of Appeal then turned to *Meyers v. Freeholders Oil* and observed that the Supreme Court of Canada there held that breach of the provision prohibiting a salesman from selling securities at a residence did not void the contract of purchase and sale because it was not part of the "general pattern" of protection. The Court of Appeal referred to specific provisions in the British Columbia Securities Act, 1967 which provided a cause of action for rescission by the purchaser which bears some resemblance to Part XXII of the Ontario Securities Act; that remedy is provided, so far as appears from the reasons for judgment, to cases where a prospectus has been filed and contains untrue or misleading statements of fact or a material omission. The nub of the Court of Appeal's reasons on this point [at p. 618] is essentially the *expressio unius* rule:

In my opinion a contract for purchase of shares in contravention of s. 37 is not voidable at the election of the purchaser except in the circumstances described in the Act itself. In other circumstances the consequence of failure to comply with s. 37 is liability to the statutory penalties.

The Court of Appeal also stated at p. 618, that the transaction is not void for breach of s. 37:

It is evident that the object of the statute is to regulate and control the business of trading in securities in order to protect the public. The statute does not prohibit trading in securities or declare contracts for sale of shares void or unlawful. I cannot, on a consideration of it, impute to the Legislature an intention to prevent the enforcement of contracts made in contravention of it as against the persons who are required to comply with it. Applying the test described by Martland, J., I do not believe it was intended to allow companies which agree to issue shares in violation of s. 37 to escape their obligations to perform their agreements. This would be the result if such agreements are void. Looking, for example, at s. 51 I do not think it was the intention that a purchaser of shares from a person or company which has failed to give a notice required by that section should be prevented from enforcing the purchase or from recovering damages for failure to deliver. I am, therefore, of the opinion that the contract in this case made in contravention of s. 37 is not rendered void by the statute.

I am puzzled by this *rationale* for two reasons: first it seems clear to me that s. 37 (the section breached) clearly prohibits trading; second it seems equally clear that s. 37 goes to the core of the scheme of protection of the public investing in mutual fund securities—it is part of the "general pattern" to use the expression of Martland J. in *Meyers v. Freeholders.* The Court of Appeal however appears to place it in the subsidiary or ancillary category which Martland J. held decisive in that case; or else they say that as a matter of judicial policy the breach ought not to void the transaction or to make it voidable by the purchaser. Whatever the *rationale* of the Court of Appeal's decision I do not regard it as applicable in the case at Bar. Rather, I consider that I am bound by the Supreme Court of Canada's decisions referred to as falling within *Re Northwestern Trust* and upon a review of the objects as a whole, not within the *ratio* of *Meyers* in that s. 52(1) of the Ontario Securities Act is clearly part of the "general pattern" referred to by Martland J.

(a) No prospectus was filed with the Ontario Securities Commission and the sale by Deacon was in breach of s. 52(1) which is a fundamental element of the statutory scheme of full disclosure and regulation by the commission for protection of the investing public in cases not exempt by the Act from the prospectus requirements.

(b) Section 70 does not here create a remedy for the plaintiff because that section applies only where a prospectus has been filed and a receipt obtained from the director.

(c) Breach of s. 52(1) does not "trigger" an offence under s. 70(1) where no prospectus is filed; the limitation in s. 135 does not apply because no cause of action is here created by Part XXII.

(d) Breach of s. 52(1) stands on its own; it is subject to a quasi-criminal penalty and regulatory action under Part XXI. The general rule, however, is that the sale is void in common law. That principle requires a clear expression by the Legislature if it was intended to abrogate it—there is none here.

While the court should be reluctant to interfere with contracts freely made, in this case the overriding consideration is the need to support the fundamental purpose of the statute as a matter of public policy to protect the integrity of the regulatory scheme of the Act; contractual integrity must give way; the penalty alone and the remedies available to the commission, in my opinion, ought not to be the only deterrent or remedy. Moreover, the scheme would be seriously impaired were the court to preserve the legal transaction and deprive the purchaser of a remedy where no prospectus has been filed at all and to recognize his only civil remedy as that created by s. 70 and other provisions of Part XXII all of which are limited to cases where s. 52 has been complied with; that would ignore the fundamental breach and support only the remedies provided in cases in which the prospectus has been filed and accepted as required.

(e) I am aware that while my decision precludes the dealer from enforcing an illegal contract against the purchaser, the purchaser cannot enforce it against the vendor should he prefer to do so; he, of course, may prefer not to exercise his remedy and continue to hold the shares. It seems to me, however, that the purchaser otherwise may maintain an action for a declaration that the contract is void and that he is entitled to recover the price paid for the shares as a form of unjust enrichment in the hands of the vendor. The court ought to provide him with that remedy at least as an innocent party (so far as this motion is concerned). On the other hand, I should deem it sound judicial policy for the court to refuse to entertain an action by the vendor (or allow it a defence), in reliance on the void transaction on the ground that to do so would enable the vendor to profit by his illegal conduct. This latter point I am frank to say is *obiter* as I am not obliged to decide it.

The defendant's motion is for an order dismissing the action. For the reasons I have outlined the motion must fail.

Rescissionary Remedies. Under *Jones*, the defences that an issuer may assert on non-compliance with prospectus requirements differ when (1) a prospectus is not filed and (2) a prospectus is filed but not delivered to the investor. In the former case, the transaction is void, with the result that the limitation period noted above (ASA s. 175; BCSA s. 124; OSA s. 138(a)) does not apply. In the second case, the transaction is not void but voidable, and the investors' remedies are restricted by the limitation period. Apart from limitation periods, the availability of legal and equitable defenses of waiver, estoppel, ratification and laches may depend upon whether the transaction is characterized as void or voidable. For example, rescissionary rights were held to have been waived in *Dorsch v. Freeholders Oil Co.*, [1965] S.C.R. 670. Dorsch was a Saskatchewan farmer with a grade 9 education who assigned his rights in an oil and gas lease to Freeholders in return for an issue of its shares. While Freeholders had filed a prospectus in Saskatchewan, it did not offer one to Dorsch. Nearly six years later Dorsch sued to set aside the agreement for misrepresentation and *non est factum*. The Court held that a breach of the requirement to provide a registered prospectus to an investor rendered the transaction at most voidable. Martland J. stated per curiam at pages 680-81 that:

Even if Dorsch had the right to avoid his share purchase, he could not exercise it when he purported to do so because, having entered into the contract on August 3, 1950, and having received his share certificate in the following year, he took no step to repudiate until June 21, 1956, and, in the meantime, had been in receipt of communications sent to him as a shareholder by Freeholders, and had attended and voted at two annual meetings. This, in my opinion, is ample evidence of his election to retain the shares, and of his waiver of any right to have the allotment of shares to him rescinded.

An investor who sits on his rights for a long period of time would not appear to be a particularly meritorious plaintiff. "The purpose of the Securities Exchange Act is to protect the innocent investor, not one who loses his innocence and then waits to see how his investment turns out before he decides to invoke the provisions of the Act." *Royal Air Properties, Inc. v. Smith*, 312 F.2d 210, 213-14 (9th Cir. 1962). In addition, the possibility of long-lasting rescissionary rights will impose a cost upon the issuer, which may have to stay liquid in anticipation of a claim that the allotment be set aside. This uncertainty will also increase the issuer's cost of capital, for creditors will fear that the business may unwind through an assertion of rescissionary remedies. Requiring an investor to litigate with diligence may then serve an economic purpose in reducing these costs. On the other hand, maintaining an action even where the plaintiff seems unmeritorious may be defended insofar as it advances the prophylactic goals of securities legislation.

A judgment based on the 1933 Act performs a dual function. It redresses a private wrong and enforces public policy. Since one of the essential purposes of the Act is to protect investors by requiring publication of information about a security through its registration, enforcement of the Act by private litigation ordinarily should not be encumbered by defenses for which the statute makes no provision.

Lawler v. Gilliam, 569 F.2d 1283, 1291 (4th Cir. 1978). More recently, the United States Supreme Court held that the *in pari delicto* defence was inapplicable in an action for a breach of S.E.C. rule 10b-5. However, an exception would arise where the plaintiff and defendant were equally culpable for the violation and the Act's purposes would not be frustrated by allowing the defence to succeed. A private securities action might then be barred on the ground of the plaintiff's own culpability where:

(1) as direct result of his own actions, the plaintiff bears at least substantially equal responsibility for the violations he seeks to redress, and (2) preclusion of suit would not significantly interfere with the effective enforcement of the securities laws and protection of the investing public.

Bateman Eichler, Hill Richards, Inc. v. Berner, 105 S. Ct. 2622, 2629 (1985). In decisions since *Berner*, however, the exception has been interpreted narrowly. For example, in *Dahl v. Pinter*, 787 F.2d 985 (5th Cir. 1986), the Court held that the *in pari delicto* defence applies "only when some unconscionable act of one coming for relief has immediate and necessary relation to the equity that he seeks in respect of the matter in litigation." *Id.* at 988 (adopting *Keystone Miller Co. v. General Excavator Co.*, 290 U.S. 240, 245 (1933)).

Investors have at times relied upon rescissionary remedies to elevate themselves to the preferred status of creditors when insolvency looms. See *Re British Canadian Commodity Options Ltd.* (1979), 22 O.R. (2d) 278. If creditors cannot easily evaluate the possibility of rescissionary remedies, this may give rise to screening inefficiencies. American decisions "seem to have a peculiar flavor" in such cases, such that equitable defenses are more likely to succeed. 3 L. Loss, *Securities Regulation* 1679-80 (2d ed. 1961).

7. Statutory Civil Liability for Misrepresentations

The Statutory Civil Action. In addition to the remedies for a failure to deliver a prospectus and a failure to file a prospectus, Canadian securities acts contain a statutory civil remedy for misrepresentations in a prospectus. A remedy of rescission or damages is available against the issuer, selling security holder or underwriter and a remedy of damages is available against certain other named defendants. See, e.g., ASA s. 168; BCSA s. 114; OSA s. 130. The statutory civil action for a misrepresentation in a prospectus goes beyond the common law action of negligent misrepresentation under *Hedley Byrne & Co. v. Heller & Partners Ltd.*, [1964] A.C. 465 (H.L.). Under the statutory civil action the plaintiff need only show that: (1) he or she purchased the security offered under the prospectus; (2) the purchase was made during the period of distribution; and (3) that there was a misrepresentation in the prospectus. See, e.g., ASA s. 168(1); BCSA s. 114(1); OSA s. 130(1). The plaintiff does not have to prove reliance. Instead, the plaintiff is deemed to have relied on the misrepresentation if it was a misrepresentation at the time the security was purchased. See, e.g., ASA s. 168(1);

BCSA s. 114(1)(a); OSA s. 130(1). However, the defendants are entitled to the defence that the plaintiff had knowledge of the misrepresentation. Unlike the common law action, the plaintiff also does not have to show that the defendant failed to meet the standard of care or that the misrepresentation caused the loss incurred. Instead, the exercise of due diligence and showing that the misrepresentation did not cause the loss are defences under the statutory civil liability provision.

The Definition of "Misrepresentation." A "misrepresentation" is broadly defined to mean an untrue statement of a material fact or an omission to state a material fact that is either required to be stated or is necessary to prevent a statement that is made from being false or misleading in the circumstances in which it was made. See, e.g., ASA s. 1(1); BCSA s. 1(1); OSA s. 130(1). A "material fact" is typically defined as a fact that significantly affects, or could reasonably be expected to significantly affect, the market price or value of the securities. See, e.g., ASA s. 1(1); BCSA s. 1(1); OSA s. 1(1).

The Potential Defendants. The statutory provisions also set out the potential defendants under the statutory civil action. The action can be brought against the issuer, or, in the case of a sale by a control person, the selling security holder. The action can also be brought against the underwriter, every director of the issuer at the time the prospectus was filed, every expert who gave her or his consent to the use of all or part of her or his opinion or report, and every person who signed the prospectus. Normally the chief executive officer and the chief financial officer of the issuer must sign the prospectus along with any promoters of the issuer.

The Available Defences. The statutory civil liability provisions set out certain defences. As noted above, there are the defences of showing the plaintiff had knowledge of the misrepresentation and that the misrepresentation did not cause the loss. See ASA ss. 168(3), (8); BCSA ss. 114(4), (10); OSA ss. 130(2), (7). There is also the defence that the misrepresentation was not made by the particular defendant and that the defendant had no reason to believe and did not believe that the statement was false. For instance, a director or officer may be able to argue that the misrepresentation was contained in a part of the prospectus that consisted of an opinion or report of an expert. A further defence is that the defendant either did not consent to the filing of the prospectus or withdrew her or his consent prior to the purchase of the securities by the purchaser.

By far the most important defence is the defence of due diligence. Under the due diligence defence the defendant must show that he or she conducted a reasonable investigation to provide reasonable grounds for a belief that there was no misrepresentation and that he or she did not believe that there was misrepresentation. ASA ss. 168(4)-(6); BCSA ss. 114(5)-(7); OSA ss. 130(3)-(5). The defendant can take steps to set up the due diligence defence beforehand by conducting a "reasonable investigation" to avoid misrepresentations in the prospectus. The standard of reasonableness is that required of a prudent person in the circumstances of the particular case. See, e.g., BCSA s. 116; OSA 131; (there is no corresponding ASA provision).

Experts are held to a duty of reasonable investigation with respect to that part of the prospectus prepared on their own authority as experts. While the distinction between experts and non-experts is of great importance in due diligence defences, these terms are not defined. The expertised portion of a prospectus would appear to include the audited financial statements as well as those parts of the "company story" prepared by engineers or geologists, but it is not clear who else might be considered an expert. This issue is discussed in *Escott v. BarChris Construction Corp.* (set out below). A further issue canvassed in the *Escott v. BarChris* case is whether some non-experts, such as inside directors, are held to a higher standard of care than others.

The issuer of the securities is not entitled to claim the defence of due diligence, the defence of not having consented to the prospectus, or the defence that the misrepresentation was not made by the issuer. See ASA ss. 158(4)-(6); BCSA s. 114(10); OSA ss. 130(3)-(5). Thus the issuer is effectively strictly liable for misrepresentations in a prospectus.

Limitation. There is a relatively short limitation period for an action based on the statutory civil liability provisions. An action for rescission must be brought within 180 days from the date of the transaction giving rise to the cause of action. In the case of an action for damages the action must be brought from the earlier of 180 days from the date the plaintiff had knowledge of the facts giving rise to the cause of action and three years from the date of the transaction. See, e.g., ASA s.175; BCSA s. 124; OSA s. 138.

Interpretation of the Statutory Civil Action for Misrepresentations in a Prospectus.
The statutory civil action provisions for a misrepresentation in a prospectus contained in most Canadian securities acts are based upon s. 11 of the Securities Act of 1933 in the United States. As s. 11 has been interpreted in the United States, the standard of care to be observed in the preparation of a prospectus or registration statement is particularly high, and stands in marked contrast to the somewhat related obligations imposed on management under the general corporate duty of care of CBCA s. 122, a topic discussed in Chapter Seven.

Escott v. BarChris Construction is a seminal case in the interpretation of s. 11 of the U.S. Securities Act of 1933. Under s. 11 of the 1933 Act, the test is that of a prudent person in the management of his or her own property. Is this a more onerous standard than that of the statutory provisions in Canada?

Escott v. BarChris Construction Corp.
United States District Court, Southern District of New York
283 F. Supp. 643 (1968)

McLEAN J.: This is an action by the purchasers of 5½ per cent convertible subordinated fifteen year debentures of BarChris Construction Corporation (BarChris). Plaintiffs purport to sue on their own behalf and "on behalf of all other and present and former holders" of the debentures. When the action was begun on October 25, 1962, there were nine plaintiffs. Others were subsequently permitted to intervene. At the time of the trial, there were over sixty.

The action is brought under Section 11 of the Securities Act of 1933 (15 U.S.C. § 77k). Plaintiffs allege that the registration statement with respect to these debentures filed with the Securities and Exchange Commission, which became effective on May 16, 1961, contained material false statements and material omissions.

Defendants fall into three categories: (1) the persons who signed the registration statement; (2) the underwriters, consisting of eight investment banking firms, led by Drexel & Co. (Drexel); and (3) BarChris's auditors, Peat, Marwick, Mitchell & Co. (Peat, Marwick).

The signers, in addition to BarChris itself, were the nine directors of BarChris, plus its controller, defendant Trilling, who was not a director. Of the nine directors, five were officers of BarChris, i.e., defendants Vitolo, president; Russo, executive vice president; Pugliese, vice president; Kircher, treasurer; and Birnbaum, secretary. Of the remaining four, defendant Grant was a member of the firm of Perkins, Daniels, McCormack & Collins, BarChris's attorneys. He became a director in October 1960. Defendant Coleman, a partner in Drexel, became a director on April 17, 1961, as did the other two, Auslander and Rose, who were not otherwise connected with BarChris.

Defendants, in addition to denying that the registration statement was false, have pleaded the defenses open to them under Section 11 of the Act, plus certain additional defenses, including the statute of limitations. Defendants have also asserted cross-claims against each other, seeking to hold one another liable for any sums for which the respective defendants may be held liable to plaintiffs.

This opinion will not concern itself with the cross-claims or with issues peculiar to any particular plaintiff. These matters are reserved for later decision. On the main issue of liability, the questions to be decided are (1) did the registration statement contain false statements of fact, or did it omit to state facts which should have been stated in order to prevent it from being misleading; (2) if so, were the facts which were falsely stated or omitted "material" within the meaning of the Act; (3) if so, have defendants established their affirmative defenses?

Before discussing these questions, some background facts should be mentioned. At the time relevant here, BarChris was engaged primarily in the construction of bowling alleys, somewhat euphemistically referred to as "bowling centers." These were rather elaborate affairs. They contained not only a number of alleys or "lanes," but also, in most cases, bar and restaurant facilities.

BarChris was an outgrowth of a business started as a partnership by Vitolo and Pugliese in 1946. The business was incorporated in New York in 1955 under the name of B & C Bowling Alley Builders, Inc. Its name was subsequently changed to BarChris Construction Corporation.

The introduction of automatic pin setting machines in 1952 gave a marked stimulus to bowling. It rapidly became a popular sport, with the result that "bowling centers" began to appear throughout the country in rapidly increasing numbers. BarChris benefited from this increased interest in bowling. Its construction operations expanded rapidly. It is estimated that in 1960 BarChris installed approximately three per cent of all lanes built in the United States. It was thus a significant factor in the industry, although two large established companies, American Machine & Foundry Company and Brunswick, were much larger factors. These two companies manufactured bowling equipment, which BarChris did not. They also built most of the bowling alleys, 97 per cent of the total, according to some of the testimony.

BarChris's sales increased dramatically from 1956 to 1960. According to the prospectus, net sales, in round figures, in 1956 were some $800,000, in 1957 $1,300,000, in 1958 $1,700,000. In 1959 they increased to over $3,300,000, and by 1960 they had leaped to over $9,165,000.

For some years the business had exceeded the managerial capacity of its founders. Vitolo and Pugliese are each men of limited education. Vitolo did not get beyond high school. Pugliese ended his schooling in seventh grade. Pugliese devoted his time to supervising the actual construction work. Vitolo was concerned primarily with obtaining new business. Neither was equipped to handle financial matters.

Rather early in their career they enlisted the aid of Russo, who was trained as an accountant. He first joined them in the days of the partnership, left for a time, and returned as an officer and director of B & C Bowling Alley Builders, Inc. in 1958. He eventually became executive vice president of BarChris. In that capacity he handled many of the transactions which figure in this case.

In 1959 BarChris hired Kircher, a certified public accountant who had been employed by Peat, Marwick. He started as controller and became treasurer in 1960. In October of that year, another ex-Peat, Marwick employee, Trilling, succeeded Kircher as controller. At approximately the same time Birnbaum, a young attorney, was hired as house counsel. He became secretary on April 17, 1961.

In general, BarChris's method of operation was to enter into a contract with a customer, receive from him at that time a comparatively small down payment on the purchase price, and proceed to construct and equip the bowling alley. When the work was finished and the building delivered, the customer paid the balance of the contract price in notes, payable in installments over a period of years. BarChris discounted these notes with a factor and received part of their face amount in cash. The factor held back part as a reserve.

In 1960 BarChris began a practice which has been referred to throughout this case as the "alternative method of financing." In substance this was a sale and leaseback arrangement. It involved a distinction between the "interior" of a building and the building itself, i.e., the outer shell. In instances in which this method applied, BarChris would build and install what it referred to as the "interior package." Actually this amounted to constructing and installing the equipment in a building. When it was completed, it would sell the interior to a factor, James Talcott Inc. (Talcott), who would pay BarChris the full contract price therefor. The factor then proceeded to lease the interior either directly to BarChris's customer or back to a subsidiary of BarChris. In the latter case, the subsidiary in turn would lease it to the customer.

Under either financing method, BarChris was compelled to expend considerable sums in defraying the cost of construction before it received reimbursement. As a consequence, BarChris was in constant need of cash to finance its operations, a need which grew more pressing as operations expanded.

In December 1959, BarChris sold 560,000 shares of common stock to the public at $3.00 per share. This issue was underwritten by Peter Morgan & Company, one of the present defendants.

By early 1961, BarChris needed additional working capital. The proceeds of the sale of the debentures involved in this action were to be devoted, in part at least, to fill that need.

The registration statement of the debentures, in preliminary form, was filed with the Securities and Exchange Commission on March 30, 1961. A first amendment was filed on May 11 and a second on May 16. The registration statement became effective on May 16. The closing of the financing took place on May 24. On that day BarChris received the net proceeds of the financing.

By that time BarChris was experiencing difficulties in collecting amounts due from some of its customers. Some of them were in arrears in payments due to factors on their discounted notes. As time went on those difficulties increased. Although BarChris continued to build alleys in 1961 and 1962, it became increasingly apparent that the industry was overbuilt. Operators of alleys, often inadequately financed, began to fail. Precisely when the tide turned is a matter of dispute, but at any rate, it was painfully apparent in 1962.

In May of that year BarChris made an abortive attempt to raise more money by the sale of common stock. It filed with the Securities and Exchange Commission a registration statement for the stock issue which it later withdrew. In October 1962 BarChris came to the end of the road. On October 29, 1962, it filed in this court a petition for an arrangement under Chapter XI of the Bankruptcy Act. BarChris defaulted in the payment of the interest due on November 1, 1962 on the debentures. [In an extremely lengthy recitation of the facts of the case, the Court found a large number of misrepresentations in the BarChris prospectus. Those misrepresentations which the Court ultimately found to be material included the following:

A. *The 1960 balance sheet (audited):*
   1. overstatement of current assets by $609,689. This resulted in turn from
      (a) an overstatement of the cash account by $145,000, being an amount held by the factor, Talcott, as security for payments by BarChris's customers, which Talcott released temporarily to BarChris on the condition that BarChris would repay it to Talcott immediately after the audit. Ultimately BarChris would be entitled to this money, but only on condition that all its customers should pay off their notes. This type of transaction in which a temporary cash infusion is made immediately before an audit—to be removed thereafter—is known as "window dressing";
      (b) overstatement of trade accounts receivable by $150,000, an amount allegedly owed by a bowling center (Howard Lanes) which had not in fact been sold to an outside buyer;
      (c) failure to provide for any reserve (the Court found that $50,000 would have been reasonable) for a highly doubtful account receivable;
      (d) treatment as current of an asset labeled "Financial Institutions on Notes Discounted" in the amount of $264,689. This was the amount of the reserves withheld by factors on customers' notes discounted with them by BarChris. While this money was definitely an asset of BarChris, the Court found that, since the customers' notes were of a term longer than one year, release of this reserve to BarChris could not be anticipated within a year and therefore the asset was not current.

2. understatement of liabilities by $325,000, of which $65,000 was a current liability. This $325,000 represented, in effect, the amount owed to the factor, Talcott, by Capitol Lanes on Capitol's notes. Capitol Lanes was a subsidiary of BarChris.

Had the current assets and current liabilities been correctly stated, the current ratio would have been reduced from a bad 1.9 : 1 to a worse 1.6 : 1.

B. Contingent Liabilities as of April 30, 1961 (unaudited): In the prospectus they were stated to be $825,000, which the Court found to be understated by $618,000. This resulted from an error in computing BarChris's liability to Talcott in the event that certain customers to whom BarChris had leased bowling lanes on the "alternative method of financing" should default on their notes payable.

C. Earnings for the Quarter Ending March 31, 1961 (unaudited): Sales, which were stated to be $2,138,455, were found to be overstated by $519,810. Gross profit, stated as $483,121, was found to be overstated by $230,755. These overstatements resulted from the inclusion in sales (and profits) of certain "sales" of lanes which were not in fact sold but rather were operated by BarChris subsidiaries.

D. Backlog as of March 31, 1961 (unaudited): BarChris claimed to have a backlog of unfilled orders in the amount of $6,905,000, which the Court found to be an overstatement of $4,490,000. Many of the "contracts" to build bowling centers were not executed until after March 31, 1961 or were never executed, and some of the centers were never built.

E. Loans from Officers: The prospectus recited that while the company from time to time made advances to its company officers and vice versa, all such advances had been repaid. In fact, on the effective date of the prospectus there were $386,615 outstanding in loans from officers to the company. The company had issued cheques in repayment of these loans but had instructed the officers not to cash them until after the company received the proceeds of the debenture offering (since not until then would the company have sufficient funds in its chequing account to cover the cheques).

F. Use of Proceeds of Offering: The prospectus stated that proceeds of the offering would be used in various ways to expand the company's business; it failed to disclose that over one-third of the proceeds would be devoted to payment of overdue debts.

G. Customer Delinquencies: The prospectus stated that "since 1965, the Company has been required to repurchase less than one-half of one per cent of promissory notes" of customers discounted at financial institutions, such as Talcott. In fact, by the effective date of the prospectus, Talcott had indicated to BarChris that the customer default problem had become so serious that BarChris might have to repurchase at their face value $1,350,000 in bad notes.

H. Description of Business: The prospectus stated that BarChris was in the business of constructing bowling alleys. It failed to disclose that, owing to customer defaults, BarChris was also increasingly in the business of operating bowling alleys.]

Materiality

It is a prerequisite to liability under Section 11 of the Act that the fact which is falsely stated in a registration statement, or the fact that is omitted when it should have been stated to avoid misleading, be "material." The regulations of the Securities and Exchange Commission pertaining to the registration of securities define the word as follows (17 C.F.R. § 230.405(l)):

> The term "material," when used to qualify a requirement for the furnishing of information as to any subject, limits the information required to those matters as to which an average prudent investor ought reasonably to be informed before purchasing the security registered.

What are "matters as to which an average prudent investor ought reasonably to be informed"? It seems obvious that they are matters which such an investor needs to know before he can make an intelligent, informed decision whether or not to buy the security.

• • •

The average prudent investor is not concerned with minor inaccuracies or with errors as to matters which are of no interest to him. The facts which tend to deter him from purchasing a security are facts which have an important bearing upon the nature or condition of the issuing corporation or its business.

Judged by this test, there is no doubt that many of the misstatements and omissions in this prospectus were material. This is true of all of them which relate to the state of affairs in 1961, i.e., the overstatement of sales and gross profit for the first quarter, the understatement of contingent liabilities as of April 30, the overstatement of orders on hand and the failure to disclose the true facts with respect to officers' loans, customers' delinquencies, application of proceeds and the prospective operation of several alleys.

• • •

The "Due Diligence" Defenses

Section 11(b) of the Act provides that:

> ... no person, other than the issuer, shall be liable ... who shall sustain the burden of proof—
>
> ...
>
> (3) that (A) as regards any part of the registration statement not purporting to be made on the authority of an expert ... he had, after reasonable investigation, reasonable ground to believe and did believe, at the time such part of the registration statement became effective, that the statements therein were true and that there was no omission to state a material fact required to be stated therein or necessary to make the statements therein not misleading; ... and (C) as regards any part of the registration statement purporting to be made on the authority of an expert (other than himself) ... he had no reasonable ground to believe and did not believe, at the time such part of the registration statement became effective, that the statements therein were untrue or that there was an omission to state a material fact required to be stated therein or necessary to make the statements therein not misleading. ...

Section 11(c) defines "reasonable investigation" as follows:

In determining, for the purpose of paragraph (3) of subsection (b) of this section, what constitutes reasonable investigation and reasonable ground for belief, the standard of reasonableness shall be that required of a prudent man in the management of his own property.

Every defendant, except BarChris itself, to whom, as the issuer, these defenses are not available, and except Peat, Marwick, whose position rests on a different statutory provision, has pleaded these affirmative defenses. Each claims that (1) as to the part of the registration statement purporting to be made on the authority of an expert (which, for convenience, I shall refer to as the "expertised portion"), he had no reasonable ground to believe and did not believe that there were any untrue statements or material omissions, and (2) as to the other parts of the registration statement, he made a reasonable investigation, as a result of which he had reasonable ground to believe and did believe that the registration statement was true and that no material fact was omitted. As to each defendant, the question is whether he has sustained the burden of proving these defenses. Surprising enough, there is little or no judicial authority on this question. No decisions directly in point under Section 11 have been found.

Before considering the evidence, a preliminary matter should be disposed of. The defendants do not agree among themselves as to who the "experts" were or as to the parts of the registration statement which were expertised. Some defendants say that Peat, Marwick was the expert, others say that BarChris's attorneys, Perkins, Daniels, McCormack & Collins, and the underwriters' attorneys, Drinker, Biddle & Reath, were also the experts. On the first view, only those portions of the registration statement purporting to be made in Peat, Marwick's authority were expertised portions. On the other view, everything in the registration statement was within this category, because the two law firms were responsible for the entire document.

The first view is the correct one. To say that the entire registration statement is expertised because some lawyer prepared it would be an unreasonable construction of the statute. Neither the lawyer for the company nor the lawyer for the underwriters is an expert within the meaning of Section 11. The only expert, in the statutory sense, was Peat, Marwick, and the only parts of the registration statement which purported to be made upon the authority of an expert were the portions which purported to be made on Peat, Marwick's authority.

The parties also disagree as to what those portions were. Some defendants say that it was only the 1960 figures (and the figures for prior years, which are not in controversy here). Others say in substance that it was every figure in the prospectus. The plaintiffs take a somewhat intermediate view. They do not claim that Peat, Marwick expertised every figure, but they do maintain that Peat, Marwick is responsible for a portion of the text of the prospectus, i.e., that pertaining to "Methods of Operation," because a reference to it was made in footnote 9 to the balance sheet.

Here again, the more narrow view is the correct one. The registration statement contains a report of Peat, Marwick as independent public accountants dated February 23, 1961. This relates only to the consolidated balance sheet of BarChris and consolidated subsidiaries as of December 31, 1960, and the related statement of earnings and retained earnings for the five years then ended. This is all that Peat, Marwick purported to certify.

It is perfectly clear that it did not purport to certify the 1961 figures, some of which are expressly stated in the prospectus to have been unaudited.

Moreover, plaintiffs' intermediate view is also incorrect. The cross reference in footnote 9 to the "Methods of Operation" passage in the prospectus was inserted merely for the convenience of the reader. It is not a fair construction to say that it thereby imported into the balance sheet everything in that portion of the text, much of which had nothing to do with the figures in the balance sheet.

I turn now to the question of whether defendants have proved their due diligence defenses. The position of each defendant will be separately considered.

[The Court held that five insider directors or officers, Russo, Vitolo, Pugliese, Kircher and Trilling, were liable for misrepresentations in the registration statements. Russo, in effect the chief executive officer, was personally fraudulent. Vitolo and Pugliese, president and vice-president, respectively, could not have believed that the registration statement was wholly true, notwithstanding their defence of illiteracy. Kircher, the chief financial officer, and Trilling, the controller, did not have a reasonable belief that the registration statement was true.]

Birnbaum

Birnbaum was a young lawyer, admitted to the bar in 1957, who, after brief periods of employment by two different law firms and an equally brief period of practicing in his own firm, was employed by BarChris as house counsel and assistant secretary in October 1960. Unfortunately for him, he became secretary and a director of BarChris on April 17, 1961, after the first version of the registration statement had been filed with the Securities and Exchange Commission. He signed the later amendments, thereby becoming responsible for the accuracy of the prospectus in its final form.

Although the prospectus, in its description of "management," lists Birnbaum among the "executive officers" and devotes several sentences to a recital of his career, the fact seems to be that he was not an executive officer in any real sense. He did not participate in the management of the company. As house counsel, he attended to legal matters of a routine nature. Among other things, he incorporated subsidiaries, with which BarChris was plentifully supplied. Among the subsidiaries which he incorporated were Capitol Lanes, Inc. which operated Capitol, Yonkers Lanes, Inc. which eventually operated Yonkers, and Parkway Lanes, Inc. which eventually operated Bridge. He was thus aware of that aspect of the business.

Birnbaum examined contracts. In that connection he advised BarChris that the T-Bowl contracts were not legally enforceable. He was thus aware of that fact.

One of Birnbaum's more important duties, first as assistant secretary and later as full-fledged secretary, was to keep the corporate minutes of BarChris and its subsidiaries. This necessarily informed him to a considerable extent about the company's affairs. Birnbaum was not initially a member of the executive committee, however, and did not keep its minutes at the outset. According to the minutes, the first meeting which he attended, "upon invitation of the Committee," was on March 22, 1961. He became a member shortly thereafter and kept the minutes beginning with the meeting of April 24, 1961.

It seems probable that Birnbaum did not know of many of the inaccuracies in the prospectus. He must, however, have appreciated some of them. In any case, he made no investigation and relied on the others to get it right. Unlike Trilling, he was entitled to rely upon Peat, Marwick for the 1960 figures, for as far as appears, he had no personal knowledge of the company's books of account or financial transactions. But he was not entitled to rely upon Kircher, Grant and Ballard for the other portions of the prospectus. As a lawyer, he should have known his obligations under the statute. He should have known that he was required to make a reasonable investigation of the truth of all the statements in the unexpertised portion of the document which he signed. Having failed to make such an investigation, he did not have reasonable ground to believe that all these statements were true. Birnbaum has not established his due diligence defenses except as to the audited 1960 figures.

Auslander

Auslander was an "outside" director, i.e., one who was not an officer of BarChris. He was chairman of the board of Valley Stream National Bank in Valley Stream, Long Island. In February 1961 Vitolo asked him to become a director of BarChris. Vitolo gave him an enthusiastic account of BarChris's progress and prospects. As an inducement, Vitolo said that when BarChris received the proceeds of a forthcoming issue of securities, it would deposit $1,000,000 in Auslander's bank.

In February and early March 1961, before accepting Vitolo's invitation, Auslander made some investigation of BarChris. He obtained Dun & Bradstreet reports which contained sales and earnings figures for periods earlier than December 31, 1960. He caused inquiry to be made of certain of BarChris's banks and was advised that they regarded BarChris favorably. He was informed that inquiry of Talcott had also produced a favorable response.

On March 3, 1961, Auslander indicated his willingness to accept a place on the board. Shortly thereafter, on March 14, Kircher sent him a copy of BarChris's annual report for 1960. Auslander observed that BarChris's auditors were Peat, Marwick. They were also the auditors for the Valley Stream National Bank. He thought well of them.

Auslander was elected a director on April 17, 1961. The registration statement in its original form had already been filed, of course without his signature. On May 10, 1961, he signed a signature page for the first amendment to the registration statement which was filed on May 11, 1961. This was a separate sheet without any document attached. Auslander did not know that it was a signature page for a registration statement. He vaguely understood that it was something "for the SEC."

Auslander attended a meeting of BarChris's directors on May 15, 1961. At that meeting he, along with the other directors, signed the signature sheet for the second amendment which constituted the registration statement in its final form. Again, this was only a separate sheet without any document attached. Auslander never saw a copy of the registration statement in its final form.

At the May 15 directors' meeting, however, Auslander did realize that what he was signing was a signature sheet to a registration statement. This was the first time that he had appreciated that fact. A copy of the registration statement in its earlier form as amended on May 11, 1961 was passed around at the meeting. Auslander glanced at it briefly. He did not read it thoroughly.

At the May 15 meeting, Russo and Vitolo stated that everything was in order and that the prospectus was correct. Auslander believed this statement.

In considering Auslander's due diligence defenses, a distinction is to be drawn between the expertised and non-expertised portions of the prospectus. As to the former, Auslander knew that Peat, Marwick had audited the 1960 figures. He believed them to be correct because he had confidence in Peat, Marwick. He had no reasonable ground to believe otherwise.

As to the non-expertised portions, however, Auslander is in a different position. He seems to have been under the impression that Peat, Marwick was responsible for all the figures. This impression was not correct, as he would have realized if he had read the prospectus carefully. Auslander made no investigation of the accuracy of the prospectus. He relied on the assurance of Vitolo and Russo, and upon the information he had received in answer to his inquiries back in February and early March. These inquiries were general ones, in the nature of a credit check. The information which he received in answer to them was also general, without specific reference to the statements in the prospectus, which was not prepared until some time thereafter.

It is true that Auslander became a director on the eve of the financing. He had little opportunity to familiarize himself with the company's affairs. The question is whether, under such circumstances, Auslander did enough to establish his due diligence defense with respect to the non-expertised portions of the prospectus.

Although there is a dearth of authority under Section 11 on this point, an English case under the analogous Companies Act is of some value. In *Adams v. Thrift*, [1915] 1 Ch. 557, aff'd, [1915] 2 Ch. 21, it was held that a director who knew nothing about the prospectus and did not even read it, but who relied on the statement of the company's managing director that it was "all right," was liable for its untrue statements. See also *In the Matter of Interstate Hosiery Mills, Inc.*, 4 S.E.C. 706 (1939).

Section 11 imposes liability in the first instance upon a director, no matter how new he is. He is presumed to know his responsibility when he becomes a director. He can escape liability only by using that reasonable care to investigate the facts which a prudent man would employ in the management of his own property. In my opinion, a prudent man would not act in an important matter without any knowledge of the relevant facts, in sole reliance upon representations of persons who are comparative strangers and upon general information which does not purport to cover the particular case. To say that such minimal conduct measures up to the statutory standard would, to all intents and purposes, absolve new directors from responsibility merely because they are new. This is not a sensible construction of Section 11, when one bears in mind its fundamental purpose of requiring full and truthful disclosure for the protection of investors.

I find and conclude that Auslander has not established his due diligence defense with respect to the misstatements and omissions in those portions of the prospectus other than the audited 1960 figures.

• • •

Grant

Grant became a director of BarChris in October 1960. His law firm was counsel to BarChris in matters pertaining to the registration of securities. Grant drafted the registration statement for the stock issue in 1959 and for the warrants in January 1961. He also drafted the registration statement for the debentures. In the preliminary division of work between him and Ballard, the underwriters' counsel, Grant took initial responsibility for preparing the registration statement, while Ballard devoted his efforts in the first instance to preparing the indenture.

Grant is sued as a director and as a signer of the registration statement. This is not an action against him for malpractice in his capacity as a lawyer. Nevertheless, in considering Grant's due diligence defenses, the unique position which he occupied cannot be disregarded. As the director most directly concerned with writing the registration statement and assuring its accuracy, more was required of him in the way of reasonable investigation than could fairly be expected of a director who had no connection with this work.

There is no valid basis for plaintiffs' accusation that Grant knew that the prospectus was false in some respects and incomplete and misleading in others. Having seen him testify at length, I am satisfied as to his integrity. I find that Grant honestly believed that the registration statement was true and that no material facts had been omitted from it.

In this belief he was mistaken, and the fact is that for all his work, he never discovered any of the errors or omissions which have been recounted at length in this opinion, with the single exception of Capitol Lanes. He knew that BarChris had not sold this alley and intended to operate it, but he appears to have been under the erroneous impression that Peat, Marwick had knowingly sanctioned its inclusion in sales because of the allegedly temporary nature of the operation.

Grant contends that a finding that he did not make a reasonable investigation would be equivalent to a holding that a lawyer for an issuing company, in order to show due diligence, must make an independent audit of the figures supplied to him by his client. I do not consider this to be a realistic statement of the issue. There were errors and omissions here which could have been detected without an audit. The question is whether, despite his failure to detect them, Grant made a reasonable effort to that end.

Much of this registration statement is a scissors and paste-pot job. Grant lifted large portions from the earlier prospectuses, modifying them in some instances to the extent that he considered necessary. But BarChris's affairs had changed for the worse by May 1961. Statements that were accurate in January were no longer accurate in May. Grant never discovered this. He accepted the assurances of Kircher and Russo that any change which might have occurred had been for the better, rather than the contrary.

It is claimed that a lawyer is entitled to rely on the statements of his client and that to require him to verify their accuracy would set an unreasonably high standard. This is too broad a generalization. It is all a matter of degree. To require an audit would obviously be unreasonable. On the other hand, to require a check of matters easily verifiable is not unreasonable. Even honest clients can make mistakes. The statute imposes liability for untrue statements regardless of whether they are intentionally untrue. The way to prevent mistakes is to test oral information by examining the original written record.

There were things which Grant could readily have checked which he did not check. For example, he was unaware of the provisions of the agreements between BarChris and Talcott. He never read them. Thus, he did not know, although he readily could have ascertained, that BarChris's contingent liability on Type B lease-back arrangements was 100 per cent, not 25 per cent. He did not appreciate that if BarChris defaulted in repurchasing delinquent customers' notes upon Talcott's demand, Talcott could accelerate all the customer paper in its hands, which amounted to over $3,000,000.

As to the backlog figure, Grant appreciated that scheduled unfilled orders on the company's books meant firm commitments, but he never asked to see the contracts which, according to the prospectus, added up to $6,905,000. Thus, he did not know that this figure was overstated by some $4,490,000.

Grant was unaware of the fact that BarChris was about to operate Bridge and Yonkers. He did not read the minutes of those subsidiaries which would have revealed that fact to him. On the subject of minutes, Grant knew that minutes of certain meetings of the BarChris executive committee held in 1961 had not been written up. Kircher, who had acted as secretary at those meetings, had complete notes of them. Kircher told Grant that there was no point in writing up the minutes because the matters discussed at those meetings were purely routine. Grant did not insist that the minutes be written up, nor did he look at Kircher's notes. If he had, he would have learned that on February 27, 1961 there was an extended discussion in the executive committee meeting about customers' delinquencies, that on March 8, 1961 the committee had discussed the pros and cons of alley operation by BarChris, that on March 18, 1961 the committee was informed that BarChris was constructing or about to begin constructing twelve alleys for which it had no contracts, and that on May 13, 1961 Dreyfuss, one of the worst delinquents, had filed a petition in Chapter X.

Grant knew that there had been loans from officers to BarChris in the past because that subject had been mentioned in the 1959 and January 1961 prospectuses. In March Grant prepared a questionnaire to be answered by officers and directors for the purpose of obtaining information to be used in the prospectus. The questionnaire did not inquire expressly about the existence of officers' loans. At approximately the same time, Grant prepared another questionnaire in order to obtain information on proxy statements for the annual stockholders' meeting. This questionnaire asked each officer to state whether he was indebted to BarChris, but it did not ask whether BarChris was indebted to him.

Despite the inadequacy of these written questionnaires, Grant did, on March 16, 1961, orally inquire as to whether any officers' loans were outstanding. He was assured by Russo, Vitolo and Pugliese that all such loans had been repaid. Grant did not ask again. He was unaware of the new loans in April. He did know, however, that, at Kircher's request, a provision was inserted in the indenture which gave loans from individuals priority over the debentures. Kircher's insistence on this clause did not arouse his suspicions.

It is only fair to say that Grant was given to understand Kircher that there were no new officers' loans and that there would not be any before May 16. It is still a close question, however, whether, under all the circumstances, Grant should have investigated further, perhaps by asking Peat, Marwick, in the course of its S-1 review, to look at the books on this particular point. I believe that a careful man would have checked.

There is more to the subject of due diligence than this, particularly with respect to the application of proceeds and customers' delinquencies.

The application of proceeds language in the prospectus was drafted by Kircher back in January. It may well have expressed his intent at that time, but his intent, and that of the other principal officers of BarChris, was very different in May. Grant did not appreciate that the earlier language was no longer appropriate. He never learned of the situation which the company faced in May. He knew that BarChris was short of cash, but he had no idea how short. He did not know that BarChris was withholding delivery of checks already drawn and signed because there was not enough money in the bank to pay them. He did not know that the officers of the company intended to use immediately approximately one-third of the financing proceeds in a manner not disclosed in the prospectus, including approximately $1,000,000 in paying old debts.

In this connection, mention should be made of a fact which has previously been referred to only in passing. The "negative cash balance" in BarChris's Lafayette National Bank account in May 1961 included a check dated April 10, 1961 to the order of Grant's firm, Perkins, Daniels, McCormack & Collins, in the amount of $8,711. This check was not deposited by Perkins, Daniels until June 1, after the financing proceeds had been received by BarChris. Of course, if Grant had knowingly withheld deposit of this check until that time, he would be in a position similar to Russo, Vitolo and Pugliese. I do not believe, however, that that was the case. I find that the check was not delivered by BarChris to Perkins, Daniels until shortly before June 1.

This incident is worthy of mention, however, for another reason. The prospectus stated on page 10 that Perkins, Daniels had "received fees aggregating $13,000" from BarChris. This check for $8,711 was one of those fees. It had not been received by Perkins, Daniels prior to May 16. Grant was unaware of this. In approving this erroneous statement in the prospectus, he did not consult his own bookkeeper to ascertain whether it was correct. Kircher told him that the bill had been paid and Grant took his word for it. If he had acquired and had found that this representation was untrue, this discovery might well have led him to a realization of the true state of BarChris's finances in May 1961.

As far as customers' delinquencies is concerned, although Grant discussed this with Kircher, he again accepted the assurances of Kircher and Russo that no serious problem existed. He did not examine the records as to delinquencies, although BarChris maintained such a record. Any inquiry on his part of Talcott or an examination of BarChris's correspondence with Talcott in April and May 1961 would have apprised him of the true facts. It would have led him to appreciate that the statement in this prospectus, carried over from earlier prospectuses, to the effect that since 1955 BarChris had been required to repurchase less than one-half of one per cent of discounted customers' notes could no longer properly be made without further explanation.

Grant was entitled to rely on Peat, Marwick for the 1960 figures. He had no reasonable ground to believe them to be inaccurate. But the matters which I have mentioned were not within the expertised portion of the prospectus. As to this, Grant was obliged to make a reasonable investigation. I am forced to find that he did not make one. After making all due allowances for the fact that BarChris's officers misled him, there are too many instances in which Grant failed to make an inquiry which he could easily have made which, if pursued, would have put him on his guard. In my opinion, this finding on the evidence in this case does not establish an unreasonably high standard in other cases for company counsel who are also directors. Each case must rest on its own facts. I conclude that Grant has not established his due diligence defenses except as to the audited 1960 figures.

The Underwriters and Coleman

The underwriters other than Drexel made no investigation of the accuracy of the prospectus. One of them, Peter Morgan, had underwritten the 1959 stock issue and had been a director of BarChris. He thus had some general familiarity with its affairs, but he knew no more than the other underwriters about the debenture prospectus. They all relied upon Drexel as the "lead" underwriter.

Drexel did make an investigation. The work was in charge of Coleman, a partner of the firm, assisted by Casperson, an associate. Drexel's attorneys acted as attorneys for the entire group of underwriters. Ballard did the work, assisted by Stanton.

On April 17, 1961 Coleman became a director of BarChris. He signed the first amendment to the registration statement filed on May 11 and the second amendment, constituting the registration statement in its final form, filed on May 16. He thereby assumed a responsibility as a director and signer in addition to his responsibility as an underwriter.

The facts as to the extent of the investigation that Coleman made may be briefly summarized. He was first introduced to BarChris on September 15, 1960. Thereafter he familiarized himself with general conditions in the industry, primarily by reading reports and prospectuses of the two leading bowling alley builders, American Machine & Foundry Company and Brunswick. These indicated that the industry was still growing. He also acquired general information on BarChris by reading the 1959 stock prospectus, annual reports for prior years, and an unaudited statement for the first half of 1960. He inquired about BarChris of certain of its banks and of Talcott and received favorable replies.

The purpose of this preliminary investigation was to enable Coleman to decide whether Drexel would undertake the financing. It did not have direct reference to any specific registration statement for at that time, of course, none had been prepared. Coleman was sufficiently optimistic about BarChris's prospects to buy 1,000 shares of its stock, which he did in December 1960.

On January 24, 1961, Coleman held a meeting with Ballard, Grant and Kircher, among others. By that time Coleman had about decided to go ahead with the financing, although Drexel's formal letter of intent was not delivered until February 9, 1961 (subsequently revised on March 7, 1961). At this meeting Coleman asked Kircher how BarChris intended to use the proceeds of the financing. In reply to this inquiry, Kircher wrote a letter to Coleman dated January 30, 1961 outlining BarChris's plans. This eventually formed the basis of the application of proceeds section in the prospectus.

Coleman continued his general investigation. He obtained a Dun & Bradstreet report on BarChris on March 16, 1961. He read BarChris's annual report for 1960 which was available in March.

By mid-March, Coleman was in a position to make more specific inquiries. By that time Grant had prepared a first draft of the prospectus, consisting of a marked-up copy of the January 1961 warrant prospectus. Coleman attended three meetings to discuss the prospectus with BarChris's representatives. The meetings were held at Perkins, Daniel's office on March 20, March 23 and March 24, 1961. Those present included Grant or his partner McCormack and Kircher for the company, and Coleman, Casperson and Ballard for the underwriters. Logan, Peat, Marwick's manager of the 1960 audit, was present at one of the meetings.

At these discussions, which were extensive, successive proofs of the prospectus were considered and revised. At this point the 1961 figures were not available. They were put in the prospectus in May.

Coleman and Ballard asked pertinent questions and received answers which satisfied them. Among other things, the following transpired.

Logan explained some of the 1960 figures, including the reserve for bad debts, which he considered adequate.

There was a discussion of the application of proceeds section. It was not changed in any respect material here.

As to the backlog of orders on hand, Ballard said that the figure, not then available, must be "hard and fast," not "puffy." Grant and Kircher "concurred."

There was talk about the 15 to 25 per cent down payment figure. Kircher said that this was accurate.

More important for our purposes, there was a discussion of the one-half of one per cent figure with respect to BarChris's past experience in repurchasing discounted customers' notes. Kircher said that this figure was "conservative." Ballard inquired whether, regardless of what past experience had been, there was "any real chance that you see of being forced to take any [alleys] back in the future?" Kircher's answer was "negative."

The alternative method of financing was explained. Kircher said that BarChris's contingent liability was only 25 per cent.

There was talk about operating alleys. Kircher said that BarChris did not operate any. Coleman and Ballard inquired whether BarChris built alleys on speculation, i.e., without any customer's contract for them. Kircher said BarChris did not.

There was discussion of officers' loans. Kircher said that the $155,000 had been repaid and that no further officers' loans were contemplated. Coleman said that this was wise, for loans from officers "indicated financial instability of the company."

Coleman did not participate personally in any further meetings of this sort. Casperson attended some and reported to Coleman. Ballard advised Coleman as to what he was doing.

After Coleman was elected a director on April 17, 1961, he made no further independent investigation of the accuracy of the prospectus. He assumed that Ballard was taking care of this on his behalf as well as on behalf of the underwriters.

In April 1961 Ballard instructed Stanton to examine BarChris's minutes for the past five years and also to look at "the major contracts of the company."[23] Stanton went to

---

23 Stanton was a very junior associate. He had been admitted to the bar in January 1961, some three months before. This was the first registration statement he had ever worked on.

BarChris's office for that purpose on April 24. He asked Birnbaum for the minute books. He read the minutes of the board of directors and discovered interleaved in them a few minutes of executive committee meetings in 1960. He asked Kircher if there were any others. Kircher said that there had been other executive committee meetings but that the minutes had not been written up.

Stanton read the minutes of a few BarChris subsidiaries. His testimony was vague as to which ones. He had no recollection of seeing the minutes of Capitol Lanes, Inc. or Biel or Parkway Lanes, Inc. He did not discover that BarChris was operating Capitol or that it planned to operate Bridge and Yonkers.

As to the "major contracts," all that Stanton could remember seeing was an insurance policy. Birnbaum told him that there was no file of major contracts. Stanton did not examine the agreements with Talcott. He did not examine the contracts with customers. He did not look to see what contracts comprised the backlog figure. Stanton examined no accounting records of BarChris. His visit, which lasted one day, was devoted primarily to reading the directors' minutes.

On April 25 Ballard wrote to Grant about certain matters which Stanton had noted on his visit to BarChris the day before, none of which Ballard considered "very earth shaking." As far as relevant here, these were (1) Russo's remark as recorded in the executive committee minutes of November 3, 1960 to the effect that because of customers' defaults, BarChris might find itself in the business of operating alleys; (2) the fact that the minutes of Sanpark Realty Corporation were incomplete; and (3) the fact that minutes of the executive committee were missing.

On May 9, 1961, Ballard came to New York and conferred with Grant and Kircher. They discussed the Securities and Exchange Commission's deficiency letter of May 4, 1961 which required the inclusion in the prospectus of certain additional information, notably net sales, gross profits and net earnings figures for the first quarter of 1961. They also discussed the points raised in Ballard's letter to Grant of April 25. As to the latter, most of the conversation related to what Russo had meant by his remark on November 3, 1960. Kircher said that the delinquency problem was less severe now than it had been back in November 1960, that no alleys had been repossessed, and that although he was "worried about one alley in Harlem" (Dreyfuss), that was a "special situation." Grant reported that Russo had told him that his statement on November 3, 1960 was "merely hypothetical." On the strength of this conversation, Ballard was satisfied that the one-half of the one per cent figure in the prospectus did not need qualification or elaboration.

As to the missing minutes, Kircher said that those of Sanpark were not significant and that the executive committee meetings for which there were no written minutes were concerned only with "routine matters."

It must be remembered that this conference took place only one week before the registration statement became effective. Ballard did nothing else in the way of checking during that intervening week.

Ballard did not insist that the executive committee minutes be written up so that he could inspect them, although he testified that he knew from experience that executive committee minutes may be extremely important. If he had insisted, he would have found the minutes highly informative, as has previously been pointed out. Ballard did not ask to see BarChris's schedule of delinquencies or Talcott's notices of delinquencies, or BarChris's correspondence with Talcott.

Ballard did not examine BarChris's contracts with Talcott. He did not appreciate what Talcott's rights were under those financing agreements or how serious the effect would be upon BarChris of any exercise of those rights. Ballard did not investigate the composition of the backlog figure to be sure that it was not "puffy." He made no inquiry after March about any new officers' loans, although he knew that Kircher had insisted on a provision in the indenture which gave loans from individuals priority over the debentures. He was unaware of the seriousness of BarChris's cash position and of how BarChris's officers intended to use a large part of the proceeds. He did not know that BarChris was operating Capitol Lanes.[24]

Like Grant, Ballard, without checking, relied on the information which he got from Kircher. He also relied on Grant who, as company counsel, presumably was familiar with its affairs.

The formal opinion which Ballard's firm rendered to the underwriters at the closing on May 24, 1961 made clear that this is what he had done. The opinion stated ([italics] supplied):

In the course of the preparation of the Registration Statement and Prospectus by the Company, we have had numerous conferences with representatives of and counsel for the Company and with its auditors and we have raised many questions regarding the business of the Company. Satisfactory answers to such questions were in each case given us, and all other information and documents we requested have been supplied. We are of the opinion that the *data presented* to us are accurately reflected in the Registration Statement and Prospectus and that there has been omitted from the Registration Statement no material facts *included in such data*. Although *we have not otherwise verified* the completeness or accuracy of the information furnished to us, on the basis of the foregoing and with the exception of the financial statements and schedules (which this opinion does not pass upon), we have no reason to believe that the Registration Statement or Prospectus contains any untrue statement or any material fact or omits to state a material fact required to be stated therein or necessary in order to make the statements therein not misleading.

Coleman testified that Drexel had an understanding with its attorneys that "we expect them to inspect on our behalf the corporate records of the company including, but not limited to, the minutes of the corporation, the stockholders and the committees of the board authorized to act for the board." Ballard manifested his awareness of this understanding by sending Stanton to read the minutes and the major contracts. It is difficult to square this understanding with the formal opinion of Ballard's firm which expressly disclaimed any attempt to verify information supplied by the company and its counsel.

In any event, it is clear that no effectual attempt at verification was made. The question is whether due diligence required that it be made. Stated another way, is it sufficient to ask questions, to obtain answers which, if true, would be thought satisfactory, and to let it go at that, without seeking to ascertain from the records whether the answers in fact are true and complete?

---

24 Stanton was also unaware of this, although there was a reference to it in the minutes of the board of directors' meeting of November 22, 1960, which he presumably read.

I have already held that this procedure is not sufficient in Grant's case. Are underwriters in a different position, as far as due diligence is concerned?

The underwriters say that the prospectus is the company's prospectus, not theirs. Doubtless this is the way they customarily regard it. But the Securities Act makes no such distinction. The underwriters are just as responsible as the company if the prospectus is false. And prospective investors rely upon the reputation of the underwriters in deciding whether to purchase the securities.

There is no direct authority on this question, no judicial decision defining the degree of diligence which underwriters must exercise to establish their defense under Section 11.

There is some authority in New York for the proposition that a director of a corporation may rely upon information furnished him by the officers without independently verifying it. See *Litwin v. Allen*, 25 N.Y.S.2d 667 (Sup.Ct. 1940).

In support of that principle, the court in *Litwin* (25 N.Y.S.2d at 719) quoted from the opinion of Lord Halsbury in *Dovey v. Cory*, [1901] App.Cas. 477, 486, in which he said:

The business of life could not go on if people could not trust those who are put into a position of trust for the express purpose of attending to details of management.

Of course, New York law does not govern this case. The construction of the Securities Act is a matter of federal law. But the underwriters argue that *Litwin* is still in point, for they say that it establishes a standard of reasonableness for the reasonably prudent director which should be the same as the standard for the reasonably prudent underwriter under the Securities Act.

In my opinion the two situations are not analogous. An underwriter has not put the company's officers "into a position of trust for the express purpose of attending to details of management." The underwriters did not select them. In a sense, the positions of the underwriter and the company's officers are adverse. It is not unlikely that statements made by company officers to an underwriter to induce him to underwrite may be self-serving. They may be unduly enthusiastic. As in this case, they may, on occasion, be deliberately false.

The purpose of Section 11 is to protect investors. To that end the underwriters are made responsible for the truth of the prospectus. If they may escape that responsibility by taking at face value representations made to them by the company's management, then the inclusion of underwriters among those liable under Section 11 affords the investors no additional protection. To effectuate the statute's purpose, the phrase "reasonable investigation" must be construed to require more effort on the part of the underwriters than the mere accurate reporting in the prospectus of "data presented" to them by the company. It should make no difference that this data is elicited by questions addressed to the company officers by the underwriters, or that the underwriters at the time believe that the company's officers are truthful and reliable. In order to make the underwriters' participation in this enterprise of any value to the investors, the underwriters must make some reasonable attempt to verify the data submitted to them. They may not rely solely on the company's officers or on the company's counsel. A prudent man in the management of his own property would not rely on them.

It is impossible to lay down a rigid rule suitable for every case defining the extent to which such verification must go. It is a question of degree, a matter of judgment in each case. In the present case, the underwriters' counsel made almost no attempt to verify management's representations. I hold that that was insufficient.

On the evidence in this case, I find that the underwriters' counsel did not make a reasonable investigation of the truth of those portions of the prospectus which were not made on the authority of Peat, Marwick as an expert. Drexel is bound by their failure. It is not a matter of relying upon counsel for legal advice. Here the attorneys were dealing with matters of fact. Drexel delegated to them, as its agent, the business of examining the corporate minutes and contracts. It must bear the consequences of their failure to make an adequate examination.

The other underwriters, who did nothing and relied solely on Drexel and on the lawyers, are also bound by it. It follows that although Drexel and the other underwriters believed that those portions of the prospectus were true, they had no reasonable ground for that belief, within the meaning of the statute. Hence, they have not established their due diligence defense, except as to the 1960 audited figures.[26]

The same conclusions must apply to Coleman. Although he participated quite actively in the earlier stages of the preparation of the prospectus, and contributed questions and warnings of his own, in addition to the questions of counsel, the fact is that he stopped his participation toward the end of March 1961. He made no investigation after he became a director. When it came to verification, he relied upon his counsel to do it for him. Since counsel failed to do it, Coleman is bound by that failure. Consequently, in his case also, he has not established his due diligence defense except as to the audited 1960 figures.

Peat, Marwick

Section 11(b) provides:

Notwithstanding the provisions of subsection (a) no person ... shall be liable as provided therein who shall sustain the burden of proof—

...

(3) that ... (B) as regards any part of the registration statement purporting to be made upon his authority as an expert ... (i) he had, after reasonable investigation, reasonable ground to believe and did believe, at the time such part of the registration statement became effective, that the statements therein were true and that there was no omission to state a material fact required to be stated therein or necessary to make the statements therein not misleading. ...

This defines the due diligence defense for an expert. Peat, Marwick has pleaded it.

The part of the registration statement purporting to be made upon the authority of Peat, Marwick as an expert was, as we have seen, the 1960 figures. But because the statute requires the court to determine Peat, Marwick's belief, and the grounds thereof, "at the time such part of the registration statement became effective," for the purposes of this affirmative defense, the matter must be viewed as of May 16, 1961, and the question

---

26 In view of this conclusion, it becomes unnecessary to decide whether the underwriters other than Drexel would have been protected if Drexel had established that as lead underwriter, it made a reasonable investigation.

is whether at that time Peat, Marwick, after reasonable investigation, had reasonable ground to believe and did believe that the 1960 figures were true and that no material fact had been omitted from the registration statement which should have been included in order to make the 1960 figures not misleading. In deciding this issue, the court must consider not only what Peat, Marwick did in its 1960 audit, but also what it did in its subsequent "S-1 review." The proper scope of that review must also be determined.

• • •

The 1960 Audit

Peat, Marwick's work was in general charge of a member of the firm, Cummings, and more immediately in charge of Peat, Marwick's manager, Logan. Most of the actual work performed by a senior accountant, Berardi, who had junior assistants, one of whom was Kennedy.

Berardi was then about thirty years old. He was not yet a C.P.A. He had had no previous experience with the bowling industry. This was his first job as a senior accountant. He could hardly have been given a more difficult assignment.

After obtaining a little background information on BarChris by talking to Logan and reviewing Peat, Marwick's work papers on its 1959 audit, Berardi examined the results of test checks of BarChris's accounting procedures which one of the junior accountants had made, and he prepared an "internal control questionnaire" and an "audit program." Thereafter, for a few days subsequent to December 30, 1960, he inspected BarChris's inventories and examined certain alley construction. Finally, on January 13, 1961, he began his auditing work which he carried on substantially continuously until it was completed on February 24, 1961. Toward the close of the work, Logan reviewed it and made various comments and suggestions to Berardi.

It is unnecessary to recount everything that Berardi did in the course of the audit. We are concerned only with the evidence relating to what Berardi did or did not do with respect to those items which I have found to have been incorrectly reported in the 1960 figures in the prospectus. More narrowly, we are directly concerned only with such of those items as I have found to be material.

Capitol Lanes

First and foremost is Berardi's failure to discover that Capitol Lanes had not been sold. This error affected both the sales figure and the liability side of the balance sheet. Fundamentally, the error stemmed from the fact that Berardi never realized that Heavenly Lanes and Capitol were two different names for the same alley. In the course of his audit, Berardi was shown BarChris's contract file. He examined the contracts in the file and made a list of them. The file must have included a contract with an outside purchaser for Heavenly Lanes, although no such contract was ever produced at the trial, for Berardi included Heavenly on his list. Apparently there was no contract in the file for a lane named Capitol because that name did not appear on Berardi's list.

Kircher also made a list of jobs. Heavenly was on his list. Capitol was not. Berardi compared the two lists and satisfied himself that he had the proper jobs to be taken into account. Berardi assumed that Heavenly was to be treated like any other completed job. He included it in all his computations.

The evidence is conflicting as to whether BarChris's officers expressly informed Berardi that Heavenly and Capitol were the same thing and that BarChris was operating Capitol and had not sold it. I find that they did not so inform him.

Berardi did become aware that there were references here and there in BarChris's records to something called Capitol Lanes. He also knew that there were indications that at some time BarChris might operate an alley of that name. He read the minutes of the board of directors' meeting of November 22, 1960 which recited that:

... the Chairman recommended that the Corporation operate Capitol Lanes, 271 Main Street, East Haven, Connecticut, through a corporation which would be a subsidiary of Sanpark Realty Corp.

The minutes further recorded that:

... it was unanimously agreed that the officers of the Corporation exercise their discretion as to operating Capitol Lanes through the aforesaid subsidiary on an experimental basis.

The junior accountant, Kennedy, read the minute book of Capitol Lanes, Inc., a Connecticut corporation organized in December 1960. The book contained a certificate of incorporation which empowered the corporation, among many other things, to own and manage bowling alleys. There was no minute in the book, however, that indicated that the corporation actually did own or manage one.

Berardi knew from various BarChris records that Capitol Lanes, Inc. was paying rentals to Talcott. Also, a Peat, Marwick work paper bearing Kennedy's initials recorded that Capitol Lanes, Inc. held certain insurance policies, including a fire insurance policy on "contents," a workmen's compensation and a public liability policy. Another Peat, Marwick work paper also bearing Kennedy's initials recorded that Capitol Lanes, Inc. had $1,000 in a fund in Connecticut. A note on this paper read: "Traced to disbursements book—advanced for operation of alley—not expensed at 12/31/60."

Logan's written comments upon the audit contained an entry reading as follows:

When talking to Ted Kircher in latter part of '60 he indicated one subsidiary is leasing alley built by BarChris—the profit on this job should be eliminated as its ownership is within the affiliated group.

Opposite this note is an entry by Berardi reading as follows: "Properties sold to others by affiliates. Capitol Lanes is paying currently lease rentals which amount to a lease purchase plan."

This note is somewhat ambiguous. If by "others" Berardi meant outside buyers, then it would seem that he should have accounted in some way for this sale, which he did not do. Presumably, by "others" he meant "other affiliates." Hence, he regarded the transaction, whatever he thought it to have been, as an intercompany one. Apparently Logan so understood Berardi's explanation.

Berardi testified that he inquired of Russo about Capitol Lanes and that Russo told him that Capitol Lanes, Inc. was going to operate an alley some day but as yet it had no alley. Berardi testified that he understood that the alley had not been built and that he believed that the rental payments were on vacant land.

I am not satisfied with this testimony. If Berardi did hold this belief, he should not have held it. The entries as to insurance and as to "operation of alley" should have alerted him to the fact that an alley existed. He should have made further inquiry on the subject. It is apparent that Berardi did not understand this transaction.

In any case, he never identified this mysterious Capitol with the Heavenly Lanes which he had included in his sales and profit figures. The vital question is whether he failed to make a reasonable investigation which, if he had made it, would have revealed the truth.

Certain accounting records of BarChris, which Berardi testified he did not see, would have put him on inquiry. One was a job cost ledger card for job no. 6036, the job number which Berardi put on his own work sheet for Heavenly Lanes. This card read "Capitol Theatre (Heavenly)." In addition, two accounts receivable cards each showed both names on the same card, Capitol and Heavenly. Berardi testified that he looked at the accounts receivable records but that he did not see these particular cards. He testified that he did not look on the job cost ledger cards because he took the costs from another record, the costs register.

The burden of proof on this issue is on Peat, Marwick. Although the question is a rather close one, I find that Peat, Marwick has not sustained that burden. Peat, Marwick has not proved that Berardi made a reasonable investigation as far as Capitol Lanes was concerned and that his ignorance of the true facts was justified.

● ● ●

This disposes of the inaccuracies in the 1960 sales figures. I turn now to the errors in the current assets which involve four items: cash, reserve for Federal Lanes, factors' reserves and Howard Lanes Annex, which latter I have already covered.

As to cash, Berardi properly obtained a confirmation from the bank as to BarChris's cash balance on December 31, 1960. He did not know that part of this balance had been temporarily increased by the deposit of reserves returned by Talcott to BarChris conditionally for a limited time. I do not believe that Berardi reasonably should have known this. Although Peat, Marwick's work papers record the fact that these reserves were returned, there was nothing to indicate that the payment was conditional. Russo obviously did not reveal this fact. It would not be reasonable to require Berardi to examine all of BarChris's correspondence files when he had no reason to suspect any irregularity.

As to the reserve on Federal Lanes, there is little to add to the earlier discussion of this subject in this opinion. I appreciate that in that instance the court has substituted its judgment for that of Russo and Berardi. For the reasons previously mentioned, I believe that their judgment was clearly wrong.

As to factors' reserves, it is hard to understand how Berardi could have treated this item as entirely a current asset when it was obvious that most of the reserves would not be released within one year. If Berardi was unaware of that fact, he should have been aware of it.

The net result, as far as current assets are concerned, is that Peat, Marwick is responsible for the errors as to reserves but not for those involving the cash item and the receivable from Howard Lanes Annex.

● ● ●

The S-1 Review

The purpose of reviewing events subsequent to the date of a certified balance sheet (referred to as an S-1 review when made with reference to a registration statement) is to ascertain whether any material change has occurred in the company's financial position which should be disclosed in order to prevent the balance sheet figures from being misleading. The scope of such a review, under generally accepted auditing standards, is limited. It does not amount to a complete audit.

Peat, Marwick prepared a written program for such a review. I find that this program conformed to generally accepted auditing standards. Among other things, it required the following:

1. Review minutes of stockholders, directors and committees. ...

2. Review latest interim financial statements and compare with corresponding statements of preceding year. Inquire regarding significant variations and changes.

...

4. Review the more important financial records and inquire regarding material transactions not in the ordinary course of business and other significant items.

...

6. Inquire as to changes in material contracts. ...

...

10. Inquire as to any significant bad debts or accounts in dispute for which provision has not been made.

...

14. Inquire as to ... newly discovered liabilities, direct or contingent. ...

Berardi made the S-1 review in May 1961. He devoted a little over two days to it, a total of 20½ hours. He did not discover any of the errors or omissions pertaining to the state of affairs in 1961 which I have previously discussed at length, all of which were material. The question is whether, despite his failure to find out anything, his investigation was reasonable within the meaning of the statute.

What Berardi did was to look at a consolidating trial balance as of March 31, 1961 which had been prepared by BarChris, compare it with the audited December 31, 1960 figures, discuss with Trilling certain unfavorable developments which the comparison disclosed, and read certain minutes. He did not examine any "important financial records" other than the trial balance. As to minutes, he read only what minutes Birnbaum gave him, which consisted only of the board of directors' minutes of BarChris. He did not read such minutes as there were of the executive committee. He did not know that there was an executive committee, hence he did not discover that Kircher had notes of executive committee minutes which had not been written up. He did not read the minutes of any subsidiary.

In substance, what Berardi did is similar to what Grant and Ballard did. He asked questions, he got answers which he considered satisfactory, and he did nothing to verify them. For example, he obtained from Trilling a list of contracts. The list included Yonkers and Bridge. Since Berardi did not read the minutes of subsidiaries, he did not learn that Yonkers and Bridge were intercompany sales. The list also included

Woonsocket and the six T-Bowl jobs, Moravia Road, Milford, Groton, North Attleboro, Odenton and Severna Park. Since Berardi did not look at any contract documents, and since he was unaware of the executive committee minutes of March 18, 1961 (at that time embodied only in Kircher's notes), he did not learn that BarChris had no contracts for these jobs. Trilling's list did not set forth contract prices for them, although it did for Yonkers, Bridge and certain others. This did not arouse Berardi's suspicion.

Berardi noticed that there had been an increase in notes payable by BarChris. Trilling admitted to him that BarChris was "a bit slow" in paying its bills. Berardi recorded in his notes of his review that BarChris was in a "tight cash position." Trilling's explanation was that BarChris was experiencing "some temporary difficulty."

Berardi had no conception of how tight the cash position was. He did not discover that BarChris was holding up checks in substantial amounts because there was no money in the bank to cover them.[27] He did not know of the loan from Manufacturers Trust Company or of the officers' loans. Since he never read the prospectus, he was not even aware that there had ever been any problem about loans from officers.

During the 1960 audit Berardi had obtained some information from factors, not sufficiently detailed even then, as to delinquent notes. He made no inquiry of factors about this in his S-1 review. Since he knew nothing about Kircher's notes of the executive committee meetings, he did not learn that the delinquency situation had grown worse. He was content with Trilling's assurance that no liability theretofore contingent had become direct.

Apparently the only BarChris officer with whom Berardi communicated was Trilling. He could not recall making any inquiries of Russo, Vitolo or Pugliese. As to Kircher, Berardi's testimony was self-contradictory. At one point he said that he had inquired of Kircher and at another he said that he could not recall making any such inquiry.

There had been a material change for the worse in BarChris's financial position. That change was sufficiently serious so that the failure to disclose it made the 1960 figures misleading. Berardi did not discover it. As far as results were concerned, his S-1 review was useless.

Accountants should not be held to a standard higher than that recognized in their profession. I do not do so here. Berardi's review did not come up to that standard. He did not take some of the steps which Peat, Marwick's written program prescribed. He did not spend an adequate amount of time on a task of this magnitude. Most important of all, he was too easily satisfied with glib answers to his inquiries.

This is not to say that he should have made a complete audit. But there were enough danger signals in the materials which he did examine to require some further investigation on his part. Generally accepted accounting standards required such further investigation under these circumstances. It is not always sufficient merely to ask questions.

Here again, the burden of proof is on Peat, Marwick. I find that that burden has not been satisfied. I conclude that Peat, Marwick has not established its due diligence defense.

---

27 One of these checks was a check to the order of Peat, Marwick in the amount of $3,000. It was dated April 4, 1961. It was deposited by Peat, Marwick on May 29, 1961.

The Causation Defense

Section 11(a) provides that when a registration statement contains an untrue statement of a material fact or omits to state a material fact, "any person acquiring such security ... may ... sue." Section 11(e) provides that:

The suit authorized under subsection (a) may be to recover such damages as shall represent the difference between the amount paid for the security (not exceeding the price at which the security was offered to the public) and (1) the value thereof as of the time such suit was brought, or (2) the price at which such security shall have been disposed of in the market before suit, or (3) the price at which such security shall have been disposed of after suit but before judgment if such damages shall be less than the damages representing the difference between the amount paid for the security (not exceeding the price at which the security was offered to the public) and the value thereof as of the time such suit was brought. ...

Section 11(e) then sets forth a proviso reading as follows:

Provided, that if the defendant proves that any portion or all of such damages represents other than the depreciation in value of such security resulting from such part of the registration statement, with respect to which his liability is asserted, not being true or omitting to state a material fact required to be stated therein or necessary to make the statements therein not misleading, such portion of or all such damages shall not be recoverable.

Each defendant in one form or another has relied upon this proviso as a complete defense. Each maintains that the entire damage suffered by each and every plaintiff was caused by factors other than the material falsities and omissions of the registration statement. These factors, in brief, were the decline in the bowling industry which came about because of the fact that the industry was overbuilt and because popular enthusiasm for bowling diminished.

These adverse conditions had begun before these debentures were issued, as evidenced by the growing defaults in customers' notes discounted with Talcott. Talcott did not discount any new notes for BarChris after April 1961. BarChris's financial position, as we have seen, was materially worse in May 1961 than it had been on December 31, 1960.

As time went on, conditions grew worse, both for BarChris and the industry. The receipts of alley operators diminished. New construction of alleys fell off. By 1962 it had almost ceased. There is a wide disparity in the factual pattern of purchases and sales of BarChris debentures by the plaintiffs in this action. Some plaintiffs bought theirs when the debentures were first issued on May 16, 1961. Others bought theirs later in 1961. Still others purchased theirs at various dates in 1962, some even as late as September 1962, shortly before BarChris went into Chapter XI. In at least one instance, a plaintiff purchased debentures after BarChris was in Chapter XI.

There is a similar disparity as to sales. Some plaintiffs sold their debentures in 1961. Others sold theirs in 1962. Others never sold them.

The position taken by defendants in their affirmative defenses is an extreme one which cannot be sustained. I cannot say that the entire damage suffered by every plaintiff was caused by factors other than the errors and omissions of the registration statement for which these defendants are responsible. As to some plaintiffs, or as to part of the damage sustained by others, that may be true. The only practicable course is to defer decision of this issue until the claim of each individual plaintiff is separately considered. As stated at the outset, this opinion is devoted only to matters common to all plaintiffs.

• • •

Plaintiffs' motion is denied.

NOTE

Few recent decisions have had as great an impact upon corporate practice as *BarChris*. Canadian and American securities lawyers now routinely conduct extensive "due diligence" reviews and meetings to ensure that full compliance is made with the duty of reasonable investigation. A material contracts review is conducted to examine the principal agreements between the issuer and its lenders, suppliers and customers, and corporate minute books are read carefully. Detailed questionnaires are sent to directors and senior officers in order to verify the information contained in the prospectus. Finally, lengthy meetings are conducted, with lawyers, underwriters, auditors and management poring over the prospectus. A second major consequence of BarChris is the rapid development of directors' and officers' insurance, a subject discussed in Chapter Seven.

The question of the liability of a BarChris director arose again in *Lanza v. Drexel & Co.*, 479 F.2d 1277 (2d Cir. 1973), where Coleman was found not liable under Rule 10b-5 of the Securities Exchange Act of 1934, reproduced in Chapter Eight, Section A. (A s. 11 claim was not asserted here since no public offering was involved.) Unlike s. 11, Rule 10b-5 does not expressly refer to duty of reasonable investigation. The Court stated that:

[N]either the language nor intent of Section 10(b) or Rule 10b-5 would justify a holding (1) that a director is an insurer of the honesty of individual officers of the corporation in their negotiations which involve the purchase or sale of the corporation's stock or (2) that, although he does not conduct the negotiations, participate therein, or have knowledge thereof, he is under a duty to investigate each such transaction and to enquire as to what representations had been made, by whom and to whom, and then independently check on the truth or falsity of every statement made and document presented.

. . .

A director may have an obligation to maintain an awareness of significant corporate developments and to consider any material, adverse developments which come to his attention. But Coleman, in our view, more than met his standard of responsibility. [*Id.* at 1281, 1296]

See further Folk, *Civil Liabilities Under the Federal Securities Acts: The BarChris Case*, 55 Va. L. Rev. 1. (1969), and *The BarChris Case: Prospectus Liability*, 24 Bus. Law. 523 (1969).

Feit v. Leasco Data Processing Equipment Corp. The second major case on s. 11 liability is *Feit v. Leasco Data Processing Equipment Corp.*, 332 F. Supp. 544 (E.D.N.Y. 1971), which involved misrepresentations in a take-over bid circular. The Court adopted *BarChris* and stated that it imposed "such stringent requirements of knowledge of corporate affairs on inside directors that one is led to the conclusion that liability will lie in practically all cases of misrepresentation. Their liability approaches that of the issuer as guarantor of the accuracy of the prospectus" (*Id.* at 578).

The specific misrepresentation in *Feit v. Leasco* concerned a failure by the defendant offeror to disclose fully material facts concerning the target corporation for whose shares the offer was made. The target corporation, Reliance Insurance Co., had accumulated a large amount of "surplus surplus," being the highly liquid assets of an insurance company which cannot be invested in non-regulated enterprises. Since Reliance was not itself permitted to engage in non-insurance business activities, such surplus surplus was of value only if it could be separated from the insurance operation. While Reliance could not do so alone, Leasco could on acquiring control of Reliance. The Leasco take-over bid was therefore primarily motivated by a desire to make use of this fund. However, the registration statement made only a passing reference to the surplus surplus, and did not disclose the approximate value of the fund, which was known to Leasco.

The Court concluded that this information was material since, even if the fund could not be used by Reliance, it affected the value of Reliance shares to outside tender offerors. "Knowledge of the intensity of demand is essential to determination of a fair price in a market economy" (*Id.* at 572).

The ultimate goal of the Securities Act is, of course, investor protection. Effective disclosure is merely a means. The entire legislative scheme can be frustrated by technical compliance with the requirements of the Securities and Exchange Commission's Form S-1 for preparation of registration statements in the absence of any real intent to communicate. It is for this reason that the SEC, through its rule making power, has consistently required "clearly understandable" prospectuses. The Wheat Report at 78.

Unfortunately, the results have not always reflected these efforts. "[E]ven when an investor [is] presented with an accurate prospectus prior to his purchase, the presentation in most instances tend[s] to discourage reading by all but the most knowledgeable and tenacious." Knauss, A Reappraisal of the Role of Disclosure, 62 Mich.L.Rev. 607, 618-619 (1964). These documents are often drafted so as to be comprehensible to only a minute part of the investing public.

> There are also the perennial questions of whether prospectuses, once delivered to the intended reader, are readable, and whether they are read. The cynic's answer to both questions is "No"; the true believer's is "Yes"; probably a more accurate answer than either would be: "Yes"—by a relatively small number of professionals or highly sophisticated non-professionals; "No"—by the great majority of those investors who are not sophisticated and, within the doctrine of *SEC v. Ralston Purina Co.* [346 U.S. 119, 73 S.Ct. 981, 97 L.Ed. 14941, are not "able to fend for themselves" and most "need the protection of the Act." Cohen, "Truth in Securities" Revisited, 79 Harv. L. Rev. 1340, 1351-1352 (1966).

See also The Wheat Report at 77-78.

In at least some instances, what has developed in lieu of the open disclosure envisioned by the Congress is a literary art form calculated to communicate as little of the essential information as possible while exuding an air of total candor. Masters of this medium utilize turgid prose to enshroud the occasional critical revelation in a morass of dull, and—to all but the sophisticates—useless financial and historical data. In the face of such obfuscatory tactics the common or even the moderately well-informed investor is almost as much at the mercy of the issuer as was his pre-SEC parent. He cannot by reading the prospectus discern the merit of the offering.

. . .

The view that prospectuses should be intelligible to the average small investor as well as the professional analyst, immediately raises the question of what substantive standard of disclosure must be maintained. The legal standard is that all "material" facts must be accurately disclosed. But to whom must the fact have material significance?

In an industry in which there is an unmistakable "trend toward a greater measure of professionalism ... with the accompanying demand for more information about issuers" "a pragmatic balance must be struck between the needs of the unsophisticated investor and those of the knowledgeable student of finance." The Wheat Report at 9-10. There are three distinct classes of investors who must be informed by the prospectus: (1) the amateur who reads for only the grosser sorts of disclosures; (2) the professional advisor and manager who studies the prospectus closely and makes his decisions based on the insights he gains from it; and (3) the securities analyst who uses the prospectus as one of many sources in an independent investigation of the issuer.

The proper resolution of the various interests lies in the inclusion of a clearly written narrative statement outlining the major aspects of the offering and particularly speculative elements, as well as detailed financial information which will have meaning only to the expert. Requiring inclusion of such technical data benefits amateurs, as well as experts, because of the advice many small investors receive and the extent to which the market reflects professional judgments. The Wheat Report at 52. Such "[e]xpert sifters, distillers, and weighers are essential for an informed body of investors." Cohen, "Truth in Securities" Revisited, 79 Harv.L.Rev. 1340, 1353 (1966).

. . .

The Wheat Report further notes:

> that a fully effective disclosure policy would require the reporting of complicated business facts that would have little meaning for the average investor. Such disclosures reach average investors through a process of filtration in which intermediaries (brokers, bankers, investment advisors, publishers of investment advisory literature, and occasionally lawyers) play a vital role. The Wheat Report at 52.

> The significance of disclosures which have an initial impact at the professional level has been heightened by recent changes in the securities business. Most important of these is the enormous growth of intermediation in investment. The relative importance of such professional money managers as bank trust departments, pension fund managers, investment counseling firms and investment advisors to mutual funds and other investment companies is greater than ever before. The Wheat Report at 54.

> The significance of these observations is that the objectives of full disclosure can be fully achieved only by complete revelation of facts which would be material to the sophisticated investor or the securities professional, not just the average common shareholder. But, at the same time, the prospectus must not slight the less experienced. They are entitled to have within the four corners of the document an intelligible description of the transaction. [Id. at 564-66]

One of the few Canadian decisions to consider standards of disclosure in a prospectus is In the Matter of A.E. Ames & Co., [1972] O.S.C.B. 98. Ames was lead underwriter on a public issue of shares of Kaiser Resources Ltd. Since the prospectus would not be qualified by the S.E.C., American counsel insisted that the prospectus bear a statement that the underwriters agreed that the shares would not be offered, sold or delivered "to or for the account of residents" of that country. However, many of the directors and senior officers of Kaiser and its American parent wished to subscribe for the Kaiser shares, and a plan was devised to enable them to do so. A new Canadian private holding company called KRL Investments Ltd. was incorporated to purchase the Kaiser shares. Shares in KRL were allotted to Kaiser's in-house counsel on behalf of the American directors and senior officers. Ames was advised by the in-house counsel that Kaiser shares might be issued to KRL as part of the distribution, notwithstanding the statement in the prospectus that no Kaiser shares would be sold to an American. On these facts, the O.S.C. held that the responsible Ames officer had breached the "full, true and plain disclosure" requirements of the OSA, and suspended him as a trading officer for a one-week period. If the overriding standard of disclosure is materiality, was the fact that the shares of one of the purchasers were beneficially owned by Americans in any sense material to the other Canadian purchasers of Kaiser shares?

An Analysis of the Effects of the Statutory Civil Action. The possibility of fraud by firm managers in their preparation of a prospectus means that it is a less credible document, and the resulting cost will be borne by the issuing firm in efficient capital markets. The firm will then wish to reduce fraud costs, and one strategy it might employ as a bonding device is an assumption of legal responsibility for fraud. Like any promise, a statement is more credible when the stakes are raised by the imposition of legal liability for a misrepresentation. Issuer liability may not, however, eliminate all incentive costs, if liability for fraud would bankrupt the issuer.

One response to the deterrence gap might be to widen the net of liability to embrace other contracting parties, such as underwriters and outside directors. The talents of these efficient monitors are harnessed by requiring the issuer to obtain their approval of the prospectus, with statutory civil liability for misrepresentations imposed on them for negligence. The imposition of a damages remedy against the parties, other than the issuer, listed in the statutory civil liability provision is an example of what Reinier Kraakman refers to as "gatekeeper liability"—a sanction imposed on one who is not the primary cause of the harm, but who is in a position to have prevented it. Kraakman, *Gatekeepers: The Anatomy of a Third-Party Enforcement Strategy*, 2 J.L. Econ. & Org. 53 (1986). The full costs of fraud will then be imposed on issuers, either directly through issuer liability under the statutory civil action or indirectly when liability is imposed on gatekeepers in a contractual nexus with the issuer. This is because gatekeepers will require that they be compensated by the issuer for their added risks. Do these efficiency explanations justify the mandatory nature of the statutory civil action for misrepresentations in a prospectus? Audited financial statements, antedated securities Act disclosure requirements and gatekeeper regimes might be instituted by issuers without legal compulsion. Recovery in damages is restricted under the statutory civil action to the depreciation in value of the security as a result of the misrepresentation. On a falling market, a plaintiff will often not be put in as good a position as he would have been had he not purchased the security, and he may therefore prefer to assert rescissionary remedies. The amount recoverable may not exceed the price at which the securities were offered to the public. The limitation period in a damages claim may be as long as three years from the transaction if the purchaser did not have knowledge of the facts giving rise to the cause of action.

The near-abolition of reliance might be thought to raise the possibility of over-deterrence, with issuers liable to purchasers who might have bought even without the misrepresentation. But if these concerns might seem compelling in garden varieties of fraud, they are less so when fraud is committed in efficient market transactions. Since an uninformed purchaser will free ride on screening by investment intermediaries, he may be prejudiced by an unread prospectus's misrepresentations. In determining how much care to take in producing a truthful prospectus, an issuer may underinvest in harm prevention if no liability is owed to such free riders. A "fraud on the market" approach, with reliance standards relaxed in favour of materiality requirements, may then be defended on allocational grounds. See, e.g., Fischel, *The Use of Modern Finance Theory in Securities Fraud Cases Involving Actively Traded Securities*, 38 Bus. Law. 1 (1982).

D. CONTINUOUS DISCLOSURE

Continuous disclosure consists of periodic reports, such as financial reports, proxy circulars and insider trading reports, and timely reports of material information concerning the issuer by way of press releases. A more recent addition to the continuous disclosure requirements is the requirement for many issuers to file an annual information form (or "AIF").

Continuous disclosure has been an important theme of securities regulation in Canada over the past 25 years. Continuous disclosure requirements were introduced in Canadian securities acts following the recommendations of the Kimber Report (*Report of the Attorney General's Committee on Securities Legislation in Ontario*, Part I, paras. 1.11, 1.12, 1.16 and Parts II, IV and VI (1965)). According to the Merger Report (*Report of the Committee of the Ontario Securities Commission on the Problems of Disclosure for Investors by Business Combinations and Private Placements* 15 (1972)), the purpose of continuous disclosure is to provide all investors in the market place with equal access to information and thus equal access to the opportunities that information provides. Continuous disclosure is central to the concept of the "closed system" (discussed below) and to prompt offering and shelf offering prospectuses (also discussed below).

1. "Reporting Issuers"

Most securities acts in Canada distinguish between so-called reporting issuers and non-reporting issuers. It is reporting issuers that are subject to the continuous disclosure requirements under most Canadian securities acts. Normally a reporting issuer is an issuer that has issued securities under a prospectus in the applicable jurisdiction or has securities listed and posted for trading on a stock exchange in the jurisdiction. See, e.g., ASA s. 1(t.1); BCSA s. 1(1); OSA s. 1(1). The definition is intended to identify issuers the securities of which are available for trading by the general investing public who presumably need to know the kind of information that would be contained in continuous disclosure documents.

2. Financial Statements

Most securities acts in Canada require issuers to provide financial statements on a regular basis. Issuers must distribute annual financial statements to shareholders and file the statements with the securities administrators in the jurisdictions in which they are reporting issuers. The annual financial statements consist of a balance sheet, an income statement, a statement of retained earnings, and a statement of changes in financial position. They must be audited and must contain comparative figures for the previous financial year. See, e.g., ASA s. 121 and ASA Reg. s. 151; BCSA Reg. ss. 4(4) and 136; OSA s. 78 and OSA Reg. s. 10.

Interim financial statements are also required. These are normally prepared for each quarter of the financial year and must be distributed to shareholders and filed with the securities administrators in the jurisdictions in which the issuer is a reporting issuer. The interim financial statements need only consist of an income statement and a statement of changes in financial position and the statements need not be audited. See, e.g., ASA ss. 120, 122, and ASA Reg. ss. 146, 148; BCSA Reg. ss. 135, 141; OSA ss. 77, 79, and OSA Reg. ss. 7, 9.

3. Proxy Solicitation

Most Canadian securities acts require the management of a reporting issuer to send a form of proxy and an information circular (or "proxy circular") to security holders within the jurisdiction whenever voting security holders are given notice of a meeting of voting security holders. See, e.g., ASA s. 127; BCSA s. 101; OSA s. 85. The information circular must contain certain specific information such as the interests of directors and officers in the matters to be voted on, the names and holdings of persons having direct or indirect beneficial ownership of more than 10% of the voting rights, information on persons proposed for election as directors, details of executive compensation, indebtedness of directors and senior officers to the issuer or its subsidiaries and the interests of directors and officers in material transactions involving the issuer. The information circular must also provide information in sufficient detail on the matters to be voted on to permit security holders to make a reasoned judgment on the matters. See, e.g., ASA Reg. s. 163 and Form 30; BCSA Reg. Form 30; OSA Reg. s. 157 and Form 30. Proxy solicitation is discussed in more detail in Chapter Six.

4. Insider Reports

Most Canadian securities acts also require reports of trades by insiders of reporting issuers. Persons who become an insider of a reporting issuer are required to file a report within 10 days of becoming an insider. The report must indicate any direct or indirect beneficial ownership of, or control or direction over, securities of the reporting issuer. Changes in the insider's direct or indirect ownership of, or control or direction over, securities of the reporting issuer must be reported within 10 days of the end of the month in which the change occurs. See, e.g., ASA s. 147; BCSA s. 70; OSA s. 107.

An "insider" includes a director or senior officer of the issuer. It also includes persons having direct or indirect beneficial ownership, or control or direction over, securities of the issuer which carry more than 10% of the voting rights attached to all the outstanding voting securities of the issuer. Directors or senior officers of persons having beneficial ownership of voting securities carrying more than 10% of the voting rights attached to the issuer's securities are also considered insiders of the reporting issuer. The issuer itself can be an insider if it holds its own voting securities. See, e.g., ASA s. 1(i); BCSA s. 1(1); OSA s. 1(1).

5. Timely Disclosure

Timely disclosure provides the securities market with information on significant events concerning the reporting issuer as soon as possible after the event occurs. Canadian securities acts typically require timely disclosure by requiring reporting issuers to disclose "material changes" in the affairs of the reporting issuer. Under the OSA a "material change" is defined as:

... a change in the business, operations or capital of an issuer that would reasonably be expected to have a significant effect on the market price or value of any of the securities of the issuer and includes a decision to implement such a change made by the board of directors of the issuer or by senior management of the issuer who believe that confirmation of the decision by the board of directors is probable.

See OSA s. 1(1); see also, e.g., ASA s. 1(k.1); BCSA s. 1(1). When a material change occurs the reporting issuer must file a press release disclosing the nature and substance of the change as soon as practicable after the change. The reporting issuer must also file a report of the material change as soon as practicable (and in any event within 10 days) in each jurisdiction in which it is a reporting issuer. See ASA s. 118(1); BCSA s. 67(1); OSA ss. 75(1), (2).

In some circumstances the material change can be reported on a confidential basis without issuing a press release. This involves sending a report marked "confidential" to the securities administrators in the jurisdictions in which the issuer is a reporting issuer. The issuer must provide written reasons for the confidential report. A confidential report may be made where, in the opinion of the reporting issuer, disclosure would be unduly detrimental to the interests of the issuer, or, where the material change involves a decision to implement a change made by senior management of the issuer who believe that confirmation of the decision by the directors is probable and senior management have no reason to believe that persons with knowledge of the material change have made use of that knowledge in purchasing or selling securities of the issuer.

National Policy No. 40 purports to extend the timely disclosure obligation to material facts in addition to material changes. As noted above, a "material fact" is typically defined to mean a fact that significantly affects, or could reasonably be expected to significantly affect, the market price or value of the securities of the issuer. National Policy No. 40 also attempts to give a sense of the kinds of situations in which disclosure is required. There is some doubt as to whether Canadian securities administrators can effectively extend the scope of the timely disclosure obligation in a way that is tantamount to an amendment to securities legislation without seeking the approval of the legislature. However, the courts appear to be willing to allow securities commissions considerable latitude in determining the scope of the definition of "material change."

This may allow securities administrators to achieve much the same result as National Policy No. 40 by giving a broad scope to the definition of "material change." See, e.g., *Pezim v. British Columbia Securities Commission*, [1994] 2 S.C.R. 557.

6. Annual Information Forms

Issuers that wish to make use of prompt offering prospectuses or shelf prospectuses (discussed below) must file an annual information form ("AIF"). The AIF must be filed within 140 days of the end of the issuer's financial year. Under Ontario Policy 5.10 reporting issuers having shareholder's equity of more than $10,000,000 or revenues of more than $10,000,000 must file an AIF.

The AIF includes information such as information on the incorporation of the issuer, a narrative description of the business, the development of the business of the issuer over the previous five years, financial information, information about the directors and officers and their ownership of securities of the issuer, information about the subsidiaries of the issuer and other information about the issuer. It can incorporate by reference information contained in the issuer's financial statements and proxy circular for the year.

The AIF must also include a section called "management's discussion and analysis" of the financial condition and results of operations of the issuer (otherwise known as MD & A). MD & A is intended to allow the investor "to look at the business through the eyes of management." It requires management to discuss the dynamics of the business and to analyze the financial statements. MD & A discusses and compares the issuer's financial condition, changes in financial condition and results of operations for the last two completed financial years. The discussion focuses on explaining why changes have or have not occurred in the financial condition and results of operations of the issuer. Management must disclose known material trends, commitments, events or uncertainties that are reasonably expected to have a material impact on the issuer's business, financial condition or results of operations. See Ontario Policy 5.10, Part III, National Policy No. 47, Appendix A, Schedule 2.

7. Liability for Misrepresentations in Continuous Disclosure Documents

Securities acts in Canada do not provide for statutory civil liability for misrepresentations in continuous disclosure documents. Instead investors must base a claim concerning a misrepresentation in continuous disclosure documents on the common law action for negligent misrepresentation. A significant hurdle for investors in such an action would be proving that they relied on the misrepresentation. In similar actions in the United States courts have accepted proof of reliance on the basis of a "fraud-on-the-market" theory. The "fraud-on-the-market" theory is based on the assumption that the market is efficient in the semi-strong form (see Chapter One on the ECMH). Thus the market price will quickly reflect information contained in continuous disclosure documents. The investor is said to rely on the market price and thus implicitly relies on any misrepresentations in continuous disclosure documents that are reflected in the market price. See, e.g., *Peit v. Speiser*, 806 F.2d 1154 (1986); *Blaikie v. Barrack*, 524 F.2d 891 (9th Cir. 1975); and *Basic v. Levinson*, 108 S. Ct. 978, 99 L. Ed. 2d 194 (U.S. Ohio, 1988). It has been argued that the theory should not be based on the efficiency of the market but on whether a misstatement distorted the price of the security. See J.R. Macey et al., *Lessons from Financial Economics: Materiality, Reliance, and Extending the Reach of Basic v. Levinson,* 77 Virg. L.R. 1017 (1991).

E. EXEMPTIONS AND THE CLOSED SYSTEM

1. Concepts Behind the Exemptions

In the past securities acts in Canada required a prospectus where there was a "primary distribution to the public." One could thus avoid the prospectus requirement where the distribution did not involve a distribution "to the public." Uncertainty over the meaning of "to the public" led to the adoption of an approach where all distributions would require a prospectus unless a specific exemption from the prospectus requirement were available. Thus the term "primary distribution to the public" was replaced in most Canadian securities legislation with the term "distribution" (discussed in Section C above).

Under this revised approach a more extensive set of exemptions from the prospectus requirement was provided. However, for the most part, the exemptions were still based on the concepts that had been developed in interpreting the meaning of the expression "to the public." Also, the phrase "to the public" was retained in an exemption for "securities of a private company where [the securities] are not offered for sale to the public." Thus it continues to be useful to have an understanding of the interpretation of the phrase "to the public."

The "Need to Know" Test. The following case is a widely cited case on the meaning of "to the public."

Securities & Exchange Comm'n v. Ralston Purina Co.
United States Supreme Court
346 U.S. 119, 73 S.Ct. 981, 97 L.Ed. 1494 (1953)

MR. JUSTICE CLARK delivered the opinion of the Court: Section 4(1) of the Securities Act of 1933 exempts "transactions by an issuer not involving any public offering" from the registration requirements of § 5.[2] We must decide whether Ralston Purina's

---

2   Sec. 5.(a) Unless a registration statement is in effect as to a security, it shall be unlawful for any person, directly or indirectly—

        (1) to make use of any means or instruments of transportation or communication in interstate commerce or of the mails to sell or offer to buy such security through the use or medium of any prospectus or otherwise; or

        (2) to carry or cause to be carried through the mails or in interstate commerce, by any means or instruments of transportation, any such security for the purpose of sale or for delivery after sale ... (48 Stat. 77, 15 U.S.C. § 77e).

offerings of treasury stock to its "key employees" are within this exemption. On a complaint brought by the Commission under § 20(b) of the Act seeking to enjoin respondent's unregistered offerings, the District Court held the exemption applicable and dismissed the suit. The Court of Appeals affirmed. The question had arisen many times since the Act was passed; an apparent need to define the scope of the private offering exemption prompted *certiorari*. 345 U.S. 903.

Ralston Purina manufactures and distributes various feed and cereal products. Its processing and distribution facilities are scattered throughout the United States and Canada, staffed by some 7,000 employees. At least since 1911 the company has had a policy of encouraging stock ownership among its employees; more particularly, since 1942 it has made authorized but unissued common shares available to some of them. Between 1947 and 1951, the period covered by the record in this case, Ralston Purina sold nearly $2,000,000 of stock to employees without registration and in so doing made use of the mails.

In each of these years, a corporate resolution authorized the sale of common stock "to employees ... who shall, without any solicitation by the Company or its officers or employees, inquire of any of them as to how to purchase common stock of Ralston Purina Company." A memorandum sent to branch and store managers after the resolution was adopted advised that "The only employees to whom this stock will be available will be those who take the initiative and are interested in buying stock at present market prices." Among those responding to these offers were employees with the duties of artist, bakeshop foreman, chow loading foreman, clerical assistant, copywriter, electrician, stock clerk, mill office clerk, order credit trainee, production trainee, stenographer, and veterinarian. The buyers lived in over fifty widely separated communities scattered from Garland, Texas, to Nashua, New Hampshire, and Visalia, California. The lowest salary bracket of those purchasing was $2,700 in 1949, $2,435 in 1950 and $3,107 in 1951. The record shows that in 1947, 243 employees bought stock, 20 in 1948, 414 in 1949, 411 in 1950, and the 1951 offer, interrupted by this litigation, produced 165 applications to purchase. No records were kept of those to whom the offers were made; the estimated number in 1951 was 500.

The company bottoms its exemption claim on the classification of all offerees as "key employees" in its organization. Its position on trial was that "A key employee ... is not confined to an organization chart. It would include an individual who is eligible for promotion, an individual who especially influences others or who advises others, a person whom the employees look to in some special way, an individual, of course, who carries some special responsibility, who is sympathetic to management and who is ambitious and who the management feels is likely to be promoted to a greater responsibility." That an offering to all of its employees would be public is conceded.

The Securities Act nowhere defines the scope of § 4(1)'s private offering exemption. Nor is the legislative history of much help in staking out its boundaries. The problem was first dealt with in § 4(1) of the House Bill, H.R. 5480, 73d Cong., 1st Sess., which exempted "transactions by an issuer not with or through an underwriter ... ." The bill, as reported by the House Committee, added "and not involving any public offering." H.R. Rep. No. 85, 73d Cong., 1st Sess. 1. This was thought to be one of those transactions "where there is no practical need for [the bill's] application or where the public benefits are too remote." *Id.*, at 5.[5] The exemption as thus delimited became law. It assumed its present shape with the deletion of "not with or through an underwriter" by § 203(a) of the Securities Exchange Act of 1934, 48 Stat. 906, a change regarded as the elimination of superfluous language. H.R. Rep. No. 1838, 73d Cong., 2d Sess. 41.

Decisions under comparable exemptions in the English Companies Acts and state "blue sky" laws, the statutory antecedents of federal securities legislation, have made one thing clear—to be public an offer need not be open to the whole world.[7] In *Securities and Exchange Comm'n v. Sunbeam Gold Mines Co.*, 95 F.2d 699 (C.A. 9th Cir. 1938), this point was made in dealing with an offering to the stockholders of two corporations about to be merged. Judge Denman observed that:

In its broadest meaning the term "public" distinguishes the populace at large from groups of individual members of the public segregated because of some common interest or characteristic. Yet such a distinction is inadequate for practical purposes; manifestly, an offering of securities to all red-headed men, to all residents of Chicago or San Francisco, to all existing stockholders of the General Motors Corporation or the American Telephone & Telegraph Company, is no less "public," in every realistic sense of the word, than an unrestricted offering to the world at large. Such an offering, though not open to everyone who may choose to apply, is none the less "public" in character, for the means used to select the particular individuals to whom the offering is to be made bear no sensible relation to the purposes for which the selection is made. ... To determine the distinction between "public" and "private" in any particular context, it is essential to examine the circumstances under which the distinction is sought to be established and to consider the purposes sought to be achieved by such distinction (95 F.2d, at 701).

The courts below purported to apply this test. The District Court held, in the language of the *Sunbeam* decision, that "The purpose of the selection bears a 'sensible relation' to the class chosen," finding that "The sole purpose of the 'selection' is to keep part stock ownership of the business within the operating personnel of the business and to spread ownership throughout all departments and activities of the business" [102 F. Supp., at 968, 969]. The Court of Appeals treated the case as involving "an offering, without solicitation, of common stock to a selected group of key employees of the issuer, most of whom are already stockholders when the offering is made, with the sole purpose of enabling them to secure a proprietary interest in the company or to increase the interest already held by them" [200 F.2d, at 91].

---

5   "... the bill does not affect transactions beyond the need of public protection in order to prevent recurrences of demonstrated abuses." *Id.*, at 7. In a somewhat different tenor, the report spoke of this as an exemption of transactions by an issuer unless made by or through an underwriter so as to permit an issuer to make a specific or an isolated sale of its securities to a particular person, but insisting that if a sale of the issuer's securities should be made generally to the public that the transaction shall come within the purview of the Act." *Id.*, at 15, 16.

7   *Nash v. Lynde*, [1929] A.C.158; *In re South of England Natural Gas and Petroleum Co. Ltd.*, [1911] 1 Ch. 573; cf. *Sherwell v. Combined Incandescent Mantles Syndicate, Ltd.*, 23 T.L.R. 482 (1907). See 80 Sol. J. 785 (1936). ...

Exemption from the registration requirements of the Securities Act is the question. The design of the statute is to protect investors by promoting full disclosure of information thought necessary to informed investment decisions. The natural way to interpret the private offering exemption is in light of the statutory purpose. Since exempt transactions are those as to which "there is no practical need for [the bill's] application," the applicability of § 4(1) should turn on whether the particular class of persons affected needs the protection of the Act. An offering to those who are shown to be able to fend for themselves is a transaction "not involving any public offering."

The Commission would have us go one step further and hold that "an offering to a substantial number of the public" is not exempt under § 4(1). We are advised that "whatever the special circumstances, the Commission has consistently interpreted the exemption as being inapplicable when a large number of offerees is involved." But the statute would seem to apply to a "public offering" whether to few or many.[11] It may well be that offerings to a substantial number of persons would rarely be exempt. Indeed nothing prevents the Commission, in enforcing the statute, from using some kind of numerical test in deciding when to investigate particular exemption claims. But there is no warrant for superimposing a quantity limit on private offerings as a matter of statutory interpretation.

The exemption, as we construe it, does not deprive corporate employees, as a class, of the safeguards of the Act. We agree that some employee offerings may come within § 4(1), e.g., one made to executive personnel who because of their position have access to the same kind of information that the Act would make available in the form of a registration statement.[12] Absent such a showing of special circumstances, employees are just as much members of the investing "public" as any of their neighbors in the community. Although we do not rely on it, the rejection in 1934 of an amendment which would have specifically exempted employee stock offerings supports this conclusion. The House Managers, commenting on the Conference Report, said that "the participants in employees' stock-investment plans may be in as great need of the protection afforded by availability of information concerning the issuer for which they work as are most other members of the public." H.R. Rep. No. 1838, 73d Cong., 2d Sess. 41.

Keeping in mind the broadly remedial purposes of federal securities legislation, imposition of the burden of proof on an issuer who would plead the exemption seems to

---

11   See Viscount Sumner's frequently quoted dictum in Nash v. Lynde: " 'The public' ... is of course a general word. No particular numbers are prescribed. Anything from two to infinity may serve: perhaps even one, if he is intended to be the first of a series of subscribers, but makes further proceedings needless by himself subscribing the whole." [1929] A.C. 158, 169.

12   This was one of the factors stressed in an advisory opinion rendered by the Commission's General Counsel in 1935. "I also regard as significant the relationship between the issuer and the offerees. Thus, an offering to the members of a class who should have special knowledge of the issuer is less likely to be a public offering than is an offering to the members of a class of the same size who do not have this advantage. This factor would be particularly important in offerings to employees, where a class of high executive officers would have a special relationship to the issuer which subordinate employees would not enjoy." 11 Fed. Reg. 10952.

us fair and reasonable. *Schlemmer v. Buffalo, R. & P.R. Co.*, 205 U.S. 1, 10 (1907). Agreeing, the court below thought the burden met primarily because of the respondent's purpose in singling out its key employees for stock offerings. But once it is seen that the exemption question turns on the knowledge of the offerees, the issuer's motives, laudable though they may be, fade into irrelevance. The focus of inquiry should be on the need of the offerees for the protections afforded by registration. The employees here were not shown to have access to the kind of information which registration would disclose. The obvious opportunities for pressure and imposition make it advisable that they be entitled to compliance with § 5.

The CHIEF JUSTICE and MR. JUSTICE BURTON dissent.

[MR. JUSTICE JACKSON took no part in the consideration or decision of this case.]

Reversed.

The "need to know" test in *S.E.C. v. Ralston Purina* has been approved of in several Canadian decisions and is the leading Canadian test on the meaning of "to the public." See, e.g., *R. v. McKillop*, [1972] 1 O.R. 164; *In the Matter of Shelter Corporation of Canada Ltd.*, [1977] O.S.C.B. 6. The kinds of factors considered in determining whether a distribution is made "to the public" were also considered at some length in the following case.

Doran v. Petroleum Management Corp.
United States Court of Appeals, Fifth Circuit
545 F.2d 893 (1977)

[Doran purchased a limited partnership interest in an oil and gas venture. He agreed to contribute $125,000, which was paid by paying $25,000 down and assuming responsibility for a debt of an organizing partner represented by a promissory note in the amount of $113,643.

The wells of the limited partnership were deliberately overproduced, which led to the wells being sealed for a period of 338 days by the Wyoming Oil and Gas Conservation Commission. Subsequent yields from the wells decreased and the promissory note for which Doran was responsible went into default. The creditor obtained a judgment against Doran on the note.

Doran filed a suit in federal district court seeking damages for breach of contract, rescission of contract on the basis of violations of the Securities Acts of 1933 and 1934, and a judgment declaring the defendants liable for payment of the judgment obtained on the note.

The lower court found the offer and sale of the limited partnership interest to be a private offering because Doran was a sophisticated investor who did not need the protection of the Securities Acts. The lower court found that there was no evidence of any misrepresentations or omissions of material facts made to Doran. The court also found that the overproduction of the wells was not in violation of the partnership agreement and that there was no evidence that Doran suffered any losses as a result of the overproduction. The court thus concluded that the relief requested by Doran should be denied. Doran appealed.]

[Before GOLDBERG, DYER and SIMPSON JJ.]

GOLDBERG J.:

• • •

II. The Private Offering Exemption

No registration statement was filed with any federal or state regulatory body in connection with the defendants' offering of securities. ...

The defendants do not contest the existence of the elements of plaintiffs prima facie case but raise an affirmative defense that the relevant transactions came within the exemption from registration found in § 4(2), 15 U.S.C. § 77d(2). Specifically, they contend that the offering of securities was not a public offering. The defendants, who of course bear the burden of proving this affirmative defense, must therefore show that the offering was private. See *SEC v. Ralston Purina Co.*, 346 U.S. 119, 126, 73 S.Ct. 981, 985, 97 L.Ed. 1494 (1953); *Hill York Corp. v. American International Franchises, Inc.*, supra, 448 F.2d at 690; *Lively v. Hirschfeld*, 440 F.2d 631, 632 (10th Cir. 1971); *United States v. Custer Channel Wing Corp.*, 376 F.2d 675, 678 (4th Cir.), cert. denied, 389 U.S. 850, 88 S.Ct. 38, 19 L.Ed.2d 119 (1967).

This court has in the past identified four factors relevant to whether an offering qualifies for the exemption. The consideration of these factors, along with the policies embodied in the 1933 Act, structure the inquiry. *Hill York Corp. v. American International Franchises, Inc.*, supra, 448 F.2d at 687-88; *Henderson v. Hayden, Stone Inc.*, 461 F.2d 1069, 1071 (5th Cir. 1972); *SEC v. Continental Tobacco Co. of South Carolina*, 463 F.2d 137, 158 (5th Cir. 1972); see also *Woolf v. S.D. Cohn & Co.*, 515 F.2d 591, 609 (5th Cir. 1975), vacated on other grounds, 426 U.S. 944, 96 S.Ct. 3161, 49 L.Ed.2d 1181 (1976). The relevant factors include the number of offerees and their relationship to each other and the issuer, the number of units offered, the size of the offering, and the manner of the offering. Consideration of these factors need not exhaust the inquiry, nor is one factor's weighing heavily in favor of the private status of the offering sufficient to ensure the availability of the exemption. Rather, these factors serve as guideposts to the court in attempting to determine whether subjecting the offering to registration requirements would further the purposes of the 1933 Act.

• • •

In the case at bar, the defendants may have demonstrated the presence of the latter three factors. A small number of units offered, relatively modest financial stakes, and an offering characterized by personal contract between the issuer and the offerees free of public advertising or intermediaries such as investment bankers or securities exchanges— these aspects of the instant transaction aid the defendants' search for a § 4(2) exemption.

• • •

A. *The Number of Offerees*

• • •

The number of offerees, not the number of purchasers, is the relevant figure in considering the number of persons involved in an offering. *Hill York Corp. v. American International Franchises, Inc.*, supra, 448 F.2d at 691. A private placement claimant's failure to adduce any evidence regarding the number of offerees will be fatal to the claim. *SEC v. Continental Tobacco Co.*, supra, 463 F.2d at 161; *Henderson v. Hayden, Stone Inc.*, supra, 461 F.2d at 1071-72; *Repass v. Rees*, 174 F.Supp. 898, 904 (D.Colo. 1959). The number of offerees is not itself a decisive factor in determining the availability of the private offering exemption. Just as an offering to few may be public, so an offering to many may be private. *SEC v. Ralston Purina Co.*, supra, 346 U.S. at 125, 73 S.Ct. at 984-85. Nevertheless, "the more offerees, the more likelihood that the offering is public." *Hill York Corp. v. American International Franchises, Inc.*, supra, 448 F.2d at 688. In the case at bar, the record indicates that eight investors were offered limited partnership shares in the drilling program—a total that would be entirely consistent with a finding that the offering was private.

The defendants attempt to limit the number of offerees even further, however. They argue that Doran was the sole offeree because all others contacted by PMC were offered "participant" rather than "special participant" interests. The district court, which did not issue a finding of fact or conclusion of law with respect to this argument, appears to have assumed that there were eight offerees.[8]

The argument is, in any event, unsupported by the record. The only evidence that the defendants adduced to show the number of offerees established merely that offers of "participant" interests were made to four investors who accepted, and that offers of "limited partnership" interests were made to three other prospective investors who declined. Because both "participant" and "special participant" interests were limited partnership interests, we are unable to discern from the record whether the three declining investors were offered "special participant" interests. Moreover, we have no evidence that the four "participants" were not also offered "special participant" interests. The defendants have the burden of proof regarding the number of offerees. We must therefore reject the argument that Doran was [the] sole offeree.[9]

---

8   The Court below noted as a matter of fact that there were three declining "offerees" and four "participants" of the limited partnership. Although it thus appears to have assumed there were eight "offerees," the lower court also concluded as a matter of law that the offer of a special participant interest to Doran was private because Doran did not need the protections of the federal securities acts. Assuming the court did find that there were eight offerees, it thus ignored the interests of all but Doran in determining whether the single offering was private. On the other hand, it is possible that the court supposed that Doran was the sole offeree, although it offered no reasons for severing Doran's limited partnership interest from that offered to or purchased by the other investors. Nor does the record support such a distinction.

9   Even had the defendants shown that Doran was the only investor to have been offered a "special participant" interest, however, it is doubtful that the defendants would thereby have established that

(The footnote is continued on the next page.)

In considering the number of offerees solely as indicative of the magnitude or scope of an offering, the difference between one and eight offerees is relatively unimportant. Rejecting the argument that Doran was the sole offeree is significant, however, because it means that in considering the need of the offerees for the protection that registration would have afforded we must look beyond Doran's interests to those of all his fellow offerees. Even the offeree-plaintiff's 20-20 vision with respect to the facts underlying the security would not save the exemption if any one of his fellow offerees was in a blind.

B. The Offerees' Relationship to the Issuer

• • •

It is important, in light of our rejection of the argument that Doran was the sole offeree, that the district court also found that all four "participants" and all three declining offerees were sophisticated investors with regard to oil ventures.

• • •

1. The role of investment sophistication: The lower court's finding that Doran was a sophisticated investor is amply supported by the record, as is the sophistication of the other offerees. Doran holds a petroleum engineering degree from Texas A & M University. His net worth is in excess of $1,000,000. His holdings of approximately twenty-six oil and gas properties are valued at $850,000.

Nevertheless, evidence of a high degree of business or legal sophistication on the part of all offerees does not suffice to bring the offering within the private placement exemption. We clearly established that proposition in *Hill York Corp. v. American International Franchises, Inc.*, supra, 448 F.2d at 690. We reasoned that "if the plaintiffs did not possess the information requisite for a registration statement, they could not bring their sophisticated knowledge of business affairs to bear in deciding whether or not to invest. ..." Sophistication is not a substitute for access to the information that registration would disclose. *United States v. Custer Channel Wing Corp.*, supra, 376 F.2d at 678. As we said in *Hill York*, although the evidence of the offerees' expertise "is certainly

---

9   Continued ...

   Doran was the sole offeree with respect to the security in question. The two kinds of limited partnership interests were (1) offered as part of a single scheme of financing contemplated by the limited partnership agreement; (2) they appear to have been offered within a time span of a few months (3) for the same kind of consideration (4) and for the same general purpose. The only difference between the two kinds of limited partnership interests that appears on the record was that the "participants" were able to take a greater portion of intangible drilling deductions. Otherwise, according to the limited partnership agreement, the two kinds of limited partnership interests were identical. Accordingly, on the present state of the record we shall treat the eight offers of limited partnership shares in the Wyoming drilling venture as an integrated offering for purposes of determining the availability of the § 4(2) exemption. See generally Schwartz, *The Private Offering Exemption—Recent Developments*, 37 Ohio St. L.J. 1, 8-11 (1976).

favorable to the defendants, the level of sophistication will not carry the point. In this context, the relationship between the promoters and the purchasers and the 'access to the kind of information which registration would disclose' become highly relevant factors." 448 F.2d at 690.[10]

In short, there must be sufficient basis of accurate information upon which the sophisticated investor may exercise his skills. ...

2. The requirement of available information: The interplay between two factors, the relationship between offerees and issuer and the offerees' access to information that registration would disclose, has been a matter of some conceptual and terminological difficulty. For purposes of this discussion, we shall adopt the following conventions: We shall refer to offerees who have not been furnished registration information directly, but who are in a position relative to the issuer to obtain the information registration would provide, as having "access" to such information. By a position of access we mean a relationship based on factors such as employment, family, or economic bargaining power that enables the offeree effectively to obtain such information. See SEC Rule 146(e), 17 C.F.R. § 280.146(e) (1976). When offerees, regardless of whether they occupy a position of access, have been furnished with the information a registration statement would provide, we shall say merely that such information has been disclosed. When the offerees have access to or there has been disclosure of the information registration would provide, we shall say that such information was available.

• • •

In *Hill York Corp. v. American International Franchises, Inc.*, supra, 448 F.2d at 689, this court approved jury instructions that "correctly stated the ultimate test ... that every offeree had to have information equivalent to that which a registration statement would disclose." In subsequent cases we have adhered to the test. See *Woolf v. S.D. Cohn & Co.*, supra, 515 F.2d at 613; *SEC v. Continental Tobacco Co.*, supra, 463 F.2d at 158-61; *Henderson v. Hayden, Stone Inc.*, supra, 461 F.2d at 1071.[11]

Because the district court failed to apply this test to the case at bar, but rather inferred from evidence of Doran's sophistication that his purchase of a partnership share

---

10   We do not intimate that evidence of the offerees' sophistication is required in all cases to establish a private offering exemption under § 4(2). Indeed, we have said that SEC Rule 146, 17 C.F.R. § 230.146 (1976), is "more restrictive than the cases in this Curcuit in that it requires that the offeree either be sophisticated or advised by an offeree representative who is, in addition to the requirement that offerees receive or have access to information that registration would disclose." *Woolf v. S.D. Cohn & Co.*, supra, 515 F.2d at 611-12 n. 14. In other words, in *Hill York* we said that the "sophistication" of the offerees was not a sufficient condition for the availability of the private offering exemption; Rule 146 says that "sophistication" is a necessary but not a sufficient condition.

11   In *Henderson v. Hayden, Stone Inc.*, supra, the district court held that a transaction was not part of a public offering because "(1) the number of people involved in this capital venture was small, and all were sophisticated investors, (2) none of the defendants 'solicited for the sale of stock,' and (3) the amount of money invested by [plaintiff] was small vis-à-vis his total investment portfolio." We reversed

(The footnote is continued on the next page.)

was incident to a private offering, we must remand so that the lower court may determine the extent of the information available to each offeree.

More specifically, we shall require on remand that the defendants demonstrate that all offerees, whatever their expertise, had available the information a registration statement would have afforded a prospective investor in a public offering. Such a showing is not independently sufficient to establish that the offering qualified for the private placement exemption, but it is necessary to gain the exemption and is to be weighed along with the sophistication and number of the offerees, the number of units offered, and the size and manner of the offering. See *SEC v. Continental Tobacco Co.*, supra, 463 F.2d at 160; see also *Woolf v. S.D. Cohn & Co.*, supra, 515 F.2d at 610-613. Because in this case these latter factors weigh heavily in favor of the private offering exemption, satisfaction of the necessary condition regarding the availability of relevant information to the offerees would compel the conclusion that this offering fell within the exemption.

The cornerstone of the regulatory structure envisaged by the authors of the Securities Act is disclosure. That Act is practical and pragmatic, not dogmatic and doctrinaire. It is designed to give a panoply of protection to the investor, but also to allow play in the marts of trade for offers of securities that do not require the oversight of the Securities and Exchange Commission. In suggesting the scope of that exemption, we cannot divine all the variables of a formula that might enable a trial court precisely to determine whether a given offering falls within or without its perimeter. There are few certitudes, and in interpreting the statute we must permit ourselves room for the ifs, the perhapses, and the maybes in commercial relationships and variegated investor postures. The question of exemption remains one of fact reserved in the first instance for the trial court. Nevertheless, it cannot be doubted that within or without the perimeter of the private offering exemption, the policies of the Securities Act mandate that the courts focus on the information available to the offerees of a security.

C. On Remand: The Issuer-Offeree Relationship

In determining on remand the extent of the information available to the offerees, the district court must keep in mind that the "availability" of information means either disclosure of or effective access to the relevant information. The relationship between issuer and offeree is most critical when the issuer relies on the latter route.

---

11 Continued ...

because the defendants had failed to prove either the number of offerees or the offerees' relationship to the issuer. We said in part:

[T]he relationship between the offerees and the issue is not known. Did the offerees have any knowledge of the business affairs of [the issuer]? Did they possess the same information as would be found in a registration statement? Did they have access to such information?

461 F.2d at 1072. Although we were troubled by the fact that prior to his retirement plaintiff had been responsible for the investment portfolio of a loan company he owned and that this thoroughly sophisticated investor knew the stock was unregistered at the time of his purchase, we nevertheless permitted him to rescind.

To begin with, if the defendants could prove that all offerees were actually furnished the information a registration statement would have provided, whether the offerees occupied a position of access pre-existing such disclosure would not be dispositive of the status of the offering. If disclosure were proved and if, as here, the remaining factors such as the manner of the offering and the investment sophistication of the offerees weigh heavily in favor of the private status of the offering, the absence of a privileged relationship between offeree and issuer would not preclude a finding that the offering was private. ...

Alternatively it might be shown that the offeree has access to the files and records of the company that contained the relevant information. Such access might be afforded merely by the position of the offeree or by the issuer's promise to open appropriate files and records to the offeree as well as to answer inquiries regarding material information. In either case, the relationship between offeree and issuer now becomes critical, for it must be shown that the offeree could realistically have been expected to take advantage of his access to ascertain the relevant information.[12] Similarly the investment sophistication of the offeree assumes added importance, for it is important that he could have been expected to ask the right questions and seek out the relevant information.

• • •

1. Disclosure or access: a disjunctive requirement: ...

Both the Second and the Fourth Circuits, however, have interpreted *Ralston Purina* as embodying a disjunctive requirement. Thus, for example, in *Gilligan, Will & Co. v. SEC*, 267 F.2d 461, 466 (2nd Cir. 1959), cert. denied, 361 U.S. 896, 80 S.Ct. 200, 4 L.Ed.2d 152 (1960), the court observed that *Ralston Purina* "held that the governing fact is whether the persons to whom the offering is made are in such a position with respect to the issuer that they either actually have such information as a registration would have disclosed, or have access to such information." See also *SEC v. Tax Service, Inc.*, 357 F.2d 143, 144 (4th Cir. 1966).

• • •

2. The role of insider status: Once the alternative means of coming within the private placement exemption are clearly separated, we can appreciate the proper role to be accorded the requirement that the offerees occupy a privileged or "insider" status relative to the issuer. That is to say, when the issuer relies on "access" absent actual disclosure, he must show that the offerees occupied a privileged position relative to the issuer that afforded them an opportunity for effective access to the information registration would otherwise provide.[18] When the issuer relies on actual disclosure to come within the exemption, he need not demonstrate that the offerees held such a privileged position.

• • •

---

12 For example, the offeree's ability to compel the issuer to make good his promise may depend on the offeree's bargaining power or on his family or employment relationship to the issuer.

18 That all offerees are in certain respects "insiders" does not ensure that the issuer will gain the private placement exemption. An insider may be an insider with respect to fiscal matters of the company, but an

(The footnote is continued on the next page.)

We think that any such requirement would inhibit the ability of business to raise capital without the expense and delay of registration under circumstances in which the offerees did not need the protection of registration. The enactment of Rule 146 represents the SEC's recognition of this legitimate business need. We think that it would be unwise to adopt in this circuit a requirement of insider status notwithstanding disclosure or that of actual disclosure notwithstanding effective access. Such requirements would constrict the scope of the private offering exemption more narrowly than does Rule 146 and would retard necessary capital investment without a corresponding benefit to those investors who need the protection of registration.

* * *

The privileged status of the offerees must be demonstrated only when it is necessary to the claimant's efforts to establish that the requisite information was in fact available.

III. Breach of Contract

We affirm that portion of the district court's judgment rejecting Doran's claim that he was damaged by the defendants' overproduction of the wells in breach of the partnership agreement.

* * *

IV. Conclusion

An examination of the record and the district court's opinion in this case leaves unanswered the central question in all cases that turn on the availability of the § 4(2) exemption. Did the offerees know or have a realistic opportunity to learn facts essential to an investment judgment? We remand so that the trial court can answer that question.

This opinion focuses on facts because the Securities Act focuses on facts—facts disclosed, facts known, or access to facts. "Insider" or "outsider" labels are not determinative. Traditional forms are not determinative. In adjusting the generalities of § 4(2) to the realities of the contemporary market, we have seized on the availability to all offerees of pertinent facts. We have conditioned the private offering exemption on either actual disclosure of the information registration would provide or the offerees' effective access to such information. If the issuer has not disclosed but instead relies on the offerees' access, the privileged status of the offerees relative to the issuer must be shown.

---

18   Continued ...

outsider with respect to a particular issue of securities. He may know much about the financial structure of the company but his position may nonetheless not allow him access to a few vital facts pertaining to the transaction at issue. If Doran had effective access to all information that registration would provide, he would be a transactional insider. That is all we require regarding the availability of information. If, on the other hand, his inside knowledge was incomplete or his access ineffective, he would be a transactional outsider despite the fact that we might consider him an "insider" for other purposes.

We are conscious of the difficulty of formulating black letter law in this area in light of the multiplicity of security transactions and their multifarious natures. Securities regulation is often a matter of the hound chasing the hare as issuers devise new ways to issue their securities and the definition of a security itself expands. We do not want the private offering exemption to swallow the Securities Act, and we must resolve doubtful cases against the private placement claimant and in favor of the Act's paramount value of disclosure. By the same token, we must heed the existence and purposes of the exemption, and be cautious lest we discourage private avenues for raising capital. Our present emphasis on the availability of information as the *sine qua non* of the private offering is an attempt to steer a middle course.

We must reverse in part the judgment of the district court and remand for proceedings not inconsistent with this opinion.

Affirmed in part, reversed in part and remanded.

The "Friends and Associates" or "Common Bonds" Test. In *R. v. Piepgrass* (1959), 29 W.W.R. 218, 23 D.L.R. (2d) 220 a promoter sought funds by soliciting farmers in the province of Alberta, most, but not all, of whom were known to the promoter from prior business dealings. The Alberta Court of Appeal upheld the trial decision that found the solicitations involved distributions to the public. The Court set out a test known as the "friends and associates" or "common bonds" test. According to MacDonald, J.A.:

It is one thing for an individual or group of individuals to disclose information to friends or associates, seeking support for a private company being formed or in existence ... but it is quite another thing for a private company to go out on the highways and byways seeking to sell securities ... .

It is clear ... that it is impossible to define with any degree of precision what is meant by the term "offer for sale to the public." It follows that in each instance the Court will be called upon to determine whether or not the sale of securities to a private company transcended the ordinary sales of a private domestic concern to a person or persons having common bonds of interest or association. [23 D.L.R. (2d) at 227-28]

MacDonald went on to note that the persons sold to "were not in any sense friends or associates of the accused or persons having common bonds of interest or association" [29 W.W.R. 228].

2. Exemptions Based on No Need to Know the Information Contained in a Prospectus

Several of the exemptions from the prospectus requirement might be characterized as being based on the concept that the prospective investor has no need to know the kind of information that would be contained in a prospectus. For instance, the investor may be considered relatively sophisticated. The degree of sophistication is generally based on a combination of the dollar volume of securities to be purchased or the expertise of the particular investor. Purchasers of large dollar volumes of securities are often in a position to demand information from the issuer of the securities. A large dollar volume purchase also justifies expenditures on gathering information and having the information analyzed. An investor who has some expertise in the analysis of securities will also be better equipped to assess any information obtained from the issuer or gathered independently.

On this justification distributions of securities to financial institutions such as banks, insurance companies and trust companies are exempt from the prospectus requirement. See, e.g., ASA s. 107(1)(a); BCSA s. 55(2)(1); OSA s. 72(1)(a). Other organizations, such as mutual funds or pension funds, may also have sufficient securities expertise and buy securities in sufficient volumes to justify an exemption. These organizations can apply to securities administrators to be designated as exempt institutions such that distributions of securities to them will be exempt from the prospectus requirement. See, e.g., ASA s. 107(1)(c); BCSA s. 55(2)(3); OSA s. 71(1)(c).

Distributions of securities to purchasers who purchase a large dollar volume of securities are also exempt from the prospectus requirement. See ASA s. 107(1)(d) and ASA Reg. s. 122.1 (which provides that the minimum amount is $97,000); BCSA s. 55(2)(4) and BCSA Reg. s. 118(1) (which provides that the minimum amount is $97,000); OSA s. 72(1)(d) and OSA Reg. s. 27 (which provides that the minimum amount is $150,000). If there is advertising in connection with a distribution relying on the large dollar purchase exemption the issuer must provide investors with an offering memorandum that contains information similar to that contained in a prospectus and that provides the purchaser with a contractual right of action similar to the statutory civil right of action for misrepresentations in a prospectus. See, e.g., ASA Reg. s. 125; BCSA Reg. ss. 126, 127; OSA Reg. s. 32. A problem may arise where several individuals, each of whom has less than $150,000 to invest, combine to form a single enterprise whose sole purpose is to claim the exemption. The O.S.C. regards this as beyond the scope of the large dollar purchase exemption. See O.S.C. Policy s. 6.1(11)(B)(4).

Also, sales of securities by the issuer to an underwriter or by one underwriter to another in the course of a distribution are also exempt from the prospectus requirement. See ASA s. 107(1)(u.1); BCSA s. 55(2)(15); OSA s. 72(1)(r). These exemptions require that the purchaser of the securities is acting as principal in the purchase so that the purchaser is not acting as a conduit for distributions to persons who are presumed to need to know the kind of information that would be contained in a prospectus.

Sales of securities under the exemption for financial institutions, the exemption for designated exempt purchasers or the large dollar volume purchase exemption are referred to as private placements. Private placements have become an increasingly common way of distributing securities in Canada.

3. Common Bonds Exemptions

Persons who have so-called common bonds with the issuer may be in a position where they have access to information concerning the issuer, have some degree of control over the issuer or have some relationship with the issuer which reduces the need for protection in the form of disclosure by way of a prospectus. For instance, promoters of the issuer have access to information concerning the issuer and may have some influence with the issuer. Consequently there is an exemption from the prospectus requirement where a trade is made by an issuer to a promoter of the issuer. See ASA s. 107(1)(o); BCSA s. 55(2)(16); OSA s. 72(1)(o). Similarly, an exemption is provided where the person purchasing the securities is a "control person" with respect to the issuer. See, e.g., ASA s. 107(1)(v); BCSA s. 55(2)(17); OSA Reg. s. 14(b)(i). A control person is a person who holds a sufficient number of the voting securities attached to voting securities of the issuer to materially affect the control of the issuer. See, e.g., ASA s. 1(c.2); BCSA s. 1(1); OSA s. 1(1) "distribution."

4. Seed Capital Exemptions

Seed Capital Exemptions Generally. Canadian securities acts typically contain so-called seed capital exemptions that provide some scope for small issuers to raise capital. Compared to other aspects of securities legislation in Canada there is a substantial degree of variation in the available seed capital exemptions. In addition to providing some assistance to small issuers in raising capital, the seed capital exemptions incorporate an amalgam of the need to know and common bonds rationales for exemptions from the prospectus requirement.

Seed Capital Exemptions Under the OSA. For instance, under the OSA s. 72(1)(p) an exemption is available where the purchaser is a senior officer or director of the issuer, a spouse, parent, brother, sister, or child of a senior officer or director of the issuer, or a person who, by virtue of net worth or investment experience, or by virtue of consultation with or advice from a registered adviser or dealer who is not a promoter of the issuer, is able to evaluate the prospective investment on the basis of information respecting the investment presented by the issuer. The exemption is only available where solicitations are made to not more than 50 prospective purchasers and sales are made to not more than 25 purchasers. The transaction can not be accompanied by an advertisement or selling or promotional expenses other than for the professional services of a registered dealer. Each purchaser must purchase as principal and must be given access to "substantially the same information concerning the issuer that a prospectus filed under [the] Act would provide." The prospectus-like information is provided in the a document called an offering memorandum which must provide the purchaser with a contractual right of action substantially similar to the statutory civil right of action for misrepresentations in a prospectus. See OSA Reg. s. 32. Perhaps the most significant constraint on the OSA s. 72(1)(p) exemption is that an issuer may only rely it once.

A similar exemption is provided in OSA Reg. s. 14(f) with respect to "government incentive securities" with the modification that the issuer can solicit up to 75 prospective purchasers with sales to up to 50 purchasers. A "government incentive security" is one that is designed to allow the holder of the security to receive a grant, or a deduction or credit for tax purposes provided by the federal government, the government of Ontario or, pursuant to a designation of the O.S.C., the government of another province or territory.

Seed Capital Exemptions Under the ASA. ASA ss. 107(1)(p), (q) and (z)(v) provide a very similar exemption to the exemption under OSA s. 72(1)(p) described above. However, the exemption under the ASA is not limited to a one-time use but can be used once in every 12-month period. Also, under the ASA exemption the issuer can sell to up to 50 purchasers (see ASA Reg. s. 122.1(3)-(5)) and there is no limit on the number of prospective purchasers solicited. However, as under OSA s. 72(1)(p), the issuer must provide the purchaser with an offering memorandum containing information similar to the information that would be contained in a prospectus and must provide a contractual right of action to the purchaser that is substantially similar to the statutory civil right of action for misrepresentations in a prospectus.

Seed Capital Exemptions Under the BCSA. A similar seed capital exemption is provided under BCSA Reg. s. 117(a) for sophisticated investors and relatives of directors and senior officers. The exemption is available for up to 50 purchasers in every 12-month period. In addition, BCSA Reg. s. 117(b) provides an exemption for sales to an unlimited number of sophisticated investors who purchase at least $25,000 worth of the securities. Both exemptions require the issuer to provide the purchaser with an offering memorandum that contains information substantially similar to the information that would be contained in a prospectus and must provide the purchaser with a contractual right of action that is substantially similar to the statutory civil right of action for misrepresentations in a prospectus. See BCSA Reg. s. 126 and Form 43.

Criticisms of the Seed Capital Exemptions. These exemptions and the financing constraints imposed on small issuers by the limited scope of these exemptions is discussed in J.G. MacIntosh, *Legal and Institutional Barriers to Financing Innovative Enterprise in Canada* (1994). See also Buckley, *Small Issuers Under the Ontario Securities Act 1978: A Plea for Exemptions*, 29 U. of Toronto L.J. 309 (1979); Emerson, *Vendor Beware: The Issue and Sale of Securities Without a Prospectus Under the Securities Act, 1978 (Ontario)*, 57 Can. Bar Rev. 195 (1979); Grover & Baillie, *Disclosure Requirements*, in *Proposals for a Securities Market Law for Canada*, Vol. 3 379 (1979).

These seed capital exemptions were based on Rule 146 under the Securities Act of 1933. Rule 146 was subjected to severe criticism for substantially reducing the access of small issuers to capital markets. See, e.g., Campbell, *The Plight of Small Issuers Under the Securities Act of 1933: Practical Foreclosure from the Capital Market*, [1977] Duke L.J. 1139; Marsh, *Who Killed the Private Offering Exemption? A Legal Whodunit*, 71 Nw. U. L. Rev. 470 (1976). The Rule has therefore been repealed by Regulation D, which also restates several other small offering exemptions. Rule 504 of Regulation D exempts offerings not exceeding $1,000,000 unaccompanied by general advertising. Rule 505 provides an exemption for offerings of up to $5,000,000 without any required disclosure if all purchasers are "accredited investors," and with specified disclosure if there are unaccredited investors. "Accredited investors" are defined to include financial institutions such as banks and insurance companies, directors or senior officers of the issuer and individuals whose net worth exceeds $1,000,000 or whose income exceeds $200,000 a year. No more than 35 purchasers may be unaccredited. Finally, Rule 506, which replaces Rule 146, permits trades to no more than 35 purchasers if the issuer reasonably believes that each purchaser who is not an unaccredited investor has such knowledge and experience in financial and business matters that he is capable of evaluating the merits and risks of the prospective investment. Certain information must be disclosed if the purchaser is not an "accredited investor." See T.L. Hazen, *The Law of Securities Regulation*, 178-82 (1990).

5. Private Issuer Exemption

A private issuer exemption is available where the issuer is not a reporting issuer or a mutual fund and its issued and outstanding securities are subject to a restriction on transfer. Its securities must not be directly or indirectly beneficially owned by more than 50 persons and it must not have distributed any of its securities "to the public." The exemption is available "where the securities are not offered for sale to the public." Thus under this exemption the interpretation of the meaning of "to the public" remains relevant. See ASA ss. 1(1)(p.1), 66(j) and 115(1)(a); BCSA ss. 1(1) "private issuer," 32(j) and 58(1)(a); OSA ss. 1(1) "private issuer," 35(2) and 73(1).

Use of the private issuer exemption can avoid the offering memorandum requirements of the seed capital exemption. However, use of the private issuer exemption does entail risks. The primary difficulty with the private offering exemption is that it applies only when all investors are able to fend for themselves. For example, the exemption might be unavailable on an issue of shares to 10 investors, because one or two of them lack financial sophistication. The unsophisticated purchasers could then rescind. But so too could the sophisticated investors, for they did not receive a prospectus either. *Henderson v. Hayden, Stone Inc.*, 461 F.2d 1069 (5th Cir. 1972). Unless all offerees qualify under the exemption, any one of them would be able to rescind. The domino effect of rescinding investors might place much of the capital of the small issuer at risk.

In considering the need of investors for protection, the focus of attention in the United States has generally been on offerees rather than on purchasers, even if "it is difficult to see how an offeree who does not buy is hurt." See American Law Institute Federal Securities Code, s. 227(b)(1)(A), Comment 2, 16. Since the onus of proof is on the party who relies on the exemption, it is unlikely to be available when there are many offerees and quite out of the question when their number is not known. Any form of general advertising is therefore incompatible with a private offering. In the same way, the basic prohibition in the OSA is against trading in unregistered securities, with trading defined to include mere solicitation. One offer, even without a subsequent sale, may then be a trade. As a consequence, the ability of offerees as well as purchasers to fend for themselves would appear relevant in Ontario as in the United States.

What kind of sophistication must offerees have for the private offering exemption to be available? In *Andrews v. Blue*, 489 F.2d 367, 373 n.3 (10th Cir. 1973), the District Court stated that although the offeree "was a sophisticated real estate investor, he was a babe in the woods when it came to stocks." Sophistication is not fungible, and a firm that claims the exemption may then have to show that its investors were sophisticated for that particular kind of investment. Is the wealth of the offerees of relevance in determining their need for protection, if not of their financial sophistication?

6. Other Exemptions

There are also a variety of other exemptions for various purposes. For instance, certain exemptions are provided on the basis that a prospectus would provide little or no information that was not already provided to investors in an earlier prospectus or through various continuous disclosure documents. Exemptions of this sort include exemptions with respect to stock dividends, rights offerings, the exercise of conversion privileges or purchase rights, or plans under which the investor can direct that dividends or interest to which the investor is entitled be reinvested in securities of the issuer that are of the same type as those the investor already owns.

In other cases the exemption is provided because some document other than a prospectus will provide essentially the same information a prospectus does. For instance, a proxy circular used in connection with an amalgamation or reorganization would provide information similar to that required for a prospectus. Similarly, a take-over bid circular used in connection with a take-over bid in which the bidder offers its securities in exchange for securities of the target corporation must contain prospectus-type disclosure with respect to the securities being offered.

While the sale of securities to employees on a broad scale was not permitted in the *Ralston Purina* case, Canadian securities acts generally provide an exemption for distributions of securities of an issuer to employees of the issuer or an affiliate of the issuer. The employee can not be induced to purchase by expectation of employment or continued employment. ASA s. 107(1)(n); BCSA s. 55(2)(9)(i); OSA s. 72(1)(n). A proposal that the U.S. Securities Act of 1933 be amended to permit various trades to employees was rejected in 1934: "The conferees eliminated the ... amendment ... on the ground that the participants in employee stock-investment plans may be in as great need of the protection afforded by availability of information concerning the issuer for which they work as are most other members of the public." H.R. Rep. No. 1838, 73d Cong., 2d Sess., at 41 (1934). The employee exemption in Canada is founded instead on a belief that "[i]t is desirable that employees should be readily permitted to invest in the company in which they are employed." See the *Report of the Committee of the Ontario Securities Commission on the Problems of Disclosure Raised for Investors by Business Combinations and Private Placements* (the Merger Report) 108 (1970). The denial of the exemption in cases where employees are "induced to purchase by expectation of employment or continued employment" will prevent the grossest abuses of the employer's bargaining leverage.

7. Exemption Orders

While the securities acts and regulations set out several exemptions from the prospectus requirement there can be other situations in which the costs of compliance with the prospectus requirement will be considered excessive relative to the benefits the prospectus is presumed to provide. Securities acts in Canada provide securities administrators with the power to grant exemptions where they consider it "in the public interest" to do so. See ASA s. 116(1); BCSA s. 59; OSA s. 74.

8. Integration of Trades

Suppose that securities are issued under more than one exemption to different groups of investors. Thus shares may be taken up by employees under s. 71(1)(n) and non-employees under s. 71(1)(p). Must all trades be exempted by one provision, such that registration in the above case is required if there are more than 25 purchasers? The O.S.C. has announced that it will not integrate trades in this fashion, permitting, with minor exceptions, concurrent reliance on different exemptions. See Ont. Policy s. 6.1, Part IIA.

F. RESALES AND THE CLOSED SYSTEM

As noted above, most Canadian securities acts have adopted the closed system. Prior to the adoption of the closed system there were situations in which securities could be sold pursuant to an exemption or on the basis that the offering of the securities did not constitute a "primary distribution to the public." The purchasers of the securities might then sell the securities to other investors who were of the type that would normally be considered to need the protection afforded by the securities acts. If the initial purchaser were a mere conduit for a broader distribution to the ultimate purchasers in the resale, the distribution would be considered to embrace "the entire process by which in the course of a public offering the block of securities is dispersed and ultimately comes to rest in the hands of the investing public." *In the Matter of Ira Haupt & Co.*, 23 S.E.C. 589 (1946). The initial purchaser might then be found to be an "underwriter" under s. 2(11) of the 1993 Act unless he purchased with the requisite "investment intent." What this requirement came to mean is discussed in the following excerpt from Buckley, *Small Issuers Under the Ontario Securities Act, 1978: A Plea for Exemptions*, 29 U. of Toronto L.J. 309, 339-41 (1979):

While "distribution" is not defined in the 1933 act, the term is considered synonymous with public offering. The obligation to file a prospectus on a "distribution to the public" in the 1966 act was therefore an attempt to reproduce American practice. Practice offerings were then not in the course of a "distribution" or "distribution to the public" under the two statutes. A resale of securities taken under the exemption may, however, result in a distribution under the 1933 act. One "who has purchased from an issuer with a view to ... the distribution of any security" is an underwriter. On a re-sale by him, the exemption under section 4(1) for "transactions by any person other than an issuer, underwriter, or dealer" will be unavailable. And since the participation of an underwriter in an issue of securities gives rise to a distribution, the private offering exemption of section 4(2) will be retro-actively lost on a reoffer by the underwriter to an investor who is unable to find for himself. An issuer relying on the exemption must therefore ensure that at the time of acquisition each purchaser takes the securities for investment and not with a view to their further distribution.

Notwithstanding admonitions against self-serving statements, it was for some time thought that an issuer might insulate itself from liability by requiring each purchaser to sign a letter stating that he intended to hold the securities for investment. These assumptions were exploded in *Crowell-Collier Publishing Co.*: "An issuer may not establish a claim to [the private offering exemption] merely by collecting so-called 'investment representations' from a limited group of purchasers if in fact a distribution by such persons occurs. ... Counsel, issuers and underwriters, who rely on investment representations ... as a basis for claim to non-public offering exemption ... do so at their peril."[176] But if not conclusive, investment letters are still evidence of the purchaser's

---

176 Securities Act Release No. 3825 (12 August 1957), CCH Fed. Sec. L. Rep. para. 76,539 [1957-8 Transfer Binder.]. See also *U.S. v. Custer Channel Wing Corp.*, 376 F.2d 675, at 679 (4th Cir. 1967).

investment intent. So too are restrictive legends on share certificates and stop-transfer instructions to transfer agents. The length of time during which the securities are held is also useful evidence of investment intent. A quick resale suggests that they were taken for speculation and not investment. A purchaser who takes securities with the intention of retaining them may, of course, experience a "change of circumstances" which requires him to sell them after a short holding period. The change must, however, be unforeseen and not related to the normal investment risks borne by the purchaser. As a result, most events which would lead an investor to sell his securities would not permit a plea of changed circumstances: "[A]n advance or decline in market price or a change in the issuer's operating results do not usually provide an acceptable basis for such claim. ... Possible inability of the purchaser to pay off loans incurred in connection with the purchase of the stock would ordinarily not be deemed an unforeseeable change of circumstances" [Securities Act Release No. 4552 (6 November 1962), 1 CCH Fed. L. Rep. para. 2,779]. Counsel for the issuer must therefore make certain that all investors are able to bear the investment risk without selling the securities. The exemption may even be lost if one of the purchasers asks how long he must hold them, since the question presupposes an interest in trading them.

Canadian lawyers may readily sympathize with the perplexity felt by their American brethren in exploring investors' motives. Investment intent was expressly required upon a private placement in the 1966 act [sections 19(3) and 58(1)(a)]. It was initially believed that the securities might be resold with a six-month period prescribed by the Toronto Stock Exchange. These views were however rejected by the OSC in *In the Matter of Warren Explorations Ltd.* [1976 O.S.C.B. 111], which adopted the subjective American test. The OSC subsequently announced that it would make enquiries on a resale within two years of the original purchase. But "whatever the duration of the holding period, the placee should furnish a detailed and reasonable explanation for the change in investment intent." If Americans found the test unclear, the Disclosure Report stated that "[t]here appears to be the same genuine confusion among Canadian legal practitioners."*

Investment intent would also appear to have been necessary under the private offering exemption, though little attention was paid to the requirement and investment letters were never prepared. A purchaser who took securities with a view to their distribution to the public was an underwriter, and, as in the 1933 act, his resale to one not able to fend for himself excluded the exemption on the initial allotment. Moreover, securities taken under the private offering exemption could not be resold to a member of the public without a prospectus. The 1966 act defined a "distribution to the public" as "trades that are made for the purpose of distributing to the public securities issued by a company and not previously distributed to the public." The Disclosure Report stated that securities taken under most exemptions, were distributed to the public. A resale of such securities to one not able to fend for himself would therefore not result in a distribution to the public. Securities issued under the private offering exemption were, however, "not previously distributed to the public," and a resale to a member of the public would require a prospectus.

If the secondary market transactions did not involve a "primary distribution to the public" there was no requirement to provide a prospectus. Further, if the issuer had not made a distribution to the public and the issuer's securities were not listed on a stock

---

*   *Report of the Committee of the Ontario Securities Commission on the Problems of Disclosure Raised for Investors by Business Combinations and Private Placements* 68 (1979) ("Disclosure Report").

exchange, the continuous disclosure requirements normally did not apply. Thus some secondary market trades might not be supported by a build-up of information about the issuer and its securities through continuous disclosure requirements.

The closed system approach addresses the uncertainty associated with whether resales might be construed as being part of a "primary distribution to the public" and the potential gap in the availability of information about the issuer and its securities if the resales were not construed as part of a primary distribution to the public. The system is closed in that a person who purchases securities pursuant to an exemption can only resell the security within a closed market of persons who do not need the protection a prospectus would provide unless information about the issuer and its securities has been provided by way of a prospectus or a build up of continuous disclosure. The purchaser of a security pursuant to an exemption from the prospectus requirement thus has three options. One is to sell to a person in respect of whom an exemption from the prospectus requirement is available. The second option is to provide a prospectus and the third is to hold the security for a prescribed period of time to allow a sufficient build-up of information by way of continuous disclosure to protect investors who need prospectus-like disclosure.

The securities acts bring the closed system into effect by deeming sales of securities purchased by a person pursuant to an exemption to be distributions. ASA ss. 109, 109.1, 110 and 111; BCSA Reg. ss. 133, 134; OSA ss. 72(4), (5), and (6) and OSA Reg. ss. 17, 19a. As a "distribution" the transaction will be subject to the prospectus requirement (see Section C above). Thus the seller of the security must either provide the prospectus as required or rely on an exemption from the prospectus requirement. The securities acts bring the third option into effect by providing that the sale of securities purchased by a person pursuant to an exemption is a distribution unless the transaction meets certain requirements that are intended to assure an adequate build-up of information about the securities and the issuer.

The conditions under which the resale of the securities will not be deemed to be a "distribution" are that (1) the issuer must be a reporting issuer (and thus subject to the continuous disclosure requirements (see Section D above)); (2) if the reporting issuer is in default of any of its reporting requirements, the seller is not an insider of the issuer; (3) the seller must have held the securities for a prescribed period of time from the later of the date the issuer became a reporting issuer and the date the seller acquired the securities; and (4) there has been no unusual effort to prepare the market or create a demand for the securities and no extraordinary commission or consideration has been paid in respect of the trade.

The applicable hold periods vary from jurisdiction to jurisdiction. In British Columbia the hold period is 12 months from the later of the date the issuer became a reporting issuer and the date the seller acquired the securities. See, e.g., BCSA s. 133(2). Ontario and Alberta have hold periods of 6, 12 and 18 months depending on the nature of the securities. See, e.g., ASA s. 109(3); OSA s. 72(4)(b).

As noted above (see Section C), the sale of securities by a control person also constitutes a distribution. Thus a control person selling securities is required either to provide a prospectus or to rely on an exemption from the prospectus requirement. However, sales of securities by control persons can also be made upon compliance with certain resale conditions. For instance, the OSA provides an exemption from the prospectus requirement for control persons if the issuer has been a reporting issuer for a period of 18 months and the control person files a notice of intention to sell at least 7 days, and no more than 14 days, before the trade. The control person must certify that she, he or it has no knowledge of any material change that has occurred in the affairs of the issuer which has not been generally disclosed. Further, there can be no unusual effort to prepare the market or create a demand for the securities and no extraordinary commission or consideration can be paid in respect of the trade. See OSA s. 72(7)(b); and see also, e.g., ASA s. 112; BCSA Reg. ss. 117(d), (c) and (e).

G. THE POP SYSTEM, SHELF OFFERINGS AND THE PREP PROCEDURES

As a consequence of regulatory competition from other markets, securities commissions in Canada were subjected to considerable pressure to streamline their prospectus review procedures. While the review of a preliminary prospectus normally takes four to six weeks, the unregulated Eurodollar market can be accessed by large Canadian issuers in a few days. In addition, regulatory restraint in the United States caused the S.E.C. to decide, in 1980, that it was no longer able to provide a detailed review of all registration statements, and opted for selective review. Senior Canadian issuers could then file a prospectus with the S.E.C. and issue securities within a few days if the S.E.C. informed the issuer that a detailed review would be waived. Further, in 1982, the S.E.C. adopted a "shelf registration" system, which greatly shortened the time needed to prepare an offering document in the case of issuers that had complied with the continuous disclosure requirements.

With these developments major Canadian issuers found it much easier to take advantage of market "windows" when their securities were issued offshore in the United States or Europe. Canadian securities administrators responded in 1982 with the introduction of the Prompt Offering Prospectus (or "POP"). The POP system is designed to reduce the time required to vet a preliminary prospectus. In 1983, after the first full year of operation of the POP system, it accounted for 33% of the total dollar value of all registered issues in Ontario. By 1985 this had increased to 62%. See Steen & McKee, *The Prompt Offering Qualification System (1981-1985)*, [1986] 9 O.S.C.B. 1-97. Competitive pressures also eventually led to the adoption of a shelf offering system in 1991. A system to allow the pricing of securities after a receipt is given for the final prospectus was also introduced in conjunction with the shelf offering system in response to concerns with respect to the exposure to market price fluctuations between the time the final prospectus is filed and the time a receipt for the final prospectus is given.

1. The POP System

The system allowing for the use of a prompt offering prospectus (the "POP system") is brought into effect by legislation in Alberta and Quebec. However, in the other provinces the POP system relies on a National Policy statement (National Policy No. 47), which is brought into effect by securities administrators by way of a blanket order using the power to grant an exemption from the prospectus requirements.

The idea behind the POP system is that it takes advantage of the continuous disclosure documents that provide information on the issuer and its financial status. The prospectus can then simply contain information on the particular security to be offered and incorporate by reference the information on the issuer and its financial status contained in the continuous disclosure documents. The prospectus under the POP system is referred to as the short form prospectus and, because it is a shorter document, it can be vetted more quickly by securities administrators. Documents incorporated by reference in the prompt offering short form prospectus are deemed to be part of the prospectus for the purpose of the statutory civil action for misrepresentations in a prospectus.

Continuous disclosure under the POP system is supplemented by an annual information form (or "AIF"—discussed Section D above). The AIF includes information such as information on the incorporation of the issuer, a narrative description of the business, the development of the business of the issuer over the previous five years, financial information, information about the directors and officers and their ownership of securities of the issuer, information about the subsidiaries of the issuer and other information about the issuer. It can incorporate by reference information contained in the issuer's financial statements and proxy circular for the year.

Not every issuer can distribute securities using a prompt offering prospectus. One of the important concepts behind the POP system is that there must be a sufficient build up of information by way of continuous disclosure to allow the market to assess the value of securities offered by the issuer. Thus under National Policy 47 one test of eligibility to qualify for the POP system is that the issuer must have been a reporting issuer in a jurisdiction in Canada for at least 12 months. The issuer must also not be in default of any of its continuous disclosure obligations. This is intended to provide a build-up of information consisting of one year of interim financial statements together with an annual financial statement, one proxy circular, an annual information form and any material change reports during the year.

Another important concept behind the POP system is that there must be a sufficient market following of the issuer that information contained in the continuous disclosure documents will be reflected in the market price of the securities reasonably quickly. Thus another test of eligibility to use the POP system is a test of market following. One test of market following is that the issuer has a "public float" of equity securities having a value of at least $75,000,000. The securities of holders of 10% or more the issuer's equity securities are not counted in the public float on the assumption that these securities are not likely to be traded on a regular basis. The volume of securities available for trading is a common rule of thumb test used by investment analysts to determine whether there is potential for sufficient trading gains to cover the costs of gathering and assessing information with respect to the issuer. Another test of market following relies on the issuer's having an approved rating for offerings of non-convertible debt or preferred shares. This test substitutes rating organization analysis for the public float test of market following. The rating serves as a signal from the rating organization as to the value of the securities. The dependability of the ratings is protected by rating organization's reputation, which will depend on the quality of its ratings.

2. Shelf Offerings

Shelf offerings are provided for under National Policy No. 44. In a shelf offering the issuer files a short form prompt offering prospectus for a specified number of securities of a particular type that it expects to distribute over the ensuing two year period. The short form prospectus omits information that relates to the separate issues of the securities that will occur over the ensuing two years. Later, when the issuer chooses to issue some of the securities qualified under the short form shelf prospectus, it provides the omitted information in a prospectus supplement. The short form shelf prospectus is vetted by securities administrators, but the prospectus supplements, giving the information relating to each separate distribution of the securities, are not normally vetted by securities administrators. Thus when an issuer chooses to issue securities that have been qualified under a shelf prospectus, the securities can be brought to market in a very short space of time.

To be eligible to file a short form shelf prospectus the issuer must be eligible to use the POP system. These eligibility criteria are intended to assure that the market has a base of information from continuous disclosure incorporated by reference in the short form shelf prospectus and that there is a sufficient market following to assimilate the information in both the shelf prospectus and the prospectus supplement reasonably quickly.

Under the shelf offering procedures an issuer can also issue variable term debt where terms such as interest rates, price, denominations and currency will be determined at the time of sale. The issuer files the short form shelf prospectus for the debt security and issues a prospectus supplement when an issue of the securities is proposed. Terms determined at the time of sale are then set out in a pricing supplement. An issuer can also use the shelf offering procedures to make a non-fixed price issue of equity securities.

As with the POP system, continuous disclosure, the annual information form and the prospectus supplement incorporated by reference are deemed to be part of the prospectus for the purpose of the statutory civil action for misrepresentations in a prospectus.

3. Post Receipt Pricing Procedures

The post receipt pricing procedures ("PREP Procedures") are set out along with the shelf offering procedures in National Policy No. 44. These procedures are intended to reduce the risk of fluctuations in the market price of securities between the time the final prospectus is filed and the time a receipt is given for the final prospectus. While this may only take a few days it creates an added risk for the issuer or underwriter since, under the normal prospectus procedures, the final prospectus must set out the price at which the securities will be offered. While this concern might be addressed by preparing and filing an amended prospectus, this step can be costly and potentially dilatory. The PREP procedures reduce this risk by allowing the issuer to file a final prospectus that does not set out the price and any price related information. The issuer is then allowed to price the issue after receiving the receipt for the final prospectus. The price and price-related information are released in a "supplemented PREP prospectus" within five business days of receiving a receipt for the final prospectus.

As with the POP system, the eligibility of issuers for the PREP procedures is based on a sufficient market following of the issuer for the price related information to be quickly assimilated by the market when the price and price related information are provided. Thus an issuer is eligible to use the PREP procedures if it is eligible to use the POP system. Presumably since the amount and nature of the information that the market must assimilate under the PREP procedures is less significant than under the POP system, there is a more lenient eligibility requirement for use of the PREP procedures. An issuer is eligible to use the PREP procedures if it has equity securities outstanding that are listed and posted for trading on a recognized stock exchange. The recognized stock exchanges include the Toronto Stock Exchange, the Montreal Exchange, the senior board of the Vancouver Stock Exchange, the New York Stock Exchange and the American Stock Exchange.

H. A RECONSIDERATION OF THE NEED FOR MANDATORY DISCLOSURE

As seen above, securities regulation in both Canada and the United States mandates disclosure when securities are distributed to the investing public. This approach to securities regulation has been subject to question. First, studies of the effects of the introduction of mandatory disclosure under the U.S. Securities Act of 1933 suggest that mandatory disclosure in a prospectus on the distribution of securities had no statistically significant effect on the prices of new issues of securities. These studies also found that the risk of new issues of securities went down after the enactment of the Securities Act of 1933. See G.J. Stigler, *Public Regulation of Securities Markets*, 37 J. of Bus. 117 (1964); G.A. Jarrell, *The Economic Effects of Federal Regulation of the Market for New Security Issues*, 24 J. of Law and Eco. 613 (1981); C.J. Simon, *The Effect of the 1933 Securities Act on Investor Information and the Performance of New Issues*, 79 Am. Econ. Rev. 295 (1989). For a critical comment on the study by Stigler see I. Friend & E.S. Herman, *The S.E.C. Through a Glass Darkly*, 37 J. of Bus. 382 (1964). While the reduction in risk might be considered a benefit derived from the Securities Act of 1933, it has been suggested that this reduction in risk was largely the result of rejections of new issues of securities in riskier industries such as mining, oil and gas and merchandising with no evidence that these issues were overpriced before the enactment of the Securities Act of 1933. Similarly, there appeared to be a shift of riskier bond issues to the unregulated market of private placements. See *id.*, Jarrell.

A study of the effects of mandated disclosure of financial information also suggested that there were no statistically significant effects on the prices. The study compared firms that had voluntarily disclosed sales information prior to the U.S. Securities Exchange Act of 1934 with firms that had not disclosed sales information. It was hypothesized that if mandatory disclosure under the Securities Exchange Act of 1934 was beneficial, the prices of securities of the non-disclosing firms would go up relative to firms that had voluntarily disclosed the information. However, there was no statistically significant difference in the effects on the prices or risk of securities in the two groups of firms. See Benston, *Required Disclosure and the Stock Market: An Evaluation of the Securities Exchange Act of 1934*, 63 Am. Econ. Rev. 132 (1973). For a critical comment on Benston's study see I. Friend & R. Westerfield, *Required Disclosure and the Stock Market: Comment*, 65 Am. Econ. Rev. 467 (1975).

The following excerpts reassess the usefulness of mandatory disclosure after several years of experience with mandatory disclosure under U.S. securities laws.

Beaver, The Nature of Mandated Disclosure
Report of the Advisory Committee on Corporate Disclosure to the SEC,
95th Cong., 1st Sess. 618-56 (House Comm. Print 95-29 1977)

When the Securities Act of 1933 was enacted, Congress felt that a mandated disclosure system was needed to protect the public against fraud in the sale of securities. The Securities Exchange Act of 1934 adopted a year later continued to reflect this philosophy. ...

The current mandated disclosure system consists of a series of highly technical documents which are filed with the SEC and reside in its archives. Many investors, the intended beneficiaries of the Securities Acts, usually do not read and, in the case of 10-K, 10-Q and 8-K filings under the 1934 Act, do not usually even receive copies of these filings. There is an implicit reliance on the functioning of the professional investment community in order to justify the current system as an effective mechanism for disclosure. Moreover, this community often relies on investment information that is more comprehensive and in some cases more timely than that contained in the mandated filings. Under these conditions, the question arises concerning the role of the SEC and its mandated disclosure system in the entire framework. Why is it desirable to have a portion of that disclosure system contain a mandated set of disclosures?

There have been two common forms of justification for the desirability of disclosure regulation.

The first approach consists of citing a litany of perceived abuses. Several questions can be raised in connection with such an approach. Were the actions in question in fact "abuses"? What one person might label "manipulation" another might label "arbitrage." In particular, what harm was inflicted as a result of such actions? Was inadequate disclosure a contributing factor to the abuses? In other words, will mandating disclosure of some form deter or reduce such activities? What was the frequency of abuses relative to some measure of total activity? This is potentially important because mandated disclosure tends to be imposed on broad classes of corporations, not merely those who committed the perceived abuse.

However, more fundamentally, the point is that perfection is unattainable. Any corporate disclosure system, even one with a mandated portion, will incur some frequency of abuse. It is not clear that there has been a decline in the frequency of abuse over the 44 years since the inception of the Acts, and in the presence of increased regulation of corporate disclosure. Moreover, it is as inappropriate to judge a disclosure system solely on the basis of its perceived abuses as it would be to judge the merits of a public agency, such as the SEC, solely on the basis of its perceived worst regulations. The central issue is whether there is some flaw in the private sector forces that would lead to the conclusion that governmental regulation is a more desirable solution.

A second approach is to define the objectives of the corporate disclosure system and by implication the role of mandated disclosure. For example, "informed, rational investment decisions" is one frequently cited objective. However, again the central issue is why is governmental regulation necessary or desirable to achieve this objective?

Rationale for Disclosure Regulation

This section will attempt to develop a framework for the consideration of issues regarding disclosure regulation. In order to do so, the nature of economic problems and the purpose of government with respect to those problems will be briefly discussed.

Economic issues fall into two major categories: issues of efficiency and issues of equity. The first category is concerned with the most efficient means of achieving some specified result, where movement to a more efficient solution could in principle result in everyone in the economy being in a more preferred position (or at least as preferred a position) with no one being in a less preferred position (often called a Pareto-optimal solution). The second category deals with the choice among efficient solutions, where each solution will leave some individuals better off but others worse off. Issues as to how wealth should be distributed among individuals in the economy would be one example of an issue of equity. The government becomes involved in both types of issues. However, the rationale for governmental intervention can vary considerably depending upon the type of issue involved. Therefore it is imperative to state the extent to which the rationale for disclosure regulation rests on efficiency or equity considerations.

In general, the government has a variety of means available to deal with these issues, including the enforcement of private contracts, the definition and enforcement of property rights, taxation, regulation, and direct ownership. The Securities Acts provide two primary methods by which the flow of information to investors is effected. First are the general anti-fraud provisions; the second is the power to explicitly mandate corporate disclosure via the SEC filings and annual reports to shareholders.

With respect to the first method, the Securities Acts provide that it is unlawful to make a false or misleading statement or to omit a material fact in connection with the sale of a security. Laws against fraud are commonplace in the sale of a variety of commodities and they reflect concern over the pervasive problem that the quality of the product or service being sold is uncertain. Moreover, often one party to the transaction may naturally be in a position of superior information regarding the quality. Under anti-fraud provisions, certain parties to the transaction face the prospect of civil or criminal penalties when and if the quality of the commodity is eventually discovered and their behavior is deemed "fraudulent."

While the deterrence of fraud via legal liability is fairly commonplace, the presence of a regulatory mechanism that explicitly mandates the nature of what must be disclosed is a rather special feature of securities regulations. For example, neither federal nor state laws require filing a prospectus when an individual sells a home, even though the seller is in a potentially superior position with respect to information regarding the quality of the home.

The [next] subsection deals with arguments that potentially provide a rationale for disclosure regulation, which by implication asserts that reliance solely on the anti-fraud provisions is inadequate. The arguments fall into three major categories. (1) Corporation disclosures induce externalities and therefore have aspects of a public good. (2) Left unregulated, market forces would lead to an asymmetrical or uneven possession of information among investors. (3) Corporate management has incentives to suppress unfavorable information.

Corporate Disclosure Externalities

An externality exists when the actions of one party have effects on other parties, who are not charged (or compensated) via the price mechanism. While in principle it would be possible to conceive of an elaborate price system that would charge or compensate the third parties for these effects, it may be undesirable to do so because it is too costly or simply unfeasible.

However, without some form of collective action, the party undertaking the action has no incentive to internalize the effects on third parties, and it may lead to an inefficiency. For example, in the classic public good analysis with positive external effects on third parties, there will be an underproduction of the public good in the absence of a collective action that incorporates the third parties, who benefit from the public good but do not participate in the decision to produce or pay for it. For this reason, these third parties are often referred to as "free riders." In this situation, the private incentives are less than the social incentives to produce the public good.

In the disclosure context, two examples are frequently offered. Externalities could occur when information about the productive opportunities of one firm convey information about the productive opportunities of other firms. Shareholders in the disclosing firm pay the costs of disclosure but shareholders in other firms do not, even though they are affected by the disclosure. For example, disclosure by a firm about its success (or lack thereof) with respect to some product development may provide information to other firms about their chances of success in similar product developments. In fact, it might even obviate their having to expend resources on product developments. Thus the familiar objection to disclosure on grounds of competitive disadvantage is one form of externality. In this setting there will be a lack of incentive to fully disclose because of the benefits of disclosure to other firms for which the disclosing firm is not being compensated.

The second example deals with positive external effects on prospective shareholders. Investors demand information in order to assess the risks and rewards (i.e., the array of potential future cash flows) associated with alternative portfolios of securities. In making consumption and investment decisions, the investor finds information about a security useful whether or not that particular security ultimately is one of the securities in the portfolio chosen by the investor. The process of selecting the "best" portfolio inherently involves a consideration of investment alternatives (i.e., alternative portfolios). Therefore information on securities in these alternative portfolios may be valuable at the decision making stage, even though after-the-fact some of those securities may not be included in the portfolio chosen. In this setting, current shareholders bear the costs of disclosure, yet prospective shareholders share in the benefits of disclosure (i.e., they are free riders). If the prospective shareholders neither participate in the decision to disclose nor share in bearing the costs, there will tend to be less disclosure than there would be under a collective agreement which included them. They would be willing to pay for additional disclosure such that everyone (both current and prospective shareholders) would be in a more preferred position (i.e., a more efficient solution would be attained).

There are a number of additional issues to be introduced in considering an externality or public good approach to disclosure regulation.

• • •

First, what is the materiality of the externality or public good aspects to corporate disclosure? Currently, little empirical evidence exists to assess the importance of potential externalities.

Second, issues of cost must be introduced. These include the direct costs of disclosure, the indirect costs of disclosure, and the costs of regulation. The direct costs of disclosure include the costs of the production, certification, dissemination, processing, and interpretation of disclosures. These costs are borne by the corporations and the analyst community and ultimately by investors. The indirect costs include the adverse effects of disclosure on competitive advantage (e.g., creating a disincentive to innovate or invest in product development) and legal liability, which may induce an inefficient bearing of risk by management and auditors, among others. The costs of regulation include the costs involved in the development, compliance, enforcement, and litigation of disclosure regulations. These costs are borne by taxpayers and by shareholders (and perhaps indirectly by consumers and employees).

Third, there are issues related to the information demanded by the regulatory agency in order to develop and monitor the regulations. In the context of disclosure regulation, the SEC attempts to determine the amount and nature of corporate disclosure that would take place, absent the inefficiencies induced by the externalities. In the case where the prospective shareholders are free riders, this involves an attempt to determine their demand for information. In general, investor demand for information will be influenced by the wealth, risk preferences, and beliefs of investors, which is a nontrivial demand for information by the regulatory agency. Economic analyses which show the attainment of a more efficient solution via governmental regulation typically assume perfect knowledge on the part of the regulatory body, which is obviously an unrealistic assumption. Where it is too costly or simply unfeasible to obtain the desired information, implementation error by the regulatory agency due to imperfect information may occur.

For example, individuals may not have incentives to honestly reveal their preference for corporate disclosure. They may understate or overstate the desirability of additional disclosure depending on the extent to which they perceive their indication of preference will be used as a basis to assess their share of the costs. A clear illustration is provided when there is no attempt to include the free riders in sharing in the costs of disclosures. In other words, suppose some groups are invited to participate in the process that determines the quantity and nature of corporate disclosure but are not invited to share in bearing the costs of those additional disclosures (e.g., financial analysts). In this situation, the result may be excessive disclosure, rather than inadequate disclosure as suggested by the standard public good analysis. Issues of efficiency and equity are raised by such a process.

Fourth, there are issues that relate to the incentives of the regulatory agency itself. The economics of regulation offers two primary views of regulatory behavior.

The first is the "public interest" view, which states that regulatory behavior is directed toward furthering the public interest. This view implicitly assumes the incentives of regulators are aligned so as to further the public interest and that the concept of public interest is well-defined. The second view is known as the "capture theory" and states that the prime beneficiaries of regulation are not the public (or investors, in the case of the Securities Acts) but rather those being regulated. This has led critics of the Securities Acts, such as Stigler, to argue that the primary beneficiaries of the Acts are various members in the professional investment industry rather than investors at large.

Fifth, there is the issue of alternatives to governmental regulation, such as private sector collective agreements. For example, many goods with externalities are dealt with in the private sector. Newspapers and television are two examples. The issue of whether to deal with the problem collectively in the private or public sector revolves around the issue of relative costs of the alternative approaches. It is generally felt that the government has a comparative advantage in dealing with certain types of collective agreements. In particular, where it would be extremely costly or unfeasible to preclude free riders or where it would be extremely costly or unfeasible to attempt to charge them, it is intuitively felt the comparative advantage favors government action.

Uneven Possession of Information Among Investors

A second major argument for disclosure regulation is that, left unregulated, market forces would lead to an uneven possession of information among investors. Selective disclosure is one example. In other words, the result would be a continuum of informed investors ranging from well informed to ill informed. It is further argued that such asymmetry of access to information is inherently unfair and violates the meaning of "fair" disclosure under the Securities Acts. Hence the basis of the argument is typically one of equity rather than efficiency. Simply stated, it is only fair that the less informed be protected from the more informed.

Recent economic analysis of the demand for privately held information suggests that considerable incentives exist to expend efforts searching for and obtaining non-publicly available information for trading purposes. Studies described elsewhere in the Report document the existence of a large informal information network, where information flows from management to the analysts. However, the unfairness of such a process is not self-evident.

Presumably, the analysts pass along the benefits of the information search to their clients, either directly or indirectly. In this sense, the clients of analysts become more informed investors. However, they pay for the analysts' services either directly or indirectly. As long as the services are available to anyone willing to pay for them, there is no obvious way in which harm is occurring. At the margin, investors will purchase analysts' services to that point where investors are indifferent between being more informed or less informed, given the costs of becoming more informed. In other words, the expected benefits of being more informed (e.g., in the form of expected superior returns due to better information) are equal to (or offset by) the costs incurred to obtain the additional information. A common argument is that some investors cannot afford to purchase the services of analysts. However, the existence of financial intermediaries makes the force of this argument unclear. Moreover, it ignores several alternatives open to relatively less informed investors. One such alternative is to partially insulate themselves from more informed traders via buy-and-hold strategies and index funds. Also the actions of the more informed may signal their information to the less informed and as a result prices may partially (in the limit, fully) reflect the information.

The purchase of analysts' information can be viewed as the decision to purchase a higher quality product (in this case, superior information). In general, quality differences exist with respect to any commodity, and usually it is not thought to be unfair when one consumer chooses to purchase a higher quality product while another chooses a lower quality item. The purchase of automobiles is one example, but illustrations could be provided for almost any commodity.

While selective disclosure is commonly cast as an equity issue, there are grounds for considering it on the basis of efficiency. For example, Hirshleifer argues that the social value is zero to the acquisition of private information for trading purposes. If there were no costs to forming private-sector collective agreements, investors would agree among themselves not to privately seek information. Everyone would gain in that society would no longer incur the costs of private search for information, whose sole purpose is to redistribute wealth among investors via trading on superior information. In other words, the trading gains in the form of superior returns due to privately held information net out to zero across all investors. It is a zero-sum game in that every investor with superior returns is offset by other investors with inferior returns. However, to the extent that such search causes investors to incur real costs, it is not a zero-sum game but these costs constitute dead weight losses to investors as a whole. Investors would be better off to avoid such costs.

However, reaching and enforcing such a collective agreement might be extremely costly or simply unfeasible. In the absence of effective enforcement, the agreement would rapidly deteriorate, because there would always be a private incentive to cheat on the agreement. Therefore the SEC may have a comparative advantage in effectively eliminating private search for information. It could be accomplished by either or both of its two major means of regulation. (1) It could preempt private search by mandating the disclosure of the item in public filings or annual reports. (2) It could impose sufficient legal liability on transmittal of information from management to analysts such that information flows would be deterred (or in the limit eliminated).

This poses a dilemma. This argument suggests there will be a tendency for an excessive amount of information, as analysts and others privately search for information and disseminate it. However, this is the converse of the public good argument which implies an inadequate amount of disclosure. There are opposing forces operating. In one case the private incentives for disclosure fall short, while in the second case the private incentives are excessive. To the extent the former exists, it might be desirable to permit a certain amount of private search to compensate for the otherwise inadequate incentives to publicly disclose. However, permitting too much will lead to the inefficiencies described above.

Management Incentives to Disclose

A third major argument for disclosure regulation is that management has incentives to suppress unfavorable information. While there may be a general awareness of this potential among investors, investors would not know specifically the nature or materiality of the suppressed information. As a result, investors will be unable to distinguish quality differences among stocks to the same extent they would under fuller disclosure. Hence, security prices will not fully reflect quality differences among stocks and there will be uncertainty regarding the quality of each stock. There may be a tendency for lower quality stocks to be selling at a higher price than would prevail under fuller disclosure and conversely for the higher quality stocks. This can lead to a phenomenon known as adverse selection, where the managements of poorer quality stocks have greater incentives to offer additional shares for sale than the managements of higher quality stocks.

Firms will tend to respond to this problem in a number of ways. (1) Higher quality firms will attempt to signal their higher quality by undertaking actions that would be irrational unless they were in fact of higher quality. The effectiveness of this signaling behavior will be influenced by the extent to which the lower quality firms can imitate the signaling behavior. Moreover, signaling may be a costly activity with no rewards beyond those of signaling. (2) Managements will offer to have their disclosure system monitored and certified by an independent party, leading to a demand for auditing services. (3) Managements may offer warranties to shareholders whereby they will incur penalties if it is eventually discovered that unfavorable information was suppressed. In fact, managements' willingness to be audited and to offer warranties can be signals in themselves. Obviously both auditing services and warranty contracts are not costless. One of the most important costs in the warranty is that management may end up bearing more risk than that associated with failure to disclose.

After-the-fact it may be difficult to disentangle the deterioration in the stock price that was due to correcting inadequate disclosure as opposed to other unfavorable events. As a result, management may become an insurer for events in addition to those induced by management's disclosure policy. This may lead to an inefficient sharing of risks, relative to that that would attain if there were no uncertainty about the quality of the stocks. The costs may be so prohibitive that such warranties would not be offered.

The anti-fraud provisions can be viewed as requiring firms to provide disclosure warranties to investors, where presumably the legal liability is sufficient to offset the incentives of management to suppress unfavorable information. The argument for governmental intervention as opposed to private sector contracting would be that the SEC has a comparative (cost) advantage in achieving the same result. However, while this argument forms a basis for anti-fraud statutes, it is not clear why a mandated disclosure system is desirable. In other words, why is reliance upon anti-fraud statutes deemed to be inadequate? ...

... Recent securities price research in the areas of portfolio theory and efficient markets provides a framework within which to view the investor demand for information. These areas represent an important part of what is currently known about the investment decision and the environment within which that decision is made.

Portfolio Theory

Portfolio theory characterizes the investment decision as a trade-off between expected return and risk (i.e., as measured by the extent to which the actual return may differ from the expected return). Each portfolio of securities offers the investor a given combination of risk and expected return. Given the risk attitudes of the investor, the best portfolio is one that is the most preferred combination of risk and expected return. There are two immediate implications of portfolio theory for corporate disclosure. (1) Each individual security cannot be viewed in isolation but must be evaluated in the context of its membership in a portfolio consisting of other securities. The individual security is irrelevant, *except* insofar as it contributes to the overall risk and expected return of the portfolio. (2) The investor is concerned with risk as well as expected return (sometimes referred to as performance). Hence, corporate disclosure is concerned with the assessment of risk as well as the assessment of performance.

However, portfolio theory distinguishes between two types of risk. The first type is called unsystematic or diversifiable risk, because it can be virtually eliminated by diversification. The second type is called systematic or nondiversifiable risk, because it cannot be eliminated via diversification. The basis for this distinction rests on the view that two types of events affect the price of a security. There are economy-wide events, such as changes in anticipated inflation and interest rates, which affect the fortunes (and hence prices) of all securities with varying sensitivity. However, there are other events whose implications are largely firm-specific, such as changes in management, contract awards, and litigation. Unsystematic events by their very nature tend to be uncorrelated among firms at any point in time. To the extent that prices reflect only unsystematic or firm-specific events, returns among securities would be uncorrelated, and risk of the portfolio of such securities could be driven to zero via diversification across securities. However, to the extent that prices vary due to systematic events, security returns would be perfectly correlated, and diversification would not reduce the risk. Portfolio theory states that each security's return is subject to both types of risk. However, at the portfolio level only the systematic risk prevails, because the unsystematic risk has been diversified away. The investor is unnecessarily incurring unsystematic risk by failing to diversify. Therefore, there is a basic presumption in favor of diversification, unless the investor has some justification for choosing to remain undiversified. One reason for doing so would be superior information.

Investor Demand for Firm-Specific Information

Portfolio theory stresses the importance of diversification in the reduction of much of the risk associated with holding a single security. It is unrealistic to believe that investors hold only one security (e.g., the one being described in a registration statement). In fact, investors have the opportunity to purchase well diversified portfolios through financial intermediaries. The recent trend toward index funds is but one manifestation of the realization of the desirability of diversification. If the investor holds a well diversified portfolio, how, if at all, does this alter the way disclosure is viewed? It has been argued that diversification may substantially reduce the investor's demand for firm-specific information. The investor is concerned with firm-specific information only insofar as it is useful in assessing the portfolio attributes. While the investor may have considerable uncertainty about the risks and rewards associated with any one security, this uncertainty is considerably reduced at the portfolio level because of the effects of diversification. For example, while there may be considerable uncertainty as to the riskiness of any one security, typically the riskiness of the portfolio can be assessed with much greater confidence. In other words, an overestimate of the risk of one security will tend to be offset by an underestimation of the risk of another security. The effects of diversification are potentially powerful, and the benefits from incremental improvements in the precision of firm-specific information may be minimal.

In another context, suppose the investor is concerned that the security being purchased is mispriced, relative to the price at which it would sell if additional disclosures were available. From the point of view of the additional disclosure, some of the securities will be overpriced but some will be underpriced. A diversified portfolio will likely contain some of each and their effects will tend to be offsetting. Hence, the net effects of additional disclosure may differ considerably from the effects analyzed on a security-by-security basis.

This is not to suggest that portfolio theory implies that additional disclosure is valueless, but only that it can alter the way in which disclosure issues are viewed. There are a number of obvious additional considerations. (1) Many investors may choose not to diversify, even though they have the opportunity to do so. These investors, for one reason or another, perceive that the disadvantages of diversification outweigh the advantages. The SEC faces a social choice question of to what extent to impose disclosure requirements on companies (and hence impose costs on all investors) in order to accommodate investors who have chosen not to diversify. (2) Not all investors may have access to a given item (i.e., a problem of selective disclosure). (3) Management may use nondisclosure to obtain greater compensation than otherwise would be the case. (4) There may be effects on resource allocation that are ignored when the investor setting is narrowly viewed.

Efficient Security Markets

A securities market is said to be *efficient* with respect to some defined information if the security prices in that market "fully reflect" that information. The term, "fully reflect," is not a precise term. Operationally, if prices fully reflect a given set of information, then investors are playing a "fair game" with respect to that information. This means that all trading strategies based on that information will yield only the normal, expected return, commensurate with the risk involved.

A more precise definition is that the market is efficient with respect to a given piece of information if prices act *as if* everyone possessed that information and were able to interpret its implications for security prices. For example, several empirical studies have examined market efficiency with respect to changes in accounting methods. To say the market is efficient with respect to changes in accounting methods is to say that the stock prices behave as if all investors had knowledge of the change in method and knew how to interpret it.

The term, *market efficiency*, is unfortunate in some respects, because it may convey normative or value-laden connotations which have nothing to do with the concept itself. The concept of market efficiency refers to a relationship between stock prices and some defined information set. It is not to be confused with other uses of the term, *efficiency*, such as those which refer to how resources are allocated in the economy. It can also be misleading to use the term, *market efficiency*, without also specifying the information set. For example, to say simply that the market is efficient is an incomplete statement unless the intended implication is that the market is efficient with respect to any or all information. However, such an implication usually is not intended. Typically, when market efficiency is used in an unqualified manner, it is intended to imply that the market is efficient with respect to publicly available data, since most of the empirical research has been concerned with market efficiency of this form. Three major forms of market efficiency have been delineated: (1) weak form efficiency, which refers to market efficiency with respect to past security prices, (2) semi-strong form efficiency, which defines market efficiency with respect to publicly available information, and (3) strong form efficiency, which is concerned with market efficiency with respect to all information, including inside in formation.

There are several potential implications of market efficiency with respect to publicly available data. (1) Disclosure may still be a substantive issue. Merely because prices fully reflect publicly available information does not imply that prices necessarily reflect nonpublicly available information. (2) Once disclosure is provided, the method of formatting is unlikely to have an impact on stock prices. (3) Given the large, active private sector information system, many items may be reflected in prices even though they are not reported in annual reports, SEC filings, or any publicly available document. Moreover, any one type of data may have a number of substitutes which can provide similar information. Therefore, before proceeding to mandate any given item, it would be appropriate to consider if that item would be a material addition given the other data effectively being disseminated to the investment community and reflected in prices.

There is one nonimplication of the efficient market that deserves explicit recognition. Merely because prices reflect a broad information set does not preclude or presume the desirability of mandated disclosures. With respect to certain types of information, there still may be inadequate private incentives to gather and disseminate such data. Moreover, even if it is being disseminated via the private sector system, it may be deemed more efficient (i.e., less costly) to have it disseminated via public disclosure by the corporation rather than via the private search activities for the reasons discussed earlier. ...

Empirical research ... may be useful in dealing with some aspects of mandated disclosure. If the particular item is being mandated because it is expected to add to the information used by the market, it seems reasonable to expect the disclosure of such data to impact on stock prices. If no stock price reaction is observed, then the question must be asked—what are the effects, if any, of requiring disclosure of that item? For example, one effect could be a lower cost to investors via mandating disclosure rather than relying on the private sector's informal information network.

In other words, it is virtually inconceivable that the SEC would not be able to find some disclosures that would have a price effect. ... However, this is not the issue. Merely because the private sector has chosen not to disseminate a given item cannot be taken as prima facie evidence that the incentives to disclose are inadequate. It may be that the "benefits" of disclosure of that item are perceived to be not commensurate with the costs, such that disclosure is not worthwhile. The crucial issue is how to distinguish nondisclosure on the basis of perceived insufficient benefits from nondisclosure due to some inadequacy in the market system.

Similarly, the observation that the current system incurs a certain level of abuse is a slim basis on which to justify the desirability of mandated disclosure. Other issues must be considered. (1) To what extent, if any, would abuse be reduced by mandating additional disclosure? (2) What are the additional costs associated with mandated disclosure? (3) Are there alternative methods of dealing with the problem that might be more effective and/or less costly? Reliance on anti-fraud statutes and private sector collective agreements are two possibilities. In any event, no system, even a mandated one, is likely to drive the level of abuse to zero nor is it likely such a result would be desirable, even if it were feasible, because of the costs of achieving that result. Implementation error caused by a lack of evidence on investors' demand for information and/or biases induced by reliance on vested interests must also be considered.

Currently, there is little or no evidence that bears on these questions. As a result, the desirability of a mandated disclosure system is still an open issue. However, the issues raised here provide a framework within which to structure future research by the Commission and others. Elsewhere I have called for an increased reporting by the SEC as to the intended and actual effects of disclosure regulations. This proposal was based on the notion that the SEC, as a public agency, has a stewardship responsibility at least as great as any corporation and hence has a commensurate reporting responsibility. While it is premature to conclude that such a proposal is clearly desirable, it is not unreasonable to suggest that an effort be made, at least on an experimental basis. Such efforts may provide some evidence on the fundamental issue of the desirability of a public agency that has been regulating disclosure for over forty years.

Kripke, The Myth of the Informed Layman
28 Bus. Law. 631 (1973)

For the past several years, I have taught Securities Regulation and also Accounting for Lawyers, which is almost a branch of Securities Regulation. Each year I distribute a prospectus to my students and say, "Let's see what we can learn about the desirability of an investment in this company." I have reluctantly come to the conclusion that the Securities Act of 1933 is not operating as it should and that the prospectus has become a routine, meaningless document which does not serve its purpose. Trying to keep from going entirely academic on the ivory shelf by maintaining my contacts with the practising bar, I have reached the conclusion that most lawyers agree with me, and think of the registration process as simply a useless, but lucrative, bit of paper work.

• • •

If one searches for a clue, a single thread appears. Of course, it is oversimplification to ascribe everything to a simple cause, but I suggest that this one thread will prove to form much of the pattern. That thread is simply that the Commission has misconceived its market.

It has never admitted any hypothesis other than that the prospectus is intended for the man in the street, the unsophisticated lay investor. My theme is that the theory that the prospectus can be and is used by the lay investor is a myth. It is largely responsible for the fact that the securities prospectus is fairly close to worthless.

The Securities Act was sold to the Congress on the theory that securities are "intricate merchandise," and there is no doubt that this is so. They are becoming more intricate all the time.

We have novel packages of securities, like units of a bond or convertible debenture plus a stock or a warrant—"funny money," as we were saying a few years ago. We have particular companies with very sophisticated tax positions: now again the investment tax credit, percentage depletion, tax loss carry forwards, tax-sheltered distributions other than from earnings and profits.

We have the fact that many of the companies coming to market are very high technology companies. No layman could really understand either the products or their technical competitive positions; nor could even an expert get a solid understanding as long as disclosure is circumscribed by the push to make the prospectus short and readable for the layman.

Accounting, the basic mechanism of financial disclosure, is getting more complicated all the time. Professor Chambers, the Australian who lectured in the United States a few years ago, computed that a net income statement might represent one out of a million possible variations in the treatment of accounting items. While the Accounting Principles Board has limited the number of choices, a large number of choices do exist as to reporting the amount of the net income of a corporation. Most of us know the tremendous accounting choice between purchase and pooling. Many of us know the enormous assumptions that go into the computation of earnings per share, so that the American Institute of Accountants has had to issue numerous interpretations of its controlling opinion.

●   ●   ●

This myth that it is the layman to whom the prospectus is addressed permeates the SEC's concept of disclosure. It limits the usefulness of disclosure to those who should be its proper objective, the sophisticated investor and professional through whom information ought to filter down to the layman.

●   ●   ●

We find oversimplification for the layman working in many other fields of SEC law. The myth forces the Commission to forbid the disclosure in a prospectus of estimated values that might exist in excess of cost, e.g., in real estate, for fear that the lay investor could not be properly skeptical of an appraisal. The same myth induces the SEC to conceal potential mineral values, both oil and ore minerals, if they don't meet the Commission's concept of proven or probable minerals, for fear that the layman could not appraise, for instance, such information as the fact that oil has been discovered on the adjoining parcel of land. We read again and again in statements of Commission spokesmen that once the Commission permits something to be said in a document filed with the Commission, there is a danger that the investor will accept these assertions as gospel truth, despite all the disclaimers on the first page.

But this concern is only for the lay investor, not the professional who would be grateful for the opportunity to receive value estimates, and to consider them skeptically.

Our recurring myth and the same fear force the suppression of what should be the absolute key piece of information to any prospective securities investor, that is, information on management projections as to the registrant's future, *i.e.*, projections as to future earnings.

● ● ●

These factors have pushed the SEC into a perpetually negativistic, pessimistic approach. The prospectuses of the real estate investment trusts, coming out today one after another in rapid succession, all read the same way. Each one has a list of 50 items, more or less, in the business of the company on which cold water is thrown. Each prospectus is such a tale of potential calamity that none of them does a proper job of disclosing the really serious risk that ought to be emphasized but is submerged in this tale of woe—the very substantial risk necessarily involved in construction financing, plus the risk that the take-out commitment might not be earned or might not eventuate.

We could parody all prospectuses of promotional companies in one sentence: "Our competition is too much for us, and no representation is made that we will stay out of bankruptcy after the closing date." A prospectus loses its effect if every prospectus cries "wolf" all the time.

● ● ●

If we could get away from the assumption that the lay investor keeps his mind blank to everything except what is in the document that the Commission permits to be handed to him with its name on it, a serious new effort could be made to make securities disclosures meaningful. The present system does not address itself to the realities by which judgments on securities are formed. While for a new company coming to market for the first time, the prospectus is likely to be the only available written source of information, the situation is entirely different for the regularly reporting company, the one for which the prospects for rational judgment are best. The primary document which communicates information to investors in the established company in the real world is not the prospectus nor the annual report on Form 10K which gets buried in the Commission's files, but the annual report to stockholders. The way to do a real job of disclosure to the investing public is through the improvement of the information in the annual report to stockholders.

● ● ●

If we explode the myth and are not hampered by the necessity of writing down to the layman, what should be the future goals of disclosure? Our discussion must necessarily assume that the market is rational and that market value will fluctuate around enterprise value as the norm.

Ultimately enterprise value, which is therefore what the rational investor is searching for, is a subjective thing. Like beauty, it is in the eye of the beholder.

The fact that we have 20 million shares traded daily on the New York Stock Exchange means that people differ as to whether any security is a good buy or a good sell. Every analyst forms his own judgment as to the value of a company and of its securities, not only from judgment factors relating to the particular company and the particular industry, but also from judgment factors as to the appropriate discount rate for future earnings because of the future course of money rates, of the whole economy, of the political situation, and indeed of the international situation.

Given all of these variables of the future that affect a company, enterprise value is not a thing or a fact. It is a judgment.

Disclosure should be oriented to disclosing what the informed investor may think is important to that judgment: value estimates, earnings projections, probable and potential minerals—not exclusively what is in the past and not limited to what the layman can handle. The significant items all point to the future, and the uncomfortable reality is that they are all possibilities and probabilities, not certainties. But the Commission should not for that reason suppress the estimates for the future which really make the value of a security. The Commission's function should be to give the information to the people straight and let them make their own judgments in their own way. As I have argued elsewhere,[15] those who try to use disclosure rationally are going to use professional help in doing so anyway.

How does this concept affect accounting, the present principal repository for financial information? I think that we may have been on the wrong track in trying to reduce accounting to single numbers whose derivations are found in an Opinion of the Accounting Principles Board, because there are many aspects of financial events on which different people have different judgments. Perhaps accounting should move backwards somewhat in the direction of disclosing more detail, more information, and letting the analyst or the informed investor make his own decisions as to what is significant.

•   •   •

Although the SEC in my day as a staff member used to preach the necessity for firm rules to avoid burying the meat of a financial statement in pages of explanatory footnotes, we may have to produce more complete disclosure of the elements that go into the conclusions of financial data. I realize that we could go too far. If you just drown people in information, you can overwhelm even the professional portfolio manager who has a problem of forming a judgment on several hundred companies.

But what we need is a new departure, with disclosure oriented towards the sophisticated person able to handle it, through whom suggestions for action will filter down to the layman.

Further Notes on Mandatory Disclosure. Hirshleifer's argument, as discussed in the Beaver excerpt, about excessive production of information by market intermedi-

---

15   Kripke, *The SEC, The Accountants, Some Myths and Some Realities*, 45 N.Y.U. L. Rev. 1151, 1169-70 (1970).

aries is found in Hirshleifer, *The Private and Social Value of Information and the Reward to Inventive Activity*, 61 Am. Econ. Rev. 561 (1971). Market intermediaries will invest resources to produce and digest new information, with their reward coming in the form of profits on trading. Once the market has fully adjusted to such information, no further trading profits are available. It might then seem, as Hirshleifer suggests, that all parties would be better off with prompt disclosure which extinguishes the profit opportunity, since a wasteful investment in information production would be eliminated.

This argument is, however, weakened by recent studies on the economics of information. Even prompt disclosure of information will not lead to efficient capital markets unless the information is studied and digested. But this will not happen unless some prospect of compensation for the costs of such analysis is held out. Informed investors must therefore be able to use their information to take positions in the market that are consistently superior to those of the uninformed investors who have not absorbed screening costs. This means, as Professors Grossman and Stiglitz have demonstrated, that assumptions of perfect capital markets and of competitive equilibria for costly information are inconsistent. If capital markets were perfectly efficient, there would be no incentive for market professionals to absorb screening costs. The information production by market intermediaries is then not simply a wasteful investment in foreknowledge but a social good, since it permits free riding by uninformed investors who may rely on a more accurate price for the securities than would obtain without such screening. Hirshleifer's argument therefore fails unless, somehow, it can be demonstrated that the benefits of screening by institutional investors to the non-screening lay investor are exceeded by the costs of "excessive" screening. See further Grossman & Stiglitz, *On the Impossibility of Informationally Efficient Markets*, 70 Am. Econ. Rev. 93 (1980). The "efficiency paradox" is also discussed in Gilson & Kraakman, *The Mechanisms of Market Efficiency*, 70 Va. L. Rev. 549, 577-78, 622-26 (1984).

The usefulness of mandatory disclosure requirements are discussed further in F.H. Easterbrook & D.R. Fischel, *Mandatory Disclosure and the Protection of Investors*, 70 Va. L. Rev. 669 (1984); and J.C. Coffee, Jr., *Market Failure and the Economic Case for a Mandatory Disclosure System*, 70 Va. L. Rev. 717 (1984) (excerpts from these articles are set out in R. Romano, *Foundations of Corporate Law*, 303 and 309 (1993)). Easterbrook and Fischel note an argument in favour of mandatory disclosure based on the notion of "adverse selection." The concept of adverse selection as applied to securities markets is that investors will not be able to distinguish between honest issuers and dishonest issuers. Dishonest issuers will thus be able to convince investors that investments in their business activities are more valuable and will thus attract more of the available investment dollars than honest issuers. This competitive advantage of dishonest issuers will eventually drive out the honest issuers, which may result in a misallocation of resources and an overall reduced level of investment. See Easterbrook & Fischel, supra at 674-77.

Easterbrook and Fischel question the force of the adverse selection argument. They note that issuer management can engage in a wide variety of practices to signal to investors their commitment to act in the interests of investors and otherwise signal the accuracy of their disclosures. For instance, they can purchase shares in the issuer to align their interests more closely with the interests of investors. They can take on debt exposing management to a greater threat to the loss of their careers in the event of bankruptcy thereby strengthening their incentive to maximize the value of the issuer. They can adopt a policy of paying out a substantial portion of the issuer's profits in dividends so that they are forced to return to the capital market to raise funds on a regular basis and will thus have a stronger incentive to keep security prices high in order to raise capital on favourable terms. Management can signal the accuracy of their disclosures to investors by seeking independent reviews of their disclosures by persons such as auditors, engineers, underwriters and rating organizations. The business of auditors, engineers, underwriters, rating organizations and others who are called upon to verify the issuer's disclosures will depend on their reputation and thus they will have an incentive to be effective in their verification efforts. See *id.* at 675-76.

Disclosures by management of the issuer and the techniques used by management to signal their incentive to act in the interests of security holders and the accuracy of their disclosures will involve costs. According to Easterbrook and Fischel, management will have an incentive to engage in these activities to the point that the cost of the last dollar spent on these activities (the marginal cost) will just equal the benefit derived from these activities (the marginal gain). Incurring a marginal cost that is greater than the marginal gain to the issuer reduces the value of the issuer and is thus a net cost ultimately born by the issuer's security holders. Mandatory disclosure has the effect of requiring management to make disclosures they would not have made otherwise. They would not have chosen to make these disclosures otherwise since the marginal cost of the disclosure outweighed the marginal gain. Thus where mandatory disclosure causes management to make disclosures they would otherwise not have made it results in the incurance of costs that outweigh the gains resulting in a loss to investors. See *id.* at 680-85.

However, if the issuer does not reap all the potential gains from disclosure, it would not produce the optimal level of disclosure since, in deciding whether to disclose, it would be comparing its marginal gains (which would be less than the marginal gains to investors as a whole) with the marginal cost of disclosure. Mandatory disclosure would then be a method of requiring the issuer to disclose information to the level it would if it was comparing the marginal gains to investors as a whole with its marginal costs. It has been noted that too little information may be produced because information disclosed by an issuer may reveal information that is useful for the purpose of valuing the securities of other issuers. See *id.* Easterbrook & Fischel, at 685-87. For instance, disclosures by one issuer may provide information that is useful in valuing the securities of other issuers in the same industry. Thus the issuer making the disclosure will not capture all the gains from the disclosure and will thus have less of an incentive to disclose. Indeed, the issuer may have an incentive to free ride by waiting for other issuers to disclose first. An issuer may also choose not to disclose information that would be beneficial to investors as a whole where the information would assist competitors of the issuer (for instance, where it is information about a new product line or new technology). By requiring issuers to disclose mandatory disclosure can correct this sub-optimal incentive to disclose.

Another argument in favour of mandatory disclosure suggests that securities analysts may have a less than optimal incentive to gather and assess information because they also cannot reap the full benefits of their information gathering and assessment efforts. Once the information has been gathered individuals involved in the gathering of the information will have an incentive to leak the information. Also, once the information is used for the purpose of trading some of the information will be revealed simply by the process of trading. There will be a price response and others may also be able to discern who is trading and on what and thus make assessments as to the nature of the information being traded on. Mandatory disclosure causes the issuer to reveal information that might otherwise have to be gathered by securities analysts. Thus it can correct for the less than optimal incentive of security analysts to gather information about securities and issuers. This argument is discussed in Coffee, supra at 725-33.

A further argument in favour of mandatory disclosure is that while securities analysts may have a less than optimal incentive to gather information, the information gathering they do is excessive in the sense that each one is gathering much the same information. Thus the cost of gathering the information is being unnecessarily repeated. Mandatory disclosure can avoid this cost by forcing issuers to incur the cost of producing the information once and make it available to all investors so they do not engage in repetitive gathering of the same information. *Id.*, Coffee, at 733-34.

Easterbrook and Fischel have responded to these arguments by noting that market mechanisms exist which respond to problems in a way that brings the marginal cost of the production of information into line with the marginal gain from the production of information. One such market mechanism is the use of informational intermediaries such as underwriters, auditors, engineers and rating organizations engaged by the issuer. This can help overcome the problem of investors engaging in repetitive gathering and assessment of the same information by having the intermediary gather and assess the information once for the benefit of investors as a whole. Another market mechanism is a stock exchange. Issuers have an incentive to become listed on a stock exchange because it makes the issuers' securities more marketable thus making the securities more valuable to investors. Stock exchanges can, and usually do, require issuers to disclose information as a condition of listing. The stock exchange has an incentive to do this to increase the value of securities traded on the exchange and thereby attract investment in the securities listed and posted for trading on the exchange. Disclosure required by a stock exchange is a market response to the problem that the issuer may have a less than optimal incentive to disclose information and to the problem that securities analysts may have a less than optimal incentive to gather and assess information. See Easterbrook and Fischel, supra, at 687-90.

Merit Discretion. With respect to merit discretion there is reason to be skeptical about the benefit it provides to investors. A former Commissioner stated that:

The practical difficulty of course, is that if the [Commission] were to attempt to pass judgment in detail on the viability of the new enterprise, [it] would have to have at [its] disposal a staggering number of highly sophisticated experts from various disciplines. The result would be an economy heavily subject to public regulation, to a much greater extent than Canadians have been accustomed. [D. Johnston, *Canadian Securities Regulation* 160 (1977)]

Even if substantial blue sky screening were provided by securities commissions, it is by no means clear that public investors would thereby be made better off. If the effect of the screening is to foreclose investments in speculative firms, established firms would be protected from competition (as the capture theory of regulation would predict). In addition, public investors would be prevented from purchasing shares in successful as well as unsuccessful ventures. One example of this was the decision of the Massachusetts securities commission in December 1980 barring the first offering of securities in Apple Computer Inc. See R. Brealey & S. Myers, *Principles of Corporate Finance* 301 n. 6 (2d ed. 1984). For differing perspectives on the utility of blue sky regulation, see Campbell, *An Open Attack on the Nonsense of Blue Sky Regulation*, 10 J. Corp. L. 553 (1985); *Report on State Merit Regulation of Securities Offerings*, 41 Bus. Law. 785 (1986).

I. PUBLIC CHOICE THEORIES

One possible explanation for the existence of and staying power of mandatory disclosure is that it is the result of the relative influence of various special interest groups. This type of explanation normally posits that regulators do not necessarily make decisions for the public good, but rationally seek to maximize the level of their political support from these special interest groups. The regulators' decisions allocate wealth to the interest groups that provide the greatest level of support to the regulators. See, e.g., Stigler, *The Theory of Economic Regulation*, 2 Bell J. of Econ. and Mgnt. Sci. 3 (1971); and Peltzman, *Toward a More General Theory of Regulation*, 19 J.L. and Eco. 211 (1976) on "public choice" or interest group theories.

One interest group explanation of mandatory disclosure is that it is the result of pressure from securities analysts and institutional investors. According to Phillips and Zecher the securities laws in the United States have resulted in a subsidy of more than U.S. $1 billion by requiring issuers to provide information in a set format that securities analysts and institutional investors would otherwise have to obtain and organize at their own expense. See S. Phillips & J. Zecher, *The SEC and the Public Interest* (1981).

Another explanation of the disclosure requirements of the Securities Act of 1933 is that the requirements would not have imposed substantial burdens on major public corporations (which already provided similar information to securities exchanges and market professionals) but would have imposed substantial burdens on smaller corporations. Compliance with a single standard of disclosure would impose similar costs on all corporations, whatever the size of the issue. Consequently, public issues of stock after 1933 became considerably more costly for smaller corporations. See H.G. Manne, *Economic Aspects of Required Disclosure Under Federal Securities Law*, in H. Manne & E. Solomon, *Wall Street in Transition*, 21, 28-36 (1974).

An interest group explanation has also been offered for the development of merit regulation in the United States. It has been argued that merit regulation served the interests of small banks that had lost deposits to higher yield debt and equity securities that had grown in popularity. State merit regulation that discouraged issues of debt and equity securities would reduce the alternatives to deposits as modes of saving. Local industries and farmers may have enhanced their access to capital by excluding competition from out-of-state borrowers. Elite investment banking firms that distributed securities opposed the increased administrative burdens and the likely local bias of state merit regulation. Firms in industries that raised significant amounts of capital through bond issues, such as manufacturing firms, railroads and public utilities, opposed state merit regulation. Larger banks, the deposits of which were not affected by the growth of high yield debt and equity securities, and which engaged in securities business including the underwriting of bond issues, also opposed state merit regulation. In spite of this opposition to merit regulation it was adopted in states where the interests of small banks, local businesses and farmers outweighed the interests of those opposed to merit regulation. See J.R. Macey & G.P. Miller, *Origin of the Blue Sky Laws*, 70 Texas L.R. 347 (1991).

Several other interest group explanations of the behaviour of the SEC in the United States have been given. For instance, in 1975 Congress requested that the SEC use its authority to promote the establishment of a national market system for securities, by among other things, promoting fair competition between brokers and dealers and between exchanges and markets. One anti-competitive tactic used by stock exchanges employs a rule that prohibits exchange members from trading listed stocks where the trade was not effected through the exchange. This prevents exchange members using another exchange to trade in securities listed on the exchange on which they are a member. The SEC did not exercise its authority to remove these rules and according to Macey and Haddock this was because although support for a national market system came from brokerage firms that were not exchange members, their support was overwhelmed by opposition from the much larger number of brokerage firms that were exchange members. See J.R. Macey & D.D. Haddock, *Shirking at the SEC: The Failure of the National Market System*, [1985] U. Ill. L. Rev. 315.

Another interest group explanation of the behaviour of the SEC dealt with the abolition of fixed-rate commissions on the New York Stock Exchange ("NYSE"). Jarrell noted that the increase in trading by institutions led to increased political opposition by institutions to fixed-rate commissions. The NYSE was forced to give in to pressure to abandon fixed rate commissions for fear that it would lose income from institutional trading as institutions would find ways of avoiding trading through the NYSE to avoid fixed-rate commissions See G.A. Jarrell, *Changes at the Exchange: The Causes and Effects of Deregulation*, 27 J.L. and Eco. 273 (1984).

There is also an interest group explanation of the pattern of insider trading restrictions in the United States that argues that the interests of professional traders and insiders coalesced to bring about the particular pattern of insider trading restrictions. See D.D. Haddock & J.R. Macey, *Regulation on Demand: A Private Interest Model, with an Application to Insider Trading Regulation*, 30 J. L. and Eco. 311 (1987). This is discussed further in Chapter Eight.

Another explanation for the SEC's behaviour focuses on interests that are internal to the SEC itself. This approach offers an explanation of an extent of regulation and extensiveness of disclosure requirements that is likely to be beyond what industry participants would want. Under this approach the SEC is viewed as an organization having diffuse individual interests and attitudes with dispersed informational sources and a loss of control over the organization that is especially pronounced given the lack of discipline from a competitive marketplace. A proponent of this approach, D.C. Langevoort, argues that individuals at the SEC will seek to maximize their own utility and this utility maximization:

... can readily be understood in terms of that which serves as reward or compensation for certain behavior and runs the gamut from external "bribes" (e.g., promises of future employment in the private sector for key officials) through ego gratification (e.g., favourable publicity) to institutional self-preservation or internal consumption (e.g., enlarged or preserved turf or budget, more leisure time for the staff)—even the sense of pride or satisfaction that comes from doing a task well. [See D.C. Langevoort, *The SEC as a Bureaucracy: Public Choice, Institutional Rhetoric, and the Process of Policy Formulation*, 47 Wash. and Lee L. Rev. 527 at 529-30 (1990)]

On this view it is suggested that SEC behaviour will be primarily inner-directed "until external stimuli change in a sufficiently compelling fashion so as to draw a critical mass of attention outward" (*id.* at 530) and will tend toward risk avoidance and turf protection.

The internal interests of the SEC are also said to cause it to be reluctant to set out clear rules or standards so that it can preserve a broad scope to its discretion. As regulators the SEC is said to have a natural bias toward more regulation and increasingly complex regulation. The SEC is largely staffed by lawyers inclined toward the creation of arcane, open-ended and technical rules. See *id.* at 531. Indeed, a former SEC staff member has said that his impression of the measure of performance at the SEC is the amount of new rules one has created over a given period of time. See N. Wolfson, *A Critique of the Securities and Exchange Commission*, [1981] Emory L.J. 119.

Langevoort has also suggested that the bureaucratic nature of the SEC has created a set of rhetorical conventions that operate as a means of forming consensus among the various divisions of the SEC in the formulation of policy. According to Langevoort,

What we have, then, is a highly complex coordination problem: potentially scores of individual negotiations would have to occur to build consensus from a clean slate. This, of course, would be immensely time-consuming (and typically frustrating in a hierarchical setting because other sources of power have a fairly low cost ability to block a significant initiative). Here, it seems, is where rhetorical conventions gain their power. A person charged with formulating or reformulating the initiative is likely to mold the proposal based on rhetoric previously agreed to in earlier negotiations, if only to reduce both the risk and the transactions costs attendant to gaining each successive level of approval. In this way, each new initiative is influenced heavily by the perception of the past. [*Id.* at 532-33]

One such type of rhetoric is the claim that individual investors "add depth and liquidity" to the market. Langevoort suggests that this rhetoric has been employed by the SEC in actions to limit the economic advantage of institutional investors which threatens the basis of securities regulation since it depends on protecting individual investors who play a progressively less important role in securities markets. It is also a rhetorical convention that is likely to be supported by brokerage firms that profit from trading by individual investors and from corporate managers whose control is enhanced where the shares of the corporation are in the hands of a disperse and unorganized group of individual investors rather than concentrated in the hands of institutional investors.

J. REGISTRATION

1. The Registration Requirement

As noted above in the introduction to the prospectus requirement, a person who trades in securities is required to be registered for trading. Registration is also required where a person acts as an underwriter or acts as an adviser with respect to investment in securities. See ASA s. 54(1); BCSA s. 20(1); OSA s. 25(1). Persons who trade in securities, or act as an underwriter or adviser without being registered are subject to penal sanctions. See, e.g., ASA s. 161(1)(c); BCSA s. 138(1)(c); OSA s. 122(1)(c). In this way, entry into the securities industry is restricted in order to assert controls over industry participants. This is intended to address concerns with respect to such matters as the financial stability and competence of industry participants, and potential conflicts of interest between industry participants and their clients. For a discussion of these concerns see M.Q. Connelly, *The Licensing of Securities Market Actors*, in *Proposals for a Securities Market Law for Canada* 1269 (1979). Compliance with the requirements intended to address these concerns is enforced through penal sanctions and a variety of administrative sanctions including reprimand, suspension or cancellation of registration and restrictions on the registrant. See, e.g., ASA s. 56(1); BCSA s. 144(1)(f); OSA s. 127(1).

2. Screening Securities Industry Participants

A variety of mechanisms are used to address the concern for the financial stability of securities industry participants. For instance, in order to be registered an applicant for registration is required to have a minimum net free capital to meet its obligations. See, e.g., ASA Reg. s. 23; BCSA Reg. ss. 20-22; OSA Reg. s. 107. Securities administrators may also require the registrant to post a bond in an amount considered appropriate to protect the interests of the registrant's clients. See, e.g., ASA Reg. s. 25; BCSA Reg. s. 23; OSA Reg. s. 108. Registrants involved in trading in securities must contribute to a contingency fund that is intended to provide protection to clients in the event of a business failure of the registrant. See, e.g., ASA Reg. s. 28; BCSA Reg. s. 25; OSA Reg. s. 110.

The competence of registrants is addressed through educational and apprenticeship requirements. Courses are offered by associations such as the Canadian Securities Institute, the Investment Dealers Association and the Institute of Chartered Financial Analysts. See, e.g., ASA Reg. ss. 41-45; BCSA Reg. ss. 59-62; OSA Reg. ss. 124, 125.

Concerns with respect to the honesty of securities industry participants such as problems with conflicts of interest are also addressed with a variety of mechanisms. Conflicts of interest are in part addressed by the common remedies for breach of contract between the industry participant and the client or remedies for a breach of fiduciary duties. Securities regulation in Canada also addresses conflicts of interest in a variety of ways. For instance, portfolio managers paid a commission on individual trades may have an incentive to engage in an excessive number of trades (known as "churning" the account). Consequently securities acts often provide that portfolio managers may not base their fees on the value or volume of transactions initiated for the client. See, e.g., ASA Reg. s. 31; BCSA Reg. s. 47; OSA Reg. 115(2).

Several provinces have also passed extensive regulations imposing disclosure requirements and restrictions on the activities of registrants where they have a conflict of interest due to their relationship with other persons. See, e.g., BCSA Reg. ss. 167.1-167.12; OSA Reg. ss. 219-233. For instance, there can be a conflict of interest where a person acts as an underwriter for an issuer that has a substantial loan from another person (e.g., a bank) having a substantial interest in the underwriter. From the bank's perspective it may not be as keen to have the underwriter be especially vigilant against concerns that would discourage a public offering of securities since the public offering of securities can provide funds to pay off the loan. The bank might exercise its influence over the underwriter to protect the interests of the bank. Regulations covering this sort of situation require disclosure of the relationship, the use of an independent underwriter to underwrite a portion of the issue and that the underwriter's certificate on the prospectus (to the effect that the prospectus contains full, true and plain disclosure to the best of the underwriter's knowledge and belief) is signed by the independent underwriter. See, e.g., BCSA Reg. s. 167.4; OSA Reg. s. 199.

3. Exemptions from the Registration Requirement

There are several exemptions from the registration requirement. Most of these exemptions correspond to the exemptions from the prospectus requirement. When an issuer of securities sells securities in a distribution the issuer is trading in securities and must be registered for trading. It would be tedious and costly for an issuer to register for trading every time the issuer engaged in a distribution of securities that was exempt from the prospectus requirement. Indeed, the concerns with respect to securities industry participants do not arise when the issuer engages in an isolated trade in a distribution and does not regularly engage in trading on behalf of clients. Consequently, Canadian securities acts provide a series of exemptions from the requirement to register for trading that correspond to the exemptions from the prospectus requirement. See, e.g., ASA s. 65; BCSA s. 31; OSA s. 35. When an issuer does make a distribution that is not exempt from the prospectus requirement the issuer is required to register for trading. However, in the normal case where an issuer engages an underwriter, the issuer is exempt from the registration requirement for trades between the issuer and the underwriter or trades effected by the underwriter on behalf of the issuer. See, e.g., ASA ss. 65(1)(i), (j); BCSA ss. 31(2)(7), (16); OSA ss. 31(1)(9), (10).

Governance Structures

We have already seen in Chapter One how a firm may be viewed as an agency relationship in which one party delegates authority to a second. A breach of that authority by the second party will then impose an agency cost on the first. This chapter considers how firms may respond to agency costs in their choice of governance structures—the techniques by which managerial and supervisory roles are assigned to participants in a firm. Section A notes the concept of agency costs in the context of corporations and strategies for controlling agency costs in corporations. Sections B to F examine corporate governance structures in the context of the roles of directors and officers, shareholders' rights and powers, shareholders' meetings, proxy solicitation, the right to financial statements and access to corporate records. Section G highlights some ongoing debates on corporate governance. Sections A through G focus on corporate governance in the context of widely held corporations, while Section H notes differences in corporate governance in the context of closely held corporations.

A. AGENCY COSTS

1. The Nature of Agency Costs

Agency costs are a useful concept for analyzing corporate governance structures. At the outset it is important to note that the agency cost concept used by economists is based on a broader concept of agency than the legal concept of agency. What might be considered an agency relationship by an economist, for the purpose of an agency cost analysis, may not constitute an agency relationship in law.

Agency costs arise when one person relies on another to do something on her or his behalf. Consider the case of a retail store owner, Jane, who has no employees or creditors. Everything that is done in the store is done by Jane herself. Jane is the sole owner and has not borrowed any of the capital of the business. If she takes time off, reduces her efforts in running the store or consumes some of the store's goods, she will bear the entire cost of these activities. A one dollar loss of profit to the store will be a one dollar loss to her personally. However, if Jane employs another person to take care of the store while she is out on other business there will be an agency cost. If the employee chooses not to devote his best efforts to running the store or consumes the store's products, the employee, not being a sole owner of the store, will not bear the full cost of any lost profit. Instead, Jane will bear the cost of such activities by the employee.

Jane can control for this by monitoring the activities of the employee and taking disciplinary action against the employee. However, monitoring the employee will involve costs—so-called monitoring costs. The employee will be affected by these monitoring costs since the compensation Jane will be willing to pay the employee (usually in the form of wages) will be reduced by the amount of the monitoring costs. To avoid this the employee may try to give some assurance to Jane that he will not engage in activities that will be costly to her (i.e. he will "signal" that he will act in the interests of Jane or "bond" himself to act in the interests of Jane). For instance, he might post a bond protecting Jane against theft by him. Efforts to give such assurances to the principal also involve costs referred to as "bonding costs."

The principal will only engage in efforts to monitor the agent to the point that the marginal cost of monitoring just equals the marginal gain from controlling the activities of the agent. Similarly, the agent will only engage in bonding to the point that the marginal cost of bonding efforts just equals the marginal gain. Thus some potential for actions by the agent that are not in the interests of the principal will remain where the marginal costs of monitoring or bonding outweigh the marginal gains from such activities. This residual potential for activities of the agent contrary to the interests of the principal imposes costs referred to as "residual costs." Agency costs are then the sum of the monitoring costs, the bonding costs and the residual costs. See, e.g., M.C. Jensen & W.H. Meckling, *Theory of the Firm: Managerial Behavior, Agency Costs, and Ownership Structure*, 3 J. of Fin. Econ. 305 (1976); E. Fama, *Agency Problems and the Theory of the Firm*, 88 J. Pol. Econ. 288 (1980).

2. Agents and Principals in the Context of a Firm

The agents of a firm are those who have responsibility to make or to ratify decisions on behalf of the firm, and the principals are those who are thereby affected. If Jane gets others to join in providing equity investments while Jane continues to manage the firm, Jane will be acting on behalf of the other equity investors. Since Jane is no longer the sole investor she will not reap 100% of the profits of the firm. Consequently, Jane will no longer bear the full cost of taking time off, reducing her efforts in running the store or consuming some of the store's goods. Thus, in the relationship between Jane and the other investors, agency costs will be incurred. Similarly, if Jane borrows funds by way of a bank loan or buys goods on credit there will be agency costs in the relationship between Jane and the bank or other creditors.

3. Agents and Principals in the Context of Corporations

In the context of corporations with widely held shares, the agents will usually be its managers, and the principals will be various claimholders such as its outside shareholders, debt holders, suppliers, customers, employees and even involuntary tort creditors. However, these categories are not fixed. For instance, shareholders might be thought of as agents when their ratification of a business decision imposes external costs on other parties, such as debt holders. Also, managers, in some instances, may be thought of as principals instead of agents, such as when some firm policies, like the bankruptcy decision, are assigned to secured lenders.

4. A Hypothetical Claimholders' Bargain in the Context of Corporations

In a hypothetical claimholders' bargain, managers would agree to be bound by policies which maximize the wealth of the firm and all its participants. If the managers announced that they would make self-interested business decisions that were Kaldor-Hicks inefficient, the other claimholders could pay them more to abstain from that policy than they would make by adhering to it, since abandoning it would increase total firm wealth.

5. Enforcement Problems in a Hypothetical Claimholders' Bargain

However, the hypothetical claimholders' bargain may be difficult to maintain over time. Although the agents can be "bribed" to agree in a hypothetical bargain, they may lack the incentive to live up to the bargain thereafter. An agent would agree, for example, to take no greater compensation from the firm than is sufficient to compensate him for his managerial services, but may still be tempted to "loot" the firm thereafter, transferring wealth from other participants to himself beyond the agreed-on measure of managerial compensation. Agency costs will thus arise because of the difficulty in enforcing the claimholders' bargain over time.

6. Strategies to Reduce Agency Costs

As an initial strategy to reduce these agency costs, the firm might consider ending the agency relationship associated with outside equity or debt, as could be done through a management buyout of outside claims, by retirement of the debt, or by firing the agent (as when a secured creditor appoints a receiver over the debtor). However, parties only enter into an agency relationship because it is more efficient than competing forms of organization. By hypothesis, then, it is inefficient to eliminate the agency costs by ending the agency relationship, and it is therefore important to distinguish the strategies that would reduce agency costs through agency supervision from those that would simply reduce the scope of the agent's authority. For this reason, it is assumed that the agency cost problem of widely held firms cannot be solved by transferring power from management to another corporate constituency. Such strategies, which might include a requirement of ratification by principals on a business decision, cannot eliminate the risk of agent misbehaviour, assuming that some delegation of authority is efficient.

While retaining the agency relationship, a firm may adopt harm prevention measures aimed at lowering agency costs, with an efficient investment in harm reduction being one where the sum of prevention (monitoring and bonding) and of residual agency costs is minimized. *Governance strategies* then are harm prevention devices that reduce agency costs by attributing *monitoring* duties to claimholders or related parties. For example, the decision to grant voting rights to one set of claimholders, or to impose gatekeeping responsibilities on directors and auditors, implicates governance strategies.

Among harm prevention measures, liability strategies may be distinguished from governance structures. Liability strategies are bonding tactics in which firm managers promise efficient performance, with the promise made more creditable through the imposition of liability on breach of the promise. The manager's assets then serve as a bond of its fidelity to the promise. Governance structures are the subject of this chapter and liability strategies are considered in Chapter Seven.

The two kinds of strategies frequently overlap. Thus governance structures will often implicate liability rules under which (1) monitors may be sued for misbehaviour, such as their failure to monitor, or (2) agents may be sued if they interfere with the monitors in the course of the performance of their functions. For example, voting rules would not be worth much if managers were not bound by the results of a vote. Monitoring strategies need not, however, rest on liability rules. Thus a firm might seek to reduce agency costs through its internal monitoring of employees, with the sanction for employer misbehaviour found in the firm's hierarchical structures rather than in an action for breach of contract.

A further technique to reduce agency costs involves the firm's compensation decision. Some varieties of agent misbehaviour may be minimized *ex ante* through special forms of executive compensation, such as bonus plans, which tie the manager's salary to firm performance. (Compensation strategies are discussed in Chapter Seven.)

7. Agency Cost Strategies and Efficient Capital Markets

In a hypothetical claimholders' bargain, a firm would agree to adopt all efficient governance, liability and compensation strategies to reduce agency costs. Whether the firm will actually do so, however, may depend on how closely the market for firm claims approximates the ideal of efficient capital markets, to which information about agency costs has been fully disclosed. If capital markets are efficient, then the firm will bear all agency costs and it would voluntarily agree to adopt optimal harm prevention strategies. But the firm may lack an adequate incentive to do so if capital markets are inefficient and the probability of manager misbehaviour is not fully known by investors.

The question is then to what extent capital markets for widely traded firms are efficient. You may here wish to review the discussion of the Efficient Capital Market Hypothesis in Chapter One, Section A. According to Michael Jensen, "there is no other proposition in economics which has more empirical evidence supporting it" than the ECMH. Jensen, *Some Anomalous Evidence Regarding Market Efficiency*, 6 J. Fin. Econ. 95, 96 (1978). The Canadian evidence of stock market efficiency is somewhat more ambiguous, as might be expected where more listed firms have thinly traded shares. The evidence is reviewed in MacIntosh, *The Shareholders' Appraisal Right in Canada: A Critical Reappraisal*, 24 Osgoode Hall L.J. 201, 275 at n. 197 (1987); and R.J. Daniels & J.G. MacIntosh, *Toward a Distinctive Canadian Corporate Law Regime*, 29 Osgoode Hall L.J. 863, 872-74 (1991).

If capital markets are informed of the agency costs of a particular firm, then that firm will bear them itself in its cost of capital and debt. As a consequence, the firm will wish to take efficient preventive measures to reduce agency costs, seeking the lowest level of total agency and prevention costs.

However, scholars have challenged the assumption of efficient capital markets and have criticized hypothetical bargain models of corporate governance. See, e.g., Eisenberg, *The Structure of Corporate Law*, 89 Col. L. Rev. 1461, 1488-1524 (1989). However, even where evidence indicates that inefficiencies in the management of a particular firm may not be perceived by the market, the firm's choice of governance structures is more likely to be reflected in stock prices. For example, while shirking by managers may escape the attention of the market, the firm's decision to appoint outside directors not affiliated with management is highly public. Further, even if it could be shown that inefficient governance strategies are in fact selected by firms in real world conditions the claimholders' bargain therefore remains a useful heuristic device.

This chapter will first review corporate management structures as set out in corporations statutes, with the delineation of the respective roles of the board of directors and of the shareholders. The legal structure has been criticized for its failure to mirror the reality of control in many public corporations, with the fear expressed that shareholders are no longer in a position to monitor a management that is self-entrenched through its control of the techniques of shareholder democracy, such as the corporation's proxy machinery. These concerns may lead in either of two directions. First, it may be desired to make managers more responsible to shareholders, under the clarion call of "shareholder democracy." Second, it might be suggested that management privileges be detached from the shareholders inasmuch as the firm's principals include other parties such as employees and debt holders. The two critiques are fundamentally incompatible, although the differences between them are not always clearly articulated.

B. DIRECTORS AND OFFICERS

1. The Role of Directors

Under corporations statutes, management is identified with the directors. CBCA s. 102 states that "the directors shall manage the business and affairs of the corporation." See also ABCA s. 97(1); BCCA s. 141(1) (which provides that the directors manage *or supervise* subject to the articles of the company); and OBCA s. 115(1) (which provides that directors manage *or supervise*). This is the separation of powers clause in the corporation's constitution, and it means what it says: the directors, and not the shareholders, manage. The statutory provision is in fact declaratory of many years practice, long antedating the CBCA. See *Automatic Self-Cleansing Filter Syndicate Co. v. Cunninghame* (set out in Section C below).

2. Qualification Requirements for Directors

Legal Status, Age, Mental Competence and Financial Status. In modern corporations legislation, directors' mandatory qualification requirements are minimal. They must be natural persons, over 18 years of age and not adjudicated mental incompetents or bankrupts. CBCA s. 105(1); ABCA s. 100; BCCA s. 138(1); OBCA s. 118(1). While for many years directors had to be shareholders of the corporation (hence the expression "director's qualifying share"), most Canadian statutes no longer impose such a requirement. CBCA s. 105(2); ABCA s. 100(2); BCCA s. 139; OBCA s. 118(2). Publicly held corporations must have at least three directors, while closely held corporations may have as few as one. CBCA s. 102(2); ABCA s. 97(2); BCCA s. 132; OBCA s. 115(2).

Residency Requirements. Under CBCA s. 105(3) [ABCA s. 100(3); BCCA s. 133(1); OBCA s. 118(3)] a majority of the directors must be "resident Canadians," which includes citizens of Canada ordinarily resident in Canada, landed immigrants except those eligible for Canadian citizenship who have chosen not to apply for it, and certain citizens of Canada ordinarily resident abroad. CBCA s. 2(1) and CBCA Reg. s. 11; ABCA s. 1(t); OBCA s. 1(1) and Reg. s. 26.

The underlying notion appears to be that Canadian citizens will be more responsive to Canadian national interests in the operation of a corporation's affairs than non-citizens would be. (If this were in fact the result, do you think it desirable?) The promotion of Canadian national interests is not, however, made a statutory duty of directors, who presumably are to manage the corporation for the purpose of maximizing shareholder wealth consistently with the dictates of the law. A non-Canadian parent corporation may then quite easily appoint as directors Canadians who lack the nationalism of those who drafted the CBCA.

Furthermore, the thrust of the Canadian majority requirements might be entirely avoided in the case of wholly owned Canadian subsidiaries (a class of corporations that must have been among the prime objects of the requirement). The parent could appoint a majority or even all Canadians to the subsidiary board and then, by a unanimous shareholder agreement under CBCA s. 146(2) [see also ABCA s. 140(1)(c); OBCA s. 108(3)], strip the board of any real power (although in doing so it may be found that the persons to whom the powers are given are in fact "directors" as that term is defined in CBCA s. 2(1) (see also CBCA s. 146(5)).

In fact, the proportion of resident Canadians on boards of directors is considerably higher than the majority required by the CBCA. The Conference Board reports that the proportion increased from 84% to 87% from 1977 to 1982. *Canadian Directorship Practices: A Profile 1984*, 27 (1984).

For the better protection of provincial interests (and perhaps provincial law firms), the BCCA requires that at least one director of a corporation incorporated under the BCCA be a resident of that province. BCCA s. 133(2).

3. Election and Removal of Directors

Election. When a CBCA corporation is formed, a notice of the first directors of the corporation is sent to the Director (the person responsible for the administration of the CBCA). CBCA s. 106(1); ABCA s. 101(1). Under the BCCA the subscribers to the memorandum are the first directors of the company. CBCA s. 106(2) [ABCA s. 101(2); OBCA s. 119(1)] provides that the first directors hold office from the date of incorporation to the date of the first meeting of shareholders which (pursuant to CBCA s. 133(a); ABCA s. 127(1)(a); OBCA s. 94(a)) must be held within 18 months of incorporation. Thereafter directors are elected by an "ordinary resolution" of the shareholders. CBCA s. 106(3); ABCA s. 101(3); OBCA s. 119(4). An "ordinary resolution" is a resolution passed by a majority of the votes cast by shareholders who voted on the resolution. CBCA s. 2(1); ABCA s. 1(m); OBCA s. 1(1).

CBCA s. 106(3) provides that shareholders must elect directors at each annual meeting of the corporation, and CBCA s. 133(a) requires the directors to call an annual meeting not later than 15 months after the last preceding annual meeting. See also ABCA ss. 101(3), 127; BCCA s. 163(1) (meeting within 13 months of last meeting) and Table A Part 11; OBCA ss. 94, 119(4). The requirement of shareholder election of directors apparently may not be waived, not even where the authority of the board of directors has been sterilized in a unanimous shareholder agreement under s. 146(2).

The election of directors is one of the most important matters on which the shareholders vote. Since the directors manage the corporation, the election of directors is a significant method by which shareholders can exercise some control over the way in which the corporation is managed. It can be a useful control mechanism even for shareholders whose shareholdings are too small to influence the outcome of the election of directors. This is because their right to vote can be acquired by others who can accumulate sufficient voting rights to influence the outcome of an election of directors and thereby replace directors where the corporation is not being effectively managed. The potential for such a change in control of the voting rights gives management an incentive to act in the interests of shareholders.

Term of Office. Most commonly, the term of a director begins with the annual shareholder meeting at which she or he is elected and runs until the next annual meeting. However, the articles may provide for directors' terms of up to three years. CBCA ss. 106(3), (5); ABCA s. 101(9); [the BCCA imposes no limit on the terms of directors]; OBCA s. 119(4). Directors may also be re-elected without limit. If no directors are elected at a meeting where directors should be elected, the incumbents remain in office until successors are chosen. CBCA s. 106(6); ABCA s. 101(7); OBCA s. 119(7).

Rather than providing that all of the directors are to be elected at the same time, the corporation's articles may "classify" the board and provide that directors' terms are to be staggered. Suppose, for example, that a corporation had a nine-person board. The articles might provide for three-year terms with one-third of the directors to be elected each year.

Under CBCA s. 145, a corporation, shareholder or director may apply to court to resolve any controversy with respect to an election or appointment of a director, and the court may make "any order it thinks fit," including one restraining the person whose election or appointment is disputed from serving and ordering a new election under judicial supervision. See also ABCA s. 139; OBCA s. 107.

Filling of Vacancies. Generally, directors have the power to fill vacancies on the board. CBCA s. 111(1); ABCA s. 106(1); BCCA s. 155(1), Table A, Art. 11.4; OBCA s. 124(1). However, this rule is subject to numerous exceptions. For instance, the directors may not fill a vacancy in their number that results from an increase in the number or minimum number of directors or from the failure by the shareholders to elect the number or minimum number of directors required by the articles. CBCA s. 111(1); ABCA s. 106(1); OBCA s. 124(1).

Where the vacancy results from the removal of a director, it may be filled at the same shareholders' meeting that approved the removal. CBCA s. 109(3); ABCA s. 104(3); OBCA s. 122(3). The directors may fill the vacancy caused by the removal if the shareholders do not do so, but that is an unlikely event.

Ceasing to Hold Office. A director ceases to hold office during her or his term of office when she dies, resigns, becomes disqualified or is removed from office upon a resolution of the shareholders. CBCA s. 108; ABCA s. 103; BCCA s. 154(1); OBCA s. 121.

Removal. At common law, it was unclear whether directors could be removed for cause unless the corporation's constating documents so provided. See *Lawrence Report* 74-77; M. Eisenberg, *The Structure of the Corporation* 2, 86 (1976). However, CBCA s. 109(1) now guarantees that shareholders have the right to remove directors by ordinary resolution. See also ABCA s. 104(1); BCCA s. 154(3) (requires a special resolution); OBCA s. 122(1). The shareholders' meeting that approves the removal of a director may also fill the vacancy that results from the removal of a director. CBCA s. 109(3); ABCA s. 104(3); OBCA s. 122(3). As noted above, the directors may fill the vacancy caused by the removal in the unlikely event the shareholders fail to do so.

CBCA s. 6(4) makes the removal of directors the only matter of shareholder action for which the articles may not require a majority higher than the statute sets out. See also ABCA s. 6(4); OBCA s. 5(5). However, the following case suggests that, at least in some circumstances, this constraint can be avoided.

Bushell v. Faith
House of Lords
[1970] A.C. 1099

[The company, Bush Court (Southgate) Ltd., owned a block of flats in London. The company had three shareholders, the plaintiff, the defendant and their sister. Each held 100 shares. The plaintiff and the defendant were the directors. The plaintiff and her sister, being dissatisfied with the defendant's conduct as a director, requisitioned a meeting of shareholders for the purpose of removing him. The plaintiff and her sister voted in favour of the resolution and the defendant against. The company's article 9 provided:

In the event of a resolution being proposed at any general meeting of the company for the removal from office of any director, any shares held by that director shall carry the right to three votes per share. ...

The plaintiff issued a writ to enforce her contention that the resolution had passed by 200 votes to 100. The defendant argued that it had been defeated by 300 votes to 200. The trial Court held for the plaintiff on the basis that article 9 contravened s. 184(1) of the Companies Act, 1948 (discussed later) but the Court of Appeal reversed. The plaintiff appealed.]

LORD UPJOHN: ... The company adopted Table A in the First Schedule to the Companies Act, 1948, with variations which are immaterial for present purposes. The relevant articles of Table A are:

2. Without prejudice to any special rights previously conferred on the holders of any existing shares or class of shares, any share in the company may be issued with such preferred, deferred or other special rights or such restrictions, whether in regard to dividend, voting, return of capital or otherwise as the company may from time to time by ordinary resolution determine.

62. Subject to any rights or restrictions for the time being attached to any class or classes of shares, on a show of hands every member present in person shall have one vote, and on a poll every member shall have one vote for each share of which he is the holder.

Special article 9 is as follows:

In the event of a resolution being proposed at any general meeting of the company for the removal from office of any director, any shares held by that director shall on a poll in respect of such resolution carry the right to three votes per share and regulation 62 of Part 1 of Table A shall be construed accordingly.

Article 96 of Table A, which empowers a company to remove a director by ordinary resolution is excluded by the articles of the company so that the appellant relies on the mandatory terms of section 184(1) of the Companies Act, 1948, which so far as relevant is in these terms:

A company may [by] ordinary resolution remove a director before the expiration of his period of office, notwithstanding anything in its articles or in any agreement between it and him. ...

It is not in doubt that the requirements of subsection (2) have been satisfied. So the whole question is whether special article 9 is valid and applicable, in which case the resolution was rejected by 300 votes to 200, or whether that article must be treated as overridden by section 184 and therefore void, in which case the resolution was passed by 200 votes to 100. So to test this matter the appellant began an action for a declaration that the respondent was removed from office as a director by the resolution of November 22, 1968, and moved the court for an interlocutory injunction restraining him from acting as a director. This motion comes by way of appeal before your Lordships.

•   •   •

My Lords, when construing an Act of Parliament it is a canon of construction that its provisions must be construed in the light of the mischief which the Act was designed to meet. In this case the mischief was well known; it was a common practice, especially in the case of private companies, to provide in the articles that a director should be irremovable or only removable by an extraordinary resolution; in the former case the articles would have to be altered by special resolution before the director could be removed and of course in either case a three-quarters majority would be required. In many cases this would be impossible, so the Act provided that notwithstanding anything in the articles an ordinary resolution would suffice to remove a director. That was the mischief which the section set out to remedy; to make a director removable by virtue of an ordinary resolution instead of an extraordinary resolution or making it necessary to alter the articles.

An ordinary resolution is not defined nor used in the body of the Act of 1948 though the phrase occurs in some of the articles of Table A in the First Schedule to the Act. But its meaning is, in my opinion, clear. An ordinary resolution is in the first place passed by a bare majority on a show of hands by the members entitled to vote who are present personally or by proxy and on such a vote each member has one vote regardless of his shareholding. If a poll is demanded then for an ordinary resolution still only a bare majority of votes is required. But whether a share or class of shares has any vote upon the matter and, if so, what is its voting power upon the resolution in question depends entirely upon the voting rights attached to that share or class of shares by the articles of association.

I venture to think that Ungoed-Thomas J. overlooked the importance of article 2 of Table A which gives to the company a completely unfettered right to attach to any share or class of shares special voting rights upon a poll or to restrict those rights as the company may think fit. Thus, it is commonplace that a company may and frequently does preclude preference shareholders from voting unless their dividends are in arrear or their class rights are directly affected. It is equally commonplace that particular shares may be issued with specially loaded voting rights which ensure that in all resolutions put before the shareholders in general meeting the holder of those particular shares can always be sure of carrying the day, aye or no, as the holder pleases.

Mr. Dillon, for the appellant, felt, quite rightly, constrained to admit that if an article provided that Mr. Faith's shares should, on every occasion when a resolution was for consideration by a general meeting of the company, carry three votes such a provision would be valid on all such occasions including any occasion when the general meeting was considering a resolution for his removal under section 184.

My Lords, I cannot see any difference between that case and the present case where special voting rights are conferred only when there is a resolution for the removal of a director under section 184. Each case is an exercise of the unfettered right of the company under article 2 whereby

any share in the company may be issued with such ... special rights ... in regard to ...voting ... as the company may from time to time by ordinary resolution determine.

Parliament has never sought to fetter the right of the company to issue a share with such rights or restrictions as it may think fit. There is no fetter which compels the company to make the voting rights or restrictions of general application and it seems to me clear that such rights or restrictions can be attached to special circumstances and to particular types of resolution. This makes no mockery of section 184; all that Parliament was seeking to do thereby was to make an ordinary resolution sufficient to remove a director. Had Parliament desired to go further and enact that every share entitled to vote should be deprived of its special rights under the articles it should have said so in plain terms by making the vote on a poll one vote one share. Then, what about shares which had no voting rights under the articles? Should not Parliament give them a vote when considering this completely artificial form of ordinary resolution? Suppose there had been some preference shares in the name of Mr. Faith's wife, which under the articles had in the circumstances no vote; why in justice should her voice be excluded from consideration in this artificial vote?

I only raise this purely hypothetical case to show the great difficulty of trying to do justice by legislation in a matter which has always been left to the corporators themselves to decide.

I agree entirely with the judgment of the Court of Appeal, and would dismiss this appeal.

LORD MORRIS OF BORTH-Y-GEST: My Lords, it is provided by section 184(1) that a company may by ordinary resolution remove a director before the expiration of his period of office. The company may do so notwithstanding anything to the contrary in its articles. So if an article provided that a director was irremovable he could nevertheless be removed if an ordinary resolution to that effect was passed. So also if an article provided that a director could only be removed by a resolution carried by a majority greater than a simple majority he would nevertheless be removed if a resolution was passed by a simple majority.

Some shares may, however, carry a greater voting power than others. On a resolution to remove a director shares will therefore carry the voting power that they possess. But this does not, in my view, warrant a device such as article 9 introduces. Its unconcealed effect is to make a director irremovable. If the question is posed whether the shares of the respondent possess any added voting weight the answer must be that they possess none whatsoever beyond, if valid, an ad hoc weight for the special purpose of circumventing section 184. If article 9 were writ large it would set out that a director is not to be removed against his will and that in order to achieve this and to thwart the express provision of section 184 the voting power of any director threatened with removal is to be deemed to be greater than it actually is. The learned judge thought that to sanction this would be to make a mockery of the law. I think so also.

I would allow the appeal.

[The judgments of LORDS DONOVAN, GUEST and REID, agreeing in substance with that of LORD UPJOHN, have been omitted.]

Appeal dismissed.

All of the Law Lords who upheld the validity of special article 9 cited the fact that the Companies Act did not prevent firms from issuing shares or classes of shares with specially weighted voting rights. But is that the same thing as permitting the number of votes attached to otherwise fungible shares of a single class to fluctuate depending solely on who owns the shares for the time being?

4. Authority and Powers of Directors

As noted above, it is the directors that have the authority to manage the corporation. CBCA s. 102; ABCA s. 97(1); BCCA s. 141; OBCA s. 115(1). Corporate statutes often specifically allocate other powers to the directors.

Adoption, Amendment or Repeal of the By-Laws. For instance, the CBCA also gives the directors the power to adopt, amend or repeal by-laws. CBCA s. 103; ABCA s. 98; OBCA s. 116. However, this is only a default allocation in favour of the directors since the power of the directors to adopt, amend or repeal by-laws is subject to the articles, the by-laws or a unanimous shareholder agreement. The power of the directors with respect to the by-laws is also qualified by the requirement that any change the directors make in the by-laws must be put before the shareholders at the next annual meeting of shareholders. A change in the by-laws made by the directors is effective until the shareholder meeting and is effective thereafter only if approved by the shareholders or approved as amended. By contrast, under the BCCA the "articles" are the rough equivalent of the by-laws under the CBCA and can only be amended by a special resolution of the shareholders.

The Power to Borrow. The directors also have the power to borrow subject to the articles, the by-laws or a unanimous shareholder agreement. CBCA s. 189(1); ABCA s. 98.1; BCCA Table A Arts. 6, 10.1; OBCA s. 184(1). The directors may also delegate the power to borrow to a director, a committee of directors or an officer subject to any restriction on this in the articles, by-laws or a unanimous shareholder agreement. CBCA s. 189(2); ABCA s. 98.1(2); OBCA s. 184(2).

Declaration of Dividends. Directors also have the power to declare dividends and under the CBCA this is a power that can not be delegated. CBCA s. 115(3)(d); ABCA s. 110(3)(d); OBCA s. 127(3)(d). See also BCCA Table A, Art. 15.1.

Appointment and Compensation of Officers and the Delegation of Powers. One of the most significant powers of the directors is their power to appoint officers of the corporation, determine the compensation of officers and delegate management powers to officers. CBCA s. 121 provides that, subject to the articles, by-laws or a unanimous shareholder agreement, the directors designate the offices of the corporation, appoint officers and delegate powers. See also ABCA s. 116; BCCA s. 157; OBCA s. 133.

As noted below, widely held corporations are typically managed by officers appointed by the directors leaving the directors in a largely supervisory role. However, the power of directors to appoint officers who manage the corporation remains a significant device since shareholders can exercise their voting powers to replace the directors who can then replace the officers of the corporation.

The effectiveness of replacing the directors of a corporation as a control device would be seriously hampered if the directors had delegated all of their powers. Consequently the directors may not delegate all, or virtually all, of their powers. See, e.g., *Hayes v. Canada-Atlantic & Plant S.S. Co.*, 181 F. 289 (1st Cir. 1910). CBCA s. 115(3) provides that the directors can not delegate their powers with respect to certain matters such as filling a vacancy among the directors, issuing securities, declaring dividends, purchasing, redeeming or otherwise acquiring the shares issued by the corporation, or adopting, amending or repealing by-laws of the corporation. See also ABCA s. 110(3); OBCA s. 127(3).

Removal of Officers. Directors may also remove officers. The power to remove officers is key to the effectiveness of the election and removal of directors as a shareholder control device. However, removing the officers may permit them to assert actions for wrongful dismissal.

There is a trade-off between preserving the removal of managers as a shareholder control device and providing managers with long-term contracts and compensation in the event the long-term contract is terminated. It may be beneficial to the corporation and its officers to provide officers with the security of long-term contracts. The officer will probably value the security of a long-term contract and the corporation will benefit if the officer is willing to accept less compensation in return for the security of a long-term contract.

With the hope of a long-term reward, managers may be more willing to invest their human capital in the firm. Cutting this off by firing them might be seen as shareholder opportunism. This would not have distributional effects if managers were informed of this threat. But it may lead to inefficiencies, since informed managers would react to the threat by underinvesting in firm-specific human capital. Offering them a long-term employment contract, with damages for premature termination, might then be an efficient response to this problem, since the managers would have been given a greater incentive to seek long-term rewards in the firm.

In this context, consider the following case.

Re Paramount Publix Corp.
United States Court of Appeals, Second Circuit
90 F.2d 441 (1937)

Before MANTON, L. HAND, and SWAN, Circuit Judges.

SWAN, Circuit Judge: Under a written contract dated January 1, 1932, Sam Katz was employed by the debtor in an executive capacity for a term of three years. His duties were to be such as should be assigned to him from time to time by the board of directors or its executive committee and were to be of a dignity substantially equivalent to those he had performed under a prior contract; his compensation was to be a weekly cash salary of $2,500 and the option to purchase at stipulated prices a block of the debtor's stock at the end of each six months of service. Execution of the contract was authorized by the directors and ratified by the stockholders. The proof of claim filed by Katz alleged a wrongful discharge on October 28, 1932 (prior to the filing of the petition under section 77B, Bankr.Act, 11 U.S.C.A. § 207), and claimed damages in the amount of $265,498.18 with interest. The trustees of the debtor filed objections to the claim and brought on for hearing before a special master the objection based on section 60 of the New York Stock Corporation Law (Consol.Laws, c. 59). The special master upheld the objection and recommended that the claim be expunged, but the District Court sustained the claimant's exceptions to the special master's report and ruled that section 60 afforded no defense to the claim.

It is to be observed that the order of the District Court does not allow the claim; it is yet to be determined whether Katz was wrongfully discharged and, if so, in what amount he was damaged.

Section 60 of the New York Stock Corporation Law reads as follows:

§ 60. *Officers*. The directors of a stock corporation may appoint or elect from their number a president, and may appoint or elect one or more vice-presidents, a secretary, a treasurer, and other officers, agents and employees, who shall respectively have such powers and perform such duties in the management of the property and affairs of the corporation, subject to the control of the directors, as may be prescribed by them or in the by-laws. The directors may require any such officer, agent or employee to give security for the faithful performance of his duties, and may remove him at pleasure.

The first sentence clearly embraces such an officer as the appellee, who served as managing head of the debtor's theater department; and the sole question is whether the last sentence exempts the corporation from liability for discharging him without cause during the term of his contract of employment. The appellant contends that the District Court erred in answering that question in the negative.

The consequences of accepting the opposite view are startling. It would mean that no New York stock corporation could make a binding contract of employment for a definite term; all officers, agents and employees would be dischargeable at will without liability on the part of the corporation, and it would follow that any of them could leave at will without incurring liability on their part, no matter how essential their services might be to the interests of the corporation. The announcement of such a doctrine would certainly cause surprise and consternation to the business world, for the statute has stood on the books since 1890 without any court decision to that effect and it is common knowledge that many contracts of term employment have been made by New York corporations on the assumption of their validity. The appellant suggests that the contract might bind the corporate agent for the stated term, although the corporation were left free to discharge him at will. But, if one of the parties may perform or not in its discretion, we do not see how the other can be bound. ... It is suggested also that the section should be construed to apply only to executives who exercise managerial powers. Such a limitation seems scarcely justified. The reasonable way to read the language is that the directors may appoint the specifically named officers and "other officers, agents and employees," and that each "shall have such powers and perform such duties in the management of the property and affairs of the corporation" as the directors may see fit to assign or the by-laws prescribe. So we think the appellant's contention must really go to the extreme we have indicated. Unless forced to it by controlling New York decisions, we should hesitate to adopt a construction of the statute which would bring about results so contrary to the general business practice.

It must be conceded, however, that the appellant makes a strong argument for its contention. Section 24 of the National Banking Act (12 U.S.C.A. § 24, par. 5),which is verbally similar to section 60 of the New York Stock Corporation Law, has been uniformly construed as permitting the removal of bank officers without subjecting the corporation to liability, despite the existence of an employment contract for a definite term.

• • •

Despite this array of authority we do not think we are constrained to give to section 60 the same construction as section 24 of the National Banking Act has received. No New York court has so construed section 60 or its predecessor provision, section 27 of the Stock Corporation Law of 1890. On the contrary, such authority as there is has taken the opposite view. In *Abbott v. Stern Bros.*, 248 App.Div. 161, 288 N.Y.S. 394, it was expressly ruled that section 60 afforded no defense to an action for breach of a term contract of employment. Abbott, the plaintiff, was employed as general merchandise manager of the defendant corporation for a term of two years. Before expiration of the term he was discharged and sued for damages for unlawful dismissal. Among the defenses interposed was section 60. The trial court directed a verdict for the plaintiff, which the appellate court reversed because there was enough evidence of the plaintiff's incompetence to require the jury to pass upon whether he was discharged without cause; but the opinion of the majority stated that the fifth and sixth defenses (which pleaded section 60) were insufficient, and one justice dissented for the very reason that section 60 barred recovery. Whether decision of the majority could and should have gone on the ground of res judicata, as the appellant contends, it certainly did not rest on that ground but expressly ruled on the exact point now presented to us. It is worthy of note that the *Abbott Case* was decided by the same Appellate Division that had previously construed section 24 of the National Banking Act to preclude recovery by a bank official discharged without cause during his term of employment. *Copeland v. Melrose Nat. Bank of New York*, 229 App. Div. 311, 241 N.Y.S. 429, affirmed 254 N.Y. 632, 173 N.E. 898. The case of *Usher v. New York Central & H.R.R. Co.*, 76 App.Div. 422, 78 N.Y.S. 508, affirmed without opinion in 179 N.Y. 544, 71 N.E. 1141, gives some reason for thinking that the Court of Appeals entertains the same view, for the dissent in the court below had relied on section 60. Numerous cases both in the highest court of New York and in intermediate courts have assumed without discussion of the statute the validity and enforceability of corporate term employment contracts. ... While this group of cases cannot be treated as deciding the question, they are not without significance in showing that neither bench nor bar has entertained the view that the statute should be construed as the appellant now contends, although on numerous occasions such a construction would have been determinative of the litigation. We conclude, therefore, that the New York decisions do not compel us to adopt the appellant's construction of section 60 but support rather the construction adopted by Judge Coxe.

As a matter of independent construction we should reach the same result. ... Section 60 of the Stock Corporation Law we do not regard as a limitation upon corporate powers to make contracts of employment. It is one of the sections in article 6 entitled "Directors and Officers," and its purpose, we believe, was to declare that a corporation, through its directors, should have the same power to revoke an agency as an individual principal has. In the case of an individual the agency and the contract of hiring are distinct. When the statute was enacted, it was not certain that this was equally true of a corporate officer or agent, and particularly if he held an office fixed and regulated by the corporate charter. See Morawetz, *Private Corporations* (1886 Ed.) §§ 541 (p. 515) and 544. Section 60 declared that the directors had this power of revocation. To so construe it gives it sufficient scope and meaning, and accords with the ideas of corporate policy now currently held. See section 32(4), Uniform Business Corporation Act. There would seem to be no more reason to hold that section 60 was intended to relieve the corporation from the obligation to pay damages for breach of contract than to construe in that way a by-law empowering the directors to remove an officer at pleasure. Such a by-law came before the Court of Appeals in *Cuppy v. Stollwerck Bros.*, 216 N.Y. 591, at page 597, 111 N.E. 249, 250, where the court said:

The power to remove him from the office to which he had been elected did not carry with it the right to discharge him from the employment of the defendant in view of the special contract for a fixed term under which he was employed.

• • •

Nor can we see that a construction of the statute in a manner that permits the board of directors to bind the corporation by an employment contract for a fixed term "sterilizes" a succeeding board any more than does the admitted power to bind the corporation by a long-term lease or any other kind of contract extending over a term of years.

For the foregoing reasons we think the statute was correctly construed by the District Judge.

Order affirmed.

NOTES

1) How convincing do you find the Court's distinction between revocation of the contract of agency and revocation of the contract of employment under s. 60 of the New York statute? If the corporation had not been bankrupt and Mr. Katz had sued for reinstatement, how would the Court have held? Would the Court have enjoined the corporation from breaching its contract? For other cases taking a similar approach see, e.g., *Short v. Columbia Rubber and Gasket Company, Inc.*, 535 So.2d. 61 (Miss. 1988); *Nelson v. WEB Water Development Association*, 507 N.W. 2d. 691 (S.D. 1993).

2) In *Montreal Public Service Co. v. Champagne* (1916), 33 D.L.R. 49 (P.C.), the plaintiff was hired as general manager of the defendant corporation, and his contract gave him the control of "all the administration of the business of the company ... subject only to such direction and control as it is the duty of the directors to exercise." After the plaintiff had entered upon the employment, the corporation appointed a president under whose close supervision they placed the plaintiff. It was held that the plaintiff was entitled to damages for breach of contract.

3) In *Shindler v. Northern Raincoat Co. Ltd.*, [1960] 2 All E.R. 239, the plaintiff had been the managing director and controlling shareholder of the Raincoat company. He sold out to Loyds Retailers Ltd., a public corporation, and Loyds agreed to retain the plaintiff as managing director of the subsidiary for a period of 10 years. The Raincoat company's articles included art. 68 of Table A of the Companies Act, 1929, to the following effect:

The directors may from time to time appoint one or more of their body to the office of managing director or manager for such term and at such remuneration ... as they may think fit ...; but his appointment shall be subject to determination *ipso facto* if he ceases from any cause to be a director, or if the company in general meeting resolve that his tenure of office of managing director or manager be determined.

During the term of plaintiff's employment, Loyds decided to sell the Raincoat company to another public company, which did not wish to retain the plaintiff as managing director. After protracted negotiations between the plaintiff and Loyds concerning comparable alternative employment proved unsuccessful, the plaintiff was removed as a director, and therefore as managing director, of the Raincoat company by an extraordinary resolution approved by the Raincoat company's shareholders (that is, by Loyds). The plaintiff was held to be entitled to damages for wrongful dismissal. The Court rejected the company's claim that the contract of employment would be *ultra vires* if interpreted to exclude a power in the company's general meeting to terminate it for whatever reasons seemed sufficient to the shareholders. The Court held that the principle to be applied in resolution of the controversy was that, where a party enters into an arrangement whose effectiveness requires continuance of an existing state of circumstances, there is an implied engagement on his part that he shall do nothing of his own motion to put an end to that state of circumstances. See also *Read v. Astoria Garage (Streatham) Ltd.*, [1952] 1 Ch. 637; *Southern Foundries (1926) Ltd. v. Shirlaw*, [1940] A.C. 701 (H.L.).

5. Directors' Meetings

The mechanics of calling and holding board meetings are usually specified in the corporation's by-laws. Subject to the articles or by-laws, the quorum is a majority of the board or a majority of the minimum number of directors in the articles. CBCA s. 114(2); ABCA s. 109(2); BCCA Table A Art. 12; OBCA s. 126(3). Notice to the directors is mandated by s. 114(5) [ABCA s. 109(5); OBCA s. 126(9)], but can be waived by s. 114(6) [ABCA s. 109(6); OBCA s. 126(10)]. Meetings by conference call are permitted by s. 114(9) [ABCA s. 109(9); BCCA s. 149(2); OBCA s. 126(13)] and no meeting need be held to transact business where all of the directors sign a written resolution in lieu of the meeting. CBCA s. 117; BCCA s. 149(3); ABCA s. 112; OBCA s. 129. Meetings of one-person boards are validated by section 114(8), without which a meeting would require at least two persons. ABCA s. 109(8); OBCA s. 126(12).

According to a 1984 Conference Board report, widely held corporations have an average of eight board meetings a year, and the average for all corporations is six meetings a year. *Canadian Directorship Practices: A Profile 1984* 14 (1984). While the CBCA does not prescribe how frequent directors' meetings should be, at some point the failure to hold meetings might give rise to liability for breach of the duty of care under s. 122(1)(b) [ABCA s. 117(1)(b); OBCA s. 134(1)(b)], a subject considered in Chapter Seven.

6. How Boards of Public Corporations Operate

In his pioneering study of practices in boards of directors of publicly held corporations in the United States, *Directors: Myth and Reality* (1971), Myles Mace found that boards in his sample did not manage the corporation, and usually did not have much of a role in setting corporate strategy or in monitoring the performance of the management. He concluded, however, that directors do have a useful function. The fact that the chief executive has to appear before the board was seen as a discipline upon him, and directors either individually or (more rarely) in groups gave useful advice and counsel to the chief executive. In rare cases, when a chief executive's management became insupportably bad, the board would fire and replace him. See also Mace, *Directors: Myth and Reality—Ten Years Later*, 32 Rudgers L. Rev. 293 (1979), confirming the findings in the earlier work.

In the Conference Board of Canada, *Canadian Directorship Practices: A Critical Self-Examination* (1977), the results of lengthy interviews with 50 persons holding among themselves some 265 directorships in over 130 Canadian public corporations were published. The consensus among these directors in their self-evaluation included the following points:

(1) management often controls the board rather than the other way around and the board's effectiveness is often a function of the chief executive's desire for or tolerance of its informed input;

(2) boards are excessively hesitant to fire top management;

(3) a person with a full-time job cannot adequately attend to directorship duties if he holds more than two to six outside directorships.

A more recent study by the Conference Board, however, suggests a greater degree of board independence from management. For 93% of firms reporting, including small to large corporations, the nomination of new directors is a board prerogative. *Canadian Directorship Practices: A Profile 1984* 31 (1984). In addition, the majority of board members are "outside" directors and not affiliated with management. *Id.* at 19-21.

In *The Structure of the Corporation* (1976), Melvin Eisenberg argues that, rather than attempting to upgrade the functioning of boards to the legal model wherein they "manage" or even "supervise the management of the corporation," it would be preferable to identify what it is that boards may reasonably be expected to do and then to adjust both the legal model and the structure of boards to such expectations. The role that Professor Eisenberg believes the board is uniquely suited to perform is the selection, monitoring and, if need be, removal of the chief executive. Professor Eisenberg's views were influential in the preparation of the American Law Institute's recommendations on corporate governance the current version of which recommends as follows:

§3.01 Management of the Corporation's Business: Functions and Powers of Principal Senior Executives and Other Officers
The management of the business of a publicly held corporation [§1.31] should be conducted by or under the supervision of such principal executives [§1.30] as are designated by the board of directors, and by those other officers [§1.27] and employees to whom the management function is delegated by the board or those executives, subject to the functions and powers of the board under §3.02.

§3.02 Functions and Powers of the Board of Directors
Except as otherwise provided by statute:

(a) The board of directors of a publicly held corporation [§1.31] should perform the following functions:

(1) Select, regularly evaluate, fix the compensation of, and, where appropriate, replace the principal senior executives [§1.30];

(2) Oversee the conduct of the corporation's business to evaluate whether the business is being properly managed;

(3) Review and, where appropriate, approve the corporation's financial objectives and major corporate plans and actions;

(4) Review and, where appropriate, approve major changes in, and determinations of other major questions of choice respecting, the appropriate auditing and accounting principles and practices to be used in the preparation of the corporation's financial statements;

(5) Perform such other functions as are prescribed by law, or assigned to the board under a standard of the corporation [§1.36].

(b) A board of directors also has power to:

(1) Initiate and adopt corporate plans, commitments, and actions;

(2) Initiate and adopt changes in accounting principles and practices;

(3) Provide advice and counsel to the principal senior executives;

(4) Instruct any committee, principal senior executive, or other officer [§1.27], and review the actions of any committee, principal senior executive, or other officer;

(5) Make recommendations to shareholders;

(6) Manage the business of the corporation;

(7) Act as to all other corporate matters not requiring shareholder approval.

(c) Subject to the board's ultimate responsibility for oversight under Subsection (a)(2), the board may delegate to its committees authority to perform any of its functions and exercise any of its powers.

(Principles of Corporate Governance: Analysis and Recommendations, May 13, 1992)

A report prepared for the Toronto Stock Exchange, *Where Were the Directors?* (1995), recommended that the overall responsibility of the board should consist of:

(i) adoption of a strategic planning process;

(ii) identification of the principal risks of the corporation's business and ensuring the implementation of appropriate systems to manage these risks;

(iii) succession planning including appointment, training and monitoring senior management;

(iv) implementation of a communications policy for the corporation; and

(v) ensuring the integrity of the corporation's internal control and management information systems.

In order to fulfill the role of selecting, monitoring and possibly removing the chief executive, Professor Eisenberg believes that the board should be controlled by non-management outsiders, that the board's audit committee be made up exclusively of outsiders and that the outsiders on the board be in sole control of the corporation's proxy machinery. As appears more fully in the succeeding parts of this chapter, the proxy process is the means through which the corporation communicates with its shareholders, especially concerning nominees to the board. The proxy process has in fact largely replaced the meeting itself as the focus for shareholder voting rights. The audit committee is the principal means through which the corporation's outside auditors communicate with the board.

7. Outside Directors

As noted above, Professor Eisenberg's views were highly influential in the preparation of the American Law Institute's *Principles of Corporate Governance and Structure: Restatement and Recommendations* (Tentative Draft No. 1, 1982). This would have required that a majority of the directors of public corporations be independent of the firm. These proposals were controversial, and in a subsequent draft many of the mandatory provisions on board structure were changed to voluntary recommendations. American Law Institute, *Principles of Corporate Governance: Analysis and Recommendations* (Tentative Draft No. 2, 1984). The most recent version of the American Law Institute's *Principles of Corporate Governance: Analysis and Recommendatons* (May 13, 1992) also simply recommended that the board of a public corporation be composed of a majority of independent directors (see s. 3A.01). The American Law Institute proposals do require large publicly held corporations (2,000 or more shareholders and $100 million or more in total assets) to have an audit committee consisting of at least three members and composed exclusively of directors who are not employees of the corporation. *Id.* s. 3.05. Thus it would effectively require large publicly held corporations to have at least three outside directors. Although a majority of outside directors is not mandatory in the United States, 74% of the directors of publicly held corporations in the United States were not employees of the corporation as of 1987. See J.W. Lorsch, *Pawns or Potentates: The Reality of America's Corporate Boards* 17 (1989).

CBCA s. 102(2) requires that at least two directors of a public corporation be outsiders. ABCA s. 97(2); BCCA s. 132; OBCA s. 115(3). Though the requirement is mandatory, the requirement is considerably less exacting than the American Law Institute's Corporate Governance project, since a majority of directors in public corporations would usually number more than eight.

The Toronto Stock Exchange report, *Where Were the Directors?* (1995), recommended that the T.S.E. adopt non-binding guidelines that, among other matters, would suggest that the boards of T.S.E. listed corporations consist of a majority of "unrelated" directors. An "unrelated" director would be "a director who is free from any interest in any business or other relationship which could, or could reasonably be perceived to, materially interfere with the director's ability to act with a view to the best interests of the corporation, other than interests and relationships arising from shareholding." The report noted that a management director would not be an "unrelated" director. The corporation would have to describe its system of corporate governance in its annual report or information circular including the analysis of who constituted an "unrelated" director. The report also suggested that the audit commitee should consist exclusively of outside directors. It further recommended that the corporation should enable individual directors to engage outside advisers at the expense of the corporation in appropriate circumstances. In May 1995, the T.S.E. adopted a by-law requiring disclosure of corporate governance practices for T.S.E. listed companies. See TSE by-law s. 19.17.

Should CBCA outside director requirements be strengthened? If better quality monitoring is available through independent directors, a firm may appoint more than two outside directors as a strategy to reduce agency costs. Indeed, the Conference Board suggests that just this has happened, since "independent" outside directors now comprise the majority of board memberships in Canadian public corporations, and only one-quarter of board members of firms of all asset sizes are employees of the firm. The larger the firm, the higher the proportion of outside directors. On a narrower definition of outside director, excluding non-employee directors with a business or family relationship to the firm, they still amount to 55% of board membership, with a higher proportion for Canadian-owned, widely held corporations. *Canadian Directorship Practices: A Profile 1984* 19-21 (1984). A subsequent Conference Board study found evidence of an increase in the number of outside directors, with 64% of directors being neither full-time current or former employees nor representatives of parent shareholders. *Canadian Directorship Practices: Compensation of Boards of Directors* 9-11 (1985).

These outside directors will frequently have had some business relationship with the firm prior to their appointment. The statutory standard of what constitutes an outside director in CBCA s. 102(2) is persons who are "not officers or employees of the corporation or its affiliates," and this would be met by the corporation's retired executives, by its outside counsel and other retained advisers such as investment bankers. Such directors are likely not wholly independent of management's influence, and this has led to suggestions that the definition of who is an outside director be narrowed. However, the most useful kind of outside director is likely one with some relation to the firm, since the flow of information between the firm and its bankers, underwriters and lawyers is thereby facilitated. If the argument for mandatory outside director requirements is that this will maximize firm wealth, do you think board membership decisions might be left with the firm? If board composition may affect firm wealth, it should not be supposed that one kind of board is optimal for every firm. The best board composition would then be more easily achieved with a minimum of mandatory rules.

The Conference Board reports that among all outside directors, the most frequently mentioned occupational categories are (1) independent businessmen, financiers and consultants (21%); (2) business executives (19%); (3) executives of banks or service industries (14%); (4) practising lawyers (12%); (5) executives of non-bank financial institutions (11%); and (6) educators, union officials, lobbyists and government officials (6%). *Canadian Directorship Practices: A Profile 1984* 21-22 (1984).

The effectiveness of outside directors in monitoring corporate management has been questioned. First, outside directors are often not truly independent of management since they are often selected by management. Second, outside directors are often executives of other businesses themselves and thus share similar perspectives to management on just how closely managers should be monitored. Third, many outside directors will have similar backgrounds to management and share similar views. Fourth, outside directors also lack the information, staff, expertise or time to effectively monitor management. Fifth, while the outside directors are expected to monitor the managers, who monitors the outside directors. The market is unlikely to monitor outside directors any better than it monitors the inside directors. See, e.g., R.J. Gilson & R. Kraakman, *Reinventing the Outside Director: An Agenda for Institutional Investors*, 43 Stan. L.R. 863, 872-76 (1991); and V. Brudney, *The Independent Director—Heavenly City or Potemkin Village?* 95 Harv. L.R. 597 (1982). See further McDougall & Fogelberg, *Corporate Boards in Canada: How Sixty-Four Boards Function* (1968); White, *Powers or Pawns: Boards of Directors in Canadian Corporations* (1977); Baysinger & Butler, *Corporate Governance and the Board of Directors: Performance Effects of Changes in Board Composition*, 1 J.L. Econ. & Org. 101 (1985); Baysinger & Zardkoohi, *Technology, Residual Claimants, and Corporate Control*, 2 J.L. Econ. & Org. 339 (1986); Romano, *Metapolitics and Corporate Law Reform*, 36 Stan. L. Rev. 923 (1984).

In recognition of some of the concerns with respect to the effectiveness of outside directors the American Law Institute proposals allow outside directors to retain legal counsel, accountants or other experts at the corporation's expense on approval by the board, or by a court where the board declines to give its approval. See American Law Institute, *Principles of Corporate Governance: Analysis and Recommendations* s. 3.04 (May 13, 1992).

Professors Gilson and Kraakman have recommended the reinventing of the outside director as a full-time professional director who would have the requisite expertise and would serve on the boards of perhaps six corporations. As full-time directors of a limited number of corporations they would have a focused mandate and the time to familiarize themselves with the corporations on which they serve as board members. These professional directors would be chosen by institutional investors who might organize a separate clearinghouse to coordinate action among institutional investors for the selection of directors. See R.J. Gilson & R. Kraakman, *Reinventing the Outside Director: An Agenda for Institutional Investors*, 43 Stan. L.R. 863 (1991).

Professors Rock and Coffee have questioned the effectiveness of having institutional investors choose and monitor professional directors. Institutional investors also have managers who are separate from the owners of the institutional investor's funds. The managers of institutional investors may thus not have a sufficient incentive to effectively monitor the professional directors (or take the steps to put professional managers in place to begin with). The institutional investors would also face a conflict of interest since the corporations on the boards of which professional directors would serve would often be clients or potential clients of the institutional investor. See B. Rock, *The Logic and (Uncertain) Significance of Institutional Shareholder Activism*, 79 Georgetown L.J. 445, 453-78 (1991); J.C. Coffee, *Liquidity Versus Control: The Institutional Investor as Corporate Monitor*, 91 Col. L.R. 1277, 1329-36 (1991).

C. SHAREHOLDERS' VOTING RIGHTS

1. Shareholder Control Over Directors: Shareholder Residual Powers

The Power to Manage. Although shareholders have the power to elect the directors, they do not normally have the power to manage the corporation. As noted above, it is the directors of the corporation who "manage the business and affairs of the corporation." CBCA s. 102(1). As the following case suggests, this is an apparent codification of a long accepted practice.

Automatic Self-Cleansing Filter Syndicate Co. v. Cunninghame
English Court of Appeal
[1906] 2 Ch. 34

[The plaintiff company was incorporated in 1896, with objects in its memorandum that included the sale of the undertaking of the company. The articles provided as follows:

81. The company may by special resolution remove any director before the expiration of his period of office and appoint another qualified person in his stead. ...

96. The management of the business and the control of the company shall be vested in the directors, who, in addition to the powers and authorities by these presents expressly conferred upon them, may exercise all such powers and do all such acts and things as may be exercised or done by the company, and are not hereby or by statute expressly directed or required to be exercised or done by the company in general meeting; but subject nevertheless to the provisions of the statutes and of these presents, and to such regulations, not being inconsistent with these presents,

as may from time to time be made by extraordinary resolution, but no regulation shall invalidate any prior act of the directors which would have been valid if such regulation had not been made.

97. Without prejudice to the general powers conferred by the last preceding clause, and to the other powers and authorities conferred as aforesaid, it is hereby expressly declared that the directors shall be entrusted with the following powers, namely, power—

(1.) To purchase or otherwise acquire for the company any property, letters patent, rights or privileges which the company is authorized to acquire, at such price, and generally on such terms and conditions, as they think fit; also to sell, lease, abandon, or otherwise deal with, any property, rights, or privileges to which the company may be entitled, on such terms and conditions as they may think fit ...

(16.) To enter into all such negotiations and contracts and rescind and vary all such contracts, and execute and do all such acts, deeds, and things in the name or on behalf of the company as they might consider expedient for or in relation to any of the matters aforesaid, or otherwise for the purposes of the company.

The plaintiff, McDiarmid, wished the assets of the company to be sold, and he arranged a contract for that purpose with a purchaser. At a meeting of the shareholders of the company which had been requisitioned by McDiarmid and others, a resolution to sell the assets on the terms of the proposed contract was passed by a vote of 1502 for and 1198 against. The directors were of the opinion that the proposed contract was not in the company's best interests, and they declined to carry out the resolution.

This was a motion by the plaintiff company and by McDiarmid, suing on behalf of himself and all other shareholders in the company, to compel the defendant directors to cause the resolution to be carried out. Warrington J. held for the defendants. The plaintiff appealed.]

COLLINS M.R.: This is an appeal from a decision of Warrington J., who has been asked by the plaintiffs, Mr. McDiarmid and the company, for a declaration that the defendants, as directors of the company, are bound to carry into effect a resolution passed at a meeting of the shareholders in the company on January 16. There are a number of other incidental reliefs asked—for instance, that they be ordered to affix the seal of the company, and that they may be restrained by injunction from dealing with the assets of the company in any manner inconsistent with the agreement.

The point arises in this way. At a meeting of the company a resolution was passed by a majority—I was going to say a bare majority, but it was a majority—in favour of a sale to a purchaser, and the directors, honestly believing, as Warrington J. thought, that it was most undesirable in the interests of the company that that agreement should be carried into effect, refused to affix the seal of the company to it, or to assist in carrying out a resolution which they disapproved of; and the question is whether under the memorandum and articles of association here the directors are bound to accept, in substitution of their own view, the views contained in the resolution of the company. Warrington J. held that the majority could not impose that obligation upon the directors, and that on the true construction of the articles the directors were the persons authorized by the articles to effect this sale, and that unless the other powers given by the memorandum were invoked by a special resolution, it was impossible for a mere majority at a meeting to override the views of the directors. That depends, as Warrington J. put it, upon the construction of the articles. First of all there is no doubt that the company under its memorandum has the power in clause (3)(k) to sell the undertaking of the company or any part thereof. In this case there is some small exception, I believe, to that which is to be sold, but I do not think that that becomes material. We now come to clause 81 of the articles, which I think it is important to refer to in this connection. [His Lordship read the clause.] Then come the two clauses which are most material, 96 and 97, whereby the powers of the directors are defined. [His Lordship read clause 96 and clause 97(1.).] Therefore in the matters referred to in article 97(1.) the view of the directors as to the fitness of the matter is made the standard; and furthermore, by article 96 they are given in express terms the full powers which the company has, except so far as they "are not hereby or by statute expressly directed or required to be exercised or done by the company," so that the directors have absolute power to do all things other than those that are expressly required to be done by the company; and then comes the limitation on their general authority— "subject to such regulations as may from time to time be made by extraordinary resolution." Therefore, if it is desired to alter the powers of the directors that must be done, not by a resolution carried by a majority at an ordinary meeting of the company, but by an extraordinary resolution. In these circumstances it seems to me that it is not competent for the majority of the shareholders at an ordinary meeting to affect or alter the mandate originally given to the directors, by the articles of association. It has been suggested that this is a mere question of principal and agent, and that it would be an absurd thing if a principal in appointing an agent should in effect appoint a dictator who is to manage him instead of his managing the agent. I think that that analogy does not strictly apply to this case. No doubt for some purposes directors are agents. For whom are they agents? You have, no doubt, in theory and law one entity, the company, which might be a principal, but you have to go behind that when you look to the particular position of directors. It is by the consensus of all the individuals in the company that these directors become agents and hold their rights as agents. It is not fair to say that a majority at a meeting is for the purposes of this case the principal so as to alter the mandate of the agent. The minority also must be taken into account. There are provisions by which the minority may be over-borne, but that can only be done by special machinery in the shape of special resolutions. Short of that the mandate which must be obeyed is not that of the majority— it is that of the whole entity made up of all the shareholders. If the mandate of the directors is to be altered, it can only be under the machinery of the memorandum and articles themselves. I do not think I need say more.

One argument used by Warrington J. strongly supports that view. He says in effect: "There is to be found in these articles a provision that a director can only be removed by special resolution. What is the use of that provision if the views of the directors can be overridden by a mere majority at an ordinary meeting? Practically you do not want any special power to remove directors if you can do without them and differ from their opinion and compel something other than their view to be carried into effect." That argument appears to me to confirm the view taken by the learned judge. ... I am of opinion that this appeal fails.

COZENS-HARDY L.J.: I am of the same opinion. It is somewhat remarkable that in the year 1906 this interesting and important question of company law should for the first time arise for decision, and it is perhaps necessary to go back to the root principle which governs these cases under the Companies Act, 1862. It has been decided that the articles of association are a contract between the members of the company inter se. That was settled finally by the case of *Browne v. La Trinidad* [37 Ch. D. 1], if it was not settled before. We must therefore consider what is the relevant contract which these shareholders have entered into, and that contract, of course, is to be found in the memorandum and articles. I will not again read articles 96 and 97, but it seems to me that the shareholders have by their express contract mutually stipulated that their common affairs should be managed by certain directors to be appointed by the shareholders in the manner described by other articles, such directors being liable to be removed only by special resolution. If you once get a stipulation of that kind in a contract made between the parties, what right is there to interfere with the contract, apart, of course, from any misconduct on the part of the directors? There is no such misconduct in the present case. Is there any analogy which supports the case of the plaintiffs? I think not. It seems to me the analogy is all the other way. Take the case of an ordinary partnership. If in an ordinary partnership there is a stipulation in the partnership deed that the partnership business shall be managed by one of the partners, it would be plain that in the absence of misconduct, or in the absence of circumstances involving the total dissolution of the partnership, the majority of the partners would have no right to apply to the Court to restrain him or to interfere with the management of the partnership business. I would refer to what is said in Lindley on Partnership, 7th ed. p. 574: "Where, however, the partner complained of has by agreement been constituted the active managing partner, the Court will not interfere with him unless a strong case be made out against him"— that is to say, unless there is some case of fraud or misconduct to justify the interference of the Court. Nor is this doctrine limited to a case of co-partners. It is not a peculiar incident of co-partnership: it applies equally to cases of co-ownership. I think in some of the earlier cases before Lord Eldon with reference to the co-owners of one of the theatres, he laid down the principle that when the co-owners had appointed a particular member as manager the Court would not, except in the case of misconduct, interfere with him. And why? Because it is a fallacy to say that the relation is that of simple principal and agent. The person who is managing is managing for himself as well as for the others. It is not in the least a case where you have a master on the one side and a mere servant on the other. You are dealing here, as in the case of a partnership, with parties having individual rights as to which there are mutual stipulations for their common benefit, and when you once get that, it seems to me that there is no ground for saying that the mere majority can put an end to the express stipulations contained in the bargain which they have made. Still less can that be so when you find in the contract itself provisions which shew an intention that the powers conferred upon the directors can only be varied by extraordinary resolution, that is to say, by a three-fourths majority at one meeting, and that the directors themselves when appointed shall only be removed by special resolution, that is to say, by three-fourths majority at one meeting and a simple majority at a confirmatory meeting. That being so, if you once get clear of the view that the directors are mere agents of the company, I cannot see anything in principle to justify the contention that the directors are bound to comply with the votes or the resolutions of a simple majority at an ordinary meeting of the shareholders. I do not think it true to say that the directors are agents. I think it is more nearly true to say that they are in the position of managing partners appointed to fill that post by a mutual arrangement between all the shareholders. So much for principle. On principle I agree entirely with what the Master of the Rolls has said, agreeing as he does with the conclusions of Warrington J.

When we come to the authorities there is, I think, nothing even approaching to an authority in favour of the appellants' case. *Isle of Wight Ry. Co. v. Tahourdin* [25 Ch. D. 320] at the utmost contained a dictum which at first sight looked in favour of appellants; but, treating it as an authority, it was an authority upon an Act which differed in a vital point from the Act which we are now considering, because although by s. 90 of the Companies Clauses Act the directors have powers of management and superintendence very similar to those found in Table A, article 55, and in articles 96 and 97, that section contains these vital words: "And the exercise of all such powers shall be subject also to the control and regulation of any general meeting specially convened for the purpose." If those words had been found in the present Act of Parliament the appellants' case would have been comparatively clear. I see no ground for reading them into the Companies Act, 1862, or into the memorandum and articles of association of this company. For these reasons I think that the appeal must be dismissed.

Cunninghame is the leading case sustaining the authority of the board of directors as against the shareholders-in-meeting. See also *Kelly v. Electrical Construction Co.* (1907), 16 O.L.R. 232 (H.C.); *Scott v. Scott*, [1943] 1 All E.R. 582 (Ch.). Within its realm of authority, as established in the incorporating statute or unanimous shareholder agreement, the board may act independently of the views of the majority of shareholders and indeed in a manner opposed by a majority. CBCA s. 102(1) would therefore appear to codify the result in *Cunninghame*. See also ABCA s. 97(1); BCCA s. 141(1); OBCA s. 115(1).

While the CBCA says that "directors shall manage," it is in fact more usual for the corporation's senior officers to manage, and for directors, at most, to supervise the officers. OBCA s. 115 acknowledges in words the fact that directors typically "supervise the management of the business and affairs of a corporation" (see also BCCA s. 141(1)), but even that standard is not entirely descriptive of what many boards do. In fact, directors of many public corporations exercise only the most general supervision. Nevertheless, CBCA s. 102 is of continued importance, for the formal grant of authority to directors implicitly removes power from shareholders, as was held in *Cunninghame*. In addition, s. 102 focuses battles for control of the corporation around the shareholders' right to elect directors.

For public corporations, CBCA s. 102 is undoubtedly a rule of economic efficiency. By giving managerial authority to a separate class of managers, the CBCA facilitates specialization economies in the firm's business decisions. In that sense, Richard Posner is correct to note that "[t]he separation of ownership and control is a false issue. Separation is efficient, and indeed inescapable, given that for most shareholders the opportunity costs of active participation in the management of the firm would be prohibitively high." R. Posner, *Economic Analysis of Law* 411 (4th ed. 1992).

While specialization suggests that it is normally preferable to leave most decisions concerning the business of the corporation to management, does it mean that shareholders should not retain a residual power? Professor Gordon claims traditional justifications for restrictions on shareholder involvement in day-to-day management do not show why shareholders would not retain a current power to control corporate business decisions. However, shareholder voting on a wider range of day-to-day business decisions may lead to costs such as shareholders pursuing private interests not consistent with the interest of shareholders as a whole, or seeking side payments from management to discourage one or more shareholders from pursuing a particular resolution. See J.N. Gordon, *Shareholder Initiative: A Social Choice and Game Theoretic Approach to Corporate Law*, 60 U. Cin. L. Rev. 347 (1991). It has also been suggested that limits on shareholder decisions concerning day-to-day management may play a role in stock market liquidity and facilitating take-overs that operate to control management behaviour. See P.V. Letsou, *Shareholder Voice and the Market for Corporate Control*, 70 Wash. Univ. L.Q. 755 (1992).

Specialization economies are less likely to arise in small, closely held corporations, and for this reason CBCA s. 102 states that it is subject to a unanimous shareholder agreement. The shareholders might therefore agree to strip the board of directors of all authority and give primary managerial responsibility to shareholders, pursuant to CBCA s. 146(2). See also ABCA s. 140; OBCA s. 108. The directors are then absolved from managerial duties, which devolve upon the shareholders. The requirement that the shareholder agreement be unanimous effectively restricts its scope to small issuers. The problems of corporate governance structures for closely held corporations is deferred until Section H.

Apart from CBCA s. 146, it is not clear to what extent, if any, a corporation's articles may alter the statutory allocation of authority between directors and shareholders. ABCA s. 140; OBCA s. 108. For example, may the articles provide for additional types of action that may not be taken by the directors until they have submitted them to the shareholders? CBCA s. 6(2) states that "[t]he articles may set out any provisions permitted by this Act or by law to be set out in the by-laws of the corporation." ABCA s. 6(2); OBCA s. 5(3). While many substantive provisions of the CBCA include the phrase "unless the articles otherwise provide," s. 102 seems to contemplate that the only exception to it will be a unanimous shareholder agreement.

The Contract Between the Shareholders. It is established, at least in memorandum of association jurisdictions, and perhaps in letters patent jurisdictions as well, that the incorporating documents "are a contract between the members [shareholders] of the company *inter se*," as Cozens-Hardy L.J. states in *Cunninghame*. Of course, there is effectively a consensual relationship between shareholders and their corporation, however it is incorporated, but to find that at law a contract exists means something more than this. It recognizes the possibility that shareholders will be permitted to enjoin the corporation from breaching its charter. For example, in *Salmon v. Quin & Axtens Ltd.*, [1909] 1 Ch. 311 (C.A.), aff'd, [1909] A.C. 442, the corporation's articles provided that the directors could take certain actions only if two directors, Axtens and Salmon, had been notified and neither one had dissented from the proposal. The directors proposed to take action within one of the listed categories and Salmon dissented in writing. At an

extraordinary shareholders' meeting the proposed action was approved by simple majority of the votes cast, which majority would not have sufficed to amend the corporation's
articles. Salmon sued successfully to enjoin the action. Farwell L.J. observed that the
shareholders' resolution was "an attempt to alter the terms of the contract between the
parties by a simple resolution instead of by a special resolution," which would have
been required to amend the corporation's articles. [1909] 1 Ch. at 319.

On the other hand, a contractarian analysis may also be applied to restrict shareholder rights, and this is how the articles were interpreted in *Cunninghame*. By purchasing shares in the corporation, the shareholders had consented to the division of powers
of article 96. In addition, it is certainly not the case that every breach of the articles will
ground shareholder litigation, for a "mere irregularity" will not be actionable. See Chapter Seven. As a result, it is not clear that anything is clarified by labeling the corporate
charter a contract. See *Edmonton Country Club Ltd. v. Case*, [1975] 1 S.C.R. 534,
552-53 per Laskin J. (dissenting in part) (importance of contractual aspect of public
memorandum corporations minimized).

Shareholder Powers in Cases of Deadlock. Though management duties are assigned
to directors, shareholders enjoy special powers in cases of deadlock. In *Barron v. Potter*,
[1914] 1 Ch. 895, the corporation's articles stated that its two directors were required for
a quorum at a board meeting. The articles also provided that its chairman, Canon
Barron, had a second vote in the case of a tie, and that the directors should have the
power between ordinary general meetings to appoint additional directors. For sometime,
the conduct of the corporation's business had been at a standstill because Barron and the
other director, Potter, were not on speaking terms.

On February 9, 1914, pursuant to the provisions of the Companies Act, 1908,
Barron issued a notice to convene an extraordinary general meeting of shareholders for
3:00 p.m. on February 24 at the corporation's offices. The purpose of the meeting was
stated to be the addition of certain named individuals as directors and the removal of
Potter as managing director. On February 21, Potter sent to Barron a notice of a meeting
of the board to be held at 2:40 p.m. on the date of the shareholders' meeting and at the
same place. This notice did not reach Barron.

Upon his arrival at Paddington Station on February 24, Barron was greeted on the
platform by Potter, who proceeded to convene the directors' meeting right there. Barron
wanted none of this and stalked off, whereupon Potter declared various additional persons to have been appointed as directors. A similar purported directors' meeting was
held when Barron arrived at the corporation's offices. At the shareholders' meeting, the
resolution to remove Potter as managing director passed, as did the resolution to add
more named individuals as directors.

The upshot was a pair of writs. Barron's writ alleged that the board meetings had
been invalidly convened since he had not received notice and had had no intention of
attending any such meetings. Potter claimed in his writ that the appointment of additional directors at the extraordinary shareholders' meeting was invalid as contravening
the corporation's articles, which gave the power to add directors between ordinary
shareholders' meetings to the board. In the litigation Barron prevailed. Warrington J.
held the directors' meetings to have been invalidly convened since Barron had insisted

all along that he would not attend one. The judge reserved judgment on whether, if Barron had actually received the notice of the board meeting, he could have appeared at the appointed time and place without having been held to have attended the meeting. As for the shareholders electing new directors at an extraordinary meeting, Warrington J. held that "for practical purposes [there was] no board at all" and that, to avoid an ongoing deadlock in the conduct of the corporation's affairs, the shareholders had the power to do what the directors were unable to do.

2. Election of Directors

While shareholder voting rights do not normally extend to a residual power to manage the corporation, shareholders do have other significant voting rights. As noted above, perhaps the most important is the right of shareholders to elect directors of the corporation. The shareholders also have a right to vote in other situations discussed below.

3. Amendment of By-Laws

The default rule under the CBCA is that the directors have the power to initiate changes in the by-laws. CBCA s. 103(1); ABCA s. 98(1); OBCA 116(1). However, this is subject to the articles, the by-laws or a unanimous shareholder agreement. *Id.* Consequently, it is possible under the CBCA to put the power to change the by-laws in the hands of the shareholders.

Even where the power to initiate changes in the by-laws is left in the hands of the directors, the shareholders can make proposals for changes in the by-laws (CBCA s. 103(5); ABCA s. 98(5); OBCA s. 116(5)) and, as noted above, changes initiated by the directors must be approved by the shareholders (CBCA s. 103(2); ABCA s. 98(2); OBCA s. 116(2)).

In a memorandum jurisdiction, such as British Columbia, it is the articles that roughly correspond to the by-laws under the BCCA and, as noted above, the articles can only be amended by a special resolution of the shareholders (three quarters of the votes cast). BCCA ss. 1(1) "special resolution," 243. Normally it is the directors who would put amendments to the articles before a meeting of shareholders.

4. Fundamental Changes and Class Voting Rights

Fundamental Changes. Shareholders are typically given the right to vote in respect of certain changes concerning the corporation which are considered "fundamental." CBCA s. 173(1) provides that a "special resolution" (two-thirds of the votes cast at a meeting of shareholders (CBCA s. 2(1)) is required to amend the articles. See also ABCA s. 167(1); OBCA s. 168(1). For instance, a special resolution to amend the articles is required to change the name of the corporation, change any restriction on the businesses that the corporation may carry on, change the registered office of the corporation, create a new class of shares, increase or decrease the number of directors or the minimum or maximum number of directors or change restrictions on the issue, transfer or ownership of shares of the corporation.

Similarly, under the BCCA a "special resolution" (three quarters of the votes cast— BCCA s. 1(1)) is required to approve amendments to the memorandum or articles.

BCCA ss. 240, 241 and 243. The memorandum can only be amended where the Act specifically permits it to be amended and the Act only permits it to be amended to alter any restriction on the businesses the company can carry on (BCCA s. 245), to change its name (BCCA s. 247), to increase or decrease the company's authorized capital (BCCA ss. 254, 256) or to subdivide or consolidate shares (BCCA s. 255).

Other fundamental changes also require shareholder approval. For instance, a special resolution of shareholders is required to approve an amalgamation of the corporation with another corporation (CBCA s. 183(5); ABCA s. 177; BCCA s. 272(4); OBCA s. 176); the sale or lease of all or substantially all of the corporation's assets (CBCA ss. 189(3), (8); ABCA s. 183; BCCA s. 150; OBCA ss. 184(3), (7)); a continuance of the corporation under the laws of another jurisdiction (CBCA s. 188; ABCA s. 182; BCCA s. 37; OBCA s. 181); or a liquidation and dissolution of the corporation (CBCA s. 211; ABCA s. 204; BCCA s. 291; OBCA s. 193). On these particular fundamental changes shareholders are generally entitled to vote whether or not the shares of the class they hold otherwise carry the right to vote. CBCA ss. 183(3), 188(4), 189(6), 211(3); ABCA ss. 177(3), 182(3), 183(4), 204(3); OBCA ss. 176(3), 184(6).

Shareholders who dissent from a resolution to amalgamate, sell, lease or exchange all or substantially all of the corporation's assets, have the corporation continued under the laws of another jurisdiction, or change any restriction on the businesses that the corporation may carry on are entitled have their shares purchased by the corporation at an appraised value. CBCA s. 190(1); see also ABCA s. 184(1); BCCA s. 231; OBCA s. 185(1). This "appraisal right" of shareholders is discussed in Chapter Eleven.

Class Voting Rights. Some changes also require approval from individual classes of shares, or, in some instances, a particular series of shares. These class voting rights generally apply where the proposed change is a change in the rights or restrictions attached to a particular class of shares (or series of shares) or where the change can have a significant impact on the particular class of shares.

CBCA s. 176(1) sets out several situations in which a class of shares is entitled to vote separately as a class. See also ABCA s. 179(1); BCCA s. 250; OBCA s. 170(1). For instance, a separate vote of a class is required where it is proposed to amend the articles to increase or decrease the number of authorized shares of the class; to add, change or remove the rights, privileges, restrictions or conditions attached to the class of shares; to increase the authorized number of shares of a class having rights equal or superior to the particular class; to increase the rights or privileges of any class of shares having rights or privileges equal or superior to the shares of the particular class; to create a new class of shares having rights equal or superior to the shares of the particular class; or to make a class of shares having inferior rights or privileges equal or superior to the particular class.

A separate vote of a series of shares is required where the series of shares is affected differently from other shares of the same class. CBCA s. 176(4); ABCA s. 170(2); BCCA s. 250; OBCA s. 170(2). Where there is a right of a class or series of shares to vote separately, the right applies whether or not the shares otherwise carry the right to vote. CBCA s. 176(5); ABCA 170(3); OBCA s. 170(3). Where separate class or series voting rights apply a proposed amendment to the articles is not adopted unless each class or series of shares entitled to vote separately has approved the amendment by a special resolution. CBCA s. 176(6); ABCA s. 170(4); OBCA s. 170(4).

The BCCA provides a similar separate class or series voting right where a "right or special right attached to issued shares [will be] prejudiced or interfered with." In such circumstances a special resolution of three-quarters majority of the votes cast in the separate class or series vote is required to approve the resolution. BCCA s. 250.

Class voting rights also apply to certain other fundamental changes. For instance, a class or series voting right may apply in the context of an amalgamation where the amalgamation agreement contains a provision that would entitle a class or series of shares to vote separately as a class or series if the provision were contained in a proposed amendment to the articles. See CBCA s. 183(4); see also ABCA s. 177(4); BCCA s. 274(4)(b); OBCA s. 176(3). Similarly, a sale, lease or exchange of all or substantially all of the assets of the corporation requires separate class or series voting where the rights of a class or series will be affected in a way that is different from another class or series. CBCA s. 189(7); ABCA s. 183(5); OBCA s. 184(6). A liquidation and dissolution of the corporation also requires a special resolution of each class of shares of the corporation whether or not they otherwise carry the right to vote. CBCA s. 211(3); ABCA s. 204(3). Under the BCCA a separate class or series vote may be required in the case of a sale, lease, or exchange of all or substantially all of the assets of the corporation, a continuance, or a liquidation and dissolution where any right or special right of the class or series will be prejudiced or interfered with. See BCCA s. 250.

Shareholders entitled to vote separately as a class or series may also be entitled to a right to have the corporation purchase their shares at an appraised value where they dissent to the resolution. See CBCA s. 190(2); ABCA s. 184(2); OBCA s. 185(2). BCCA s. 251 also provides for a dissent procedure and a potential appraisal right on a much more constrained basis. Appraisal rights are discussed in Chapter Eleven, Section C.

5. The Distribution of Voting Rights

The Presumption of One Share, One Vote. There is no requirement that equity interests must always bear voting rights. Preferred shares are usually non-voting, and even common shareholders may be disenfranchised. There are, however, some corporate decisions on which all shareholders are permitted to vote. As noted above, corporations statutes typically provide that, irrespective of their voting rights generally, the holders of each class of shares are entitled to vote on "fundamental" structural changes.

(a) Development of the Use of "Restricted" (Non-Voting, Non-Preferred) Shares

Though corporate statutes permit a firm to restrict the voting rights of a class of common shares, in recent years dual class shares, with one class of voting and one of non-voting common shares, have been viewed with suspicion. Non-voting common shares are not preferred, having no priority claim to earnings or assets, but carry either no voting rights or limited voting rights. This type of equity security was frequently issued after the late 1970s as a result of (1) legislation such as the National Energy Policy and statutes governing the banking and communications industries that encourage corporations to keep voting control firmly in Canadian hands, and (2) a desire on the part of some corporations to go (or remain) public while keeping voting power exclusively in the hands of existing control groups.

(b) *Restricted Shares in the United States*

Non-voting shares are less common in the United States, since the New York Stock Exchange (N.Y.S.E.) has not listed firms with an outstanding class of such shares. See New York Stock Exchange, Inc. *Company Manual* s. A. 15, at A-280. In the face of competition from other exchanges and quotation systems that list firms with dual class stock, the N.Y.S.E. in 1987 applied to the S.E.C. for rule changes under which it would be permitted to list such firms. In July of 1988, after a critical study of dual class stock, the S.E.C. adopted a rule in which no exchange or quotation system would be permitted to list the equity securities of any issuer that issued any class of security, or took other corporate measures that nullified, restricted, or disparately reduced the per share voting rights of the holders of an outstanding class of common shares. Securities Exchange Act of 1934, Rule 19c-4. However, this did not extend to a new public issue of non-voting shares. Rule 19c-4(d). In June of 1990 Rule 19c-4 was ruled invalid on the basis that it dealt with a matter of state law and thus, in creating the Rule, the Securities Exchange Commission had exceeded the statutory authority delegated to it by Congress. See *Business Roundtable v. SEC*, 905 F.2d 406 (D.C. Cir. 1990). To avoid the constitutional limitations the chair of the S.E.C. has since asked the New York Stock Exchange, the American Stock Exchange and the National Association of Securities Dealers to adopt a rule similar to Rule 19c-4. See S.M. Bainbridge, *Revisiting the One Share/One Vote Controversy: The Exchanges Uniform Voting Rights Policy*, 22 Sec. Reg. L.J. 175, 176 (1994).

(c) *Restricted Shares in Canada*

After lengthy proceedings, the Ontario Securities Commission in 1982 decided to permit issuers subject to its jurisdiction to continue to issue dual class common shares. However, the non-voting shares must be clearly described in selling documents as "restricted" and not as common shares, and the creation of the restricted shares must be approved by a majority of the votes of minority shareholders (i.e. shareholders who are not affiliated with the issuer and who do not effectively control the issuer). See OSC Policy s. 1.3. In the same year the Toronto Stock Exchange strongly encouraged issuers of restricted shares to provide for "coattail" rights, under which the shares would be convertible into voting shares on a take-over bid for the voting shares unless an offer is made for all the restricted shares on terms identical to the offer for the voting shares. The Toronto Stock Exchange, *Policy Statement on Restricted Shares* (April 1982). After a highly publicized dispute in 1987 concerning the coattail provisions in the share conditions of the restricted shares of Canadian Tire, the T.S.E. mandated coattail provisions as a condition of listing on the exchange. See Toronto Stock Exchange, *Policy Statement on Restricted Shares* s. 1.09. This policy does not apply to firms with dual class stock that were listed on the T.S.E. prior to August 1, 1987. On the development of the regulation of restricted shares in Ontario see C.T. Hay, *Restricted Shares in Ontario*, 14 C.B.L.J. 257, 282-90 (1988).

Since the principal economic distinction between restricted and voting common shares is that the restricted shares cannot participate in a take-over bid and share in the premium price offered for the shares, this comes close to a prohibition of non-voting common shares for listed firms that were not "grandfathered" as of that date.

(d) Should Restricted Shares Be Prohibited?

Should restricted shares in fact be prohibited? The case for mandatory coattails on distributional grounds may not appear compelling, since restricted shares normally are issued and traded at a discount to reflect the fact that they will not participate on a take-over bid. An efficiency argument for a presumption of one share, one vote has, however, been made by Frank Easterbrook and Daniel Fischel. The two authors argue that voting rights should be allocated to the group that holds the residual claim at any given time so as to align management incentives with the goal of maximizing firm value. They then argue that unless each element of the residual interest carries an equal voting right, a needless agency cost of management will arise. "Those with disproportionate voting power will not receive shares of the residual gains or losses from new endeavors and arrangements commensurate with their control; as a result they will not make optimal decisions." Easterbrook & Fischel, *Voting in Corporate Law*, 26 J.L. & Econ. 395, 409 (1983). Is this view persuasive if, in all other respects, non-voting common shares are identical to voting common shares? Voting common shareholders might then be suitable proxies for their non-voting brethren, who could free ride on the other class's voting.

In addition, even where different incentives might be observed, as where voting shares are held by an inside group of managers, the Easterbrook and Fischel argument incorrectly focuses upon *ex post* agency costs rather than the *ex ante* decision to issue non-voting shares. For this reason, the authors fail to consider the benefits some firms will find in non-voting shares. These are detailed in a subsequent article by Daniel Fischel, who concludes that firms should not be hindered in their allocation of voting rights. Fischel, *Organized Exchanges and the Regulation of Dual Class Common Stock*, 54 U. Chi. L. Rev. 119 (1987).

The first advantage noted by Fischel is that a retention of control by management may encourage efficient investments by managers in firm-specific human capital. Where a small firm decides to go public, the distribution of voting shares to outsiders may act as a bonding mechanism, with management staking its performance on the market for corporate control. The promise of good management is then made more creditable through the mechanism for replacing inefficient managers. But take-over bids may also result in shareholder opportunism, with management's anticipated long-term rewards cut off when it is dismissed after a control change. Managers will then be more willing to invest in firm-specific human capital where its control cannot be challenged. This suggests that the optimal voting rights decision might reasonably be left with firm managers at issuance, in the absence of an argument that they have an insufficient incentive to maximize firm wealth.

In addition, managers in some firms will simply value control more highly than outsiders. This is particularly true of family firms, many of which issue restricted shares when they need new equity financing. Were restricted shares prohibited, family firms might then issue a minority block of voting shares to the public, with control remaining in family hands. The outsiders who purchased the shares would realize that the family would continue in control, nor can it reasonably be suggested that the family has an obligation to issue further voting shares to the public so as to surrender control.

The hypothesis that dual class shares serve efficiency goals must compete against less benign explanations of their popularity. The principal rival theory focuses on distributional gains and losses from the creation of a class of non-voting common shares. On this hypothesis, public shareholders pay a premium for their shares if they expect that they may subsequently be sought in a take-over bid. The expected premium price that the tender offeror would pay then justifies a higher purchase price for the shares on their issuance. Public shareholders may even be prepared to pay a premium where a control block remains in management's hands, so long as it is anticipated that such voting control will be lost on a subsequent issue by the firm of voting shares.* A subsequent issue by the firm of non-voting common shares in these circumstances would then defeat these expectations, and effect a wealth transfer from outside shareholders to managers. Secondary distributional effects will also arise if the issue of non-voting shares insulates inefficient managers from the threat of a loss of control.

Distributional theories of non-voting shares are, however, subject to difficulties. First, when public shareholders react to the possibility of the firm's financing through the issue of non-voting claims, or through retained earnings, they will not overpay for their shares and distributional effects will be minimized. Second, the empirical evidence does not suggest that existing public voting shareholders are harmed by the creation of a new class of non-voting or limited voting common shares. On the distributional hypothesis, one would expect common share prices to decline on the announcement of the new class of shares. A study by Partch found that the market does not greet such announcements with statistically significant negative changes. Partch, *The Creation of a Class of Limited Voting Common Stock and Shareholder Wealth*, 18 J. Fin. Econ. 33 (1987). However, a subsequent study by Gordon did not find positive share price effects overall and found significant negative share price effects where a family or management block of shares had sufficient votes to force a dual class recapitalization. See J.N. Gordon, *Ties that Bond: Dual Class Common Stock and the Problem of Shareholder Choice*, 76 Cal. L.R. 1, 26-30 (1988) (Gordon also reviews two other studies of dual class recapitalizations that yield conflicting results).

A dual class recapitalization may, however, seem less benign than a dual class issuance. In a recapitalization, the share condition provisions of outstanding voting shares are amended to restrict voting rights. Here it may be feared that the recapitalization will transfer wealth from outside public shareholders to an inside group of voting shareholders or managers, as where existing common shareholders forgo possible take-over bid premiums when they lose their voting rights. Adding such provisions to the articles will require shareholder ratification, but this may not be thought strong

---

*   Or if minority shareholders are entitled to share in the premium paid on a sale of control block shares. See Chapter Eleven.

evidence of the proposal's reasonableness if the vote is not contested by insurgents. In addition, the significance of a shareholder vote may be highly muted if the choice offered is between non-voting shares with a promise of a high dividend payout and low dividend voting shares. However, these distributional effects are not to be feared on dual class issuances, where new non-voting common shares are allotted, for here the market price of the shares would reflect the absence of voting rights. Moreover, the dual class stock may serve the efficiency goals described by Fischel. Because of this, Ronald Gilson would permit dual class issuances while prohibiting dual class recapitalizations. Gilson, *Evaluating Dual Class Common Stock: The Relevance of Substitutes*, 73 Va. L. Rev. 807 (1987); and J.N. Gordon, *Ties that Bond: Dual Class Common Stock and the Problem of Shareholder Choice*, 76 Cal. L.R. 1 (1988). Professor Gilson's distinction between firms that alter the existing rights of common shareholders and those that issue non-voting common shares to new shareholders was adopted by the S.E.C. in Rule 19c-4, which would deny listing privileges to only the first class of firms (see above).

Professor Gordon argues that the rule the N.Y.S.E. had against non-voting common shares provided a means by which corporate insiders could bond against dual class recapitalizations having the distributional effects noted above. The protection of shareholders provided by such a bonding mechanism would allow corporations to raise capital at lower cost since investors would pay more for stock that protected against the negative distributional effects of a subsequent dual class recapitalization. Presumably corporations would choose to list on an exchange that had a rule that allowed corporate insiders to bond against future dual class recapitalizations and competition among exchanges would lead to the adoption of a rule such as the N.Y.S.E. had. However, Gordon argues that there are an insufficient number of stock exchanges in the United States to provide the competition necessary to force exchanges to adopt restictions against dual class recapitalizations. He thus argues in favour of an S.E.C. rule that would force exchanges to adopt a rule on dual class recapitalizations. J.N. Gordon, *Ties That Bond: Dual Class Common Stock and the Problem of Shareholder Choice*, 76 Cal. L.R. 1 (1988). For a contrary view that not having an S.E.C. rule restricting dual class recapitalizations would promote competition among exchanges see S.M. Bainbridge, *Revisiting the One Share/One Vote Controversy: The Exchanges Uniform Voting Rights Policy*, 22 Sec. Reg. L.J. 175, 190-94 (1994).

O.S.C. Policy s. 1.3 does not distinguish between a new public issue of non-voting restricted shares and a reorganization in which existing common shareholders are disenfranchised. Where shareholder approval is sought either to an amendment to the articles to create a new class of restricted shares or to a reorganization, which results in restricted shares, a majority of the minority shareholders must approve the change. But while managers cannot vote their own shares to satisfy this "majority of the minority" test, in many cases it may not be found particularly onerous.

Voting Restrictions. One person, one vote policies are also violated when special voting rights are attached to one group within a special class of shares. Such provisions might either limit the voting rights of large shareholders (capped voting rights) or endow a class of shares held by firm insiders with more than one vote per share (supervoting rights). These provisions are often even more clearly directed at preventing a successful take-over bid than are non-voting shares, and indeed are called "shark repellents" for that reason. However, when such provisions are adopted by a corporation on incorporation, as in *Bushell v. Faith* (see Section B above), distributional effects are unlikely. The restrictions may also be justified on efficiency grounds, as argued by Fischel. But where the provisions are adopted after the issuance of shares pursuant to an amendment of the articles, as in *Jacobsen* below, they are more troubling. Not merely may take-over bid premiums be lost, but the restricted voting rights may also immunize inefficient management.

Jacobsen v. United Canso Oil & Gas Ltd.
Alberta Court of Queen's Bench
(1980), 113 D.L.R. (3d) 427, [1980] 6 W.W.R. 38, 11 B.L.R. 313

FORSYTH J.: This matter came before me for determination of a preliminary point of law on a peremptory basis to determine the following question:

Does the Defendant's By-Law (By-Law No. 6) which provides that no person shall be entitled to vote more than 1,000 shares of the Defendant notwithstanding the number of shares actually held by him contravene the provisions of the Canada Business Corporations Act.

The determination of this issue involves not only consideration of the present provisions of the Canada Business Corporations Act, 1974-75-76 (Can.) c. 33, but also the provisions of the applicable legislation at the time the by-law was enacted.

The defendant United Canso Oil & Gas Ltd. (hereinafter referred to as "United Canso") was incorporated by letters patent on April 13, 1954, pursuant to the Companies Act, R.S.C. 1952, c. 53. By-law No. 1, the general by-law of the company, was duly enacted on April 15, 1954, and provided, inter alia, as follows:

Upon a show of hands each shareholder present in person shall have one vote and upon a poll each shareholder present in person or by proxy shall have one vote for each share held by such shareholder unless the letters patent, supplementary letters patent or by-laws of the Company otherwise provide in respect of the shares of any particular class.

I would note here that there is no dispute between the parties that at the time of incorporation and up to the present time United Canso has had only one class of shares, the present capitalization being 12 million common shares.

By-law No. 6 of the company was duly enacted on March 19, 1964, and provided, inter alia, as follows:

With respect to any matter to be voted upon at any meeting of shareholders called after the final adjournment of the meeting at which this By-Law Number 6 is ratified, any one person as hereinafter defined shall be entitled to vote:

(i) with respect to shares registered in his name on the books of the Company which are beneficially owned by him, the number of such shares, but in no event more than 1,000;

(ii) with respect to shares registered in his name on the books of the Company which he holds as a trustee other than as a nominee, the number of such shares but in no event more than 1,000; and

(iii) with respect to shares registered in his name as nominee and on instructions from each one person who is the owner thereof a number of shares owned by each such one person but in no event more than 1,000 with respect to each such one person, provided that no such one person shall vote or give instructions as to the voting of more than 1,000 shares in the aggregate.

The relevant legislation applicable at the time that by-law was enacted was again the Companies Act [superseded by the Canada Corporations Act, 1964-65 (Can.), c. 52 [now R.S.C. 1985, c. C-44]]. This change of by-law with respect to voting procedure, however, was not reflected in any supplementary letters patent until July 25, 1974, when supplementary letters patent were issued to United Canso amending the letters patent of the company by adding thereto the voting limitations contained in By-law No. 6. These supplementary letters patent were issued by the Minister of Consumer and Corporate Affairs by virtue of the powers vested in him by the Canada Corporations Act, which Act replaced the Companies Act. The Canada Corporations Act itself was subsequently replaced [in part] by the Canada Business Corporations Act.

• • •

The issue before the Court raises certain fundamental questions with respect to the rights of shareholders of a corporation. It was argued by the plaintiff that there is a presumption of equality between shareholders and the voting restriction in question contravenes this presumption. In this regard reference was made to Palmer's Company Law (22nd ed., 1976), vol. 1, p. 334, where the learned author states:

Prima facie the rights carried by the shares rank *pari passu*, *i.e.*, the shareholders participate in the benefits of membership equally. It is only when a company divides its share capital into different classes with different rights attached to them that the prima facie presumption of equality of shares may be displaced.

Gower, on Modern Company Law (3rd ed., 1969), at p. 349, expresses a similar sentiment where the learned author states:

The typical company—one limited by shares—must issue some shares, and the initial presumption of the law is that all shares confer equal rights and impose equal liabilities. As in partnership equality is assumed in the absence of evidence to the contrary. Normally the shareholders' rights will fall under three heads: (i) dividends, (ii) return of capital on a winding up (or authorised reduction of capital) and (iii) attendance at meetings and voting, and unless there is some indication to the contrary all the shares will confer the like rights to all three. So far as voting is concerned this is a comparatively recent development, for, on the analogy of the partnership rule, it was long felt that members' rights to control through voting should be divorced from their purely financial interests in respect of dividend and capital, so that the equality should be between members rather than between shares. ... It is now recognised that *if voting rights are to vary, separate classes of shares must be created so that the different number of votes can be attached to the shares themselves and not to the holder*. (The italics are mine.)

It is to be noted that the learned author of course was dealing with the development of company law in England, but nevertheless there are many parallels to be drawn between the evolution of company law in England and that in Canada.

[There is omitted that part of Forsyth J.'s judgment in which the learned judge concluded that By-law No. 6 was invalid under the Companies Act, R.S.C. 1952, c. 53, and that it was equally invalid as incorporated into the company's supplementary letters patent issued under the provisions of the Canada Corporations Act, R.S.C. 1985, c. C-44, which replaced the Companies Act. Forsyth J.'s reasoning concerning these earlier statutes was very similar to that concerning the CBCA, which follows.]

This does not end the matter. A certificate of continuance for United Canso was issued on October 24, 1979, pursuant to s. 181 of the Canada Business Corporations Act and the articles of continuance contained, attached as Sched. 2, the same voting restriction previously set forth in By-law No. 6. Accordingly, it is necessary to consider the provisions of the Canada Business Corporations Act and, in particular, whether or not by virtue of the fact that the limitation was contained in the articles of continuance, that limitation became effective on the issuance of the certificate of continuance and is, accordingly, still in force.

It should be first noted that the authority for continuance of United Canso under the Canada Business Corporations Act is contained in s. 181.

Section 181 [am. 1978-79, c. 9, s. 57, now s. 187 of R.S.C. 1985, c. C-44] of the Canada Business Corporations Act provides in part as follows:

181. (1.1) A body corporate that applies for continuance under subsection (1) may, without so stating in its articles of continuance, effect by those articles any amendment to its Act of incorporation, articles, letters patent or memorandum or articles of association *if the amendment is an amendment a corporation incorporated under this Act may make to its articles.*

(2) Articles of continuance in prescribed form shall be sent to the Director together with the documents required by sections 19 and 101.

(3) Upon receipt of articles of continuance, the Director shall issue a certificate of continuance in accordance with section 255.

(4) On the date shown in the certificate of continuance

(a) the body corporate becomes a corporation to which this Act applies as if it had been incorporated under this Act;

(b) the articles of continuance are deemed to be the articles of incorporation of the continued corporation; and

(c) the certificate of continuance is deemed to be the certificate of incorporation of the continued corporation.

...

(7) Subject to subsection 45(8), a share of a body corporate issued before the body corporate was continued under this Act is deemed to have been issued in compliance with this Act and with the provisions of the articles of continuance irrespective of whether the share is fully paid or irrespective of any designation, rights, privileges, restrictions or conditions set out on or referred to in the certificate representing the share; and continuance under this section does not deprive a holder of any right or privilege that he claims under, or relieve him of any liability in respect of, an issued share. (The italics are mine.)

Subsection (7) is quoted, as it was referred to in argument on several occasions, but it would appear clear that the relevancy of that subsection would only come into play if it had been found that By-law No. 6 or the supplementary letters patent issued relating to By-law No. 6 were in fact valid. Having found to the contrary in that regard it is difficult to see that subs. (7) renders any assistance in the consideration of this matter. It is to be noted, however, that it is clear pursuant to subs. (1.1) of s. 181 that an amendment to the letters patent can be effected in the articles of continuance with respect to any corporation applying for continuance under the Canada Business Corporations Act, if the amendment is an amendment a corporation incorporated under this Act may make to its articles. Does the Canada Business Corporations Act contemplate an amendment of the nature set forth in the articles of continuance? Section 6 [am. 1978-79, c. 9, s. 3] of the Act provides in part as follows:

   6. (1) Articles of incorporation shall follow the prescribed form and shall set out, in respect of the proposed corporation,

   ...

      (c) the classes and any maximum number of shares that the corporation is authorized to issue, and

         (i) if there will be two or more classes of shares, the rights, privileges, restrictions and conditions attaching to each class of shares, and

         (ii) if a class of shares may be issued in series, the authority given to the directors to fix the number of shares in, and to determine the designation of, and the rights, privileges, restrictions and conditions attaching to, the shares of each series;

      ...

   (2) The articles may set out any provisions permitted by this Act or by law to be set out in the by-laws of the corporation.

   (3) Subject to subsection (4), if the articles or a unanimous shareholder agreement require a greater number of votes of directors or shareholders than that required by this Act to effect any action, the provisions of the articles or of the unanimous shareholder agreement prevail.

Again it is to be noted that particular provisions come into play where there are two or more classes of shares requiring the setting forth of rights, privileges, etc., attaching to such shares. Thus, the distinction is clearly made between that situation and the situation where there is only one class of shares where it must be assumed there are no rights, restrictions, etc., attaching to such shares. Section 134(1) [now s. 140] is similar to the previously quoted provisions of the Canada Corporations Act and the Companies Act and provides as follows:

   134. (1) Unless the articles otherwise provide each share of a corporation entitles the holder thereof to one vote at a meeting of shareholders.

However, that section must be read in relation to s. 24 [am. 1978-79, c. 9, s. 9] of the Act which provides as follows [subs. (3), (4)]:

   (3) Where a corporation has only one class of shares, the rights of the holders thereof are equal in all respects and include the rights

      (a) to vote at any meeting of shareholders of the corporation;

      (b) to receive any dividend declared by the corporation; and

      (c) to receive the remaining property of the corporation on dissolution.

(4) the articles may provide for more than one class of shares and, if they so provide,

(a) the rights, privileges, restrictions and conditions attaching to the shares of each class shall be set out therein; and

(b) the rights set out in subsection (3) shall be attached to at least one class of shares but all such rights are not required to be attached to one class.

It seems abundantly clear on a reading of s. 24(3) as well as the reading of the entire Act that again Parliament has even more clearly specified that it is only when there is more than one class of shares that different rights, privileges, restrictions and conditions attaching to shares may arise.

It is argued that subs. (3) of s. 24 must be read as being subject to subs. 168(5)(c) [now s. 176(4)(c)] of the Act which reads as follows:

(5) Subject to subsections 254(2) and (3), the Governor in Council may make regulations with respect to a corporation that constrains the issue or transfer of its shares prescribing

...

(c) the limitations on voting rights of any shares held contrary to the articles of the corporation.

In short, s. 24(3) must not be read in the absolute sense but is subject to other provisions in the Act which may change the basic position established by s. 24. Section 168(5)(c), however, clearly has a very restricted application and only applies to corporations which constrain the issue or transfer of their shares for the particular purposes as set out in s. 168.

It is also argued that s. 24(3) is not inconsistent with the provisions of By-law No. 6 as continued under the articles of continuance of United Canso in that it deals with the right to vote but not in any way with the number of votes. The voting limitations in the articles of continuance clearly do not affect the right of a shareholder to vote and apply equally to all shareholders. It is only when their shareholdings exceed 1,000 shares that they are restricted from voting any shares in excess of 1,000. I am not satisfied this is an interpretation which can be put on s. 24(3). In effect it is argued that the rights of the holders of the shares are equal in that all shareholders can only vote a maximum of 1,000 shares regardless of the number of shares held. It might similarly be argued that they would be equal if all shareholders could only receive dividends to a maximum of 1,000 shares regardless of the number of shares held or receive the remaining property of the corporation on the basis of a 1,000 share maximum regardless of the number of shares held. It seems to me reading s. 24 as a whole, each shareholder has the right to vote at any meeting of shareholders on the basis of the number of shares held where the corporation only has one class of shares and that this presumption can only be upset where there are more [than] one class of shares established in which case the provisions of subs. (4) come into play. That position in this regard is in my opinion fortified by the provisions of subs. 4(b) of s. 24 which makes it clear that all of the rights set forth in subs. (3) must, where there is more than one class of shares, be attached to at least one class of shares.

In the result for the reasons aforesaid the answer to the preliminary point of law put before the Court is that the defendant's By-law No. 6 which provides that no person shall be entitled to vote more than 1,000 shares of the defendant notwithstanding the number of shares actually held by him does, in fact, contravene the provisions of the Canada Business Corporations Act and is invalid.

The parties may speak to me in the question of costs if so desired on this matter.

Order accordingly.

NOTES

1) *Jacobsen* suggests that, under the CBCA, rights must be attached to shares once and for all and cannot be made to depend upon the identity of the owner of the shares for the time being. This conclusion does not in fact follow inexorably from the literal wording of the CBCA. Would it be strengthened with a provision such as OBCA s. 22(6), under which "each share of a class shall be the same in all respects as every other share of that class" except where a class of shares is issued in more than one series (not the case of United Canso)?

2) As Forsyth J. states, different voting rights may be attached to different classes of shares. Would United Canso, by using different classes of shares, have been able to prevent an aggregation of voting power in the hands of a single person? Could United Canso have prohibited any single person from owning more than 1,000 shares of a class to which voting rights were attached? See CBCA s. 49(9). For some period prior to the *Jacobsen* litigation, United Canso had been the object of numerous pitched battles for control (see, for example, *Brown v. Duby*, in Section E), and the threat of losing control cannot have been far from management's mind in enacting By-law No. 6.

3) A matter of days before the judgment in *Jacobsen* was rendered, United Canso had surrendered its charter as a CBCA corporation and had been continued under the Nova Scotia Companies Act. See *Jacobsen v. United Canso Oil & Gas Ltd.* (1980), 12 B.L.R. 113 (N.S.), where the Court declined to rule on the validity under the Nova Scotia statute of the voting restriction.

4) The validity of a voting restriction was sustained in *Providence & Worcester Co. v. Baker*, 378 A.2d 121 (Del. 1977). Unlike *Jacobsen*, the voting restriction in *Baker* had been adopted on incorporation. Relevant provisions of the Delaware statute were as follows:

151. Classes and series of stock; rights.

(a) Every corporation may issue 1 or more classes of stock or 1 or more series of stock within any class thereof, any or all of which classes may be of stock with par value or stock without par value and which classes or series may have such voting powers, full or limited, or no voting powers, and such designations, preferences and relative, participating, optional or other special rights, and qualifications, limitations or restrictions thereof, as shall be stated and expressed in the certificate of incorporation or of any amendment thereto. ...

212. Voting rights of stockholders; proxies, limitations.

(a) Unless otherwise provided in the certificate of incorporation ... each stockholder shall be entitled to 1 vote for each share of capital stock held by such stockholder. ...

The Court first held that any limitation upon the power of corporations to create restrictions on the voting rights of large shareholders had to be found "primarily" in Del.

s. 212 rather than in s. 151. It found in s. 212 no evidence of legislative intent to forbid such restrictions, especially as they were in relatively common use in Delaware corporations when the earliest predecessor to s. 212 was enacted.

5) Is *Bushell v. Faith* (set out in Section B above) consistent with *Jacobsen*? Bush (Southgate) Ltd. was a typical closely held corporation, with all of its shares held by a few members of one family. Article 9 had been consented to by all parties. Is there any reason why shareholders should not be permitted to arrange the firm's internal governance structures exactly as they please? By contrast, it would likely be harder to find an informed consent by all parties to the shark repellant in *Jacobsen*.

6) In *Re Bowater Canada Ltd. and R.L. Crain Inc.* (1987), 62 O.R. (2d) 752 (Ont. C.A.) (see Chapter Four, Section A) the articles gave ten votes per share to a class of special common shares as long as the shares were held by the person to whom they were originally issued but only one vote per share if the shares were held by any other person. The Ontario Court of Appeal upheld the decision of the trial court to the effect that this "step down" provision in the voting rights attached to the shares was invalid but was severable with the result that the special common shares carried ten votes per share regardless of whether they were held by the person to whom they were originally issued or by a transferee. Bowater may stand simply for the proposition that the rights of a given class of shares must be equal in all respects (subject to the separate rights that may be assigned to series within a class of shares). It may stand for a broader proposition that all shareholders of a class of shares must be treated equally.

Equal Treatment. The following case addresses the broader question of equal treatment of shareholders holding shares of the same class. Although the case deals with dividend rights, the judgment of La Forest also raises the question of equal treatment in context of voting rights.

The Queen v. McClurg
[1990] 3 S.C.R. 1020, (1990) 76 D.L.R. (4th) 217

DICKSON C.J.C.:—This is an income tax case. The question in the appeal is whether certain dividends received by the wife of the respondent, Jim A. McClurg, in the years 1978, 1979 and 1980 in respect of Class B common shares of Northland Trucks (1978) Ltd. (hereafter Northland Trucks) should be attributed in part to the respondent, an officer and director of Northland Trucks and the holder of the controlling Class A common shares in the capital stock of that company.

I. Background

1. Relevant legislation

Income Tax Act, S.C. 1970-71-72, c. 63:

56(2) A payment or transfer of property made pursuant to the direction of, or with the concurrence of, a taxpayer to some other person for the benefit of the taxpayer or as a benefit that the taxpayer desired to have conferred on the other person ... shall be included in computing the tax-payer's income to the extent that it would be if the payment or transfer had been made to him.

Saskatchewan Business Corporations Act, R.S.S. 1978, c. B-10:

24(4) The articles may provide for more than one class of shares and, if they so provide,

(a) the rights, privileges, restrictions and conditions attaching to the shares of each class shall be set out therein; and

(b) the rights set out in subsection (3) shall be attached to at least one class of shares but all such rights are not required to be attached to one class.

...

40. A corporation shall not declare or pay a dividend if there are reasonable grounds for believing that:

(a) the corporation is, or would after the payment be, unable to pay its liabilities as they become due; or

(b) the realizable value of the corporation's assets would thereby be less than the aggregate of its liabilities and stated capital of all classes.

...

97(1) Subject to any unanimous shareholder agreement, the directors of a corporation shall:

(a) exercise the powers of the corporation directly or indirectly through the employees and agents of the corporation; and

(b) direct the management of the business and affairs of the corporation.

...

234(1) A complainant may apply to a court for an order under this section.

(2) If, upon an application under subsection (1), the court is satisfied that in respect of a corporation or any of its affiliates:

(a) any act or omission of the corporation or any of its affiliates effects a result;

(b) the business or affairs of the corporation or any of its affiliates are or have been carried on or conducted in a manner, or

(c) the powers of the directors of the corporation or any of its affiliates are or have been exercised in a manner;

that is oppressive or unfairly prejudicial to or that unfairly disregards the interests of any security holder, creditor, director, or officer, the court may make an order to rectify the matters complained of.

2. *The facts*

The respondent is president of Northland Trucks, a company incorporated under the Saskatchewan Business Corporations Act. The company was established in 1978 upon purchase of an ongoing business, a dealership in International Harvester trucks. The respondent and his partner, Veryle Ellis, are the only directors of the company. The articles of incorporation provide for three categories of shares: Class A which are common, voting and participating shares; Class B which are common, non-voting and participating where authorized by the directors; and Class C which are preferred, non-voting shares. The articles deal with the entitlement to dividends as follows:

Class A Common:
Common, voting and shall be participating shares carrying the distinction and right to receive dividends exclusive of the other classes of shares in the said corporation.

Class B Common:

Common, non-voting and shall be participating shares where authorized to be participating shares by unanimous consent of the Directors and the said shares shall carry the distinction and right to receive dividends exclusive of other classes of shares in the said corporation.

Class C Preferred:

Preferred, non-voting shares which carry the distinction and right to receive dividends exclusive of other classes of shares in the said corporation, if the said dividends are authorized by unanimous resolution of the directors.

Each class of shares has the right to receive dividends exclusive of other classes of shares in the company and the company is authorized to issue an unlimited number of shares in each class.

The clause "the distinction and right to receive dividends exclusive of other classes of shares in the said corporation" in the definition of the share classes is crucial to the analysis in this case; a primary question is whether the clause, which gives to the directors unfettered discretion as to the allocation of dividends among classes of shares, constitutes a valid derogation to the common-law rule of equality of distribution of dividends. For the sake of simplicity, I will refer to it as the "discretionary dividend class" throughout these reasons.

Shares in the company were issued at a price of $1 each, and the distribution of shares demonstrates the closely held nature of the company:

Name	Class A Common	Class B Common	Class C Preferred
Jim McClurg	400	—	37,500
Veryle Ellis	400	—	37,500
Wilma McClurg (wife of Jim McClurg)	—	100	—
Suzanne Ellis (wife of Veryle Ellis)	—	100	—

In the years 1978, 1979 and 1980, the directors, McClurg and Ellis, voted a declaration and distribution of dividends as follows:

Name	1978	1979	1980
Jim McClurg	—	—	—
Veryle Ellis	—	—	—
Wilma McClurg	$10,000	$10,000	$10,000
Suzanne Ellis	$10,000	$10,000	$10,000

The form of resolution declaring the dividends was as follows:

It was noted and unanimously agreed by all the Directors that Class "B" Shareholders receive dividends in the amount of $100.00 per share for each issued share they hold.

Be It Resolved

that payment of dividends to Class "B" Shareholders are made as follows:

Class "B" Shareholder	Number of Issued Shares	Dividend Per Share	Total Paid
Wilma McClurg	100	$100.00	$10,000.00
Suzanne Ellis	100	$100.00	$10,000.00

• • •

On January 14, 1982, by notices of reassessment, the Minister of National Revenue reassessed the respondent's income for 1978, 1979 and 1980. The basis for the reassessment was that in each of those years $8,000 of the $10,000 dividends attributed to Wilma McClurg on her Class B shares was properly attributable instead to the respondent pursuant to s. 56(2) of the Income Tax Act. The Minister made this reallocation on the basis of the number of Class A shares owned by the respondent in relation to the number of Class B shares owned by Wilma McClurg. The position of the Minister is that the dividends declared in each of the years in question should be attributed equally to all of the common shares, no matter of what class and notwithstanding the express condition attaching to the Class B shares that they shall carry the right to receive dividends exclusive of other classes of shares in the company.

• • •

II. Analysis

This appeal raises issues relating both to corporate law and the law of income taxation.

• • •

1. Corporate law issues

I begin the analysis with a statement of the obvious. The decision to declare a dividend lies within the discretion of the directors of a company, subject to any restrictions which have been included in the articles of incorporation. This principle has long been accepted at common law ... .

• • •

With the advent of statutory regulation of corporations, the authority to pay dividends, recognized at common law as part of the internal management of the company, has been given statutory recognition. In the case at bar, the governing legislation is the Saskatchewan Business Corporations Act (hereafter S.B.C.A.). In my view, it cannot be disputed that the power to pay dividends is an internal component of the broad grant of managerial power for directors found in s. 97(1) of the Act, cited earlier. I take it, both from an observation of the workings of corporations, and from other provisions in the statute, that the section embraces the common-law power of directors. The power to declare dividends is expressly limited in the Act, in much the same way as it was at common law. For example, s. 40 of the S.B.C.A., also cited earlier, prohibits the declaration of a dividend if there exists reasonable grounds to believe that to do so would leave the corporation unable to pay its debts (s. 40(1)); or, if the payment of a dividend would render the realizable value of the assets of the corporation less than the aggregate of its liabilities and stated capital of all classes of shares (s. 40(2)). Although these restrictions are not brought into play by the declarations of dividends in issue in this appeal, the presence of those limitations in the Act suggests that the power to declare dividends is statutorily limited only by restrictions expressly stated.

Of course, the power to declare dividends is further qualified by the fact that the law has for many years recognized that the general managerial power which rests in the directors of a company is fiduciary in nature. The declaration of dividends, which is subsumed within that power, therefore is limited legally in that it must be exercised in good faith and in the best interests of the company.

$\bullet \quad \bullet \quad \bullet$

Having reviewed the legal basis for the payment of a dividend by a company, another fundamental principle of corporate law can be restated. The appellant argues, and it is conceded by the respondent, that the rights carried by all shares to receive a dividend declared by a company are equal unless otherwise provided in the articles of incorporation. This principle, like the managerial power to declare dividends, has been well accepted at common law. The principle, or more accurately, the presumption of equality amongst shares and the prerequisites required to rebut that presumption, are described in *Palmer's Company Law*, 23rd ed., vol. 1 (London: Stevens & Sons, 1982), C.M. Schmitthoff, ed. (at p. 387, para. 33-06):

Prima facie the rights carried by the shares rank *pari passu*, i.e. the shareholders participate in the benefits of membership equally. It is only when a company divides its share capital into different classes with different rights attached to them that the *prima facie* presumption of equality of shares may be displaced.

In my view, a precondition to the derogation from the presumption of equality, both with respect to entitlement to dividends and other shareholder entitlements, is the division of shares into different "classes." The rationale for this rule can be traced to the principle that shareholder rights attach to the shares themselves and not to shareholders. The division of shares into separate classes, then, is the means by which shares (as opposed to shareholders) are distinguished, and in turn allows for the derogation from the presumption of equality: *Bowater Canadian Ltd. v. R.L. Crain Inc.* (1987), 46 D.L.R. (4th) 161 at p. 163, 39 B.L.R. 34, 62 O.R. (2d) 752 (C.A.), per Houlden J.A.

The concept of share "classes" is not technical in nature, but rather is simply the accepted means by which differential treatment of shares is recognized in the articles of incorporation of a company. As Professor Welling succinctly explains, "a class is simply a sub-group of shares with rights and conditions in common which distinguish them from other shares" (p. 583). Indeed, the use of the share class is recognized in the S.B.C.A. as the means by which derogation from the principle of equality is to be achieved. The statute thus explicitly requires that "the rights, privileges, restrictions and conditions attaching to the shares of each class" must be expressly stated in the articles of incorporation: s. 24(4)(a).

Having outlined the underlying principles of corporate law relevant to the issues raised on this appeal, the application of those principles to the facts can be attempted. The appellant, the Minister of National Revenue, argues that the discretionary dividend clause in the articles of incorporation of Northland Trucks does not create discrete classes of shares with different rights to dividends. Furthermore, the Minister contends that the clause creates no right to dividends at all and, therefore, does not comply with the statutory requirement in s. 24(4)(a). Consequently, the allocation of a dividend made pursuant to the discretionary dividend clause must be disregarded because of its failure to comply with the S.B.C.A. and with the principles of corporate and common law. As a result, the presumption of equality has not been rebutted and equality of distribution amongst the share classes prevails.

• • •

The respondent argues, on the other hand, that the discretionary dividend clause is a valid exercise of contractual rights between the company and its shareholders in accordance with the common law and statute. Moreover, the right to receive dividends in potentially unique amounts gives each share class different rights. It is argued that this is a material distinction sufficient to create separate share classes with differentiated dividend entitlements which, in turn, validly derogates from the principle of equality.

I agree with the arguments which the respondent has raised in this regard. In my opinion, the discretionary dividend clause is both a valid means of allocating declared dividends and is sufficient to rebut the presumption of equality amongst shares. I find this determination, with respect to the presumption of equality, to be a simple factual inquiry. In my view, the presence of a discretionary dividend clause can only be interpreted as creating differences between share classes, since that is the rationale for the clause. As far as the statutory requirements are concerned, the purpose of s. 24(4)(a) is to ensure that shareholders are fully aware of their entitlements and privileges to the extent that the presumption of equality is rendered inapplicable. To my mind, that purpose has been met since the dividend entitlements are clearly set out in the description of the share classes. In this regard, I find the argument of Pierre Quessy in his article "Les aspects corporatifs et fiscaux des actions à dividends discrétionnaire," *Revue de Planification Fiscale et Successorale* (1985, vol. 7, No. 1, 31 at p. 45) to be persuasive (translation):

... the inclusion in the articles of a discretionary dividend clause expressly establishes that the corporation intends to derogate from the principle of equality among shareholders. The provision included in the articles alters the division of profits, which in the absence of such a provision would have to be made in accordance with the principle of equality among shareholders.

... In my view, then, the presumption of equality manifestly has been rebutted.

I find the appellant's arguments as they relate to the validity of a discretionary dividend clause in terms of general corporate law and the requirements of the S.B.C.A. to be equally unpersuasive. Counsel for the appellant placed considerable emphasis in his arguments upon the nature of a shareholder "right," arguing that for the purposes of the statute and common law, a right to a dividend comprises a right to a portion of the total dividend declared, calculated according to the terms set out in the share description if and when the directors decide to make a distribution of the profits of the company. The appellant argues that the insertion of a discretionary dividend clause in the articles of incorporation is insufficient to confer a "right" since no corresponding "duty" is imposed on the company to pay dividends on that class once a dividend has been declared. ... The appellant argues that this unconstrained discretion cannot be considered a "right" which is conferred by the shares.

I disagree with this analysis. In my opinion, the fact that dividend rights are contingent upon the exercise of the discretion of the directors to allocate the declared dividend between classes of shares does not render entitlement to a dividend any less a "right." Rather, it is the entitlement to be considered for a dividend which is more properly characterized in those terms. I agree with the respondent that the Class B common shareholders of the company have an entitlement comparable to that of a fixed dividend holder to receive a dividend if the company's directors declare one. As well, the appellant's argument that there is no corresponding "duty" on directors as regards the "right" of shareholders is, in my view, specious. The directors are bound by their fiduciary duty to act in good faith for the best interests of the company in the declaration and allocation of any dividend. That duty is in no way circumvented by the presence of a discretionary dividend clause. Finally, I think that it should be borne in mind that many shareholder rights may be qualified and contingent (voting rights, the right to transfer shares, preferential rights to dividends, participation rights); yet the mere fact that these rights are fettered does not render them anything less than shareholder rights.

In a similar vein, I do not agree that the absence of a mathematical formula for the allocation of declared dividends in the articles of incorporation of the company is dispositive of the issue of the validity of the discretionary dividend clause. As the decision to declare a dividend and the determination of the funds available for a dividend are already within the discretion of the directors, it seems to me that a discretionary dividend clause is not a significant departure or extension of that discretion: *De Vall v. Wainwright Gas Co.*, [1932] 2 D.L.R. 145, [1932] 1 W.W.R. 281, 26 Alta. L.R. 274 (C.A.). If shares are divided into separate classes, one of which contains a preferred entitlement to dividends declared by the company, the directors effectively have the discretion to allocate dividends only to that preferred class. Thus, the respondent could have achieved precisely the same allocation of dividends by structuring the company so that Wilma McClurg and Suzanne Ellis constituted a preferred class of shareholders with first entitlement to dividends. Such a structure would be unimpeachable in terms of the principles of corporate law.

Furthermore, it cannot reasonably be maintained that the presence of a discretionary dividend clause inherently leads to a conflict of the duty of directors and their self-interest any more than does the discretion to declare a dividend in any company. Consequently, I cannot agree with those authors who take the position that the allocation of dividends by directors, pursuant to a discretionary dividend clause, inherently cannot be exercised in the best interests of the company: see Maurice Martel and Paul Martel, "La compagnie au Québec, Les aspects juridiques," vol. I (Montreal: Wilson & Lafleur Ltée, 1987), at pp. 18-10-14C; Michelle Boivin, "Le droit aux dividendes et le dividende 'discrétionnaire'" (1987), 47 R. du B. 73. I agree with the argument of the respondent that it is unrealistic to think that directors will not pay heed to the identity of shareholders and the contribution to the company of those shareholders any time a decision is made as to whether dividends of any sort should be declared. The fact that directors may consider the identity of shareholders does not necessarily render the declaration invalid on the basis of a conflict of duty and self-interest. For example, the discretion could be exercised for the purpose of rewarding a group of employees who comprise a preferred class of shareholders and who have been encouraged to invest in a company. Surely the fact that the identity of the holders of that class of shares was considered in the decision to declare a dividend and in the determination of the quantum of the dividend would not render the decision invalid. To reiterate, the limitation on the decision is purely a fiduciary one and the entitlement of a shareholder is "to share in the profits of the company when these are declared as dividends in respect of the shares of the class of which his share forms a part": R.M. Bryden, "The Law of Dividends," *Studies in Canadian Company Law*, Jacob S. Ziegel, ed. (Toronto: Butterworths, 1967), at p. 270. That right is in no way undermined by the presence of a discretionary dividend clause.

In other words, the clause simply divides conceptually into two components—declaration and allocation—what has been, traditionally, one decision. In substance, though, the discretion which lies in the hands of the directors has always included both, subject to the provisions of the articles of incorporation. In this regard, the only other limitation upon the directors of which I am aware is that "if a dividend is declared by a corporation ... there must be some shares entitled to receive the dividend": Welling, pp. 588-9. The principle has been given statutory recognition in s. 24(4)(b) of the S.B.C.A. In my view, this rule is not defeated by the presence of the discretionary dividend clause because the identity of the class eligible for a dividend simply remains unknown until the allocation takes place. This conceptual division into declaration and allocation is not substantively different from any derogation from the presumption of equality in the payment of dividends. Consequently, for this court to find that the use of a discretionary dividend clause on these facts was an invalid exercise of the discretion of the directors, would be to defeat the substance of what was achieved solely on the basis of its form.

Finally, I question whether it would be appropriate for this court to determine that the use of a discretionary dividend clause is invalid in the context of an income tax appeal. The purpose of the governing statute, the S.B.C.A., is facilitative—that is, it allows parties, with certain explicit restrictions, to structure bodies corporate as they wish. As well, the Act provides the means for an aggrieved party—security holder, creditor, director or officer—whose interests have not been regarded fairly by the corporation, to seek redress through the oppression remedy in s. 234 of the Act. No such complaint has been lodged by any interested party in this case, presumably because all those involved in this company are satisfied with the way in which the directors are conducting its affairs. Furthermore, at common law it is a well-established principle that where shareholders are unanimously agreed to a transaction, inequality of treatment does not render it *ultra vires* the company: F.W. Wegenast, *The Law of Canadian Companies* (Toronto: Carswells, 1979), at pp. 321-2. As I have found that the use of a discretionary dividend clause is not prohibited expressly by the Act, nor contrary to common law or corporate law principles, I think the permissive spirit of the Act demands that a conclusion be reached that the use of the clause is valid. As Pierre Quessy, supra, explained, the use of the clause represents a legitimate exercise of the contractual rights between shareholders and a company (translation, at p. 48):

... the declaration and payment of a dividend by the directors on discretionary dividend shares is a legal act under the Corporations Acts when the articles contain a provision conferring greater discretion on them. We then have shares of the capital stock carrying the right to receive any dividend declared. Moreover, the articles contain an express provision indicating that the parties intend to derogate from the principle of equality among shareholders. Accordingly, as the parties to the contract are not acting contrary to public order and not infringing the law, we are of the view that the terms of the agreement concluded by them should be observed.

I agree with this conclusion. Professor Melvin Eisenberg, more than two decades ago, in his work on modern corporate law, "The Legal Roles of Shareholders and Management in Modern Corporate Decisionmaking" (1969), 57 Cal. L. Rev. 1 at p. 180, reasoned that "[i]n the case of the privately held corporation, legal rules governing internal decision-making should be suppletory in nature and based on the shareholders' probable expectations." Given that the legislature has not chosen to disallow the discretionary dividend clause, and no shareholder has taken remedial action against its use (presumably because shareholder expectations have been realized by its exercise), it would be paternalistic in the extreme for this court to invalidate the clause at the behest of the appellant Minister of National Revenue. If the legislature determines that the use of the discretionary dividend clause undermines the reasonable expectations of shareholders or is in some way unfair to an interested party, then it is up to the legislature to limit the use of this means of structuring corporate affairs.

In conclusion, then, I find nothing untoward in the use of the discretionary dividend clause in the allocation of corporate dividends. There is nothing in the S.B.C.A. or at common law that prohibits this dividend allocation technique.

• • •

LA FOREST J. (dissenting):

• • •

Corporate law issues

• • •

In a certain sense, the term "discretionary dividend" is a misnomer, since it is a well-accepted principle of common law that the directors of a corporation have the discretion to determine if and when a dividend should be declared, and in what amount. This discretion is, of course, subject to certain reasonable limitations. For example, s. 40(a) of the Saskatchewan Business Corporations Act provides that a dividend may not be declared if there are reasonable grounds to believe such declaration would render the corporation unable to pay its debts. As well, there is the overriding principle that the discretion must always be exercised in a manner which is in the best interests of the corporation: see Bruce Welling, *Corporate Law in Canada: The Governing Principles* (Toronto: Butterworths, 1984), at p. 614.

Although the term "discretionary dividend" may be somewhat misleading, it is none the less not difficult to understand how the label itself was first chosen. Clauses such as the one contained in the articles of incorporation of Northland Trucks give directors a power of discretion that they never previously had: the power to discriminate between different classes of shares when determining how a dividend should be distributed. Is this allocation of power to the directors valid under the Saskatchewan Business Corporations Act? To answer this question, it is necessary to examine both the principles at common law and the statute itself.

The common law

Since the famous decision of the House of Lords in *Salomon v. A. Salomon & Co., Ltd.*, [1897] A.C. 22, it has been a settled proposition of law that a corporation has a separate legal existence, independent from that of its shareholders. Even before *Salomon*, it had been said that it was this proposition that lay at the "root" of corporate law: *Farrar v. Farrars, Ltd.* (1888), 40 Ch. D. 395 at pp. 409-10.

The independent legal existence of the corporation means that, while the shareholder remains a proportionate owner of the corporation, he does not actually own its assets. These assets belong to the corporation itself, as a separate legal entity; Clive M. Schmitthoff, *Palmer's Company Law*, 23rd ed., vol. 1 (London: Stevens & Sons, 1982), at p. 384, para. 33-01. Management of the corporation is entrusted to its officers and directors with the shareholder's interest protected through the distribution of shareholder votes. Thus, the corporate entity is unique in that it allows the shareholder to alienate ownership of property by placing it in a structure where the ownership of the property is separated from the effective control over that property: see Welling, at p. 81. The sole link between the shareholder and the company is the share, which provides both a measure of the shareholder's interest in the company, as well as of the extent of the shareholder's liability for the actions of that company: see *Borland's Trustee v. Steel Brothers & Co. Ltd.*, [1901] 1 Ch. 279 at p. 288.

This separation of ownership and control provides the basis for many of the fundamental principles of corporate law. One example is the principle that the directors and officers of a corporation owe a fiduciary duty to the corporation: see *Canadian Aero Service Ltd. v. O'Malley* (1973), 40 D.L.R. (3d) 371, 11 C.P.R. (2d) 206, [1974] S.C.R. 592.

•   •   •

Another principle that I believe also stems logically from the separation of ownership and control inherent in the corporation is the principle of equality of shares. Since the shareholders are only proportionate owners of the company, if their interest is to be adequately and fairly protected, those in the position of control must treat all the shareholders, or more accurately, all the shares, equally. Thus, see Schmitthoff, at p. 387, para. 33-06:

Prima facie the rights carried by the shares rank *pari passu*, i.e. the shareholders participate in the benefits of membership equally. It is only when a company divides its share capital into different classes with different rights attached to them that the *prima facie* presumption of equality of shares may be displaced.

In my opinion, the principle of equality of shares, like the principle of fiduciary duty, developed as more than just a mere contractual right—*it was a measure of protection for the shareholder that arose as a practical consequence of the unique nature of the corporate structure itself.* This is so even though the parties could contract out of it to the extent that shares could be created that did not themselves have equal rights. In such a situation, the shareholder was still protected by virtue of the common law rule that shareholder rights had to be attached to the share itself, and not to the individual shareholder. Thus, while the shares had differentiated rights depending upon the particular class to which they belonged, the shareholder himself could not be discriminated against. For example, even when different classes of shares were created, the shares within the various classes themselves still had to be treated on an equal basis. It is thus put by F.W. Wegenast, *The Law of Canadian Companies* (Toronto: Carswells, 1979), at pp. 320-1:

Apart from provisions, duly adopted, for preferences as between different classes of shares, and, where there are such preferences, then as amongst the members in each respective class, shareholders are entitled to be treated on a basis of equality. Shareholders may differ as to the wisdom of a particular course of action, but once adopted *it must be carried out without discrimination amongst the shareholders* or, as it is said in some of the cases, "for the benefit of the company as a whole."

(Emphasis added.)

More significantly, even when more than one class of shares was created, the directors were not free to discriminate arbitrarily between the classes when awarding a dividend. As Fraser states in *Company Law of Canada*, 5th ed. (by J.L. Stewart and M. Laird Palmer (Toronto: Carswells, 1962), at p. 532, quoting Lord Cranworth L.C. in *Henry v. Great Northern R. Co.* (1857), 1 De G. & J. 606 at p. 638, 44 E.R. 858 at p. 871:

Where there is more than one class of shareholders "it will be [always] the duty of the directors to fix the amount of the fund retained with reference to the general interest of all classes of shareholders, and not to favour any one class at the expense of the other."

The few Canadian cases that appear to have considered the issue have all held that, even when the shareholders agree to do so, a company may not validly be structured so as to derogate from the common-law principle that shareholder rights must attach to the shares themselves. When I speak of shareholder rights, I include at least those three categories of rights that are considered to be fundamental: the right to a dividend, the right to vote, and the right to participate in the distribution of assets upon dissolution of the corporation.

In *Jacobsen v. United Canso Oil & Gas Ltd.* (1980), 113 D.L.R. (3d) 427, 11 B.L.R. 313, [1980] 6 W.W.R. 38 (Alta, Q.B.), the defendant company passed a by-law to the effect that no one person was entitled to vote more that 1,000 shares, notwithstanding the number of shares actually held by that person. The company had originally been incorporated under the Companies Act, R.S.C. 1952, c. 53. The court found the by-law invalid since the Companies Act recognized the common-law presumption of equality "that all shares confer equal rights and impose equal liabilities and that if voting rights are to vary separate classes of shares must be created *so that the different numbers of votes can be attached to the shares themselves and not to the holder*" (at p. 433) (emphasis added). The court also held that the by-law was invalid under the Canada Business Corporations Act (S.C. 1974-75, c. 33, which superseded the Companies Act), the Act upon which the Saskatchewan Business Corporations Act is based.

In *Bowater Canadian Ltd. v. R.L. Crain Inc.* (1987), 46 D.L.R. (4th) 161, 39 B.L.R. 34, 62 O.R. (2d) 752, the Ontario Court of Appeal held invalid a "step-down" provision contained in the respondent Crain Inc.'s articles of incorporation. The provision provided for a special class of common shares that carried ten votes per share while in the possession of the original shareholder, but that would carry only one vote per share if transferred to another. The Court of Appeal followed the reasoning of McRae J. in the court below, who, at p. 163, held that:

... although there was no express prohibition in the CBCA against a step-down provision, *s. 24(4) of the Act should be interpreted in accordance with the general principles of corporation law* with the result that the rights which are attached to a class of shares must be provided equally to all shares of that class, this interpretation being founded on the principle that *rights, including votes, attach to the share and not to the shareholder*.

(Emphasis added.)

Both *Jacobsen* and *Bowater* recognize that the principle that shareholder rights must attach to the corporation's shares is more than a mere contractual right: even the shareholders themselves may not agree to circumvent this principle.

• • •

In my view, a discretionary clause such as the one in this case, that permits the directors of a corporation to choose which class is entitled to receive dividends to the exclusion of the other classes, would be invalid at common law. It contravenes the principle that the directors are not permitted to favour one class at the expense of the others; see Fraser and Stewart, at p. 532. Further, and the respondent does not dispute this point, if dividends are allocated to the different classes on a discretionary basis, then the directors will be making this allocation primarily on the basis of the identity of the shareholders in the various classes. While the respondent contends that this does not represent a significant departure from the existing state of the law, I disagree, for it means, in effect, that the right to the dividend attaches not to the shares, but to the shareholder: see Michelle Boivin, "Le droit aux dividendes et le dividende 'discrétionnaire'" (1987), 47 R. du B. 73 at p. 92.

Again, in my view, the rule that shareholder rights must attach to the shares themselves is a principle which has its roots in the very nature of the corporate structure. When the articles of incorporation create classes of shares that have different rights, this normally does not require the directors to discriminate between the shareholders—the mode of distribution is set out in the shares themselves. To allow discrimination on the basis of the identity of those possessing the shares ignores the separation that is supposed to exist between the corporation and its shareholders: see Maurice Martel and Paul Martel, *La compagnie au Québec: Les aspects juridiques*, vol. I (Montreal: Wilson & Lafleur Ltée, 1987), at p. 18-14B.

The respondent, however, contends that, even in a situation where no discretionary dividend clause exists, in a corporation with at least one class of preferred shares, the directors of a corporation effectively have the power to choose which classes will receive dividends. They can do so by declaring dividends in an amount small enough that only the preferred shares will partake. This, however, is a discretion that is expressly limited by the terms of the articles of incorporation. The need for protection is not as great, for the common shareholder is not placed in a position where the director can award dividends of any amount to a class other than his or her own. That shareholder knows that if dividends are declared in excess of a specified amount, then his or her class of shares will participate. If dividends are never declared in excess of that amount, then at least the money is retained by the corporation. Where there is a discretionary dividend clause, however, the shareholder is completely dependent on the goodwill of the directors. The minority shareholder is placed in a near impossible position if this goodwill turns against her: see Martel and Martel, at p. 18-14A. It is interesting to note that at least one commentator who writes in favour of the discretionary dividend clause suggests that each shareholder's "informed" consent to this sort of arrangement be obtained in advance in writing, presumably to guard against just such an eventuality: see Pierre Quessy, "Les aspects corporatifs et fiscaux des actions à dividende discrétionnaire," *Revue de Planification Fiscale et Successorale* (1985), vol. 7, no. 1, 31, at pp. 42-3.

In my opinion, a second reason why the discretionary dividend clause is invalid at common law is because it places the director in a position where he cannot fulfill his fiduciary obligations to the corporation as a whole. The interests of different classes of shareholders, where a discretionary declaration of dividends is concerned, are necessarily divergent, since a dividend will be declared for the benefit of one class of shareholders at the expense of the others.

● ● ●

The conflict of interest is heightened when the director happens to be a shareholder himself. When the discretionary dividend clause is utilized to award dividends to a class in which the director holds shares, or from which he derives some personal benefit, the situation can be compared to the usurpation of a corporate opportunity properly belonging to the company. As Laskin J. observed in *Canadian Aero Service Ltd. v. O'Malley*, supra, at p. 382, the fiduciary duty, at the very least, precludes the director

... from obtaining for himself, either secretly or without the approval of the company (which would have to be properly manifested upon full disclosure of the facts), any property or business advantage either belonging to the company or for which it has been negotiating; and especially is this so where the director or officer is a participant in the negotiations on behalf of the company.

A discretionary dividend clause gives the director a licence to secure, by virtue of his position, a personal benefit at the expense of the corporation and its shareholders without having to seek shareholder approval. By contrast, requiring the mode of distribution to be expressly set out in the article of incorporation, which can only be amended by approval of the shareholders, is consistent with the fiduciary obligation as described in the *Canadian Aero* case. I note that, in the usual case, if the directors themselves hold preferred shares, this does not present a problem, for the common shareholders will have agreed to subordinate their dividend interest to the preferred class of shares based upon "full disclosure" of the maximum amount to which these preferred shares will enjoy priority. With a discretionary dividend clause, there is no such disclosure, since the amount and priority is left to be determined in the future, wholly at the directors' discretion.

The Chief Justice states that the fact that the directors take into account the identity of shareholders when declaring a dividend does not necessarily create a conflict of duty. As an example, he suggests that the directors could validly exercise their discretion to allocate dividends so as to reward a group of employees who comprise a class of preferred shareholders. With respect, it seems to me that even this would constitute an improper exercise of the discretionary dividend power. If the employees truly merit some additional reward, the proper course would be to achieve this through some other form of compensation, for example, a bonus. A dividend is supposed to be a return on an investment. On this point, I adopt the words of Desjardins J.A. of the Federal Court of Appeal ([1988] 2 F.C. 356 at p. 370, [1988] 1 C.T.C. 75, 88 D.T.C. 6047):

> But surely, there is no relationship, in company law, between the work and services a shareholder brings to a company and his or her entitlement to a dividend if declared. The dividends come as a return on his or her investment and not on account of work and services he or she may render to the company. The dividend attaches to the share and not to the shareholder.

In any event, even if I did not find that the discretionary dividend clause was itself invalid under the common law, I would find that the clause, at least as designed in the present case, is insufficient to rebut the common-law presumption of equality. As earlier noted, it is well accepted that in the absence of some differentiation between the shares, all shares must be treated equally: see *Birch v. Cropper; Re Bridgewater Navigation Co. Ltd.* (1889), 14 App. Cas. 525 (H.L.). The respondent contends that the fact that the class of shares has the potential to receive dividends in potentially different amounts is sufficient to differentiate them. The fact remains, however, that all three classes of Northland Trucks' shares are defined in substantially the same manner with respect to their entitlement to dividends. Each class carries "the distinction and right to receive dividends exclusive of other classes of shares in the said corporation."

• • •

Any difference between the shares concerning their right to receive dividends that does exist clearly does not derive from any differentiation between the shares, but would have to stem from the actions of the directors of the corporation. This would, however, be a right that does not derive from the share itself, and as such be invalid at common law.

Having found that the discretionary dividend clause contained in the articles of incorporation of Northland Trucks was an invalid allocation of power at common law, it remains to examine the Saskatchewan Business Corporations Act to see if the statute changes this result.

The Saskatchewan Business Corporations Act

Section 24(4)(a) of the Saskatchewan Business Corporations Act provides that the corporation may derogate from the common-law rule of equality, by creating more than one class of shares:

> 24(4) The articles may provide for more than one class of shares and, if they so provide:
> (a) the rights, privileges, restrictions and conditions attaching to the shares of each class shall be set out therein ...

See also s. 6(1)(c)(i).

The question becomes whether the allocation of power to the directors of a corporation to determine each class of shares' right to a dividend, once one has been declared, is consistent with s. 24(4)(a), which provides that such rights must be "set out" in the articles of incorporation. There are two possible interpretations. The first is that it is sufficient if the articles "set out" that the different classes of shares have the "right" to receive a dividend that has been declared, wholly at the discretion of the directors. The second is that the requirement that the rights be "set out" requires that the mode of distribution of the dividends be expressly provided for in the articles themselves.

I start from the premise that s. 24(4)(a) must, of course, be interpreted in accordance with the principles of the common law; see *Bowater*, supra, at p. 754. It should be apparent from the preceding analysis that, in my opinion, this would inevitably lead one towards the second interpretation, since, at common law, shareholder rights had to be expressly provided for in the shares themselves. If the Saskatchewan legislature intended to depart from this principle, it could have stated so explicitly. In my view, s. 24(4)(a) falls far short of providing the clear expression necessary to indicate an intent to provide the directors of a corporation with a power which they did not otherwise have at common law.

I note that this interpretation of s. 24(4)(a) appears to be the most consistent with other provisions of the Act as well. For example, s. 27 provides for the possibility of creating different "series" within a class of shares, which may themselves be structured so as to possess different rights. In contrast to its treatment of classes of shares, the Act expressly provides that the directors of a corporation may be given the discretion to determine the rights attaching to these series. Section 27(1) reads:

> 27(1) The articles may authorize the issue of any class of shares in one or more series and may authorize the directors to fix the number of shares in and to determine the designation, rights, privileges, restrictions and conditions attaching to the shares of each series, subject to the limitations set out in the articles.

It is significant that, even when the Act specifically provides that the directors may be given the discretion to determine the rights to be assigned to a series, this discretion is not unlimited: see s. 27(2) to (4). In particular, the directors may not assign to a series a higher priority in respect of dividends or return of capital over any other series of the class that are still outstanding: s. 27(3). Thus, even though under the Act the shareholders can give the directors the power to issue series within a class and assign rights to those series, the shareholders may not agree to give the directors the discretion to interfere with their right to dividends or a return of capital by choosing to give another series priority. Why would the legislature find it necessary to protect the shareholders by restricting the directors' discretion in this manner? In my view, the answer lies in the fact that the rights assigned to series, unlike classes of shares, may be altered without amending the corporate constitution.

• • •

Because s. 27 allows the shareholders to give directors the power to discriminate between series of shares, while leaving the directors with the ability to "supply the details" of this discrimination themselves at a later date, the legislature apparently found it necessary to limit this power, by preventing the directors from discriminating in certain areas, specifically with respect to priority over dividends. This attempt at protection would be rendered futile if it were permissible for shareholders to give to directors the same power to discriminate with respect to priority over dividends where shareholder classes are concerned, through the use of a discretionary dividend clause.

A more reasonable interpretation of the statute is that it contemplates that shareholders will be protected from changes being made to the rights attached to different classes of shares by virtue of the fact that such rights may only be amended by altering the corporate constitution. Section 170(1)(c) of the Saskatchewan Business Corporations Act provides that:

170(1) ... the holders of shares of a class or ... of a series are entitled to vote separately as a class or series upon a proposal to amend the articles to:

> ...

(c) add, change or remove the rights, privileges, restrictions or conditions attached to the shares of such class ...

The protection afforded by s. 170 for dividend rights can only be meaningful if the mode of distribution must itself be set out in the articles of incorporation. Otherwise, the section can effectively be circumvented because the directors will have the power to change each class's allocation of dividends at will, without the need for a shareholder vote. The importance of s. 170(1) as a mechanism for protecting shareholder interests is evidenced by the fact that each class of shares is entitled to vote, regardless of whether the shares normally carry this right or not: s. 170(3).

I also find the use of the discretionary dividend clause in the present case to be inconsistent with the requirement of the Act that at least one class of shares must be entitled "to receive any dividend declared by the corporation": s. 24(3)(b).

• • •

In essence, the argument of the respondent distills down to a single point: the Saskatchewan Business Corporations Act does not appear to specifically prohibit the use of a discretionary dividend clause, and in the absence of such explicit prohibition, the parties must be left free to contract at will. If one were to carry this argument to its logical conclusion, there would be nothing to prevent shareholders from passing a "discretionary voting" clause, giving the directors the power to exercise all of their votes as they see fit. Indeed, during the oral argument, counsel for the respondent appeared to suggest that this, too, would be a permissible allocation of power. I find that such an arrangement, which would leave the directors in complete control of the corporation, with the power to prolong their tenure indefinitely, to be completely unacceptable in that it would undermine virtually all of the protection afforded to shareholders by the Act.

It is true, of course, that the actions of the directors will always be subject to the qualification that they are acting as fiduciaries for the corporation. Thus, in theory, it is always open for a shareholder to bring a suit if he feels the directors are exercising their discretion improperly. In reality, however, one cannot overlook the significant burden and expense that this remedy entails. In my view, placing the onus on share-holders to bring a suit to vindicate their rights is an inadequate means of protecting them from the potential for abuse created by the presence of a discretionary dividend clause.

If this protectionist view seems somewhat patronizing, I would point out that other provisions of the Saskatchewan Business Corporations Act provide, in a similar manner, for the protection of shareholders from arrangements to which they might otherwise agree. One example already referred to is s. 27, which restricts the power that can validly be allocated to directors to determine the rights and privileges of future series of shares. I also note that the protection of the individual shareholder was one of the major driving forces behind the extensive statutory reform that took place in Canadian corporate law in the 1970s; see Welling, at p. 502. The Saskatchewan Business Corporations Act is a product of that reform, as is the Canada Business Corporations Act, S.C. 1974-75, c. 33, upon which the Saskatchewan Business Corporations Act is modeled. Corporate law has not yet evolved to the point where the freedom to contract at any cost has become paramount to all other concerns.

The need for shareholder protection from abuse of the discretionary dividend clause becomes all the more apparent when one considers the possibility that such a clause could be inserted in the articles of incorporation of a large, publicly-held corporation. I recognize that in this case we are dealing with a closely held corporation, where there has been no allegation of a breach of fiduciary duty by the directors, but the Saskatch-ewan Business Corporations Act applies to large and small corporations equally. One rule of law must stand for both. I hasten to add that, in my view, the primary reason that the discretionary dividend clause is invalid is that it offends the principle that the corporation has a separate legal existence from the shareholder. Since the shareholders of closely held corporations are given preferential treatment, such as limited liability, based upon the notion of this separation between corporation and shareholder, it is not unreasonable for the state to require them to respect this separation by structuring their corporation accordingly.

Against the weight of these arguments, I can think of no socially useful purpose, and counsel for the respondent could point to none, behind the employment of a discre-tionary dividend clause. The only apparent purpose of such a clause is to facilitate tax-avoidance through "income-splitting," which does little to persuade me of the need to allow corporations to be structured in this manner: see Boivin, at p. 106; see also comment, "McClurg v. The Queen: The Last Bastion for Income-Splitting?" (1986), 34 Canadian Tax Journal 404.

· · ·

Disposition

In the result, I would allow the appeal and uphold the Minister's reassessment.

L'HEUREUX-DUBÉ J. and WILSON J. concurred with LA FOREST J.
SOPINKA, GONTHIER and CORY JJ. concurred with DICKSON C.J.C.

NOTE

The judgments by Dickson C.J.C. on the one hand and La Forest J. on the other reflect two quite different approaches to corporate law. Dickson's approach sees corporate law as "facilitative—that is it allows parties, within certain explicit restrictions, to structure bodies corporate as they wish." La Forest, on the other hand, takes a more interventionist approach claiming that "[c]orporate law has not yet evolved to the point where the freedom of contract at any cost has become paramount to all other concerns." These contrasting approaches and how they fit into broader academic debates in corporate law are discussed in B.R. Cheffins, *Comment: The Queen v. McClurg*, 70 Can. Bar Rev. 724 (1992); see also V. Krishna & J.A. VanDuzer, *Corporate Share Capital Structures and Income Splitting: McClurg v. Canada*, 21 C.B.L.J. 335 (1993).

Cumulative Voting. If we imagine a corporation with two shareholders, one with 50.01% of the voting shares and the other owning 49.99%, the majority shareholder will be able to elect all of the directors and the minority shareholder none. If this seems unfair, it should be remembered that it is consistent with the political model in most representative democracies, including Canada. However, American legislation has often required, sometimes as a matter of state constitutional law, that business corporations have a system of proportional representation referred to as cumulative voting. The system of cumulative voting for director elections is designed to guarantee that the minority will be able to elect some members of the board of directors.

In a cumulative voting regime, a shareholder may allocate all of the votes that he would be entitled to cast for the election of all directors (the number of shares owned times number of directors to be elected, assuming one vote per share) among the different candidates in any manner he wishes. The mechanics of cumulative voting are explained in the following excerpt from the Dickerson Report:

It is obvious that [in a cumulative voting system] the smaller the number of directors in a corporation, the greater the proportional shareholding required to elect one director. The formula for determining the number of votes required to elect a single director is:

$$\frac{\text{Total number of votes that can be cast}}{\text{Number of directors to be elected} + 1} + 1 = X$$

Thus, in a corporation in which there are 9 directorships to be filled and 30,000 shares, the number of votes required to elect a single director is:

$$\frac{9 \times 30{,}000}{9 + 1} + 1 = 27{,}001$$

which is approximately 10% of the votes. If, however, the number of directors is reduced to 5, the number of votes required to elect a single director would be:

$$\frac{5 \times 30{,}000}{5 + 1} + 1 = 25{,}001$$

which is 16%; and if the number of directors is reduced to 3, the number of votes required will be 22,501 out of 90,000, that is, about 25%. Mathematically, cumulative voting will not work unless there are at least 3 directors. Reducing the number of directors thus makes it much more difficult for a minority interest to employ the right to cumulate, and dilutes its value to them. [*Id.* at 76-77]

Since reducing the number of directors to be elected at one time dilutes the benefit that cumulative voting can confer upon the minority, it follows that if a board of any given size is classified by staggered terms, that will tend to dilute the effect of cumulative voting. CBCA corporations that permit cumulative voting are not permitted to classify their boards. CBCA s. 107(f).

Cumulative voting may give minority blocks representation on the board, but majority shareholders will remain in control as long as they cast their votes wisely. Of course, management might wish to give board representation to a significant minority shareholder, but cumulative voting turns this into an entitlement. This may impose costs on a firm when the minority shareholder's interests are imperfectly correlated with those of the firm, for example when the shareholder is a competitor of the firm. Cumulative voting rights are quite rare in the United States and practically unheard of in Canada.

6. The Significance of Voting Rights

Does Voting Matter? In a closely held corporation, shareholders are often both relatively well informed about the firm and intensely interested in its affairs and governance. Indeed, as will be seen in a later in the chapter, many closely held corporations are managed by shareholders, with a substantial identity between them and management. In such cases, shareholder voting rights will certainly be exercised.

However, in widely held corporations, the shareholders, or most of them, can usually be expected to be passive. Shareholders must absorb costs in informing themselves of the corporation's activities, and will not wish to do so if the marginal benefits are exceeded by the marginal costs. Since the benefits are shared with all other shareholders, most public shareholders will prefer to free ride on monitoring by major investors or investment intermediaries. This phenomenon is described as "rational apathy" in Gilson, *The Case Against Shark Repellant Amendments: Structural Limitations on the Enabling Concept*, 34 Stan. L. Rev. 775, 829 (1982). It was also this phenomenon which led Berle and Means to the hypothesis that this created a separation of ownership and control that allowed for considerable latitude and laxity in the management of American corporations in the 1930s (see Adolf A. Berle & Gardiner C. Means, *The Modern Corporation and Private Property*, 1932).

When shareholders are mere *rentiers* of capital, management can be said to control the firm and the shareholders meeting will in most cases be an empty ritual. Management's nominees to the board will be elected and management's proposals uniformly approved by the shareholders. This has led to demands for greater "shareholder democracy," a subject taken up in the following sections. However, other writers have suggested that the "corporate Jacksonians" are fundamentally misguided and assert that little would be lost if form followed what these commentators see as substance and shareholders' voting rights were eliminated. See, e.g., Manning, *Book Review*, 67 Yale L.J. 1477 (1958). These commentators emphasize that under the "Wall Street Rule" disaffected holders of shares in publicly traded corporations have a much easier and faster route than corporate suffrage to express their displeasure with management: they can sell their shares.

Shareholder Monitoring. In *The Structure of the Corporation* (1976), Professor Eisenberg set out to debunk the debunkers by showing that, in all but a small handful of the largest American widely held firms, there is usually at least one shareholder or an identifiable group of shareholders with a sufficiently large block of shares to have a realistic expectation of a meaningful voice in the conduct of corporate affairs. In very few corporations is the pattern of share ownership so diffuse that management can entirely count on the passivity of shareholders. Indeed, an S.E.C. survey in 1984 showed that in approximately 20% of firms listed on the New York Stock Exchange or the American Stock Exchange, or traded over-the-counter, at least one non-officer owned more than 10% of the common shares and in approximately 15% at least one officer owned more than 10% of the common shares. While premiums paid in block trades suggest private benefits may accrue to large block holders, evidence of overall share price increases and management turnover suggest large block holders do assert influence over the management of the corporation. See, e.g., C.G. Holderness & D.P. Sheehan, *The Role of Majority Shareholders in Publicly Held Corporations*, 20 J. of Fin. Econ. 317 (1988). M.J. Barclay & C.G. Holderness, *Private Benefits from Control of Public Corporations*, 25 J. of Fin. Econ. 371 (1989) (noting premiums on trades involving blocks of 5% or more of the common shares average 20%); and M.J. Barclay & C.G. Holderness, *Negotiated Block Trades and Corporate Control*, 46 J. of Fin. 861 (1991) (noting average significant share price gains on block trades and replacement of 33% of chief executive officers within one year of block trades).

The notion that in the typical publicly held corporation there are individuals or groups of shareholders that care intensely about the corporation's ongoing performance and that have clout with management as a result of the size of their interest, although based on American data, is particularly applicable to Canada. This is because, even when the shares of a Canadian corporation are widely traded within Canada, so many large Canadian business corporations are dominated by a foreign parent or by another significant holder of controlling block of shares. It would appear obvious that the foreign owner with a 25%, 50% or 75% interest will keep the closest of tabs on the Canadian corporation's activities. On the extent of control block or significant corporate share ownership in Canada see R.J. Daniels & J.G. MacIntosh, *Toward a Distinctive Canadian Corporate Law Regime*, 29 Osgoode Hall L.J. 863, 884 (1991). On the role of institutional investors as significant shareholders in Canadian corporations and how the law has interfered with the role they play in monitoring the corporation see J.G. MacIntosh, *The Role of Institutional and Retail Investors in Canadian Capital Markets*, 31 Osgoode Hall L.J. 371 (1993).

In addition, one study found that shareholder-controlled firms are more likely to be encountered in industries where major shareholders may be useful monitors. Demsetz & Lehn, *The Structure of Corporate Ownership: Causes and Consequences*, 93 J. Pol. Econ. 1155 (1985). For example, firms in stable markets are easier to monitor and are more likely to be manager-controlled. Volatile industries offer more opportunities for manager misbehaviour, and here a greater proportion of firms are shareholder-controlled. Regulated firms are more likely to be manager-controlled, in part because of the subsidized monitoring performed by the regulator. On the other hand, firms where managers might have a greater temptation to indulge their personal preferences, such as sports clubs and mass media firms, are more frequently shareholder-controlled. In reviewing the evidence, the two authors suggest that firm ownership structures are in general efficient.

The Market for Control. Even where no shareholder holds more than a small fraction of the shares of a public corporation, voting rights remain important because they facilitate take-overs. Among the techniques for winning control of a corporation, take-overs or tender offers for voting shares have to a very great extent replaced proxy battles, in which two sides compete for the votes of current shareholders. On a take-over, the acquirer assumes control of the target corporation by purchasing a majority or a significant block of its voting shares, with the right to displace incumbent management by exercising the votes attached to the acquired shares. Such acquisitions are usually made at a substantial premium over market price. As a result, voting shares are frequently observed to trade at a premium over non-voting shares, even where no take-over bid is being made, with the possibility of an offer in the future accounting for the difference. See e.g., Lease, McConnell & Mikkleson, *The Market Value of Control in Publicly-Traded Corporations*, 11 J. Fin. Econ. 439 (1983) (where firms had issued voting and non-voting common stock, the voting common stock traded at a 5.44% premium over the non-voting common shares).

Since share price premiums are available to offeree shareholders of target firms on take-over bids, tactics by the target to defeat a bid will likely reduce shareholder wealth. See, e.g., Jensen & Ruback, *The Market for Corporate Control: The Scientific Evidence*, 11 J. Fin. Econ. 5, 35-37 (1983); G.A. Jarrell, J.A. Brickley & J.M. Netter, *The Market for Corporate Control: The Empirical Evidence Since 1980*, 2 J. of Econ. Perspectives 49; and R. Romano, *A Guide to Takeovers: Theory, Evidence and Regulation*, 9 Yale Journal on Regulation, 119 (1992). When a shareholder has purchased voting shares, paying a premium for them in anticipation of a possible take-over bid, defensive tactics by management whose effect is to lessen the probability that the offer will succeed may then be viewed as fraudulent.

This does not, however, explain why voting rights are important. After all, if managers had sought to remain in control of the firm by financing with non-voting shares, the shareholders would not have paid a premium in anticipation of a take-over bid, and would not be defrauded by the absence of a bid. What then is needed is an efficiency argument for voting shares, and this was provided by Henry Manne in two highly influential articles. Manne, *Some Theoretical Aspects of Share Voting*, 64 Colum. L. Rev. 1427 (1964); Manne, *Mergers and the Market for Corporate Control*, 73 J. Pol. Econ. 110 (1965). Manne's argument is that voting rights operate as an incentive to managerial honesty and efficiency. Where firm wealth is dissipated by management, either by looting (excessive consumption of wealth) or shirking (excessive consumption of leisure), the firm's shares will decline in value and the firm will become a more attractive candidate for a take-over bid by those who believe they can manage it more efficiently. Thus viewed, an issue of voting stock by a publicly held corporation is a bonding technique to reduce agency costs. The firm "promises" competent management, backing up the promise with a technique by which it can be displaced if it fails to live up to expectations.

A further result of the attribution of voting rights to shareholders is to align management's interests with those of the firm's residual claimants. This is likely efficient, provided that solvency problems do not intrude, since management will then be led to maximize firm value in seeking the highest possible value of the residual claims. (You may here wish to refer to the discussion of incentive costs in Chapter One, Section C, and consider the effect on firm value if management's primary incentive in all circumstances was to maximize the value of the firm's debt claims.)

On a claimholders' bargain model, all parties affected by a firm would agree to Kaldor-Hicks efficient governance structures. But if all stakeholders would be represented in an implicit contract, the bargain need not provide for formal representation of all classes of claimholders in governance structures. While all parties would agree to devices to maximize the wealth of the firm, this does not necessarily implicate political rights for all claimholders in firm governance. Thus, as we have seen in Chapter One, Section C, the firm value of a solvent corporation is more likely to be maximized when managers are allied to equity holders rather than to debt holders. A claimholder's bargain would then endow the former but not the latter with voting rights in elections of directors, except in near-insolvency circumstances where the agency costs of equity are likely to be high.

Transaction Cost Theories. Other insights into the issues that underlie the attribution of voting rights in corporations are provided by transaction cost economics. Transactions themselves impose costs, which include not merely the expenses of negotiating and preparing an agreement but also costs associated with opportunism by the parties. One risk of opportunism arises where one of the parties has invested assets in the bargain itself, such as the cost associated with the production of information concerning the transaction (e.g., creditors' costs in determining a debtor's creditworthiness). This information is a "transaction-specific" asset, inasmuch as it cannot be transferred to another transaction and will be lost if one of the parties abandons the bargain. The party that has made the investment will then run the risk of a shakedown by the other party if a termination of the relationship is less costly for him. The possibility of termination threats may of course be reflected in the bargain *ex ante*, so that distributional effects are dissipated.

However, the possibility of opportunism may lead to an underinvestment in transaction-specific assets, and both parties may therefore seek to limit strategic behaviour. One way of doing so is through the acquisition of a cooperative reputation, and the temptation to defect is in fact considerably chilled if one ultimately "pays" for defection through an *ex post* adjustment to one's reputation. A second way is through a "hostage" strategy, in which both parties make an equal investment in transaction-specific assets, such that a termination threat by either is less creditable.

Participation in voting may also serve to reduce opportunism that would reduce the incentive to invest in transaction specific assets. Participation in the voting process can provide a source of information which can allow one to anticipate future developments and plan investments in transaction-specific assets accordingly. It can also give a measure of control against changes that would substantially reduce the value of transaction-specific assets. However, voting can be a costly governance mechanism to control against changes that substantially lower the value of transaction-specific assets. To be used effectively the participants will have to incur the costs of becoming well informed about the corporation. There is also the risk that someone who has committed transaction-specific assets will use participation in voting as leverage to capture a greater degree of the gain to be derived from use of the transaction-specific asset. Thus voting will not be the preferred technique where other less costly techniques to protect transaction-specific assets are available.

Voting may be particularly useful to shareholders who, unlike other corporate constituencies, do not have their relationship with the corporation regularly come up for renewal. The risk of non-renewal and the development of a reputation for opportunistic behaviour can discourage management from making decisions that reduce the value of transaction-specific assets. Also, unlike a creditor who can take a security interest in an asset of the corporation to protect itself, the shareholder has no claim to the assets of the corporation and is the last to be compensated out of the assets of the corporation on a liquidation. Thus other controls to protect against management opportunism may be less readily available for shareholders and some participation in decision making through voting rights may be a more important device for shareholders in controlling against management opportunism.

This use of transaction cost analyses of the usefulness of voting was suggested in Williamson, *Corporate Governance*, 93 Yale L.J. 1197 (1984). Its application to constituencies other than shareholders is discussed in Section G below.

D. SHAREHOLDERS' MEETINGS

1. Meetings Called by Directors

Annual Meetings. CBCA corporations are required to hold annual meetings of shareholders to elect directors (CBCA s. 106(3); ABCA s. 101(3); BCCA Table A Articles Part 11; OBCA s. 119(4)); appoint auditors (s. 162(1); ABCA s. 156(1); BCCA s. 202(3); OBCA s. 149(1)); and receive the financial statements of the corporation (s.155(1); ABCA s, 149(1); BCCA s. 169(1); OBCA s. 154(1)). The meeting must be held not later than 18 months after the corporation comes into existence and subsequently not later than 15 months after the last annual meeting. CBCA s. 133(a); ABCA s. 127(a); OBCA s. 94(a). Under the BCCA the first annual meeting of shareholders must be held within 15 months of incorporation and thereafter in each calendar year not more than 13 months after the previous annual meeting (BCCA s. 163). Where a challenge to management's control is expected, its ability to choose the date of the annual meeting gives it an important strategic advantage over insurgents, as is the case for incumbent governments in parliamentary democracies.

Special Meetings. Shareholders' meetings called at other times, usually to approve some transaction not in the ordinary course and for which the incorporating statute or the corporation's constitutive documents requires shareholder approval, are called "special" meetings. CBCA s. 133(b); ABCA s. 127(b); OBCA s. 94(b). Sometimes, especially in England (and under the BCCA Table A, Part 7), a meeting of shareholders, whether annual or special, is referred to as a "general" meeting (or the "company in general meeting") to distinguish it from a meeting of the directors. Under the BCCA general meetings other than annual meetings are referred to as "extraordinary general meetings" (similar to special meetings under the CBCA).

Ordinary and Special Resolutions. To confuse matters further, the terms "ordinary resolution" and "special resolution" are used to describe the quantum of majority approval required for different shareholder actions. An ordinary resolution is one for which the requisite approval is a simple majority, while a special resolution requires the affirmative vote of more than a simple majority of the votes cast—usually two-thirds in Canada. CBCA s. 2(1); ABCA ss. 1(m), (y); BCCA s. 1(1) (three-quarters for a special resolution); OBCA s. 1(1).

Generally the matters dealt with at the annual meeting call for an ordinary resolution, and the matters customarily the subject of a special meeting of shareholders require special resolutions for passage. The latter are "fundamental" changes (discussed in Section C above) such as an amendment to the articles of incorporation, a restructuring of capital, a sale of assets, an amalgamation or a dissolution. However, the correlation between special meetings and special resolutions is not exact since a proposal recommending a fundamental change, which requires a special resolution, may be made at the annual meeting. Finally, one proposal that would almost always be the subject of a special rather than an annual meeting of shareholders—removal of directors before their terms are up—can be approved by ordinary resolution. CBCA s. 109; ABCA s. 104; OBCA s. 122 (cf. BCCA s. 154(3), which requires a special resolution).

Place of Meeting. The CBCA provides that the meeting is to be held at a place within Canada designated in the by-laws, or, in the absence of such a provision, in the place determined by the directors. CBCA s. 132; ABCA s. 126 (within Alberta) (cf. OBCA s. 93). A BCCA company meeting must be held within the province unless the registrar approves of the holding of a meeting outside of British Columbia. BCCA s. 170. Otherwise the standard form articles provide that meetings are to be held at a time and place decided on by the directors. BCCA Table A, para. 7.1.

Quorum. Typically the by-laws of a CBCA corporation will provide a quorum requirement for a shareholder meeting. Otherwise, the CBCA provides that, subject to the by-laws, a quorum is present at a meeting of shareholders if holders of a majority of the shares entitled to vote at the meeting are present or are represented by proxy. CBCA s. 139(1); see also ABCA s. 133(1); OBCA s. 101(1). Unless the by-laws otherwise provide, it is not necessary that the a quorum continue to be present throughout the meeting in order for business to be transacted at the meeting. It is sufficient that there be a quorum at the start of the meeting. CBCA s. 139(2); ABCA s. 133(2); OBCA s. 101(2). Where a quorum is not present at the opening of a meeting the shareholders present may adjourn the meeting to a fixed time and place but cannot transact any other business. CBCA s. 139(3); ABCA s. 133(3); OBCA s. 101(3).

Under BCCA s. 168 the quorum requirement is two persons unless the articles otherwise provide.

The Principle of Notice. When the directors propose to call a meeting of shareholders, they will generally first fix a "record date," not more than 50 nor less than 21 days before the meeting is to be held, for determining who is entitled to receive notice of the meeting. CBCA s. 134; ABCA s. 128; OBCA s. 95. Notice of the record date must also be given at least seven days prior to it under CBCA s. 128(4); ABCA s. 128(4); OBCA s. 95(4). Notice of the meeting will then be mailed to all those listed as shareholders in the records of the corporation on the record date.

The actual notice of the meeting must be sent to shareholders between 50 and 21 days before the meeting is to be held. CBCA s. 135(1); ABCA s. 129(1); OBCA s. 96(1). The most critical part of the notice provision is s. 135(6), which provides that "[n]otice of a meeting of shareholders at which special business is to be transacted shall state (a) the nature of that business in sufficient detail to permit the shareholder to form a reasoned judgment thereon ... ." See also ABCA s. 129(7); OBCA s. 96(6). "Special business" includes all business to be transacted at a special meeting and all business to be transacted at an annual meeting except consideration of the financial statements and the auditors' report, reappointment of the incumbent auditor and election of directors. CBCA s. 135(5); ABCA s. 129(6); OBCA s. 96(5). If the notice is defective, then the action taken at the meeting may be set aside at the instance of a dissenting shareholder. Judicial standards for what constitutes adequate disclosure will be discussed in the next section as an aspect of proxy regulation.

Under the BCCA notice of a meeting of shareholders must be given at least 21 days before the meeting. BCCA s. 167. Where directors are to be elected at the meeting (as is usually the case at annual meetings) a notice inviting nominations must be given at least 56 days before the meeting. BCCA s. 135.

In most publicly held corporations it will appear from the corporation's record that a securities depository institution or stock brokerage firms own large numbers of shares. Since the corporation is concerned with shareholders as identified in its records, notice will go to the securities depository institution or brokerage firms. In reality, however, the securities depository institution is usually a nominee owner for brokerage firms and brokerage firms, for the most part, are mere nominee owners of their customers, the beneficial non-registered holders of the shares. The customers of the brokerage firms leave the shares with the broker registered in the broker's name, or the name of the securities depository institution, for custodial purposes and to facilitate trading in the securities. National Policy No. 41 now requires public issuers and investment intermediaries to establish systems to ensure that the non-registered holders receive proxy materials and an opportunity to vote through the intermediary.

Under National Policy No. 41 public corporations with security holders in Canada must set a record date between 35 and 60 days in advance of the meeting. At least 25 days before the record date the corporation must request the names of beneficial owners of the shares of the corporation entitled to vote at the meeting from securities depository institutions. This normally will identify a number of brokerage firms who hold the shares as nominee owners. The corporation must then send a search card to these nominee owners giving information about the date of the meeting, the record date for the meeting and the classes of shares entitled to vote at the meeting. At least 33 days before the meeting the corporation must then send to the nominee owners the number of sets of meeting materials requested by the nominee owners. This is to allow nominee owners to send the materials to the beneficial owners of the shares at least 25 days before the meeting. The corporation is required to pay the costs of having the nominee owners transmit the meeting materials. Brokers holding shares as nominee owners must communicate with their clients to obtain the clients' instruction on whether the clients want to have the meeting materials forwarded to them.

Conduct of Meetings. The chair of the meeting of shareholders, who is very often the president of the corporation, is under a general duty to assist the meeting in achieving its objectives. To this end the chair's duties are: (1) to preserve order; (2) to see that the proceedings are regularly conducted; (3) to take care that the sense of the meeting is properly ascertained with regard to any question properly before it; and (4) to decide incidental questions arising for decision during the meeting. In exercising the duties of the chair the chair is to act "in good faith and in an impartial manner."

Ordinarily, concerns about the conduct of meetings will arise only where control is disputed. Because control at a shareholders' meeting in a public corporation will vest in the party that has secured the most proxies, the chair's conduct has most often been challenged where he or she has rejected proxies.

There are a number of formalities in the execution of proxies that must be complied with. For example, the board of directors of a corporation that owns shares in another corporation must either itself determine how to vote those shares or delegate such decision to a committee or an officer. A question may then arise about whether the chair may or should attempt to ascertain whether a proxy appointed by a corporate shareholder or by a stockbroker has been lawfully appointed. This question was stated but not answered by the Ontario Court of Appeal in *Murphy v. Lindzon*, [1969] 2 O.R. 704. It is one of some difficulty because the chair, who is usually the corporation's president and virtually always the director, would hardly be a neutral party if at the particular meeting an effort was being made to unseat management.

Re Marshall
Ontario High Court
(1981), 129 D.L.R. (3d) 378

CALLAGHAN J. (orally): This is an application by William C. Marshall, a director and shareholder of Marshall Boston Iron Mines Limited (the Company) for an order under s. 252 of the Business Corporations Act, R.S.O. 1980, c. 54 (the Act), directing the chairman of the adjourned annual and general meeting of the shareholders of the Company to tabulate the votes of 405,001 escrowed common shares of the Company in accordance with certain written directions of the beneficial owners thereof and not as voted by the registered owners of the said shares. The vote in issue relates to the election of the board of directors of the Company. If the vote is tabulated on the basis of the escrowed shares being counted as cast by the registered shareholders, the Company's slate of directors continues in office. If the vote is tabulated in accordance with the written directions given by some of the acknowledged beneficial owners under the escrow agreement then there will be a switch of approximately 36,500 votes resulting in a slate of directors nominated by the applicant.

The annual meeting has been adjourned until tomorrow, October 15, 1981, and a ruling is sought today so that the tabulation of the votes can be completed in the light of this ruling. Voluminous material has been filed from which it appears there are other groups of votes in issue. However, the parties to this application have agreed that if the Court either affirms the proposed method of tabulation of the respondent or orders that the tabulation be governed by the written directions of the beneficial owners of the shares, then the matter will be resolved as the outstanding issues relating to the other groups of shares will not affect the outcome of the balloting.

The capital of the Company includes 405,001 common shares held in escrow by the Royal Trust Company pursuant to an agreement dated February 10, 1970. These shares are separately registered in the names of Raymond J. Marshall as to 202,501 and Charles Marshall Jr. as to 202,500. It is common ground that the beneficial ownership of the shares is divided amongst six directors of the Company and five other persons named in the material filed herein.

The escrow agreement provides that the shares are not to be released without the consent of the Ontario or Quebec Securities Commission. This agreement apparently follows upon an earlier agreement dated January 5, 1964, which was a vendor's agreement attendant upon the incorporation of the Company.

In August, 1971, the registered owners of the escrowed shares executed an acknowledgment that these shares were held in trust in proportionate amounts for the named persons in the said acknowledgment. That agreement is set forth in the supplementary record at p. 89.

The annual meeting was held on October 8, 1981. Prior thereto the applicant and two other beneficial owners of a number of these shares signed a written direction to Raymond J. Marshall, Charles Marshall Jr. and the Royal Trust Company to the effect that the escrowed shares beneficially owned by each were to be voted in favour of the slate of directors nominated by the applicant. At the meeting this direction was delivered to the chairman and the scrutineers of the voting. It should be noted that the chairman is the president of the Company and supports the management slate of candidates. On October 8th, a poll was taken at the meeting to determine the distribution of votes among the various candidates for election as directors. Charles Marshall Jr. voted all 202,500 escrowed shares, registered in his name, in favour of the applicant's slate of candidates. Raymond J. Marshall voted 202,501 escrowed shares, registered in his name, in favour of the existing board of directors. Raymond J. Marshall did not execute a form of proxy in favour of the applicant's slate for 36,750 escrowed shares representing the excess of the sum of the beneficial holdings pursuant to the above-mentioned written directions of those in favour of the applicant's slate over the 202,500 escrowed shares registered in the name of Charles Marshall Jr.

It is clear on the material before me that the chairman of the meeting, as well as the scrutineers, were aware of the written directions of the beneficial owners (see the affidavit of William Marshall, para. 9 and the affidavit of Rosemary Millan, paras. 18 and 19). It is the contention of the applicant on this proceeding that to ignore the written direction of the beneficial owners would violate and disenfranchise the vote of the beneficial owners of the escrowed shares relevant to that direction. The applicant relies on paras. 41 and 44 of the general by-laws of the Company which provide as follows:

41. *Votes to Govern.* At all meetings of shareholders every question shall, unless otherwise required by the letters patent or by-laws of the company or by law, be decided by the majority of the votes duly cast on the question.

44. *Votes on Polls.* Upon a poll each shareholder who is present in person or represented by proxy shall be entitled to one vote for each share in respect of which he is entitled to vote at the meeting and the result of the poll shall be the decision of the company in annual or special meeting, as the case may be, upon that question.

It is the submission of the applicant that to ignore the written direction of the beneficial owners and only accept the vote as cast by Raymond J. Marshall, is contrary to the provisions of para. 41 of the by-law, in that the tabulation of votes thereby ignores "*votes duly cast,*" as required by this provision. The applicant submits that the Company is bound to protect the rights of a beneficial owner where it has notice the shares of such owner are held in trust: see Fraser & Stewart, *Company Law of Canada*, 5th ed. (1962), p. 230. The applicant also relies on the authority of *Elliot v. Hatzic Prairie Ltd.* (1912), 6 D.L.R. 9, 21 W.L.R. 897, wherein on an application for an interim injunction Mr. Justice Murphy of the British Columbia Supreme Court restrained directors of a company from allowing trust shares to be voted against the wish of the *cestui que trust*, in circumstances which he concluded were designed to make the exercise of such voting power utterly useless.

There is no dispute in the application before this Court that Raymond J. Marshall is registered as the owner of 202,501 common shares of the Company. This appears clear from the share register filed herein (see p. 40 of the supplementary record). It is also clear that he is presently so registered and was on the date of voting, October 8, 1981.

Paragraph 36 of the general by-law of the Company provides as follows:

Right to Vote. At each meeting of shareholders every shareholder shall be entitled to vote who is at the proper time entered in the books of the company as the holder of one or more shares carrying the right to vote at such meeting and who is not in arrear in respect of any call; save that, if the share or shares in question have been mortgaged or hypothecated, the person who mortgaged or hypothecated such share or shares (or his proxy) may nevertheless represent the shares at meetings and vote in respect thereof unless in the instrument creating the mortgage or hypothec he has expressly empowered the holder of such mortgage or hypothec to vote thereon, in which case such holder (or his proxy) may attend meetings and vote in respect of such shares upon filing with the Secretary of the meeting sufficient proof of the terms of such instrument.

It would appear that Raymond J. Marshall was, at the time of the vote, the person entered in the books of the Company as the holder of these shares and, accordingly, he was entitled to vote for each share so held. The provisions of this by-law are consistent with s. 110, s-s. (2) of the Act which in turn is consistent with the general rule in company law that the persons entitled to vote as a shareholder are those shown on the company's books to be shareholders.

The narrow issue before me, as I see it, is whether or not the chairman of this annual meeting is required to go behind the share register, and, in case of dispute, accept written directions from beneficial owners as to the manner in which their vote shall be cast. In my view I think he is not so required. The Company has no right whatsoever to enter into disputes between the beneficial owners as to the manner in which escrowed shares or shares held in trust should be voted. To do so would require the chairman to go behind the share register and to enter into legal questions of beneficial ownership, and in this case, the question of the propriety of a trustee of a private trust acting separately from his co-trustee. Such issues generally speaking are matters that a chairman would neither have the training nor the time to consider at a general meeting. This issue, in part, was considered at length by Mr. Justice Kelly in the case referred to by the respondent herein, *Tough Oakes Gold Mines Ltd. v. Foster* (1917), 39 O.L.R. 144, 34 D.L.R. 748. At pp. 154-5 O.L.R., pp. 757-8 D.L.R., Mr. Justice Kelly reviews the judgment of the Master of the Rolls, Jessel, in the case of *Pender v. Lushington* (1877), 6 Ch. D. 70 at pp. 77-8. The general principles as established by the Master of the Rolls were applied by Mr. Justice Kelly in *Tough Oakes* and the practicalities of what is sought herein were dealt with by him at pp. 157-8 O.L.R., p. 761 D.L.R.:

... it was not within the province of the president or presiding officer to sit in judgment in respect of that right as between them [joint shareholders] and any others claiming these shares, and to declare against the right of these two holders to attend or be represented and to vote at such meetings. If that course were permissible, then how would it be possible to carry on such business of a company as must necessarily be transacted at a meeting of its shareholders? for never would there be certainty as to who is properly entitled to appear at a shareholders' meeting and take part in its deliberations.

This view was accepted and followed in a series of cases quoted by counsel for the respondent and most recently in the *Re Manitoba Securities Com'n and Versatile Cornat Corp.* (1979), 97 D.L.R. (3d) 45, [1979] 2 W.W.R. 714, 7 B.L.R. 38, wherein the principle of *Tough Oakes* was applied by Mr. Justice Hewak, who in dealing with the practicalities of the situation stated, at pp. 54-5 D.L.R., p. 725 W.W.R.:

... the American decisions favour the interpretation that when statutes refer to stockholders they refer to stockholders of record as they appear on the register of the company books. To me, that is only reasonable. It would cause utter chaos in the world of commerce to hold otherwise and to expect corporations to deal with past shareholders, prospective shareholders, or simply share "holders" in their attempt to run the business of the companies.

(See also *People v. Botts* (1941), 34 N.E. 2d 476, a judgment of Chief Justice Gunn of the Supreme Court of Illinois at p. 406, paras. 7 and 8.)

In my view the chain of authority from the *Pender* case through *Tough Oakes v. Foster*, to the present time is clear. A chairman at an annual general meeting is not to be placed in the position of determining the legal rights of beneficial owners of shares registered in the name of others. He is entitled to rely on the votes as cast by the registered owner of those shares. In result, therefore, I am of the view that the chairman of the meeting herein should count the votes cast by the registered owners of the escrowed shares as voted and, accordingly, the application is dismissed with costs.

Application dismissed.

NOTE

While the chair of the meeting need not become involved in questions between the registered owner and the beneficial owner of shares, the chair may be called upon to decide who is in fact the registered owner and thus who is entitled to vote the shares. See *Heil v. T.E.N. Private Cable Systems Inc.* (1993), 11 B.L.R. 54 in which the petitioner challenged the decision of the chair of a shareholders meeting with respect to who the registered owner was where there was a transfer before the record date that was not registered before the record date.

Overreaching by a chair was successfully impeached in *Re United Canso Oil & Gas Ltd.* (1980), 41 N.S.R. (2d) 282. That litigation was one of many growing out of the bitter battle for United Canso, in which the insurgents finally won control from the Buckley family. At the shareholders' meeting at which the Buckley board was deposed in favour of the insurgents' slate, the chair (John Buckley) had: (1) refused to accept the proxies of corporate shareholders that had been executed with a facsimile signature; (2) refused to accept the proxies of corporate shareholders without proof that their boards of directors had approved the proxies; (3) refused to accept proxies executed by stockbrokers holding securities on behalf of clients without clients' authorizations; and (4) refused to accept the tabulation of votes of the professional tabulators hired by management. The chair ruled that a quorum was not present, and adjourned the meeting for a judicial resolution of the dispute. Hallett J. held that in all of these respects the chair had acted in bad faith in an unlawful effort to retain control of the corporation.

See also *Johnson v. Hall* (1957), 10 D.L.R. (2d) 243 (B.C.); *Bluechel v. Pre-fabricated Bldgs. Ltd.*, [1945] 2 D.L.R. 725 (B.C.); *Re Versatile Cornat Corp.* (1979), 97 D.L.R. (3d) 45 (Man.); *Pender v. Lushington* (1877), 6 Ch. Div. 70; *Cohen-Herrendorf v. Army & Navy Department Store Holdings Limited* (1986), 55 Sask. R. 134 (Q.B.). But see *Elliot v. Hatzic Prairie Ltd.* (1912), 6 D.L.R. 9 (B.C.).

As noted above, the chair of the meeting is very often the president of the corporation. Thus when there is a battle for control the chair of the meeting will be put in a position where his or her interests conflict with the interests of certain other shareholders. Should such a conflict of interest of the chair disqualify the chair from exercising the "quasi-judicial" functions of the chair of a shareholders meeting? Can the chair avoid being found to have breached the duty of good faith and impartiality if the chair relies on legal advice in making a ruling? These questions were addressed in the following case.

Blair v. Consolidated Enfield Corp.
Ontario Court of Appeal
(1993), 15 O.R. (3d) 783

[Blair was the president and chair of Consolidated Enfield. Blair took legal advice with respect to proxies submitted on behalf of Canadian Express Ltd. The solicitors expressed the view that the proxies could only be voted for the management slate of directors and could not be voted to replace Blair. At the meeting the majority of votes were cast in favour of replacing Blair. Blair asked the solicitors for Consolidated Enfield whether he could make a ruling where his own election would be affected. The solicitors said that Blair had a duty to make a ruling. Blair, acting on the advice given by the solicitors for Consolidated Enfield, then declared that he and the rest of the management slate of directors had been elected.

Canadian Express then brought an action for a declaration that the ballot cast for Canadian Express was validly cast in favour of the replacement slate of directors. The court determined that the ballot was legally cast in favour of the replacement slate and ordered costs against both Consolidated Enfield and Blair. Since Canadian Express now had control of Consolidated Enfield it sought recovery of costs in the amount of over $165,000 against Blair only. Blair then sought indemnity for costs from Consolidated Enfield under s. 136(1) of the OBCA. Under s. 136(1) of the OBCA a director can be indemnified against the costs of an action if the director acted honestly and in good faith with a view to the best interests of the corporation. The indemnity was refused and Blair then applied to court for a declaration that he was entitled to indemnification. The court refused the declaration on the basis that Blair had not acted in the best interests of the corporation. Blair appealed. The judgment of the court was delivered by Carthy J.A. who made the following comments on the good faith duties of the chair of a meeting in the situation in which Blair found himself.]

CARTHY J.A.: In the present case there is nothing controversial about Blair's ballot directed to preserve his control by voting in favour of himself—that was fully expected. At issue is his ruling on the overall balloting, and to conclude that his ruling was made *male fide* because the result favoured him is to conclude that he was compelled to rule the other way, or give up the chair, no matter what advice he received. Aside from the question of giving up the chair, the real test should be whether the ruling was made with the *bona fide* intent that the company have a lawfully elected board of directors.

Johnson v. Hall (1957), 10 D.L.R. (2d) 243, 23 W.W.R. 228 (B.C.S.C.) and *Re United Canso Oil & Gas Ltd.* (1980), 12 B.L.R. 130, 41 N.S.R. (2d) 282 (T.D.), are examples of trial judgments where the rulings of chairpersons have been set aside as being in bad faith and intended to preserve control rather than serve the interest of the company. In neither is there any discussion concerning solicitors' advice nor the tension that exists between admitted self-interest and the duty of a chairman sitting in what is termed a quasi-judicial role.

In *Bomac Batten Ltd. v. Pozhke* (1983), 43 O.R. (2d) 344, 1 D.L.R. (4th) 435 (H.C.J.), the chairman of a shareholders meeting declared certain proxies invalid because of lack of evidence that they were authorized by resolution of the shareholder. The ruling was supported by legal advice and the result of the ruling preserved the chairman's position on the board. When the chairman adjourned the meeting, the dissident shareholders appointed a new chairman who allowed the disputed proxy to be exercised and a new board was put in place. Cromarty J., without discussing the effect of the legal advice, found that a resolution was not required, that one existed in any event, and that the chairman breached his duty to act quasi-judicially by failing to hear both sides of the argument before coming to a decision.

• • •

There is thus little guidance in the Canadian authorities on the extent to which legal advice affects the assessment of good faith conduct. Nor have we been directed to any settled views expressed in other jurisdictions. I have already concluded that, on a proper reading of ss. 130 to 136 of the Ontario Business Corporations Act, legal advice does not automatically sanctify conduct based upon it as honest and in good faith for purposes of claiming indemnity under s. 136. It is, however, an ingredient to be considered and one should not be dismissive of it simply because it favours the election of the chair person or, as in many such situations, because it comes from a law firm whose own retainer is at stake. It must be considered in the context in which it was given and alongside the duty of the chairperson to act fairly.

The authorities referred to above generally describe the chairperson's duty as quasi-judicial without defining what that means in this context. It is confusing to me to use, and seek to define, the word judicial or quasi-judicial in this context because an adjudicator or judge can never have a personal interest in the issue. A chairperson who is more than a nominal shareholder of a public company, on the other hand, always has a personal interest in everything that affects the company, which includes all of the rulings of the chair. If that distinction is not recognized the reflex reaction is to assume that a decision which benefits the chair personally is non-judicial and thus not *bona fide*. In my view, it is preferable to describe the duty as one of honesty and fairness to all individual interests, and directed generally to the best interests of the company.

The events that lead up to the meeting of July 20 created an aggressively competitive atmosphere. Blair felt very strongly that the shareholders as a whole should be fully informed of a change in control. He undoubtedly resented the surprise nomination of Price and was pleased with Osler's advice. That makes him very much a protagonist in the duel for control. However, that is the position of any chairperson dependent for his position upon proxy support and threatened by contrary votes.

The ballots cast were in accordance with the instructions in the proxies or they were not. An experienced team of lawyers gave an opinion the evening before and, broadening their inquiries to even more lawyers when the event occurred, they remained of the same view. They also told Blair that it was his duty to make the ruling despite his interest in the outcome. Following the sequence of events I do not see that he had a choice. It would have appeared more fair if he had not closed debate, but the result could not have been different. If lawyers for Canadian Express had expressed a contrary view, he would then have two opinions on a complicated legal problem. Given the necessity of determining who the legal directors of the company were, so that business could be carried on in a regular fashion, some decision had to be made. Even if a disinterested chairperson could have been found in the room, he or she would, in the circumstances, have had to look to the corporation's solicitors for an answer to this purely legal issue of interpretation.

• • •

No matter what debate might have ensued on July 20 and no matter who the chairperson might have been, there was no obvious error or oversight which would enable the chairperson to turn away from the advice of the company's solicitors.

No one suggested that the Osler opinion and advice was other than totally professional or that there was any qualification in that advice. Osler was fully advised of all facts bearing on the issuer. A layperson reading the rather confused language of Note 3 would, in my view, treat the opinion as ostensibly credible and thus, I am satisfied that Blair was acting honestly and in good faith and in the best interests of the corporation in accepting and implementing that advice.

Counsel for Canadian Express focused on the lack of fairness shown by Blair in knowing that a mistake had been made and giving no opportunity to correct it. They argue that when the nomination of Price was made from the floor that Blair, in fairness, should have alerted Walt and Boultbee that they would not be able to vote for Price. Presumably, Walt would then have executed a new proxy on behalf of Canadian Express but Boultbee would have had to return to the shareholders he represented to obtain new proxies, on the assumption that it would be their desire to change them. It must be remembered that there is another faction deserving fairness from the chairman—the 15 per cent of shareholders who decided not to be represented on the basis of what they read in the management information circular, or for whatever other reason. If the meeting was to be adjourned to accommodate Walt and Boultbee, should these shareholders not be informed that a battle for control was on and that their votes could determine the result? In my view it goes too far to say that the duty of fairness means that Blair must selectively assist those who attend to vote in the process leading to the vote. His duty of fairness relates to the decision-making process and the conduct of a proper corporate meeting. His taunting remark to Timothy Price did not distinguish him, but I am satisfied that the evidence shows that he properly performed his duty as chairman of the meeting.

Shareholders are entitled to speak to any matter before the meeting of shareholders. However, if the right to speak at the meeting were unconstrained it could frustrate the completion of the business of the meeting. This could be particularly problematic in the case of meetings for widely held corporations if it led to adjournments of the meeting since it could significantly add to the cost of the meeting. Thus the chair of the meeting, acting in good faith and an impartial manner, must allow shareholders to speak to the matters before the meeting but need not allow more than a reasonable time for reasonable arguments. See, e.g., *Wall v. London and Northern Assets Corporation*, [1898] 2 Ch. 469 (C.A.). For a discussion of how control over the agenda and the power of the chair to recognize speakers can have a significant effect on the outcome of voting see S. Levmore, *Parliamentary Law, Majority Decisionmaking, and the Voting Paradox*, 75 Virg. L.R. 971 (1989).

2. Meetings Requisitioned by Shareholders

Meetings of shareholders, whether annual or special, are generally called by the directors. A residual possibility for the exercise of shareholder initiative is provided for in corporations statutes that permit the holders of a certain proportion of voting shares to requisition the board to call a shareholders' meeting. Without such a right, it would be difficult to remove the board of directors before the end of its term, since the directors might be expected to refrain from calling a shareholders' meeting for such a purpose.

Under CBCA s. 143, the holders of not less than 5% of the shares that carry the right to vote at the meeting sought to be held (including shares enfranchised only for that vote) may requisition a meeting of the shareholders for the purposes stated in the requisition. See also ABCA s. 137; BCCA s. 171; OBCA s. 105. The directors have then a duty to call a meeting, and if they do not do so, then any one of the requisitioning shareholders may call it. Where the shareholders themselves are forced to call the meeting in this way, the corporation must reimburse the requisitioning shareholders for expenses reasonably incurred by them "in requisitioning, calling and holding a meeting," unless the shareholders resolve otherwise at the meeting.

What proposals may be dealt with at a requisitioned meeting? It will be recalled that CBCA s. 102 stated a fundamental principle of constitutionality, with management of the business and affairs of the corporation removed from the purview of shareholders' meetings. Does the right of shareholders under CBCA s. 143 to requisition a meeting "for the purposes stated" in the requisition reverse the division of powers in s. 102 in such meetings? If not, the scope of shareholder initiatives at requisitioned meetings would be limited to removal and replacement of directors (which is in fact almost always the purpose for which such meetings are called), and possibly those precatory resolutions whose purpose is not to require but rather to request the directors to consider a specific business decision. The draft CBCA that accompanied the Dickerson Report more clearly restricted the scope of requisitioned meetings in this way. Section 11.05(5) of the draft, the precursor of CBCA s. 137(5), provided that management did not have to circulate for a shareholders' meeting any shareholder proposal that "is not a proper subject for action by shareholders or is a recommendation or request that the directors act in respect of a matter relating to the conduct of the ordinary business operations of the corporation."

3. Meetings by Order of Court

Upon an application by shareholders under CBCA s. 144, a court may order a shareholders' meeting to be called. See also ABCA s. 138; BCCA s. 173; OBCA s. 106. Such order may be made either if it is "impracticable" to call or conduct a meeting in another way or "if for any other reason a court thinks fit." Section 144 is based upon s. 135 of the English Companies Act, 1984. Not surprising, it is often not easy to say what "impracticable" means in these provisions.

Re El Sombrero Ltd.
English Chancery Division
[1958] Ch. 900

[The applicant held 900 of the corporation's 1,000 issued shares and the rest were held by the respondents, who had been the firm's directors even before the applicant had bought his shares. No meeting of shareholders had ever been held. The corporation's articles provided that the quorum for a shareholders' meeting was two, and the applicant asked the court to reduce this to one when ordering the meeting.]

WYNN-PARRY J. stated the facts and continued: The first point of law which arises involves the construction of section 135(1) of the Companies Act, 1948, the examination being directed to consider the scope of the phrase "If for any reason it is impracticable to call a meeting of a company in any manner in which meetings of that company may be called, or to conduct the meeting of the company in manner prescribed by the articles or this Act. ..." It is to be observed that the section opens with the words "If for any reason," and therefore it follows that the section is intended to have, and, indeed, has by reason of its language, a necessarily wide scope. The next words are "... it is impracticable to call a meeting of a company ..." The question then arises, what is the scope of the word "impracticable"? It is conceded that the word "impracticable" is not synonymous with the word "impossible"; and it appears to me that the question necessarily raised by the introduction of that word "impracticable" is merely this: examine the circumstances of the particular case and answer the question whether, as a practical matter, the desired meeting of the company can be conducted, there being no doubt, of course, that it can be convened and held. Upon the face of the section there is no express limitation which would operate to give those words "is impracticable" any less meaning than that which I have stated, and I can find no good reason in the arguments which have been addressed to me on behalf of the respondents for qualifying in any way the force of that word "impracticable" or the interpretation which I have placed upon it, and therefore upon that point I am in favour of the applicant.

It was contended that the court could not or ought not to direct a meeting under this section where there was, as there is here, opposition, and, indeed, strong opposition; and in the course of his judgment the registrar said: "So far as I am aware there has never been a case where the court has made an order under section 135 in the face of opposition to such an order. ..." It will be observed that the registrar is careful not to go so far as to say as a conclusion that the court has no jurisdiction to make an order under the section in the face of opposition. There is nothing I can find in the language of the section which would even indicate that the jurisdiction can only be invoked if, at least, there is no opposition, and I hold that, on the true construction of the section, there is nothing to prevent the court intervening in a proper case and where the application before it is opposed by other shareholders.

It is interesting to see that the registrar, having made the observation which I have quoted as to the absence of any authority for the proposition that an order could be made under the section in the face of opposition, goes on to say: "... and I do not consider that under the circumstances of this case the court ought to exercise its discretion by making such an order." What, as I read his judgment, really operated in his mind was this, that the two respondents had the power to prevent the desired meeting being held and, as he puts it in one passage of his judgment, having considered the Scottish case of *Edinburgh Workmen's Houses Improvement Co. Ltd.*:

That case affords me some guidance as to the meaning of "impracticable" in section 135 in relation to the quorum provisions of articles and perhaps would justify me in holding that it is impracticable in the circumstances of the present case to conduct a meeting of the company in the manner prescribed by the articles for the purpose of passing the resolutions mentioned in the schedule to the originating summons since the personal respondents will see to it that a quorum is never present at a meeting convened for that purpose; but beyond that the case does not assist me for it is clearly distinguishable from the facts of the present case in that there the court made an order in relation to a public company to enable resolutions to be passed which an overwhelming majority of the shareholders in number and value wanted passed, to which no member had expressed dissent and in circumstances in which the three non-assenting shareholders with their 48 shares would still have an opportunity, if so minded, of coming before the court to express their views and oppose any order which would render the resolutions effective. Whereas in the present case I am asked to make an order in relation to a private company at the request of one member (the applicant) in the face of strenuous opposition from the other two (the personal respondents) to enable the one to remove the other two from their directorships, notwithstanding that under the terms of the contract by which their respective rights are governed the two respondents are entitled to prevent the applicant from removing them at a meeting requisitioned by him. [1935 S.C. 56; 1934 S.L.T. 513]

Later, referring to an argument which had been put before him by Mr. Cohen on behalf of the applicant, namely, that the applicant, as a majority shareholder, is entitled to remove the personal respondents from the board under section 184, and that the court would be stultifying the applicant's statutory powers if he refused to make the order which was asked for, the registrar said this: "I cannot accept that proposition as correct. His power of removing a director under section 184 is limited to doing so by ordinary resolution and under the terms of his contract with the respondents they have power to prevent him from passing such a resolution if they wish to do so. I do not consider that the court ought to exercise its powers under section 135 in such a way as to deprive the respondents against their will of that power."

With all respect to the registrar, I think those passages proceed upon a misconception. It was conceded by Mr. Lindner, and, in my view, very properly conceded, that it was not possible to say that the respondents, by virtue of the articles, had such right as is implicit in the use of the word "entitled" by the registrar, to prevent the applicant from holding and conducting the meeting. They have, it is true, a power to prevent him from doing so, but that power is not derived from the articles; it is derived from the accidental distribution of the shareholding in this company, and that, to my mind, explains the whole difficulty which has arisen.

I therefore arrive at the stage where I hold that I have jurisdiction in this case, and there is nothing to prevent me exercising the discretion which is given under the section if I choose to exercise it. It is true that I am sitting as an appellate court, but I am entitled to consider the question of discretion, because, in my view, as I have held, the registrar has misdirected himself on a question of law. In my judgment, this is eminently a case in which the court ought to exercise its discretion; first, because if the court were to refuse the application it would be depriving the applicant of a statutory right, which, through the company, he is entitled to exercise under section 184(1), to remove the respondents as directors; secondly (and I think this is a proper matter to take into account as part of the reasons for deciding to exercise my discretion), the evidence disclosed that the respondents are failing to perform their statutory duty to call an annual general meeting. The period within which they should have held an annual general meeting expired at some date in October, 1957. Their excuse in the evidence is that there would be no use in convening and holding an annual general meeting, because the accounts for the first period of the company's history are not yet available. I have read the evidence with care, and I do not accept it as bona fide evidence. There is a clear statutory duty on the directors to call the meeting whether or not the accounts, the consideration of which is only one of the matters to be dealt with at an annual general meeting, are ready or not. It cannot possibly serve as an excuse for failing to perform that statutory duty. It is quite obvious that the only reason why the respondents refuse to call an annual general meeting is because the inevitable result of convening and holding that meeting would be that they would find that they had ceased to be directors. ...

For these reasons, therefore, I propose to accede to this application and to direct a meeting of the company to be held under the power given me by section 135 of the Companies Act, 1948.

(After a discussion it was agreed that the order should direct that one member of the company present in person or by proxy should be deemed to constitute a quorum and that the meeting should be held at the offices of the appellant's solicitors.)

Order accordingly.

Court Ordered Meetings in Cases of Deadlock. In *Re El Sombrero Ltd.* Wynn-Parry J. made short shrift of the respondents' argument that the predicament in which the applicant found himself, owning 90% of the shares and yet unable to remove directors, was one to which he had consented. However, the applicant had indeed become a shareholder on the basis of the firm's articles, which included the quorum requirement. The effect of the decision was therefore to nullify a contractual provision that had been meant for the protection of the parties. No annual general meetings of El Sombrero Ltd. had ever been called and, as Wynn-Parry J. stated, this was a clear breach of their statutory duty by the directors. Yet the directors might have called meetings of shareholders and then, in their capacity as shareholders, have failed to attend. Thus no meetings would have been held and the directors would have remained secure in their position. Though directors have a duty to call a meeting, shareholders have no duty to attend, and the quorum requirement would seem to have contemplated non-attendance as a veto mechanism by shareholders.

A situation in which attempts to convene a meeting were foiled by the lack of a quorum due to the non-attendance of a shareholder occurred in *Re Opera Photographic*

Ltd., [1989] 1 W.L.R. 634 (Ch. D.). The company had two shareholders, one holding 51% and the other holding 49% of the 100 issued shares. The quorum for meetings of directors or shareholders was two. There was a falling out between the parties. The 51% shareholder requisitioned a meeting but the 49% shareholder refused to attend. The 51% shareholder also convened a meeting under provisions of the U.K. Companies Act but the 49% shareholder did not attend so that there was no quorum. The 51% shareholder then sought a court ordered meeting which the court granted citing *El Sombrero*. The judge concluded as follows:

In this case Mr. Instone, on behalf of the second respondent, submits that there is no allegation of breach of duty against the second respondent; that the second respondent was acting within his rights; and that the company is what is conventionally described as a quasi-partnership case in which each of the individuals had an equity of equal participation. He submits that *In re El Sombrero Ltd.* [1958] Ch. 900 is of no assistance because in 1958 it was considered that 51 per cent. gave an absolute right to remove a director and, as he submits, that has been overtaken by events in the form of a decision of the House of Lords in *In re Westbourne Galleries Ltd.* [1973] A.C. 360 to the effect that the legal rights of the parties may be overlaid by equitable considerations arising out of the constitution and their agreement.

The plain fact of the matter is that deadlock exists between the two individuals which has to be resolved one way or another. It is either capable of being resolved by ordering a meeting, at which no doubt Mr. Martin will be removed, and which will then no doubt result either in him exercising the pre-emption rights under the articles of selling his shares, or presenting a petition for the winding-up of the company, or presenting a petition under section 459 of the Act of 1985 based on unfair prejudice to him. Equally, if no order is made the deadlock will continue because no meetings can be conducted which are going effectively to manage or procure the management of this company, and if that persists for any length of time then no doubt one or other of the individuals will again be presenting a petition based on that deadlock in order to provide some form of resolution.

In the circumstances I do not think that the distinction which Mr. Instone seeks to draw is a valid one. The point still remains that the applicant, as the 51 per cent. shareholder, has the statutory right under the Companies Act 1985 to remove the second respondent as a director. As Brightman J.'s decision in *In re H.R. Paul & Son Ltd.*, 118 S.J. 166 shows, the quorum provisions cannot be regarded as conferring upon the second respondent some form of veto as being his entitlement ... .

In those circumstances I see no reason not to exercise the discretion which it is accepted exists in this case and I will accordingly make the order sought.

Such cases may appear paradoxical if the choice is seen as one between enforcing a bargain and promoting efficient behaviour. However, a policy of judicial non-intervention does not necessarily spell the doom of the firm. Instead, the parties might themselves resolve the dispute, compromising their differences. Quorum requirements of the kind found in *El Sombrero* are in fact not uncommon, and most disputes are undoubtedly settled sooner or later by the parties on their own. While this is not to suggest that such negotiations are costless, or that some firms might in fact fail without an order under s. 144, a right to a court ordered meeting on every deadlock would sterilize unanimity requirements that the parties have bargained for.

Intervening in Battles for Control. The Ontario Court of Appeal refused to order a shareholders' meeting in *Re Morris Funeral Service Ltd.* (1957), 7 D.L.R. (2d) 642. The corporation had 278 outstanding shares, held as follows: the Morris estate—147; the widow Morris—98; the Morris's son, Donald—30; their son, Arthur—1; the managing director, Kelly—1; and McPhee—1.

All the individual shareholders were directors. The executors of the estate were the widow Morris, Kelly and McPhee. Donald and his mother wished to remove Kelly as manager and substitute Donald. The other three were opposed. The law of estates requires the executors to act unanimously. Since they were deadlocked, the estate could not be present at a shareholders' meeting. Therefore no shareholders' meeting could be held under the company's quorum rule of three shareholders holding not less than 60% of the shares. Donald and his mother requisitioned a meeting of the shareholders and, before such a meeting could be convened, applied to the court to order a meeting for the purpose of removing and replacing one or more directors. They asked that the quorum requirement be reduced by the court to two shareholders with at least 120 shares. The lower Court ordered the meeting on those terms, but the Court of Appeal reversed.

The powers of the Court under s. 309 of the Act are, of course, discretionary. It is to be noted that in none of the reported decisions was the Court requested by one faction among the shareholders to intervene as against some other faction; on the contrary, in each case the Court was requested to remove some obstacle making it impracticable for the shareholders as a whole, or for an overwhelming majority thereof to call or conduct a meeting in accordance with the requirements in that behalf of the company's Articles of Association. It is further to be observed, as illustrated in the *Pall Mall Building Society's* case, [*Re Pall Mall Building Society's Deed of Dissolution,* [1947] W.N. 143] that the Court, when ordering the calling of a meeting or directing the conduct of a meeting, was careful to do as little violence as possible to the corporate articles or regulations and, in fact, was careful to see that any meeting ordered to be held should be called and conducted in conformity with such articles or regulations as far as practicable.

Applying—as I do—these principles to the application of s. 309 of the Act to the facts as revealed in this case, the order appealed from must be set aside. The alleged difficulty is an artificial one, caused in great part at least by the respondents, who seek to invoke the section. In my opinion, except in extraordinary circumstances—none of which are present here—the section may not be invoked successfully for the express and sole purpose of placing in control of the company's directorate and affairs one of two or more contending factions among the shareholders. The present disagreement, among the three executors jointly entitled under the will to registration in their names of 147 shares, renders those shares ineffective so far as voting is concerned. It is the championing by the widow of the cause of her fellow respondent which has brought about that disagreement. She and he ought not to be allowed to capitalize upon that fact by securing, through the Court's intervention under s. 309 of the Act, the ouster of *bona fide* directors who may not see fit to agree with them and the substitution in their place of directors more malleable to their will. The present difficulty remains to be solved either amicably—which certainly ought to be the case—or by other means to ensure the carrying out of the testator's intentions, but with that the Court cannot be concerned upon this application. [*Id.* at 647-81]

While it is true that a court in exercising its discretion to call a shareholders meeting will do so in a manner consistent with the corporation's rules so far as possible, there is no doubt that the court has jurisdiction to alter quorum and notice requirements, for example, where necessary to grant full relief. Is it any more true of *Morris Funeral Service* than of *El Sombrero* that the court was being asked to intervene to place in control of the corporation one of two contending factions of shareholders?

A narrow view of the court's discretion to order a meeting was also taken in *Re Barsh* (1986), 54 O.R. (2d) 340, where the last meeting of shareholders or of directors of Feldbar Construction Co. had been held in 1966. Feldman, Barsh and Barsh's son each subscribed for one common share on incorporation in 1954. Feldbar Construction was a real estate development corporation that became relatively inactive in 1966, though it continued to own two vacant parcels of land. In 1983, Barsh died and his son wished to see the land developed. Feldman showed little interest in these plans, and Barsh's son applied under OBCA s. 106(1) for an order varying the quorum requirement for a shareholders' meeting. At trial, Feldman gave an undertaking to sign a resolution for the annual meeting, which obviated the necessity of calling the meeting. However, Madame Justice Van Camp was apparently of the opinion that the case would not have been an appropriate one for a s. 106 order.

I am of the opinion that the facts do not support the exercise of discretion to change the quorum. The result would be that one of three equal shareholders was effectively locked into a company in which he had no control. The quorum here was not to permit attendance of a shareholder, but to ensure that there would be no corporate action, except on the consent of all. Each shareholder had an equal interest. If there is no such consent obtainable, then there are provisions for the winding-up of the Corporation. None of the shareholders wish a winding-up, but unless they can agree it is the only alternative. The corporation was carefully structured that no shareholder could control it. ...

The answer to the problem of disagreement among the shareholders is not to compel a meeting whereby two of the three equal shareholders may outvote the third. The answer is the winding-up of the corporation. When none of them wish that winding-up, they can find a compromise. [*Id.* at 342-43]

These cases might be thought to ignore the possibility of strategic behaviour by the party who relies on veto rights. While veto rights offer useful protection to shareholders, they also introduce a possibility of shareholder opportunism. If the insistence on veto rights would lower firm value and the burden of the loss would fall unequally on the parties, the party with less to lose may then threaten to assert such rights unless he is given his way. The possibility of strategic behaviour is in fact a principal reason to eschew veto rights in corporate governance. But in a small firm greater opportunism might be anticipated without veto rights, with minority shareholders at the mercy of a majority coalition. Refusing to enforce all veto rights in order to minimize strategic behaviour then seems a species of the "Nirvana" fallacy, where second-best strategies are criticized for lingering inefficiencies but are still allocatively superior to alternative strategies under real world conditions.

This is not, however, to say that veto rights should always be enforced. The parties will adopt a variety of techniques to avert strategic behaviour, and might for this reason prefer to deal only with people in whom they may repose confidence, such as family members. See, e.g., Kronman, *Contract Law in the State of Nature*, 1 J.L. Econ. & Org.

5, 20-24 (1985) (risk of opportunism may be reduced through "union" strategies based on bonds of common interest or affection). A further device that might be used to reduce opportunism costs is binding good faith norms, in the form of legal sanctions for breaches of commitments to cooperative norms. Where the court is prepared to take sides in a dispute, one form that judicial intervention might then take is a release from a veto right, as in *El Sombrero*.

Intervention on the Basis of Fault. Should a court be more ready to intervene in circumstances where one of the parties seems more at fault than the other? Judicial neutrality might then seem less necessary, even if courts ought normally to be reluctant to take sides in the dispute. Moreover, it is not always difficult to apportion blame. One such case was perhaps *Re Routley's Holdings Ltd.*, [1960] O.W.N. 160. The corporation had four holders of its 158 outstanding shares: J.F. Boland—26; Bertha Boland—1; Clara May Routley—1; and Routley's Ltd.—130. The three individual shareholders were the directors and J.F. Boland was the president. No annual meeting had been held for many years until Clara Routley and Routley's Ltd. threatened litigation unless a meeting was called. Boland thereupon called a shareholders' meeting to be held at the corporation's headquarters, which was his law office. At it he rejected the proxies of Routley's Ltd. and of Clara Routley despite the fact that they were valid. Boland then continued with the meeting even though there was no quorum once the proxies were rejected, because a quorum was three shareholders with at least 50% of the shares. The Court ordered a meeting to be convened at a neutral locale, and lowered the quorum to two shareholders with 50% of the shares lest the Bolands attempt to thwart the meeting by refusing to attend. The Court emphasized J. F. Boland's clear breaches of law in his conduct of the previous shareholders' meeting. So too, an application for a court ordered meeting succeeded in *Re B. Love Ltd.* (1982), 141 D.L.R. (3d) 621 (Ont.), where the applicant also obtained an interlocutory injunction restraining a director from certain breaches of fiduciary duty. In ordering the shareholders' meeting, Gray J. gave very serious consideration to "the substantial case of prejudice" to the corporation occasioned by the director's improper conduct. *Id.* at 630.

Court Ordered Meeting Where the Shareholder Could Requisition a Meeting. Should a court refuse to order a meeting under CBCA s. 144 where the applicant possesses a sufficient number of shares to requisition a meeting himself under s. 143? In *Athabasca Holdings Ltd. v. ENA Datasystems Inc.* (1980), 30 O.R. (2d) 527, it was held that a meeting might be ordered where the requisition procedure would be futile to secure a meeting that would actually be held, as opposed to merely called.

Widely Held Corporations. The cases discussed thus far have all involved closely held corporations, but s. 144 is not so limited, and courts have ordered shareholders' meetings in publicly held corporations. In *Re Canadian Javelin Ltd.* (1976), 69 D.L.R. (3d) 439 (Que.), the corporation, whose shares were widely held in Canada and the United States, effectively had two boards of directors. At the June 1975 annual meeting, 11 men were elected to the board. A deep split of 6 versus 5 developed. At a meeting of the 6, those among the 5 who were officers were dismissed from such positions. A meeting of the 5 was then held at which some of the 6 were found no longer to be qualified to serve as directors and others were appointed in their places, so as to make a quorum. Affairs proceeded in this manner with the two boards each purporting to act for the corporation. It was important that the corporation have an annual meeting in order to satisfy S.E.C. requirements. Failure to do so could have made it difficult for the corporation to obtain further financing in the United States.

On application to court by one of the 5, a meeting of shareholders was ordered for the purpose of electing a board of directors. Even though the petitioning shareholders owned a sufficient number of shares to entitle them to requisition a meeting, the Court still found that it would be "impracticable" to conduct a meeting fairly except under court order. The Court appointed a neutral chairman and made numerous orders as to the solicitation and receipt of proxies, including that no person or group would be allowed to solicit proxies under the name of "management."

Constitutionality Requirements. Could a court-ordered meeting consider a matter assigned to the competence of the board by CBCA s. 102(1)? This question is considered in the following case, which may also provide a suggestion as to how constitutionality requirements would be interpreted in the case of shareholder-requisitioned meetings under CBCA s. 143.

Charlebois v. Bienvenu
Ontario Court of Appeal
[1968] 2 O.R. 217, 68 D.L.R. (2d) 578

AYLESWORTH J.A.: Appellants appeal from the order of Fraser J., dated November 17, 1967, ordering the calling, holding and conducting of a general meeting of the shareholders of British International Finance (Canada) Limited (which was incorporated in 1960) for the principal purpose of electing directors of the company, hereinafter referred to as "B.I.F." The order was made in reliance upon the provisions of s. 310 of the Corporations Act, R.S.O. 1960, c. 71, as amended, which section reads:

310. If for any reason it is impracticable to call a meeting of shareholders or members of the corporation in any manner in which meetings or shareholders or members may be called or to conduct the meeting in the manner prescribed by this Act, the letters patent, supplementary letters patent or by-laws, the court may, on the application of a director or a shareholder or member who would be entitled to vote at the meeting, order a meeting to be called, held and conducted in such manner as the court thinks fit, and any meeting called, held and conducted in accordance with such an order shall for all purposes be deemed to be a meeting of shareholders or members of the corporation duly called, held and conducted.

• • •

The personal appellants were shareholders and directors of B.I.F. for some years prior to July 28, 1967, when an annual meeting of the company purportedly was held at which a new board of directors, omitting the personal appellants, purportedly was elected. Members of the old board other than appellants were purportedly re-elected and an existing vacancy filled; the "new" directors purportedly elected were the respondents Brillant, Hamilton, Woods and Morissette. In August, 1967, the plaintiff-appellants instituted this action challenging the validity of the July meeting and of the election of directors thereat, claiming an injunction and interim injunction restraining the then elected directors from acting as such, claiming a declaration of such invalidity and damages and other relief. Fraser J., on September 8, 1967 [[1967] 2 O.R. 635, 64 D.L.R. (2d) 683], granted plaintiff-appellants an interim injunction until trial and directed expedition of the trial; little success in such expedition has been achieved.

B.I.F.'s dilemma stems from the issue raised in the action and from the granting of the interim injunction for, as stated by Fraser J. "until this action is tried no one will know with certainty which is, in law, the board entitled to control the affairs of this company." Action taken by the "new" board, including its appointment of officers, likewise is subject to uncertainty. Fraser J. concluded that, in the circumstances, the impracticability of calling or conducting a meeting of shareholders as referred to in s. 310 had been made out by the applicants and with this I respectfully agree; in fact, I did not understand counsel for the appellants to argue otherwise. There really are only two issues in the appeal, namely (1) are the provisions of s. 310 wide enough to sanction an order for the calling and conducting of a shareholders meeting to achieve some purpose thereat beyond the powers of shareholders at a meeting called in any other manner "in which meetings of shareholders may be called," and (2) on the facts of the case and the law applicable thereto, is the proposed election of directors for which the meeting is called such a purpose beyond the powers of the shareholders.

As to the first of these issues, s. 310, in my view, is incapable of the broad construction for which the respondents contend. The section is aimed at and limited to the removal of difficulties militating against the calling of a shareholders meeting or militating against the conducting of business which lawfully might come before the meeting. When such difficulties render lawful action in securing a meeting or in conducting it "impracticable" unless the difficulties are solved by an order of the Court, then such an order properly may be made. Once such difficulties have been removed by the provisions of the order however, it is open to the shareholders present at the meeting to conduct only such business thereat which could have been conducted at a meeting legally called "in any other manner." In my view, the only phrase in the section lending any plausibility to a broader construction is the concluding phrase thereof "and any meeting called, held and conducted in accordance with such an order shall for all purposes be deemed to be a meeting of shareholders or members of the corporation duly called, held and conducted." The wording in that phrase "for all purposes" when read in the context of the whole section clearly is limited in application to establishing the legality of the meeting so far as the calling, holding and conducting thereof as a meeting is concerned. This interpretation of the section would seem to bestow full effect on its complete wording. I hold that further specific provision, which is absent from the section, would be required to support a construction sanctioning the Court to "order," as it were, shareholders to do in a meeting what they otherwise would have no power to do simply because it had been established that without the help of the Court it was "impracticable" to call, hold or conduct the meeting.

As to the second issue raised in the appeal, the salient fact, of course, is the uncertainty as to the present composition of B.I.F.'s board of directors. If the contention of the plaintiffs in the action as to the purported election of directors in the July meeting be upheld, then the board of directors of the company as the same existed prior to that meeting is still B.I.F.'s board, s. 300(4); if the action, however, fails in this respect then the board elected in the July meeting is still in office and their term of office has not expired, s. 300(2).

Respondents argue that B.I.F.'s By-law 1, cl. 5, provides for an "uncertain" term of office for directors and that another election of the board within one year is contemplated and sanctioned thereby. That clause provides:

5. *Term of Office.* The directors' term of office (subject to the provisions, if any, of the letters patent and any supplementary letters patent of the Company) shall be from the date of the meeting at which they are elected or appointed until the annual meeting next following or until their successors are elected or appointed. As long as there is a quorum of directors in office, any vacancy occurring in the board of directors may be filled for the remainder of the term by the directors then in office.

I do not agree with the contention. I construe that clause to be in harmony with s. 300(4) of the Act:

(4) If an election of directors is not held at the proper time, the directors continue in office until their successors are elected.

Nor subject to the provisions of s. 66 of the Act do I think it competent for B.I.F. to hold what in effect amounts to a second election of an entire board of directors within one year. Section 300(2) provides:

(2) Unless the letters patent or supplementary letters patent otherwise provide, the election of directors shall take place yearly. ...

And see *Stephenson v. Vokes* (1896), 27 O.R. 691, and *London Finance Corp. v. Banking Service Corp.*, 23 O.W.N. 138, [1925] 1 D.L.R. 319.

The first provision in our statutes for recall of directors was inserted in the Corporations Act, 1953 (Ont.), c. 19, as s. 66. It also appears in the present Act as s. 66 and reads as to s-s. (1) thereof:

66. (1) Where the letters patent, supplementary letters patent or by-laws of a company do not provide for cumulative voting under section 64, the letters patent, supplementary letters patent or by-laws may provide that the shareholders may, by a resolution passed by at least two-thirds of the votes cast at a general meeting of which notice specifying the intention to pass such resolution has been given, remove any director before the expiration of his term of office, and may, by a majority of the votes cast at that meeting, elect any person in his stead for the remainder of his term.

Had the application to the Court under s. 310 been made on proper material for an order directing a meeting to consider action thereat by the shareholders pursuant to s. 66 and had the application been made by shareholders "holding not less than one-tenth of the issued shares ... that carry the right to vote at the meeting proposed to be held"

(s. 308(1)) other considerations doubtless would apply. That, however, was not the application before Fraser J. and such an application is in no sense the subject-matter of adjudication in this appeal.

I would allow the appeal with costs here and below, set aside the order in appeal and direct that an order go dismissing the application.

Appeal allowed; application dismissed.

---

4. Access to the List of Shareholders

Modern corporations statutes require corporations to keep extensive records and generally to make those records available to inspection by directors and shareholders and sometimes by creditors and, in the case of publicly held companies, by "any other person." CBCA ss. 20, 21; ABCA ss. 20, 21; BCCA ss. 187, 188; OBCA ss. 140, 141, 144, 145. For present purposes the most important of these records is the list of shareholders. Access to it will be critical for any shareholder who wishes to communicate with his fellow shareholders concerning the management of the corporation or his desire to change management. For example, if a disgruntled shareholder wished to rally others to remove the directors he might want access to the shareholder list to put together the owners of 5% of the voting shares to requisition a special meeting. Access to the list of shareholders is also of paramount importance in a take-over bid.

Under CBCA s. 21(3) a corporation must furnish a current list of shareholders, together with addresses and numbers of shares owned, to "shareholders and creditors ..., their agents and legal representatives, the Director and, where the corporation is a distributing corporation, ... any other person, upon payment of a reasonable fee. ..." The only limitation upon this right is that the request must be accompanied by the requestor's affidavit stating that the list will not be used "except in connection with ... [a] matter relating to the affairs of the corporation" (CBCA s. 21(9) or "for corporate purposes" (BCCA s. 191(d)(iii)). See also ABCA s. 21; OBCA s. 146. It is an offence to use the list for other than authorized purposes. Is there any practical difference between the formulations in the British Columbia statute and the CBCA? Consider this after reading the next case.

State ex rel. Pillsbury v. Honeywell Inc.
Minnesota Supreme Court
191 N.W.2d 406 (1971)

KELLY, JUSTICE: Petitioner appeals from an order and judgment of the district court denying all relief prayed for in a petition for writs of mandamus to compel respondent, Honeywell, Inc., (Honeywell) to produce its original shareholder ledger, current shareholder ledger, and all corporate records dealing with weapons and munitions manufacture. We must affirm.

The issues raised by petitioner are ... whether petitioner, who bought shares in respondent corporation for the purpose of changing its policy of manufacturing war munitions, had a proper purpose germane to a shareholder's interest. ...

Petitioner attended a meeting on July 3, 1969, of a group involved in what was known as the "Honeywell Project." Participants in the project believed that American involvement in Vietnam was wrong, that a substantial portion of Honeywell's production consisted of munitions used in that war, and that Honeywell should stop this production of munitions. Petitioner had long opposed the Vietnam war, but it was at the July 3rd meeting that he first learned of Honeywell's involvement. He was shocked at the knowledge that Honeywell had a large government contract to produce anti-personnel fragmentation bombs. Upset because of knowledge that such bombs were produced in his own community by a company which he had known and respected, petitioner determined to stop Honeywell's munitions production.

On July 14, 1969, petitioner ordered his fiscal agent to purchase 100 shares of Honeywell. He admits that the sole purpose of the purchase was to give himself a voice in Honeywell's affairs so he could persuade Honeywell to cease producing munitions. Apparently not aware of that purpose, petitioner's agent registered the stock in the name of a Pillsbury family nominee—Quad & Co. Upon discovering the nature of the registration, petitioner bought one share of Honeywell in his own name on August 11, 1969. In his deposition testimony petitioner made clear the reason for his purchase of Honeywell's shares:

Q. ... [D]o I understand that you requested Mr. Lacey to buy these 100 shares of Honeywell in order to follow up on the desire you had to bring to Honeywell management and to stockholders these theses that you have told us about here today? A. Yes. That was my motivation.

The "theses" referred to are petitioner's beliefs concerning the propriety of producing munitions for the Vietnam war.

During July 1969, *subsequent* to the July 3, 1969, meeting and after he had ordered his agent to purchase the 100 shares of Honeywell stock, petitioner inquired into a trust which had been formed for his benefit by his grandmother. The purpose of the inquiry was to discover whether shares of Honeywell were included in the trust. It was then, *for the first time*, that petitioner discovered that he had a contingent beneficial interest under the terms of the trust in 242 shares of Honeywell.

Prior to the instigation of this suit, petitioner submitted two formal demands to Honeywell requesting that it produce its original shareholder ledger, current shareholder ledger, and all corporate records dealing with weapons and munitions manufacture. Honeywell refused.

•   •   •

Honeywell is a Delaware corporation doing business in Minnesota. Both petitioner and Honeywell spent considerable effort in arguing whether Delaware or Minnesota law applies. The trial court, applying Delaware law, determined that the outcome of the case rested upon whether or not petitioner has a proper purpose germane to his interest as a shareholder. Del.Code Ann. tit. 8, § 220 (Supp. 1968). This test is derived from the common law and is applicable in Minnesota. ... We need not rule on whether the lower court applied the right state law since the test used was correct.

• • •

The trial court ordered judgment for Honeywell, ruling that petitioner had not demonstrated a proper purpose germane to his interest as a stockholder. Petitioner contends that a stockholder who disagrees with management has an absolute right to inspect corporate records for purposes of soliciting proxies. He would have this court rule that such solicitation is per se a "proper purpose." Honeywell argues that a "proper purpose" contemplates concern with investment return. We agree with Honeywell.

This court has had several occasions to rule on the propriety of shareholders' demands for inspection of corporate books and records. Minn.St. 300.32, not applicable here, has been held to be declaratory of the common-law principle that a stockholder is entitled to inspection for a proper purpose germane to his business interests. While inspection will not be permitted for purposes of curiosity, speculation, or vexation, adverseness to management and a desire to gain control of the corporation for economic benefit does not indicate an improper purpose.

Several courts agree with petitioner's contention that a mere desire to communicate with other shareholders is, per se, a proper purpose. *Lake v. Buckeye Steel Castings Co.*, 2 Ohio St.2d 101, 206 N.E.2d 566 (1965). This would seem to confer an almost absolute right to inspection. We believe that a better rule would allow inspections only if the shareholder has a proper purpose for such communication. This rule was applied in *McMahon v. Dispatch Printing Co.*, 101 N.J.L. 470, 129 A. 425 (1925), where inspection was denied because the shareholder's objective was to discredit politically the president of the company, who was also the New Jersey secretary of state.

The act of inspecting a corporation's shareholder ledger and business records must be viewed in its proper perspective. In terms of the corporate norm, inspection is merely the act of the concerned owner checking on what is in part his property. In the context of the large firm, inspection can be more akin to a weapon in corporate warfare. The effectiveness of the weapon is considerable:

Considering the huge size of many modern corporations and the necessarily complicated nature of their bookkeeping, it is plain that to permit their thousands of shareholders to roam at will through their records would render impossible not only any attempt to keep records efficiently, but the proper carrying on of their businesses. [*Cooke v. Outland*, 265 N.C. 601, 611, 144 S.E.2d 835, 842 (1965).]

See, also, *Matter of Pierson*, 28 Misc. 726, 59 N.Y.S. 1003 (Sup. Ct. 1899), affirmed, 44 App.Div. 215, 60 N.Y.S. 671 (1899). Because the power to inspect may be the power to destroy, it is important that only those with a bona fide interest in the corporation enjoy that power.

That one must have proper standing to demand inspection has been recognized by statutes in several jurisdictions. Courts have also balked at compelling inspection by a shareholder holding an insignificant amount of stock in the corporation.

Petitioner had utterly no interest in the affairs of Honeywell before he learned of Honeywell's production of fragmentation bombs. Immediately after obtaining this

knowledge, he purchased stock in Honeywell for the sole purpose of asserting ownership privileges in an effort to force Honeywell to cease such production. We agree
with the court in *Chas. A. Day & Co. v. Booth*, 123 Maine 443, 447, 123 A. 557, 558
(1924) that "where it is shown that such stockholding is only colorable, or solely for
the purpose of maintaining proceedings of this kind, [we] fail to see how the petitioner can be said to be a 'person interested,' entitled as of right to inspect. ..." But
for his opposition to Honeywell's policy, petitioner probably would not have bought
Honeywell stock, would not be interested in Honeywell's profits and would not desire
to communicate with Honeywell's shareholders. His avowed purpose in buying
Honeywell stock was to place himself in a position to try to impress his opinions
favoring a reordering of priorities upon Honeywell management and its other shareholders. Such a motivation can hardly be deemed a proper purpose germane to his
economic interest as a shareholder.

The fact that petitioner alleged a proper purpose in his petition will not necessarily
compel a right to inspection. "A mere statement in a petition alleging a proper purpose is
not sufficient. The facts in each case may be examined." *Sawers v. American Phenolic
Corp.*, 404 Ill. 440, 449, 89 N.E.2d 374, 379 (1949). Neither is inspection mandated by
the recitation of proper purpose in petitioner's testimony. Conversely, a company cannot
defeat inspection by merely alleging an improper purpose. From the deposition, the trial
court concluded that petitioner had already formed strong opinions on the immorality
and the social and economic wastefulness of war long before he bought stock in
Honeywell. His sole motivation was to change Honeywell's course of business because
that course was incompatible with his political views. If unsuccessful, petitioner indicated that he would sell the Honeywell stock.

We do not mean to imply that a shareholder with a bona fide investment interest
could not bring this suit if motivated by concern with the long- or short-term economic
effects on Honeywell resulting from the production of war munitions. Similarly, this suit
might be appropriate when a shareholder has a bona fide concern about the adverse
effects of abstention from profitable war contracts on his investment in Honeywell.

In the instant case, however, the trial court, in effect, has found from all the facts
that petitioner was not interested in even the long-term well-being of Honeywell or the
enhancement of the value of his shares. His sole purpose was to persuade the company
to adopt his social and political concerns, irrespective of any economic benefit to himself or Honeywell. This purpose on the part of one buying into the corporation does not
entitle the petitioner to inspect Honeywell's books and records.

Petitioner argues that he wishes to inspect the stockholder ledger in order that he
may correspond with other shareholders with the hope of electing to the board one or
more directors who represent his particular viewpoint. On p. 30 of his brief he states that
this purpose alone compels inspection:

... [T]his Court has said that a stockholder's motives or "good faith" are not a test of his right of inspection, except as "bad faith" actually manifests some recognized "improper purpose"—such as
vexation of the corporation, or purely destructive plans, or *nothing specific*, just pure idle curiosity,
or necessarily illegal ends, or *nothing germane to his interests*. [*State ex rel. G.M. Gustafson Co. v.
Crookston Trust Co.* [222 Minn. 17, 22 N.W.2d 911 (1946)]. ...] (Italics supplied.)

While a plan to elect one or more directors is specific and the election of directors normally would be a proper purpose, here the purpose was not germane to petitioner's or Honeywell's economic interest. Instead, the plan was designed to further petitioner's political and social beliefs. Since the requisite propriety of purpose germane to his or Honeywell's economic interest is not present, the allegation that petitioner seeks to elect a new board of directors is insufficient to compel inspection.

•   •   •

The order of the trial court denying the writ of mandamus is affirmed.

Proper Purpose to Inspect the List. Pillsbury clearly was not an average shareholder since his concern was not to increase the value of his investment but to convince the company to alter its business. Does that mean that his desire to communicate with the other shareholders was not "a proper purpose germane to a shareholder's interest"? Did his purpose have to do with "the affairs of the corporation"? Did he plan to use the shareholders' list "for corporate purposes"? Suppose Pillsbury had not had to communicate with the other shareholders because he had succeeded in convincing the board of directors of Honeywell to stop making fragmentation bombs for use in the Vietnam War. Assuming that the manufacture of such bombs had been profitable, could a shareholder whose interest in Honeywell was more profit-centered than Pillsbury's have succeeded in a suit against the directors asserting that their actions were beyond their authority? Would a shareholder resolution requiring Honeywell to leave the bomb business have been within the shareholders' competence?

See also *Credit Bureau of St. Paul, Inc. v. Credit Bureau Reports, Inc.*, 290 A.2d 691 (Del. 1972), aff'g, 290 A.2d 689 (shareholder list ordered disclosed for likely benefit of competing corporation which sought to acquire control of the firm); *Re MacMillan Bloedel Ltd.*, [1976] 6 W.W.R. 475 (B.C.) (shareholder list ordered for agent of undisclosed principal upon receipt of undertaking that list to be used only for permissible purposes).

Mechanics of Access. The CBCA provides two devices whereby a shareholder or other party might gain access to the list of shareholders. First, he might assert a right to examine the list and to take extracts from it under CBCA ss. 21(1) and 138(4). See also ABCA ss. 21, 132; BCCA s. 188; OBCA ss. 145(1), 100. Second, he might require the corporation, on 10 days' notice, to provide him with a copy of the list of shareholders, saving him from the trouble of making extracts. This latter device would seem more convenient, but it suffers from the drawback that the corporation is given 10 days' notice that something is up. On the other hand, where the corporation has thousands of shareholders, this may be the only practicable method of obtaining the list. In addition, since a shareholder's desire to communicate with other shareholders frequently indicates discontent with management, it is not surprising that corporate officials might seek to place a variety of obstacles in the way of a shareholder who wishes to inspect the list, as is illustrated by the following case.

Cooper v. Premier Trust Co.
Ontario Court of Appeal
[1945] O.R. 35, [1945] 1 D.L.R. 376

[Before ROBERTSON C.J.O., GILLANDERS and ROACH J.J.A.]

ROBERTSON C.J.O.: An appeal by the plaintiff in the action from the judgment of Hogg J., dated September 14, 1944, after the trial of the action before him, without a jury, at Toronto.

The action, in brief, was for a mandatory order that the defendant (the present respondent) keep open its share register for the plaintiff's inspection, at its head office, during reasonable business hours of every day except Sundays and holidays, and permit the plaintiff to make extracts therefrom. The action was dismissed, with costs.

The respondent is a company incorporated by special Act of the Parliament of Canada (c. 179, 3-4 Geo. V). By the Act of incorporation certain parts of the general Companies Act of Canada then in force were made applicable to the respondent, including two sections since carried into the Companies Act, 1934 (24-25 Geo. V, c. 33), and being ss. 166 and 169 thereof. These sections are as follows:

166. The company shall cause a book or books to be kept by the secretary, or by some other officer specially charged with that duty, wherein shall be kept recorded

　　(a) the names, alphabetically arranged, of all persons who are or have been shareholders;

　　(b) the address and calling of every such person, while such shareholder. ...

169. Such books shall, during reasonable business hours of every day, except Sundays and holidays, be kept open for the inspection of shareholders and creditors of the company, and their personal representatives, at the head office or chief place of business of the company, and every shareholder, creditor or personal representative may make extracts therefrom.

The appellant is the holder of 21 shares of the capital stock of the respondent, and has respondent's certificate, dated March 21, 1944, that she is such shareholder. On April 11, 1944 the appellant attended at the respondent's head office, and said to the respondent's secretary that she would like to examine the respondent's share register. She produced to him her share certificate, and the secretary asked her whether she could identify herself as the shareholder in fact. He suggested her National Registration card as a means of proving her identity. The appellant produced her National Registration card, but, on inspection, it was observed that her name appeared thereon as Janet Deborah Cooper, while her share certificate bore the name Janet Cooper. The secretary was not satisfied with this as identification, and the appellant went out, saying she would get something further.

The appellant returned the next day, April 12, and brought with her means of identification satisfactory to the respondent's secretary. He did not, however, permit her to inspect the share register on that day, but suggested that she come at three o'clock on the next day. The appellant duly appeared at 3 p.m. on April 13th—a Thursday—and the share register was made available to her. She was accommodated with a chair at the secretary's desk, and proceeded, for about one hour, with the copying of extracts from the register. She was then interrupted by the secretary, who asked whether she would be much longer, to which she replied that she would like to make a full list of shareholders, and had not nearly finished, having only got as far as the letter "B" or "C." The secretary informed her that certain transfers of shares had come in, and that he would like to record them, and the appellant asked whether she could arrange another time. The following Monday was arranged between them, for her to proceed with her inspection, and she was to telephone the secretary on that morning, and agree upon a time mutually convenient.

The appellant thereupon left respondent's office, it being then about 4 p.m. At 4:15 p.m. respondent's secretary was informed by telephone, by a member of the firm who are the appellant's solicitors herein, and in whose office the appellant is employed, that he was not satisfied to have the inspection of the register continue on the following Monday, and that the appellant would attend at respondent's head office at 10 a.m. on the following day—Friday, April 14th—and that if the register was not made available then, a writ would be issued at once. A letter was also sent on the same afternoon by the appellant's solicitors to the respondent, but although tendered in evidence for the appellant, the learned trial Judge, on objection by respondent's counsel, refused to admit it.

On Friday, April 14th, the appellant, accordingly, again attended at respondent's head office at 10 a.m., and asked to inspect the share register. She was not permitted to do so, the secretary giving her as the reason that he thought they had arranged to make the register available to her on the following Monday, and that that was mutually satisfactory to them.

The writ of summons in this action was issued on the same day, and appellant's action must, therefore, be founded upon what had occurred to this time. She did not go to the respondent's head office on the following Monday, nor did she again communicate with respondent's secretary to say that she wanted to see the share register.

Before proceeding to discuss the result of the facts in evidence, I should add that the transfers of shares, for the entry of which appellant's inspection of the register was interrupted by the secretary on April 13th, were, in one case, a transfer from Thomas B. Holmes, the respondent's general manager, to Thomas B. Holmes in trust, and in another, a transfer to the secretary himself. We are asked by the appellant to infer that the presentation of these transfers at this time for entry in the register was part of a scheme of the company's officers to prevent, hinder or delay the inspection of the register by the appellant. This will have to be considered with the other facts in evidence, but it will be well first to consider the legal relations of the parties in respect to the keeping and inspection of the share register.

It would seem to be a clear duty owed by the company to its shareholders to keep such book or books as s. 166 provides for. It would appear to be equally the clear duty of the company "during reasonable business hours of every day, except Sundays and holidays" to keep such books "open for the inspection of shareholders and creditors of the company, and their personal representatives, at its head office or chief place of business, and to permit every shareholder, creditor or other personal representative to make extracts therefrom." There is not much to be found in the way of reported decisions upon these provisions of the Companies Act of Canada, nor upon more or less similar provisions in the Companies Acts of the Provinces. There are, however, a number of reported decisions in England upon comparable provisions there, and a reference to some of these decisions will indicate how such provisions have been regarded judicially, and the importance that has been given to their enforcement.

• • •

In another case in the same year, *Mutter v. Eastern & Midlands R. Co.* (1888), 38 Ch. D. 92, 57, L.J.Ch. 615 at pp. 617-8, the questions principally in issue were as to the status of the plaintiff, who sought an injunction to restrain the company from preventing his access to the register, and taking extracts therefrom, and as to the right to take copies and extracts. In dealing with the objection that the plaintiff had bought stock, not in his own interest but in that of some other person, Chitty J. said that the company could look only at the register and could not go behind it, and that the Court could not refuse to accord to the shareholder rights which the Legislature had given him. He continued, "the object of the Act of Parliament was plainly this, that every shareholder should be able to see not merely the register so far as it related to himself, but to see it with reference to those who also stand upon the register with him—and the object, I take it, was that he might, if he thought fit, have communications with them. Unquestionably, as a matter of fact, directors of a company are not disposed to allow shareholders too much inspection, when it comes to a question that is going to be decided at one of the general meetings. The directors have the advantage of being able themselves, or by their officers, to refer to the register and send out circulars to canvas all the stockholders, and I think this section was intended to put the stockholder in a similar position, that each stockholder might see who were entitled to the stocks of which he had a part, and what interest they had."

In the course of a judgment dismissing an appeal from the order granting an injunction in the foregoing case, Lindley L.J. said (p. 621), "When the right to inspect and take a copy is expressly conferred by statute, the limit of the right depends on the true construction of the statute." Later in his judgment he said, "It is obvious that a shareholder or debenture stockholder may desire to consult the whole of the debenture stockholders on some matter which concerns them all, and it is reasonable to suppose that the right to inspect the debenture stock register is conferred to enable him to do this as well as for other purposes."

This case was followed in *Nelson v. Anglo-American Land, etc. Co.*, [1897] 1 Ch. 130. See also *Board v. African Cons. Land & Trading Co.*, [1897] W.N. 174.

Having regard to the terms of s. 169 of the Companies Act already quoted, there is no room for doubting the right of the appellant "during reasonable business hours of every day except Sundays and holidays" to inspect the share-register of the respondent. She sought to exercise her right to inspect the register at the respondent's head office, where the register is kept, at 10 o'clock on Friday, April 14, 1944, in accordance with notice given by telephone to the respondent's secretary on the preceding afternoon. She was not permitted to inspect the register on that day, and the reason given for refusing permission to inspect on that day was that she and the company's secretary had arranged to make the register available to her on the following Monday. It was not, and is not, alleged that any other ground existed for refusing inspection on April 14th. Respondent's secretary was the only witness called. He did not say at the time of the refusal, nor did he say in his evidence, that the register was otherwise in use when the appellant came, or was expected to be in use, or that any inconvenience whatsoever or disturbance of respondent's business would have been occasioned by permitting appellant the in-spection she requested.

In my opinion what occurred on Friday, April 14th, was a refusal of inspection, and that refusal was unwarranted. The right of inspection that a shareholder has is a right vested in him personally, to be exercised independently of the consent of the company. It is not something for which it is necessary that he should make arrangements with the company. It may well be that he will make better progress if he does so, and I confess that on the argument I was doubtful whether the appellant had not been too precipitate here. Upon reflection, however, I am of the opinion that the appellant was entitled, if so advised, to put her right of inspection to the test by a demand to inspect on the Friday. While it is not necessary, nor perhaps right, to conclude that the respondent was design-edly putting the appellant off from time to time, yet it was obvious to her legal advisers that unless they did something about it, she would have only one hour's inspection in five days. Appellant's solicitor may have been wise to put an end to nice courtesies, and to assert his client's rights. The propriety of so doing is supported by the position taken by the respondent in its statement of defence. In para. 6 the respondent denies prevent-ing the appellant from inspecting the books it is required to keep open for its sharehold-ers "at such reasonable times as would not interfere with its business." The words of the statute are "during reasonable business hours of every day except Sundays and holi-days." Again, in para. 7 respondent states that the appellant may still "during reasonable business hours on any day at the reasonable convenience of both parties inspect the said books."

The understanding, such as it was, that existed between the appellant and the re-spondent's secretary when she departed on the afternoon of April 13th, did not amount to a contract or a waiver by the appellant of any of her rights. The secretary gave nothing and promised nothing. If the appellant telephoned him on Monday morning, they were to see what they could arrange. There was nothing in that to deprive the appellant of her statutory right to demand inspection of the register on the 14th, as she in fact did. The ground put forward on behalf of the respondent for refusing the appellant inspection on the 14th, was available to the respondent only so long as the appellant recognized it, and the respondent's secretary had notice within 15 minutes after the appellant's departure on the 13th, that she proposed to exercise her right of inspection on the 14th. I can see no answer to her claim.

I would allow the appeal and direct judgment to be entered for the appellant for the relief claimed, with costs of action and of the appeal.

Appeal allowed.

E. PROXY SOLICITATION IN THE PUBLIC CORPORATION

1. Reasons for Proxies

Since many corporations have very large numbers of shareholders, numbering often in the thousands or even the tens of thousands, it is not practicable for all or even a very large number of them to attend meetings in person. With quorum requirements typically running at levels of fifty per cent or more of voting shares, it becomes obvious that meetings must in fact be conducted by means of the appointment of proxies.

2. Proxies and the Proxy Process

The term proxy is commonly used to refer to a person appointed to represent a shareholder at a meeting. However, statutory provisions in Canada use the term "proxy" to refer to the form or instrument by which such person is appointed. CBCA s. 147; ABCA s. 141; BCCA s. 1(1); OBCA s. 109. The proxy process is the manner in which proxies for meetings are solicited from shareholders and information is provided to them in connection with the solicitation.

3. The Proxy Process Prior to Regulation by Statute

It is only since the 1960s that the proxy process has been extensively regulated by statute. However, even before that time it was established that where the information circular sent by management did not give shareholders sufficient relevant particulars to enable the shareholders to form a reasoned judgment on matters to be dealt with at the meeting then the results of the meeting would be set aside. Further, courts might not approve of management's form of proxy if it did not enable the shareholder to exercise a real choice, although this did not necessarily invalidate the meeting. *Re Langley's Ltd.*, [1938] O.R. 123, [1938] 3 D.L.R. 230 (C.A.); *Re National Grocers Co.*, [1938] O.R. 142, [1938] 3 D.L.R. 106: *Re Dairy Corp. of Canada,* [1934] O.R. 436, [1934] 3 D.L.R. 347.

Getz, The Alberta Proxy Legislation: Borrowed Variations on an Eighteenth Century Theme
8 Alta. L. Rev. 18, 19-22 (1970)

At common law, shareholders in a business corporation had no right to vote by proxy. The common law rule was apparently derived from an earlier rule concerning the rights of members in the quasi-public medieval corporation in which membership "was coupled with no pecuniary interest. The voting privilege was in the nature of a personal trust, committed to the discretion of the member as an individual, and hence not susceptible of exercise through delegation."[13] Despite obvious differences in character and social function between the two types of corporation, no legal distinction was made. Indeed, one American court, when invited to differentiate, declared roundly that "the fact that it is a business corporation in no wise dispenses with the obligation for all members to assemble together, unless otherwise provided, for the exercise of a right to participate in the election of directors."[14]

---

13 *Walker v. Johnson* (1900), 17 D.C. App. 14, cited by Axe, *Corporate Proxies*, (1942) 41 Mich. L. Rev. 38, at 39.

14 *Commonwealth ex. rel. Verree v. Bringhurst* (1883), 103 Pa. St. 134 at 138.

If there was to be a right to vote by proxy, special authority had to be found for it in the corporate constitution; as, in the memorandum jurisdictions at least, the rights created by the corporate constitution are contractual in character, there seemed no limits to the extent to which the right, if granted, could be contractually circumscribed. Frequently, for example, a shareholder could only appoint as his proxy another shareholder—a practice sanctioned by the "model" provisions of Table A. Since, especially in a company whose shares were widely dispersed, the only other shareholders known to the persons giving the proxy were the directors from whom they received the forms, this device often had the effect of placing considerable voting power in the hands of the latter—in addition, of course, to preventing members from being represented by competent professional advisers.

Moreover, it was for the directors to determine what form the proxy instrument should take, and, therefore, what authority it conferred. In *Re National Grocers Co. Ltd.* [[1938] 3 D.L.R. 106 (Ont. H.C.)], for example, Roach J. described as "commonly used" a form of proxy in which the name of the management's nominee had already been filled in when received by the shareholder. The learned judge went on to remark that "very often unthinking shareholders more or less automatically sign these forms ... and therefore the vote recorded under such circumstances cannot always be considered as reflecting the considered opinion of the absent shareholder" [at 112]. Yet, although the practice was condemned by one Canadian judge as "vicious"[22] and described by another as "not good corporate practice,"[23] it was not considered sufficient ground to invalidate the proxy.[24] Further, there was no general requirement that a two-way proxy form be used— that is, one worded in such a way as to permit the shareholder, through his nominee, to vote either for or against any proposal or group of related proposals. While some Stock Exchanges required this for listed companies, the model proxy form in Table A merely authorised the nominee to vote "for me and on my behalf," thus in effect conferring *carte blanche* upon the nominee, frequently a director, to vote as he thought fit and, if he thought fit, perhaps not to vote at all.

• • •

[T]he only obligation imposed upon those responsible for summoning company meetings was to give adequate notice, and, with one exception, the contents of the notice were left to be regulated by the articles of the company and by the rules of equity and the common law. It is true that in those cases in which judicial approval was essential to the validity of some corporate act, the courts as a matter of practice insisted upon full and fair disclosure, generally by means of an explanatory circular, of all relevant facts,

---

22 *Re Dairy Corporation of Canada Ltd.*, [1934] 3 D.L.R. 347 at 349, per Middleton J.A. The form of proxy in this case included the marginal note: "If you desire to nominate any other person your proxy, strike out the printed name and fill in the name of your nominee."

23 Spence J. in *Garvie v. Axmith* (1961), 31 D.L.R. (2d) 65 at 77 (Ont. H.C.).

24 *Re Langley's Ltd.*, [1938] 3 D.L.R. 230 (Ont.); *Re English, Scottish & Australian Chartered Bank* [1893] Ch. 385; but cf. *McDougall v. Black Lake Asbestos & Chrome Co. Ltd.* (1920), 47 O.L.R. 328 which, however, probably turned on inadequate disclosure.

but there was no statutory obligation to follow this procedure. Moreover, it has been held to be a part of the duty of directors to explain and defend to the membership, and where appropriate to solicit its support for, their conduct of the company's business, and also that it is proper to use company funds for the purpose; and it has also been held that the management is under no obligation, moral or legal, to circulate a contrary case or to include in the notice of meeting any reference to proposals other than those emanating from the management itself. This, of course, might be critical, for the general meeting cannot effectively do anything that is not fairly comprehended in the notice of meeting.

---

4. Legislative Developments

The chief impetus for the modern Canadian proxy legislation was the Kimber Report in 1965. The authors of the Kimber Report were in turn influenced heavily in their recommendations by the proxy soliciting pattern established in s. 14 of the American Securities Exchange Act of 1934.*

Proxies and Proxyholders. Under the legislation a "proxy" is defined as a form signed by a shareholder that appoints a proxyholder. CBCA s. 147; ABCA s. 141; BCCA s. 1(1); OBCA s. 109. A "proxyholder" is defined as a person appointed to act on behalf of a shareholder. A proxyholder can be appointed by a shareholder entitled to vote at a meeting of shareholders. CBCA s. 148(1); ABCA s. 142(1); BCCA s. 175(1); OBCA s. 110(1). The proxyholder has the same rights as a shareholder. However, the shareholder can limit the rights of the proxyholder in the grant of authority given by the shareholder. CBCA ss. 148(1), 152(2); ABCA ss. 142(1), 146(2); BCCA ss. 175(1), (2); OBCA ss. 110(1), 114(2).

At a meeting the proxyholder may be constrained on the exercise of a vote by a show of hands where the proxyholder holds proxies for more than one shareholder and has conflicting instructions from different shareholders. Thus a proxyholder cannot vote on a show of hands where the proxyholder has conflicting instructions from different shareholders. However, a proxyholder may register votes on conflicting instructions where a ballot is taken. This would allow the proxyholder to record votes for the resolution on the basis of a proxy given by one shareholder while recording votes against the resolution on the basis of a proxy given by another shareholder. See CBCA s. 152(2); ABCA s. 146(2); BCCA s. 175(2); OBCA s. 114(2).

A ballot may be demanded by a shareholder in person or by a proxyholder. Otherwise the vote can be conducted by a show of hands unless there are proxies representing more than 5% of all the voting rights of securities entitled to be represented and voted at

---

* In the United States there is no federal corporations statue, and the various state corporations statutes are virtually silent on the proxy soliciting process. Hence, as a practical matter (if not as a constitutional matter as a result of the country's pre-emption doctrine), the proxy soliciting field in the United States is occupied wholly by the federal Securities Exchange Act as regards corporations subject to it— generally those having assets of over $1 million and at least 500 shareholders.

the meeting which require that the securities represented by the proxies be voted against what would otherwise be the decision of the meeting. CBCA s. 152(3); ABCA s. 146(3); OBCA s. 114(3); cf. BCCA s. 182.

Requirements for the Form of Proxy. Regulation 32 under the CBCA requires that any form of proxy, whether used by management or by others, must state that the shareholder may appoint as proxy a person other than the one pre-designated on the form and must provide a space to do so. The form must either state clearly how the pre-designated individual intends to vote on the business to be brought before the meeting or provide a means for the shareholder to specify how his shares shall be voted. With regard to the appointment of the auditor and the election of directors, for which the voting is not for or against but rather granted or withheld, the proxy form must provide a means for the shareholder to instruct whether or not his shares shall be voted for the nominees. See also ABCA Reg. s. 8 (referring to the ASA requirements, ASA Reg. s. 164); BCCA s. 181; OBCA Reg. s. 27.

In *Re Goldhar and D'Aragon Mines Ltd.* (1977), 15 O.R. (2d) 80, dissidents had requisitioned a meeting of shareholders for the purposes of removing the incumbent board and electing a new one. Management's proxy form designated a named individual as proxy and provided a place for the shareholder to instruct the proxy to vote for or against the removal resolution. The form stated that if the removal resolution were passed the person designated on the form would vote all shares for which he held proxies in favour of the re-election of the existing board. In the result, "so long as the company nominee is inserted in the company proxy it makes little practical difference which box the shareholder marks either for or against the resolution removing a director" (*id.* at 81). The Court declared the proxy form to be "null and void" because it "is not only unfair but also ... does not permit the shareholders to exercise their choice in connection with the transaction of the business stated in the requisition" (*id.* at 82).

Who Must Solicit Proxies. Management of a publicly held corporation must, concurrently with giving notice of a shareholders' meeting, send a form of proxy to each shareholder entitled to receive notice of the meeting. CBCA s. 149; ABCA s. 143; BCCA s. 177; OBCA s. 111. Anyone who solicits proxies, including both management and dissenters, must send an information circular. The information circular provides information such as the interest of persons making the solicitation in the matters to be voted upon (which, in the case of a management solicitation, must note the interests of directors and senior officers), information concerning persons proposed as directors, information on executive compensation, the interest of insiders in material transactions, the indebtedness of directors and senior officers to the corporation or its subsidiaries, details of management contracts under which a substantial degree of management functions are performed by persons other than the directors and senior officers. Further, with respect to any special matters to be voted on, such as fundamental changes, the information circular must provide information in sufficient detail to permit security holders to form a reasoned judgment concerning the matter.

As noted above, management must solicit proxies and thus must also send an information circular. Mandatory solicitation by management is the linchpin of the modern proxy rules because the most complete disclosure regulations would not work if management was free to ignore them by not soliciting proxies or by soliciting them only from sufficient friendly shareholders to constitute a quorum. Where management fails to send a required information circular, then a court will nullify the results of the shareholders' meeting. *Babic v. Milinkovic* (1971), 22 D.L.R. (3d) 732 (B.C.), aff'd, (1972), 25 D.L.R. (3d) 752 (C.A.).

Compliance with More Than One Set of Proxy Solicitation Rules. When American-style proxy legislation was introduced in Ontario in 1966, it appeared in both The Corporations Act and The Securities Act (OSA). Since proxy provisions are found in the OSA, the effect is that an issuer incorporated elsewhere than in Ontario but which has issued securities traded in Ontario is *prima facie* subject to Ontario's proxy soliciting rules. However, where a corporation subject to the OSA complies with the proxy soliciting law of its incorporating jurisdiction, and such law is substantially similar to that of Ontario, then OSA s. 88 exempts the corporation from that statute's proxy rules. Since the CBCA proxy rules are substantially similar to those in the OSA, CBCA corporations with securities publicly traded in Ontario need not comply with the OSA proxy rules.

Many Canadian public corporations have a class of securities traded in American markets. Such corporations must comply with the proxy rules under the Securities Exchange Act of 1934, at least if they solicit American resident shareholders. This is ordinarily required, since management of a CBCA corporation must solicit proxies from all holders of voting shares (ss. 149(1), 135(1)). Compliance with the American proxy rules is, if anything, more onerous than compliance with the CBCA.

5. The Meaning of "Solicitation"

Proxy solicitation provisions in corporation statutes and securities legislation in Canada contain very broad definitions of "solicitation" which can have significant implications concerning the potential for the expression of dissident shareholder views. The following case highlights some of these concerns.

Brown v. Duby
Ontario High Court
(1980), 28 O.R. 745, 111 D.L.R. (3d) 418, 11 B.L.R. 129

CRAIG J.: ... I will deal first with the application for an interlocutory injunction restraining the defendants from soliciting proxies from shareholders of United Canso Oil & Gas Ltd. without the dissident proxy circular required by the Canada Business Corporations Act, 1974-75-76 (Can.), c. 33 (the Act).

The plaintiff, United Canso Oil & Gas Ltd. (Canso), is a company incorporated under the laws of Canada; it has its head office in the City of Calgary in the Province of Alberta. Its co-plaintiff is a shareholder and officer of Canso.

The defendants, except for D.F. King & Co. Inc., are all shareholders of the company. They are also members of a shareholders' committee (dissident shareholders) formed in December, 1979. This committee is opposed to the present management of the company. The defendant D.F. King & Co. Inc. is a limited company carrying on business in New York City. Part of its business is the solicitation of proxies on behalf of companies and individuals.

Canso is engaged in the exploration for and development of oil and gas properties and mineral deposits, located principally in Western Canada, the United States of America and Australia. It is publicly owned and its common shares are listed for trading in Canada on the Toronto and Montreal Stock Exchanges. They are traded in the United States of America on the Boston and Pacific Stock Exchanges.

The majority of the shareholders holding the majority of shares reside in the United States of America. I was informed by counsel that the largest number of Canadian shareholders are resident in Ontario and that they hold a majority of the Canadian shares. For reasons which I need not repeat I have dismissed the defendants' motion to dismiss this application upon the ground of lack of jurisdiction.

The plaintiffs claim that the individual defendants caused two letters to be sent by D.F. King & Co. Inc. to certain shareholders and stockbrokers. The first letter was dated March 7, 1980, and was sent only to the shareholders of Canso resident in the United States of America. The second letter was dated March 30, 1980, and was sent to all shareholders. The plaintiffs claim that both letters constitute a solicitation of proxies within the meaning of s. 144(1) [now CBCA s. 150(1)] of, and in breach of, the Act which provides in part as follows:

Soliciting proxies.
    144. (1) A person shall not solicit proxies unless

    ...

    (b) in the case of any other solicitation, a dissident's proxy circular in prescribed form stating the purposes of the solicitation is sent to the auditor of the corporation, to each shareholder whose proxy is solicited and, if paragraph (b) applies, to the corporation.

I will return to the "dissident's proxy circular" in a moment.

Section 141 [now CBCA s. 147] provides in part:

    141. In this Part, ... "solicit" or "solicitation" includes
        (a) a request for a proxy whether or not accompanied by or included in a form of proxy,
        (b) a request to execute or not to execute a form of proxy or to revoke a proxy,
        (c) the sending of a form of proxy or other communication to a shareholder under circumstances reasonably calculated to result in the procurement, withholding or revocation of a proxy. ...

In my opinion the letter of March 30th is not a solicitation for proxies within the meaning of s. 144(1) [150(1)] but is directed to requesting the shareholders to sign a requisition requiring the calling of a meeting of shareholders "for the election of directors" pursuant to s. 137 [now CBCA s. 143], which provides:

Requisition of meeting.
    137. (1) The holders of not less than five per cent of the issued shares of a corporation that carry the right to vote at a meeting sought to be held may requisition the directors to call a meeting of shareholders for the purposes stated in the requisition.

Turning now to the letter of March 7th, I quote it in full (except for the "proxy circular" attached to it giving the names, addresses, principal occupations and shareholdings of the shareholders' committee):

United Canso Oil & Gas Ltd. Shareholders Committee

335-8th Avenue
Calgary, Alberta
T2P IC9
(403) 269-8221

2810 Glenda Avenue
Fort Worth, Texas
76117
(817) 831-0761

March 7, 1980

Dear Fellow United Canso Shareholder:

We believe it's time for a change in the management of your Company.

As substantial shareholders of United Canso Oil & Gas Ltd. we have formed this Committee because of our serious concern about your Company's past operating record and its future prospects under a board of directors led by the incumbent president, John W. Buckley.

In our view, the Buckley-headed management has failed to achieve the Company's potential for growth. The history of your Company's management, as we see it, has been marked by conflicts of interest and little progress. Your Company lost $272,079 for the fiscal year ended September 30, 1979 and $1,056,533 for the quarter ended December 31, 1979. Instead of a record of earnings growth, the Buckley management—as it has done in the past—offers you promises for the future.

We intend to solicit proxies at the next meeting of shareholders for the election of an entirely new Board of Directors, committed to managing the Company for the benefit of all its shareholders.

The members of the Committee together own more than 394,000 shares—over twenty times the amount owned by the present board, which together owns fewer than 18,000 shares, or less than one-third of 1% of your Company. We believe we share with you a common interest in the Company and its future.

We are writing to you now to introduce the Committee. We enclose a description of the Committee members, including their present principal occupations and their shareholders in United Canso.

We are not requesting proxies at this time. The Shareholders Committee will ask for your proxy only after we have prepared a definitive proxy statement, which cannot be done for the next shareholders' meeting until the incumbents' materials have been sent out. At present, we do not know the date of the meeting, the incumbent slate, or, indeed, what matters are to be considered at the meeting.

If the experience of the past two shareholder meetings is any guide, the present management will mail their materials to you not more than 30 days before the meeting date. *We urge you not to send in any management proxy before you have received and considered our proxy materials.*

In their proxy materials, management may well attempt to win your vote by attacking the Committee and its members. We also expect that the incumbents will attempt to divert your attention from their record in recent years by promises of future growth. You should know that Mr. Buckley has already begun to make vague promises for the future: "record fiscal 1980 operating revenues" and a "turnaround in profitability." We ask you to consider what these promises really mean. Operating revenues are not necessarily any measure of profitability: remember fiscal 1979, a year in which, despite record operating revenues, your Company suffered a sizeable loss. Moreover, any profit—however small—would fulfill Mr. Buckley's promise of a "turnaround in profitability," after the loss the Company sustained last year.

Management may also attempt to point with pride to the recent rise in the price of United Canso stock—even though the stock has only recently sold at the levels it reached in 1974.

Do not be misled by these tactics. We ask you not to sign any proxy for the Buckley slate of directors, but to consider, in your own best interests, the information we will be reporting to you.

If you are undecided, we suggest you consult your broker, banker or investment advisor.

We Welcome Your Comments

We hope you, as an owner of United Canso, will share with us your concerns about the Company, and your hopes and thoughts for the Company's future. *Please write us at either of the addresses shown on our letterhead, or call us collect at the numbers shown there.*

For those of you whose stock is held of record by a broker, bank or other nominee, we enclose a postage prepaid card which will enable you to furnish your name, address and telephone number so that we may contact you directly should you so desire.

We look forward to hearing from you and to working together toward a new management for United Canso.

Sincerely yours,

United Canso Oil & Gas Ltd.
Shareholders Committee

It is my view that, while this letter states that "we are not requesting proxies at this time," it appears to be a solicitation within the meaning of the definition of "solicit" or "solicitation" in s. 141(b) and (c) [now 147] in that it is a "request not to execute a form of proxy" for management and/or a "withholding" of proxies from management.

The proxy circular giving a description of the committee members, including occupations and their shareholders in Canso, does not meet the requirements of a "dissident's proxy circular" referred to in s. 144(1)(b) [150(1)(b)].

The requirements of a dissident's proxy circular are provided by s. 38 of the Regulations, SOR/79-316. I quote only those parts of s. 38 that are relied on by counsel for the plaintiff in this case:

38. A dissident's proxy circular shall contain the following information:

   ...

(c) details of the identity and background of each dissident, including

   ...

(iii) all material occupations, offices or employments during the preceding 5 years, with starting and ending dates of each and the name, principal business and address of the body corporate or other business organization in which each such occupation, office or employment was carried on,

   ...

(v) convictions in criminal proceedings during the preceding 10 years for which a pardon has not been granted, other than in respect of traffic violations and similar offences, and the date and nature of the conviction, the name and location of the court and the sentence imposed;

(d) the circumstances under which each dissident became involved in the solicitation and the nature and extent of his activities as a dissident;

...

(f) details of the interest of each dissident in the securities of the corporation to which the solicitation relates, including

...

(ii) the dates on which securities of the corporation were purchased or sold during the preceding 2 years, the amount purchased or sold on each date and the price at which they were purchased or sold,

(iii) if any part of the purchase price or market value of any of the securities specified in subparagraph (ii) is represented by funds borrowed or otherwise obtained for the purpose of acquiring or holding the securities, the amount of the indebtedness as of the latest practicable date and a brief description of the transaction including the names of the parties. ...

...

(i) details of any contract, arrangement or understanding, including the names of the parties, between a dissident or his associates and any person with respect to

(i) future employment by the corporation or any of its affiliates, or

(ii) future transactions to which the corporation or any of its affiliates will or may be a party.

It is my opinion that the background information required by the above-quoted Regulation is obviously important material to be considered by shareholders along with other information in deciding whether to support management or the dissidents, and that the Regulation was framed with that in mind.

Because the shares of Canso are listed for trading on certain U.S. exchanges, Canso is required to meet certain requirements of the Securities Exchange Act, 1934 (U.S.) (SEC), including its proxy provisions. The evidence before me indicates that the March 7th letter was also sent to the SEC and to the Boston and Pacific Stock Exchanges pursuant to the requirements of the SEC. There is evidence before me that United States counsel for the shareholders committee advises that the March 7th letter complied in full with the SEC requirements.

The letter of March 7th was sent from the United States and it was not sent to Canadian shareholders. It is suggested by counsel for the defendants that the provisions of the Act relating to proxy solicitation do not have extraterritorial effect in this situation. I disagree. The status of a corporation is to be determined by the law of the incorporating jurisdiction: see *Cheshire's Private International Law*, 8th ed., p. 191, and 20 C.J.S. p. 12, § 1788. The general rules are stated in *Corpus Juris Secundum* (pp. 21, 22, 23):

1802. Every corporation necessarily carries its charter wherever it goes, for that is the law of its existence. Whatever disabilities are thereby placed upon the corporation at home it retains abroad, and whatever legislative control it is subject to at home must be recognized and submitted to by those who deal with it elsewhere with knowledge of such limitations.

Apart from burdens which may be imposed upon them by the laws of a state which a foreign corporation enters and in which it undertakes to do business ... the rights and liabilities of stockholders and directors are determined by the charter and governing laws of the state in which the corporation is created.

The general rules stated above are subject to exceptions. Upon principles of comity, a corporation which establishes or seeks to establish a business domicile in a State other than that of its creation takes that domicile subject to the responsibilities and burdens imposed by the laws in force there; it becomes amenable to the laws of the latter State: see *Corpus Juris Secundum*, p. 27, § 1807. In the absence of this last-mentioned rule, the principles of comity could invite abuse from individuals choosing to incorporate a company in a country having lax corporation laws and then carrying on the corporation's business in a jurisdiction having stricter corporation laws, all the while shielded by the cloak of the law of the corporation's domicile: Gower, *The Principles of Modern Company Law*, 3rd ed. (1969), p. 669. To prevent or at least discourage such abuse, the host State very often prescribes certain terms and conditions upon which foreign corporations will be permitted to carry on business in the host State. However, a corporation remains subject to the law of its incorporating jurisdiction notwithstanding that its business and centre of administration may be in another jurisdiction: cf. Gower, p. 668; 9 Hals., 4th ed., p. 732, para. 1227. Thus a corporation which carries on operations outside the jurisdiction in which it was incorporated will be subject to the requirements of its incorporating statute as well as those imposed by the laws of the host State.

In the instant case, as a condition of registration of its shares in the United States Canso is obliged to comply with the trading rules and regulations of the SEC. These rules and regulations apply irrespective of the incorporating statute but these do not supplant the Canadian Act and its requirements. That is, the provisions of the Act relating to proxy solicitation apply to Canso and its shareholders wherever Canso carries on business, even though they are also required to comply with the laws of the host jurisdiction. Therefore if the letter of March 7th is interpreted as a solicitation of proxies then it was written in contravention of the Act and its Regulations. In my opinion the plaintiffs have established a *prima facie* case of solicitation, or at least there is a serious question to be tried as to that issue: *Yule Inc. v. Atlantic Pizza Delight Franchise (1968) Ltd. et al.* (1977), 17 O.R. (2d) 505, 80 D.L.R. (3d) 725, 35 C.P.R. (2d) 273.

In my opinion the object of the Act and the provisions in question are for the benefit of the shareholders and to protect them from possible harm. The Act provides for offences and penalties for breach. It is my view that these penalties are not the sole remedies available, but that this legislation gives rise to rights enforceable by action: *Direct Transport Co. Ltd. v. Cornell*, [1938] O.R. 365, [1938] 3 D.L.R. 456; also the comments of Duff J. in *Orpen v. Roberts et al.*, [1925] S.C.R. 364 at pp. 369-70, [1925] 1 D.L.R. 1101 at pp. 1105-6, and *Cunningham et al. v. Moore*, [1972] 3 O.R. 369, 28 D.L.R. (3d) 277 [affirmed [1973] 1 O.R. 357, 31 D.L.R. (3d) 149]. Also the action is based on the alleged tort of conspiracy; that is, an agreement of two or more shareholders to breach the provisions of the statute: *Posluns v. Toronto Stock Exchange et al.*, [1964] 2 O.R. 547, 46 D.L.R. (2d) 210 [affirmed [1965] 1 O.R. 428, 48 D.L.R. (2d) 299].

Upon the application in this action the question of the appropriateness of interlocutory injunction remains. There is very little Canadian jurisprudence in matters involving proxy solicitation disputes between shareholders of a corporation. Undoubtedly the next meeting of shareholders will be held before the trial of the action, so that an interlocutory injunction is almost tantamount to a final judgment after trial. The annual meeting is required by law to be held within 15 months of the last annual meeting—which now means that it must be held on or before June 28, 1980; counsel for the plaintiffs advises me that an undertaking has been given to the Toronto Stock Exchange that it will be held on or before that date.

In my view damages in lieu of injunction would not be an adequate remedy to either side in this case, so that the question of balance of convenience arises. Also injunction is an extraordinary remedy and in my view it ought not to be ordered in this case solely because of the breach mentioned unless it can be said that is clearly required to protect the shareholders in the circumstances. I was referred to American authorities which indicate that United States Courts are generally unwilling to tip the scales toward one shareholders' group or the other in a proxy contest: *Cook United, Inc. v. Stockholders Protective Committee of Cook United, Inc. et al.* (1979), Fed. Sec. L. Rep. (C.C.H.) 95,576 (S.D.N.Y.); *McConnell v. Lucht et al.* (1970), 320 F. Supp. 1162 (S.D.N.Y.), and *Kennecott Copper Corp. v. Curtiss-Wright Corp.* (1978), 584 F.2d 1195 (U.S.C.A., 2nd Cir.).

In *General Time Corp. v. Talley Industries, Inc.* (1968), 403 F.2d 159 (U.S.C.A., 2nd Cir.), the United States Court of Appeals, Second Circuit, dealt with a case involving use of proxies allegedly obtained in violation of the SEC regulations including allegations of false or misleading statements with respect "to any material fact, or which omits to state any material fact," contrary to regulation. Judge Friendly stated, at p. 162:

The standard of materiality is somewhat more elusive in relation to statements issued in a contested election than in regard to a prospectus or other representation designed to induce the purchase or sale of securities, or a proxy statement seeking approval of a proposed corporate transaction—the situation in *Borak*. ... No one knows just what motivates stockholders in choosing between slates. Those experienced in contested elections are likely to doubt whether proxy statements are read with much precision, and determination of the innocence of a particular omission or even misstatement is almost sheer guesswork. The past record of the management, the market performance of the stock, the lustre of the opposition, and the recommendations of brokers and investment advisors based on such considerations, are likely to be much more influential than tired-eye scrutiny of the proxy statements. Still, issuers of such statements should be held to fair accuracy even in the hurly-burly of election contests.

The test, we suppose, is whether, taking a properly realistic view, there is a substantial likelihood that the misstatement or omission may have led a stockholder to grant a proxy to the solicitor or to withhold one from the other side, whereas in the absence of this he would have taken a contrary course. This latter circumstance—that there is another side—has a bearing on materiality in a case where, as here, the facts have been disclosed to it in ample time for comment.

• • •

In the instant case there is some (but not much) evidence that some shareholders have already decided to support the dissidents, but it is not shown that it would be otherwise but for the breach. In the light of my decision the defendants will be required to comply with the solicitation rules of the Act. Here the letter of March 7, 1980, was critical of management, also the material before me alleges specific instances of mismanagement. The dissident shareholders are entitled to be critical and to communicate their criticisms to other shareholders. Here, however, their letter of March 7, 1980, gives rise to a *prima facie* case that it solicits proxies contrary to s. 144. It might be said that the real breach was one of omission to provide the required background information as to the members of the committee by way of "dissident's proxy circular." It is apparent to me ... that there will be an active proxy contest. Ample time remains within which to make full presentation of the relevant information and conflicting contentions of both sides, and the shareholders will have the particulars omitted from the March 7th letter. It seems unlikely to this Court that the shareholders will not be fully exposed to the issues involved.

Counsel for the defendants submits that the defendants will be seriously harmed by an interlocutory injunction far more than the plaintiffs will be aided. The balance of convenience element in a proxy battle was considered in *D-Z Investment Co. v. Holloway* (1974), Fed. Sec. L. Rep. (C.C.H.) 96,057 (S.D.N.Y.), at p. 96,061:

Additionally, and in balancing the hardships, the Court finds that the equities of the present situation tip decidedly in defendants' favor, rather than that of the plaintiff. If a preliminary injunction were to issue, no matter how such was explained to the shareholders by the present management, a substantial number of shareholders would regard its issuance as a determination of the alleged Securities Act violations on the merits and a finding that the incumbent management had acted improperly with regard to the trust. Again, as this Court had opportunity to state in *Sherman v. Posner*, supra:

Conversely, if the preliminary injunction were granted at this time, irreparable injury would accrue to the defendants. Beyond a peradventure, the issuance of an injunction would come to the attention of the stockholders ... And no matter how clearly it was indicated otherwise, the issuance of the injunction undoubtedly would be viewed by some as a favourable adjudication of the claims of the plaintiff. This would be tantamount to a determination of wrongdoing on the part of the [present] management. *Just how this result could be remedied in the event it was found at a full hearing that the claims of the plaintiff here unfounded is not readily perceptible to this Court.*" [emphasis added]

See also *Kass et al. v. Arden-Mayfair, Inc.* (1977), 431 F. Supp. 1037 (C.D. Calif.), where the Court stated (at p. 1041):

In addition, the issuance of a preliminary injunction now would undoubtedly come to the attention of all stockholders. No matter how clearly it was indicated that the issuance was in no way an adjudication on the merits, it would be inevitable that at least a substantial number of stockholders would reach the conclusion that such a holding was tantamount to final determination of wrongdoing on the part of management. *Kauder v. United Board and Carton Corp.*, 199 F. Supp. 420, 423 (S.D.N.Y., 1961).

For these reasons it is my opinion that the balance of convenience favours the defendants; the extraordinary remedy of injunction is not appropriate. The application is dismissed. Having reached this decision it is unnecessary for me to deal with any of the other interesting points raised by counsel on this application.

Application dismissed.

The statutory definition of "solicitation" is designed to bring within the regulatory scheme certain communications made with a view toward procuring the giving or withholding of a proxy but which do not do so explicitly. In other words, communications a step or two before the actual solicitation are caught by the statutory definition. In *Securities and Exchange Commission v. Okin*, 132 F.2d 784 (2d Cir. 1943), a case very similar on its facts to *Brown v. Duby*, Learned Hand J. stated that the issue was whether the power of the S.E.C.

extends to any ... writings which are part of a continuous plan ending in solicitation and which prepare the way for its success. We have no doubt that the power extends to such writings; were it not so, an easy way would be open to circumvent the statute; one need only spread the misinformation adequately before beginning to solicit, and the Commission would be powerless to protect shareholders. The earlier stages in the execution of such a continuous purpose must be subject to regulation, if the purpose of Congress is to be fully carried out. [132 F.2d at 786]

Could a newspaper advertisement constitute a solicitation of proxies? In *Brown v. Chicago, Rock Island & Pacific R.R. Co.*, Rock Island Railroad (RI) and Union Pacific Railroad (UP) planned to merge. On May 23, 1963, management of the RI and UP announced that they would submit a plan for merger of the two companies to their respective boards of directors. On June 24, the Chicago & North Western Railway Company (North Western) announced a tender offer by which it sought to acquire a controlling interest in RI. If successful, the tender offer would defeat the proposed merger between RI and UP. On June 27, the boards of RI and of UP formally adopted the plan of merger. The plan would become effective, however, only upon the approval of the shareholders of RI. On July 26, UP published an advertisement in 45 newspapers across the United States praising the RI-UP merger proposal, criticizing North Western's offer for RI shares and urging its rejection by RI shareholders. The RI shareholders meeting to consider the RI-UP merger was not called until October 1; it was scheduled for November 15. Was UP's newspaper advertisement a solicitation of proxies? See *Brown v. Chicago, Rock Island & Pacific R.R. Co.*, 328 F.2d 122 (7th Cir. 1964).

Would a court be more willing to find that a borderline communication was a solicitation if it contained a misrepresentation?

The statement in *Brown v. Duby* that "[t]here is evidence ... that United States counsel for the shareholders committee advises that the March 7 letter complied in full with the SEC requirements" is somewhat surprising since, at the time, the definition of "solicitation" in Rule 14a-1(f) was essentially the same as that of CBCA s. 141. In fact, the proxy rules under the CBCA were derived in large measure from the rules under the Exchange Act. A narrower approach to the definition of "solicitation" was taken in *Western Mines Ltd. v. Sheridan* (unreported judgment, B.C. 1975). See Getz, *Note*, 1 C.B.L.J. 472 (1976).

Does a Request to Join in Requisitioning a Meeting Constitute a "Solicitation"? In *Brown v. Duby* the Court held that the Duby letter in which he sought to convince other shareholders to join with him in forming a 5% block to requisition a shareholders' meeting of Canso was not a proxy solicitation. If a meeting were requisitioned, then the requisitionists would solicit proxies in favour of the proposals to be considered at the meeting. Suppose a person were to send a letter to his fellow shareholders urging them to join with him in bringing derivative litigation under CBCA s. 239 [ABCA s. 232; BCCA s. 225; OBCA s. 246]. Would such a letter be treated as a solicitation under the CBCA?

In *Brown v. Duby*, management of United Canso (the Buckley family) sought an interlocutory injunction restraining the dissidents from soliciting proxies without a dissident proxy circular. However, the dissidents in their letter to American shareholders stated that they intended to solicit proxies, and no doubt planned to prepare a dissident proxy circular in due course. How then do you explain the decision by United Canso management to seek the interlocutory injunction? Why did Craig J. not grant the injunction, even though the dissidents were found in breach of the statute? Would an overbroad definition of solicitation have a chilling effect on dissenters? In particular, might proxy solicitation rules immunize management from the threat of a proxy contest if informal communications among institutional investors were characterized as solicitations?

Revisions to Proxy Solicitation Rules in the United States. The proxy rules in the United States were amended in 1992 to reduce the constraints on shareholder communications associated with the broad scope of the term "solicitation." In introducing the new rules the S.E.C., stated that

the demonstrated effect of the current rules is contrary to Congress' intent that the rules assure fair, and effective shareholder suffrage. ... [T]o the degree the current rules inhibit the ability of shareholders not seeking proxy authority to analyze and discuss issues pertaining to the operation of a company and its performance, these rules may in fact run exactly contrary to the best interests of shareholders. [Final Proxy Rule Amendments, Exchange Act Release No. 31, 326, (transfer Binder) Fed. Sec. L. Rep. (CCH) para. 83,355 as cited in N.M. Sharara & A.E. Hoke-Witherspoon, *The Evolution of the 1992 Shareholder Communication Proxy Rules and Their Impact on Corporate Governance*, 49 Bus. Lawyer 327 (1993)]

The revised rules also allow shareholders to announce publicly how they intend to vote, along with reasons for their intended vote, without triggering the proxy solicitation requirements. SEC Rule 14a-1(l)(2)(iv)(a). The revised rules also allow a shareholder to communicate with other shareholders without triggering the proxy solicitation requirements if the person is not seeking proxy authority. There are limitations on this exemption from the proxy solicitation requirements. Certain persons are not entitled to the exemption, such as the corporation and its affiliates, an officer or director of the corporation engaging in a solicitation, any nominee for the position of director with respect to whom proxies are being solicited, any person seeking to oppose a merger, recapitalization, reorganization, sale of assets or other extraordinary transaction approved by the directors of the corporation where the person intends to propose an alternative transaction, and any person who, "because of a substantial interest in the subject matter of the solicitation, is likely to receive a benefit from a successful solicitation that would not be shared *pro rata* by all other holders of the same class of securities." See SEC Rule 14a-2(b)(1). The list of non-exempt persons does not include most institutional and individual investors who thus have a freer reign than under the former rules to communicate with other shareholders for the purpose of expressing concerns about management performance or other issues concerning the corporation.

There is also a notice requirement where a written soliciation is made and the person making the solicitation beneficially owns over $5 million worth of shares of the class which are the subject of the written solicitation. See SEC Rule 14a-6(g)(1). Where the notice requirement applies the written solicitation material must be filed with the S.E.C. and with each national securities exchange on which the shares are listed. The notice requirement does not apply to oral solicitations, speeches delivered in a public forum, press releases, published or broadcast opinions, statements, or advertisements in broadcast media, newspapers or magazines. SEC Rule 14a-6(g)(2). According to the S.E.C., written commications were subject to the notice requirement while oral communications were not because written communications are longer and more complex and can be republished while the burden of recording and filing an oral communication is greater than for written communications.

Changes to the proxy solicitation rules allegedly came about in the United States in response to changes in the market and the nature of corporate governance. Institutional investors were continuing to grow in size and importance in capital markets. The size of institutional investor holdings also made it difficult for them to unload their shares in particular corporations without having a negative impact on the price of the shares. Consequently, institutional investors often found themselves stuck with their investments in particular corporations and thus had a greater desire to have a say in how the corporations were managed. At the same time corporate managers had become increasingly immune from take-overs with the adoption and acceptance of certain poison pill take-over defences and the enactment of state anti-take-over statutes. This made the institutional investor desire to have increased say in corporate governance that much stronger. However, features of corporate and securities laws, and the legal regime in which institutional investors operate, make it difficult for institutions to respond to inefficient management performance. Pressure from insitutional investors to address these concerns appear to have led to changes in the proxy solicitation rules. On the problems faced by institutional investors in having a stronger say in corporate management see, e.g., B.S. Black, *Shareholder Passivity Reexamined*, 89 Mich. L.R. 520 (1990); M.J. Roe, *A Political Theory of American Corporate Finance*, 91 Col. L.R. 10 (1991); and A.F. Conrad, *Beyond Managerialism: Investor Capitalism?* 22 Univ. Mich. J.L. Ref. 117 (1988).

The changes in the proxy solicitation rules are said to have led to an increased influence by shareholders in the shareholder meeting. See R.S. Frenchman, *The Recent Revisions to Federal Regulations: Lifting the Ban on Shareholder Communications*, 68 Tulane L.R. 161, 180 (n. 128) (1993). However, there continues to be concern that giving reasons as to why a shareholder plans to vote a certain way will be construed as a "solicitation" on the basis that it will amount to a communication to security holders "under circumstances reasonably calculated to result in the procurement of a proxy." Subject to judicial clarification or clarification from the S.E.C., this uncertainty is said to cause a continued chilling effect on shareholder communications. See N.M. Sharara & A.E. Hoke-Witherspoon, *The Evolution of the 1992 Shareholder Communication Proxy Rules and Their Impact on Corporate Governance*, 49 Bus. Lawyer 327 (1993). For other comments on the revised S.E.C. proxy rules see, e.g., B.S. Black, *Next Steps in Proxy Reform*, 18 J. of Corp. L. 1 (1992); J.A. Hornstein, *Proxy Solicitation Redefined:*

The SEC Takes an Incremental Step Toward Effective Corporate Governance, 71 Wash. Univ. Law Quarterly 1129 (1993); C. Goforth, *Proxy Reform as a Means of Increasing Shareholder Participation in Corporate Governance: Too Little, But Not Too Late*, 43 Am. Univ. L.R. 379 (1994).

6. Adequacy of Disclosure

When a widely held corporation solicits proxies for a shareholders' meeting, it must comply with three separate statutory disclosure standards. First, it must give shareholders sufficient information of "special business" to permit a "reasoned judgment" to be formed thereon. CBCA s. 135(6). See also ABCA s. 129(7); BCCA Form 24, Item 11; OBCA s. 96(6). All business transacted at a special meeting of shareholders and all business transacted at an annual meeting except consideration of the financial statements, auditor's report, election of directors and reappointment of the auditor is deemed to be "special business." CBCA s. 135(5). See also ABCA s. 129(6); BCCA Table A, Part 8.1; OBCA s. 96(5). Second, a similar "materiality" requirement is imposed on management when it solicits proxies, with the general requirement in CBCA Reg. s. 35(jj) that "the substance of each such matter or group of related matters" be disclosed "in sufficient detail to permit shareholders to form a reasoned judgment concerning the matter." Finally, CBCA Reg. ss. 32-43 (and OSA Form 30) prescribe detailed disclosure of certain items, whether or not they might be considered material under s. 35(jj). See also ASA Form 30; BCCA Form 24.

Materiality Standards. Even prior to statutory disclosure requirements, courts sought to ensure that adequate disclosure was provided to shareholders by nullifying the effects of a shareholders' meeting where inadequate disclosure had been made to them. The judicial principle of notice has now been codified, but the pre-statute decisions are still of interest with respect to the definition of materiality. The leading such decision is *Pacific Coast Coal Mines Ltd. v. Arbuthnot*, [1917] A.C. 607 (P.C.), where there was a falling out between two groups of Pacific shareholders, each of whom held large blocks of shares. The group based in New York brought suit against the British Columbia group, which was in control of the corporation and against which allegations of serious breaches of fiduciary duty were made. In order to settle the litigation, the parties agreed that the British Columbia group should retire from management and should be given debentures in lieu of their shares. A shareholders' meeting was called to approve the capital restructuring required to carry out the agreement, and approval by the requisite majority was secured. However, it was held that the shareholder approval was invalid since the notice of the shareholders' meeting failed to reveal that debentures were to be issued to the British Columbia group, and that completion of the transaction would extinguish any claims of the corporation against the British Columbia group for mismanagement. Viscount Haldane said:

Their Lordships are of opinion that to render the notice a compliance with the Act under which it was given it ought to have told the shareholders, including those who gave proxies, more than it did. It ought to have put them in a position in which each of them could have judged for himself whether he would consent, not only to buying out the shares of directors, but to releasing possible claims against them. Now this is just what it did not do, and therefore, quite apart from the fact that the meeting was held in half an hour from the time the Act passed and before the shareholders could have had a proper opportunity of learning the particulars of what the legislature had authorized, their Lordships are of opinion that the notice was bad, and that what was done was consequently ultra vires. [*Id.* at 618]

In reviewing the adequacy of disclosure, should information that likely would not have altered the result of the vote had it been disclosed be found immaterial? If the standard of adequacy of disclosure is unrelated to whether disclosure might have affected the outcome of the vote, then the circular would be very long indeed. Could *any* information concerning the corporation safely be omitted under such a standard?

A notice of meeting was struck down in *Garvie v. Axmith*, [1962] O.R. 65, notwithstanding that the omitted disclosure would likely have had no effect on the outcome of the vote. Plaintiff was a shareholder of Rockwin Mines Ltd., which proposed to purchase all of the assets of Trans-Canada Explorations Ltd. In soliciting shareholder approval of the transaction, Rockwin provided its shareholders with the financial statements of both corporations. However, these did not permit shareholders to understand how Rockwin had arrived at the ratios according to which shares of the old enterprises would be exchanged for shares of the new combined enterprise. Pursuant to the reorganization, 10 old shares of Rockwin would be exchanged for one new share of the combined enterprise, with 2 1/4 Trans-Canada shares being exchanged for one new share. However, the book value of the shares, according to the financial statements presented to shareholders, indicated that 10 Rockwin shares were worth $4.08, while 2 1/4 Trans-Canada shares were worth $3.04, and shareholders could not have guessed how the same valuation was given to the two blocks of shares. According to the information available to them, the Rockwin shareholders would then have concluded that the transaction was a better deal for Trans-Canada shareholders than for themselves. The reorganization was nevertheless approved by the Rockwin shareholders, and plaintiff sued to enjoin it on the basis that proper notice had not been given to them. The injunction was granted, even though Rockwin shareholders had overwhelmingly approved the transaction, which looked far less attractive to them than it would have based on the method of evaluation used by the directors and which Spence J. said should have been supplied to the shareholders. Was the disclosure in *Garvie* so inadequate that concerns about causation might reasonably be discounted? In what sense can information be said to be material if it cannot be expected to have an effect on the vote? Should information be held material under OSA s. 1(1) if disclosure could reasonably be expected to have an effect on the market price of the securities, even if the shareholder's vote would be unaffected? If so, proxy disclosure would itself be a proxy for disclosure to the market, with attention shifting beyond the vote by shareholders to "fraud on the market," where the loss is one suffered by traders in a market from which information is withheld.

A less rigorous standard of materiality was applied in *Wotherspoon v. Canadian Pacific Ltd.* (1982), 35 O.R. (2d) 449, 483-91 (C.A.), aff'd (1987), 39 D.L.R. (4th) 169, 232-33 (S.C.C.). Plaintiff, a minority shareholder of the Ontario and Quebec Railway Co. (O & Q), sought to have the result of an O & Q shareholders' meeting set aside on the grounds of inadequacy of notice. Eighty percent of O & Q's shares were owned by CP, and the O & Q meeting had been called to secure shareholder approval of the sale of certain parcels of real estate by O & Q to a wholly owned subsidiary of CP (Marathon). The notice of meeting stated that the transaction price, $8.8 million dollars, was "somewhat in excess" of the values of the properties according to appraisals done for O & Q. The gist of the complaint was that, while that was indeed true, the appraisals themselves, consisting of lengthy reports, were not, but should have been, provided to the O & Q shareholders. Furthermore, the O & Q shareholders were not told that appraisals had been obtained for Marathon that were substantially higher (the reported judgments do not state how much higher) than the O & Q appraisals. However, the Court of Appeal held that the disclosure was adequate on the basis that the price had been found to be fair by the trial Court and that the appraisal reports were too voluminous to be sent to O & Q shareholders. This decision was affirmed by the Supreme Court.

A basis for a more rigorous standard was provided in the following case.

Mills v. Electric Auto-Lite Co.
United States Supreme Court
396 U.S. 375 (1970)

MR. JUSTICE HARLAN delivered the opinion of the Court.

I

Petitioners were shareholders of the Electric Auto-Lite Company until 1963, when it was merged into Mergenthaler Linotype Company. They brought suit on the day before the shareholders' meeting at which the vote was to take place on the merger, against Auto-Lite, Mergenthaler, and a third company, American Manufacturing Company, Inc. The complaint sought an injunction against the voting by Auto-Lite's management of all proxies obtained by means of an allegedly misleading proxy solicitation; however, it did not seek a temporary restraining order, and the voting went ahead as scheduled the following day. Several months later petitioners filed an amended complaint, seeking to have the merger set aside and to obtain such other relief as might be proper.

In Count II of the amended complaint, which is the only count before us, petitioners predicated jurisdiction on § 27 of the 1934 Act, 15 U.S.C. § 78aa. They alleged that the proxy statement sent out by the Auto-Lite management to solicit shareholders' votes in favor of the merger was misleading, in violation of § 14(a) of the Act and SEC Rule 14a-9 thereunder. (17 CFR § 240.14a-9). Petitioners recited that before the merger Mergenthaler owned over 50% of the outstanding shares of Auto-Lite common stock, and had been in control of Auto-Lite for two years. American Manufacturing in turn owned about one-third of the outstanding shares of Mergenthaler, and for two years had been in voting control of Mergenthaler and, through it, of Auto-Lite. Petitioners charged that in light of these circumstances the proxy statement was misleading in that it told Auto-Lite shareholders that their board of directors recommended approval of the merger without also informing them that all 11 of Auto-Lite's directors were nominees of Mergenthaler and were under the "control and domination of Mergenthaler." Petitioners asserted the right to complain of this alleged violation both derivatively on behalf of Auto-Lite and as representatives of the class of all its minority shareholders.

On petitioners' motion for summary judgment with respect to Count II, the District Court for the Northern District of Illinois ruled as a matter of law that the claimed defect in the proxy statement was, in light of the circumstances in which the statement was made, a material omission. The District Court concluded, from its reading of the *Borak* opinion, that it had to hold a hearing on the issue whether there was "a causal connection between the finding that there has been a violation of the disclosure requirements of § 14 (a) and the alleged injury to the plaintiffs" before it could consider what remedies would be appropriate. (Unreported opinion dated February 14, 1966.)

After holding such a hearing, the court found that under the terms of the merger agreement, an affirmative vote of two-thirds of the Auto-Lite shares was required for approval of the merger, and that the respondent companies owned and controlled about 54% of the outstanding shares. Therefore, to obtain authorization of the merger, respondents had to secure the approval of a substantial number of the minority shareholders. At the stockholders' meeting, approximately 950,000 shares, out of 1,160,000 shares outstanding, were voted in favor of the merger. This included 317,000 votes obtained by proxy from the minority shareholders, votes that were "necessary and indispensable to the approval of the merger." The District Court concluded that a causal relationship had thus been shown, and it granted an interlocutory judgment in favor of petitioners on the issue of liability, referring the case to a master for consideration of appropriate relief. (Unreported findings and conclusions dated Sept. 26, 1967; opinion reported at 281 F. Supp. 826 (1967).)

The District Court made the certification required by 28 U.S.C. § 1292 (b), and respondents took an interlocutory appeal to the Court of Appeals for the Seventh Circuit. That court affirmed the District Court's conclusion that the proxy statement was materially deficient, but reversed on the question of causation. The court acknowledged that, if an injunction had been sought a sufficient time before the stockholders' meeting, "corrective measures would have been appropriate." 403 F.2d 429, 435 (1968). However, since this suit was brought too late for preventive action, the courts had to determine "whether the misleading statement and omission caused the submission of sufficient proxies," as a prerequisite to a determination of liability under the Act. If the respondents could show, "by a preponderance of probabilities, that the merger would have received a sufficient vote even if the proxy statement had not been misleading in the respect found," petitioners would be entitled to no relief of any kind. *Id.*, at 436.

The Court of Appeals acknowledged that this test corresponds to the common-law fraud test of whether the injured party relied on the misrepresentation. However, rightly concluding that "[r]eliance by thousands of individuals, as here, can scarcely be inquired into" (*id.*, at 436 n. 10), the court ruled that the issue was to be determined by proof of the fairness of the terms of the merger. If respondents could show that the merger had merit and was fair to the minority shareholders, the trial court would be justified in concluding that a sufficient number of shareholders would have approved the merger had there been no deficiency in the proxy statement. In that case respondents would be entitled to a judgment in their favor.

Claiming that the Court of Appeals has construed this Court's decision in *Borak* in a manner that frustrates the statute's policy of enforcement through private litigation, the petitioners then sought review in this Court. We granted certiorari, 394 U.S. 971 (1969), believing that resolution of this basic issue should be made at this stage of the litigation and not postponed until after a trial under the Court of Appeals' decision.[4]

II

As we stressed in *Borak*, § 14(a) stemmed from a congressional belief that "[f]air corporate suffrage is an important right that should attach to every equity security bought on a public exchange." H.R. Rep. No. 1383, 73d Cong., 2d Sess., 13. The provision was intended to promote "the free exercise of the voting rights of stockholders" by ensuring that proxies would be solicited with "explanation to the stockholder of the real nature of the questions for which authority to cast his vote is sought." *Id.*, at 14; S. Rep. No. 792, 73d Cong., 2d Sess., 12; see 377 U.S., at 431. The decision below, by permitting all liability to be foreclosed on the basis of a finding that the merger was fair, would allow the stockholders to be bypassed, at least where the only legal challenge to the merger is a suit for a retrospective relief after the meeting has been held. A judicial appraisal of the merger's merits could be substituted for the actual and informed vote of the stockholders.

The result would be to insulate from private redress an entire category of proxy violations—those relating to matters other than the terms of the merger. Even outrageous misrepresentations in a proxy solicitation, if they did not relate to the terms of the transaction, would give rise to no cause of action under § 14(a). Particularly if carried over to enforcement actions by the Securities and Exchange Commission itself, such a result would subvert the congressional purpose of ensuring full and fair disclosure to shareholders.

Further, recognition of the fairness of the merger as a complete defense would confront small shareholders with an additional obstacle to making a successful challenge to a proposal recommended through a defective proxy statement. The risk that they would be unable to rebut the corporation's evidence of the fairness of the proposal, and thus to establish their cause of action, would be bound to discourage such shareholders from the private enforcement of the proxy rules that "provides a necessary supplement to Commission action." *J.I. Case Co. v. Borak*, 377 U.S., at 432.[5]

• • •

---

4   Respondents ask this court to review the conclusion of the lower courts that the proxy statement was misleading in a material repsect. Petitioners naturally did not raise this question in their petition for certiorari, and respondents filed no cross-petition. Since reversal of the Court of Appeals' ruling on this question would not dictate affirmance of that court's judgment, which remanded the case for proceedings to determine causation, but rather elimination of petitioners' rights thereunder, we will not consider the question in these circumstances.

5   The Court of Appeals' ruling that "causation" may be negated by proof of the fairness of the merger also rests on a dubious behavioral assumption. There is no justification for presuming that the share-

(The footnote is continued on the next page.)

Where the misstatement or omission in a proxy statement has been shown to be "material," as it was found to be here, that determination itself indubitably embodies a conclusion that the defect was of such a character that it might have been considered important by a reasonable shareholder who was in the process of deciding how to vote. This requirement that the defect have a significant *propensity* to affect the voting process is found in the express terms of Rule 14a-9, and it adequately serves the purpose of ensuring that a cause of action cannot be established by proof of a defect so trivial, or so unrelated to the transaction for which approval is sought, that correction of the defect or imposition of liability would not further the interests protected by § 14(a).

There is no need to supplement this requirement, as did the Court of Appeals, with a requirement of proof of whether the defect actually had a decisive effect on the voting. Where there has been a finding of materiality, a shareholder has made a sufficient showing of causal relationship between the violation and the injury for which he seeks redress if, as here, he proves that the proxy solicitation itself, rather than the particular defect in the solicitation materials, was an essential link in the accomplishment of the transaction. This objective test will avoid the impracticalities of determining how many votes were affected, and, by resolving doubts in favor of those the statute is designed to protect, will effectuate the congressional policy of ensuring that the shareholders are able to make an informed choice when they are consulted on corporate transactions. Cf. *Union Pac. R. Co. v. Chicago & N.W.R. Co.*, 226 F. Supp. 400, 411 (D.C.N.D. Ill. 1964); 2 L. Loss, *Securities Regulation* 962 n. 411 (2d ed. 1961); 5 *id.*, at 2929-2930 (Supp. 1969).[7]

III

Our conclusion that petitioners have established their case by showing that proxies necessary to approval of the merger were obtained by means of a materially misleading

---

5 Continued ...

holders of every corporation are willing to accept any and every fair merger offer put before them; yet such a presumption is implicit in the opinion of the Court of Appeals. That court gave no indication of what evidence petitioners might adduce, once respondents had established that the merger proposal was equitable, in order to show that the shareholders would nevertheless have rejected it if the solicitation had not been misleading. Proof of actual reliance by thousands of individuals would, as the court acknowledged, not be feasible, see R. Jennings & H. Marsh, *Securities Regulation, Cases and Materials* 1001 (2d ed. 1968) and reliance on the *nondisclosure* of a fact is a particularly difficult matter to define or prove, see 3 L. Loss, Securities Regulation 1766 (2d ed. 1961). In practice, therefore, the objective fairness of the proposal would seemingly be determinative of liability. But, in view of the many other factors that might lead shareholders to prefer their current position to that of owners of a larger, combined enterprise, it is pure conjecture to assume that the fairness of the proposal will always be determinative of their vote. Cf. *Wirtz v. Hotel, Motel & Club Employees Union*, 391 U.S. 492, 508 (1968).

7 We need not decide in this cas whether causation could be shown where the management controls a sufficient number of shares to approve the transaction without any votes from the minority. Even in that situation, if the management finds it necessary for legal or practical reasons to solicit proxies from minority shareholders, at least one court has held that the proxy solicitation might be sufficiently related to the merger to satisfy the causation requirement, ...

solicitation implies nothing about the form of relief to which they may be entitled. We held in *Borak* that upon finding a violation the courts were "to be alert to provide such remedies as are necessary to make effective the congressional purpose," noting specifically that such remedies are not to be limited to prospective relief. 377 U.S., at 433, 434. In devising retrospective relief for violation of the proxy rules, the federal courts should consider the same factors that would govern the relief granted for any similar illegality or fraud. One important factor may be the fairness of the terms of the merger. Possible forms of relief will include setting aside the merger or granting other equitable relief, but, as the Court of Appeals below noted, nothing in the statutory policy "requires the court to unscramble a corporate transaction merely because a violation occurred." 403 F.2d, at 436. In selecting a remedy the lower courts should exercise "the sound discretion which guides the determinations of courts of equity," keeping in mind the role of equity as "the instrument for nice adjustment and reconciliation between the public interest and private needs as well as between competing private claims." *Hecht Co. v. Bowles*, 321 U.S. 321, 329-330 (1944), quoting from *Meredith v. Winter Haven*, 320 U.S. 228, 235 (1943).

• • •

Monetary relief will, of course, also be a possibility. Where the defect in the proxy solicitation relates to the specific terms of the merger, the district court might appropriately order an accounting to ensure that the shareholders receive the value that was represented as coming to them. On the other hand, where, as here, the misleading aspect of the solicitation did not relate to terms of the merger, monetary relief might be afforded to the shareholders only if the merger resulted in a reduction of the earnings or earnings potential of their holdings. In short, damages should be recoverable only to the extent that they can be shown. If commingling of the assets and operations of the merged companies makes it impossible to establish direct injury from the merger, relief might be predicated on a determination of the fairness of the terms of the merger at the time it was approved. These questions, of course, are for decision in the first instance by the District Court on remand, and our singling out of some of the possibilities is not intended to exclude others.

• • •

For the foregoing reasons we conclude that the judgment of the Court of Appeals should be vacated and the case remanded to that court for further proceedings consistent with this opinion.

It is so ordered.

NOTES

Upon the remand of *Mills*, the trial Court found the terms of the merger to have been unfair. It did not order the merger undone, but instead awarded substantial monetary damages. The Court of Appeals reversed, holding that the terms of the merger were fair and that the plaintiff had been, if anything, overcompensated. 552 F.2d 1239 (7th Cir.), cert. denied, 434 U.S. 922 (1977). As a consequence, it took seven years to determine that a cause of action existed, and a further seven years to determine that no damages would be awarded. Is this an argument for denying a cause of action in cases where the Court determines that the transaction is fair, as the Ontario Court of Appeal did in *Wotherspoon*?

Could the finding that materiality standards had not been satisfied be justified on a "fraud-on-the-market" theory? Under the "fraud-on-the-market" theory the investor is presumed to have relied on a misrepresentation where the misrepresentation would have affected the price of the shares given the efficiency of the market. In *Mills*, unlike *Garvie*, the omitted fact was one that market professionals must have been well aware of. An explicit disclosure that the Auto-Lite board was controlled by Mergenthaler would have been unlikely to have had a significant effect on Auto-Lite's stock price, the test of materiality for prospectus disclosure under OSA s. 1(1).

The *Mills* disclosure standard has subsequently been narrowed, as discussed in the following case.

Harris v. Universal Explorations Ltd.
Alberta Court of Appeal
(1982), 17 B.L.R. 135

[Before MOIR, KERANS and STEVENSON JJ.A.]

KERANS J.A.: This is an appeal from an order by Miller J. approving an amalgamation, pursuant to s. 156(8) of the Companies Act, R.S.A. 1970, c. 60, between two Alberta companies.

• • •

Upon the application it was the duty of the learned Chambers Judge to approve or not the amalgamation agreement. The statute directs that he was to have regard to "the rights and interests of all parties including the dissentient shareholders and creditors" [s. 156(8)].

There was much discussion before us as to the extent of this responsibility. But, it was common ground that he be satisfied that there had been compliance with the principle stated in item 10 in Form 3 to Reg. 227/67 which is enacted under s. 144 of The Companies Act. This provides in part that:

If action is to be taken on any matter to be submitted to the meeting of shareholders ... the substance of each such matter, or related groups of matters, should be briefly described, ... in sufficient detail to permit shareholders to form a reasoned judgment concerning any such matter.

The question arises what is the proper test for sufficient detail. In our view, the answer was supplied by the Supreme Court of Canada in *Rathie v. Montreal Trust Co.*, [1953] 2 S.C.R. 204, [1953] 4 D.L.R. 289 where, at p. 213 [S.C.R.], Mr. Justice Rand speaks of the need to supply to the shareholders "... the controlling facts ... to enable them to come to a decision one way or the other." What is a controlling fact? In this regard we adopt the statement by Marshall J. in the Supreme Court of the United States in *T.S.C. Indust Inc. v. Northway Inc.*, CCH Fed. Sec. L. Rep. ¶90,069 U.S.S.C., June 14, 1976, where he says:

Some information is of such dubious significance that insistence on its disclosure may accomplish more harm than good. The potential liability for a Rule 14A-9 violation [apparently similar to that under consideration] can be great indeed, and if the standard of materiality is unnecessarily low, not only may the corporation and its management be subjected to liability for insignificant omissions or mis-statements, but also management's fear of exposing itself to substantial liability may cause it simply to bury the shareholder in an avalanche of trivial information—a result that is hardly conducive to informed decision-making. Precisely these dangers are presented, we think, [by] the definition of a material fact adopted by the Court of Appeals in this case—a fact which a reasonable shareholder *might* consider important. ... The general standard of materiality which we think best comports with the policies of Rule 14A-9 is as follows: an omitted fact is material if there is a substantial likelihood that a reasonable shareholder would consider it important in deciding how to vote.

We now turn to the information circular before us. This circular proposes an amalgamation based on a share ratio of four shares in the new company for each share in Petrol, one of the amalgamated companies, and one share in the amalgamated company for each share in Universal, the other amalgamated company. The applicants (appellants here dissentient shareholders on the merger) are shareholders in Petrol. They rightly assert that they, and all shareholders in Petrol, have a right to be told all facts respecting which it might be said that there is a substantial likelihood that a reasonable Petrol shareholder would consider the fact important in deciding how to vote. Moreover, they had a right to be told accurately, or as this Court said in *Norcan* [*Fogler v. Norcan Oils Ltd.* (1964), 47 W.W.R. 257, 43 D.L.R. (2d) 508, reversed (sub nom. *Norcan Oils Ltd. v. Fogler*) [1965] S.C.R. 36, 49 W.W.R. 321, 46 D.L.R. (2d) 630] "candidly."

The purpose of the information circular was to explain to the shareholders how the directors (the majority of whom are common to both companies and not at arm's length) settled on the proposed share ratios. The circular says:

The share exchange ratios were negotiated on the basis of many factors after receiving input from the directors of Universal and Petrol, examination of *independent valuations* of Universal and Petrol, examination of the respective market values, consideration of the Western Decalta Petroleum (1977) Ltd. and Universal Explorations Ltd. agreement, and in consultation with Wood Gundy Ltd. Wood Gundy Ltd., after examinations subscribed in their letter attached hereto as Schedule B as well as the historical market prices of both Petrol and Universal shares, offered their opinion that the proposed exchange ratio for the amalgamation is fair and reasonable to the shareholders of both Petrol and Universal. Wood Gundy letter refers both to the history of prices of stock of the two companies on the stock market, but also to a study of the assets of the two companies.

Before us, it was argued that the comparative material before the learned Chambers Judge on the subject of stock exchange prices was sufficient to justify the proposed share ratios. In our view, the proponents of the amalgamation cannot, in view of the position taken in the information circular, be now heard to deny the materiality of an analysis of the value of the assets of the two companies. In any event, it was put to the shareholders that this analysis was one reasonable means to support the proposal. In companies in the resource ownership field, this would appear to be important. It therefore is material.

The preliminary comment about the comparative analysis of the assets of the two companies begins with this statement:

A comparative valuation of the net assets has been carried out using the following material:

(i) an evaluation of Universal's oil and gas reserves and undeveloped acreage prepared by D & S Petroleum Consultants (1974) Ltd. and dated July 1, 1981;

(ii) an evaluation of Universal's Jackson Lovett Hill placer gold project prepared in February 1981 by Colt Engineering Corporation;

(iii) an evaluation of Universal Gas (Montana) Inc's Monarch gold deposit prepared by Tetreau & Associates Ltd. and dated January 1, 1981;

(iv) an evaluation of Petro[l]'s Canadian oil and gas reserves prepared by McDaniel & Associates Consultants Ltd. and dated December 31, 1980.

In our view, a fair reading of the information circular leads one inevitably to the conclusion that this statement was inserted to offer assurance to the shareholders that the values thereafter expressed had been fixed by independent experts.

We are of the view that there is a substantial likelihood that a reasonable shareholder would consider it important in deciding how to vote whether the valuations had been fixed by independent experts in a case where, as here, a majority of the shares in Petrol were already owned by Universal and where the majority of the board of directors were common to both companies and where, therefore, it could be said that the transaction was not at arm's length.

Before the learned Chambers Judge, it became clear that the "evaluation" of Universal's placer gold project prepared in February 1981 by Colt Engineering Corporation was in fact an analysis of the mining operation of Universal. Universal had started a project of placer mining of old gravel tailings in the Yukon. This project was analyzed by Colt. The general thrust of the report is an analysis from an operational point of view: it makes certain suggestions for improved operations and comments on the economic viability of the project. It in no way attempts to put a market value on the project, or settle or value the ore reserves. On the contrary, it recommends some effort be made to establish the reserves. In this context, there is appended a projection of future revenues based on an assumption as to future rises in the price of gold and other assumptions. The projected profit on these assumptions is then capitalized, that is given a present value. This present value is inserted in the pro forma balance sheet of the amalgamated company as the value of the "project" for the purposes of the amalgamation. The learned Chambers Judge describes the Colt report in these words [at pp. 210-11 B.L.R.]:

It would appear that prior to February 1981 a company called Colt Engineering Ltd. was retained by Unex to make a "study" of the 1980 operation of the Jackson-Lovett Hill Placer gold project. They completed their work and submitted a written report in February of 1981. Their recommendations and conclusions were based on certain assumptions and information supplied to Colt by Unex, one of which was an assumption that there was a ten-year supply of ore available at the site. Colt did not attempt to verify this information and so referred to this fact in their report. A table of calculations is part of the Colt report and it indicates that, if the assumptions are accurate, the present worth of this property could be from $8,000,000 to $10,000,000 and Unex's 50% share would be half of this figure.

In our view, the Colt report is not an independent and expert valuation of this asset. Indeed, when Colt discovered that its report had been used as a basis for an evaluation, they wrote a letter of protest.

In our view, the fact that the Colt report was not an independent and expert attempt to value the property, and that any valuation contained therein was only incidental to its main purpose is a material fact having regard to the suggestion, implicit if not explicit in the information circular, that the report is something other than what it is. In our view, this information is the sort of information that a shareholder would consider important in deciding how to vote. In other words, we are not saying that it is necessary in an information circular to produce independent valuations. But, if it is sought to leave the impression with the shareholders that the figures used are based on valuations by independent experts, this must be true.

The learned Chambers Judge dealt at some length with this problem. He says [at pp. 211-12]:

I am satisfied that the use and description of the material and the work done by Colt and Tetreau could have been more accurately described in the joint information circular, and with the benefit of hindsight, no doubt Mr. Buchanan wishes he had done so. However that, to my mind, is not the crucial issue. Much seems to turn around the meaning to be ascribed to the word "evaluation." If there is some special meaning or custom to be attached to this [word] in the context of an information circular, the same was not brought to my attention by counsel. Failing some well-established usage of the trade or custom, I can only assume that the word is to be given its normal, everyday meaning.

Webster's Third New International Dictionary defines the term "evaluation" to be: "A judgment, appraisal, rating, interpretation. ..."

It seems to me that the work done by Colt Engineering Ltd. and Tetreau & Associates Ltd. could fall under one or more of these headings, forming part of a judgment, appraisal, rating or interpretation of some of the items that must be considered in arriving at a guesstimate of the value of the gold mining properties.

With respect, we disagree. In the context in which it is found, the word means, as we have said, much more than that. It must be taken as a statement that there have been independent expert evaluations.

Further, the learned Chambers Judge says [at p. 213]:

In general I found the joint information circular to be quite straightforward and intelligible even for a relatively unsophisticated shareholder. It appears to comply with the statutory requirements. I am not prepared to find that the misdescription of the Colt and Tetreau material was sufficient to render the whole document such that a shareholder would have been prevented from forming a reasoned opinion as to whether the proposal was, or was not, in his best interests. The dissentient shareholders have failed to meet the burden thrust upon them to rebut the initial presumption of reasonable disclosure.

We cannot agree, for the reasons we have already given. The learned Chambers Judge also says [at p. 212]:

There is no evidence that, prior to the meeting, any shareholders of either company examined the Colt and Tetreau material and was misled by it or objected to it being used as some basis for placing a value on the gold properties.

This is not the correct test. The correct test is not whether somebody in fact was misled but whether there is a substantial likelihood that someone was misled by the appellant.

The misdescription of the support for the value might be excused as immaterial if the actual figures are demonstrably correct. But, here, the figures are open to serious attack. There are allegations of double counting which could result in errors of more than $5,000,000. There are other criticisms. We have not been satisfied that the figures supplied to the shareholders are necessarily correct, and we note that the learned Chambers Judge made no such finding. On the contrary, he sought to avoid the issue.

He sought to avoid such a finding by going on to consider that, in any event, the proposal was a fair one and the Petrol shareholders would receive full value on an amalgamation because the 4:1 share ratio was generous and even if the property in question was treated as having no value at all the proposed share ratio would be fair. In our view, this is an error. The accuracy of the information circular is a threshold issue; one cannot validate an agreement in respect of which the voting shareholders might reasonably have been misled on a point where there was a substantial likelihood of their relying on the misinformation. Indeed, the very fact of some misdescription would be of significance to a shareholder as reflecting on the reliability of the whole proposal.

Therefore, without passing on the question whether or not this was a fair offer, we are of the view that the information circular was in breach of the required duty and, therefore, the proposal cannot be approved.

We accordingly set aside the decision of the learned Chambers Judge and make an order that the application is dismissed with costs here and in Chambers. ...

Appeal allowed.

NOTES

1) After the *Harris* decision was rendered, a new meeting of Petrol shareholders was called. Again the requisite majority approved the amalgamation, and again the Court withheld approval. This time the notice of meeting was found to be inadequate because the balance sheets provided to the shareholders were out of date. *Re Universal Explorations Ltd.*, [1983] 1 W.W.R. 542 (Alta). According to reports in the financial press, the amalgamation was finally consummated in November 1983.

2) The remainder of the paragraph from *TSC Industries Inc. v. Northway Inc.*, 426 U.S. 438, 449 (1976), quoted by Kerans J.A. in Harris is as follows:

This standard is fully consistent with *Mills's* [*Mills v. Electric Auto-Line Co.*, 396 U.S. 375 (1970)] general description of materiality as a requirement that "the defect have a significant propensity to affect the voting process." It does not require proof of a substantial likelihood that disclosure of the omitted fact would have caused the reasonable investor to change his vote. What the standard does contemplate is a showing of a substantial likelihood that, under all the circumstances, the omitted fact would have assumed actual significance in the deliberations of the reasonable shareholder. Put another way, there must be a substantial likelihood that the disclosure of the omitted fact would have been viewed by the reasonable investor as having significantly altered the "total mix" of information made available.

The Express Statutory Remedy. An express statutory remedy for non-disclosure in a proxy circular is provided by CBCA s. 154, which permits an "interested person" to apply to court for a restraining order where a form of proxy or a management or dissident proxy circular "makes an untrue statement of a material fact or omits to state a material fact required therein or necessary to make a statement contained therein not misleading." See also ABCA s. 240; OBCA s. 253.

Would this provision be applicable in cases such as *Brown v. Duby*, where the dissidents did not prepare a form of proxy or proxy circular? In that case an implied civil cause of action was recognized in favour of both the corporation for whose meeting the proxies were being solicited and the individual plaintiff, without regard to remedies under s. 154. The Court did not specify whether the individual plaintiff's standing followed from his status as an officer who would likely be removed by the directors whom the dissidents would elect, or a shareholder, or both.

(a) *Limitation to Material Misstatements or Omissions*

CBCA s. 154 provides an express cause of action for non-disclosure in a proxy circular. However, the remedy exists only for misstatements and omissions that are material. It will be recalled that the CBCA requires disclosure of a considerable amount of information in Reg. ss. 32-43, not all of which may be determined to be material. Suppose, for example, that management omits to disclose the high and low sale prices for each quarterly period during the previous two years, as prescribed by CBCA Reg. s. 35(ff)(vii). This might not ordinarily seem a particularly important item of disclosure, and in any event the omitted disclosure would already be as public as any information could be. Is there, however, a risk that a court would find it material on the basis that, were it not so, it would not have been mandated by the regulations? What do you think of the absolutist argument that if *any* of the information prescribed by the regulations is omitted, the document is not a proxy circular, with the result that a corporation will be in breach of CBCA s. 150(1)(a) for soliciting proxies without a circular?

(b) *Remedies Other Than a Restraining Order*

Upon an application under s. 154, "the court may make any order it thinks fit." Could such an order include damages? If an interested person could bring a s. 154 application after the meeting to which the misleading proxy circulars related had been held, it is possible that substantial damages might be claimed.

How likely do you think it that a Canadian court would interpret the phrase "any other order it thinks fit" in s. 154 to include the power to unwind an amalgamation?

While the quoted phrase is said not to be limited to the list of specific orders which follows it, nonetheless the three types of relief listed are all prospective in operation.

An argument that an amalgamation should be set aside failed in *Norcan Oils Ltd. v. Fogler*, [1965] S.C.R. 36. Two Alberta corporations, Gridoil and Norcan, amalgamated under the Alberta Companies Act, which provided that the agreement had to be approved by three-fourths of the shareholders of each amalgamated corporation and then submitted for the approval of the court. Once these approvals had been obtained, the Registrar of Companies would issue a certificate of amalgamation. The shareholders of both Gridoil and Norcan approved the proposal by the requisite majorities, and the Court of Queen's Bench gave its approval over the objection of a minority Gridoil shareholder, who claimed that the information circular for the Gridoil shareholders meetings was materially defective in understating Gridoil's assets. The minority shareholder appealed, but the filing of the notice of appeal did not automatically stay the effectiveness of the order appealed from nor did the shareholder move for such a stay. The Registrar issued the certificate of amalgamation before the appeal was heard and the amalgamated entity entered into numerous transactions with third parties. The Alberta Appellate Division allowed the appeal on the basis that the Gridoil information circular was fatally defective. It ordered that the lower court order be set aside. The Supreme Court, per Martland J., allowed the appeal, reasoning that there was no judicial authority to revoke the certificate of amalgamation and that therefore the order of the Appellate Division setting aside that of the lower court was a nullity. (But see now ABCA s. 234(3)(j).) Spence J. dissented. He held that because the proxy materials were misleading the Appellate Division was correct in holding that the lower court order had been improperly made.

7. Access to Management's Proxy Soliciting Materials: Shareholder Proposals

Under CBCA s. 137 shareholders are entitled to submit proposals for consideration at shareholders meetings. See also ABCA s. 131; OBCA s. 99. Management is obligated to give notice of such a proposal in management's proxy soliciting materials and to include a brief statement in support of the proposal if the shareholder supplies such a statement. There is no corresponding provision under the BCCA. However, under the BCCA s. 171 shareholders owning 5% or more of the shares could requisition a meeting and would then be entitled (under BCCA s. 180) to put a 1,000-word statement in the proxy circular for the requisitioned meeting.

A well-heeled shareholder, or, more usually, a group of shareholders, doubtless would prefer to do his or its own soliciting in order to preserve an element of surprise and to avoid having the proposal go out in a single document with management's objections to it. Nonetheless, access to management's proxy circular can be very useful for shareholders without large amounts of funds. If management refuses to include a shareholder proposal in management's proxy soliciting materials, then the battle lines will be drawn around the issue of whether the particular proposal is one that falls within the class of proposals that can be excluded pursuant to s. 137(5) (ABCA s. 131(5); OBCA s. 99(5)).

The main class of proposals that a corporation is not required to include under s. 137(5) are those that are primarily for the purpose of enforcing a personal claim or

redressing a personal grievance against the corporation or its directors, officers or security holders, or primarily for the purpose of promoting general economic, political,
racial, religious, social or similar causes. The proposal can also be rejected by the
corporation if it is being used to secure publicity, is not submitted at least 90 days before
the anniversary date of the previous annual meeting, the corporation included a proposal
from the shareholder in the management proxy circular within the previous two years
and the shareholder failed to present the proposal at the meeting, or substantially the
same proposal was included in a proxy circular in the previous two years and the
proposal was defeated.

The following case considers this issue in the context of similar rules for excluding
shareholder proposals under the Securities Exchange Act in the United Sates.

Medical Committee for Human Rights v. Securities & Exchange Comm'n
United States Court of Appeals, District of Columbia Circuit
432 F.2d 659 (1970), vacated and dismissed as moot, 404 U.S. 403 (1972)

Before McGOWAN, TAMM, and ROBINSON, Circuit Judges.

TAMM C.J.: ... On March 11, 1968, Dr. Quentin D. Young, National Chairman of the
Medical Committee for Human Rights wrote to the Secretary of the Dow Chemical
Company, stating that the Medical Committee had obtained by gift several shares of
Dow stock and expressing concern regarding the company's manufacture of the chemi-
cal substance napalm. In part, Dr. Young's letter said:

After consultation with the executive body of the Medical Committee, I have been instructed to
request an amendment to the charter of our company, Dow Chemical. We have learned that we
are technically late in asking for an amendment at this date, but we wish to observe that it is a
matter of such great urgency that we think it is imperative not to delay until the shareholders'
meeting next year.

. . .

We respectfully propose the following wording to be sent to the shareholders:
"RESOLVED, that the shareholders of the Dow Chemical Company request the Board of Directors, in accordance with the laws of the State of Delaware, and the Composite Certificate
of Incorporation of the Dow Chemical Company, to adopt a resolution setting forth an
amendment to the Composite Certificate of Incorporation of the Dow Chemical Company
that napalm shall not be sold to any buyer unless that buyer gives reasonable assurance that
the substance will not be used on or against human beings."

(App. 1a–2a.) The letter concluded with the following statement:

Finally, we wish to note that our objections to the sale of this product [are] primarily based on the
concerns for human life inherent in our organization's credo. However, we are further informed
by our investment adviser that this product is also bad for our company's business as it is being
used in the Vietnamese War. It is now clear from company statements and press reports that it is
increasingly hard to recruit the highly intelligent, well-motivated. young college men so impor-

tant for company growth. There is, as well, an adverse impact on our global business, which our advisers indicate, suffers as a result of the public reaction to this product.

(App. 2a) Copies of this letter were forwarded to the President and the General Counsel of Dow Chemical Company, and to the Securities and Exchange Commission. (App. 3a.)

By letter dated March 21, 1968, the General Counsel of Dow Chemical replied to the Medical Committee's letter, stating that the proposal had arrived too late for inclusion in the 1968 proxy statement, but promising that the company would "study the matter and ... communicate with you later this year" regarding inclusion of the resolution in proxy materials circulated by management in 1969. (App. 4a.) Copies of this letter, and of all subsequent correspondence, were duly filed with the Commission.

The next significant item of record is a letter dated January 6, 1969, noting that the Medical Committee was "distressed that 1968 has passed without our having received a single word from you on this important matter," and again requesting that the resolution be included in management's 1969 proxy materials. (App. 7a-8a.) The Secretary of Dow Chemical replied to this letter on January 17, informing the Medical Committee that Dow intended to omit the resolution from its proxy statement and enclosing an opinion memorandum from Dow's General Counsel, the contents of which will be discussed in detail infra. (App. 9a-12a.) On February 3 the Medical Committee responded to Dow's General Counsel, asserting that he had misconstrued the nature of their proposal in his opinion memorandum, and averring that the Medical Committee would not "presume to serve as draftsmen for an amendment to the corporate charter." (App. 15a.) The letter continued:

We are willing to bend ... to your belief that the management should be allowed to decide to whom and under what circumstances it will sell its products. Nevertheless, we are certain that you would agree that the company's owners have not only the legal power but also the historic and economic obligation to determine what products their company will manufacture. Therefore, [we submit] ... our revised proposal ... requesting the Directors to consider the advisability of adopting an amendment to the corporate charter, forbidding the company to make napalm (any such amendment would, of course, be subject to the requirements of the "Defense Production Act of 1950," as are the corporate charters and management decisions of all United States Corporations), [and] we request that the following resolution be included in this year's proxy statement: "RESOLVED, that the shareholders of the Dow Chemical Company request that the Board of Directors, in accordance with the laws [sic] of the Dow Chemical Company, consider the advisability of adopting a resolution setting forth an amendment to the composite certificate of incorporation of the Dow Chemical Company that the company shall not make napalm."

(App. 16a.) On the same date, a letter was sent to the Securities and Exchange Commission, requesting a staff review of Dow's decision if it still intended to omit the proposal, and requesting oral argument before the Commission if the staff agreed with Dow. (App. 17a.)

On February 7, 1969, Dow transmitted to the Medical Committee and to the Commission a letter and memorandum opinion of Counsel, which in essence reiterated the previous arguments against inclusion of the proposal and stated the company's intention to omit it from the proxy statement (App. 18a-19a.) Shortly thereafter, on February 18,

1969, the Commission's Chief Counsel of the Division of Corporation Finance sent a letter to Dow, with copies to the Medical Committee, concluding that "[f]or reasons stated in your letter and the accompanying opinion of counsel, both dated January 17, 1969, this Division will not recommend any action ... if this proposal is omitted from the management's proxy material. ..." (App. 20a.) In a letter dated February 28—which contains the first indications of record that petitioners had retained counsel—the Medical Committee again renewed its request for a Commission review of the Division's decision. (App. 24a.) On the same day, the Medical Committee filed with the Commission a memorandum of legal arguments in support of its resolution, urging numerous errors of law in the Division's decision. (App. 26a-32a.) Several other documents were filed by both the company and the Medical Committee; finally, on April 2, 1969, both parties were informed that "[t]he Commission has approved the recommendation of the Division of Corporation Finance that no objection be raised if the Company omits the proposals from its proxy statements for the forthcoming meeting of shareholders." (App. 44a-45a.) The petitioners thereupon instituted the present action, and on July 10, 1969, the Commission moved to dismiss the petition for lack of jurisdiction. On October 13 we denied the motion "without prejudice to renewal thereof in the briefs and at the argument on the merits."

In its briefs and oral argument, the Commission has consistently and vigorously urged, to the exclusion of all other contentions, that this court is without jurisdiction to review its action. We find this argument unpersuasive.

[The Court's discussion of its jurisdiction to review the Commission's order has been omitted. The Commission urged strenuously that the petition for review was out of time and that its order lacked sufficient formality and finality to be susceptible of judicial review. The Court rejected these arguments. While it assumed, from the Supreme Court's opinion in *J.I. Case Co. v. Borak*, that the Medical Committee could bring suit against Dow asserting that the company had violated the rules for inclusion of shareholder proposals (without speculating upon the effect that the Commission's support of the company's position would have upon the likely success of such a suit), the Court held that it was likely to be cheaper and quicker, and therefore more consonant with the over-all legislative scheme, to give shareholders meaningful access to and review of the Commission's action in deciding not to compel management to include a particular shareholder proposal.]

The Medical Committee's sole substantive contention in this petition is that its proposed resolution could not, consistently with the Congressional intent underlying section 14(a), be properly deemed a proposal which is either motivated by *general* political and moral concerns, or related to the conduct of Dow's ordinary business operations. These criteria are two of the established exceptions to the general rule that management must include all properly submitted shareholder proposals in its proxy materials. They are contained in Rule 14a-8(c), 17 C.F.R. § 240.14a-8(c) (1970), which provides in relevant part:

... [M]anagement may omit a proposal ... from its proxy statement and form of proxy under any of the following circumstances:

...

(2) If it clearly appears that the proposal is submitted by the security holder ... primarily for the purpose of promoting general economic, political, racial, religious, social or similar causes; or
...
(5) If the proposal consists of a recommendation or request that the management take action with respect to a matter relating to the conduct of the ordinary business operations of the issuer.

Despite the fact that our October 13 order in this case deferred resolution of the jurisdictional issue pending full argument on the merits, the Commission has not deigned to address itself to any possible grounds for allowing management to exclude this proposal from its proxy statement. We confess to a similar puzzlement as to how the Commission reached the result which it did, and thus we are forced to remand the controversy for a more illuminating consideration and decision. Cf. *Environmental Defense Fund, Inc. v. Hardin*, supra. In aid of this consideration on remand, we feel constrained to explain our difficulties with the position taken by the company and endorsed by the Commission.

It is obvious to the point of banality to restate the proposition that Congress intended by its enactment of section 14 of the Securities Exchange Act of 1934 to give true vitality to the concept of corporate democracy. ...

In striving to implement this open-ended mandate, the Commission has gradually evolved its present proxy rules. Early exercises of the rule-making power were directed primarily toward the achievement of full and fair corporate disclosure regarding management proxy materials (see, e.g., 3 Fed. Reg. 1991 (1938); 5 Fed. Reg. 174 (1940)); the rationale underlying this development was the Commission's belief that the corporate practice of circulating proxy materials which failed to make reference to the fact that a shareholder intended to present a proposal at the annual meeting rendered the solicitation inherently misleading. See Hearings on Security and Exchange Commission Proxy Rules Before the House Comm. on Interstate and Foreign Commerce, 78th Cong., 1st Sess., pt. 1, at 169-170 (1943) [hereinafter "House Hearings"]. From this position, it was only a short step to a formal rule requiring management to include in its proxy statement any shareholder proposal which was "a proper subject for action by the security holders." 7 Fed. Reg. 10,659 (1942). It eventually became clear that the question of what constituted a "proper subject" for shareholder action was to be resolved by recourse to the law of the state in which the company had been incorporated; however, the paucity of applicable state law giving content to the concept of "proper subject" led the Commission to seek guidance from precedent existing in jurisdictions which had a highly developed commercial and corporate law and to develop its own "common law" relating to proper subjects for shareholder action. See generally II L. Loss, Securities Regulation 905-906 (1961); Hearings on SEC Enforcement Problems Before a Subcom. of the Senate Comm. on Banking and Currency, 85th Cong., 1st Sess., pt. 1, at 118 (1957) [hereinafter "Senate Hearings"].

Further areas of difficulty became apparent as experience was gained in administering the "proper subject" test, and these conflicts provided the Commission with opportunities to put a detailed gloss upon the general phraseology of its rules. Thus, in 1945 the Commission issued a release containing an opinion of the Director of the Division of Corporation Finance that was rendered in response to a management request to omit shareholder resolutions which bore little or no relationship to the company's affairs; for example, these shareholder resolutions included proposals "that the anti-trust laws and the enforcement thereof be revised," and "that all Federal legislation hereafter enacted providing for workers and farmers to be represented should be made to apply equally to investors." The Commission's release endorsed the Director's conclusion that "proposals which deal with general political, social or economic matters are not, within the meaning of the rule, 'proper subjects for action by security holders.' " The reason for this conclusion was summarized as follows in the Director's opinion:

Speaking generally, *it is the purpose of Rule X-14A-7 to place stockholders in a position to bring before their fellow stockholders matters of concern to them as stockholders in such corporation*; that is, such matters relating to the affairs of the company concerned as are proper subjects for stockholders' action under the laws of the state under which it was organized. It was not the intent of Rule X-14A-7 to permit stockholders to obtain the consensus of other stockholders with respect to matters which are of a general political, social or economic nature. *Other forums exist for the presentation of such views.*

Several years after the Commission issued this release, it was confronted with the same kind of problem when the management of a national bus company sought to omit a shareholder proposal phrased as "A Recommendation that Management Consider the Advisability of Abolishing the Segregated Seating System in the South"—a proposal which, on its face, was ambiguous with respect to whether it was limited solely to company policy rather than attacking all segregated seating, and which quite likely would have brought the company into violation of state laws then assumed to be valid. The Commission staff approved management's decision to omit the proposal, and the shareholder then sought a temporary injunction against the company's solicitation in a federal district court. The injunction was denied because the plaintiff had failed to exhaust his administrative remedies or to show that he would be irreparably harmed by refusal to grant the requested relief. *Peck v. Greyhound Corp.*, 97 F. Supp. 679 (S.D.N.Y. 1951). The Commission amended its rules the following year to encompass the above-quoted exception for situations in which "it clearly appears that the proposal is submitted by the security holder ... primarily for the purpose of promoting general economic, political, racial, religious, social or similar causes." 17 Fed. Reg. 11,433 (1952); see also *id.* at 11,431. So far as we have been able to determine, the Commission's interpretation or application of this rule has not been considered by the courts.

The origins and genesis of the exception for proposals "relating to the conduct of the ordinary business operations of the issuer" are somewhat more obscure. This provision was introduced into the proxy rules in 1954, as part of amendments which were made to clarify the general proposition that the primary source of authority for determining whether a proposal is a proper subject for shareholder action is state law. See 19 Fed. Reg. 246 (1954). Shortly after the rule was adopted, the Commission explained its purpose to Congress in the following terms:

The policy motivating the Commission in adopting the rule ... is basically the same as the underlying policy of most State corporation laws to confine the solution of ordinary business problems to the board of directors and place such problems beyond the competence and direction of the shareholders. The basic reason for this policy is that it is manifestly impracticable in most cases for stockholders to decide management problems at corporate meetings. ...

These two exceptions are, on their face, consistent with the legislative purpose underlying section 14; for it seems fair to infer that Congress desired to make proxy solicitations a vehicle for *corporate* democracy rather than an all-purpose forum for malcontented shareholders to vent their spleen about irrelevant matters, and also realized that management cannot exercise its specialized talents effectively if corporate investors assert the power to dictate the minutiae of daily business decisions. However, it is also apparent that the two exceptions which these rules carve out of the general requirement of inclusion can be construed so as to permit the exclusion of practically any shareholder proposal on the grounds that it is either "too general" or "too specific." Indeed, in the present case Dow Chemical Company attempted to impale the Medical Committee's proposal on both horns of this dilemma: in its memorandum of counsel, it argued that the Medical Committee's proposal was a matter of ordinary business operations properly within the sphere of management expertise and, at the same time, that the proposal clearly had been submitted primarily for the purpose of promoting general political or social causes. (App. 9a-10a; see also *id.* at 19a.) As noted above, the Division of Corporation Finance made no attempt to choose between these potentially conflicting arguments, but rather merely accepted Dow Chemical's decision to omit the proposal "[f]or reasons stated in [the company's] letter and the accompanying opinion of counsel, both dated January 17, 1969"; this determination was then adopted by the full Commission. Close examination of the company's arguments only increases doubt as to the reasoning processes which led the Commission to this result.

In contending that the Medical Committee's proposal was properly excludable under Rule 14a-8(c)(5), Dow's counsel asserted:

It is my opinion that *the determination of the products which the company shall manufacture,* the customers to which it shall sell the products, and the conditions under which it shall make such sales are related to the conduct of the ordinary business operations of the Company and that any attempt to amend the Certificate of Incorporation to define the circumstances under which the management of the Company shall make such determinations is contrary to the concept of corporate management, which is inherent in the Delaware General Corporation Act under which the Company is organized.

In the first place, it seems extremely dubious that this superficial analysis complies with the Commission's longstanding requirements that management must sustain the burden of proof when asserting that a shareholder proposal may properly be omitted from the proxy statement, and that "[w]here management contends that a proposal may be omitted because it is not proper under State law, it will be incumbent upon management to refer to the applicable statute or case law." 19 Fed. Reg. 246 (1954). As noted above, the Commission has formally represented to Congress that Rule 14a-8(c)(5) is intended to make state law the governing authority in determining what matters are ordinary business operations immune from shareholder control; yet, the Delaware General Corporation law provides that a company's Certificate of Incorporation may be amended to "change, substitute, enlarge or diminish the nature of [the company's] business." If there are valid reasons why the Medical Committee's proposal does not fit within the language and spirit of this provision, they certainly do not appear in the record.

The possibility that the Medical Committee's proposal could properly be omitted under Rule 14a-8(c)(2) appears somewhat more substantial in the circumstances of the instant case, although once again it may fairly be asked how Dow Chemical's arguments on this point could be deemed a rational basis for such a result: the paragraph in the company's memorandum of counsel purporting to deal with this issue, which is set forth in the margin,[30] consists entirely of a fundamentally irrelevant recitation of some of the political protests which had been directed at the company because of its manufacture of napalm, followed by the abrupt conclusion that management is therefore entitled to exclude the Medical Committee's proposal from its proxy statement. Our own examination of the issue raises substantial questions as to whether an interpretation of Rule 14a-8(c)(2) which permitted omission of this proposal as one motivated primarily by *general* political or social concerns would conflict with the congressional intent underlying section 14(a) of the Act.

As our earlier discussion indicates, the clear import of the language, legislative history, and record of administration of section 14(a) is that its overriding purpose is to assure to corporate shareholders the ability to exercise their right—some would say their duty—to control the important decisions which affect them in their capacity as stockholders and owners of the corporation. ... Here, in contrast to the situations detailed above which led to the promulgation of Rule 14a-8(c)(2), the proposal relates solely to a matter that is completely within the accepted sphere of corporate activity and control. No reason has been advanced in the present proceedings which leads to the conclusion that management may properly place obstacles in the path of shareholders who wish to present to their co-owners, in accord with applicable state law, the question of whether they wish to have their assets used in a manner which they believe to be more socially responsible but possibly less profitable than that which is dictated by present company policy. Thus, even accepting Dow's characterization of the purpose and intent of the Medical Committee's proposal, there is a strong argument that permitting the company to exclude it would contravene the purpose of section 14(a).

However, the record in this case contains indications that we are confronted with quite a different situation. The management of Dow Chemical Company is repeatedly quoted in sources which include the company's own publications as proclaiming that the

---

30 App. 10a: "It is a well-known fact that the Company has been the target of protests and demonstrations for the past few years at its office and plant locations, and on the occasion of recruiting on college and university campuses, as well as at its annual meeting of stockholders held May 8, 1968. The various protests and demonstrations are a reflection of opposition on the part of certain segments of the population against the policy of the United States Government in waging the war in Vietnam. Although the Dow Chemical Company was not among the 100 largest prime contractors with the Department of Defense during the 1967-68 Government fiscal year and was only 75th on the list in the 1966-67 fiscal year, it appears to have been singled out symbolically by the protestors. Under all of these circumstances it is my opinion that it clearly appears that the proposal is primarily for the purpose of promoting a general political, social or similar cause."

decision to continue manufacturing and marketing napalm was made not *because* of business considerations, but *in spite* of them; that management in essence decided to pursue a course of activity which generated little profit for the shareholders and actively impaired the company's public relations and recruitment activities because management considered this action morally and politically desirable. (App. 40a-43a; see also *id.* at 33.) The proper political and social role of modern corporations is, of course, a matter of philosophical argument extending far beyond the scope of our present concern; the substantive wisdom or propriety of particular corporate political decisions is also completely irrelevant to the resolution of the present controversy. What *is* of immediate concern, however, is the question of whether the corporate proxy rules can be employed as a shield to isolate such managerial decisions from shareholder control. After all, it must be remembered that "[t]he control of great corporations by a very few persons was the abuse at which Congress struck in enacting Section 14(a)." *SEC v. Transamerica Corp.*, supra, 163 F.2d at 518. We think that there is a clear and compelling distinction between management's legitimate need for freedom to apply its expertise in matters of day-to-day business judgment, and management's patently illegitimate claim of power to treat modern corporations with their vast resources as personal satrapies implementing personal political or moral predilections. It could scarcely be argued that management is more qualified or more entitled to make these kinds of decisions than the shareholders who are the true beneficial owners of the corporation; and it seems equally implausible that an application of the proxy rules which permitted such a result could be harmonized with the philosophy of corporate democracy which Congress embodied in section 14(a) of the Securities Exchange Act of 1934.

In light of these considerations, therefore, the cause must be remanded to the Commission so that it may reconsider petitioner's claim within the proper limits of its discretionary authority as set forth above, and so that "the basis for [its] decision [may] appear clearly on the record, not in conclusory terms but in sufficient detail to permit prompt and effective review."

Remanded for further proceedings consistent with this opinion.

NOTES

Note that the Court of Appeals did not rule that Dow had to include the Medical Committee's proposal in its proxy materials. Rather, it remanded the case to the S.E.C. for a reconsideration of the Committee's claims and for a detailed restatement of the Commission's conclusions, if indeed they remained the same. The Commission petitioned for review to the United States Supreme Court. In the meantime Dow agreed to include the Committee's proposal in the notice for the company's next annual meeting (by this time the 1971 meeting, whereas originally the petition was submitted for the 1968 meeting). The Supreme Court therefore held the case to be moot.

A few years after the *Medical Committee* decision, the S.E.C. revised the categories of shareholder proposals that management could exclude from its proxy materials. The permissible exclusion for proposals that promote "general economic, political, racial, religious, social or similar causes" was eliminated. Such an exclusion does appear, however, in CBCA s. 137(5)(b) (although not in OBCA s. 99). See also ABCA s. 131(5)(b).

Both Rule 14a-8 under the Securities Exchange Act and CBCA s. 137(5) permit the exclusion of proposals relating primarily to redress of a personal grievance and proposals "not related in any significant way to the business ... of the corporation." A proposal might well be put forward for the purpose of promoting a political or social cause and yet be very significant for the issuer's business. The *Medical Committee* case provides an excellent illustration. Furthermore, while ending the Vietnam War was presumably "beyond [Dow's] power to effectuate," ending its own manufacture of napalm surely was not.

The basis for exclusion in Rule 14a-8(c)(5)—that the proposal relate to "the ordinary business operations of the issuer"—was inserted to preserve the integrity of the division of authority in state corporations statutes between directors, who are made responsible for the conduct of the ordinary business operations, and shareholders, who are excluded from that sphere. In addition, rule 14a-8(c)(1) permits the deletion of a proposal which is "not a proper subject for action by securities holders." However, a note to this provision validates precatory resolutions:

Whether a proposal is a proper subject for action by security holders will depend on the applicable state law. Under states' laws, a proposal that mandates certain action by the registrant's board of directors cannot be a proper subject matter for shareholder action, while a proposal recommending or requesting such action of the board may be proper under such state law. ...

By revisions made to Rule 14a-8 in 1983, the S.E.C. made it generally easier for corporations to exclude shareholder proposals from management's proxy materials. The Commission did this not by expanding the grounds for exclusion but by creating more conditions that shareholders have to satisfy in order to have proposals included. See *Proxy Communications and Management Disclosure*, Fed. Sec. L. Rep. (CCH), Special Report No. 1046 (November 1983).

You will recall that a similar issue arose in the *Honeywell* decision in the previous section. Do you agree that, as in *Honeywell*, the shareholders' concern in the *Medical Committee* case about the affairs of Dow Chemicals was "only colorable"? To what extent did the Medical Committee's concern stem from a desire to maximize the value of Dow Chemicals?

As a focus for political protest, shareholder proposals were less frequently used by dissenters once management began to carry the proposals in their proxy circulars, together with contrary arguments from management's point of view. After this development, which followed the *Medical Committee* decision, politically inspired proposals were routinely rejected by the vast majority of shareholders, and dissenters took to making their points by attending the shareholders' meeting to ask pointed questions of the chair. Does this suggest that the S.E.C. was correct in restricting access to management's proxy materials? Might such proposals be excluded under CBCA s. 137(5)(e)?

Suggestions have been made for amendments to the shareholder proposal rules in the United States to complement the changes to the proxy solicitation rules noted above and thereby increase shareholder control over the management of the corporation. See, e.g., E.A. Welter, *The Shareholder Proposal Rule: A Change to Certainty*, 60 Geo. Wash. L.R. 1980 (1992); and J.E. Fisch, *From Legitimacy to Logic: Reconstructing Proxy Regulation*, 46 Vanderbuilt L.R. 1129 (1993).

Canadian Cases on Shareholder Proposals. There appears to be a more restrictive approach to shareholder proposals in Canada than that taken by the court in Medical Committee.

In *Varity Corp. v. Jesuit Fathers of Upper Canada* (1987), 59 O.R. (2d) 459, aff'd (1987), 60 O.R. (2d) 640 (C.A.) Varity Corporation applied to exclude a shareholder proposal that requested that the corporation: (1) take immediate steps to terminate Varity's investments in South Africa; (2) take immediate steps to terminate a licence agreement with Atlantis Diesel Engines; and (3) announce publicly to the South African government Varity's plans to leave South Africa as soon as possible. The preamble to the proposed resolution, among other things, noted the Commonwealth Eminent Persons Group conclusion that the South African Government was not prepared to negotiate the dismantling of apartheid and that economic measures might offer the last opportunity to compel change. The proposal noted support for disinvestment from South Africa by foreign enterprises in an effort to achieve a peaceful elimination of apartheid. It noted Varity's interest in a particular South African corporation and the connection between Atlantis Diesel Engines and an arrangement "established by the South African government to ensure South African self-sufficiency in diesel engines for agricultural, commercial and military needs." The preamble further noted that conditions in South Africa made continued viable economic investments risky.

In support of the proposal it was argued that because the resolution involved specific goals or purposes it did not fall within s. 137(5)(b) even if the purpose was also an economic, political, racial, religious or social purpose. The court accepted that the resolution was specific to Varity but concluded that "[a]s I read the legislation, the fact that there may be a more specific purpose or target does not save the proposal. ... The legislation makes it clear that if the primary purpose is one of those listed, however commendable either the specific or the general purpose may be, the company cannot be compelled to pay for taking the first step towards achieving it."

In *Greenpeace Foundation of Canada v. Inco Ltd.* (unreported, Feb. 23, 1984, Ont. H.C.J.), Greenpeace submitted a proposal under CBCA s. 137 to be put before the shareholders at Inco's annual meeting scheduled for March 1984. The proposal was a resolution to "request the board of directors to carry out ... pollution control measures at the corporation's Sudbury complex and to 'further request the board of directors to consult' with government as to sources of funding for the pollution abatement efforts." To reduce acid rain the resolution called for a reduction of sulpher dioxide emissions to 274 tonnes per day. Montgomery J. sustained Inco's refusal to include the proposal on three grounds: (1) Greenpeace was not a shareholder of record 90 days before the date scheduled for the meeting (CBCA s. 137(5)(a)); (2) the proposal was substantially the same as one submitted by Greenpeace the preceding year, which had sought a reduction of sulpher dioxide emissions to 43 tonnes per day and which had been defeated (s. 137(5)(d)); and (3) the proposal had been submitted by Greenpeace "primarily for the purpose of promoting general economic, political, racial, religious, social or similar causes" (s. 137(5)(b)). The Court of Appeal affirmed the decision on the basis of non-compliance with s. 137(5)(a).

8. Proxy Solicitation Expenses

Normally the costs of proxy solicitation by management are paid by the corporation. Are there instances when management should not be allowed to pay proxy solicitation expenses out of the assets of the corporation? Should dissident proxy solicitation expenses be paid for by the corporation? The following case raises these issues.

Rosenfeld v. Fairchild Engine and Airplane Corp.
New York Court of Appeals
128 N.E.2d 291 (1955)

FROESSEL, Judge: In a stockholder's derivative action brought by plaintiff, an attorney, who owns 25 out of the company's over 2,300,000 shares, he seeks to compel the return of $261,522, paid out of the corporate treasury to reimburse both sides in a proxy contest for their expenses. The Appellate Division, 284 App.Div. 201, 132 N.Y.S.2d 273, has unanimously affirmed a judgment of an Official Referee, Sup., 116 N.Y.S.2d 840, dismissing the plaintiffs complaint on the merits, and we agree. Exhaustive opinions were written by both courts below, and it will serve no useful purpose to review the facts again.

Of the amount in controversy $106,000 was spent out of corporate funds by the old board of directors while still in office in defense of their position in said contest; $28,000 were paid to the old board by the new board after the change of management following the proxy contest, to compensate the former directors for such of the remaining expenses of their unsuccessful defense as the new board found was fair and reasonable; payment of $127,000, representing reimbursement of expenses to members of the prevailing group, was expressly ratified by a 16 to 1 majority vote of the stockholders.

The essential facts are not in dispute, and, since the determinations below are amply supported by the evidence, we are bound by the findings affirmed by the Appellate Division. The Appellate Division found that the difference between plaintiff's group and the old board "went deep into the policies of the company," and that among these Ward's contract was one of the "main points of contention." The Official Referee found that the controversy "was based on an understandable difference in policy between the two groups, at the very bottom of which was the Ward employment contract" [116 N.Y.S.2d 844].

By way of contrast with the findings here, in *Lawyers' Advertising Co. v. Consolidated Ry., Lighting & Refrigerating Co.*, 187 N.Y. 395, at page 399, 80 N.E. 199, at page 200, which was an action to recover for the cost of publishing newspaper notices not authorized by the board of directors, it was expressly found that the proxy contest there involved was "by one faction in its contest with another for the control of the corporation ... a contest for the perpetuation of their offices and control." We there said by way of *dicta* that under *such* circumstances the publication of certain notices on behalf of the management faction was not a corporate expenditure which the directors had the power to authorize.

Other jurisdictions and our own lower courts have held that management may look to the corporate treasury for the reasonable expenses of soliciting proxies to defend its position in a *bona fide* policy contest. *Peel v. London & North Western Ry. Co.*, [1907] 1 Ch. 5; [remaining citations omitted].

It should be noted that plaintiff does not argue that the aforementioned sums were fraudulently extracted from the corporation; indeed, his counsel conceded that "the charges were fair and reasonable," but denied "they were legal charges which may be reimbursed for." This is therefore not a case where a stockholder challenges specific items, which, on examination, the trial court may find unwarranted, excessive or otherwise improper. Had plaintiff made such objections here, the trial court would have been required to examine the items challenged.

If directors of a corporation may not in good faith incur reasonable and proper expenses in soliciting proxies in these days of giant corporations with vast numbers of stockholders, the corporate business might be seriously interfered with because of stockholder indifference and the difficulty of procuring a quorum, where there is no contest. In the event of a proxy contest, if the directors may not freely answer the challenges of outside groups and in good faith defend their actions with respect to corporate policy for the information of the stockholders, they and the corporation may be at the mercy of persons seeking to wrest control for their own purposes, so long as such persons have ample funds to conduct a proxy contest. The test is clear. When the directors act in good faith in a contest over policy, they have the right to incur reasonable and proper expenses for solicitation of proxies and in defense of their corporate policies, and are not obliged to sit idly by. The courts are entirely competent to pass upon their *bona fides* in any given case, as well as the nature of their expenditures when duly challenged.

It is also our view that the members of the so-called new group could be reimbursed by the corporation for their expenditures in this contest by affirmative vote of the stockholders. With regard to these there was, of course, "no duty ... to set forth the facts, with corresponding obligation of the corporation to pay for such expense." However, where a majority of the stockholders chose—in this case by a vote of 16 to 1—to reimburse the successful contestants for achieving the very end sought and voted for by them as owners of the corporation, we see no reason to deny the effect of their ratification nor to hold the corporate body powerless to determine how its own moneys shall be spent.

The rule then which we adopt is simply this: In a contest over policy, as compared to a purely personal power contest, corporate directors have the right to make reasonable and proper expenditures, subject to the scrutiny of the courts when duly challenged, from the corporate treasury for the purpose of persuading the stockholders of the correctness of their position and soliciting their support for policies which the directors believe, in all good faith, are in the best interests of the corporation. The stockholders, moreover, have the right to reimburse successful contestants for the reasonable and *bona fide* expenses incurred by them in any such policy contest, subject to like court scrutiny. That is not to say, however, that corporate directors can, under any circumstances, disport themselves in a proxy contest with the corporation's moneys to an unlimited extent. Where it is established that such moneys have been spent for personal power, individual gain or private advantage, and not in the belief that such expenditures are in the best interests of the stockholders and the corporation, or where the fairness and reasonableness of the amounts allegedly expended are duly and successfully challenged, the courts will not hesitate to disallow them.

The judgment of the Appellate Division should be affirmed, without costs.

DESMOND, Judge (concurring): Plaintiff asserts that it was illegal for the directors (unless by unanimous consent of stockholders) to expend corporate moneys in the proxy context beyond the amounts necessary to give to stockholders bare notice of the meeting and of the matters to be voted on thereat. Defendants say that the proxy context revolved around disputes over corporate policies and that it was, accordingly, proper not only to asses against the corporation the expense of serving formal notices and of routine proxy solicitation, but to go further and spend corporate moneys, on behalf of each group, thoroughly to inform the stockholders. The reason why that important question, is, perhaps, not directly before us in this lawsuit is because, as the Appellate Division properly held, [284 App. Div. 201, 132 N.Y.S.2d 280] plaintiff failed "to urge liability as to specific expenditures." The cost of giving routinely necessary notice is, of course, chargeable to the corporation. It is just as clear, we think, that payment by a corporation of the expense of "proceedings by one faction in its contest with another for the control of the corporation" is *ultra vires*, and unlawful. *Lawyers' Advertising Co. v. Consolidated Ry., Lighting & Refrigerating Co.*, 187 N.Y. 395, 399, 80 N.E. 199, 200. Approval by directors or by a majority stock vote could not validate such gratuitous expenditures. *Continental Securities Co. v. Belmont*, 206 N.Y. 7, 99 N.E. 138, 51 L.R.A., N.S., 112. Some of the payments attacked in this suit were, on their face, for lawful purposes and apparently reasonable in amount but, as to others, the record simply does not contain evidentiary bases for a determination as to either lawfulness or reasonableness. Surely, the burden was on plaintiff to go forward to some extent with such particularization and proof. It failed to do so, and so failed to make out a prima facie case.

We are, therefore, reaching the same result as did the Appellate Division but on one only of the grounds listed by that court, that is, failure of proof. We think it not inappropriate, however, to state our general views on the question of law principally argued by the parties, that is, as to the validity of corporate payments for proxy solicitations and similar activities in addition to giving notice of the meeting, and of the questions to be voted on. For an answer to that problem we could not do better than quote from this court's opinion in the *Lawyers' Advertising Co.* case, 187 N.Y. 395, 399, 80 N.E. 199, 200, supra:

The remaining notices were not legally authorized and were not legitimately incidental to the meeting or necessary for the protection of the stockholders. They rather were proceedings by one faction in its contest with another for the control of the corporation, and the expense thereof, as such, is not properly chargeable to the latter. This is so apparent as to the last two notices that nothing need be said in reference to them; but a few words may be said in regard to the first one, calling for proxies. It is to be noted that this is not the case of an ordinary circular letter sent out with and requesting the execution of proxies. The custom has become common upon the part of corporations to mail proxies to their respective stockholders, often accompanied by a brief circular of directions, and such custom when accompanied by no unreasonable expenditure, is not without merit in so far as it encourages voting by stockholders, through making it convenient and ready at hand. The notice in question, however, was not published until after proxies had been sent out. It simply amounted to an urgent solicitation that these proxies should be executed and returned for use by one faction in its contest, and we think there is no authority for imposing the expense of its publication upon the company. ... It would be altogether too dangerous a rule to permit directors in control of a corporation and engaged in a contest for the perpetuation of their offices and control, to impose upon the corporation the unusual expense of publishing advertisements or, by analogy, of dispatching special messengers for the purpose of procuring proxies in their behalf.

A final comment: since expenditures which do not meet that test of propriety are intrinsically unlawful, it could not be any answer to such a claim as plaintiff makes here that the stockholder vote which purported to authorize them was heavy or that the change in management turned out to be beneficial to the corporation.

The judgment should be affirmed, without costs.

VAN VOORHIS, Judge (dissenting): The decision of this appeal is of far-reaching importance insofar as concerns payment by corporations of campaign expenses by stockholders in proxy contexts for control. This is a stockholder's derivative action to require directors to restore to a corporation moneys paid to defray expenses of this nature, incurred both by an incumbent faction and by an insurgent faction of stockholders. The insurgents prevailed at the annual meeting, and payments of their own campaign expenses were attempted to be ratified by majority vote. It was a large majority, but the stockholders were not unanimous. Regardless of the merits of this contest, we are called upon to decide whether it was a corporate purpose (1) to make the expenditures which were disbursed by the incumbent or management group in defense of their acts and to remain in control of the corporation, and (2) to defray expenditures made by the insurgent group, which succeeded in convincing a majority of the stockholders. The Appellate Division held that stockholder authorization or ratification was not necessary to reasonable expenditures by the management group, the purpose of which was to inform the stockholders concerning the affairs of the corporation, and that, although these incumbents spent or incurred obligations of $133,966 (the previous expenses of annual meetings of this corporation ranging between $7,000 and $28,000), plaintiff must fail for having omitted to distinguish item by item between which of these expenditures were warranted and which ones were not; and the Appellate Division held that the insurgents also should be reimbursed, but subject to the qualification that "The expenses of those who were seeking to displace the management should not be reimbursed by the corporation except upon approval by the stockholders." It was held that the stockholders had approved.

No resolution was passed by the stockholders approving payment to the management group. It has been recognized that not all of the $133,966 in obligations paid or incurred by the management group was designed merely for information of stockholders. This outlay included payment for all of the activities of a strenuous campaign to persuade and cajole in a hard-fought contest for control of this corporation. It included, for example, expenses for entertainment, chartered airplanes and limousines, public relations counsel and proxy solicitors. However legitimate such measures may be on behalf of stockholders themselves in such a controversy, most of them do not pertain to a corporate function but are part of the familiar apparatus of aggressive factions in corporate contests. In *Lawyers' Advertising Co. v. Consolidated Ry., Lighting & Refrigerating Co.*, 187 N.Y. 395, 399, 80 N.E. 199, 201, this court said:

The notice in question, however, was not published until after proxies had been sent out. It simply amounted to an urgent solicitation that these proxies should be executed and returned for use by one faction in its contest, and we think there is no authority for imposing the expense of its publication upon the company. It may be conceded that the directors who caused this publication acted in good faith, and felt that they were serving the best interests of the stockholders; but it would be altogether too dangerous a rule to permit directors in control of a corporation and engaged in a contest for the perpetuation of their offices and control, to impose upon the corporation the unusual expense of publishing advertisements, or, by analogy, of dispatching special messengers for the purpose of procuring proxies in their behalf.

The Appellate Division acknowledged in the instant case that "It is obvious that the management group here incurred a substantial amount of needless expense which was charged to the corporation," but this conclusion should have led to a direction that those defendants who were incumbent directors should be required to come forward with an explanation of their expenditures under the familiar rule that where it has been established that directors have expended corporate money for their own purposes, the burden of going forward with evidence of the propriety and reasonableness of specific items rests upon the directors. ... The complaint should not have been dismissed as against incumbent directors due to failure of plaintiff to segregate the specific expenditures which are *ultra vires*, but, once plaintiff had proved facts from which an inference of impropriety might be drawn, the duty of making an explanation was laid upon the directors to explain and justify their conduct.

The second ground assigned by the Appellate Division for dismissing the complaint against incumbent directors is stockholder ratification of reimbursement to the insurgent group. Whatever effect or lack of it this resolution had upon expenditures by the insurgent group, clearly the stockholders who voted to pay the insurgents entertained no intention of reimbursing the management group for their expenditures. The insurgent group succeeded as a result of arousing the indignation of these very stockholders against the management group; nothing in the resolution to pay the expenses of the insurgent group purported to authorize or ratify payment of the campaign expenses of their adversaries, and certainly no inference should be drawn that the stockholders who voted to pay the insurgents intended that the incumbent group should also be paid. Upon the contrary, they were removing the incumbents from control mainly for the reason that they were charged with having mulcted the corporation by a long-term salary and pension contract to one of their number, J. Carlton Ward, Jr. If these stockholders had been presented with a resolution to pay the expenses of that group, it would almost certainly have been voted down. The stockholders should not be deemed to have authorized or ratified reimbursement of the incumbents.

There is no doubt that the management was entitled and under a duty to take reasonable steps to acquaint the stockholders with essential facts concerning the management of the corporation, and it may well be that the existence of a contest warranted them in circularizing the stockholders with more than ordinarily detailed information. As this court said in *Lawyers' Advertising Co. v. Consolidated Ry., Lighting & Refrigerat-*

ing Co., supra, 187 N.Y. at page 399, 80 N.E. at page 200: "Proper and honest corporate management was subserved by widespread notice to stockholders of questions affecting the welfare of the corporation, and there is no impropriety in charging the latter with any expenses within reasonable limits which were incurred in giving sufficient notice of a special meeting at which the stockholders would be called upon to decide these questions."

What expenses of the incumbent group should be allowed and what should be disallowed should be remitted to the trial court to ascertain, after taking evidence, in accordance with the rule that the incumbent directors were required to assume the burden of going forward in the first instance with evidence explaining and justifying their expenditures. Only such as were reasonably related to informing the stockholders fully and fairly concerning the corporate affairs should be allowed. The concession by plaintiff that such expenditures as were made were reasonable in amount does not decide this question. By way of illustration, the costs of entertainment for stockholders may have been, and it is stipulated that they were, at the going rates for providing similar entertainment. That does not signify that entertaining stockholders is reasonably related to the purposes of the corporation. The Appellate Division, as above stated, found that the management group incurred a substantial amount of needless expense. That fact being established, it became the duty of the incumbent directors to unravel and explain these payments.

Regarding the $127,556 paid by the new management to the insurgent group for their campaign expenditures, the question immediately arises whether that was for a corporate purpose. The Appellate Division has recognized that upon no theory could such expenditures be reimbursed except by approval of the stockholders and, as has been said, it is the insurgents' expenditures alone to which the stockholders' resolution of ratification was addressed. If *unanimous* stockholder approval had been obtained and no rights of creditors or of the public intervened, it would make no practical difference whether the purpose were *ultra vires*—i.e., not a corporate purpose. *Kent v. Quicksilver Min. Co.*, 78 N.Y. 159; *Capitol Wine & Spirit Corp. v. Pokrass*, 277 App.Div. 184, 187, 98 N.Y.S.2d 291, 294, affirmed 302 N.Y. 734, 98 N.E.2d 704. Upon the other hand, an act which is *ultra vires* cannot be ratified merely by a majority of the stockholders of a corporation. *Continental Securities Co. v. Belmont*, 206 N.Y. 7, 99 N.E. 138. ...

The familiar rule, applied in those and other decisions, is that merely voidable acts of the directors of a corporation can be ratified by majority stockholder approval, such as contracts between corporations having interlocking directorates, *Continental Ins. Co. v. New York & H.R. Co.*, 187 N.Y. 225, 79 N.E. 1026, loans of surplus funds by a trading corporation, *Murray v. Smith*, 166 App.Div. 528, 152 N.Y.S. 102—although not in the case of loans to stockholders in violation of the Stock Corporation Law, Consol. Laws, c. 59, § 59, and other irregularities involving acts which are neither *ultra vires*, fraudulent or illegal.

In considering this issue, as in the case of the expenses of the incumbents, we begin with the proposition that this court has already held that it is beyond the power of a corporation to authorize the expenditure of mere campaign expenses in a proxy contest. *Lawyers' Advertising Co. v. Consolidated Ry., Lighting & Refrigerating Co.*, supra. That decision is not distinguishable upon the ground that those expenditures were made by the secretary of that corporation without previous authorization by its directors. That point was involved, but this court said: "Thus we have it that the publication of the last three notices was not authorized by the board of directors, *and that it could not have been lawfully authorized, even if the attempt were made. They bore upon their face sufficient notice to the plaintiff [the printer suing for printing fees] that they were of a character beyond the limit of anything which could be published in behalf of or at the expense of the corporation*" 187 N.Y. at page 400, 80 N.E. at page 201; (italics supplied). The decision was placed upon both grounds. The statement in the carefully considered opinion written by Judge Hiscock was not dictum that "it would be altogether too dangerous a rule to permit directors, in control of a corporation and engaged in a contest for the perpetuation of their offices and control, to impose upon the corporation the unusual expense." In that case, and in all of the other decisions which have been cited with the single exception of a Federal district court decision, *Steinberg v. Adams, D.C.*, 90 F. Supp. 604, 606, the question concerned reimbursement of a management group. Moreover, with the exception of an English decision, *Peel v. London & North Western Ry. Co.*, [1907] 1 Ch. 5, all of the appellate court cases which have been cited, and *Steinberg v. Adams*, were decided under the law of the State of Delaware. The Delaware law contains more latitude than in New York State, as was recognized by Judge Rifkind in his opinion in *Steinberg v. Adams*, supra, who said, 90 F. Supp. at page 607: "The instant case is concerned with a Delaware corporation and the law of that state determines the scope of the corporation's powers. Both parties, as I have indicated, agree that this case is governed by a less stringent rule" than the ruling by this court in *Lawyers' Advertising Co. v. Consolidated Ry., Lighting & Refrigerating Co.*, supra. We are called upon to decide whether to abandon the rule as previously established in this State and adopt the less strict doctrine of the State of Delaware . ...

The case most frequently cited and principally relied upon from among these Delaware decisions is *Hall v. TransLux Daylight Picture Screen Corp.*, supra. There the English case was followed of *Peel v. London & North Western Ry. Co.*, supra, which distinguished between expenses merely for the purpose of maintaining control, and contests over policy questions of the corporation. In the *Hall* case the issues concerned a proposed merger, and a proposed sale of stock of a subsidiary corporation. These were held to be policy questions, and payment of the management campaign expenses was upheld.

In our view, the impracticability of such a distinction is illustrated by the statement in the *Hall* case, supra, 20 Del.Ch. at page 85, 171 A. at page 229, that "It is impossible in many cases of intracorporate contests over directors, to sever questions of policy from those of persons." This circumstance is stressed in Judge Rifkind's opinion in the *Steinberg* case, supra, 90 F. Supp. at page 608: "The simple fact, of course, is that generally policy and personnel do not exist in separate compartments. A change in personnel is sometimes indispensable to a change of policy. A new board may be the symbol of the shift in policy as well as the means of obtaining it."

That may be all very well, but the upshot of this reasoning is that inasmuch as it is generally impossible to distinguish whether "policy" or "personnel" is the dominant factor, any averments must be accepted at their face value that questions of policy are dominant. Nowhere do these opinions mention that the converse is equally true and more pervasive, that neither the "ins" nor the "outs" ever say that they have no program to offer to the shareholders, but just want to acquire or to retain control, as the case may be. In common experience, this distinction is unreal. ...

The main question of "policy" in the instant corporate election, as is stated in the opinions below and frankly admitted, concerns the long-term contract with pension rights of a former officer and director, Mr. J. Carlton Ward, Jr. The insurgents' chief claim of benefit to the corporation from their victory consists in the termination of that agreement, resulting in an alleged actuarial saving of $350,000 to $825,000 to the corporation, and the reduction of other salaries and rent by more than $300,000 per year. The insurgents had contended in the proxy contest that these payments should be substantially reduced so that members of the incumbent group would not continue to profit personally at the expense of the corporation. If these charges were true, which appear to have been believed by a majority of the shareholders, then the disbursements by the management group in the proxy contest fall under the condemnation of the English and the Delaware rule.

These circumstances are mentioned primarily to illustrate how impossible it is to distinguish between "policy" and "personnel," as Judge Rifkind expressed it, but they also indicate that personal factors are deeply rooted in this contest. That is certainly true insofar as the former management group is concerned. It would be hard to find a case to which the careful reservation made by the English Judge in the *Peel* case, supra, was more directly applicable.

Some expenditures may concededly be made by a corporation represented by its management so as to inform the stockholders, but there is a clear distinction between such expenditures by management and by mere groups of stockholders. The latter are under no legal obligation to assume duties of managing the corporation. They may endeavour to supersede the management for any reason, regardless of whether it be advantageous or detrimental to the corporation but, if they succeed, that is not a determination that the company was previously mismanaged or that it may not be mismanaged in the future. A change in control is in no sense analogous to an adjudication that the former directors have been guilty of misconduct. The analogy of allowing expenses of suit to minority stockholders who have been successful in a derivative action based on misconduct of officers or directors, is entirely without foundation.

Insofar as a management group is concerned, it may charge the corporation with any expenses within reasonable limits incurred in giving widespread notice to stockholders of questions affecting the welfare of the corporation. *Lawyers' Advertising Co. v. Consolidated Ry., Lighting & Refrigerating Co.*, supra. Expenditures in excess of these limits are *ultra vires*. The corporation lacks power to defray them. The corporation lacks power to defray the expenses of the insurgents in their entirety. The insurgents were not charged with responsibility for operating the company. No appellate court case is cited from any jurisdiction holding otherwise. No contention is made that such disbursements could be made, in any event, without stockholder ratification; they could not be ratified except by unanimous vote if they were *ultra vires*. The insurgents, in this instance, repeatedly announced to the stockholders in their campaign literature that their proxy contest was being waged at their own personal expense. If reimbursement of such items were permitted upon majority stockholder ratification, no court or other tribunal could pass upon which types of expenditure were "needless," to employ the characterization of the Appellate Division in this case. Whether the insurgents should be paid would be made to depend upon whether they win the stockholders election and obtain control of the corporation. It would be entirely irrelevant whether the corporation is "benefitted" by their efforts or by the outcome of such an election. The courts could not indulge in a speculative inquiry into that issue. That would truly be a matter of business judgment. In some instances corporations are better governed by the existing management and in others by some other group which supersedes the existing management. Courts of law have no jurisdiction to decide such questions, and successful insurgent stockholders may confidently be relied upon to reimburse themselves whatever may be the real merits of the controversy. The losers in a proxy fight may understand the interests of the corporation more accurately than their successful adversaries, and agitation of this character may ultimately result in corporate advantage even if there be no change in management. Nevertheless, under the judgment which is appealed from, success in a proxy contest is the indispensible condition upon which reimbursement of the insurgents depends. Adventurers are not infrequent who are ready to take advantage of economic recessions, reduction of dividends or failure to increase them, or other sources of stockholder discontent to wage contests in order to obtain control of well-managed corporations, so as to divert their funds through legal channels into other corporations in which they may be interested, or to discharge former officers and employees to make room for favored newcomers according to the fashion of political patronage, or for other objectives that are unrelated to the sound prosperity of the enterprise. The way is open and will be kept open for stockholders and groups of stockholders to contest corporate elections, but if the promoters of such movements choose to employ the costly modern media of mass persuasion, they should look for reimbursement to themselves and to the stockholders who are aligned with them. If the law be that they can be recompensed by the corporation in case of success, and only in that event, it will operate as a powerful incentive to persons accustomed to taking calculated risks to increase this form of high-powered salesmanship to such a degree that, action provoking reaction, stockholders' meetings will be very costly. To the financial advantages promised by control of a prosperous corporation, would be added the knowledge that the winner takes all insofar as the campaign expenses are concerned. To the victor, indeed, would belong the spoils.

The questions involved in this case assume mounting importance as the capital stock of corporations becomes more widely distributed. To an enlarged extent the campaign methods consequently come more to resemble those of political campaigns, but, as in the latter, campaign expenses should be borne by those who are waging the campaign and their followers, instead of being met out of the corporate or the public treasury. Especially is this true when campaign promises have been made that the expenses would not be charged to the corporation.

Nothing which is said in this opinion is intended as any reflection upon the motives of the insurgent group in instigating this corporate contest, nor upon the management group. Questions of law are involved which extend beyond the persons and the corporation presently before the court. It is the established law of this State that expenditures may be incurred by management limited to informing the stockholders fully and fairly concerning the affairs and policies of the corporation, which may well include an explanation of the reasons on account of which its policies have been undertaken, nor is there any reason on account of which stockholders who have neglected to sign proxies through apathy may not be solicited so as to insure a quorum, which would ordinarily occur in instances where there is no contest, but beyond measures of this character, the purely campaign expenses of a management group do not serve a corporate purpose, and paying them is *ultra vires*. The same is true of all of the expenses of insurgent stockholders.

The release given to J. Carlton Ward, Jr., by the authority of his codirectors, could not have the effect of discharging liability to which they were otherwise subject upon the theory that it operated to release them as joint tort-feasors.

The judgment appealed from should be reversed. ...

CONWAY C.J. and BURKE J. concur with FROESSEL J.; DESMOND J. concurs in part in a separate opinion; VAN VOORHIS J. dissents in an opinion in which DYE and FULD JJ. concur.

Judgment affirmed.

NOTES

The *Rosenfeld* case appears to have gone well beyond any earlier authority, at least outside Delaware, in allowing liberal payment out of corporate funds for the very substantial expenses typically involved in proxy battles.

In *Lawyers' Advertising Co. v. Consol. Ry. Lighting & Refrigerating Co.*, 80 N.E. 199 (N.Y. 1907), discussed in all three opinions in the main case, a publisher sued to recover the cost of advertisements from the defendant corporation. A majority of the corporation's directors had caused the advertisements to be published in connection with an upcoming shareholders' meeting called to resolve a bitter dispute between the directors and the corporation's president. The Court of Appeals held that the plaintiff could recover from the corporation the cost of the first advertisement, giving notice of the meeting. The plaintiff was held not to be entitled to recover from the corporation the cost of three additional advertisements. One of these was an urgent request that proxies which had been sent out should be returned, and the remaining two argued the views of the directors against those of the president. The passage denying recovery for the last three notices is set out in the opinion of Desmond J. in *Rosenfeld*.

Peel v. London and Northwestern Ry. Co., [1907] 1 Ch. 5 (C.A.) was a suit by a minority shareholder to recover for the corporation expenses incurred by the directors, and charged by them to the corporation, in successfully defending their management policies against a challenge launched by the plaintiff. The expenses were for printing and mailing: (1) a notice of the meeting with a defence of the directors' policies; and (2) a form of proxy with suggested nominees. The directors included in the mailing a stamped envelope for return of the proxies. Not only were the directors successful in garnering a heavy majority of shareholder support for their policies, but their expenditure of corporate funds on the proxy solicitation was also approved by the shareholders. The English Court of Appeal sustained the propriety of the expenditures in all respects. Vaughan Williams L.J. stated:

What one has to consider here is that there is an attack upon the policy of the railway company. The attack in this particular case happens to be an attack by an association of high-minded gentlemen who only have the interests of the company at heart; but, in the principle that one has to deal with here, one must contemplate the possibility of an attack being made by persons who have not the interests of the company so much at heart—attacks, it may be, by others who have a deeper interest in other and competing undertakings. Under those circumstances I ask myself, have the directors of the company the right to take steps that there shall be a full attendance of shareholders at the next meeting? I say it is their positive duty, if they think that there is a serious attack being made upon their policy which is likely to jeopardize the interest of the company in the future, to take care that there is a meeting at which there shall be a full attendance of shareholders. I cannot doubt myself but that, if it is their duty to take care that there are plenty of shareholders present at the meeting, it is also their duty to take care that there are a sufficient number of shareholders put into a position to vote for those who personally are unable to attend the meeting. It is not denied that it is right, under those circumstances, to spend the funds of the company in printing proxy papers. There can be no doubt that it is also their duty to take care that a sufficient statement of the facts which will have to be considered by the shareholders at the coming meeting is also placed before the shareholders. Indeed, the expense of printing the proxy papers and the postage stamps is not in question. The only question is whether the directors have a right to stamp the proxies. All I can say there is that, in my judgment, when once you admit the duty of the board of directors to be of the character which I have described, namely, that of informing, and advising the shareholders, I cannot help thinking that, inasmuch as this stamping is not prohibited, it is fairly to be held incidental to and consequential upon the duties of the directors as servants of the company, and by no means ultra vires of the company itself. [*Id.* at 13-14]

Buckley L.J., who agreed with Vaughan Williams L.J., added the following caveat to his judgment:

[C]ases often arise in which the board in power are anxious to maintain themselves in power, to procure their own re-election, or to drive a policy not really in the interests of the corporation, but for some private purpose of their own, down the throats of the corporators at a general meeting, and in which they issue at the expense of the company circulars and proxy papers for the purpose of attaining that object. When a case of that kind comes before the Court, I sincerely trust that the decision of this Court in this case will not be cited as any authority for justifying the action of the directors. The point here decided is that directors bona fide acting in the interests of the corporation, and not to serve their own interests, are entitled and bound to inform and guide the corporators in matters affecting the corporate interests, and any expenses reasonably incurred in so doing may be borne out of the funds of the company. [*Id.* at 21]

The result in *Rosenfeld* might seem uncomfortably close to pure vote-buying. On the other hand, can you articulate precisely why, as a technique of acquiring control of a corporation, vote-buying should be prohibited? At present, control can be acquired through an attempt to persuade shareholders to vote for one's slate in a proxy battle, or by purchasing the shares with the votes attached. However, Robert Clark has suggested that a third technique for acquiring control might be permitted: the purchase of the votes attached to a share without buying the underlying stock interest. See Clark, *Vote Buying and Corporate Law*, 29 Case Western L. Rev. 776 (1978-79). The purchaser may be prepared to bid for votes in this way if, by installing new management, he can increase the value of his shares by an amount exceeding the price of the votes he purchased.

This argument is criticized in Easterbrook & Fischel, *Voting in Corporate Law*, 26 J.L. & Econ. 395 (1983), which argues that shareholders might be willing to pay a substantial premium to acquire control if, once elected, they are able to loot the corporation. These premiums may be greater than those that a bidder who was solely interested in efficiency gains might pay, and the result might be a bidding war in which only looters could afford to compete. (For an argument that similar pathologies would attend vote-buying in political elections, see Epstein, *Why Restrain Alienation?* 85 Colum. L. Rev. 970, 987-88 (1985).) Might the same consequences be feared from a decision like *Rosenfeld*? On the other hand, might it be argued that this problem will be more severe if management is not permitted to reimburse itself for expenses associated with defeating insurgents?

F. ACCESS TO RECORDS AND FINANCIAL DISCLOSURE

1. Access to Records

Access to corporate records can provide information for the purpose of monitoring the performance of the corporation's management. Thus, in addition to maintaining and providing access to shareholder lists, corporations are typically required to maintain and provide access to other corporate records. For instance, in addition to a shareholders list a CBCA corporation must maintain adequate accounting records and records containing (1) the articles and by-laws of the corporation and amendments thereto; (2) any unanimous shareholder agreement; (3) minutes of shareholder meetings and shareholder resolutions; (4) minutes of meetings of the directors and resolutions of the directors; (5) copies of notices of who the directors of the corporation are and of any changes in the members of the board of directors. See CBCA ss. 20(1), (2); ABCA ss. 20(1), (2); OBCA ss. 140(1), (2). Similar records maintenance requirements are set out in the BCCA ss. 187, 195.

The accounting records are normally kept at the registered office of the corporation but may be kept at another place as the directors think fit. CBCA s. 20(4); ABCA s. 20(7); OBCA s. 140(1); cf. BCCA ss. 39, 40, 187. Where accounting records are maintained outside Canada the corporation must keep sufficient accounting records at a place in Canada that will allow directors to determine the financial position of the corporation with reasonable accuracy. CBCA s. 20(5); see also ABCA s. 20(8). Records other than accounting records must be kept either at the registered office of the corporation or at another place in Canada chosen by the directors. CBCA s. 20(1); see also ABCA s. 19(7); OBCA s. 140(1); cf. BCCA ss. 39, 40, 187.

Access to the minutes of directors meetings, resolutions of directors and accounting records must be open to inspection by directors at reasonable times. CBCA s. 20(4); ABCA s. 20(7); BCCA s. 188(1); OBCA s. 144(1). Minutes of directors' meetings, directors' resolutions and accounting records are not available to shareholders, creditors or the general public. CBCA ss. 20(2), (4), 21(1); ABCA ss. 20(1), 21; BCCA s. 188(2); OBCA ss. 140(1), 145(1).

Shareholders and creditors (and their agents or representatives) have access to the articles, by-laws, any unanimous shareholder agreement, minutes of shareholder meetings, shareholder resolutions, notices of directors, and the securities register. CBCA s. 21(1); ABCA s. 21; OBCA s. 145(1). They can examine and take extracts of the records free of charge during the usual business hours of the corporation. CBCA s. 21(1); ABCA s. 21; BCCA s. 188; OBCA s. 145.

Where the corporation has made a distribution of shares to the public the general public has access to the same records that shareholders and creditors do. Members of the general public can examine the records and may take extracts from the records for a reasonable fee. CBCA s. 21; see also BCCA s. 188(3).

2. Financial Reports

The financial statements for the preceding year must be placed before the annual meeting and mailed to shareholders no less than 21 days before the meeting. CBCA ss. 155, 159; ABCA ss. 149, 153 (no less than 10 days); BCCA s. 196 (no less than 10 days); OBCA s. 154. In the case of widely held corporations, the financial statements will be included in the proxy circular, and will contain a balance sheet, income statement, statement of retained earnings and a statement of changes in financial position. CBCA Reg. s. 46; ABCA Reg. s. 9; BCCA s. 169; OBCA Reg. s. 42. These "financials" must be prepared in accordance with the standards of the Canadian Institute of Chartered Accounts. CBCA Reg. ss. 44-45; ABCA Reg. s. 9(2); OBCA Reg. ss. 40, 41. If the corporation is a public corporation the financial statements must be filed and thus available for public scrutiny. See CBCA s. 160; ABCA s. 154; OBCA s. 156. Securities acts contain similar financial statement filing requirements (these are briefly noted in Chapter Five).

3. Auditing of Financial Statements

The use of auditors antedates statutes mandating their use. This can be explained in terms of the concept of bonding—the auditor's report serves as a signal of the accuracy of the financial statements. See Watts & Zimmerman, *Agency Problems, Auditing, and the Theory of the Firm: Some Evidence,* 26 J.L. & Econ. 613 (1983). CBCA s. 161 now requires the financials to be reported upon by an auditor who is "independent" of the corporation. See also ABCA s. 155; BCCA s. 207; OBCA s. 152. There is, however, an exemption for small firms that permits corporations which are not publicly held to dispense with the requirement of an auditor with the unanimous consent of shareholders. CBCA s. 163; ABCA s. 157; BCCA s. 203; OBCA s. 148.

It is important to remember that, while the financial statements are reported upon by the auditor, they are the *corporation's* statements, and are not issued by it until they have been approved by its directors. CBCA s. 158; ABCA s. 152; BCCA s. 198; OBCA s. 159. Unless exempted, the board of directors of a publicly held corporation must appoint an audit committee, a majority of whose members must not be employees of the corporation or an affiliate. CBCA s. 171; ABCA s. 165; BCCA s. 211; OBCA s. 158. The audit committee serves generally as a go-between for the board and the auditors, and is charged with examining the financial statements before they are submitted to the board for approval.

Although the CBCA-based statutes do not specify what manner of report the corporation's auditor is to make upon the corporation's financial statement (contrast in this regard BCCA s. 212), the following, or words of similar purport, is the customary form of a "clean" auditor's report:

We have examined the [list of financial statements]. Our examination included a general review of the accounting procedures and such tests of accounting records and other supporting evidence as we considered necessary in the circumstances.

In our opinion these financial statements present fairly the financial position of the company as at [year end] and the results of their operations for the year then ended in accordance with generally accepted accounting principles.

In a clean opinion the auditor generally opines as to two matters: that the financial statements have been set out in accordance with "generally accepted accounting principles" and that they "present fairly" the financial position of the corporation. Generally accepted accounting principles include at least those principles so recognized in the *CICA Handbook*. See Timbrell, *When Are Accounting Principles Generally Accepted?* 2 C.B.L.J. 77 (1977). There is often more than one accounting principle that could be applied to a given situation, and the results may differ depending upon which principle is used. Usually it is management's prerogative in such a case to choose among applicable principles, and an auditor is not obliged to qualify his opinion simply because he does not feel that the most appropriate principle was chosen. At some point, however, the issue of choosing among accounting principles begins to shade into the "fairness" with which the financial position is being presented. For an illustration of how financial statements prepared in accordance with generally accepted accounting principles nevertheless might not "present fairly" the company's financial position, see *United States v. Simon*, 425 F.2d 796 (2d Cir. 1969), cert. denied, 397 U.S. 1006 (1970).

In a given situation, the auditor may not feel able to give a clean opinion, in which case he may note that the opinion is "subject to" one or more qualifications. These qualifications may be required either because the auditor was unable to verify certain accounts in accordance with the standards for testing ordinarily applied to an audit, or because of the existence of certain "contingencies." The latter are customarily the subject of footnote disclosure. In an extreme case, the auditor might refuse to issue any opinion at all. Of course, it will be very damaging to the corporation's reputation if the auditor fails to issue an opinion or issues one subject to serious qualifications.

Like a director, the auditor may be removed by ordinary resolution of the shareholders. The vacancy may be filled either by the shareholders at the meeting where it is created or, if not filled then, by the directors. At the end of his term, an auditor may in effect be removed by the directors if they fail to renominate him. The CBCA-based statutes attempt to preserve some measure of true independence for the auditor, in the light of management's practical ability to remove the auditor, by giving the auditor the right to attend and to speak at all meetings of the audit committee and of the shareholders. Whenever it is proposed to remove the auditor or to nominate another instead, or whenever the auditor proposes to resign, the auditor may submit to management a written statement of position that must be sent to the shareholders with management's proxy solicitation materials. In addition, corporations statutes often provide that no person is to accept an appointment as a corporation's auditor until the auditor has received from the predecessor auditor a written statement of the circumstances surrounding the predecessor's departure.

G. SOME REFLECTIONS ON CORPORATE GOVERNANCE

This chapter has introduced many key aspects of corporate governance structures. With a knowledge of corporate governance structures in mind, this section canvasses several debates concerning corporate governance. In particular, it notes the debate over whether corporate law should be mandatory or enabling in nature, the corporate chartering competition debate, the reassessment of the shareholder passivity theory in the light of the growth of institutional investment, interest group theories of corporate governance, issues of corporate social responsibility and the stakeholder debate.

1. Mandatory Versus Enabling Corporate Law

Many provisions of the CBCA are enabling in nature. That is, they set out default rules that will apply unless the corporation specifies otherwise. For example, CBCA s. 103(1) provides that the directors may make, amend or repeal by-laws of the corporation "unless the articles, by-laws or a unanimous shareholder agreement otherwise provide." See also ABCA s. 98(1); OBCA s. 116(1). For a list of other enabling provisions under the ABCA and evidence on the extent to which corporations opt out of the default provisions see R.J. Wood, M.T. Brown & R.W. Bauman, *Modifications to Constitutions in Alberta: An Empirical Study*, 31 Alta. L.R. 263 (1993). Other provisions of the CBCA are mandatory in nature setting out rules that the corporation *must* follow. For example, voting on fundamental changes (CBCA s. 173) and class voting rights (CBCA s. 176) are, with a few exceptions with respect to class voting, mandatory in nature.

Should corporate law be primarily mandatory in nature, or should it be primarily enabling in nature? This question has been the subject of a considerable amount of academic debate.

The Argument for Enabling Corporate Law. Those who argue for a primarily enabling form of corporate laws note that market mechanisms will create an incentive for managers to adopt corporate charter provisions that minimize agency costs. Market mechanisms will cause corporate managers to bear the costs of failing to minimize agency costs by making the cost of finance and risk of take-over higher for such managers. The optimal corporate contract for all corporations is not likely to be obtained under a corporate law statute consisting exclusively, or primarily, of mandatory provisions since the optimal corporate contract is likely to vary from one business enterprise to another. Thus corporate law which is enabling in nature allows corporations to set their own corporate rules in a way that best allows the particular corporation to minimize its agency costs.

Under an enabling approach a corporate statute would serve as a standard form contract that would minimize the transactions costs of incorporation. Much of the incorporating statute could be adopted thereby avoiding costly negotiation over and drafting of many of the corporate law rules. The corporation would just have to deal with the more significant aspects for the particular corporation and opt out of some provisions of the incorporating statute by drafting separate rules on certain matters. The corporate statute would then be designed to approximate the corporate rules that most corporations would prefer to have. In this way the total amount of transactions costs for corporate charters could be minimized. On the enabling corporate law approach see, e.g., F.H. Easterbrook & D.R. Fischel, *The Corporate Contract*, 89 Col. L.R. 1416 (1989); R.C. Clark, *Contracts, Elites, and Traditions in the Making of Corporate Law*, 89 Col. L.R. 1703 (1989); and H.N. Butter & L.E. Ribstein, *Opting Out of Fiduciary Duties: A Response to the Anti-Contractarians*, 65 Wash. L.R. 1, 7-18 (1990). For a succinct review of arguments for and against mandatory corporate laws see L.E. Ribstein, *The Mandatory Nature of the ALI Code*, 61 Geo. Wash. L.R. 984, 987-998 (1993).

Arguments for Mandatory Laws. Several arguments have been made in response to the enabling corporate law argument.

(a) *Market Mechanisms Inadequate*

One such argument questions the effectiveness of market mechanisms in causing corporate managers to adopt a value-maximizing corporate charter. The product market, it is said, is not characterized by perfect competition. Rather, it is primarily oligopolistic, generating profits in excess of those that would obtain in perfectly competitive markets. This allows management some slack to provide a less than optimal corporate contract.

Proponents of mandatory corporate law argue that corporate managers are not significantly affected by capital markets because they obtain new finance primarily from retained earnings and seldom go to equity capital markets for further finance. The efficiency of capital markets has also been questioned noting that while capital markets may react very quickly to new information, they may not necessarily be pricing securities on the basis of their underlying values based on the present value of projected cash flows. It is suggested that the capital market is least likely to be efficient in the market for initial public offerings of new corporations where corporate charters are first assessed. The market for initial public offerings lacks established market pices and may consist primarily of relatively unsophisticated investors who can not effectively price corporate charter provisions. These alleged weaknesses in capital markets, it is argued, give corporate management scope to adopt less than optimal corporate charters.

With respect to the market for corporate control, critics of the enabling approach to corporate law note that the high premiums that are paid for corporations in take-overs implies that take-overs will only occur when management deviations from the optimum corporate contract are quite substantial. Again the market for corporate control, it is said, allows considerable slack for management to adopt a less than optimal corporate charter.

It is further contended that there is a very weak link between performance and removal of managers in the market for corporate managers. Thus the market for corporate managers will also not provide a sufficient incentive for corporate managers to adopt an optimal corporate contract.

These concerns with respect to the effectiveness of markets in giving corporate managers the incentive to adopt value maximizing corporate contracts are reviewed in M.A. Eisenberg, *The Structure of Corporate Law*, 89 Col. L.R. 1461 (1989). See also L.A. Kornhauser, *The Nexus of Contracts Approach to Corporations: A Comment on Easterbrook and Fischel*, 89 Col. L.R. 1449 (1989).

One response to these criticisms of the effectiveness of market mechanisms challenges the claims that these markets are ineffective. Firstly, there is a substantial body of empirical evidence supporting the claim that capital markets react very quickly to new information (see the discussion of the ECMH in Chapter One). With respect to initial public offerings it is argued that there is a significant institutional component among purchasers in initial public offerings. The institutional purchasers are sophisticated investors and the price will be set to sell the shares to these sophisticated investors. Other less sophisticated investors can benefit from the institutional investor effect on the price. Underwriters involved in the issue have their reputations to protect and may discourage overpricing of issues. Further, the evidence on initial public offerings is that they are typically underpriced. See, e.g., J.N. Gordon, *The Mandatory Structure of Corporate Law*, 89 Col. L.R. 1549 (1989); L.A. Ribstein, *The Mandatory Nature of the ALI Code*, 61 Geo. Wash. L.R. 984, 993-95 (1993). Further, it is argued that managements are subject to capital market discipline even if they finance with retained earnings rather than by selling shares. If the market requires a return of 10% on the corporation's securities then 10% is the cost of investment for the corporation. A corporation that can earn 12% on a given project will invest in the project if the required return on the market is 10%. A less efficient corporation that can only earn 8% on the same project will not invest if the required return on the market is 10%. The less efficient corporation's managers will have a reduced potential for earnings out of which management compensation can be paid. See, e.g., R.A. Winter, *Comment on Eisenberg*, 89 Col. L.R. 1526, 1527 (1989).

Another response to criticisms of the effectiveness of market mechanisms is that the argument in favour of enabling corporate law is not based on the existence of perfect markets. Indeed, the argument for enabling corporate law is that it allows corporations to adopt charter provisions that minimize agency costs. But agency costs would not exist in perfect markets. The enabling corporate law argument calls for flexibility in corporate charters so that market participants can engage in techniques to reduce market imperfections to the point that the marginal costs of such techniques just equal the marginal gains derived. Enacting mandatory provisions on the basis of the existence of market imperfections would, under the enabling corporate law argument, either prevent corporations from reducing the extent of such imperfections, or cause corporations to adopt techniques to minimize market imperfections which impose costs that outweigh the gains. Thus mandatory terms only make sense if the costs of enabling terms exceed the costs of mandatory terms. In addition, the legislative process by which mandatory laws would be produced may be subject to interest group pressures (see the section on Interest Group Theories below), which could lead to less than optimal mandatory provisions. In other words, it is wrong to assume that legislated mandatory provisions represent some form of "Nirvana" compared to the alleged failures of market mechanisms. F.S. McChesney, *Economics,*

Law, and Science in the Corporate Field: A Critique of Eisenberg, 89 Col. L.R. 1530 (1989); and H.N. Butter & L.E. Ribstein, *Opting Out of Fiduciary Duties: A Response to the Anti-Contractarians*, 65 Wash. L.R. 1, 53-58 (1990).

Stronger arguments in favour of legislated mandatory provisions would be ones that show that legislatures can provide lower cost mechanisms to respond to market imperfections or that legislated mandatory provisions can overcome market failures that prevent corporations from adopting agency cost reducing techniques to the point that the marginal costs equal the marginal benefits to society as a whole. Several such arguments are reviewed in J.N. Gordon, *The Mandatory Structure of Corporate Law*, 89 Col. L.R. 1549 (1989); see also R. Romano, *Answering the Wrong Question: The Tenuous Case for Mandatory Corporate Laws*, 89 Col. L.R. 1599 (1989). These arguments are considered in subsections (b) to (f) below.

(b) *Adverse Selection*

Another argument in favour of mandatory provisions is an adverse selection argument. The concept of adverse selection is that poor quality products will drive out good quality products. This might occur when consumers, to some extent, are unable to make distinctions in the quality of products. In the context of corporate charters, corporate managers might gain by putting in suboptimal terms that favour corporate management which will not be detected by investors. Because investors may not be able to detect some types of suboptimal charter provisions, capital markets will not cause corporate managers to bear the costs of suboptimal terms. Indeed, corporate managers that attempt to provide optimal terms not recognized as such by investors may risk incurring costs associated with such terms without deriving compensating benefits. Consequently suboptimal terms may eventually dominate the market. While investors may not be able to identify some suboptimal terms in individual corporate charters, they may observe their long-run returns and thus may eventually apply a discount on all corporate investments. Mandatory corporate law provisions might prevent corporate managers from adopting such suboptimal terms and thereby reduce the adverse selection problem and the overall discounting of corporate investments.

Corporate managers may be able to take steps to reduce the adverse selection problem by attempting to indicate to the market the superior quality of their corporate charter provisions. They could do so to the point that the marginal costs of attempting to so indicate just equal the marginal gains. Other market mechanisms might also respond to the adverse selection problem. For instance, corporations may find it beneficial to list securities on stock exchanges. Stock exchanges could impose standard minimum charter requirements that reduce management opportunism. While investors might not be able to assess the effect of individual standardized minimum charter provisions for individual corporations, they will probably be able to assess the overall effect on returns on investments in securities listed on the exchange. Competition between stock exchanges could result in experimentation with standardized minimum charter provisions in a search for the most efficient charter terms. In other words, the mandatory terms need not necessarily come in the form of legislated mandatory corporate law. See also the discussion of mandatory disclosure in Chapter Five.

(c) *Uncertainty of Customized Terms and the Public Good Hypothesis*

Another argument in favour of mandatory corporate law is based on the uncertainty that may be created by having enabling corporate law. Enabling corporate law would allow corporations to opt out of statutory provisions and create customized terms. This may lead to uncertainty because investors may not have enough experience with the customized terms to assess effectively the affect of such terms. A set of primarily mandatory corporate law provisions might allow investors to assess the effect of the terms for numerous corporations. The corporate charter of a new corporation might then be assessed at relatively low cost because investors may be able to extrapolate from their experience with other corporations which were required to have largely similar corporate charter provisions.

The uncertainty argument has been criticized for failing to take account of the extent to which market mechanisms may constrain the degree of uncertainty created by allowing customized corporate charter provisions. Corporate managers may bear the costs of uncertainty created by corporate charter provisions because the market will apply a discount to the price of the securities of corporations adopting corporate charter provisions of uncertain effect. Thus corporate managers may have an incentive to adopt standardized terms to the extent that the costs (or market discount) due to uncertainty outweighs the gains from customized terms.

A further argument in favour of mandatory provisions extends the uncertainty argument by arguing that market forces may not cause corporate managers to adopt standard form provisions to the optimal extent. The argument is that standard form terms have a public goods quality in that every corporation benefits from the build-up of court decisions on, and experience with, standardized terms. However, individual corporations may not have a sufficient incentive to adopt standard form terms to the optimal extent because they can not capture all of the benefits from standard form terms. Other corporations may benefit from the court decisions on, and experience with, the standard form terms adopted by an individual corporation and that individual corporation may not be able to charge other corporations a fee for the benefit that such other corporations receive. Thus the individual firm may only adopt standard provisions to the extent that the benefits it receives just equal the costs of adopting such terms (as opposed to customized terms). If the decision were made from the perspective of corporations and investors as a whole, the individual corporation might be more likely to adopt standard terms because the gains to corporations and investors as a whole from the adoption of standardized terms are greater then they are for the individual corporation. A corporate law regime with more mandatory provisions might then force individual corporations to adopt standardized terms to an extent more in accord with the benefits to corporations and investors as a whole.

One counterargument to this public goods hypothesis is that the public goods effect could run the other way. Individual corporations may not be able to capture all the benefits of experimentation with innovative customized terms. In other words, an individual corporation takes the risk of the uncertain effect of an innovative term. If it is unsuccessful other corporations could benefit from knowing that the term did not work effectively. If it is a successful innovation other corporations could copy the innovative term at no cost. The corporation that experimented with the innovative term may not be able to capture the benefits other corporations derive from its experiment with the innovative term.

Another counterargument is that the market might provide standardized forms through enterprises that can capture the benefits of such terms. For instance, standard debenture and stock terms are sold commercially and stock exchanges can require standardized terms and reap the benefits through listing fees and the trading profits of member brokers.

(d) *Innovation Hypothesis*

Responses to many of the arguments in favour of mandatory corporate law claim that market mechanisms exist for addressing the concerns raised. However, the innovation hypothesis posits that legislatures have a competitive advantage in providing innovative corporate charter terms. Here it is argued that legislatures can better signal the benefits of innovative corporate charter provisions because the adoption of similar provisions by individual corporations will be viewed with suspicion in the market for fear that corporate managers will be engaged in some form of opportunism transferring wealth from investors.

The criticism of this argument is that it depends on investors believing that the legislative response is more likely to be the result of a deliberative process that considers the interests of investors. However, the legislature may be dominated by, or heavily influenced by, a narrow set of interests which, in the context of corporate law, is likely to include well organized interests of corporate managers who have a significant stake in the outcome of the legislative process on matters of corporate law. It is also argued that the legislative process may be less responsive to market changes and thus less innovative than individual corporations or market intermediaries such as stock exchanges.

This "innovation" argument operates at cross-purposes to the "public goods" argument noted above. The innovation argument suggests the market will underproduce innovative terms while the public goods argument suggests the market will overproduce innovative terms. The question then is one of promoting the optimal amount of innovation. If mandatory terms are used to achieve an optimal trade-off between standardization and innovation then just how does one tell what the level is? If one cannot determine this optimal level than do either the innovation or the public goods argument provide any assistance in determining whether corporate laws should be mandatory or enabling?

The inadequacy of market mechanisms, adverse selection, uncertainty/public goods and innovation arguments suggest the use of legislated mandatory terms as a response to market failure problems. However, as noted above, in order to assess whether a legislative outcome would be superior to the market outcome one should also assess the potential failures of the legislative outcome. The influences exerted by various interest groups on legislative processes may cause legislative outcomes to deviate from optimal solutions even more than market outcomes.

(e) *Opportunistic Amendment Hypothesis*

Even if corporate charters can be effectively assessed in the market when they are first introduced, there may still be a concern that subsequent opportunistic changes will be made to the charter which could reduce the value of an investment based on the initial charter terms. Corporations will of course have to make changes in response to changing circumstances. Shareholders may be protected by supermajority voting requirements and class voting requirements but these may not fully protect them due to "rational shareholder apathy" and interested shareholder voting. Mandatory corporate provisions might thus serve as an additional protection against subsequent opportunistic changes in the corporate charter. In addition to the discussion in Gordon, *id.*, on this argument see, e.g., L.A. Bebchuk, *The Debate on Contractual Freedom in Corporate Law*, 89 Col. L.R. 1395 (1989).

As the enabling argument suggests, there can be costs to such mandatory provisions. Mandatory provisions may restrict the ability of corporations to adjust their corporate structures over time and may constrain the ability of corporations to adopt different corporate structures more suitable to the particular industry and the circumstances in which the corporation finds itself.

Is Corporate Law Trivial? A further note to provide food for thought in the context of the mandatory/enabling debate is the suggestion by Professor Black that corporate law may be trivial. B.S. Black, *Is Corporate Law Trivial? A Political and Economic Analysis*, 84 Nw. Univ. L.R. 542 (1990). Black questions the extent to which allegedly mandatory rules are really mandatory in practice. He notes four different types of mandatory corporate law rules: (1) market mimicking rules; (2) avoidable rules; (3) changeable rules; and (4) unimportant rules.

Market mimicking rules are rules that most corporations would have chosen in any case. They are the types of rules that market mechanisms would have given corporations an incentive to adopt. Mandatory corporate law rules of this type have little or no real mandatory bite since most corporations would have followed the rule regardless of whether legislation mandated it.

Avoidable rules are rules that may appear mandatory but which the corporation can avoid by simply structuring the transaction in a different way. For instance, to amalgamate corporations A and B, shareholder approval by way of a supermajority vote at a shareholders meeting will be required from both corporation A and corporation B. If it was felt that corporation A shareholder approval had to be avoided this could be done in any of a number of ways. Corporation A could make a take-over bid for the shares of corporation B and then use its controlling position to wind up corporation B. This would not require a vote from the shareholders of corporation A or the shareholders of corporation B (although corporation B shareholders could decide whether or not to tender their shares under the bid of corporation A). Corporation A could also incorporate a subsidiary, have the subsidiary amalgamate with corporation B and then wind up the amalgamated subsidiary corporation. The amalgamation between A-sub and corporation B would require the approval of corporation B shareholders but it would not require the vote of corporation A shareholders. Corporation B could also sell its assets to corporation A. This would require the approval of corporation B shareholders but not the approval of corporation A shareholders.

Changeable rules are rules that while mandatory on their face can be changed over time by political pressure. The political pressure will not necessarily result in provisions that maximize the value of corporations if the political process is dominated by particular interest groups. One such interest group may be corporate managers themselves and thus could lead to downstream changes that effect wealth transfers to management from other corporate constituents.

Unimportant mandatory rules are rules that would not be chosen by the corporation but are of little or no significance. One example of such a rule is the statutory minimum quorum rule under section 168 of the BCCA, which provides that the minimum quorum for a shareholder meeting is two persons unless the corporation only has one shareholder, in which case the quorum is one person. A minimum quorum requirement of two persons where a corporation has two or more shareholders is not likely to have a binding effect in most cases.

In addition to these claims that the mandatory effect of corporate laws may be rather limited, corporations can be incorporated in any of a number of jurisdictions both domestically and internationally and still carry on business in other jurisdictions. This choice of corporate laws, and the ability to change the statute under which a corporation is incorporated, limits the extent to which corporate laws can be mandatory since corporations that do not like a particular set of mandatory rules can change jurisdiction and adopt a competing set of mandatory rules. On the effect of forum shopping on the mandatory nature of corporate laws and a discussion of several mandatory laws that are not truly binding in effect see R. Romano, *Answering the Wrong Question: The Tenuous Case for Mandatory Corporate Laws*, 89 Col. L.R. 1599 (1989). This potential for competition in corporate laws is the subject of the next subsection.

2. Corporate Charter Competition

It was noted in Chapter Three that a corporation could be incorporated in any of several jurisdictions in Canada and yet operate in other jurisdictions upon the payment of an extra-provincial registration fee and compliance with extra-provincial licensing requirements. This potential to choose the jurisdiction of incorporation allows for competition between jurisdictions for incorporation revenues. Evidence of this form of competition in the United States has provoked considerable debate as to the efficacy of such competition.

The Potential for Corporate Chartering Competition in the United States. In the United States there is no federal incorporation statute. Corporate statutes are a matter of state jurisdiction. Further, in the United States (as in Canada) the general conflict of laws rule regarding corporate law is that the corporate law of the statute of incorporation governs. This allows incorporators to choose which of the various state corporate statutes the corporation should be incorporated under. This choice of incorporating statutes creates the potential for competition among the various states for incorporation fees from incorporations.

Delaware as the Winner in the Competition. A curious feature of this competition in the United States is that approximately one-half of the largest U.S. industrial firms are incorporated in Delaware. For firms listed on national securities exchanges, more are incorporated in Delaware than in any other state. Further, of corporations that change their state of incorporation by reincorporating in another state, by far the vast majority reincorporate in Delaware. See R. Romano, *The Genius of American Corporate Law*, 6 (1993).

The Race to the Bottom. This so-called competition for corporate chartering was characterized by Professor Cary as a "race to the bottom," which Delaware is winning. In Cary's view it is race to bottom because Delaware's success, he claimed, came from having a lax statute that allowed corporate managers to take advantage of shareholders more effectively than the statutes of other states. Given the separation of ownership and control, it was management that would decide the state of incorporation or reincorporation and management could thus choose the most lax statute. W.L. Cary, *Federalism and Corporate Law: Reflections Upon Delaware*, 88 Yale L.J. 663 (1974). Under Cary's characterization of the competition Delaware's success came not from offering a more efficient corporate statute for management and shareholders alike, but from permitting managers to effect a wealth transfer from shareholders to themselves.

The Race to the Top. Professor Winter subsequently suggested a different characterization of the success of Delaware. According to Professor Winter, Delaware is winning the "race to the top." While Professor Winter agreed with Professor Cary that states were responding to the demands of corporate managers, corporate managers were, he noted, constrained by market forces in the product market, capital markets and the market for corporate control. These market constraints forced managers to seek a corporate law regime that would maximize the value of the corporation. In Winter's view shareholder demand would drive corporate charter competition because market constraints would reduce the agency problem associated with the separation of ownership and control. R.K. Winter, *State Law, Shareholder Protection and the Theory of the Corporation*, 6 J. of Legal Studies 251 (1977).

The Empirical Evidence. Proponents of the race-to-the-bottom view challenged Winter's assertion on the basis that the market constraints are imperfect and the slack in market constraints allows managements to engage in non-value maximizing, wealth-transferring behaviour. This left an empirical question that has been addressed in several studies. Of five studies examining the share price effect of reincorporations in the state of Delaware none found negative effects while four found significant positive share price effects. On the face of it the results do not support the race-to-the-bottom hypothesis. This and other evidence is reviewed in Romano, *id.* at 17-24.

The usefulness of these empirical studies has been challenged on the basis that there may be confounding effects of a reincorporation given that the reincorporation may be done for a variety of reasons. For instance, the reincorporation may be done to facilitate corporate acquisitions, which may be viewed as value maximizing to shareholders. See L.A. Bebchuk, *Federalism and the Corporation: The Desirable Limits on State Competition in Corporate Law*, 105 Harv. L.R. 1435 (1992) and M.A. Eisenberg, *The Structure of Corporation Law*, 89 Col. L.R. 1461 (1989). However, Professor Romano has argued that it is unlikely that these confounding wealth increasing effects would swamp the negative effects of wealth transfers if the race-to-the-bottom hypothesis were correct. In particular, she argues that one should observe significant negative share price consequences for corporations that reincorporate to engage in activities that are perceived as favouring managers over shareholders. since there would be no offsetting price effect. However, the share price effect does not appear to be affected by the purpose of the reincorporation. *Id.*, Romano, at 18-19.

Why Is Delaware Winning the Race? Professor Romano argues that Delaware is winning the corporate chartering competition because it can offer a credible commitment to abstain from altering the attractive conditions it has provided once it has obtained the corporate fee revenues from a reincorporation. It does this by investing in so-called transaction-specific assets. A transaction-specific asset is one that derives a much higher value from a particular use than can be obtained in any other use. The transaction-specific asset that Romano claims Delaware has developed is the intangible asset of its reputation for responsiveness to corporate concerns. It is committed to being responsive because of the importance of incorporation fee revenues in the state's budget. Delaware has a much higher ratio of incorporation fee revenues to other revenues than other states. It would be difficult for the state to maintain its level of services without continued incorporation fee revenues. As Professor Romano puts it, Delaware is "hostage to its success in the chartering market." Other transaction-specific intangible assets that Delaware has committed to incorporations are said to be a judicial expertise in corporate law, a comprehensive body of case law and expertise in processing corporate filings. These intangible assets can not be readily redeployed to other profitable uses. *Id.*, Romano, at 37-44.

Delaware also maintains a commitment not to alter the corporate laws that were the basis for incorporation in Delaware by a constitutional provision that requires a two-thirds vote in both houses of the state legislature to change the Delaware corporate statute. While this may slow the rate of corporate reform, it protects against volatility due to changes in the corporate laws that form the basis of a reincorporation in Delaware. *Id.*, Romano, at 41-42.

Corporate Charter Competition in Canada. As was noted in Chapter Three, there are 13 potential incorporation statutes in Canada—the federal CBCA and the incorporation statutes of the 10 provinces and the 2 territories. As in the United States, the applicable conflict of law rules with respect to corporate law is that the applicable corporate law is the corporate law of the statute of incorporation. Thus there appears to be the same scope for corporate charter competition in Canada. However, there is no clear winner of a corporate chartering competition in Canada and corporate chartering competition appears to be less pronounced in Canada than it is in the United States (if it exists at all). See R.J. Daniels, *Should Provinces Compete? The Case for a Competitive Corporate Law Market*, 36 McGill L.J. 130 (1991); and J.G. MacIntosh, *The Role of Interjurisdictional Competition in Shaping Canadian Corporate Law: A Second Look* (1993). In the following excerpt Professor Romano reviews both the Daniels and MacIntosh articles on corporate chartering competition in Canada and comments on why there may be less corporate chartering competition in Canada than in the United States.

R. Romano, The Genius of American Corporate Law
American Enterprise Institute Studies in Regulation and Federalism, 1993
Chapter 6, pp. 118-28

There are two interesting studies of corporate charter competition in Canada, a pioneering study by Ronald Daniels and a careful critique of it by Jeffrey MacIntosh.[1] Daniels contends that enactment of the Canada Business Corporations Act provoked a competitive reaction by provinces, creating uniform code provisions, similar to the situation in the United States.[2] MacIntosh disagrees, maintaining that the diffusion of the CBCA across the provinces is a function of the preferences of the administrators who initiate corporate law reform, rather than charter competition: administrators either strongly prefer uniform laws or develop a consensus view on what constitutes a good law.

Daniels develops his thesis by showing that the role of the Canadian national government in charter competition has been analogous to Delaware's: besides the rapid diffusion of CBCA reform provisions across the provinces, the predominant choice of reincorporating firms is national.[3] Many firms also initially incorporate under the CBCA, with the bulk coming from businesses located in one province, Quebec. Daniels suggests that this phenomenon is a function of special political concerns and incorporation fee structure. Changes in incorporation levels across the two regimes (Quebec and Canadian) are related to the growing political success of the separatist party in Quebec and to changes in franchise fees. Quebec's fees are calculated on a scale graduated according to a firm's capital, which imposes a higher charge than other provinces and the CBCA, which assess a small flat fee.[4] In 1985, national incorporation fees were increased from $200 to $500 (Canadian); thereafter national incorporations by Quebec firms slowed, and the total number of national incorporations decreased. Presumably, by 1985, with the union still intact, the Quebec business community was less concerned over the separatist movement, so that price became the determinative factor in an incorporation decision. Recent events reviving the issue of separation (the rejection in 1992 of a proposed constitutional provision concerning Quebec's distinctive status) may induce a reversion to national incorporation.

---

1   Ronald J. Daniels, "Should Provinces Compete? The Case for a Competitive Corporate Law Market,"
    McGill Law Journal, vol. 36 (1991), p. 130; Jeffrey MacIntosh, "The Role of Interjurisdictional Competition in Shaping Canadian Corporate Law: A Second Look," University of Toronto Law and Economics
    Working Paper 18 (Toronto, 1993).

2   Daniels, "Should Provinces Compete?" pp. 151-55. The national corporation statute was introduced in
    1975. Daniels does not indicate the reason for this enactment (that is, whether firms or regulators were
    dissatisfied with provincial regimes). He does note that the national government sought provincial input
    into the drafting process but because the provinces were reluctant to participate, it acted unilaterally;
    ibid., p. 151 n. 49.

3   Ibid., pp. 152, 157, 165 n. 69. Moreover, like the development of Delaware's code, some of the Canadian government's reforms in the CBCA had previously been enacted by provinces; ibid., p. 154.

4   Ibid., pp. 167-69. Other provinces abandoned graduated fee systems by the beginning of the 1980s.

Canada's 1985 fee increase, Daniels suggests, had a political source: Quebec politicians lobbied for a national fee increase to improve their market share of incorporations.[5] He does not, however, address why the national government acceded to such a request. If the national government was competing for corporate charters, then it is difficult to explain why it acquiesced to Quebec's lobbying for higher national incorporation fees. In fact, this datum seems to provide evidence that the national government was not seriously attempting to compete with the provinces, consistent with MacIntosh's view of Canadian corporate law reform, which treats the innovative features of the CBCA as either a random event or a function of bureaucratic preferences rather than a response to corporate demands.

Alternatively, the national government might have been competing for charters, but administrators thought that they offered a sufficiently superior product that firms would be willing to pay a premium for a national domicile, just as U.S. firms are willing to pay higher franchise fees for a Delaware address. Such an explanation—miscalculation of the price sensitivity of firms—is not compelling, however, because the government did not respond to the significant decline in incorporations after the rate change with a rate reduction to recoup its market position. Another explanation that partially reconciles Daniels's and MacIntosh's competing views of the Canadian charter market is that, whatever its motivation when it adopted the innovative CBCA, the national government simply decided to stop competing for charters when it decided to raise incorporation fees: presumably Quebec was willing to provide the national government with greater benefits than it received from charter revenues, such as support on policy issues unrelated to corporate law, in compensation for the franchise fee revision.

Whether or not supported by Quebec's lobbying, the national government's fee increase underscores the feebleness of a national government's incentive to compete for charters. A national government's ability to commit itself credibly to a responsive corporation code is limited, despite pioneering efforts at corporate law reform, because firms understand that such a government faces a minimal financial penalty from failure to continue to innovate. Franchise fee revenues are an insignificant percentage of a national government's budget.[6] Hence, such a government is far less motivated than a small state, such as Delaware, to be responsive to firms. The decrease in national incorporations after the fee increase is, then, not simply a function of the sensitivity of firms to charter prices. Rather, it is a function of price and an additional factor, the

---

5   Ibid., pp. 168-69. None of the provinces raised their fees in response to the national fee increase.

6   A crude estimate, providing an order of magnitude, can be extrapolated from Daniels's data on new incorporations under the CBCA and Canada's gross domestic product; ibid., pp. 158, 160 (tables 2 and 3). In 1988, the national government earned approximately $6 million in fees from new incorporations, compared to approximately $4 million in 1984; these amounts are less than 0.5 percent of Canada's gross domestic product. MacIntosh indicated that at the current fee level the national government obtains $6 million from franchise fees, an amount equal to $1/25,000$ of the national budget; MacIntosh, "Role of Interjurisdictional Competition," p. 11. He further suggested that were the national government to recruit an incorporation business more actively, the additional revenues would still be insignificant, amounting to approximately $1/10,000$ of the national budget.

government's reputation for responsiveness. Action with an adverse effect on the government's reputation will reduce the number of new incorporations, as will an increase in price. In this scenario, firms perceived the national government's fee increase as an indication that it would also capitulate to provincial pressure concerning substantive code content. As a consequence, national incorporations declined as firms realized that it was too costly to run the risk of a national domicile.

To bolster this explanation for the decrease in national incorporations, it would be useful to know whether there were contemporaneously important national issues on which Quebec's support was key and which led to the increase in the national government's incorporation fee. Quebec's desire for separation may have been one such issue: if raising the CBCA incorporation fee disproportionately subsidized Quebec because it was the only province losing corporate revenues under the old rate structure, then the change could route additional national funds to Quebec and mollify separatist impulses. It certainly would be plausible for a national government to place priority on preserving the union over maintaining a reputation as a reliable sovereign for corporations, especially given the infinitesimal revenues that it obtained from corporate chartering.

Daniels concludes that state competition is far less effective in Canada than in the United States, and MacIntosh contends that it does not exist, because several factors important to Delaware's success are lacking, in particular the development of a comprehensive and specialized corporate law jurisprudence, as well as a significant dependence on franchise revenues. The best explanation for the more limited Canadian competition for charters, which both Daniels and MacIntosh emphasize, is that provinces do not control their corporation codes: authority is shared with independent provincial regulators and national judges. In particular, securities law administrators, whose jurisdiction is based on the residence of the investor rather than on the domicile of the issuing firm, are able to regulate corporate governance and thereby override provincial corporate law regimes.[7] The Ontario Securities Commission, for example, imposes fiduciary obligations on majority shareholders under its public interest powers.[8] Securities commissions also regulate shareholder communications, going-private transactions, attendance at shareholder meetings, and receipt of financial statements.[9] As long as a firm has a shareholder in Ontario (a probable event, as it is the most populous province), its corporate law can be dictated by the Ontario Securities Commission rather than the legislature or court of its province of incorporation. This authority has even been exercised over stock transactions involving solely non-Ontario investors.[10] In the United States, by contrast, the Supreme Court has refused to expand the reach of the national securities laws to include traditional fiduciary duties, and it has preserved the states' jurisdiction over corporate governance even in the one area of overlapping jurisdiction,

---

7   Daniels, "Should Provinces Compete?" pp. 182-84.

8   Ibid., p. 183 n. 119.

9   MacIntosh, "Role of Interjurisdictional Competition," p. 30.

10   Ronald J. Daniels and Jeffrey G. MacIntosh, "Toward a Distinctive Canadian Corporate Law Regime,"
     Osgoode Law Journal, vol. 29 (1991), pp. 1, 37.

takeover regulation.[11] The Securities and Exchange Commission has also been prevented by the courts from forays into corporate governance.[12]

In addition, the Supreme Court of Canada reviews all provincial appellate courts.[13] This feature of jurisdictional spillover may be less important than the activities of securities law administrators, however, for Daniels states that in recent years the Supreme Court of Canada has reviewed few provincial decisions involving corporate or commercial matters.[14] Business appeals became discretionary in 1974, when the automatic appeal right for cases whose amount in controversy exceeded $10,000 was eliminated and the court's docket changed considerably, as constitutional cases increased throughout the 1980s with the adoption of the Canadian Charter of Rights and Freedoms.[15] Still, in the United States there is little if any basis for the U.S. Supreme Court to review a Delaware court's corporate law decision.

A further difference between the United States and Canada affecting corporate law jurisdiction is that all Canadian judges are federal appointees with life tenure. As MacIntosh notes, even a province that sought to create a special corporate law court along the lines of Delaware cannot do so as effectively as Delaware: the provincial judicial nominees must be appointed through a national process, which is not conditioned on the provincial government's approval.[16] In addition, life tenure diminishes the judge's incentive, provided by the need for reappointment, to be responsive to changing business conditions. Thus, the ability of Canadian provinces to deliver a predictable and stable corporation code like Delaware is attenuated further, because they do not exercise complete control over judicial appointments.

A province's control over what is ostensibly its substantive law and the judges who interpret that law is, then, highly circumscribed. This weakens the incentive to invest in assets that maintain a responsive corporate law regime because the value of such assets can be dramatically impaired by the actions of securities regulators in other provinces or by the Canadian judiciary.[17] The inability of provinces to commit credibly to a responsive corporate law regime, given overlapping jurisdiction, also renders firms less willing

---

11   *Santa Fe Industries v. Green*, 430 U.S. 462 (1977); *CTS Corp. v. Dynamics Corp. of America*, 481 U.S. 69 (1987).

12   *Business Roundtable v. SEC*, 905 F.2d 406 (D.C. Cir. 1990) (striking down SEC regulation of shareholder voting).

13   Daniels, "Should Provinces Compete?" pp. 186-87.

14   Ibid., p. 187 n. 132 (from 1986 to 1989, only 14 of 304 cases heard by the Canadian Supreme Court could be classified as corporate or commercial).

15   Ibid., p. 187.

16   MacIntosh, "Role of Interjurisdictional Competition," p. 37.

17   I have no explanation for why Canadians tolerate such interference in corporate governance by securities administrators; neither Daniels nor MacIntosh provides one. To the extent that provincial securities administrators cannot discriminate against foreign-incorporated firms, the overlapping jurisdiction

(The footnote is continued on the next page.)

to invest in optimizing incorporation decisions, which has a feedback effect, further reducing provincial incentives to compete.

A second important distinguishing institutional feature, besides control of the code, contributes to the difference in competition for charters between the United States and Canada. Large Canadian corporations have greater concentration of stock ownership than their U.S. counterparts. Daniels and MacIntosh note that more than half the firms in the Toronto Stock Exchange 300 Composite Index are owned by a single shareholder with holdings exceeding 50 percent of the votes, whereas only 12 percent of the U.S. Fortune 500 firms are controlled by a 50 percent shareholder or shareholder group.[18] As ownership concentration increases, the choice of legal regime declines in importance: management with voting control does not need statutory discretion to operate a firm because it has the votes to change statutory default rules as it pleases. A firm with a concentrated ownership structure is therefore not likely to pay a premium willingly for a corporate law regime that is superior on several Delaware dimensions, such as organizational flexibility and managerial discretion.

Self-dealing issues are, however, more important from the public shareholders' perspective when ownership is concentrated than when it is diffuse. If insiders need outside equity capital, they then have an incentive to lower cost of capital to incorporate in a province whose regime best protects minority interests against self-dealing. But this involves a far more limited area of corporation laws on which provinces could compete in comparison with U.S. law, and thus even vigorous Canadian charter competition would be more circumscribed than that of the United States.

Jurisdictions such as Canadian provinces that are populated by firms with concentrated stock ownership, then, have less to gain from corporate charter competition than those whose firms are more widely held, such as U.S. states. Hence, any economic return from provincial competition for chartering would be far lower than the return in the United States. Causality, however, could run in the opposite direction: in the absence of vigorous competition for corporate charters, equity investments of public firms could become more concentrated, as investors compensate for less responsive legal regimes with more immediate monitoring of management. We do not have data to test the direction of causality in the relation between corporate ownership and charter competition, and I am uncertain whether an adequate test could be constructed.

Differentiation of which shareholder issues matter when ownership composition varies is borne out in a comparison of the two countries' shareholder litigation rules.

---

17   Continued . . .

  problem may be mitigated if all provinces are interested in charter revenue maximization: top provincial authorities could rein in their securities administrators from rendering decisions that undercut the province's corporation laws, and other provinces' laws would, derivatively, be protected. Overlapping oversight still adds unnecessary friction to a competitive system, which may slow the introduction and diffusion of corporate law reforms, as one province's innovation may run into difficulty with administrators in another province that has yet to adopt the reform provision.

18   Ronald J. Daniels and Jeffrey G. MacIntosh, "Capital Markets and the Law: The Peculiar Case of Canada," Canada Investment Review, vol. 3 (1990), pp. 77, 80-81.

Shareholder litigation is more easily undertaken in the United States than Canada. Canada follows the British cost rule, in which a losing party pays the other's costs (costs follow the event), although the losing plaintiff-shareholder in a derivative suit can petition the court for indemnification from the corporation.[19] Furthermore, contingent fees are not as prevalent in Canada; they are not permitted in Ontario, require local bar society approval in other provinces, and are legislatively capped, typically at 25 percent.[20] In addition, class action rules, following British procedure, are more restrictive than in the United States.[21] The Canadian cost and class action rules severely restrict the incentive for a shareholder to bring a lawsuit against management, an incentive that is weak to begin with, because litigation costs typically exceed the plaintiff's pro rata benefit. The U.S. solution to the collective action problem of shareholder litigation is to create an incentive for attorneys, who are paid on a contingent fee basis, to bring shareholder suits by offering the prospect of recovery of a substantial legal fee from the defendant corporation.[22] The Canadian rules eliminate the U.S. solution.

Why don't Canadian provinces seek to compete in the dimension of lawsuit accessibility, as U.S. states do? One explanation is that greater concentration of ownership affects litigation patterns and reduces the need for more accommodating access rules. In particular, controlling shareholders have superior incentives to monitor managers for breach of the duty of care[23] compared with dispersed shareholders with small holdings, and their managers rarely engage in unilateral action to thwart a takeover because firms with controlling owners are not subject to hostile bids. Two common categories of U.S.

19　See Frank H. Buckley and Mark Q. Connelly, Corporations: Principles and Policies, 2d ed. (Toronto: Emond Montgomery, 1988), p. 615; Jeffrey G. MacIntosh, "The Oppression Remedy: Personal or Derivative?" Canadian Bar Review, vol. 70 (1991), pp. 29, 56.

20　I would like to thank Jeffrey MacIntosh for explaining to me how contingency fees are used in Canada.

21　Unlike U.S. class actions, the British rules require that an amount in liquidated damages be specified and that class members have identical claims. These requirements discourage suits. Consequently, most shareholder suits that are not brought under the derivative statutes are individual (personal) actions. There is, however, proposed legislation in Ontario to change class action rules; Quebec has, in fact, departed from the British practice. The greater difficulty in pursuing a class action may not be as consequential as it appears. Canadian securities administrators have much greater discretion than the SEC in affecting firms' governance, so shareholder claims that in the United States are pursued as class actions may be undertaken, at the government's expense, by securities regulators in Canada. I would like to thank Jeffrey MacIntosh for explaining these differences to me.

22　See John C. Coffee, "The Unfaithful Champion: The Plaintiff as Monitor in Shareholder Litigation," Law and Contemporary Problems, vol. 48 (1985), p. 5. As Coffee and others have detailed, there are serious problems with such an incentive scheme, including conflict of interest between shareholders and attorney and the possibility of frivolous litigation.

23　See Romano, "The Shareholder Suit," pp. 81-82 (U.S. firms with lower management stock ownership sued more frequently for breach of duty of care, whereas those with high management stock ownership more frequently sued for breach of duty of loyalty).

shareholder suits are therefore of little concern to the vast majority of Canadian firms.[24] This reduces the need for increased access to the courts.

A less efficiency-centered explanation of Canadian shareholder litigation rules is that controlling shareholders and their counsel have exerted influence on Canadian corporation codes to obtain laws that make shareholder litigation difficult in order to enrich themselves at the minority's expense. This, however, is not a persuasive explanation because, in contrast to U.S. corporation codes, Canadian codes have statutory oppression remedies, which entail simplified filing procedures compared with derivative and individual (personal) shareholder actions in the United States. These provisions are aimed at providing relief against corporate action detrimental to the minority.[25] Moreover, if provinces are not competing for charters in the first place, this would also answer the question why they do not compete on the dimension of lawsuit accessibility, without need of recourse to a controlling shareholder-political conspiracy explanation.

The Canadian experience is not clearly analogous to the close corporation context in the United States, where charter competition is arguably anemic; Canadian firms differ significantly from U.S. close corporations. In contrast to close corporations, Canadian corporations with concentrated ownership are publicly traded, and thus stock market signals are available to price the legal regime for the minority shareholders. In addition, Canadian firms with controlling owners are typically much larger than U.S. close corporations. They are consequently more likely to engage in repetitive transactions for which the product of charter competition—standard form contracts—is of value.

There is, however, a simpler answer to the claim that there is little competition for corporate charters in Canada compared with the United States than the story developed thus far. Such an explanation involves numbers: there are far fewer provinces than states, and industrial organization theorists conventionally link competition to market structure (that is, number of producers as well as barriers to entry).[26] Although there are five times as many states as provinces, the credible commitment explanation of Delaware's success, built on transaction-specific assets that create a reputation for responsiveness, suggests that competition is viable only for a subset of states, those small enough for franchise revenues to make a budgetary difference. Accordingly, it is questionable whether the smaller number of provinces accounts for the absence of vigorous competition, as opposed to the barrier created by overlapping jurisdictional authority and the more limited demands placed on corporation codes because of the concentration of equity ownership of publicly traded Canadian firms.

----

24   Ibid., p. 60.

25   For a discussion of the oppression remedy, and the extent to which courts have interpreted it to cover derivative claims, see MacIntosh, "The Oppression Remedy." MacIntosh is skeptical of the efficacy of the remedy.

26   The earliest work along these lines is associated with Joe Bain. See Jean Tirole, The Theory of Industrial Organization (Cambridge: MIT Press, 1988), p. 1.

NOTES

What effect would growing international competition in the trade in goods and services and the internationalization of capital markets have on corporate charter competition within Canada itself and between corporate law jurisdictions around the world? How would a corporate seat conflict of laws rule (i.e. the applicable corporate law is the law of the jurisdiction where the corporation's top-level management decisions are made) affect the competition in corporate chartering?

3. Shareholder Passivity and the Growth of Institutional Investment

Shareholder Passivity. The nature of the public corporation as it was described by Adolph Berle and Gardiner Means in *The Modern Corporation and Private Property* (1932) consists of managers controlling corporations in which they have little or no ownership interest and are subject to little or no control by the large and disperse group of shareholder "owners" of the corporation. This lack of control over managers by the disperse group of shareholders, or "shareholder passivity" was later explained as "rational shareholder apathy." Shareholder apathy is rational where there is a large and disperse group of shareholders because their individual small stakes in the corporation make the gains from monitoring the managers small relative to the costs. Further, the rational shareholder would rather free ride on the monitoring efforts of others, receiving the benefits of monitoring without incurring the costs.

The Large Stake Shareholder Incentive to Be Active. However, shareholder passivity becomes progressively less rational as the shareholder's stake in the corporation increases. As the shareholder's stake increases the gains from monitoring become more significant relative to the costs. At the same time the likelihood of being able to free ride on the monitoring efforts of others diminishes. Thus a shareholder with a significant stake in the corporation has an incentive to become actively involved in monitoring the performance of the corporation rather than to remain passive. See further, B.S. Black, *Shareholder Passivity Reexamined*, 89 Mich. L.R. 520 (1990). Evidence suggesting that large block shareholders do have an effect on the monitoring of corporate managers is reviewed in, e.g., J.G. MacIntosh, *The Role of Institutional and Retail Investors in Canadian Capital Markets*, 31 Osgoode Hall L.J. 371 (1993); and B.S. Black, *The Value of Institutional Investor Monitoring: The Empirical Evidence*, 39 UCLA L.R. 895, 917-27 (1992).

Potential for Large Stake Shareholders. Shareholders having relatively small stakes in corporations supposedly came about as a natural development in response to demands for large amounts of capital to take advantage of economies of scale while allowing investors the benefits of diversification and liquidity (see the discussion of limited liability in Chapter Three). However, this need not be the pattern of investment. Indeed, in Japan and Germany quite a different pattern of investment developed in response to demand for large amounts of capital. In Japan and Germany large financial institutions developed with large stakes in the corporations they provided financial assistance to. These financial institutions play an important role in corporate governance in those countries. See, e.g., M.J. Roe, *Some Differences in Corporate Structure in Germany, Japan, and the United States*, 102 Yale L.J. 1927 (1993); Mark Roe, *Strong Managers, Weak Owners* (1994); Gilson & Roe, *Understanding the Japanese Kieretsu: Overlaps Between Corporate Governance and Industrial Organization*, 102 Yale L.J. 871 (1993); B.S. Black, *The Value of Institutional Investor Monitoring: The Empirical Evidence*, 39 UCLA L.R. 895, 927-31 (1992). See also the discussion in subsection 4 below.

In recent years changes in capital markets in North America have created the potential for shareholders with large stakes in corporations. Institutional investors (such as banks, trust companies, pension funds, insurance companies and mutual funds) have grown significantly in size and importance in recent years in both Canada and the United States. See, e.g., B.S. Black, *Shareholder Passivity Reexamined*, 89 Mich. L.R. 520, 567-70 (1990) with respect to the United States; and see J.G. MacIntosh, *The Role of Institutional and Retail Investors in Canadian Capital Markets*, 31 Osgoode Hall L.J. 371 (1993) with respect to Canada. These institutional investors can and have had an increasing influence on corporate decision making. See, e.g., *id.*, MacIntosh, 377-78; and B.S. Black, *The Value of Institutional Investor Monitoring: The Empirical Evidence*, 39 UCLA L.R. 895, 925-27 (1992). However, they are subject to a variety of legal constraints that limit their ability to exert influence over corporate decision making.

Constraints on Institutional Investor Monitoring. While institutional shareholders holding large stakes can play a significant role in monitoring corporate performance, it has been argued that several features of the existing law keep even institutional owners relatively passive by putting constraints on institutions acquiring substantial stakes in corporations and discouraging institutions from voicing concerns about corporate performance or influencing shareholder voting. The kinds of constraints discussed below are addressed in detail in the Canadian context in J.G. MacIntosh, *The Role of Institutional and Retail Investors in Canadian Capital Markets*, 31 Osgoode Hall L.J. 371 (1993). Similar constraints in the U.S. context are discussed in, e.g., B.S. Black, *Shareholder Passivity Reexamined*, 89 Mich. L.R. 520, 567-70 (1990); M.J. Roe, *A Political Theory of American Corporate Finance*, 91 Col. L.R. 10 (1991); and A.F. Conard, *Beyond Managerialism: Investor Capitalism?* 22 J. of Law Reform 117 (1988). See also the discussion in subsection 4 below.

(a) *Constraints on Large Stake Shareholding*

For instance, institutions are constrained in the acquisition of substantial stakes in corporations by laws that impose ownership limits on banks, trust companies and insurance companies. See, e.g., the Bank Act, S.C. 1991, c. 46, s. 466(1); the Insurance Companies Act, S.C. 1991, c. 47, s. 493(1); and the Trust and Loan Companies Act, S.C. 1991, c. 45, s. 451(1). Mutual funds are also subject to laws that limit the size of the stakes they can take in any individual corporation. See National Policy No. 39, s. 2.04. Trust companies and insurance funds are subject to rules either constraining the kinds of corporate shareholdings they can have (see, e.g., the Ontario Loan and Trust Companies Act, R.S.O. 1990, c. L.25, s. 162(1)(c) and the Ontario Insurance Act, R.S.O. 1990, c. I.8, s. 433(1)(n)) or subjecting them to a prudence standard that militates against taking a substantial position in the shares of any given corporation.

Securities laws also put significant constraints on the extent of share ownership an institution takes. Securities laws require the disclosure of shareholdings as soon as a person acquires 10% or more of the voting securities of a corporation. Additional acquisitions of 2% or more of the voting securities of the corporation must also be disclosed. A person is deemed to be an insider on the acquisition of 10% or more of the voting securities of a corporation. This triggers insider reporting obligations and the restrictions on insider trading (see Chapter Eight). The restrictions on insider trading puts constraints on the institution's ability to sell the shares of corporations of which it is an insider since an insider cannot trade when the insider is in possession of undisclosed material information concerning the corporation. If the institution acquires 20% or more of a class of shares of a corporation then it is subject to take-over bid requirements (see Chapter Eleven) which, subject to limited exceptions, require it to make an offer to buy the shares of all holders of shares of that class. If an institutional investor acquires 20% or more of the voting shares of a corporation it is deemed to be a "control person" (see Chapter Five) and will be subject to rules that constrain the sale of the shares. The control person constraints on the sale of shares may apply with ownership of even less than 20% of the voting shares of the corporation since a person can be a "control person" if the person is in a position to "affect materially the control of the [corporation]." These constraints are discussed in J.G. MacIntosh, *Role of Institutional and Retail Investors in Canadian Capital Markets*, 31 Osgoode Hall L.J. 371 (1993).

(b) *Constraints on Large Stakeholders Exerting Influence*

Although institutional investors with substantial stakes in the corporation have an incentive to exert influence over corporate governance, it has been argued that there are laws that constrain their ability to exert such an influence.

As discussed in Section E, the wide scope of the term "solicitation" can constrain communications between shareholders because of the risk that those communications will subject them to very costly proxy solicitation requirements. The constraints on the sale of shares by a "control person" also raise concerns with respect to shareholder communications. A person can also be a "control person," and therefore subject to constraints on the sale of shares, if the person is "acting in concert" with other persons and together they hold a sufficient number of shares "to affect materially the control of [a corporation]." Persons "acting in concert" are deemed to be control persons if together they hold 20% or more of the voting shares of the corporation. Thus persons (normally institutional investors) holding substantial stakes in a corporation (although less than 20% of the voting shares) must be careful in their communications with other shareholders that they do not appear to have reached "an agreement, arrangement, commitment or understanding" to vote their shares in the same way on a given issue since they may appear to be "acting in concert" in a way that "affect[s] materially the control of the [corporation]." Communications with shareholders can also be frustrated, or at least made significantly more costly, because of efforts by corporations to resist access to the list of shareholders. Thus attempts by an institutional investor to contact fellow shareholders (including other institutional investors) to express concerns about corporate performance are inhibited.

If large stakeholders such as institutional investors do engage in a proxy solicitation campaign it is unlikely that they will be able to recoup their proxy solicitation expenses. Although shareholder proposals could provide a means of exerting some influence on corporate governance, the constraints on shareholder proposals coupled with the problems of shareholder communications (noted above) in seeking shareholder support for the proposals make shareholder proposals an ineffective mechanism for influencing corporate governance.

Although a person is deemed to be a control person if he or she owns 20% or more of the voting shares of a corporation, a person can be a control person with an even smaller portion of the voting shares if the person is in a position to "affect materially the control of the [corporation]." Thus an institutional investor may need to exercise caution in having one or more directors on the board of directors of a corporation since it could result in a finding that the institutional investor is in a position "to affect materially the control of the [corporation]." An institutional investor may also be reluctant to put an employee of the institution on the board of directors of a corporation since it can make the institution subject to insider trading restrictions thereby constraining its ability to sell the shares (although this can be controlled to some extent by restricting the flow of information between the institution's appointed director and the trading department of the institution—a so-called Chinese wall).

Institutions such as securities firms, banks, trust companies and insurance companies also often have contractual relationships with corporations in which they have made an investment. This gives managers of the corporation some leverage over the institutional investor in that they can threaten to take their business elsewhere if the institutional investor does not vote in a particular way. The lack of confidentiality in voting allows managers to exert this influence.

In the shareholder meeting process itself corporate management has several advantages. They control the meeting agenda. They can get votes in the proxy solicitation process from apathetic shareholders who simply sign and return the proxy form in favour of the management nominee without considering the issues involved. Management nominees also decide on the acceptance or non-acceptance of proxies and tabulate the votes at shareholder meetings.

(c) Doubts as to the Benefits of an Expanded Role for Institutional Investors

Evidence that institutional investors often take lesser stakes in corporations than they otherwise might legally take suggests that there are trade-offs between exerting control and maintaining liquidity (i.e. the ability to sell shares quickly without significantly affecting the market price of the shares). Consequently, removing barriers to the taking of large shareholding stakes by insitutional investors may not necessarily result in a substantial increase in the size of insitutional investor stakes in corporations or in increased institutional investor monitoring. See J.C. Coffee, *Liquidity Versus Control: The Institutional Investor as Corporate Monitor*, 91 Col. L.R. 1277, 1318-29 (1991). Institutional investors also have managements with the inherent agency costs. The question then is who monitors the institutional monitors of corporate managements. Institutional investors can be subject to conflicts of interest where the corporations in which they have a substantial stakes are also their clients. They may side with management at the expense of minority shareholders. These and other concerns with respect to institutional investors as monitors of corporate management are raised in Coffee, *id.*, 1329-36; see also, e.g., E.B. Rock, *The Logic and (Uncertain) Significance of Institutional Shareholder Activism*, 79 Georgetown L.J. 445 (1991); and B.S. Black, *Agents Watching Agents: The Promise of Institutional Investor Voice*, 39 UCLA L.R. 811 (1992) (concluding that constraints on institutional investor managers will mitigate these problems and that the risks of institutional investor monitoring of corporate management are limited); see also MacIntosh, *id.*, 430-33.

Professor Roe takes an intermediate position on the effectiveness of institutional investors. While acknowledging problems with institutional investor activism he suggests that they could play an effective role in making managers more accountable for their performance. Having to justify plans to institutional investors having an economic interest in the firm would clarify and improve the work of corporate managers. Institutional investors would be more familiar with the workings of the corporation and would be able to respond to a crisis immediately without having to build up information on the corporation almost from scratch in the event of a crisis. Although the managers of institutional investors are subject to the same agency cost problems as corporate managers, their formal duties and the economic interest of investors in the institution would provide some incentive to monitor corporate managers resulting in an overall improvement in the monitoring of corporate managers. Having multiple institutional investors with a significant economic interest in a corporation could also improve corporate decision making through the input of multiple monitors reducing errors (much as several high-quality lawyers in a law firm cooperating and conversing can do a better job than one high-quality lawyer working alone). Institutional investors with significant economic interests in a corporation could also have access to information that would allow them to better assess the long-term benefits of investments in human capital (perhaps through training programs or other human capital development projects). This could reduce the alleged short-term focus that capital markets with dispersed investors are said to have because of their inability to assess long-term investments. Investors may be unable to assess long-term investments if managers are unable to disclose the nature of long-term investments for fear that doing so would allow competitors to compete away the expected gains from long-term investments. See M.J. Roe, *Strong Managers, Weak Owners: The Political Roots of American Corporate Finance*, 233-47 (1994).

4. Interest Group Theories

Public choice theories provide a very useful perspective on the development of corporate governance rules. Such theories analyze legal rules as the output of a political process in which politicians maximize political advantage and interest groups compete for rules that transfer wealth to themselves. In particular, interest group theories predict that a state will adopt rules that transfer wealth from less to more powerful coalitions, from more dispersed to more concentrated groups. For an introduction to public choice scholarship, most closely associated with George Mason's Public Choice Center, see James Buchanan & Gordon Tullock, *The Calculus of Consent* (1962); Dennis C. Mueller, *Public Choice II* (1989).

Interest Group Theories of Corporate Law. The interest group analysis of corporate law therefore suggests an explanation for legal rules that entrench corporate managers in power, and weaken rival claimholders such as shareholders and creditors. Corporate managers are a concentrated constituency, whose ability to make political contributions from corporate coffers may buy them considerable political clout. By contrast, shareholders might be thought more dispersed, particularly on the Berle-Means model. Creditors are more concentrated than shareholders, even in the United States with its continued barriers to interstate banking. But in any contest between management and banker in the United States, managers could count on a strong populist antibank settlement. As well, bankers were more dependent on regulatory approval, and thus more susceptible to political pressure, than most firm managers.

Interest group theories might therefore explain a host of rules in corporate, bankruptcy and financial intermediary law. The tender offer requirements we shall see in Chapter Eleven, passed ostensibly to benefit shareholders, make it more difficult for bidders to take over a firm, and thus serve management interests. Barriers to creditor repossessory or receivership remedies, such as Chapter 11 of the U.S. Bankruptcy Code, also insulate managers from control challenges, as we shall see in Chapter Ten. Proxy regulation, the subject of Section E of this chapter, may also advantage managers by chilling discussions between dissenters and by imposing burdensome disclosure duties on them. Similarly, Bank Act barriers to shareholder ownership serve to prevent the creation of monitoring blocks of shareholders, and to increase the Berle-Means agency cost of separation of management and control. In the United States, banks are not permitted to own more than 5% of the shares of any non-bank firm, and a plethora of tax and state law barriers inhibit the creation of effective voting blocks by other financial institutions, such as insurance companies, mutual funds and pension plans. So too, barriers to lender monitoring, in the form of lender liability laws, also chill creditor monitoring, as we saw in Chapter One, Section C. See further Romano, *The Political Economy of Takeover Statutes*, 73 Va. L. Rev. 111 (1987); Black, *Shareholder Passivity Reexamined*, 89 Mich. L. Rev. 520 (1992); Macey & Miller, *Toward an Interest Group Theory of Delaware Corporate Law*, 65 Tex. L. Rev. 469 (1987) (discussing the influence of the Delaware corporate bar on the development of Delaware corporate law); Buckley, *The American Stay*, 3 S. Cal. Interdisciplinary L.J. (forthcoming 1995).

Interest group explanations of legal rules are tautological where the only evidence of interest group clout is the legal rules themselves. A full interest group theory must therefore be able to account for how legal rules developed, as a matter of legal history. Such an explanation is offered by Mark Roe in *Strong Managers, Weak Owners* (1994), which promises to be the decade's most influential book on corporate law. Roe describes the very different monitoring regime that obtains in Germany, where banks are permitted to own substantial blocks of firm stock, and in Japan, where cross-holdings among a group of firms is commonplace. As Roe notes, none of the 15 largest U.S. firms has an institution or group holding more than 20% of its stock, while all of the largest Japanese firms have an institution or group holding a 20% block. Roe attributes the very different corporate structures in the United States to American populism, which advantaged firm managers in their battles with Wall Street. A shift in popular sentiment, such as occurred at Populist moments in 1776, 1832, the "money trust" era of 1890-1914, and the Great

Depression, could shatter an interest group equilibrium, and shift power decisively away from creditors or financiers.

An Interest Group Theory in Canadian Corporate Law. Many of the legal barriers to shareholder control examined by Roe have a parallel in Canada as noted in subsection 3 above. Canadians also insisted on the segregation of banks from insurance, trust and brokerage business. In other respects, however, there are important differences between the Canadian and American pictures. Bay Street never attracted the opprobrium of Wall Street, and Canada never banned inter-provincial banking. As a consequence, a small number of banks dominate the Canadian financial landscape. Nor did Canadians stay the receivership remedies of secured lenders, in the manner of Chapter 11 of the U.S. Bankruptcy Code, until the recent BIA. The BIA's stay is in any event considerably milder than that of Chapter 11, as will be seen in Chapter Nine. More important still are differences between blockholder stock ownership in the two countries. As Daniels and MacIntosh note, only 14% of the firms that comprise the TSE 300 are widely held. Over 60% of the firms are controlled by a single shareholder with more than 50% of the voting shares. There is also a greater degree of cross-ownership, with nearly 45% of the 100 most profitable firms owning more than 10% of the stock of another firm on the list. See Daniels & MacIntosh, *Toward a Distinctive Canadian Corporate Law Regime*, 29 Osgoode Hall L.J. 863 (1991).

The result is a distinctively Canadian system of financial management, more closely resembling that of the United States, but not entirely dissimilar from that of Japan either. With the United States, Canada shares a similar legal culture and scheme of financial regulation, as well as nearly identical corporate and securities laws. With Japan, Canada shares a concentrated financial establishment. All three countries restrict bank ownership of non-bank stock. In Canada and Japan, however, a small number of relatively very large banks stand at the apex of a financial hierarchy. Before the 1980s, each major Canadian bank had its stable of major clients, all sharing the services of the same law, accounting and underwriting firms. By relying on a single major lender, a firm strengthened the bank's voice in setting corporate policies. Without a Chapter 11 to stay bank receivership remedies, the firm was dependent on its bank in a financial crisis. Even if solvent, the firm would look to the bank for a continued source of credit. The result was something like the Japanese keiretsu, a group of allied industrial firms and financial intermediaries, with cross-ownership of stock. After the recession of the early 1980s, when industrial firms saw a value in alternative sources of credit, the alliances weakened, and indeed were never so strong as the Japanese keiretsu. However, Canadian financial structures have always been more concentrated and hierarchical than those of the United States, at least since the end of the money trust period in that country in 1914.

As Daniels and MacIntosh note, cross-border differences in financial structure may reasonably lead one to wonder whether American corporate and securities law provides an entirely suitable model for the Canadian lawyer. Benignly neglected by the American theorist, Canadian firms may have quietly worked out their own solution to the agency costs of the separation of management and control. And while agency costs undoubtedly remain, American solutions may not be apposite. For example, one might ask whether rules ostensibly designed to enfranchise a voiceless American shareholder are needed in

Canada. With respect to shareholder litigation, discussed in the next chapter, one might also wonder whether management misbehaviour in Canada is more effectively policed through the quiet influence of blockholders and bankers than through noisy proceedings in court.

In particular, American-style barriers to insider trading might inefficiently chill the club-like techniques of blockholder monitoring in Canada. A spectacular example of this might be found in the facts of an Ontario Securities Commission administrative proceeding from the early 1980s, *Royal Trust Co. Ltd. v. O.S.C.* (1983), 42 O.R. (2d) 147 (Div. Ct.). Robert Campeau sought to break into the Toronto business establishment through a take-over bid for the shares of Royal Trust, one of the country's leading trust companies. Before publicly disclosing the bid, Campeau arrived unannounced at the country estate of the Royal Trust president, whom he told of the bid. The Royal Trust president told Campeau that the bid would fail and unceremoniously ordered him off the estate. Royal Trust officials thereupon contacted their network of allies in the Toronto financial establishment, who lined up to oppose the bid, which did indeed fail.

One of the consequences of the bid was an O.S.C. proceeding against two Royal Trust principals to sanction them for failing to make a public disclosure of material information. While drumming up opposition to the Campeau bid, they told the Toronto-Dominion Bank that the bid would likely fail because voting control was in the hands of Trustco allies who had agreed not to tender their shares to Campeau. This was material information, the O.S.C. held, and private disclosure to the bank was not the kind of public disclosure mandated by the OSA. The decision of the Divisional Court, affirming the finding that the Royal Trust officials had violated OSA disclosure requirements, is discussed further in Chapter Eight, Section D.

The Royal Trust proceedings serve to explain why one feature of the Japanese scheme of corporate governance has not been adopted in Canada. This is the Presidents' Council, monthly meetings of the heads of financial intermediaries and industrial firms, who share information and set policy goals, which they appear to feel are binding. As the meetings of the Presidents' Council are private, they would likely contravene OSA continuous disclosure requirements were they attempted in Canada. Quite apart from this, the benefits of any attempt to formalize Bay Street's control of Canadian finance would very possibly be exceeded by the costs politicians might impose on the financial establishment. This plausibly explains why formal monitoring structures, such as the Presidents' Council, were never adopted in Canada, even before modern securities regulation. Of course, bank and blockholder influence may be exerted, possibly as effectively, through more private and informal avenues of persuasion.

Another consequence of the bid was Campeau's decision to decamp for the less concentrated financial pastures in the United States. There Campeau launched another hostile take-over bid, this time against Federal Department Stores. After a bidding war with rival offerors, in which the offer price increased substantially, Campeau emerged the winner. The victory, however, was pyrrhic. To pay the U.S. $8 billion acquisition price, Campeau financed 97% of that amount with debt. Two years later, unable to meet its debt payments, Federated sought the protection of Chapter 11. This might appear to have justified *Fortune* magazine's criticism of the Federated take-over, in a story entitled *The Biggest, Looniest Deal Ever*, Loomis, *Fortune*, June 18, 1990. Equally, the

Federated bankruptcy might be thought to have justified the defensive tactics of the Toronto financial community, and to cast doubt on the efforts of the O.S.C. to cast itself in the role of financial trust-buster.

History teaches one, however, to guard against premature judgments. Is it perhaps too early to say whether the French Revolution was a good or bad thing? Campeau may have overpaid in his bid, but the net value of Federated assets (including the acquiring firm's assets) increased by $3.1 billion in 1992 U.S. dollars between the time of the offer and the time it emerged from bankruptcy. See Kaplan, *Campeau's Acquisition of Federated: Post-bankruptcy Results*, 35 J. Fin. Eco. 123 (1994). It is difficult, therefore, to say that the hierarchical structure of Canadian finance must necessarily be preferred to the more fragmented American regime. The Canadian system economizes on information production costs, and might police some forms of management misbehavior quite effectively. At the same time, however, borrowing from a single bank increases the possibility of bank opportunism. The increase in shareholder voice in Canada might also be accompanied by a weakening in alternative monitoring strategies, such as the take-over bids discussed in Chapter Eleven. Even with the benefit of hindsight, we might regret Campeau's decision to depart for the United States.

This suggests that reasonable people might differ on the optimal set of financial regulation laws. It also suggests that lawyers might usefully exercise a degree of Burkean caution in proposing changes to Canadian corporate and securities law. Financial regulation, corporate and securities laws do not exist in watertight compartments, but in part exist as a response to each other. Thus a rule that appears inefficient from the perspective of corporate or securities law might be thought justified from the perspective of financial regulation law. For example, the *Royal Trust* proceedings, which might seem suspect from a securities law perspective, may yet commend themselves as an effort to open up a Toronto financial cartel.

Other Constituencies. Besides managers, other constituencies might be served by management entrenchment devices. Where managers can delay bankruptcy reorganization for a lengthy period of time, as they can under Chapter 11, firm employees retain their jobs along with the managers. If the delay is value-decreasing, the number of old jobs saved is likely exceeded by forgone new jobs. However, the old employees are concentrated, particularly if unionized, while new employees cannot even be identified. Thus interest group theories predict net employee pressure for delay and the stay of Bankruptcy proceedings. See Eskridge, *Overriding Supreme Court Statutory Interpretation Decisions*, 101 Yale L.J. 331, Tables 7 and 9 (1991) (finding that organized labor is as successful as private industry in obtaining legislative overrides of Supreme Court decisions). If anything, labour unions are a stronger constituency in Canada than in the United States.

The corporate and bankruptcy bars are also powerful interest groups. Not merely do lawyers contribute heavily to political parties, but they also represent a mediating constituency, articulating broad public needs. The public interest is not discovered or stated without cost, and society must free ride on mediating groups to identify efficient means to desirable ends. In a stable equilibrium, the marginal cost to mediating lawyers (in articulating public policy) will equal their marginal returns (in the creation or defence of rules that transfer wealth to themselves). Up to that point, the publicly minded lawyer need not wait till the next world for his reward; but thereafter a cynical public will discount the lawyer's advice, and refuse to permit him to shape legal rules. For a similar model of investment intermediation, see Grossman & Stiglitz, *On the Impossibility of Informationally Efficient Markets*, 70 Am. Econ. Rev. 393 (1980).

While lawyers are not a homogenous interest group, we might expect a net legal preference for complexity. For litigation lawyers, complexity will likely mean more litigation, as more deals unwind. Complexity might also benefit corporate planners, particularly sophisticated ones who can specialize in complex transactions. When fewer and fewer transactions are plain vanilla, clients have a greater need to retain the full-service major law firm. In particular, the rise of the Ontario Securities Commission as an arbiter of Canadian corporate governance has greatly benefitted a small group of Toronto law firms. Apart from this, corporate lawyers in well-diversified major law firms share in the gains complexity provides members of the firm's litigation department. Of course, the costs of inefficiently complex rules represent a smaller future client base, and forgone future revenue. However, such losses will be shared with future planners not yet in law school, and lawyers might thus have a net preference for value-decreasing complexity.

Regulators, particularly securities regulators, are also an important interest group, and can be expected to seek to enlarge the scope of their authority. For any regulator, more authority means more power, greater prestige, more staff, more interesting work and better pay. See Niskanen, *Bureaucracy and Representative Government* (1971). For agencies such as the Ontario Securities Commission, which trade off staff with prestigious law firms, the human capital gains from regulation may be enormous. This might explain the O.S.C.'s hostility to rival monitors, such as the blockholders and banks in the *Royal Trust* decision.

Courts are also an interest group, nor should we expect that agency costs problems can be solved by assigning them to a party that lacks an equity interest in the outcome. Charged with the duty of promoting an optimal set of strict legal norms, then, courts might misbehave by promoting less rigorous fairness norms. Fairness norms, being uncertain, can be expected to increase the volume of litigation, and this will benefit the litigators from which class the judges arose and to whom they may feel continued loyalty. Fairness norms, being fact-sensitive, are also less likely to be overturned on appeal, and this will appeal to a risk averse judge. Finally, prestige-seeking judges can be expected to adopt fairness norms. We all seek prestige, and judges possibly more than the rest of us. The willingness to accept a pay cut on a judicial appointment suggests a marginal preference for prestige over income, rather like the purchase of a peerage in the Age of Walpole. Among judges, a love of prestige is value-increasing when only efficient judgments are respected. In such cases, promoting competition for litigation among judges usefully stimulates a race for the top. When efficiency norms are not strongly respected, however, the race may be to the bottom. A judge might adopt inefficient fairness norms because these will appeal to litigators. They will cite him more frequently in their legal briefs and law review articles, for his inventiveness offers them more business. In addition, the innovator, more ready than his colleagues to cut through legal barriers to advance broad political goals, can expect to be lionized by the press and by liberal interest groups. None of us is immune to flattery, and the innovator not infrequently comes to regard himself as wiser and more caring than his more traditional colleagues.*

This analysis of trial judge misbehaviour suggests an explanation for appellate courts. If trial judges did not systematically err in the direction of fairness norms, there might be little reason to grant leave to appeal. Given the first instance bias toward fairness norms, however, appellate courts might usefully uphold the integrity of the legal system's strict rules. In this century, however, many appellate judges have come to share the liberal sentiments that they were appointed to monitor. Such judges became popular heroes, and often appeared immensely pleased at this. If fairness norms are value-decreasing, however, the expansion of fairness norms to the appellate bench is the traison des clercs.

5. Corporate Social Responsibility

This section on corporate social responsibility begins by noting the goal for which the corporation has traditionally been said to be run. It notes criticisms of this traditionally accepted goal and its alleged consequences and then presents one of several typologies of different approaches to corporate social responsibility.

The Goal for Which the Corporation Is Run. The following case indicates the view courts have taken to the purpose for which a corporation is normally to be run.

Dodge v. Ford Motor Co.
Michigan Supreme Court
170 N.W. 668 (1919)

[This was a suit to compel the declaration and payment of dividends by, and to enjoin the expansion of the physical facilities of, the defendant Ford Motor Company. Plaintiffs, the brothers John F. and Horace B. Dodge, owned 10% of the shares of Ford Motor. The defendant Henry Ford owned 58% of the shares and was *de facto* in sole control of the management of the corporation. The corporation was formed in 1903 with an issued capital of about $44,000, and was fabulously successful. By 1916, when the suit was brought, it had a paid-up capital of $2,000,000, upon which a regular dividend of 60 per cent per annum had consistently been paid. Special dividends amounting to several million dollars per year were also paid through 1915. In the summer of 1916 Henry Ford announced that no further special dividends would be paid and that the company's retained earnings would henceforth be used exclusively to finance expansion of the business. At July 31, 1916, the company had cash and marketable securities on hand of about $54,000,000 and retained earnings of about $112,000,000, of which some $60,000,000 had been earned in the year just ended.

---

* For an early recognition of the agency costs of judicial misbehavior, see Buchanan, *Good Economics—Bad Law*, 60 Va. L. Rev. 483 (1974) (reviewing the first edition of Posner).

The trial Court ordered that approximately two-fifths of the cash on hand be paid out as a special dividend and enjoined the defendants from carrying out their expansion plans. The defendants appealed to the Supreme Court of Michigan.]

OSTRANDER J. [after stating the facts and disposing of plaintiffs' argument that the company's paid-in capital exceeded the maximum permitted under the statute]: The rule which will govern courts in deciding these questions is not in dispute. It is, of course, differently phrased by judges and by authors, and, as the phrasing in a particular instance may seem to lean for or against the exercise of the right of judicial interference with the actions of corporate directors, the context, or the facts before the court, must be considered. This court, in *Hunter v. Roberts, Throp & Co.*, 83 Mich. 63, 71, 47 N. W. 131, 134, recognized the rule in the following language:

It is a well-recognized principle of law that the directors of a corporation, and they alone, have the power to declare a dividend of the earnings of the corporation, and to determine its amount. 5 Amer. & Eng. Enc. Law, 725. Courts of equity will not interfere in the management of the directors unless it is clearly made to appear that they are guilty of fraud or misappropriation of the corporate funds, or refuse to declare a dividend when the corporation has a surplus of net profits which it can, without detriment to its business, divide among its stockholders, and when a refusal to do so would amount to such an abuse of discretion as would constitute a fraud, or breach of that good faith which they are bound to exercise towards the stockholders.

• • •

When plaintiffs made their complaint and demand for further dividends, the Ford Motor Company had concluded its most prosperous year of business. The demand for its cars at the price of the preceding year continued. It could make and could market in the year beginning August 1, 1916, more than 500,000 cars. Sales of parts and repairs would necessarily increase. The cost of materials was likely to advance, and perhaps the price of labor; but it reasonably might have expected a profit for the year of upwards of $60,000,000. It had assets of more than $132,000,000, a surplus of almost $112,000,000, and its cash on hand and municipal bonds were nearly $54,000,000. Its total liabilities, including capital stock, was a little over $20,000,000. It had declared no special dividend during the business year except the October, 1915, dividend. It had been the practice, under similar circumstances, to declare larger dividends. Considering only these facts, a refusal to declare and pay further dividends appears to be not an exercise of discretion on the part of the directors, but an arbitrary refusal to do what the circumstances required to be done. These facts and others call upon the directors to justify their action, or failure or refusal to act. In justification, the defendants have offered testimony tending to prove, and which does prove, the following facts: It had been the policy of the corporation for a considerable time to annually reduce the selling price of cars, while keeping up, or improving, their quality. As early as in June, 1915, a general plan for the expansion of the productive capacity of the concern by a practical duplication of its plant had been talked over by the executive officers and directors and agreed upon: not all of the details having been settled, and no formal action of directors having been taken. The erection of a smelter was considered, and engineering and other data in connection therewith secured. In consequence, it was determined not to reduce the selling price of cars for the year beginning August 1, 1915, but to maintain the price and to accumulate a large surplus to pay for the proposed expansion of plant and equipment, and perhaps to build a plant for smelting ore. It is hoped, by Mr. Ford, that eventually 1,000,000 cars will be annually produced. The contemplated changes will permit the increased output.

The plan, as affecting the profits of the business for the year beginning August 1, 1916, and thereafter, calls for a reduction in the selling price of the cars. It is true that this price might be at any time increased, but the plan called for the reduction in price of $80 a car. The capacity of the plant, without the additions thereto voted to be made (without a part of them at least), would produce more than 600,000 cars annually. This number, and more, could have been sold for $440 instead of $360, a difference in the return for capital, labor, and materials employed of at least $48,000,000. In short, the plan does not call for and is not intended to produce immediately a more profitable business, but a less profitable one: not only less profitable than formerly, but less profitable than it is admitted it might be made. The apparent immediate effect will be to diminish the value of shares and the returns to shareholders.

It is the contention of plaintiffs that the apparent effect of the plan is intended to be the continued and continuing effect of it, and that it is deliberately proposed, not of record and not by official corporate declaration, but nevertheless proposed, to continue the corporation henceforth as a semi-eleemosynary institution and not as a business institution. In support of this contention, they point to the attitude and to the expressions of Mr. Henry Ford.

Mr. Henry Ford is the dominant force in the business of the Ford Motor Company. No plan of operations could be adopted unless he consented, and no board of directors can be elected whom he does not favor. One of the directors of the company has no stock. One share was assigned to him to qualify him for the position, but it is not claimed that he owns it. A business, one of the largest in the world, and one of the most profitable, has been built up. It employs many men, at good pay. [Said Mr. Ford:]

My ambition is to employ still more men, to spread the benefits of this industrial system to the greatest possible number, to help them build up their lives and their homes. To do this we are putting the greatest share of our profits back in the business.

With regard to dividends, the company paid sixty per cent. on its capitalization of two million dollars, or $1,200,000, leaving $58,000,000 to reinvest for the growth of the company. This is Mr. Ford's policy at present, and it is understood that the other stockholders cheerfully accede to this plan.

He had made up his mind in the summer of 1916 that no dividends other than the regular dividends should be paid, "for the present."

Q. For how long? Had you fixed in your mind any time in the future, when you were going to pay— A. No.

Q. That was indefinite in the future? A. That was indefinite; yes, sir.

The record, and especially the testimony of Mr. Ford, convinces that he has to some extent the attitude towards shareholders of one who has dispensed and distributed to them large gains and that they should be content to take what he chooses to give. His testimony creates the impression, also, that he thinks the Ford Motor Company has made too much money, has had too large profits, and that, although large profits might be still earned, a sharing of them with the public, by reducing the price of the output of the company, ought to be undertaken. We have no doubt that certain sentiments, philanthropic and altruistic, creditable to Mr. Ford, had large influence in determining the policy to be pursued by the Ford Motor Company—the policy which has been herein referred to.

It is said by his counsel that—

Although a manufacturing corporation cannot engage in humanitarian works as its principal business, the fact that it is organized for profit does not prevent the existence of implied powers to carry on with humanitarian motives such charitable works as are incidental to the main business of the corporation.

And again:

As the expenditures complained of are being made in an expansion of the business which the company is organized to carry on, and for purposes within the powers of the corporation as hereinbefore shown, the question is as to whether such expenditures are rendered illegal because influenced to some extent by humanitarian motives and purposes on the part of the members of the board of directors.

In discussing this proposition, counsel have referred to decisions such as *Hawes v. Oakland*, 104 U.S. 450, 26 L. Ed. 827; *Taunton v. Royal Ins. Co.*, 2 Hem. & Miller 135; *Henderson v. Bank of Australia*, L.R. 40 Ch. Div. 170; *Steinway v. Steinway & Sons*, 17 Misc. Rep. 43, 40 N.Y. Supp. 718; *People v. Hotchkiss*, 136 App. Div. 150, 120 N.Y. Supp. 649. These cases, after all, like all others in which the subject is treated, turn finally upon the point, the question, whether it appears that the directors were not acting for the best interests of the corporation. We do not draw in question, nor do counsel for the plaintiffs do so, the validity of the general proposition stated by counsel nor the soundness of the opinions delivered in the cases cited. The case presented here is not like any of them. The difference between an incidental humanitarian expenditure of corporate funds for the benefit of the employees, like the building of a hospital for their use and the employment of agencies for the betterment of their condition, and a general purpose and plan to benefit mankind at the expense of others, is obvious. There should be no confusion (of which there is evidence) of the duties which Mr. Ford conceives that he and the stockholders owe to the general public and the duties which in law he and his codirectors owe to protesting, minority stockholders. A business corporation is organized and carried on primarily for the profit of the stockholders. The powers of the directors are to be employed for that end. The discretion of directors is to be exercised in the choice of means to attain that end, and does not extend to a change in the end itself, to the reduction of profits, or to the nondistribution of profits among stockholders in order to devote them to other purposes.

There is committed to the discretion of directors, a discretion to be exercised in good faith, the infinite details of business, including the wages which shall be paid to employees, the number of hours they shall work, the conditions under which labor shall be carried on, and the price for which products shall be offered to the public.

It is said by appellants that the motives of the board members are not material and will not be inquired into by the court so long as their acts are within their lawful powers. As we have pointed out, and the proposition does not require argument to sustain it, it is not within the lawful powers of a board of directors to shape and conduct the affairs of a corporation for the merely incidental benefit of shareholders and for the primary purpose of benefiting others, and no one will contend that, if the avowed purpose of the defendant directors was to sacrifice the interests of shareholders, it would not be the duty of the courts to interfere.

We are not, however, persuaded that we should interfere with the proposed expansion of the business of the Ford Motor Company. In view of the fact that the selling price of products may be increased at any time, the ultimate results of the larger business cannot be certainly estimated. The judges are not business experts. It is recognized that plans must often be made for a long future, for expected competition, for a continuing as well as an immediately profitable venture. The experience of the Ford Motor Company is evidence of capable management of its affairs. It may be noticed, incidentally, that it took from the public the money required for the execution of its plan, and that the very considerable salaries paid to Mr. Ford and to certain executive officers and employees were not diminished. We are not satisfied that the alleged motives of the directors, in so far as they are reflected in the conduct of the business, menace the interests of shareholders. It is enough to say, perhaps, that the court of equity is at all times open to complaining shareholders having a just grievance.

Assuming the general plan and policy of expansion and the details of it to have been sufficiently, formally, approved at the October and November, 1917, meetings of directors, and assuming further that the plan and policy and the details agreed upon were for the best ultimate interest of the company and therefore of its shareholders, what does it amount to in justification of a refusal to declare and pay a special dividend or dividends? The Ford Motor Company was able to estimate with nicety its income and profit. It could sell more cars than it could make. Having ascertained what it would cost to produce a car and to sell it, the profit upon each car depended upon the selling price. That being fixed, the yearly income and profit was determinable, and, within slight variations, was certain.

There was appropriated—voted—for the smelter $11,325,000. As to the remainder voted, there is no available way for determining how much had been paid before the action of directors was taken and how much was paid thereafter; but assuming that the plans required an expenditure sooner or later of $9,895,000 for duplication of the plant, and for land and other expenditures $3,000,000, the total is $24,220,000. The company was continuing business, at a profit—a cash business. If the total cost of proposed expenditures had been immediately withdrawn in cash from the cash surplus (money and bonds) on hand August 1, 1916, there would have remained nearly $30,000,000.

Defendants say, and it is true, that a considerable cash balance must be at all times carried by such a concern. But, as has been stated, there was a large daily, weekly, monthly, receipt of cash. The output was practically continuous and was continuously, and within a few days, turned into cash. Moreover, the contemplated expenditures were not to be immediately made. The large sum appropriated for the smelter plant was payable over a considerable period of time. So that, without going further, it would appear that, accepting and approving the plan of the directors, it was their duty to distribute on or near the 1st of August, 1916, a very large sum of money to stockholders.

In reaching this conclusion, we do not ignore, but recognize, the validity of the proposition that plaintiffs have from the beginning profited by, if they have not lately, officially, participated in, the general policy of expansion pursued by this corporation. We do not lose sight of the fact that it had been, upon an occasion, agreeable to the plaintiffs to increase the capital stock to $100,000,000 by a stock dividend of $98,000,000. These things go only to answer other contentions now made by plaintiffs, and do not and cannot operate to estop them to demand proper dividends upon the stock they own. It is obvious that an annual dividend of 60 percent. upon $2,000,000, or $1,200,000, is the equivalent of a very small dividend upon $100,000,000, or more.

The decree of the court below fixing and determining the specific amount to be distributed to stockholders is affirmed. In other respects, except as to the allowance of costs, the said decree is reversed. Plaintiffs will recover interest at 5 per cent. per annum upon their proportional share of said dividend from the date of the decree of the lower court. Appellants will tax the costs of their appeal, and two-thirds of the amount thereof will be paid by plaintiffs. No other costs are allowed.

STEERE, FELLOWS, STONE and BROOKE JJ. concurred with OSTRANDER J.

[The concurring opinion of MOORE J., with whom BIRD C.J. and KUHN J. concurred, has been omitted.]

According to the evidence, the market for automobiles in 1919 was not competitive—Ford Motor Co. was not a price-taker, forced to sell at average cost so as to eliminate economic profits. Instead, it could set its own prices, and in fact chose to sell its cars at $360 each when it could have sold all of them at $440 each. If the competitive price of the cars had been $360, the exercise in corporate altruism (were it that) would have had the effect of transferring monopolistic profits from shareholders to customers in the same way that this would have happened in competitive markets. On the other hand, it might be argued that pricing at less than the traffic would bear was a sophisticated strategy by an oligopolist to drive competitors out of business or prevent their entry in the market.

Would the case have been decided differently without Henry Ford's testimony that the corporation would not declare anything other than regular dividends for the indefinite future?

Excessive corporate charity was also impeached in exceptional circumstances in *Parke v. Daily News Ltd.*, [1962] Ch. 927. The defendant owned two newspapers as the major part of its business. For some years prior to October 1960 both newspapers had been losing substantial amounts of money, and in that month the defendant agreed to sell them to a larger chain, Associated Newspapers Ltd., for a price of about £2,000,000. The directors of the defendant determined to apply the entire proceeds to about 2,700 employees whose jobs would be terminated as a result of the transaction. About £500,000 would go for the payment of various entitlements of those employees who were to be terminated, and the remaining £1,500,000 would be voluntary (from the corporation's perspective) severance compensation to them. The plaintiff, a minority shareholder, sued for a declaratory order that the proposed payments were beyond the powers of the corporation and could not be ratified by a majority of the shareholders. In granting the order, Plowman J. stated that:

the defendants were prompted by motives which, however laudable, and however enlightened from the point of view of industrial relations, were such as the law does not recognize as a sufficient justification. Stripped of all its side issues, the essence of the matter is this, that the directors of the defendant company are proposing that a very large part of its funds should be given to its former employees in order to benefit those employees rather than the company, and that is an application of the company's funds which the law, as I understand it, will not allow. [*Id.* at 963]

Note that, since the defendant was going out of business, it was not subject to the same discipline from capital markets that going concerns would be. In the absence of such "end game" strategies, management of a going concern might have worried that the destruction of equity claims through the gift would render it impossible for the firm subsequently to raise capital by a sale of equity interests.

Notwithstanding cases such as *Dodge v. Ford Motor Co.* and *Parke v. Daily News*, courts have consistently upheld the power of corporations to make charitable contributions on the basis of "enlightened self-interest." For example, in *Hutton v. West Cork. Ry. Co.* (1883), 23 Ch. D. 654, 673 (C.A.), Bowen L.J. stated:

The law does not say that there are to be no cakes and ale, but there are to be no cakes and ale except such as are required for the benefit of the company ... Now that I think is the principle to be found in the case of *Hampson v. Price's Patent Candle Co.* The Master of the Rolls there held that the company might lawfully expend a week's wages as gratuities for their servants; because that sort of liberal dealing with servants eases the friction between masters and servants, and is, in the end, a benefit to the company. It is not charity sitting at the board of directors, because as it seems to me charity has no business to sit at boards of directors *qua* charity. There is, however, a kind of charitable dealing which is for the interest of those who practice it, and to that extent and in that garb (I admit not a very philanthropic garb) charity may sit at the board, but for no other purpose.

An even more expansive standard of enlightened self-interest was adopted in *A.P. Mfg. Co. v. Barlow*, 98 A.2d 581 (N.J. 1953), where, in the course of sustaining the propriety of a gift of $1,500 to Princeton University over the objection of a minority shareholder, the Court said:

More and more [corporations] have come to recognize that their salvation rests upon sound economic and social environment which in turn rests in no insignificant part upon free and vigorous nongovernmental institutions of learning. It seems to us that just as the conditions prevailing when corporations were originally created required that they serve public as well as private interests, modern conditions require that corporations acknowledge and discharge social as well as private responsibilities as members of the communities within which they operate. Within this broad concept, there is no difficulty in sustaining, as incidental to their proper objects and in aid of the public welfare, the power of corporations to contribute corporate funds within reasonable limits in support of academic institutions. But even if we confine ourselves to the terms of the common-law rule in its application to current conditions, such expenditures may likewise readily be justified as being for the benefit of the corporation; indeed if need be the matter may be viewed strictly in terms of actual survival of the corporation in a free enterprise system. [*Id.* at 586]

Theories of Corporate Charity. On distributional theories of corporate charity, the effect of a donation is to transfer wealth from one corporate constituency (shareholders) to the recipients of corporate charity. Even distributional theorists will wish to set limits on this, since it is perhaps a little too easy to be charitable with other people's money. Indeed, from the point of view of shareholders, corporate charity which exceeds that which the shareholders themselves would have approved is indistinguishable from any other kind of self-dealing by management.

The removal of legal obstacles to corporate donations need not, however, result in increased corporate altruism. The actual ratio of corporate contributions to earnings is low in the United States, and lower still in Canada. As a percentage of profits after tax in Canadian corporations, corporate donations declined from 1.8% in 1959 to 0.8% in 1980. Webster, *Public and Private Philanthropy in the Eighties*, 4 Philanthropist 32, 50 (1984). Low rates of giving by corporations are no doubt a consequence of their accountability in competitive capital and product markets. Thus firms in oligopolistic industries on average make higher-than-average contributions than firms in competitive industries. Johnson, *Corporate Philanthropy: An Analysis of Corporate Contributions*, 39 J. Bus. 489 (1966). Given the low rates of corporate charity, legal rules facilitating charitable contributions by corporations may have little effect, and those opposed to distributional theories might even regard legal barriers to excessive corporate charity as unnecessary except in cases such as *Dodge* and *Parke* where management's incentives to maximize shareholder wealth are weak.

Suppose, however, that charitable donations by a particular firm are substantial. A further objection to distributional theories of corporate social responsibility is then that tax-financed welfare schemes may be a superior technique of distributional justice. Even if the recipients of corporate charity are considered worthy of some form of public support, this does not imply that the burden should fall upon shareholders. If, as a class, shareholders were wealthier than other members of society, corporate charity might be considered a disguised form of progressive taxation. But many shareholders are not particularly wealthy, being holders of interests in pension and mutual funds, for example. A taxation system calibrated to income levels might then better accord with theories of distributive justice.

On the other hand, corporations may in some circumstances be better providers of distributional justice than the state because of efficiencies in information production. While distributional justice is commonly believed to be exclusively the province of the state, this view is inconsistent with the charitable gift deductibility provisions of the Income Tax Act, which contemplate that private givers will be enlisted in public wealth transfer schemes. The result is a mixed system of distributional justice, with state recognition that the choice of suitable beneficiaries should rest in part with private groups. On a principle of *subsidiarity*, non-state donors may economize on the costs of production of information with respect to the identity of deserving candidates for charity. Not all such wisdom resides in government, and frequently those closest to the donees may be in the best position to recognize their needs or to arbitrate among rent-seeking donees. On this explanation, better "quality" donees might be found through a mixed system of giving, which might also result in lower screening and administrative expenses than would obtain under purely public systems of social welfare. In addition, more money might in total be devoted to charitable purposes under charitable gift deductibility. The supply of corporate charity is generally thought elastic, in the sense that for every dollar lost to tax authorities through charitable gift deductibility, more than $1 is given to charity.

A less plausible defence of corporate charity is that it lessens free rider problems of giving. If shareholders as individuals desire a certain amount of private charity in their society, they might prefer that the decision to donate be made by intermediaries like a public corporation than by themselves, since if charity is left solely to individuals some people would free ride on donations by others. Free riding concerns might then be dissipated when intermediaries make the donation, leading to a level of giving more attuned to that which individuals would desire. The difficulty with this argument is that free riding is still possible if individuals might transfer their investments to corporations that have a record of low charitable contributions.

Corporate charity is not simply a matter of donations, but also implicates "excessive" precaution costs incurred by a corporation to reduce anticipated harm. In defining charity, there is, after all, no reason to distinguish between outright gifts and corporate decisions animated by altruistic motives, which reduce firm wealth through a failure to extract all possible profits. One example of the second kind of altruism may arise on a harm prevention decision. Where its products threaten to cause harm, a firm will maximize its profits by achieving the lowest possible level of anticipated damages and harm prevention costs. This would mean, for example, reducing pollution to the level where the marginal benefits to the firm of the polluting activity equal the marginal cost of the anticipated damages award. But as noted in Chapter Two, Section B, liability strategies may not suffice to lead the firm to efficient levels of harm prevention. For example, because of high costs of detection or the transactions costs associated with litigation, a deterrence gap will arise such that insufficient levels of care are taken. This might seem to call for a levering up of the level of sanctions, with greater penalties imposed when enforcement is less likely. However, there are barriers to the level of penalties that might be imposed, which Reinier Kraakman calls *sanction insufficiency*. Kraakman, *Corporate Liability Strategies and the Costs of Legal Controls*, 93 Yale L.J. 857, 881-84 (1984). Thus, in the case of serious harm that is virtually undetectable, we might shrink from imposing the maximum possible punishment. In addition, if individuals react to extremely small probabilities of detection in a myopic fashion, they will be underdeterred by extreme penalties. Finally, if extreme penalties might not deter some managers, others might be overdeterred, particularly ordinary, risk-averse managers.

If liability rules are unlikely to suffice to redress these incentive failures, they may perhaps be supplemented through social or ethical norms. This theory is first suggested, then criticized, by David Engel in *An Approach to Corporate Social Responsibility*, 32 Stan. L. Rev. 1 (1979). Engel argues that where the underdeterrence arises from undetected conduct, the problem could more readily be cured by disclosure of the harm than by altruistic investments in harm prevention. Where, on the other hand, the difficulty of enforcement is a result of expenses related to litigation, Engel argues that management is ill-equipped to estimate external social costs. *Id.* at 52-54. However, as a supplement to legal sanctions, it is difficult to contest the utility of social sanctions. A society's response to failures in legal rules through its ethical norms might also be seen to reflect a broader understanding of social costs than that possessed by a single manager.

See further R. Nader, M. Green & J. Seligman, *Taming the Giant Corporation* (1976); Arrow, *Social Responsibility and Economic Efficiency*, 21 Pub. Pol'y 303 (1973); Manne, *The Limits and Rationale of Corporate Altruism: An Individualistic Model*, 59 Va. L. Rev. 708 (1972); Mundheim, *A Comment on the Social Responsibilities of Life Insurance Companies as Investors*, 61 Va. L. Rev. 1247 (1975).

Alleged Consequences of the Profit Calculus. The generally assumed corporate goal of profit (subject to a limited scope for charitable contributions) has been criticized on the basis that it is the corporate profit goal that leads to socially unacceptable behaviour by corporations. Such criticisms point to corporate acts such as locating a gas tank in a car in a place that was known to run a relatively high risk of explosion even though the cost to move it to a safer location would have been only $9 per car. A similar attack has been made with respect to an alleged cover-up of the risks of asbestos by Johns Manville Inc. which it is said to have had evidence of early on. See P. Brodeur, *Outrageous Misconduct: The Asbestos Industry on Trial* (1985). Other alleged consequences of the profit motive include disregard for the impact of plant closings on local communities, knowingly producing dangerous products or using dangerous production methods, ignoring the effects of pollution caused by the corporation to the environment and the local community, engaging in anti-competitive practices at the expense of consumers, shipping toxic wastes to foreign countries and bribing foreign officials. For a criticism of the profit motive and its effects on corporate behaviour see, e.g., H. Glasbeek, *Why Corporate Deviance is not Treated as a Crime—The Need to Make "Profits" a Dirty Word*, 22 Osgoode Hall L.J. 393 (1984). Would the result be different if the goal of profit maximization were replaced with the goal of keeping costs down? What should one make of the evidence of poor product quality and environment degredation in former Communist countries where producers were presumably not subject to the goal of profit maximization?

A Typology of Approaches to Corporate Social Responsibility. A wide range of different approaches to corporate social responsibility are possible. A typology of approaches has been provided by Professor Clark. The typology identifies several possible approaches to corporate social responsibility that he has labeled dualism, monism, modest idealism and high idealism. Clark's typology is briefly summarized below. See R.C. Clark, *Corporate Law*, 677-94 (1986). For a similar typology see, e.g., L.D. Solomon & K.J. Collins, *Humanistic Economics: A New Model for the Corporate Social Responsibility Debate*, 12 J. of Corp. L. 337 (1987).

(a) *Dualism*

Under the dualist (or traditionalist) approach there are public and private spheres having distinct functions. Following this approach in the context of corporations directors and officers should maximize the profit of the corporation (thereby maximizing shareholder wealth) while the interests of other constituents, such as consumers, employees, suppliers and society generally, are protected through a range of legal controls such as contract law, tort law, consumer protection laws, labour laws, health and safety standards, bankruptcy laws and environmental laws. This approach is reflected in the dicta of cases like *Dodge v. Ford Motor Co.* and *Parke v. Daily News*, which suggest that the goal for which the corporation is to be run is profit.

The rationale for the dualist approach is that it allows corporate managers to concentrate on a single goal on which they can focus their energies more efficiently than they could if they pursued numerous goals reflecting the interests of several different constituencies. Further, no one need necessarily be worse off under this approach since the interests of other constituencies can be protected by regulatory controls on the corporation.

As Clark notes, criticisms of the dualist approach include a concern for the failures of government regulation of corporations. Critics question whether government regulation can be an effective way of protecting the interests of other corporate constituencies, particularly in the light of the potential for corporations controlling assets of substantial value to influence the political process.

Government regulation is also constrained by the deterrence trap or "sanction insufficiency" (discussed in Chapter Two, Section B and under "Theories of Corporate Charities" above).

(b) *Monism*

The monist approach sees the goal of profit maximization in a broader perspective considering some socially responsible corporate activities as conducive to profit maximization. For instance, certain activities may have a favourable reputational affect on the corporation, which may lead to improved sales and improved profits. As noted above (see the notes after *Dodge v. Ford Motor Co.*) courts have generally provided some scope for the monist approach by allowing, for instance, charitable contributions in reasonable amounts.

One concern with the monist approach (noted above under "Theories of Corporate Charity") is that the potential for management to justify their acts on the basis that they may ultimately redound to the benefit of the corporation gives corporate managers additional slack to act contrary to the interests of shareholders. Another concern is that the monist approach gives relatively little scope for corporate response to non-shareholder constituencies.

(c) *Modest Idealism*

Under the modest idealist approach corporate managers would make decisions based on the spirit of laws rather than follow a strict profit maximization calculus. The law would be complied with even if non-compliance would increase the value of the corporation. Following this approach a corporate management could decide to move the gas tank in a car to a location that would reduce the risk of injury or loss of life even if the cost of doing so outweighed any profits to the corporation or losses avoided. Under this approach the corporate manager does not make the political decisions associated with the protection of various non-shareholder constituencies but simply carries out the public policy created through other political mechanisms.

Presumably a court would not sanction a decision by corporate management to ignore a regulatory provision on the basis of a cost-benefit analysis nor is it likely to allow an action by shareholders on the basis that the corporate management chose to follow a regulation even though a cost-benefit analysis would suggest it should not have followed the regulation.

Rationales in favour of this approach suggest that the negative effects of profit maximization could be reduced and that the costs of enforcement of laws protecting corporate constituents would be substantially reduced. One problem with this approach is that it is difficult to bring it about because corporations that do not follow the modest idealist approach will have a competitive advantage over corporations that do—they will maximize firm value by non-compliance where the costs of compliance exceed the benefits. Competitive pressures in the product market, capital markets and the market for corporate control will ultimately discourage corporate managers from acting as modest idealists.

(d) *High Idealism*

Under the high idealist approach corporations would more directly respond to a wider range of interests than just those of shareholders. One conception of the high idealist approach would be to expand the purpose of the corporation to include the interests of groups other than shareholders. Another conception of the high idealist approach would have other interest groups directly represented in the corporate decision making process, perhaps though representation on the board of directors or through an expanded form of corporate meeting.

In support of such an approach it is said that it would respond to concerns for the failure of government regulation and provide for a more disperse, decentralized form of government. It would also increase participation in the corporate decision making process by persons who should have a voice in corporate decisions because they are directly affected by them.

The American Law Institute, *Principles of Corporate Governance: Analysis and Recommendations* (May 13, 1992) recommended the following corporate code provision:

§2.01 The Objective and Conduct of the Corporation

(a) Subject to the provisions of Subsection (b) and §6.02 (Action of Directors That Has the Foreseeable Effect of Blocking Unsolicited Tender Offers), a corporation [§1.12] should have as its objective the conduct of business activities with a view to enhancing corporate profit and shareholder gain.

(b) Even if corporate profit and shareholder gain are not thereby enhanced, the corporation, in the conduct of its business:

(1) Is obliged, to the same extent as a natural person, to act within the boundaries set by law;

(2) May take into account ethical considerations that are reasonably regarded as appropriate to the responsible conduct of business; and

(3) May devote a reasonable amount of resources to public welfare, humanitarian, educational, and philanthropic purposes.

How does this fit into Clark's typology? This ALI recommendation has been criticized for not requiring the corporation to take into account ethical considerations and devote a reasonable amount of resources to public welfare, etc. See D.J. Morrissey, *Toward a New/Old Theory of Corporate Social Responsibility*, 40 Syracuse L. Rev. 1005 (1991) (suggesting that the word "may" in (b)(2) and (3) be replaced with the word "shall").

6. The Corporate Stakeholder Debate

As noted above, the high idealism approach to corporate social responsibility would either expand the purpose of the corporation to include the interests of groups other than shareholders or have other interest groups directly represented in the corporate decision making process though representation on the board of directors or through an expanded form of corporate meeting. These approaches to corporate social responsibility have been debated in the context of the so-called stakeholder debate. In the corporate stakeholder debate the shareholders are seen as a group of stakeholders in the corporation along with other stakeholders such as creditors, employees, suppliers, customers and the local communities in which the corporation's offices or production facilities are located.

The corporate stakeholder debate has been around for some time. With the book *The Modern Corporation and Private Property*, published in 1932, Adolph Berle and Gardner Means sparked a major debate about corporate governance structures which focused on the agency cost problem of management power without apparent accountability. In addition, they raised issues as to who were the proper constituents to whom directors ought to owe duties. The following excerpt summarizes the now classic debate between Berle and Dodd over the issue of to whom the directors owe their duties.

Katz, Responsibility and the Modern Corporation
3 J.L. & Econ. 75, 75-78 (1960)

For whom are corporate managers trustees? The traditional answer has been that corporate directors and officers are trustees for the stockholders and that the basic management objective is therefore the earning of profit for the benefit of the stockholders. This responsibility has been viewed as resulting partly from the typical reservation of residual control to the stockholders; stockholder votes are the source of management power and are necessary for continuance of that power. Furthermore, management responsibility to stockholders has been legally enforced in suits brought by individual stockholders. And the traditional belief has been that the actual behavior of corporate managers is, by and large, in the interests of stockholders.

This view of management responsibility has been under attack for a generation. The attack has had many spokesmen but it has most vigorously been expressed in the writings of Adolph A. Berle, Jr. In Berle's books[1] it is asserted that conditions prevailing in

---

1   A.A. Berle, Jr. & G.C. Means, *The Modern Corporation and Private Property* (1932); A.A. Berle, Jr., *The 20th Century Capitalist Revolution* (1954); A.A. Berle, Jr., *Power Without Property* (1959).

the modern giant corporation are incompatible with the traditional view of management responsibility. With varying emphasis, the critics have found this view both misleading as a description and indefensible as a matter of social policy.

The great theme of *The Modern Corporation and Private Property*, by Berle and Gardner C. Means (1932), was separation of ownership from control associated with the wide dispersion of stock ownership. No showing was made that stockholders in corporations with widely dispersed ownership had actually fared worse than those in corporations with concentrated ownership. It was urged, however, that typical passivity of scattered stockholders makes it unbelievable that management responsibility is promoted by the voting rights of stockholders. Stockholders of the modern corporation think of themselves as passive investors, like bondholders, and not as owners. Most of them have no thought of actually participating in the selection of management. In the modern corporation, management is in practice a self-perpetuating oligarchy. It is management which selects the board of directors and not the other way around. Meetings of stockholders and the proxy solicitation machinery are no more than elaborate rituals by which management nominations for the board are ratified. The rare outbreak of a proxy war and the even rarer unseating of management serve only to highlight the absence of political responsibility in most modern corporations. The result, as Berle has put it, is that management is left with "substantially absolute power."[2]

It must be noted that Berle's concern with power was not a fear of social consequences of inefficiency where management is free from responsibility to stockholders. And while the divergence of interest between stockholders and management was discussed, the primary concern was not that the profits of stockholders might be reduced. Quite the contrary, Berle, and other critics as well, argued that it would be undesirable for the modern corporation to be managed so as to maximize stockholder profit. What Berle primarily saw in the separation of ownership from control was a basis for arguing that stockholders' interests should not be the exclusive concern of management. His premise was that true ownership involves not only risk but active participation in management. A passive investor who abdicates management responsibility has no justifiable claim to the full fruits of the enterprise.

A second ground for criticizing the goal of maximizing corporate profits has recently been given more emphasis. It is argued that under modern conditions of imperfect competition, vigorous management in the interest of stockholders would leave other groups without adequate protection. The typical large corporation is an oligopolist. It is one of a very small number of firms which together produce the bulk of the industry volume. In such markets entry of new firms is difficult. Each of the industry leaders is so large that its decisions as to output have a substantial effect upon prices. Under these conditions, it can not be assumed that the efforts of management in the interests of stockholders will be forced into patterns of social responsibility.

It must be noted that the ambit of this argument is different from that of the preceding criticism based upon separation of ownership from control. The present argument would cover corporations like the Ford Motor Company whose stockholders have exercised active control.

---

2   A.A. Berle, Jr., *The 20th Century Capitalist Revolution* 180 (1954).

The principal critics disagreed as to the desirability of legal change. Professor E. Merrick Dodd, Jr., asked that corporate managers be recognized as legally free from an obligation to maximize profit, free to recognize "social responsibility" on the part of the corporation.[4] He cited leading businessmen as expressing a sense of professional responsibility. In 1929 Owen D. Young (a lawyer who became president of General Electric) had spoken of a rising notion that managers are "no longer attorneys for stockholders" but are becoming "trustees of an institution," owing obligations to employees, customers, stockholders, and the general public. Dodd's article was written in 1932; his primary concern was apparently with economic instability and unemployment.

The Berle and Means book showed similar concern. Its concluding point was that claims of stockholders to ownership rights should not prevent the carrying out of a community program "comprising fair wages, security to employees, reasonable service to their public, and stabilization of business." To Berle it seemed conceivable—indeed "almost essential if the corporate system is to survive—that the 'control' of the great corporations should develop into a purely neutral technocracy, balancing a variety of claims by various groups in the community and assigning to each a portion of the income stream on the basis of public policy rather than private cupidity."[5]

Berle, however, did not approve the freeing of management to experiment with this role. Answering Dodd, he wrote:

I submit that you cannot abandon the emphasis on the view that business corporations exist for the sole purpose of making profits for their stockholders until such time as you are prepared to offer a clear and reasonably enforceable scheme of responsibilities to someone else.

One might have expected that a new scheme of responsibilities, "clear and reasonably enforceable" would in due time have been suggested by Mr. Berle. Such suggestions, however, were never forthcoming. He never associated himself with those who suggested formal redefinition of the goal of management. Nor did he support the reconstitution of the board of directors to include representatives of workers, consumers, etc.

By 1954, however, Berle was asserting that Dodd's goal of freeing management to be socially responsible had been fulfilled. He described the change as a "20th Century Capitalist Revolution." In the book to which he gave this title, Berle spoke eloquently of the conscience of the corporation. In his latest book, *Power Without Property*, he described the modern corporation as an Economic Republic, with management power somehow held responsible to a "public concensus," a body of opinion led by informed critics (such as Mr. Berle himself). For the last chapter of *The 20th Century Capitalist Revolution*, Berle took the title "The Modern Corporation and the City of God." But notwithstanding the exuberant optimism of these books, Berle has recently insisted that he is not convinced that the modern development is desirable, that he has merely been

---

4   Dodd, *For Whom Are Corporate Managers Trustees?* 45 Harv. L. Rev. 1145, 1157 (1932).

5   A.A. Berle, R. & G.C. Means, *The Modern Corporation and Private Property* 356 (1932).

describing the change and "endeavoring to seek the best use of a social and legal situation whose existence can neither be denied nor changed."9

The Berle and Means analysis of modern, public corporations sought an answer to two related questions: (1) Which corporate constituency controls them? and (2) For whose benefit should they be run? In both cases, the answers given to the questions de-emphasized the importance of the corporation's shareholders. Public corporations were found to be controlled by a class of professional managers rather than by shareholders, and the two authors argued that firms should be run for the benefit not merely of shareholders but of all parties with a stake in the firm, including employees, consumers and community members. The two answers were related in another way, for Berle and Means believed that broader stakeholder interests were more likely to be considered when firms were managed by an independent class of public-spirited managers.

At the time of its publication, *The Modern Corporation and Private Property* aroused considerable opposition, not the least of which was from Marxists whose demonology required a class of oppressive capitalists in control of the economy. Other critics questioned whether a Berle and Means apparachik would be any less self-interested than other kinds of managers. Today, the idea of a benign managerial class whose primary commitment is to the public interest seems a little naive, like the ideal vision of the New Deal reformer whose enemy is local prejudice and who himself is entirely uninfluenced by interest group coalitions.

Notwithstanding this, the theory that the efficiency of firm structures is to be judged by examining their effects on all interested parties is no longer controversial. From an economic perspective, there is no basis for distinguishing between "internal" shareholders and "external" stakeholders in assessing cost and benefits. This has led some commentators to propose that the interests of non-shareholder claimants be more explicitly recognized in corporate law. It might thus be argued that stakeholders should be permitted to participate in firm governance through such devices as special seats on the board of directors. In addition, in setting business policies managers might be encouraged to take account of stakeholder interests in making corporate decisions.

Corporate Constituency Statutes. Several states in the United States have added provisions to their statutes which allow corporations to take the interests of non-shareholder interests into account. For example, the Illinois statute provides as follows:

Directors and Officers—Considering Best Interests of Corporation. In discharging the duties of their respective positions, the board of directors, committees of the board, individual directors and individual officers may, in considering the best interests of the corporation, consider the effects of any action upon employees, suppliers and customers of the corporation, communities in which offices or other establishments of the corporation are located and all other pertinent factors. [Illinois Ann. Stat. ch. 32, para. 8.85]

---

9   See E.S. Mason, *The Corporation in Modern Society* xii (1960) (Foreword by A.A. Berle, Jr.).

For a discussion of non-shareholder constituency statutes see, e.g., ABA Committee on Corporate Laws, *Other Constituencies Statutes: Potential for Confusion*, 45 Bus. Lawyer 2253 (1990); and the symposium in 21 Stetson L.R. 1-252 (1991). Several corporate constituency statutes are set out in 21 Stetson L.R. 279-93 (1991).

Corporate constituency statutes in the United States generally do not mandate that directors of the corporation take the various non-shareholder interests into account. Instead, like the Illinois provision noted above, they typically provide that the directors "may" take the interests of non-shareholder constituents into account. Corporate constituency statutes in the United States also do not give non-shareholder interests a legal right of action against the directors of a corporation for failing to take their interests into account. The New York State provision in fact provides that "[n]othing in this paragraph shall create any duties owed by any director to any person or entity to consider or afford any particular weight to any of the foregoing or abrogate any duty of the directors either statutory or recognized by common law or court decisions." These constraints on constituency statutes have led critics to suggest that these statutes have come into existence not because of a desire to protect non-shareholder interest groups but rather as an additional device in the arsenal of corporate managers to avoid being sued for a breach of their fiduciary duties when they engage in defences designed to block take-overs. The constituency statutes will allow managers to point to non-shareholder interests to justify defences to block take-overs that cannot be justified from the perspective of shareholders. See, e.g., ABA Committee on Corporate Laws, *Other Constituencies Statutes: Potential for Confusion*, 45 Bus. Lawyer 2253 (1990); J.R. Macey & G.P. Miller, *Corporate Stakeholders: A Contractual Perspective*, 43 U. of Toronto L.J. 401 (1993); and J.R. Macey, *An Economic Analysis of the Various Rationales for Making Shareholders the Exclusive Beneficiaries of Corporate Fiduciary Duties*, 21 Stetson L.R. 23 (1991).

Another criticism of constituency statutes is that spreading fiduciary duties over several constituencies reduces the overall benefit of fiduciary duties. This may be the case with constituency statutes in that they may make it difficult for any group to succeed in a claim for a breach of fiduciary duties by the directors and officers since they can more easily justify their actions by pointing to the interests of any of a number of other corporate constituencies. If the benefits of fiduciary duties are greatest when allocated to one constituency then it may be worthwhile for the constituency that reaps the greatest benefit from fiduciary duties to pay other constituencies for the right to have the exclusive benefit of fiduciary duties. For example, the bondholders of solvent firms may be willing to relinquish the benefit of fiduciary duties to shareholders in return for higher interest payments (on fiduciary duties and bondholders in insolvent firms, see Chapter Nine). See J.R. Macey & G.P. Miller, *Corporate Stakeholders: A Contractual Perspective*, 43 U. of Toronto L.J. 401 (1993); see also J.R. Macey, *An Economic Analysis of the Various Rationales for Making Shareholders the Exclusive Beneficiaries of Corporate Fiduciary Duties*, 21 Stetson L.R. 23 (1991). See also the discussion on this point in Chapter Seven.

Macey and Miller challenge the argument that shareholders have to be the exclusive beneficiaries of fiduciary duties since otherwise managers would have to serve too many masters with multiple objectives making monitoring of management difficult. They note that corporations often have more than one class of shares each with differing interests in a given decision. Thus in acting in the interests of shareholders alone, directors must serve more than one master with different interests. However, Macey and Miller argue that the shareholders derive the greatest benefit from fiduciary duties of directors in part because they are owners of the residual interest in the corporation, and because they have a greater need for fiduciary duties as a method of filling gaps in their contractual relationship with the corporation. As owners of the residual interest, shareholders face most of the marginal costs and most of the marginal gains associated with a corporate decision. Thus focusing on the shareholder perspective, they suggest, will lead to allocatively efficient incentives in most instances. They note that there will be instances in which a decision from the perspective of the shareholders will have negative impact on other constituencies. However, they suggest that other constituencies can better control against opportunistic behaviour through contractual provisions. For instance, bondholders and employees can be protected through bond covenants and collective agreement provisions. Gaps that remain in such contracts can be filled in by courts. On the other hand, shareholders, they argue, do not have the same contractual backdrop against which courts can fill gaps. They need the protection of fiduciary duties as a means of gap filling. *Id.*, Macey & Miller.

Proponents of non-shareholder constituency fiduciary duties claim that non-shareholder constituencies can not properly protect themselves through contractual provisions. In particular, employees have "implicit" long-term arrangements with corporations that are not legally recognized and that can be opportunistically breached by corporations. For instance, it is argued corporations pay workers less than they are worth to the corporation in early years and more than they are worth to the corporation in later years. This encourages workers to make a long-term commitment to the corporation by investing in firm-specific human capital. However, the corporation may take advantage of this by dismissing more senior workers to avoid the higher payments in their senior years. This type of opportunistic behaviour is more likely to occur in the context of a change in control of the corporation. Employees that are not unionized, it is argued, cannot fully protect themselves against this kind of opportunistic behaviour, and even where they are unionized they cannot fully protect themselves because of the difficulties in drafting severance provisions that take account of all the events that could trigger dismissals. See K. Stone, *Employees as Stakeholders Under State Nonshareholder Constituency Statutes*, 21 Stetson L.R. 45 (1991); K. Stone, *Policing Employment Contracts Within the Nexus-of-Contracts Firm*, 43 U. of Toronto L.J. 353 (1993).

In Canada directors are generally said to owe their duties to the company. However, there is some judicial dicta in support of a broader approach to the fiduciary duties of directors. In *Teck Corp. v. Millar* (1972), 33 D.L.R. (3d) 228 (B.C.), a case involving management's defensive tactics to a take-over bid, Berger J. stated:

If today the directors of a company were to consider the interests of its employees no one would argue that in doing so they were not acting *bona fide* in the interests of the company itself. Similarly, if the directors were to consider the consequences to the community of any policy that the company intended to pursue, and were deflected in their commitment to that policy as a result, it could not be said that they had not considered *bona fide* the interests of the shareholders.

I appreciate that it would be a breach of their duty for directors to disregard entirely the interests of a company's shareholders in order to confer a benefit on its employees: *Parke v. Daily News Ltd.* ... But if they observe a decent respect for other interests lying beyond those of the company's shareholders in a strict sense, that will not, in my view, leave directors open to the charge that they have failed in their fiduciary duty to the company. [*Id.* at 314]

In spite of the general legal position, many directors appear to view themselves as having broader fiduciary duties. According to the Conference Board's *1977 Report*, directors of Canadian public corporations believe that "they ought not to represent ... shareholders at the expense of employees, customers, local communities and the company at large." Instead, "the board should regard the balancing of these interests and the provision of wider and longer term perspectives as integral parts of their tasks." The directors were not reported as having addressed themselves to how or to whom they should be accountable for the balancing of these various and often conflicting interests, and were generally unenthusiastic about the notion of special interest group representation on boards of directors. *Canadian Directorship Practices: A Critical Self-Examination* ix, 94-109 (1977).

Representation of Non-Shareholder Constituents on the Board. An alternative approach to having the interests of non-shareholder constituents taken into account would be to have other stakeholders represented on the board of directors. Representation of various non-shareholder constituents on the board of directors might be considered consistent with notions of democracy and could provide a means for non-shareholder constituents to better protect their interests. However, representation of various constituencies on the board of directors may involve costs. There would be substantial information costs for constituency representatives to become informed participants on the board. Participation by various constituencies, especially employees, may direct the attention of the board to day-to-day operating-level concerns at the expense of focus on strategic concerns. There may also be potential for opportunistic behaviour by constituencies that have contractual arrangements with the corporation and who use participation on the board to gain leverage to extract additional concessions from the board during the life of the contract. With many constituency participants on the board there would also be opportunities for constituencies to support each other in decisions that would reduce the value of the corporation but would lead to wealth transfers in their favour from other constituents.

One often suggested form of non-shareholder constituency representation on the board of directors is a employee representation. The most frequently cited example of employee representation on the board of directors is the approach to employee co-determination in Germany. In Germany public corporations (Aktiengesellschaft—or AGs) have a mandatory two-tiered board system consisting of a management board and a supervisory board of non-management directors. In businesses other than the coal, iron and steel industries (for which there is a separate co-determination statute) one-third of the supervisory board must consist of employee representatives in AGs having fewer than 2,000 employees, and one-half of the supervisory board must be employee representatives in AGs with more than 2,000 employees.

There is no requirement for employee co-determination in most incorporation statutes in Canada. Aspects of both corporate law and labour law in Canada may frustrate attempts to provide for employee representation on boards of directors in Canada. See, e.g., C.S. Axworthy, *Corporation Law as if Some People Mattered*, 36 U. of Toronto L.J. 392, 399-404 (1986); and C.S. Axworthy & D. Perry, *The Law of Worker Ownership*, 27 Osgoode Hall L.J. 647, 648-49 (1989). However, ABCA ss. 101(9) and 117(4) provide that the articles or a unanimous shareholder agreement may provide for the election or appointment of directors by creditors or employees of the corporation. Similarly section 101(8) of the Saskatchewan Business Corporations Act provides that the articles can provide for the election or appointment of directors by creditors or employees of the corporation.

Participation on the board of directors may be an effective technique for protecting employees where, as noted above, they make firm-specific human capital investments. An employee representative on the board of directors may also assist in overcoming informational astmmetries between corporate management and employees, particularly during periods when management alleges that the corporation is experiencing financial difficulties. See O. Williamson, *Corporate Governance*, 93 Yale L.R. 1197, 1207-9 (1984).

Creditors of the corporation might also be represented on the board of directors. Representation of creditors could protect firm-specific investments by creditors such as the cost of assessing the credit worthiness of the particular corporation. However, creditors typically have defined terms for their loans and can protect their interests through a variety of contractual devices such as taking security interests in assets of the corporation or creating various legal rights when the corporation fails to meet tests of financial soundness. They have less need for the protection that representation on the board of directors may afford. Where higher debt-equity ratios expose creditors to more substantial risks representation on the board of directors may be a more effective device than available contractual devices to protect the interests of creditors. See *id.*, Williamson, 1211-12. Indeed, creditors occasionally reserve a right to representation on the board of directors when the corporation is in financial distress.

Similarly suppliers can normally use a variety of contractual devices to protect firm-specific investments but, like creditors, may find representation on the board a useful device where they have a substantial volume of business with the corporation and information about the corporation through representation on the board can assist the supplier in planning its investments in supplying the corporation. *Id.*, Williamson, 1212-13.

Consumer representation on the board might assist consumers in addressing problems such as the health hazards associated with a corporation's products. However, there are the difficulties of determining who would be representative of consumers and how consumer representatives would communicate with a large and dispersed group of consumers. Given these difficulties, consumer representation on the board may only be practical for a particularly large customer of the corporation. *Id.*, Williamson, 1213-14.

H. CLOSELY HELD CORPORATIONS

1. The Nature of Closely Held Corporations

There is no universally accepted definition of a closely held—or simply "close"—corporation. However, a closely held corporation is normally considered to have the following characteristics: (1) relatively few shareholders; (2) most or all of the shareholders participate actively in the management of the corporation; and (3) no established market for the shares of the corporation. In addition, closely held corporations typically have a restriction on the transfer of the shares of the corporation.

When "private corporation" was defined in Canadian corporations statutes, the upper limit on the number of shareholders was usually set between 25 and 50. However, the ceiling on the number of individual shareholders that a corporation might have and still maintain a substantial identity between owners and managers is probably more like 10 or 12. Most closely held corporations have a lower value than widely held ones, but that is not universally true. The T. Eaton Co., to cite but one well-known example, is anything but small and yet is closely held by members of the Eaton family and the family trust.

2. Corporate Governance Modifications for Closely Held Corporations

Reasons for Different Treatment. Given the nature of closely held corporations the corporate governance structures suitable for such corporations may be different than those suitable for widely held corporations. With fewer shareholders and most or all of the shareholders taking part in the management of the corporation, there may be less need for devices imposed in the context of widely held corporations (such as mandatory proxy solicitation and the distribution of audited financial statements) to facilitate the monitoring of management. The efficiencies achieved by allocating the management of the business and affairs of the corporation to directors and their delegated officers are not as significant where there are only a few shareholders. A small group of shareholders may more readily assemble to deal with an array of matters of a more day-to-day management nature. Indeed, with relatively few shareholders in a closely held corporation, the individual shareholders usually have a significant stake in the corporation and have an incentive to protect their investments through more active participation in the day-to-day affairs of the corporation.

Attempts to Provide for Different Treatment. Because of these differences corporate laws typically provide for different treatment for closely held corporations. Many other countries (such as France, Germany and Japan) have a separate statute for closely held corporations. In Canada the early corporate statutes did not distinguish between closely held corporations and widely held corporations. However, in 1910 British Columbia adopted a "private company" concept that had been adopted a few years earlier in England. The term "private company" attempted to define corporations having characteristics of closely held corporations and generally provided relief from financial disclosure requirements. Subsequently most Canadian jurisdictions also adopted this approach.

When changes were made to Canadian corporate statutes in the 1970s and 1980s the private company concept was eliminated in most jurisdictions on the basis that it was difficult to precisely define a closely held corporation. The "private company" distinction was generally replaced with a series of permitted modifications to the basic legislative framework which were of a kind most likely to be used only by a closely held corporation.

Different Treatment Under Modern Canadian Statutes. The following modifications are available to closely held corporations:

(1) *Waiver of Notice to Shareholder Meetings.* A shareholder can waive notice to a shareholder meeting. CBCA s. 136; ABCA s. 130; BCCA s. 167; OBCA s. 98. While shareholders in widely held corporations can waive notice to meetings under this provision, it is most likely to be used by closely held corporations where shareholders can be more readily contacted with respect to a meeting.

(2) *Resolutions by Unanimous Consent in Lieu of Meeting.* In lieu of having shareholder resolutions passed at a meeting of shareholders, shareholders' resolutions can be passed by having the resolution in writing signed by all the shareholders entitled to vote on the resolution. Unanimous consent to the resolution in writing would be difficult to obtain in the context of a widely held corporation and is thus an option that is normally limited to a closely held corporation. CBCA s. 142; ABCA s. 136; BCCA s. 164; OBCA s. 104.

(3) *Avoiding Proxy Solicitation Requirements.* The expense of proxy solicitation and the preparation of a proxy circular is likely to substantially outweigh any possible gains for shareholders in closely held corporations when the shareholders have a sufficient stake in the corporation to keep themselves well informed and to exercise their voting rights. Thus OBCA s. 111 and BCCA s. 177 provide that corporations that have not made a distribution of their shares to the public are not subject to the mandatory proxy solicitation requirements. CBCA s. 149(2) and ABCA s. 143(2) exempt a corporation from mandatory proxy solicitation if the corporation does not have more than 15 shareholders (the ABCA also requires that the shareholders waive their right to proxy solicitation).

(4) *Dispensing with an Auditor.* The shareholders of a corporation that has not made a distribution of its shares to the public can also dispense with the requirement of having an auditor. CBCA s. 163; ABCA s. 157; BCCA s. 203; OBCA s. 148 (limited to corporations with assets not exceeding $2,500,000 and gross operating revenues not exceeding $5,000,000). This provision will most often be used by closely held corporations where possible to avoid what can be substantial costs of having a full audit conducted.

(5) *Financial Disclosure.* A corporation that has not made a distribution of its shares to the public can also avoid having to publicly file its financial statements. See CBCA s. 160; ABCA s. 154; OBCA s. 156. Under the BCCA the scope of financial disclosure for a company that has not made a distribution of its shares to the public is reduced. See BCCA ss. 169, 197.

The CBCA also explicitly recognizes single shareholder corporations and provides that where the corporation has only one shareholder the shareholder's presence in person or by proxy constitutes a meeting. CBCA s. 139(4); ABCA s. 133(4); BCCA ss. 165, 168(b); OBCA s. 101(4).

Shareholder Agreements. As noted above, shareholders in closely held corporations will typically want to become more involved in the day-to-day running of the business. Thus perhaps the most significant modification for closely held corporations is that which allows a closely held corporation to modify the default allocation of the power to manage the business and affairs of the corporation to the directors. Section 102 of the CBCA allocates the power to manage to the directors, but this is subject to a unanimous shareholder agreement. See ABCA s. 97; OBCA s. 115.

Shareholders can enter into agreements whereby they agree as to how they will vote their shares. Such agreements are now explicitly recognized in the CBCA. CBCA s. 146(1); see also ABCA s. 139.1; OBCA s. 108(1). Section 146(2) of the CBCA allows shareholders to remove management powers from directors and allocate them to the shareholders. See also ABCA s. 140(1); OBCA s. 108(2). This requires a unanimous agreement among the shareholders of the corporation. It is thus not an agreement that is likely to be achieved in the context of a widely held corporation. The explicit authority given in CBCA s. 146(2) for the use of a shareholders' agreement to reallocate the powers assigned to directors responded to the concern raised by the following case

Ringuet v. Bergeron
Supreme Court of Canada
[1960] S.C.R. 672, 24 D.L.R. (2d) 449

JUDSON J. (by whom the judgment of ABBOTT, JUDSON and RITCHIE JJ. was delivered): The respondent sued the appellants for a declaration that against each of them, he was entitled to certain shares of the St. Maurice Knitting Mills Limited registered in their names. In the Superior Court the learned trial judge dismissed the action. The Court of Queen's Bench (Appeal Side) allowed the appeal and maintained the action. The two unsuccessful shareholders now appeal to this Court.

The action was brought on an agreement dated August 3, 1949, between the respondent and the appellants. At that time these parties and four other persons each held 50 shares of the St. Maurice Knitting Mills Limited, a company incorporated by letters patent under Part I of the Quebec Companies Act. These shares constituted all the issued capital stock of the company. The purpose of the agreement was to provide for the acquisition of 50 shares from one Frank Spain and the division of these shares among the parties. With these 50 shares divided among them the parties then had control of the company and they agreed, among other matters to vote for their election to the Board of Directors; to ensure the election of the appellant Ringuet as president of the company, of the appellant Pagé as vice-president and general manager, and of the respondent Bergeron as secretary-treasurer and assistant general manager of the company, all at stated and agreed salaries. They also agreed to vote unanimously at all meetings of the company and provided for a penalty for breach of the contract in the following terms:

11. Dans toutes assemblées de la dite Compagnie, les parties aux présentes s'engagent et s'obligent à voter unanimement sur tout objet qui nécessite un vote. Aucune des parties aux présentes ne pourra différer d'opinion avec ses co-parties contractantes en ce qui concerne le vote. Le vote prépondérant du Président devra toujours être en faveur des deux parties contractantes.

12. Si l'une des parties ne se conforme à présente convention, ses actions seront cédées et transportées aux deux autres parties contractantes en parts égales, et ce gratuitement.

Tel est la sanction de la non exécution d'aucune des clauses de la présente convention par l'une des parties contractantes.

Two or three months later the parties also purchased the shares of another share-holder Robert Sevigny and divided them among themselves in accordance with the agreement. On the completion of this purchase, there remained only five shareholders in the company: the two appellants, the respondent, the mis-en-cause Gerard Jean, and Zénon Bachand. On February 3, 1950, the three parties to the first agreement entered into another agreement and included in this one the mis-en-cause Gerard Jean. The purpose of this agreement was to provide for the admission of Gerard Jean into the controlling group and for the acquisition of the shares of Zénon Bachand, the last of the minority shareholders. Two shares were issued from the treasury and the total issued shares were equally divided among the four individuals with the result that each held 88 shares. The contract of February 3, 1950, to which Jean was a party, contains no provision corresponding to clause 12 of the contract of August 3, 1949. It does not purport to replace or alter the earlier contract, which remains in full force and effect.

From August 3, 1949 to June 14, 1952 the three parties to the first contract observed its terms. There had during this period been certain increases in salary which were properly authorized and fixed by mutual consent. On June 14, 1952 the appellant Maurice Pagé, at a directors' meeting, began to take steps to oust the respondent from the management of the company, and at a shareholders' meeting held on July 21, 1952, the appellants and Jean voted themselves in as a new board of directors. The respondent says that he had no notice of this meeting and did not attend. He was not nominated and no votes were cast for his election as director of the company. The new board of directors held a meeting following the shareholders' meeting. Ringuet was elected president, Pagé was elected vice-president and Jean, secretary-treasurer. The respondent was thus completely excluded from the management of the company. He brought his action alleging that the appellants in failing to vote for his election to the board of directors and in not ensuring that he be appointed assistant general manager and secretary-treasurer, had violated the contract of August 3, 1949, and that he was entitled to enforce the penalty provided in clause 12 of the agreement. He claimed a transfer of 88 shares from each defendant. The facts were admitted in the pleadings and the sole defence was that the contract was contrary to public order.

The Superior Court rejected the action on the very narrow ground that clause 12 had no application when one party was suing the other two. No opinion delivered in the Court of Queen's Bench accepted this interpretation of clause 12 and no attempt was made in this Court to support the judgment at trial on this ground. In the Court of Queen's Bench the learned Chief Justice and Mr. Justice Owen found for the respondent, with Mr. Justice Pratte dissenting. The Chief Justice found nothing illegal in the agreement and decided that it should be given its full effect. The ratio of the dissenting opinion is to be found in the distinction drawn between the rights of a shareholder and the obligations assumed on becoming a director. While majority shareholders may agree to vote their shares for certain purposes, they cannot by this agreement tie the hands of directors and compel them to exercise the power of management of the company in a particular way. This appears in the following extract from the reasons of Pratte J:

Mais la situation des directeurs est bien différente de celle des actionnaires. Le directeur est désigné par les actionnaires, mais il n'est pas à proprement parler leur mandataire; il est un administrateur chargé par la loi de gérer un patrimoine qui n'est ni le sien, ni celui de ses codirecteurs, ni celui des actionnaires, mais celui de la compagnie, une personne juridique absolument distincte à la fois de ceux qui la dirigent et de ceux qui en possèdent le capital actions. En cette qualité, le directeur doit agir en bonne conscience, dans le seul intérêt du patrimoine confié à sa gestion. Cela suppose qu'il a la liberté de choisir, au moment d'une décision à prendre, celle qui lui paraît la plus conforme aux intérêts sur lesquels la loi lui impose le devoir de veiller.

There can be no objection to the general principle stated in this passage, but, in my view, it was not offended by this agreement. However, the conclusion of Pratte J. was that a director who has bound himself as this contract bound the parties has rendered himself incapable of doing what the law requires of him and that clause 11 requiring unanimity at all meetings had that effect. He also held that clause 11 was not severable and that therefore the agreement was invalidated in its entirety.

Owen J. agreed that the undertaking of unanimity at the directors' meetings which he considered was required by clause 11 might be contrary to public order but that it was not necessary to decide this since the clause was severable from the other provisions of the agreement to which he gave full effect. The defendants had failed to comply with other clauses in the contract—the voting of Bergeron's salary, the election of Bergeron as a director of the company and his appointment as secretary-treasurer and assistant general manager.

The point of the appeal is therefore whether an agreement among a group of shareholders providing for the direction and control of a company in the circumstances of this case is contrary to public order, and whether it is open to the parties to establish whatever sanction they choose for a breach of such agreement.

Did the parties of this agreement tie their hands in their capacity as directors of the company so as to contravene the requirements of the Quebec Companies Act, which provides (s. 80) that "the affairs of the company shall be managed by a board of not less than three directors"? I agree with the reasons of the learned Chief Justice that this agreement does not contravene this or any other section of the Quebec Companies Act. It is no more than an agreement among shareholders owning or proposing to own the majority of the issued shares of a company to unite upon a course of policy or action and upon the officers whom they will elect. There is nothing illegal or contrary to public order in an agreement for achieving these purposes. Shareholders have the right to combine their interests and voting powers to secure such control of a company and to ensure that the company will be managed by certain persons in a certain manner. This is a well-known, normal and legal contract and one which is frequently encountered in current practice and it makes no difference whether the objects sought are to be achieved by means of an agreement such as this or a voting trust. Such an arrangement is not prohibited either by law, by good morals or public order.

It is important to distinguish the present action, which is between contracting parties to an agreement for the voting of shares, from one brought by a minority shareholder demanding a certain standard of conduct from directors and majority shareholders. Nothing that can arise from this litigation and nothing that can be said about it can touch on that problem. The fact that this agreement may potentially involve detriment to the minority does not render it illegal and contrary to public order. If there is such injury, there is a remedy available to the minority shareholder who alleges a departure from the standards required of the majority shareholders and the directors. The possibility of such injurious effect on the minority is not a ground for illegality.

I think that this litigation can be decided on the simple ground that clause 11 has no reference to directors' meetings. Clause 11 refers to meetings of the company, that is, shareholders' meetings, and not to meetings of the board of directors. On this point I agree with the Chief Justice, who stated his opinion in the following terms:

Au surplus, y a-t-il quelque chose qui répugne à la loi, à l'ordre public et aux bonnes moeurs qu'un groupe d'actionnaires s'entendent pour contrôler et diriger une compagnie, pour devenir ses administrateurs, ses principaux officiers? Il n'était sûrement pas besoin d'un contrat écrit pour pareille entente qui intervient chaque jour dans le monde des compagnies, étant notoire qu'un grand nombre d'entre elles sont contrôlées par un groupe d'actionnaires qui souvent même ne représentent pas la majorité des actions.

L'engagement des co-contractants à voter unanimement leurs actions dans les assemblées de la compagnie ne saurait lui-même, à mon avis, être invalide; après tout, chacun des comparants n'a pas renoncé à la délibération, à la discussion, au droit de faire triompher son opinion avant de se ranger à l'avis de la majorité qui en principe doit gouverner.

I have the greatest difficulty in seeing how any question of public order can arise in a private arrangement of this kind. The possibility of injury to a minority interest cannot raise it. If this were not so, every arrangement of this kind would involve judicial enquiry. Minority rights have the protection of the law without the necessity of invoking public order. This litigation is between shareholders of a closely held company. The agreement which the plaintiff seeks to enforce damages nobody except the unsuccessful party to the agreement. No public interest or illegality is involved.

I would dismiss the appeal with costs.

As Judson J. noted, there is nothing illegal at common law in an agreement among shareholders on how they will vote their shares. This does not offend fiduciary ideology, since shareholders could ordinarily vote in accordance with their own interests. They might then have agreed to bind their discretion with respect to future shareholders' meetings. See *Pender v. Lushington* (1877), 6 Ch. Div. 70, 75-76 (C.A.); Iacobucci & Johnston, *The Private or Closely Held Corporation*, in 2 Ziegel 68, 109. In this way, a bargain as to who will be a director of the firm was always enforceable under pre-CBCA law.

In the United States, these agreements sometimes take a more complicated form. For example shareholders might be required to execute a form of proxy in favour of a nominee who is a party to the agreement. In Canada this would not be a convenient mechanism, standing by itself, since under CBCA s. 148 a proxy is valid only for the meeting for which it is given and is revocable. Another device used in the United States is a voting trust. Here the parties transfer legal ownership of the shares to a trustee who votes them in accordance with the terms of the trust deed and otherwise holds them for their beneficial owners. This obviates the possibility of a party selling his shares out from under the voting trust. A simpler device for achieving the same end might be to print on any share certificates a legend indicating that the shares are subject to restrictions on transfer in a shareholder agreement. The transferee of shares is bound by the agreement if the share certificate bears a legend referring to the shareholder agreement, or if he has actual notice of it. CBCA ss. 146(3), 49(8). When the certificates bear a restrictive legend, the shares are called "letter stock."

If the agreement is not unanimous, however, it is not so clear that actual notice of it will bind the purchaser of the shares. In *Greenhalgh v. Mallard*, [1943] 2 All E.R. 234 (C.A.), certain of the corporation's shareholders had entered into an agreement to vote so as to give the plaintiff effective control of the corporation. Shortly thereafter, certain of the parties sold their shares to someone not a party to the agreement. The plaintiff sued for a declaration that the purchaser was bound by the voting agreement. The Court held that no intention was revealed on the face of the agreement either that its duration should be longer than the period during which a particular party would continue to own his shares, or that a party was to be restrained from selling his shares. Therefore the Court did not have to decide whether: (1) the "restrictive covenant" could run with the shares; (2) the shares could be held to be impressed with a constructive trust that would bind purchasers with notice; or (3) the purchasers (who in fact knew of the voting agreement) could be held to have induced a breach of contract. Lord Greene M.R., who delivered the judgment of the Court, did, however, express doubts that any of these theories was correct. In such cases, a voting trust might be a more secure device to ensure that transferees will be bound.

Binding the Directors' Discretion. While shareholders were generally free to agree on how they would vote to elect directors, an agreement that fettered the discretion of directors might be impeached. For this reason, the interpretation of clause 11 in *Ringuet v. Bergeron* was all important. If "assemblé" included directors' meetings then the provision might be illegal, and Fauteux J. would indeed have held it so. The underlying notion appeared to be that the directors' fiduciary duty to advance the best interests of the firm required that the directors be free to assess that interest and to act upon their assessment from time to time. As in Rousseau's paradox of freedom, the directors were forced to be free.

The argument for holding such agreement is illegal is not, however, a strong one. Management's discretion is fettered by any long-term contract—for example, one retaining the services of a senior executive in a multi-year contract, with a right of damages for wrongful dismissal. See Section B. These contracts are upheld on the basis that the decision whether firm value will be advanced through a long-term contract is one of business judgment best left to management. These agreements are not very different from shareholder agreements that provide for the appointment of officers or for their remuneration. If the purpose behind policies restricting directors' agreements is to maximize firm value, is there any reason why investors require mandatory rules to achieve this end?

Even before enabling statutory legislation, American courts began to enforce agreements binding directors. In *Clark v. Dodge*, 199 N.E. 641 (N.Y. 1936), the Court enforced an agreement specifying that a minority shareholder would remain as an officer and receive one-fourth of the firm's net income as salary or dividends.

"The business of a corporation shall be managed by its board of directors." General Corporation Law (Consol. Laws, c. 23) § 27. That is the statutory norm. Are we committed ... to the doctrine that there may be no variation, however slight or innocuous, from that norm, where salaries or policies or the retention of individuals in office are concerned? There is ample authority supporting that doctrine, ... and something may be said for it, since it furnishes a simple, if arbitrary, test. Apart from its practical administrative convenience, the reasons upon which it is said to rest are more or less nebulous. Public policy, the intention of the Legislature, detriment to the corporation, are phrases which in this connection mean little. Possible harm to *bona fide* purchasers of stock or to creditors or to stockholding minorities have more substance; but such harms are absent in many instances. If the enforcement of a particular contract damages nobody—not even, in any perceptible degree, the public—one sees no reason for holding it illegal, even though it impinges slightly upon the broad provision of section 27. Damage suffered or threatened is a logical and practical test, and has come to be the one generally adopted by the courts. ... Where the stockholders are the sole stockholders, there seems to be no objection to enforcing an agreement among them to vote for certain people as officers. [Id. at 642]

See also *Galler v. Galler*, 203 N.E. 2d 577 (Ill. 1964).

Could CBCA s. 146 be interpreted as an exclusive safe harbour in the case of shareholder agreements? In other words, would a court refuse to enforce a non-unanimous shareholder agreement of the kind that was upheld in *Ringuet*? A unanimity requirement may be thought desirable if it is feared that a non-unanimous agreement may impose costs on excluded shareholders which exceed the gain to parties to the agreement. But this only makes sense if enforcing non-unanimous agreements will result in more self-dealing than would arise if they were proscribed. This might reasonably be thought unlikely, since an informal coalition of controlling shareholders would still be possible, and in any event shareholders might not wish to evidence self-dealing projects in a formal agreement. The parties to a non-unanimous coalition of shareholders might also want to reduce an informal and fair non-unanimous pact to a written agreement in order to reduce uncertainty concerning business policies. Assuming that minority shareholders thus excluded from governance have not themselves bargained for management rights, is there a compelling reason why such an agreement should not be upheld?

Under the BCCA the directors manage or supervise the affairs and business of the company subject to the articles. The standard form articles give the directors the powers of the company subject to those powers that the Act or the articles assign to the shareholders in general meeting. Thus under the BCCA the powers of the directors can be proscribed and assigned to shareholders in the articles—a unanimous shareholders' agreement is not necessary. However, it is common to use a unanimous shareholders' agreement for companies incorporated under the BCCA on the basis that the unanimous shareholders' agreement is easier and cheaper to amend, is not publicly filed and can also be used to control how shareholder votes will be exercised. When a unanimous shareholders' agreement is used the articles provide that the directors powers are subject to the unanimous shareholder agreement.

There is broad scope for devising innovative management structures through a unanimous shareholder agreement. At the same time, the ability to sterilize the board is not a right to abolish it, so that the requirement to elect directors in s. 106(3) remains. While this might seem simply a matter of internal housekeeping, a disregard of these corporate formalities carries with it the risk of veil piercing. See Chapter Two, Section B. The modern trend is, however, toward allowing closely held corporations maximum flexibility in their structures. See *Report of Committee on Corporate Laws, Proposed Statutory Close Corporations Supplement to the Model Business Corporations Act*, 37 Bus. Law. 269 (1981); *Report of Committee on Corporate Laws, Statutory Close Corporations Supplement to the Model Business Corporations Act*, 38 Bus. Law. 1031 (1983). Today, the restrictions on the scope of shareholder agreements under pre-CBCA law may seem anomalous, but these barriers have not wholly been eliminated.

3. Share Transfer Restrictions

A small firm may have a considerable stake in the identities of its members. Where shareholders are not passive investors, but are expected to take part in management, the identity of the shareholders will affect firm value. Even where active management duties are not contemplated, shareholders in closely held corporations will be greatly interested in the identities of the other members of the group because of the heightened possibility of hold-out strategies when decisions are made in small groups. For these reasons, a closely held corporation's charter will frequently provide for share transfer restrictions.

Transfer restrictions can achieve other aims. They may make it possible for the owners to maintain their relative share ownership, and therefore relative power, within the entity. In this way, they are analogous to pre-emptive rights upon a new share issuance. Transfer restrictions are also required if a firm is to take advantage of the OSA private offering exemption. Without them, prospectus requirements might also be triggered where securities of control persons are resold under OSA s. 72(7). In addition, they may be drafted so as to provide liquidity to the estate of a deceased owner or to an owner who simply wishes to retire from the corporation. Finally, they may also reduce the likelihood of a deadlock by providing that one or more of the owners will then become obligated to offer his shares to the others or to the corporation under a pre-arranged formula.

At least five types of transfer restrictions may be identified. These are:

(1) *Absolute restrictions.* Under these restrictions the shareholder simply cannot sell. Because of their Draconian effect, they are rarely used, except possibly in the start-up phase of a new corporation.

(2) *Consent restrictions.* With these restrictions, a transfer of shares may be made only upon the approval of the corporation's board.

(3) *First option restrictions*. This is the most commonly encountered type. Although a first option restriction can be quite complex in its drafting and mechanics, the notion is basically simple. The shareholder may not sell her or his shares or may not sell them to any person not already a shareholder of the corporation without first offering them to the corporation or to the remaining shareholders. They would then have an option to buy the shares, either at the price that has been offered by the proposed purchaser or at the price fixed by a valuer, who is often the corporation's auditor.

(4) *Buy-sell agreements*. This is like a first option restriction except that, as the name implies, the corporation or the other shareholders must buy the shares of the selling shareholders when the triggering event occurs. These provisions are very popular as a form of protection against the death of a shareholder. The estate of the deceased shareholder would then be obliged to sell her or his shares, and the corporation or the other shareholders would be obliged to buy them. In this way, a shareholder is able to make better provision for her or his family on death than were he simply to leave them her or his shares in the firm. The transaction will frequently be financed through an insurance policy taken out on the life of the shareholder. Another triggering transaction might be deadlock.

(5) *Buyback rights*. Here the corporation is given the right to repurchase shares on the occurrence of certain events, even if the shareholder does not want to sell. A typical event would be the termination of the shareholder's employment with the firm.

In general, a share transfer restriction may not be adopted by a firm that has made a public distribution of its shares. CBCA s. 49(9). However, under amendments made to the CBCA in 1982, a public corporation may constrain the issuance or transfer of shares to, or their ownership by, persons who are not resident Canadians, in order to qualify under any federal or provincial law making a specified level of Canadian ownership a prerequisite for receipt of a licence or other benefit. See CBCA ss. 46, 47, 49(9)-(11), 174. A constrained share provision can be quite drastic in its operation because the directors are authorized to sell, "as if [the corporation] were the owner thereof, any of such constrained shares that are owned, or that the directors determine ... may be owned, contrary to the constraints" (CBCA s. 46(1)). The shares to be sold must be selected by the directors "in good faith," and the proceeds of sale are to be held in trust for the benefit of the exshareholders, who must, however, bear the costs of administration of the trust fund. CBCA s. 47.

Validity. American courts, when confronted with share transfer restrictions, tend to emphasize shares-as-property and therefore to view transfer restrictions as falling into the suspect legal category of restraints upon the alienation of property. American courts would be likely to hold any absolute share transfer restriction invalid, and the validity of consent-type restrictions at common law depends upon the jurisdiction, as well as upon the features of the particular restriction, although many states have legislation governing share transfer restrictions. First option restrictions have been upheld at common law if "reasonable." See generally *Allen v. Biltmore Tissue Corp.*, 141 N.E.2d 812 (N.Y. 1957); Bradley, *Stock Transfer Restrictions and Buy-Sell Agreements*, 1969 Ill. L.F. 139. English Courts, in contrast, tend to view shares as predominantly contractual in nature and have been relatively untroubled by doubts as to the validity of transfer restrictions. See generally Gower, *Some Contrasts between British and American Corporation Law*, 69 Harv. L. Rev. 1369, 1377-78 (1956).

In 1918 the Privy Council held *ultra vires* a by-law of a company incorporated under special Act of the Parliament of Canada which gave the corporation's directors an absolute discretion to approve transfers to new shareholders or not. *Canada National Fire Ins. Co. v. Hutchings*, [1918] A.C. 451. The decision turned on a distinction posited between "companies in the United Kingdom which are formed by contract, whether it be under deed of settlement or under memorandum and articles of association ... and Canadian companies which are formed under the Canadian Companies Act, either by letters patent or by special Act." The latter companies were said to be "pure creatures of statute [with] their powers and duties ... to be found in the two Acts" ([1918] A.C. at 456). Their Lordships were unable to find in the Acts in question any power to adopt a by-law restricting share transfers. Since all of the Canadian letters patent jurisdictions except for Prince Edward Island have now adopted the articles of incorporation form of statute, the present day applicability of *Hutchings* in Canada is very limited. It may be imprudent, however, to grant to the directors of a closely held corporation an extremely broad discretion in regard to share transfers.

In *Edmonton Country Club v. Case*, [1975] 1 S.C.R. 534, the club was incorporated as a public corporation (because its articles did not restrict to 50 the maximum number of shareholders) and one of its articles prohibited the transfer of shares to anyone without the consent of the directors, who might withhold consent "in their unfettered discretion." A shareholder claimed that the article was *ultra vires*. Justice Dickson rejected the attack, but with the observation that:

[b]efore we move to strike down such a power on the ground that it is unreasonable, we should, in my view, have some factual support for that conclusion. There is no evidence before us, nor is it alleged, that the directors have at any time in the almost thirty-year history of the company acted in bad faith or arbitrarily or otherwise abused the power. [*Id.* at 550]

Laskin J., dissenting, would have struck out the article. He explained the difference of opinion between himself and Dickson J. as follows:

The difference between us is whether this arbitrary power, not related to any standard for the exercise of an unfettered discretion, should be controlled only in the context of a particular case requiring its exercise (as he would have it), or whether it should be struck out simply because it is on its face utterly arbitrary (as I would have it). [*Id.* at 551]

It is not clear whether Laskin J. would have found arbitrariness to be as fatal to a restriction in a private corporation as in a public one. After quoting various American authorities dealing with restrictions in closely held corporations, he concluded: "[a] test of reasonableness commends itself to me" (*id.* at 554). Today in Alberta, as federally, the statute does not permit a share transfer restriction in a public corporation.

The English Court of Appeal has held that where a transfer restriction on its face gives the directors an unfettered discretion to approve a transfer or not, the only restraint upon the directors is that "[t]hey must exercise their discretion *bona fide* in what they consider—not what a court may consider—is in the interests of the company, and not for any collateral purpose" (*Re Smith and Fawcett Ltd.*, [1942] 1 Ch. 304, 306). This formula is not much of a constraint upon the directors' arbitrary exercise of power, as the result in that case amply demonstrated. The burden of proof of improper purpose will be on the plaintiff, who is not in the best position to know what motivated the directors, and the court is likely to pay the utmost deference to the purposes as stated by the directors. It is not impossible, however, for a shareholder to convince a court in a given case that the directors' refusal to transfer was motivated by bad faith. *Re Shoal Harbour Marine Service Ltd.* (1956), 20 W.W.R. 312 (B.C.).

When a share transfer restriction is incorporated into a firm's charter, a possibility exists that it may be invoked in circumstances in which the benefit to the firm in relying upon it is less than the harm suffered by the would-be selling shareholder. In these circumstances, the refusal to register the transfer is opportunistic, with one group of shareholders using a veto power to prevent an efficient transaction. This possibility may suggest the desirability of a judicial review of the decision under norms of good faith bargaining or proper purposes. Even then, it will not be easy for a court to distinguish between a legitimate exercise of contract rights and opportunistic behaviour. One possible response to this problem may be to place the onus of resolving the informational problem on the parties, who might provide an express statement of what constitutes strategic behaviour in a shareholder agreement. On the other hand, given the impossibility of indicating precisely all of the circumstances in which it may be inappropriate to rely on a share transfer restriction, it may be desirable to leave some of these gaps to be filled in by a court through the application of good faith norms. See further Aivazian, Trebilcock & Penny, *The Law of Contract Modifications: The Uncertain Quest for a Benchmark of Enforceability*, 22 Osgoode Hall L.J. 173 (1974); Muris, *Opportunistic Behaviour and the Law of Contracts*, 65 Minn. L. Rev. 521 (1981).

A CBCA corporation that desires share transfer restrictions must include them in its articles. CBCA s. 6(d). The restriction thereby becomes part of the corporation's internal law, and transfers in contravention of it will not be registered by the corporation or its transfer agent. In addition, the restriction or a reference to it must be noted conspicuously on all share certificates. Otherwise, the restriction is ineffective against transferees without actual knowledge of it. CBCA s. 49(8).

See further Clark 763-72; Coates, *Share Transfer and Transmission Restrictions in the Close Corporation*, 3 U.B.C. L. Rev. 96 (1968).

4. The Choice Between a Closely Held and a Widely Held Corporation

Whether a firm will become closely or widely held will depend on a variety of economic considerations. A firm will go public only when doing so increases the value of the shares which were issued prior to the public distribution. If, instead, the firm is worth more as a closely held corporation it will refrain from a public issue of its shares, or if it has already made a public issue of shares it will seek to repurchase them from outside shareholders in a buyout transaction. The techniques by which a public firm may eliminate minority shareholders, and legal restrictions on such transactions, are discussed in Chapter Eleven.

One of the principal advantages of a public market arises through efficiencies in information production. Competitive markets may exist only if some consumers bear the screening costs associated with comparing the price and quality of the product against that of similar products. In the case of consumer product markets, the screeners include those who shop around to determine whether bargains are available, while in capital markets screening costs are absorbed by investment intermediaries. In both cases, the screening would not be undertaken unless some reward, in the form of bargain prices, was available to the screeners. What this means is that, so long as any cost is associated with screening, it is impossible that a single competitive price could be available to screeners and non-screeners alike. Yet the activity of the screeners reduces dispersion in prices of similar products, so that "untalented" screeners may free ride on the activities of screeners. See Schwartz & Wilde, *Intervening in Markets on the Basis of Imperfect Information: A Legal and Economic Analysis*, 127 U. Pa. L. Rev. 630 (1979). In efficient capital markets, this free riding takes the form of trading in widely held shares by lay investors who do not investigate share quality and seek only to craft a suitably diversified portfolio of securities. The free rider may then assume that the price of the security as quoted in the financial pages of a newspaper reflects all publicly available and digested information.

In its information about firm value, an efficient market provides monitoring services. Anticipated management misbehaviour will be reflected in the price of the firm securities, with the agency cost ultimately borne by the firm in the issue price of its securities. In addition, the firm's promise of efficient management is made more creditable when, on breach of the promise, it becomes a candidate for take-over bid. No doubt, some form of a market for control also exists in the case of a closely held corporation, with efficient trades possible where purchasers believe they can manage the firm at lower cost. However, the market for corporate control is broader for widely held firms. This is because small firms are more likely to be dependent upon the services of a particular manager than large firms, for which managerial services more closely resemble fungible inputs.

The availability of a resale market in securities of widely held firms is of course an advantage to investors. Shares in a closely held corporation are often made inalienable by the firm's charter. Moreover, even if the firm agrees to permit a resale, the shares will be very difficult to dispose of because of the closed system (Chapter Five) and, most crucially, the absence of demand for the securities. These barriers to profitable resales will then render the securities of a closely held corporation less valuable.

A further advantage of widely held corporations is easier access to capital markets, given the substantial costs of a public issue. As a firm grows in value, it becomes harder to obtain financing solely through injections of equity from present shareholders. They may simply lack the assets to finance the acquisition of all available opportunities, and even were they able to do so they might still prefer to diversify their investments, rather than let their entire fortune ride with a single firm. So long as a management's private funds plus the firm's internally generated funds do not enable it to accept all opportunities with a positive net present value, public markets in securities facilitate wealth creation.

Against these advantages of going public, the primary reason to remain or to become a closely held corporation, other than the potential tax advantages of closely held corporations, is to economize on agency costs. Since such costs arise as a consequence of the separation of ownership and control, one technique for reducing them is to assign to management a portion of the firm's residual value as part of its compensation package (e.g., in the form of stock options). Pushed to its extreme, this strategy would assign to managers the entire residual value, with the agency relationship effectively terminated. This indeed is what buyouts amount to.

While agency costs will normally be greater in widely held firms, a special concern arises for the protection of minority shareholders in closely held corporations. One reason for this is their inability to sell their shares, which heightens concerns for strategic behaviour. In the absence of a market for their securities, shareholders of a closely held corporation face each other in a bilateral monopoly, with attendant risks of opportunism. However, too much emphasis may be placed on the lack of resale opportunities. Even were a market available, shareholders in a closely held corporation might reasonably wish to restrict share transfers, since firm value will be tied to the identity of shareholders.

Instead, management opportunism is more to be feared as a consequence of the greater valuation uncertainties surrounding closely held corporations. This is a principal reason for small firms to adopt broadly based governance structures in which all shareholders participate in management decisions. For example, shareholders in a closely held corporation will often agree to restrict the power of a majority of the board of directors, even giving veto rights to individual shareholders on some decisions. Although this strategy introduces a possibility of shareholder opportunism, it will also lower the agency costs of management misbehaviour. The firm will then adopt management structures that give rise to the lowest net opportunism costs, and these structures often differ in important respects from those of widely held firms.

Closely held corporations may also wish to adopt different liability rules than those for widely held firms. Certain transactions that might pass scrutiny if effected by a widely held firm might be proscribed if attempted by a closely held corporation. For example, matters left to management's business judgment in a public corporation might be subjected to strict, prophylactic rules in a closely held corporation. Once again, however, the benefits of such rules must be weighed against the resultant loss of opportunities with a positive net present value.

For a general discussion of issues animating closely held corporation principles, see Easterbrook & Fischel, *Close Corporations and Agency Costs*, 38 Stan. L. Rev. 271 (1986).

Closely held corporations also face lower costs of disclosure given the reduced proxy solicitation and disclosure obligations discussed above.

There are also tax advantages to closely held corporations. See generally, e.g., V. Krishna, *The Fundamentals of Canadian Income Tax*, 757-819, 4th ed. (1993); and B.J. Arnold, D.K. McNair & C.F.L. Young, *Taxation of Corporations and Shareholders*, 43-52 (1986).

CHAPTER SEVEN

Liability Strategies

Reference is often made in the literature on corporations to the proposition that as corporations have emerged as the dominant form of business organization, investors and managers have become increasingly distinct groups. See, e.g., Chapter Four, Section A. One of the major challenges for corporate law has been to develop strategies designed to address problems of accountability associated with having a group of professional managers running a corporation. In other words, the challenge has been to develop strategies designed to reduce agency costs within the firm. Chapter Six examined how governance structures might be used to address this challenge. However, as was noted in Chapter Three, Section I. B., the history of modern corporations law is one of a reduction of restrictions on management's ability to manage and an expansion of remedies for claimholders whose interests are prejudiced by management's actions. It is therefore necessary to examine attempts to influence management through the imposition of liability. This will be the focus of the first part of this chapter. As you consider the issues raised in the first part of the chapter, you should ask yourself whether Canada has a satisfactory balance of governance and liability strategies.

The second part of this chapter examines related problems that flow from questions raised in Chapter Six and that promise to be some of the thornier issues that Canadian corporate law must confront in the years to come. In the same way that the stakeholder debate raises difficult issues with respect to the design of governance structures, so too it raises difficult issues with respect to liability strategies. Questions arise concerning whether it is necessary to provide constituencies other than shareholders with techniques for imposing liability on the corporation and its managers. At the same time, it is necessary to consider whether different constituencies should in any way be accountable to each other and, if so, whether liability strategies have a role to play in enhancing this accountability.

There is another dimension to these problems that must also be borne in mind. Specifically, thought needs to be given to the institutions that are best placed to develop standards of conduct and to impose liability when those standards are breached. Traditionally, the legislature and the courts were on the front lines. But in recent years securities commissions have found it increasingly tempting to participate in this debate, particularly when they have concluded that the corporate law that the legislature has put in place or the judiciary's application of that corporate law is not doing a satisfactory job. See, e.g., *Standard Trustco Limited et al.* (1992), 15 O.S.C.B. 4322. Yet securities commissions have typically concentrated their attention on relations between the corporation and its shareholders and, more recently, on relations between shareholders (see OSC Policy 9.1, discussed in Chapter Eleven, Section D). Whether one thinks that securities commissions are well equipped to venture into this area may therefore depend in part on one's views about whether constituencies other than shareholders have interests that need to be protected through governance structures and liability strategies. Of course, even if one were to conclude that shareholders are the only constituency whose interests warrant protection, there would still be plenty of room to debate the mix of corporate law and securities law that should be used in order to implement governance structures and liability strategies.

The third and final part of this chapter examines what happens when governance and liability strategies have proven unattractive or unsuccessful and parties conclude that the only option is to dissolve the corporation.

I. LIABILITY STRATEGIES AND MANAGEMENT MISBEHAVIOUR

A. INTRODUCTION

In a claimholders' bargain, managers would be given broad authority to make business decisions on behalf of the firm, but would also commit to standards of care and loyalty in the discharge of their responsibilities. In order to make these commitments more credible, the parties would agree that liability be imposed on breach.

Liability strategies impose costs and therefore assume a failure in alternative devices to cure management misbehaviour, such as governance techniques. A firm is, however, unlikely to find that agency costs can be eliminated solely through the structure of corporate democracy, since few shareholders will have an incentive to absorb the substantial costs associated with (1) producing information of management misbehaviour, and (2) contesting management control. Henry Manne's theory of the market for corporate control, discussed in Chapter Six, Section C, provides an alternative explanation of how inefficient managers may be displaced, but once again residual agency costs will remain. Because take-over bids are costly to mount, and because the information with respect to management misbehaviour may not be public, an optimal deterrence policy is unlikely to arise solely through the market for corporate control. Liability standards will then be applied in aid of monitoring strategies, and may economize on monitoring costs borne by the firm.

Though liability strategies may serve to reduce agency costs, at some point liability rules become excessive. Overly strict standards can reduce firm wealth by preventing the firm from taking up positive net present value investment opportunities.* On a claimholders' bargain, then, liability rules will be critically compared with substitute

---

* The present value of an investment opportunity, written as PVo, is calculated in the same way as a firm's present value in Chapter One, Section A. The opportunity's net present value, or $NPVo$, is equal to PVo less the cost Co of the opportunity. Co will include not merely the direct costs of purchasing the opportunity but also opportunity costs of passing up other opportunities. The opportunity is then an attractive one if it has a positive net present value, defined as $NPVo > 0$.

governance and compensation strategies, which may render costly legal duties unnecessary. The extent to which a liability rule is efficient may therefore depend upon the kind of managerial self-dealing at issue.

At least four different kinds of self-dealing may be identified. Management's decision to *shirk*, or to underinvest in managerial competence and care, can be distinguished from fraud even if managers in effect transfer wealth to themselves by consuming excessive leisure. Second, managers may exhibit *excessive risk aversion* in their investment decisions as a consequence of a conflict of interest between themselves and other claimholders. Third, garden varieties of fraud are described as *looting*, though this term also embraces more innocuous breaches of strict equitable rules. Finally, a special concern for self-dealing arises in *control transactions*, where an insurgent seeks to wrest the levers of corporate power from incumbent management.

1. Shirking

On a liability strategy, managers would first warrant the quality and quantity of their services, promising not to shirk through an underinvestment in skill and care. However, anti-shirking policies would likely not be particularly demanding, since an exacting care standard might easily be costly for the firm. For example, management would lose the advantages of speed and flexibility in responding to rapidly changing business circumstances through mandatory procedural requirements of due care, such as due diligence meetings of the board, and fairness opinions and comfort letters from outside experts prior to major transactions. In addition, managers may generally be adequately motivated to take care through the firm's compensation policies. The temptation to shirk will in most cases not survive these extralegal incentives to take due care.

2. Excessive Risk Aversion

Shareholders of a widely held firm will seek to bargain for a risk neutral investment strategy for the firm, even if individually they are risk averse. This is because the shareholders will have a small proportion of their wealth invested in the firm, and the diversification of their holdings across many kinds of securities and forms of investments will dissipate their concerns with respect to those risks that are idiosyncratic to any one firm. On the other hand, managers will likely be considerably more sensitive than shareholders to firm-specific risk. Their expectations of future earnings from the firm are a non-diversifiable human capital investment, and represent a proportionately far greater stake in the firm than that of outside shareholders. With more to lose, managers may exhibit greater risk aversion in firm investment decisions than shareholders might wish. Given two investment opportunities, managers might then prefer the one offering a lower *EMV* but greater security, with the result that firm value is reduced. This loss is an adverse incentive cost, which the firm would bear on issuing securities in efficient capital markets.

On this analysis, managers would be expected to bind themselves to risk-neutral investment policies. In other words, among new investment opportunities, managers would promise to select the one with the highest *EMV* (so long as its promised return exceeds that of the firm's existing investments). Risk averse investment decisions would therefore breach the claimholders' bargain. There are, however, several reasons why legal rules have virtually never been applied in aid of this incentive failure. First, judicial review of management decisions would be restricted to alternatives of which the court is aware, and would not include those known only to management. As such, managers could safely pass up secret high-risk, high-return opportunities. It would therefore be extraordinarily difficult, after the fact, to arrive at a proper standard to judge management's investment decisions. Second, the imposition of personal liability on managers would exacerbate adverse incentives, since managers would have even more to lose if their personal assets were held hostage. Lastly, the firm has a variety of extralegal techniques that it might adopt to address the incentive problem. These include, for example, internal monitoring strategies and special incentive provisions in management's compensation package. In addition, risk averse investment strategies may be self-defeating. As a firm becomes less valuable through risk averse investment strategies, it becomes a more attractive candidate for a take-over bid. While the possibility of bankruptcy is reduced, the likelihood of a take-over bid is then increased. Since management's human capital may be as threatened by a take-over as by bankruptcy, the temptation to pass up a high-return, high-risk investment is weakened through the market for corporate control.

3. Looting

The claimholders' bargain will also prohibit looting, which includes not merely the expropriation of corporate assets, but also all direct and indirect compensation which exceeds that to which the manager is entitled. Under perfect bargaining conditions, the manager's compensation would be tied directly to the value of his productivity within the firm, and the form of compensation would itself be measurable without cost. But both ends of the compensation equation are blurred in real world conditions. What a manager contributes to the firm will not be immediately measurable, nor is the form of managerial compensation always clearly observable. For example, the compensation decision will implicate not merely direct salary benefits, but also the perquisites of office. These would include, for example, the thickness of the carpet in the executive offices, and the value of discretionary power in such matters as charitable contributions. Further afield, a manager's right to extract a profit in collateral dealings with his firm, or to take up a business opportunity, which in other circumstances might have gone to the firm, can be seen as an element in the compensation decision.

Anti-looting policies are directed at any device used by the managers to transfer to themselves a portion of the residual value of the firm beyond their agreed-on compensation level. Bright-line standards of adequacy of compensation are then impossible unless the firm can discriminate perfectly between the value of managerial and capital contributions. Since clear standards as to managerial inputs are not to be found, a variety of second-best techniques may be suggested, including prophylactic rules whose effect is to prevent managers from indulging in a particular activity even if in some circumstances it might be benign.

4. Control Transactions

Fourth, the claimholders' bargain will contain special terms with respect to strategies managers might adopt in the context of control transactions. Governance structures provide techniques whereby incumbent managers can be replaced by a group of insurgent shareholders. Since these devices likely serve efficiency goals (see Chapter Six), the claimholders' bargain will limit the discretion of managers to adopt defensive tactics to defeat the insurgents. These policies are described as the *proper purposes doctrine*, and impeach transactions to defeat insurgents that are motivated by management's improper purpose of retaining control.

This first part of this chapter considers liability strategies aimed at management shirking or looting. The proper purposes doctrine has already been seen in the previous chapter in the context of proxy battles, and will again be studied in Chapter Eleven, Section E, when we turn to take-over bids. Though insider trading liability may be seen to serve anti-looting policies, arguments for and against insider trading have a life of their own and will therefore be considered in the next chapter. Before embarking on the details of liability strategies aimed at management shirking or looting, it is worth spending a few moments examining the role of executive compensation as a technique for controlling management behaviour.

B. THE COMPENSATION DECISION

1. Human Capital Theories

As an alternative to liability strategies, a solution to agency cost problems might be sought in management's compensation policy. First, any incentive to loot or shirk would be lost if the manager ultimately bore the costs of misbehaviour through depreciation of his human capital. See Fama, *Agency Problems and the Theory of Firm*, 88 J. Pol. Econ. 288, 304-6 (1980). The possibility of human capital losses, as happens where a reputation of dishonesty renders one unemployable, may then be a manager's strongest incentive to honesty. These arguments have strong intuitive appeal, and in addition are supported by empirical studies indicating that a manager's lifetime earnings are closely correlated to long-term firm value. See Jensen & Zimmerman, *Managerial Compensation and the Managerial Labor Market*, 7 J. Acc. & Econ. 3 (1985); Murphy, *Corporate Performance and Managerial Regulation: An Empirical Analysis* 7 J. Acc. & Econ. 11 (1985). However, it is unlikely that agency costs could be entirely eliminated through human capital considerations, since a manager may still find the temptation to defect too strong in the case of spectacular, one-shot looting. In addition, "end game" shirking prior to retirement is unlikely to be cured, and a full settling up of management misbehaviour may in any event not occur when it is impossible to trace declining firm value to the actions of a particular manager. Nevertheless, human capital theories are of interest in suggesting that liability strategies are not the only, or even the primary, device to minimize agency costs.

2. Incentive Provisions

Apart from *ex post* human capital theories, an *ex ante* compensation strategy would seek to alleviate agency costs through incentive features in the compensation package offered to managers. Where (1) managers are risk neutral, and (2) their efforts can be observed with certainty, the optimal compensation package would be one in which managers would absorb all variations of profits, becoming in effect the holders of a portion of the firm's residual value. Managers could then be expected to adhere to proper levels of care and to adopt investment policies which maximized firm value. In most corporations such a strategy is not feasible (although it is worth noting that in 1994 NOVA Corporation, one of Canada's largest public companies, announced that its CEO would receive his compensation in the form of shares in the corporation). The best compensation package is then one in which management and equity holders share firm risk, even though such risk sharing does not eliminate adverse incentive costs. This would implicate bonus strategies in which, in addition to a manager's direct salary, he is awarded further compensation if the firm is profitable. At the same time, the manager will share the risk of firm losses, since the bonus plan will then be valueless. See Holmstrom, *Moral Hazard and Observability*, 10 Bell. J. Econ. & Mgt. 74 (1979); Ramakrishnan & Thakor, *The Valuation of Assets Under Moral Hazard*, 39 J. Fin. 229 (1984); Shavell, *Risk Sharing Incentives in the Principal Agent Relationship*, 10 Bell J. Econ. & Mgt. 55, 56 (1979).

3. Excessive Compensation

In publicly held firms it is important to distinguish compensation for directorial services from executive compensation. The former is modest; the latter may not be. The most common form of compensation for directors' services is a combination of annual retainer plus a fee per meeting attended. Most public corporations do not compensate inside directors separately for board service. Compensation for outside directors in public corporations is typically in the $10,000-30,000 range, which reflects the limited demands of board membership on the time of directors. See *Canadian Directorship Practices: Compensation of Boards of Directors* 17-49, 20, 27, 52 (6th ed. 1985).

CBCA s. 125 provides that, subject to the corporation's articles and by-laws, the directors may fix the remuneration of the corporation's directors, officers and employees. One constraint upon board discretion inheres in the concept of waste: the directors may not give away the corporation's assets. The compensation decision may therefore be impeached in circumstances where no services have been provided by the managers, as where the payment is made for past services for which the managers have already been compensated. See *Re Dorenwends* (Chapter Four, Section C); *Re Lee, Behrens & Co.*, [1932] 2 Ch. 46. But where the services are not entirely fictitious, the valuation problem facing courts when compensation is challenged as excessive may seem wholly intractable. No Thomistic standard for the just price of managerial services has been suggested, and fears of excessive compensation are somewhat dissipated by the existence of a market for managerial services. For example, where a firm acquires a senior executive by raiding him from another corporation, using the services of a head-hunter, the salary will have been the product of an arm's-length bargain, however high it might be. Moreover, these bargains may be taken as a measure for executive compensation even where the executive has not been raided. See Note, *The Executive Compensation Contract: Creating Incentives to Reduce Agency Costs*, 37 Stan L. Rev. 1147 (1985) (courts should conclusively presume the validity of compensation plans that are comparable to those of related firms). Evidence of the value of top executives to a firm is also provided by studies on abnormal stock price declines on their unexpected deaths. See

Johnson, Magee, Nagarajan & Newman, *An Analysis of the Stock Price Reaction to Sudden Executive Deaths*, 7 J. Acc. & Econ. 151 (1985).

Legal concerns about excessive compensation have been most evident in the case of stock option plans, and many of the American state corporations statutes require shareholder approval to validate such provisions. Similarly, the Toronto Stock Exchange has adopted policies requiring companies listed on that exchange to obtain shareholder approval of stock option plans. See Toronto Stock Exchange, *Revised Policy on Listed Company Share Incentive Arrangements* (March 22, 1994). Further restrictions are added by the case law. First, there must be a "reasonable relationship" between the benefit to the corporation and the value of the options. Second, the plan must be designed so as to make it probable that the corporation will actually receive the benefit supposedly passing to it. See *Beard v. Elster*, 160 A.2d 731 (Del. 1960). Although the "reasonable relationship" requirement is not applied very rigorously, it is troublesome in theory. The value of the option is a function of price movements of the optioned shares during the option's lifetime, but it is virtually impossible to link any particular executive's performance to changes in the market price of the corporation's shares. Indeed, there may in a given case be no correlation between share price movements and the performance of the corporation's executives as a group because many factors external to the corporation can dramatically affect the price of its shares.

The reason for the paucity of reported decisions challenging executive compensation is not hard to find. The market for top executives is a highly specialized one, and there is no ready yard-stick by which to measure the worth of an executive. This point has been made nowhere better than in a decision arising out of shareholder litigation in the United States involving bonus compensation paid to top executives of the American Tobacco Company. The formula under which the payments were made, a percentage of profits over a stipulated amount, had been established in a by-law approved by the shareholders many years before the litigation. As the profits of the corporation swelled enormously, so did the payments. The United States Supreme Court held that, even though the by-law was valid, still the payments under it might not be if they could be found to have grown so huge as to constitute waste. *Rogers v. Hill*, 289 U.S. 582 (1933). But when the issue of waste came to be tried, the plaintiffs failed. Collins J. put the issue as follows:

Is the plan moral and to the interest of the stockholders in lean years, but immoral and subversive in fat times? Just how much prosperity must be achieved to convert the compensation from legitimate to illegitimate? What is the saturation point? Where does adequacy end and waste begin? Under the plan the stockholders prosper with the officers, the increased earnings of the stockholders work increased earnings for the officers. The plan is by no means one-sided; it is largely contingent upon and measured by success. ...

Yes, the Court possesses the power to prune these payments, but openness forces the confession that the pruning would be synthetic and artificial rather than analytic or scientific. Whether or not it would be fair and just, is highly dubious. Yet, merely because the problem is perplexing is no reason for eschewing it. It is not timidity, however, which perturbs me. It is finding a rational or just gauge for revising these figures were I inclined to do so. No blueprints are furnished. The elements to be weighed are incalculable; the imponderables, manifold. To act out of whimsy or caprice or arbitrariness would be more than inexact—it would be the precise antithesis of justice; it would be a farce.

If comparisons are to be made, with whose compensation are they to be made—executives? Those connected with the motion picture industry? Radio artists? Justices of the Supreme Court of the United States? The President of the United States? Manifestly, the material at hand is not of adequate plasticity for fashioning into a pattern or standard. Many instances of positive underpayment will come to mind, just as instances of apparent rank overpayment abound. Haplessly, intrinsic worth is not always the criterion. A classic might perhaps produce trifling compensation for its author, whereas a popular novel might yield a titantic fortune. Merit is not always commensurately rewarded, whilst mediocrity sometimes unjustly brings incredibly lavish returns. Nothing is so divergent and contentious and inexplicable as values.

Courts are ill-equipped to solve or even to grapple with these entangled economic problems. Indeed, their solution is not within the juridical province. Courts are concerned that a corporation be honestly and fairly operated by its directors, with the observance of the formal requirements of the law; but what is reasonable compensation for its officers is primarily for the stockholders. This does not mean that fiduciaries are to commit waste, or misuse or abuse trust property, with impunity. A just cause will find the Courts at guard and implemented to grant redress. But the stockholder must project a less amorphous plaint than is here presented. [*Heller v. Boylan*, 29 N.Y.S.2d 653, 679-80 (S. Ct., Special Term 1941)]

The judge went on to emphasize that he was not "approving" the payments in question but merely declaring that he could find no standard by which to call them "waste."

Outside claimants likely have less to fear from excessive salaries or bonus plans than from indirect benefits, such as the taking of corporate business opportunities. If a widely held corporation discloses the salaries and bonuses it pays to top executives, distributional effects are unlikely and the compensation decision would *prima facie* appear to be Kaldor-Hicks efficient. S.E.C. reporting requirements in fact mandate disclosure of compensation paid to top officers on an individualized basis and in October 1993, the government of Ontario introduced analogous regulations. See Securities Exchange Act of 1934, ss. 12, 14(a), Schedule 14A, Reg. S-K; Ontario Securities Act, Form 40. With respect to CBCA corporations see paragraph 35(1)(t) of the Canada Business Corporations Regulations.

In addition, recent studies of the effect of the announcement of bonus plans for top executives on stock prices suggest that they serve efficiency goals. On a self-dealing hypothesis, stock option plans will be created by managers to transfer part of the residual value of the firm to themselves. Proponents of such theories point to the fact that the compensation thereby received may greatly exceed the actual fixed salaries paid to the executives, with procedural and substantive safeguards suggested to circumvent this. See Vagts, *Challenges to Executive Compensation: For the Markets or the Courts?* 8 J. Corp. Law 231 (1983). If this is why such plans are adopted, common shareholders ought reasonably to fear them, with news of their announcement greeted unfavourably. However, studies indicate that common share prices *increase* when such plans are announced. See Brickley, Bhagat & Lease, *The Impact of Long-Range Managerial Compensation Plans on Shareholder Wealth*, 7 J. Acc. & Econ. 115 (1985); Tehranian & Waegelein, *Market Reaction to Short-Term Executive Compensation Plan Adoption*, 7 J. Acc. & Econ. 132 (1985). One explanation for this is that the market views bonus plans as a desirable incentive feature in management contracts, reducing the likelihood that risk averse managers will prefer secure investments to more valuable high risk, high return ones.

The strength of the incentive effect of bonus plans is, however, unclear, since bonus plans might also be adopted for signalling reasons. Managers might be expected to initiate a bonus plan at the most favourable possible time to themselves, that is immediately prior to an anticipated increase in firm value. The announcement of the plan may then be interpreted by the market as a signal that good news is forthcoming, with a resultant increase in share prices. It has, however, been argued that at least part of the reason for adopting a bonus plan is for its incentive effects. See Bhagat, Brickley & Lease, *Incentive Effects of Stock Purchase Plans,* 14 J. Fin. Econ. 195 (1985) (bonus plans adopted in closely held firms where the need to signal information to outside investors is absent).

Specialized compensation features might also be applied to other kinds of incentive problems—for example, those relating to management's time frame. It is sometimes feared that managers lack an adequate time perspective, being more concerned to maximize short-term profits than the firm's long-run earnings. If compensation is tied to immediate performance this might be anticipated, particularly with older employees who do not expect to be with the firm for many years. As a response to such end-game problems, the firm might then adopt delayed compensation strategies (e.g., pension plans), which postpone a component of compensation if future indicators of executive performance are more informative than present ones. Empirical studies suggest that firms do tailor their compensation plans with these problems in mind, with delayed compensation plans used more for older than younger executives. In addition, deferred compensation plans are used more by firms with relatively high investments in research and development, where time frame issues may seem more pressing. See Eaton & Rosen, *Agency, Delayed Compensation, and the Structure of Executive Compensation,* 38 J. Fin. 1489 (1983).

4. Golden Parachutes

In the take-over fever of the 1980's, corporate managers sometimes resorted to "golden parachute" severance arrangements. These are employment contracts in which, if control of the corporation is transferred to new owners and an incumbent executive leaves, the corporation will be obligated to pay him a lump sum, possibly three or four times his annual compensation. The aggregate golden parachute liabilities of a given corporation can easily run into many millions of dollars.

Critics of golden parachutes have raised two objections to them. First, they have been alleged to amount to excessive compensation, with the officers receiving considerably more than they would have got in an action for wrongful dismissal. It is, moreover, noted that golden parachutes are triggered by the voluntary decision of the executive who leaves the firm, without an actual dismissal by new management. The second criticism of golden parachutes is that they amount to a form of "poison pill"—a device used by managers to render their firm a less desirable take-over target by conditioning an event that makes the firm less valuable on a change of control. In this way, the likelihood that managers will lose their jobs through a take-over bid is lessened. Because of this, golden parachutes may sap incentives to due care that arise when inefficiently managed firms become candidates for acquisition in the market for corporate control.

The case against golden parachutes is, however, not proven. Though large in size, it does not follow that they amount to excessive compensation. Since managers may suffer a considerable decline in the value of their human capital on a change of control of the firm, it is not unreasonable for them to bargain for a substantial severance payment. In addition, the executive will want a parachute that opens on his voluntary jump, without his waiting to be fired, since the change of control might substantially affect his prospects within the firm even if he is kept on. In this sense, the golden parachute is a constructive dismissal provision in a labour contract. The argument for golden parachutes is then like the argument for long-term employment contracts for officers, considered in Chapter Six, Section B, in that both may dissipate fears of shareholder opportunism through take-over bids that cut off management's expectation of long-term compensation. More efficient investment by managers in firm-specific human capital may then result if they seek damages for wrongful dismissal. See Knoeber, *Golden Parachutes, Shark Repellents, and Hostile Tender Offers*, 76 Am. Econ. Rev. 155 (1986). In addition, it has not been demonstrated that large severance payments for managers deter potential bidders from attempting to acquire control of a firm. While golden parachutes will be of great importance to individual managers, even in the aggregate they may amount to only a small percentage of the merger gains anticipated from an acquisition. See R. Gilson, *The Law and Finance of Corporate Acquisitions* 670-72 (1986).

Arguments against golden parachutes will then largely rest on incentive costs that arise when managers need no longer fear take-over bids. These must, however, be balanced against management's lessened incentive to defeat profitable take-over bids. When a bid is made to acquire shares at a premium over market price, the outside shareholders will usually want it to succeed in order to share in the premium. But if the success of the bid means the loss of employment by incumbent management, it might respond with defensive tactics in order to defeat the bid. This agency cost problem might be mitigated with golden parachutes that reduce management incentives to defeat a bid. See further Note, *Golden Parachutes and the Business Judgment Rule: Toward a Proper Standard of Review*, 94 Yale L.J. 909 (1985). Empirical evidence that these incentive strategies may have an effect on resistance to take-over bids is provided by studies which indicate that higher degrees of resistance are correlated with a lower equity interest in the firm. See Walkling & Long, *Agency Theory, Managerial Welfare, and Takeover Bid Resistance*, 15 Rand J. Econ. 54 (1984). Even as managers are less likely to oppose a bid when they may gain on tendering their shares, the same result may be anticipated where the gain comes from a golden parachute. However, this argument for golden parachutes amounts to a second-best strategy, which will not be persuasive if a first-best prohibition of defensive tactics by management can be adopted. See Chapter Eleven, Section E, on defensive maneouvres.

5. Compensation in the Closely Held Corporation

Where the firm is closely held, the owners have an incentive to pay themselves salaries rather than dividends to the extent that the income tax laws effectively impose a double tax upon dividends, once as net income to the corporation and then as income to the recipient. This preference causes no particular corporate law problem where all the owners are active in management, but it could be oppressive where that is not the case.

Thus, in *Nolan v. Parsons*, [1942] O.R. 358 (C.A.), the corporation had five shareholders. Four of them were directors; the fifth, who was the plaintiff, was not. In each of the years 1939 and 1940 the corporation had profits before the disputed payments in the neighborhood of $20,000, and in each year the defendants voted and caused the corporation to pay to each of themselves directors' fees of $2,000. At this time the defendants had apparently been seeking without success to purchase the plaintiff's shares "at a bargain price." The plaintiff sued to recover the directors' fees for the corporation. He succeeded at trial and on appeal. Masten J.A. held that "the time, attention and services of the individual appellants as directors ... was wholly incommensurate with the fees which they appropriated to themselves" and that the defendants' action in so doing was "fraudulently oppressive ... as against the plaintiff." *Id.* at 362. See also *National Building Maintenance Ltd. v. Dove*, [1972] 5 W.W.R. 41O (B.C.C.A.).

C. SHIRKING

1. Duty of Skill

CBCA s. l05 prescribes certain qualifications for corporate directors. They must be: (1) at least 18 years of age; (2) not found to be of unsound mind by any court; (3) individuals; and (4) not bankrupt. These requirements establish minimum standards that a person must attain before he can take his seat on the board. Can a further threshold requirement be found in CBCA s. 122(1)(b), which imposes a duty of skill on directors and officers? Consider *Re Cariff Savings Bank*, [1892] 2 Ch. 100. At the age of six months, the Marquis of Bute succeeded to that title and to the presidency of the bank. Twenty-one years later he attended his first meeting of bank managers, at which he presided.

With reference to this the Marquis said, in his evidence, "I cannot recollect the circumstances under which I attended the meeting, but I suppose that, happening to be at Cardiff at the time, it was suggested to me that I should attend, and, considering the bank as a charity and worthy of support, I acted as above stated." From that time until the stoppage of the bank the Marquis never attended a meeting, and he said, "The circumstances had so entirely faded from my recollection that I was much surprised after the stoppage of the bank to find my name connected with it." [*Id.* at 102]

The Court held that the Marquis was not in breach of his duty of care for failing to attend bank meetings. This decision is now suspect. But even had he attended meetings diligently, do you think that the 21-year-old peer should have been held in breach of his duty of skill for his complete ignorance of business?

Consider next *Re Brazilian Rubber Plantations and Estates, Ltd.*, [1911] 1 Ch. 425. The company issued a prospectus containing serious misrepresentations in 1906 and became insolvent two years later. The directors were not aware of the misrepresentations.

The directors of the company, Sir Arthur Aylmer, Bart., Hendry William Tugwell, Edward Barber, and Edward Henry Hancock, were all induced to become directors by [company promoters]. Sir Arthur Aylmer was absolutely ignorant of business. He only consented to act because he was told the office would give him a little pleasant employment without his incurring any responsibility. H.W. Tugwell was a partner in a firm of bankers in a good position in Bath; he was seventy-five years of age and very deaf. ... Barber was a rubber broker and was told that all he would have to do would be to give an opinion as to the value of rubber when it arrived in England. Hancock was a man of business who said he was induced to join by seeing the names of Tugwell and Barber, whom he considered good men. [*Id.* at 427]

Neville J. absolved the directors from liability.

A director's duty has been laid down as requiring him to act with such care as is reasonably to be expected from him, having regard to his knowledge and experience. He is, I think, not bound to bring any special qualifications to his office. He may undertake the management of a rubber company in complete ignorance of everything connected with rubber, without incurring responsibility for the mistakes which may result from such ignorance. [*Id.* at 437]

See also *Re City Equitable Fire Ins. Co.*, [1925] 1 Ch. 407, 427-28 (C.A.) per Romer J.

According to the Dickerson Report, CBCA s. 122(1)(b) was intended to upgrade directors' duties of skill and care. However, even without legal duties, market forces will ordinarily impel a corporation to select as competent a management team as possible, since the cost of hiring inefficient monitors to serve as directors will be borne by the firm in efficient markets. Suppose, for example, that inside directors of a widely held firm are parties to a fraudulent scheme, and "shut-eyed sentries" are sought to serve as outside directors. Even if outside investors are unaware of the fraud, they may react to the choice of directors by discounting any possibility of monitoring by the board and adjusting claim values as a consequence.

The Lawrence Report proposed a duty of skill "which a reasonably prudent director would exercise in comparable circumstances." Lawrence Report 53. On this test, might an unskilled outside director have been liable even if he had logged a respectable number of hours at his post? The proposal contemplated a class of professional directors and was rejected in the Ontario Business Corporations Act, where the word "person" was substituted for "director," as in the CBCA. R.S.O. 1970, c. 53, s. 144.

One problem in defining a duty of skill is in determining who should be excluded from the board. It is excessive to require that directors of a rubber company have expertise in the rubber business. With conglomerates, it is quite impossible to expect directors to be skilled in all of the diverse operations carried on by the corporation. Bankers, underwriters, accountants and lawyers may then be useful to have as board members, both for their professional skills and for their role as conduits of information between the firm and its relational contractors. However, what about consumer spokespersons and community leaders whose presence on the board is sometimes championed by advocates of corporate social responsibility? Would it be better to nullify skill requirements in CBCA s. 122?

2. Duty of Care

Like duties of skill, the need for legal requirements of care by managers may reasonably be questioned. Management's temptation to shirk by taking inadequate care or spending insufficient time in managing the corporation is subject to strong extralegal sanctions. Shirking may readily be noted by co-workers on a team, and the threatened depreciation of a manager's human capital may be more than sufficient to instill in him an incentive to take care. In addition, group shirking may attract offers from the market for corporate control, discussed in Chapter Six, Section C. Liability rules may also be expensive in inducing excessive caution by managers in their investment decisions. Where managers may already be thought overcautious as a consequence of differential risk aversion, the prospect of having ordinary business decisions second-guessed (with the benefit of hindsight) is likely inefficient.

For these reasons, courts have been loath to find that managers have breached their duty of care or to award damages on a finding of breach. Moreover, even if they have, a plaintiff shareholder would ordinarily not have had standing to complain of a breach of the duty of care under the rule in *Foss v. Harbottle* (1843), 2 Hare 461, 67 E.R. 189. That case restricted the circumstances in which an individual shareholder could sue on management misbehaviour, and though some "exceptions" remained where shareholder litigation was permitted, these did not include cases of simple negligence. For example, in *Pavlides v. Jensen*, [1956] Ch. 565, the plaintiff, a minority shareholder in Tunnel Asbestos Cement Co., brought an action on behalf of the corporation seeking damages from its directors who, the plaintiff alleged, had negligently caused the corporation to sell for £180,000 a mine worth about £1,000,000. Danckwerts J. held that the rule in *Foss v. Harbottle* precluded the suit, since the plaintiffs did not allege fraud. For arguments that shareholders should not be permitted to litigate alleged breaches of negligence standards, see Scott, *The Role of Preconceptions in Policy Analysis in Law: A Response to Fischel and Bradley*, 71 Cornell L. Rev. 299 (1986); *Edited Transcript of Proceedings of the Business Roundtable*, 71 Cornell L. Rev. 357, 369-70 (1986) (remarks of K. Scott).

These considerations do not, however, apply quite so readily to the firm's gatekeepers, including its outside directors and auditors. While ordinary business judgments should not be second-guessed, the firm's promise of diligent monitoring is more creditable when the monitors bear liability on breach. Even here, however, the threat of personal liability may lead to inefficiencies associated with excessive caution and formalization of decision processes.

Barnes v. Andrews
United States District Court, Southern District of New York
298 F. 614 (1924)

Final hearing on a bill in equity, under section 91-a of the General Corporation Law of New York (Consol. Laws, c. 23), to hold liable the defendant as director for misprision of office. The corporation was organized under the laws of that state to manufacture starters for Ford motors and aeroplanes. On October 9, 1919, about a year after its organization, the defendant took office as a director, and served until he resigned on June 21, 1920. During that period over $500,000 was raised by the sales of stock of the company, made through an agent working on commission. A force of officers and employees was hired at substantial salaries, and the factory, already erected when the defendant took office, was equipped with machinery. Starter parts were made in quantity, but delays were experienced in the production of starters as a whole, and the funds of the company were steadily depleted by the running charges.

After the defendant resigned, the company continued business until the spring of 1921, when the plaintiff was appointed receiver, found the company without funds, and realized only a small amount on the sale of its assets. During the incumbency of the defendant there had been only two meetings of directors, one of which (i.e., that of October 9, 1919) he attended; the other happening at a day when he was forced to be absent because of his mother's death. He was a friend of the president, who had induced him as the largest stockholder to become a director, and his only attention to the affairs of the company consisted of talks with the president as they met from time to time.

LEARNED HAND, District Judge (after stating the facts as above): This cause may be divided into three parts: First, the defendant's general liability for the collapse of the enterprise; second, his specific liability for overpayments made to Delano; third, his specific liability for the expenses of printing pamphlets and circulars used in selling the corporate shares.

The first liability must rest upon the defendant's general inattention to his duties as a director. He cannot be charged with neglect in attending directors' meetings, because there were only two during his incumbency, and of these he was present at one and had an adequate excuse for his absence from the other. His liability must therefore depend upon his failure in general to keep advised of the conduct of the corporate affairs. The measure of a director's duties in this regard is uncertain; the courts contenting themselves with vague declarations, such as that a director must give reasonable attention to the corporate business. While directors are collectively the managers of the company, they are not expected to interfere individually in the actual conduct of its affairs. To do so would disturb the authority of the officers and destroy their individual responsibility, without which no proper discipline is possible. To them must be left the initiative and the immediate direction of the business; the directors can act individually only by counsel and advice to them. Yet they have an individual duty to keep themselves informed in some detail, and it is this duty which the defendant in my judgment failed adequately to perform.

All he did was to talk with Maynard as they met, while commuting from Flushing, or at their homes. That, indeed, might be enough, because Andrews had no reason to suspect Maynard's candor, nor has any reason to question it been yet disclosed. But it is plain that he did not press him for details, as he should. It is not enough to content oneself with general answers that the business looks promising and that all seems prosperous. Andrews was bound, certainly as the months wore on, to inform himself of what was going on with some particularity, and, if he had done so, he would have learned that there were delays in getting into production which were putting the enterprise in most serious peril. It is entirely clear from his letters of April 14, 1920, and June 21, 1920, that he had made no effort to keep advised of the actual conduct of the corporate affairs, but had allowed himself to be carried along as a figurehead, in complete reliance upon Maynard. In spite of his own substantial investment in the company, which I must assume was as dear to him as it would be to other men, his position required of him more than this. Having accepted a post of confidence, he was charged with an active duty to learn whether the company was moving to production, and why it was not, and to consider, as best he might, what could be done to avoid the conflicts among the personnel, or their incompetence, which was slowly bleeding it to death.

Therefore I cannot acquit Andrews of misprision in his office, though his integrity is unquestioned. The plaintiff must, however, go further than to show that he should have been more active in his duties. This cause of action rests upon a tort, as much though it be a tort of omission as though it had rested upon a positive act. The plaintiff must accept the burden of showing that the performance of the defendant's duties would have avoided loss, and what loss it would have avoided. ...

When the corporate funds have been illegally lent, it is a fair inference that a protest would have stopped the loan, and that the director's neglect caused the loss. But when a business fails from general mismanagement, business incapacity, or bad judgment, how is it possible to say that a single director could have made the company successful, or how much in dollars he could have saved? Before this cause can go to a master, the plaintiff must show that, had Andrews done his full duty, he could have made the company prosper, or at least could have broken its fall. He must show what sum he could have saved the company. Neither of these has he made any effort to do.

The defendant is not subject to the burden of proving that the loss would have happened, whether he had done his duty or not. If he were, it would come to this: That, if a director were once shown slack in his duties, he would stand charged prima facie with the difference between the corporate treasury as it was, and as it would be, judged by a hypothetical standard of success. How could such a standard be determined? How could any one guess how far a director's skill and judgment would have prevailed upon his fellows, and what would have been the ultimate fate of the business, if they had? How is it possible to set any measure of liability, or to tell what he would have contributed to the event? Men's fortunes may not be subjected to such uncertain and speculative conjectures. It is hard to see how there can be any remedy, except one can put one's finger on a definite loss and say with reasonable assurance that protest would have deterred, or counsel persuaded, the managers who caused it. No men of sense would take the office, if the law imposed upon them a guaranty of the general success of their companies as a penalty for any negligence.

It is, indeed, hard to determine just what went wrong in the management of this company. Any conclusion is little better than a guess. Still some discussion of the facts is necessary, and I shall discuss them. The claim that there were too many general employees turned out to be true, but, so far as I can see, only because of the delay in turning out the finished product. Had the factory gone into production in the spring of 1920, I cannot say, and the plaintiff cannot prove, that the selling department would have been prematurely or extravagantly organized. The expense of the stock sales was apparently not undue, and in any event Andrews was helpless to prevent it, because he found the contract an existing obligation of the company. So far as I can judge, the company had a fair chance of life, if the factory could have begun to turn out starters at the time expected. Whether this was the fault of Delano, as I suspect, is now too uncertain to say. It seems to me to make no difference in the result whether Delano, through inattention, or through sickness, or through contempt for Taylor, or for all these reasons, did not send along "Van Dycks," or whether Taylor should have got along without them, or should have shown more initiative and competence than he did. Between them the production lagged, until it was too late to resuscitate the dying company; its funds had oozed out in fixed payments, till there was nothing left with which to continue the business.

Suppose I charge Andrews with a complete knowledge of all that we have now learned. What action should he have taken, and how can I say that it would have stopped the losses? The plaintiff gives no definite answer to that question. Certainly he had no right to interject himself personally into the tangle; that was for Maynard to unravel. He would scarcely have helped to a solution by adding another cook to the broth. What suggestion could he have made to Maynard, or to his colleagues? The trouble arose either from an indifferent engineer, on whom the company was entirely dependent, or from an incompetent factory manager, who should have been discharged, or because the executives were themselves inefficient. Is Andrews to be charged for not insisting upon Taylor's discharge, or for not suggesting it? Suppose he did suggest it; have I the slightest reason for saying that the directors would have discharged him? or, had they discharged him, is it certain that a substitute employed in medias res would have speeded up production? Was there not a fair chance that Delano and Taylor might be brought to an accommodation as there was in putting in a green man at that juncture? How can I, sitting here, lay it down that Andrews' intervention would have brought order out of this chaos, or how can I measure in dollars the losses he would have saved? Or am I to hold Andrews because he did not move to discharge Maynard? How can I know that a better man was available? It is easy to say that he should have done something, but that will not serve to harness upon him the whole loss, nor is it the equivalent of saying that, had he acted, the company would now flourish.

True, he was not very well-suited by experience for the job he had undertaken, but I cannot hold him on that account. After all, it is the same corporation that chose him which now seeks to charge him. I cannot agree with the language of *Hun v. Cary* [82 N.Y. 65 (1880)] that in effect he gave an implied warranty of any special fitness. Directors are not specialists, like lawyers or doctors. They must have good sense, perhaps they must have acquaintance with affairs; but they need not—indeed, perhaps, they should not—have any technical talent. They are the general advisers of the business, and if they faithfully give such ability as they have to their charge, it would not be lawful to hold them liable. Must a director guarantee that his judgment is good? Can shareholders call him to account for deficiencies which their votes assured him did not disqualify him for his office? While he may not have been the Cromwell for that Civil War, Andrews did not engage to play any such role.

I conclude, therefore, as to this first claim that there is no evidence that the defendant's neglect caused any losses to the company, and that, if there were that loss cannot be ascertained.

[The remainder of Judge Hand's opinion, in which he held Andrews not liable for the overpayments to Delano and the cost of printing the false circulars, has been omitted.]

Bill dismissed.

Statutory Standard of Care. Judicial statements of the duty of care in English cases did not impose heavy standards on management. Thus it was said in *Overend & Gurney Co. v. Gibb* (1872), L.R. 5 H.L. 480, 486-87, that the criterion of liability is:

[w]hether or not the directors exceeded the power entrusted to them, or whether if they did not so exceed their powers they were cognisant of circumstances of such a character, so plain, so manifest, and so simple of appreciation, that no men with any ordinary degree of prudence, acting on their own behalf, would have entered into such a transaction as they entered into?

It was even suggested that the test is one of gross negligence.*

In holding that Andrews had breached his duty of care owed to the corporation by failing "to inform himself of what was going on with some particularity," Judge Hand in *Barnes* appears to have gone further than the English cases in imposing upon a director a duty of diligence, especially when it is borne in mind that Andrews had no reason to suspect that all was not going well. But the point is that he had no reason to suspect that all *was* going well, apart from very general assurances from Maynard, which the Court held were not enough.

It will be recalled that the Dickerson Report sought to upgrade the duty of care from that required by English common law through a statutory formulation that became CBCA s. 122(1)(b). One may be skeptical, however, as to whether a few ambiguous words will by themselves effect a profound change. For some years the Pennsylvania Business Corporation Law (Pa. B.C.L.) provided that directors were to discharge their duties "with that diligence, care and skill which ordinarily prudent men would exercise under similar circumstances in their personal business affairs." This is the standard of care generally imposed in England and North America upon trustees, upon whom the law imposes the most exacting standards demanded of any fiduciaries. Following upon litigation in which the Pennsylvania Supreme Court noted that the statutory standard was much more stringent than had theretofore prevailed for directors and held directors personally liable for spectacular corporate losses, *Selheimer v. Manganese Corp. of America*, 224 A.2d 634 (1966), the Pennsylvania corporate bar prevailed upon the legislature to remove the last five words from the quoted language. See Pa. B.C.L. 408. It was implicit in this amendment, as in *Selheimer*, that one takes more care in one's personal business affairs than in other circumstances. However, Neville J. stated in *Re Brazilian Rubber Plantations and Estates Ltd.*, [1911] 1 Ch. 425, 437 that the duty of care imposed on directors is measured by the care an ordinary man might be expected to take in the same circumstances on his own behalf. Was the lax English standard of care in fact the same as the upgraded Pennsylvania one? Perhaps the intensity of the duty of care to which judges will hold directors is not dependent ultimately upon the formulation of the statutory standard.

---

* "Gross negligence" is a civilian term. The qualifying adjective suggests a particularly lax duty, not a boorish tortfeasor. See *Re Brazilian Rubber Plantations and Estates Ltd.*, [1911] 1 Ch. 425, 436-37; *Re City Equitable Fire Insurance Co.*, [1925] 1 Ch. 407, 427-28. A gross negligence standard was adopted in *Smith v. Van Gorkom*, excerpted below.

The statutory standard of care imposed by s. 122(1) cannot be made less demanding in the corporation's articles or by-laws. CBCA s. 122(3). This is significant when it is recalled that in the two leading English cases on directors' duties of care, the articles had contained exculpatory clauses, and the courts held that these clauses encompassed part of the terms on which the directors had agreed to serve. *Re Brazilian Rubber Plantation. and Estates, Ltd.*, [1911] 1 Ch. 425; *Re City Equitable Fire Ins. Co.*, [1925] 1 Ch. 407, aff'd, [1925] 1 Ch. 500. In *Brazilian Rubber* the directors' liability was limited by the articles to cases of "dishonesty," and in *City Equitable* it was limited to "wilful neglect or default."

Causation of Loss. Before a director's negligence can result in liability to the corporation for loss, the plaintiff must show that the breach of duty was a proximate cause of the loss. And while it might often seem appropriate that where the plaintiff proves the defendant to have breached a duty the burden should be on the defendant to show that observance of the duty would not have prevented the loss, such "burden shifting" does not appear to be the law. It may be, then, that the causation barrier masks more fundamental questions about the desirability of anti-shirking liability rules.

Sometimes the causation barrier to recovery by the corporation against its director can be a high one indeed. In *Allied Freightways Inc. v. Cholfin*, 91 N.E.2d 765 (Mass. 1950), the corporation's receiver in bankruptcy sought to hold its two directors, a husband and wife, jointly and severally liable for certain payments wrongfully made by the corporation. Most of them had been made to discharge the personal debts of the husband; some were for the benefit of the wife. The husband ran the corporation and owned all its shares. The wife was a "dummy" director. In considering her liability, Ronan J. stated:

Mrs. Cholfin, however, did not supervise the conduct of the business or the management of the corporate affairs. She was apparently content to entrust her husband with the carrying on of the business. She seemed to have been hardly any more than a nominal director. She might have been an ordinary housewife with no business experience, so far as anything appears in the evidence. She could, or course, have made inquiries of her husband or of the bookkeeper. She might have examined the books but it is doubtful whether, unless she was skilled in accounting, she could have derived much information from the books, which were not well kept and which contained twenty-five or more slips of paper containing tabulations made by the bookkeeper in attempting to ascertain how certain entries, some of which pertained to major transactions of the corporation, should be posted. Indeed, the bookkeeper in some instances had to rely upon Cholfin as to the nature of the transaction to be recorded in the books and they did not always agree as to the information given by him to her. ...

The directors of a business corporation other than a bank are not to be held responsible for mere errors of judgment or want of prudence short of clear and gross negligence. ... A director of a corporation cannot avoid liability for losses sustained by the wrongful conduct of corporate officers by showing that he had abandoned his duties as director or that his ignorance of such conduct was due to what amounted to wilful neglect of his duties. ... Mrs. Cholfin apparently did not appreciate the responsibilities connected with her position as a director, but whether, if she had acted with due diligence in supervising the conduct of the corporate business, the improper disbursements of the funds now complained of, other than those used for her personal benefit, would have been prevented is a matter of surmise and conjecture. Of the nine checks issued for her personal use, only three were issued before the corporation decided to close its business. Cholfin alone disposed of the property of the corporation and attempted to wind up its affairs. No one other than he seems to know with any degree of certainty the various transactions in which he engaged in closing up the corporation. Even the bookkeeper was not familiar with the details of what he was doing. There was considerable confusion concerning the financial affairs of the corporation. It is doubtful whether, if Mrs. Cholfin had taken steps, as soon as the first check was issued, to familiarize herself with the conduct of the business by her husband, she could have changed the situation, and it is more doubtful whether, if she even attempted to supervise the closing up of the affairs of the corporation, she could have prevented her husband from proceeding in the manner in which he did. Of course, she should not have permitted checks to be issued for her benefit, and she is liable to account to the corporation. Upon a careful reading of the evidence, we do not think that it can quite be said that the neglect of her official duties as a director was a contributing cause of the loss sustained by the corporation by the wrongful withdrawal of its funds, save only the amounts used for her personal benefit. [*Id.* at 768-69]

Does the Court seem too willing to absolve Mrs. Cholfin from most of the claim against her on the basis that she "might have been an ordinary housewife with no business experience"? Assuming that she did breach a duty of care, as the Court seems to have found, would it not be just as reasonable to surmise that she might have persuaded her husband to stop the wrongful payments? Would it be correct to justify the result of *Allied Freightways* on the basis that, since Mr. Cholfin owned all of the corporation's shares, he was the only one hurt if the "dummy" director was indeed that?

Not all American courts recognize a "housewife's defence." In *Francis v. United Jersey Bank*, 432 A.2d 814 (N.J. 1981), the trustee in bankruptcy of a casualty reinsurance broker sued the estate of the founder's widow, a director, for negligence in failing to discover and attempt to prevent a massive misappropriation of funds by the couple's two sons, who managed the business after their father's death. As a reinsurance broker, the corporation was in the business of syndicating casualty insurance risks among a large number of insurance underwriters. The Court characterized the business as a trust business since at any given time the broker was in possession of large quantities of client funds. These were payable either by the originating underwriter to the reinsurers as the latter's share of premiums or by the reinsurers to the originating underwriter to cover losses. The sons misappropriated these client funds to their personal uses. The statutory standard for directors in New Jersey is the care "which ordinarily prudent men would exercise under similar circumstances in like positions." The Court said that to comply with this standard a director "should acquire at least a rudimentary understanding of the business of the corporation," is "under a continuing obligation to keep informed about the activities of the corporation," "should attend meetings regularly" and "should maintain familiarity with the financial status of the corporation by a regular review of financial statements [that] may give rise to a duty to inquire further into matters revealed by those statements." The widow had done none of those things and she was held to have breached her duty as a director. An examination of the corporation's financial statements would have made the misappropriations apparent. On the issue of causation, she was held liable on the basis that "[t]he actions of the sons were so blatantly wrongful that it is hard to see how they could have resisted any moderately firm objection to what they were doing." [*Id.* at 827]

Suppose that a director of a corporation learns of seriously questionable management behaviour. The matter is brought to the board, and the director dissents. Is he thereafter excused from all liability arising from such mismanagement? Must the director carry his dissent further, beyond the forum of a board meeting? Whistleblowing requirements were discussed in *Joint Stock Discount Co. v. Brown* (1869), L.R. 8 Eq. 381, where the plaintiff investment company held a great deal of commercial paper from a bank in serious financial difficulties. A scheme was devised to prop up the bank by having the plaintiff and another creditor underwrite a public issue of its securities. The scheme was presumably to the advantage of the inside group of monitoring creditors, but not to the other creditors of the bank who relied on its solvency and who assumed that the major creditors would see that the bank was wound up if insolvent. The case is then an excellent example of how, when one group of claimants free rides on the monitoring services provided by a second group, a risk of monitor misbehaviour may arise through a coalition between monitor and agent. James V.C. in fact suggested that the scheme was criminal.

It is a very singular thing that persons should be found to join in a scheme of this kind, which, beyond all question, was to operate as a delusion and a snare upon the innocent persons who were to be tempted, by this representation of a large amount of applications that had been made, to accept shares in the company. [*Id.* at 399]

One director, Brown, had supported a preliminary resolution with respect to the subscription of shares in the bank. Ultimately he objected to the scheme, although he was absent from the crucial board meetings where it was approved. However, he wrote a letter to the board to explain the reasons for his dissent. At trial he argued that there was thereafter nothing he could do. This defence did not succeed. James V.C. indeed called it "a singularly frank, *naive*, and startling confession of dereliction of duty and breach of trust ..." (*id.* at 402). The letter of protest would not have come to the attention of directors who did not attend the meeting at which it was read.

Then it is said, "What was he to do? Was he to have filed a bill to prevent the directors carrying out what they thought was authorized by the first resolution?" All I can say is this, if he could have done it in no other way, it was his duty as a director, knowing what was going on, not to have remained quiescent, or acquiescent, which is much the same thing, in what his brother directors were doing; but to have filed a bill, supposing that a bill was necessary. But can anybody suppose that a bill would have been necessary? If he had simply called the directors together, put on the minutes of the company the letters that he wrote ... , and insisted on taking the vote of the directors upon those letters, I am satisfied the matter would never have gone beyond that. But if that had not been done, if he had found that his brother directors insisted on misappropriating the money of the company, and bringing them under what might have been a very onerous engagement as to these shares in spite of his protest, he might have sent a general circular to every one of the shareholders to tell them what the directors were doing; or, in the last resort, he might have come to the Court of Chancery and stopped this thing in a moment. [*Id.* at 403]

Even if Brown did not protest overmuch, were the affirmative duties imposed on him excessive? Outside directors today have in fact easier methods of alerting the public of dishonesty than those discussed by James V.C.—they might now call up a journalist.

Would it then be desirable to impose liability on outside directors for not blowing the whistle in circumstances where a possibility of third party harm might arise, as in *Joint Stock Discount Co.*? However, limits to whistleblowing strategies are noted by Reinier Kraakman. For example, corporate insiders might respond to the threat of whistleblowing by withholding information from those of suspect loyalty, and the breakdown in trust will impose its own costs. See Kraakman, *Gatekeepers: The Anatomy of a Third-Party Enforcement Strategy*, 2 J.L. Econ. & Org. 53 (1986). In addition, anecdotal evidence suggests that whistleblowing is extremely costly to the whistleblower, whose career in the firm or even the industry may be brought to an abrupt end.

Non-Attendance at Meetings. In *Re Dominion Trust Co.* (1916), 32 D.L.R. 63 (B.C. C.A.), the trial judge's dismissal of an action for negligence against those directors who attended no board meetings was upheld, while directors who did attend were found negligent for failing to ensure that trust moneys were segregated from corporate funds. See also *Joint Stock Discount Co. v. Brown* (1869), L.R. 8 Eq. 381, 401. This seems an odd result. Directors who do nothing are immunized, while those who do something but not enough are liable. There is an analogy here to the topic of rescue in tort law. There is no duty to rescue, but one who undertakes a rescue will be liable for failure to exercise reasonable care. Similarly, it might be inferred from cases like *Dominion Trust* that directors are under no duty to attend board meetings but must take care if they do. In reality, however, the analogy between the duty to rescue and the duty to direct is not very close since rescuers do not stand for election. Affirmative duties might then be imposed on one who voluntarily occupies the position of director, knowing that with it comes active monitoring duties, on whose performance others rely. Moreover, if liability rules are related to the terms of a claimholders' bargain, affirmative duties might be placed on outside directors simply because they are efficient monitors.

Non-attendance at board meeting is more likely to ground liability in negligence today. In *Re City Equitable Fire Ins. Co.*, [1925] 1 Ch. 407, 429, Romer J. stated that, while a director is not bound to attend all meetings of the board, "he ought to attend whenever, in the circumstances, he is reasonably able to do so." In addition, the CBCA may impose liability on non-attending directors through deemed assent provisions. CBCA s. 123(3) provides that a director who is not present at a meeting at which a resolution was passed or an action was taken is deemed to have consented to it unless, within seven days after he becomes aware of it, he notes his dissent. It is conceivable that a director would never become aware of a resolution passed at a board meeting for which he was absent, but that is unlikely because a corporation will ordinarily send minutes of the board meetings to all directors, present and absent. Where the director assents to a resolution in this way, liability may follow if the resolution was an illegal transaction under s. 118. This includes the payment of dividends and redemption of shares in violation of insolvency rules, and the issuance of watered stock.

Directors of Financial Institutions. In the United States, directors of banks and of other financial institutions are apparently held to a more exacting standard of care than directors of industrial corporations. See W. Cary & M. Eisenberg, *Cases and Materials on Corporations* 523 (5th ed. 1980). It is appropriate to impose higher duties of care on monitors where substantial assets are in "liquid" form, since the danger of agent misbehaviour is greatest in such cases. A similar policy animates bulk sales legislation, whose purpose is to ensure that creditors of a firm that sells its assets outside of the ordinary course of business are protected against the risk that managers will abscond with the cash proceeds of the sale.

Reliance by the Directors Upon the Officers. Many or most of the reported cases where directors are sought to be made liable for alleged lack of proper diligence involve fraudulent activities of the corporate manager—who has usually absconded and is always judgment-proof by the time of the litigation—that the defendant directors fail to detect. Courts generally are sympathetic to the defendants in such cases, often citing Lord Halsbury's statement in *Dovey v. Cory*, [1901] A.C. 477, 486 (H.L.), that "[t]he business of life could not go on if people could not trust those who are put into a position of trust for the express purpose of attending to the details of management." See *Re City Equitable Fire Ins. Co.*, [1925] 1 Ch. 407, 430, aff'd, [1925] 2 Ch. 500; *Barnes v. Andrew*, 298 F. 614 at 615; and *Litwin v. Allen*, 25 N.Y.S.2d 667 (S. Ct., Special Term 1940). Conceding, however, that in general directors are entitled to trust the corporation's officers, the more difficult point is to determine whether the directors must demand full accounts of their activities from management and verify what management has to say. In general, judging from the cases, the directors appear to be under a duty to do neither the first nor, unless their suspicions have been aroused, the second.

A defence of reliance upon management may not succeed in respect of the liability of directors for misrepresentations in a prospectus under OSA s. 130. In such a case, directors may be liable to purchasers of securities if the directors fail to conduct a reasonable investigation of the facts.

The liability imposed by CBCA s. 118(2) upon a director for certain improper corporate payments (for example, improper dividends) is absolute except for the defence provided by s. 123(4). This provision shields a director who relies in good faith upon financial statements of the corporation that were represented by an officer or auditor of the corporation fairly to reflect its financial position or upon a report of a lawyer, accountant, engineer, appraiser or other person whose profession lends credibility to statements made by him.

Shlensky v. Wrigley
Appellate Court of Illinois, First District
237 N.E.2d 776 (1968)

SULLIVAN, Justice: This is an appeal from a dismissal of plaintiff's amended complaint on motion of the defendants. The action was a stockholders' derivative suit against the directors for negligence and mismanagement. The corporation was also made a defendant. Plaintiff sought damages and an order that defendants cause the installation of lights in Wrigley Field and the scheduling of night baseball games.

Plaintiff is a minority stockholder of defendant corporation, Chicago National League Ball Club (Inc.), a Delaware corporation with its principal place of business in

Chicago, Illinois. Defendant corporation owns and operates the major league professional baseball team known as the Chicago Cubs. The corporation also engages in the operation of Wrigley Field, the Cubs' home park, the concessionaire sales during Cubs' home games, television and radio broadcasts of Cubs' home games, the leasing of the field for football games and other events and receives its share, as visiting team, of admission moneys from games played in other National League stadia. The individual defendants are directors of the Cubs and have served for varying periods of years. Defendant Philip K. Wrigley is also president of the corporation and owner of approximately 80% of the stock therein.

Plaintiff alleges that since night baseball was first played in 1935 nineteen of the twenty major league teams have scheduled night games. In 1966, out of a total of 1620 games in the major leagues, 932 were played at night. Plaintiff alleges that every member of the major leagues, other than the Cubs, scheduled substantially all of its home games in 1966 at night, exclusive of opening days, Saturdays, Sundays, holidays and days prohibited by league rules. Allegedly this has been done for the specific purpose of maximizing attendance and thereby maximizing revenue and income.

The Cubs, in the years 1961-65, sustained operating losses from its direct baseball operations. Plaintiff attributes those losses to inadequate attendance at Cubs' home games. He concludes that if the directors continue to refuse to install lights at Wrigley Field and schedule night baseball games, the Cubs will continue to sustain comparable losses and its financial condition will continue to deteriorate.

Plaintiff alleges that, except for the year 1963, attendance at Cubs' home games has been substantially below that at their road games, many of which were played at night.

Plaintiff compares attendance at Cubs' games with that of the Chicago White Sox, an American League club, whose weekday games were generally played at night. The weekend attendance figures for the two teams was similar; however, the White Sox week-night games drew many more patrons than did the Cubs' weekday games.

Plaintiff alleges that the funds for the installation of lights can be readily obtained through financing and the cost of installation would be far more than offset and recaptured by increased revenues and incomes resulting from the increased attendance.

Plaintiff further alleges that defendant Wrigley has refused to install lights, not because of interest in the welfare of the corporation but because of his personal opinions "that baseball is a 'daytime sport' and that the installation of lights and night baseball games will have a deteriorating effect upon the surrounding neighborhood." It is alleged that he has admitted that he is not interested in whether the Cubs would benefit financially from such action because of his concern for the neighborhood, and that he would be willing for the team to play night games if a new stadium were built in Chicago.

Plaintiff alleges that the other defendant directors, with full knowledge of the foregoing matters, have acquiesced in the policy laid down by Wrigley and have permitted him to dominate the board of directors in matters involving the installation of lights and scheduling of night games, even though they knew he was not motivated by a good faith concern as to the best interests of defendant corporation, but solely by his personal views set forth above. It is charged that the directors are acting for a reason or reasons contrary and wholly unrelated to the business interests of the corporation; that such arbitrary and capricious acts constitute mismanagement and waste of corporate assets, and that the directors have been negligent in failing to exercise reasonable care and prudence in the management of the corporate affairs.

The question on appeal is whether plaintiff's amended complaint states a cause of action. It is plaintiff's position that fraud, illegality and conflict of interest are not the only bases for a stockholder's derivative action against the directors. Contrariwise, defendants argue that the courts will not step in and interfere with honest business judgment of the directors unless there is a showing of fraud, illegality or conflict of interest.

The cases in this area are numerous and each differs from the others on a factual basis. However, the courts have pronounced certain ground rules which appear in all cases and which are then applied to the given factual situation. The court in *Wheeler v. Pullman Iron and Steel Company*, 143 Ill. 197, 207, 32 N.E. 420, 423, said:

It is, however, fundamental in the law of corporations, that the majority of its stockholders shall control the policy of the corporation, and regulate and govern the lawful exercise of its franchise and business. ... Every one purchasing or subscribing for stock in a corporation impliedly agrees that he will be bound by the acts and proceedings done or sanctioned by a majority of the shareholders, or by the agents of the corporation duly chosen by such majority, within the scope of the powers conferred by the charter, and courts of equity will not undertake to control the policy or business methods of a corporation, although it may be seen that a wiser policy might be adopted and the business more successful if other methods were pursued. The majority of shares of its stock, or the agents by the holders thereof lawfully chosen, must be permitted to control the business of the corporation in their discretion, when not in violation of its charter or some public law, or corruptly and fraudulently subversive of the rights and interests of the corporation or of a shareholder.

The standards set in Delaware are also clearly stated in the cases. In *Davis v. Louisville Gas & Electric Co.*, 16 Del.Ch. 157, 142 A. 654, a minority shareholder sought to have the directors enjoined from amending the certificate of incorporation. The court said on page 659:

We have then a conflict in view between the responsible managers of a corporation and an overwhelming majority of its stockholders on the one hand and a dissenting minority on the other—a conflict touching matters of business policy, such as has occasioned innumerable applications to courts to intervene and determine which of the two conflicting views should prevail. The response which courts make to such applications is that it is not their function to resolve for corporations questions of policy and business management. The directors are chosen to pass upon such questions and their judgment *unless shown to be tainted with fraud is* accepted as final. The judgment of the directors of corporations enjoys the benefit of a presumption that it was formed in good faith and was designed to promote the best interests of the corporation they serve. (Emphasis supplied.)

• • •

Plaintiff argues that the allegations of his amended complaint are sufficient to set forth a cause of action under the principles set out in *Dodge v. Ford Motor Co.*, 204 Mich. 459, 170 N.W. 668. In that case plaintiff, owner of about 10% of the outstanding stock, brought suit against the directors seeking payment of additional dividends and the enjoining of further business expansion. In ruling on the request for dividends the court indicated that the motives of Ford in keeping so much money in the corporation for expansion and security were to benefit the public generally and spread the profits out by means of more jobs, etc. The court felt that these were not only far from related to the good of the stockholders, but amounted to a change in the ends of the corporation and that this was not a purpose contemplated or allowed by the corporate charter. The court relied on language found in Hunter v. Roberts, Throp & Co., 83 Mich. 63, 47 N.W. 131, 134, wherein it was said:

Courts of equity will not interfere in the management of the directors unless it is clearly made to appear that they are guilty of fraud or misappropriation of the corporate funds, or refuse to declare a dividend when the corporation has a surplus of net profits which it can, without detriment to its business, divide among its stockholders, and when a refusal to do so would amount to such an abuse of discretion as would constitute a fraud or breach of that good faith which they are bound to exercise toward the stockholders.

From the authority relied upon in that case it is clear that the court felt that there must be fraud or a breach of that good faith which directors are bound to exercise toward the stockholders in order to justify the courts entering into the internal affairs of corporations. This is made clear when the court refused to interfere with the directors' decision to expand the business. ...

Plaintiff in the instant case argues that the directors are acting for reasons unrelated to the financial interest and welfare of the Cubs. However, we are not satisfied that the motives assigned to Philip K. Wrigley, and through him to the other directors, are contrary to the best interests of the corporation and the stockholders. For example, it appears to us that the effect on the surrounding neighborhood might well be considered by a director who was considering he patrons who would or would not attend the games if the park were in a poor neighborhood. Furthermore, the long run interest of the corporation in its property value at Wrigley Field might demand all efforts to keep the neighborhood from deteriorating. By these thoughts we do not mean to say that we have decided that the decision of the directors was a correct one. That is beyond our jurisdiction and ability. We are merely saying that the decision is one properly before directors and the motives alleged in the amended complaint showed no fraud, illegality or conflict of interest in their making of that decision.

While all the courts do not insist that one or more of the three elements must be present for a stockholder's derivative action to lie, nevertheless we feel that unless the conduct of the defendants at least borders on one of the elements, the courts should not interfere. The trial court in the instant case acted properly in dismissing plaintiff's amended complaint.

We feel that plaintiff's amended complaint was also defective in failing to allege damages to the corporation. ...

There is no allegation that the night games played by the other nineteen teams enhanced their financial position or that the profits, if any, of those teams were directly related to the number of night games scheduled. There is an allegation that the installation of lights and scheduling of night games in Wrigley Field would have resulted in large amounts of additional revenues and incomes from increased attendance and related sources of income. Further, the cost of installation of lights, funds for which are allegedly readily available by financing, would be more than offset and recaptured by increased revenues. However, no allegation is made that there will be a net benefit to the corporation from such action, considering all increased costs.

Plaintiff claims that the losses of defendant corporation are due to poor attendance at home games. However, it appears from the amended complaint, taken as a whole, that factors other than attendance affect the net earnings or losses. For example, in 1962, attendance at home and road games decreased appreciably as compared with 1961, and yet the loss from direct baseball operation and of the whole corporation was considerably less.

The record shows that plaintiff did not feel he could allege that the increased revenues would be sufficient to cure the corporate deficit. The only cost plaintiff was at all concerned with was that of installation of lights. No mention was made of operation and maintenance of the lights or other possible increases in operating costs of night games and we cannot speculate as to what other factors might influence the increase or decrease of profits if the Cubs were to play night home games.

•   •   •

Finally, we do not agree with plaintiff's contention that failure to follow the example of the other major league clubs in scheduling night games constituted negligence. Plaintiff made no allegation that these teams' night schedules were profitable or that the purpose for which night baseball had been undertaken was fulfilled. Furthermore, it cannot be said that directors, even those of corporations that are losing money, must follow the lead of the other corporations in the field. Directors are elected for their business capabilities and judgment and the courts cannot require them to forgo their judgment because of the decisions of directors of other companies. Courts may not decide these questions in the absence of a clear showing of dereliction of duty on the part of the specific directors and mere failure to "follow the crowd" is not such a dereliction.

For the foregoing reasons the order of dismissal entered by the trial court is affirmed.

DEMPSEY P.J. and SCHWARTZ J. concur.

Affirmed

NOTES

1) Would you expect that Wrigley's sensitivity to preservation of the amenities of the neighbourhood was as acute in the operation of his business, Wrigley's Chewing Gum, as in the operation of his gentlemen's pastime, the Chicago Cubs?

2) Of what dereliction of duty did the plaintiff accuse the defendant directors of the Chicago Cubs? Why was the plaintiff unable to bring his case within the rule in *Dodge* (Chapter Six) in which the Court intervened where the directors' motives in operating the company "amounted to a change in the ends of the corporation and ... not a purpose contemplated or allowed by the corporate charter"?

The Business Judgment Rule. The rule announced by the Court in *Shlensky*, that courts will not interfere in the management of a corporation in the absence of an allegation that the directors' actions have been tainted with fraud, illegality or conflict of interest, is known as the "business judgment rule." It is adhered to by all the American jurisdictions. While the approach has not been specifically adopted in Canada, it has clearly had an impact on the approach that Canadian courts have taken to the analysis of fiducary law and the oppression remedy: see, for example, *Brant Investments v. KeepRite Inc.* (1991), 3 O.R. (3d) 289 (Ont. C.A.), excerpted in Part II of this chapter. Corporate litigation often turns then on the question what constitutes a substantial allegation of fraud, illegality or conflict of interest. Were any of these alleged by the plaintiff in *Shlensky*?

The business judgment rule has also been applied in some American courts when firm management is charged with improper defensive manoeuvres on a take-over bid for the firm. These defensive strategies, discussed in Chapter Eleven, Section E, may be harmful to an ordinary shareholder, since take-over bids are made at offering prices that exceed market value, and the defeat of the bid means the loss of this premium for shareholders. Because the result of a successful take-over bid is often to dislodge management from its position of control, defensive strategies may amount to self-dealing by management. If this kind of case is seen as an appropriate one for a business judgment standard, the effect is to widen considerably the scope of permitted defensive manoeuvres that the target firm may adopt to defeat the take-over bid. The prior question may therefore be whether defensive tactics should be proscribed in all cases, without enquiring into management's business judgment. Might such considerations inform judicial standards with respect to Phil Wrigley's views about nighttime ball games? Even if defensive tactics are not uniformly prohibited, one might also expect that a heavier standard of care would be imposed on directors who seek to defeat a take-over bid. See *Hanson Trust PLC v. ML SCM Acquisitions Inc.*, 781 F.2d 264 (2d Cir. 1986) (discussed in Chapter Eleven, Section E).

Because of barriers to litigation, few claims for breach of the duty of care have succeeded. In Canada as in the United States, "the search for cases in which directors of industrial corporations have been held liable in derivative suits for negligence uncomplicated by self-dealing is a search for a very small number of needles in a very large haystack." Bishop, *Sitting Ducks and Decoy Ducks: New Trends in the Indemnification of Corporate Directors and Officers*, 77 Yale L.J. 1078, 1099 (1986). However, decisions imposing liability for negligence may eventually become more frequent as a consequence of the following case, one which resonated through the boardrooms of corporate North America.

Smith v. Van Gorkom
Delaware Supreme Court
488 A.2d 858 (1985)

Before HERRMANN, C.J., and McNEILLY, HORSEY, MOORE and CHRISTIE, JJ., constituting the Court en banc.

HORSEY, Justice (for the majority): This appeal from the Court of Chancery involves a class action brought by shareholders of the defendant Trans Union Corporation ("Trans

Union" or "the Company"), originally seeking rescission of a cash-out merger* of Trans Union into the defendant New T Company ("New T"), a wholly-owned subsidiary of the defendant, Marmon Group, Inc. ("Marmon"). Alternate relief in the form of damages is sought against the defendant members of the Board of Directors of Trans Union, Net T, and Jay A. Pritzker and Robert A. Pritzker, owners of Marmon.[1]

Following trial, the former Chancellor granted judgment for the defendant directors by unreported letter opinion dated July 6, 1982.[2] Judgment was based on two findings: (1) that the Board of Directors had acted in an informed manner so as to be entitled to protection of the business judgment rule in approving the cash-out merger; and (2) that the shareholder vote approving the merger should not be set aside because the stockholders had been "fairly informed" by the Board of Directors before voting thereon. The plaintiffs appeal.

Speaking for the majority of the Court, we conclude that both rulings of the Court of Chancery are clearly erroneous. Therefore, we reverse and direct that judgment be entered in favor of the plaintiffs and against the defendant directors for the fair value of the plaintiffs' stockholdings in Trans Union, in accordance with *Weinberger v. UOP, Inc.*, Del.Supr., 457 A.2d 701 (1983).[3]

We hold: (1) that the Board's decision, reached September 20, 1980, to approve the proposed cash-out merger was not the product of an informed business judgment; (2) that the Board's subsequent efforts to amend the Merger Agreement and take other curative action were ineffectual, both legally and factually; and (3) that the Board did not deal with complete candor with the stockholders by failing to disclose all material facts, which they knew or should have known, before securing the stockholders' approval of the merger.

I.

The nature of this case requires a detailed factual statement. The following facts are essentially uncontradicted:

---

* A merger in which all outside shares, including those held by dissenting shareholders, are exchanged for cash. See Chapter Eleven, Section D.

1 The plaintiff, Alden Smith, originally sought to enjoin the merger; but, following extensive discovery, the Trial Court denied the plaintiff's motion for preliminary injunction by unreported letter opinion dated February 3, 1981. On February 10, 1981, the proposed merger was approved by Trans Union's stockholders at a special meeting and the merger became effective on that date. Thereafter, John W. Gosselin was permitted to intervene as an additional plaintiff; and Smith and Gosselin were certified as representing a class consisting of all persons, other than defendants, who held shares of Trans Union common stock on all relevant dates. At the time of the merger, Smith owned 54,000 shares of Trans Union stock, Gosselin owned 23,600 shares, and members of Gosselin's family owned 20,000 shares.

2 Following trial, and before decision by the Trial Court, the parties stipulated to the dismissal, with prejudice, of the Messrs. Pritzker as parties defendant. However, all references to defendants hereinafter are to the defendant directors of Trans Union, unless otherwise noted.

3 It has been stipulated that plaintiffs sue on behalf of a class consisting of 10,537 shareholders (out of a total of 12,844) and that the class owned 12,734,404 out of 13,357,758 shares of Trans Union outstanding.

– A –

Trans Union was a publicly-traded, diversified holding company, the principal earnings of which were generated by its railcar leasing business. During the period here involved, the Company had a cash flow of hundreds of millions of dollars annually. However, the Company had difficulty in generating sufficient taxable income to offset increasingly large investment tax credits (ITCs). Accelerated depreciation deductions had decreased available taxable income against which to offset accumulating ITCs. The Company took these deductions, despite their effect on usable ITCs, because the rental price in the railcar leasing market had already impounded the purported tax savings.

In the late 1970s, together with other capital-intensive firms, Trans Union lobbied in Congress to have ITCs refundable in cash to firms which could not fully utilize the credit. During the summer of 1980, defendant Jerome W. Van Gorkom, Trans Union's Chairman and Chief Executive Officer, testified and lobbied in Congress for refundability of ITCs and against further accelerated depreciation. By the end of August, Van Gorkom was convinced that Congress would neither accept the refundability concept nor curtail further accelerated depreciation.

Beginning in the late 1960's, and continuing through the 1970's, Trans Union pursued a program of acquiring small companies in order to increase available taxable income. In July 1980, Trans Union Management prepared the annual revision of the Company's Five Year Forecast. This report was presented to the Board of Directors at its July, 1980 meeting. The report projected an annual income growth of about 20%. The report also concluded that Trans Union would have about $195 million in spare cash between 1980 and 1985, "with the surplus growing rapidly from 1982 onward." The report referred to the ITC situation as a "nagging problem" and, given that problem, the leasing company "would still appear to be constrained to a tax breakeven." The report then listed four alternative uses of the projected 1982-1985 equity surplus: (1) stock repurchase; (2) dividend increases; (3) a major acquisition program; and (4) combinations of the above. The sale of Trans Union was not among the alternatives. The report emphasized that, despite the overall surplus, the operation of the Company would consume all available equity for the next several years, and concluded: "As a result, we have sufficient time to fully develop our course of action."

– B –

On August 27, 1980, Van Gorkom met with Senior Management of Trans Union. Van Gorkom reported on his lobbying efforts in Washington and his desire to find a solution to the tax credit problem more permanent than a continued program of acquisitions. Various alternatives were suggested and discussed preliminarily, including the sale of Trans Union to a company with a large amount of taxable income.

Donald Romans, Chief Financial Officer of Trans Union, stated that his department had done a "very brief bit of work on the possibility of a leveraged buy-out."* This work

---

*   An acquisition of outside equity interests financed by an issue of debt interests. See Chapter Eleven, Section A.

had been prompted by a media article which Romans had seen regarding a leveraged buy-out by management. The work consisted of a "preliminary study" of the cash which could be generated by the Company if it participated in a leveraged buy-out. As Romans stated, this analysis "was very first and rough cut at seeing whether a cash flow would support what might be considered a high price for this type of transaction."

On September 5, at another Senior Management meeting which Van Gorkom attended, Romans again brought up the idea of a leveraged buy-out as a "possible strategic alternative" to the Company's acquisition program. Romans and Bruce S. Chelberg, President and Chief Operating Officer of Trans Union, had been working on the matter in preparation for the meeting. According to Romans: They did not "come up" with a price for the Company. They merely "ran the numbers" at $50 a share and at $60 a share with the "rough form" of their cash figures at the time. Their "figures indicated that $50 would be very easy to do but $60 would be very difficult to do under those figures." This work did not purport to establish a fair price for either the Company or 100% of the stock. It was intended to determine the cash flow needed to service the debt that would "probably" be incurred in a leveraged buy-out, based on "rough calculations" without "any benefit of experts to identify what the limits were to that, and so forth." These computations were not considered extensive and no conclusion was reached.

At this meeting, Van Gorkom stated that he would be willing to take $55 per share for his own 75,000 shares. He vetoed the suggestion of a leveraged buy-out by Management, however, as involving a potential conflict of interest for Management. Van Gorkom, a certified public accountant and lawyer, had been an officer of Trans Union for 24 years, its Chief Executive Officer for more than 17 years, and Chairman of its Board for 2 years. It is noteworthy in this connection that he was then approaching 65 years of age and mandatory retirement.

For several days following the September 5 meeting, Van Gorkom pondered the idea of a sale. He had participated in many acquisitions as a manager and director of Trans Union and as a director of other companies. He was familiar with acquisition procedures, valuation methods, and negotiations; and he privately considered the pros and cons of whether Trans Union should seek a privately or publicly-held purchaser.

Van Gorkom decided to meet with Jay A. Pritzker, a well-known corporate takeover specialist and a social acquaintance. However, rather than approaching Pritzker simply to determine his interest in acquiring Trans Union, Van Gorkom assembled a proposed per share price for sale of the Company and a financing structure by which to accomplish the sale. Van Gorkom did so without consulting either his Board or any members of Senior Management except one: Carl Peterson, Trans Union's Controller. Telling Peterson that he wanted no other person on his staff to know what he was doing, but without telling him why, Van Gorkom directed Peterson to calculate the feasibility of a leveraged buy-out at an assumed price per share of $55. Apart from the Company's historic stock market price,[5] and Van Gorkom's long association with Trans Union, the

---

5   The common stock of Trans Union was traded on the New York Stock Exchange. Over the five year period from 1975 through 1979, Trans Union's stock had traded within a range of a high of $39 1/2 and a low of $24 1/4. Its high and low range for 1980 through September 19 (the last trading day before announcement of the merger) was $38 1/4 – $29 1/2.

record is devoid of any competent evidence that $55 represented the per share intrinsic value of the Company.

Having thus chosen the $55 figure, based solely on the availability of a leveraged buy-out, Van Gorkom multiplied the price per share by the number of shares outstanding to reach a total value of the Company of $690 million. Van Gorkom told Peterson to use this $690 million figure and to assume a $200 million equity contribution by the buyer. Based on these assumptions, Van Gorkom directed Peterson to determine whether the debt portion of the purchase price could be paid off in five years or less if financed by Trans Union's cash flow as projected in the Five Year Forecast, and by the sale of certain weaker divisions identified in a study done for Trans Union by the Boston Consulting Group ("BCG study"). Peterson reported that, of the purchase price, approximately $50-80 million would remain outstanding after five years. Van Gorkom was disappointed, but decided to meet with Pritzker nevertheless.

Van Gorkom arranged a meeting with Pritzker at the latter's home on Saturday, September 13, 1980. Van Gorkom prefaced his presentation by stating to Pritzker: "Now as far as you are concerned, I can, I think, show how you can pay a substantial premium over the present stock price and pay off most of the loan in the first five years. ... If you could pay $55 for this Company, here is a way in which I think it can be financed."

Van Gorkom then reviewed with Pritzker his calculations based upon his proposed price of $55 per share. Although Pritzker mentioned $50 as a more attractive figure, no other price was mentioned. However, Van Gorkom stated that to be sure that $55 was the best price obtainable, Trans Union should be free to accept any better offer. Pritzker demurred, stating that his organization would serve as a "stalking horse" for an "auction contest" only if Trans Union would permit Pritzker to buy 1,750,000 shares of Trans Union stock at market price which Pritzker could then sell to any higher bidder. After further discussion on this point, Pritzker told Van Gorkom that he would give him a more definite reaction soon.

On Monday, September 15, Pritzker advised Van Gorkom that he was interested in the $55 cash-out merger proposal and requested more information on Trans Union. Van Gorkom agreed to meet privately with Pritzker, accompanied by Peterson, Chelberg, and Michael Carpenter, Trans Union's consultant from the Boston Consulting Group. The meetings took place on September 16 and 17. Van Gorkom was "astounded that events were moving with such amazing rapidity."

On Thursday, September 18, Van Gorkom met again with Pritzker. At that time, Van Gorkom knew that Pritzker intended to make a cash-out merger offer at Van Gorkom's proposed $55 per share. Pritzker instructed his attorney, a merger and acquisition specialist, to begin drafting merger documents. There was no further discussion of the $55 price. However, the number of shares of Trans Union's treasury stock to be offered to Pritzker was negotiated down to one million shares; the price was set at $38—75 cents above the per share price at the close of the market on September 19. At this point, Pritzker insisted that the Trans Union Board act on his merger proposal within the next three days, stating to Van Gorkom: "We have to have a decision by no later than Sunday [evening, September 21] before the opening of the English stock exchange on Monday morning." Pritzker's lawyer was then instructed to draft the merger documents, to be reviewed by Van Gorkom's lawyer, "sometimes with discussion and sometimes not, in the haste to get it finished."

On Friday, September 19, Van Gorkom, Chelberg, and Pritzker consulted with Trans Union's lead bank regarding the financing of Pritzker's purchase of Trans Union. The bank indicated that it could form a syndicate of banks that would finance the transaction. On the same day, Van Gorkom retained James Brennan, Esquire, to advise Trans Union on the legal aspects of the merger. Van Gorkom did not consult with William Browder, a Vice-President and director of Trans Union and former head of its legal department, or with William Moore, then the head of Trans Union's legal staff.

On Friday, September 19, Van Gorkom called a special meeting of the Trans Union Board for noon the following day. He also called a meeting of the Company's Senior Management to convene at 11:00 a.m., prior to the meeting of the Board. No one, except Chelberg and Peterson, was told the purpose of the meetings. Van Gorkom did not invite Trans Union's investment banker, Salomon Brothers or its Chicago-based partner, to attend.

Of those present at the Senior Management meeting on September 20, only Chelberg and Peterson had prior knowledge of Pritzker's offer. Van Gorkom disclosed the offer and described its terms, but he furnished no copies of the proposed Merger Agreement. Romans announced that his department had done a second study which showed that, for a leveraged buy-out, the price range for Trans Union stock was between $55 and $65 per share. Van Gorkom neither saw the study nor asked Romans to make it available for the Board meeting.

Senior Management's reaction to the Pritzker proposal was completely negative. No member of Management, except Chelberg and Peterson, supported the proposal. Romans objected to the price as being too low;[6] he was critical of the timing and suggested that consideration should be given to the adverse tax consequences of an all-cash deal for low-basis shareholders; and he took the position that the agreement to sell Pritzker one million newly-issued shares at market price would inhibit other offers, as would the prohibitions against soliciting bids and furnishing inside information to other bidders. Romans argued that the Pritzker proposal was a "lock up"* and amounted to "an agreed merger as opposed to an offer." Nevertheless, Van Gorkom proceeded to the Board meeting as scheduled without further delay.

Ten directors served on the Trans Union Board, five inside (defendants Bonser, O'Boyle, Browder, Chelberg, and Van Gorkom) and five outside (defendants Wallis, Johnson, Lanterman, Morgan and Reneker). All directors were present at the meeting, except O'Boyle who was ill. Of the outside directors, four were corporate chief executive officers and one was the former Dean of the University of Chicago Business School. None was an investment banker or trained financial analyst. All members of the Board were well informed about the Company and its operations as a going concern. They were familiar with the current financial condition of the Company, as well as operating

---

6   Van Gorkom asked Romans to express his opinion as to the $55 price. Romans stated that he "thought the price was too low in relation to what he could derive for the company in a cash sale, particularly one which enabled us to realize the values of certain subsidiaries and independent entities."

*   An option given in the context of a control contest which has the effect of "locking up" control of the target firm in the hands of a particular bidder.

and earnings projections reported in the recent Five Year Forecast. The Board generally received regular and detailed reports and was kept abreast of the accumulated investment tax credit and accelerated depreciation problem.

Van Gorkom began the Special Meeting of the Board with a twenty-minute oral presentation. Copies of the proposed Merger Agreement were delivered too late for study before or during the meeting.[7] He reviewed the Company's ITC and depreciation problems and the efforts theretofore made to solve them. He discussed his initial meeting with Pritzker and his motivation in arranging that meeting. Van Gorkom did not disclose to the Board, however, the methodology by which he alone had arrived at the $55 figure, or the fact that he first proposed the $55 price in his negotiations with Pritzker.

Van Gorkom outlined the terms of the Pritzker offer as follows: Pritzker would pay $55 in cash for all outstanding shares of Trans Union stock upon completion of which Trans Union would be merged into New T Company, a subsidiary wholly-owned by Pritzker and formed to implement the merger; for a period of 90 days, Trans Union could receive, but could not actively solicit, competing offers; the offer had to be acted on by the next evening, Sunday, September 21; Trans Union could only furnish to competing bidders published information, and not proprietary information; the offer was subject to Pritzker obtaining the necessary financing by October 10, 1980; if the financing contingency were met or waived by Pritzker, Trans Union was required to sell to Pritzker one million newly-issued shares of Trans Union at $38 per share.

Van Gorkom took the position that putting Trans Union "up for auction" through a 90-day market test would validate a decision by the Board that $55 was a fair price. He told the Board that the "free market will have an opportunity to judge whether $55 is a fair price." Van Gorkom framed the decision before the Board not as whether $55 per share was the highest price that could be obtained, but as whether the $55 price was a fair price that the stockholders should be given the opportunity to accept or reject.[8]

Attorney Brennan advised the members of the Board that they might be sued if they failed to accept the offer and that a fairness opinion was not required as a matter of law.

Romans attended the meeting as chief financial officer of the Company. He told the Board that he had not been involved in the negotiations with Pritzker and knew nothing about the merger proposal until the morning of the meeting; that his studies did not indicate either a fair price for the stock or a valuation of the Company; that he did not see his role as directly addressing the fairness issue; and that he and his people "were trying to search for ways to justify a price in connection with such a [leveraged buy-out] transaction, rather than to say what the shares are worth." Romans testified:

---

7   The record is not clear as to the terms of the Merger Agreement. The Agreement, as originally presented to the Board on September 20, was never produced by defendants despite demands by the plaintiffs. Nor is it clear that the directors were given an opportunity to study the Merger Agreement before voting on it. All that can be said is that Brennan had the Agreement before him during the meeting.

8   In Van Gorkom's words: The "real decision" is whether to "let the stockholders decide it" which is "all you are being asked to decide today."

I told the Board that the study ran the numbers at 50 and 60, and then the subsequent study at 55 and 65, and that was not the same thing as saying that I have a valuation of the company at X dollars. But it was a way—a first step towards reaching that conclusion.

Romans told the Board that, in his opinion, $55 was "in the range of a fair price," but "at the beginning of the range."

Chelberg, Trans Union's President, supported Van Gorkom's presentation and representations. He testified that he "participated to make sure that the Board members collectively were clear on the details of the agreement or offer from Pritzker;" that he "participated in the discussion with Mr. Brennan, inquiring of him about the necessity for valuation opinions in spite of the way in which this particular offer was couched;" and that he was otherwise actively involved in supporting the positions being taken by Van Gorkom before the Board about "the necessity to act immediately on this offer," and about "the adequacy of the $55 and the question of how that would be tested."

The Board meeting of September 20 lasted about two hours. Based solely upon Van Gorkom's oral presentation, Chelberg's supporting representations, Romans' oral statement, Brennan's legal advice, and their knowledge of the market history of the Company's stock,[9] the directors approved the proposed Merger Agreement. However, the Board later claimed to have attached two conditions to its acceptance: (1) that Trans Union reserved the right to accept any better offer that was made during the market test period; and (2) that Trans Union could share its proprietary information with any other potential bidders. While the Board now claims to have reserved the right to accept any better offer received after the announcement of the Pritzker agreement (even though the minutes of the meeting do not reflect this), it is undisputed that the Board did not reserve the right to actively solicit alternate offers.

The Merger Agreement was executed by Van Gorkom during the evening of September 20 at a formal social event that he hosted for the opening of the Chicago Lyric opera. Neither he nor any other director read the agreement prior to its signing and delivery to Pritzker.

•   •   •

On Monday, September 22, the Company issued a press release announcing that Trans Union had entered into a "definitive" Merger Agreement with an affiliate of the Marmon Group, Inc., a Pritzker holding company. Within 10 days of the public announcement, dissent among Senior Management over the merger had become widespread. Faced with threatened resignations of key officers, Van Gorkom met with

---

9   The Trial Court stated the premium relationship of the $55 price to the market history of the Company's stock as follows:

   ... the merger price offered to the stockholders of Trans Union represented a premium of 62% over the average of the high and low prices at which Trans Union stock had traded in 1980, a premium of 48% over the last closing price, and a premium of 39% over the highest price at which the stock of Trans Union had traded any time during the prior six years.

Pritzker who agreed to several modifications of the Agreement. Pritzker was willing to do so provided that Van Gorkom could persuade the dissidents to remain on the Company payroll for at least six months after consummation of the merger.

Van Gorkom reconvened the Board on October 8 and secured the directors' approval of the proposed amendments—sight unseen. The Board also authorized the employment of Salomon Brothers, its investment banker, to solicit other offers for Trans Union during the proposed "market test" period.

The next day, October 9, Trans Union issued a press release announcing: (1) that Pritzker had obtained "the financing commitments necessary to consummate" the merger with Trans Union; (2) that Pritzker had acquired one million shares of Trans Union common stock at $38 per share; (3) that Trans Union was now permitted to actively seek other offers and had retained Salomon Brothers for that purpose; and (4) that if a more favorable offer were not received before February 1, 1981, Trans Union's shareholders would thereafter meet to vote on the Pritzker proposal.

It was not until the following day, October 10, that the actual amendments to the Merger Agreement were prepared by Pritzker and delivered to Van Gorkom for execution. As will be seen, the amendments were considerably at variance with Van Gorkom's representations of the amendments to the Board on October 8; and the amendments placed serious constraints on Trans Union's ability to negotiate a better deal and withdraw from the Pritzker agreement. Nevertheless, Van Gorkom proceeded to execute what became the October 10 amendments to the Merger Agreement without conferring further with the Board members and apparently without comprehending the actual implications of the amendments.

• • •

Salomon Brothers' efforts over a three-month period from October 21 to January 21 produced only one serious suitor for Trans Union—General Electric Credit Corporation ("GE Credit"), a subsidiary of the General Electric Company. However, GE Credit was unwilling to make an offer for Trans Union unless Trans Union first rescinded its Merger Agreement with Pritzker. When Pritzker refused, GE Credit terminated further discussions with Trans Union in early January.

In the meantime, in early December, the investment firm of Kohlberg, Kravis, Roberts & Co. ("KKR"), the only other concern to make a firm offer for Trans Union, withdrew its offer under circumstances hereinafter detailed.

On December 19, this litigation was commenced and, within four weeks, the plaintiffs had deposed eight of the ten directors of Trans Union, including Van Gorkom, Chelberg and Romans, its Chief Financial Officer. On January 21, Management's Proxy Statement for the February 10 shareholder meeting was mailed to Trans Union's stockholders. On January 26, Trans Union's Board met and, after a lengthy meeting, voted to proceed with the Pritzker merger. The Board also approved for mailing, "on or about January 27," a Supplement to its Proxy Statement. The Supplement purportedly set forth all information relevant to the Pritzker Merger Agreement, which had not been divulged in the first Proxy Statement.

• • •

On February 10, the stockholders of Trans Union approved the Pritzker merger proposal. Of the outstanding shares, 69.9% were voted in favor of the merger, 7.25% were voted against the merger; and 22.85% were not voted.

II.

We turn to the issue of the application of the business judgment rule to the September 20 meeting of the Board.

The Court of Chancery concluded from the evidence that the Board of Directors' approval of the Pritzker merger proposal fell within the protection of the business judgment rule. The Court found that the Board had given sufficient time and attention to the transaction, since the directors had considered the Pritzker proposal on three different occasions, on September 20, and on October 8, 1980 and finally on January 26, 1981. On that basis, the Court reasoned that the Board had acquired, over the four-month period, sufficient information to reach an informed business judgment on the cash-out merger proposal. The Court ruled:

... that given the market value of Trans Union's stock, the business acumen of the members of the board of Trans Union, the substantial premium over market offered by the Pritzkers and the ultimate effect on the merger price provided by the prospect of other bids for the stock in question, that the board of directors of Trans Union did not act recklessly or improvidently in determining on a course of action which they believed to be in the best interest of the stockholders of Trans Union.

The Court of Chancery made but one finding; i.e., that the Board's conduct over the entire period from September 20 through January 26, 1981 was not reckless or improvident, but informed. This ultimate conclusion was premised upon three subordinate findings, one explicit and two implied. The Court's explicit finding was that Trans Union's Board was "free to turn down the Pritzker proposal" not only on September 20 but also on October 8, 1980 and on January 26, 1981. The Court's implied, subordinate findings were: (1) that no legally binding agreement was reached by the parties until January 26; and (2) that if a higher offer were to be forthcoming, the market test would have produced it,[10] and Trans Union would have been contractually free to accept such higher offer. However, the Court offered no factual basis or legal support for any of these findings; and the record compels contrary conclusions.

This Court's standard of review of the findings of fact reached by the Trial Court following full evidentiary hearing is as stated in *Levitt v. Bouvier*, Del.Supr., 287 A.2d 671, 673 (1972):

[In an appeal of this nature] this court has the authority to review the entire record and to make its own findings of fact in a proper case. In exercising our power of review, we have the duty to review

---

10   We refer to the underlined portions of the Court's ultimate conclusion (previously stated): "that given the market value of Trans Union's stock, the business acumen of the members of the board of Trans Union, the substantial premium over market offered by the Pritzkers *and the ultimate effect on the merger price provided by the prospect* or *other bids for the stock in question*, that the board of directors of Trans Union did not act recklessly or improvidently. ..."

the sufficiency of the evidence and to test the propriety of the findings below. We do not, however, ignore the findings made by the trial judge. If they are sufficiently supported by the record and are the product of an orderly and logical deductive process, in the exercise of judicial restraint we accept them, even though independently we might have reached opposite conclusions. It is only when the findings below are clearly wrong and the doing of justice requires their overturn that we are free to make contradictory findings of fact.

Applying that standard and governing principles of law to the record and the decision of the Trial Court, we conclude that the Court's ultimate finding that the Board's conduct was not "reckless or imprudent" is contrary to the record and not the product of a logical and deductive reasoning process.

The plaintiffs contend that the Court of Chancery erred as a matter of law by exonerating the defendant directors under the business judgment rule without first determining whether the rule's threshold condition of "due care and prudence" was satisfied. The plaintiffs assert that the Trial Court found the defendant directors to have reached an informed business judgment on the basis of "extraneous considerations and events that occurred after September 20, 1980." The defendants deny that the Trial Court committed legal error in relying upon post-September 20, 1980 events and the directors' later acquired knowledge. The defendants further submit that their decision to accept $55 per share was informed because: (1) they were "highly qualified"; (2) they were "well-informed"; and (3) they deliberated over the "proposal" not once but three times. On essentially this evidence and under our standard of review, the defendants assert that affirmance is required. We must disagree.

Under Delaware law, the business judgment rule is the offspring of the fundamental principle, codified in 8 *Del.C.* § 141(a), that the business and affairs of a Delaware corporation are managed by or under its board of directors.[11] *Pogostin v. Rice*, Del.Supr., 480 A.2d 619, 624 (1984); *Aronson v. Lewis*, Del.Supr., 473 A.2d 805, 811 (1984); *Zapata Corp. v. Maldonado*, Del.Supr., 430 A.2d 779, 782 (1981). In carrying out their managerial roles, directors are charged with an unyielding fiduciary duty to the corporation and its shareholders. *Loft, Inc. v. Guth*, Del.Ch., 2 A.2d 225 (1938), aff'd, Del.Supr., 5 A.2d 503 (1939). The business judgment rule exists to protect and promote the full and free exercise of the managerial power granted to Delaware directors. *Zapata Corp. v. Maldonado*, supra at 782. The rule itself "is a presumption that in making a business decision, the directors of a corporation acted on an informed basis, in good faith and in the honest belief that the action taken was in the best interests of the company." *Aronson*, supra at 812. Thus, the party attacking a board decision as uninformed must rebut the presumption that its business judgment was an informed one. *Id.*

---

11   8 *Del.C.* § 141 provides, in pertinent part:

(a) The business and affairs of every corporation organized under this chapter shall be managed by or under the direction of a board of directors, except as may be otherwise provided in this chapter or in its certificate of incorporation. If any such provision is made in the certificate of incorporation, the powers and duties conferred or imposed upon the board of directors by this chapter shall be exercised or performed to such extent and by such person or persons as shall be provided in the certificate of incorporation.

The determination of whether a business judgment is an informed one turns on whether the directors have informed themselves "prior to making a business decision, of all material information reasonably available to them." *Id.*[12]

Under the business judgment rule there is no protection for directors who have made "an unintelligent or unadvised judgment." *Mitchell v. Highland-Western Glass*, Del.Ch., 167 A. 831, 833 (1933). A director's duty to inform himself in preparation for a decision derives from the fiduciary capacity in which he serves the corporation and its stockholders. *Lutz v. Boas*, Del.Ch., 171 A.2d 381 (1961). *See Weinberger v. UOP, Inc.*, supra; *Guth v. Loft*, supra. Since a director is vested with the responsibility for the management of the affairs of the corporation, he must execute that duty with the recognition that he acts on behalf of others. Such obligation does not tolerate faithlessness or self-dealing. But fulfillment of the fiduciary function requires more than the mere absence of bad faith or fraud. Representation of the financial interests of others imposes on a director an affirmative duty to protect those interests and to proceed with a critical eye in assessing information of the type and under the circumstances present here. *See Lutz v. Boas*, supra; *Guth v. Loft*, supra at 510. *Compare Donovan v. Cunningham*, 5th Cir., 716 F.2d 1455, 1467 (1983); *Doyle v. Union Insurance Company*, Neb.Supr., 277 N.W.2d 36 (1979); *Continental Securities Co. v. Belmont*, N.Y. App., 99 N.E. 138, 141 (1912).

Thus, a director's duty to exercise an informed business judgment is in the nature of a duty of care, as distinguished from a duty of loyalty. Here, there were no allegations of fraud, bad faith, or self-dealing, or proof thereof. Hence, it is presumed that the directors reached their business judgment in good faith, *Allaun v. Consolidated Oil Co.*, Del.Ch., 147 A. 257 (1929), and considerations of motive are irrelevant to the issue before us.

The standard of care applicable to a director's duty of care has also been recently restated by this Court. In *Aronson*, supra, we stated:

While the Delaware cases use a variety of terms to describe the applicable standard of care, our analysis satisfies us that under the business judgment rule director liability is predicated upon concepts of gross negligence. (footnote omitted)

473 A.2d at 812.

We again confirm that view. We think the concept of gross negligence is also the proper standard for determining whether a business judgment reached by a board of directors was an informed one.[13]

---

12   See *Kaplan v. Centex Corporation*, Del.Ch., 284 A.2d 119, 124 (1971), where the Court stated:

Application of the [business judgment] rule of necessity depends upon a showing that informed directors did in fact make a business judgment authorizing the transaction under review. And, as the plaintiff argues, the difficulty here is that the evidence does not show that this was done. There were director-committee-officer references to the realignment but none of these singly or cumulative showed that the director judgment was brought to bear with specificity on the transactions.

13   Compare *Mitchell v. Highland-Western Glass*, supra, where the Court posed the question as whether the board acted "so far without information that they can be said to have passed an unintelligent and
(The footnote is continued on the next page.)

In the specific context of a proposed merger of domestic corporations, a director has a duty under 8 *Del.C.* 251(b),[14] along with his fellow directors, to act in an informed and deliberate manner in determining whether to approve an agreement of merger before submitting the proposal to the stockholders. Certainly in the merger context, a director may not abdicate that duty by leaving to the shareholders alone the decision to approve or disapprove the agreement. See *Beard v. Elster*, Del.Supr., 160 A.2d 731, 737 (1960). Only an agreement of merger satisfying the requirements of 8 *Del. c. § 251*(b) may be submitted to the shareholders under § 251(c). See generally *Aronson v. Lewis*, supra at 811-13; see also *Pogostin v. Rice*, supra.

It is against those standards that the conduct of the directors of Trans Union must be tested, as a matter of law and as a matter of fact, regarding their exercise of an informed business judgment in voting to approve the Pritzker merger proposal.

III.

The defendants argue that the determination of whether their decision to accept $55 per share for Trans Union represented an informed business judgment requires considera-tion, not only of that which they knew and learned on September 20, but also of that which they subsequently learned and did over the following four-month period before the shareholders met to vote on the proposal in February, 1981. The defendants thereby seek to reduce the significance of their action on September 20 and to widen the time

---

13   Continued ...

unadvised judgment." 167 A. at 833. Compare also *Gimbel v. Signal Companies, Inc.*, 316 A.2d 599, aff'd per curiam Del.Supr., 316 A.2d 619 (1974), where the Chancellor, after expressly reiterating the *Highland-Western Glass* standard, framed the question, "Or to put the question in its legal context, did the Signal directors act without the bounds of reason and recklessly in approving the price offer of Burmah?" *Id.*

14   8 *Del.C.* § 251(b) provides in pertinent part:

(b) The board of directors of each corporation which desires to merge or consolidate *shall adopt a resolution approving an agreement of merger* or consolidation. The agreement shall state: (1) the terms and conditions of the merger or consolidation; (2) the mode of carrying the same into effect; (3) such amendments or changes in the certificate of incorporation of the surviving corpo-ration as are desired to be effected by the merger or consolidation, or, if no such amendments or changes are desired, a statement that the certificate of incorporation of one of the constituent cor-porations shall be the certificate of incorporation of the surviving or resulting corporation; (4) the manner of converting the shares of each of the constituent corporations ... and (5) such other de-tails or provisions as are deemed desirable. ... The agreement so adopted shall be executed in ac-cordance with section 103 of this title. *Any of the terms of the agreement of merger or consolidation may be made dependent upon facts ascertainable outside of such agreement, pro-vided that the manner in which such facts shall operate upon the terms of the agreement is clearly and expressly set forth in the agreement of merger or consolidation.* ([italics] added for emphasis) frame for determining whether their decision to accept the Pritzker proposal was an informed one. Thus, the defendants contend that what the directors did and learned subsequent to September 20 and through January 26, 1981, was properly taken into account by the Trial Court in determining whether the Board's judgment was an informed one. We disagree with this *post hoc* approach.

The issue of whether the directors reached an informed decision to "sell" the Company on September 20, 1980 must be determined only upon the basis of the information then reasonably available to the directors and relevant to their decision to accept the Pritzker merger proposal. This is not to say that the directors were precluded from altering their original plan of action, had they done so in an informed manner. What we do say is that the question of whether the directors reached an informed business judgment in agreeing to sell the Company, pursuant to the terms of the September 20 Agreement presents, in reality, two questions: (A) whether the directors reached an informed business judgment on September 20, 1980; and (B) if they did not, whether the directors' actions taken subsequent to September 20 were adequate to cure any infirmity in their action taken on September 20. We first consider the directors' September 20 action in terms of their reaching an informed business judgment.

– A –

On the record before us, we must conclude that the Board of Directors did not reach an informed business judgment on September 20, 1980 in voting to "sell" the Company for $55 per share pursuant to the Pritzker cash-out merger proposal. Our reasons, in summary, are as follows:

The directors (1) did not adequately inform themselves as to Van Gorkom's role in forcing the "sale" of the Company and in establishing the per share purchase price; (2) were uninformed as to the intrinsic value of the Company; and (3) given these circumstances, at a minimum, were grossly negligent in approving the "sale" of the Company upon two hours' consideration, without prior notice, and without the exigency of a crisis or emergency.

As has been noted, the Board based its September 20 decision to approve the cash-out merger primarily on Van Gorkom's representations. None of the directors, other than Van Gorkom and Chelberg, had any prior knowledge that the purpose of the meeting was to propose a cash-out merger of Trans Union. No members of Senior Management were present, other than Chelberg, Romans and Peterson; and the latter two had only learned of the proposed sale an hour earlier. Both general counsel Moore and former general counsel Browder attended the meeting, but were equally uninformed as to the purpose of the meeting and the documents to be acted upon.

Without any documents before them concerning the proposed transaction, the members of the Board were required to rely entirely upon Van Gorkom's 20-minute oral presentation of the proposal. No written summary of the terms of the merger was presented; the directors were given no documentation to support the adequacy of $55 price per share for sale of the Company; and the Board had before it nothing more than Van Gorkom's statement of his understanding of the substance of an agreement which he admittedly had never read, nor which any member of the Board had ever seen.

Under 8 *Del.C.* § 141(e),[15] "directors are fully protected in relying in good faith on reports made by officers." *Michelson v. Duncan*, Del.Ch., 386 A.2d 1144, 1156 (1978); aff'd in part and rev'd in part on other grounds, Del.Supr., 407 A.2d 211 (1979). See also *Graham v. Allis-Chalmers Mfg. Co.*, Del. Supr., 188 A.2d 125, 130 (1963); *Prince v. Bensinger*, Del.Ch., 244 A.2d 89, 94 (1968). The term "report" has been liberally construed to include reports of informal personal investigations by corporate officers, *Cheff v. Mathes*, Del.Supr., 199 A.2d 548, 556 (1964). However, there is no evidence that any "report," as defined under § 141(e), concerning the Pritzker proposal, was presented to the Board on September 20.[16] Van Gorkom's oral presentation of his understanding of the terms of the proposed Merger Agreement, which he had not seen, and Romans' brief oral statement of his preliminary study regarding the feasibility of a leveraged buy-out of Trans Union do not qualify as § 141(e) "reports" for these reasons: The former lacked substance because Van Gorkom was basically uninformed as to the essential provisions of the very document about which he was talking. Romans' statement was irrelevant to the issues before the Board since it did not purport to be a valuation study. At a minimum for a report to enjoy the status conferred by § 141(e), it must be pertinent to the subject matter upon which a board is called to act, and otherwise be entitled to good faith, not blind, reliance. Considering all of the surrounding circumstances—hastily calling the meeting without prior notice of its subject matter, the proposed sale of the Company without any prior consideration of the issue or necessity therefor, the urgent time constraints imposed by Pritzker, and the total absence of any documentation whatsoever—the directors were duty bound to make reasonable inquiry of Van Gorkom and Romans, and if they had done so, the inadequacy of that upon which they now claim to have relied would have been apparent.

The defendants rely on the following factors to sustain the Trial Court's finding that the Board's decision was an informed one: (1) the magnitude of the premium or spread between the $55 Pritzker offering price and Trans Union's current market price of $38 per share; (2) the amendment of the Agreement as submitted on September 20 to permit the Board to accept any better offer during the "market test" period; (3) the collective

---

15 Section 141(e) provides in pertinent part:

> A member of the board of directors ... shall, in the performance of his duties, be fully protected in relying in good faith upon the books of accounts or reports made to the corporation by any of its officers, or by an independent certified public accountant, or by an appraiser selected with reasonable care by the board of directors ... , or in relying in good faith upon other records of the corporation.

16 In support of the defendants' argument that their judgment as to the adequacy of $55 per share was an informed one, the directors rely on the BCG study and the Five Year Forecast. However, no one even referred to either of these studies at the September 20 meeting; and it is conceded that these materials do not represent valuation studies. Hence, these documents do not constitute evidence as to whether the directors reached an informed judgment on September 20 that $55 per share was a fair value for sale of the Company.

experience and expertise of the Board's "inside" and "outside" directors;[17] and (4) their reliance on Brennan's legal advice that the directors might be sued if they rejected the Pritzker proposal. We discuss each of these grounds *seriatim*:

(1)

A substantial premium may provide one reason to recommend a merger, but in the absence of other sound valuation information, the fact of a premium alone does not provide an adequate basis upon which to assess the fairness of an offering price. Here, the judgment reached as to the adequacy of the premium was based on a comparison between the historically depressed Trans Union market price and the amount of the Pritzker offer. Using market price as a basis for concluding that the premium adequately reflected the true value of the Company was a clearly faulty, indeed fallacious, premise, as the defendants' own evidence demonstrates.

The record is clear that before September 20, Van Gorkom and other members of Trans Union's Board knew that the market had consistently undervalued the worth of Trans Union's stock, despite steady increases in the Company's operating income in the seven years preceding the merger. The Board related this occurrence in large part to Trans Union's inability to use its ITCs as previously noted. Van Gorkom testified that he did not believe the market price accurately reflected Trans Union's true worth; and several of the directors testified that, as a general rule, most chief executives think that the market undervalues their companies' stock. Yet, on September 20, Trans Union's Board apparently believed that the market stock price accurately reflected the value of the Company for the purpose of determining the adequacy of the premium for its sale.

In the Proxy Statement, however, the directors reversed their position. There, they stated that, although the earnings prospects for Trans Union were "excellent," they found no basis for believing that this would be reflected in future stock prices. With regard to past trading, the Board stated that the prices at which the Company's common stock had traded in recent years did not reflect the "inherent" value of the Company. But having referred to the "inherent" value of Trans Union, the directors ascribed no number to it. Moreover, nowhere did they disclose that they had no basis on which to fix "inherent" worth beyond an impressionistic reaction to the premium over market and an unsubstantiated belief that the value of the assets was "significantly greater" than book value. By their own admission they could not rely on the stock price as an accurate measure of value. Yet, also by their own admission, the Board members assumed that Trans Union's market price was adequate to serve as a basis upon which to assess the adequacy of the premium for purposes of the September 20 meeting.

The parties do not dispute that a publicly-traded stock price is solely a measure of the value of a minority position and, thus, market price represents only the value of a single share. Nevertheless, on September 20, the Board assessed the adequacy of the

---

17   We reserve for discussion under Part III hereof, the defendants' contention that their judgment, reached on September 20, if not then informed became informed by virtue of their "review" of the Agreement on October 8 and January 26.

premium over market, offered by Pritzker, solely by comparing it with Trans Union's current and historical stock price. (See supra note 5 at 866.)

Indeed, as of September 20, the Board had no other information on which to base a determination of the intrinsic value of Trans Union as a going concern. As of September 20, the Board had made no evaluation of the Company designed to value the entire enterprise, nor had the Board ever previously considered selling the Company or consenting to a buy-out merger. Thus, the adequacy of a premium is indeterminate unless it is assessed in terms of other competent and sound valuation information that reflects the value of the particular business.

Despite the foregoing facts and circumstances, there was no call by the Board, either on September 20 or thereafter, for any valuation study or documentation of the $55 price per share as a measure of the fair value of the Company in a cash-out context. It is undisputed that the major asset of Trans Union was its cash flow. Yet, at no time did the Board call for a valuation study taking into account that highly significant element of the Company's assets.

We do not imply that an outside valuation study is essential to support an informed business judgment; nor do we state that fairness opinions by independent investment bankers are required as a matter of law. Often insiders familiar with the business of a going concern are in a better position than are outsiders to gather relevant information; and under appropriate circumstances, such directors may be fully protected in relying in good faith upon the valuation reports of their management. See 8 *Del.C.* § 141(e). See also *Cheff v. Mathes*, supra.

Here, the record establishes that the Board did not request its Chief Financial Officer, Romans, to make any valuation study or review of the proposal to determine the adequacy of $55 per share for sale of the Company. On the record before us: The Board rested on Romans' elicited response that the $55 figure was within a "fair price range" within the context of a leveraged buy-out. No director sought any further information from Romans. No director asked him why he put $55 at the bottom of his range. No director asked Romans for any details as to his study, the reason why it had been undertaken or its depth. No director asked to see the study; and no director asked Romans whether Trans Union's finance department could do a fairness study within the remaining 36-hour[18] period available under the Pritzker offer.

Had the Board, or any member, made an inquiry of Romans, he presumably would have responded as he testified: that his calculations were rough and preliminary; and, that the study was not designed to determine the fair value of the Company, but rather to assess the feasibility of a leveraged buy-out financed by the Company's projected cash flow, making certain assumptions as to the purchaser's borrowing needs. Romans would have presumably also informed the Board of his view, and the widespread view of Senior Management, that the time of the offer was wrong and the offer inadequate.

---

18 Romans' department study was not made available to the Board until circulation of Trans Union's Supplementary Proxy Statement and the Board's meeting of January 26, 1981, on the eve of the shareholder meeting; and, as has been noted, the study has never been produced for inclusion in the record in this case.

The record also establishes that the Board accepted without scrutiny Van Gorkom's presentation as to the fairness of the $55 price per share for sale of the Company—a subject that the Board had never previously considered. The Board thereby failed to discover that Van Gorkom had suggested the $55 price to Pritzker and, most crucially, that Van Gorkom had arrived at the $55 figure based on calculations designed solely to determine the feasibility of a leveraged buy-out.[19] No questions were raised either as to the tax implications of a cash-out merger or how the price for the one million share option granted Pritzker was calculated.

We do not say that the Board of Directors was not entitled to give some credence to Van Gorkom's representation that $55 was an adequate or fair price. Under § 141(e), the directors were entitled to rely upon their chairman's opinion of value and adequacy, provided that such opinion was reached on a sound basis. Here, the issue is whether the directors informed themselves as to all information that was reasonably available to them. Had they done so, they would have learned of the source and derivation of the $55 price and could not reasonably have relied thereupon in good faith.

None of the directors, Management or outside, were investment bankers or financial analysts. Yet the Board did not consider recessing the meeting until a later hour that day (or requesting an extension of Pritzker's Sunday evening deadline) to give it time to elicit more information as to the sufficiency of the offer, either from inside Management (in particular Romans) or from Trans Union's own investment banker, Salomon Brothers, whose Chicago specialist in merger and acquisitions was known to the Board and familiar with Trans Union's affairs.

Thus, the record compels the conclusion that on September 20 the Board lacked valuation information adequate to reach an informed business judgment as to the fairness of $55 per share for sale of the Company.[20]

(2)

This brings us to the post-September 20 "market test" upon which the defendants ultimately rely to confirm the reasonableness of their September 20 decision to accept the Pritzker proposal. In this connection, the directors present a two-part argument: (a) that by making a "market test" of Pritzker's $55 per share offer a condition of their Septem-

---

19   As of September 20 the directors did not know: that Van Gorkom had arrived at the $55 figure alone, and subjectively, as the figure to be used by Controller Peterson in creating a feasible structure for a leveraged buy-out by a prospective purchaser; that Van Gorkom had not sought advice, information or assistance from either inside or outside Trans Union directors as to the value of the Company as an entity or the fair price per share for 100% of its stock; that Van Gorkom had not consulted with the Company's investment bankers or other financial analysts; that Van Gorkom had not consulted with or confided in any officer or director of the Company except Chelberg; and that Van Gorkom had deliberately chosen to ignore the advice and opinion of the members of his Senior Management group regarding the adequacy of the $55 price.

20   For a far more careful and reasoned approach taken by another board of directors faced with the pressures of a hostile tender offer, see *Pogostin v. Rice*, supra at 623-627.

ber 20 decision to accept his offer, they cannot be found to have acted impulsively or in an uninformed manner on September 20; and (b) that the adequacy of the $17 premium for sale of the Company was conclusively established over the following 90 to 120 days by the most reliable evidence available—the marketplace. Thus, the defendants impliedly contend that the "market test" eliminated the need for the Board to perform any other form of fairness test, either on September 20, or thereafter.

Again, the facts of record do not support the defendants' argument. There is no evidence: (a) that the Merger Agreement was effectively amended to give the Board freedom to put Trans Union up for auction sale to the highest bidder; or (b) that a public auction was in fact permitted to occur. The minutes of the Board meeting make no reference to any of this. Indeed, the record compels the conclusion that the directors had no rational basis for expecting that a market test was attainable, given the terms of the Agreement as executed during the evening of September 20. We rely upon the following facts which are essentially uncontradicted:

The Merger Agreement, specifically identified as that originally presented to the Board on September 20, has never been produced by the defendants, notwithstanding the plaintiffs' several demands for production before as well as during trial. No acceptable explanation or this failure to produce documents has been given to either the Trial Court or this Court. Significantly, neither the defendants nor their counsel have made the affirmative representation that this critical document has been produced. Thus, the Court is deprived of the best evidence on which to judge the merits of the defendants' position as to the care and attention which they gave to the terms of the Agreement on September 20.

Van Gorkom states that the Agreement as submitted incorporated the ingredients for a market test by authorizing Trans Union to receive competing offers over the next 90-day period. However, he concedes that the Agreement barred Trans Union from actively soliciting such offers and from furnishing to interested parties any information about the Company other than that already in the public domain. Whether the original Agreement of September 20 went so far as to authorize Trans Union to receive competitive proposals is arguable. The defendants' unexplained failure to produce and identify the original Merger Agreement permits the logical inference that the instrument would not support their assertions in this regard. *Wilmington Trust Co. v. General Motor. Corp.*, Del.Supr., 51 A.2d 584, 593 (1947); II *Wigmore on Evidence* § 291 (3d ed. 1940). It is a well established principle that the production of weak evidence when strong is, or should have been, available can lead only to the conclusion that the strong would have been adverse. *Interstate Circuit v. United States*, 306 U.S. 208, 226, 59 S.Ct. 467, 474, 83 L.Ed. 610 (1939); *Deberry v. State*, Del.Supr., 457 A.2d 744, 754 (1983). Van Gorkom, conceding that he never read the Agreement, stated that he was relying upon his understanding that, under corporate law, directors always have an inherent right, as well as a fiduciary duty, to accept a better offer notwithstanding an existing contractual commitment by the Board. (See the discussion infra, part III B(3) at p. 55.)

The defendant directors assert that they "insisted" upon including two amendments to the Agreement, thereby permitting a market test: (1) to give Trans Union the right to accept a better offer; and (2) to reserve to Trans Union the right to distribute proprietary information on the Company to alternative bidders. Yet, the defendants concede that they did not seek to amend the Agreement to permit Trans Union to solicit competing offers.

Several of Trans Union's outside directors resolutely maintained that the Agreement as submitted was approved on the understanding that, "if we got a better deal, we had a right to take it." Director Johnson so testified: but he then added, "And if they didn't put that in the agreement, then the management did not carry out the conclusion of the Board. And I just don't know whether they did or not." The only clause in the Agreement as finally executed to which the defendants can point as "keeping the door open" is the following underlined statement found in subparagraph (a) of section 2.03 of the Merger Agreement as executed:

The Board of Directors shall recommend to the stockholders of Trans Union that they approve and adopt the Merger Agreement ("the stockholders' approval") and to use its best efforts to obtain the requisite votes therefor. *GL acknowledges that Trans Union directors may have a competing fiduciary obligation to the shareholders under certain circumstances.*

Clearly, this language on its face cannot be construed as incorporating either of the two "conditions" described above: either the right to accept a better offer or the right to distribute proprietary information to third parties. The logical witness for the defendants to call to confirm their construction of this clause of the Agreement would have been Trans Union's outside attorney, James Brennan. The defendants' failure, without explanation, to call this witness again permits the logical inference that his testimony would not have been helpful to them. The further fact that the directors adjourned, rather than recessed, the meeting without incorporating in the Agreement these important "conditions" further weakens the defendants' position. As has been noted, nothing in the Board's Minutes supports these claims. No reference to either of the so-called "conditions" or of Trans Union's reserved right to test the market appears in any notes of the Board meeting or in the Board Resolution accepting the Pritzker offer or in the Minutes of the meeting itself. That evening, in the midst of a formal party which he hosted for the opening of the Chicago Lyric opera, Van Gorkom executed the Merger Agreement without he or any other member of the Board having read the instruments.

The defendants attempt to downplay the significance of the prohibition against Trans Union's actively soliciting competing offers by arguing that the directors "understood that the entire financial community would know that Trans Union was for sale upon the announcement of the Pritzker offer, and anyone desiring to make a better offer was free to do so." Yet, the press release issued on September 22, with the authorization of the Board, stated that Trans Union had entered into "definitive agreements" with the Pritzkers; and the press release did not even disclose Trans Union's limited right to receive and accept higher offers. Accompanying this press release was a further public announcement that Pritzker had been granted an option to purchase at any time one million shares of Trans Union's capital stock at 75 cents above the then-current price per share.

Thus, notwithstanding what several of the outside directors later claimed to have "thought" occurred at the meeting, the record compels the conclusion that Trans Union's Board had no rational basis to conclude on September 20 or in the days immediately following, that the Board's acceptance of Pritzker's offer was conditioned on (1) a "market test" of the offer; and (2) the Board's right to withdraw from the Pritzker Agreement and accept any higher offer received before the shareholder meeting.

(3)

The directors' unfounded reliance on both the premium and the market test as the basis for accepting the Pritzker proposal undermines the defendants' remaining contention that the Board's collective experience and sophistication was a sufficient basis for finding that it reached its September 20 decision with informed, reasonable deliberation.[21] Compare *Gimbel v. Signal Companies, Inc.*, Del.Ch., 316 A.2d 599 (1974), aff'd per curiam, Del.Supr., 316 A.2d 619 (1974). There, the Court of Chancery preliminary enjoined a board's sale of stock of its wholly-owned subsidiary for an alleged grossly inadequate price. It did so based on a finding that the business judgment rule had been pierced for failure of management to give its board "the opportunity to make a reasonable and reasoned decision." 316 A.2d at 615. The Court there reached this result notwithstanding: the board's sophistication and experience; the company's need of immediate cash; and the board's need to act promptly due to the impact of an energy crisis on the value of the underlying assets being sold—all of its subsidiary's oil and gas interests. The Court found those factors denoting competence to be outweighed by evidence of gross negligence; that management in effect sprang the deal on the board by negotiating the asset sale without informing the board; that the buyer intended to "force a quick decision" by the board; that the board meeting was called on only one-and-a-half days' notice; that its outside directors were not notified of the meeting's purpose; that during a meeting spanning "a couple of hours" a sale of assets worth $480 million was approved; and that the Board failed to obtain a *current* appraisal of its oil and gas interests. The analogy of *Signal* to the case at bar is significant.

(4)

Part of the defense is based on a claim that the directors relied on legal advice rendered at the September 20 meeting by James Brennan, Esquire, who was present at Van Gorkom's request. Unfortunately, Brennan did not appear and testify at trial even though his firm participated in the defense of this action. There is no contemporaneous evidence of the advice given by Brennan on September 20, only the later deposition and trial testimony of certain directors as to their recollections or understanding of what was said at the meeting. Since counsel did not testify, and the advice attributed to Brennan is hearsay received by the Trial Court over the plaintiffs' objections, we consider it only in the context of the directors' present claims. In fairness to counsel, we make no findings

---

21 Trans Union's five "inside" directors had backgrounds in law and accounting, 116 years of collective employment by the Company and 68 years of combined experience on its Board. Trans Union's five "outside" directors included four chief executives of major corporations and an economist who was a former dean of a major school of business and chancellor of a university. The "outside" directors had 78 years of combined experience as chief executive officers of major corporations and 50 years of cumulative experience as directors of Trans Union. Thus, defendants argue that the Board was eminently qualified to reach an informed judgment on the proposed "sale" of Trans Union notwithstanding their lack of any advance notice of the proposal, the shortness of their deliberation, and their determination not to consult with their investment banker or to obtain a fairness opinion.

that the advice attributed to him was in fact given. We focus solely on the efficacy of the defendants' claims, made months and years later, in an effort to extricate themselves from liability.

Several defendants testified that Brennan advised them that Delaware law did not require a fairness opinion or an outside valuation of the Company before the Board could act on the Pritzker proposal. If given, the advice was correct. However, that did not end the matter. Unless the directors had before them adequate information regarding the intrinsic value of the Company, upon which a proper exercise of business judgment could be made, mere advice of this type is meaningless; and, given this record of the defendants' failures, it constitutes no defense here.[22]

• • •

We conclude that Trans Union's Board was grossly negligent in that it failed to act with informed reasonable deliberation in agreeing to the Pritzker merger proposal on September 20; and we further conclude that the Trial Court erred as a matter of law in failing to address that question before determining whether the directors' later conduct was sufficient to cure its initial error.

A second claim is that counsel advised the Board it would be subject to lawsuits if it rejected the $55 per share offer. It is, of course, a fact of corporate life that today when faced with difficult or sensitive issues, directors often are subject to suit, irrespective of the decisions they make. However, counsel's mere acknowledgement of this circumstance cannot be rationally translated into a justification for a board permitting itself to be stampeded into a patently unadvised act. While suit might result from the rejection of a merger or tender offer, Delaware law makes clear that a board acting within the ambit of the business judgment rule faces no ultimate liability. *Pogostin v. Rice*, supra. Thus, we cannot conclude that the mere threat of litigation, acknowledged by counsel, constitutes either legal advice or any valid basis upon which to pursue an uninformed course.

Since we conclude that Brennan's purported advice is of no consequence to the defense of this case, it is unnecessary for us to invoke the adverse inferences which may be attributable to one failing to appear at trial and testify.

– B –

We now examine the Board's post-September 20 conduct for the purpose of determining first, whether it was informed and not grossly negligent; and second, if informed, whether it was sufficient to legally rectify and cure the Board's derelictions of September 20.[23]

---

22   Nonetheless, we are satisfied that in an appropriate factual context a proper exercise of business judgment may include, as one of its aspects, reasonable reliance upon the advice of counsel. This is wholly outside the statutory protections of 8 *Del.C.* § 141(e) involving reliance upon reports of officers, certain experts and books and records of the company.

23   As will be seen, we do not reach the second question.

(1)

First, as to the Board meeting of October 8: Its purpose arose in the aftermath of the September 20 meeting: (1) the September 22 press release announcing that Trans Union "had entered into definitive agreements to merge with an affiliate of Marmon Group, Inc."; and (2) Senior Management's ensuing revolt.

Trans Union's press release stated:

FOR IMMEDIATE RELEASE:

CHICAGO, IL—Trans Union Corporation announced today that it had entered into definitive agreements to merge with an affiliate of The Marmon Group, Inc. in a transaction whereby Trans Union stockholders would receive $55 per share in cash for each Trans Union share held. The Marmon Group, Inc. is controlled by the Pritzker family of Chicago.

The merger is subject to approval by the stockholders of Trans Union at a special meeting expected to be held sometime during December or early January.

Until October 10, 1980, the purchaser has the right to terminate the merger if financing that is satisfactory to the purchaser has not been obtained, but after that date there is no such right.

In a related transaction, Trans Union has agreed to sell to a designee of the purchaser one million newly-issued shares of Trans Union common stock at a cash price of $38 per share. Such shares will be issued only if the merger financing has been committed for no later than October 10, 1980, or if the purchaser elects to waive the merger financing condition. In addition, the New York Stock Exchange will be asked to approve the listing of the new shares pursuant to a listing application which Trans Union intends to file shortly.

Completing of the transaction is also subject to the preparation of a definitive proxy statement and making various filings and obtaining the approvals or consents of government agencies.

The press release made no reference to provisions allegedly reserving to the Board the rights to perform a "market test" and to withdraw from the Pritzker Agreement if Trans Union received a better offer before the shareholder meeting. The defendants also concede that Trans Union never made a subsequent public announcement stating that it had in fact reserved the right to accept alternative offers, the Agreement notwithstanding.

The public announcement of the Pritzker merger resulted in an "en masse" revolt of Trans Union's Senior Management. The head of Trans Union's tank car operations (its most profitable division) informed Van Gorkom that unless the merger were called off, fifteen key personnel would resign.

Instead of reconvening the Board, Van Gorkom again privately met with Pritzker, informed him of the developments, and sought his advice. Pritzker then made the following suggestions for overcoming Management's dissatisfaction: (1) that the Agreement be amended to permit Trans Union to solicit, as well as receive, higher offers; and (2) that the shareholder meeting be postponed from early January to February 10, 1981. In return, Pritzker asked Van Gorkom to obtain a commitment from Senior Management to remain at Trans Union for at least six months after the merger was consummated.

Van Gorkom then advised Senior Management that the Agreement would be amended to give Trans Union the right to solicit competing offers through January, 1981, if they would agree to remain with Trans Union. Senior Management was temporarily mollified; and Van Gorkom then called a special meeting of Trans Union's Board for October 8.

Thus, the primary purpose of the October 8 Board meeting was to amend the Merger Agreement, in a manner agreeable to Pritzker, to permit Trans Union to conduct a "market test."[24] Van Gorkom understood that the proposed amendments were intended to give the Company an unfettered "right to openly solicit offers down through January 31." Van Gorkom presumably so represented the amendments to Trans Union's Board members on October 8. In a brief session, the directors approved Van Gorkom's oral presentation of the substance of the proposed amendments, the terms of which were not reduced to writing until October 10. But rather than waiting to review the amendments, the Board again approved them sight unseen and adjourned, giving Van Gorkom authority to execute the papers when he received them.[25]

Thus, the Court of Chancery's finding that the October 8 Board meeting was convened to *reconsider* the Pritzker "proposal" is clearly erroneous. Further, the consequence of the Board's faulty conduct on October 8, in approving amendments to the Agreement which had not even been drafted, will become apparent when the actual amendments to the Agreement are thereafter examined.

The next day, October 9, and before the Agreement was amended, Pritzker moved swiftly to off-set the proposed market test amendment. First, Pritzker informed Trans Union that he had completed arrangements for financing its acquisition and that the parties were thereby mutually bound to a firm purchase and sale arrangement. Second, Pritzker announced the exercise of his option to purchase one million shares of Trans Union's treasure stock at $38 per share—75 cents above the current market price. Trans Union's Management responded the same day by issuing a press release announcing: (1) that all financing arrangements for Pritzker's acquisition of Trans Union had been completed; and (2) Pritzker's purchase of one million shares of Trans Union's treasury stock at $38 per share.

The next day, October 10, Pritzker delivered to Trans Union the proposed amendments to the September 20 Merger Agreement. Van Gorkom promptly proceeded to

---

24   As previously noted, the Board mistakenly thought that it had amended the September 20 draft agreement to include a market test.

 A secondary purpose of the October 8 meeting was to obtain the Board's approval for Trans Union to employ its investment advisor, Salomon Brothers, for the limited purpose of assisting Management in the solicitation of other offers. Neither Management nor the Board then or thereafter requested Salomon Brothers to submit its opinion as to the fairness of Pritzker's $55 cash-out merger proposal or to value Trans Union as an entity.

 There is no evidence of record that the October 8 meeting had any other purpose; and we also note that the Minutes of the October 8 Board meeting, including any notice of the meeting, are not part of the voluminous records of this case.

25   We do not suggest that a board must read *in haec verba* every contract or legal document which it approves, but if it is to successfully absolve itself from charges of the type made here, there must be some credible contemporary evidence demonstrating that the directors knew what they were doing, and ensured that their purported action was given effect. That is the consistent failure which cast this Board upon its unredeemable course.

countersign all the instruments on behalf of Trans Union without reviewing the instruments to determine if they were consistent with the authority previously granted him by the Board. The amending documents were apparently not approved by Trans Union's Board until a much later date, December 2. The record does not affirmatively establish that Trans Union's directors ever read the October 10 amendments.[26]

The October 10 amendments to the Merger Agreement did authorize Trans Union to solicit competing offers, but the amendments had more far-reaching effects. The most significant change was in the definition of the third-party "offer" available to Trans Union as a possible basis for withdrawal from its Merger Agreement with Pritzker. Under the October 10 amendments, a better *offer* was no longer sufficient to permit Trans Union's withdrawal. Trans Union was now permitted to terminate the Pritzker Agreement and abandon the merger only if, prior to February 10, 1981, Trans Union had either consummated a merger (or sale of assets) with a third party or had entered into a "definitive" merger agreement more favorable than Pritzker's and for a greater consideration—subject only to stockholder approval. Further, the "extension" of the market test period to February 10, 1981 was circumscribed by other amendments which required Trans Union to file its preliminary proxy statement on the Pritzker merger proposal by December 5, 1980 and use its best efforts to mail the statement to its shareholders by January 5, 1981. Thus, the market test period was effectively reduced, not extended. *See* infra note 29 at 886.

In our view, the record compels the conclusion that the directors' conduct on October 8 exhibited the same deficiencies as did their conduct on September 20. The Board permitted its Merger Agreement with Pritzker to be amended in a manner it had neither authorized nor intended. The Court of Chancery, in its decision, overlooked the significance of the October 8-10 events and their relevance to the sufficiency of the directors' conduct. The Trial Court's letter opinion ignores: the October 10 amendments; the manner of their adoption; the effect of the October 9 press release and the October 10 amendments on the feasibility of a market test; and the ultimate question as to the reasonableness of the directors' reliance on a market test in recommending that the shareholders approve the Pritzker merger.

We conclude that the Board acted in a grossly negligent manner on October 8; and that Van Gorkom's representations on which the Board based its actions do not constitute "reports" under § 141(e) on which the directors could reasonably have relied. Further, the amended Merger Agreement imposed on Trans Union's acceptance of a third party offer conditions more onerous than those imposed on Trans Union's acceptance of Pritzker's offer on September 20. After October 10, Trans Union could accept from a third party a better offer only if it were incorporated in a definitive agreement between the parties, and not conditioned on financing or on any other contingency.

The October 9 press release, coupled with the October 10 amendments, had the clear effect of locking Trans Union's Board into the Pritzker Agreement. Pritzker had

---

26 There is no evidence of record that Trans Union's directors ever raised any objections, procedural or substantive, to the October 10 amendments or that any of them, including Van Gorkom, understood the opposite result of their intended effect—until it was too late.

thereby foreclosed Trans Union's Board from negotiating any better "definitive" agreement over the remaining eight weeks before Trans Union was required to clear the Proxy Statement submitting the Pritzker proposal to its shareholders.

(2)

Next, as to the "curative" effects of the Board's post-September 20 conduct, we review in more detail the reaction of Van Gorkom to the KKR proposal and the results of the Board-sponsored "market test."

The KKR proposal was the first and only offer received subsequent to the Pritzker Merger Agreement. The offer resulted primarily from the efforts of Romans and other senior officers to propose an alternative to Pritzker's acquisition of Trans Union. In late September, Romans' group contacted KKR about the possibility of a leveraged buy-out by all members of Management, except Van Gorkom. By early October, Henry R. Kravis of KKR gave Romans written notice of KKR's "interest in making an offer to purchase 100%" of Trans Union's common stock.

Thereafter, and until early December, Romans' group worked with KKR to develop a proposal. It did so with Van Gorkom's knowledge and apparently grudging consent. On December 2, Kravis and Romans hand-delivered to Van Gorkom a formal letter-offer to purchase all of Trans Union's assets and to assume all of its liabilities for an aggregate cash consideration equivalent to $60 per share. The offer was contingent upon completing equity and bank financing of $650 million, which Kravis represented as 80% complete. The KKR letter made reference to discussions with major banks regarding the loan portion of the buy-out cost and stated that KKR was "confident that commitments for the bank financing ... can be obtained within two or three weeks." The purchasing group was to include certain named key members of Trans Union's Senior Management, excluding Van Gorkom, and a major Canadian company. Kravis stated that they were willing to enter into a "definitive agreement" under terms and conditions "substantially the same" as those contained in Trans Union's agreement with Pritzker. The offer was addressed to Trans Union's Board of Directors and a meeting with the Board, scheduled for that afternoon, was requested.

Van Gorkom's reaction to the KKR proposal was completely negative; he did not view the offer as being firm because of its financing condition. It was pointed out, to no avail, that Pritzker's offer had not only been similarly conditioned, but accepted on an expedited basis. Van Gorkom refused Kravis' request that Trans Union issue a press release announcing KKR's offer, on the ground that it might "chill" any other offer.[27] Romans and Kravis left with the understanding that their proposal would be presented to Trans Union's Board that afternoon.

Within a matter of hours and shortly before the scheduled Board meeting, Kravis withdrew his letter-offer. He gave as his reason a sudden decision by the Chief Officer of Trans Union's rail car leasing operation to withdraw from the KKR purchasing group.

---

27   This was inconsistent with Van Gorkom's espousal of the September 22 press release following Trans Union's acceptance of Pritzker's proposal. Van Gorkom had then justified a press release as encouraging rather than chilling later offers.

Van Gorkom had spoken to that officer about his participation in the KKR proposal immediately after his meeting with Romans and Kravis. However, Van Gorkom denied any responsibility for the officer's change of mind.

At the Board meeting later that afternoon, Van Gorkom did not inform the directors of the KKR proposal because he considered it "dead." Van Gorkom did not contact KKR again until January 20, when faced with the realities of this lawsuit, he then attempted to reopen negotiations. KKR declined due to the imminence of the February 10 stockholder meeting.

GE Credit Corporation's interest in Trans Union did not develop until November; and it made no written proposal until mid-January. Even then, its proposal was not in the form of an offer. Had there been time to do so, GE Credit was prepared to offer between $2 and $5 per share above the $55 per share price which Pritzker offered. But GE Credit needed an additional 60 to 90 days; and it was unwilling to make a formal offer without a concession from Pritzker extending the February 10 "deadline" for Trans Union's stockholders meeting. As previously stated, Pritzker refused to grant such extension; and on January 21, GE Credit terminated further negotiations with Trans Union. Its stated reasons, among others, were its "unwillingness to become involved in a bidding contest with Pritzker in the absence of the willingness of [the Pritzker interests] to terminate the proposed $55 cash merger."

· · ·

In the absence of any explicit finding by the Trial Court as to the reasonableness of Trans Union's directors' reliance on a market test and its feasibility, we may make our own findings based on the record. Our review of the record compels a finding that confirmation of the appropriateness of the Pritzker offer by an unfettered or free market test was virtually meaningless in the face of the terms and time limitations of Trans Union's Merger Agreement with Pritzker as amended October 10, 1980.

(3)

Finally, we turn to the Board's meeting of January 26, 1981. The defendant directors rely upon the action there taken to refute the contention that they did not reach an informed business judgment in approving the Pritzker merger. The defendants contend that the Trial Court correctly concluded that Trans Union's directors were, in effect, as "free to turn down the Pritzker proposal" on January 26, as they were on September 20.

Applying the appropriate standard of review set forth in *Levitt v. Bouvier*, supra, we conclude that the Trial Court's finding in this regard is neither supported by the record nor the product of an orderly and logical deductive process. Without disagreeing with the principle that a business decision by an originally uninformed board of directors may, under appropriate circumstances, be timely cured so as to become informed and deliberate, *Muschel v. Western Union Corporation*, Del.Ch., 310 A.2d 904 (1973),[28] we find that the record does not permit the defendants to invoke that principle in this case.

---

28 The defendants concede that *Muschel* is only illustrative of the proposition that a board may reconsider a prior decision and that it is otherwise factually distinguishable from this case.

The Board's January 26 meeting was the first meeting following the filing of the plaintiffs' suit in mid-December and the last meeting before the previously-noticed shareholder meeting of February 10.[29] All ten members of the Board and three outside attorneys attended the meeting. At that meeting the following facts, among other aspects of the Merger Agreement, were discussed:

(a) The fact that prior to September 20, 1980, no Board member or member of Senior Management, except Chelberg and Peterson, knew that Van Gorkom had discussed a possible merger with Pritzker;

(b) The fact that the price of $55 per share had been suggested initially to Pritzker by Van Gorkom;

(c) The fact that the Board had not sought an independent fairness opinion;

(d) The fact that, at the September 20 Senior Management meeting, Romans and several members of Senior Management indicated both concern that the $55 per share price was inadequate and a belief that a higher price should and could be obtained;

(e) The fact that Romans had advised the Board at its meeting on September 20 that he and his department had prepared a study which indicated that the Company had a value in the range of $55 to $65 per share, and that he could not advise the Board that the $55 per share offer made by Pritzker was unfair.

The defendants characterize the Board's Minutes of the January 26 meeting as a "review" of the "entire sequence of events" from Van Gorkom's initiation of the negotiations on September 13 forward.[30] The defendants also rely on the testimony of several of

---

29   This was the meeting which, under the terms of the September 20 Agreement with Pritzker, was scheduled to be held January 10 and was later postponed to February 10 under the October 8-10 amendments. We refer to the document titled "Amendment to Supplemental Agreement" executed by the parties "as of" October 10, 1980. Under new Section 2.03(a) of Article A VI of the "Supplemental Agreement," the parties agreed, in part, as follows:

> "The solicitation of such offers or proposals [i.e., 'other offers that Trans Union might accept in lieu of the Merger Agreement'] by TU ... shall not be deemed to constitute a breach of this Supplemental Agreement or the Merger Agreement provided that ... [Trans Union] shall not (1) delay promptly seeking all consents and approvals required hereunder ... [and] shall be deemed [in compliance] if it files its Preliminary Proxy Statement by December 5, 1980, uses its best efforts to mail its Proxy Statement by January 5, 1981 and holds a special meeting of its Stockholders on or prior to February 10, 1981 ...

> • • •

> It is the present intention of the Board of Directors of TU to recommend the approval of the Merger Agreement to the Stockholders, unless another offer or proposal is made which in their opinion is more favorable to the Stockholders than the Merger Agreement."

30   With regard to the Pritzker merger, the recently filed shareholders' suit to enjoin it, and relevant portions of the impending stockholder meeting of February 10, we set forth the Minutes in their entirety:

> The Board then reviewed the necessity of issuing a Supplement to the Proxy Statement mailed to stockholders on January 21, 1981, for the special meeting of stockholders scheduled to be held on

(The footnote is continued on the next page.)

the Board members at trial as confirming the Minutes.[31] On the basis of this evidence, the defendants argue that whatever information the Board lacked to make a deliberate and informed judgment on September 20, or on October 8, was fully divulged to the entire Board on January 26. Hence, the argument goes, the Board's vote on January 26

---

30   Continued ...

February 10, 1981, to vote on the proposed $55 cash merger with a subsidiary of GE Corporation. Among other things, the Board noted that subsequent to the printing of the Proxy Statement mailed to stockholders on January 21, 1981, General Electric Company had indicated that it would not be making an offer to acquire the Company. In addition, certain facts had been adduced in connection with pretrial discovery taken in connection with the lawsuit filed by Alden Smith in Delaware Chancery Court. After further discussion and review of a printer's proof copy of a proposed Supplement to the Proxy Statement which had been distributed to Directors the preceding day, upon motion duly made and seconded, the following resolution was unanimously adopted, each Director having been individually polled with respect thereto:

RESOLVED, that the Secretary of the Company be and he hereby is authorized and directed to mail to the stockholders a Supplement to Proxy Statement, substantially in the form of the proposed Supplement to Proxy Statement submitted to the Board at this meeting, with such changes therein and modifications thereof as he shall, with the advice and assistance of counsel, approve as being necessary, desirable, or appropriate.

The Board then reviewed and discussed at great length the entire sequence of events pertaining to the proposed $55 cash merger with a subsidiary of GE Corporation, beginning with the first discussion on September 13, 1980, between the Chairman and Mr. Jay Pritzker relative to a possible merger. Each of the Directors was involved in this discussion as well as counsel who had earlier joined the meeting. Following this review and discussion, such counsel advised the Directors that in light of their discussions, they could (a) continue to recommend to the stockholders that the latter vote in favour of the proposed merger, (b) recommend that the stockholders vote against the merger, or (c) take no position with respect to recommending the proposed merger and simply leave the decision to stockholders. After further discussion, it was moved, seconded, and unanimously voted that the Board of Directors continue to recommend that the stockholders vote in favour of the proposed merger, each Director being individually polled with respect to his vote.

31   In particular, the defendants rely on the testimony of director Johnson on direct examination:

Q. Was there a regular meeting of the board of Trans Union on January 26, 1981?

A. Yes.

Q. And what was discussed at that meeting?

A. Everything relevant to this transaction.

You see, since the proxy statement of the 19th had been mailed, see, General Electric had advised that they weren't going to make a bid. It was concluded to suggest that the shareholders be advised of that, and that required a supplemental proxy statement, and that required authorization of the board, and that led to a total review from beginning to end of every aspect of the whole transaction and all relevant developments.

(The footnote is continued on the next page.)

to again "approve" the Pritzker merger must be found to have been an informed and deliberate judgment.

On the basis of this evidence, the defendants assert: (1) that the Trial Court was legally correct in widening the time frame for determining whether the defendants' approval of the Pritzker merger represented an informed business judgment to include the entire four-month period during which the Board considered the matter from September 20 through January 26; and (2) that, given this extensive evidence of the Board's further review and deliberations on January 26, this Court must affirm the Trial Court's conclusion that the Board's action was not reckless or improvident.

We cannot agree. We find the Trial Court to have erred, both as a matter of fact and as a matter of law, in relying on the action on January 26 to bring the defendants' conduct within the protection of the business judgment rule.

Johnson's testimony and the Board Minutes of January 26 are remarkably consistent. Both clearly indicate recognition that the question of the alternative courses of action, available to the Board on January 26 with respect to the Pritzker merger, was a legal question, presenting to the Board (*after* its review of the full record developed through pre-trial discovery) *three* options: (1) to "continue to recommend" the Pritzker merger; (2) to "recommend that the stockholders vote against" the Pritzker merger; or (3) to take a noncommittal position on the merger and "simply leave the decision to [the] shareholders."

We must conclude from the foregoing that the Board was mistaken as a matter of law regarding its available courses of action on January 26, 1981. Options (2) and (3) were not viable or legally available to the Board under 8 *Del. C.* § 251(b). The Board could not remain committed to the Pritzker merger and yet recommend that its stockholders vote it down; nor could it take a neutral position and delegate to the stockholders the unadvised decision as to whether to accept or reject the merger. Under § 251(b), the Board had but two options: (1) to proceed with the merger and the stockholder meeting, with the Board's recommendation of approval; *or* (2) to rescind its agreement with Pritzker, withdraw its approval of the merger, and notify its stockholders that the proposed shareholder meeting was cancelled. There is no evidence that the Board gave any consideration to these, its only legally viable alternative courses of action.

---

31   Continued ...

      Since that was occurring and a supplemental statement was going to the shareholders, it also was obvious to me that there should be a review of the board's position again in the light of the whole record. And we went back from the beginning. Everything was examined and reviewed. Counsel were present. And the board was advised that we could recommend the Pritzker deal, we could submit it to the shareholders with no recommendation, or we could recommend against it.

      The board voted to issue the supplemental statement to the shareholders. It voted unanimously—and this time we had a unanimous board, where one man was missing before—to recommend the Pritzker deal. Indeed, at that point there was no other deal. And, in truth, there never had been any other deal. And that's what transpired: a total review of the GE situation, KKR and everything else that was relevant.

But the second course of action would have clearly involved a substantial risk—that the Board would be faced with suit by Pritzker for breach of contract based on its September 20 agreement as amended October 10. As previously noted, under the terms of the October 10 amendment, the Board's only ground for release from its agreement with Pritzker was its entry into a more favorable definitive agreement to sell the Company to a third party. Thus, in reality, the Board was not "free to turn down the Pritzker proposal" as the Trial Court found. Indeed, short of negotiating a better agreement with a third party, the Board's only basis for release from the Pritzker Agreement without liability would have been to establish fundamental wrongdoing by Pritzker. Clearly, the Board was not "free" to withdraw from its agreement with Pritzker on January 26 by simply relying on its self-induced failure to have reached an informed business judgment at the time of its original agreement.

See *Wilmington Trust Company v. Coulter*, Del.Supr., 200 A.2d 441, 453 (1964), aff'g *Pennsylvania Company v. Wilmington Trust Company*, Del.Ch., 186 A.2d 751 (1962).

Therefore, the Trial Court's conclusion that the Board reached an informed business judgment on January 26 in determining whether to turn down the Pritzker "proposal" on that day cannot be sustained. The Court's conclusion is not supported by the record; it is contrary to the provisions of § 251(b) and basic principles of contract law; and it is not the product of a logical and deductive reasoning process.

• • •

Upon the basis of the foregoing, we hold that the defendants' post-September conduct did not cure the deficiencies of their September 20 conduct; and that, accordingly, the Trial Court erred in according to the defendants the benefits of the business judgment rule.

• • •

REVERSED and REMANDED for proceedings consistent herewith.

McNEILLY, Justice, dissenting: The majority opinion reads like an advocate's closing address to a hostile jury. And I say that not lightly. Throughout the opinion great emphasis is directed only to the negative, with nothing more than lip service granted the positive aspects of this case. In my opinion Chancellor Marvel (retired) should have been affirmed. The Chancellor's opinion was the product of well reasoned conclusions, based upon a sound deductive process, clearly supported by the evidence and entitled to deference in this appeal. Because of my diametrical opposition to all evidentiary conclusions of the majority, I respectfully dissent.

It would serve no useful purpose, particularly at this late date, for me to dissent at great length. I restrain myself from doing so, but feel compelled to at least point out what I consider to be the most glaring deficiencies in the majority opinion. The majority has spoken and has effectively said that Trans Union's Directors have been the victims of a "fast shuffle" by Van Gorkom and Pritzker. That is the beginning of the majority's comedy of errors. The first and most important error made is the majority's assessment of the directors' knowledge of the affairs of Trans Union and their combined ability to act in this situation under the protection of the business judgment rule.

Trans Union's Board of Directors consisted of ten men, five of whom were "inside" directors and five of whom were "outside" directors. The "inside" directors were Van Gorkom, Chelberg, Bonser, William B. Browder, Senior Vice-President-Law, and Thomas P. O'Boyle, Senior Vice-President-Administration. At the time the merger was proposed the inside five directors had collectively been employed by the Company for 116 years and had 68 years of combined experience as directors. The "outside" directors were A. W. Wallis, William B. Johnson, Joseph B. Lanterman, Graham J. Morgan and Robert W. Reneker. With the exception of Wallis, these were all chief executive officers of Chicago based corporations that were at least as large as Trans Union. The five "outside" directors had 78 years of combined experience as chief executive officers, and 53 years cumulative service as Trans Union directors.

The inside directors wear their badge of expertise in the corporate affairs of Trans Union on their sleeves. But what about the outsiders? Dr. Wallis is or was an economist and math statistician, a professor of economics at Yale University, dean of the graduate school of business at the University of Chicago, and Chancellor of the University of Rochester. Dr. Wallis had been on the Board of Trans Union since 1962. He also was on the Board of Bausch & Lomb, Kodak, Metropolitan Life Insurance Company, Standard Oil and others.

William B. Johnson is a University of Pennsylvania law graduate, President of Railway Express until 1966, Chairman and Chief Executive of I.C. Industries Holding Company, and member of Trans Union's Board since 1968.

Joseph Lanterman, a Certified Public Accountant, is or was President and Chief Executive of American Steel, on the Board of International Harvester, Peoples Energy, Illinois Bell Telephone, Harris Bank and Trust Company, Kemper Insurance Company and a director of Trans Union for four years.

Graham Morgan is a chemist, was Chairman and Chief Executive Officer of U.S. Gypsum, and in the 17 and 18 years prior to the Trans Union transaction had been involved in 31 or 32 corporate takeovers.

Robert Reneker attended University of Chicago and Harvard Business Schools. He was President and Chief Executive of Swift and Company, director of Trans Union since 1971, and member of the Boards of seven other corporations including U.S. Gypsum and the Chicago Tribune.

Directors of this caliber are not ordinarily taken in by a "fast shuffle." I submit they were not taken into this multi-million dollar corporate transaction without being fully informed and aware of the state of the art as it pertained to the entire corporate panoroma of Trans Union. True, even directors such as these, with their business acumen, interest and expertise, can go astray. I do not believe that to be the case here. These men knew Trans Union like the back of their hands and were more than well qualified to make on the spot informed business judgments concerning the affairs of Trans Union including a 100% sale of the corporation. Lest we forget, the corporate world of then and now operates on what is so aptly referred to as "the fast track." These men were at the time an integral part of that world, all professional business men, not intellectual figureheads.

The majority of this Court holds that the Board's decision, reached on September 20, 1980, to approve the merger was not the product of an *informed* business judgment, that the Board's subsequent efforts to amend the Merger Agreement and take other curative action were *legally and factually* ineffectual, and that the Board did *not deal with complete candor* with the stockholders by failing to disclose all material facts, which they knew or should have known, before securing the stockholders' approval of the merger. I disagree.

At the time of the September 20, 1980 meeting the Board was acutely aware of Trans Union and its prospects. The problems created by accumulated investment tax credits and accelerated depreciation were discussed repeatedly at Board meetings, and all of the directors understood the problem thoroughly. Moreover, at the July, 1980 Board meeting the directors had reviewed Trans Union's newly prepared five-year forecast, and at the August, 1980 meeting Van Gorkom presented the results of a comprehensive study of Trans Union made by The Boston Consulting Group. This study was prepared over an 18 month period and consisted of a detailed analysis of all Trans Union subsidiaries, including competitiveness, profitability, cash throwoff, cash consumption, technical competence and future prospects for contribution to Trans Union's combined net income.

At the September 20 meeting Van Gorkom reviewed all aspects of the proposed transaction and repeated the explanation of the Pritzker offer he had earlier given to senior management. Having heard Van Gorkom's explanation of the Pritzker's offer, and Brennan's explanation of the merger documents the directors discussed the matter. Out of this discussion arose an insistence on the part of the directors that two modifications to the offer be made. First, they required that any potential competing bidder be given access to the same information concerning Trans Union that had been provided to the Pritzkers. Second, the merger documents were to be modified to reflect the fact that the directors could accept a better offer and would not be required to recommend the Pritzker offer if a better offer was made. The following language was inserted into the agreement:

"Within 30 days after the execution of this Agreement, TU shall call a meeting of its stockholders (the 'Stockholder's Meeting') for the purpose of approving and adopting the Merger Agreement. The Board of Directors shall recommend to the stockholders of TU that they approve and adopt the Merger Agreement (the 'Stockholders' Approval') and shall use its best efforts to obtain the requisite vote therefor; *provided, however, that GL and NTC acknowledge that the Board of Directors of TU may have a competing fiduciary obligation to the Stockholders under certain circumstances.*" (Emphasis added)

While the language is not artfully drawn, the evidence is clear that the intention underlying that language was to make specific the right that the directors assumed they had, that is, to accept any offer that they thought was better, and not to recommend the Pritzker offer in the face of a better one. At the conclusion of the meeting, the proposed merger was approved.

At a subsequent meeting on October 8, 1981 the directors, with the consent of the Pritzkers, amended the Merger Agreement so as to establish the right of Trans Union to *solicit* as well as to receive higher bids, although the Pritzkers insisted that their merger proposal be presented to the stockholders at the same time that the proposal of any third party was presented. A second amendment, which became effective on October 10, 1981, further provided that Trans Union might unilaterally terminate the proposed merger with the Pritzker company in the event that prior to February 10, 1981 there existed a definitive agreement with a third party for a merger, consolidation, sale of assets, or purchase or exchange of Trans Union stock which was more favorable for the stockholders of Trans Union than the Pritzker offer and which was conditioned upon receipt of stockholder approval and the absence of an injunction against its consummation.

Following the October 8 board meeting of Trans Union, the investment banking firm of Salomon Brothers was retained by the corporation to search for better offers than that of the Pritzkers, Salomon Brothers being charged with the responsibility of doing "whatever possible to see if there is a superior bid in the marketplace over a bid that is on the table for Trans Union." In undertaking such project, it was agreed that Salomon Brothers would be paid the amount of $500,000 to cover its expenses as well as a fee equal to ⅜ths of 1% of the aggregate fair market value of the consideration to be received by the company in the case of a merger or the like, which meant that in the event Salomon Brothers should find a buyer willing to pay a price of $56.00 a share instead of $55.00, such firm would receive a fee of roughly $2,650,000 plus disbursements.

As the first step in proceeding to carry out its commitment, Salomon Brothers had a brochure prepared, which set forth Trans Union's financial history, described the company's business in detail and set forth Trans Union's operating and financial projections. Salomon Brothers also prepared a list of over 150 companies which it believed might be suitable merger partners, and while four of such companies, namely, General Electric, Borg-Warner, Bendix, and Genstar, Ltd. showed some interest in such a merger, none made a firm proposal to Trans Union and only General Electric showed a sustained interest.[1] As matters transpired, no firm offer which bettered the Pritzker offer of $55 per share was ever made.

On January 21, 1981 a proxy statement was sent to the shareholders of Trans Union advising them of a February 10, 1981 meeting in which the merger would be voted. on January 26, 1981 the directors held their regular meeting. At this meeting the Board discussed the instant merger as well as all events, including this litigation, surrounding it. At the conclusion of the meeting the Board unanimously voted to recommend to the

---

[1] Shortly after the announcement of the proposed merger in September senior members of Trans Union's management got in touch with KKR to discuss their possible participation in a leverage buyout scheme. on December 2, 1980 KKR through Henry Kravis actually made a bid of $60.00 per share for Trans Union stock on December 2, 1980 but the offer was withdrawn three hours after it was made because of complications arising out of negotiations with the Reichman family, extremely wealthy Canadians and a change of attitude toward the leveraged buyout scheme, by Jack Kruzenga, the member of senior management of Trans Union who most likely would have been President and Chief Operating Officer of the new company. Kruzenga was the President and Chief Operating Officer of the seven subsidiaries of Trans Union which constituted the backbone of Trans Union as shown through exhaustive studies and analysis of Trans Union's intrinsic value on the market place by the respected investment banking firm of Morgan Stanley. It is interesting to note that at no time during the market test period did any of the 150 corporations contacted by Salomon Brothers complain of the time frame or availability of corporate records in order to make an independent judgment of market value of 100% of Trans Union.

stockholders that they approve the merger. Additionally, the directors reviewed and approved a Supplemental Proxy Statement which, among other things, advised the stockholders of what had occurred at the instant meeting and of the fact that General Electric had decided not to make an offer. On February 10, 1981 the stockholders of Trans Union met pursuant to notice and voted overwhelmingly in favor of the Pritzker merger, 89% of the votes cast being in favor of it.

I have no quarrel with the majority's analysis of the business judgment rule. It is the application of that rule to these facts which is wrong. An overview of the entire record, rather than the limited view of bits and pieces which the majority has exploded like popcorn, convinces me that the directors made an informed business judgment which was buttressed by their test of the market.

At the time of the September 20 meeting the 10 members of Trans Union's Board of Directors were highly qualified and well informed about the affairs and prospects of Trans Union. These directors were acutely aware of the historical problems facing Trans Union which were caused by the tax laws. They had discussed these problems *ad nauseam*. In fact, within two months of the September 20 meeting the board had reviewed and discussed an outside study of the company done by The Boston Consulting Group and an internal five year forecast prepared by management. At the September 20 meeting Van Gorkom presented the Pritzker offer, and the board then heard from James Brennan, the company's counsel in this matter, who discussed the legal documents. Following this, the Board directed that certain changes be made in the merger documents. These changes made it clear that the Board was free to accept a better offer than Pritzker's if one was made. The above facts reveal that the Board did not act in a grossly negligent manner in informing themselves of the relevant and available facts before passing on the merger. To the contrary, this record reveals that the directors acted with the utmost care in informing themselves of the relevant and available facts before passing on the merger.

• • •

The dissenting opinion of CHRISTIE J. is omitted.

NOTES

On the assumption that the facts were as stated in the majority opinion, consider what steps the board should have taken to avoid liability. How close would this come to the due diligence review contemplated in *Escott v. BarChris*? If many of the procedures suggested by the majority seem reasonable, do you think that such standards should be prescribed by a court, with liability for breach?

According to Judge McNeilly, "[t]he majority opinion reads like an advocate's closing address to a hostile jury." Certainly, the majority's statement of the procedural requirements for board approval of a cash-out merger caught the corporate bar and directors by surprise. On the other hand, it can be argued that, in some respects, the majority lowered the standard of care by adopting a gross negligence test. The result of *Van Gorkom* could therefore be that, once the board has satisfied the due diligence requirements, its decisions will essentially be unimpeachable. On the other hand, where a breach of care is alleged, the only issue is ordinarily the adequacy of the due diligence review, so that the effect of *Van Gorkom* will likely be to require more from directors (particularly outside board members) in the performance of their duties.

Would the Delaware Supreme Court have applied a less exacting standard had the transaction in question not been a cash-out merger, but rather an ordinary investment decision? The more momentous the decision, the more care will generally be required of board members. In addition, considerable judicial attention has focused on buyout transactions, and it would therefore not be surprising if duties of care were levered up in these cases. See Chapter Eleven, Section D.

One advantage of the merger in *Van Gorkom* would appear to have been the reduction of agency costs associated with "free cash flow." During the period in question, Trans Union had an annual cash flow of hundreds of millions of dollars. To the extent that such amounts were in excess of that required to fund all profitable opportunities, this was free cash flow, and Jensen has noted that self-dealing may take the form of an investment of such moneys at less than the cost of capital, rather than distributing them to shareholders as dividends. Jensen, *Agency Costs of Free Cash Flow, Corporate Finance, and Takeovers*, 98 Am. Econ. Rev. 323 (1986). For example, if the cost of capital is 10%, an opportunity with an anticipated 9% return has a negative net present value and management's decision to take it up will reduce firm value. Management would then commit to pay out free cash flow to shareholders in a claimholders' bargain. These problems, are, however, reduced or eliminated in a leveraged buyout where the acquirer finances the purchase largely through borrowings, with the free cash flow disappearing in interest payments on the debt.

Suppose you sat on the Chancery Court on remand. Just what would you do to find the intrinsic value of the shares?

It is not an overstatement to say that *Smith v. Van Gorkom* had a bombshell effect in U.S. boardrooms. One result was apparently to make it harder to interest people in serving as outside directors. See, e.g., *The Job Nobody Wants*, Bus. Week, Sept. 8, 1986, at 56. Another was to push up rates for director and officer insurance. Even in Canada, one study found an average 686% increase in premiums from 1985 to 1986, the period immediately following *Van Gorkom*. Toronto *Globe and Mail* Report on Business, Nov. 7, 1986. A third consequence of *Van Gorkom* might be to inhibit firm growth by inducing excessive caution and investment in the trappings of procedural fairness (e.g., fairness opinions on the transaction from investment bankers or valuers). See Herzel & Katz, *Smith v. Van Gorkom: The Business of Judging Business Judgment*, 41 Bus. Law. 1187 (1986).

Further fallout from *Van Gorkom* was an amendment to the Delaware corporations statute permitting a corporation's charter to limit or eliminate the personal liability of directors for specified breaches. The text of new Del. s. 102(b)(7), which came into force on July 1, 1986, is as follows:

A provision eliminating or limiting the personal liability of a director to the corporation or its stockholders for monetary damages for breach of fiduciary duty as a director, provided that such provision shall not eliminate or limit the liability of a director (i) for any breach of the director's duty of loyalty to the corporation or its stockholders, (ii) for acts or omissions not in good faith or which involve intentional misconduct or a knowing violation of law, (iii) under section 174 of this Title,* or (iv) for any transaction from which the director derived an improper personal benefit. ...

The effect of this provision is to leave to the corporation the decision of how much monitoring from directors it wishes. If the standard in *Van Gorkom is* indeed perceived as excessive, substantial reliance by firms on Del. s. 102(b)(7) can be expected. In the 18 months after its passage, the Delaware statute inspired similar legislation in seven other states, while other states lowered the standard of care to cases of wilful or reckless misbehaviour. See Note, *Limiting Corporate Directors' Liability: Delaware's Section 102(b)(7) and the Erosion of the Directors' Duty of Care*, 136 U. Pa. L. Rev. 239, 242-43 nn. 12-13 (1987). For widely traded firms, accountability on capital markets could be presumed to deter reliance on Del. s. 102(b)(7) when this would sap efficient monitoring incentives. Thus a firm would not wish to limit directors' liability if the full liability rule was efficient in the first place, since the benefits of limited liability would be exceeded by the increase in the firm's cost of capital. Limited liability for managers is however prohibited by CBCA s. 122(3).

3. Shiftable Liability: Indemnity and Insurance

Shiftable liability, or the combination of the imposition of primary duties on managers and devices like indemnification or insurance to pass on the burden of such liability to other parties, may appear to undercut the distributional and efficiency motives for imposing liability in the first place. For example, the distributional effects of shiftable liability will be puzzling when (1) a manager transfers moneys from the firm to himself through looting, (2) the transfer is reversed through a damages award, and (3) the damages award is undone through indemnification. In addition, the incentive goals of management liability strategies may seem frustrated if a manager may pass liability on to the firm or to an insurance company. For this reason, an underwriter who had been sued for misrepresentations in a prospectus was not permitted to seek an indemnity against the issuer pursuant to a contractual indemnification right in *Globus v. Law Research Service, Inc.*, 418 F.2d 1276 (2d Cir. 1969), cert. denied, 397 U.S. 913 (1970). The issuer (LRS) had promised to indemnify the underwriter for any loss arising out of defects in the prospectus, except for those attributable to the underwriter's "wilful misfeasance, bad faith or gross negligence ... or ... reckless disregard of its obligations under the agreement." *Id.* at 1287. The Court found that the underwriter had actual knowledge of material misstatements in the prospectus, and denied the cross-claim both because it fell within the exception to the agreement and because it offended public policy:

Given this state of the record, we concur in Judge Mansfield's ruling that to tolerate indemnity under these circumstances would encourage flouting the policy of the common law and the Securities Act. It is well established that one cannot insure himself against his own reckless, wilful or criminal misconduct.

· · ·

---

* Del. s. 174 provides for director liability on unlawful dividend payments or stock repurchases.

Although the 1933 Act does not deal expressly with the question before us, provisions in that Act confirm our conclusion that Blair should not be entitled to indemnity from LRS. See generally Note, Indemnification of Underwriters and § 11 of the Securities Act of 1933, 73 Yale L.J. 406. For example, § 11 of the Act, 15 U.S.C. § 77k, makes underwriters jointly liable with directors, experts and signers of the registration statement. And, the SEC has announced its view that indemnification of directors, officers and controlling persons for liabilities arising under the 1933 Act is against the public policy of the Act. 17 C.F.R. § 230.460. If we follow the syllogism through to its conclusion, underwriters should be treated equally with controlling persons and hence prohibited from obtaining indemnity from the issuer. See 72 Yale, supra, at 411. But see 3 Loss, supra, at 1834 (1961).

Civil liability under section 11 and similar provisions was designed not so much to compensate the defrauded purchaser as to promote enforcement of the Act and to deter negligence by providing a penalty for those who fail in their duties. And Congress intended to impose a "high standard of trusteeship" on underwriters. Kroll, supra, at 687. Thus, what Professor Loss terms the *"in terrorem* effect" of civil liability, 3 Loss, supra, at 1831, might well be thwarted if underwriters were free to pass their liability on to the issuer. Underwriters who knew they could be indemnified simply by showing that the issuer was "more liable" than they (a process not too difficult when the issuer is inevitably closer to the facts) would have a tendency to be lax in their independent investigations. [*Id.* at 1288]

Does indemnification for liability under negligence stand on the same footing as indemnification for liability under fraud? In looting breaches, indemnification operates as a wash trade, permitting the errant manager to expropriate firm value without regard to liability rules. On the other hand, distributional effects are less to be feared when a manager seeks to be indemnified for breach of an anti-shirking covenant. In *Globus*, for example, the third party plaintiffs would have been able to recover from either the issuer or the underwriter. If the issuer were insolvent, then, the plaintiffs would still have been able to recover against the underwriter, and here the rights of indemnification would have been valueless. Moreover, indemnification and insurance reduce the possibility that compensation policies will fail because of the defendant's bankruptcy.

This suggests that, but for efficiency concerns, there will be little reason to restrict rights of indemnification or insurance for breaches of due care standards. However, shiftable liability of this kind would indeed be troubling from an efficiency perspective if it sapped incentives to take care. For example, if the point of imposing liability on outside directors is to enlist their aid as efficient gatekeepers, this policy may seem subverted by indemnification or insurance. Nevertheless, shiftable liability may be defended on a variety of arguments.

One unsatisfactory defence of shiftable liability is that it provides a safety valve against the possibility that excessively high duties will be imposed on managers. For example, if care standards in *Van Gorkom* are inefficient because they lead managers to adopt an overcautious investment policy, director and officer (D & O) insurance might be purchased to realign management incentives with those of the firm. This does not, however, provide a plausible justification for shiftable liability, since errors in liability standards could more easily be cured by a firm through limited liability provisions such as Del. s. 102(b)(7). If Canadian firms insure or indemnify for this reason, it is only because limitations of liability are prohibited by CBCA s. 122(3).

Limited liability strategies are, however, inappropriate where liability is imposed on the manager in the first instance as a response to incentive costs of limited shareholder liability. How the possibility of bankruptcy may warp manager incentives was considered in *Walkovszky v. Carlton* in Chapter Two. Where the full costs of the harm it produces are not borne by the firm, as where bankruptcy may cut off non-consensual claims, a firm will in some circumstances underinvest in harm prevention. This possibility may be addressed through the imposition of liability on managers as well as the firm, for under such dual liability regimes managers may be expected to force the firm to take the full costs of harm into account in its investment in care. This is because the managers will be unwilling to incur the risk of enormous personal liability associated with inefficient care levels. Barriers to risk shifting may then reduce firm value, since managerial risk aversion may lead to an excessive investment in care (where $1 invested in harm prevention reduces anticipated harm costs by less than $1). But, as was seen in Chapter Two, this possibility may be addressed with D & O insurance, under which (1) the firm would still be led to efficient harm prevention decisions, and (2) managerial risk aversion would not increase through personal liability. In such cases, shiftable liability is superior to both limited liability and unshiftable dual liability. See Kraakman, *Corporate Liability Strategies and the Costs of Legal Controls*, 93 Yale L.J. 857 (1984). D & O insurance may also reduce agency costs if the insurer is an efficient monitor.

D & O insurance will, however, be inappropriate in the case of breaches of anti-looting policies. Liability for overt self-dealing should therefore be non-shiftable when the purpose of the duty is to prevent management from expropriating the firm's residual value. Otherwise, managers might loot the firm in the knowledge that if their actions are impeached they will ultimately succeed through indemnification. Non-shiftable liability then operates as a me-first rule, protecting the integrity of residual claims.

The distinction between fraud and negligence is observed in CBCA s. 124, which governs the circumstances in which managers may seek indemnification or insurance. In no case may liability be shifted if the manager has not acted honestly and in good faith with a view to the best interest of the corporation. As such, indemnification and insurance are largely restricted to (1) breaches of due care standards under the CBCA, and (2) breaches of statutory duties (such as those of the OSA) imposed on managers for harm done to parties other than the firm.

In some circumstances, indemnification by the firm is mandatory. Under Del. s. 145(c), for example, a director or officer is entitled to indemnity as of right where he is "successful on the merits or otherwise" in the litigation. What this might mean is something less than substantive vindication. See *Dornan v. Humphrey*, 106 N.Y.S.2d 142, 144 (1951), modified, 112 N.Y.S.2d 585 (1952) (defendants are "successful" under the New York Business Corporation Law when the complaint is dismissed under the statute of limitations). Mandatory indemnification under CBCA s. 124(3) is, however, narrower in scope. There a director or officer is entitled to indemnity as of right only where he "was substantially successful on the merits in his defense." Would a director be entitled to indemnity under this provision where the action is so unmeritorious that it is discontinued by the plaintiff without any form of adjudication?

Where a manager is not entitled to indemnity as of right under s. 124(3), the firm may still indemnify him pursuant to ss. 124(1)-(2). Though indemnification is merely permissive here, the manager might nevertheless bargain for indemnity rights in his employment contract, such that, from the firm's perspective, it would be no less mandatory than statutory indemnity rights under s. 124(3). But permissive indemnification under ss. 124(1)-(2), whether pursuant to a contractual right or not, is not permitted in certain circumstances. A manager may only be indemnified if:

(1) he acted honestly and in good faith with a view to the best interests of the corporation; and

(2) in the case of a criminal or administrative action or proceeding that is enforced by a monetary penalty, he had reasonable grounds for believing that his conduct was lawful.

CBCA s. 124(2) sets higher standards for indemnification in derivative action than does s. 124(1) for non-derivative claims. As will be seen in the next section, derivative claims are shareholder actions brought with respect to a breach of a duty to the firm, on whose behalf the shareholder sues. If damages are awarded, they are paid to the firm. In a non-derivative (or personal) claim, the action is brought by the individual shareholder (or group of shareholders) suing on his own behalf, and recovery is paid personally to the shareholder. A plaintiff shareholder's incentive to litigate would then be far more weakened through indemnification in a derivative than a non-derivative action, and this explains the special hurdles in the former case. First, indemnification in derivative actions under s. 124(2), unlike s. 124(1), requires court approval. Moreover, s. 124(2) does not appear to contemplate indemnification for an amount paid in settlement of an action, as under s. 124(1). See also *Denton v. Equus Petroleum Corp.* (1986), 33 B.L.R. 314 (B.C.) (no indemnification permitted for expenses incurred in an investigation where no charges laid).

According to The Conference Board's study of 365 firms of all sizes, about 71% of Canadian corporations carry liability insurance for directors, and this figure increases to 100% for manufacturing firms with assets exceeding $1.4 billion. About 82% of the firms that insured paid the entire premium themselves, with a median coverage of $15 million. Where managers do incur liability in the course of their activities for the firm, 93% of all firms indemnify the managers, and 100% of large manufacturing firms. Where indemnification is paid, 98% of all firms indemnify to the full extent. *Canadian Directorship Practices: Compensation of Boards of Directors* 65-67 (1985).

See further J. Bishop, *Law of Corporate Officers and Directors: Indemnification and Insurance* (1982); Bishop, *New Problems in Indemnifying and Insuring Directors*, [1972] Duke L.J. 1153; Bishop, *Sitting Ducks and Decoy Ducks: New Trends in the Indemnification of Corporate Directors and Officers*, 77 Yale L.J. 1078 (1968); Oesterle, *Limits on a Corporation's Protection of Its Directors and Officers from Personal Liability*, [1983] Wisc. L. Rev. 513.

D. LOOTING: INTERESTED DIRECTORS' CONTRACTS

In addition to wishing to ensure that managers work in the best interests of the corporation, courts have been concerned to ensure that managers not engage in looting. The material set out below examines how this particular liability strategy has evolved.

Aberdeen Ry. Co. v. Blaikie Brothers
House of Lords
(1854), 1 Macq. (H.L.) 461, [1843-60] All E.R. Rep. 249

[The railway contracted to purchase a quantity of chairs from Blaikie Brothers. (A chair is an iron plate used to secure a rail to a tie.) Thomas Blaikie, the chairman of the railway, was also a partner in Blaikie Brothers. Some of the chairs were delivered, but for reasons not appearing in the reports, the railway refused to accept delivery of the rest. Blaikie Brothers sued for specific performance. The railway defended on the ground that it could avoid the contract because its chairman had a pecuniary interest in the contract as a partner in the vendor firm. The Court of Session in Scotland rejected the defence on the law, and the railway appealed. The House of Lords reversed.]

LORD CRANWORTH L.C.: ... This, therefore, brings us to the general question, whether a director of a railway company is or is not precluded from dealing on behalf of the company with himself or with a firm in which he is a partner. The directors are a body to whom is delegated the duty of managing the general affairs of the company. A corporate body can only act by agents, and it is, of course, the duty of those agents so to act as best to promote the interests of the corporation whose affairs they are conducting. Such an agent has duties to discharge of a fiduciary character towards his principal, and it is a rule of universal application that no one having such duties to discharge shall be allowed to enter into engagements in which he has or can have a personal interest conflicting or which possibly may conflict with the interests of those whom he is bound to protect. So strictly is this principle adhered to that no question is allowed to be raised as to the fairness or unfairness of a contract so entered into. It obviously is, or may be, impossible to demonstrate how far in any particular case the terms of such a contract have been the best for the cestui que trust which it was impossible to obtain. It may sometimes happen that the terms on which a trustee has dealt or attempted to deal with the estate or interests of those for whom he is a trustee have been as good as could have been obtained from any other person; they may even at the time have been better. But still so inflexible is the rule that no inquiry on that subject is permitted.

The English authorities on this subject are numerous and uniform. The principle was acted on by Lord King in *Keech v. Sandford* [(1726), Sel. Cas. Ch. 61, 25 E.R. 223], and by Lord Hardwicke, in *Whelpdale v. Cookson* [(1747), 1 Ves. Sen. 9, 27 E.R. 856], and the whole subject was considered by Lord Eldon on a great variety of occasions. It is sufficient to refer to what fell from that very able and learned judge in *Ex parte James* [(1803), 8 Ves. 337, 32 E.R. 385]. It is true that the questions have generally arisen on agreements for purchases or leases of land, and not, as here, on a contract of a mercantile character. But this can make no difference in principle. The inability to contract depends not on the subject-matter of the agreement, but on the fiduciary character of the contracting party, and I cannot entertain a doubt of its being applicable to the case of a party who is acting as manager of a mercantile or trading business for the benefit of others no less than to that of an agent or trustee employed in selling land.

Was, then, Mr. Blaikie so acting in the case now before us? If he was, did he, while so acting, contract, on behalf of those for whom he was acting, with himself? Both these questions must obviously be answered in the affirmative. Mr. Blaikie was not only a director, but, if that was necessary, the chairman of the directors. In that character it was his bounden duty to make the best bargains he could for the benefit of the company. While he filled that character, viz., on Feb. 6, 1846, he entered into a contract on behalf of the company with his own firm for the purchase of a large quantity of chairs at a certain stipulated price. His duty to the company imposed on him the obligation of obtaining these iron chairs at the lowest possible price. His personal interest would lead him in an entirely opposite direction—would induce him to fix the price as high as possible. This is the very evil against which the rule in question is directed; and I see nothing whatever to prevent its application here. I observe that Lord Fullerton seemed to doubt whether the rule would apply where the party whose act or contract is called in question, is only one of a body of directors not a sole trustee or manager. But, with all deference, this appears to me to make no difference. It was Mr. Blaikie's duty to give to his co-directors, and through them to the company, the full benefit of all the knowledge and skill which he could bring to bear on the subject. He was bound to assist them in getting the articles contracted for at the cheapest possible rate. As far as related to the advice he should give them, he put his interest in conflict with his duty, and whether he was the sole director, or only one of many, can make no difference in principle. The same observation applies to the fact, that he was not the sole person trading with the company. He was one of the firm of Blaikie Brothers with whom the contract was made, and so was interested in driving as hard a bargain with the company as he could induce them to make.

· · ·

I have therefore satisfied myself that the Court of Session came to a wrong conclusion; and that the third plea was a sufficient answer to the plaintiff's case. I, therefore, move that the judgment of the court below be reversed.

NOTES

A rule of inalienability, such as was set forth in *Aberdeen Ry.*, will impose costs on corporations, since valuable business opportunities may thereby be lost. On the other hand, the presumption that no one will enter into a contract in which he is made worse off cannot be extended to bargains induced by fraud or duress. In the case of interested directors' contracts, the fear is that management will cause the firm to enter into bargains that transfer wealth to the directors. Of course, not every contract between management and firm will be Pareto-inferior for the firm, but in some the fear of self-dealing will be real. If (1) a substantial number of such agreements are unfair, and (2) it is too costly to screen fair from unfair contracts, a prophylactic rule, such as that of *Aberdeen Ry.*, may be justified. Do you think that valuation problems in screening fair from unfair contracts call for a prophylactic rule in the case of interested directors' contracts? Consider this after you have read the following case.

North-West Transportation Co. v. Beatty
Privy Council
(1887), 12 App. Cas. 589

SIR RICHARD BAGGALLAY (by whom the judgment of their Lordships was delivered): The action, in which this appeal has been brought, was commenced on the 31st of May, 1883, in the Chancery Division of the High Court of Justice in Ontario. The plaintiff, Henry Beatty, is a shareholder in the North-West Transportation Company, Limited, and he sues on behalf of himself and all other shareholders in the company, except those who are defendants. The defendants are the company and five shareholders, who, at the commencement of the action, were the directors of the company. The claim in the action is to set aside a sale made to the company by James Hughes Beatty, one of the directors, of a steamer called the *United Empire*, of which previously to such sale he was sole owner.

The general principles applicable to cases of this kind are well established. Unless some provision to the contrary is to be found in the charter or other instrument by which the company is incorporated, the resolution of a majority of the shareholders, duly convened, upon any question with which the company is legally competent to deal, is binding upon the minority, and consequently upon the company, and every shareholder has a perfect right to vote upon any such question, although he may have a personal interest in the subject-matter opposed to, or different from, the general or particular interests of the company.

On the other hand, a director of a company is precluded from dealing, on behalf of the company, with himself, and from entering into engagements in which he has a personal interest conflicting, or which possibly may conflict, with the interests of those whom he is bound by fiduciary duty to protect; and this rule is as applicable to the case of one of several directors as to a managing or sole director. Any such dealing or engagement may, however, be affirmed or adopted by the company, provided such affirmance or adoption is not brought about by unfair or improper means, and is not illegal or fraudulent or oppressive towards those shareholders who oppose it.

The material facts of the case are not now in dispute.

• • •

The company commenced business shortly after its incorporation, and acquired for its purposes a fleet of several steamers. In the autumn of 1882, one of its steamers, the *Asia*, was lost, and another, the *Sovereign*, was deemed unsuitable for the company's business. At this time the steamer *United Empire* was in process of building for the defendant James Hughes Beatty, and was approaching completion; the contract for her construction had been entered into in December, 1880, and she was in fact completed on the 20th of May, 1883, a few days before the commencement of the action. The acquisition of the *United Empire* by the company had been suggested to the directors and had been the subject of consideration by them and others interested in the company as early as the close of the year 1881; the loss of the *Asia* led to the matter being further considered, and the sale to the company was brought about in the following manner.

The annual meeting for the year 1883 was held on the 7th of February, and, at such meeting, the defendants were elected directors for the ensuing year; at the same meeting, a discussion took place as to the suggested purchase of the *United Empire*, and it was resolved that a special meeting of the shareholders should be held on the 16th for the purpose of having submitted to them a bye-law for the purchase of the steamer *United Empire*, and also to consider the advisability of selling the steamer *Sovereign*.

At a meeting of the directors held on the 10th of February, 1883, and at which all the directors except the defendant William Beatty were present, it was resolved that a bye-law, which was read to the meeting, for the purchase of the *United Empire* should pass. It is unnecessary to refer in detail to the terms in which this bye-law was expressed; it is sufficient to state that, after reciting an agreement between the company and the defendant James Hughes Beatty, that the company should buy and the defendant should sell the steamer *United Empire* for the sum of $125,000, to be in part paid in cash and in part secured, as therein mentioned, it was enacted that the company should purchase the steamer from the defendant upon those terms, with various directions for giving effect to the terms of the contract.

The agreement recited in the bye-law was executed at the same meeting.

At a meeting of shareholders, held, as arranged, on the 16th of February, 1883, the bye-law which had been enacted by the directors was read by the secretary, and, after being modified in its terms, with respect to the price, was adopted by a majority of votes.

The *United Empire*, on her completion, was delivered to the company, and has ever since been employed in the ordinary business of the company.

It is proved by uncontradicted evidence, and is indeed now substantially admitted, that at the date of purchase the acquisition of another steamer to supply the place of the *Asia* was essential to the efficient conduct of the company's business; that the *United Empire* was well adapted for that purpose; that it was not within the power of the company to acquire any other steamer equally well adapted for its business; and that the price agreed to be paid for the steamer was not excessive or unreasonable.

Had there been no material facts in the case other than those above stated, there would have been, in the opinion of their Lordships, no reason for setting aside the sale of the steamer; it would have been immaterial to consider whether the contract for the purchase of the *United Empire* should be regarded as one entered into by the directors and confirmed by the shareholders, or as one entirely emanating from the shareholders; in either view of the case, the transaction was one which, if carried out in a regular way, was within the powers of the company; in the former view, any defect arising from the fiduciary relationship of the defendant James Hughes Beatty to the company would be remedied by the resolution of the shareholders, on the 16th of February, and, in the latter, the fact of the defendant being a director would not deprive him of his right to vote, as a shareholder, in support of any resolution which he might deem favourable to his own interests.

There is, however, a further element for consideration, arising out of the following facts, which have been relied upon in the arguments on behalf of the plaintiff, as evidencing that the resolution of the 16th of February was brought about by unfair and improper means.

It appears that, at the commencement of the year 1883, 595 of the 600 shares into which the capital of the company was divided were held by seven living shareholders, and five belonged to the estate of a deceased shareholder; that of the seven living shareholders,

The defendant J.H. Beatty held	200 shares.
The plaintiff	120 „
S. Neelon (then a director)	101 „
F.S. Hankey	71 „
The defendant J.D. Beatty	59 „
J.C. Graham	39 „
The defendant W. Beatty	5 „

It further appears that the defendant J.H. Beatty purchased the 101 shares of S. Neelon, and that they were transferred to him on the last day of January, 1883, the number of shares held by the defendant being thus raised to 301, an actual majority of all the shares in the company; that on the morning of the 7th of February, before the annual meeting of that day, the defendant J.H. Beatty transferred five of his shares to the defendant Rose, and the like number to the defendant Laird, whereby they respectively became qualified to be elected directors; and that on the same day they were elected directors.

The defendants Rose and Laird deny, and their denial is unimpeached, that there was any agreement or understanding between them or either of them and the defendant J.H. Beatty that they would support his views in respect of the sale of his steamer to the company; they both, however, admit that, previously to the transfers of the shares to them, they considered that the purchase of the steamer would be beneficial to the company, that they accepted the transfer with the view of becoming directors, and that the defendant was well aware of the opinions and views entertained by them. Indeed, the defendant Rose states that he would not have joined the company but for the intention to purchase the steamer.

By the transfers to the defendants Rose and Laird, the number of shares held by the defendant J.H. Beatty was reduced to 291, but the united voting power of the three last-named defendants was such that they could command a majority at any meeting of the shareholders.

Though there was a discussion, at the annual meeting on the 7th of February, as to the expediency of purchasing the steamer, the resolution directing a bye-law to be prepared appears to have been passed without any division.

At the meeting of directors of the 10th, the same three defendants were in a position to carry any resolution or to pass any bye-law upon which they were agreed.

At the shareholders' meeting of the 16th the voting was as follows:

For the confirmation of the bye-law,

	Votes.
The defendant J.H. Beatty	291
The defendant J.E. Rose	5
The defendant R. Laird	5
The defendant William Beatty	5
Total	306

Against the confirmation,

	Votes.
John C. Graham	39
F.L. Hankey	71
The plaintiff	120
The defendant John D. Beatty	59
Total	289

It follows that the majority of votes in favour of the confirmation of the bye-law was due to the votes of the defendant J.H. Beatty.

[The plaintiff sued in the Ontario courts to have the contract set aside on the ground that J.H. Beatty's involvement in the transaction constituted a breach of fiduciary duty. The Chancellor ruled for the plaintiff, but the Ontario Court of Appeal reversed. The Supreme Court of Canada reversed the Court of Appeal and reinstated the Chancellor's order. The Supreme Court held that the interested director's contract could be ratified effectively only by a disinterested majority of the shareholders and that there was no such ratification since without the votes of J.H. Beatty the shareholder majority would have been against ratification.]

From this decision of the Supreme Court of Canada the appeal has been brought with which their Lordships have now to deal. The question involved is doubtless novel in its circumstances, and the decision important in its consequences; it would be very undesirable even to appear to relax the rules relating to dealings between trustees and their beneficiaries; on the other hand, great confusion would be introduced into the affairs of joint stock companies if the circumstances of shareholders, voting in that character at general meetings, were to be examined, and their votes practically nullified, if they also stood in some fiduciary relation to the company.

It is clear upon the authorities that the contract entered into by the directors on the 10th of February could not have been enforced against the company at the instance of the defendant J.H. Beatty, but it is equally clear that it was within the competency of the shareholders at the meeting of the 16th to adopt or reject it. In form and in terms they adopted it by a majority of votes, and the vote of the majority must prevail, unless the adoption was brought about by unfair or improper means.

The only unfairness or impropriety which, consistently with the admitted and established facts, could be suggested, arises out of the fact that the defendant J.H. Beatty possessed a voting power as a shareholder which enabled him, and those who thought with him, to adopt the bye-law, and thereby either to ratify and adopt a voidable contract, into which he, as a director, and his co-directors had entered, or to make a similar contract, which latter seems to have been what was intended to be done by the resolution passed on the 7th of February.

It may be quite right that, in such a case, the opposing minority should be able, in a suit like this, to challenge the transaction, and to shew that it is an improper one, and to be freed from the objection that a suit with such an object can only be maintained by the company itself.

But the constitution of the company enabled the defendant J.H. Beatty to acquire this voting power; there was no limit upon the number of shares which a shareholder might hold, and for every share so held he was entitled to a vote; the charter itself recognised the defendant as a holder of 200 shares, one-third of the aggregate number; he had a perfect right to acquire further shares, and to exercise his voting power in such a manner as to secure the election of directors whose views upon policy agreed with his own, and to support those views at any shareholders' meeting; the acquisition of the *United Empire* was a pure question of policy, as to which it might be expected that there would be differences of opinion, and upon which the voice of the majority ought to prevail; to reject the votes of the defendant upon the question of the adoption of the bye-law would be to give effect to the views of the minority, and to disregard those of the majority.

The judges of the Supreme Court appear to have regarded the exercise by the defendant J.H. Beatty of his voting power as of so oppressive a character as to invalidate the adoption of the bye-law; their Lordships are unable to adopt this view; in their opinion the defendant was acting within his rights in voting as he did, though they agree with the Chief Justice in the views expressed by him in the Court of Appeal, that the matter might have been conducted in a manner less likely to give rise to objection.

Their Lordships will humbly advise Her Majesty to allow the appeal; to discharge the order of the Supreme Court of Canada; and to dismiss the appeal to that Court with costs; the respondent must bear the costs of the present appeal.

NOTES

Today, a company that is subject to the jurisdiction of the Ontario Securities Commission and that enters into a transaction with a majority shareholder to buy or sell an asset that has a value greater than 25% of that company's market capitalization would have to comply with OSC Policy 9.1. The policy is applicable to "related party transactions" of this kind and it requires that there be: (1) a formal valuation of the asset (to ensure that a fair price is being obtained); and (2) approval by a majority of the shareholders other than the interested majority shareholder (known as "majority of the minority" approval). Do you think that there should be a requirement of the kind seen in OSC Policy 9.1? Is it appropriate for securities commissions to impose requirements with respect to the conduct of a company's affairs? Who is better positioned to pursue this kind of liability strategy: courts or securities commissions?

Ratification and Derivative Actions. The plaintiff in *North-West Transportation* brought his action on behalf of himself and all other shareholders, except the defendants, alleging a breach by them of their duties to the firm. This was then a *derivative* action, since the plaintiff's standing derived from a wrong to the corporation. The question when an individual shareholder may litigate on behalf of the firm is one of the most vexed in corporate law. It has bedeviled the courts for close to a century and a half, since the first modern case to announce it, *Foss v. Harbottle* (1843), 2 Hare 461, 67 E.R. 189. There two minority shareholders of the Victoria Park Company, a real estate development corporation in modern parlance, sued various of the directors to recover damages for the company. In an extremely lengthy bill of complaint, the directors were alleged to have committed a variety of wrongs. Principal among these were that: (1) immediately before incorporation they secretly purchased for themselves certain lands essential to the corporation's purposes which they then sold to the corporation at an exorbitant profit; and (2) they made unauthorized dispositions of the corporation's lands to secure financing. Wigram V.C. dismissed the bill. He first observed that "the conduct with which the Defendants are charged in this suit is an injury not to the plaintiffs exclusively; it is an injury to the whole corporation by individuals whom the corporation entrusted with powers to be exercised only for the good of the corporation" (67 E.R. at 202). He concluded that the bill had to be dismissed for reasons stated in the following passage:

The corporation, in a sense, is undoubtedly the *cestui que trust*; but the majority of the proprietors at a special general meeting assembled, independently of any general rules of law upon the subject, by the very terms of the incorporation in the present case, has power to bind the whole body, and every individual corporator must be taken to have come into the corporation upon the terms of being liable to be so bound. How then can this Court act in a suit constituted as this is, if it is to be assumed, for the purposes of the argument, that the powers of the body of the proprietors are still in existence, and may lawfully be exercised for a purpose like that I have suggested? Whilst the Court may be declaring the acts complained of to be void at the suit of the present Plaintiffs, who in fact may be the only proprietors who disapprove of them, the governing body of proprietors may defeat the decree by lawfully resolving upon the confirmation of the very acts which are the subject of the suit. The very fact that the governing body of proprietors assembled at the special general meeting may so bind even a reluctant minority is decisive to shew that the frame of this suit cannot be sustained whilst the body retains its functions. In order then that this suit may be sustained it must be shewn either that there is no such power as I have supposed remaining in the proprietors, or, at least, that all means have been resorted to and found ineffectual to set that body in motion: this latter point is nowhere suggested in the bill: there is no suggestion that an attempt has been made by any proprietor to set the body of proprietors in motion, or to procure a meeting to be convened for the purpose of revoking the acts complained of. [*Id.* at 203-4]

The principle that the corporation and not a shareholder is the proper plaintiff in an action to vindicate corporate rights has come to be known as "the rule in *Foss v. Harbottle.*" The rule may be stated as follows:

A suit to redress a wrong done to a corporation may not be brought by a shareholder thereof, and can be brought only by the corporation itself, in any case where the wrong may be ratified by an ordinary majority of the shareholders in general meeting.

The doctrine of ratification was then closely related to shareholder standing to bring a derivative action. Derivative actions were non-ratifiable, and ratifiable breaches would not support derivative actions. Under the rule in *Foss v. Harbottle*, for example, the action in *North-West Transportation* should have failed not only because the breach was ratified but because it might have been ratified. The fundamental principle was one of futility: so long as the breach might have been ratified it would be futile for a court to consider it, since in the midst of its deliberations the shareholders might absolve the errant managers. *North-West Transportation* is in fact an example of this: because the vote of ratification was effective to terminate proceedings against the director, the litigation was futile (though it would have been otherwise had Beatty been barred from voting his shares).

In some cases absolution decision may reasonably be delegated from courts to shareholders. If shareholders are capable of distinguishing between serious and trivial breaches, the substitution of shareholder ratification for detailed judicial scrutiny may be defended on the basis that investors are best able to look after their own interests. In particular, the evidentiary value of the judgment of shareholders of closely held corporations may reasonably be thought high. But in widely held corporations, management often has substantial influence on the results of a shareholder vote, such that ratification may be an ineffective screening device except where a group of insurgents actively oppose management.

This is not, however, to suggest that in public firms ratification should always be ineffective, or that every breach should support a derivative action. The decision to commence litigation by or on behalf of a corporation is a business one, and there may be a number of reasons why it is not desirable that breaches should invariably be the subject of court proceedings. In some cases, the offence may be trivial and adequately sanctioned by internal firm procedures. In other cases, the probability of success or of recovery against an impecunious manager may be low. The corporation must also weigh the benefits it will receive against the costs it must absorb in pursuing the action and in any possible loss of reputation. For this reason, the litigation decision is unambiguously assigned to management under CBCA s. 102(1) when no issue of self-dealing arises. See *Macson Dev. Co. v. Gordon* (1959), 19 D.L.R. (2d) 465 (N.S.); *John Shaw & Sons (Salford) Ltd. v. Shaw*, [1935] 2 K.B. 113 (C.A.).

However, when the decision is whether to sue a manager, the possibility of self-dealing may suggest that management's discretion should be second-guessed. Yet even here it is excessive to require that trivial breaches be litigated. The common law technique of resolving this problem in *Foss v. Harbottle* was to give managers the primary responsibility of determining whether the corporation would sue errant managers, while permitting shareholders to bring an action in the name of the corporation in certain circumstances if the corporation had not sued. As a technique of distinguishing cases where such derivative actions might or might not be maintained, the rule in *Foss v. Harbottle* focused attention on the formal legal nature of the allegations. Derivative actions were permitted in at least four types of cases under *Foss v. Harbottle*.* These were actions challenging:

(1) *ultra vires* transactions;
(2) actions that could validly be taken only with the approval of a special majority of shareholders;
(3) actions in contravention of the personal rights of shareholders; and
(4) "fraud on the minority" by a majority that was still in control at the time of the proposed litigation and that therefore would not cause the corporation to sue.

---

*   This list is given in *Edwards v. Halliwell*, [1950] 2 All E.R. 1064 (C.A.).

While these four categories were sometimes described as "exceptions" to the rule in *Foss v. Harbottle*, this was misleading. That rule provided only that ratifiable breaches would not support a derivative action. The "exceptions" to the rule were then cases where ratification was ineffective and where shareholders had standing to sue on behalf of the firm. Some examples of the fourth category, fraud on the minority, were possibly the only true exceptions to the rule, since shareholder actions were found to co-exist with ratifiable breaches.

For the purpose of the offences detailed in this chapter, the relevant exception to *Foss v. Harbottle* was fraud on the minority, which came to mean a quite specialized variety of self-dealing. Not every kind of breach of fiduciary duties would ground a derivative action, but only one in which the managers had expropriated assets that at law or in equity belonged to the firm. The distinction was explained in *Cook v. Deeks*, [1916] 1 A.C. 554 (P.C.), in which three shareholders of a four-man corporation formed a new corporation to compete with the first corporation. The Canadian Supreme Court held that the expropriation of the corporate opportunity could be made regular by resolutions of shareholders of the first corporation which were passed by the votes of the three defendants. The Privy Council reversed. Lord Buckmaster stated:

In their Lordships' opinion the Supreme Court has insufficiently recognized the distinction between two classes of case and has applied the principles applicable to the case of a director selling to his company property which was in equity as well as at law his own, and which he could dispose of as he thought fit, to the case of a director dealing with property which, though his own at law, in equity belonged to his company. The cases of *North-West Transportation Co. v. Beatty* and *Burland v. Earle* both belonged to the former class. In each, directors had sold to the company property in which the company had no interest at law or in equity. If the company claimed any interest by reason of the transaction, it could only be by affirming the sale, in which case such sale, though initially voidable, would be validated by subsequent ratification ...

If, as their Lordships find on the facts, the contract in question was entered into under such circumstances that the directors could not retain the benefit of it for themselves, then it belonged in equity to the company and ought to have been dealt with as an asset of the company. Even supposing it be not ultra vires of a company to make a present to its directors, it appears quite certain that directors holding a majority of votes would not be permitted to make a present to themselves. This would be to allow a majority to oppress the minority. To such circumstances the cases of *North-West Transportation Co. v. Beatty* and *Burland v. Earle* have no application. [*Id.* at 563-64]

A similar example of expropriation of corporate assets arose in *Menier v. Hooper's Telegraph Works* (1874), L.R. 9 Ch. App. 350. The plaintiff was a minority shareholder and the defendant a majority shareholder of the European and South American Telegraph Co. The corporation had been granted a franchise to construct a telegraph line between Portugal and Brazil, but its chairman appropriated the franchise for himself, and the corporation sued to regain it. The chairman and the defendant entered into an arrangement to terminate the litigation against the chairman and to share the franchise between themselves individually. When the plaintiff discovered this he sued the defendant to recover the profits for the corporation. It was held that "the majority have put something into their pockets at the expense of the minority" and that the case was, therefore, "precisely one of the exceptions" to the rule in *Foss v. Harbottle*.

Framed in this way, fraud on the minority could not be extended to breaches that did not involve the taking of corporate property. One example of this, considered in the last section, was *Pavlides v. Jensen*, where the plaintiff complained of negligence on the part of directors but did not allege fraud. Similarly, a manager's sale of this own property to his corporation, as in *North-West Transportation*, could not amount to an expropriation of corporate property. The result was a criterion of when a derivative action might be brought which did not appear to depend on the seriousness of the breach from an economic point of view. For example, an interested director's contract may give rise to serious financial loss, while the loss associated with looting corporate assets might be trivial, but these considerations ostensibly counted for little in *Foss v. Harbottle*.

One of the policies behind *Foss v. Harbottle* was a judicial reluctance to intervene in corporate management. For example, Lord Davey stated in *Burland v. Earle*, [1902] A.C. 83, 93 (P.C.), that:

> the court will not interfere with the internal management of companies acting within their powers ... [I]t is clear law that in order to redress the wrong done to the company, or to recover moneys or damages alleged to be due to the company, the action should *prima facie* be brought by the company itself.

This principle may be seen as a application of a more general judicial reluctance to apply standards of substantive fairness, with norms of procedural unconscionability preferred. For example, by foreclosing an enquiry into the fairness of a transaction, the prophylactic rule in *Aberdeen Ry.* was considerably easier to apply than one that would have required a court to determine whether the contract was in reality in the interests of the corporation. Similarly, the criterion as to standing to bring a derivative action would seem ridiculously easy to apply when a director sells his assets to his firm: since no corporate property is expropriated, a derivative action may never be maintained. In addition, a strict equitable standard as to duties of loyalty in *Aberdeen Ry.* is rendered more palatable by the barriers to derivative actions.

More recently, English courts have tempered the strictness of the rule of non-standing in the case of contracts with the corporation. In *Daniels v. Daniels*, [1978] 1 Ch. 406, a corporation sold land for £4,250 to one of its directors in October 1970, who resold it four years later for £120,000. The statement of claim alleged that the 1970 price was one which the defendants knew or ought to have known was less than the current value of the land at that time. The plaintiff shareholders did not allege fraud, and the defendants brought an application to strike out the claim for failing to state a cause of action. Since the breach did involve the sale of corporate assets, it might perhaps have been found to constitute an expropriation of corporate property, and thus to amount to fraud on the minority even without a specific allegation of fraud. However, Templeman J. preferred to rest the right of the plaintiff's to bring the action on broader grounds.

> The authorities which deal with simple fraud on the one hand and gross negligence on the other do not cover the situation which arises where, without fraud, the directors and majority shareholders are guilty of a breach of duty which they owe to the company, and that breach of duty not only harms the company but benefits the directors. In that case it seems to me that different considerations apply. If minority shareholders can sue if there is fraud, I can see no reason why they cannot sue where the action of the majority and the directors, though without fraud, confers some

benefit on those directors and majority shareholders themselves. It would seem to me quite monstrous—particularly as fraud is so hard to plead and difficult to prove—if the confines of the exception to *Foss v. Harbottle* … were drawn so narrowly that directors could make a profit out of their negligence. … To put up with foolish directors is one thing; to put up with directors who are so foolish that they make a profit of £115,000 odd at the expense of the company is something entirely different. [*Id.* at 413-14]

A greater judicial readiness to examine issues of substantive fairness was also evident in *Wedge v. McNeill* (1981), 126 D.L.R. (3d) 596, rev'd (1982),142 D.L.R. (3d) 133 (P.E.I. S.C.), where C Ltd. owned 99% of the shares of Hillcrest Housing Ltd., a Prince Edward Island corporation. C Ltd. was in turn owned in equal proportions by W Ltd., B Ltd. and G Ltd. W Ltd. was owned by the plaintiff Wedge, B Ltd. by the defendant McNeill, and G Ltd. by the defendant MacDonald. Wedge, McNeill and MacDonald were directors of Hillcrest. In the law suit, Wedge alleged that McNeill and MacDonald had caused Hillcrest to enter into transactions with Arcona, a corporation wholly owned by McNeill and MacDonald, which had the effect of diverting to Arcona large amounts of profits that rightfully belonged to Hillcrest. The transactions had been ratified by Hillcrest's 99% shareholder, C Ltd., as a result of the defendants' indirect control of C Ltd. On a stated case, the trial judge found the contracts to have been unfair to Hillcrest, and held that the ratification was a nullity because it had been procured by the indirect ownership by the defendants of the majority of Hillcrest shares. In his decision, Large J. adopted the following passage from Wegenast 237-38:

It comes back … to a question of the equities of the particular transaction which is impeached. Thus in the case of *North-West Transportation Co. v. Beatty*, it is easy to infer that if the purchase price of the boat sold to the company by the respondent director had not been a reasonable price, the fact that the respondent had at a directors' meeting voted for the adoption of the contract would have rendered it invalid and a ratification of the contract by a majority vote of the shareholders would not have availed to cure the invalidity. It would seem, therefore, that the real question in each case is as to the equity and good faith of the transaction and that it would not be safe to rely upon the rule in *Foss v. Harbottle* except in cases of purely technical irregularity.

The Prince Edward Island Supreme Court, sitting *en banc*, allowed the defendants' appeal on the basis that the facts as submitted did not support the trial judge's conclusion that the contracts were unfair.

The CBCA has now substantially altered the circumstances in which shareholders have standing to bring a derivative action. A "complainant," as defined in s. 238, may bring a derivative action upon obtaining leave of the court under s. 239. In screening claims to determine when a derivative action may be brought, the CBCA has substituted for the pigeonholes of *Foss v. Harbottle* a more flexible standard geared to such questions as the good faith of the complainant and the interests of the corporation. The effect of CBCA s. 239 is to make it easier to commence a derivative action in circumstances that formerly fell without the rule in *Foss v. Harbottle*, but it is also more difficult to sue derivatively in those cases that formerly would have amounted to an exception to the rule, since leave of a court to litigate is now required under s. 239(2). Even with s. 239, common law standards of when a derivative action could be brought might well have survived if ratification continued to cure a breach, and CBCA s. 242 therefore provides that shareholder ratification will not suffice to stay a derivative action. Evidence of shareholder approval may, however, be taken into account by the court in granting a remedy for a derivative action. When the vote of ratification is effected through the vote of the errant director, as in *North-West Transportation*, its evidentiary value may then be slight. See *Re Northwest Forest Products Ltd.*, infra Section F.

See further Beck, *The Shareholders' Derivative Action*, 52 Can. Bar Rev. 159 (1974); Beck, *An Analysis of Foss v. Harbottle*, in 2 Ziegel 545; Buckley, *Ratification and the Derivative Action under the Ontario Business Corporations Act*, 22 McGill L.J. 167 (1976); Wedderburn, *Shareholders' Rights and the Rule in Foss v. Harbottle*, [1957] Camb. L.J. 194 (pt. 1), [1958] Camb. L.J. 93 (pt. 2).

Safe Harbour for Interested Contracts. The harshness of strict equitable rules under pre-CBCA law is mitigated by s. 120, which provides a mechanism whereby interested contracts may be upheld on a review of their substantive fairness. A contract in which a director or officer has a material interest is not voidable "by reason only of that relationship" where (1) the director or officer has made written disclosure of his interest in the contract; (2) after such disclosure the contract has been approved either by a disinterested majority of the board or by a majority of the shareholders; and (3) the contract was reasonable and fair to the corporation at the time it was approved. Apart from the criterion of substantive fairness, the procedural requirements of s. 120 may not be onerous where the approval is by the directors (presumably in most cases). On board ratification the interest directors may be counted toward a quorum, not an insignificant matter.

Other than these ratification requirements, CBCA s. 120 does not set down any procedural standards for the determination of the fairness of the contract. However, managers will often wish to adopt some of the techniques of directorial review discussed in *Van Gorkom*. In particular, major interested contracts will often be approved by a committee of independent directors and certified as fair in a fairness opinion from a securities firm or investment banker. Indeed, in the case of transactions that are subject to OSC Policy 9.1, the OSC has stated that it "is good practice" to make use of such a committee. Though these devices have been criticized as rubber stamps (and expensive ones in the case of fairness opinions), they might also serve to reduce management misbehaviour.

It has been argued that the evidential weight of independent directors' committees and of fairness opinions is weakened by the absence of clear standards of what constitutes an adequate fairness review. See Guiffra, *Investment Bankers' Fairness Opinions in Corporate Control Transactions*, 96 Yale L.J. 119 (1986) (advocating strict judicial scrutiny of directors' reliance on fairness opinions and judicial recognition of the duty of investment bankers to act with care when giving fairness opinions). If levering up the standards of a fairness review in this way produced a better quality review, courts would likely respond by relying to a greater extent on the review as a badge of fairness. This would assist in resolving uncertainty as to whether the transaction might be impeached under s. 120. This benefit must, however, be weighed against the cost of more formal review structures. In addition, arguments for legal rules on the basis of externalities seem inappropriate here, since the full costs of a shoddy review will be borne by the firm that commissioned it. The risk that a court will not place much weight upon a hastily prepared review might thus provide the firm and its investment banker or securities firm with an adequate incentive to take care in a fairness review, without the need for liability on breach of due care standards. The scope of the review to be conducted by the investment banker or securities firm will have been specified by the firm commissioning the opinion, and will be described in the opinion. Since it bears the costs of an inadequate review, the scope of the review might then perhaps be left to the determination of the firm.

CBCA s. 120(8) provides that where the director or officer fails to make the required disclosure, the corporation or a shareholder may apply to a court, which may "set aside the contract on such terms as it thinks fit." If it is not feasible to avoid the contract, may the court order the director to account for his profits? Is s. 120(8) self-executing or must a shareholder applicant comply with s. 239 (derivative actions)? See *Churchill Pulpmill Ltd. v. Manitoba*, [1977] 6 W.W.R. 109 (C.A.). What happens where the director does make the required disclosure but either the contract is not fair or approval by the board or the shareholders is not forthcoming? Note that the failure of the board to approve does not necessarily mean that the contract cannot be carried out because many contracts, even material ones, can be carried out on the authority of an officer. Section 120 is not a code for interested directors' contracts but rather a safe harbour rule. Where its terms are met, certain common law consequences, which would ordinarily attach to such transactions, do not apply. Where its terms are not met, then presumably the common law rules apply. In this regard, OBCA s. 132 is more comprehensive in its terms than CBCA s. 120.

State ex rel. Hayes Oyster Co. v. Keypoint Oyster Co.
Washington Supreme Court
391 P.2d 979 (1964)

DENNEY, Judge: This is an action to determine ownership of an interest in the capital stock of a corporation under circumstances requiring consideration of corporate morality and ethics in the conduct of the president, manager and director of a corporation in the sale of corporate assets.

The parties are Hayes Oyster Company, an Oregon corporation, hereinafter called Hayes Oyster; Coast Oyster Company, a Washington corporation, hereinafter called Coast; Keypoint Oyster Company, a Washington corporation, hereinafter called Keypoint; Joseph W. Engman, his wife, Edith M. Engman; Verne Hayes and Sam Hayes. Verne Hayes will be referred to as Hayes unless designated otherwise.

The action was commenced against Keypoint to require transfer of 50 per cent of its stock to Hayes Oyster. Keypoint disclaimed ownership of the stock and interpleaded other parties heretofore mentioned.

Hayes was one of the founders of Coast which, over the years, became a public corporation and acquired several large oyster property holdings, among which were oyster beds and facilities for harvesting oysters located at Allyn and Poulsbo, Washington. These properties will hereafter be referred to as Allyn and Poulsbo. Hayes was an officer and director of Coast from its incorporation and was president and manager and owner of 23 per cent of its stock in the year 1960, and a portion of 1961, during which time the events leading to this litigation occurred.

On October 21, 1958, Coast and Hayes entered into a full employment contract by which Hayes was to act as president and manager of Coast for a 10-year period and to refrain directly or indirectly from taking part in any business which would be in competition with the business of Coast, except Hayes Oyster.

Hayes Oyster was a family-owned corporation in which Sam Hayes owned about 75 per cent and Verne Hayes about 25 per cent of its stock.

[By the spring of 1960 Coast was in need of immediate cash. Hayes suggested that it sell the Allyn and Poulsbo beds. In June Hayes suggested to Engman, a long-time Coast employee, that Engman might wish to purchase them. Engman was interested but told Hayes that he would need capital to commence operations. He suggested that Hayes might wish to go in on the deal with him. On August 11, the board of Coast voted to sell the beds to Engman. Engman caused Keypoint Oyster Co. to be incorporated on October 1 to carry out his part of the bargain. On September 1 Engman and Hayes had agreed that Hayes would co-sign a bank note of Keypoint and in return Hayes Oyster would receive 50% of the shares in Keypoint. Keypoint issued 50% of its shares to Mrs. Engman, who agreed to hold them beneficially for Hayes Oyster. On October 21, a Coast shareholders meeting was held to approve the sale of beds to Engman/Keypoint. Hayes held proxies which, with his own stock, authorized him to vote a majority of Coast stock in favour of the resolution, which he did.]

Hayes made no mention at the meeting in Long Beach on August 4, 1960, or at the Coast directors' meeting on August 11, 1960, that Hayes or Hayes Oyster might acquire some interest in Keypoint. Hayes made no disclosure to any officer, director, stockholder or employee of Coast at the shareholders' meeting or at the time Hayes signed the contract for Coast on October 21, 1960, that Hayes or Hayes Oyster were to participate in or have a financial interest in Keypoint. Indeed, Coast acquired no knowledge of the Engman-Hayes deal until subsequent to the termination of Hayes' administrative duties as president and general manager of Coast in May, 1961; and subsequent to the time Hayes sold his stock in Coast and the execution of an agreement on March 7, 1962, between Hayes and Coast, by which Hayes' rights and obligations under the 1958 full-employment contract were settled.

[In June, 1962 Hayes demanded that the shares of Keypoint held by Mrs. Engman should be transferred on Keypoint's books into the name of Hayes Oyster. Engman refused and informed Coast for the first time of Hayes's involvement in Keypoint. In the ensuing litigation, Hayes, Hayes Oyster, Engman, Keypoint and Coast were all parties. Hayes demanded that the Keypoint shares be registered in the name of Hayes Oyster; Coast asserted that the shares should be transferred, to it. At trial, Hayes prevailed and Coast appealed.]

Coast does not seek a rescission of the contract with Keypoint, nor does it question the adequacy of the consideration which Keypoint agreed to pay for the purchase of Allyn and Poulsbo, nor does Coast claim that it suffered any loss in the transaction. It does assert that Hayes, Coast's president, manager and director, acquired a secret profit and personal advantage to himself in the acquisition of the Keypoint stock by Hayes or Hayes Oyster in the side deal with Engman; and that such was in violation of his duty to Coast, and that, therefore, Hayes or Hayes Oyster should disgorge such secret profit to Coast.

Certain basic concepts have long been recognized by courts throughout the land on the status of corporate officers and directors. They occupy a fiduciary relation to a private corporation and the shareholders thereof akin to that of a trustee, and owe undivided loyalty, and a standard of behavior above that of the workaday world. ...

This concept is confirmed by the enactment of RCW 23.01.360, which provides:

Officers and directors shall be deemed to stand in a fiduciary relation to the corporation, and shall discharge the duties of their respective positions in good faith, and with that diligence, care and skill which ordinarily prudent men would exercise similar circumstances in like positions.

Directors and other officers of a private corporation directly or indirectly acquire a profit for themselves or acquire any other personal advantage in dealings with others on behalf of the corporation. ...

Respondent is correct in his contention that this court has abolished the mechanical rule whereby any transaction involving corporate property in which a director has an interest is voidable at the option of the corporation. Such a contract cannot be voided if the director or officer can show that the transaction was fair to the corporation. However, nondisclosure by an interested director or officer is, in itself, unfair. This wholesome rule can be applied automatically without any of the unsatisfactory results which flowed from a rigid bar against any self-dealing. ...

The trial court found that any negotiations between Hayes and Engman up to the time of the loan by the Poulsbo Bank on September 1, 1960, resulted in no binding agreement that Hayes would have any personal interest for himself or as a stockholder in Hayes Oyster in the sale of Allyn and Poulsbo. The undisputed evidence, however, shows that Hayes knew he might have some interest in the sale. It would have been appropriate for Hayes to have disclosed his possible interest at the informal meeting in Long Beach on August 4, 1960, and particularly at the meeting of Coast's board of directors on August 11, 1960. It is not necessary, however, for us to decide this case on a consideration of Hayes' obligation to Coast under the circumstances obtaining at that time.

Subsequent to the agreement with Engman, Hayes attended the meeting of Coast stockholders on October 21, 1960, recommended the sale, and voted a majority of the stock, including his own, in favor of the sale to Keypoint. On the same day, as president of Coast, he signed the contract which, among other things, required Keypoint to pay 10 monthly payments amounting to $25,000 per year, to pay interest on deferred balance at 5 per cent, to make payments on an option agreement which Coast had with one Smith, to plant sufficient seed to produce 45,000 gallons of oysters per year, inform Coast of plantings, furnish annual reports to Coast, operate the oysterlands in good workmanlike manner, keep improvements in repair, pay taxes, refrain directly or indirectly from engaging in growing, processing or marketing dehydrated oysters or oyster stew, give Coast first refusal on purchase of Keypoint oysters of 10,000 gallons per year or one-fourth of Keypoint's production. Title was reserved in Coast until payment in full of the purchase price of $250,000 and was subject to forfeiture for failure to pay installments or to fulfill any of the conditions of the contract.

At this juncture, Hayes was required to divulge his interest in Keypoint. His obligation to do so arose from the possibility, even probability that some controversy might arise between Coast and Keypoint relative to the numerous provisions of the executory contract. Coast shareholders and directors had the right to know of Hayes' interest in Keypoint in order to intelligently determine the advisability of retaining Hayes as president and manager under the circumstances, and to determine whether or not it was wise to enter into the contract at all, in view of Hayes' conduct. In all fairness, they were entitled to know that their president and director might be placed in a position where he must choose between the interest of Coast and Keypoint in conducting Coast's business with Keypoint.

Furthermore, after receipt of the Keypoint stock, Hayes instructed the treasurer of Coast to make a payment on the Smith lease-option agreement which Keypoint was required to pay under the provisions of the contract. This action by Hayes grew out of a promise which Hayes made to Engman during their negotiations before the sale to reduce the sale price because of mortality of oysters on Allyn and Poulsbo. There was a clear conflict of interest.

The cases relied upon by respondent are not opposed to the rule condemning secrecy when an officer or director of a corporation may profit in the sale of corporate assets. In *Leppaluoto v. Eggleston* [357 P.2d 725 (Wash. 1960)], Eggleston secretly chartered his own equipment to a corporation in which he had one-half interest, for $25,000, without the knowledge of the owner of the remaining stock. We held that Eggleston was not required to return the $25,000 to the corporation because there was no proof that the charter arrangement was unfair or unreasonable and no proof that Eggleston made any profit on the transaction and that, absent proof of loss to the corporation or profit to Eggleston, no recovery could be had. In the case before us, profit to Hayes or Hayes Oyster in acquiring 50 per cent of Keypoint stock is clear and undisputed.

● ● ●

It is true that Hayes hypothecated his stock in Coast in one of Coast's creditors in early August, 1960. Undoubtedly, this aided Coast in placating its creditors at that time and showed absence of an intent to defraud Coast. It is not necessary, however, that an officer or director of a corporation have an intent to defraud or that any injury result to the corporation for an officer or director to violate his fiduciary obligation in secretly acquiring an interest in corporate property.

In quoting from 13 Am.Jur. § 1002, p. 955, in the case of *Lycette v. Green River Gorge, Inc.*, 21 Wash. 2d 859, p. 865, 153 p. 2d 873, p. 876, we said:

Actual injury is not the principle upon which the law proceeds in condemning such contracts. Fidelity in the agent is what is aimed at, and as a means of securing it, the law will not permit the agent to place himself in a situation in which he may be tempted by his own private interest to disregard that of his principal. ...

Respondent asserts that action by Coast shareholders was not necessary to bind Coast to the sale because it had already been approved by Coast's board of directors.

Assuming this to be true, Hayes' fiduciary status with Coast did not change. He could not place himself in an adverse position to Coast by acquiring an interest in the executory contract before the terms of said contract have been performed by Keypoint.

The trial court found that Coast's release of Hayes on March 7, 1962, was not binding on Coast because there was no disclosure of Hayes' or Hayes Oyster's interest in Keypoint. We agree. A corporation cannot ratify the breach of fiduciary duties unless full and complete disclosure of all facts and circumstances is made by the fiduciary and an intentional relinquishment by the corporation of its rights. ...

Coast had the option to affirm the contract or seek rescission. It chose the former and can successfully invoke the principle that whatever a director or officer acquires by virtue of his fiduciary relation, except in open dealings with the company, belongs not to such director or officer, but to the company. Nothing less than this satisfies the law. 3 Fletcher, Cyclopedia of Corporations (1947 ed.) § 888, p. 289.

2 Thompson on Corporations (3d ed.) § 1339, p. 822, has this to say:

The corporation may compel a director to account for all profits made by him in dealings with the corporation and this without disaffirming the contract under which the profits were made.

This rule appears to have universal application and is recognized in this state. *Leppaluoto v. Eggleston*, supra; *Kane v. Klos* [314 P.2d 672 (Wash. 1957)].

The trial court's finding that Hayes acted on behalf of Hayes Oyster in all of his negotiations with Engman subsequent to July, 1960, does not alter the situation. Sam Hayes knew that Verne Hayes was president and manager of Coast and owed complete devotion to the interests of Coast at the time Verne Hayes first approached him on the subject of sharing with Engman in the purchase of Allyn and Poulsbo. Sam Hayes knew and agreed that any interest of Verne Hayes or Hayes Oyster in Keypoint was to be kept secret and revealed to no one, including Coast. Sam Hayes authorized Verne Hayes to proceed with the deal on behalf of Hayes Oyster on this basis. Verne Hayes became the agent of Hayes Oyster in negotiating with Engman.

It is well settled that a corporation is chargeable with constructive notice of facts acquired by an agent while acting within the scope of his authority. *Post v. Maryland Casualty Co.*, 2 Wash. 2d 21, 97 P.2d 173. Verne Hayes was the moving spirit in the transaction with Engman. Hayes Oyster cannot claim immunity from Verne Hayes' fiduciary breach to Coast.

Hayes Oyster gave no consideration for any interest in Keypoint. It did not even become liable on the Poulsbo Bank note. Every sound consideration of equity affects Hayes Oyster as well as Verne Hayes. Neither can profit by the dereliction of Verne Hayes.

• • •

The decree ordering issuance of a new certificate stock for 250 shares of Keypoint Oyster Company to Hayes Oyster Company is reversed with direction to order Keypoint Oyster Company to issue a new certificate for 250 shares of its stock to Coast Oyster Company and cancel the certificates heretofore standing in the name of or assigned to Hayes Oyster Company.

Appellant Coast Oyster Company will recover costs against Verne Hayes, Sam Hayes and Hayes Oyster Company.

WEAVER, HUNTER, HAMILTON and HALE JJ. concur.

NOTES

1) The Court said that the "profit to Hayes or Hayes Oyster in acquiring 50% of Keypoint stock is clear and undisputed." Treating Hayes and Hayes Oyster as one, how would you calculate their profits? Did they give any consideration for the 50% interest in Keypoint? As a result of the judgment, Coast got this 50% interest for no consideration.

2) Hayes claimed that his failure to disclose his interest in Keypoint at the Coast shareholders' meeting was unimportant because Coast's shareholders did not have to approve the sale. Whether shareholder approval would be necessary would generally depend upon characterizing the sale of the oyster beds either as within the "ordinary course" of Coast's business, in which case it would fall within the directors' power to manage the corporation, or as a sale of all or substantially all of the corporation undertaking, for which most jurisdictions would require approval by two-thirds of the shares voting. See, for example, CBCA ss. 189(3)-(8). Assuming, that the sale was not of "substantially all" of Coast's undertaking, it may be that Coast's articles or by-laws required shareholder approval of the transaction or that the directors considered it prudent to secure shareholder approval for the sale of a substantial income producing asset. Obviously the shareholders' meeting was not called to approve an interested officer's or director's transaction—unless Engman was himself a sufficiently senior employee of Coast that it was thought necessary for the shareholders to approve a sale to him.

3) If by the time the corporation discovers a director's interest, the contract has already been performed and it cannot be rescinded because the parties cannot be restored to their former positions, can the corporation recover the director's profits? If the applicable analogy is that of trustees buying from or selling to the trust, the answer would appear to be "yes." See *Gray v. New Augarita Porcupine Mines Ltd.*, [1952] 3 D.L.R. 1 (P.C.). However, it has been said that to rescind a contract is one thing but that to hold the director liable for profits is in effect to re-write the contract at a different price. *Burland v. Earle*, [1902] A.C. 83, 99 (P.C.); *Re Cape Breton Co.* (1885), 29 Ch. D. 795, 812 (C.A.), aff'd, sub nom. *Cavendish Bentinck v. Fenn* (1887), 12 App. Cas. 652 (H.L.). In *Burland*, at least, the director was forthright in declaring his interest. Possibly the director's accountability for profits if the contract cannot be rescinded will depend upon the fairness to the corporation of the contract price and the director's openness in dealing with the corporations.

The result in *Hayes Oyster* has the appeal of rough justice to it: if a director fails to reveal his interest in the contract to the relevant body in the corporation—the other directors or the shareholders, as the case may be—then he is accountable for his profits in the transaction, assuming they can be measured. This is a strong prophylactic rule. The directors will be careful to make full disclosure of their interests if failure to do so entails loss of profits. But is this excessive? In *Hayes Oyster*, Coast was apparently fully satisfied with the deal it got from Keypoint and was not interested in rescission of the contract. Compare the judgments in *Hely-Hutchinson v. Brayhead Ltd.*, [1968] 1 Q.B. 549, aff'd, [1968] 1 Q.B. 573 (C.A.) (where, however, the non-disclosure appears to have been more innocent than in *Hayes Oyster*). Is the result in *Hayes Oyster* contemplated by CBCA s. 120(8)? By OBCA s. 132(9)?

How "Interested" Does the Director Have to Be? The interest does not have to be pecuniary. It has been held that where a director of a corporation holds shares in another corporate party to a contract as trustee, rather than beneficially, that interest is sufficient to attract the conflict of interest prohibition. *Transvaal Lands Co. v. New Belgium (Transvaal) Land and Development Co.*, [1914] 2 Ch. 488 (C.A.). CBCA s. 120(1)(b) provides that a directorship in another corporate party to the transaction is an interest. CBCA s. 120(1)(a) refers more generally to material interests of officers and directors in material contracts with the corporation. The term material is not defined. It presumably means substantial or significant.

Material interests of directors must be disclosed in proxy circulars. CBCA Reg. s. 35(bb) requires disclosure of any material interest of officers and directors in respect of "any matter to be acted upon at the meeting" of shareholders for which the proxies are circulated, other than election of directors and appointment of the auditor. If shareholders are being asked at the meeting to approve a transaction for the purposes of s. 120, Reg. 35(bb) governs. Even if action is not to be taken at the meeting, Reg. 35(w) requires disclosure of material interests of officers and directors in material contracts. Reg. 35(w) permits numerous omissions, however. These include contracts in which the officer's or director's interest derives solely from his being a director of another corporate party, contracts wherein the price is fixed by law or by competitive bidding, contracts for banking or other depository services and contracts (not involving remuneration for services) made in the ordinary course of the corporation's business that do not involve more than 10% of its sales or purchases and in which the interest of the officer or director results from his ownership of not more than 10% of the shares of the other party to the transaction. The first and third exceptions are of great practical importance because of the degree to which interlocking directorates among large corporations characterize the Canadian economy and the high degree of concentration in the banking industry. Reg. 35(w) does not state that its exceptions to mandatory disclosure are based on non-materiality, but that may be a fair inference. Does Reg. 35(w) aid in the interpretation of materiality in s. 120?

E. LOOTING: CORPORATE OPPORTUNITIES

In a hypothetical bargain between managers and residual owners of firm value, the right to take advantage of a particular business opportunity would be assigned to the party that values it most highly. In dealings between managers and firms, an asset may be either *firm-specific* (valued more highly by the firm) or *manager-specific* (valued more highly by the manager). With firm-specific opportunities, the parties would provide through non-competition provisions that managers should not pursue the opportunity themselves. On the other hand, where the opportunity is manager-specific, the parties would not wish to assign it to the corporation. A justification of a strict prohibition against the expropriation of a corporate opportunity by a manager therefore requires a demonstration that (1) such opportunities are never manager-specific or (2) if some are, the majority are not and the screening costs, which must be absorbed to distinguish the two kinds of opportunities, are so great that prophylactic rules are warranted. However, both propositions are controversial.

First, some opportunities are likely manager-specific. One reason for this is that agency costs are the lowest when an opportunity is unambiguously assigned to a manager. If the risk of agent misbehaviour is a function of the separation of ownership from control, then giving sole ownership of an opportunity to a manager will eliminate agency costs associated with outside equity interests. Manager-specific opportunities may also arise through the firm's decision not to hire 100% of the manager's time. If a firm, in an exercise of business judgment, decides that it is best served by part-time managerial services, it may then be expected that the managers will seek out their own opportunities for the balance of their working hours. If the manager's expertise relates to only one industry, this may result in competition between him and the firm. In other cases, the firm may be unable to exploit an opportunity through impecuniosity, as where it is on the verge of insolvency or where it is merely financially overextended. A dog-in-the-manger restriction on the manager taking up a positive net present value opportunity that the firm cannot profit from itself may then reduce firm wealth because of the higher managerial compensation the firm will be called on to pay. See further Easterbrook & Fischel, *Corporate Control Transactions*, 91 Yale L.J. 698, 733-35 (1982).

The case for a strict prohibition against assigning a corporate opportunity to a manager must then rest upon a fear that, without a prophylactic rule, management will appropriate firm-specific as well as manager-specific opportunities, and that informational barriers will prevent a court from distinguishing between the two kinds of opportunities. Consider how difficult you think this problem to be after reading the following cases.

Regal (Hastings) Ltd. v. Gulliver
House of Lords
[1942] 1 All E.R. 378

LORD RUSSELL OF KILLOWEN: My Lords, the very special facts which have led up to this litigation require to be stated in some detail, in order to make plain the point which arises for decision on this appeal.

The appellant is a limited company called Regal (Hastings), Ltd., and may conveniently be referred to as Regal. Regal was incorporated in the year 1933 with an authorised capital of £20,000 divided into 17,500 preference shares of £1 each and 50,000 ordinary shares of one shilling each. Its issued capital consisted of 8,950 preference shares and 50,000 ordinary shares. It owned, and managed very successfully, a freehold cinema theatre at Hastings called the Regal. In July, 1935, its board of directors consisted of one Walter Bentley and the respondents Gulliver, Bobby, Griffiths and Bassett. Its shareholders were twenty in number. The respondent Garton acted as its solicitor.

In or about that month, the board of Regal formed a scheme for acquiring a lease of two other cinemas (viz., the Elite at Hastings, and the Cinema de Luxe at St. Leonards), which were owned and managed by a company called Elite Picture Theatres (Hastings & Bristol), Ltd. The scheme was to be carried out by obtaining the grant of a lease to a subsidiary limited company, which was to be formed by Regal, with a capital of 5,000 £1 shares, of which Regal was to subscribe for 2,000 in cash, the remainder being allotted to Regal or its nominees as fully paid for services rendered. The whole beneficial interest in the lease would, if this scheme were carried out, enure solely to the benefit of Regal and its shareholders, through the shareholding of Regal in the subsidiary company. The respondent Garton, on the instructions of Regal, negotiated for the acquisition of the lease, with the result that an offer to take a lease for 35 or 42 years at a rent of £4,600 for the first year, rising in the second and third years up to £5,000 in the fourth and subsequent years, was accepted on behalf of the owners on Aug. 21, 1935, subject to mutual approval of the form of the lease. Subsequently, the owners of the two cinemas required the rent under the proposed lease to be guaranteed.

On Sept. 11, 1935, Walter Bentley died; and on Sept. 18, 1935, his son, the respondent Bentley, who was one of his executors, was appointed a director of Regal. It should now be stated that, concurrently with the negotiations for the acquisition of a lease for the two cinemas, Regal was contemplating a sale of its own cinema, together with the leasehold interest in the two cinemas which it was proposing to acquire. On Sept. 18, 1935, at a board meeting of Regal, the respondent Garton was instructed that the directors were prepared to give a joint guarantee of the rent of the two cinemas, until the subscribed capital of the proposed subsidiary company amounted to £5,000. He was further instructed to deal with all offers received for the purchase of Regal's own assets. On Sept. 26, 1935, the proposed subsidiary company was registered under the name Hastings Amalgamated Cinemas, Ltd., which may, for brevity, be referred to as Amalgamated. Its directors were the five directors of Regal, and in addition the respondent Garton.

• • •

On Oct. 2, 1935, an offer was received from would-be purchasers offering a net sum of £92,500 for the Regal cinema and the lease of the two cinemas. Of this sum £77,500 was allotted as the price of Regal's cinema, and £15,000 as the price of the two leasehold cinemas. This splitting of the price seems to have been done by the purchasers at the request of the respondent Garton; but it must be assumed in favour of the legal directors that they were satisfied that £77,500 was not too low a price to be paid for their company's cinema, with the result that £15,000 cannot be taken to have been in excess of the value of the lease which Amalgamated was about to acquire. On the afternoon of Oct. 2, the six respondents met at 62, Shaftesbury Avenue, London, the registered offices of Regal. Various matters were mentioned and discussed between them, and they came to certain decisions. Subsequently, minutes were prepared which record the different matters as having been transacted at two separate and distinct board meetings, viz., a meeting of the board of Regal, and a meeting of the board of Amalgamated. The respondent Gulliver stated in his evidence that two separate meetings were held, that of the Amalgamated board being held and concluded before that of the Regal board was begun. On the other hand, the respondent Bentley says: "It was more or less held in one lump, because we were talking about selling the three properties." The respondent Garton states that, after it was decided that Regal could only afford to put up £2,000 in Amalgamated, which was purely a matter for the consideration of the Regal board, the next matter discussed was one which figures in the minutes of the Amalgamated board meeting. Moreover, both meetings are recorded in the minutes as having been held at 3 p.m.

Whatever may be the truth as to this, the matters discussed and decided included the following: (i) Regal was to apply for 2,000 shares in Amalgamated; (ii) the offer of £77,500 for the Regal cinema and £15,000 for the two leasehold cinemas was accepted; (iii) the solicitor reporting that completion of the lease was expected to take place on Oct. 7, it was resolved that the seal of Amalgamated be affixed to the engrossment when available; and (iv) the respondent Gulliver having objected to guaranteeing the rent it was resolved "... that the directors be invited to subscribe for 500 shares each and that such shares be allotted accordingly." On Oct. 7, 1935, a lease of the two cinemas was executed in favour of Amalgamated, for the term of 35 years from Sept. 29, 1935, in accordance with the agreement previously come to. The shares of Amalgamated were all issued, and were allotted as follows: 2,000 to Regal, 500 to each of the respondents Bobby, Griffiths, Bassett, Bentley and Garton, and (by the direction of the respondent Gulliver) 200 to a Swiss company called Seguliva A.G., 200 to a company called South Downs Land Co., Ltd., and 100 to a Miss Geering.

In fact, the proposed sale and purchase of the Regal cinema and the two leasehold cinemas fell through. Another proposition, however, took its place, viz., a proposal for the purchase from the individual shareholders of their shares in Regal and Amalgamated. This proposal came to maturity by agreements dated Oct. 24, 1935, as a result of which the 3,000 shares in Amalgamated held otherwise than by Regal were sold for a sum of £3 16s. 1d. per share, or in other words at a profit of £2 16s. 1d. per share over the issue price of par.

As a sequel to the sale of the shares in Regal, that company came under the management of a new board of directors, who caused to be issued the writ which initiated the present litigation. By this action Regal seeks to recover from its five former directors and its former solicitor a sum of £8,142 10s. either as damages or as money had and received to the plaintiffs' use. The action was tried by Wrottesley J., who entered judgment for all the defendants with costs. An appeal by the plaintiffs to the Court of Appeal was dismissed with costs.

My Lords, those are the relevant facts which have led up to the debate in your Lordships' House, and I now proceed to consider whether the appellants are entitled to succeed against any and which of the respondents. The case has, I think, been complicated and obscured by the presentation of it before the trial judge. If a case of wilful misconduct or fraud on the part of the respondents had been made out, liability to make good to Regal any damage which it had thereby suffered could, no doubt, have been established; and efforts were apparently made at the trial, by cross-examination and otherwise, to found such a case. It is, however, due to the respondents to make it clear at the outset that this attempt failed. The case was not so presented to us here. We have to consider the question of the respondents' liability on the footing that, in taking up these shares in Amalgamated, they acted with *bona fides*, intending to act in the interest of Regal.

Nevertheless, they may be liable to account for the profits which they have made, if, while standing in a fiduciary relationship to Regal, they have by reason and in course of that fiduciary relationship made a profit. This aspect of the case was undoubtedly raised before the trial judge, but, in so far as he deals with it in his judgment, he deals with it on a wrong basis. Having stated at the outset quite truly that what he calls "this stroke of fortune" only came the way of the respondents because they were the directors and solicitor of the Regal, he continues thus:

But in order to succeed the plaintiff company must show that the defendants both ought to have caused and could have caused the plaintiff company to subscribe for these shares, and that the neglect to do so caused a loss to the plaintiff company. Short of this, if the plaintiffs can establish that, though no loss was made by the company, yet a profit was corruptly made by the directors and the solicitor, then the company can claim to have that profit handed over to the company, framing the action in such a case for money had and received by the defendants for the plaintiffs' use.

Other passages in his judgment indicate that, in addition to this "corrupt" action by the directors, or, perhaps, alternatively, the plaintiffs in order to succeed must prove that the defendants acted *mala fide*, and not *bona fide* in the interests of the company, or that there was a plot or arrangement between them to divert from the company to themselves a valuable investment. However relevant such considerations may be in regard to a claim for damages resulting from misconduct, they are irrelevant to a claim against a person occupying a fiduciary relationship towards the plaintiff for an account of the profits made by that person by reason and in course of that relationship.

In the Court of Appeal, upon this claim to profits, the view was taken that in order to succeed the plaintiff had to establish that there was a duty on the Regal directors to obtain the shares for Regal. ... Other portions of the judgment appear to indicate that upon this claim to profits, it is a good defence to show *bona fides* or absence of fraud on the part of the directors in the action which they took, or that their action was beneficial to the company, and the judgment ends thus:

That being so, the only way in which these directors could secure that benefit for their company was by putting up the money themselves. Once that decision is held to be a *bona fide* one, and fraud drops out of the case, it seems to me there is only one conclusion, namely, that the appeal must be dismissed with costs.

My Lords, with all respect I think there is a misapprehension here. The rule of equity which insists on those, who by use of a fiduciary position make a profit, being liable to account for that profit, in no way depends on fraud, or absence of *bona fides*; or upon such questions or considerations as whether the profit would or should otherwise have gone to the plaintiff, or whether the profiteer was under a duty to obtain the source of the profit for the plaintiff, or whether he took a risk or acted as he did for the benefit of the plaintiff, or whether the plaintiff has in fact been damaged or benefited by his action. The liability arises from the mere fact of a profit having, in the stated circumstances, been made. The profiteer, however honest and well-intentioned, cannot escape the risk of being called upon to account.

The leading case of *Keech v. Sandford* [(1726), Sel. Cas. Ch. 61] is an illustration of the strictness of this rule of equity in this regard, and of how far the rule is independent of these outside considerations. A lease of the profits of a market had been devised to a trustee for the benefit of an infant. A renewal on behalf of the infant was refused. It was absolutely unobtainable. The trustee, finding that it was impossible to get a renewal for the benefit of the infant, took a lease for his own benefit. Though his duty to obtain it for the infant was incapable of performance, nevertheless he was ordered to assign the lease to the infant, upon the bare ground that, if a trustee on the refusal to renew might have a lease for himself, few renewals would be made for the benefit of *cestui que trust.* Lord King L.C. said, at p. 62:

This may seem hard, that the trustee is the only person of all mankind who might not have the lease: but it is very proper that the rule should be strictly pursued, and not in the least relaxed ...

One other case in equity may be referred to in this contention, viz., *Ex p. James* [(1803), 8 Ves. 337], decided by Lord Eldon L.C. That was a case of a purchase of a bankrupt's estate by the solicitor to the commission, the Lord Eldon L.C. refers to the doctrine thus, at p. 354:

This doctrine as to purchases by trustees, assignees, and persons having a confidential character, stands much more upon general principles than upon the circumstances of any individual case. It rests upon this: that the purchase is not permitted in any case however honest the circumstances; the general interests of justice requiring it to be destroyed in every instance; as no court is equal to the examination and ascertainment of the truth in much the greater number of cases.

Let me now consider whether the essential matters, which the plaintiff must prove, have been established in the present case. As to the profit being in fact made there can be no doubt. The shares were acquired at par and were sold three weeks later at a profit of £2 16s. 1d. per share. Did such of the first five respondents as acquired these very profitable shares acquire them by reason and in course of their office of directors of Regal? In my opinion, when the facts are examined and appreciated, the answer can only be that they did. The actual allotment no doubt had to be made by themselves and Garton (or some of them) in their capacity as directors of Amalgamated; but this was merely an executive act, necessitated by the alteration of the scheme for the acquisition of the lease of the two cinemas for the sole benefit of Regal and its shareholders through Regal's shareholding in Amalgamated. That scheme could only be altered by or with the consent of the Regal board. Consider what in fact took place on Oct. 2, 1935. The position immediately before that day is stated in Garton's letter of Sept. 26, 1935. The directors were willing to guarantee the rent until the subscribed capital of Amalgamated reached £5,000. Regal was to control Amalgamated and own the whole of its share capital, with the consequence that the Regal shareholders would receive their proportion of the sale price of the two new cinemas. The respondents then meet on Oct. 2, 1935. They have before them an offer to purchase the Regal cinema for £77,500, and the lease of the two cinemas for £15,000. The offer is accepted. The draft lease is approved and a resolution for its sealing is passed in anticipation of completion in five days. Some of those present, however, shy at giving guarantees, and accordingly the scheme is changed by the Regal directors in a vital respect. It is agreed that a guarantee shall be avoided by the six respondents bringing the subscribed capital up to £5,000. I will consider the evidence and the minute in a moment. The result of this change of scheme (which only the Regal directors could bring about) may not have been appreciated by them at the time; but its effect upon their company and its shareholders was striking. In the first place, Regal would no longer control Amalgamated, or own the whole of its share capital. The action of its directors had deprived it (acting through its shareholders in general meeting) of the power to acquire the shares. In the second place, the Regal shareholders would only receive a largely reduced proportion of the sale price of the two cinemas. The Regal directors and Garton would receive the moneys of which the Regal shareholders were thus deprived. This vital alteration was brought about in the following circumstances—I refer to the evidence of the respondent Garton. He was asked what was suggested when the guarantees were refused, and this is his answer:

Mr. Gulliver said "We must find it somehow. I am willing to find £500. Are you willing," turning to the other four directors of Regal, "to do the same?" They expressed themselves as willing. He said, "That makes £2,500," and he turned to me and said, "Garton, you have been interested in Mr. Bentley's companies; will you come in to take £500?" I agreed to do so.

Although this matter is recorded in the Amalgamated minutes, this was in fact a decision come to by the directors of Regal, and the subsequent allotment by the directors of Amalgamated was a mere carrying into effect of this decision of the Regal board. The resolution recorded in the Amalgamated minute runs thus: "After discussion it was resolved that the directors be invited to subscribe for 500 shares each, and that such shares be allotted accordingly." As I read that resolution, and my reading agrees with Garton's evidence, the invitation is to the directors of Regal, and is made for the purpose of effectuating the decision which the five directors of Regal had made, that each should take up 500 shares in the Amalgamated. The directors of Amalgamated were not conveying an "invitation" to themselves. That would be ridiculous. They were merely giving effect to the Regal directors' decision to provide £2,500 cash capital themselves, a decision which had been followed by a successful appeal by Gulliver to Garton to provide the balance.

My Lords, I have no hesitation in coming to the conclusion, upon the facts of this case, that these shares, when acquired by the directors, were acquired by reason, and only by reason of the fact that they were directors of Regal, and in the course of their execution of that office.

It now remains to consider whether in acting as directors of Regal they stood in a fiduciary relationship to that company. Directors of a limited company are the creatures of statute and occupy a position peculiar to themselves. In some respects they resemble trustees, in others they do not. In some respects they resemble agents, in others they do not. In some respects they resemble managing partners, in others they do not.

[Lord Russell reviewed many cases.]

In the result, I am of opinion that the directors standing in a fiduciary relationship to Regal in regard to the exercise of their powers as directors, and having obtained these shares by reason and only by reason of the fact that they were directors of Regal and in the course of the execution of that office, are accountable for the profits which they have made out of them. The equitable rule laid down in *Keech v. Sandford* and *Ex p. James*, and similar authorities applies to them in full force. It was contended that these cases were distinguishable by reason of the fact that it was impossible for Regal to get the shares owing to lack of funds, and that the directors in taking the shares were really acting as members of the public. I cannot accept this argument. It was impossible for the *cestui que trust* in *Keech v. Sandford* to obtain the lease, nevertheless the trustee was accountable. The suggestion that the directors were applying simply as members of the public is a travesty of the facts. They could, had they wished, have protected themselves by a resolution (either antecedent or subsequent) of the Regal shareholders in general meeting. In default of such approval, the liability to account must remain. The result is that, in my opinion, each of the respondents Bobby, Griffiths, Bassett and Bentley is liable to account for the profit which he made on the sale of his 500 shares in Amalgamated.

* * *

There remains to consider the case of Garton. He stands on a different footing from the other respondents in that he was not a director of Regal. He was Regal's legal adviser; but, in my opinion, he has a short but effective answer to the plaintiffs' claim. He was requested by the Regal directors to apply for 500 shares. They arranged that they themselves should each be responsible for £500 of the Amalgamated capital, and they appealed, by their chairman, to Garton to subscribe the balance of £500 which was required to make up the £3,000. In law his action, which has resulted in a profit, was taken at the request of Regal, and I know of no principle or authority which would justify a decision that a solicitor must account for profit resulting from a transaction which he has entered into on his own behalf, not merely with the consent, but at the request of his client.

My Lords, in my opinion the right way in which to deal with this appeal is (i) to dismiss the appeal as against the respondents Gulliver and Garton with costs, (ii) to allow it with costs as against the other four respondents, and (iii) to enter judgment as against each of these four respondents for a sum of £1,402 1s. 8d. with interest at 4 per cent from Oct. 25, 1935, as to £1,300 part thereof and from Dec. 5, 1935, as to the balance. As regards the liability of these four respondents for costs, I have read the shorthand notes of the evidence at the trial, and it is clear to me that the costs were substantially increased by the suggestions of *mala fides* and fraud with which the cross-examination abounds, and from which they have been exonerated. In my opinion a proper order to make would be to order these four respondents to pay only three-quarters of the appellants' taxed costs of the action. The taxed costs of the appellants in the Court of Appeal and in this House they must pay in full.

One final observation I desire to make. In his judgment Lord Greene M.R. stated that a decision adverse to the directors in the present case involved the proposition that, if directors *bona fide* decide not to invest their company's funds in some proposed investment, a director who thereafter embarks his own money therein is accountable for any profits which he may derive therefrom. As to this, I can only say that to my mind the facts of this hypothetical case bear but little resemblance to the story with which we have had to deal.

[The judgments of Lords MACMILLAN, WRIGHT, PORTER and VISCOUNT SANKEY, all of which were to the same effect as that of LORD RUSSELL, have been omitted.]

Appeal allowed.

NOTES

1) The action was dismissed against Gulliver because he bought no shares himself but instead procured others to buy his allotment. Any profits were made by them and not by him.

2) What did Lord Russell mean when he said that the case had to be decided on the basis that the directors in purchasing the shares of Amalgamated for themselves had acted with *bona fides*? Presumably, *bona fides* would mean that the directors had no intention to make a profit for themselves by depriving Regal of a profitable opportunity. On one view, the case for the directors could be put even higher. They were clearly under no obligation personally to guarantee Regal's payments on the leases. Had they not purchased the shares for themselves, Regal would have lost the opportunity to make the profit that it did make. So viewing the facts, why were the directors held liable? Why must courts apply with uncompromising rigidity the rule that prohibits a fiduciary from making a profit for himself in the course of carrying out his fiduciary office, if to do so would deprive the corporation of a profitable opportunity? If *everyone* is better off in such cases, should the transactions still be prohibited because greater profits go to some people than to others? Is Lord Eldon's answer in *Ex p. James* convincing? Are courts any less able to ascertain the truth in this category of cases than in others?

3) How likely do you think it is that at the October 2 meeting the directors would have been able to make a decision totally untainted by self-interest? At that point Regal had received an offer to purchase the assets of Amalgamated at a price yielding a 200% profit over that which Amalgamated was about to pay for the same assets. The directors knew that for every pound which they determined was in excess of what Regal could invest in Amalgamated, one or another of themselves would be able to earn a two pound profit. Might Regal have been able to secure a loan for the £3,000 that the directors determined it was unable to supply from its own resources? What did Lord Russell mean when he said that a hypothetical in which directors decided *bona fide* not to invest company funds in a proposed transaction in which thereafter one of the directors invests his own funds "would bear but little resemblance to the story with which we have had to deal"? Is that the story of *Regal*? Did Lord Russell actually doubt the directors' good faith but feel constrained not to say so? The trial judge in commenting upon the evidence remarked:

All this subsequent history does not help me to decide whether the action of the directors of the plaintiff company and their solicitor on Oct. 2 was *bona fide* in the interests of the company and not *mala fide* and in breach of their duty to the company. ... I must take it that, in the realization of those facts, it means that I cannot accept what has to be established by the plaintiff, and that is that the defendants here acted in ill faith. ... Finally, I have to remind myself, were it necessary, that the burden of proof, as in a criminal case, is the plaintiffs', who must establish the fraud they allege. On the whole, I do not think the plaintiff company succeeds in doing that and, therefore, there must be judgment for the defendants. [Quoted by Viscount Sankey, [1942] 1 All. E.R. at 380]

4) Why was the solicitor, Garton, absolved of liability in *Regal*? Was it because as a solicitor he did not stand in a fiduciary relationship toward his client, Regal? See *Boardman v. Phipps*, [1967] 2 A.C. 46 (H.L.). Who do you think was more familiar with the old chestnuts from the law of trusts, Garton or the non-lawyer directors?

5) Lord Russell's test of what constitutes a corporate asset amounts to something less than a rule that prohibits all possible conflicts of interest between managers and their firms, since a breach arises only when managers make a profit "by reason and in the course of" their managerial duties. This suggests that, had the information come to the Regal directors otherwise than in the course of their duties, they might have retained any resulting profits.

6) Note that Lord Russell stated that the directors would have been absolved of liability to the corporation had they secured approval of their conduct from the Regal shareholders. By the time Regal's action was commenced, however, it was too late for ratification. The defendants were by then the former directors, and the new owners of Regal were not the owners at the time of the conduct in question. They were, in fact, the persons who had bought the shares of Regal and of Amalgamated in the transaction that yielded the profit in question. There is no suggestion that in purchasing the shares they did not receive full value for their money. The recovery by Regal was then a windfall for its new owners. That fact by itself does not indicate that the case was wrongly decided if its facts called for the application of a strong prophylactic rule. This subject is taken up in more detail, in Section F of this part of the chapter, in connection with the *Abbey Glen* case.

Peso Silver Mines Ltd. v. Cropper
Supreme Court of Canada
[1966] S.C.R. 673, 58 D.L.R. (2d) 1, 56 W.W.R. 641

[This was an action by Peso against Cropper, one of its founding directors, for a declaration that shares owned by Cropper in Cross Bow Mines Ltd. and Mayo Silver Mines Ltd. were held by him as trustee for Peso or, in the alternative, that Cropper was liable to account to Peso for the proceeds of those shares. At the end of the trial the action was dismissed, a result upheld in the British Columbia Court of Appeal, with one judge dissenting. Peso appealed to the Supreme Court of Canada.]

CARTWRIGHT J. (by whom the judgment of the Court was delivered): The findings of fact made by the learned trial judge were concurred in by the Court of Appeal and were not challenged before us. In order to appreciate the questions to be decided it is necessary to set out the facts in some detail.

The respondent resides in Vancouver. At the date of the trial, in December 1964, he stated that he had had twenty years of successful business experience. He was then president of Traders Investment Limited in Vancouver and of several mining companies. He has a practical knowledge of mining and had done some prospecting for himself in 1958 and 1959.

In 1959, R. Verity, D. Ross and the respondent caused a company, Tanar Gold Mines Limited, hereinafter referred to as "Tanar" to be incorporated and became its first directors. At the invitation of the respondent C.S. Walker also became a shareholder and director of Tanar.

On March 17, 1961, Tanar caused the appellant to be incorporated as a private company. Walker, Verity and the respondent were its first directors and a month later three additional directors, Whittal, Lennox and Hodges were duly appointed. Tanar transferred to the appellant a number of claims in the Mayo district in the Yukon Territory which it had acquired from one C.D. Poli together with additional claims which had been staked on Tanar's instructions. In return for these, shares in the appellant were issued to Tanar.

On September 18, 1961, the appellant was converted into a public company and from time to time a considerable number of its shares were sold to raise funds to explore, develop and add to its properties. Until the commencement of the action the appellant, Tanar and CalMac Gold Mines Ltd., another company which Tanar had caused to be incorporated, had their offices in the same suite in Vancouver.

By the end of 1961 or early in 1962 the appellant had acquired, in addition to the claims which it had been formed to take over, a further 128 claims from the Barker Estate. In the result in the spring of 1962 it held about 20 square miles of mineral claims in the Yukon and was doing field work and exploration thereon. It had strained the financial resources of the appellant to take over the Barker claims. The appellant had been advised by its engineers that it should spend on the properties it then held from $40,000 to $50,000 per month during 1962. The acquisition of additional claims would have involved increased expenditures and the appellant neither needed nor wanted more ground at this time.

On April 20, 1961, the respondent was appointed managing director of the appellant at a monthly salary of $750 which was increased to $11,000 per annum in June 1962.

Early in the spring of 1962 a prospector, Dickson, was endeavouring to sell three groups of claims in the Mayo district totalling 126 claims. One group was contiguous to the appellant's ground, a second was about five miles to the north-east and the third about eleven miles to the north-east. The claims were unproven and of speculative value. Dickson's asking price was some $31,000 in cash together with a block of shares in a public company to be formed to take over the property. Dickson approached Dr. Aho, a consulting geologist who was retained by the appellant and by many other mining companies. Dr. Aho suggested that Dickson should offer the claims to the appellant and he did so. Dickson's offer was considered by the full board of directors to the appellant in March 1962, and was rejected. On this point there are concurrent findings of fact which were expressed as follows in the reasons of Bull J.A.:

It was common ground, and so found by the learned trial Judge, that this decision rejecting the acquisition was an honest and considered decision of the appellant's board of directors as a whole and done in the best of faith and solely in the interest of the appellant, and not from any personal or ulterior motive on the part of any director, including the respondent.

During the time that the respondent was an officer of the appellant there were between 200 and 300 mining properties offered to it; it was usual for it to receive two or three of such offers a week.

After the appellant had rejected Dickson's offer and the matter had passed out of the respondent's mind, Dr. Aho came to the respondent and suggested the possibility of a group being formed to acquire Dickson's claims. After some discussion it was agreed that Dr. Aho, Walker, Verity and the respondent would take up these claims and they did so, each contributing an equal amount to finance the purchase. Dr. Aho who knew the property advised his associates that he was unaware of any specific mineralization thereon and it is common ground that the purchase was a highly speculative venture.

In May 1962, Cross Bow was incorporated to make the purchase, the four partici- pants put up in equal shares the money necessary to have the intervening ground be- tween the groups of claims "staked blind" by Dickson thus increasing the total holdings to approximately 326 claims. Shortly afterwards Mayo was incorporated as a public company to take over, finance and develop the properties and Cross Bow received 600,000 escrowed shares of Mayo for the properties out of which Dickson received his agreed proportion. Later the respondent and his associates bought for cash about 50,000 free treasury shares of Mayo at 10 cents to 12 cents per share. The respondent was at all relevant times a director of both Cross Bow and Mayo.

In November 1963, Charter Oil Company Limited, hereinafter referred to as "Char- ter," offered to purchase 1,000,000 shares of the capital stock of the appellant at the price of $1 per share, payable $200,000 on the date of closing and $200,000 on or before the tenth days of February, April, June and August, 1964.

[At the end of 1963, five Charter nominees, including one Berliz, joined the Peso board. The officers then included: Berliz, Chairman; Walker, President; and Cropper, Executive Vice-President.]

According to the evidence of Mr. Walker, who was called by the plaintiff, there was a disagreement between Berliz and the respondent in regard to the making of the payment of $200,000 from Charter to the appellant which fell due in February 1964 and this resulted in "a spirit of unfriendliness between the two of them." On Febru- ary 26, 1964, Berliz sent a memorandum to the respondent reading in part: "It is imperative that all officers of Peso Silver Mines make full disclosure of their connec- tion with other mining companies." At a meeting of the executive committee of the appellant on March 6, 1964, the respondent disclosed his interest in Cross Bow and Mayo and repeated this at a meeting of the directors of the appellant on March 16, 1964. At the last-mentioned meeting Berliz asked the respondent if he was prepared to turn over his interest in Cross Bow (and two other companies with which we are not now concerned) at cost. The respondent stated that he would give the matter further consideration. The meeting was later adjourned to the following day. When it reconvened Berliz repeated his request and the respondent refused. Thereupon a mo- tion was passed rescinding the appointment of the respondent as Executive Vice-President and as a member of the Executive Committee. The respondent was asked "to vacate the offices of the Company" and Berliz asked him to resign as a director. The respondent refused to resign as a director but did so later and his resignation was accepted at a meeting of the directors on April 8, 1964.

The action was commenced on March 19, 1964.

The appellant submits that the shares in Cross Bow and Mayo held by the respondent are property obtained by him as a result of his position as a director of the appellant, without the approval of the latter's shareholders, and that equity imposes upon him an obligation to account to the appellant for that property which is unaffected by the circumstances that he acted throughout in good faith, that the appellant had decided for sound business reasons not to acquire the property and had suffered no loss by reason of the respondent's actions.

Counsel for the appellant founded his argument on the decision of the House of Lords in *Regal (Hastings), Ltd. v. Gulliver et al.* [[1942] 1 All. E.R. 378], in which the principles of equity relating to the liability of a person who acquires property in regard to which a fiduciary relationship exists are considered and the leading cases are reviewed. The judgment in *Regal* has been followed by this court in *Zwicker v. Stanbury* [[1953] 2 S.C.R. 438] and in *Midcon Oil & Gas Ltd. v. New British Dominion Oil Co. Ltd. et al.* [[1958] S.C.R. 314]. Counsel for the respondent accepts the statements of the law contained in *Regal* and submits that their application to the facts of the case at bar does not result in imposing liability on the respondent.

It is not necessary to review the somewhat complicated facts of the *Regal* case. While each of the Law Lords stated his reasons in his own words, there was no difference in substance between their statements of the test to be applied in determining whether or not the directors were liable to account for the profit which they personally had made on the purchase and resale of shares in a subsidiary of *Regal*. It will be of assistance to consider the actual words which were used.

• • •

Lord Russell of Killowen, with whose reasons Lord Macmillan, Lord Wright and Lord Porter agreed, said at p. 385:

We have to consider the question of the respondents' liability on the footing that, in taking up these shares in Amalgamated, they acted with *bona fides*, intending to act in the interest of Regal.

Nevertheless they may be liable to account for the profits which they have made, if, while standing in a fiduciary relationship to Regal, they have *by reason and in course of that fiduciary relationship* made a profit.

• • •

In the course of his short concurring speech Lord Macmillan said at p. 391:

The sole ground on which it was sought to render them accountable was that, being directors of the plaintiff company and therefore in a fiduciary relationship to it, they entered *in the course of their management* into a transaction in which *they utilised the position and knowledge possessed by them in virtue of their office as directors*, and that the transaction resulted in a profit to themselves.

and at pp. 391 and 392:

This issue thus becomes one of fact. The plaintiff company has to establish two things, (i) that what the directors did was *so related to the affairs of the company that it can properly be said to have been done in the course of their management and in utilisation of their opportunities and special knowledge as directors*; and (ii) that what they did resulted in a profit to themselves.

• • •

Lord Porter said at p. 395:

The legal proposition may, I think, be broadly stated by saying that one occupying a position of trust must not make a profit which he can acquire *only by use of his fiduciary position*, or, if he does, he must account for the profit so made.

and on the same page:

Directors, no doubt, are not trustees, but they occupy a fiduciary position towards the company whose board they form. Their liability in this respect does not depend upon breach of duty but upon the proposition that a director must not make a profit *out of property acquired by reason of his relationship to the company of which he is a director.*

The phrases which I have italicized in some of the passages quoted above appear to me to state in varying words the principle which Lord Russell of Killowen laid down, at p. 389 of the *Regal* judgment, in the passage quoted above which was adopted by Locke J. in the *Midcon* case.

On the facts of the case at bar I find it impossible to say that the respondent obtained the interests he holds in Cross Bow and Mayo by reason of the fact that he was a director of the appellant and in the course of the execution of that office.

When Dickson, at Dr. Aho's suggestion, offered his claims to the appellant it was the duty of the respondent as director to take part in the decision of the board as to whether that offer should be accepted or rejected. At that point he stood in a fiduciary relationship to the appellant. There are affirmative findings of fact that he and his co-directors acted in good faith, solely in the interests of the appellant and with sound business reasons in rejecting the offer. There is no suggestion in the evidence that the offer to the appellant was accompanied by any confidential information unavailable to any prospective purchaser or that the respondent as director had access to any such information by reason of his office. When, later, Dr. Aho approached the appellant it was not his capacity as a director of the appellant, but as an individual member of the public whom Dr. Aho was seeking to interest as a co-adventurer.

The judgements in the *Regal* case in the Court of Appeal are not reported but counsel were good enough to furnish us with copies. In the course of his reasons Lord Greene M.R. said:

To say that the Company was entitled to claim the benefit of those shares would involve this proposition: Where a Board of Directors considers an investment which is offered to their company and *bona fide* comes to the conclusion that it is not an investment which their Company ought to make, any Director, after that Resolution is come to and *bona fide* come to, who chooses to put up the money for that investment himself must be treated as having done it on behalf of the Company, so that the Company can claim any profit that results to him from it. That is a proposition for which no particle of authority was cited; and goes, as it seems to me, far beyond anything that has ever been suggested as to the duty of directors, agents, or persons in a position of that kind.

In the House of Lords, Lord Russell of Killowen concluded his reasons, at p. 391, with the following paragraph:

One final observation I desire to make. In his judgment Lord Greene M.R. stated that a decision adverse to the directors in the present case involved the proposition that, if directors *bona fide* decide not to invest their company's funds in some proposed investment, a director who thereafter embarks his own money therein is accountable for any profits which he may derive therefrom. As to this, I can only say that to my mind the facts of this hypothetical case bear but little resemblance to the story with which we have had to deal.

I agree with Bull J.A. when after quoting the two above passages he says:

As Greene M.R. was found to be in error in his decision, I would think that the above comment by Lord Russell on the hypothetical case would be superfluous unless it was intended to be a reservation that he had no quarrel with the proposition enunciated by the Master of the Rolls, but only that the facts of the case before him did not fall within it.

As Bull J.A. goes on to point out, the same view appears to have been entertained by Lord Denning M.R. in *Phipps v. Boardman* [(1965)] 1 All. E.R. 849 at 856].

If the members of the House of Lords in *Regal* had been of the view that in the hypothetical case stated by Lord Greene the director would have been liable to account to the company, the elaborate examination of the facts contained in the speech of Lord Russell of Killowen would have been unnecessary.

The facts of the case at bar appear to me in all material respects identical with those in the hypothetical case stated by Lord Greene and I share the view which he expressed that in such circumstances the director is under no liability. I agree with the conclusion of the learned trial judge and of the majority in the Court of Appeal that the action fails. ...

NOTES

1) What did Cartwright J. mean when he found that it was "impossible to say" that Cropper obtained his shares "in Cross Bow and Mayo by reason of the fact that he was a director of [Peso] and in the course of the execution of that office"? Could it not as easily have been said that the Regal directors were not acting as such when they decided to purchase Amalgamated shares for themselves? Peso's argument was precisely that once Cropper had dealt with the Dickson claims in his capacity as a Peso director, he would retain that capacity in any further dealings with them.

2) The judgment of Bull J.A. in the British Columbia Court of Appeal states that Cropper first learned of the availability of the Dickson claims when Dickson approached Dr. Aho, who sent him to Peso's offices to discuss the matter. Thus Cropper learned of the opportunity because of his position with Peso. Where a director, acting in that capacity, learns of an opportunity within the corporation's line of business, he must offer the opportunity to the corporation, as Cropper did here. The Supreme Court appears to have held that where the corporation determines not to pursue the opportunity, the director is free to pursue it on his own. It apparently does not matter whether the director acted gratuitously or out of fiduciary obligation in bringing the opportunity to the corpo-

ration's attention. If the result is viewed in terms of a fiduciary competing with his beneficiary, it may seem odd. There is, however, no prohibition at common law or by statute against a person being a director of competing corporations. In *Peso* Cropper was involved in a number of different mining ventures simultaneously, a common pattern in the junior mining industry. The decision in *Peso is* therefore consistent with the accepted norm in that industry.

3) A number of facts not mentioned in Mr. Justice Cartwright's opinion emerge from the dissenting judgment in the British Columbia Court of Appeal. 56 D.L.R (2d) at 120. First, Verity, Walker and Cropper, the three Peso directors who together with Dr. Aho formed Cross Bow to purchase the Dickson claims, in general dominated the affairs of Peso at the relevant time, and each had voted against acquisition of those claims by Peso. Second, when Berliz challenged the interest of the Peso directors in Cross Bow, Verity and Walker turned over their Cross Bow shares to Peso. Third, shortly after Cross Bow bought the Dickson claims, Walker wrote to the Superintendent of Brokers (the government official in British Columbia charged with overseeing the public issuance of securities) stating that he and the other Peso directors had considered it important that the Dickson claims, which were contiguous to those of Peso, be in hands friendly to Peso. Do these additional facts put Cropper's activities in a different perspective from that in which they were viewed by the Supreme Court? See Beck, *The Saga of Peso Silver Mines: Corporate Opportunity Reconsidered*, 49 Can. Bar Rev. 80 (1971).

4) In *Zwicker v. Stanbury*, [1953] 2 S.C.R. 438, the first case in which the Supreme Court of Canada adopted the judgments of the Law Lords in *Regal*, the defendants were directors of the corporation (LNH Ltd.) that owned the Lord Nelson Hotel in Halifax. LNH Ltd. had issued common and preferred shares, first mortgage bonds in the amount of $600,000 which at the relevant time were about to become due, and a second mortgage on the hotel with a face amount of about $240,000. The Canadian Pacific Railway (CP) held about 50% of both classes of the shares. It also owned the second mortgage and had guaranteed the payment of interest on the bonds. It was urgent to refinance the bonds if LNH Ltd. was to continue in business. CP told the defendant directors that it was not willing to make any further commitment to LNH Ltd. and that it had written off its investment as a loss. The directors thereupon promised CP that they would come up with a scheme to refinance the bonds if CP would turn over to them *gratis* the railroad's shares in LNH Ltd. CP was willing to donate the shares (just why does not appear in the report), but it suggested that the shares should be distributed among all of the LNH shareholders proportionately. The defendants refused to do this, so CP turned over its shares to them personally. The refinancing of the bonds succeeded, and thereafter in a separate transaction the defendants bought the second mortgage from CP for $120,000. Ultimately LNH Ltd. prospered, and the shares rose greatly in value. The Supreme Court decided that the defendants held the shares obtained from CP in trust for LNH Ltd. As regards the mortgage, the Supreme Court held, reversing the lower courts in this respect, that the corporation would be entitled to cancel it upon payment to the defendants of the price they had paid for it plus interest.

With respect to the share transaction in *Zwicker*, it is not difficult to see how the directors breached their fiduciary duty. Since the directors were acting for the corporation in their dealings with CP on the refinancing, any consideration that CP was willing to part with to achieve the result should have gone to the corporation and not to the directors personally. Turning the shares over to the corporation would have been equivalent to distributing them among the shareholders proportionately to their shareholdings.

The analysis of the mortgage transaction is not quite so straightforward, and unfortunately the judgments in the Supreme Court are not very clear on this aspect. Kellock J. held that the directors should not be permitted to profit from the mortgage transaction because it was while acting in their capacity as directors that they learned of "the small value placed by [CP] upon its security." There is no reason to believe that the directors got any bargain from CP in their purchase of the mortgage. While they paid only half the face value of the mortgage, it was not due for another 20 years and it bore a very low rate of interest. Furthermore, the interest was payable exclusively out of profits, and the enterprise was hardly prosperous at the relevant time. Finally, the second mortgage could not be foreclosed so long as the first mortgage bonds were outstanding. Does *Zwicker* hold that directors may never purchase the corporation's debt instruments in the secondary market at a discount from face value? See also *Martin v. Columbia Metals Corp.* (1980), 12 B.L.R. 72 (Ont.); *Manufacturers Trust Co. v. Becker*, 338 U.S. 304 (1949).

Corporate Opportunity and Corporate Impossibility. In *Zwicker*, Rand J. considered it "quite irrelevant" that LNH Ltd. had no money to buy back the second mortgage at the time the defendants acquired it from CP. In *Regal* the House of Lords was prepared to assume that it would have been impossible or at least imprudent for Regal to have invested in Amalgamated the £3,000 that the directors invested. While the Supreme Court in *Peso* considered Peso's straitened circumstances relevant in determining whether Cropper should be held accountable for taking up the investment that Peso rejected, the weight of authority appears to be with *Regal* and *Zwicker* on the point. Often the courts do not satisfactorily explain why they make short shrift of the impossibility argument. Probably it is because the defendants are usually in control of the corporate possibilities. If the opportunity has a positive net present value, the presumption as to the availability of financing may not seem unreasonable. But if the opportunity's *NPV* is approximately equal to 0, as may be the case if the firm is in constant receipt of new proposals, the presumption as to financing may seem less plausible.

In *Irving Trust Co. v. Deutsch*, 73 F.2d 121 (2d Cir. 1934), cert. denied, 294 U.S. 708 (1935), Acoustic Products Co. had agreed to purchase from Reynolds & Co. a controlling block of shares of the De Forest Radio Co. De Forest owned valuable patent rights for the manufacture of radios that it was deemed essential for Acoustic to obtain. At the last moment, Deutsch, Acoustic's President, announced that he had been unable to obtain sufficient funds for Acoustic to enable it to purchase the De Forest stock. In the result, it was purchased by a group including Deutsch and two other Acoustic directors, and they arranged for Acoustic to work the De Forest patents. The defendants were held liable to account to Acoustic for their profits. The Court rejected the defence that Acoustic lacked the necessary funds:

If directors are permitted to justify their conduct on such a theory, there will be a temptation to refrain from exerting their strongest efforts on behalf of the corporation since, if it does not meet the obligations, an opportunity of profit will be open to them personally. ... Indeed, in the present suit it is at least open to question whether a stronger effort might not have been made on the part of the management to procure for Acoustic the necessary funds or credit. Thus it appears that Deutsch owed Acoustic $125,000 on his note due February 2, 1928, and secured by collateral. No effort was made to collect it or to realize on the collateral. The directors contend that they took no action because Deutsch thought that he had a defense to his note; but the validity of such defense, as well as whether the possibility of resorting to his asset was actually considered, is very doubtful. After April 9th no efforts appear to have been made to raise for Acoustic the $100,000 required for the De Forest stock. Moreover, Acoustic did have substantial banking accommodations on June 6th, and, if these had been made available a few weeks earlier, it would have been able to perform its contract with Reynolds & Co. While these facts raise some question whether Acoustic actually lacked the funds or credit necessary for carrying out its contract, we do not feel justified in reversing the District Court's finding that it did. Nevertheless, they tend to show the wisdom of a rigid rule forbidding directors of a solvent corporation to take over for their own profit a corporate contract on the plea of the corporation's financial inability to perform. If the directors are uncertain whether the corporation can make the necessary outlays, they need not embark it upon the venture; if they do, they may not substitute themselves for the corporation any place along the line and divert possible benefits into their own pockets. [*Id.* at 124]

In *Abbey Glen Property Corp. v. Stumborg* (1978), 85 D.L.R. (3d) 35, [1978] 4 W.W.R. 28 (Alta. App. Div.), the Stumborg brothers were officers and directors of Abbey Glen's predecessor corporation, Terra Developments. Terra was a land developer in the Edmonton area. Certain syndicates in which other Stumborg-controlled corporations were substantial participants owned two large parcels of land in Edmonton. On behalf of Terra, the Stumborgs approached Traders Financial Corp. of Toronto to attempt to arrange a joint venture between Terra and Traders for the development of the two parcels. Traders refused to deal with Terra because Terra was publicly held and it was against Traders' policy to enter into joint ventures with public corporations. (On this point Traders' officials gave unequivocal and uncontradicted evidence at trial.) In the result, the Stumborgs and Traders formed a new corporation, Green Glenn, to develop the parcels, and the venture was a great success. The Stumborgs were held accountable to Abbey Glen for their profits from Green Glenn. See also *Industrial Development Consultants Ltd. v. Cooley*, [1972] 2 All E.R. 162.

In *Robinson v. Brier*, 194 A.2d 204 (Pa. 1963), the defendant Brier owned together with the Robinsons all the shares of L Corp. Brier was also a director and the manager of L's wholly owned subsidiary, M Corp., the business of which was the assembly of soft luggage. In addition, Brier had various other business interests, as was known to the Robinsons. Brier determined that the prices paid by M Corp. for the wooden frames for the luggage were excessive. He convinced the frame suppliers to reduce their prices, but eventually he concluded that S Corp., of which he was the sole owner, could produce the frames still cheaper. S Corp. began to manufacture and sell wooden frames to M Corp. at a price lower than M Corp. had been able to obtain anywhere else. The Robinsons' suit on behalf of M Corp. to recover Brier's profits from S Corp.'s frame sales failed. The Court noted that at the time when S Corp. started manufacturing the frames, all of M Corp.'s available space was being used for luggage assembly and that M Corp. was behind in filling orders from various large customers. "Accordingly there was no usurpation of a corporate opportunity" belonging to M Corp. *Id.* at 206.

Canadian Aero Service Ltd. v. O'Malley
Supreme Court of Canada
[1974] S.C.R. 592, 40 D.L.R. (3d) 371

LASKIN J. (by whom the judgment of the Court was delivered): This appeal arises out of a claim by the plaintiff-appellant (hereinafter referred to as Canaero) that the defendants had improperly taken the fruits of a corporate opportunity in which Canaero had a prior and continuing interest. The allegation against the defendants O'Malley and Zarzycki is that while directors or officers of Canaero they had devoted effort and planning in respect of the particular corporate opportunity as representatives of Canaero, but had subsequently wrongfully taken the benefit thereof in breach of a fiduciary duty to Canaero. The defendant Wells, who had been a director of Canaero but never an officer, was brought into the action as an associate of the other individual defendants in an alleged scheme to deprive Canaero of the corporate opportunity which it had been developing through O'Malley and Zarzycki; and the defendant Terra Surveys Limited was joined as the vehicle through which the individual defendants in fact obtained the benefit for which Canaero had been negotiating.

Canaero failed before Grant J., whose judgment on October 8, 1969 [61 C.P.R. 1] was affirmed by the Ontario Court of Appeal [4 C.P.R. (2d) 136, 23 D.L.R. (3d) 632, [1972] 1 O.R. 592], speaking through MacKay J.A. on June 18, 1971. The trial Judge fixed the damages at $125,000 in the event of a successful appeal, and this determination was implicitly endorsed by the Ontario Court of Appeal. The appeal to this Court is taken in the light of concurrent findings of fact on all points touching the course of events, but the Ontario Court of Appeal did not agree with Grant J. that the relationship of O'Malley and Zarzycki to Canaero, by reason of their positions as senior managerial officers, was of a fiduciary character, like that existing between directors and a company; rather, it was of the view that the relationship was simply that of employees and employer, involving no corresponding fiduciary obligations and, apart from valid contractual restriction, no limitation upon post-employment competition save as to appropriation of trade secrets and enticement of customers, of which there was no proof in this case.

Canaero was incorporated in 1948 under the Companies Act of Canada as a wholly-owned subsidiary of Aero Service Corporation, a United States company whose main business, like that of Canaero and other subsidiaries, was topographical mapping and geophysical exploration. In 1961, the parent Aero and its subsidiaries came under the control of another United States corporation, Litton Industries Inc. O'Malley joined Aero Service Corporation in 1936 and, apart from army service, remained with it until 1950 when he became general manager and president of Canaero whose head office was in Ottawa. He returned to the parent Aero company in 1957, but rejoined Canaero in 1964 as president and chief executive officer, and remained as such until he resigned on August 19, 1966. Acknowledgment and acceptance of the resignation followed on August 26, 1966.

Zarzycki, who attained a widely-respected reputation in geodesy, joined Canaero in 1953, soon becoming a chief engineer. He was named executive vice-president in 1964 and made a director in March 1965. He resigned these posts on August, 22, 1966 and received the acknowledgment and acceptance of his resignation in a letter of August 29, 1966.

Wells, a solicitor in Ottawa, knowledgeable about external aid programmes and the opportunities open in that connection to aeroplane companies, became a director of Canaero on March 15, 1950 at the same time as O'Malley. He was never an officer and was, on the evidence, an inactive director. When Survair Limited was incorporated in 1960, at Canaero's instance to provide it with flying services at first, exclusively, but not so after February 1, 1966), Wells became a shareholder by reason of his association with Canaero. He submitted his resignation as a director of Canaero at the request of Litton Industries Inc., when the latter took control, the resignation to be effective at its pleasure. No such pleasure was indicated, and Wells submitted a resignation on his own on February 5, 1965. There is an uncontested finding that he ceased to be a director after that date.

The defendant Terra Surveys Limited was incorporated on August 6, 1966, following a luncheon meeting of O'Malley, Zarzycki and Wells on August 6, 1966, at which the suggestion to form a company of their own was made by Wells to O'Malley and Zarzycki. To Wells' knowledge, the latter were discontented at Canaero by reason of the limitations upon their authority and the scope of independent action imposed by the Litton company, and they also feared loss of position if Canaero should fail to get contracts. Nominal directors and officers of the new company were appointed, but O'Malley and Zarzycki became major shareholders when common stock was issued on September 12, 1966. One share was issued to Wells at this time but he made a further investment in the new company on November 6, 1966. There is no doubt that Terra Surveys Limited was conceived as a company through which O'Malley and Zarzycki could pursue the same objects that animated Canaero. O'Malley became president of Terra Surveys Limited and Zarzycki became executive vice-president shortly after its incorporation.

The legal issues in this appeal concern what I shall call the Guyana project, the topographical mapping and aerial photographing of parts of Guyana (known as British Guiana until its independence on May 25, 1965) to be financed through an external aid grant or loan from the Government of Canada under its programme of aid to developing countries.

• • •

Canaero's interest in promoting a project in Guyana for the development of its natural resources, and in particular electrical energy, began in 1961. It had done work in nearby Surinam (or Dutch Guiana) where conditions were similar. It envisaged extensive aerial photography and mapping of the country which, apart from the populated coastal area, was covered by dense jungle. Promotional work to persuade the local authorities that Canaero was best equipped to carry out the topographical mapping was done by O'Malley and by another associate of the parent Aero. A local agent, one Gavin B. Kennard, was engaged by Canaero. In May, 1962, Zarzycki spent three days in Guyana in the interests of Canaero, obtaining information, examining existing geographical surveys and meeting government officials. He submitted a report on his visit to Canaero and to the parent Aero company.

Between 1962 and 1964, Canaero did magnetometer and electromagnetometer surveys in Guyana on behalf of the United Nations, and it envisaged either the United Nations or the United States as the funding agency to support the topographical mapping project that it was evolving as a result of its contracts in Guyana and Zarzycki's visit and report. Political conditions in Guyana after Zarzycki's visit in May, 1962, did not conduce to furtherance of the project and activity thereon was suspended.

It was resumed in 1965, when it appeared that funds for it might be made available under Canada's external aid programme. The United States had adopted a policy in this area of awarding contracts to United States firms. The record in this case includes a letter of October 22, 1968, after the events which gave rise to this litigation, in which the Canadian Secretary of State for External Affairs wrote that Canada's external aid policy was to require contractors to be incorporated in Canada, managed and operated from Canada and to employ Canadian personnel; and although preference in awarding external aid contracts was given to Canadian controlled firms, this was not an absolute requirement of eligibility to obtain such contracts. Canaero would hence have been eligible at that time for an award of a contract and, inferentially, in 1966 as well.

Zarzycki returned to Guyana on July 14, 1965 and remained there until July 18, 1965. By July 26, 1965, he completed a proposal for topographical mapping of the country, a proposal that the Government thereof might use in seeking Canadian financial aid. Copies went to Guyana cabinet minister, to the Canadian High Commissioner there and to the External Aid Office in Ottawa. Zarzycki in his evidence described the proposal as more sales-slanted than technical. The technical aspects were nonetheless covered; for example, the report recommended the use of an aerodist, a recently invented airborne electronic distance-measuring device. Zarzycki had previously urged that Canaero purchase one as a needed piece of equipment which other subsidiaries of Litton Industries Inc. could also use. Canaero placed an order for an aerodist, at a cost of $75,000, on or about July 15, 1966.

A few days earlier, on July 10, 1966, to be exact, an internal communication to the acting director-general of the Canadian External Aid Office, one Peter Towe, informed him that the Governments of Guyana and Canada had agreed in principle on a loan to Guyana for a topographical survey and mapping. The Prime Minister of Guyana had come to Ottawa early in July, 1966, for discussion on that among other matters. O'Malley had felt that if the assistance from Canada was by way of a loan Guyana would have the major say in naming the contractor, and this would make Canaero's chances better than if the assistance was by way of grant because then the selection would be determined by Canada. Although a loan was authorized, its terms were very liberal, and it was decided that Canada would select the contractor with the concurrence of Guyana, after examining proposals from a number of designated companies which would be invited to bid. An official of the Department of Mines and Technical Surveys visited Guyana and prepared specifications for the project which was approved by the Cabinet on August 10, 1966. Towe was informed by department letter of August 18, 1966, of a recommendation that Canaero, Lockwood Survey Corporation, Spartan Air Services Limited and Survair Limited be invited to submit proposals for the project. There was a pencilled note on the side of the letter, apparently added later, of the following words: "general photogramy Terra Ltd."

The Canadian External Aid Office by letter of August 23, 1966, invited five companies to bid on the Guyana project, Survair Limited was dropped from the originally recommended group of four companies, and Terra Surveys Limited and General Photogrammetric Services Limited was added. A briefing on the specifications for the project was held by the Department of Mines and Technical Surveys on August 29, 1966. Zarzycki and another represented Terra Surveys Limited at this briefing.

O'Malley and Zarzycki pursued the Guyana project on behalf of Canaero up to July 25, 1966, but did nothing thereon for Canaero thereafter. On July 9, 1966, they had met with the Prime Minister of Guyana during his visit to Ottawa, and on July 13, 1966, they had met with Towe (who had previously been informed of the intergovernmental agreement in principle on the Guyana project) and learned from him that the project was on foot. O'Malley had written to Kennard, Canaero's Guyana agent, on July 15, 1966, that he felt the job was a certainty for Canaero. By letter of the same date to Towe, O'Malley wrote that Zarzycki had spent about 20 days in Georgetown, Guyana on two successive visits to inventory the data available and determine the use to which the control survey and mapping would be put, and that he had subsequently prepared a proposal for a geodetic network and topographical mapping which was submitted to the Honourable Robert Jordan (the appropriate Guyanese Cabinet Minister) on July 27, 1965. On July 22, 1966, O'Malley wrote to an officer of the parent company that the Prime Minister of Guyana had advised him that "the Canadian Government would honour the project." Finally, on July 25, 1966, O'Malley wrote to Kennard to ask if he could learn what position Guyana was taking on the selection of a contractor, that is whether it proposed to make the selection with Canada's concurrence or whether it would leave the selection to Canada subject to its concurrence.

Thereafter the record of events, subject to one exception, concerns the involvement of O'Malley and Zarzycki with Wells in the incorporation of Terra Surveys Limited, their resignations from their positions with Canaero and their successful intervention through Terra Surveys Limited into the Guyana project. As of the date of O'Malley's letter of resignation, August 19, 1966, Terra Surveys Limited had a post office box and a favourable bank reference. Zarzycki had then not yet formally resigned as had O'Malley but had made the decision to do so. O'Malley informed the Canadian External Aid Office on August 22, 1966, of the new company which he, Zarzycki and Wells had formed.

The exception in the record of events just recited concerns a visit of Zarzycki, his "regular trip to the External Aid Office" (to use his own words), to the man in charge of the Caribbean area. This was on or about August 13, 1966, after his return from holidays and after the luncheon meeting with O'Malley and Wells that led to the incorporation of Terra. The purpose of the visit related to two project possibilities in the Caribbean area for Canaero, that in Guyana and one in Ecuador. Zarzycki then received confirmation of what he had earlier learned from Towe, namely, that the Guyana project had been approved in principle.

Despite having lost O'Malley and Zarzycki and also a senior employee Turner (who joined the Terra venture and attended the briefing session on August 29, 1966, on its behalf with Zarzycki), Canaero associated itself with Spartan Air Services Limited in the latter's proposal on the Guyana project which was submitted under date of September

12, 1966. Prior to this submission, representatives of these two companies visited Guyana to assure officials there that Canaero was involved in the preparation of the Spartan proposal and was supporting it.

Terra Surveys Limited submitted its proposal on September 12, 1966, through Zarzycki, having sent a letter on that date to the External Aid Office setting out its qualifications. A report on the various proposals submitted was issued on September 16, 1966, by the Canadian Government officer who had visited Guyana and had prepared the specifications for the project. He recommended that Terra Surveys Limited be the contractor, and included in his report the following observations upon its capabilities:

•   •   •

Although Terra, like other Canadian companies, has had no practical experience in planning and executing a similar type of Aerodist project, the proposal indicates that its authors have studied the subject very thoroughly and in preparing their plan of operation have also taken conditions peculiar to Guyana into account. ...

Dr. J.M. Zarzycki is named as the project manager. He is known internationally as an outstanding photogrammetric engineer and has developed and successfully used an aerial triangulation procedure utilizing superwide angle photography, the Wild B.8 and auxiliary data. Like most photogrammetric operations it requires good work by technicians but its success or failure hinges on the professional judgment and supervision of the engineer. Dr. Zarzycki has demonstrated this ability most clearly in past years.

Mr. M.H. Turner is to assist Dr. Zarzycki. He gained extensive experience in different field operations in Africa and has shown his ability to establish excellent working relationships with the senior survey officials as well as carrying out very difficult survey tasks. The Aerodist project will call for a high degree of theoretical knowledge in geodesy as well as practical management ability. This can be provided by Messrs. Turner and Zarzycki. ...

The proposal submitted by Terra Surveys Limited covered the operation in much greater detail than might normally be expected. However, the suggestions put forward indicate that all aspects of the operation have been most carefully reviewed and the plan of operation well thought out. The sections of the Terra proposal dealing with Aerodist indicate a more complete understanding of the problems in the field and subsequent operations than the other two proposals.

The treatment of many aspects of the project varies very little in the three proposals. However, appreciable differences do appear in the key phases of aerial photography and Aerodist control as explained in the preceding paragraphs. My assessment is that Terra Surveys Limited, in combination with Survair Limited and General Photogrammetric Services Limited, is best fitted to undertake this very difficult operation.

In the result, Terra Surveys Limited negotiated a contract with the External Aid Office, and on November 26, 1966, entered into an agreement with the Government of Guyana to carry out the project for the sum of $2,300,000. This was the amount indicated in the proposal of July 26, 1965, prepared by Zarzycki on behalf of Canaero.

There is no evidence that either Zarzycki or any other representative of Terra visited Guyana between August 23, 1966, the date when the invitations to submit proposals went out, and September 12, 1966, the date of the Terra proposal. The reference in the report of September 16, 1966, to the fact that the Terra proposal "covered the operation in much greater detail than might normally be expected" is a tribute to Zarzycki that owed much to his long involvement in the Guyana project on behalf of Canaero. From the time of his contact with certain Guyana officials in Canada in July, 1966, Zarzycki had no relationship with them or any others until he went to Guyana to sign the contract which had been awarded to Terra.

There are four issues that arise from consideration on the facts so far recited. There is, first, the determination of the relationship of O'Malley and Zarzycki to Canaero. Secondly, there is the duty or duties, if any, owed by them to Canaero by reason of the ascertained relationship. Thirdly, there is the question whether there has been any breach of duty, if any is owing, by reason of the conduct of O'Malley and Zarzycki in acting through Terra to secure the contract for the Guyana project; and, fourthly, there is the question of liability for breach of duty if established.

Like Grant J., the trial Judge, I do not think it matters whether O'Malley and Zarzycki were properly appointed as directors of Canaero or whether they did or did not act as directors. What is not in doubt is that they acted respectively as president and executive vice-president of Canaero for about two years prior to their resignations. To paraphrase the findings of the trial Judge in this respect, they acted in those positions and their remuneration and responsibilities verified their status as senior officers of Canaero. They were "top management" and not mere employees whose duty to their employer, unless enlarged by contract, consisted only of respect for trade secrets and for confidentiality of customer lists. Theirs was a larger, more exacting duty which, unless modified by statute or by contract (and there is nothing of this sort here), was similar to that owed to a corporate employer by its directors. I adopt what is said on this point by Gower, *Principles of Modern Company Law*, 3rd ed. (1969), at p. 518 as follows:

... these duties, except in so far as they depend on statutory provisions expressly limited to directors, are not so restricted but apply equally to any officials of the company who are authorised to act on its behalf, and in particular to those acting in a managerial capacity.

The distinction taken between agents and servants of an employer is apt here, and I am unable to appreciate the basis upon which the Ontario Court of Appeal concluded that O'Malley and Zarzycki were mere employees, that is servants of Canaero rather than agents. Although they were subject to supervision of the officers of the controlling company, their positions as senior officers of a subsidiary, which was a working organization, charged them with initiatives and with responsibilities far removed from the obedient role of servants.

It follows that O'Malley and Zarzycki stood in a fiduciary relationship to Canaero, which in its generality betokens loyalty, good faith and avoidance of a conflict of duty and self-interest. Descending from the generality, the fiduciary relationship goes at least this far: a director or a senior officer like O'Malley or Zarzycki is precluded from obtaining for himself, either secretly or without the approval of the company (which would have to be properly manifested upon full disclosure of the facts), any property or business advantage either belonging to the company or for which it has been negotiating; and especially is this so where the director or officer is a participant in the negotiations on behalf of the company.

An examination of the case law in this Court and in the Courts of other like jurisdictions on the fiduciary duties of directors and senior officers shows the pervasiveness of a strict ethic in this area of the law. In my opinion, this ethic disqualifies a director or senior officer from usurping for himself or diverting to another person or company with whom or with which he is associated a maturing business opportunity which his company is actively pursuing; he is also precluded from so acting even after his resignation where the resignation may fairly be said to have been prompted or influenced by a wish to acquire for himself the opportunity sought by the company, or where it was his position with the company rather than a fresh initiative that led him to the opportunity which he later acquired.

It is this fiduciary duty which is invoked by the appellant in this case and which is resisted by the respondents on the grounds that the duty as formulated is not nor should be part of our law and that, in any event, the facts of the present case do not fall within its scope.

This Court considered the issue of fiduciary duty of directors in *Zwicker v. Stanbury et al.*, [1954] 1 D.L.R. 257, [1953] 2 S.C.R. 438 where it found apt for the purposes of that case certain general statements of law by Viscount Sankey and by Lord Russell of Killowen in *Regal (Hastings) Ltd. v. Gulliver et al.*, [1942] 1 All E.R. 378, at pp. 381 and 389. These statements reflecting basic principle which is not challenged in the present case, are represented in the following passages, per Viscount Sankey:

In my view, the respondents were in a fiduciary position and their liability to account does not depend upon proof of *mala fides*. The general rule of equity is that no one who has duties of a fiduciary nature to perform is allowed to enter into engagements in which he has or can have a personal interest conflicting with the interests of those whom he is bound to protect. If he holds any property so acquired as trustee, he is bound to account for it to his *cestui que trust*. The earlier cases are concerned with trusts of specific property: *Keech v. Sandford* ((1726), Sel. Cas. Ch. 61) per Lord King, L.C. The rule, however, applies to agents, as, for example, solicitors and directors, when acting in a fiduciary capacity.

Per Lord Russell of Killowen:

In the result, I am of opinion that the directors standing in a fiduciary relationship to Regal in regard to the exercise of their powers as directors, and having obtained these shares by reason and only by reason of the fact that they were directors of Regal and in the course of the execution of that office, are accountable for the profits which they have made out of them. The equitable rule laid down in *Keech v. Sandford* [supra] and *Ex p. James* ((1803), 8 Ves. 337), and similar authorities applies ... in full force. It was contended that these cases were distinguishable by reason of the fact that it was impossible for Regal to get the shares owing to lack of funds, and that the directors in taking the shares were really acting as members of the public. I cannot accept this argument. It was impossible for the *cestui que trust* in *Keech v. Sandford* to obtain the lease, nevertheless the trustee was accountable. The suggestion that the directors were applying simply as members of the public is a travesty of the facts. They could, had they wished, have protected themselves by a resolution (either antecedent or subsequent) of the Regal shareholders in general meeting. In default of such approval, the liability to account must remain.

I need not pause to consider whether on the facts in *Regal (Hastings) Ltd. v. Gulliver* the equitable principle was overzealously applied; see, for example, Gower, op. cit., at pp. 535-7. What I would observe is that the principle, or indeed, principles, as stated, grew out of older cases concerned with fiduciaries other than directors or managing officers of a modern corporation, and I do not therefore regard them as providing a rigid measure whose literal terms must be met in assessing succeeding cases. In my opinion, neither the conflict test, referred to by Viscount Sankey, nor the test of accountability for profits acquired by reason only of being directors and in the course of execution of the office, reflected in the passage quoted from Lord Russell of Killowen, should be considered as the exclusive touchstones of liability. In this, as in other branches of the law, new fact situations may require a reformulation of existing principle to maintain its vigour in the new setting.

The reaping of a profit by a person at a company's expense while a director thereof is, of course, an adequate ground upon which to hold the director accountable. Yet there may be situations where a profit must be disgorged, although not gained at the expense of the company, on the ground that a director must not be allowed to use his position as such to make a profit even if it was not open to the company, as for example, by reason of legal disability, to participate in the transaction. An analogous situation, albeit not involving a director, existed for all practical purposes in the case of *Boardman et al. v. Phipps*, [1967] 2 A.C. 46 which also supports the view that liability to account does not depend on proof of an actual conflict of duty and self-interest. Another, quite recent, illustration of a liability to account where the company itself had failed to obtain a business contract and hence could not be regarded as having been deprived of a business opportunity is *Industrial Development Consultants Ltd. v. Cooley*, [1972] 2 All E.R. 162, a judgment of a Court of first instance. There, the managing director, who was allowed to resign his position on a false assertion of ill health, subsequently got the contract for himself. That case is thus also illustrative of the situation where a director's resignation is prompted by a decision to obtain for himself the business contract denied to his company and where he does obtain it without disclosing his intention.

What these decisions indicate is an updating of the equitable principle whose roots lie in the general standards that I have already mentioned, namely, loyalty, good faith and avoidance of a conflict of duty and self-interest. Strict application against directors and senior management officials is simply recognition of the degree of control which their positions give them in corporate operations, a control which rises above day to day accountability to owning shareholders and which comes under some scrutiny only at annual general or at special meetings. It is a necessary supplement, in the public interest, of statutory regulation and accountability which themselves are, at one and the same time, an acknowledgment of the importance of the corporation in the life of the community and of the need to compel obedience by it and by its promoters, directors and managers to norms of exemplary behaviour.

A particular application of the equitable principle against a director is found in an early Australian case, appealed unsuccessfully to the Privy Council, where there was a refusal to permit a director to carry out a scheme for acquiring a mining claim of the company, through unopposed enforcement of a forfeiture, on his undertaking to give all shareholders save a pledgee bank the benefit of his purchase according to their shareholdings: see *Smith v. Harrison et al.* (1872), 27 L.T.R. 188. The High Court of Australia applied the equitable principle on a conflict of duty and self-interest basis in a case where a director, who was empowered to sell a branch of his company's business with which he was particularly associated (which would result in loss of his position), arranged with the purchaser to enter its employ, doing so with the approval of the chairman of the board of the seller company, he having consulted with his fellow directors: see *Furs Ltd. v. Tomkies et al.* (1936), 54 C.L.R. 583. As was there pointed out, there was failure to make full disclosure to the shareholders of the financial arrangements made by the director, and it was no answer to the breach of fiduciary duty that no loss was caused to the company or that any profit made was of a kind which the company could not have obtained.

In the same vein is the New Zealand case of *G.E. Smith, Ltd. v. Smith; Smith v. Solnik*, [1952] N.Z.L.R. 470, which founded itself not only on *Regal (Hastings) Ltd. v. Gulliver*, supra, but as well on the proposition stated by Lord Cranworth in *Aberdeen R. Co. v. Blaikie Bros.* (1854), 1 Macq. 461, that a possible conflict of personal interest and duty will establish a basis for relief. The case concerned acquisition by a company director in his own right of an import licence (which had been refused to the company) for goods in which the company dealt, this being done at a time when liquidation of the company was contemplated by him and the other principal shareholder but before an agreement was concluded by which the defendant sold his interest in the company to that other shareholder.

Cases in the United States show that early enunciations of principle, resting on particular fact situations, have been broadened to cover succeeding cases, but one cannot pretend that there is any one consistent line of approach among the different state jurisdictions: see James c. Slaughter, "The Corporate Opportunity Doctrine," 18 Southwestern L.J. 96 (1964). What emerges from a review of the American case law is an imprecise ethical standard "which prohibits an 'executive'—here defined to include either a director or an officer—from appropriating to himself a business opportunity which in fairness should belong to the corporation": see Note, "Corporate Opportunity," 74 Harv. L. Rev. 765 (1961).

• • •

That the rigorous standard of behaviour enforced against directors and executives may survive their tenure of such offices was indicated as early as *Ex p. James* (1803), 8 Ves. Jun. 337, 32 E.R. 385, where Lord Eldon, speaking of the fiduciary in that case who was a solicitor purchasing at a sale, said (at p. 352, pp. 390-1 E.R.):

With respect to the question now put, whether I will permit *Jones* to give up the office of solicitor, and to bid, I cannot give that permission. If the principle is right, that the solicitor cannot buy, it would lead to all the mischief of acting up to the point of the sale, getting all the information that may be useful to him, then discharging himself from the character of solicitor, and buying the property. ... On the other hand I do not deny, that those interested in the question may give the permission.

• • •

In so far as the trial Judge, founding himself upon what Lord Russell of Killowen said in *Regal (Hastings) Ltd. v. Gulliver*, would limit the liability of directors or senior officers to the case where they obtained a contract "in the course of their duties as such," I regard his position as too narrowly conceived. *Raines v. Toney* [(1958) 313 S.W.2d 802] does not support the trial Judge's view, as is evident from the assertion of the Supreme Court of Arkansas that the fiduciary duty of a director or officer does not terminate upon resignation and that it cannot be renounced at will by the termination of employment: see also *Mile-O-Mo Fishing Club Inc. v. Noble et al.* (1965), 210 N.E. 2d 12. The passage quoted by Grant J. from *Raines v. Toney* was directed to a different point, namely, that of a right to compete with one's former employer unless restricted by contract.

The view taken by the trial Judge, and affirmed by the Court of Appeal (which quoted the same passage from the reasons of Lord Russell of Killowen in *Regal (Hastings) Ltd. v. Gulliver*), tended to obscure the difference between the survival of fiduciary duty after resignation and the right to use non-confidential information acquired in the course of employment and as a result of experience. I do not see that either the question of the confidentiality of the information acquired by O'Malley and Zarzycki in the course of their work for Canaero on the Guyana project or the question of copyright is relevant to the enforcement against them of a fiduciary duty. The fact that breach of confidence or violation of copyright may itself afford a ground of relief does not make either one a necessary ingredient of a successful claim for breach of fiduciary duty.

Submissions and argument were addressed to this Court on the question whether or how far Zarzycki copied Canaero's documents in preparing the Terra proposal. The appellant's position is that Zarzycki was not entitled to use for Terra what he compiled for Canaero; and the respondents contended that, although Zarzycki was not entitled to use for Terra the 1965 report or proposal as such that he prepared for Canaero, he was entitled to use the information therein which came to him in the normal course and by reason of his own capacity. It was the respondents' further submission that Zarzycki did not respond in 1966, on behalf of Terra on the basis of his 1965 report as an officer of and for Canaero; and they went so far as to say that it did not matter that O'Malley and Zarzycki worked on the same contract for Terra as they had for Canaero, especially when the project was not exactly the same.

In my opinion, the fiduciary duty upon O'Malley and Zarzycki, if it survived their departure from Canaero, would be reduced to an absurdity if it could be evaded merely because the Guyana project had been varied in some details when it became the subject of invited proposals, or merely because Zarzycki met the variations by appropriate changes in what he prepared for Canaero in 1965, and what he proposed for Terra in 1966. I do not regard it as necessary to look for substantial resemblances. Their presence would be a factor to be considered on the issue of breach of fiduciary duty but they are not a *sine qua non*. The cardinal fact is that the one project, the same project which Zarzycki had pursued for Canaero, was the subject of his Terra proposal. It was that business opportunity, in line with its general pursuits, which Canaero sought through O'Malley and Zarzycki. There is no suggestion that there had been such a change of objective as to make the project for which proposals were invited from Canaero, Terra and others a different one from that which Canaero had been developing with a view to obtaining the contract for itself.

Again, whether or not Terra was incorporated for the purpose of intercepting the contract for the Guyana project is not central to the issue of breach of fiduciary duty.

Honesty of purpose is no more a defence in that respect than it would be in respect of personal interception of the contract by O'Malley and Zarzycki. This is fundamental in the enforcement of fiduciary duty where the fiduciaries are acting against the interests of their principal. Then it is urged that Canaero could not in any event have obtained the contract, and that O'Malley and Zarzycki left Canaero as an ultimate response to their dissatisfaction with that company and with the restrictions that they were under in managing it. There was, however, no certain knowledge at the time O'Malley and Zarzycki resigned that the Guyana project was beyond Canaero's grasp. Canaero has not abandoned its hope of capturing it, even if Wells was of opinion, expressed during his luncheon with O'Malley and Zarzycki on August 6, 1966, that it would not get a foreign aid contract from the Canadian Government. Although it was contended that O'Malley and Zarzycki did not know of the imminence of the approval of the Guyana project, their ready run for it, when it was approved at about the time of their resignations and at a time when they knew of Canaero's continuing interest, are factors to be considered in deciding whether they were still under a fiduciary duty not to seek to procure for themselves or for their newly-formed company the business opportunity which they had nurtured for Canaero.

Counsel for O'Malley and Zarzycki relied upon the judgment of this Court in *Peso Silver Mines Ltd. (N.P.L.) v. Cropper* (1966), 58 D.L.R. (2d) 1, [1966] S.C.R. 673, 56 W.W.R. 641, as representing an affirmation of what was said in *Regal (Hastings) Ltd. v. Gulliver* respecting the circumscription of liability to circumstances where the directors or senior officers had obtained the challenged benefit by reason only of the fact that they held those positions and in the course of execution of those offices. In urging this, he did not deny that leaving to capitalize on their positions would not necessarily immunize them, but he submitted that in the present case there was no special knowledge or information obtained from Canaero during their service with that company upon which O'Malley and Zarzycki had relied in reaching for the Guyana project on behalf of Terra.

There is a considerable gulf between the *Peso* case and the present one on the facts as found in each and on the issues that they respectively raise. In *Peso*, there was a finding of good faith in the rejection by its directors of an offer of mining claims because of its strained finances. The subsequent acquisition of those claims by the managing director and his associates, albeit without seeking shareholder approval, was held to be proper because the company's interest in them ceased. There is some analogy to *Burg v. Horn* because there was evidence that Peso had received many offers of mining properties and, as in *Burg v. Horn*, the acquisition of the particular claims out of which the litigation arose could not be said to be essential to the success of the company. Whether evidence was overlooked in *Peso* which would have led to the result reached in *Regal (Hastings) Ltd. v. Gulliver* (see the examination by Beck, "The Saga of Peso Silver Mines: Corporate Opportunity Reconsidered," 49 Can. Bar Rev. 80 (1971), at p. 101) has no bearing on the proper disposition of the present case. What is before this Court is not a situation where various opportunities were offered to a company which was open to all of them, but rather a case where it had devoted itself to originating and bringing to fruition a particular business deal which was ultimately captured by former senior officers who had been in charge of the matter for the company. Since Canaero had been invited to make a proposal on the Guyana project, there is no basis for contending that it could not, in any event, have obtained the contract or that there was any unwillingness to deal with it.

It is a mistake, in my opinion, to seek to encase the principle stated and applied in *Peso*, by adoption from *Regal (Hastings) Ltd. v. Gulliver*, in the strait-jacket of special knowledge acquired while acting as directors or senior officers, let alone limiting it to benefits acquired by reasons of and during the holding of those offices. As in other cases in this developing branch of the law, the particular facts may determine the shape of the principle of decision without setting fixed limits to it. So it is in the present case. Accepting the facts found by the trial Judge, I find no obstructing considerations to the conclusion that O'Malley and Zarzycki continued, after their resignations, to be under a fiduciary duty to respect Canaero's priority, as against them and their instrument Terra, in seeking to capture the contract for the Guyana project. They entered the lists in the heat of the maturation of the project, known to them to be under active Government consideration when they resigned from Canaero and when they proposed to bid on behalf of Terra.

In holding that on the facts found by the trial Judge, there was a breach of fiduciary duty by O'Malley and Zarzycki which survived their resignations I am not to be taken as laying down any rule of liability to be read as if it were a statute. The general standards of loyalty, good faith and avoidance of a conflict of duty and self-interest to which the conduct of a director or senior officer must conform, must be tested in each case by many factors which it would be reckless to attempt to enumerate exhaustively. Among them are the factor of position or office held, the nature of the corporate opportunity, its ripeness, its specificness and the director's or managerial officer's relation to it, the amount of knowledge possessed, the circumstances in which it was obtained and whether is was special or, indeed, even private, the factor of time in the continuation of fiduciary duty where the alleged breach occurs after termination of the relationship with the company, and the circumstances under which the relationship was terminated, that is whether by retirement or resignation or discharge.

Wells stands on a different footing from O'Malley and Zarzycki. The case put against Wells in the submissions to this Court is not that he personally owed a fiduciary duty to Canaero in respect of the Guyana project from the time it took shape but rather that he was a party to a conspiracy with O'Malley and Zarzycki to convert Canaero's business opportunity in respect of the Guyana project to personal benefit in breach of fiduciary obligation. Although Wells was associated with his co-defendants beyond the role of their solicitor, and was a director and substantial shareholder of Survair Limited, which was among the original intended invitees to submit proposals for the Guyana project but was dropped when the formal invitations were issued, there is no reason to interfere with the concurrent findings of fact upon which the action against Wells was dismissed and the dismissal affirmed on appeal. Unlike the case with O'Malley and Zarzycki, the findings of fact do not admit of a conclusion of law by which to fix Wells with liability.

There remains the question of the appropriate relief against O'Malley and Zarzycki, and against Terra through which they acted in breach of fiduciary duty. In fixing the damages at $125,000, the trial Judge based himself on a claim for damages related only to the loss of the contract for the Guyana project, this being the extent of Canaero's claim as he understood it. No claim for a different amount or for relief on a different basis, as, for example, to hold Terra as constructive trustee for Canaero in respect of the execution of the Guyana contract, was made in this Court. Counsel for the respondents, although conceding that there was evidence of Terra's likely profit from the Guyana contract, emphasized the trial Judge's finding that Canaero could not have obtained the contract itself in view of its association with Spartan Air Services Limited in the submission of a proposal. It was his submission that there was no evidence that that proposal would have been accepted if Terra's had been rejected and, in any event, there was no evidence of Canaero's likely share of the profit.

Liability of O'Malley and Zarzycki for breach of fiduciary duty does not depend upon proof by Canaero that, but for their intervention, it would have obtained the Guyana contract; nor is it a condition of recovery of damages that Canaero establish what its profit would have been or what it has lost by failing to realize the corporate opportunity in question. It is entitled to compel the faithless fiduciaries to answer for their default according to their gain. Whether the damages awarded here be viewed as an accounting of profits or, what amounts to the same thing, as based on unjust enrichment, I would not interfere with the quantum. The appeal is, accordingly, allowed against all defendants save Wells, and judgment should be entered against them for $125,000. The appellant should have its costs against them throughout. I would dismiss the appeal as against Wells with costs.

Appeal allowed as against all defendants save one.

American and Canadian Standards. The oldest test in the United States of what constitutes a corporate opportunity is the *present interest or expectancy* standard. This would prohibit a manager from competing with his corporation for an opportunity in which the corporation had either a present interest or an expectancy growing out of an existing right. See *Lagarde v. Anniston Lime & Stone Co.*, 28 So. 199 (Ala. 1900). On this definition of corporate opportunities, the manager's action in *Canaero* would likely have been wrongful. Liability in that case was indeed unexceptional, since the opportunity was clearly firm-specific. Of course, when the bids were submitted in *Canaero*, the opportunity might have been worth more to Terra Surveys since it stood a greater chance of getting the contract. However, the proper time to determine who is best able to take up an opportunity is not when the manager begins to compete for it but when the firm does. This is because a firm's incentives to compete for a possible opportunity would be considerably altered were it possible for the manager hired to oversee the project to expropriate it in the way O'Malley did. There may, however, be other circumstances where the present interest test does not so clearly discriminate between firm- and manager-specific opportunities. Even when judged at the time when the firm begins to compete for it, an opportunity may be worth more to the manager.

A broader *line of business* test of what constitutes a corporate opportunity was established by the Delaware Supreme Court in *Guth v. Loft, Inc.*, 5 A.2d 503 (1939). Loft manufactured and distributed beverages, including soft drinks. Its president, Guth, acquired a personal interest in the secret formula and trademark of Pepsi Cola, and sold large quantities of Pepsi to Loft. The Court held that this represented a corporate opportunity.

[W]here a corporation is engaged in a certain business, and an opportunity is presented to it embracing an activity as to which it has fundamental knowledge, practical experience and ability to pursue, which, logically and naturally, is adaptable to its business having regard for its financial position, and is one that is consonant with its reasonable needs and aspirations for expansion, it may be properly said that the opportunity is in the line of the corporation's business. [*Id.* at 514]

The line of business test might in many cases appear to provide a more suitable definition of a corporate opportunity than the present interest or expectancy standard, since an opportunity may be firm-specific even if the firm has not indicated a present interest in it. However, there are circumstances where the line of business test will be either insufficiently exacting or too strict. It may firstly be too lax for conglomerates which carry on business in a variety of different industries, where the fact that the opportunity is not related to businesses in which the firm is presently engaged is not particularly compelling. So long as the firm is diversified over a broad range of industries, an opportunity might easily be firm-specific even if it represents a new line of business. On the other hand, the line of business standard may be excessively harsh, particularly for close corporations, if all parties have agreed that the firm will not exploit every opportunity in its line of business. Taking its facts at face value, *Peso* would appear to be one such case. Another was *Burg v. Horn*, 380 F.2d 897 (2d Cir. 1967). The plaintiff was a one-third shareholder of Darand Realty Corp., which owned and operated low-rent residential buildings in Brooklyn. The defendants George and Max Horn had already acquired other buildings in Brooklyn before joining forces with Burg and her husband. The Court rejected the Burgs' claim that residential properties privately acquired by the Horns after the incorporation of Darand were corporate opportunities of Darand, since there was no agreement that all low-rent buildings found by the Horns should be offered to Darand. The Burgs had indeed been aware of some of the Horn's acquisitions after the incorporation of Darand in 1953. Lumbard C.J. stated:

A director may be barred from competing with his corporation even though he does not by doing so appropriate a corporate opportunity. ... but the duty not to compete, like the duty to offer opportunities to the corporation, is measured by the circumstances of each case. ... [*Id.* at 901]

More recently, American courts have applied a more open-ended *fairness* standard which, as in *Canaero*, eschews exclusive touchstones in favour of a review of all the facts surrounding the corporate opportunity. See, e.g., *Miller v. Miller*, 222 N.W.2d 71 (Minn. 1974). A fairness standard would appear to amount to a flat rejection of prophylactic standards, since what is contemplated is a case-by-case review of all the relevant circumstances, precisely what prophylactic rules were designed to avoid. The "let's look at the facts" approach of Laskin J. does not, however, appear to offer an unbiased fairness standard. In approaching a corporate opportunity case, Laskin J. would have combined a rejection of narrowly formulated rules with an alertness to the possibility of self-dealing. In the end, it is not clear whether what is proposed is a continuation of prophylactic rules or their replacement by a fairness standard coupled with a deep suspicion of managerial self-dealing. Those who believe that prophylactic rules survive may point to Laskin's statement that "there may be situations where a profit must be disgorged, although not gained at the expense of the company, on the ground that a director must not be allowed to use his position as such to make a profit even if it was not open to the company. ... to participate in the transaction." Those who think that prophylactic rules must now be re-examined will instead focus on Laskin J.'s emphasis on close attention to factual circumstances, and to his critical remarks about *Regal*.

For a discussion of corporate opportunities in the United States, see Clark 223-34.

Fiduciary Duties of High-Level Corporate Employees. Generally, an employee is free to resign one day and to compete against the employer the next, provided the employee has not entered into an enforceable covenant not to do so. The only thing the employee may not do after termination of his employment, irrespective of any covenant, is to use the employer's trade secrets or confidential commercial information (including confidential customer lists) in the employee's competitive activities. *Canaero* has been interpreted as altering that rule where the employee is a high level officer or director of a corporate employer.

In *W.J. Christie & Co. Ltd. v. Creer* (1981), 121 D.L.R. (3d) 472 (Man. C.A.), the defendant had been director, secretary and "a key management person" of the plaintiff, a corporation controlled by one McKinnon and engaged in a general real estate and insurance brokerage business. The defendant quit these positions and immediately thereafter began soliciting the plaintiff's customers. After stating that generally ex-employees had a broad freedom to compete with their former employers, Huband J.A. went on:

But it is different for a director/officer/key management person who occupies a fiduciary position. Upon his resignation and departure, that person is entitled to accept business from former clients, but direct solicitation of that business is not permissible. Having accepted a position of trust, the individual is not entitled to allow his own self-interest to collide and conflict with fiduciary responsibilities. The direct solicitation of former clients traverses the boundary of acceptable conduct. [*Id.* at 477 (citing *Canaero*)]

The broad fiduciary duty imposed upon corporate functionaries by *Canaero* has been extended to high level employees who are neither officers nor directors. *MacMillan Bloedel Ltd. v. Binstead* (1983), 22 B.L.R. 255 (B.C.); *Humboldt Industries Ltd. v. Chester Basin Hydraulics & Machine Ltd.* (1983), 22 B.L.R. 215 (N.S.).

The Director of Many Corporations. In *Johnston v. Greene*, 121 A.2d 919 (Del. 1956), the plaintiff, a shareholder of Airfleets Inc., sued Odlum, Airfleets's President and "dominating director," alleging that Odlum had diverted to his personal benefit a corporate opportunity belonging to Airfleets. Airfleets had been organized to finance aircraft sales but in fact it never engaged in that business. At the relevant time, Airfleets was cash rich and looking for profitable investment of whatever type. Odlum was a director of Airfleets, of Atlas, which was Airfleets's largest single shareholder, and of numerous other business corporations. One Hutson owned a patent for the manufacture of self-locking nuts used in the manufacture of airplanes and also all the outstanding shares of Nutt-Shel Company, the exclusive licensee of the patents. Hutson wished to sell both of these assets, and to that end he approached Odlum, whom he knew by reputation to be a prominent financier. Odlum thought favourably of the purchases. He was advised by counsel that for tax reasons it would be undesirable for the shares in the patent licensee and the patents themselves to be under common ownership. Odlum caused the stock to be offered to Airfleets. That corporation's board decided to buy the shares of Nutt-Shel but not the patents. Although Odlum refrained from voting, it was found that he dominated the other directors and that the board's decision not to buy the patents was in fact his. Subsequently Odlum bought the patents for a syndicate of 35 individual investors including himself. The Chancellor found the purchase of the patents to be an opportunity belonging to Airfleets, diverted by Odlum. The Delaware Supreme Court reversed. The following is excerpted from the Supreme Court's opinion at 923-25:

The first important fact that appears is that Hutson's offer, which was to sell the patents and at least part of the stock, came to Odlum, not as a director of Airfleets, but in his individual capacity. The Chancellor so found. The second important fact is that the business of Nutt-Shel—the manufacture of self-locking nuts—had no direct or close relation to any business that Airfleets was engaged in or ever had been engaged in, and hence its acquisition was not essential to the conduct of Airfleets' business. Again, the Chancellor so found. The third fact is that Airfleets had no interest or expectancy in the Nutt-Shel business, in the sense that those words are used in the decisions dealing with the law or corporate opportunity.

. . .

It is one thing to say that a corporation with funds to invest has a general interest in investing those funds; it is quite another to say that such a corporation has a specific interest attaching in equity to any and every business opportunity that may come to any of its directors in his individual capacity. This is what the Chancellor appears to have held. Such a sweeping extension of the rule of corporate opportunity finds no support in the decisions and is, we think, unsound.

It is, of course, entirely possible that a corporate opportunity might in some cases arise out of a corporate need to invest funds and the duty of the president or any other director to seek such an opportunity. But, whether it does arise, in any particular case, depends on the facts—upon the existence of special circumstances that would make it unfair for him to take the opportunity for himself.

We cannot find any such circumstances in this case. At the time when the Nutt-Shel business was offered to Odlum, his position was this: He was the part-time president of Airfleets. He was also president of Atlas—an investment company. He was a director of other corporations and a trustee of foundations interested in making investments. If it was his fiduciary duty, upon being offered any investment opportunity, to submit it to a corporation of which he was a director, the question arises, Which corporation? Why Airfleets instead of Atlas? Why Airfleets instead of one of the foundations? So far as appears, there was no specific tie between the Nutt-Shel business and any of these corporations or foundations. Odlum testified that many of his companies had money to invest, and this appears entirely reasonable. How, then, can it be said that Odlum was under any obligation to offer the opportunity to one particular corporation? And if he was not under such an obligation, why could he not keep it for himself?

Plaintiff suggests that if Odlum elects to assumed fiduciary relationships to competing corporations he must assume the obligations that are entailed by such relationships. So he must, but what are the obligations? The mere fact of having funds to invest does not ordinarily put the corporations "in competition" with each other, as that phrase is used in the law of corporate opportunity. There is nothing inherently wrong in a man of large business and financial interests serving as a director of two or more investment companies, and both Airfleets and Atlas (to mention only two companies) must reasonably have expected that Odlum would be free either to offer to any of his companies any business opportunity that came to him personally, or to retain it for himself—provided always that there was no tie between any of such companies and the new venture or any specific duty resting upon him with respect to it. 3 Fletcher, Cyclopedia Corporations, § 862.

It is clear to us that the reason why the Nutt-Shel business was offered to Airfleets was because Odlum, having determined that he did not want it for himself, chose to place the investment in that one of his companies whose tax situation was best adapted to receive it. He chose to do so, although he could probably have sold the stock to an outside company at a profit to himself. If he had done so, who could have complained? If a stockholder of Airfleets could have done so, why not a stockholder of Atlas as well?

It is unnecessary to labor the point further. We are of opinion that the opportunity to purchase the Nutt-Shel business belonged to Odlum and not to any of his companies.

If Airfleets had been the only corporation of which Odlum had been a director, would the Court have held that the opportunity belonged to it? How can a director of many corporations ever decide whether a given opportunity belongs in equity to one or another of them? If a trustee manages many investment funds, how ought he to allocate favourable investment opportunities among them? How should a parent corporation allocate a given investment opportunity among its various partially owned subsidiaries? For a recent discussion of the problems that directors who sit on interlocking boards must confront, see *PWA Corp. v. Gemini Group Automated Distribution Systems Inc.* (1994), 15 O.R. (3d) 730.

Sinclair Oil Corp. v. Levien
Supreme Court of Delaware
280 A.2d 717 (1971)

WOLCOTT C.J., CAREY J. and CHRISTIE Judge, sitting.

WOLCOTT, Chief Justice: This is an appeal by the defendant, Sinclair Oil Corporation (hereafter Sinclair), from an order of the Court of Chancery, 261 A.2d 911 in a derivative action requiring Sinclair to account for damages sustained by its subsidiary, Sinclair Venezuelan Oil Company (hereafter Sinven), organized by Sinclair for the purpose of operating in Venezuela, as a result of dividends paid by Sinven, the denial to Sinven of industrial development, and a breach of contract between Sinclair's wholly-owned subsidiary, Sinclair International Oil Company, and Sinven.

Sinclair, operating primarily as a holding company, is in the business of exploring for oil and of producing and marketing crude oil and oil products. At all times relevant to this litigation, it owned about 97% of Sinven's stock. The plaintiff owns about 3000 of 120,000 publicly held shares of Sinven. Sinven, incorporated in 1922, has been engaged in petroleum operations primarily in Venezuela and since 1959 has operated exclusively in Venezuela.

Sinclair nominates all members of Sinven's board of directors. The Chancellor found as a fact that the directors were not independent of Sinclair. Almost without exception, they were officers, directors, or employees of corporations in the Sinclair complex. By reason of Sinclair's domination, it is clear that Sinclair owed Sinven a fiduciary duty. ... Sinclair concedes this.

The Chancellor held that because of Sinclair's fiduciary duty and its control over Sinven, its relationship with Sinven must meet the test of intrinsic fairness. The standard of intrinsic fairness involves both a high degree of fairness and a shift in the burden of proof. Under this standard the burden is on Sinclair to prove, subject to careful judicial scrutiny, that its transactions with Sinven were objectively fair. ...

Sinclair argues that the transactions between it and Sinven should be tested, not by the test of intrinsic fairness with the accompanying shift of the burden of proof, but by the business judgment rule under which a court will not interfere with the judgment of a board of directors unless there is a showing of gross and palpable overreaching. *Meyerson v. El Paso Natural Gas Co.*, 246 A.2d 789 (Del.Ch. 1967). A board of directors enjoys a presumption of sound business judgment, and its decisions will not be disturbed if they can be attributed to any rational business purpose. A court under such circumstances will not substitute its own notions of what is or is not sound business judgment.

We think, however, that Sinclair's argument in this respect is misconceived. When the situation involves a parent and a subsidiary, with the parent controlling the transaction and fixing the terms, the test of intrinsic fairness, with its resulting shifting of the burden of proof, is applied. ... The basic situation for the application of the rule is the one in which the parent has received a benefit to the exclusion and at the expense of the subsidiary.

• • •

A parent does indeed owe a fiduciary duty to its subsidiary when there are parent-subsidiary dealings. However, this alone will not evoke the intrinsic fairness standard. This standard will be applied only when the fiduciary duty is accompanied by self-dealing—the situation when a parent is on both sides of a transaction with its subsidiary. Self-dealing occurs when the parent, by virtue of its domination of the subsidiary, causes the subsidiary to act in such a way that the parent receives something from the subsidiary to the exclusion of, and detriment to, the minority stockholders of the subsidiary.

We turn now to the facts. The plaintiff argues that, from 1960 through 1966, Sinclair caused Sinven to pay out such excessive dividends that the industrial development of Sinven was effectively prevented, and it became in reality a corporation in dissolution.

From 1960 through 1966, Sinven paid out $108,000,000 in dividends ($38,000,000 in excess of Sinven's earnings during the same period). The Chancellor held that Sinclair caused these dividends to be paid during a period when it had a need for large amounts of cash. Although the dividends paid exceeded earnings, the plaintiff concedes that the payments were made in compliance with 8 Del.C. § 170, authorizing payment of dividends out of surplus or net profits. However, the plaintiff attacks these dividends on the ground that they resulted from an improper motive—Sinclair's need for cash. The Chancellor, applying the intrinsic fairness standard, held that Sinclair did not sustain its burden of proving that these dividends were intrinsically fair to the minority stockholders of Sinven.

Since it is admitted that the dividends were paid in strict compliance with 8 Del.C. § 170, the alleged excessiveness of the payments alone would not state a cause of action. Nevertheless, compliance with the applicable statute may not, under all circumstances, justify all dividend payments. If a plaintiff can meet his burden of proving that a dividend cannot be grounded on any reasonable business objective, then the courts can and will interfere with the board's decision to pay the dividend.

Sinclair contends that it is improper to apply the intrinsic fairness standard to dividend payments even when the board which voted for the dividends is completely dominated. In support of this contention, Sinclair relies heavily on *American District Telegraph Co. [ADT] v. Grinnell Corp.*, (N.Y.Sup.Ct. 1969) aff'd. 33 A.D.2d 769, 306 N.Y.S.2d 209 (1969). Plaintiffs were minority stockholders of ADT, a subsidiary of Grinnell. The plaintiffs alleged that Grinnell, realizing that it would soon have to sell its ADT stock because of pending antitrust action, caused ADT to pay excessive dividends. Because the dividend payments conformed with applicable statutory law, and the plaintiffs could not prove an abuse of discretion, the court ruled that the complaint did not state a cause of action. ...

We do not accept the argument that the intrinsic fairness test can never be applied to a dividend declaration by a dominated board, although a dividend declaration by a dominated board will not inevitably demand the application of the intrinsic fairness standard. ...

If such a dividend is in essence self-dealing by the parent, then the intrinsic fairness standard is the proper standard. For example, suppose a parent dominates a subsidiary and its board of directors. The subsidiary has outstanding two classes of stock, X and Y. Class X is owned by the parent and Class Y is owned by the minority stockholders of the subsidiary. If the subsidiary, at the direction of the parent, declares a dividend on its Class X stock only, this might well be self-dealing by the parent. It would be receiving something from the subsidiary to the exclusion of and detrimental to its minority stockholders. This self-dealing, coupled with the parent's fiduciary duty, would make intrinsic fairness the proper standard by which to evaluate the dividend payments.

Consequently it must be determined whether the dividend payments by Sinven were, in essence, self-dealing by Sinclair. The dividends resulted in great sums of money being transferred from Sinven to Sinclair. However, a proportionate share of this money was received by the minority shareholders of Sinven. Sinclair received nothing from Sinven to the exclusion of its minority stockholders. As such, these dividends were not self-dealing. We hold therefore that the Chancellor erred in applying the intrinsic fairness test as to these dividend payments. The business judgment standard should have been applied.

We conclude that the facts demonstrate that the dividend payments complied with the business judgment standard and with 8 Del.C. § 170. The motives for causing the declaration of dividends are immaterial unless the plaintiff can show that the dividend payments resulted from improper motives and amounted to waste. The plaintiff contends only that the dividend payments drained Sinven of cash to such an extent that it was prevented from expanding.

The plaintiff proved no business opportunities which came to Sinven independently and which Sinclair either took to itself or denied to Sinven. As a matter of fact, with two minor exceptions which resulted in losses, all of Sinven's operations have been conducted in Venezuela, and Sinclair had a policy of exploiting its oil properties located in different countries by subsidiaries located in the particular countries.

From 1960 to 1966 Sinclair purchased or developed oil fields in Alaska, Canada, Paraguay, and other places around the world. The plaintiff contends that these were all opportunities which could have been taken by Sinven. The Chancellor concluded that Sinclair had not proved that its denial of expansion opportunities to Sinven was intrinsically fair. He based this conclusion on the following findings of fact. Sinclair made no real effort to expand Sinven. The excessive dividends paid by Sinven resulted in so great a cash drain as to effectively deny to Sinven any ability to expand. During this same period Sinclair actively pursued a company-wide policy of developing through its subsidiaries new sources of revenue, but Sinven was not permitted to participate and was confined in its activities to Venezuela.

However, the plaintiff could point to no opportunities which came to Sinven. Therefore, Sinclair usurped no business opportunity belonging to Sinven. Since Sinclair received nothing from Sinven to the exclusion of and detriment to Sinven's minority stockholders, there was no self-dealing. Therefore, business judgment is the proper standard by which to evaluate Sinclair's expansion policies.

Since there is no proof of self-dealing on the part of Sinclair, it follows that the expansion policy of Sinclair and the methods used to achieve the desired result must, as far as Sinclair's treatment of Sinven is concerned, be tested by the standards of the business judgment rule. Accordingly, Sinclair's decision, absent fraud or gross overreaching, to achieve expansion through the medium of its subsidiaries, other than Sinven, must be upheld.

Even if Sinclair was wrong in developing these opportunities as it did, the question arises, with which subsidiaries should these opportunities have been shared? No evidence indicates a unique need or ability of Sinven to develop these opportunities. The decision of which subsidiaries would be used to implement Sinclair's expansion policy was one of business judgment with which a court will not interfere absent a showing of gross and palpable overreaching. *Meyerson v. El Paso Natural Gas Co.*, 246 A.2d 789 (Del.Ch. 1967). No such showing has been made here.

• • •

We will therefore reverse that part of the Chancellor's order that requires Sinclair to account to Sinven for damages sustained as a result of dividends paid between 1960 and 1966, and by reason of the denial to Sinven of expansion during that period.

NOTES

Even if Sinclair's motives in causing the directors of Sinven to issue huge dividends were improper, Sinven was not damaged unless it had business uses for the cash. Sinclair, however, had allegedly foreclosed that possibility by its policy of forming a different subsidiary to engage in the oil business in each foreign country. It was this policy, if anything, which damaged Sinven and its minority shareholders, but the policy was reviewed only cursorily by the Court. As the Court said, when a parent has one opportunity and many subsidiaries that could profitably exploit it, how is the parent to determine to which subsidiary the opportunity belongs?

When an investment opportunity might be exploited by both a parent corporation and its partially owned subsidiary, Brudney and Clark propose that the opportunity be given to the one which can most effectively exploit it. Brudney & Clark, *A New Look at Corporate Opportunities*, 94 Harv. L. Rev. 998 (1981). Where, on the other hand, the opportunity's value does not depend on whether the parent or subsidiary owns it or does not give rise to anything other than normal profits, the parent's taking cannot be seen as an injury to the subsidiary. Finally, where the opportunity is equally valuable to both firms and is available at a bargain price, Brudney and Clark propose that the opportunity should be deemed to belong to the subsidiary unless the parent shows by clear and convincing evidence that it is parent-specific. Here, the authors reject a sharing rule, in which the benefits of the opportunity are shared *pro rata* by the two firms. Such a sharing rule was proposed by Brudney and Chirlstein in *Fair Shares and Corporate Mergers and Takeovers*, 88 Harv. L. Rev. 297 (1977) for the allocation of synergistic benefits on parent-subsidiary mergers. However, Brudney and Clark argue that this is inappropriate for corporate opportunities because of greater valuation uncertainties. Given these enforcement costs, a substantial problem of undetected unfairness would remain, and for this reason Brudney and Clark propose a prophylactic rule.

The Brudney and Clark argument is criticized in Easterbrook & Fischel, *Corporate Control Transactions*, 91 Yale L.J. 698, 734 (1982):

The argument is defective because it ignores the possibility of side payments. Assume that a corporate opportunity is worth $100 to a 70% owned subsidiary but only $80 to the parent. It might appear that the parent would allocate the opportunity to itself even though it could use the opportunity less profitably, because the $80 gain is greater than the $70 (70% times $100) gained if the opportunity is allocated to the subsidiary. But the parent corporation could gain more than $80 by allocating the opportunity to the subsidiary and charging it some amount between $11 and $30. The charge could be explicit or implicit. That is, the parent's other dealings with the subsidiary could somehow be adjusted to compensate it for the release of the opportunity—transfer pricing between parents and subsidiaries is extremely flexible.

F. SHAREHOLDER AND CORPORATE REMEDIES

1. The Statutory Derivative Action

CBCA ss. 238-40, 242 codify the rules governing shareholder derivative actions. A "complainant" under s. 238 may commence a derivative action with leave of court under s. 239. The court will only permit the action to be brought under s. 239(2) if:

(a) the complainant has given reasonable notice to the directors ... of his intention to apply to the court [for leave] if the directors do not bring [or] diligently prosecute ... the action;

(b) the complainant is acting in good faith; and

(c) [the action] appears to be in the best interests of the corporation. ...

It is not clear what condition (b) adds to (c). While an honest but misguided complainant might wish to bring an action that would not be in the best interests of the corporation, it is hard to imagine the reverse.

Under s. 240 the court may make a variety of orders to govern the conduct of the action, including that the corporation should pay the complainant's reasonable legal fees and that the amount of any recovery should be paid not to the corporation but to its present or former security holders. The effect of the latter type of order is not to convert a derivative into a personal action but rather to avoid what would otherwise be an incongruous result where either the defendants are major shareholders in the corporation or the shareholders at the time of the injury are not the shareholders at the time of the action. Under s. 242 of the statute, the court may order the corporation to pay the complainant's interim costs, including legal fees and disbursements, but such interim award would be without prejudice to an allocation of costs as between the corporation and the complainant upon final disposition of the action.

A derivative action may not be settled except upon approval of the court. CBCA s. 242(2). This provision is of American origin. See Federal Rules of Civil Procedure s. 23.1. It is designed to obviate the possibility of collusive settlements between a derivative plaintiff and the corporation whereby the corporation might buy off the plaintiff to settle a nuisance suit. Suits brought by plaintiffs precisely for the purpose of settlement (often by the corporation buying the plaintiff's shares at an exorbitant price) came to be known as "strike suits."

One American device specifically not permitted under the CBCA is the requirement that the plaintiff give security for the corporation's costs. It can be appreciated that these costs, and hence the cost of a bond to cover them, can be substantial owing to the number of parties who may require separate representation in the litigation and the corporation's obligation to indemnify such of them as are its officers or directors in the event that claims against them prove not well-founded. The need to require derivative plaintiffs to post security for costs is more pressing in the United States than in Canada because in that country there is not the inherent discipline against litigiousness that exists in our loser-pay-all costs rules. Generally in the United States, subject to a number of statutory exceptions, each party bears his own costs, including legal fees, irrespective of the outcome of the litigation.

The rule in *Foss v. Harbottle* is changed by s. 242(1) of the CBCA which provides that derivative litigation shall not be dismissed by reason only that the conduct complained of has been or may be ratified by the shareholders. Ratification may, however, be taken into account by the court as a factor in determining whether the proposed litigation would be in the best interests of the corporation. See *Re Northwest Forest Products Ltd.* (this section). Shareholder ratification may also be taken into account by the court in proceedings under CBCA s. 214 (just and equitable winding up) and s. 241(oppression). See Part II of this chapter.

While the derivative action often goes by the name "shareholder's derivative action," in fact the class of persons who may be complainants under CBCA s. 238 is a good deal broader. It includes a registered or beneficial owner of a security (not just shares) of the corporation or any of its affiliates; a former owner (contrast the American rule, which ordinarily requires the plaintiff to have been a shareholder both at the time of the wrong and at the time of the complaint); a director or officer, present or former, of the corporation or of any of its affiliates; the Director of Corporations appointed under CBCA s. 260; and, finally, any other person the court deems "proper" (see *First Edmonton Place*, in Part II of this chapter).

The origins of the CBCA provisions governing the derivative action can be found, according to the Dickerson Report, in three sources: Professor Gower's disapproval of the rule in *Foss v. Harbottle*, the Report of the Jenkins Committee in the United Kingdom recommending (without success to date) the creation of a statutory derivative action there and s. 99 of the Ontario Business Corporations Act, R.S.O. 1970, c. 53, which became effective in 1971. Section 99 lacked the broad definition of "complainant" and did not address the effect of ratification or ratifiability. In other respects it was similar to CBCA s. 239. It was in turn based in large measure upon American state precedents. The Americans do not, however, require leave of court for the commencement of a derivative action. The CBCA model has been most innovative, and is formally a good deal more liberal than the American statutes, in the recognition of a broad class of possible complainants, the abolition of the contemporaneous ownership rule, the provision for the possibility of recovery by shareholders of derivative action damages and the recognition of the "double derivative" action. The latter term denotes a suit on behalf of a subsidiary of the corporation in which the plaintiff holds shares.

Where provision is made for a statutory derivative action, it is the exclusive method by which a shareholder can vindicate corporate rights. *Churchill Pulpmill Ltd. v. Manitoba*, [1977] 6 W.W.R. 109, 115-20 (Man. C.A.) (Manitoba Corporations Act); *Shield Development Co. Ltd. v. Snyder*, [1976] 3 W.W.R. 44, 48-52 (B.C.) (BCCA); *Farnham v. Fingold*, [1973] 2 O.R. 132, 135 (C.A.) (Ontario Business Corporations Act). That is, a shareholder cannot avoid the requirement that leave of court be obtained before an action may be commenced on behalf of a corporation by attempting to bring the action under one of the so-called exceptions to the rule in *Foss v. Harbottle*. As will be seen, however, actions brought to vindicate not corporate but personal claims do not require leave of the court under s. 239.

There have been relatively few reported applications to commence statutory derivative actions since the Ontario Business Corporations Act introduced the concept to Canada. The following case is a typical example of the hospitable attitude that Canadian courts have shown to applications for leave.

Re Northwest Forest Products Ltd.
British Columbia Supreme Court
[1975] 4 W.W.R. 724

CASHMAN L.J.S.C.: This is an application under s. 222 of The Companies Act, 1973 (B.C.), c. 18, that leave be given to the applicants to commence an action in the name of and on behalf of Northwest Forest Products Ltd. against five directors of that company for an accounting of what but for their wilful default or negligence the company's shareholdings in the Fraser Valley Pulp and Timber Ltd. ought to be worth and payment of the amount found due, or alternatively for damages for misfeasance.

• • •

The requirements of subs. (3) [of s. 222 of the British Columbia Companies Act, 1973] are:

1. That the applicant had made reasonable efforts to cause the directors of the company to commence the action;
2. That the applicant is acting in good faith;
3. That it is shown that it is prima facie in the interests of the company that the action be brought; and
4. That the applicant was a member of the company at the time of the transaction giving rise to the cause of action.

Before I consider the specific criteria for granting leave sought I turn to the facts of this application.

The applicant, Reginal William John Burleigh, is represented by Howard Victor Ross who was appointed committee of Mr. Burleigh by an order made 22nd April 1971. Mr. Burleigh is the registered holder of 804 shares of Northwest Forest Products Ltd. (hereinafter referred to as "the company"). The other applicant, David A. Bone, is the registered holder of 400 shares in the company. By order of this Court made 25th November 1974 Mr. Ross was given leave to bring this motion.

The company was incorporated on 11th March 1950. Fraser Valley Pulp and Timber Ltd. (hereinafter referred to as "Fraser Valley") was incorporated on 9th August 1965. Both companies are incorporated under The Companies Act of British Columbia.

The persons against whom leave is sought to commence an action were at all material times and still are directors of the company. They are: J. Arthur Wood, Norman M. Wood, Louis Clarke, J. McLallen, Leonard F. Wright.

The company owned 51 per cent of the issued shares of Fraser Valley.

The basis of the action which the applicants ask leave to commence concerns the sale of the entire undertaking of Fraser Valley to Green River Log Sales Ltd. (hereinafter referred to as "Green River"), also a company incorporated under the laws of British Columbia. This sale is evidenced by an agreement in writing dated 30th June 1972 (which I shall hereinafter refer to as "the agreement").

The agreement was signed on behalf of the company by J.A. Wood and Louis Clarke. The purchase price is shown as $199,813.99 to be paid by the assumption of current and long term liabilities totalling $120,813.99 and by two debentures: one to the company for $30,000 and one to Phillip Louis Clarke of $30,000. Phillip Louis Clarke and Frederick W. Clark were at all material times the members of Green River and between them held all 20 of the issued shares in that company.

The sale was concluded by a deed of land and bill of sale (absolute) and presumably by the debentures specified in the agreement.

By a debenture executed also on 30th June 1972 Green River pledged the assets acquired from Fraser Valley to the Royal Bank of Canada for $290,500.

It will be readily seen that on the fact of the documents the assets purchased by Green River enhanced in value by an amount approximating $91,700 on the day of the sale. There may be some reasonable explanation for this but if there is it does not appear in the material filed. Mr. Wood's affidavit says simply that Fraser Valley was in an insolvent condition and its assets had to be liquidated. That however does not in my respectful opinion explain the large increase in the value of Fraser Valley's assets on the same day.

• • •

By letter dated 3rd April 1974 Mr. Ross wrote to the president and directors of the company requesting the company take the action sought in this application and the last paragraph on page one of the letter, continuing on the top of page two, says this:

I further request and require you as Directors of Northwest Forest Products Ltd. to cause the shares of Fraser Valley Pulp and Timber Ltd. held by the company to be voted at a meeting of Fraser Valley Pulp and Timber Ltd. to bring action to set aside the sale by Fraser Valley to Green River on the ground that the assets of Fraser Valley in such sale were so grossly undervalued to the knowledge of the Directors of both Fraser Valley and Green River as to amount to a fraud on the shareholders of Fraser Valley.

No response to that letter appears to have been forthcoming.

On 6th May 1974 Mr. Ross requisitioned a meeting to pass a resolution to commence an action. At the meeting held pursuant to that requisition that motion was defeated.

Counsel for the company submits that in this case I must be governed by the fact that what was done by the directors in selling Fraser Valley's assets was done with the approval of the majority of the shareholders and indeed the various minutes filed would tend to show that that is correct.

Section 222(7) says that this is a factor that "may" be taken into account by the Court.

However here it should be noted that the company had issued 4,125 shares. J.A. Wood and Norman Wood between them owned 1,570 shares which were less than 50 per cent of the issued shares. The other three directors owned no shares in the company. On the other hand no minutes have been produced to indicate how many shareholders or how many shares were represented at that meeting. In this connection it should be borne in mind that Vancouver Island Utilities Ltd. owns 1,090 shares. There is no evidence as to who voted those shares or indeed whether any shares were voted by proxy.

For these reasons I do not take into account the apparent approval of the members of the company.

Mr. McConnell submits that when viewed as a whole the affidavit and material in support of the motion does not disclose a prima facie case and furthermore that the directors were never informed of the specification they were requested to take prior to this motion and indeed he questions whether the motion itself discloses an action.

As I understand his submission it appears that while he does not necessarily agree that the applicants are acting in good faith as required by subs. (3)(b) or that both were members of the company within the meaning of subs. (3)(d) he does not seriously contend that these things are not so.

Accordingly I find that the applicants have satisfied the requirements of s. 222(3)(b) and (d).

He does however submit that while the applicants did make a reasonable effort to cause the directors to commence an action the applicants failed to specify the precise nature of the action. In making this submission he relies upon the United States case of *Halprin v. Babbit* (1962), 303 F. 2nd 138 at 141. He submits that there is no evidence that the directors had full knowledge of the basis of the claim.

It is in my view that that is the correct interpretation of the requirement of s. 222(3)(a). The directors could hardly bring any action whether by their own initiative or on the requisition of a minority shareholder without knowing the specific cause of action. However I would think that no more would be required than that sufficient to found an endorsement on a generally endorsed writ of summons.

Mr. McConnell submits that there is a difference between the relief sought in the motion and that set out in the requisition, the two paragraphs of which read as follows:

1. To pass a resolution that the Company take action against the persons who were directors of the Company during the time when certain shares of Fraser Valley Pulp & Timber Ltd. owned by the Company were voted for a special resolution to sell the assets of Fraser Valley Pulp & Timber Ltd. to Green River Log Sales Ltd., and against the person who held the proxy for the said shares and cast them for such special resolution.

2. To pass a resolution that the directors of the Company cause the shares of Fraser Valley Pulp & Timber Ltd., held by the Company be voted at a meeting of Fraser Valley Pulp & Timber Ltd. to bring action to set aside the sale by Fraser Valley Pulp & Timber Ltd., to Green River Log Sales Ltd., on the ground that the assets of Fraser Valley Pulp & Timber Ltd., in such sale were so grossly undervalued to the knowledge of the directors of both Fraser Valley Pulp & Timber Ltd. and Green River Log Sales Ltd., as to amount to a fraud on the shareholders of Fraser Valley Pulp & Timber Ltd.

In my view that notice sufficiently specifies the cause of action and contains sufficient information to found an endorsement on a writ.

While there are some differences between the wording of the requisition and that relief sought in the motion, which is conceded by Miss Southin, I do note that Mr. Ross's letter of 3rd April 1974 sets out the relief sought in substantially the same words as contained in the motion. Those words I have set out heretofore in this judgment.

Furthermore the relief sought is in the nature of equitable relief and there is in my view no substantial difference between the requisition and the motion as both refer to fraud. Furthermore there is no evidence that the directors refused to commence the action in the terms specifically set out in either the letter or the requisition. All the directors did was defeat the motion.

Accordingly I find that the applicants have satisfied the requirements of s. 222(3)(a).

The real question here is whether in the circumstances of this case "it is prima facie in the interests of the company that the action be brought" (s. 222(3)(c)). It will be noted that the Legislature has said that it is sufficient to show that the action sought is prima facie in the interests of the company and does not appear to require that the applicants prove a prima facie case. Presumably the authors of that legislation had in mind that a minority shareholder being in a real sense on the outside is often not in a position to obtain evidence such as that that the Crown would be expected to put forward to found a prima facie case in a criminal matter.

In a criminal case the Crown is not required to do more than produce evidence which if unanswered and believed is sufficient to raise a prima facie case upon which the jury might be justified in finding a verdict: *Girvin v. The King* (1911), 45 S.C.R. 167, 20 W.L.R. 130; *Rex v. Scott*, [1919] 2 W.W.R. 227, 14 Alta. L.R. 439, 31 C.C.C. 399 (C.A.).

The words "prima facie" are not defined in any statute of which I am aware. "Prima facie" is defined as "at first sight," "on the face of" in Jowitt's Dictionary of English Law and Black's Law Dictionary. The latter volume also contains the definition "so far as can be judged from the first disclosure."

It should be borne in mind that an application such as this is in the nature of an interlocutory application because it decides nothing more than that an action may or may not be commenced.

That being so then the various civil cases set out in Cross on Evidence, 2nd ed., at pp. 24-26, and Phipson on Evidence, 11th ed., p. 103, are of small assistance. The cases set out in these volumes are concerned with "prima facie evidence" upon the trial of an issue. The definition of "prima facie evidence" when used in English statutes usually has that meaning attributed to it by Statford J.A. in *Regina v. Jabobson and Levy*, [1931] App. D. 466 at 478 (South Africa), where he said this:

... "*prima facie* evidence" in its usual sense is used to mean *prima facie* proof of an issue, the burden of proving which is upon the party giving that evidence. In the absence of further evidence from the other side, the *prima facie* proof becomes conclusive proof and the party giving it discharges his onus.

It will be seen that that definition is not particularly helpful because such a criterion must be for proof upon trial. This application decides nothing more than whether the applicant has adduced sufficient evidence which on the face of that evidence discloses that it is, so far as can be judged from the first disclosure, in the interests of the company to pursue the action.

Adopting that definition one must then consider what disclosures are contained in the evidence which might warrant a Court exercising its discretion to allow the minority shareholders here to commence an action against the directors for fraud in the name of and on behalf of the company.

The principle matters relied upon by the applicants are:

1. The sale to Green Valley of the entire undertaking of Fraser Valley for a price of approximately $91,700 less than its apparent value for lending purposes, both transactions having been concluded on the same day.
2. The apparent failure of the directors to seek out any bids from other persons, bearing in mind that Louis Clarke as a director of both companies appears on the face of the documents to have derived a benefit from this transaction.
3. The apparent failure of the directors to find out the current market value of the lands sold as it appears in the notes of Mr. Ross that the directors did not rely upon the appraisal made 31st December 1971 when consummating the sale to Green River.

4. The possible loss or diminution of the water lot.
5. The question as to the authority of the directors to make the sale to Green River in the absence of any evidence as to voting authority or the presence or absence of sufficient members to pass the resolutions.
6. The acceptance of a promissory note in substitution for a debenture and an account receivable.

In my view these are matters which concern the interests of the company as the major shareholders of Fraser Valley within the meaning of s. 222(3)(c). These may also be matters of moment and concern to the individual shareholders of the company, but that, in my view, does not detract from the derivative nature of the action sought to be commenced.

Miss Southin submits that the question is whether there is evidence that discloses a case that should be dealt with. Mr. McConnell who relies in his argument essentially on majority rule points out that a court must give careful consideration to the possible consequences of such an order. There can be no question but that that is an important consideration.

The standard of care required of a director of a company is that set out in 6 Hals. (3d) 309, para. 619:

A director is liable for negligence if he fails to exercise such degree of care as a reasonable man might be expected to take in the circumstances on his own behalf, and the company in consequence suffers loss.

Bearing that standard in mind it is my view that the applicants have put forward sufficient evidence which on the face of it discloses a failure on the part of the directors to take that degree of care required of them and accordingly I grant leave to the applicants to bring the action set out in the motion in the name of and on behalf of Northwest Forest Products Ltd. against the five persons named in the motion.

The motion also claims security for costs and disbursements. It is conceded that that application is premature and cannot as appears by s. 222(4) be brought until the action is commenced.

NOTES

1) Would shareholders have been permitted to maintain a derivative action at common law on the facts of *Northwest Forest Products Ltd.*?

2) The plaintiff's theory was not so much that the corporation had wrongfully disposed of one of its assets, but that its subsidiary (Fraser Valley) had done so. In this sense, the claim sought a "double derivative" recovery. This is expressly permitted by CBCA s. 239(1) (cause of action may be brought on behalf of the firm "or any of its subsidiaries"). Harm to a subsidiary also injures its parent, however, so that this provision is unremarkable. In fact, at the time of the *Northwest Forest Products* case, the BCCA did not include this provision, nor does it today.

Shareholder Ratification. In *Northwest Forest Products*, Cashman J., construing a provision of the BCCA nearly identical to CBCA s. 242(1), stated that he would not "take into account the apparent approval of the members of the company" of the challenged conduct in the absence of evidence as to whether the shareholder majority included shares voted by the defendant directors. The inference is that the only kind of shareholder approval that would bar a derivative plaintiff would be approval by a disinterested shareholder majority, one that included votes cast neither by the proposed defendant directors nor by shareholders with a direct pecuniary interest in the conduct complained of. It is clear that the intent of the statutory provisions for derivative actions is to liberalize the availability of redress for corporate wrongs at the instance of a minority shareholder. See Lawrence Report 55-64, Dickerson Report 160-65. It seems just as clear, however, that the intent was not to make irrelevant the views of the shareholder majority as to whether the corporation should pursue claims against its managers. The value of shareholder ratification under s. 242 is that it may be evidence of the fairness of the transaction or of the desirability of forgiving a breach. The persuasiveness of such evidence may depend upon many factors, such as the adequacy of proxy disclosure, how outside shareholders have voted, and the nature of the impeached transaction. Would ratification of directorial conduct by a shareholder majority including the directors in question preclude minority shareholder challenges to the transaction if the transaction is apparently fair, as in *North-West Transportation Co.*? Even if the fairness of the transaction was open to question, would approval by a majority of outside shareholders suggest that it should be upheld? Would such a ratification have evidentiary value in respect of breaches which formerly constituted "fraud on the minority"?

The question of shareholder ratification is really two questions which, although related, can usefully be thought of separately: (1) must a minority shareholder make a demand on the shareholders either to join him or to attempt to cause the company to sue, as a condition of being permitted to maintain a derivative action? and (2) what effect is to be given to ratification by a shareholder majority?

At common law, if a minority shareholder sought to sue the directors on behalf of the corporation under the "fraud on the minority" exception to the rule in *Foss v. Harbottle*, he would have to show either that he had put to the corporation in general meeting a motion that the action should be commenced or that such a demand would have been futile because the wrongdoers were in control of the share majority. *Burrows v. Becker* (1967), 63 D.L.R. (2d) 100 (B.C.C.A.), aff'd, [1969] S.C.R. 162, 70 D.L.R. (2d) 433. If the alleged wrongdoers were not in control of the share majority and therefore a demand upon the shareholders had to be made, a negative decision by the general meeting would preclude further litigation. This is consistent with the policy behind the rule in *Foss v. Harbottle*. The corporation's causes of action, like other assets, belong to it and not to the shareholders. If a cause of action is to be asserted, it is the corporation itself that must do so unless it cannot because the wrongdoers will not permit it to proceed against themselves.

In considering whether a derivative plaintiff should be required to make a demand to sue upon his fellow shareholders, it should be remembered that shareholder solicitation, in publicly held corporations at least, is expensive and that control of the proxy machinery is usually control of the outcome.

Finally, consider CBCA s. 122(3) (to which there are substantially equivalent provisions in most of the provincial acts):

[N]o provision in a contract, the articles, the by-laws or a resolution relieves a director or officer from the duty to act in accordance with this Act or the regulations or relieves him from liability for a breach thereof.

While this provision, literally construed, would simply nullify any and all ratifications, it seems unlikely that it was intended to have that effect. It seems designed, rather, to reach blanket attempts to relieve directors and officers by way of contract or by-law from the normal obligations of their fiduciary status. Furthermore, it may point toward a distinction between the evidentiary value of a vote of ratification and the preclusive effect against litigation that the common law gave to a resolution absolving directors.

2. The Role of the Board in Derivative Litigation

Demand Upon the Directors. CBCA s. 239(2)(a) provides that leave to bring a derivative action shall not be granted unless the plaintiff has "given reasonable notice to the directors of the corporation ... of his intention to apply to the court under subsection (1) if the directors of the corporation ... do not bring, diligently prosecute or defend or discontinue the action." A demand requirement was never particularly difficult to comply with in Canada, and one or two letters to the corporation's solicitor to complain about the transaction might well suffice. See *Armstrong v. Gardner* (1978), 20 O.R. (2d) 648. on the other hand, the notice should at least give details of the nature of the claim to be asserted. *Re Daon Dev. Corp.* (1984), 10 D.L.R. (4th) 216, 221-22 (B.C.).

Demand requirements are more onerous in the United States, though derivative plaintiffs have been excused from the requirement where the demand could be said in advance to be futile. One example of this occurs when all of the directors are under the domination of the wrongdoers. *Papilsky v. Berndt*, 59 F.R.D. 95 (S.D.N.Y. 1973), aff'd, 503 F.2d 554 (2d Cir.), cert. denied, 419 U.S. 1048 (1974); *de Haas v. Empire Petroleum Co.*, 286 F. Supp. 809 (D. Colo. 1968), modified, 435 F.2d 1223 (10th Cir. 1970). In other cases the plaintiff had sought to challenge an underlying transaction as an unlawful interested directors' transaction, and had named as defendants in the derivative action not only the interested directors, as to whom the complaint was akin to an allegation of fraud, but also the remaining board members, on the basis that they were negligent in permitting the main defendants to act as they did. There is a difference of opinion on whether a demand on the board should be excused in such a case. Compare *Barr v. Wackman*, 329 N.E.2d 180 (N.Y. 1975) (demand excused) with *In Re Kauffman Mutual Fund Actions*, 479 F.2d 257 (1st Cir.), cert. denied, 414 U.S. 857 (1973) (demand required).

The most obvious purpose of the notice-to-directors requirement is to give the corporation the opportunity to sue on its own behalf. But suppose that the directors consider the matter and decline to cause the corporation to sue. Does that decision simply clear away the hurdle, automatically allowing the derivative plaintiffs to go forward? Or is the decision of the directors not to bring the action itself a factor for the court to consider in determining whether maintenance of the action is *prima facie* in the best interests of the corporation? Does s. 239(2)(a) give the board, on receipt of the demand from shareholders, the discretion to "discontinue the action"? Suppose that the directors do not simply ignore the plaintiff's notice but rather respond with reasons why they are not causing the corporation to sue. They may argue that in their considered judgment maintenance of the action would not serve the corporation's interests. The directors might conclude that the underlying claim is not well founded or that, even though it might prove meritorious, the likely recovery would not justify the direct and indirect costs to the corporation. These costs might include not only reputational costs and the corporation's own legal fees, but also an indemnity to the defendant directors and officers if the action does succeed. The directors might then decide that the present value of the anticipated recovery does not equal its costs. These are all reasons why an individual may decide not to assert a personal action, and because of them the directors may determine that the game is not worth the candle. How should a court deal with such assertions by the directors?

A decision to sue or not to sue is ordinarily a matter of business judgment, like the decision to buy or not to buy a new truck. It is different, however, when the litigation concerns a member of the management team. Can a business judgment standard be applied uncritically to decisions to absolve a fellow member of the team? Suppose that maintaining the action would really not be in the best interests of the corporation. How able is a court to determine such questions under CBCA s. 239(2)(c)?

Auerbach v. Bennett
New York Court of Appeals
393 N.E.2d 994 (1979)

JONES, Judge: While the substantive aspects of a decision to terminate a shareholders' derivative action against defendant corporate directors made by a committee of disinterested directors appointed by the corporation's board of directors are beyond judicial inquiry under the business judgment doctrine, the court may inquire as to the disinterested independence of the members of that committee and as to the appropriateness and sufficiency of the investigative procedures chosen and pursued by the committee. In this instance, however, no basis is shown to warrant either inquiry by the court. Accordingly we hold that it was error to reverse the lower court's dismissal of the shareholders' derivative action.

In the summer of 1975 the management of General Telephone & Electronics Corporation, in response to reports that numerous other multinational companies had made questionable payments to public officials of political parties in foreign countries, directed that an internal preliminary investigation be made to ascertain whether that corporation had engaged in similar transactions. On the basis of the report of this survey, received in October, 1975, management brought the issue to the attention of the corporation's board of directors. At a meeting held on November 6 of that year the board referred the matter to the board's audit committee. The audit committee retained as its special counsel the Washington, D.C., law firm of Wilmer, Cutler & Pickering which had not previously acted as counsel to the corporation. With the assistance of such special counsel and Arthur Andersen & Co., the corporation's outside auditors, the audit committee engaged in an investigation into the corporation's worldwide operations, focusing on whether, in the period January 1, 1971 to December 31, 1975, corporate funds had been (1) paid directly or indirectly to any political party or person or to any officer, employee, shareholder or director of any governmental or private customer, or (2) used to reimburse any officer of the corporation or other person for such payments.

On March 4, 1976 the audit committee released its report which was filed with the Securities and Exchange Commission and disclosed to the corporation's shareholders in a proxy statement prior to the annual meeting of shareholders held in April, 1976. The audit committee reported that it had found evidence that in the period from 1971 to 1975 the corporation or its subsidiaries had made payments abroad and in the United States constituting bribes and kickbacks in amounts perhaps totaling more than 11 million dollars and that some of the individual defendant directors had been personally involved in certain of the transactions.

Almost immediately Auerbach, a shareholder in the corporation, instituted the present shareholders' derivative action on behalf of the corporation against the corporation's directors, Arthur Andersen & Co. and the corporation. The complaint alleged that in connection with the transactions reported by the audit committee defendants, present and former members of the corporation's board of directors and Arthur Andersen & Co., are liable to the corporation for breach of their duties to the corporation and should be made to account for payments made in those transactions.

On April 21, 1976, the board of directors of the corporation adopted a resolution creating a special litigation committee "for the purpose of establishing a point of contract between the Board of Directors and the Corporation's General Counsel concerning the position to be taken by the Corporation in certain litigation involving shareholder derivative claims on behalf of the Corporation against certain of its directors and officers" and authorizing that committee "to take such steps from time to time as it deems necessary to pursue its objectives including the retention of special outside counsel." The special committee comprised three disinterested directors who had joined the board after the challenged transactions had occurred. The board subsequently additionally vested in the committee "all of the authority of the Board of Directors to determine, on behalf of the Board, the position that the Corporation shall take with respect to the derivative claims alleged on its behalf" in the present and similar shareholder derivative actions.

The special litigation committee reported under date of November 22, 1976. It found that defendant Arthur Andersen & Co. had conducted its examination of the corporation's affairs in accordance with generally accepted auditing standards and in good faith and concluded that no proper interest of the corporation or its shareholders would be served by the continued assertion of a claim against it. The committee also concluded that none of the individual defendants had violated the New York State statutory standard of care, that none had profited personally or gained in any way, that the claims asserted in the present action are without merit, that if the action were allowed to proceed the time and talents of the corporation's senior management would be wasted on lengthy pretrial and trial proceedings, that litigation costs would be inordinately high in view of the unlikelihood of success, and that the continuing publicity could be damaging to the corporation's business. The committee determined that it would not be in the best interests of the corporation for the present derivative action to proceed, and, exercising the authority delegated to it, directed the corporation's general counsel to take that position in the present litigation as well as in pending comparable shareholders' derivative actions.

[The defendants and the corporation moved to dismiss the complaint or for summary judgment. The trial court granted the motion, and the Appellate Division of the Supreme Court reversed. The defendants and the corporation appealed to the Court of Appeals, New York's highest court.]

As all parties and both courts below recognize, the disposition of this case on the merits turns on the proper application of the business judgment doctrine, in particular to the decision of a specially appointed committee of disinterested directors acting on behalf of the board to terminate a shareholders' derivative action. That doctrine bars judicial inquiry into actions of corporate directors taken in good faith and in the exercise of honest judgment in the lawful and legitimate furtherance of corporate purposes. "Questions of policy of management, expediency of contracts or action, adequacy of consideration, lawful appropriation of corporate funds to advance corporate interests, are left solely to their honest and unselfish decision, for their powers therein are without limitation and free from restraint, and the exercise of them for the common and general interests of the corporation may not be questioned, although the results show that what they did was unwise or inexpedient." (*Pollitz v. Wabash R.R. Co.*, 207 N.Y. 113, 124, 100 N.E. 721, 724.)

In this instance our inquiry, to the limited extent to which it may be pursued, has a two-tiered aspect. The complaint initially asserted liability on the part of the defendants based on the payments made to foreign governmental customers and privately owned customers, some unspecified portions of which were allegedly passed on to officials of the customers, i.e., the focus was on first-tier bribes and kickbacks. Then subsequent to the service of the complaint there came the report of a special litigation committee, particularly appointed by the corporation's board of directors to consider the merits of the present and similar shareholders' derivative actions, and its determination that it would not be in the best interests of the corporation to press claims against defendants based on their possible first-tier liability. The motions for summary judgment were predicated principally on the report and determination of the special litigation committee and on the contention that this second-tier corporate action insulated the first-tier trans-actions from judicial inquiry and was itself subject to the shelter of the business judgment doctrine. The disposition at Special Term was predicated on this analysis; its decision focused on the actions of the special litigation committee, and the motions for summary judgment were granted on the ground that the business judgment doctrine precluded the courts from going back on the decision of the special litigation committee on behalf of the corporation not to pursue the claims alleged in the complaint. Similarly the reversal at the Appellate Division was based on that court's perception of the proper application of the business judgment rule to the actions and determination of the special litigation committee. We proceed on the same analysis, concluding, however, on the record before us, at variance with the Appellate Division, that the determination of the special litigation committee forecloses further judicial inquiry in this case.

· · ·

Derivative claims against corporate directors belong to the corporation itself. As with other questions of corporate policy and management, the decision whether and to what extent to explore and prosecute such claims lies within the judgment and control of the corporation's board of directors. Necessarily such decisions must be predicated on the weighing and balancing of a variety of disparate considerations to reach a considered conclusion as to what course of action or inaction is best calculated to protect and advance the interests of the corporation. This is the essence of the responsibility and role of the board of directors, and courts may not intrude to interfere.

In the present case we confront a special instance of the application of the business judgment rule and inquire whether it applies in its full vigor to shield from judicial scrutiny the decision of a three-pension minority committee of the board acting on behalf of the full board not to prosecute a shareholder's derivative action. The record in this case reveals that the board is a 15-member board, and that the derivative suit was brought against four of the directors. Nothing suggests that any of the other directors participated in any of the challenged first-tier transactions. Indeed the report of the audit committee on which the complaint is based specifically found that no other directors had any prior knowledge of or were in any way involved in any of these transactions. Other directors had, however, been members of the board in the period during which the transactions occurred. Each of the three director members of the special litigation committee joined the board thereafter.

The business judgment rule does not foreclose inquiry by the courts into the disinterested independence of those members of the board chosen by it to make the corporate decision on its behalf—here the members of the special litigation committee. Indeed the rule shields the deliberations and conclusions of the chosen representatives of the board only if they possess a disinterested independence and do not stand in a dual relation which prevents an unprejudicial exercise of judgment. (Cf. *Koral v. Savory, Inc.*, 276 N.Y. 215, 11 N.E.2d 883.)

We examine then the proof submitted by defendants. It is not disputed that the members of the special litigation committee were not members of the corporation's board of directors at the time of the first-tier transactions in question. ... None of the three had had any prior affiliation with the corporation. Notwithstanding the vigorous and imaginative hypothesizing and innuendo of counsel there is nothing in this record to raise a triable issue of fact as to the independence and disinterested status of these three directors.

The contention of Wallenstein that any committee authorized by the board of which defendant directors were members must be held to be legally infirm and may not be delegated power to terminate a derivative action must be rejected. In the very nature of the corporate organization it was only the existing board of directors which had authority on behalf of the corporation to direct the investigation and to assure the cooperation of corporate employees, and it is only that same board by its own action—or as here pursuant to authority duly delegated by it—which had authority to decide whether to prosecute the claims against defendant directors. The board in this instance, with slight adaptation, followed prudent practice in observing the general policy that when individual members of a board prove to have personal interests which may conflict with the interests of the corporation, such interested directors must be excluded while the remain-

ing members of the board proceed to consideration and action. (Cf. Business Corporation Law, § 713, which contemplates such situations and provides that the interested
directors may nonetheless be included in the quorum count.) Courts have consistently
held that the business judgment rule applies where some directors are charged with
wrongdoing, so long as the remaining directors making the decision are disinterested
and independent.

To accept the assertions of the intervenor and to disqualify the entire board would
be to render the corporation powerless to make an effective business judgment with
respect to prosecution of the derivative action. The possible risk of hesitancy on the part
of the members of any committee, even if composed of outside, independent, disinterested directors, to investigate the activities of fellow members of the board where personal liability is at stake is an inherent, inescapable, given aspect of the corporation's
predicament. To assign responsibility of the dimension here involved to individuals
wholly separate and apart from the board of directors would, except in the most extraordinary circumstances, itself be an act of default and breach of the nondelegable fiduciary
duty owed by the members of the board to the corporation and to its shareholders,
employees and creditors. For the courts to preside over such determinations would
similarly work an ouster of the board's fundamental responsibility and authority for
corporate management.

We turn then to the action of the special litigation committee itself which comprised
two components. First, there was the selection of procedures appropriate to the pursuit
of its charge, and second, there was the ultimate substantive decision, predicated on the
procedures chosen and the data produced thereby, not to pursue the claims advanced in
the shareholders' derivative actions. The latter, substantive decision falls squarely within
the embrace of the business judgment doctrine, involving as it did the weighing and
balancing of legal, ethical, commercial, promotional, public relations, fiscal and other
factors familiar to the resolution of many if not most corporate problems. To this extent
the conclusion reached by the special litigation committee is outside the scope of our
review. Thus, the courts cannot inquire as to which factors were considered by that
committee or the relative weight accorded them in reaching that substantive decision—
"the reasons for the payments, the advantages or disadvantages accruing to the corporation by reason of the transactions, the extent of the participation or profit by the
respondent directors and the loss, if any, of public confidence in the corporation which
might be incurred" (64 A.D.2d, at p. 107, 408 N.Y.S.2d at pp. 87-88). Inquiry into such
matters would go to the very core of the business judgment made by the committee. To
permit judicial probing of such issues would be to emasculate the business judgment
doctrine as applied to the actions and determinations of the special litigation committee.
Its substantive evaluation of the problems posed and its judgment in their resolution are
beyond our reach.

As to the other component of the committee's activities, however, the situation is
different, and here we agree with the Appellate Division. As to the methodologies and
procedures best suited to the conduct of an investigation of facts and the determination
of legal liability, the courts are well equipped by long and continuing experience and
practice to make determinations. In fact they are better qualified in this regard than are
corporate directors in general. Nor do the determinations to be made in the adoption of

procedures partake of the nuances or special perceptions or comprehensions of business judgment or corporate activities or interests. The question is solely how appropriately to set about to gather the pertinent data.

While the court may properly inquire as to the adequacy and appropriateness of the committee's investigative procedures and methodologies, it may not under the guise of consideration of such factors trespass in the domain of business judgment. At the same time those responsible for the procedures by which the business judgment is reached may reasonably be required to show that they have pursued their chosen investigative methods in good faith. What evidentiary proof may be required to this end will, of course, depend on the nature of the particular investigation, and the proper reach of disclosure at the instance of the shareholders will in turn relate inversely to the showing made by the corporate representatives themselves. The latter may be expected to show that the areas and subjects to be examined are reasonably complete and that there has been a good-faith pursuit of inquiry into such areas and subjects. What has been uncovered and the relative weight accorded in evaluating and balancing the several factors and considerations are beyond the scope of judicial concern. Proof, however, that the investigation has been so restricted in scope, so shallow in execution, or otherwise so *pro forma* or halfhearted as to constitute a pretext or sham, consistent with the principles underlying the application of the business judgment doctrine, would raise questions of good faith or conceivably fraud which would never be shielded by that doctrine.

• • •

On the submissions made by defendants in support of their motions, we do not find either insufficiency or infirmity as to the procedures and methodologies chosen and pursued by the special litigation committee. That committee promptly engaged eminent special counsel to guide its deliberations and to advise it. The committee reviewed the prior work of the audit committee, testing its completeness, accuracy and thoroughness by interviewing representatives of Wilmer, Cutler & Pickering, reviewing transcripts of the testimony of 10 corporate officers and employees before the Securities and Exchange Commission, and studying documents collected by and work papers of the Washington law firm. Individual interviews were conducted with the directors found to have participated in any way in the questioned payments, and with representatives of Arthur Andersen & Co. Questionnaires were sent to and answered by each of the corporation's nonmanagement directors. At the conclusion of its investigation the special litigation committee sought and obtained pertinent legal advice from its special counsel. The selection of appropriate investigative methods must always turn on the nature and characteristics of the particular subject being investigated, but we find nothing in this record that requires a trial of any material issue of fact concerning the sufficiency or appropriateness of the procedures chosen by this special litigation committee. Nor is there anything in this record to raise a triable issue of fact as to the good-faith pursuit of its examination by that committee.

• • •

For the reasons stated the order of the Appellate Division should be modified, with costs to defendants, by reversing so much thereof as reversed the order of Supreme Court, and, as so modified, affirmed.

JASEN, WACHTLER, FUCHESBERG and MEYER JJ. concurred with JONES J.

[The dissenting opinion of COOKE C.J. has been omitted.]

Zapata Corp. v. Maldonado
Delaware Supreme Court
430 A.2d 779 (1981)

Before DUFFY, QUILLEN and HORSEY JJ.

QUILLEN, Justice: ... In June, 1975, William Maldonado, a stockholder of Zapata, instituted a derivative action in the Court of Chancery on behalf of Zapata against ten officers and/or directors of Zapata, alleging, essentially, breaches of fiduciary duty.

[Plaintiff alleged that Zapata's directors were optionees under a corporate stock option plan and that they caused the date on which the options could be exercised to be advanced in order to save themselves tax liability. The options would produce taxable income to the directors based upon the difference between the option exercise price and the market price of the underlying securities on the date of exercise. The directors had determined that the corporation should make a tender offer for its own shares. The effect of the tender offer would be to raise the market price of Zapata shares. The directors determined to move up the option exercise date by about a month in order to exercise them before the tender offer was announced. The plaintiff alleged that the tax saving to the directors represented an increased tax burden to the corporation, the tax liability of which was, in respect of the option transaction, the obverse of that of the directors.]

Maldonado did not first demand that the board bring this action, stating instead such demand's futility because all directors were named as defendants and allegedly participated in the acts specified. ...

By June, 1979, four of the defendant-directors were no longer on the board, and the remaining directors appointed two new outside directors to the board. The board then created an "Independent Investigation Committee" (Committee), composed solely of the two new directors, to investigate Maldonado's actions, as well as a similar derivative action then pending in Texas, and to determine whether the corporation should continue any or all of the litigation. The Committee's determination was stated to be "final, ... not ... subject to review by the Board of Directors and ... in all respects ... binding upon the Corporation."

[The Committee moved in the Court of Chancery to have the action dismissed on the ground that its continued maintenance was inimical to the best interests of the corporation. The Chancellor denied the motion, and the Committee appealed to the Delaware Supreme Court.]

We begin with an examination of the carefully considered opinion of the Vice Chancellor which states, in part, that the "business judgment" rule does not confer power "to a corporate board of directors to terminate a derivative suit," 413 A.2d at 1257. His conclusion is particularly pertinent because several federal courts, applying Delaware law, have held that the business judgment rule enables boards (or their committees) to terminate derivative suits, decisions now in conflict with the holding below.

• • •

The corporate power inquiry then focuses on whether the board, tainted by the self-interest of a majority of its members, can legally delegate its authority to a committee of two disinterested directors. We find our statute clearly requires an affirmative answer to this question. As has been noted, under an express provision of the statute, § 141(c), a committee can exercise all of the authority of the board to the extent provided in the resolution of the board. Moreover, at least by analogy to our statutory section on interested directors, 8 *Del.C.* § 141, it seems clear that the Delaware statute is designed to permit disinterested directors to act for the board. Compare *Puma v. Marriott*, Del.Ch., 283 A.2d 693, 695-96 (1971).

We do not think that the interest taint of the board majority is per se a legal bar to the delegation of the board's power to an independent committee composed of disinterested board members. The committee can properly act for the corporation to move to dismiss derivative litigation that is believed to be detrimental to the corporation's best interest.

Our focus now switches to the Court of Chancery which is faced with a stockholder assertion that a derivative suit, properly instituted, should continue for the benefit of the corporation and a corporate assertion, properly made by a board committee acting with board authority, that the same derivative suit should be dismissed as inimical to the best interests of the corporation.

At the risk of stating the obvious, the problem is relatively simple. If, on the one hand, corporations can consistently wrest bona fide derivative actions away from well-meaning derivative plaintiffs through the use of the committee mechanism, the derivative suit will lose much, if not all, of its generally-recognized effectiveness as an intra-corporate means of policing boards of directors. ... If, on the other hand, corporations are unable to rid themselves of meritless or harmful litigation and strike suits, the derivative action, created to benefit the corporation, will produce the opposite, unintended result. It thus appears desirable to us to find a balancing point where bona fide stockholder power to bring corporate causes of action cannot be unfairly trampled on by the board of directors, but the corporation can rid itself of detrimental litigation.

As we noted, the question has been treated by other courts as one of the "business judgment" of the board committee. If a "committee, composed of independent and disinterested directors, conducted a proper review of the matters before it, considered a variety of factors and reached, in good faith, a business judgment that [the] action was not in the best interest of [the corporation]," the action must be dismissed. See, e.g.,

Maldonado v. Flynn, 485 F.Supp. at 282, 286. The issues become solely independence, good faith, and reasonable investigation. The ultimate conclusion of the committee, under that view, is not subject to judicial review.

We are not satisfied, however, that acceptance of the "business judgment" rationale at this stage of derivative litigation is a proper balancing point. While we admit an analogy with a normal case respecting board judgment, it seems to us that there is sufficient risk in the realities of a situation like the one presented in this case to justify caution beyond adherence to the theory of business judgment.

The context here is a suit against directors where demand on the board is excused. We think some tribute must be paid to the fact that the lawsuit was properly initiated. It is not a board refusal case. Moreover, this complaint was filed in June of 1975 and, while the parties undoubtedly would take differing views on the degree of litigation activity, we have to be concerned about the creation of an "Independent Investigation Committee" four years later, after the election of two new outside directors. Situations could develop where such motions could be filed after years of vigorous litigation for reasons unconnected with the merits of the lawsuit.

Moreover, notwithstanding our conviction that Delaware law entrusts the corporate power to a properly authorized committee, we must be mindful that directors are passing judgment on fellow directors in the same corporation and fellow directors, in this instance, who designated them to serve both as directors and committee members. The question naturally arises whether a "there but for the grace of God go I" empathy might not play a role. And the further question arises whether inquiry as to independence, good faith and reasonable investigation is sufficient safeguard against abuse, perhaps subconscious abuse.

There is another line of exploration besides the factual context of this litigation which we find helpful. The nature of this motion finds no ready pigeonhole, as perhaps illustrated by its being set forth in the alternative. It is perhaps best considered as a hybrid summary judgment motion for dismissal because the stockholder plaintiff's standing to maintain the suit has been lost. But it does not fit neatly into a category described in Rule 12(b) of the Court of Chancery Rules nor does it correspond directly with Rule 56 since the question of genuine issues of fact on the merits of the stockholder's claim are not reached.

It seems to us that there are two other procedural analogies that are helpful in addition to reference to Rules 12 and 56. There is some analogy to a settlement in that there is a request to terminate litigation without a judicial determination of the merits. See *Perrine v. Pennroad Corp.*, Del.Supr., 47 A.2d 479, 487 (1946). "In determining whether or not to approve a proposed settlement of a derivative stockholders' action [when directors are on both sides of the transaction], the Court of Chancery is called upon to exercise its own business judgment." *Neponsit Investment Co. v. Abramson*, Del.Supr., 405 A.2d 97, 100 (1979) and cases therein cited. In this case, the litigating stockholder plaintiff facing dismissal of a lawsuit properly commenced ought, in our judgment, to have sufficient status for strict Court review.

Finally, if the committee is in effect given status to speak for the corporation as the plaintiff in interest, then it seems to us there is an analogy to Court of Chancery Rule 41(a)(2) where the plaintiff seeks a dismissal after an answer. Certainly, the position of record of the litigating stockholder is adverse to the position advocated by the corporation in the motion to dismiss. Accordingly, there is perhaps some wisdom to be gained by the direction in Rule 41(a)(2) that "an action shall not be dismissed at the plaintiff's instance save upon order of the Court and upon such terms and conditions as the Court deems proper."

Whether the Court of Chancery will be persuaded by the exercise of a committee power resulting in a summary motion for dismissal of a derivative action, where a demand has not been initially made, should rest, in our judgment, in the independent discretion of the Court of Chancery. We thus steer a middle course between those cases which yield to the independent business judgment of a board committee and this case as determined below which would yield to unbridled plaintiff stockholder control. In pursuit of the course, we recognize that "[t]he final substantive judgment whether a particular lawsuit should be maintained requires a balance of many factors—ethical, commercial, promotional, public relations, employee relations, fiscal as well as legal." *Maldonado v. Flynn,* supra, 485 F.Supp. at 285. But we are content that such factors are not "beyond the judicial reach" of the Court of Chancery which regularly and competently deals with fiduciary relationships, disposition of trust property, approval of settlements and scores of similar problems. We recognize the danger of judicial overreaching but the alternatives seem to us to be outweighed by the fresh view of a judicial outsider. Moreover, if we failed to balance all the interests involved, we would in the name of practicality and judicial economy foreclose a judicial decision on the merits. At this point, we are not convinced that is necessary or desirable.

After an objective and thorough investigation of a derivative suit, an independent committee may cause its corporation to file a pretrial motion to dismiss in the Court of Chancery. The basis of the motion is the best interests of the corporation, as determined by the committee. The motion should include a thorough written record of the investigation and its findings and recommendations. Under appropriate Court supervision, akin to proceedings on summary judgment, each side should have an opportunity to make a record on the motion. As to the limited issues presented by the motion noted below, the moving party should be prepared to meet the normal burden under Rule 56 that there is no genuine issue as to any material fact and that the moving party is entitled to dismiss as a matter of law. The Court should apply a two-step test to the motion.

First, the Court should inquire into the independence and good faith of the committee and the bases supporting its conclusions. Limited discovery may be ordered to facilitate such inquiries. The corporation should have the burden of proving independence, good faith and a reasonable investigation, rather than presuming independence, good faith and reasonableness. If the Court determines either that the committee is not independent or has not shown reasonable bases for its conclusions, or, if the Court is not satisfied for other reasons relating to the process, including but not limited to the good faith of the committee, the Court shall deny the corporation's motion. If, however, the Court is satisfied under Rule 56 standards that the committee was independent and showed reasonable bases for good faith findings and recommendations, the Court may proceed, in its discretion, to the next step.

The second step provides, we believe, the essential key in striking the balance between legitimate corporate claims as expressed in a derivative stockholder suit and a corporation's best interests as expressed by an independent investigating committee. The Court should determine, applying its own independent business judgment, whether the motion should be granted.[18] This means, of course, that instances could arise where a committee can establish its independence and sound bases for its good faith decisions and still have the corporation's motion denied. The second step is intended to thwart instances where corporate actions meet the criteria of step one, but the result does not appear to satisfy its spirit, or where corporate actions would simply prematurely terminate a stockholder grievance deserving of further consideration in the corporation's interest. The Court of Chancery of course must carefully consider and weigh how compelling the corporate interest in dismissal is when faced with a non-frivolous lawsuit. The Court of Chancery should, when appropriate, give special consideration to matters of law and public policy in addition to the corporation's best interests.

If the Court's independent business judgment is satisfied, the Court may proceed to grant the motion, subject, of course, to any equitable terms or conditions the Court finds necessary or desirable.

The interlocutory order of the Court of Chancery is reversed and the cause is remanded for further proceedings consistent with this opinion.

Independent Litigation Committees. In *Re Bellman* (1981), 130 D.L.R. (3d) 193 (B.C.C.A.), the Court did not have to determine what weight to accord to the committee's views because it found that the committee's members were not independent of the defendants and that the issues which they had commissioned an auditing firm to investigate were not the ones germane to the complaint. The underlying allegations of the minority shareholder-complainants in the derivative suit were that the defendant directors, in order to finance their purchase of shares of the corporation, Western Approaches Ltd., had borrowed money from the Toronto-Dominion Bank. In negotiating for the loan, they had allegedly disclosed confidential corporate information and had promised to cause Western to become a public corporation, without regard to whether that would be in the corporation's best interests. The defendants had allegedly promised that, if they could not make good on this commitment, they would pay a fee to another corporation calculated on the basis of Western's gross revenues (thus giving those directors an incentive to keep Western's revenues down). The members of the litigation committee had, like all the directors of Western, been appointed to the board by the defendants. In addition the defendants had promised the bank (at least by inference) that the directors who eventually were appointed to the litigation committee were under their control.

Suppose that in a Canadian derivative action there is no quorum of disinterested directors, either because most of the directors are named as defendants or because, as in *Bellman*, those who are not defendants were placed on the board by those who are. May the board validly appoint a committee of disinterested directors to review the merits of the litigation and to determine what the corporation's position is to be with respect to it

---

18   This step shares some of the same spirit and philosophy of the statement by the Vice Chancellor: "Under our system of law, courts and not litigants should decide the merits of litigation." 413 A.2d at 1263.

and, as in *Zapata*, make such committee's determination final and not subject to review by the full board, so as not to infect the determination with the germ of "interest"? Recall that in *Peso Silver Mines* the Supreme Court of Canada held in effect that the board could ratify in advance action by some of its members, which might otherwise have been a breach of those members' fiduciary duties, and the Court did not even address the question of the board's independence.

How independent can independent directors be when the question is whether their colleagues on the board should be sued? Consider in this connection the following comments based on a review of the extensive American literature on directors' independence.

The independence of outside directors also may be compromised in many ways. The selection of outside directors is usually controlled by the senior management of the corporation, which seeks to name individuals who will not "rock the boat." Most outside directors share similar social and professional backgrounds and general attitudes with their inside director colleagues. Most are themselves corporate executives, often with firms that do business with the corporation, and thus are unlikely to look favorably on shareholder interference with management generally, or on derivative suits seeking to foist liability on corporate directors. Outside directors are often friends of high executives in the corporation before becoming directors, and even if not, friendships among directors naturally grow during their tenures on the board. Furthermore, the outside director is indebted to his fellow directors for the income and prestige he derives from his position, and he depends on those same directors for the continued receipt of these benefits.

Both inside and outside directors are discouraged from independence by pressures to conform, sometimes referred to as "group-think." The pressure to conform is great enough in ordinary matters of corporate planning, where board rejection of a management proposal would produce nothing more than annoyance. The pressure is much more onerous when the directors are asked to subject a fellow director to a suit that could lead to major financial liability, loss of job, and public humiliation. When a minority of directors is asked to sue the majority, the pressure may be unbearable. Abstention by or recusal of the interested directors does not solve the problem. [Dent, *The Power of Directors to Terminate Shareholder Litigation: The Death of the Derivative Suit*, 75 Nw. U. L. Rev. 96, 111-13 (1980)]

As his title suggests, Professor Dent sees cases like *Auerbach* as presaging the end of derivative litigation in the United States. Critics of *Auerbach* suggest that it invites a procedure to which defendant directors will always have resort, secure in the knowledge that their independent brethren will almost always find that litigation is not in the corporation's best interests. So long as the special litigation committee is competently advised, it should be able to produce a sufficiently weighty report to satisfy a court that a reasonable investigation has been made of the merits of the plaintiff's allegations and of the advantages and disadvantages to the corporation of litigating the claims. Dent proposes that, where a majority of the directors are named as defendants, the special litigation committee should never be able to secure dismissal. Where only a minority of the directors are named as defendants, then Dent proposes rules similar in outline to the *Zapata* decision.

The *Auerbach* rule, that there can be no judicial scrutiny of a decision made after a reasonable investigation by a committee of independent directors to seek dismissal of derivative litigation, has been criticized as inconsistent with a closely analogous area of corporate law, that of interested directors' transactions. Such transactions, even after approval by the disinterested directors, are still subject to judicial review for fairness, and the majority American rule appears to place the burden of proving fairness upon the proponents of the transaction. See Buxbaum, *Conflict of Interests Statutes and the Need for a Demand on Directors in Derivative Actions*, 68 Calif. L. Rev. 1122 (1980). Upon whom should the burden of proof lie in the matters of independence of the special litigation committee and adequacy of investigation? As between the derivative plaintiff and the directors, who has better access to the facts relevant to these issues? Who is advocating the inherently less likely proposition? Upon whom was the burden placed by the New York Court in *Auerbach*? By the Delaware Court in *Zapata*?

Should the evidentiary value given to the findings of an independent litigation committee depend upon the nature of the alleged breach? The revelation in the early 1970s of the prevalence of the payment by American multinational corporations of bribes in foreign countries, sometimes running into several millions of dollars, produced a spate of derivative litigation, *Auerbach* being a prime example. For a number of reasons courts have generally been hostile to shareholder litigation concerning these payments. At least until the passage in 1977 of the Foreign Corrupt Practices Act, it was far from clear that such payments were unlawful under American law. They were not designed to benefit the corporate officials who made them, and they may well have benefitted the corporations themselves. In short, they were probably not the sort of corporate "fraud" the prevention of which is the ultimate rationale for minority shareholder litigation.

Insofar as a trend among the American decisions has emerged, the jurisdictions seem fairly evenly divided between adherence to the New York position in *Auerbach* and the Delaware position in *Zapata*. California, for example, follows *Auerbach* (*Lewis v. Anderson*, 615 F.2d 778 (9th Cir. 1979)), while Connecticut follows *Zapata* (*Joy v. North*, 692 F.2d 880 (2d Cir. 1982), cert. denied, 103 S.Ct. 1498 (1983)).

See further Coffee & Schwartz, *The Survival of the Derivative Suit: An Evaluation and a Proposal for Legislative Reform*, 81 Colum. L. Rev. 261 (1981) (proposing legislation to decrease the power of the board to terminate derivative suits); Cox, *Compensation, Deterrence, and the Market as Boundaries for Derivative Suit Procedures*, 52 Geo. Wash. L. Rev. 745 (1985); Fischel & Bradley, *The Role of Liability Rules and the Derivative Suit in Corporate Law: A Theoretical Analysis*, 71 Cornell L. Rev. 261 (1986) (evidence suggests that derivative suits do not play a fundamental role in aligning the interests of managers and investors); Scott, *Corporation Law and the American Law Institute Corporate Governance Project*, 35 Stan. L. Rev. 927 (1983).

3. Personal Actions

Derivative actions must be distinguished from personal claims, brought when managers breach duties formally owed to shareholders individually, for in the latter case the shareholder's standing to sue does not derive from the corporation. Prior to the CBCA, the principal distinction between personal and derivative actions was that (1) amounts recovered went to the plaintiffs directly in a personal action and to the corporation in a derivative action, and (2) as a matter of pleading, it was unnecessary to join the corporation in a personal action, while the corporation was ordinarily sued as a party defendant in a derivative action. With the CBCA, a further difference arises: in the case of a derivative, but not personal action, it is necessary to obtain leave of a court to commence proceedings under s. 239. This is likely now the greatest strategic advantage to claiming that a breach is personal. Whether or not the corporation is joined in the action is not in itself of any importance. Moreover, apart from tax considerations, a shareholder will not much care whether per share recovery of $1 is received in cash on a personal claim or through an increase in stock value on a derivative claim.*

These differences apart, however, the circumstances that will support the two kinds of actions may look very similar. For example, a misleading proxy circular will likely ground either a personal or derivative claim. In both cases, the plaintiff may sue on behalf of all other shareholders (save the defendants). Personal claims may therefore be asserted as class actions in circumstances very similar to those of derivative wrongs. See *Goldex Mines Ltd. v. Revill* (1974), 7 O.R. (2d) 216 (C.A.).

One of the fullest discussions of the distinction between personal and derivative claims is contained in the following case, the analysis of which was discussed approvingly by the Ontario Court of Appeal in *Goldex Mines Ltd. v. Revill*.

Jones v. H.F. Ahmanson & Co.
Supreme Court of California
60 P.2d 464 (1969)

TRAYNOR, Chief Justice: June K. Jones, the owner of 25 shares of the capital stock of United Savings and Loan Association of California brings this action on behalf of herself individually and of all similarly situated minority stockholders of the Association. The defendants are United Financial Corporation of California, fifteen individuals, and four corporations, all of whom are present or former stockholders or officers of the Association. Plaintiff seeks damages and other relief for losses allegedly suffered by the minority stockholders of the Association because of claimed breaches of fiduciary responsibility by defendants in the creation and operation of United Financial, a Delaware holding company that owns 87 percent of the outstanding Association stock.

Plaintiff appeals from the judgment entered for defendants after an order sustaining defendants' general and special demurrers to her third amended complaint without leave to amend. Defendants have filed a protective cross-appeal. We have concluded that the allegations of the complaint and certain stipulated facts sufficiently state a cause of action and that the judgment must therefore be reversed.

The following facts appear from the allegations of the complaint and stipulation.

United Savings and Loan Association of California is a California chartered savings and loan association that first issued stock on April 5, 1956. Theretofore it had been

---

* In addition, CBCA s. 240(c) now contemplates the possibility of personal recovery in a derivative action. This might be appropriate when it is sought to exclude wrongdoing managers from recovering as shareholders, or where former shareholders are permitted to sue. On non-*pro rata* payouts, personal recovery may be more advantageous than derivative recovery.

owned by its depositors, who, with borrowing members, elected the board of directors. No one depositor had sufficient voting power to control the Association.

The Association issued 6,568 shares of stock on April 5, 1956. No additional stock has been issued. Of these shares, 987 (14.8 percent) were purchased by depositors pursuant to warrants issued in proportion to the amount of their deposits. Plaintiff was among these purchasers. The shares allocated to unexercised warrants were sold to the then chairman of the board of directors who later resold them to defendants and others. The stockholders have the right to elect a majority of the directors of the Association.

The Association has retained the major part of its earnings in tax-free reserves with the result that the book value of the outstanding shares has increased substantially.[2] The shares were not actively traded. This inactivity is attributed to the high book value, the closely held nature of the Association, and the failure of the management to provide investment information and assistance to shareholders, brokers, or the public. Transactions in the stock that did occur were primarily among existing stockholders. Fourteen of the nineteen defendants comprised 95 percent of the market for Association shares prior to 1959.

In 1958 investor interest in shares of savings and loan associations and holding companies increased. Savings and loan stocks that were publicly marketed enjoyed a steady increase in market price thereafter until June 1962, but the stock of United Savings and Loan Association was not among them. Defendants determined to create a mechanism by which they could participate in the profit taking by attracting investor interest in the Association. They did not, however, undertake to render the Association shares more readily marketable. Instead, the United Financial Corporation of California was incorporated in Delaware by all of the other defendants except defendant Thatcher on May 8, 1959. On May 14, 1959, pursuant to a prior agreement, certain Association stockholders who among them owned a majority of the Association stock exchanged their shares for those of United Financial, receiving a "derived block" of 250 United Financial shares for each Association share.

After the exchange, United Financial held 85 percent of the outstanding Association stock. More than 85 percent of United Financial's consolidated earnings and book value of its shares reflected its ownership of this Association stock. The former majority stockholders of the Association had become the majority shareholders of United Financial and continued to control the Association through the holding company. They did not offer the minority stockholders of the Association an opportunity to exchange their shares.

The first public offering of United Financial stock was made in June 1960. To attract investor interest, 60,000 units were offered, each of which comprised two shares of United Financial stock and one $100, 5 percent interest-bearing, subordinated, convertible debenture bond. The offering provided that of the $7,200,000 return from the sale of these units, $6,200,000 would be distributed immediately as a return of capital to the original shareholders of United Financial, i.e., the former majority stockholders of the Association.[6] To obtain a permit from the California Corporations Commissioner for

---

2   Between 1959 and 1966 the book value of each share increased from $1,131 to $4,143.70.

6   This distribution was equivalent to a $927.50 return of capital on each derived block of shares.

the sale, United Financial represented that the financial reserve requirement for debenture repayment established by Commissioner's Rules 480 subdivision (a) and 486 would be met by causing the Association to liquidate or encumber its income producing assets for cash that the Association would then distribute to United Financial to service and retire the bonds.

In the Securities and Exchange Commission prospectus accompanying this first public offering, United Financial acknowledged that its prior earnings were not sufficient to service the debentures and noted that United Financial's direct earnings would have to be augmented by dividends from the Association.

A public offering of 50,000 additional shares by United Financial with a secondary offering of 600,000 shares of the derived stock by the original investors was made in February 1961 for a total price of $15,275,000. The defendants sold 568,190 shares of derived stock in this secondary offering. An underwriting syndicate of 70 brokerage firms participated. The resulting nationwide publicity stimulated trading in the stock until, in mid-1961, an average of 708.5 derived blocks were traded each month. Sales of Association shares decreased during this period from a rate of 170 shares per year before the formation of United Financial to half that numer. United Financial acquired 90 percent of the Association shares that were sold.

Shortly after the first public offering of United Financial shares, defendants caused United Financial to offer to purchase up to 350 shares of Association stock for $1,100 per share. The book value of each of these shares was $1,411.57, and earnings were $301.15 per share. The derived blocks of United Financial shares then commanded an aggregate price of $3,700 per block exclusive of the $927.50 return of capital. United Financial acquired an additional 130 shares of Association stock as a result of this offer.

In 1959 and 1960 extra dividends of $75 and $57 per share had been paid by the Association, but in December 1960, after the foregoing offer had been made, defendants caused the Association's president to notify each minority stockholder by letter that no dividends other than the regular $4.00 per share annual dividend would be paid in the near future. The Association president, defendant M.D. Jameson, was then a director of both the Association and United Financial.

Defendants then proposed an exchange of United Financial shares for Association stock. Under this proposal each minority stockholder would have received approximately 51 United Financial shares of a total value of $2,400 for each Association share. When the application for a permit was filed with the California Corporations Commissioner on August 28, 1961, the value of the derived blocks of United Financial shares received by defendants in the initial exchange had risen to approximately $8,800.[9] The book value of the Association stock was in excess of $1,700 per share, and the shares were earning at an annual rate of $615 per share. Each block of 51 United Financial shares had a book value of only $210 and earnings of $134 per year, 85 percent of which reflected Association earnings. At the hearings held on the application by the Commissioner, representatives of United Financial justified the higher valuation of United Fi-

---

9 The derived block sold for as much as $13,127.41 during 1960-1961. On January 30, 1962, the date upon which plaintiff commenced this action, the mean value was $9,116.08.

nancial shares on the ground that they were highly marketable, whereas Association stock was unmarketable and poor collateral for loans. Plaintiff and other minority stockholders objected to the proposed exchange, contending that the plan was not fair, just, and equitable. Defendants then asked the Commissioner to abandon the application without ruling on it.

Plaintiff contends that in following this course of conduct defendants breached the fiduciary duty owed by majority or controlling shareholders to minority shareholders. She alleges that they used their control of the Association for their own advantage to the detriment of the minority when they created United Financial, made a public market for its shares that rendered Association stock unmarketable except to United Financial, and then refused either to purchase plaintiff's Association stock at a fair price or exchange the stock on the same basis afforded to the majority. She further alleges that they also created a conflict of interest that might have been avoided had they offered all Association stockholders the opportunity to participate in the initial exchange of shares. Finally, plaintiff contends that the defendants' acts constituted a restraint of trade in violation of common law and statutory antitrust laws.

I

We are faced at the outset with defendants' contention that if a cause of action is stated, it is derivative in nature since any injury suffered is common to all minority stockholders of the Association. Therefore, defendants urge, plaintiff may not sue in an individual capacity or on behalf of a class made up of stockholders excluded from the United Financial exchange, and in any case may not maintain a derivative action without complying with Financial Code, section 7616. Defendants invoke *Shaw v. Empire Savings & Loan Assn.*, 186 Cal.App. 2d 401, 9 Cal.Rptr. 204. There the defendant majority stockholder, who controlled the board of directors, had the bylaws amended to delete a provision granting preemptive rights and thereafter caused the Association to issue shares to himself at less than market or book value, thus diluting plaintiff minority stockholder's interest. Plaintiff sought a declaration that he was entitled to maintain his proportionate interest in the Association either through purchase of a proportionate number of shares from the buyer or issuance of a proportionate number of additional shares to him by the Association on the same terms. The Court of Appeal concluded that inasmuch as the injury to the plaintiff was no different from that caused other minority stockholders, relief was available only in a derivative action.

Analysis of the nature and purpose of a shareholders' derivative suit will demonstrate that the test adopted in the *Shaw* case does not properly distinguish the cases in which an individual cause of action lies. A shareholder's derivative suit seeks to recover for the benefit of the corporation and its whole body of shareholders when injury is caused to the corporation that may not otherwise be redressed because of failure of the corporation to act. Thus, "the action is derivative, *i.e.*, in the corporate right, if the gravamen of the complaint is injury to the corporation, or to the whole body of its stock or property without any severance or distribution among individual holders, or if it seeks to recover assets for the corporation or to prevent the dissipation of its assets." (*Gagnon Co., Inc. v. Nevada Desert Inn*, 45 Cal.2d 448, 453, 289 P.2d 466, 471: *Sutter v. General*

Petroleum Corp., 28 Cal.2d 525, 530, 170 P.2d 898, 167 A.L.R. 271; see Ballantine & Sterling, California Corporation Laws (4th ed. 1968) 168B.)

A stockholder's derivative suit is brought to enforce a cause of action which the corporation itself possesses against some third party, a suit to recompense the corporation for injuries which it has suffered as a result of the acts of third parties. The management owes to the stockholders a duty to take proper steps to enforce all claims which the corporation may have. When it fails to perform this duty, the stockholders have a right to do so. Thus, although the corporation is made a defendant in a derivative suit, the corporation nevertheless is the real plaintiff and it alone benefits from the decree; the stockholders derive no benefit therefrom except the indirect benefit resulting from a realization upon the corporation's assets. The stockholder's individual suit, on the other hand, is a suit to enforce a right against the corporation which the stockholder possesses as an individual. [Rules of Civ. Proc. for U.S. District Courts, Advisory Committee Notes (1966) H.R. Doc. No. 391, 89th Cong., 2d Sess. 40.]

It is clear from the stipulated facts and plaintiff's allegations that she does not seek to recover on behalf of the corporation for injury done to the corporation by defendants. Although she does allege that the value of her stock has been diminished by defendants' actions, she does not contend that the diminished value reflects an injury to the corporation and resultant depreciation in the value of the stock. Thus the gravamen of her cause of action is injury to herself and the other minority stockholders.

In *Shaw v. Empire Savings & Loan Assn.*, supra, 186 Cal.App.2d 401, 9 Cal.Rptr. 204, the court noted the "well established general rule that a stockholder of a corporation has no personal or individual right of action against third persons, including the corporation's officers and directors, for a wrong or injury to the corporation which results in the destruction or depreciation of the value of his stock, since the wrong thus suffered by the stockholder is merely incidental to the wrong suffered by the corporation and affects all stockholders alike." (186 Cal.App.2d 401, 407, 9 Cal.Rptr. 204, 208.) From this the court reasoned that a minority shareholder could not maintain an individual action unless he could demonstrate the injury to him was somehow different from that suffered by other *minority* shareholders. (186 Cal.App.2d 401, 408, 9 Cal.Rptr. 204.) In so concluding the court erred. The individual wrong necessary to support a suit by a shareholder need not be unique to that plaintiff. The same injury may affect a substantial number of shareholders. If the injury is not incidental to an injury to the corporation, an individual cause of action exists. To the extent that *Shaw v. Empire Savings & Loan Assn.* is inconsistent with the opinion expressed herein, it is disapproved.

II

Defendants take the position that as shareholders they owe no fiduciary obligation to other shareholders, absent reliance on inside information, use of corporate assets, or fraud. This view has long been repudiated in California. The Courts of Appeal have often recognized that majority shareholders, either singly or acting in concert to accomplish a joint purpose, have a fiduciary responsibility to the minority and to the corporation to use their ability to control the corporation in a fair, just, and equitable manner. Majority shareholders may not use their power to control corporate activities to benefit themselves alone or in a manner detrimental to the minority. Any use to which they put the corporation or their power to control the corporation must benefit all shareholders proportionately and must not conflict with the proper conduct of the corporation's business. (*Brown v. Halbert*, 271 A.C.A. 307, 316, 76 Cal.Rptr. 781; *Burt v. Irvine Co.*, 237 Cal.App.2d 828, 47 Cal.Rptr. 392; *Efron v. Kalmanovitz*, 226 Cal.App.2d 546, 38 Cal.Rptr. 148; *Remillard Brick Co. v. Remillard-Dandini*, 109 Cal.App.2d 405, 241 P.2d 66.)

· · ·

Defendants assert, however, that in the use of their own shares they owed no fiduciary duty to the minority stockholders of the Association. They maintain that they made full disclosure of the circumstances surrounding the formation of United Financial, that the creation of United Financial and its share offers in no way affected the control of the Association, that plaintiff's proportionate interest in the Association was not affected, that the Association was not harmed, and that the market for Association stock was not affected. Therefore, they conclude, they have breached no fiduciary duty to plaintiff and the other minority stockholders.

· · ·

The extension of fiduciary obligations to controlling shareholders in their exercise of corporate powers and dealings with their shares is not a recent development. The Circuit Court for the Southern District of New York said in 1886 that "when a number of stockholders combine to constitute themselves a majority in order to control the corporation as they see fit, they become for all practical purposes the corporation itself, and assume the trust relation occupied by the corporation towards its stockholders." (*Ervin v. Oregon Ry. & Nav. Co.* (C.C.S.D.N.Y. 1886) 27 F. 625, 631.) Professor Lattin has suggested that "the power to control, or rather its use, should be considered in no lesser light than that of a trustee to deal with the trust estate and with the beneficiary. Self-dealing in whatever form it occurs should be handled with rough hands for what it is—dishonest dealing. And while it is often difficult to discover self-dealing in mergers, consolidations, sale of all the assets or dissolution and liquidation, the difficulty makes it even more imperative that the search be thorough and relentless." (Lattin, Corporations (1959) 565.)

The increasingly complex transactions of the business and financial communities demonstrate the inadequacy of the traditional theories of fiduciary obligation as tests of majority shareholder responsibility to the minority. These theories have failed to afford adequate protection to minority shareholders and particularly to those in closely held corporations whose disadvantageous and often precarious position renders them particularly vulnerable to the vagaries of the majority. Although courts have recognized the potential for abuse or unfair advantage when a controlling shareholder sells his shares at a premium over investment value (*Perlman v. Feldmann*, 219 F.2d 173, 50 A.L.R.2d 1134 [premium paid for control over allocation of production in time of shortage]; *Gerdes v. Reynolds, Sup.*, 28 N.Y.S.2d 622 [sale of control to looters or incompetents]; *Porter v. Healy*, 244 Pa. 427, 91 A. 428; *Brown v. Halbert*, supra, 271 A.C.A. 307, 76 Cal.Rptr. 781 [sale of only controlling shareholder's shares to purchaser offering to buy assets of corporation or all shares]) or in a controlling shareholder's use of control to avoid equitable distribution of corporate assets (*Zahn v. Transamerican Corporation* (3rd Cir. 1946) 162 F.2d 36, 172 A.L.R. 495 [use of control to cause subsidiary to redeem stock prior to liquidation and distribution of assets]), no comprehensive rule has emerged in other jurisdictions. Nor have most commentators approached the problem from a perspective other than that of the advantage gained in the sale of control. Some have suggested that the price paid for control shares over their investment value be treated as an asset belonging to the corporation itself (Berle and Means, The Modern Corporation and Private Property (1932) p. 243), or as an asset that should be shared proportionately with all shareholders through a general offer (Jennings, Trading in Corporate Control (1956) 44 Cal.L.Rev. 1, 39), and another contends that the sale of control at a premium is always evil (Bayne, The Sale-of-Control Premium: the Intrinsic Illegitimacy (1969) 47 Tex.L.Rev. 215).

The additional potential for injury to minority shareholders from majority dealings in its control power apart from sale has not gone unrecognized, however. The ramifications of defendants' actions here are not unlike those described by Professor Gower as occurring when control of one corporation is acquired by another through purchase of less than all of the shares of the latter:

The [acquired] company's existence is not affected, nor need its constitution be altered; all that occurs is that its shareholders change. From the legal viewpoint this methodological distinction is formidable, but commercially the two things may be almost identical. If ... a controlling interest is acquired, the [acquired] company ... will become a subsidiary of the acquiring company ... and cease, in fact though not in law, to be an independent entity.

This may produce the situation in which a small number of dissentient members are left as a minority in a company intended to be operated as a member of a group. As such, their position is likely to be unhappy, for the parent company will wish to operate the subsidiary for the benefit of the group as a whole and not necessarily for the benefit of that particular subsidiary. [Gower, *The Principles of Modern Company Law* (2d ed. 1957 p. 561).]

Professor Eisenberg notes that as the purchasing corporation's proportionate interest in the acquired corporation approaches 100 percent, the market for the latter's stock disappears, a problem that is aggravated if the acquiring corporation for its own business purposes reduces or eliminates dividends. (Eisenberg, The Legal Role of Shareholders and Management in Modern Corporate Decision-making (1969) 57 Cal.L.Rev. 1, 132. See also, O'Neal and Derwin, Expulsion or Oppression of Business Associates (1961) passim; Leech, Transactions in Corporate Control (1956) 104 U.Pa.L.Rev. 725, 728; Comment, The Fiduciary Relation of the Dominant Shareholder to the Minority Shareholders (1958) 9 Hastings L.J. 306, 314.) The case before us, in which no sale or transfer of actual control is directly involved, demonstrates that the injury anticipated by these authors can be inflicted with impunity under the traditional rules and supports our conclusion that the comprehensive rule of good faith and inherent fairness to the minority in any transaction where control of the corporation is material properly governs controlling shareholders in this state. We turn now to defendants' conduct to ascertain whether this test is met.

III

Defendants created United Financial during a period of unusual investor interest in the stock of savings and loan associations. They then owned a majority of the outstanding stock of the Association. This stock was not readily marketable owing to a high book value, lack of investor information and facilities, and the closely held nature of the Association. The management of the Association had made no effort to create a market for the stock or to split the shares and reduce their market price to a more attractive level. Two courses were available to defendants in their effort to exploit the bull market in savings and loan stock. Both were made possible by defendants' status as controlling stockholders. The first was either to cause the Association to effect a stock split (Corp.Code, § 1507) and create a market for the Association stock or to create a holding company for Association shares and permit all stockholders to exchange their shares before offering holding company shares to the public. All stockholders would have benefited alike had this been done, but in realizing their gain on the sale of their stock the majority stockholders would of necessity have had to relinquish some of their control shares. Because a public market would have been created, however, the minority stockholders would have been able to extricate themselves without sacrificing their investment had they elected not to remain with the new management.

The second course was that taken by defendants. A new corporation was formed whose major asset was to be the control block of Association stock owned by defendants, but from which minority shareholders were to be excluded. The unmarketable Association stock held by the majority was transferred to the newly formed corporation at an exchange rate equivalent to a 250 for 1 stock split. The new corporation thereupon set out to create a market for its own shares. Association stock constituted 85 percent of the holding company's assets and produced an equivalent proportion of its income. The same individuals controlled both corporations. It appears therefrom that the market created by defendants for United Financial shares was a market that would have been available for Association stock had defendants taken the first course of action.

After United Financial shares became available to the public it became a virtual certainty that no equivalent market could or would be created for Association stock. United Financial had become the controlling stockholder and neither it nor the other defendants would benefit from public trading in Association stock in competition with United Financial shares. Investors afforded an opportunity to acquire United Financial shares would not be likely to choose the less marketable and expensive Association stock in preference. Thus defendants chose a course of action in which they used their control of the Association to obtain an advantage not made available to all stockholders. They did so without regard to the resulting detriment to the minority stockholders and in the absence of any compelling business purpose. Such conduct is not consistent with their duty of good faith and inherent fairness to the minority stockholders. Had defendants afforded the minority an opportunity to exchange their stock on the same basis or offered to purchase them at a price arrived at by independent appraisal, their burden of establishing good faith and inherent fairness would have been much less. At the trial they may present evidence tending to show such good faith or compelling business purpose that would render their action fair under the circumstances. On appeal from the judgment of dismissal after the defendants' demurrer was sustained we decide only that the complaint states a cause of action entitling plaintiff to relief.

Defendants gained an additional advantage for themselves through their use of control of the Association when they pledged that control over the Association's assets and earnings to secure the holding company's debt, a debt that had been incurred for their own benefit. In so doing the defendants breached their fiduciary obligation to the minority once again and caused United Financial and its controlling shareholders to become inextricably wedded to a conflict of interest between the minority stockholders of each corporation. Alternatives were available to them that would have benefited all stockholders proportionately. The course they chose affected the minority stockholders with no less finality than does dissolution (*In re Security Finance*, supra, 49 Cal.2d 370, 317 P.2d 1) and demands no less concern for minority interests.

In so holding we do not suggest that the duties of corporate fiduciaries include in all cases an obligation to make a market for and to facilitate public trading in the stock of the corporation. But when, as here, no market exists, the controlling shareholders may not use their power to control the corporation for the purpose of promoting a marketing scheme that benefits themselves alone to the detriment of the minority. Nor do we suggest that a control block of shares may not be sold or transferred to a holding company. We decide only that the circumstances of any transfer of controlling shares will be subject to judicial scrutiny when it appears that the controlling shareholders may have breached their fiduciary obligation to the corporation or the remaining shareholders.

IV

Plaintiff contends that she should have been afforded the opportunity to exchange her stock for United Financial shares at the time of and on the same basis as the majority exchange. She therefore proposes that upon tender of her Association stock to the defendants she be awarded the fair market value of a derived block of United Financial shares during 1960-1962 plus interest from the date of her action as well as a return of capital of $927.50 plus interest from the date the same was made to the former majority shareholders. In addition she seeks exemplary damages and other relief.

Defendants, on the other hand, claim that plaintiff seeks a "free ride" after they have taken all of the risks in creating United Financial and marketing its stock. They maintain that plaintiff has not been damaged by their conduct and that they have breached no duty owed to plaintiff and the other minority stockholders. We are thus without guidance from defendants as to the remedy that a court of equity might appropriately fashion in these circumstances.

From the perspective of the minority stockholders of the Association, the transfer of control under these circumstances to another corporation and the resulting impact on their position as minority stockholders accomplished a fundamental corporate change as to them. Control of a closely held savings and loan association, the major portion of whose earnings had been retained over a long period while its stockholders remained stable, became an asset of a publicly held holding company. The position of the minority shareholder was drastically changed thereby. His practical ability to influence corporate decisionmaking was diminished substantially when control was transferred to a publicly held corporation that was in turn controlled by the owners of more than 750,000 shares.[15] The future business goals of the Association could reasonably be expected to reflect the needs and interest of the holding company rather than the aims of the Association stockholders thereafter. In short, the enterprise into which the minority stockholders were now locked was not that in which they had invested.

• • •

If, after trial of the cause, plaintiff has established facts in conformity with the allegations of the complaint and stipulation, then upon tender of her Association stock to defendants she will be entitled to receive at her election either the appraised value of her shares on the date of the exchange, May 14, 1959, with interest at 7 percent a year from the date of this action or a sum equivalent to the fair market value of a "derived block" of United Financial stock on the date of this action with interest thereon from that date, and the sum of $927.50 (the return of capital paid to the original United Financial shareholders) with interest thereon from the date United Financial first made such payments to its original shareholders, for each share tendered. The appraised or fair market value shall be reduced, however, by the amount by which dividends paid on Association shares during the period from May 14, 1959 to the present exceeds the dividends paid on a corresponding block of United Financial shares during the same period.

• • •

The judgment appealed from by plaintiff is reversed. ...

PETERS, TOBRINER, BURKE, SULLIVAN and COUGHLIN JJ. concur. McCOMB J. dissents.

NOTES

Under pre-CBCA law, a personal action would ordinarily not lie for looting or breaches of due care standards. For example, in *Prudential Assurance Co. v. Newman Industries Ltd. (No. 2)*, [1982] 2 W.L.R. 71, it was claimed that Newman's shareholders had been fraudulently induced to approve a purchase by Newman of the assets of another corporation, in which certain Newman directors were interested, at a price greatly in excess of the true value. The English Court of Appeal held that the claim against the interested directors was derivative only and not personal to the plaintiff, a Newman shareholder.

[W]hat [a shareholder] cannot do is to recover damages merely because the company in which he is interested has suffered damage. He cannot recover a sum equal to the diminution in the market value of his share, or equal to the likely diminution in dividend because such a "loss" is merely a reflection of the loss suffered by the company. The shareholder does not suffer any personal loss. His only "loss" is through the company, in the diminution in the value of the net assets of the

---

15   Although the H.F. Ahmanson & Co. owned a majority of the Association stock prior to the exchange, it appears that this company was privately held for the benefit of the Ahmanson family.

company, in which he has (say) a 3 per cent shareholding. The plaintiff's shares are merely a right of participation in the company on the terms of the articles of association. The shares themselves, his right of participation, are not directly affected by the wrongdoing. The plaintiff still holds all the shares as his own absolutely unencumbered property. The deceit practised upon the plaintiff does not affect the shares; it merely enables the defendant to rob the company. A simple illustration will prove the logic of this approach. Suppose that the sole asset of a company is a cash box containing £100,000. The company has an issued share capital of 100 shares, of which 99 are held by the plaintiff. The plaintiff holds the key of the cash box. The defendant by a fraudulent misrepresentation persuades the plaintiff to part with the key. The defendant then robs the company of all its money. The effect of the fraud and the subsequent robbery, assuming that the defendant successfully flees with his plunder, is (i) to denude the company of all its assets; and (ii) to reduce the sale value of the plaintiff's shares from a figure approaching l00,000 pounds to nil. There are two wrongs, the deceit practised on the plaintiff and the robbery of the company. But the deceit on the plaintiff causes the plaintiff no loss which is separate and distinct from the loss to the company. The deceit was merely a step in the robbery. The plaintiff obviously cannot recover personally some £100,000 damages in addition to the £100,000 damages recoverable by the company. [*Id.* at 48-49]

On the other hand, personal actions were more frequently permitted in matters pertaining to control. *Goldex Mines Ltd. v. Revill* (1974), 7 O.R. (2d) 216 (misleading proxy circular); *Baillie v. Oriental Telephone Co.*, [1915] 1 Ch. 503 (C.A.) (defective notice of shareholders' meeting). Such breaches would not, however, support a personal action in all cases, and the wrong was sometimes only derivative. See *Watt v. Commonwealth Petroleum Ltd.*, [1938] 4 D.L.R. 701 (miscount of votes for election of directors). In addition, trivial breaches were usually held to be "mere irregularities," and not a breach of any kind. *Mozley v. Alston* (1847), 1 Ph. 790, 41 E.R. 833.

Since the consequences of labelling a claim as personal or derivative have changed with leave requirements of CBCA s. 239, it may be that the criteria for distinguishing between the two kinds of actions will change as well. Formerly it did not matter much whether an action was personal or derivative. Since derivative claims were easier for a court to administer, a rule which precluded personal recovery when the harm was felt by all shareholders in the same way made eminent sense. However, the principal advantage of asserting a personal claim is now that it is unnecessary to obtain leave of a court, and the need for the s. 239(2) screening procedure may therefore come to define the circumstances when a personal action is available. Even if leave to commence a derivative action under s. 239(2) is usually granted, the procedure is costly for plaintiffs. The most egregious kinds of wrongdoing might then be labelled as personal, and exempted from judicial screening. Less troubling kinds of misbehaviour would then constitute screenable, derivative wrongs. On this analysis, how in fact should a court distinguish among claims? The seriousness of the breach's economic consequences will frequently be a matter of dispute until the court has heard the evidence. Should the court then distinguish among the claims on the basis of formal legal categories of wrongdoing? If so, would this amount to a return to *Foss v. Harbottle*?

Personal actions have greatly expanded under the CBCA, with specific personal remedies created for certain kinds of offences. Examples of this are found in CBCA s. 120(8) (interested directors' contracts); s. 205 (take-over bids); s. 241 (the oppression remedy, discussed at length in Part II of this chapter); and s. 247 (restraining order on a violation of the CBCA). Do these describe cases where derivative screening under CBCA s. 239(2) is not desirable? Occasionally, judicial resistance to the recognition of broad personal remedies in a corporate context is encountered. See, e.g., *Re Goldhar* (1975), 9 O.R. (2d) 740, where the Court held that a claim that corporate directors had breached the statutory duty of care could not be litigated in the guise of an application for compliance order, but only as a derivative action.

In considering an alleged personal breach, should a court take account of shareholder ratification or the report of an independent directors' committee? On what basis might the court do so?

4. Corporate Actions

On distributional theories, the party who recovers should be the one who suffered the loss. In corporate actions brought by or on behalf of a corporation, however, the parties who were injured may not see the recovery. The corporation's owners when a corporate claim is litigated are not necessarily the same persons as when the wrong was done, but only the former ordinarily share in the recovery. For example, a derivative action may be asserted by a shareholder who did not hold his shares at the time of the breach. This is permitted since there is no "contemporaneous ownership" requirement in the CBCA as there is in many state corporations statutes in the United States. Moreover, even if the action is brought by a contemporaneous shareholder, a subsequent purchaser of the securities will be benefitted by recovery if it is paid to the corporation, and this too may seem like a windfall. An extreme example of this arises in actions brought by a corporation when all of the shares have been sold between the time of the breach and the time of the action. Such an action cannot be justified on distributional theories.

The facts of *Regal* are a good illustration of this last problem. In that case, the directors were held accountable for an unlawful profit on the purchase of Amalgamated shares. They had gained this profit by selling their shares to those persons who caused Regal to initiate the action. From the latter's perspective, Regal's recovery was an unbargained for discount off the purchase price of the stock, and this likely explains Laskin J.'s difficulty with *Regal* in *Canaero*. It is of course true that if the alleged wrong by the Regal directors had been known, the price received by the selling shareholders would have included a premium for the possibility of a recovery in subsequent litigation. However, the existence of such knowledge seems highly unlikely in many circumstances.

Even if the distributional consequences of a case like *Regal* are not particularly compelling, can the result be justified on efficiency grounds? An action by the purchasers of securities in such cases will serve to vindicate norms of corporate behaviour, with the corporate action providing a supplement to shareholder litigation. If all that counts is the deterrence effect of corporate sanctions, it does not much matter who recovers, except insofar as the possibility of recovery will provide an incentive to sue. Consider, in this context, the likely effect of a rule that required the purchaser in a case like *Regal* to share the damages with former outside Regal shareholders. What would this do to the corporation's desire to sue? Of course, the outside shareholders could, if they banded together, pay the corporation to commence the action, but such an agreement would be unlikely because of free rider problems and transaction cost barriers. The effect of a case like *Regal* is therefore to provide higher incentives to vindicate corporate law norms, particularly in circumstances where a take-over of the firm is possible. On the other hand, it should not be assumed that the "right" amount of litigation will be commenced when corporate actions are permitted in cases like *Regal*. Where no change in control has occurred, a corporation may reasonably decide.not to litigate when the breach was a violation of a strict equitable rule and did not harm the firm. But these considerations may mean little after a change of control, since the firm and its former managers will no longer be bound in a long-term relationship.

Abbey Glen Property Corp. v. Stumborg
Alberta Supreme Court, Appellate Division
(1978), 85 D.L.R. (3d) 35, [1978] 4 W.W.R. 28

[The facts of this case are set out in Section E of this chapter. The trial Court had held that two brothers, Clarence and Jerome Stumborg, who were officers and directors of Terra Developments Ltd., were accountable to Abbey Glen, a corporation formed after the events in question by an amalgamation between Terra and Western Realty Projects Ltd., for profits earned by the Stumborgs in a joint venture with Traders Finance Corporation. The brothers' liability was founded upon principles of the *Regal* and *Canaero* cases.

The Stumborgs appealed; reproduced here is that part of the appellate Court judgments that dealt with their argument that, because no shareholder of Terra at the time of the transaction giving rise to liability was a shareholder of Abbey Glen at the time of the litigation, recovery by Abbey Glen would amount to unjust enrichment.]

CLEMENT J.A. (with whom HADDAS J.A. concurs): ... This brings me to the same principle of unjust enrichment, but raised in this Court as a defence by the Stumborgs. I have had the advantage of reading the judgment proposed by my brother McDermid, and, as he points out, the issue was not specifically pleaded in the statement of defence nor put forward at the trial. It was argued here on the basis of evidence adduced in the course of the trial. This is perhaps less than satisfactory in dealing with a matter of some difficulty as it gives no assurance that all relevant facts have been adequately explored. Nevertheless, the issue should not be rejected on this ground in the absence of objection as to evidentiary matters. In *Moses v. Macferlan* (1760), 1 Wm Bl. 219, 97 E.R. 676, a case that has been taken as a progenitor of this developing branch of jurisprudence, Lord Mansfield noted, at p. 679 that, when a claim is made in equity the defendant "may go into every equitable defence, upon the general issue."

McDermid J.A., in his consideration of unjust enrichment put forward in defence by the Stumborgs, has taken into account a "windfall" resulting to the new shareholder of Terra by reason of the decreed accounting, it presumably having bought the shares in 1969 without reference to, or knowledge of, the accountability of the Stumborgs. On this basis he denied an accounting. With respect, I have some difficulty with the application of the principle in this context. At the moment in July, 1965, when Terra was put aside and replaced by Stumborgs in the agreement the obligation to account arose, and I am unable to see how a change in the shareholders some four years later diminished that obligation. The accounting is in respect of a beneficial interest owned by Terra and traced into the shares. Its probable existence came to the attention of the new officers of Terra, and by their enterprise in legal proceedings the beneficial interest has been declared and the net advantage to be gained by it is directed to Terra. The book values of the shares may now be increased thereby, but assuming that to be so, there is no evidence in the record other than of a speculative nature as to what effect knowledge of the existence of this claim in equity would have had on the purchase price of the shares in 1969. I find it somewhat difficult to categorize such an amorphous situation as a "windfall" for the new shareholder. It must be noted that whatever gain there may be will not be a windfall for Terra, since the decree did no more than accord to it restitution by means of accounting of its beneficial interest in the original trust *res*.

Nor do I think that whatever gain may result to the new shareholder through increase in the value of its shares, can serve to invoke the principle of unjust enrichment to defeat the remedy of accounting based on unjust enrichment properly granted to Terra against the Stumborgs. The duty on a fiduciary is strict. In *Regal (Hastings), Ltd.*, supra, Lord Porter said at p. 394:

This, it seems, may be an unexpected windfall, but whether it be so or not, the principle that a person occupying a fiduciary relationship shall not make a profit thereof is of such vital importance that the possible consequence in the present case is in fact as it is in law an immaterial consideration.

The emphasis here is on the enforcement of the fiduciary obligation in order to maintain the underlying principle that a fiduciary shall not profit.

A change in shareholders of itself cannot diminish the rigour of the obligation to account to the company, which remains unchanged in its character of a corporate entity. Essentially what is invoked here is the assertion of a defence which, if successful, would result in the Stumborgs retaining the gain which the law says plainly they are not to keep. In a word, the Stumborgs point to the assumed unjust enrichment of a new shareholder, which was not in a fiduciary relationship with the Stumborgs, as a ground to defeat an accounting for their own unjust enrichment. In my opinion the principle is not designed for such purpose. If it were to be extended to have such a startling effect, then in logic the consequences would vary with the proportion of new shareholders in the company. If, say, one-half were new shareholders, the defence would be halfway successful, the company would receive an accounting for only one-half of its equitable interest, and the fiduciary would keep the rest. The remedy of restitution would fail in part or in whole, as it would here if the defence were to succeed. With the failure of the remedy the principle itself is compromised. I cannot accept such a defence.

I should say a word about *Bangor Punta Operations, Inc. et al. v. Bangor & Aroostook R. Co.* (1974), 417 U.S. 703, 41 L.Ed. 2d 418, 94 S.Ct. 2578, in which the opening sentence of the judgment of Powell J., delivering the opinion of the majority, is in these words:

This case involves an action by a Maine railroad corporation seeking damages from its former owners for violations of federal antitrust and securities laws, applicable states' statutes, and common-law principles.

The facts of the case, and the interrelation of the legal components with the facts, afford little assistance in the reasons for judgment on the point in issue here. For these reasons I differ, with respect, from the conclusion reached by my brother McDermid. I would dismiss the appeal with costs in double column 5. ...

McDERMID J.A. (dissenting): ... If it were not for one defence argument, which I shall now deal with, I would be in agreement with the result arrived at by the trial Judge. It is that none of the present shareholders of Abbey Glen was a shareholder of Terra at the time of the breaches of fiduciary duty. The defence was not pleaded in the defence but there was evidence led setting it out. It was not dealt with by the trial Judge in his judgment, nor was it set out in the appellant's factum. However, it was argued before this Division. This defence was accepted by the Supreme Court of the United States in *Bangor Punta Operations, Inc. et al. v. Bangor & Aroostook R. Co.* (1974), 417 U.S. 703, 41 L.Ed. 2d 418, 94 S.Ct. 2578. However, in the argument before us this case was not referred to. We brought it to the attention of counsel and asked them whether they would like to present further submissions to us concerning this case. Counsel for the respondent asked that he be given the opportunity of presenting further argument, and we have now had further oral argument from both counsel.

As I have said, since the breaches of fiduciary obligations of the Stumborgs for which the trial Judge found they were liable to account, there has been a complete change in the ownership of the shares of Terra. None of the shareholders of Terra at the time the breaches occurred now owns his shares. The result would be that the shareholders of Abbey Glen, who were not shareholders at the time the breaches occurred, would receive a windfall profit by having the value of their shares increased as a result of the moneys recovered by Abbey Glen.

When the Stumborgs and the other shareholders whom the Stumborgs represented in the sale sold their shares of Terra to Western Realty Projects Ltd. on September 8, 1969, the purchase price was based on the value of the assets less the liabilities of Terra. This is of course the usual procedure when a large block of stock is purchased from controlling shareholders. The corporate entity is disregarded and it is the assets which are brought through the medium of the company. When shares are purchased on a stock exchange, the purchaser by obtaining his shares obtains whatever they represent. If in fact there are undisclosed liabilities his shares are worth less, and he has no recourse against the vendor; likewise, if there are undisclosed assets he obtains the benefit of them and the vendor cannot demand a higher purchase price. However, in this case, the vendor and purchaser of the shares disregarded the corporate entity and set the price to be paid for the shares on the value of the assets less the liabilities. Although the members of the financial community, in negotiating the price to be placed on the shares, look through the corporate entity, it is argued the Courts should not do so.

The respondent submits that *Salomon v. Salomon & Co. Ltd.*, [1897] A.C. 22, applies, and it matters not that the purchasers, in setting the price to be paid for the shares, did not pay any value for such an action as the present one or that the vendors had no intention of selling the same. The contention is that the right is that of the company and the position of the shareholders should be disregarded.

In *Pound on Jurisprudence*, vol. IV, p. 252, the author says:

On the other hand, there are cases, and they have become somewhat numerous in the United States in recent years, in which it becomes necessary to look behind the corporate entity to the actual beneficiaries. In general, where a corporation seeks relief in equity and it appears to grant it would result in unjust enrichment of or inequitable benefit to the stockholders, who will be the real beneficiaries ... the courts have looked through the corporate entity to the individuals behind it.

The problem has been recently dealt with by the Supreme Court of the United States in *Bangor Punta Operations, Inc. et al. v. Bangor & Aroostook R. Co.*, supra. The Court divided five to four, the majority judgment being given by Mr. Justice Powell. I quote the following from his judgment in which I have deleted references to other U.S. authorities.

At p. 422:

This case involves an action by a Maine railroad corporation seeking damages from its former owners for violations of federal antitrust and securities laws, applicable state statutes, and common-law principles. The complaint alleged that former owners had engaged in various acts of corporate waste and mismanagement during the period of their control. The shareholder presently in control of the railroad acquired more than 99% of the railroad's shares from the former owners long after the alleged wrongs occurred. We must decide whether equitable principles applicable under federal and state law preclude recovery by the railroad in these circumstances.

At p. 424:

The District Court granted petitioners' motion for summary judgment and dismissed the action. 353 F. Supp 724 (1972). The court first observed that although the suit purported to be a primary action brought in the name of the corporation, the real party in interest and hence the actual beneficiary of any recovery, was Amoskeag, the present owner of more than 99% of the outstanding stock of BAR. The court then noted that Amoskeag had acquired all of its BAR stock long after the alleged wrongs occurred and that Amoskeag did not contend that it had not received full value for its purchase price, or that the purchase transaction was tainted by fraud or deceit. Thus, any recovery on Amoskeag's part would constitute a windfall because it had sustained no injury.

At pp. 425-6:

We first turn to the question whether respondent corporations may maintain the present action under s. 10 of the Clayton Act. ... The resolution of this issue depends upon the applicability of the settled principle of equity that a shareholder may not complain of acts of corporate mismanagement if he acquired his shares from those who participated or acquiesced in the allegedly wrongful transactions. ... This principle has been invoked with special force where a shareholder purchases all or substantially all the shares of a corporation from a vendor at a fair price, and then seeks to have the corporation recover against that vendor for prior corporate mismanagement. ... The equitable considerations precluding recovery in such cases were explicated long ago by Dean (then Commissioner) Roscoe Pound in *Home Fire Ins. Co. v. Barber* (1903), 93 N.W. 1024 supra. Dean Pound, writing for the Supreme Court of Nebraska, observed that the shareholders of the plaintiff corporation in that case had sustained no injury since they had acquired their shares from the alleged wrongdoers after the disputed transactions occurred and had received full value for their purchase price. Thus, any recovery on their part would constitute a windfall, for it would enable them to obtain funds to which they had no just title or claim. Moreover, it would in effect allow the shareholders to recoup a large part of the price they agreed to pay for their shares, notwithstanding the fact that they received all they had bargained for. Finally, it would permit the shareholders to reap a profit from wrongs done to others, thus encouraging further such speculation. Dean Pound stated that these consequences rendered any recovery highly inequitable and mandated dismissal of the suit.

At p. 427:

We are met with the argument, however, that since the present action is brought in the name of respondent corporations, we may not look behind the corporate entity to the true substance of the claims and the actual beneficiaries. The established law is to the contrary. Although a corporation and its shareholders are deemed separate entities for most purposes, the corporate form may be disregarded in the interests of justice where it is used to defeat an overriding public policy. ... In such cases, courts of equity, piercing all fictions and disguises, will deal with the substance of the action and not blindly adhere to the corporate form. Thus, where equity would preclude the shareholders from maintaining an action in their own right, the corporation would also be precluded.

There is as divided an opinion in the cases in the United States as there was in the Supreme Court. The cases are discussed in Fletchers' *Cyclopedia of the Law of Private Corporations*, vol. 3A, para. 1287, and vol. 13, para. 5981, and in an annotation in 148 A.L.R. 1090.

In England in *Regal (Hastings), Ltd. v. Gulliver et al.*, [1942] 1 All E.R. 378 at p. 394, Lord Porter said:

My Lords, I am conscious of certain possibilities which are involved in the conclusion which all your Lordships have reached. The action is brought by the Regal company. Technically, of course, the fact that an unlooked for advantage may be gained by the shareholders of that company is immaterial to the question at issue. The company and its shareholders are separate entities. One cannot help remembering, however, that in fact the shares have been purchased by a financial group who were willing to acquire those of the Regal and the Amalgamated at a certain price. As a result of your Lordships' decision the group will, I think, receive in one hand part of the sum which has been paid by the other. For the shares in Amalgamated they paid £3 16s. 1d. per share, yet part of that sum may be returned to the group, though not necessarily to the individual shareholders by reason of the enhancement in value of the shares in Regal—an enhancement brought about as a result of the receipt by the company of the profit made by some of its former directors on the sale of Amalgamated shares. This, it seems, may be an unexpected windfall, but whether it be so or not, the principle that a person occupying a fiduciary relationship shall not make a profit by reason thereof is of such vital importance that the possible consequence in the present case is in fact as it is in law an immaterial consideration.

The other Law Lords did not mention it but the effect of the judgment was to give a windfall profit to the new shareholders. This has been commented on by various text book writers. In Ziegel, *Studies in Canadian Company Law* (1967), at p. 598:

Where the control of the company has passed, as in *Regal Hastings Ltd. v. Gulliver*, it means the purchasers receive an unwarranted reduction in the purchase price. The statute should provide that the court may, if justice so required, order restoration of any property or payment of damages in favour of the shareholders or former shareholders. This solution has been judicially fashioned in the United States *(Perlman v. Feldman* (1957), 219 F. (2d) 173) and ought to be provided for by statute.

See also Pennington's *Company Law*, 3rd ed., p. 514. There are of course cases in England where the corporate entity has been looked through. In *Scottish Cooperative Wholesale Society Ltd. v. Meyer* [1959] A.C. 324 at p. 343, per Viscount Simonds, quoting from Lord Cooper's words on the first hearing of the case: "In my view he said the section warrants the court in looking at the business realities of a situation and does not confine them to a narrow legalistic view." In *D.H.N. Food Distributors Ltd. v. Tower Hamlets London Borough Council*, [1976] 1 W.L.R. 852, the Court of Appeal treated three companies as being one for the purpose of deciding what compensation was available to them. Lord Justice Goff, at p. 861, said:

Secondly, on the footing, this is not in itself sufficient, still, in my judgment, this is a case in which one is entitled to look at the realities of the situation and to pierce the corporate veil.

In Gower's *Principles of Modern Company Law*, 3rd ed. (1969), at p. 189, it is stated there are no consistent principles that the courts have applied in departing from the principle of *Salomon's* case.

I find no Canadian case specifically on point. There are cases where the Courts have gone behind the corporate entity, for example, in *Palmolive Mfg. Co. (Ontario) Ltd. v. The King*, [1933] 2 D.L.R. 81, [1933] S.C.R. 131.

What must be weighed in each case is whether a Court of Equity should by its order grant an unjust enrichment unless there is some public purpose to be served by it so doing. A somewhat similar situation was referred to by Martland J., in *Rur. Mun. of Shorthoaks v. Mobil Oil Canada Ltd.* (1975), 55 D.L.R. (3d) 1 at pp. 12-3, [1976] 2 S.C.R. 147 at p. 163, [1975] 4 W.W.R. 591, where he said:

American authority has recognized that the rule that money paid under a mistake is recoverable "is equitable and may be defeated where to allow the recovery would be inequitable" *(U.S. v. National Park Bank of New York* (1881), 6 F. 852 at pp. 853-4).

This is not a case of fraud. Where there has been fraud by an officer or director the Court may well consider that it is more important that there by a penalty exacted from the wrongdoer than that it prevent a windfall profit from being obtained. In this case the breach of the fiduciary duty was of a technical kind and the penalty is imposed by the Courts because of the difficulty of ascertaining whether or not the principal has suffered any damage. See Lord Wright quoting James L.J. in *Regal (Hastings)*, supra, at p. 393. The parties who gave evidence all stated that Traders would not have dealt with Terra; yet, as I have previously related, the Courts should not accept such a position. It is not a case where the Stumborgs were fraudulent, but a case where, having started to negotiate for Terra, they were disqualified from usurping for themselves a business opportunity of the company, even although they came to the conclusion it was useless for Terra to pursue the same. As was stated in the *Canadian Aero* case, the ethic applied by the Court may be stricter than that imposed by the business community, who would consider such "a dog in the manger" attitude unreasonable. The original approach to Traders was made by the Stumborgs on behalf of Terra. If they made it on their own behalf the position might have been different.

I would again emphasize that this is a case where the shares were purchased on the basis of what were the assets and liabilities of the company; the purchasers looked through the corporate entity and a substantial number of the shares were purchased from the very persons who are now being sued for an asset they were not paid for; all of the persons who were shareholders at the time of the breach of the fiduciary duty are no longer such, and would receive no benefit from this action. If the damages recoverable were to be received by the persons who were shareholders at the time, then there would be no unjust enrichment and no reason to dismiss the company's action. If Abbey Glen could show any damages it received were to be distributed to the shareholders entitled, then the action should succeed. I recognize there may be great, if no insurmountable corporate difficulties in Abbey Glen so doing, but it is the party asking for equitable relief and so it has the problem of showing that it would likewise do equity. In short, I am of the opinion that it is no proper function of a Court of Equity to unjustly enrich a litigant unless there be some public purpose served in so doing.

I would allow the appeal and dismiss the action, and dismiss the cross-appeal. Under all the circumstances there will be no costs of the trial or of the appeal.

Appeal dismissed.

NOTES

1) In *Abbey Glen*, unlike *Bangor Punta*, by the time of the litigation there was no shareholder of Terra who had been such at the time of the transaction complained of. The absence of contemporaneous ownership would be fatal to the possibility of derivative litigation in the United States and probably in British Columbia. However, under CBCA s. 238(a) a former shareholder may be a "complainant," and s. 240(c) permits a court to order direct recovery in a derivative action.

2) In *Bangor Punta* Powell J. relied heavily upon the analysis of Roscoe Pound, sitting as Chief Justice of Nebraska, in the case of *Home Fire Ins. Co. v. Barber*, 93 N.W. 1024 (1903). An excerpt from that analysis follows:

But it is said the defendant Barber, by reason of his delinquencies, is in no position to ask that the court look behind the corporation to the real and substantial parties in interest. ... We do not think such a proposition can be maintained. It is not the function of courts of equity to administer punishment. When one person has wronged another in a matter within its jurisdiction, equity will spare no effort to redress the person injured, and will not suffer the wrongdoer to escape restitution to such person through any device or technicality. But this is because of its desire to right wrongs, not because of a desire to punish all wrongdoers. If a wrongdoer deserves to be punished, it does not follow that others are to be enriched at his expense by a court of equity. A plaintiff must recover on the strength of his own case, not on the weakness of the defendant's case. It is his right, not the defendant's wrongdoing, that is the basis of recovery. When it is disclosed that he has no standing in equity, the degree of wrongdoing of the defendant will not avail him. [*Id.* at 1035]

II. THE STATUTORY OPPRESSION REMEDY

A. INTRODUCTION

1. United Kingdom

The statutory oppression remedy in the CBCA is derived from s. 210 of the U.K. Companies Act, 1948, whose purpose was to provide a more flexible remedy than that available through a winding up action. Section 210 provided that "any member of a company" might apply to a court to show that "the affairs of the company are being conducted in a manner oppressive to some part of the members (including himself)." If the court was satisfied that such was the case and that a "just and equitable" winding up would be in order except that it would unfairly prejudice the oppressed members, then the court might make an order "regulating the conduct of the company's affairs in the future, or for the purchase of the shares of any members ... by other members ... or by the company." An identical provision was adopted as s. 185 of the British Columbia Companies Act, R.S.B.C. 1960, c. 67.

This original version of the oppression remedy came to be seen as having three major shortcomings. Because the conduct had to be oppressive against a person in his capacity as member (shareholder), the remedy did not reach one of the prototypical fact situations, exclusion of a director or manager. Section 210 was also read as requiring a continuous course of oppressive conduct rather than a single oppressive transaction. *Re H.R. Harmer Ltd.*, [1958] 3 All. E.R. 689 (C.A.). Finally, the conduct had to be serious enough to warrant a winding up before the courts could exercise remedial powers under the oppression remedy. The latter two conditions were amended in s. 75 of the U.K. Companies Act, 1980.

2. Canada

Outside of British Columbia, the oppression remedy was introduced into Canadian statutes by the CBCA in 1975. This remedy is broader than that of the old English s. 210. Under CBCA s. 241 any "complainant" may make an application for the remedy—the term "complainant" including any present or former security (not just share) holder, an officer or director of the corporation or of any of its affiliates, plus any person who, in the discretion of the court, is a proper person to be a complainant. The conduct complained of may be "oppressive" or "unfairly prejudicial" to, or may simply "unfairly disregard" the interests of, any security holder, creditor, director or officer. Moreover, the act or omission about which one is complaining may be that of the corporation, any of its affiliates or that of the corporation's directors. The statute provides a long list of possible remedial orders, and the list is without prejudice to the ability of a court to make such further orders as it thinks fit. The introduction of the oppression remedy in the CBCA led to several provinces adopting the same provision: Alberta, Saskatchewan, Manitoba, Ontario, New Brunswick, Newfoundland and Nova Scotia. Some provinces, however, have yet to adopt the oppression remedy: Quebec and Prince Edward Island. For an example of how courts that are not able to draw on the oppression remedy must sometimes resort to the rather heavy-handed tactic of winding up a company, see *Développements Urbain Candiac Inc. c. Combest Corp.*, [1993] R.J.Q. 1321 (Que. C.A.). As you consider the material in this part of the chapter, ask yourself whether the presence or absence of the oppression remedy would have an effect on your decision about where to incorporate a company.

The broadest Canadian oppression remedy is now found in OBCA s. 248, introduced in 1982. Section 248 reaches not only conduct that has occurred or is occurring but also conduct that is "threatened." Within a few months of proclamation of the OBCA, the O.S.C., which has standing under s. 248 to apply for an oppression remedy in the case of a publicly traded corporation, successfully applied to have the entire board of Mascan Corp. replaced. *In the Matter of Mascan Corp.*, unreported order, Ont. October 6, 1983. A commentator has said of the new OBCA oppression remedy that "it is beyond question, the broadest, most comprehensive and most open-ended shareholder remedy in the common law world. It is unprecedented in its scope." Beck, *Minority Shareholders' Rights in the 1980's*, [1982] L.S.U.C. Special Lects. 311, 312.

3. Issues Raised by the Oppression Remedy

In its early days, the oppression remedy seemed particularly relevant to resolving disputes in close corporations, especially when a minority shareholder found that her fellow shareholders were systematically excluding her from management decisions. In this respect, the oppression remedy looked much like another form of liability strategy that was particularly useful in situations in which one group of shareholders threatened to hijack management of the corporation. The extensive range of powers afforded to courts under the oppression remedy continues to make it a very attractive tool for fashioning creative solutions to situations in which relations between a small group of shareholders have broken down and in which the parties are unwilling to use techniques like mediation or arbitration to resolve their problems. For recent creative uses of the remedial powers available under the oppresion remedy, see *Wittlin and Bergman* (1994), 19 O.R. (3d) 145 (use of a buzzer system in connection with an auction of the shares of a closely held corporation); and *Naneff v. Con-Crete Holdings Limited et al.* (1994), 19 O.R. (3d) 691 (order that there be a sale of a corporation on the open market and refusal to order a buyout because this would have achieved the majority shareholders' objective of forcing out the plaintiff).

One question worth asking is whether it was necessary to introduce the concept of "oppression" into the corporate law in order to deal with these kinds of disputes. After all, American courts had set about developing the proposition that majority shareholders owe fiduciary duties to minority shareholders in order to deal with situations in which majority shareholders' actions were prejudicial to the interests of minority shareholders. See, e.g., *Donahue v. Rodd Electrotype Co. of New England*, 328 N.E. 2d 505 (1975) and J. MacIntosh, J. Holmes & S. Thompson, *The Puzzle of Shareholder Fiduciary Duties*, 19 Can. Bus. L.J. 86 (1991). Might it have been possible to follow the same approach in Canada? Could the legislature simply have added that the courts were hereinafter to have a broader range of remedial powers for dealing with situations in which majority shareholders were found to have breached their fiduciary duties to minority shareholders? Recent pronouncements from the Supreme Court of Canada about the analytic framework to be used in determining whether fiduciary obligations exist might well be able to accommodate the idea that a majority shareholder owes a fiduciary duty to a minority shareholder. See *Lac Minerals Ltd. v. International Corona Resources Ltd.*, [1989] 2 S.C.R. 574, in which the Court asserted that a fiduciary obligation may arise in relationships that involve three general characteristics: (1) the fiduciary has scope for the exercise of some discretion or power; (2) the fiduciary can unilaterally exercise that power or discretion so as to affect the beneficiary's legal or practical interests; and (3) the beneficiary is particularly vulnerable to the fiduciary's holding the discretion.

Be that as it may, the proposition that majority shareholders owe fiduciary duties has not been well received in Canadian courts. However, it has not always been easy to determine whether this is: (1) because there is a principled argument against extending fiduciary duties in this way; or (2) because the presence of the oppression remedy is thought to make the exercise redundant (a proposition that is far from self-evident). See *Brant Investments v. KeepRite Inc.* (1991), 3 O.R. (3d) 289 (Ont. C.A.), excerpted below, and *Bell v. Source Data Control Ltd.* (1988), 66 O.R. (2d) 78 (Ont. C.A.), from which an extract is reproduced in Chapter Eight.

Although early analyses of the oppression remedy in Canada focused on the relationship between shareholder and corporation (see, e.g., M. Waldron, *Corporate Theory and the Oppression Remedy*, 6 Can. Bus. L.J. 129 (1981-82)), the oppression remedy harbours the potential to be much more than a device for resolving disputes between shareholders in closely held corporations. Thus, in recent years the remedy has not only been invoked in the context of publicly held corporations, but debt holders, creditors and even employees have looked to the remedy as a vehicle to advance claims against shareholders or the corporation. As you review the caselaw in this chapter on the use that these constituencies have made of the oppression remedy, ask yourself whether these same claims could have been made under the law on fiduciary duties or only under the oppression remedy. Similarly, ask yourself whether securities commissions are particularly well positioned to offer alternative ways of looking after these constituencies.

As was suggested at the beginning of this chapter, the use of the oppression remedy by constituencies like creditors and shareholders raises difficult issues that require careful analysis of the nature of the corporation in order to determine what interests these constituencies have in the corporation and whether they are worthy of judicial protection. In this respect, the conclusion reached with respect to the stakeholder debate examined in Chapter Six is extremely pertinent to how liberally the oppression remedy should be construed. In reflecting on this issue, you may also wish to revisit the discussion of the "nexus of contracts" view of the firm found in Chapter One, Section B and of the question whether a shareholder is an "owner" raised in Chapter Four.

The answer to the question whether it is best to see the corporation's directors as agents mandated to act solely on behalf of the "owners" or as having a responsibility to advance a more complex web of interests is likely to colour assessments about whether a board of directors' actions are "oppressive" or whether they unfairly disregarded the interests of a complainant that is not a shareholder. In other words, one's vision of the corporation is likely to have a profound impact on the way in which one thinks liability strategies that involve claimholders other than shareholders should be structured. Nowhere is this more obvious than with the oppression remedy.

The rest of this chapter examines the way in which the oppression remedy has developed to date, looking first at its use by shareholders and then at how other kinds of complainants have fared. Additionally, the chapter examines some of the tensions in Canada's business law framework that the remedy's introduction has generated.

B. SHAREHOLDERS AS COMPLAINANTS UNDER THE OPPRESSION REMEDY

Scottish Co-operative Wholesale Society Ltd. v. Meyer
House of Lords
[1959] A.C. 324

[The Co-operative Society was anxious to enter the rayon trade in 1946. It felt that the aid of Meyer and Lucas and their technical experts were desirable or essential to make the venture successful. The Society incorporated a subsidiary, 4,000 shares in which were issued to the Society and 3,900 of which were issued to Meyer and Lucas together. These gentlemen also occupied two of the five seats on the subsidiary's board.

By about 1952 the Society had apparently decided that the participation of Meyer and Lucas in the subsidiary had become dispensable. It offered to buy their shares in the subsidiary, but this offer was rejected, apparently upon the ground that the price was inadequate. Thereafter, the Society established an internal department that entered upon the rayon trade to the great diminution of the subsidiary's profits. The Society's nominees on the subsidiary's board (who were also directors of the Society) sat by mutely.

Meyer and Lucas petitioned for an order to be made under s. 210 of the Companies Act, by which the Society would have to buy up their shares in the subsidiary at a price to be determined without reference to the damage that had recently been inflicted upon the subsidiary by the Society's competition.

Section 210 of the Companies Act, 1948 provided: "(1) Any member of a company who complains that the affairs of the company are being conducted in a manner oppressive to some part of the members (including himself) ... may make application to the court by petition for an order under this section. (2) If on any such petition the court is of opinion—(a) that the company's affairs are being conducted as aforesaid; and (b) that to wind up the company would unfairly prejudice that part of the members, but otherwise the facts would justify the making of a winding-up order on the ground that it was just and equitable that the company should be wound up, the court may, with a view to bringing to an end the matters complained of, make such order as it thinks fit, whether for regulating the conduct of the company's affairs in future, or for the purchase of the shares of any members of the company by other members of the company, or by the company, and, in the case of a purchase by the company, for the reduction accordingly of the company's capital, or otherwise."]

LORD DENNING: ... The complaints which were established were, I think, these: The co-operative society set up a competing business. It established its own merchant converting department, engaged in the rayon trade itself, and quoted more favourable terms to its own department than it did to the textile company. It is said that the co-operative society did this with intent to injure the textile company—to depress the value of its shares so that the co-operative society could get them cheap—but I would not myself go as far as this. It seems to me that the co-operative society all the time was seeking to promote its own interests. It was ready in 1946 to enlist the co-operation of Dr. Meyer and Mr. Lucas when they were useful to it—so as to get an introduction into the rayon trade—but it was ready to throw them over when they were no longer useful. By which I mean that it was ready to withdraw all support from them. That was, I think, the state of mind of the co-operative society right from the moment in November, 1951, when Dr. Meyer and Mr. Lucas refused to realign the shares at par. At that time the rayon trade was in a recession and Dr. Meyer and Mr. Lucas were not of so much use to the society as they had been. By the time the rayon trade revived, the controls were off and the co-operative society was able to engage in rayon production itself—and it had no further need of Dr. Meyer and Mr. Lucas or of the textile company. It had its own department for rayon. So the textile company could go to the wall. It had "served its purpose"—or rather the purpose of the co-operative society—and could be let go into liquidation. The co-operative society had not the voting power to put it into voluntary liquidation. But liquidation might come about by sheer inanition. So it came about, that, when Dr. Meyer and Mr. Lucas in January, 1953, offered to sell their shares to the co-operative society at a price to be negotiated (mentioning 96s.), the co-operative society refused "at the present time." The co-operative society thought, perhaps, that, if they waited, sooner or later liquidation would come about, or that terms of purchase would be arranged later more favourable to the co-operative society than paying 96s. a share.

Such being "the matters complained of" by Dr. Meyer and Mr. Lucas, it is said: "Those are all complaints about the conduct of the co-operative society. How do they touch the real issue—the manner in which the affairs of the textile company were being conducted?" The answer is, I think, by their impact on the nominee directors. It must be remembered that we are here concerned with the manner in which the affairs of the textile company were being conducted. That is, with the conduct of those in control of its affairs. They may be some of the directors themselves, or, behind them, a group of shareholders who nominate those directors or whose interests those directors serve. If those persons—the nominee directors or the shareholders behind them—conduct the affairs of the company in a manner oppressive to the other shareholders, the court can intervene to bring an end to the oppression.

What, then, is the position of the nominee director here? Under the articles of association of the textile company the co-operative society was entitled to nominate three out of the five directors, and it did so. It nominated three of its own directors and they held office, as the articles said, "as nominees" of the co-operative society. These three were therefore at one and the same time directors of the co-operative society—being three out of 12 of that company—and also directors of the textile company—three out of five there. So long as the interests of all concerned were in harmony, there was no difficulty. The nominee directors could do their duty by both companies without embarrassment. But, so soon as the interests of the two companies were in conflict, the nominee directors were placed in an impossible position. Thus, when the realignment of shareholdings was under discussion, the duty of the three directors to the textile company was to get the best possible price for any new issue of its shares ... whereas their duty to the co-operative society was to obtain the new shares at the lowest possible price—at par, if they could. Again, when the co-operative society determined to set up its own rayon department, competing with the business of the textile company, the duty of the three directors to the textile company was to do their best to promote its business and to act with complete good faith towards it; and in consequence not to disclose their knowledge of its affairs to a competitor, and not even to work for a competitor, when to do so might operate to the disadvantage of the textile company whereas they were under the self-same duties to the co-operative society. It is plain that, in the circumstances, these three gentlemen could not do their duty by both companies, and they did not do so. They put their duty to the co-operative society above their duty to the textile company in this sense, at least, that they did nothing to defend the interests of the textile company against the conduct of the co-operative society. They probably thought that "as nominees" of the co-operative society their first duty was to the co-operative society. In this they were wrong. By subordinating the interests of the textile company to those of the co-operative society, they conducted the affairs of the textile company in a manner oppressive to the other shareholders.

It is said that these three directors were at most only guilty of inaction—of doing nothing to protect the textile company. But the affairs of a company can, in my opinion, be conducted oppressively by the directors doing nothing to defend its interests when they ought to do something—just as they can conduct its affairs oppressively by doing something injurious to its interests when they ought not to do it.

The question was asked: What could these directors have done? They could, I suggest, at least on behalf of the textile company, have protested against the conduct of the co-operative society. They could have protested against the setting up of a competing business. But then it was said: What good would that have done? Any protest by them would be sure to have been unavailing, seeing that they were in a minority on the board of the co-operative society. The answer is that no one knows whether it would have done any good. They never did protest. And it does not come well from their mouths to say it would have done no good, when they never put it to the test. ... Even if they had protested, it might have been a formal gesture, ostensibly correct, but not to be taken seriously.

Your Lordships were referred to *Bell v. Lever Brothers Ltd.*, [[1932] A.C. 161, 195; 48 T.L.R. 133], where Lord Blanesburgh said that a director of one company was at liberty to become a director also of a rival company. That may have been so at that time. But it is at the risk now of an application under section 210 if he subordinates the interests of the one company to those of the other.

So I would hold that the affairs of the textile company were being conducted in a manner oppressive to Dr. Meyer and Mr. Lucas. The crucial date is, I think, the date on which the petition was lodged—July 14, 1953. If Dr. Meyer and Mr. Lucas had at that time lodged a petition to wind up the company compulsorily, the petition would undoubtedly have been granted. The facts would plainly justify such an order on the ground that it was "just and equitable" that the company should be wound up; see *In re Yenidje Tobacco Co. Ltd.* [[1916] 2 Ch. 426; 32 T.L.R. 709]. But such an order would unfairly prejudice Dr. Meyer and Mr. Lucas because they would only recover the break-up value of their shares. So instead of petitioning for a winding-up order, they seek to invoke the new remedy given by section 210 of the Companies Act, 1948. But what is the appropriate remedy? It was said that section 210 only applies as an alternative to winding up and that an order can only be made under section 210 if the company is fit to be kept alive: whereas in this case the business of the company was virtually at an end when the petition was lodged, and there was no point in keeping it alive. If the co-operative society were ordered, in these circumstances, to buy the shares of Dr. Meyer and Mr. Lucas, this would amount, it was said, to an award of damages for past misconduct—which is not the remedy envisaged by section 210.

Now, I quite agree that the words of the section do suggest that the legislature had in mind some remedy whereby the company, instead of being wound up, might continue to operate. But it would be wrong to infer therefrom that the remedy under section 210 is limited to cases where the company is still in active business. The object of the remedy is to bring "to an end the matters complained of," that is, the oppression, and this can be done even though the business of the company has been brought to a standstill. If a remedy is available when the oppression is so moderate that it only inflicts wounds on the company, whilst leaving it active, so also it should be available when the oppression is so great as to put the company out of action altogether. Even though the oppressor by his oppression brings down the whole edifice—destroying the value of his own shares with those of everyone else—the injured shareholders have, I think, a remedy under section 210.

One of the most useful orders mentioned in the section—which will enable the court to do justice to the injured shareholders—is to order the oppressor to buy their shares at a fair price: and a fair price would be, I think, the value which the shares would have had at the date of the petition, if there had been no oppression. Once the oppressor has bought the shares, the company can survive. It can continue to operate. That is the matter for him. It is, no doubt, true that an order of this kind gives to the oppressed shareholders what is in effect money compensation for the injury done to them: but I see no objection to this. The section gives a large discretion to the court and it is well exercised in making an oppressor make compensation to those who have suffered at his hands.

True it is that in this, as in other respects, your Lordships are giving a liberal interpretation to section 210. But it is a new section designed to suppress an acknowledged mischief. When it comes before this House for the first time, I believe, in accordance with long precedent ... that your Lordships should give such construction as shall advance the remedy. And that is what your Lordships do today.

I would dismiss the appeal.

Appeal dismissed.

[The Judgments of VISCOUNT SIMONDS, LORD MORTON and LORD KEITH, all of whom agreed that the appeal should be dismissed, have been omitted.]

NOTES

1) Do you understand why a winding up would have "unfairly prejudiced" the oppressed shareholders of the textile company?

2) Lord Denning's problem in granting relief to the plaintiffs, that arguably the conduct that oppressed them was occurring in the management of the Society and not in the management of the corporation in which the plaintiff's were shareholders, is obviated by the wording of CBCA s. 241. That section brings within the purview of the oppression remedy the management of the affairs not only of the corporation with which the complainant is connected but also of its affiliates.

3) To pursue Lord Denning's analysis a bit further, what might the Society's three directors, who were nominated as the majority of the textile corporation's board, have done for the textile corporation? Had they protested the diversion of business from the textile corporation at meetings of the Society's board, their protests might well have been useless. The Ontario Court of Appeal has recently discussed the potential conflict of interest that directors who sit on interlocking boards may confront and their fiduciary duties in these circumstances: see *PWA Corp. v. Gemini Group Automated Distribution Systems Inc.* (1994), 15 O.R. (3d) 730. The wrong in *Scottish Insurance*, however, was done not so much by directors of the Society as by its majority shareholder. Thus, the case may be seen to be fundamentally about relations between majority and minority shareholders, even though much of Lord's Denning's analysis focuses on the actions of the majority shareholder's nominees to the textile company's board of directors.

4) A critical question that any board of a company incorporated under a statute that embodies the oppression remedy must confront is how to ensure that its actions are not in fact oppressive. Consider what advice you would give to a board as you read the following decision.

Brant Investments v. KeepRite Inc.
Ontario Court of Appeal
(1991), 3 O.R. (3d) 289

[In late 1982, KeepRite, a company involved in the cooling business, was facing serious financial problems. In December 1982, its management proposed that KeepRite acquire certain assets from a subsidiary of KeepRite's majority shareholder, Inter-City Gas Corporation (ICG). The assets in question had to do with the heating business. Management's proposal was to combine a cyclical heating business with KeepRite's own cyclical cooling business in an effort to diversify and thereby stabilize the company's flow of revenue. KeepRite proposed to proceed with a rights offering, in part to finance the acquisition, but also because it was under substantial pressure from its bankers to shore up its debt to equity ratio. Management concluded that the acquisition would make the company more attractive to the equity markets and so saw the acquisition as part of a broad strategy to put KeepRite back on an even keel.

Because the purchase was from a related company (i.e. a subsidiary of the controlling shareholder), KeepRite set up an independent committee to review the merits of the proposed transaction. The committee was made up of directors who were independent from management of KeepRite and ICG. The independent committee concluded that KeepRite should proceed with the transaction.

A shareholders' meeting was called to approve the creation of new shares that would underlie the rights being issued to finance the acquisition. At that meeting, it became clear that some of KeepRite's minority shareholders were not happy with the proposed transaction. These minority shareholders voted against the proposal and dissented under the appraisal remedy.

The dissenting shareholders refused KeepRite's initial offer for their shares and so KeepRite moved to the next step, namely an application to the Supreme Court of Ontario to fix the fair value of the shares. At the same time, the dissenting shareholders brought an oppression action under the CBCA alleging that KeepRite and ICG had acted in a way that was unfairly prejudicial to their rights as minority shareholders.

At first instance, the trial judge dismissed the oppression action. The minority shareholders appealed.]

The judgment of the court was delivered by McKINLAY J.A.: ... In the oppression action, the plaintiffs claim payment to them of an amount equal to the value of their shares in KeepRite plus interests and costs, damages for loss caused by the allegedly oppressive and unfairly prejudicial conduct of the respondents and, in the alternative, an order appointing a receiver and a receiver-manager to manage KeepRite's affairs for such period of time as the court might direct.

The learned trial judge dismissed the oppression action on the basis that the record did not establish any of the grounds on which an oppression remedy may be granted pursuant to s. 234(2), and that no prejudicial effect on or disregard of the interests of the minority had been shown. The appellants argued three grounds of appeal:

(a) the trial judge erred in concluding that there is no fiduciary duty owed by a majority shareholder to the minority, particularly in respect of a transaction in which the majority shareholder has a clear conflict of interest with the minority;

(b) the trial judge misdirected himself with respect to the onus of proof of oppression; and

(c) the trial judge erred in failing to apply an objective test of fairness in considering whether the impugned transaction consisted of or resulted in oppression of the dissenting shareholders and, in particular:

(i) he erred in concluding that some "want of probity" or bad faith of the respondents is requisite to a finding of oppression; and

(ii) he erred in suggesting that allegations of oppressive corporate conduct can be disposed of on the basis of judicial deference to the business judgment of corporate officers and directors.

The appellants argued that all of these questions should be viewed in the light of s. 4 of the CBCA, which states:

4. The purposes of this Act are to revise and reform the law applicable to business corporations incorporated to carry on business throughout Canada, to advance the cause of uniformity of business corporation law in Canada and to provide a means of allowing an orderly transference of certain federal companies incorporated under various Acts of Parliament to this Act.

Although the appellants emphasize that the purposes of the CBCA were to revise and reform corporate law as it applied to federally incorporated companies, a number of the cases relied on by the appellants in their argument pre-date the coming into force of the CBCA in December 1975.

Fiduciary duty

The appellants argue that the issues of fiduciary duty and oppression are intertwined on the facts of this case and that, if a breach of fiduciary duty were established, that breach would necessarily result in a concurrent finding of oppression under s. 234.

The trial judge, while recognizing that the categories of fiduciary relationships are not closed and have recently been broadened, was of the view that majority shareholders owe no fiduciary duty to minority shareholders, first, because no such duty is currently recognized by Canadian authority or learned opinion and, second, because the relationship between the majority and the minority lacks any of the *indicia* which have traditionally led courts of equity to find such a duty.

The appellants cite three Ontario cases to support their position that the common law recognizes a fiduciary duty owed by a majority shareholder to the minority: *Goldex Mines Ltd. v. Revill* (1974), 7 O.R. (2d) 216, 54 D.L.R. (3d) 672 ((C.A.), at pp. 223-24 O.R.); *Ontario (Ontario Securities Commission) v. McLaughlin*, Ont. H.C.J., Henry J. December 20, 1987 [summarized at 10 A.C.W.S. (3d) 270]; and *Re Canadian Tire Corp.* (1987), 35 B.L.R. 56, 10 O.S.C.B. 857 (Securities Commission), aff'd (1987), 59 O.R. (2d) 79 sub nom. *Re C.T.C. Dealer Holdings Ltd. and Ontario Securities Commission*, 23 Admin. L.R. 285, 35 B.L.R. 117, 37 D.L.R. (4th) 94, 21 O.A.C. 216 (Div. Ct.) [leave to appeal to Ont. C.A. refused (1987), 35 B.L.R. xx].

In *Goldex Mines*, the Ontario Court of Appeal dismissed an appeal from the Divisional Court which had set aside the writs in two actions because, in the opinion of the Divisional Court [*Probe Mines v. Goldex Mines Ltd.* [1973] 3 O.R. 869, 38 D.L.R. (3d) 513], the actions were derivative in nature and the requisite leave had not been granted prior to the issuing of the writs. The proposed actions were based on allegedly false and misleading information disseminated by the company to shareholders. In the process of dismissing the appeal, the Court of Appeal made the following comment at p. 224 O.R.:

The principle that the majority governs in corporate affairs is fundamental to corporation law, but its corollary is also important—that the majority must act fairly and honestly. Fairness is the touchstone of equitable justice, and when the test of fairness is not met, the equitable jurisdiction of the Court can be invoked to prevent or remedy the injustice which misrepresentation or other dishonesty has caused. The category of cases in which fiduciary duties and obligations arise is not a closed one: *Laskin v. Bache & Co. Inc.*, [1972] 1 O.R. 465 at p. 472, 23 D.L.R. (3d) 385 at p. 392.

The Court of Appeal in that case did not hold that a fiduciary duty was owed by directors or majority shareholders to the minority shareholders, but merely commented that the category of cases in which fiduciary duties arise is not closed.

The decision of the Ontario Court of Appeal in *Laskin v. Bache & Co.*, [1972] 1 O.R. 465, 23 D.L.R. (3d) 385, cited in the *Goldex* case, involved a transaction by a stockbroker on behalf of his client in which the broker, on reporting the purchase of shares on the client's behalf, failed to inform his client that he had merely accepted the undertaking of the selling broker to exert his best efforts to deliver the shares involved, rather than obtaining actual delivery of them. The plaintiff suffered substantial loss when the selling broker failed to deliver the shares. Arnup J.A., speaking for the court, stated, at p. 472 O.R., that the categories of cases in which fiduciary duties arise are "no more 'closed' than the categories of negligence at common law." He quoted from the decision of the House of Lords in *Nocton v. Lord Ashburton*, [1914] A.C. 932, [1914-15] All E.R. Rep. 45, 83 L.J. Ch. 784, where Viscount Haldane L.C. states at p. 955 A.C.:

> ... the Courts, and especially the Court of Chancery, had to deal with ... cases raising claims of an essentially different character, which have often been mistaken for actions of deceit. Such claims raise the question whether the circumstances and relations of the parties are such as to give rise to duties of particular obligation which have not been fulfilled.
>
>   • • •
>
> Such a special duty may arise *from the circumstances and relations of the parties. These may give rise to an implied contract at law or to a fiduciary obligation in equity.*

(Emphasis added)

In *Laskin v. Bache & Co.*, the Court of Appeal was of the view that the "circumstances and relations of the parties" in the particular case before it did give rise to a fiduciary obligation on the part of the defendant broker to advise his client in advance of the method used in dealing with the selling broker.

Ontario (Ontario Securities Commission) v. McLaughlin, supra, involved motions by the defendants pursuant to rules 20.01 and 21.01 of the Rules of Civil Procedure, O. Reg. 560/84, for orders striking out statements of claim as showing no triable issue. The plaintiffs, in their statements of claim, had asserted an alternative claim for injuries they suffered as minority shareholders, through diminution of the value of their shares by reason of an alleged breach of fiduciary duty owed to them by the majority shareholders. In considering whether or not to strike this claim, Henry J. referred to the Court of Appeal decision in the *Goldex* case and also to the decision of Anderson J. in the case at bar. He concluded that there were differing views on this issue requiring legal clarification, and that the matter should be left to the trial judge. Consequently, he refused to strike the claim based on breach of fiduciary duty.

The last case cited by the appellants on this issue was *Re Canadian Tire Corp.*, supra, in which the Ontario Securities Commission decided to issue, pursuant to the provisions of s. 123 of the *Securities Act*, R.S.O. 1980, c. 466, a cease-trading order on a take-over bid and on the trade in common shares owned by the majority shareholders. In its reasons, the Commission stated that the vendors on the take-over bid were "in a fiduciary position in at least two categories—as directors of Tire and as Tire's controlling shareholders" (at p. 954 O.S.C.B., p. 110 B.L.R.), but did not explain to whom the fiduciary duty was owed. In its comments, the Commission purported to rely on the decision of the Ontario Court of Appeal in the *Goldex Mines* case. However, the Commission stated that its decision to impose a cease-trading order did not depend on finding a fiduciary duty, and that the Commission was not the proper forum "particularly in a s. 123 proceeding, to determine the question of whether or not there has been a breach of fiduciary duty" (at p. 955 O.S.C.B., p. 111 B.L.R.). What the Commission did determine in its reasons in that case was that the majority shareholders failed to act fairly and honestly and that their unfair and dishonest conduct supported facts which in themselves would have been sufficient to warrant a cease-trading order under s. 123. On appeal, the Divisional Court quite properly rejected the appellant's argument that the Commission had usurped the functions of a court in finding a breach of fiduciary duty on the part of the selling shareholders, since the Commission did not so find.

It is clear that none of the foregoing authorities imposes a fiduciary duty on majority shareholders or directors in favour of minority shareholders. The case that comes closest to doing so is the *Goldex Mines* case, which was decided prior to the coming into force of the CBCA in December of 1975, and involved facts which, if they arose at the present time, would appropriately lead to an application under s. 234 of the CBCA or its counterpart, s. 247(2) of the Ontario Business Corporations Act, 1982, S.O. 1982, c. 4 (the OBCA). The enactment of these provisions has rendered any argument for a broadening of the categories of fiduciary relationships in the corporate context unnecessary and, in my view, inappropriate.

It must be recalled that in dealing with s. 234, the impugned acts, the results of the impugned acts, the protected groups, and the powers of the court to grant remedies are all extremely broad. To import the concept of breach of fiduciary duty into that statutory provision would not only complicate its interpretation and application, but could be inimical to the statutory fiduciary duty imposed upon directors in s. 117(1) of the CBCA. That provision requires that

117.(1) Every director and officer of a corporation in exercising his powers and discharging his duties shall

    (a) act honestly and in good faith *with a view to the best interests of the corporation* ...

(Emphasis added)

Acting in the best interests of the corporation could, in some circumstances, require that a director or officer act other than in the best interests of one of the groups protected under s. 234. To impose upon directors and officers a fiduciary duty to the corporation as well as to individual groups of shareholders of the corporation could place directors in a position of irreconcilable conflict, particularly in situations where the corporation is faced with adverse economic conditions.

Courts impose fiduciary duties only in situations where someone stands in a particular position of trust by virtue of an agreement or as a result of the circumstances and relationship of the parties. In an application under s. 234, evidence of any relevant agreement between the parties and evidence of the circumstances of their relationship would appropriately be adduced to assist in determining whether the facts of the case warrant a remedy. Because the statutory scheme of s. 234 is so broadly formulated, the evidence necessary to establish a breach of fiduciary duty would be subsumed in the broader range of evidence which would be appropriately adduced on an application under the section.

In any event, on the facts of this case, I do not consider that the respondents, the board of directors of KeepRite, or the members of the independent committee owed a fiduciary duty to the appellants.

Bona fides of the impugned transaction

It was submitted before the trial judge and by the appellant before this court that the granting of a remedy under the oppression provision "does not require a finding that there has been a want of probity in those responsible for the impugned conduct," and "that oppression in the result is sufficient." The learned trial judge viewed that submission with "a measure of scepticism" because in reviewing the facts in the decisions to which he had been referred, in which a remedy had been granted, there was "always a finding of conduct clearly inconsistent with good faith and honesty" (*Brant Investments*, supra, at p. 767 O.R.).

A brief view of the authorities, some of which were undoubtedly not cited to the learned trial judge, indicates that judicial opinion on this question is mixed. A careful reading of the section itself does not indicate any statutory requirement of bad faith. In support of its submission that only conduct inconsistent with honesty and good faith can invoke a remedy under s. 234, the respondent relies primarily on the House of Lords decision in *Scottish Co-operative Wholesale Society Ltd. v. Meyer*, [1959] A.C. 324, [1958] 3 All E.R. 66, [1958] 3 W.L.R. 404, and the decision of this court in *Re Ferguson and Imax Systems Corp.* (1983), 43 O.R. (2d) 128, 150 D.L.R. (3d) 718 [leave to appeal to S.C.C. refused (1983), 52 N.R. 317n, 2 O.A.C. 158n].

In the *Scottish Co-operative* case, the appellant co-operative wished to enter into the rayon business, but a regulatory scheme prevented it from manufacturing rayon directly. Accordingly, a corporation was formed in which the co-operative was the majority shareholder and the two respondents, both experts in the rayon business, were minority shareholders. Raw materials were supplied to the corporation by the co-operative. The corporation prospered, and eventually the particular regulatory scheme was removed, resulting in the co-operative itself being able to enter the rayon manufacturing business directly, which it did. Subsequently, the co-operative withheld raw materials from the corporation to establish its own production facilities. The evidence showed that it was the effective policy of the co-operative to "destroy the company it had created, knowing that the minority shareholders alone would suffer in that process: (p. 70 All E.R., per Viscount Simonds). The House of Lords concluded that such activity was oppressive, and therefore ordered that the minority shares be purchased at a price set by the lower court.

In finding that the conduct of the co-operative was "oppressive," Lord Simonds adopted the dictionary meaning of the term—that is, "burdensome, harsh and wrongful." Lord Keith stated that oppression could take various forms, but suggested that at the least it involved "a lack of probity and fair dealing in the affairs of a company to the prejudice of some portion of its members" (at p. 86 All E.R.).

At the time of the *Scottish Co-operative* decision, s. 210 of the Companies Act, 1948 (U.K., 11 & 12 Geo. 6), c. 38, read, in part, as follows:

> 210.(1) Any member of a company who complains that the affairs of the company are being conducted *in a manner oppressive* to some part of the members ... may make an application to the court by petition for an order under this section.

(Emphasis added)

Thus, under s. 210, the conduct of corporate actors had to be found to be *oppressive* in order for the court to grant relief.

Since the *Scottish Co-operative* decision, the definitions adopted by Lord Simonds and Lord Keith have been relied upon in many cases in which oppression has been associated with a lack of probity or an absence of good faith. Such cases, however, pre-date the 1980 amendments to the English oppression provision which now resembles more closely its Canadian counterpart. That provision—the Companies Act, 1985 (U.K.), c. 6, s. 459(1)—reads as follows:

A member of a company may apply to the court by petition for an order under this Part on the ground that the company's affairs are being or have been conducted in a manner which is *unfairly prejudicial* to the interests of some part of the members (including an act or omission on its behalf) or would be so prejudicial.

(Emphasis added)

It will be noted that the main thrust of the change in the English law is to replace the requirement that the conduct complained of must be *"oppressive* to some part of the members"* with a requirement that it be *"unfairly prejudicial* to the interests of some part of the members." Since that change, the English cases have adopted the view that bad faith is not required to invoke a remedy. The test adopted in at least two decisions is whether, in considering the acts complained of, "a reasonable bystander, observing the consequences of (the majority's) conduct, would regard it as having unfairly prejudiced the petitioner's interests." See *Re Bovey Hotel Ventures Ltd.*, U.K. Ch.D., July 31, 1981.

Re Bovey Hotel Ventures Ltd. involved a small company of which the only two shareholders were husband and wife. At the time of the action, they were involved in a bitter matrimonial dispute. Mr. Bovey brought petitions under the old s. 210 of the British Companies Act, 1948, and subsequently under s. 75 of the Companies Act, 1980 (U.K.), c. 22—identical in terms to s. 459(1) of the 1985 statute quoted above. Numerous allegations of bad faith were alleged on both sides.

In dealing with the question of what constituted conduct "unfairly prejudicial," the learned trial judge expressed his view that the test of unfairness must be an objective and not a subjective one; that it is not necessary for the petitioner to show that the persons who have had *de facto* control of the company have acted in the conscious knowledge that their acts were unfair to the petitioner; and that it is not necessary for the petitioner to show bad faith.

On appeal, the Court of Appeal did not interfere with the test applied by the trial judge.

In *Re a Company*, [1989] B.C.L.C. 383 (Ch.D.), the court considered a unilateral exercise by a director of his power of allotment so as to increase his own shareholdings from 60 per cent to 96 per cent and reduce the holding of the only other shareholder accordingly. The court held that this was unfairly prejudicial conduct and, in so doing, relied on the proposition set out in *Re Bovey Hotel Ventures Inc.* The court also stated that the test is one of unfairness, not unlawfulness (see pp. 389-90 B.C.L.C.). The court went on to state, however, that if, from an objective viewpoint, the impugned conduct was performed for an improper purpose or with an improper motive, that could well be a relevant consideration in determining whether the conduct was unfairly prejudicial.

Section 234(2) of the CBCA is drafted in substantially more detail than the provisions of the English Act. Clause (a) makes specific reference to the wrongfulness of the *result* of corporate conduct. If the result is oppressive, unfairly prejudicial, or unfairly disregards the interests of the complainant, then the court may grant a remedy. Clause (b) refers to the *manner* in which the business affairs of the corporation are carried on. If they are carried on in a manner that is oppressive, unfairly prejudicial, or unfairly disregards the interests of the complainant, a remedy may be available. Clause (c) refers to the *manner* in which the powers of the directors have been exercised. If they have been exercised in a manner that is oppressive, unfairly prejudicial or that unfairly disregards the interests of the complainant, a remedy may be available. It can thus be seen that clause (a) emphasizes the *results* of behaviour whereas clause (b) and (c) emphasize the *manner* in which acts have been carried out. Although the emphasis in wording is different between clause (a) and clauses (b) and (c), I am satisfied that the difference is not significant in any practical sense in this case. It may be significant in cases where clause (a) is inapplicable because no oppressive or unfair *result* has been alleged, but where the acts complained of allegedly have been *carried out in a manner* which is oppressive or unfair so as to engage clause (b) or clause (c).

I have concluded that the evidence of bad faith or want of probity in the actions complained of is unnecessary in an application under s. 234. I should have been content to arrive at that conclusion merely on the basis of a literal reading of the provision coupled with an application of the statutory objective articulated in s. 4, "to revise and reform the law applicable to business corporations incorporated to carry on business throughout Canada," had it not been for the substantial body of conflicting opinion on this issue cited to us, involving the application of s. 234 or similarly worded provisions in provincial or Commonwealth statutes.

In considering whether conduct is "oppressive" one can appropriately look to the English cases decided before 1980 which defined that word in a similar context. Adopting the definition supplied by Lord Simonds in the *Scottish Co-operative* case—namely, "burdensome, harsh and wrongful"—it is unlikely that an act could be found to be oppressive without there being an element of bad faith involved. However, in considering the alternative question of whether any act is unfairly prejudicial to, or unfairly disregards the interests of one of the protected persons or groups, I am of the view that a requirement of lack of *bona fides* would unnecessarily complicate the application of the provision and add a judicial gloss that is inappropriate given the clarity of the words used. Of course, there may be many situations where the rights of minority shareholders have been prejudiced or their interests disregarded, without any remedy being appropriate. The difficult question is whether or not their rights have been prejudiced or their interests disregarded "unfairly." In testing the facts in a given case against the word "unfairly," evidence of bad faith as to motive could be relevant, but there may be other cases where particular acts effect an unfair result, but where there has been no bad faith whatsoever on the part of the actors. Such a case came before the Ontario Divisional Court in *Palmer v. Carling O'Keefe Breweries of Canada Ltd.* (1989), 67 O.R. (2d) 161, 41 B.L.R. 128, 56 D.L.R. (4th) 128, 32 O.A.C. 113.

The *Palmer* case involved an application pursuant to s. 247 of the OBCA. An amalgamated company took on the large acquisition debt of one of the amalgamation companies, which the parent company guaranteed under a support agreement. The increase in debt in the resulting company achieved tax savings for the parent company.

The Divisional Court found that the complaining preference shareholders has been made to suffer the risks of higher leverage without any corresponding benefit, and that the support agreement was inadequate to protect their interests. Further, the nature of their investment had changed from that of a Canadian brewing company to a diversified multi-national holding company. Thus, the amalgamation was held to be unfairly preju-dicial to the interests of the holders of preferred shares. Southey J., speaking for the court, stated at p. 172 O.R.:

I do not think that Elders or the directors of Carling O'Keefe intended to harm the preference shareholders, and I am not prepared to find that the management or directors of either Elders or Carling O'Keefe acted in bad faith. But I am satisfied they did something that violated one of the fundamental principles of our company law. They treated C.O. ... as though it was a private com-pany, when it still had other shareholders. They then tried to make amends in a fashion that those other shareholders were not required to accept.

In support of its position that bad faith or want of probity are essential ingredients of conduct which could result in a remedy under the oppression provision, the respondents cite the following cases: *Re Ferguson and Imax Systems Corp.*, supra; *Bank of Montreal v. Dome Petroleum Ltd.* (1987), 54 Alta. L.R. (2d) 289, 67 C.B.R. (N.S.) 296 (Q.B.); *Re Pizza Pizza Ltd.*, Ont H.C.J., August 14, 1987; *Cumberland Holdings Ltd. v. Washington H. Soul Pattison & Co.* (1977), 13 A.L.R. 561, 2 A.C.I.R. 307 (P.C.); *H.J. Rai Ltd. v. Reed Point Marina Ltd.*, B.C.S.C., Skipp L.J.S.C. in Chambers, May 26, 1981 [summa-rized at 9 A.C.W.S. (2d) 216]; and *Keho Holdings Ltd. v. Noble* (1987), 52 Alta. L.R. (2d) 195, 78 A.R. 131, 38 D.L.R. (4th) 368 (C.A.).

In the *Ferguson* case, supra, the Ontario Court of Appeal was dealing with a closely held corporation, the founding shareholders of which were three married couples, the men having been issued voting shares and the women non-voting shares. The complain-ant and her husband ultimately divorced and there followed what the Court of Appeal found to be a lengthy course of oppressive and unfairly prejudicial conduct including a *mala fides* exercise of the company's power to amend its articles and reorganize its capital structure. In making those findings, Brooke J.A., for the court, made the follow-ing statement (at p. 137 O.R.), on which Anderson J. relied in the judgment under appeal:

... the court must consider the *bona fides* of the corporate transaction in question to determine whether the act of the corporation or directors effects a result which is oppressive or unfairly prejudicial to the minority shareholder.

Although Brooke J.A. did state that the court *must* consider the *bona fides* of the corporate transaction in question, it must be remembered that he did so in the context of a closely held corporation involving friends and spouses where there was overwhelming evidence of lack of *bona fides* and unfairly prejudicial conduct leading inevitably to a remedy under the section. The court does not appear to have specifically directed its mind to the issue of whether lack of *bona fides* must be considered in every application for s. 234 relief. Indeed, the court states, at p. 137:

... each case turns on its own facts. What is oppressive or unfairly prejudicial in one case may not necessarily be so in the slightly different setting of another.

I do not consider the *Ferguson* decision authority for the proposition that lack of *bona fides* must be shown in all applications under s. 234.

In *Bank of Montreal v. Dome Petroleum Ltd.*, supra, Forsythe J. of the Alberta Court of Queen's Bench stated that in the case before him it was unnecessary to deal with this issue, but in an aside he referred with approval to Anderson J.'s comments in the trial judgment in this case. The decision in *Bank of Montreal v. Dome* is not of assistance on this issue.

In dealing with an application under s. 247 of the OBCA, Sutherland J. in *Pizza Pizza*, supra, seems to have held that a want of *bona fides* is a threshold requirement for success on an application under the oppression provision—primarily on the authority of this court's decision in *Ferguson*, supra, and of the trial decision in this case. To the extent that the *Pizza Pizza* case represents authority for the proposition under consideration, I would respectfully disagree. I agree, however, with the comments of the learned trial judge where he states at p. 76 of the reasons:

Obviously, not every adverse consequence to the complainant from conduct of the majority will give rise to relieve under s. 247. The term "unfairly" as much as the term "oppressive" invites and requires consideration of the *quality* of the acts of the alleged wrong doer and not merely of the adverse effects of those acts upon the interests of the complainant. Although the thresholds are clearly different for oppression and for what Anderson J. referred to ... as the "wider range of conduct" under the more modern statutory provisions and are probably different as between "conduct unfairly prejudicial" and "conduct unfairly disregarding" ... the court is required to have regard to the *propriety* of the conduct complained of where the complaint involves any of the three categories.

(Emphasis added)

Considering the "quality" or "propriety" of the conduct complained of is clearly relevant in determining whether the conduct is oppressive or unfair. However, in my view, that is substantially different from requiring that a complainant show that there was lack of *bona fides* on the part of the corporate actor.

In *Cumberland Holdings v. Washington*, supra, the Privy Council was dealing with a petition for winding up pursuant to the provisions of the Companies Act of New South Wales. Two statutory provisions were relied upon; although they were similar in some respects to s. 234 of the CBCA, they contained additional phrases not found in s. 234. In any event, their Lordships, although they stated that no lack of probity on the part of the directors was shown, did not in any way state that such a finding was a requirement under the statutory provisions involved.

In *H.J. Rai Ltd.*, supra, the British Columbia Supreme Court was dealing with an application under s. 224 of the Company Act, R.S.B.C. 1979, c. 59. Although that section is not identical to s. 234, it does allow for application to the court for an appropriate remedy where the impugned acts have been effected in a manner that is "oppressive" or that is "unfairly prejudicial" to the complainant. In that case, the learned trial judge emphasized the concept of "majority rule" in the corporate context and stated that the facts before him merely disclosed certain directors who had one view as to what was needed to ameliorate the financial plight of the company, which view was not concurred in by the petitioners. He then went on to say that he did not find *mala fides* on the part of the respondents and that he therefore declined to make the order requested. There is no analysis in his brief reasons of the prerequisites to granting relief, but merely the bald statement that there was no *mala fides*. I do not consider that case to be helpful in analyzing the provisions of s. 234.

In *Keho Holdings Ltd. v. Noble*, supra, the Alberta Court of Appeal considered a hybrid provision of the Alberta Business Corporations Act, S.A. 1981, c. B-15, which allowed for dissolution of an Alberta corporation in circumstances similar to those outlined in s. 234 of the CBCA and also in situations similar to those historically contained in corporations Acts for the winding-up of corporations when it is "just and equitable." Although the Alberta Court of Appeal in the case quoted with approval a portion of the reasons in the *Ferguson* case, supra, including that portion quoted above, it clearly did so only to show concurrence with those reasons to the following extent (*Keho*, p. 201 Alta. L.R.):

... these sections ought to be broadly and liberally interpreted. A broad interpretation will reflect the intention of the legislation to ensure settlement of intracorporate disputes on equitable principles as opposed to adherence to legal rights.

There was no discussion in the reasons in *Keho* of the *bona fides* issue.

My reason for summarizing all of the cases cited by the respondents on this question is to demonstrate that lack of *bona fides* has not been specifically addressed as an issue in any of those cases, other than in the trial decision in this case and in the decision of Sutherland J. in the *Pizza Pizza* case. Anderson J. in this case stated that he viewed with "a measure of scepticism" the submission that the granting of the oppression remedy does not require a finding that there has been a want of probity. He discussed some of the cases to which I have referred. However, it appears that the only case cited to him for the proposition that there need be no finding of bad faith was *Re R.A. Nobel & Sons (Clothing) Ltd.*, [1983] B.C.L.C. 273, which, in turn, referred to the test set out in the unreported decision in *Re Bovey Hotel Ventures Ltd.*, supra, the facts of which were not made available at trial. This court had the benefit of the unreported reasons of the learned Chancery judge in *Bovey Hotel*, and also of the English Court of Appeal reasons, both of which were referred to earlier in these reasons.

Other recent decisions have reinforced the view stated in the English cases cited above in the decision of the Divisional Court in *Palmer v. Carling O'Keefe Breweries*, supra. In *Low v. Ascot Jockey Club* (1986), 1 B.C.L.R. (2d) 123 (S.C.), Southin J., in dealing with an "oppression remedy" application pursuant to s. 224(1) of the British Columbia Company Act, stated at p. 129 B.C.L.R.:

... I see no reason why the motive or intent of those doing the things complained of should be inquired into. What is at issue is the effect of the conduct or acts complained of. Nothing is to be gained by importing notions of malice into this branch of the law. The best way to put my opinion is to say that malice or an intent of on the part of the respondents to do harm is not a necessary ingredient of the petitioner's case at least in circumstances such as those now before me. I do not doubt that there might be cases in which the purpose of the acts complained of would be relevant to determining whether it was oppressive ...

The decision of McEachern C.J.S.C. in *Nystad v. Harcrest Apartments Ltd.* (1986), 3 B.C.L.R. (2d) 39 (S.C.), is an interesting one, also involving an application under

s. 224(1) of the Company Act of British Columbia. The respondent company was incorporated to operate, as a co-operative, an apartment in west Vancouver, for the benefit of its tenant shareholders. In 1973 the petitioner purchased 28 shares in the company which shares carried with them the right to lease a bachelor suite from the company. He lived in the premises until 1978, when other tenant shareholders became concerned about his use of the suite for noisy parties. In 1981, after several warnings and extraordinary general meetings of shareholders, the petitioner was given a notice to quit, with which he complied. The petitioner continued to pay all assessments for taxes and maintenance of the apartment and made applications for reinstatement of his occupancy, which were refused.

On his petition for relief pursuant to s. 224 of the British Columbia statute, the court found that the shareholders did not act in bad faith, but rather, because of their bad experience with the petitioner they did not want his residing in the premises. The court considered that there could be no finding of oppression on the facts involved since bad faith was required for such a finding. However, the court proceeded to deal with the question of whether the acts of the company were, within the words of the British Columbia Act, "unfairly prejudicial" to the petitioner.

The petitioner has been without the use of the premises for a period of close to five years, and during that time, his shareholding rights had been sterilized. Any sale of the shares at the time of the petition would have left the petitioner in a position of having to accept a "fire sale" price for his shares. Consequently, because of what the court considered to be "unfair prejudice" to the petitioner, and absent any bad faith on the part of the corporation, an order was made that the petitioner's shares be valued objectively and that the company either purchase his shares at that value, or find a buyer, or subsidize a buyer, so that the return to the petitioner would equal fair market value of his shares.

I agree with Anderson J. in the judgment under appeal that there will be few cases where there has not been some "want of probity" on the part of the corporate actor where a remedy pursuant to s. 234 will be appropriate. However, given the wording of the section, and the broad objectives set out in s. 4 of the Act, I do not consider it necessary that a finding of want of *bona fides* be made in every case where the court is disposed to grant a remedy.

Onus of proof

The appellants submit that, in an application for relief under s. 234 (now s. 241), once a dissenting shareholder has shown that an impugned transaction involves benefits to one group of shareholders in which dissenting shareholders do not share, and a corresponding detriment to the dissenting shareholders which the other group of shareholders do not suffer, then the burden of proof rests upon the majority shareholders to demonstrate that: (a) the impugned transaction is at least as advantageous to the company and to all shareholders as any available alternative transaction; (b) that no undue pressure was applied to the company, its officers and directors, to accept the impugned transaction as proposed; and (c) that the substance of the impugned transaction and the process of decision-making leading to its acceptance were intrinsically fair to the dissenting shareholders.

No case was cited to us that would substantiate such broad and onerous legal requirements. In any event, the learned trial judge in his very careful reasons dealt with each question raised. He did not consider that there were benefits of ICG which were not shared by the dissenting shareholders, nor did he consider that the dissenting shareholders suffered a detriment which ICG did not suffer. A review of the evidence and of the trial judge's decision makes it clear that there was substantial evidence on which he could base such findings. That being so, the burden of proof which the appellants would have shifted to the respondents on the above-mentioned bases does not arise.

Anderson J. pointed out that possible solutions to KeepRite's problems suggested by the dissenting shareholders were considered and rejected by KeepRite management and by the independent committee. To suggest that directors are required, when entering into a transaction on behalf of the corporation, to consider every available alternative transaction is unrealistic. Any number of considerations may be relevant, if not vital, to the carrying out of a particular transaction at a particular time. In many cases, there will not be obvious or immediate alternatives. The extent to which directors should inquire as to alternatives is a business decision, which, if made honestly in the best interests of the corporation, should not be interfered with.

The appellants also take the position that the single fact that this was a non-arm's-length transaction shifts the burden of proof to the respondent. The only example of such a shift of onus cited to us was in *Sinclair Oil Corp. v. Levien*, 280 A.2d 717 (1971). The facts in that case were much stronger than the facts in this case. Sinclair Oil Corporation allegedly caused damage to its subsidiary, Sinclair Venezuelan Oil Company (Sinven), as a result of numerous acts, including causing the subsidiary to pay substantial dividends, denying industrial development to the subsidiary and causing breach of contract between that subsidiary and a wholly owned subsidiary of Sinclair. The case involved a derivative action by minority shareholders of Sinven for losses suffered by it as a result of its parent's actions. In that case, the fiduciary duty owed by the parent to the subsidiary resulted in a shifting of the burden of proof to Sinclair to show "intrinsic fairness" in the dealings between it and its subsidiary.

As pointed out by the appellants, courts in this jurisdiction have held that where a party who owns a fiduciary duty deals with trust property to his own personal benefit, a burden of proof, the nature of which will depend on the circumstances of the case, will rest on the fiduciary. There are undoubtedly other cases where proof of basic preliminary facts would warrant a shift of onus. Whether or not this is one of those cases we need not decide since, as pointed out by Anderson J., the respondents in this case assumed from the outside the burden of adducing evidence as to the nature of the transaction, the manner in which it was carried out, and the result. It was not merely the non-arm's-length nature of the transaction that made it, in the trial judge's words, "tactically sound" to do so. As many of the necessary facts were solely in the knowledge of the respondents, the burden of adducing evidence on those facts would have been theirs in any event.

Independent committee

The appellants attack the role of the independent committee on the basis, first, that it was not, in fact, independent, and second, that the advice given by the committee to the directors of KeepRite was not in the best interests of the company and its shareholders.

With respect to the makeup of the committee, the evidence discloses that all of its members were outside members of the board of KeepRite. None was an officer or director of ICG. The three-member committee comprised H. Purdy Crawford and John Edison, both solicitors, and Ross Hanbury, a former partner of Wood, Gundy. Mr. Crawford became involved with KeepRite in the winter of 1979 when the Odette Group retained him and the law firm in which he was a senior partner in connection with the possible acquisition of KeepRite. That group eventually became owners of approximately 50 percent of the shares of KeepRite. It was at the request of the Odette Group that Mr. Crawford became a director of KeepRite. His first encounter with ICG was at the time of its failed take-over bid for KeepRite. He continued as a member of the board after ICG acquired its interest in KeepRite in 1981. Mr. Edison had acted as legal advisor to the founder of KeepRite from its inception, and had also acted for the company over a number of years. He was a long term member of the KeepRite board. Mr. Hanbury had been involved with KeepRite since the 1960s, when Wood, Gundy was involved in a public offering of KeepRite shares. There is no evidence of any involvement with ICG by any of these individuals.

The trial judge found as a fact that the members of the committee were truly independent in the sense that they "felt at all times free to deal with the impugned transaction upon its merits" (*Brant Investments*, supra, at p. 756 O.R.). There was more than adequate evidence to substantiate such a finding.

That, of course, does not end the matter, since the appellants allege that the advice given by the committee to KeepRite was not in the best interests of KeepRite and its shareholders. With respect to those issues, the learned trial judge made the following findings, at p. 756 O.R.:

I conclude and find that the members of the committee were fully aware that the transaction was not at arm's length and that the function of the committee was to assure that the impugned transaction be fair to the minority shareholders as well as in the best interests of KeepRite as a whole. I likewise conclude and find that the advice which it gave was independent advice and had not been in any way dictated or predetermined.

The real complaint of the appellants on this appeal is that, rather than making his own assessment of the value to KeepRite of the transaction, the learned trial judge relied on the decision of the independent committee that the transaction was of value to KeepRite because of the synergies and economies of scale involved. The appellants argue that, although reliance on investigations carried out by such a committee may be appropriate in some cases, it is not appropriate in this case where, they argue, the committee itself did not adequately assess the benefits of the transaction to KeepRite. The appellants criticize work of the independent committee on the following bases:

(a) the committee did not consider whether there were alternative transactions open to KeepRite;
(b) the committee approved the transaction based upon assurances that certain "synergistic" benefits could be achieved by combining the businesses—they were aware of the need for a strategic plan to realize benefits but proceeded without obtaining one;

(c) the committee never received a final report from the consultants retained to review management's assumptions concerning the anticipated synergies; and

(d) the committee did not commission a valuation of the Inter-City businesses on a going concern basis.

(a) Possible alternative transactions

The appellants argue that there were a number of alternative transactions available to KeepRite which were not considered by the independent committee, and they point specifically to three. First, they say that Wood, Gundy, KeepRite's financial advisors, and Mr. McKay, KeepRite's chief executive officer, believed that equity could be raised in the absence of an asset purchase. Mr. S.A. Jarislowsky, called by the appellants, testified that the dissenting shareholders would have looked favourably at supporting such an offering. I do not consider that Mr. Jarislowsky's after-the-fact evidence of such a position is of assistance. There was some evidence that an alternative suggestion was made by Mr. Jarislowsky on behalf of the dissenting shareholders prior to the carrying out of the transaction. However, it is not for the minority shareholders to dictate to corporate officers the manner in which they should deal with corporate problems. Whether or not the directors or the independent committee looked favourably on any suggestion by Mr. Jarislowsky is irrelevant unless it could be shown that he presented an alternative which was definitely available and clearly more beneficial to the company than the chosen transaction. However, the suggestion made by Mr. Jarislowsky was nothing more than that—a mere suggestion.

With respect to evidence regarding the raising of equity without the asset purchase, Mr. Falconer from Wood, Gundy, opined that the raising of equity financing other than with the cooperation of ICG and the minority shareholders would be extremely difficult, particularly given the recent financial history of the company. In addition, while a public rights offering would have provided additional equity financing to KeepRite, it would not have alleviated its deteriorating competitive position as a seasonal manufacturer with a declining market share. It was the opinion of the independent committee that the synergies available in the impugned transaction would help solve that problem. Other alternatives were considered by the committee and rejected because none was considered as attractive as the integration of KeepRite's air-conditioning business with the heating business of the ICG companies.

Second, the appellants suggest that certain divisions of KeepRite had been identified as unnecessary to KeepRite's future plans: "They were profitable, and could have been sold with other redundant assets to reduce KeepRite's debt." The evidence to which we were referred on this point is of no assistance whatsoever to the appellants. Mr. McKay, the president of KeepRite during the relevant period, says that he considered the sale of these assets at some time prior to the period when the impugned transaction was under consideration. He had some discussions with an unnamed American firm which did not proceed beyond the preliminary negotiation stage.

Third, the appellants suggest that the shares of Manufacturing and of Energy Products might have been acquired in order to make tax losses in those companies available against future profits in KeepRite. The evidence indicated that such a possibility was in fact considered by the committee but rejected.

It is clear from the evidence that the independent committee did consider some alternative possibilities for solving KeepRite's problems. It did so, however, in the context of a concrete proposal for the purchase of assets from the ICG companies. The evaluation of that proposal was the purpose for which the committee was struck. I agree with the words of the trial judge where he stated at pp. 757-58 O.R.:

There is nothing inherently wrong in a parent company making such a proposal to a subsidiary. Any difficulty arises because the transaction, if carried forward, will not be at arm's length. It was because of that aspect of the transaction, and to protect against the vices which may be involved, that the Independent Committee was called into existence. In my view, the committee was not thereupon called to make a wide-ranging search for alternatives, or in other words, to determine whether the proposal which had been made was the best possible solution to the problem. Its function was to determine whether the proposed transaction was fair and reasonable and of benefit to KeepRite and its shareholders.

(b) Strategic plan

The appellants argue that, although the independent committee was aware of the need for a strategic plan to realize the synergistic benefits of the transaction, they proceeded without obtaining such a plan. First of all, the evidence referred to by the appellants on this point does not reveal that the committee considered that a comprehensive "strategic plan" to realize synergistic benefits was necessary. Mr. Purdy Crawford, a witness with broad experience in corporation matters, indicated in his evidence that it is not unusual for decisions to be made with respect to very substantial acquisitions without any previously existing strategic plan. However, in this case, the committee and the directors of KeepRite considered it absolutely necessary in the situation in which KeepRite found itself that some action be taken which would alleviate the concerns of KeepRite bankers.

Early in 1983 a task force comprised of representatives of both KeepRite and ICG was appointed to study and report on the merits of combining the air-conditioning business of KeepRite and the heating business of the Inter-City companies. In the process of the work of that task force, a background financial paper was prepared which analyzed the financial impact of combining the businesses. This financial analysis was filed as an exhibit at trial. It analyzed the anticipated synergies from the integration of the two operations, and the anticipated effect on the resulting balance sheet of KeepRite—both of which were very important for the purposes of KeepRite's bankers.

It is clear from the evidence that KeepRite did have a plan to realize the proposed benefits of the transaction, which was reviewed by the independent committee. There does not appear to have been a minutely detailed plan setting out projected day-by-day actions to be followed after closing of the transaction, but no one suggests that such a detailed plan was necessary, or even desirable.

(c) Consultants' report

The independent committee retained the firm of Crosbie, Armitage as consultants to assess the benefits of the proposed transaction to KeepRite. Crosbie, Armitage did, in fact, make an assessment of the anticipated synergistic benefits of the transaction. Allan

Crosbie presented a report dated March 23, 1983 to a meeting of the independent committee on that same date. His report contained an appendix setting forth the main elements of the proposed business plan arising out of the transaction and a reasonably detailed financial analysis of the proposed acquisition. He made it clear in his report that the assumptions on which it was based were developed by KeepRite and ICG senior operating personnel in several working sessions in which Crosbie, Armitage participated. Thus, the underlying assumptions used in the financial analysis represented a consensus view of the senior management of the two companies. On the basis of the information contained in the report, it was Mr. Crosbie's opinion that:

Not only are there important cost savings as a result of rationalization of the businesses, but in addition there are substantial increased sales opportunities.

At the meeting of the independent committee, Mr. Crosbie informed its members that the transaction appeared to him and his associates to make business sense. Mr. McKay informed the committee that senior management could successfully carry out the integration and business plan as set out in the Crosbie, Armitage report.

The appellants criticize the independent committee because it did not obtain a further final report from Crosbie, Armitage establishing their confirmation of some of the assumptions on which their original report was based. In my opinion, the fact that the committee did not require such a report in no way invalidates the opinion contained in the original report and conveyed orally to the committee by Mr. Crosbie. The learned trial judge considered it completely appropriate that the assumptions on which the report was based were developed by senior operating personnel of KeepRite and ICG, along with personnel of Crosbie, Armitage. I agree. Those individuals were not only the persons who had access to and familiarity with the relevant information, but many of them were also the officers who would be implementing the integrated business plan after the completion of the transaction. There was no suggestion that any of the information presented was inaccurate or misleading.

(d) Valuation of the Inter-City business on a going-concern basis

The appellants complain that: "The Committee did not commission a valuation of the Inter-City business on a going-concern basis, even though Mr. McKay expressed concern about their profitability. The Inter-City businesses had substantial losses in 1982, and budgeted further losses for 1983. They were reviewed by Inter-City, KeepRite and at least two members of the Committee as only marginally profitable, if at all."

None of these allegations is disputed by the respondents. The two Inter-City businesses, the major assets of which were to be purchased by KeepRite, had not recently been profitable. KeepRite itself had suffered substantial losses in the 1982 fiscal year, was experiencing a decrease in its share of the market in its field, and was under substantial pressure from its bankers to acquire new equity financing. It was not the profitability of the businesses as separate entities that was of concern to the independent committee, but the benefits to KeepRite of combining their operations. It is probably worth while at this point to quote from the summary business plan included in the Crosbie, Armitage report, since it very concisely indicates what the expected benefits to KeepRite would be:

1. KeepRite would acquire the assets and liabilities of the businesses of ICG Manufacturing and ICG Energy respectively, exclusive of the St. Catharines facility and deferred taxes.

2. ICG's sheet metal business would be wound up on an orderly basis.

3. The significant portion of ICG's St. Catharines manufacturing business would be integrated into KeepRite's Brantford manufacturing facility.

4. KeepRite and ICG's sales and distribution components would be rationalized. Also, as part of this rationalization, ICG would terminate its existing distribution business and sell direct or through other distributors in a manner similar to KeepRite. As part of the restructuring of ICG's sales and marketing network, this should enable reductions in sales personnel and the amounts of finished goods inventory that would have to be carried.

5. With the rationalization of the KeepRite and ICG selling and distribution networks, it is anticipated that sales of certain product lines in Canada, the U.S. and offshore markets would be expanded slightly. In particular, in Canada, with the rationalization of KeepRite's and ICG's sales forces, domestic sales increases are projected; in the U.S., utilizing KeepRite's existing sales and distribution network, sales increases of selected ICG products are projected.

6. As part of this overall program, provision is to be made for establishing a senior marketing group.

7. As part of the rationalization program, KeepRite and ICG Manufacturing and Engineering personnel requirements would be rationalized with attendant savings in costs.

8. As part of the rationalization program, KeepRite and ICG corporate administration, finance and EDP departments would be rationalized with attendant savings in costs.

The independent committee retained Price, Waterhouse, KeepRite's auditors, to review the statement of net book values of ICG assets as at March 31, 1983. Price, Waterhouse held discussions with Coopers & Lybrand, who had completed an audit of the Inter-City companies as at December 31, 1982. Price, Waterhouse presented its opinion to the committee that the net book values were appropriate and appeared to have been arrived at in accordance with generally accepted accounting principles.

Since KeepRite was purchasing assets for the purpose of combining the two operations, the committee did not consider a going-concern valuation to be necessary.

The trial judge was satisfied that the independent committee was aware of its mandate, was at all times conscious that this was not an arm's-length transaction, and appropriately carried out its function of assessing the benefits of the transaction to KeepRite. He was completely satisfied on the evidence that the committee carried out its function in an appropriate and independent manner. I see no reason whatever to doubt the correctness of that finding. Neither the evidence nor the argument persuades me that his findings were anything other than appropriate.

Business judgment and the oppression remedy

The appellants argue strongly that since the enactment of s. 234 of the CBCA, it is no longer appropriate for a trial judge to delegate to directors of a corporation, or to a committee such as that established in this case, judgment as to the fairness of conduct complained of by dissenting shareholders. This is particularly important, they argue, because the persons to whom that judgment is delegated are the very persons whose conduct is under scrutiny. They argue that the trial judge in this case erred in his approach to the exercise of his jurisdiction under s. 234, when he stated, at pp. 759-60 O.R.:

... the court ought not to usurp the function of the board of directors in managing the company, nor should it eliminate or supplant the legitimate exercise of control by the majority ... Business decisions, honestly made, should not be subjected to microscopic examination.

This, they argue, indicates that the trial judge declined to exercise independent judgment with respect to the fairness of essential aspects of the impugned transaction. Such a submission is, in my view, patently unfounded. The portion of the trial judge's reasons quoted above should be placed in context. The relevant portion of the reasons is quoted below (pp. 759-60 O.R.):

The jurisdiction is one which must be exercised with care. On the one hand the minority share-holder must be protected from unfair treatment; that is the clearly expressed intent of the section. On the other hand the court ought not to usurp the function of the board of directors in managing the company, nor should it eliminate or supplant the legitimate exercise of control by the major-ity. In *Re Bright Pine Mills Pty. Ltd.*, 1969 V.R. 1002 (Supreme Court of Victoria), analogous leg-islation to s. 234 was under consideration. At p. 1001 O'Bryan J., writing for the full court, says:

It is true to say, however, that it was not intended ... to give jurisdiction to the Court (a juris-diction the courts have always been loath to assume) to interfere with the internal manage-ment of a company by directors who in the exercise of the powers conferred upon them by the memorandum and articles of association are acting honestly and without any purpose of advancing the interests of themselves or others of their choice at the expense of the company or contrary to the interests of other shareholders.

Although the statute there under consideration was confined to "oppression," I consider the caveat there expressed to apply with equal force to the wider language of s. 234. Busi-ness decisions, honestly made, should not be subjected to microscopic examination. There should be no interference simply because a decision is unpopular with the minority.

There can be no doubt that on an application under s. 234 the trial judge is required to consider the nature of the impugned acts and the method in which they were carried out. That does not mean that the trial judge should substitute his own business judgment for that of managers, directors, or a committee such as the one involved in assessing this transaction. Indeed, it would generally be impossible for him to do so, regardless of the amount of evidence before him. He is dealing with the matter at a different time and place; it is unlikely that he will have the background knowledge and expertise of the individuals involved; he could have little or no knowledge of the background and skills of the persons who would be carrying out any proposed plan; and it is unlikely that he would have any knowledge of the specialized market in which the corporation operated. In short, he does not know enough to make the business decision required. That does not mean that he is not well equipped to make an objective assessment of the very factors which s. 234 requires him to assess. Those factors have been discussed in some detail earlier in these reasons.

It is important to note that the learned trial judge did not say that business decisions honestly made should not be subjected to examination. What he said was that they should not be subjected to *microscopic* examination. In spite of those words, the learned trial judge did, in fact, scrutinize, in a very detailed and careful manner, the nature of the transaction in this case and the manner in which it was executed. Having carefully reviewed the major aspects of the appellants' criticisms of the transaction, he came to the conclusion that it in no way, either substantively or procedurally, offended the provisions of s. 234. Having carefully reviewed all of the exhibits and transcribed evidence to which we were referred, I have no hesitation in agreeing with the correctness of his assessment.

The appellants refer specifically to two areas where they say the trial judge declined to exercise independent judgment with respect to the fairness of essential aspects of the transaction. These were:

1) whether the impugned transaction was, in fact, for the benefit of KeepRite as a whole, or rather beneficial to Inter-City and detrimental to KeepRite; and
2) whether the "earnings dilution" caused by the disparity in historical earnings between KeepRite and the Inter-City businesses resulted in unfairness to the dissenting shareholders.

With respect to the first argument, I can only say that the reasons of the trial judge indicate exactly the reverse. If anything, he took an excess of care in exercising independent judgment with respect to the fairness of the transaction.

With respect to the second, the trial judge in his reasons dealt with the question of the disparity in historical earnings between the ICG subsidiaries and KeepRite. He stated that the members of the independent committee and the directors were aware of these problems and considered that they had been overcome. The learned trial judge was of the view that this was a matter of business judgment and he was not disposed to intervene. The appellants argue that the disparity in historical earnings would inevitably result in an earnings dilution to the shareholders of KeepRite. Such a result was by no means inevitable. A large proportion of the assets transferred consisted of inventory and accounts receivable, the book value of which were guaranteed by ICG, and no interest was payable on the note given by KeepRite to ICG covering payment of the purchase price. The cash resulting from realization of the receivables and inventory would have the effect of reducing the bank borrowings of KeepRite, and the transaction was very favourably viewed by KeepRite's bankers. If, in addition, the anticipated synergies were realized (which it appears in retrospect they were) there would likely be an earnings enhancement per share rather than the "earnings dilution" alleged by the dissenting shareholders.

Conclusion

For the foregoing reasons, I do not consider that the impugned transaction, or the method by which it was implemented, involved oppression or unfairness within the meaning of s. 234 of the CBCA. I would dismiss the oppression appeal with costs.

NOTES

1) Do you think that McKinlay J.A.'s understanding of how the oppression remedy should interact with a board's fiduciary duties to the corporation is satisfactory? Why

would imposing a fiducary duty on a majority shareholder with respect to minority shareholders put a board of directors in a position of conflict with respect to their obligation to act in the best interests of the company? Does the answer to this question depend on one's vision of the corporation: that is, one's views about whether the board is acting as agent of the shareholders/"owners" or whether its job is to foster the interests of a broader range of constituencies? Does a clear vision of the corporation emerge from McKinlay J.A.'s analysis?

2) Would imposing a fiduciary duty on majority shareholders with respect to minority shareholders really give rise to an obligation that was any different from the obligation that has effectively been imposed through the oppression remedy? McKinlay J.A. obviously thought that there would be a difference and it would appear that he was after a legal structure that would give the board room to manoeuvre as it considers how best to deal with competing interests in the corporation. Has he crafted a structure that is compatible with the business judgment rule seen in the first part of this chapter? Would it really have been impossible to achieve the same result if one said that the majority owed a fiduciary duty to the minority?

3) *KeepRite* is a case of great interest at a number of levels. First, the case did not involve a closely held company. Thus, one sees the oppression remedy being used to address a dispute between a majority shareholder and a group of minority shareholders with respect to a publicly traded company (KeepRite was listed on the Toronto Stock Exchange).

Second, as the questions set out above suggest, the case involves an effort to sort out how best to reconcile the introduction of the oppression remedy with the pre-existing body of fiduciary law. The fact that McKinlay J.A.'s analysis of this issue gives rise to difficult questions suggests that we may need to look more deeply at whether courts are working with a unified theory of the firm as they approach the challenge of harmonizing the oppression remedy with fiduciary law.

Third, the case deals with the question whether in order to succeed under the oppression remedy one need establish not only that the actions complained of were unfair or gave rise to an unfair result, but were also motivated by bad faith. For further analysis of the proposition that bad faith need not be established, see J. MacIntosh, *Bad Faith and the Oppression Remedy: Uneasy Marriage, or Amicable Divorce?* 69 Can. Bar Rev. 276 (1990). Do you agree with McKinlay J.A.'s conclusion that a complainant should not have to establish bad faith?

Fourth, the case displays a concern that courts not second guess every aspect of a board's decision making process. The degree of deference that courts should show to a board of directors is an issue that has been seen in connection with our review of other liability strategies and it is an extremely important question when examining a board's decision with respect to phenomena like unsolicited take-over bids. McKinlay J.A. makes clear that the decision-making process that a board follows is extremely important in ensuring that a decision withstands judicial scrutiny. This is a message that emerges from other cases on the oppression remedy: see, e.g., *Westfair Foods Ltd. v. Watt*, [1991] 4 W.W.R. 695 at 711 (Alta. C.A.). In many cases a board will look to its lawyers to advise it with respect to the process that should be followed if it is to avoid having its decisions successfully challenged under the oppression remedy. What advice with respect to process would you provide to a board faced with a decision as important to the company as the one involved in *KeepRite*?

Fifth, do you think that KeepRite's board would have been subjected to a higher degree of scrutiny, with more expansive fiduciary duties, had it not gone to such lengths to seek an independent evaluation of the fairness and profitability of the transaction?

4) The Ontario Securities Commission has imposed its own set of rules with respect to the procedures that a company with a majority shareholder must follow when engaged in transactions that will affect minority shareholders (including "related party transactions" of the kind seen in *KeepRite*): OSC Policy 9.1, discussed in Chapter Eleven, Section D. Had the current version of OSC Policy 9.1 been in place when the events in *KeepRite* took place, the board would have faced a detailed code of conduct that it would have had to follow. In your view, who should be developing standards of conduct for boards faced with transactions of the kind seen in *KeepRite*: courts or securities commissions? If a board complies with the policies set out by a securities commission should this provide a complete defence to a complaint brought under the oppression remedy? Are securities commissions particularly concerned about the interests of constituencies other than security holders?

C. OTHER COMPLAINANTS UNDER THE OPPRESSION REMEDY

Scottish Insurance and *KeepRite* were both cases in which the complainants were shareholders and the disputes were between groups of shareholders with competing interests. But the oppression remedy is worded sufficiently broadly to capture other constituencies. Hence the challenge, at a practical level, of sorting out whether the oppression remedy should become a vehicle for resolving conflict between different constituencies with an interest in the corporation. As you read the next case, ask yourself whether if one allows the remedy to serve such a function it will still be possible for the oppression remedy to remain part of a well focused liability strategy. What would one expect a board to do? Achieve perfect harmony between all constituencies with an interest in the corporation? Or simply ensure that a process is in place whereby these groups' interests are borne in mind before a final decision is taken as to what was in the best interests of the corporation?

First Edmonton Place Ltd. v. 315888 Alberta Ltd.
Alberta Court of Queen's Bench
(1980), 40 B.L.R. 28

[A landlord provided a package of inducements to get a numbered company controlled by three lawyers to sign a ten year lease. The package of inducements included an 18 month rent free period, a leasehold improvement allowance of $115,900 and a cash payment of $140,126. The lawyers promptly had the cash distributed to themselves. They made use of the premises during the rent free period and for a further three months without the numbered company having entered into a formal lease. They then vacated the premises and no further rent was paid.

The landlord sought leave to bring an oppression action under s. 234 of the Business Corporations Act (Alberta) or, in the alternative, a derivative action under s. 232 and alleged that the actions of the three lawyers as directors of the numbered company were unfairly prejucial to or unfairly disregarded the landlord's interests.]

McDONALD J.: ... In *Brant Investments v. KeepRite*, supra, Anderson J. expressed the following concern (at 99 [B.L.R.]):

The jurisdiction is one which must be exercised with care. On the one hand the minority shareholder must be protected from unfair treatment; that is the clearly expressed intent of the section. On the other hand the Court ought not to usurp the function of the board of directors in managing the company, nor should it eliminate or supplant the legitimate exercise of control by the majority.

He went on to state (at 100 [B.L.R.]):

Business decisions, honestly made, should not be subjected to microscopic examination. There should be no interference simply because a decision is unpopular with the minority.

There are almost no decisions on the availability of s. 234 to *creditors*. Most applications under s. 234 are made by minority shareholders. With respect to the applicability of decisions involving minority shareholders to cases involving creditors, in *Bank of Montreal v. Dome Petroleum Ltd.* (1987), 54 Alta. L.R. (2d) 289 (Q.B.), Forsyth J. quoted the above statements of Anderson J. in *Brant Investments*. He then commented (at 298):

While Mr. Justice Anderson in that decision was dealing with the rights of minority shareholders, I fully subscribe to those views and would adopt the same approach in dealing with the rights of creditors when it is alleged same are being unfairly dealt with in some fashion and relief is sought under s. 234.

In the *Dome Petroleum* case, supra, the Bank of Montreal claimed that an arrangement agreement entered into by Dome and Amoco, coupled with certain confidentiality agreements, which effectively restricted any sale of Dome shares or assets for an indeterminate amount of time, unfairly prejudiced or unfairly disregarded the Bank of Montreal's position as a creditor. As the arrangement agreement could not go forward in the absence of the Bank of Montreal's consent, Forsyth J. could not find any oppression, unfair prejudice, or unfair disregard on the evidence before him. As such, he granted Dome Petroleum's application for summary dismissal of the application under s. 234.

• • •

Where, as in s. 234 of the ABCA, it may be used as an instrument for the protection of the interests of a creditor, the basic formula for establishing unfair prejudice or unfair disregard of the interests of the creditor should reflect as a goal the desire to seek to balance protection of the creditor's interest against the policy of preserving freedom of action for management and the right of the corporation to deal with a creditor in a way that may be to the prejudice of the interests of the creditor or that may disregard those interests so long as the prejudice or disregard is not unfair.

The s. 234 remedy would be available if the act or conduct of the directors or management of the corporation which is complained of amounted to using the corporation as a vehicle for committing fraud upon a creditor. An example might be the directors of a corporation using it to obtain credit for the purchase of goods by means which, if the credit were obtained by an individual, would be fraudulent on the part of the individual.

Assuming the absence of fraud, in what other circumstances would a remedy under s. 234 be available? In deciding what is unfair, the history and nature of the corporation, the essential nature of the relationship between the corporation and the creditor, the type of rights affected, and general commercial practice should all be material. More concretely, the test of unfair prejudice or unfair disregard should encompass the following considerations: the protection of the underlying expectation of a creditor in its arrangement with the corporation, the extent to which the acts complained of were unforeseeable or the creditor could reasonably have protected itself from such acts, and the detriment to the interests of the creditor. The elements of the formula and the list of considerations as I have stated them should not be regarded as exhaustive. Other elements and considerations may be relevant, based upon the facts of a particular case.

● ● ●

Is the Applicant a "Complainant" under S. 231(b)(iii)?

Under s. 231(b)(iii), a person may be a "complainant" if he is a person "who, in the discretion of the Court, is a proper person to make an application under this Part."

This is not so much a definition as a grant to the Court of a broad power to do justice and equity in the circumstances of a particular case where a person who otherwise would not be a "complainant" ought to be permitted to bring an action under either s. 232 or s. 234 to right a wrong done to the corporation which would not otherwise be righted, or to obtain compensation himself or itself where his or its interests have suffered from oppression by the majority controlling the corporation or have been unfairly prejudiced or unfairly disregarded, and the applicant is a "security holder, creditor, director or officer."

The report of the Institute of Law Research and Reform of Alberta had some reservations about the inclusion of such a broad power to permit a person to complain. It is stated, at p. 150:

We have some reservations about legislation which confers broad statutory discretions without guidelines. Here, however, we think such a discretion appropriate. The specific listed classes appear to us to cover all cases in which the derivative and personal remedies should be available, but foresight is necessarily imperfect, and the general discretion would allow the courts to make up for the imperfections of foresight. We think also that the courts can be relied upon to allow only proper applications. s. 231(b)(iv) of the draft Act therefore follows CBCA s. 231(d).

(It should be noted that what was s. 231(b)(iv) in the draft Act became s. 231(b)(iii) in the ABCA.) The Institute's report thus recommended that the question of who is a "proper person" be left to the discretion of the Court. Even accepting that the s. 232 and s. 234 remedies should be given a liberal interpretation, the circumstances in which a person who is not a security holder (as I have interpreted that phrase) or a director or officer should be recognized as "a proper person to make an application" must show that justice and equity clearly dictate such a result.

I turn now to an application by a person who claims to be a "proper person" to make an application under s. 234. As in the case of an application made under s. 232, an applicant for leave to bring an action under s. 234 does not have to be a security holder, director, or officer. The applicant could be a creditor, or even a person toward whom the corporation had only a contingent liability at the time of the act or conduct complained of. However, it is important to note that he would not be held to be a "proper person" to make the application under s. 234 unless he satisfied the Court that there was some evidence of oppression or unfair prejudice or unfair disregard for the interests of a security holder, creditor, director, or officer.

Having said that, *assuming* that the applicant was a creditor of the corporation at the time of the act or conduct complained of, what criterion should be applied in determining whether the applicant is "a proper person" to make the application? Once again, in my view, the applicant must show that in the circumstances of the case, justice and equity require him or it to be given an opportunity to have the claim tried.

There are two circumstances in which justice and equity would entitle a creditor to be regarded as "a proper person." (There may be other circumstances; these two are not intended to exhaust the possibilities.) The first is if the act or conduct of the directors or management of the corporation which is complained of constituted using the corporation as a vehicle for committing a fraud *upon the applicant*. In the present case there is no evidence suggesting *such* fraud, although there is some evidence of the directors having used the money paid as a cash inducement for their own personal investment purposes, and that, as I shall later explain, may constitute fraud against the corporation: see infra where *R v. Olan* is cited.

Second, the Court might hold that the applicant is a "proper person to make an application" for an order under s. 234 if the act or conduct of the directors or management of the corporation which is complained of constituted a breach of the underlying expectation of the applicant arising from the circumstances in which the applicant's relationship with the corporation arose. For example, where the applicant is a creditor of the corporation, did the circumstances which gave rise to the granting of credit include some element which prevented the creditor from taking adequate steps when he or it entered into the agreement to protect his or its interests against the occurrence of which he or it now complains? Did the creditor entertain an expectation that, assuming fair dealing, its chances of repayment would not be frustrated by the kind of conduct which subsequently was engaged in by the management of the corporation? Assuming that the evidence established the existence of such an expectation, the next question would be whether that expectation was, objectively, a reasonable one.

Thus, in the present case, an inquiry would properly be directed at trial toward whether the lessor, First Edmonton Place, at the time of entering into the lease, consciously and intentionally decided to contract only with the numbered company and not to obtain person guarantees from the three lawyers. A further proper inquiry would be into whether the lessor entered into the lease fully aware that it was not protecting itself against the possibility that the corporation might pay out the cash advance to the lawyers, leaving no other assets in the corporation, and that the corporation might permit the lawyers to occupy the space without entering into a sublease either for 10 years or for any lesser period. In the absence of evidence establishing at least a prima facie case than an injustice would be done to the lessor or that there would be inequity if the lessor were not allowed to bring its action and go to trial, leave to bring the action ought not to be granted. There is, in the present case, no evidence showing that there was an expectation on the part of the lessor that the lessee corporation would retain the funds in its hands for any set period of time or any time at all. Nor is there any evidence that there was an expectation that the lessee corporation would grant a lease for a term of 10 years or any other set term beyond the rent-free period, to the law firm or any other person or persons. It is true that the lease contemplated the possibility that the corporation would enter into a lease with the lawyers, for it specified that the lessee could do so. That falls far short of evidencing the existence of an *expectation* that there would be a lease for the entire 10 year period or for any set term longer than the rent-free period and less than 10 years. Nor does the evidence establish any inequality of bargaining power between First Edmonton Place on the one hand and the three lawyers and their corporation on the other, at the time the lease was being negotiated. If there were some circumstances evidencing such inequality of bargaining power, the result might be different.

It is not without significance that the ABCA does provide specific remedies to creditors where, for example, money is paid out of the corporation and the solvency test has not been passed, or where a director contravenes other parts of the Act (such as ss. 113(5), (6) and 240). The relevant provisions are as follows:

113 ...

(5) If money or property of a corporation was paid or distributed to a shareholder or other recipient contrary to section 32, 33, 34, 39, 40, 42, 119, 184 or 234, the corporation, any director or shareholder of the corporation, *or any person who was a creditor of the corporation at the time of payment or distribution*, is entitled to apply to the Court for an order under subsection (6).

(6) On an application under subsection (5), the Court may, if it is satisfied that it is equitable to do so, do any or all of the following:

(a) order a shareholder or other recipient to restore the corporation any money or property that was paid or distributed to him contrary to section 32, 33, 34, 39, 40, 42, 119, 184 or 234;

(b) order the corporation to return or issue shares to a person from whom the corporation has purchased, redeemed or otherwise acquired shares;

(c) make any further order it thinks fit.

. . .

240 If a corporation or any shareholder, director, officer, employee, agent, auditor, trustee, receiver, receiver-manager or liquidator of a corporation contravenes this Act, the regulations, the articles or bylaws or a unanimous shareholder agreement, *a complainant or a creditor of the corporation may*, in addition to any other right he has, apply to the Court for an order directing that person to comply with, or restraining that person from contravening any of those things, and on the application the Court may so order and make any further order it thinks fit. [emphasis added]

In these provisions, creditors are specifically mentioned as persons entitled to apply to the Court for remedies. While these sections do not preclude creditors from applying for other remedies (such as those provided for by ss. 232 and 234), the Legislature has singled out cases in which creditors generally are specifically entitled to protection.

. . .

In deciding who is a "proper person," and whether justice and equity require a particular applicant to be recognized as a "proper person," it is appropriate to bear in mind the purposes of the statutory actions provided for in ss. 232 and 234. To the extent that these actions were intended to protect minority shareholders, Professor Bruce Welling, in *Corporate Law in Canada* (Toronto: Butterworths, 1986), stated at p. 504: "A statutory representative action is the minority shareholder's sword to the majority's twin shields of corporate personality and majority rule." In addition to protecting minority shareholders, the actions provided for by ss. 232 and 234 serve the more general purpose of ensuring managerial accountability. That purpose encompasses protection of the rights of not only minority shareholders but also creditors and even the public in general. It is obvious that by permitting s. 232 and s. 234 actions to be brought by persons other than shareholders, the Legislature intended that the abuse of majority corporate power be capable of remedial action at the invocation of persons other than shareholders.

The derivative action has been characterized as "the most important procedure the law has yet developed to police the internal affairs of corporations" (Rostow, "To Whom and for What Ends is Corporate Management Responsible?" in E.S. Mason, ed., *The Corporation in Modern Society* (1959) at 48). In support of the view that the derivative action should be available to a broad base of applicants is the dominant role which corporations presently play in our society. As stated by Professor Stanley M. Beck in "The Shareholders' Derivative Action" (1974) 52 Can. Bar Rev. 159 at 159-160:

The large corporation, as the dominant economic institution of our time, is particularly being redefined. No longer is it seen as a private institution operating solely for profit or on behalf of and answerable only or its one true constituency, its shareholders. It is realized that it is a public institution in the sense that its major decisions have as significant an impact on the economy as do those of government and that its constituency, like government's, is the entire citizenry whether in the guise of shareholder, worker, consumer, supplier, or simply user and enjoyer of clean air and water.

It is arguable that the modern-day corporation, affecting as it does such a wide variety of persons and interests, must be policed in a manner to protect these other interests. By allowing a derivative action to be brought by a wider group of interested persons, the Legislature has decided that such a procedure is an effective manner in which to enhance managerial accountability by ensuring that a wrong done to a corporation is remedied. While much of the impetus for such a reform may have originated with concern for the social impact of large corporations, no attempt has been made to limit the applicability of the reform to such corporations. In her article already cited, Professor Maloney supported the availability of the derivative action on a wider basis (at 315):

Derivative actions are in effect liability rules designed to act as a deterrent and, as a necessary corollary, create incentives to engage in socially desirable conduct, in this case honest and skilful management. Facilitating such conduct must of course be done in such a manner as to avoid undue interference with managerial decision-making and risk-taking. The desire to maintain an appropriate balance between corporate self-determination and the desire to ensure, from a shareholder (and the public's) perspective, that the directors or majority shareholders do not run roughshod over minority shareholders' rights or abuse the corporate form has produced much of the tension that exists in present day statutory shareholder remedies and in the judicial decisions in this area.

And further at p. 319, she said:

Finally and importantly, the category of applicants should not remain or become static. The changing face of capitalism and the role which corporations play in furthering its aims dictate the necessity of flexibility. As the notion of which interests the corporation is working towards changes, and becomes increasingly sophisticated, so must the pool of applicants change. Any fears regarding floodgate possibilities or limitless applications can be dealt with by the other procedural or substantive requirements.

Powerful as these arguments are, the Legislature has not gone so far as expressly to permit *any* interested person to be a "complainant." However broad the discretion provided for in s. 231(b)(iii) may be, it nevertheless contemplates that a limiting line will be drawn. That line should, in my view, be drawn by application of the criteria which I have enunciated.

Is the Applicant "Acting in Good Faith," and Would the Proposed Action be "in the Interests of the Corporation"?

Even if the applicant were found to be a "complainant," s. 232(2)(b) and (c) require that the complainant "is acting in good faith" and that "it appears to be in the interests of the corporation ... that the action be brought." The respondents contend that these two conditions have not been met in the present case.

These two requirements were commented upon in the Dickerson Report (161), as follows:

By requiring good faith on the part of the complainant this provision precludes private vendettas. And by requiring the complainant to establish that the action is "prima facie in the interest of the corporation" it blocks actions to recover small amounts, particularly actions really instituted to harass or to embarrass directors or officers who have committed an act which, although unwise, is not material.

It may be noted that in the CBCA, as recommended by the Dickerson Report, the requirement is that the action be "prima facie in the interest of the corporation" whereas the ABCA requires that it be established that "it appears to be in the interests of the corporation" that the action be brought. Thus, the ABCA requires satisfaction of a stricter criterion.

Is the "good faith" requirement directed against "private vendettas"? Does this requirement merely require the Court to ensure that the action is not frivolous or vexatious? The latter proposition appears to be supported in several cases, including *Bellman v. Western Approaches Ltd.* (1981), 17 B.L.R. 117, 33 B.C.L.R. 45, 130 D.L.R. 193 (C.A.); *Armstrong v. Gardner* (1978), 20 O.R. (2d) 648 (H.C.); and *Re Marc-Jay Investments Inc. and Levy* (1974), 5 O.R. (2d) 235, 50 D.L.R. (3d) 45 (H.C.).

• • •

In the present case, it is clear that First Edmonton Place is in good faith in seeking the potential return of money paid out by the corporation, in order that the corporation will have assets with which to meet the action of First Edmonton against the corporation for breach of the lease. The proposed action to be brought under s. 232 is not designed to obtain a tactical advantage against the directors. If obtaining a tactical advantage against the directors were the motive, that might constitute lack of good faith (see *Vendova v. Garden House Inn Ltd.*, supra).

• • •

The lessor, in bringing an action on this ground, would be acting in good faith, and if successful, the action would be in the interests of the corporation because, to the extent that there would be recovery from the lawyers, the corporation would be better enabled to meet its liability to the lessor, whatever that might be.

If an Action were Brought under s. 234 on the Ground that the Conduct of the Directors was "Oppressive or Unfairly Prejudicial to" or Unfairly Disregarded "the Interests of any ... Creditor," was the Lessor a "Creditor" at the Time of the Conduct Complained of?

... I turn to the requirement of s. 234(2) that, if leave to commence the action is to be granted, it must be shown that the conducts of the directors was oppressive or unfairly prejudicial to or unfairly disregarded the interests of, inter alia, a "creditor." The applicant must have had an interest as creditor at the time the acts complained of occurred: *R v. Sands Motor Hotel Ltd.*, 28 B.L.R. 122, [1985] 1 W.W.R. 59, [1984] C.T.C. 612, 84 D.T.C. 6464, 36 Sask. R. 45 (Q.B.). The wording of s. 113(5) supports this view, at least with respect to creditors. Section 113(5) gives creditors "at the time of the payment or distribution" relief for payments or distributions contrary to certain provisions of the Act, including s. 234.

At the time of the acts complained of, there was not any rent yet due under the lease. The applicant contends that the lease obligations of the corporation were a present debt at the time of the acts complained of, citing *Re Hulbert & Mayer* (1916), 11 Alta. L.R. 239, [1917] 1 W.W.R. 380, 31 D.L.R. 330 (S.C.). According to *Re Hulbert & Mayer*, the legal liability to pay rent is incurred at time the lease is created. Thus, at the time of the acts complained of, although the corporation did not owe any rent to the applicant, it did have an obligation to the applicant in respect of future rent. Notwithstanding this obligation, it may be that the applicant was not a creditor at the relevant time as its claim was for unliquidated damages. In *Re Porcupine Gold Reef Mining Co.*, [1946] O.R. 45, 27 C.B.R. 216, [1946] 2 D.L.R. 618 at 622 (H.C.), aff'd 28 C.B.R. 105, [1947] O.W.N. 185, [1947] 1 D.L.R. 918 (C.A.), Urquhart J. defined "creditor" as "one to whom a debt is owing—correlative to debtor." In attempting to arrive at a definition for debt," Professor C.R.C. Dunlop, in his work, *Creditor-Debtor Law in Canada* (Toronto: Carswell, 1981), stated, at pp. 19-20:

The above discussion indicates that the word "debt" is not today a term of art with a clear, never-changing denotation. Instead of trying to define a core meaning, it would seem better to agree with the editors of the corpus Juris Secundum that "[the word] takes shades of meaning from the occasion of its use, and colour from accompanying use, and it is used in different statutes and constitutions in senses varying from a very restricted to a very general one." One can say that the most common use of the word "debt" is to describe an obligation to pay a sum certain or a sum readily reducible to a certainty. The obligation may or may not depend on an express or implied contract, depending on the context in which the word is used, but to this writer the essence of the term is that, if there is an obligation to pay a certain or ascertainable sum, the courts should tend not to concern themselves with the precise nature of the cause of action. Claims for unliquidated damages will generally not be describable as debts unless the context suggests otherwise.

• • •

My conclusion is that the word "creditor" as it is used in s. 234 does not include a lessor in respect of rent which is not owing at the time of the acts complained of, and that therefore the applicant could not succeed in its claim in so far as it is based upon the lease.

• • •

In the case of the application under s. 232, the applicant was not a holder of a security or a "creditor" at the time of use of the cash inducement money by the three directors. However, there is some evidence that the cash inducement money was not used for purposes of the corporation and that its use might have been a fraud upon the corporation. If it was a fraud upon the corporation, and if the corporation were entitled to recover the money from the three directors, the applicant may have a genuine interest in advancing the claim to such recovery because the corporation might be liable in damages to the applicant. Therefore, the applicant is in my opinion a proper person to make an application under s. 232 and should be granted leave to bring an action in the name and on behalf of the corporation in respect of the payment of the cash inducement money to or for the benefit of the three lawyers.

Moreover, as for the three lawyers, as directors of the corporation, permitting themselves as lawyers to occupy the leased premises without paying rent or entering into a lease, whether that conduct constitute a wrong to the corporation is a matter that should be tried. Once against, if there was a wrong, the applicant might ultimately stand to benefit from any recovery by the corporation. Therefore, the applicant is in my opinion a proper person to make an application under s. 232 in regard to this head of claim and should be granted leave in the same action to advance a claim in the name and on behalf of the corporation in respect of the occupation of the premises by the directors for their own personal purposes and in respect of the failure of the directors to obtain from themselves personally (or their law firm) a sublease for the term of the lease.

Granting leave to bring the statutory derivative action under s. 232 does not in any way imply that on the basis of the evidence placed before me I am of the view that the action is likely to succeed. As to that, of course, I offer no opinion.

During the course of argument, there was no suggestion that if leave were granted any condition or conditions would be appropriate. If counsel for the respondents wishes to make any submission in that regard now that leave has been granted, he should make this known to me without delay.

In the case of the application under s. 234, leave to bring an action in regard to either claim is denied because the applicant was not a creditor at the time of the act or conduct complained of.

Costs may be spoken to.

Application allowed in part.

NOTES

1) Are you satisfied with the balance that McDonald J. has struck between the need for management to have room to manage the company and his view that the oppression remedy should protect a creditor's "legitimate expectations"? Is this balance consistent with the approach taken in the decision seen above in *KeepRite*?

2) Has McDonald J. fashioned a test that is sufficiently precise? After all, how is a board to know what a creditor's expectations may be if not by looking at the terms of its contract with the debtor? Should a board not be able to rely on the terms of whatever contractual arrangement is in fact in place with a creditor? Why should corporations law protect a creditor that has not had the good sense to define the terms of its relationship with a debtor in writing? Or is it legitimate to say that the courts should be able to exercise a broader equitable jurisdiction to monitor creditor-debtor relationships? Should we distinguish between creditors that have entered into contractual relationships with a debtor corporation and those who could not have been expected to do so? One's vision of the corporation will again prove extremely influential in answering these questions: if one sees shareholders as the only constituency that a board is there to serve, one is more likely to conclude that creditors should rely on contractual negotiation to protect their interests; if, on the other hand, one considers that a board must take into account the interests of a broader range of constituencies, one may have more sympathy for McDonald J.'s approach.

3) Is McDonald J.'s conclusion that the landlord was not a creditor at the time of the conduct complained of entirely convincing? Is the result (no leave to proceed with the oppression action, but leave to proceed with the derivative action) satisfactory? Given the plaintiff's ability to use the derivative action is there any reason to retain the oppression remedy as a part of a statute like the Business Corporations Act (Alberta)?

4) Should courts be less ready to find a fiduciary duty where the complainant is in a clear contractual nexus with the corporation? From an economic perspective, fiduciary duties are a gap-filling device which might usefully realign management incentives in an implicit contract with shareholders. For non-shareholder constituencies, however, the gap-filling might not require a finding of fiduciary duties. When the non-shareholder is in a contractual nexus with the firm, such as the landlord in *First Edmonton Place*, the gap-filling might instead take the form of finding an implied term in an express contract. The difference might not seem to matter, since labelling someone a fiduciary does not tell one what his duties are. However, all parties appear to assume that semantics counts, and that good faith norms are levered up when fiduciary language may properly be used. For contrasting views on this problem, see Jonathan Macey & Geoffrey Miller, *Corporate Stakeholders: A Contractual Perspective*, 43 U. of Toronto L.J. 401 (1993); Jacob Ziegel, *Creditors as Corporate Stakeholders: The Quiet Revolution—An Anglo-Canadian Perspective*, 43 U. of Toronto L.J. 511 (1993).

5) The following case takes us one step further: from creditors to employee shareholders.

West v. Edson Packaging Machinery Ltd.
Ontario Court (General Division)
(1993), 16 O.R. (3d) 24

CAVARZAN J.: —These are applications under rules 14.05(3) and 38 of the Rules of Civil Procedure and under ss. 248 and 249 of the Ontario Business Corporations Act, R.S.O. 1990, c. B.16, for oppression remedies. Orders are sought directing the respondents or either of them to purchase all of the common shares of Edson Holdings owned by the applicants, requiring the respondents to pay the interest expense incurred by the applicants to purchase those shares, appointing an expert evaluator to value those shares, and directing the respondent, Edson Packaging, to pay to the applicants, on an interim basis, reasonable legal fees and disbursements. In the event that the trial of an issue is directed, an order is requested that the affidavits filed in these applications and transcripts of all cross-examinations be constituted the pleadings and discoveries, and that steps be taken to facilitate a speedy trial.

The applicants were both management employees of Edson Packaging who were dismissed on September 6, 1992. West was the plant manager; he was hired in that capacity on March 27, 1989. Dallas was the sales manager and vice-president of sales and marketing from April 1, 1987. In June 1990, each of the applicants purchased 1,150 common shares of Edson Holdings in the following circumstances.

Edson Holdings owns 100 percent of the issued shares of Edson Packaging. Trevar Gibson is the president of both respondents and owner of 54 per cent of the shares of Edson Holdings. Edson Holdings is described in an affidavit by John Dallas as a privately held corporation with a history of ensuring that the retiring employees of Edson Packaging, a wholly owned subsidiary of Edson Holdings, always received fair market value for the shares they held in Edson Holdings. This history is based upon events associated with three former employees: William Johnston, a former manager of engineering who resigned in 1988; Jim Sinclair, who retired in 1990; and James Howes, who sold his shares in June 1990, in anticipation of retirement in 1991. Trevar Gibson and Jim Sinclair purchased Johnston's 3,500 shares. Jim Sinclair's shares were purchased by Edson Holdings, and James Howes' 3,500 shares were purchased by the applicants and two other members of Edson Packaging's management group.

The applicants allege that Trevar Gibson made it clear to them in a series of meetings in early 1990 that the purchase of these shares would be a show of support for him personally as well as for the company, that a shareholders' agreement would be entered into with the purchasers of these shares, and that Edson Holdings would purchase back the shares of any former employee when he left the company. In essence, what is alleged is a "bait and switch" involving undue pressure by Trevar Gibson on the applicants to purchase the Howes shares, followed by a refusal to enter into a shareholders' agreement and a refusal to buy back the shares when the applicants were dismissed.

The position of the applicants is that, by his statements, Gibson engendered in the applicants a reasonable expectation that a shareholders' agreement would be executed within six months of the applicants' purchase of the Howes shares and, irrespective of the shareholders' agreement, Edson Holdings or other shareholders in Edson Holdings would purchase these shares upon the death or termination of the applicants. The oppression remedies sought are based on the non-fulfilment of these reasonable expectations on the part of the applicants.

Trevar Gibson denies that there was ever a firm undertaking to enter into a shareholders' agreement. He acknowledges that the applicants indicated to him that they would like a "buy-back" of the shares, but he advised them that this was not possible. Gibson concedes that he did indicate at one time that if someone purchased Jim Sinclair's shares and wanted a shareholders' agreement, he (Gibson) would make sure that they were part of any future agreement. Gibson maintains that he had always said, both before and after June 1990, that there would not be a repurchase mechanism in the shareholders' agreement. Gibson maintains that the applicants purchased the Howes' shares from another shareholder in a private transaction and that neither he nor the corporation was a direct part of those transactions.

It is the position of the respondents that these applications are improperly constituted and ought to be dismissed or, in the alternative, that the trial of an issue be directed. The respondents argue that inasmuch as the applications are based upon s. 248 of the Ontario Business Corporations Act, they are not properly constituted because the applicants do not come within the definition of "complainant" in s. 245. They argue, as well, that if the applicants rely upon rule 14.05(3) of the Rules of Civil Procedure, then this is not a matter where it is unlikely that there will be any material facts in dispute (rule 14.05(3)(h)). ...

Mr. Keesmaat, for the respondents, submitted that since the applicants were not shareholders at the time when the alleged coercion took place and when the alleged misrepresentations were made, the applicants lack status to bring an application for an oppression remedy under s. 248. ...

The course of conduct which the applicants maintain gave rise to certain reasonable expectations on their part covers a period of several months, both preceding and following their purchase of Howes' shares in June of 1990. This, in my opinion, is sufficient to qualify them as "complainants" under the Act. They are minority shareholders in Edson Holdings and have been since June of 1990. In addition, I would respectfully adopt the reasoning of D.C. McDonald J. of the Alberta Court of Queen's Bench, who considered the parallel provisions of the Alberta Business Corporations Act, 1981, S.A. 1981, c. B-15, in *First Edmonton Place Ltd. v. 315888 Alberta Ltd.* (1988), 60 Alta. L.R. (2d) 122, 40 B.L.R. 28. At p. 150, s. 231(b)(iii) of the Alberta statute is considered:

Under s. 231(b)(iii) a person may be a "complainant" if he is a person "who, in the discretion of the Court, is a proper person to make an application under this Part."

This is not so much a definition as a grant to the court of a broad power to do justice and equity in circumstances of a particular case, where a person who otherwise would not be a "complainant" ought to be permitted to bring an action under s. 232 or s. 234 to right a wrong done to the corporation which would not otherwise be righted, or to obtain compensation himself or itself where his or its interests have suffered from oppression by the majority controlling the corporation or have been unfairly prejudiced or unfairly disregarded, and the applicant is a "security holder, creditor, director or officer."

At p. 152, D.C. McDonald J. states that there are at least two circumstances in which justice and equity would entitle one to be regarded as "a proper person." The first is where the act or conduct complained of constituted using the corporation as a vehicle for committing a fraud upon the applicant. The second is where the act or conduct complained of constituted a breach of the underlying expectation of the applicant arising from the circumstances in which the applicant's relationship with the corporation arose. Although these observations were made by D.C. McDonald J. in contemplating the claim of a creditor of the corporation to be "a proper person" to make an application, I do not understand that reasoning to be limited to creditors of the corporation. I conclude, therefore, that the applicants in this case would qualify as "proper persons" under the Act if their version of the facts were accepted by the court.

This interpretation of "complainant" under the Act harmonizes with the broad and liberal interpretation given by the courts in both Alberta and Ontario to the statutory remedy against oppression; see *Ferguson v. Imax Systems Corp.* (1983), 43 O.R. (2d) 128 at p. 137, 150 D.L.R. (3d) 718 (C.A.), per Brooke J.A.; *Abraham v. Inter Wide Investments Ltd.* (1985), 51 O.R. (2d) 460 at p. 468, 20 D.L.R. (4th) 267 (H.C.J.), per Griffiths J.D.C. McDonald J. in *First Edmonton Place Ltd.*, supra, states at p. 140 that:

The introduction of a statutory remedy against oppression and unfair prejudice is a deliberate departure from the policy of judicial non-intervention in corporate affairs. Section 234 "casts the court in the role of an active 'arbiter of business policy' " (Shapira, at p. 137). It is drawn in very broad terms and as remedial legislation should be given a liberal interpretation in favour of the complainant: *Re Abraham and Inter Wide Invt. Ltd.* [supra]; *Stech v. Davies*, 53 Alta. L.R. (2d) 373, [1987] 5 W.W.R. 563, 80 A.R. 298 (Q.B.).

• • •

In my opinion, this dispute cannot be fairly and satisfactorily resolved through judicial intervention without the benefit of a trial. Accordingly, an order will issue converting these applications into actions. These actions should also be expedited; and order will issue directing that the affidavits filed and the transcripts of cross-examinations thereon and any other examinations be constituted the pleadings and discoveries in the action, and that the actions be placed on the list for the next available assignment court at Hamilton for an early trial date. ...

NOTES

1) In your view, were the plaintiffs really complaining in their capacity as shareholders? Or were they complaining in their capacity as former management employees? Put another way, was the complaint one about their "legitimate expectations" as shareholders or as employees who had agreed that as part of the employment relationship they would purhase shares that were to be repurchased upon the termination of their employment?

2) The definition of "complainant" is open-ended and employees will quite often be able to characterize themselves as being not only employees but also shareholders (as in *West v. Edson*) or creditors (see *Tavares v. Deskin* (February 1, 1993) Ont. Ct. of Justice, unreported: plaintiff alleging wrongful dismissal was granted leave to commence an

action for relief from oppression). In this way, an employee may argue that she is a proper person to bring an application and that she is entitled to relief under the oppression remedy. Should an employee have to proceed in this rather circuitous manner or should the oppression remedy be amended to say quite simply that an employee may bring an application under the oppression remedy? Would this open the floodgates to endless claims by employees? Should we prevent business corporations statutes from becoming a vehicle for dealing with issues that you might more typically see raised through labour law, or would this merely be an exercise in reinforcing an unnecessarily artificial distinction?

III. WINDING UP

The dissolution of a corporation involves the surrender of the corporate charter and the termination of the firm as a separate entity. Dissolution may occur either voluntarily, at the instance of directors, or involuntarily. While involuntary dissolution usually arises as a consequence of creditor displeasure, shareholders may seek to dissolve the firm where (1) an event has occurred that entitles the complaining shareholder to demand dissolution under a unanimous shareholder agreement (s. 214(1)(b)(i)); (2) it is "just and equitable" that the firm should be wound up (s. 214(1)(b)(ii)); or (3) the conditions for granting a s. 241 oppression remedy have been met (s. 214(1)(a)).

The following case illustrates the kind of situation in which a party may seek to have a corporation involuntarily wound up.

Ebrahimi v. Westbourne Galleries Ltd.
House of Lords
[1973] A.C. 360

LORD WILBERFORCE: My Lords, the issue in this appeal is whether the respondent company Westbourne Galleries Ltd. should be wound up by the court on the petition of the appellant who is one of the three shareholders, the personal respondents being the other two. The company is a private company which carries on business as dealers in Persian and other carpets. It was formed in 1958 to take over a business founded by the second respondent (Mr. Nazar). It is a fact of cardinal importance that since about 1945 the business had been carried on by the appellant and Mr. Nazar as partners, equally sharing the management and the profits. When the company was formed, the signatories to its memorandum were the appellant and Mr. Nazar and they were appointed its first directors. Of its issued share capital, 500 shares of £1 each were issued to each subscriber and it was found by the learned judge, after the point had been contested by Mr. Nazar, that Mr. Ebrahimi paid up his shares out of his own money. Soon after the company's formation the third respondent (Mr. George Nazar) was made a director, and each of the two original shareholders transferred to him 100 shares, so that at all materials times Mr. Ebrahimi held 400 shares, Mr. Nazar 400 and Mr. George Nazar 200. The Nazars, father and son, thus had a majority of the votes in general meeting. Until the dispute all three gentlemen remained directors.

The company made good profits, all of which were distributed as directors' remuneration. No dividends have ever been paid, before or after the petition was presented.

On August 12, 1969, an ordinary resolution was passed by the company in general meeting, by the votes of Mr. Nazar and Mr. George Nazar, removing Mr. Ebrahimi from the office of director, a resolution which was effective in law by virtue of section 184 of the Companies Act 1948 and article 96 of Part 1 of Table A. Shortly afterwards the appellant presented his petition to the court.

This petition was based in the first place upon section 210 of the Companies Act 1948, the relief sought under this section being an order that Mr. Nazar and his son be ordered to purchase the appellant's shares in the company. In the alternative it sought an order for the winding up of the company. The petition contained allegations of oppression and misconduct against Mr. Nazar which were fully explored at the hearing before Plowman J. [1970] 1 W.L.R. 1378. The learned judge found that some were unfounded and others unproved and that such complaint as was made out did not amount to such a course of oppressive conduct as to justify an order under section 210. However, he made an order for the winding up of the company under the "just and equitable" provision. I shall later specify the grounds on which he did so. The appellant did not appeal against the rejection of his case under section 210 and this House is not concerned with it. The Company and the individual respondents appealed against the order for winding up and this was set aside by the Court of Appeal. The appellant now seeks to have it restored.

My Lords, the petition was brought under section 222(f) of the Companies Act 1948, which enables a winding up order to be made if "the court is of the opinion that it is just and equitable that the company should be wound up." This power has existed in our company law in unaltered form since the first major Act, the Companies Act 1862. Indeed, it antedates that statute since it existed in the Joint Stock Companies Winding Up Act 1848. For some 50 years, following a pronouncement by Lord Cottenham L.C. [*Ex parte Spackman* (1849) 1 Mac. & G. 170, 174] in 1849, the words "just and equitable" were interpreted so as only to include matters *ejusdem generis* as the preceding clauses of the section, but there is now ample authority for discarding this limitation. There are two other restrictive interpretations which I mention to reject. First, there has been a tendency to create categories or headings under which cases must be brought if the clause is to apply. This is wrong. Illustrations may be used, but general words should remain general and not be reduced to the sum of particular instances. Secondly, it has been suggested, and urged upon us, that (assuming the petitioner is shareholder and not a creditor) the words must be confined to such circumstances as affect him in his capacity as shareholder. I see no warrant for this either. No doubt, in order to present a petition, he must qualify as a shareholder, but I see no reason for preventing him from relying upon any circumstances of justice or equity which affect him in his relations with the company, or, in a case such as the present, with the other shareholders.

One other signpost is significant. The same words "just and equitable" appear in the Partnership Act 1892, section 25, as a ground for dissolution of a partnership and no doubt the considerations which they reflect formed part of the common law of partnership before its codification. The importance of this is to provide a bridge between cases under section 222(f) of the Act of 1948 and the principles of equity developed in relation to partnerships.

The winding up order was made following a doctrine which has developed in the courts since the beginning of this century. As presented by the appellant, and in substance accepted by the learned judge, this was that in a case such as this the members of the company are in substance partners, or quasi-partners, and that a winding up may be ordered if such facts are shown as could justify a dissolution of partnership between them. The common use of the words "just and equitable" in the company and partnership law supports this approach. You Lordships were invited by the respondents' counsel to restate the principle on which this provision ought to be used; it has not been previously considered by this House. The main line of his submission was to suggest that too great a use of the partnership analogy has been made; that in the case of a company, the rights of its members are governed by the articles of association which have contractual force; that the court has no power or at least ought not to dispense parties from observing their contracts; that, in particular, when one member has been excluded from the directorate, or management, under powers expressly conferred by the Companies Act and the articles, an order for winding up, whether on the partnership analogy or under the just and equitable provision, should be made. Alternatively, it was argued that before the making of such an order could be considered the petitioner must show and prove that the exclusion was not made by *bona fide* in the interests of the company.

My Lords, I must first make some examination of the authorities in order to see how far they support the respondents' propositions and, if they do not, how far they rest upon a principle of which this House should disapprove. I will say at once that, over a period of some 60 years, they show a considerable degree of consistency, and that such criticism as may be made relates rather to the application of accepted principle to the facts than to the statements of principles themselves.

The real starting point is the Scottish decision in *Symington v. Symington's Quarries Ltd.* (1905) 8 F. 121. There had been a partnership business carried on by two brothers who decided to transfer it to a private limited company. Each brother was to hold half the shares except for a small holding for a third brother to hold balance for voting. A resolution was passed in general meeting by the votes of one brother together with other members having nominal interests that he should be sole director. The other two brothers petitioned for a winding up under the just and equitable provision and the court so ordered. The reasons for so doing, given by some of their Lordships of the First Division, are expressed in terms of lost substratum or deadlock—words clearly used in a general rather than a technical sense. The judgment of Lord M'Laren, which has proved to be the most influential as regards later cases, puts the ground more generally. He points out, at p. 130, that the company was not formed by appeal to the public: it was a domestic company, the only real partners being the three brothers:

In such case it is quite obvious that all reasons that apply to the dissolution of private companies, on the grounds of incompatibility between the views or methods of the partners, would be applicable in terms to the division amongst the shareholders of this company. ...

In England, the leading authority is the Court of Appeal's decision in *In re Yenidje Tobacco Co. Ltd.* [1916] 2 Ch. 426. This was a case of two equal director shareholders, with an arbitration provision in the articles, between whom a state of deadlock came into existence. It has often been argued, and was so in this House, that its authority is limited to true deadlock cases. I could, in any case, not be persuaded that the words "just and equitable" need or can be confined to such situations. But Lord Cozens-Hardy M.R. clearly puts his judgment on wider grounds. Whether there is deadlock or not, he says at p. 432, the circumstances

are such that we ought to apply, if necessary, the analogy of the partnership law and to say that this company is now in a state which could not have been contemplated by the parties when the company was formed. ...

Warrington L.J. adopts the same principle, treating deadlock as an example only of the reasons why it would be just and equitable to wind the company up.

In 1924, these authorities were reviewed, approved and extended overseas by the Judicial Committee of the Privy Council in an appeal from the West Indian Court of Appeal (Barbados), *Loch v. John Blackwood Ltd.* [1924] A.C. 783. The judgment of the Board delivered by Lord Shaw of Dunfermline clearly endorses, if not enlarges, the width to be given to the just and equitable clause. The case itself was of a domestic company and was not one of deadlock. One of the directors had given grounds for loss of confidence in his probity and (a matter echoed in the present case) had shown that he regarded the business as his own. His Lordship quotes with approval from the judgments of Lord M'Laren in *Symington v. Symington's Quarries Ltd.*, 8 F. 121 and of Lord Cozens-Hardy M.R. in *In re Yenidje Tobacco Co. Ltd.* [1916] 2 Ch. 426.

I note in passing the Scottish case of *Thomson v. Drysdale*, 1925 S.C. 311 where a winding up was ordered under the just and equitable clause at the instance of a holder of one share against the only other shareholder who held 1,501 shares, clearly not a case of deadlock, and come to *In re Cuthbert Cooper & Sons Ltd.* [1937] Ch. 392, a case which your Lordships must consider. The respondents relied on this case which carries the authority of Simonds J. as restricting the force of the just and equitable provision. The company was clearly a family company, the capital in which belonged to a father and his two elder sons. After the death of the father leaving his shares to his younger sons and appointing them his executors his elder sons, exercising the powers given to directors by the articles, refused to register the executors as shareholders and dismissed them from employment. The executor's petition for winding up the company was dismissed. My Lords, with respect for the eminent judge who decided it, I must doubt the correctness of this. Whether on the facts stated a case of justice and equity was made out is no doubt partly a question of fact on which, even though my own view is clear enough, I should respect the opinion of the trial judge; but, this matter apart, I am unable to agree as to the undue emphasis he puts on the contractual rights arising from the articles, over the equitable principles which might be derived from partnership law, for in the result the latter seem to have been entirely excluded in the former's favour. I think that the case should no longer be regarded as of authority.

There are three recent cases which I should mention since they have figured in the judgments below. *In re Lundie Brothers Ltd.* [1965] 1 W.L.R. 1051 was, like the present, a decision of Plowman J. This was a case where the petitioner, one of three shareholders and directors, was excluded from participation in the management and from directors' remuneration. Plowman J. applying partnership principles made a winding up order under the just and equitable clause. If that decision was right it assists the present appellant. The Court of Appeal in the present case disagreed with it and overruled it, in so far as it related to a winding up. The respondent argues that this was the first case where exclusion of a working director, valid under the articles, had been treated as a ground for winding up under the just and equitable clause and that as such it was an unjustifiable innovation.

In re Expanded Plugs Ltd. [1966] 1 W.L.R. 514 was, on the other hand, approved by the Court of Appeal in the present case. The case itself is a paradigm of obscure forensic tactics and, as such, of merely curious interest; its only importance lies in the statement, contained in the judgment, at p. 523, that since the relevant decisions were carried out within the framework of the articles the petitioner must show that they were not carried out *bona fide* in the interests of the company. I shall return, in so far as it limits the scope of the just and equitable provision, to this principle but I should say at once that I disagree with it.

In *In re K/9 Meat Supplies (Guildford) Ltd.* [1966] 1 W.L.R. 1112 there was a company of three shareholder/directors one of whom became bankrupt; the petitioner was his trustee in bankruptcy. It was contended that the company was a quasi-partnership and that since section 33 of Partnership Act 1890 provides for dissolution on the bankruptcy of one of the partners a winding up order on this ground should be made. Pennycuick J. rejected this argument on the ground that, since the "partnership" had been transformed into a company and since the articles gave no automatic right to a winding up on bankruptcy, bankruptcy of one member was not a ground for winding up of itself. He then proceeded to consider whether the just and equitable provision should be applied. In my opinion, this procedure was correct and I need not express an opinion whether, on the facts, it was right to refuse an order.

[His Lordship reviewed several more cases which in general were hospitable to the notion that exclusion of the petitioner from management could be a factor making it "just and equitable" that a company be wound up.]

My Lords, in my opinion these authorities represent a sound and rational development of the law which should be endorsed. The foundation of it all lies in the words "just and equitable" and, if there is any respect in which some of the cases may be open to criticism, it is that the courts may sometimes have been too timorous in giving them full force. The words are a recognition of the fact that a limited company is more than a mere legal entity, with a personality in law of its own: that there is room in company law for recognition of the fact that behind it, or amongst it, there are individuals, with rights, expectations and obligations *inter se* which are not necessarily submerged in the company structure. That structure is deemed by the Companies Act and by the articles of association by which shareholders agree to be bound. In most companies and in most contexts, this definition is sufficient and exhaustive, equally so whether the company is large or small. The "just and equitable" provision does not, as the respondents suggest, entitle one party to disregard the obligation he assumes by entering a company, nor the court to dispense him from it. It does, as equity always does, enable the court to subject the exercise of legal rights to equitable considerations; considerations, that is, of a personal character arising between one individual and another, which may make it unjust, or inequitable, to insist on legal rights, or to exercise them in a particular way.

It would be impossible, and wholly undesirable, to define the circumstances in which these considerations may arise. Certainly the fact that a company is a small one, or a private company, is not enough. There are very many of these where the association is a purely commercial one, of which it can safely be said that the basis of association is adequately and exhaustively laid down in the articles. The superimposition of equitable considerations requires something more, which typically may include one, or probably more, of the following elements: (i) an association formed or continued on the basis of a personal relationship, involving mutual confidence—this element will often be found where a pre-existing partnership has been converted into a limited company; (ii) an agreement, or understanding, that all, or some (for there may be "sleeping" members), of the shareholders shall participate in the conduct of the business; (iii) restriction upon the transfer of the members' interest in the company—so that if confidence is lost, or one member is removed from management, he cannot take out his stake and go elsewhere.

It is these, and analogous, factors which may bring into play the just and equitable clause, and they do so directly, through the force of the words themselves. To refer, as so many of the cases do, to "quasi-partnerships" or "in substance partnerships" may be convenient but may also be confusing. It may be convenient because it is the law of partnership which has developed the conceptions of probity, good faith and mutual confidence, and the remedies where these are absent, which become relevant once such factors as I have mentioned are found to exist: the words "just and equitable" sum these up in the law of partnership itself. And in many, but not necessarily all, cases there has been a pre-existing partnership the obligations of which it is reasonable to suppose continue to underlie the new company structure. But the expressions may be confusing if they obscure, or deny, the fact that the parties (possibly former partners) are now co-members in a company, who have accepted, in law, new obligations. A company, however small, however domestic, is a company not a partnership or even a quasi-partnership and it is through the just and equitable clause that obligations, common to partnership relations, may come in.

My Lords, this is an expulsion case, and I must briefly justify the application in such cases of the just and equitable clause. The question is, as always, whether it is equitable to allow one (or two) to make use of his legal rights to the prejudice of his associate(s). The law of companies recognises the right, in many ways, to remove a director from the board. Section 184 of the Companies Act 1948 confers this right upon the company in general meeting whatever the articles may say. Some articles may prescribe other methods: for example, a governing director may have the power to remove (compare *In re Wondoflex Textiles Pty. Ltd.* [1951] V.L.R. 458). And quite apart from removal powers, there are normally provisions for retirement of directors by rotation so that their reselection can be opposed and defeated by a majority, or even by a casting vote. In all these ways a particular director-member may find himself no longer a director, through removal, or non-re-election: this situation he must normally accept, unless he undertakes the burden of proving fraud or *mala*. The just and equitable provision nevertheless comes to his assistance if he can point to, and prove, some special underlying obligation of his fellow member(s) in good faith, or confidence, that so long as the business continues he shall be entitled to management participation, an obligation so basic that, if broken, the conclusion must be that the association must be dissolved. And the principles on which he may do so are those worked out by the courts in partnership cases where there has been exclusion from management (see *Const. v. Harris* [1824] Tur. & Rus. 496, 525) even where under the partnership agreement there is a power of expulsion (see *Blisset v. Daniel* (1853) 10 Hare 493; *Lindley on Partnership*, 13th ed. (1971), pp. 331, 595).

I come to the facts of this case. It is apparent enough that a potential basis for a winding up order under the just and equitable clause existed. The appellant after a long association in partnership, during which he had an equal share in the management, joined in the formation of the company. The inference must be indisputable that he, and Mr. Nazar, did so on the basis that the character of the association would, as a matter of personal relation and good faith, remain the same. He was removed from his directorship under a power valid in law. Did he establish a case which, if he had remained in a partnership with a term providing for expulsion, would have justified an order for dissolution? This was the essential question for the judge. Plowman J. dealt with the issue in a brief paragraph in which he said [1970] 1 W.L.R. 1378, 1389:

... while no doubt the petitioner was lawfully removed, in the sense that he ceased in law to be a director, it does not follow that in removing him the respondents did not do him a wrong. In my judgment, they did do him a wrong, in the sense that it was an abuse of power and a breach of the good faith which partners owe to each other to exclude one of them from all participation in the business upon which they have embarked on the basis that all should participate in its management. The main justification put forward for removing him was that he was perpetually complaining, but the faults were not all on one side and, in my judgment, this is not sufficient justification. For these reasons, in my judgment, the petitioner, therefore, has made out a case for a winding up order.

Reading this in the context of the judgment as a whole, which had dealt with the specific complaints of one side against the other, I take it as a finding that the respondents were not entitled, in justice and equity, to make use of their legal powers of expulsion and that, in accordance with the principles of such cases as *Basset v. Daniel*, 10 Hare 493, the only just and equitable course was to dissolve the association. To my mind, two factors strongly support this. First, Mr. Nazar made it perfectly clear that he did not regard Mr. Ebrahimi as a partner, but did regard him as an employee. But there was no possible doubt as to Mr. Ebrahimi's status throughout, so that Mr. Nazar's refusal to recognize it amounted, in effect, to a repudiation of the relationship. Secondly, Mr. Ebrahimi, through ceasing to be a director, lost his right to share in the profits through directors' remuneration, retaining only the chance of receiving dividends as a minority shareholder. It is true that an assurance was given in evidence that the previous practice (of not paying dividends) would not be continued, but the fact remains that Mr. Ebrahimi was thenceforth at the mercy of the Messrs. Nazar as to what he should receive out of the profits and when. He was, moreover, unable to dispose of his interest without the consent of the Nazars. All these matters lead only to the conclusion that the right course was to dissolve the association by winding up.

I must deal with one final point which was much relied on by the Court of Appeal. It was said that the removal was, according to the evidence of Mr. Nazar, *bona fide* in the interests of the company; that Mr. Ebrahimi had not shown the contrary; that he ought to do so or to demonstrate that no reasonable man could think that his removal was in the company's interest. This formula "*bona fide* in the interests of the company" is one that is relevant in certain contexts of company law and I do not doubt that in many cases decisions have to be left to majorities or directors to take which the courts must assume had this basis. It may, on the other hand, become little more than an alibi for a refusal to consider the merits of the case, and in a situation such as this it seems to have little meaning other than "in the interests of the majority." Mr. Nazar may well have persuaded himself, quite genuinely, that the company would be better off without Mr. Ebrahimi, but if Mr. Ebrahimi disputed this, or thought the same with reference to Mr. Nazar, what prevails is simply the majority view. To confine the application of the just and equitable clause to proved cases of *mala fides* would be negative to the generality of the words. It is because I do not accept this that I feel myself obliged to differ from the Court of Appeal. I would allow the appeal and restore the judgment of Plowman J. I propose that the individual respondents pay the appellant's costs here and in the Court of Appeal.

LORD CROSS OF CHELSEA: ... What the minority shareholder in cases of this sort really wants is not to have the company wound up—which may prove an unsatisfactory remedy—but to be paid a proper price for his shareholding. With this in mind Parliament provided by section 210 of the Companies Act 1948 that if a member of a company could show that the company's affairs were being conducted in a manner oppressive to some of the members including himself, that the facts proved would justify the making of a winding up order under the "just and equitable" clause but that to wind up the company would unfairly prejudice the "oppressed" members the court could (inter alia) make an order for the purchase of the shares of those members by other members or by the company. To give the court jurisdiction under this section the petitioner must show both that the conduct of the majority is "oppressive" and also that it affects him in his capacity as a shareholder. Mr. Ebrahimi was unable to establish either of these preconditions. But the jurisdiction to wind up under section 222(t) continues to exist as an independent remedy and I have no doubt that the Court of Appeal was right in rejecting the submissions of the respondents to the effect that a petitioner cannot obtain an order under that subsection any more than under section 210 unless he can show that his position as a shareholder has been worsened by the action of which he complains. The facts of this case are set out in detail in the judgment of Plowman J. and I need not repeat them. The essence of the matter is that Mr. Nazar and Mr. Ebrahimi had been carrying on business as partners at will in equal shares; that the business was transferred to the company in which each had 40 per cent of the capital and Nazar's son George the remaining 20 per cent; that it was not contemplated that any dividends would be paid but was contemplated that the profits of the company should be distributed by way of director's fees; and that the result of Mr. Ebrahimi's removal from the directorship was that instead of his having a share in the management of the business and an income of some £3,000 a year he was excluded from the management and deprived of any share in the profits save such dividend as might be paid on his shares if the Nazars thought fit to declare a dividend. The Court of Appeal held that Mr. Ebrahimi could not obtain a winding up order under the "just and equitable" clause unless he could show that the Nazars had not exercised the power to remove him from his directorship "*bona fide* in the interests of the company" or that their grounds for exercising the power were such that no reasonable man could think that the removal was in the interest of the company. With all respect to them I cannot agree that this is an appropriate test to apply. If one assumes that the company is going to remain in existence it may very well be that a reasonable man would say that it was in the interest of the company that Mr. Ebrahimi should cease to be a director. "These two men," he might say, "are hopelessly at logger-heads. If the business is to prosper one or other must go and the company is likely to do better without Mr. Ebrahimi than without Mr. Nazar." But these considerations have not, to my mind, anything to do with the question whether in the circumstances it is right that the company should continue in existence if Mr. Ebrahimi wishes it to be wound up. The argument upon which counsel for the respondent chiefly relied in support of the decision of the Court of Appeal was quite different. Mr. Ebrahimi, he said, consented to the conversion of the partnership into a limited company. Even though he became, because George Nazar was taken in, only a minority shareholder he could have safeguarded his position by procuring the insertion in the articles of a provision "weighting" the voting power of his shares on any question touching his retention of office as director: see *Bushell v. Faith* [1970] A.C. 1099. He must, therefore, be taken to have accepted the risk that if he and Mr. Nazar fell out he would be at Mr. Nazar's mercy. There might be force in this argument if there was any evidence to show that the minds of the parties were directed to the point; but there is no such evidence and the probability is that no one gave a moment's thought to the change in relative strength of their respective positions brought about by the conversion of the partnership into a company. It was not suggested that Mr. Ebrahimi had been guilty of any misconduct such as would justify one partner in expelling another under an expulsion clause contained in partnership articles. All that happened was that without one being more to blame than the other the two could no longer work together in harmony. Had no company been formed Mr. Ebrahimi could have had the partnership wound up and though Mr. Nazar and his son were entitled in law to oust him from his directorship and deprive him of his income they could only do so subject to Mr. Ebrahimi's right to obtain equitable relief in the form of a winding up order under section 222(t). I would, therefore, allow the appeal.

[VISCOUNT DILHORNE, LORD PEARSON and LORD SALMON agreed that the appeal should be allowed.]

Just and Equitable Winding Up. Involuntary dissolution is clearly a remedy of desperation, though pulling the trigger is unlikely to lead to the withdrawal of the firm's productive facilities. Instead, the remaining shareholders are likely to decide to continue it under the form of a new corporation so long as going concern value exceeds liquidation value. However, winding up petitions are frequently resisted, often very strenuously. One reason for this is that the dissolution of the old firm and reincorporation of the new one is not treated as a roll-over for the purposes of the Canadian Income Tax

Act, so that a duty to pay tax on any capital gain will arise. In addition, the remaining shareholders may themselves be unwilling to purchase the minority shareholder's interest at a price to be determined by the court. The uncertainty with respect to the judicial valuation of the shares will itself impose costs, and the remaining shareholders may in addition wish to avoid concentrating the better part of their wealth in a single firm.

The concern over distribution policy that arose in *Ebrahimi* is one that frequently forms the basis of allegations of unfair dealing. Because of tax considerations, investors in a close corporation often prefer to receive distributions in the form of salaries or directors' fees rather than as dividends. If this reduces the net tax burden, all investors will prefer to commit to this policy. But then the termination of a director's or employee's services may pose special problems. If a majority of shareholders might ordinarily remove a director without cause under CBCA s. 109, different considerations may apply in a case like *Ebrahimi*. Granting winding up remedies in such cases is functionally equivalent to providing directors with the protection of a buy-sell agreement in an action for wrongful dismissal. What would have been the result in *Ebrahimi* if the Nazars had excluded Ebrahimi as a director but had simultaneously caused the corporation to change the distribution policy and to begin paying dividends? If the partnership analogy is applied, Ebrahimi had a right to participate in management and not just in profits. But if, as Lord Cross implied, the parties simply could no longer work together in the corporation, then it was in the best interests of the firm to remove Ebrahimi.

What if Ebrahimi had become senile? His removal as a director would have been justified under any standard, but his income would then have been cut off if the corporation had continued to pursue the payout policy that was entirely to his satisfaction when healthy. Would it have been oppressive under CBCA s. 241 if the corporation had not changed this policy in the light of Ebrahimi's changed situation? A refusal to alter the terms of a unanimous shareholder agreement in changed circumstances was not found oppressive in *Nelkin v. H.J.R. Realty Corp.*, 255 N.E.2d 713 (N.Y. 1969). The tenants in a small office building in New York City formed H.J.R. to purchase the building from the landlord. Because each of H.J.R.'s shareholders was either a tenant in the building or financially interested in the tenant, it was unanimously agreed among the shareholders that H.J.R. should charge a break-even rather than a market value rental to all tenants affiliated with an H.J.R. shareholder. The arrangement worked satisfactorily for many years, but eventually two of H.J.R.'s shareholders, who between them held 44% of its shares, retired from the businesses that were tenants in the building. They sought unsuccessfully to convince the majority shareholders to alter the below market rental policy. In the meantime, the building had increased greatly in value. The majority offered to buy the minority out but only at the initial investment price. The minority's petition for a judicial dissolution was not granted. The New York Court of Appeals held that because the majority was simply continuing the same policy that once had been agreeable to all, they could not be said to be "guilty of looting or exploiting the corporation to the detriment of minority shareholders." *Id.* at 716. Two judges dissented. After pointing out that contributors of 44% of the corporation's capital were now earning no return whatsoever and had no prospect of earning any, they stated:

The circumstances that majority shareholders may not be "looting" the corporation or "wrongfully diverting" its assets is an insufficient basis for denying corporate dissolution. What is significant and operative is the indisputable fact that this corporation has been continued solely and exclusively for the benefit of those holding 5/9 of the company's shares. Stated somewhat differently, in the light of what has occurred, the reason for corporate existence is gone. [*Id.* at 718]

When Will a Winding Up Be "Just and Equitable"? The English and Canadian cases where a winding up order has been granted appear generally to fall into one or more of three categories, although, as Lord Wilberforce stated in *Ebrahimi*, care must be taken that categorization not lead to ossification. First, winding up has been ordered in cases of deadlock. While deadlock literally implies either an inability to elect directors, or an equal split among an even number of directors on fundamental policy so that the firm's business cannot be carried on, courts will also find deadlock where there is constant fighting and mutual sabotage among owners whose cooperation is necessary for the conduct of business. *Re Yenidje Tobacco Co.*, [1916] 2 Ch. 426 (C.A.); *Re Bondi Better Bananas Ltd.*, [1951] O.R. 845 (C.A.). Though cases of deadlock need not implicate management misbehaviour, such claims are usually asserted in the context of an allegation of management selfdealing. In the same way, a court may perhaps be more likely to order a meeting of shareholders under CBCA s. 144 on the grounds of "impracticability" where some misbehaviour is alleged. See Chapter Six, Section D.

Second, winding up has been ordered in cases, like *Ebrahimi* itself, where the firm is described as an "incorporated partnership," and there has been an irreversible breakdown in mutual trust and confidence. See, e.g., *Re Rogers* (1976), 14 O.R. (2d) 489 (C.A.). The partnership analogy may seem tempting since partners enjoy the presumptive right under PA ss. 26(1) and 32(c) to terminate the partnership unilaterally without alleging fault. However, in many respects the analogy to partnership law is inapt. One form of enterprise organization may be chosen over another for a variety of reasons, of which presumptive termination rights may not be among the most important. Even in a partnership, it is by no means clear that most partners would today wish to reserve such a right, and partnership agreements almost invariably contain a term contracting out of no-fault termination rights. At a minimum, this aspect of the partnership analogy could not reasonably apply in the case of a corporation whose participants were formerly governed by a partnership agreement in which termination rights had been waived. In addition, evidence of former partnership status is ambiguous: did the parties seek to incorporate for the purpose of avoiding the strictures of partnership law, including no-fault termination rights? What of the many close corporations that today are incorporated from the very beginning: does the trend to incorporation at the birth of a firm mean that the just and equitable winding up remedy has shrunk in recent years? So long as form does not dominate substance, what is most important are the termination rights the parties could be expected to have bargained for, and not the enterprise organization decision.

The third commonly asserted, although less commonly successful, ground for claiming that a winding up would be just and equitable is that management has demonstrated a "lack of probity" in the conduct of a corporation's affairs. The leading case is *Loch v. John Blackwood Ltd.*, [1924] A.C. 783 (P.C.), the facts of which read like a catalogue of abusive practices by an entrenched management intent upon destroying minority claims. A testator had instructed his executors to incorporate his business and to distribute half of the shares to his sister and one quarter to each of his niece and nephew. One of the executors was the sister's husband. He incorporated the business and distributed half of the shares to his wife and slightly less than one-quarter each to the niece and to the nephew. He gave the remaining few shares to his own nominees, thus guaranteeing that he and his wife could always outvote the other two. (Oddly enough, Lord Shaw referred to this distribution, which violated the terms of the will, as "quite a natural and proper arrangement." *Id.* at 786.) Under the husband's management, the corporation was highly profitable. The husband took an enormous salary for himself, but no dividends were ever paid, no shareholders meetings were ever held, and no financial accounting was ever made to the niece or nephew. After the nephew's death, the husband sought unsuccessfully to enlist the niece's aid in a scheme to purchase the shares from the nephew's estate at a grossly inadequate price. The niece's petition to have the corporation wound up was granted.

Courts almost universally refer to winding up as a "drastic remedy," and it is certainly not one lightly granted. In a number of reported cases, the petitioning shareholder had been fired as an employee of the corporation after a falling out with the controlling interest. In such a setting, courts are usually not disposed to accept a characterization of the firm as an incorporated partnership, if there is no question of deadlock and the controlling owners are guilty of nothing more than an inability to get along with the petitioner. See *Re R.C. Young Ins. Ltd.*, [1955] O.R. 598; *Re Graham* (1981), 32 O.R. (2d) 297; *B. Love Ltd. v. Bulk Steel & Salvage Ltd.* (1982), 38 O.R. (2d) 691; *Re D & D Holdings Ltd.*, [1981] 4 W.W.R. 13 (Alta.).

It will not always be easy for a court to discriminate perfectly between opportunistic behaviour by managers and wealth-maximizing decisions that have the consequence that a minority shareholder is removed as a director or an officer. Given this uncertainty, a minority shareholder might prefer rights that may be asserted without proof of management misbehaviour, such as the presumptive rule of PA ss. 26(1) and 32(c). If the winding up does not lead to the withdrawal of the productive facilities of the firm, which afterwards reincorporates under the ownership of the remaining investors, a right to a no-fault winding up would be equivalent to a unilateral buyout privilege. Indeed, because of possible unfavourable tax consequences, it would usually be better to structure such transactions as a one-step repurchase of shares by the firm, rather than as a two-step dissolution plus reincorporation. The minority shareholder might then be fully protected against the possibility of management misbehaviour even where it is difficult to demonstrate such misbehaviour. No-fault buyouts are proposed in Hetherington & Dooley, *Illiquidity and Exploitation: A Proposed Statutory Solution to the Remaining Close Corporation Problem*, 63 Va. L. Rev. 1 (1977). Similar rights are available to shareholders in both public and close corporations on the occurrence of certain "fundamental" corporate events under the appraisal remedy of CBCA s. 190. See Chapter Eleven, Section C.

The difficulty with compulsory buyout rights is that they impose a cost on the remaining shareholders of ensuring that the firm will have the cash to repurchase the shares should the buyout right be triggered. If shareholders prefer to diversify their investments, they might not wish to enter into business on those terms, and the forgone investment opportunities would represent a real loss. A further cost would arise when the remaining shareholders do effect the purchase, but are then more risk averse because of reduced diversification, with the result that they are more likely to pass up high risk, high return investments with a positive net present value. A right of unilateral termination on the part of the minority shareholders also introduces the possibility of strategic behaviour by the minority shareholder, in the same way that creditors might be guilty of premature termination through a precipitous decision to appoint a receiver. So long as the assertion of termination rights would be regretted by the remaining shareholders, minority shareholders might threaten termination unless they are assigned a disproportionate share of firm benefits. In these circumstances, investors may seek to protect themselves from minority shareholder opportunism by adopting a fault standard for dissolution. While some management misbehaviour might escape correction with a fault standard, it is important to note that, because of the possibility of strategic behaviour by minority shareholders, the most efficient management structure is not one where the costs of management misbehaviour are reduced to zero. See Baysinger & Butler, *Race for the Bottom v. Climb to the Top: The ALI Project and Uniformity in Corporate Law*, 10 J. Corp. L. 431, 451-56 (1985) (optimal governance structure seeks the lowest total prevention and agency costs for *all* claimholders).

Even if some investors might prefer no-fault buyout rights, does this provide a justification for mandatory termination rights? Investors may always craft their own form of protection against possible strategic behaviour by any party. Should no-fault buyouts then be left to private bargains in unanimous shareholder agreements? Investors generally do not provide for such rights in shareholder agreements, and usually contract around them in partnership agreements.

Is it consistent for a court in a non-CBCA jurisdiction to enforce a non-contractual undertaking as to management rights in a case like *Ebrahimi*, while at the same time refusing to uphold a shareholder agreement binding directors?

CHAPTER EIGHT

Insider Trading

Insider trading refers to trading in the securities of an issuer by its insiders, who include at a minimum its officers and directors. Insider trading legislation does two things. It requires insiders to report publicly upon their trades through reports to securities commissions; and it prohibits, through civil remedies or offences or both, the use by an insider of confidential, undisclosed information material to the value of the corporation's securities in connection with the trades.

The CBCA and the OSA each require insiders of public corporations to make public reports of their trades in securities issued by the corporation. Thus CBCA s. 127 (in combination with the definitional provisions found in s. 126) provides that an insider of a "distributing corporation" must file an initial report of his ownership of securities of the corporation within 10 days of becoming an insider, and a follow-up report of any change in his ownership of securities of the corporation within 10 days after the end of the month within which the change occurs. Canadian stock exchanges impose similar reporting requirements upon the insiders of listed corporations. Such reports enable regulators to monitor trading by insiders, insofar as abnormal intensity of trading might indicate the existence of material undisclosed facts. For example, purchases by an insider may indicate that he knows of undisclosed good news about the firm, and signal share price increases.

The prohibition of insider trading is found in civil remedies and offences under the OSA and CBCA. Civil remedies are provided to the outsider with whom the insider trades by OSA s. 134(1) and CBCA s. 131(4)(a), while corporate actions by the issuer are permitted by OSA s. 134(4) and CBCA s. 131(4)(b). Insider trading is also a quasi-criminal offense under OSA s. 76. See generally Gillen 269-81.

A. CIVIL LIABILITY

Insider trading is usually a matter of non-disclosure, not affirmative misrepresentation, since an actual misstatement in a share transaction may ground a common law fraud action without the need for insider trading remedies. Thus, if an affirmative misrepresentation is made with the intent that another should rely on it, and he does so to his detriment, then the maker of the statement is answerable at law for his fraud. However, common law antifraud standards do not ordinarily avail in the case of mere silence, and here the plaintiff must seek a remedy for insider trading. In this way, insider trading liability supplements continuous disclosure requirements in OSA s. 75. While no express statutory remedy against an issuer is provided for breach of the duty of press release disclosure on a material change under s. 75(1), an action may be asserted against insiders who trade prior to the issuance of the press release. The result is a "disclose or abstain" philosophy, in which the corporation is permitted to keep information confidential by virtue of s. 75(3), but where insiders are then barred from trading by OSA ss. 76 and 134.

Historical Development. Although insider trading was considered to be one of the evils to which securities legislation was addressed, it was not specifically proscribed by the Securities Exchange Act of 1934. Section 10(b) of that Act did provide that "it shall be unlawful for any person ... to use or employ in connection with the purchase or sale of any security ... any maunipulative or deceptive device or contrivance in contravention of such rules ... as the [Securities and Exchange] Commission may prescribe ... ," but it was not until 1942 that the S.E.C. got around to prescribing Rule 10b-5. Moreover, this was simply meant as a residual antifraud prohibition, aimed generally at deceptive contrivances that had not been specifically banned:

It shall be unlawful for any person, directly or indirectly, by the use of any means or instrumentality of interstate commerce, or of the mails, or of any facility of any national securities exchange

> (1) to employ any device, scheme, or artifice to defraud,

> (2) to make any untrue statement of a material fact or to state a material fact necessary in order to make the statements made, in the light of circumstances under which they were made, not misleading, or

> (3) to engage in any act, practice, or course of business which operates or would operate as a fraud or deceit upon any person, in connection with the purchase or sale of any security. [17 C.F.R. 240.10b-5]

Over the years, it came to be accepted in American jurisprudence that violation of s. 10b and Rule 10b-5 gave rise to an implied private cause of action for damages,* and these provisions developed as remedies for insider trading even though they made no reference to "insiders."

In 1965, the Attorney General's Committee on Securities Legislation in Ontario (Kimber Committee) reviewed what it found to be the inadequate state of the common law on insider trading and recommended the legislative creation of a cause of action in favour of a person who trades with an insider who improperly uses confidential information. The Committee reported the essence of its views on insider trading in the following paragraph:

> 2.02 In our opinion, it is not improper for an insider to buy or sell securities in his own company. Indeed, it is generally accepted that it is beneficial to a company to have officers and directors purchase securities in the company as they thereby acquire a direct financial interest in the

---

*   The earliest case holding in favour of the implied private cause of action is *Kardon v. National Gypsum, Inc.*, 73 F. Supp. 798 (E.D. Pa. 1947), but the issue was not put beyond doubt by the United States Supreme Court until *Herman & MacLean v. Huddleston*, 103 S. Ct. 683 (1983).

welfare of the company. It is impossible to justify the proposition that an investment so made can never be realized or liquidated merely because the investor is an insider. However, in our view it is improper for an insider to use confidential information acquired by him by virtue of his position as an insider to make profits by trading in the securities of his company. The ideal securities market should be a free and open market with the prices thereon based upon the fullest possible knowledge of all relevant facts among traders. Any factor which tends to destroy or put in question this concept lessens the confidence of the investing public in the market place and is, therefore, a matter of public concern.

The Committee recommended as well that the insider in such a case should be accountable to the corporation for any profits realized on the trade. These recommendations were translated into legislation in the following year in the 1966 Ontario Securities Act, the provisions of which were substantially similar to the present CBCA s. 131. Section 113 of the 1966 Act provided that "every insider of a corporation or associate or affiliate of such insider, who, in connection with a transaction" in corporate securities, "makes use of any specific, confidential information" material to the value of the securities in question was liable to compensate "any person or company for any direct loss suffered by such person or company as a result of such transaction." In addition, the defendant was "also accountable to the corporation for any direct benefit or advantge received or receivable ... as a result of such transaction." Notwithstanding that the civil remedy for insider trading in Canada is now close to 30 years old, there are only a handful of reported judgments on the merits. By contrast, in the United States there are hundreds of such reported cases.

Insiders were defined in the 1966 Ontario legislation to include directors, "senior officers," holders of more than 10% of the voting shares of the corporation and directors and senior officers of corportions that are themselves insiders (that is, more than 10% owners) of the corporation in question. The addition of "associates" to the civil liability provision caught an individual's immediate family, partners, controlled corporations and family trusts. The term "affiliates" caught corporations controlling, controlled by or under common control with a corporate insider. For civil liability purposes the CBCA defined insider more inclusively than did the 1966 Ontario Securities Act. In addition to those included in the provincial legislation, the following are insiders under CBCA s. 131: the issuer and its affiliates; all of its employees and persons "retained" by it; and, most significantly, any person who receives confidential information from an insider and who knows his mediate or immediate source to be an insider. Members of this last group are called "tippees." In the 1978 OSA, the definition of insider was expanded to embrace those who engaged or who proposed to engage in any business or professional activities with the issuer, a category that included some but not all tippees. However, 1987 amendments to the OSA extended the statute's reach to nearly all tippees. OSA ss. 76(5), 134(7).

OSA Remedies. Let us examine how OSA civil liability standards work by considering the following hypothetical. First, assume that a director of a corporation listed on the Toronto Stock Exchange hears in the course of a board meeting that the firm's major customer plans to reduce greatly his purchases from the firm. Armed with this information, the director sells 1,000 of his shares in the corporation prior to public disclosure of the news, at a time when the shares are trading at $20 each. Subsequently, the corporation makes a press release disclosure of the news under OSA s. 75(1), and the market value of the shares falls to $10 each. In this bad news scenario, the director might be liable for damages to the purchaser under s. 134(1) or to account for his gain to the corporation under s. 134(4).

Insider trading liability is imposed only on parties in a "special relationship" with a "reporting issuer." Special relationship is defined in s. 134(4) and includes "insiders," which, as defined in s. 1(1), would include directors, senior officers and 10% shareholders and the issuer itself on a stock buyback. Reporting issuers are defined in OSA s. 1(1). Civil remedies for insider trading are not available unless the information relates to a "material fact" or "material change," as those terms are defined in OSA s. 1(1). Information is material if its disclosure would reasonably be expected to have a significant effect on the market price or value of any of the issuer's securities. The insider would then be liable to the corporation and to the purchaser unless one of the defences referred to in the subsections is available. For example, the insider is permitted to trade if he proves that he reasonably believed that the information had been publicly disclosed.

The second example is one of good news. Suppose now that the director discovers that the firm has all but negotiated an output agreement under which a large number of its products will be taken up by a major purchaser over the next several years. Believing the information to be material, the insider purchases 1,000 shares of the corporation at a time when they are trading at $20. After disclosure, the price increases to $30. Provided the vendors can be identified, individual recovery may be permitted under s. 134(1), with the change in market price after disclosure taken as establishing the measure of damages. OSA s. 134(6).

See further Gillen 269-79.

B. DISTRIBUTIONAL CONCERNS

The prohibition of insider trading would appear to be premised largely on a fear of distributional consequences. However, it is important to note that the concern for a level playing field, which we now associate with securities regulation, is exceptional, and that in most other markets the common law principle that silence does not constitute fraud is the rule. Consider, for example, an insider of a major oil producer who learns that his firm has made an exceedingly rich find of new oil reserves. The insider might then make a profit either by purchasing shares of his firm, or by selling oil in futures contracts on the assumption that disclosure of the find will lower oil prices worldwide. While the first strategy may give rise to civil liability, the second will not since trading requirements are not a feature of commodities trading regulation.

This is not, however, to deny that, because of informational asymmetries between insiders and outsiders, insiders are advantaged in their trades, with an attendant transfer of wealth from one group to the other. Evidence of insiders' sustained informational advantages is provided by studies that indicate that insiders outperform the market in their reported trades. These publicly reported trades are least likely to be made with the benefit of material information because of the threat of civil liability. Where insiders do have access to undisclosed material information about the firm, they might instead be expected to trade surreptitiously in offshore markets, and report only their more innocuous trades. But even reported trades systematically outperform the market. See, e.g., Baesel & Stein, *The Value of Information: Inferences from the Probability of Insider Trading*, 14 J. Fin. & Quant. Anal. 553, 568 (1979) (reviewing Canadian evidence). These studies contradict the "strong" version of the ECMH, which holds that it is impossible over the long run for any investor to "beat the market" or to produce a rate of return in securities markets greater than that of a broadly based securities index such as the Dow Jones Industrials. The strong version of the ECMH therefore assumes that all information about securities, including all information relating to predictions of future developments concerning the firm, is already reflected in the market price of widely traded securities. But were this the case, insiders would not be able to outperform the market in the manner they do.

The Privity Requirement. Insider trading might then appear to give rise to distributional effects. If insiders are in fact able to achieve abnormal profits in their trades, outsiders as a class must systematically do worse in theirs. At first glance, the primary victims of insider trading are the outsiders who traded with the insiders, and this would suggest that remedies should be limited to those in privity with the insider. However, it is difficult to link up buyers and sellers when the trade is effected on an impersonal securities exchange. In a typical exchange trade (to simplify somewhat), the purchaser will call a stockbroker and instruct him to purchase *x* number of shares either "at market," which means at whatever the market price is on that day, or at a price not to exceed *y* dollars. The broker will take the purchase order, perhaps aggregated with others that the broker has received for the same class of shares of the same corporation, and bring it to the floor of an exchange or list it on a computer-assisted trading system. He will then trade with another broker, who has received sell orders at a compatible price, without either broker knowing who the principal on the other side is. Problems of privity are magnified when the shares trade on several exchanges and where shares are held beneficially in the names of brokers or trust companies. If a civil cause of action for insider trading is to be created, but only for the person whose actual shares were either purchased from or sold to the insider, then insiders might avoid liability by trading on an impersonal market.

Under the CBCA, an insider is liable to compensate "any person for any direct loss suffered by that person as a result of the transaction." This does not unambiguously impose a privity requirement, but in the *Green v. Charterhouse* decision considered in Section D, the Ontario Court of Appeal appeared to hold that the "direct loss" test of s. 113 of the 1966 Ontario Securities Act did require privity. OSA s. 134 would seem more clearly to impose a privity requirement, with the remedy in damages granted to "the seller or purchaser" under s. 134(1). See Getz, *Some Aspects of Corporate Share Repurchases*, 9 U.B.C.L. Rev. 9, 34 (1974); but see Anisman, *Insider Trading Under the Canada Business Corporations Act*, [1975] Meredith Mem. Lects. 151, 234-43 (arguing that privity is not necessarily required under the CBCA). Of course, privity problems would not intrude on a corporate or derivative action for an accounting of the insider's profits under OSA s. 134(4) or CBCA s. 131(4)(b).

Privity requirements may seem troubling if their effect is to facilitate insider trading. This may seem to be particularly true of the OSA, which, unlike the CBCA, restricts the outsider's remedy to trades in the securities of a "reporting issuer." In the one circumstance where insider trading liability is imposed by the OSA, the insider might easily avoid it through trading on an impersonal securities exchange. In addition, were it possible to link up who sold to whom on an exchange, becoming a competent plaintiff would be a little bit like winning a lottery. No plaintiff would know whether he had traded with an insider at the time of the trade. This might suggest relaxing the privity requirement, for example, through schemes of *pro rata* recovery for every outsider who traded on the same day as the insider. But this seems entirely artificial if liability is premised on distributional concerns. As well, consider the difficulty of determining the quantum of damages without a privity requirement. Is "direct loss" under CBCA s. 131(4) suffered by (1) only the trading outsider; (2) anyone who traded at about the same time; or (3) those who did not trade but assert that they would have if the information had been disclosed? If the availability of a remedy is not conditioned upon privity, the insider might be subject to enormous liability. These problems arose in American cases, for privity was not required in private Rule 10b-5 actions.

Fridrich v. Bradford
United States Court of Appeals, Sixth Circuit
542 F.2d 307 (1976), cert. denied, 429 U.S. 1053 (1977)

ENGEL, Circuit Judge: On April 27, 1972 J.C. Bradford, Jr. purchased 1,225 shares of common stock of Old Line Life Insurance Company (Old Line). The shares were purchased on inside information Bradford, Jr. had received on a trip from his father. The shares were purchased on the over-the-counter market from J.C. Bradford and Co., a Nashville brokerage firm of which Bradford, Jr. and his father are managing partners.* Subsequent to the purchase, Old Line stock increased in value and on July 27, 1972, Bradford, Jr. sold the 1,225 shares, reaping a profit of $13,000 on the transaction.

The Securities and Exchange Commission investigated Bradford, Jr.'s stock transaction. As a result of a consent decree entered into between the Commission and Bradford, Jr., he was required to disgorge the entire $13,000 profit, was permanently enjoined from any further violation of § 10(b) of the Securities Exchange Act of 1934 and Rule 10b-5, and was suspended from performing any business activities as a broker-dealer for twenty working days.

Thereafter plaintiffs filed this civil action, alleging that Bradford, Jr.'s trading activities violated Rule 10b-5. By the judgment of the district court appealed from

---

*   Bradford and Co. was a professional securities dealer. As such, it "made a market" in the securities of certain issuers that were traded over-the-counter, in distinction to on a securities exchange. A market-maker holds itself out to the public and to the trade as willing to buy and sell securities of particular issuers at stated prices. Market-makers' activities are essential to the depth and liquidity of an over-the-counter securities market. In the instant case, Bradford and Co.'s market-making in Old Line was not at issue. Rather the case concerned Bradford Jr.'s personal trading in Old Line shares.

here, Bradford, Jr., has been rendered jointly and severally liable to plaintiffs for the sum of $361,186.75. He has been liable, although plaintiffs never sold their stock to him or his associates, nor did they sell on the same day or even in the same month in which he bought. There was no proof that Bradford, Jr.'s trading activities had any impact upon the market price of Old Line stock or upon plaintiff's decision to trade in it. As we read the district court judgment, Bradford, Jr.'s liability would have been the same even though he had purchased only five shares of Old Line and made a profit of less than $53.00.

While Bradford, Jr. is only one of five defendants in this appeal, we have focused on his liability at the outset in order to illustrate the "Draconian liability" to which persons who trade on inside information may be subjected under the district court's interpretation of Rule 10b-5. Because we conclude that under the circumstances of this case imposition of civil liability constitutes an unwarranted extension of the judicially created private cause of action under Rule 10b-5, we reverse the judgment of the district court.

I

Of the five defendants named in the district court action, the dominant figure was James C. Bradford (Bradford). In 1961, Bradford put together a syndicate to purchase a controlling block of Old Line stock, which the syndicate continued to own through 1972. After the purchase, Bradford became a director of Old Line and upon his retirement as a director, was succeeded by Bradford, Jr., who remained a director until August 1972. Approximately once a year Bradford was visited in Nashville by Forrest Guynn, president of Old Line, who gave Bradford a personal report on the affairs of the company. After the 1961 purchase, Bradford & Co. became the principal market-maker of the stock.

Prior to 1972, Old Line was considered a prime target for merger or takeover in the insurance industry and Bradford, because of his relationship with Old Line, was often approached by companies interested in a takeover.

In October, 1971, Gordon E. Crosby, chairman of U.S. Life Corporation (USLIFE), a New York based insurance company, contacted Bradford concerning the possible acquisition of Old Line by USLIFE. Crosby was advised by Bradford that no offer would be considered unless it involved an offer of at least $50 per share for Old Line stock. Since Old Line had a market price of only $24 per share at that time, Crosby did not pursue the negotiations.

On April 19, 1972 Crosby telephoned Bradford and stated that he was then in a position to work out a deal at better than $50 per share of Old Line stock. Crosby, in effect, proposed an acquisition on the basis of one share of USLIFE stock for one share of Old Line. In a letter of April 21, 1972, Crosby agreed to negotiate the acquisition only with Bradford and agreed to pay Bradford a finder's fee equivalent to 1% of the fair market value of the USLIFE stock exchanged for the Old Line stock. On April 19, 1972 the closing bid price for Old Line stock was $33 per share and the closing price for USLIFE on the New York Stock Exchange was $61 per share. ... On April 27, 1972, after hearing of Bradford's conversation with Crosby, Bradford, Jr. purchased 1,225 shares of common stock of Old Line at $37 per share. ...

On May 15, 1972 Bradford called Crosby and told him that he had spoken to Forrest Guynn, chief executive officer of Old Line. Bradford reported that Guynn was interested in having serious negotiations concerning the merger. ...

Negotiations toward the merger continued in June, 1972. ... The June 29, 1972 press release was the first public announcement of the proposed merger. On July 7, 1972, Guynn with the authorization of Old Line's Board of Directors, agreed in principle to the merger of Old Line and USLIFE. On July 11 a press release announcing the agreement in principle was issued and this was delivered to stockholders on July 14. Because of problems concerning SEC approval of the merger, the proposed date of the merger, September, 1972, had to be delayed. ... After an investigation of several months, the SEC approved the merger on November 20, 1972 and on December 28, 1972, after approval by Old Line's stockholders, the merger became effective.

Bradford and Co. was the principal market maker in Old Line stock throughout 1972, purchasing 169,054 shares and selling 170,685 shares, for which it was paid commissions in the amount of $103,214. Approximately $75,000 of this profit was a result of trading activity of Old Line during the months of April through December, 1972.

Only July 31, 1972, Bradford, Jr. sold the 1,225 shares of Old Line stock he had purchased in April 1972 at a profit of $13,000. ...

Two of the plaintiffs (Fridrich and Kim) bought stock in Old Line in May, 1972 and sold the stock in June at a slight profit. The stock was purchased from a broker, Ken Schoen, and was sold on his advice. These transactions did not involve Bradford or any of his associates. The other plaintiffs (the Woosley family) purchased their stock from Bradford & Co. in 1967 but sold in June, 1972, through Schoen and on his advice. Schoen testified he would not have advised clients to sell their stock had he been aware that Bradford and Old Line were negotiating an agreement with USLIFE to effect a merger. Schoen did not have any information concerning the proposed merger until mid-July, 1972. He did not advise the plaintiffs to repurchase Old Line stock.

• • •

II

On April 25, 1973 a complaint was filed in the United States District Court for the Middle District of Tennessee by plaintiffs Fridrich, Kim and the Woosleys. The complaint charged defendants with violation of § 10(b) of the Securities Exchange Act of 1934 and Rule 10b-5 because of their trading in Old Line stock while in possession of material insider information.

• • •

Without making any particular distinction between the defendants, the district court found that all had violated Rule 10b-5 by trading in Old Line stock while in possession of material inside information, without first disclosing the information to the investing public trading in the same market.

• • •

The district judge thus held that insiders who buy in an impersonal market using material inside information can be liable to sellers in an impersonal market who sold without knowledge of the inside information, even though it was undisputed that the insiders did not purchase the shares sold by the plaintiff sellers. ...

... In the final analysis, the question is how far the courts are to extend the private civil right of action under Section 10(b) and Rule 10b-5 when the alleged violation is the unlawful use of inside information and the stock involved is traded upon an impersonal market.

• • •

IV

Few early cases brought under § 10(b) and Rule 10b-5 dealt with non-disclosure by insiders trading in the open market. Development of the law in this area is largely traceable to the "abstain or disclose rule" developed in *SEC v. Texas Gulf Sulphur Co.*, 401 F.2d 833 (2d Cir. 1968), cert. den., 394 U.S. 976, 89 S. Ct. 1454, 22 L.Ed.2d 765 (1969). This was an SEC enforcement action brought under 15 U.S.C. §§ 78u and 78aa against Texas Gulf Sulphur Co. (TGS) and thirteen individuals who, it was charged, purchased TGS stock or calls on the strength of undisclosed inside information of favorable exploratory drilling results by the company near Timmins, Ontario. Noting that an important purpose of Rule 10b-5 was to help insure that all persons trading on the securities markets have relatively equal access to material information, Judge Waterman observed:

The essence of the Rule is that anyone who, trading for his own account in the securities in a corporation has "access, directly or indirectly to information intended to be available only for a corporate purpose and not for the personal benefit of anyone" may not take "advantage of such information knowing it is unavailable to those with whom he is dealing," i.e., the investing public.

• • •

Thus, anyone in possession of material inside information must either disclose it to the investing public, or, if he is disabled from disclosing it in order to protect a corporate confidence, or he chooses not to do so, must abstain from trading in recommending the securities concerned while such information remains undisclosed.

SEC v. Texas Gulf Sulphur Co., 401 F.2d 833, 848. *SEC v. Texas Gulf Sulphur*, supra, involved an SEC enforcement action against the company and several corporate investors. That particular case did not involve an attempt to impose civil liability for damages upon insiders who trade in the open market without disclosure of inside information.

[The Court discussed cases in which persons who sold in the open market, that is, either an exchange market or an organized, impersonal over-the-counter market, between the time that an insider bought shares on the basis of material confidential information and the time that the information was disclosed were denied standing as Rule 10b-5 plaintiffs against the insider.]

A different result has been indicated in *Shapiro v. Merrill Lynch, Pierce, Fenner and Smith, Inc.*, 353 F. Supp. 264 (S.D.N.Y. 1973) aff'd., 495 F.2d 228 (2d Cir. 1974). In *Shapiro*, supra, plaintiffs were purchasers of common stock of Douglas Aircraft

Corporation during the period of June 20-24, 1966 on the New York Stock Exchange. On June 24, 1966, public disclosure was made by Douglas of a drastic change in its financial situation which had occurred since June 7, 1966, the date of the release of its earnings report for the first five months of 1966. That report indicated a favorable earnings picture. Between June 16 and June 20 the management of Douglas learned that, contrary to the June 7 release, Douglas would be reporting substantially lower earnings for the first six months of fiscal 1966 and that there would be little or no profit for the company during that year, with substantially reduced earnings for fiscal 1967. Defendant Merrill Lynch was engaged by Douglas as a managing underwriter for a proposed offering by Douglas of $75,000,000 in convertible debentures. Presumably because of this relationship, the information of the changed earnings picture was promptly transmitted to Merrill Lynch but without public disclosure. Plaintiffs alleged that thereafter, between June 20 and June 24, 1966, Merrill Lynch and certain of its directors and employees divulged this inside information to certain of their institutional investors who, in turn, sold their Douglas common stock on the New York Stock Exchange without disclosing the inside information to the public.

In an extensive and carefully drafted opinion, District Judge Charles H. Tenney denied a defense motion for judgment on the pleadings, holding that if the allegations were proved, they would amount to violations of Section 10(b) and Rule 10b-5 and render the defendants liable to the plaintiffs who, during the period of June 20-24, purchased Douglas stock in the open market without knowledge of the earnings information which was in the possession of the defendants.

In *Shapiro*, plaintiffs did not allege that they had actually traded with the defendants. Neither does it appear from the opinion that defendants' act of trading had any influence upon their own decision to purchase. In their motion to dismiss, defendants contended that their violation of Rule 10b-5, even if proved, did not cause any damage to plaintiffs and that since plaintiffs would have bought the stock in any event, no injury to plaintiffs was occasioned. Judge Tenney rejected this analysis:

> But therein lies the fallacy of defendants' reasoning: it is not the act of trading which causes plaintiffs' injury, *it is the act of trading without disclosing material inside information which causes plaintiffs' injury.* Had Merrill Lynch and the individual defendants refrained from divulging the earnings information to the selling defendants, or had the selling defendants decided not to trade, there would have been no liability for plaintiffs' injury due to the eventual public disclosure of Douglas' poor financial position. But defendants did not choose to follow that course of action, and by trading in Douglas stock on a national securities exchange they assumed the duty to disclose information to all potential buyers. It is the breach of this duty which gives rise to defendants' liability.

353 F. Supp. 264, 278.

The Second Circuit, in affirming the district court judgment, agreed with Judge Tenney's analysis and further concluded that any argument defendants might make that their conduct did not cause plaintiffs' damage was precluded by the Supreme Court holding in *Affiliated Ute Citizens v. United States*, 406 U.S. 128, 92 S. Ct. 1456, 31 L.Ed.2d 741 (1972):

> The short, and we believe conclusive, answer to defendants' assertion that their conduct did not "cause" damage to plaintiffs is the "causation in fact" holding by Supreme Court in *Affiliated Ute*

Citizens v. United States, 406 U.S. 128, 153-54 [92 S. Ct. 1456, 31 L.Ed.2d 741] (1972), upon the authority of which we conclude that the requisite element of causation in fact has been established here by the uncontroverted facts that defendants traded in or recommended trading in Douglas stock without disclosing material inside information which plaintiffs as reasonable investors might have considered important in making their decision to purchase Douglas stock.

495 F.2d 228, 238. While neither court endeavoured to rule upon the measure of any damages which might ultimately be allowed, the Second Circuit observed:

Moreover, we do not foreclose the possibility that an analysis by the district court of the nature and character of the Rule 10b-5 violations committed may require limiting the extent of liability imposed on either class of defendants.

Shapiro v. Merrill Lynch, supra, 495 F.2d 228, 242.

Thus it appears that both the district court and the Second Circuit in their respective opinions in *Shapiro*, supra, were ready and willing to extend the 10b-5 private right of action to accord relief to those who traded upon an impersonal market where the defendants were charged with violation of the "abstain or disclose" rule in *SEC v. Texas Gulf Sulphur*, supra.

As the foregoing cases illustrate, extension of the private civil remedy under Rule 10b-5 where shares have been traded upon an impersonal market has eluded uniform analysis by judicial writers. The courts and legal writers seem to agree that the plaintiff must establish a causal connection between the defendant's misconduct and his loss, *Bromberg*, supra, § 8.7.1 at 213-14, but what exactly plaintiff must show to establish this causal element is unclear.

V

We conclude that upon the facts of this case defendants' conduct caused no injury to plaintiffs and the judgment of the district court must be reversed. It is undisputed that defendants did not purchase any shares of stock from plaintiffs, and that defendants' acts of trading in no way affected plaintiffs' decision to sell.

We are unable to agree with the observation of the district judge in *Shapiro* that "... it is the act of trading without disclosing material inside information which causes plaintiffs' injury. ... Having breached that obligation [to abstain or disclose], the defendants are liable for plaintiffs' injuries." 353 F. Supp. 264, 278. The flaw in this logic, we conclude, is that it assumes the very injury which it then declares compensable. It does so by presupposing that the duty to disclose is absolute, and that the plaintiff is injured when the information is denied him. The duty to disclose, however, is not an absolute one, but an alternative one, that of either disclosing or abstaining from trading. We conceive it to be the act of trading which essentially constitutes the violation of Rule 10b-5, for it is this which brings the illicit benefit to the insider, and it is this conduct which impairs the integrity of the market and which is the target of the rule. If the insider does not trade, he has an absolute right to keep material information secret. *SEC v. Texas Gulf Sulphur Co.*, supra, at 848. Investors must be prepared to accept the risk of trading in an open market without complete or always accurate information. Defendants' trading did not alter plaintiffs' expectations when they sold their stock, and in no way influenced plaintiffs' trading decision. ...

We hold, therefore, the defendants' act of trading with third persons was not causally connected with any claimed loss by plaintiffs who traded on the impersonal market and who were otherwise unaffected by the wrongful acts of the insider.

Likewise, we are not persuaded, as was the Second Circuit in its decision in *Shapiro*, supra, that *Affiliated Ute Citizens v. United States*, supra, mandates a "short, and ... conclusive answer" to the contrary, 495 F.2d 228, 238.

In *Affiliated Ute*, certain members of the Ute Indian tribe brought suit against a bank and two of its employees under Rule 10b-5. The basis of the complaint was that the bank, which held certain shares of stock owned by plaintiffs, had arranged sales of the stock without disclosing to the plaintiffs certain material information, including the fact that defendants were making a market in the stock, purchasing some of it for their own account, and that the stock was sold for a substantially higher price to nonmembers of the tribe. The district judge entered judgment for plaintiffs. The Court of Appeals reversed, holding there could be no recovery under § 10(b) and Rule 10b-5 without proof that the plaintiffs had relied upon some misrepresentation by defendants. In reversing the Court of Appeals, the Supreme Court held:

> Under the circumstances of this case, involving primarily a failure to disclose, positive proof of reliance is not a prerequisite to recovery. All that is necessary is that the facts withheld be material in the sense that a reasonable investor might have considered them important in the making of this decision. See *Mills v. Electric Auto-Life Co.*, 396 U.S. 375, 384 [90 S. Ct. 616, 24 L.Ed.2d 593] (1970); *SEC v. Texas Gulf Sulphur Co.*, 401 F.2d 833, 849 (CA2 1968), cert. denied *sub nom. Coates v. SEC*, 394 U.S. 976 [89 S. Ct. 1454, 22 L.Ed.2d 756] (1969); 6 L. Loss, Securities Regulation 3876-880 (1969 Supp. to 2d ed. of Vol. 3); A. Bromberg, Securities Law, Fraud—SEC Rule 10b-5, §§ 2.6 and 8.6 (1967). This obligation to disclose and this withholding of a material fact establish the requisite element of causation in fact. *Chasins v. Smith, Barney & Co.*, 438 F.2d [1167] at 1172 (CA2).

406 U.S. 128, 153-54, 92 S. Ct. 1456, 1472, 31 L.Ed.2d 741.

It is this language which the Second Circuit, in *Shapiro*, felt to be controlling upon it. We are unable to construe the language quoted so broadly. It was shown in *Affiliated Ute* that the defendant bank employees had engaged in prior business dealings with the plaintiff Indians.[25] They entered into a deliberate scheme to induce the plaintiffs to sell their stock without disclosure of material facts which would have influenced the decision to sell. The resulting sales were a direct result of the scheme. Thus it comes as no surprise that the Supreme Court concluded that "[U]nder the circumstances of this case," 406 U.S. 128, 153, 92 S. Ct. 1456, 1472, 31 L.Ed.2d 741, all that was necessary was that the information withheld be material in order to establish the requisite causation.

• • •

---

25   It seems clear that because of their prior business dealings with plaintiffs, defendants in *Affiliated Ute* owed a duty of disclosure to them. For an extensive discussion of the case, see Comment, *Affiliated Ute Citizens v. United States—The Supreme Court Speaks on Rule 10b-5*, 1973 Utah L. Rev. 119.

Here, unlike *Affiliated Ute*, defendants did not perpetrate any scheme to induce defendants to sell their stock. Plaintiffs and defendants here had no relationship whatever during the period in question. The plaintiffs in *Affiliated Ute* had a right to expect that the defendant bank officials would fully disclose all material information concerning the stock while inducing them to sell. When defendants did not make full disclosure, they breached Rule 10b-5 and became liable for plaintiffs' foreseeable damages. The type of relationship existing between plaintiffs and defendants in *Affiliated Ute* is totally absent here.

VI

Neither do we believe that sound policy considerations support the result reached by the district court. Logic, at first blush, tends to support extension of the civil remedy to persons trading in an impersonal market in the context presented here. Congress certainly never intended § 10(b) to be limited in its scope solely to face-to-face transactions. Indeed since the Securities Exchange Act of 1934 is aimed at nationwide practices, H.R.No.1382, 73rd Cong., 2nd Sess. 11 (1934), it would be idle to exclude from its operation those over-the-counter and national stock exchange transactions which are most characteristic of the national market. *See SEC v. Texas Gulf Sulphur*, supra, 401 F.2d 833, 848.

The key issue, as we see it, is not whether the proscriptions of § 10(b) and Rule 10b-5 should encompass open market transactions, which they should, but whether the civil remedy must invariably be coextensive in its reach with the reach of the SEC, which under the Act, was designated by the Congress as the primary vehicle of its enforcement. We reject such a view where its application leads us inexorably to an unjust and unworkable result.[27] By so extending the liability of defendants here beyond that which has already been imposed through the SEC enforcement action, we believe we would be doing violence to the intent of the statute and rule, creating a windfall for those fortuitous enough to be aware of their nebulous legal rights, and imposing what essentially must be considered punitive damages almost unlimited in their potential scope.

Where private civil actions under Rule 10b-5 have been employed in essentially face-to-face situations, the potential breadth of the action was usually contained. However, extension of the private remedy to impersonal market cases where plaintiffs have neither dealt with defendants nor been influenced in their trading decisions by any act of the defendants would present a situation wholly lacking in the natural limitations on damages present in cases dealing with face-to-face transactions. We think the potential

---

27   We specifically do not reach the question of availability of the remedy to open market situations where the insider trading with resultant price changes has in fact induced the plaintiffs to buy or sell to their injury. See Painter, *Inside Information: Growing Pains for the Development of Federal Corporation Law Under Rule 10b-5*, 65 Column. L. Rev. 1361, 1370 (1965). Here there was no proof that defendants' insider trading had any impact whatever upon the value of Old Line Stock.

liability of Bradford, Jr. in this case, noted earlier, is sufficiently illustrative of the damages posed.[29]

We recognize that in precluding recovery here, it may be argued that the deterrent impact on insider trading of a large award of damages is thereby lost. A similar argument was found unpersuasive by the Supreme Court in *Bangor Punta Operations v. Bangor & A.R. Co.*, 417 U.S. 703, 94 S. Ct. 2578, 41 L.Ed.2d 418 (1974).

• • •

While we hold to the view that the private action should be compensatory, it is to be observed that in any event the 1934 Act provides a number of non-compensatory sanctions to deter insider misconduct, including SEC investigations and criminal sanctions. Further, the SEC may ask the federal district court, in the exercise of its equity jurisdiction under § 27 of the 1934 Act, to require an insider to disgorge any profits he may have made from his illegal trading, *SEC v. Texas Gulf Sulphur Co.*, 446 F.2d 1301 (2d Cir. 1971), cert. denied, 404 U.S. 1005, 92 S. Ct. 561, 30 L.Ed.2d 558 (1971), or even an amount in excess of the amount of illicit profits which the insider has made. *SEC v. Shapiro*, 494 F.2d 1301, 1309 (2d Cir. 1974). Finally, state law may provide various sanctions against insider trading.

Whether the sanctions imposed upon the defendants here together with others which were also available amount to a sufficient vindication of the public rights and to an adequate deterrent to future misconduct we need not say. We may at least observe that the impact is bound to be significant.

Finally, it has been suggested that the problem of unlimited damages can be avoided by allowing recovery to all plaintiffs who traded during the period of non-disclosure, but limiting recovery to the amount of defendants' profits from insider trading. This type of limitation has been incorporated into the proposal ALI Federal Securities Code (Tent.Draft No. 2, March 1973). In situations where the insider trades in an impersonal market on inside information, § 1402(f)(2)(B) of the proposed Code limits the damages for which he becomes liable "to the extent of the securities that the defendant sold or bought." Thus were the proposed Code in effect in this case, defendants' liability would presumably be limited to the amount by which the price of Old Line stock increased between the time they purchased and the time of public disclosure of the inside information multiplied by the number of shares defendant purchased. ...

As compared to Congress or administrative agencies such as the SEC, we think the courts are ill-fitted to the task of rulemaking which would be required. As we see no

---

29   Plaintiffs sold Old Line stock in the over-the-counter market in various lots on June 13, 14 and 15, 1972. Based upon the market data received in evidence at the trial, if all of the persons who had sold their shares of Old Line stock on those days alone had joined in the instant lawsuit, Bradford, Jr.'s potential liability in damages would have totalled approximately $800,000. If a class action had been brought which included all investors who sold Old Line stock between April 21 and June 29, 1972, the damages could have totalled approximately $3,700,000. If the class had been further expanded to those selling up to November 20, 1972 (and the holding appealed from admits of no limitations short thereof), the damages would have run in excess of $7,000,000.00. As noted earlier, Bradford, Jr.'s profit from his illegal purchases, already disgorged in an SEC proceeding, amounted to about $13,000.

connection between defendants' violation of Rule 10b-5 and plaintiffs' alleged losses, we decline to base our decision upon a rule of limitation of damages here.

• • •

Reversed and remanded for entry of judgment for defendants.

CELEBREEZE, Circuit Judge (concurring): I concur in the result reached by the Court. However, because of the importance of defining the scope of civil liability under rule 10b-5 in an open market context and the apparent divergence of today's decision and that of the Second Circuit in *Shapiro v. Merrill Lynch, Pierce, Fenner & Smith Inc.*, 495 F.2d 228 (2d. Cir. 1974), aff'g, 353 F. Supp. 264 (S.D.N.Y. 1972), I feel compelled to explain my reasons for joining in the Court's decision.

There is no doubt that Appellants, J.C. Bradford and J.C. Bradford, Jr. actively engaged in trading for their own account on the basis of material inside information which had not been disclosed to the trading public. This was a patent violation of the "disclose or abstain" rule announced in *SEC v. Texas Gulf Sulphur Co.*, 401 F.2d 833 (2nd Cir. 1968). In *Shapiro* the Second Circuit extended the rule to provide a basis for recovery in private actions for damages. 495 F.2d at 236. I do not read today's decision as a repudiation of the "disclose or abstain" rule in private damage actions. Rather, I see the Court's opinion as imposing a rational limitation on the scope of civil liability under rule 10b-5 for insiders trading in the open market.

There is an obvious need to restrict the scope of civil liability of insiders trading in the open market. If an insider trades in a widely held stock which is actively traded on a national market, the number of potential plaintiffs could be astronomical and the possible award of damages may be grossly disproportionate to the volume of the insider trading. ...

... An insider who breaches the "disclose or abstain" rule by trading in the open market should not become a virtual insurer for losses sustained by those who happen to trade in the same stock weeks after the insider has ceased his trading activities. There must be some causative link between breach of the insider's duty to disclose the withheld information before trading and the losses incurred by would-be plaintiffs. On the other hand, an insider should not escape civil liability for conduct which would clearly violate rule 10b-5 in a face-to-face transaction, by the simple expedient of restricting his trading to the open market where the mechanics of the marketplace make it difficult, if not impossible, to trace particular transactions.

It was fear of creating a loophole in the "disclose or abstain" rule which led the Second Circuit in *Shapiro* to reject the argument that the rule should be restricted to SEC injunctive actions or to private suits where the actual purchasers of the stock could be identified. 495 F.2d at 236-37. To do so, the Court reasoned, would be to circumvent the strong policy considerations supporting the rule and "make a mockery" of an insider's duty to disclose or abstain from trading.[4] *Id*. Indeed, the "disclose or abstain" rule

---

4   In this case the defendants purchased the bulk of their shares from the inventory of their own brokerage house, J.C. Bradford & Co. They were, in effect, trading with themselves. If recovery were limited to

(The footnote is continued on the next page.)

was devised to cope with the difficulty in tracing transactions in an impersonal market. Since the mechanics of the marketplace make it virtually impossible to identify the actual investors with whom an insider is trading, the duty of disclosure is owed to investors as a class who trade on the market during the period of insider trading.[5] As the Court stated in *SEC v. Texas Gulf Sulphur Co.*, 401 F.2d at 848:

[T]he Rule is based in policy on the justifiable expectations of the securities marketplace that all investors trading on impersonal exchanges have relatively equal access to material information.

The essence of the "disclose or abstain" rule is the inherent unfairness in allowing an insider to enter the open market and trade for his own account in the securities of a corporation on the basis of material inside information "'knowing [such information] is unavailable to those with whom he is dealing,' i.e., the investing public." *SEC v. Texas Gulf Sulphur Co.*, 401 F.2d at 848, *quoting Matter of Cady, Roberts & Co.*, 40 SEC 907, 912 (1961). "It is, in fact, the insider's advantage over others in trading the corporation's securities which gives rise to the duty of disclosure." Painter, 65 Colum.L.Rev. at 1384. The "disclose or abtain" rule accomplishes two salutory purposes of rule 10b-5: it insures the integrity of the marketplace and it compensates for the inequality of trading with a corporate insider who has superior access to material inside information. *See* 401 F.2d at 848.

Given the availability of the "disclose or abstain" rule to private litigants, the problem of identifying those entitled to recover for breach of that duty remains. At common law, recovery for deceit was limited to these who could show "reliance" and "privity." See generally W. Prosser, Law of Torts § 105 at 685-86, 700-02 (4th ed. 1971). Due to the impersonal nature of trading on the open market and the remedial purpose of rule 10b-5, "privity" and "reliance" as means for limiting the plaintiff class have generally fallen into disfavor. See generally Painter at 1370, 1372. Since there is no practical method for matching purchases and sales in the open market, requiring privity in the common law sense as an element of rule 10b-5 would create an insurmountable obstacle for plaintiffs.[7]

---

4   Continued ...

    those who actually sold Old Line stock to defendants, their own company would be the principal plaintiff. This would be an absurdity. An insider should not be immunized from liability simply because he trades through intermediaries. See *Strong v. Repide*, 213 U.S. 419, 29 S. Ct. 521, 53 L.Ed. 853 (1909). The real persons requiring protection are the anonymous investors whose Old Line shares were funneled to defendants through various broker-dealers.

5   "Since in any active market disclosure to a particular individual is not feasible, the duty to disclose, if such a duty exists, must be owed to all members of that ill-defined class of stockholders who, with the benefit of inside information, would alter their intention to sell. Thus, it must be concluded that all those who sold while the defendant was purchasing should be accorded equal rights of recovery." [Painter, *Inside Information: Growing Pains for the Development of Federal Corporation Law*, 65 Colum. L. Rev. 1361, 1378 (1965)].

7   Plaintiffs should not be required to prove that it was their particular stock certificates which passed through various brokerage houses and came to rest in an insider's portfolio. As the Second Circuit said in *Shapiro*, 495 F.2d at 239: "It would make a mockery of the 'disclose or abstain' rule if we were to

(The footnote is continued on the next page.)

Reliance also has little relevance to trading in the open market where there are no face-to-face negotiations as a rule, and where non-disclosure of a material fact is often the gravamen of the complaint. See e.g., *Blackie v. Barrack*, 524 F.2d 891, 905-06 (9th Cir. 1975). See also Note, *The Reliance Requirement in Private Actions under SEC Rule 10b-5*, 88 Harv.L.Rev. 584, 589-600 (1975).

Without reliance, however, there is no causative link between defendants' conduct and plaintiffs' investment decisions. And without at least a "semblance of privity" defendants' liability could extend to complete strangers. ...

In *Affiliated Ute Citizens v. United States*, 406 U.S. 128, 153-54, 92 S. Ct. 1456, 31 L.Ed.2d 741 (1972), the Supreme Court dispensed with the requirement of showing actual reliance where liability was grounded on the non-disclosure of a material fact by individuals in a fiduciary relationship to the plaintiffs. Where there is such a relationship, the Court indicated that all that need be shown to prove causation is "causation-in-fact"—an affirmative obligation of disclosure and the withholding of material information. 406 U.S. at 153-54, 92 S. Ct. 1456. Because of the materiality of the information, the Court was willing to presume that disclosure would have affected plaintiffs' investment decisions. See generally Note, *Reliance under Rule 10b-5*, 24 Case W.Res.L.Rev. 363, 385-88 (1973). In *Shapiro* the Second Circuit found *Affiliated Ute* controlling on the causation issue. 495 F.2d at 238. The Court reasoned that the duty of disclosure imposed on an insider who chooses to sell or recommend selling a certain stock on the basis of material inside information establishes the requisite element of causation-in-fact for those who purchased that stock during the same period. 495 F.2d at 240-41.

In the present case, the Court holds that persons who trade on an open market weeks after an insider has concluded his trading activity must establish more than the materiality of the undisclosed information to demonstrate that their losses were caused by defendants' trading.[9] As the Court notes, the "disclose or abstain" rule is stated in the alternative. Trading is the gravamen of the offense. The public has no absolute right to the undisclosed information. It is only when the insider enters the market and creates an informational imbalance that a duty to disclose is imposed to protect the anonymous investors trading with the insider. See *SEC v. Texas Gulf Sulphur Co.*, supra at 848. The duty of disclosure is owed to the class of investors trading contemporaneously with the insider and it is only this group who are the proper beneficiaries of the relaxed causation

---

7   Continued ...

permit the fortuitous matching of buy and sell orders to determine whether a duty of disclosure were violated." See also Painter, 65 Colum.L.Rev. at 1372, 1377-8. One commentator has suggested that courts have dismissed cases for "lack of privity" when their real concern was over the absence of causation between the insider's trading and the plaintiff's losses. Bromberg § 8.7(1) at 215 n. 68.

9   Although the Court specifically does not address the question of market manipulation, if an insider's trading affects the market price to the extent of creating an artificial market in a security, subsequent investors who were induced to trade on the basis of the price change could logically establish transactional causation without reference to an insider's duty to "disclose or abstain." See *Cochran v. Channing*, 211 F. Supp. 239 (S.D.N.Y. 1962). See generally 88 Harv.Rev. at 592-96.

standard of *Affiliated Ute*. These investors as a class are disadvantaged by the superior knowledge of the insider. The stocks they traded generate the insider's profits.[11]

There was admittedly no connection between Appellants' trading and Appellees' decision to sell their Old Line stock. Appellees are in precisely the same situation they would have been in if Appellants had chosen to abstain from trading. Since they entered the market weeks after Appellants had ceased trading, none of the shares they sold could possibly have been purchased by Appellants. When Appellees entered the market, the information available to investors had returned to equilibrium. Non-contemporaneous traders do not require the special protection of the "disclose or abstain" rule because they do not suffer the disadvantage of trading with someone who has superior access to information. Parties on both sides of the transaction have equal access to information. Of course, as a practical matter, if the insider had made full public disclosure before trading subsequent traders would have been aware of the information and able to gauge its effect on the market. In this sense, whatever losses they suffered were "caused" by the insider's failure to disclose. But, as the Court points out, that presupposes that the insider's duty of disclosure runs to investors who have no possible connection to the insider trading. I also am unwilling to extend the "disclose or abstain" rule beyond the class of investors it was designed to protect—those trading contemporaneously with the insiders.

On remand from the Second Circuit, the District Court in *Shapiro* rejected the argument that recovery should be limited to those who purchased Douglas common stock during the period when defendants were actively trading in or recommending trading in the stock. *Shapiro v. Merrill Lynch, Pierce, Fenner & Smith, Inc.*, CCH Sec. L. Rep. ¶95,377 at 98,874, 98,877-78 (1976) (Transfer Binder) (S.D.N.Y. Dec. 9, 1975). Instead, the District Court held that the duty of disclosure extends "to all purchasers trading contemporaneously with defendants' wrongdoing, that is, 'while such information remains undisclosed.' " *Id.* at 98,878. Under this view, Appellees would be able to recover their losses from Appellants even though there was no possible connection between their trading and that of the insiders. Recovery would simply be based on their sale of Old Line Stock sometime before effective public disclosure of the planned merger. While I agree with the District Court in *Shapiro* that "liability should be

---

11   As noted above, the mechanics of the market necessitate designation of the class of contemporaneous investors as surrogate plaintiffs for those who actually traded with the insiders. This class must include investors who were in no way involved in the insider transactions, and except for the time of their trading, are indiscernible from subsequent traders. However, to accomplish the deterrent and compensatory purposes of 10b-5, it is better to be overinclusive in the definition of the plaintiff class than underinclusive.

Of course, limiting the plaintiff class to contemporaneous traders does not remove the spectre of "Draconian" damages. The number of persons trading contemporaneously with an insider in the open market could still be enormous. However one may limit liability, the prospect of ruinous recovery remains until some realistic measure of damages is devised. But this question is better left to the remedy stage where a court can employ its equitable powers in shaping an award or until such time as the Congress chooses to act on this problem.

coterminous with the duty breached by the wrongdoer," *id.*, I feel that the District Court has misinterpreted the breadth of the "disclose or abstain" rule in a straight insider trading situation. To repeat, the wrong which gives rise to the duty to "disclose or abstain" is the act of trading without disclosure. Neither an insider's trading when he is not in possession of material inside information, nor the decision to abstain from trading when he does possess such information, gives rise to a duty of disclosure. That duty arises only when necessary to equalize the information available to outside investors who are actively trading with an insider who is privy to undisclosed material facts. When the insider ceases trading, the informational imbalance ends and the market returns to its normal state. However, where there is tipping in conjunction with insider trading the circumstances are significantly altered. When an insider tips material information to selected traders he is perpetuating the informational imbalance in the market and breaching a separate duty to treat all persons in the market alike. By tipping, the insider has set off a chain of events which perhaps may only be remedied by full public disclosure.[12] *Shapiro* was not a case of straight insider trading but involved tipping on a mass scale. The complaint was essentially aimed at Merrill Lynch's policy of selective leakage of information about Douglas' financial straits to favored customers who in turn unloaded their shares in the market to unwary purchasers. Under these circumstances, the District Court in *Shapiro* may have correctly defined the class of potential plaintiffs to include those in the market up to the point of effective public disclosure.

In this case, by contrast, the Bradfords engaged in a straight scheme of insider trading. While I have no doubt that they knowingly violated rule 10b-5, I believe that recovery should be limited to those who sold Old Line shares between April 21st and 27th, 1972, the period when the Bradfords were actively purchasing Old Line Stock in the over-the-counter market. Since Appellees did not sell their shares during that period, I join in the Court's reversal of the decision below.

NOTE

A privity requirement may seem attractive as a device to avoid Draconian liability. But if that is all that is wanted, there are easier ways of limiting liability. In addition, it is not even clear that a contractual nexus is a guarantee that plaintiffs will have suffered real harm. Suppose that the plaintiff would have traded anyway, if not with the insider then with another outsider. In that case it is difficult to argue that the plaintiff has been harmed by insider trading. Then there are the other outsiders who might have traded with the trading outsider, but whose place was taken by the insider. These other outsiders will have traded as well, though perhaps not at the same bargain price as the insider. Still, they too will have made a profit. It is therefore difficult to point to any but the most

---

12 Tipping because it involves a more widespread imbalance of information presents an even greater threat to the integrity of the marketplace than simple insider trading. Tipping, by its very nature, is a more open-ended violation than that of the insider who enters the market, trades on his own account and withdraws.

general kinds of wealth transfer effects which are felt by outsiders. If insiders as a class outperform the market, then outsiders as a class must systematically receive lower returns, though without any clear nexus between winners and losers.

This is not enough to demonstrate the existence of distributional effects, unless it can also be shown that the advantages of insider trading are not paid for by insiders and that outsiders are not compensated for its disadvantages. If capital markets are relatively efficient, however, the possibility of insider trading would be reflected in the prices outsiders pay on issuance for widely held securities. It is difficult to maintain that underwriters and dealers are capable of adjusting to the most complicated kind of financial disclosure, but lack the knowledge of statutory insider trading requirements possessed by a law student. On an *ex ante* perspective, then, the possibility of a transfer of wealth from outsiders to insiders when insider trading occurs would be paid for by the firm through a lower share price when the securities are first issued to outsiders. See further Scott, *Insider Trading: Rule 10b-5, Disclosure and Corporate Privacy*, 9 J. Legal Stud. 801 (1980). The effect of insider trading prohibitions may also be felt in management markets when insiders require higher levels of direct executive compensation.

Measure of Damages. Even if liability runs only to those who bought or sold the very shares that the insider traded, there are considerable difficulties in measuring damages. One possible measure would be the difference between the price of the shares in the liability triggering transaction and their price at the date of judgment. This measure would confront the defendant with a very open-ended liability indeed. It would also seem extravagant where the stock is publicly traded because once the information is publicly disclosed or the plaintiff-to-be learns of it he can mitigate by replacing the shares that he had sold or by selling the ones he had bought. Another measure would be the difference between the price of the shares in the liability triggering transaction and their true value at that date, being an imputed market price as if the information in question had been publicly disclosed. This "out-of-pocket" measure is the one preferentially adopted in OSA s. 137(6), which uses as a proxy for true value the price at which the shares were actually quoted after the true information was in fact publicly disclosed. A problem with any measure of damages based upon the price to which the shares rose (or fell) at a given date is that many factors other than disclosure of the improperly used information may have contributed to the price change. To the extent that other factors have intervened, it would be argued under the CBCA that the improper trading did not cause "direct loss" to the plaintiff.

A generally helpful discussion of this question is contained in the opinion of the United States Court of Appeals for the Second Circuit in *Elkind v. Liggett & Myers Inc.*, 635 F.2d 156 (1980). In that case, an L & M officer had tipped a securities analyst about adverse earnings information. The analyst traded and the information was publicly disclosed about one-and-a-half days later. In the class action successfully maintained on behalf of L & M share purchasers, the Court settled upon what it called a "disgorgement" measure of damages, which it characterized as:

(1) ... allow[ing] any uninformed investor, where a reasonable investor would either have delayed his purchase or not purchased at all if he had had the benefit of the tipped information, to recover any post-purchase decline in market value of his shares up to a reasonable time after he

learns of the tipped information or after there is a public disclosure of it but (2) limit[ing] his re-covery to the amount gained by the tippee as a result of this [transacting] at the earlier date rather than delaying ... until the parties could trade on an equal informational basis. [*Id.* at 172]

Note that, within the "disgorgement" limit to the defendant's liability under the *Elkind* formulation, the defendant bears the risk (or reaps the benefit) of price changes not caused by disclosure of the confidential information.

Close Corporations. If the ECMH suggests that fears of distributional consequences through insider trading may reasonably be discounted in the case of widely traded securities, a concern for wealth transfer effects in close corporations may remain. Absent a market for the securities, it is less likely that distributional consequences would be undone *ex ante* through a lower issuance price in regimes that permit insider trading. Moreover, there may be "special facts" that suggest that the trade is unfair in these cases. For this reason, even before securities legislation, higher common law disclosure duty arose in face to face transactions than in trades on public exchanges.

Of course, not every face to face trade between insiders and outsiders will twig one's fairness antennae. For example, when an outsider reasonably believes on the basis of public information that his shares are worth $20 each and is approached by an insider to sell his shares for $25, he may conclude that either (1) the insider has knowledge of undisclosed good news about the firm or (2) the insider is trying to bolster a control position, seeking, for example, to give himself 51% of the outstanding stock. In both cases, the outsider's knowledge that he is dealing with an insider is valuable information in itself: it signals two possible motives for trade, which presumably the outsider will be capable of distinguishing. If the insider does not appear to be consolidating a control position, the outsider will then conclude that the shares are worth at least $25, and indeed will suppose that the insider regards them as worth more than that. What he will not know, except through negotiations, is how much more valuable the insider considers them to be. Are they really worth $30 or $100 in the insider's view? Whatever price is arrived at, the outsider will still conclude that the shares are in fact more valuable than that from the insider's perspective.* Though every trade to the insider will leave him with a gain, the contract is not for that reason unfair, for the outsider will have consented to the transaction with the knowledge of the insider's gain.

These considerations support the traditional Anglo-Canadian rule that, absent spe-cial facts, insiders do not owe fiduciary duties to the shareholders on insider trading. For example, in *Percival v. Wright*, [1902] 2 Ch. 421, the plaintiff shareholders had ap-proached the defendant directors, wishing to sell their shares at a stated price. The

---

* In a bad news scenario, the game theoretic considerations are different. Purchasers will fear that the securities are always less valuable than the insider's asking price, and so the market for such securities may unwind. Students of finance economies will recognize this as a "lemons" market. See Akerlof, *The Market for "Lemons": Quality Uncertainty and the Market Mechanism*, 84 Q.J. Econ. 488 (1970). By contrast, securities that an insider seeks to buy are "anti-lemons"—goods always worth more than their purchase price. Of course, in a bad news scenario, where insiders sell to outsiders, it is difficult to see how common law fiduciary duties might arise.

directors eventually bought the shares at a slightly higher price also named by the plaintiffs. The directors did not disclose that, at the time, they were negotiating to sell to third parties the corporation's undertaking—which by the articles the directors were empowered to do—at a price that on a per-share basis would greatly exceed the prices asked by the plaintiffs. The sale of the undertaking ultimately fell through, but when the plaintiffs learned of these negotiations they sued to set aside their sale of shares to the directors. Swinfen Eady J. held for the defendants, on the basis that they were under no duty to disclose the negotiations to sell the undertaking because they were not in a fiduciary relationship to the shareholders, as opposed to the corporation. The judge concluded:

> There is no question of unfair dealing in this case. The directors did not approach the shareholders with a view of obtaining their shares. The shareholders approached the directors and named the price at which they were desirous of selling. [*Id.* at 427]

From the perspective of distributional concerns, the *Percival* decision seems unexceptional on its facts. Since the outsiders initiated the transaction and bid up the price, they would appear to have been satisfied with the trade. Though the insiders thought the shares were worth more than the offering price, purchasers always do. Had the outsiders wanted something more, they might have asked if any material information remained undisclosed, with a common law fraud remedy available if the insiders lied. See Levmore, *Securities and Secrets: Insider Trading and the Law of Contracts*, 68 Va. L. Rev. 117, 137-42 (1982).

In special circumstances, however, distributional concerns may seem more pressing, and here insiders have been held to owe fiduciary duties to selling shareholders. For example, where insiders purchase shares using third parties to act on their behalf, the outsiders will be unaware of the fact that they are dealing with insiders. Because the insiders are undisclosed principals, the signalling effect of a face to face dealing is lost, the courts have impeached these trades. In *Gadsden v. Bennetto* (1913), 9 D.L.R. 719 (Man. C.A.), the defendant was a member of a committee of directors appointed to solicit a buyer for the assets or shares of the corporation. After procuring an offer for the assets, the defendant employed a solicitor to act as his agent in purchasing shares from the plaintiff. The shares were purchased in this way and no disclosure was made of the offer, which was eventually accepted. The Court of Appeal, reversing the trial Court, found the non-disclosure to be a breach of duty by the defendant to the plaintiff. Perdue J.A. stated:

> The position of the members of the committee in this case is very different from that of ordinary directors of a company as regards their fiduciary relations, and is quite distinguishable from *Percival v. Wright* [1902] 2 Ch. 421. In the present case the committee were acting outside the ordinary duties of directors, they were appointed for the purpose of securing and bringing in a proposal for disposing, not only of the land which was the property of the company, but the shares which were the property of the individual shareholders. On any proposal being received by them which involved the acquisition of the shares, they were bound to disclose to the shareholders, the interested parties, the nature of the proposal and the price offered. If the proposal took the form of acquiring all the company's property and leaving the shares out of account, the shareholders would be immediately interested in that proposal, because their shares would become worthless when the property was transferred and they could only look for reimbursement to their share of

the purchase money on a distribution being made. If the committee, acting under its duties to the company and the shareholders, secured a highly advantageous offer, they were bound to make full disclosure of the offer to the company and the shareholders. The members of the committee were the confidential agents of the company and the shareholders. [*Id.* at 723]

It is not always easy to say when the special facts doctrine will be triggered. The following case tests the limits of the doctrine.

Bell v. Source Data Control Ltd.
Ontario Court of Appeal
53 D.L.R. (4th) 580; 66 O.R. (2d) 78 (1988)

CORY J.A. (dissenting): The principal issue on this appeal is whether the majority shareholder, James Hood, owed a duty to disclose to the minority shareholders, Robert Bell and Ian Stewart, that he had negotiated for the sale of his shares to McLean-Hunter Limited at a price considerably higher than they would receive.

Factual Background

The company, Source Data Control Ltd. ("S.D.C."), was established in 1968. James Hood put up the majority of the capital required for the establishment of the firm and, as well, had the original idea for the business. As a result, he received 60% of the issued shares of the company. Stewart also contributed funds and worked in the business from the outset. He received 10% of the issued shares. Hood and Stewart then brought in Bell and Wilmot. Each of these received 10% of the issued shares of the company. Soon after Pickell came into S.D.C. He sold his 10% holding to Williamson in 1975 and plays no role in these proceedings. The company struggled and then prospered until some time in 1979. Certainly, all the parties to this action worked hard and long so that the company could succeed as it did. Some time during 1979 Hood had become embroiled in matrimonial problems. His personal difficulties affected him to such an extent that at one point one of the minority shareholders wondered whether Hood was running a divorce rather than a business. At the same time the relationship between Hood and the minority shareholders deteriorated to a marked degree. The plaintiffs and Williamson, another 10% minority shareholder, began to look for a way out.

In 1980, the company registered a loss in its operations at the end of its fiscal year in September. The company was also experiencing cash-flow problems. The company's bankers were concerned with its operations. Indeed, it was known to all parties that the bank was considering placing what was termed a "soft" receiver in the company. By 1979-1980 Hood had become erratic and it was very difficult to discuss business matters with him.

From sometime in the early 1970's McLean-Hunter had expressed an interest in acquiring S.D.C. In 1980, with the deteriorating situation at S.D.C., Williamson had two telephone conversations with Greenhough, a McLean-Hunter representative. At the first occasion Williamson stated that he could deliver a total of 30% of the shares of S.D.C. for a total of $600,000. He was told by Greenhough that McLean-Hunter would only be interested in purchasing control of S.D.C. There can be no doubt that throughout 1980 Bell, Stewart and Williamson were actively attempting to find a way out and to sell their shares in S.D.C. Williamson approached McLean-Hunter as late as October 29, 1980, to see if he could sell his shares. He put forward the same price of $200,000 for 10% of the shareholdings. Once again he was advised that McLean-Hunter was only interested in purchasing controlling interest in S.D.C.

Finally on November 14, 1980, Hood called McLean-Hunter and advised Greenhough that he would be interested in selling his shares. This would, of course, entail a sale of the majority interest in the company.

Greenhough and Nymark of McLean-Hunter met with Hood on some four to six occasions between November 14, 1980 and early 1981. Hood proposed a sale based on his evaluation of the company at $3.5 million of which 60% or $2.1 million would come to him. At the outset, it was apparent that Hood was proceeding on the basis that the minority shareholders would get an equivalent amount for their shares, that is to say, $350,000 for each 10% interest in the company. However, by December, 1980, Greenhough and others at the McLean-Hunter group had obtained further financial information about S.D.C. and concluded that $3 million was the top value they could place on the company. They were not prepared to pay more than $2.7 million for 90% of the shareholdings in S.D.C. Hood was insistent that he receive $2.1 million for his shares. The situation had apparently reached an impasse. At that point Nymark, of McLean-Hunter, suggested that the minority shareholders obtain the price which they themselves had suggested to McLean-Hunter of $200,000 for each of their 10% shareholdings.

That would leave $2.1 million for Hood's 60% shares. Each of the participants in the sale would receive the price which they wished and at the same time McLean-Hunter would keep within the amount it could expend for the acquisition of the company.

It is significant that McLean-Hunter had never, at any time, dealt directly with the minority shareholders although it made an offer to do so. Hood advised McLean-Hunter that he had an understanding or arrangement with the minority shareholders and that he would deal with them. It was clear that he was worried that his wife might learn of the proposed sale and his financial status.

Hood arranged a meeting with Bell, Stewart and Wilmot on December 19, 1980. He raised with them the possibility of the sale of their shares. The trial judge found that they wished to get out of the company, to get away from Hood and were most desirous of selling their shares. The minority shareholders advised Hood that they wanted $200,000 for each of their 10% shareholdings. Both Bell and Stewart acknowledged that this figure originated with them. It was not an amount suggested by Hood, who carefully refrained from suggesting any amount to the minority shareholders. The plaintiffs agreed that there was neither influence exerted nor pressure put upon them by Hood with regard to the sale or the valuation of their shares. Nor, of course, was there any influence or pressure exerted upon them by anyone at McLean-Hunter since none of their representatives had spoken to any of the minority shareholders, with the exception of the earlier conversations between Greenhough and Williamson.

Hood wished to obtain a written commitment from the minority shareholders. He requested them to sign a document which provided that each of the minority shareholders agreed to sell their entire shareholding in S.D.C. for $200,000 to whatever purchaser

Hood would direct. Two of the minority shareholders signed the document at the meeting. Bell took his document to his own solicitor who made some changes in the form which was then signed by Bell. The revised form provided that Bell had the right to continue to look for a purchaser. The other change was that he was committed to sell his shares for $200,000 to Hood or such other purchaser as he (apparently meaning Hood) might direct.

Bell made it very clear in his evidence that he was distrustful of Hood and would not sign anything without first consulting his own solicitor. The plaintiffs stated that Hood told them that his own shares were not for sale. Hood did not give evidence at trial but in his discovery stated that he was not asked whether his own shares were for sale or not and that he could not remember saying that they were. It is of no significance whether the statement was made by Hood or not as the plaintiffs stated that their commitment to sell their shares did not come about as a result of any inquiry of Hood.

At the same meeting Hood talked of the poor financial condition of the company. The plaintiffs, who were also directors, were aware of the financial situation as they received not only the annual statement of the company but monthly operating statements. Although its sales were high the bank loan was not in good shape. All the parties were aware that the bank was, in the words of the trial judge, getting "rather nervous," and had gone so far as to speak of the possibility of putting in a "soft" receiver.

On January 22, 1981, Bell called Greenhough to advise him that the minority shareholders would sell to McLean-Hunter for $200,000 each. He did this completely unaware that Hood was dealing with McLean-Hunter. Greenhough was suspicious of the call from Bell. He was aware that Hood did not wish any disclosure of the sale for fear it would get back to his wife. He also wondered whether Bell had been put up to making the call by Hood. As a result, he was extremely guarded and did not disclose the proposed purchase by McLean-Hunter of 90% of the shares of S.D.C.

By December 22, 1980, Greenhough and Nymark had obtained approval of the transaction from the president of McLean-Hunter. On December 24, 1980, a letter of intent was drawn up whereby McLean-Hunter was to purchase 90% of the shares of S.D.C. for the total sum of $2.7 million. No breakdown of price was set out in that memorandum of intent, which expressly stated that it was not intended to be legally binding or enforceable between the parties. It was signed sometime in the next 10 days. The closing of the transaction was fixed for February 10, 1981. The trial judge accepted the evidence of the solicitor for McLean-Hunter and of Mr. Greenhough that there remained a good many matters outstanding to be resolved and that there was some doubt that the matter would close on February 10th.

The trial judge found that as a result of the circulation of documents to the plaintiffs they must have known no later than January 29th that McLean-Hunter would be the purchaser of the shares, and that they were aware that McLean-Hunter would only be interested in the purchase of the majority of the shares of S.D.C. They were thus aware before the date of closing of the identity of the purchaser and that the purchaser must have negotiated to buy a majority interest. Thus, at least some of the shares of Hood must have been included in the total price. The trial judge did not accept the evidence of Stewart and Bell that they were not aware of these facts and found that at the closing on February 10th this knowledge must have been confirmed and must have been apparent to the plaintiffs.

On January 22, 1981, the plaintiffs with their solicitors requested information with regard to the over-all transaction, but Hood and his lawyer refused to give any details at all. Sometime after the closing the plaintiffs learned the price that Hood had received for his shares. The trial judge found that at the time of closing the plaintiffs had obtained their objective to get clear of Hood and to get $200,000 in cash for their shares. The trial judge emphasized that there had been no question that at the meeting of December 19, 1980, when they undertook to sell their shares for $200,000, they had not asked Hood whether he was selling his shares or whether the sale of their shares was in any way tied to the sale of Hood's shares.

The trial judge specifically found that the plaintiffs had not placed any reliance upon Hood for guidance in making their decision either about selling their shares or about the price at which they were to be sold. He found that they had made their decision to sell long before the meeting of December 19th and had, of their own volition, fixed upon the price of $200,000. He concluded that it was quite in order for McLean-Hunter to pay a premium for the majority shares in a private company.

Decision at Trial

Based upon the findings of fact which he made [summarized 39 A.C.W.S. (2d) 62], the trial judge found that there had been no conspiracy between the defendants, that there had been no deceitful or fraudulent acts committed by the defendants, that no constructive trust existed which placed any duty upon the defendant Hood and lastly, that there was no fiduciary duty or obligation upon Hood to disclose to the plaintiffs the price at which he was selling his shares.

The appellants Stewart and Bell take issue with all these conclusions of the trial judge.

Was deceit established?

The trial judge was, in my view, correct in his conclusion that the tort of deceit had not been established. In order to establish such a claim the appellants were required to establish that a false representation of fact by words or conduct had been made by the defendants; that the representation was made with the knowledge of its falsity; that the representation was made with the intention that it be acted upon by the appellants, and that the appellants did in fact act in reliance upon the representation and that they sustained damage in so doing.

The appellants put forward as a basis for this claim the statements made by Greenhough to Bell during the telephone conversation of January 22, 1981. The trial judge was correct in his conclusion that Greenhough did not make any false representations during that conversation. Greenhough avoided volunteering information because of what the trial judge properly found to have been quite reasonable concerns. Specifically, he was worried about the motivation for the call and that if he gave any information he would be in breach of his undertaking to Hood that the nature of the transaction would be kept confidential. As well, Greenhough did not make any representations in that conversation intending that they be relied upon by the appellants. Rather, he wished to avoid saying anything that would represent a breach of his undertaking of confidentiality, or anything that Hood could use against him in the course of their negotiations should Bell be calling at Hood's request. Finally, there is no evidence that the appellants acted in reliance upon anything that was said during that telephone conversation. It was clear that they had committed their shares to Hood before they had any discussion with McLean-Hunter representatives. The appellants cannot succeed on this issue.

Was the tort of conspiracy established?

In order to establish a claim for conspiracy the appellants would have to prove the following elements:

(a) a combination or agreement (i) the predominant purpose of which is to cause injury to the appellants; or (ii) to use unlawful means directed towards the appellants in circumstances where the respondents should have known injury to the appellants was likely to result, and

(b) that the appellant suffered actual damage by reason of the acts of the respondents carried out in furtherance of the combination or agreement.

See *Canada Cement LaFarge Ltd. v. B.C. Lightweight Aggregate Ltd.* (1983), 145 D.L.R. (3d) 385 at pp. 398-9, 72 C.P.R. (2d) 1, [1983] 1 S.C.R. 452 at pp. 471-2 (S.C.C.).

It is clear that the appellants cannot establish that the predominant purpose of the agreement between Hood and McLean-Hunter was to cause injury to them. The sole purpose for which McLean-Hunter entered into the agreement was to purchase S.D.C. They were doing no more than pursuing their own business interests. Nor was there any finding or any evidence that McLean-Hunter or any of the respondents used unlawful means in promoting their business interests. I would agree with the trial judge that there is nothing improper in paying a premium to the controlling shareholder. Certainly McLean-Hunter made no misrepresentations in acquiring the shares of the appellants. The appellants cannot succeed in this ground of the appeal.

Was a constructive trust imposed on the McLean-Hunter respondents as a result of their knowingly assisting Hood in breaching his fiduciary duty?

Once again I agree with the trial judge that there was no evidence put forward which would establish such a claim. To justify the imposition of a constructive trust on McLean-Hunter, who it must be remembered are strangers to any fiduciary relationship that may exist between Hood and the appellants, the appellants would have to establish the following:

(a) that the appellants had a fiduciary relationship with Hood;

(b) that Hood breached his fiduciary duty; and

(c) that Greenhough assisted Hood in the breach of that duty (i) with actual subjective knowledge of the breach of duty; or (ii) as a result of wilfully shutting his eyes to an obvious breach of duty; or (iii) wilfully and recklessly failing to make such inquiries of Hood concerning the propriety of what Hood was doing as an honest and reasonable man would make in the circumstances.

See Oakley, *Constructive Trusts*, 2nd ed. (1987), pp. 87-102.

Assuming that Hood owed a fiduciary duty to the appellants and breached it, there was no evidence that Greenhough knew of Hood's breach or that the McLean-Hunter representatives shut their eyes to the obvious or wilfully and recklessly failed to make reasonable inquiries. It was quite appropriate for the McLean-Hunter respondents to accept Hood's statement that he had an understanding with the minority shareholders and that Greenhough was to deal exclusively with him. McLean-Hunter had no indication from the appellants that Hood was acting improperly. The evidence is really quite to the contrary. The appellants deposited their shares on January 29, 1981, after receiving independent legal advice and knowing that they were only going to receive $200,000 each. They knew that McLean-Hunter was undoubtedly the purchaser. Further, notwithstanding Hood's refusal to give any particulars of the total transaction they agreed to deposit their shares. In those circumstances this ground of appeal must fail.

Was a fiduciary duty owed by Hood to the appellants?

This is the most difficult aspect of the case. It may be helpful to review the cases which have established the common law rule as to fiduciary duty owed by directors and majority shareholders to their corporation and the minority shareholders.

At common law the rule was that directors and majority shareholders owe a fiduciary duty to the corporation itself but not to other individual shareholders: see L.C.B. Gower, *Principles of Modern Company Law*, 4th ed. (1979), p. 573, and B. Welling, *Corporate Law in Canada* (1984), pp. 380-81.

The rule is derived from the decision of the House of Lords in *Percival v. Wright*, [1902] 2 Ch. 421. In that case, the directors purchased shares from the plaintiffs while secretly negotiating to sell the company at a more favourable price. None the less, the court declined to upset the contract and observed that premature disclosure of the negotiations might well be against the "best interests of the company."

In *Wotherspoon v. C.P. Ltd.* (1982), 35 O.R. (2d) 449, 129 D.L.R. (3d) 1 (C.A.), an issue was raised as to whether C.P., the majority shareholder, had a fiduciary duty to disclose certain financial information to the O. & Q. shareholders. At p. 489 O.R., p. 44 D.L.R. of the reasons, it was stated "[I]f C.P. owed a fiduciary duty, it was owed to O. & Q. and not to O. & Q.'s shareholders."

The rule was also referred to in *Pelling v. Pelling* (1981), 130 D.L.R. (3d) 761, [1982] 2 W.W.R. 185 (B.C.S.C.). In that case, the majority shareholder purchased shares from the minority at a time when he had negotiated an arrangement to sell them for a profit to another company. Berger J. held that the minority shareholder could successfully recover his damages under British Columbia's statutory insider trading provision. None the less, he specifically found that at common law there was no fiduciary obligation as between shareholders and further that there was no general fiduciary obligation owed by a director to shareholders. He noted that a director's duty is to the company and that he has no fiduciary obligation to the shareholders. The common law thus did not provide a remedy.

In *Coleman v. Myers*, [1977] 2 N.Z.L.R. 225 (C.A.), the New Zealand Court of Appeal departed from the rule set out in *Percival v. Wright*, supra. In this case, the appellants were minority shareholders in a small family-owned private company. They sold out their interests to the company's managing director. When he had gained control the director sold some of the company's assets and distributed some of the proceeds as a dividend which in turn paid for his acquisition of control. The court set forward a test for determining whether or not a fiduciary duty existed. It provided that the standard of conduct required from a director in dealing with a shareholder would differ depending upon the surrounding circumstances and the nature of the responsibility that the director had assumed towards the shareholder. It was expressed at pp. 324-5 in the following way:

As I have indicated it is my opinion that the standard of conduct required from a director in relation to dealings with a shareholder will differ depending upon all the surrounding circumstances and the nature of the responsibility which in a real and practical sense the director has assumed towards the shareholder. In the one case there may be a need to provide an explicit warning and a great deal of information concerning the proposed transaction. In another there may be no need to speak at all. There will be intermediate situations. It is, however, an area of the law where the courts can and should find some practical means of giving effect to sensible and fair principles of commercial morality in the cases that come before them; and while it may not be possible to lay down any general test as to when the fiduciary duty will arise for a company director or to prescribe the exact conduct which will always discharge it when it does, there are nevertheless some factors that will usually have an influence upon a decision one way or the other. They include, I think, dependence upon information and advice, the existence of a relationship of confidence, the significance of some particular transaction for the parties and, of course, the extent of any positive action taken by or on behalf of the director or directors to promote it.

A similar test can be derived from some Ontario decisions. In *Laskin v. Bache & Co. Inc.*, [1972] 1 O.R. 465, 23 D.L.R. (3d) 385 (C.A.), Arnup J.A. observed that the category of fiduciary duties and obligations which may arise from the circumstances of the case and the relationship of the parties was no more closed than the categories of negligence at common law.

The potential fiduciary obligation owed by a majority shareholder to minority shareholders was considered by Morand J. in *Farnham v. Fingold*, [1972] 3 O.R. 688, 29 D.L.R. (3d) 279 (H.C.J.). Although his conclusions were overruled by the Court of Appeal, [1973] 2 O.R. 132, 33 D.L.R. (3d) 156, there were no adverse comments expressed on his very useful summary pertaining to fiduciary obligations. At pp. 696-7 O.R., pp. 287-8 D.L.R., he put forward his position in this way:

Aside from a general duty of directors to shareholders, over the past few years, a body of law has developed imposing special obligations on controlling shareholders who wish to sell their shares at a price not available to other shareholders. The duty on controlling shareholders appears to be based upon several theories:

(a) As a matter of fairness, considering the relevant positions of the parties, such an obligation should be generally imposed.

(b) The controlling shareholders derive their benefit from their special access to corporate information which is not generally available to all shareholders. This information is owned by the company and the fruits thereof should not be appropriated to specific shareholders, but should be available to all.

(c) The sale of corporate control is an intangible asset which passes with the sale of control blocks, and this asset is owned by the corporation. As such, all shareholders should benefit by its sale.

I agree with these comments.

In *Goldex Mines Ltd. v. Revill* (1974), 7 O.R. (2d) 216, 54 D.L.R. (3d) 672 (C.A.), the court considered a class action brought by minority shareholders for the wrongs allegedly inflicted upon them by the majority. At issue was whether the action was a derivative one which could not be brought without leave of the court. Although it was held that based on the pleadings the action could only be considered a derivative action, nevertheless the importance of protecting shareholders' rights was emphasized in this way at p. 224 O.R., p. 680 D.L.R.:

The principle that the majority governs in corporate affairs is fundamental to corporation law, but its corollary is also important—that the majority must act fairly and honestly. Fairness is the touchstone of equitable justice, and when the test of fairness is not met, the equitable jurisdiction of the Court can be invoked to prevent or remedy the injustice which misrepresentation or other dishonesty has caused. The category of cases in which fiduciary duties and obligations arise is not a closed one: *Laskin v. Bache & Co. Inc.*, [1972] 1 O.R. 465 at p. 472, 23 D.L.R. (3d) 385 at p. 392.

The issue of the existence of a fiduciary duty was considered as well in *Francis v. Dingman* (1983), 43 O.R. (2d) 641, 2 D.L.R. (4th) 244, 23 B.L.R. 234 (C.A.). There the court once again emphasized that the categories of fiduciary relations were not closed and that their existence might depend upon the relationship which had developed as a matter of business exigency. The position was put forward by Lacourciere J.A. in this way at pp. 647-8 O.R., p. 251 D.L.R.:

I am also prepared to find the existence of a fiduciary relationship on other, broader grounds. It is settled that the categories of fiduciary relationships should not be considered closed. ... In my view it is not necessary to strain to fit the facts into a well-established category of fiduciary obligation to find the existence of a fiduciary relationship; it is permissible to look at a relationship which has developed as a matter of business exigency and determine whether it is appropriate that fiduciary obligations attach given the attendant factual circumstances.

The principle that whether or not a fiduciary duty exists was to be determined upon the facts presented in each case was emphasized once again in *International Corona Resources v. Lac Minerals* (1987), 62 O.R. (2d) 1, 44 D.L.R. (4th) 592, 18 C.P.R. (3d) 263 (C.A.). At pp. 44-5 O.R., p. 636 D.L.R. the following appears:

It becomes a question of fact in each case whether the relationship of the parties, the one to the other, is such as to create a fiduciary relationship. The circumstances which give rise to such a relationship have not been fully defined nor are they forever closed. An example of a court finding a fiduciary relationship between parties who initially are involved at arm's length in a commercial transaction may be found in *United Dominion Corp. Ltd. v. Brian Pty. Ltd.* (1985), 59 A.L.J.R. 676.

In its early stages, the law of fiduciary relationship developed from the vesting of property in a trustee for the sole benefit of a beneficiary. The courts, concerned with the protection of the property for the benefit of the beneficiary, recognized a fiduciary relationship which carried with it an obligation on the trustee to hold the property in trust for the beneficiary. Subsequently, the classes of relationships which have been recognized by the court to be fiduciary in nature have been extended. They now include trustees, executors, administrators, assignees in bankruptcy, solicitors, accountants, banks, directors, agents, partners, senior management and persons holding public office: Waters, *Law of Trusts in Canada*, 2nd ed. (1984), at pp. 6-10 and 712-3. In *Lloyds Bank Ltd. v. Bundy*, [1975] Q.B. 326, Sir Eric Sachs said at p. 341:

> Everything depends on the particular facts, and such a relationship [fiduciary relationship] has been held to exist in unusual circumstances as between purchaser and vendor, as between great uncle and adult nephew, and in widely other different sets of circumstances. Moreover, it is neither feasible nor desirable to attempt closely to define the relationship, or its characteristics, or the demarcation line showing the exact transition point where a relationship that does not entail that duty passes into one that does (cf Ungoed-Thomas J. in *In re Craig, dec'd.* [1971] Ch. 95, 104).

A very similar factual situation to the case at bar was considered by the British Columbia Court of Appeal in *Dusik v. Newton* (1985), 62 B.C.L.R. 1. In that case, the plaintiff owned 10% of the shares in the company, the defendant through another company owned 90%. The plaintiff and defendant enjoyed a special relationship arising from their long association in the enterprise. The plaintiff was having financial difficulties and he agreed to sell his 10% for $450,000 to the purchaser. The purchaser offered the defendant $15 million for the company, that is to say, $1.5 million for each 10%. This amount was never disclosed to the plaintiff. The defendant and the purchaser agreed on a plan whereby the defendant would sell his shares for $13.5 million and the purchaser would press the plaintiff to sell for $450,000. The plaintiff discovered how he had been misled and brought the action against the defendant.

It was held that a minority shareholder could successfully sustain a personal action for breach of fiduciary duty against a director and majority shareholder who had failed to inform him of a take-over offer. It was determined that the defendant, as a director, had breached his fiduciary duty to the plaintiff by failing to inform him of the proposed sale. The court set out and relied upon the quotations set out earlier from *Goldex*, supra, and from *Francis v. Dingman*, supra. The court concluded that the rule set out in *Percival v. Wright*, supra, should no longer be strictly applied. The court held that the correct approach was that stated in the passages quoted from *Coleman v. Myers*, supra, and from *Goldex* and *Francis v. Dingman*.

It can then be seen that the original rule that individual shareholders are not owed a fiduciary duty by other directors or majority shareholders has been altered. It is now clear that the issue as to whether fiduciary obligations are owed will depend upon the facts of the particular case and will not be dependent solely upon the formal classification of the parties as majority and minority shareholders or director and shareholder.

Applying that principle to the facts of this case I have concluded that a fiduciary duty was indeed owed by Hood to the minority shareholders. This was a small, very closely held corporation. The parties had worked together very hard and in close association for a number of years. They had all dedicated themselves to the success of the company. They had, until 1978 or 1980, enjoyed a special relationship arising from their long and close association in S.D.C. In all probability they would have continued their association had it not been for the marital difficulties experienced by Hood. The fact that as a result of his personal problems he was difficult to deal with and the minority shareholders no longer trusted him nor wished to continue their association with him does not relieve him from his obligation. Where, as here, parties have worked together in a close association for some years, equitable fairness requires the majority share-holder at least to disclose the fact of the take-over.

The sale of a majority interest in a company is fundamental to its operations. If ever there is to be a duty to disclose it should arise in the circumstances of a take-over. It may well have been sufficient for Hood to disclose that he was selling his shares at a price greater than that of the minority shareholders. In a private corporation the majority interest may be entitled to receive a premium from the sale of the majority shares. Nevertheless, the fact that there is to be such a premium should be disclosed, if not the precise amount.

I am strengthened in this conclusion by reference to the provisions of both the Securities Act, R.S.O. 1980, c. 466, as amended by S.O. 1987, c. 7, and the Canada Business Corporations Act, S.C. 1974-75-76, c. 33, pertaining to take-over bids. It is clear that in a publicly held corporation there must be disclosure of the terms of any take-over bid. It would seem anomalous that there should be complete protection of minority shareholders of a publicly held corporation, and no protection in a private corporation. In circumstances where a small, closely held corporation has existed for a number of years and has been the source of livelihood for all the shareholders, common decency and elementary fairness dictate that a fiduciary obligation rests upon the major-ity shareholder to disclose the sale of the majority interest and at least whether there is to be a premium for the majority shares.

It may well be that a minority shareholder is not in any position to quarrel with the terms of the proposed sale. For instance, in this case the minority shareholders could, by refusing to go along with the transaction, have created a situation where the sale was lost. They would have been left without a buyer interested in acquiring the financially troubled company, and their shares might have become valueless. None the less, the duty remained upon Hood, the majority shareholder, to disclose the sale of his shares at a premium. ...

BROOKE J.A.: Having regard to the findings of fact made by the trial judge, I think that this case must be distinguished from cases in which the principle relied upon by my brother Cory is to be applied. In these circumstances I agree with the reasons of Mr. Justice Eberle. Therefore the appeal should be dismissed.

McKINLAY J.A. concurs with BROOKE J.A.

Appeal dismissed.

NOTES

1) At trial (39 A.C.W.S. (2d) 62), Eberle J. had held that the firm promoters had no duty to disclose details of the negotiations to the minority shareholders, who had not relied on the promoters for advice or opinion with respect to the sale of the minority shares. Nor did the representative of the prospective purchaser have a duty to disclose the negotiations to the minority shareholders. There had been no fraudulent misrepresentation or conspiracy, or any intention on part of the purchasers to injure the plaintiffs. Moreover, the majority shareholders and the purchaser were not constructive trustees for the minority shareholders.

2) On the facts, does this case more closely resemble *Percival* or *Gadsden*? The plaintiffs knew that their shares would come to rest in the hands of McLean-Hunter. They also had tried to sell their shares to McLean-Hunter for $200,000. What they did not know was the premium price at which Hall would sell his 60% block of shares to McLean-Hunter.

3) The question whether a majority shareholder is entitled to sell his shares at a control premium which he does not share with minority shareholders is discussed further in Chapter Eleven, Section F.

C. EFFICIENCY CONCERNS

On a soft defence of insider trading, the practice might be permitted if distributional effects are not troubling. On hard defences, which we now consider, an institution should be encouraged if it is Kaldor-Hicks efficient, whatever its distributional consequences. An efficiency defence of insider trading was first made by Henry Manne in his book, *Insider Trading and the Stock Market*, published in 1966. The book's vigorous attack of insider trading prohibitions was greeted with controversy, to put it mildly. Much of this controversy is detailed in Manne, *Insider Trading and the Law Professors*, 23 Vand. L. Rev. 547 (1970). In recent years, Manne's claim that a judgment of the institution depends critically upon a discriminating analysis of its allocational effects has become generally accepted by academics, though not all would agree with him that insider trading is wholly benign. At the same time, public reaction to insider trading, fuelled by sanctions imposed against market professionals like Ivan Boesky, appears more harsh than at any time since the 1930s.

1. Insider Trading as Managerial Compensation

Entrepreneurial Compensation. Dean Manne argues that the most compelling reason for permitting insider trading is that it serves as an efficient form of entrepreneurial compensation. Manne sees entrepreneurs as the agents of change in the market economy whose financial health depends upon the pure profits available to them. The pre-eminence given to entrepreneurship finds an echo in the Austrian rejection of neo-classical economics. From an Austrian perspective, economic growth is founded on an entrepreneurial "alertness" to opportunities to profit. See I. Kirzner, *Competition and Entrepreneurship* (1973).

This argument for insider trading will not, however, be persuasive unless, as a class, insiders are seen as entrepreneurs. Most commentators have rejected this premise and therefore do not accept Manne's arguments for insider trading as entrepreneurial compensation. Those with access to material undisclosed information often seem not so much risk-taking entrepreneurs as agents of a firm charged with carrying out its corporate policies. For example, profits are more readily available in widely traded firms, whose senior executives may more easily be seen as belonging to a managerial rather than to an entrepreneurial class. Moreover, the private disclosure of inside information to "tippees" may not seem to benefit a class of entrepreneurs, though tipping may perhaps serve other economic goals, as we shall see.

Managerial Risk Aversion. A further argument for insider trading as a compensation strategy is that it may serve to cure adverse incentives caused by managerial risk aversion. As discussed in Chapter Seven, managerial self-dealing may take the form of rejection by managers of positive net present value opportunities in favour of less profitable but more secure ones. If management's long-term economic prospects are correlated to the fortunes of the firm, then inefficient investment strategies might be adopted by risk-averse managers as a means of protecting their human capital. By contrast, shareholders whose investments are more highly diversified may be presumed to be risk neutral, and would therefore prefer that the firm take up the opportunity with the highest expected monetary value, whatever its risk characteristics. These incentives failures may in part be addressed through bonus plans and through the market for human capital itself, and insider trading may also be seen as a response to this form of self-dealing. The idea here is that insiders will be led to adopt only the most profitable investment opportunities, since these offer the best prospects for insider trading profits.

Insider trading may, however, be thought a crude method of addressing incentive failures, since it permits managers to profit on the basis of bad news as well as good. It might then be feared that managers will cause the firm to take up less valuable investments for the insider trading profits available on a sale of shares. Managers might also be led to maximize not share value but rather the volatility of the firm's securities. Greater profits through insider trading are available from securities that fluctuate widely in price than from those that only gradually advance in value. These concerns may, however, be effectively counterbalanced by the various other incentives managers have to maximize firm value. It must be the rare case where a manager of a public corporation would find it to his advantage to lower firm value for the purpose of insider trading. In addition, because decisions are made in groups, internal monitoring systems would appear to render it extremely difficult for an insider to reduce firm value in order to speculate on its shares.

Insider trading may also be an inefficient form of compensation because its returns are more risky (in the sense of a mean-preserving dispersion of possible outcomes) than fixed salary compensation. If managerial risk aversion is presumed, it might then be cheaper to offer managers a more traditional kind of compensation package, such as a bonus plan. In addition, the difficulty of measuring insider trading imposes its own risks on the firm, and this uncertainty will also increase the cost of insider trading as a form of compensation. With more uncertainty about the size of manager compensation, outside shareholders will also impose a higher cost of capital. See Dooley, *Enforcement of Insider Trading Restrictions*, 66 Va. L. Rev. 1 (1980). A further possible inefficiency is that permitting insider trading may allow an insider to "unbundle" other incentive policies in the compensation package. Carlton & Fischel, *The Regulation of Insider Trading*, 35 Stan. L. Rev. 857, 873-74 (1983). For example, the firm might offer the manager bonus plan compensation to align his interests with those of the firm. But if a decline in the value of a bonus plan or a fall in stock price is cushioned through the possibility of insider trading, the two kinds of compensation devices will operate at cross purposes.

These arguments might suggest that, in a legal regime that permitted insider trading, a firm might do well to prohibit insider trading in its management contracts. However, these arguments do not in themselves support mandatory prohibitions, since many other features of the compensation decision are left unregulated. Moreover, the absence of prohibitions of insider trading in management contracts prior to legislative prohibition might suggest that these inefficiencies are minor or swamped by competing efficiencies. See Dooley, *Enforcement of Insider Trading Restrictions*, 66 Va. L. Rev. 1, 48-49 (1980). But see Gilson & Kraakman, *The Mechanisms of Market Efficiency*, 70 Va. L. Rev. 549, 634 n. 224 (1984) (absence of contractual prohibitions explained by the difficulty of private monitoring of insider trading by the firm, as compared with public monitoring by securities commissions).

2. Information Costs

What is generally taken as the strongest argument for permitting insider trading is that it may have the effect of promoting market efficiency by leading share prices more quickly to reflect changes in the firm's affairs. This point may be better appreciated after reading the facts of the following decision. *S.E.C. v. Texas Gulf Sulphur Co.* was an injunctive action, rather than an action for damages, brought by the S.E.C. against the corporation and various of its insiders growing out of the defendant's activities in reaction to a spectacular copper ore discovery by T.G.S. near Timmins, Ontario.

Securities & Exchange Comm'n v. Texas Gulf Sulphur Co.
United States Court of Appeals, Second Circuit
401 F.2d 833 (2d Cir. 1968), cert. denied 394 U.S. 976 (1969)

[Before LUMBARD C.J. and WATERMAN, MOORE, FRIENDLY, SMITH, KAUFMAN, HAYS, ANDERSON and FEINBERG JJ.]

WATERMAN J.: ... This action derives from the exploratory activities of TGS begun in 1957 on the Canadian Shield in eastern Canada. In March of 1959, aerial geophysical surveys were conducted over more than 15,000 square miles of this area by a group led by defendant Mollison, a mining engineer and a Vice-President of TGS. The group included defendant Holyk, TGS's chief geologist, defendant Clayton, an electrical engineer and geophysicist, and defendant Darke, a geologist. These operations resulted in the detection of numerous anomalies, i.e., extraordinary variations in the conductivity of rocks, one of which was on the Kidd 55 segment of land located near Timmins, Ontario.

On October 29 and 30, 1963, Clayton conducted a ground geophysical survey on the northeast portion of the Kidd 55 segment which confirmed the presence of an anomaly and indicated the necessity of diamond core drilling for further evaluation. Drilling of the initial hole K-55-1, at the strongest part of the anomaly was commenced on November 8 and terminated on November 12 at a depth of 655 feet. Visual estimates by Holyk of the core of K-55-1 indicated an average copper content of 1.15% and an average zinc content of 8.64% over a length of 599 feet. This visual estimate convinced TGS that it was desirable to acquire the remainder of the Kidd 55 segment, and in order to facilitate this acquisition TGS President Stephens instructed the exploration group to keep the results of K-55-1 confidential and undisclosed even as to other officers, directors, and employees of TGS. The hole was concealed and a barren core was intentionally drilled off the anomaly. Meanwhile, the core of K-55-1 had been shipped to Utah for chemical assay which, when received in early December, revealed an average mineral content of 1.18% copper, 8.26% zinc, and 3.94% ounces of silver per ton over a length of 602 feet. These results were so remarkable that neither Clayton, an experienced geophysicist, nor four other TGS expert witnesses, had ever seen or heard of a comparable initial exploratory drill hole in a base metal deposit. ... By March 27, 1964, TGS decided that the land acquisition program had advanced to such a point that the company might well resume drilling, and drilling was resumed on March 31.

During this period, from November 12, 1963 when K-55-1 was completed, to March 31, 1964 when drilling was resumed, [T.G.S. shares or call options to purchase T.G.S. shares were purchased by Clayton, Darke, Fogarty (executive Vice President of T.G.S.), Holyk, Mrs. Holyk, Mollison and a large number of persons, otherwise unconnected to T.G.S., who had been advised of the favourable developments by Darke]. Prior to these transactions these persons had owned 1135 shares of TGS stock and possessed no calls; thereafter they owned a total of 8235 shares and possessed 12,300 calls.

On February 20, 1964, also during this period, TGS issued stock options to 26 of its officers and employees whose salaries exceeded a specified amount, five of whom were the individual defendants Stephens, Fogarty, Mollison, Holyk, and Kline. Of these, only Kline was unaware of the detailed results of K-55-1, but he, too, knew that a hole containing favourable bodies of copper and zinc ore had been drilled in Timmins. At this time, neither the TGS Stock Option Committee nor its Board of Directors had been informed of the results of K-55-1, presumably because of the pending land acquisition program which required confidentiality. All of the foregoing defendants accepted the options granted them.

[Between March 31 and April 10, drilling was carried out at three points and the visual results were uniformly encouraging. Between April 1 and April 8 T.G.S. shares were purchased by Clayton, Fogarty and Mrs. Mollison.]

Meanwhile, rumors that a major ore strike was in the making had been circulating throughout Canada. On the morning of Saturday, April 11, Stephens at his home in Greenwich, Conn. read in the New York Herald Tribune and in the New York Times unauthorized reports of the TGS drilling which seemed to infer a rich strike from the fact that the drill cores had been flown to the United States for chemical assay. Stephens immediately contacted Fogarty at his home in Rye, N.Y., who in turn telephoned and later that day visited Mollison at Mollison's home in Greenwich to obtain a current report and evaluation of the drilling progress. The following morning, Sunday, Fogarty again telephoned Mollison, inquiring whether Mollison had any further information and told him to return to Timmins with Holyk, the TGS Chief Geologist, as soon as possible "to move things along." With the aid of one Carroll, a public relations consultant, Fogarty drafted a press release designed to quell the rumors, which release, after having been channeled through Stephens and Huntington, a TGS attorney, was issued at 3:00 P.M. on Sunday, April 12, and which appeared in the morning newspapers of general circulation on Monday, April 13. It read in pertinent part as follows:

New York, April 12—The following statement was made today by Dr. Charles F. Fogarty, executive vice president of Texas Gulf Sulphur Company, in regard to the company's drilling operations near Timmins, Ontario, Canada. Dr. Fogarty said:

"During the past few days, the exploration activities of Texas Gulf Sulphur in the area of Timmins, Ontario, have been widely reported in the press, coupled with rumors of a substantial copper discovery there. These reports exaggerate the scale of operations, and mention plans and statistics of size and grade of ore that are without factual basis and have evidently originated by speculation of people not connected with TGS.

"The facts are as follows. TGS has been exploring in the Timmins area for six years as part of its overall search in Canada and elsewhere for various minerals—lead, copper, zinc, etc. During the course of this work, in Timmins as well as in Eastern Canada, TGS has conducted exploration entirely on its own, without the participation by others. Numerous prospects have been investigated by geophysical means and a large number of selected ones have been core-drilled. These cores are sent to the United States for assay and detailed examination as a matter of routine and on advice of expert Canadian legal counsel. No inferences as to grade can be drawn from this procedure.

"Most of the areas drilled in Eastern Canada have revealed either barren pyrite or graphite without value; a few have resulted in discoveries of small or marginal sulphide ore bodies.

"Recent drilling on one property near Timmins has led to preliminary indications that more drilling would be required for proper evaluation of this prospect. The drilling done to date has not been conclusive, but the statement made by many outside quarters are unreliable and include information and figures that are not available to TGS.

"The work done to date has not been sufficient to reach definite conclusions and any statement as to size and grade of ore would be premature and possibly misleading. When we have progressed to the point where reasonable and logical conclusions can be made, TGS will issue a definite statement to its stockholders and to the public in order to clarify the Timmins project."

The release purported to give the Timmins drilling results as of the release date, April 12. From Mollison Fogarty had been told of the developments through 7:00 P.M. on April 10, and of the remarkable discoveries made up to that time, detailed supra, which discoveries, according to the calculations of the experts who testified for the SEC at the hearing, demonstrated that TGS had already discovered 6.2 to 8.3 million tons of proved ore having gross assay values from $26 to $29 per ton. TGS experts, on the other hand, denied at the hearing that proven or probable ore could have been calculated on April 11 or 12 because there was then no assurance of continuity in the mineralized zone.

The evidence as to the effect of this release on the investing public was equivocal and less than abundant. On April 13 the New York Herald Tribune in an article head-noted "Copper Rumor Deflated" quoted from the TGS release of April 12 and backtracked from its original April 11 report of a major strike but nevertheless inferred from the TGS release that "recent mineral exploratory activity near Timmins, Ontario, has provided preliminary favorable results, sufficient at least to require a step-up in drilling operations." Some witnesses who testified at the hearing stated that they found the release encouraging. On the other hand, a Canadian mining security specialist, Roche, stated that "earlier in the week [before April 16] we had a Dow Jones saying that they [T.G.S.] didn't have anything basically" and a TGS stock specialist for the Midwest Stock Exchange became concerned about his long position in the stock after reading the release. The trial court stated only that "While, in retrospect, the press release may appear gloomy or incomplete, this does not make it misleading or deceptive on the basis of the facts then known."

Meanwhile, drilling operations continued. By morning of April 13, in K-55-5, the fifth drill hole, substantial copper mineralization had been encountered to the 580 foot mark, and the hole was subsequently drilled to a length of 757 feet without further results. Visual estimates revealed an average content of 0.82% copper and 4.2% zinc over a 525-foot section. Also by 7:00 A.M. on April 13, K-55-6 had found mineralization to the 946-foot mark. On April 12 a fourth drillrig began to drill K-55-7, which was drilled westerly at a 45° angle, at the eastern edge of the anomaly. The next morning the 137 foot mark had been reached, fifty feet of which showed mineralization. By 7:00 P.M. on April 15, the hole had been completed to a length of 707 feet but had only encountered additional mineralization during a 26-foot length between the 425 and 451-foot marks. A mill test hole, K-55-8, had been drilled and was complete by the evening of April 13 but its mineralization had not been reported upon prior to April 16. K-55-10 was drilled westerly at a 45° angle commencing April 14 and had encountered mineralization over 231 of its 249-foot length by the evening of April 15. It, too, was drilled at the anomaly's eastern edge.

While drilling activity ensued to completion, TGS officials were taking steps toward ultimate disclosure of the discovery. On April 13, a previously-invited reporter for The Northern Miner, a Canadian mining industry journal, visited the drillsite, interviewed Mollison, Holyk and Darke, and prepared an article which confirmed a 10 million ton ore strike. This report, after having been submitted to Mollison and returned to the reporter unamended on April 15, was published in the April 16 issue. A statement relative to the extent of the discovery, in substantial part drafted by Mollison, was given to the Ontario Minister of Mines for release to the Canadian media. Mollison and Holyk expected it to be released over the airways at 11 P.M. on April 15th, but, for undisclosed reasons, it was not released until 9:40 A.M. on the 16th. An official detailed statement, announcing a strike of at least 25 million tons of ore, based on the drilling data set forth above, was read to representatives of American financial media from 10:00 A.M. to 10:10 or 10:15 A.M. on April 16, and appeared over Merrill Lynch's private wire at 10:29 A.M. and, somewhat later than expected, over the Dow Jones ticker tape at 10:54 A.M.

Between the time the first press release was issued on April 12 and the dissemination of the TGS official announcement on the morning of April 16, the only defendants before us on appeal who engaged in market activity were Clayton and Crawford and TGS director Coates. Clayton ordered 200 shares of TGS stock through his Canadian broker on April 15 and the order was executed that day over the Midwest Stock Exchange. Crawford ordered 300 shares at midnight on the 15th and another 300 shares at 8:30 A.M. the next day, and these orders were executed over the Midwest Exchange in Chicago at its opening on April 16. Coates left the TGS press conference and called his broker son-in-law Haemisegger shortly before 10:20 A.M. on the 16th and ordered 2,000 shares of TGS for family trust accounts of which Coates was a trustee but not a beneficiary; Haemisegger executed this order over the New York and Midwest Exchanges, and he and his customers purchased 1500 additional shares.

During the period of drilling in Timmins, the market price of TGS stock fluctuated but steadily gained overall. On Friday, November 8, when the drilling began, the stock closed at $17^3/8$; on Friday, November 15, after K-55-1 had been completed, it closed at 18. After a slight decline to $16^3/8$ by Friday, November 22, the price rose to $20^7/8$ by December 12, when the chemical assay results of K-55-1 were received, and closed at a high of $24^1/8$ on February 21, the day after the stock options had been issued. It had reached a price of 26 by March 31, after the land acquisition program had been completed and drilling had been resumed; and continued to ascend to $30^1/8$ by the close of trading on April 10, at which time the drilling progress up to then was evaluated for the April 12th press release. On April 13, the day on which the April 12 release was disseminated, TGS opened at $30^1/8$, rose immediately to a high of 32 and gradually tapered off to close at $30^7/8$. It closed at $30^1/4$ the next day, and at $29^3/8$ on April 15. On April 16, the day of the official announcement of the Timmins discovery, the price climbed to a high of 37 and closed at $36^3/8$. By May 15, TGS stock was selling at $58^1/4$.

[The Court held that the insiders were in possession of undisclosed material facts from November 12, 1963, when the drilling of K-55-1 was completed. This finding was based upon the direct evidence of various witnesses familiar with the mining industry and was confirmed by "the importance attached to the drilling results by those who knew about it (401 F.2d at 851)—that is, by their substantial purchase of T.G.S. shares and call options. All of the insiders who bought T.G.S. shares or call options and who knew about the K-55-1 discovery were held to have violated Rule 10b-5. Findings of violation were made as well against Darke, for having "tipped" outsiders to buy T.G.S. shares, and against Coates, who had practically run from the room where the April 16 press release had been read to purchase shares without, as the Court found, waiting for the information to be effectively disseminated. The senior officers who accepted stock options without disclosing the full facts about the ore discoveries to the corporation's options committee (which might presumably have issued fewer options or on different terms if it had known their true value), were also held to have violated Rule 10b-5. The corporation's April 12 press release was found by the Court to be materially misleading and therefore to be an "untrue statement of material fact" in violation of Rule 10b-5. That rule's requirement that a misstatement be made "in connection with the purchase or sale of any security" was established because, the Court held, all public statements by widely traded corporations concerning their affairs are made "in connection with" trades, even though the corporation itself is not trading.]

[LUMBARD C.J. and MOORE J. dissented.]

NOTES

In another round of litigation, injunctions were granted against the corporation and most of the individual defendants. Most of the stock options were cancelled. See 312 F. Supp. 77 (S.D.N.Y. 1970), varied 446 F.2d 1301 (2d Cir. 1971). Ultimately, those who had sold T.G.S. shares on the open market between the April 12 and April 16 press releases recovered damages from the corporation in related litigation. *Mitchell v. Texas Gulf Sulphur Co.*, 446 F.2d 90 (10th Cir.), cert. denied, 404 U.S. 1004 (1971).

It is ironic that the corporate purpose that legitimated the corporation's delay in disclosing its remarkable mineral discoveries was the purchase of land from the owners who were ignorant of the riches beneath it. However, no one has suggested that the land owners should have been told of the mineral finds. This is because of economic considerations concerning the production of information about ore discoveries. Information is itself a product, with a cost associated with its production. Without a reward for producing information, mining corporations would not incur search costs in discovering it. Requiring them to share the benefits of their discoveries by extending insider trading prohibitions to the mining industry would therefore result in a decline in the level of mining.

The inefficiency of extending insider trading requirements to land transactions arises from a free rider problem. The optimal level of investment in information production is one in which marginal search costs equal the marginal benefit in the production of a new piece of information. On an ore discovery, the marginal benefits are enjoyed by a potentially large group of people, since a knowledge of mineral finds is of value not only to the immediate land owner, but also to his neighbours, under whose land ore is likely to be found as well. Were mining corporations required to disclose the existence of hidden claims when purchasing adjoining land, they would not expend the same resources in prospecting unless they could secure the cooperation of all land owners in the area before beginning. But here free rider problems might be anticipated, with land owners refusing to contribute to the common pool when risk capital is requested, yet charging full dollar for the land upon the discovery of ore.

This suggests that antifraud standards should be limited to actual misrepresentations by mining firms, without mandating disclosure of information, which indeed is the general common law rule. But this justification for non-disclosure immunity at common law may not avail if some information, like manna, does not have a cost of production. Thus several writers have argued that inside information comes to managers simply as a by-product of their insider status, and without any costs of production. If so, the shares and the land in *T.G.S.* are not analogous. See Brudney, *Insiders, Outsiders, and Informational Advantages under the Federal Securities Laws*, 93 Harv. L. Rev. 322, 353-67 (1979); Kronman, *Mistake, Disclosure, Information and the Law of Contracts*, 7 J. Legal

Stud. 1 (1978); Levmore, *Securities and Secrets: Insider Trading and the Law of Contracts*, 68 Va. L. Rev. 117 (1982).

This does not, however, conclude the debate, for even if the availability of inside information is not dependent on the legal regime regarding insider trading, at least legal prohibitions will chill the amount of insider trading. The leading defence of insider trading is in fact that it promotes efficient capital markets through share prices that react more quickly to material changes. One way this will happen is through the simple increase in demand when insiders come to the market. A potentially more important reason for share price movements is that other investors will realize that insiders are trading and will take this as a signal of inside information. That insiders are trading may be revealed when public insider trading reports are filed or when market professionals "decode" changes in demand for the shares. See Gilson & Kraakman, *The Mechanisms of Market Efficiency*, 70 Va. L. Rev. 549, 572-79 (1984) (share price changes may be an informative signal even where identity of traders is not known). Prohibitions of insider trading will then result in less efficient capital markets.

On this argument, insider trading serves the same efficiency goals as disclosure requirements in securities legislation. Why a firm would seek to disclose information about itself is discussed in the following excerpt from Carlton & Fischel, *The Regulation of Insider Trading*, 35 Stan. L. Rev. 857, 867 (1983):

One reason is that disclosure can reduce wasteful expenditures on search and reduce investor uncertainty about the firm. This may make the firm more valuable to investors. Investors expend resources to identify overvalued or undervalued securities until the next dollar they spend on information no longer produces an additional dollar of return. If the firm can produce information about itself at the lowest cost, disclosure of information by the firm will save resources by reducing the amount of expenditures on search and will lead to less investor uncertainty about the firm.

A second reason is that disclosure of information by the firm also may enable the firm's current investors to sell their shares to outsiders at a higher price, on average. If the firm discloses no information, outsiders may assume the worst and discount the price they are willing to pay for shares by a factor that reflects their uncertainty. Because every firm has an incentive to distinguish itself from those firms about which the worst is true, so that outsiders will pay a higher price for its shares, information will be produced.

Finally, accurately priced securities will enable firms to observe more accurately when corporate managers are successful. Thus, markets for managerial services and for corporate control will function more effectively. Also, the better managers will signal their quality by their willingness to tie a higher proportion of their compensation to stock performance. Accurate prices then enable these managers to receive the rewards for their superior performance. For these reasons, shareholders would want managers to disclose information about the value of the firm.

On this analysis, traders in stock markets can be divided into three groups: insiders, outsiders and investment intermediaries. Insider trading will effect a wealth transfer to insiders from members of the other two groups, though this distributional effect can be undone *ex ante* when the issue price of the shares is discounted against anticipated insider trading losses. In addition, insider trading will reduce the opportunities for profitable investments in the production of information by investment intermediaries. Since bargain opportunities will have been exploited by insiders, there will be a lessened incentive for investment intermediaries to incur screening costs.* Seen in this context, these screening costs represent a deadweight efficiency loss: markets can be equally well informed without them through insider trading. Carlton and Fischel's argument about the reduction of wasteful expenditures through insider trading is then the same as that of Hirshleifer, *The Private and Social Value of Information and the Reward to Inventive Activity*, 61 Am. Econ. Rev. 561 (1971), as discussed in the Beaver excerpt in Chapter Five, Section B.

Signalling theories of insider trading offer a fresh perspective on the distributional consequences of insider trading. Consider the shareholders who gave their brokers orders to sell T.G.S. shares on the days when the insiders had placed purchase orders, and whose shares ended up owned by the insiders. Could they be identified, these vendors would presumably have standing under either CBCA s. 131(4) or OSA s. 131(4) to bring actions for damages. They did not, however, rely on any representations of the insiders, as there were no representations made. Were they nonetheless damaged by the insiders' trades? They would have been, if the wrongful act by the insiders had been their failure to disclose the ore discoveries. However, the non-disclosure was not wrongful. In fact, by disclosing the corporation's valuable proprietary information, its insiders would have breached their duty to it.

The insiders' wrongful act, if any, was in purchasing shares. Had the insiders not been purchasing shares in the market, however, the vendors would likely have been worse off. Recall from the facts that during the five months from November 12 to April 10 the price of T.G.S. stock was rising slowly but steadily from about $17 to $30 per share. Since there was substantial insider buying activity throughout this time, it is not unreasonable to suppose that, directly or indirectly, the price was rising as a result of that activity. If the vendors would have sold whether or not the insiders were buying, either because the vendors needed cash or because they had other investment opportunities, they were helped rather than hurt by the insiders' purchases. Had the insiders stayed out of the market, the vendors would have sold their shares at lower prices to different purchasers. These purchasers, rather than the insiders, would have reaped the windfall profits after April 16, but that fact is neutral as to the vendors, for whose benefit statutory remedies are provided.

Does this ignore the possibility that, even though the insiders had no dealings with the vendors, they may nonetheless have induced the vendors to sell? The vendors individually may have been led to sell by the rising market, each vendor attempting to get out at the market peak. This argument is, however, at variance with theories of modern portfolio analysis, which suggest that the best investment strategy for an investor is to seek diversification through a broad-ranging group of shareholdings, rather than by trying to "pick" securities. In addition, if stock prices follow a random walk, a stock

---

* Evidence that insider trading cuts into profits available to investment intermediaries is provided by studies indicating a positive correlation between it and the spread between the bid and ask prices in listed securities. The bid-ask spread is the commission charged by intermediaries: with smaller profit opportunities for their own trades, the intermediaries will demand a higher spread. See, e.g., Copeland & Galai, *Information Effects on the Bid-Ask Spread*, 38 J. Fin. 1457 (1983).

price increase does not signal a market peak: after the increase, the price is as likely to continue to rise as it is to fall, so that the perception that shares should be sold after an increase, without more, appears irrational.

In *Texas Gulf Sulphur*, insiders trading opportunities arose because the firm had a business purpose in secrecy. Where this is not the case, the firm will ordinarily disclose new material changes promptly, and is in fact required to do so by OSA s. 75. A court is unlikely to accept an argument that a firm was not bound to make timely disclosure where its insiders have been trading. See *Re Pezim* (1992), 96 D.L.R. (4th) 137 (B.C.C.A.).

It has been argued that a prohibition on insider trading may further the policy of quick publication of material changes in a corporation's affairs. Since the insiders cannot make trading profits from non-disclosure, they will not have that particular incentive to keep the information secret longer than necessary for legitimate corporate purposes. Brudney, *Insiders, Outsiders and Informational Advantages under the Federal Securities Law*, 92 Harv. L. Rev. 322, 335 (1979). However, this argument likely underestimates a firm's incentives to make prompt disclosure. Firms that suppress information in order to permit insider trading will impose costs on outsiders, and this will be reflected in share values.

Insiders may be advantaged even after public disclosure of information, since processing the information is itself a costly activity. For example, market intermediaries will be called on to read the firm's financial statements with the utmost care. By contrast, managers may have been aware of the financial information well in advance of public disclosure. Managers will also know those pieces of soft information that individually do not constitute material facts but which, in the ensemble, give them a more sophisticated knowledge of firm value than that available to outside market professionals. For example, there may be no duty to reveal the marital problems of the chief executive officer under OSA s. 75(1), even if in some way they alter the firm's financial picture. A policy of full disclosure under the OSA may then still leave room for profitable trading by insiders. Such trading will reduce the expenditure on information production by market professionals without access to inside information, the first of the efficiencies described above by Carlton and Fischel.

Tippee Liability. If a firm is not permitted to signal share quality through its own trading or through insider trading, it might seek to employ disclosure strategies. These may be either general or selective. On a general disclosure policy, the firm commits to make prompt disclosure of material changes, and this strategy is in fact mandated by OSA s. 75. However, even if the firm incurred legal liability for breach of a general disclosure policy, a promise of prompt disclosure might not be wholly creditable. First, the firm might still refuse to disclose when it asserts a business purpose in secrecy, as in *Texas Gulf Sulphur*. This is permitted by OSA s. 75(3), under which the firm need only file a confidential material change statement with the O.S.C. In addition, liability will be determined in accordance with the business judgment standard, with a non-rigorous judicial review as to when to disclose. See Chapter Five, Section B. The second reason why general disclosure may not be wholly creditable is that outsiders might fear puffery, particularly with respect to impressionistic disclosure and forecasts.

In place of general disclosure, then, a firm might prefer a strategy of selective disclosure, revealing the information to small groups of market intermediaries. The advantage of selective disclosure is that of relational contracts. When a firm reveals information selectively to institutional investors, the firm's honesty may be more readily gauged than on public disclosure. For example, a broker might be told that good news is imminent without being told what it is, if the firm has a business interest in its confidentiality. On a general disclosure strategy, such an announcement might be largely discounted, but a private broker might be prepared to invest heavily in it if, on the basis of past performance, he has come to trust the firm. Concentrating the gain of disclosure in a single investor may then serve efficiency goals. The broker will not, however, scoop the exclusive benefit of the news if other market intermediaries decode the change from the fact of the broker's trading, for this too may operate as a signal to sophisticated investors.

This explanation of selective disclosure policies is, however, speculative. The cost to a firm when it defects is limited to the damage to its relationship with the particular broker, and this might seem trivial if the firm can easily choose to advantage another broker. On the other hand, the firm would not appear to have a strong temptation to defect through dishonest tips, and doing so may result in reputational losses with subsequent brokers. In addition, a firm may be motivated to make honest disclosure by the prospect of a side payment from the tippee.

Selective disclosure strategies are prohibited by modern insider trading liability. Tippee liability is discussed in the following case.

In the Matter of Cady, Roberts & Co.
Securities and Exchange Comm'n
40 S.E.C. 907 (1959)

CARY, Chairman: This is a case of first impression and one of signal importance in our administration of the Federal securities acts. It involves a selling broker who executes a solicited order and sells for discretionary accounts (including that of his wife) upon an exchange. The crucial question is what are the duties of such a broker after receiving non-public information as to a company's dividend action from a director who is employed by the same brokerage firm.

These proceedings were instituted to determine whether Cady, Roberts & Co. ("registrant") and Robert M. Gintel ("Gintel"), the selling broker and a partner of the registrant, willfully violated the "anti-fraud" provisions of Section 10(b) of the Securities Exchange Act of 1934 ("Exchange Act"), Rule 10b-5 issued under that Act, and Section 17(a) of the Securities Act of 1933 ("Securities Act") and, if so, whether any disciplinary action is necessary or appropriate in the public interest. The respondents have submitted an offer by settlement which essentially provides that the facts stipulated by respondents shall constitute the record in these proceedings for the purposes of determining the occurrence of a willful violation of the designated anti-fraud provisions and the entering of an appropriate order, on the condition that no sanction may be entered in excess of a suspension of Gintel for 20 days from the New York Stock Exchange.

The facts are as follows:

Early in November 1959, Roy T. Hurley, then President and Chairman of the Board of Curtiss-Wright Corporation, invited 2,000 representatives of the press, the military and the financial and business communities to a publuc unveiling on November 23, of a new type of internal combustion engine being developed by the company. On November 24, 1959, press announcements concerning the new engine appeared in certain newspapers. On that day Curtiss-Wright stock was one of the most active issues on the New York Stock Exchange, closing at 35 1/4, up 3 1/4 on a volume of 88,700 shares. From November 6, through November 23, Gintel had purchased approximately 11,000 shares of Curtiss-Wright stock for about 30 discretionary accounts of customers of registrant. With the rise in the price on November 24, he began selling Curtiss-Wright shares for these accounts and sold on that day a total of 2,200 shares on the Exchange.

The activity in Curtiss-Wright stock on the Exchange continued the next morning, November 25, and the price rose to 40 1/4, a new high for the year. Gintel continued sales for the discretionary accounts and, between the opening of the market and about 11:00 a.m., he sold 4,300 shares.

On the morning of November 25, the Curtiss-Wright directors, including J. Cheever Cowdin ("Cowdin"), then a registered representative of registrant,[4] met to consider, among other things, the declaration of a quarterly dividend. The company had paid a dividend, although not earned, of $.625 per share for each of the first three quarters of 1959. The Curtiss-Wright board, over the objections of Hurley, who favored declaration of a dividend at the same rate as in the prior quarters, approved a dividend for the fourth quarter at the reduced rate of $.375 per share. At approximately 11:00 a.m., the board authorized transmission of information of this action by telegram to the New York Stock Exchange. The Secretary of Curtiss-Wright immediately left the meeting room to arrange for this communication. There was a short delay in the transmission of the telegram because of a typing problem and the telegram, although transmitted to Western Union at 11:12 a.m., was not delivered to the Exchange until 12:29 p.m. It had been customary for the company also to advise the Dow Jones News Ticker Service of any dividend action. However, apparently through some mistake or inadvertence, the Wall Street Journal was not given the news until approximately 11:48 a.m. and the announcement did not appear on the Dow Jones ticker tape until 11:45 a.m.

Sometime after the dividend decision, there was a recess of Curtiss-Wright directors' meeting, during which Cowdin telephoned registrant's office and left a message for Gintel that the dividend had been cut. Upon receiving this information, Gintel entered two sell orders for execution on the Exchange, one to sell 2,000 shares of Curtiss-Wright stock for 10 accounts, and the other to sell about 5,000 shares for 11 accounts. Four hundred of the 5,000 shares were sold for three of Cowdin's customers. According to Cowdin, pursuant to directions from his clients, he had given instructions to Gintel to

---

4   Mr. Cowdin, who died in September 1960, was a registered representative of the registrant from July 1956 until March 1960, and was also a member of the board of directors of Curtiss-Wright, having first been elected in 1929.

take profits on these 400 shares if the stock took a "run-up." These orders were executed at 11:15 and 11:18 a.m. at $40^{1}/_{4}$ and $40^{3}/_{8}$, respectively.

When the dividend announcement appeared on the Dow Jones tape at 11:48 a.m., the Exchange was compelled to suspend trading in Curtiss-Wright because of the larger number of sell orders. Trading in Curtiss-Wright stock was resumed at 1:59 p.m. at $36^{1}/_{2}$, ranged during the balance of the day between $38^{1}/_{8}$ and 37, and closed at $34^{7}/_{8}$.

So many times that citation is unnecessary, we have indicated that the purchase and sale of securities is a field in special need for regulation for the protection of investors. To this end one of the major purposes of the securities acts is the prevention of fraud, manipulation or deception in connection with securities transactions. Consistent with this objective, Section 17(a) of the Securities Act, Section 10(b) of the Exchange Act and Rule 10b-5, issued under that Section, are broad remedial provisions aimed at reaching misleading or deceptive activities, whether or not they are precisely and technically sufficient to sustain a common law action for fraud and deceit. Indeed ... the securities acts may be said to have generated a wholly new and far-reaching body of Federal corporation law.

Section 17(a) and Rule 10b-5, in almost identical terms, make illegal the use of the mails or of the facilities of interstate commerce, including the facility of any national exchange, by any person who directly or indirectly engages in any of the following prohibited kinds of conduct in connection with the sale of any security:

(1) Employment of any device, scheme or artifice to defraud.
(2) The obtaining of money or property by means of, or the making of, any untrue statement of a material fact or the omission to state a material fact necessary in order to make statements made, in the light of the circumstances under which they were made, not misleading.
(3) Engaging in any act, practice or course of business which operates or would operate as a fraud or deceit upon any person.

These anti-fraud provisions are not intended as a specification of particular acts or practices which constitute fraud, but rather are designed to encompass the infinite variety of devices by which undue advantage may be taken of investors and others.

Section 17 and Rule 10b-5 apply to securities transactions by "any person." Misrepresentation will lie within their ambit, no matter who the speaker may be. An affirmative duty to disclose material information has been traditionally imposed on corporate "insiders," particularly officers, directors, or controlling shareholders. We and the courts have consistently held that insiders must disclose material facts which are known to them by virtue of their position but which are not known to persons with whom they deal and which, if known, would affect their investment judgment. Failure to make disclosure in these circumstances constitutes a violation of the anti-fraud provisions. If, on the other hand, disclosure prior to effecting a purchase or sale would be improper or unrealistic under the circumstances, we believe the alternative is to [forgo] the transaction.

The ingredients are here and we accordingly find that Gintel willfully violated Sections 17(a) and 10(b) and rule 10b-5. We also find a similar violation by the registrant, since the actions of Gintel, a member of registrant, in the course of his employment are to be regarded as actions of registrant itself. It was obvious that a reduction in the quarterly dividend by the Board of Directors was a material fact which could be expected to have an adverse impact on the market price of the company's stock. The rapidity with which Gintel acted upon receipt of the information confirms his own recognition of that conclusion.

We have already noted that the anti-fraud provisions are phrased in terms of "any person" and that a special obligation has been traditionally required of corporate insiders, e.g., officers, directors and controlling stockholders. These three groups, however, do not exhaust the classes of persons upon whom there is such an obligation. Analytically, the obligation rests on two principal elements; first, the existence of a relationship giving access, directly or indirectly, to information intended to be available only for a corporate purpose and not for the personal benefit of anyone,[15] and second, the inherent unfairness involved where a party takes advantage of such information knowing it is unavailable to those with whom he is dealing. In considering these elements under the broad language of the anti-fraud provisions we are not to be circumscribed by fine distinctions and rigid classifications. Thus our task here is to identify those persons who are in a special relationship with a company and privy to its internal affairs, and thereby suffer correlative duties in trading in its securities. Intimacy demands restraint lest the uninformed be exploited.

The facts here impose on Gintel the responsibilities of those commonly referred to as "insiders." He received the information prior to its public release from a director of Curtiss-Wright, Cowdin, who was associated with the registrant. Cowdin's relationship to the company clearly prohibited him from selling the securities affected by the information without disclosure. By logical sequence, it should prohibit Gintel, a partner of registrant. This prohibition extends not only over his own account, but to selling for discretionary accounts and soliciting and executing other orders. In somewhat analogous circumstances, we have charged a broker-dealer who effects securities transactions for an insider and who knows that the insider possesses non-public material information with the affirmative duty to make appropriate disclosures or dissociate himself from the transaction.

The three main subdivisions of Section 17 and Rule 10b-5 have been considered to be mutually supporting rather than mutually exclusive. Thus, a breach of duty of disclosure may be viewed as a device or scheme, an implied misrepresentation, and an act or practice, violative of all three subdivisions. We hold that, in these circumstances, Gintel's conduct at least violated clause (3) as a practice which operated as a fraud or deceit upon the purchasers. Therefore, we need not decide the scope of clauses (1) and (2).

We cannot accept respondents' contention that an insider's responsibility is limited to existing shareholders and that he has no special duties when sales of securities are

---

15 A significant purpose of the Exchange Act was to eliminate the idea that the use of inside information for personal advantage was a normal emolument of corporate office. See Sections 2 and 16 of the Act; H.R. Rep. No. 1383, 73rd Cong., 2d Sess. 13 (1934); S. Rep. No. 792, 73rd Cong., 2d Sess. 9 (1934); S.E.C. *Tenth Annual Report* 50 (1944).

made to non-stockholders. This approach is too narrow. It ignores the plight of buying public—wholly unprotected from the misuse of special information.

... There is no valid reason why persons who *purchase* stock from an officer, director or other person having the responsibilities of an "insider" should not have the same protection afforded by the disclosure of special information as persons who *sell* stock to them. Whatever distinctions may have existed at common law based on the view that an officer or director may stand in a fiduciary relationship to existing stockholders from whom he purchases but not to members of the public to whom he sells, it is clearly not appropriate in the securities acts.[23]

Respondents further assert that they made no express representations and did not in any way manipulate the market, and urge that in a transaction on an exchange there is no further duty such as may be required in a "face-to-face" transaction. We reject this suggestion. It would be anomalous indeed if the protection afforded by the anti-fraud provisions were withdrawn from transactions effected on exchanges, primary markets for securities transactions. If purchasers on an exchange had available material information known by a selling insider, we may assume that their investment judgment would be affected and their decision whether to buy might accordingly be modified. Consequently, any sales by the insider must await disclosure of the information.

Cases cited by respondents in which relief was denied to purchasers or sellers of securities in exchange transactions are distinguishable. The action here was instituted by the Commission, not by individuals. The cited cases concern private suits brought against insiders for violation of the anti-fraud rules. They suggest that the plaintiffs may not recover because there was lacking a "semblance of privity" since it was not shown that the buyers or sellers bought from or sold to the insiders. These cases have no relevance here as they concern the remedy of the buyer or seller *vis-à-vis* the insider. The absence of a remedy by the private litigant because of lack of privity does not absolve an insider from responsibility for fraudulent conduct.

Respondents argue that any requirement that a broker-dealer in exchange transactions make disclosure of "adverse factors disclosed by his analysis" would create uncertainty and confusion as to the duties of those who are constantly acquiring and analyzing information about companies in which they or their clients are interested. Furthermore, it is claimed, substantial practical difficulties would be presented as to the manner of making disclosures.

---

23   As Judge Learned Hand has stated in the context of Section 16(b) of the Exchange Act: "For many years a grave omission in our corporation law had been its indifference to dealings of directors or other corporate officers in the shares of their companies. When they brought shares they came literally within the conventional prohibitions of the law of trusts; yet the decisions were strangely slack in so deciding. When they sold shares, it could indeed be argued that they were not dealing with a beneficiary, but with one whom his purchase made a beneficiary. That should not, however, have obscured the fact that the director or officer assumed a fiduciary relation to the buyer by the very sale; for it would be a sorry distinction to allow him to use the advantage of his position to induce the buyer into the position of a beneficiary although he was forbidden to do so once the buyer had become one." [*Gratz v. Claughton*, 187 F.2d 46, 49 (C.A. 2, 1951), cert. denied, 341 U.S. 920 (1951).]

There should be no quandary on the facts here presented. While there may be a question as to the materiality and significance of some corporate facts and as to the necessity of their disclosure under particular circumstances, that is not the case. Corporate dividend action of the kind involved here is clearly recognizable as having a direct effect on the market value of securities and the judgment of investors. Moreover, knowledge of this action was not arrived at as a result of perceptive analysis of generally known facts, but was obtained from a director (and associate) during the time when respondents should have known that the board of directors of the issuer was taking steps to make the information publicly available but before it was actually announced.

Furthermore, the New York Stock Exchange has recognized that prompt disclosure of important corporate developments, including specifically dividend action, is essential for the benefit of stockholders and the investing public and has established explicit requirements and recommended procedures for the immediate public release of dividend information by issuers whose securities are listed on the Exchange. The practical problems envisaged by respondents in effecting appropriate disclosures in connection with transactions on the Exchange are easily avoided where, as here, all the registered broker-dealer need do is to keep out of the market until the established procedures for public release of the information are carried out instead of hastening to execute transactions in advance of, and in frustration of, the objectives of the release.

Finally, we do not accept respondents' contention that Gintel was merely carrying out a program of liquidating the holdings in his discretionary accounts—determined and embarked upon prior to his receipt of the dividend information. In this contention, it is further alleged that he had a fiduciary duty to these accounts to continue the sales, which overrode any obligations to unsolicited purchasers on the Exchange.

The record does not support the contention that Gintel's sales were merely a continuance of his prior schedule of liquidation. Upon receipt of the news of the dividend reduction, which Gintel knew was not public, he hastened to sell before the expected public announcement all of the Curtiss-Wright shares remaining in his discretionary accounts, contrary to his previous moderate rate of sales. In so doing, he also made short sales of securities which he then allocated to his wife's account and to the account of a customer whom he had never seen and with whom he had had no prior dealings. Moreover, while Gintel undoubtedly occupied a fiduciary relationship to his customers, this relationship could not justify any actions by him contrary to law.[31] Even if we assume the existence of conflicting fiduciary obligations, there could be no doubt which is primary here. On these facts, clients may not expect of a broker the benefits of his inside information at the expense of the public generally.

---

31 "But to say that a man is a fiduciary only begins analysis; it gives direction to further inquiry. To whom is he a fiduciary? What obligations does he owe as a fiduciary?" *S.E.C. v. Chenery Corporation*, 318 U.S. 80, 85-86 (1943). In the circumstances, Gintel's relationship to his customers was such that he would have a duty not to take a position adverse to them, not to take secret profits at their expense, not to misrepresent facts to them, and in general to place their interests ahead of his own.

[The Commission decided that the public interest called for a 20-day suspension of Gintel from membership on the New York Stock Exchange and no sanction against Cady, Roberts & Co.]

Who Is an Insider? While Rule 10b-5 nowhere uses the term insider, the SEC in its *Cady, Roberts* decision found it necessary to pin the label insider upon Gintel in order that his silence could be said to operate as a "fraud or deceit," the phrase employed in the third and broadest clause of Rule 10b-5. The Commission then imposed upon him fiduciary duties under which he was not privileged to remain silent in dealing with the beneficiaries of such duties.

Can you identify the critical passages in *Cady, Roberts* in which Chairman Cary explains why it is appropriate to treat Gintel as an insider of Curtiss-Wright?

A story, possibly apocryphal, is told of Gintel after the *Cady, Roberts* decision was released. His 20-day period of suspension was spent on a holiday in Florida. On his return to New York, he found himself busier than ever, pursued by clients who thought he was precisely the kind of broker they wanted.

The CBCA definition of insider for civil liability purposes differs from that used for reporting purposes. For civil liability, persons to whom insiders reveal specific confidential information ("tippees") become insiders. Section 131(1) imposes insider trading liability upon:

- the corporation itself;
- affiliates of the corporation;
- directors, officers, employees and persons "retained" by the corporation;
- a person owning or controlling more than 10% of the shares of the corporation;
- a person who receives specific confidential information from a source that he knows to be one of the foregoing or that he knows received it, mediately or immediately, from one of the foregoing.

"Corporation" for civil liability purposes means any entity incorporated under the CBCA and is not limited to distributing corporations. "Person" includes individuals, partnerships and corporations. The reference to persons "retained by the corporation" presumably includes persons, such as outside lawyers and accountants, who perform services on a contractual basis. In any event, such persons would likely be included as tippees. Indeed, because s. 131(1)(f) is a chain with infinite links, it is hard to imagine a person who is told of material non-public information and who is not a tippee.

CBCA liability arises where the insider, "in connection with a transaction in a security of the corporation ... , makes use of any specific confidential information for his own benefit or advantage." Would this include tipping? Suppose that the tip is passed on by a broker to his client, who then trades. Has the broker made use of the information for his own benefit in connection with the client's trade? See *Woods v. The Queen*, 1994 Ont. C.J. LEXIS 2002 (Div. Ct. 1993) (director who recommended a short sale of stock to a financer who had agreed to prop up a failing firm was held to have "sold" securities).

When one corporation becomes an insider or a second corporation, or merges with it, every officer of the first corporation is deemed to have been an insider of the second corporation for six months prior to the transaction. CBCA ss. 131(2) and (3). Thus insider trading liability may be imposed on X Corp. directors who purchased Y Corp. shares knowing that X Corp. planned to make a take-over bid for Y Corp.'s shares within six months.

The OSA imposes liability on insiders who purchase or sell securities with knowledge of undisclosed material information. OSA s. 134(1). Insiders are those in a "special relationship" with the issuer, as defined in s. 134(7). Under 1987 amendments, the definition of special relationship was extended to everyone who learns the material information from an insider, and who knows that his source was in a special relationship with the issuer. This provision, inspired by CBCA s. 131(1)(f), would also embrace remote tippees, who have been tipped by another tippee, as long as every tippee in the chain knew that his source was in a special relationship with the firm under s. 134(7). The OSA also imposes liability on tippers under s. 134(2) although further defences are available here if the information was given in the necessary course of business. This would include, for example, private disclosure by any issuer to a banker or underwriter in the course of preparing for a take-over bid or public issue of securities. Would it also include a broker's disclosure to his clients, as in *Cady, Roberts*? Commissioner Cary was not much impressed by the broker's argument about a conflict of duties in that decision.

In *Cady, Roberts*, the S.E.C. stated that, even if it was assumed that the persons to whom Gintel sold the shares would have no cause of action against him under Rule 10b-5 because of the absence of "privity" between him and them, he could still be found to have violated Rule 10b-5 in a Commission disciplinary proceeding. The questions whether a legal rule has been breached and who can enforce it are separate. Similarly, since the OSA (but not the CBCA) contains a general prohibition against insider trading (s. 76) as well as a provision creating civil liability (s. 134), a person might be found to have violated the rule in a securities commission disciplinary proceeding, even if a private plaintiff with standing to enforce it could not be identified in the particular instance. Furthermore, an expert body such as a securities commission is free to develop ethical standards for the industry regulated higher than those mandated by statute and to conclude from a registrant's conduct that he is unfit for registration even though he has not violated a specific statutory command. *Re Mitchell*, [1975] O.W.N. 595 (C.A., single judge).

Dirks v. Securities & Exchange Comm'n
United States Supreme Court
463 U.S. 646, 103 S. Ct. 3255 (1983)

JUSTICE POWELL delivered the opinion of the Court: Petitioner Raymond Dirks received material nonpublic information from "insiders" of a corporation with which he had no connection. He disclosed this information to investors who relied on it in trading in the shares of the corporation. The question is whether Dirks violated the antifraud provisions of the federal securities laws by this disclosure.

I

In 1973, Dirks was an officer of a New York broker-dealer firm who specialized in providing investment analysis of insurance company securities to institutional investors. On March 6, Dirks received information from Ronald Secrist, a former officer of Equity Funding of America. Secrist alleged that the assets of Equity Funding, a diversified corporation primarily engaged in selling life insurance and mutual funds, were vastly overstated as the result of fraudulent corporate practices. Secrist also stated that various regulatory agencies had failed to act on similar charges made by Equity Funding employees. He urged Dirks to verify the fraud and disclose it publicly.

Dirks decided to investigate the allegations. He visited Equity Funding's headquarters in Los Angeles and interviewed several officers and employees of the corporation. The senior management denied any wrongdoing, but certain corporation employees corroborated the charges of fraud. Neither Dirks nor his firm owned or traded any Equity Funding stock, but throughout his investigation he openly discussed the information he had obtained with a number of clients and investors. Some of these persons sold their holdings of Equity Funding securities, including five investment advisers who liquidated holdings of more than $16 million.[2]

While Dirks was in Los Angeles he was in touch regularly with William Blundell, the *Wall Street Journal's* Los Angeles bureau chief. Dirks urged Blundell to write a story on the fraud allegations. Bundell did not believe, however, that such a massive fraud could go undetected and declined to write the story. He feared that publishing such damaging hearsay might be libelous.

During the two week period in which Dirks pursued his investigation and spread word of Secrist's charges, the price of Equity Funding stock fell from $26 per share to less than $15 per share. This led the New York Stock Exchange to halt trading on March 27. Shortly thereafter California insurance authorities impounded Equity Funding's records and uncovered evidence of the fraud. Only then did the Securities and Exchange Commission (SEC) file a complaint against Equity Funding and only then, on April 2, did the *Wall Street Journal* publish a front-page story based largely on information assembled by Dirks. Equity Funding immediately went into receivership.

[The S.E.C. brought an administration proceeding against Dirks in which he was found to have violated s. 10b of the Securities Exchange Act of 1934 and Rule 10b-5 by disclosing the allegations of fraud to his clients and other investors who immediately thereupon sold their Equity Funding shares. Recognizing, however, that Dirks played an important role in bringing Equity Funding's fraud to light, the S.E.C. only censured him. The findings and penalty were affirmed by the United States Court of Appeals for the District of Columbia Circuit, per Wright J. The Supreme Court accepted the case for review.]

---

2   Dirks received from his firm a salary plus a commission for securities transactions above a certain amount that his clients directed through his firm. But "[it] is not clear how many of those with whom Dirks spoke promised to direct some brokerage business through [Dirk's firm] to compensate Dirks, or how many actually did so." 220 U.S. App. D.C. at 316, 681 F.2d at 831. The Boston Company Institutional Investors, Inc., promised Dirks about $25,000 in commissions, but it is unclear whether Boston actually generated any brokerage for his firm.

II

In the seminal case of *In re Cady, Roberts & Co.*, 40 S.E.C. 907 (1961), the SEC recognized that the common law in some jurisdictions imposes on "corporate 'insiders,' particularly officers, directors, or controlling stockholders" an "affirmative duty of disclosure ... when dealing in securities." *Id.*, at 911, and n. 13. The SEC found that not only did breach of this common-law duty also establish the elements of a Rule 10b-5 violation, but that individuals other than corporate insiders could be obligated either to disclose material nonpublic information before trading or to abstain from trading altogether. *Id.*, at 912. In *Chiarella*, we accepted the two elements set out in *Cady, Roberts* for establishing a Rule 10b-5 violation: "(i) the existence of a relationship affording access to inside information intended to be available only for a corporate purpose, and (ii) the unfairness of allowing a corporate insider to take advantage of that information by trading without disclosure." 445 U.S. at 227. In examining whether Chiarella has an obligation to disclose or abstain, the Court found that there is no general duty to disclose before trading on material nonpublic information, and held that "a duty to disclose under § 10(b) does not arise from the mere possession of nonpublic market information." *Id.*, at 235. Such a duty arises rather from the existence of a fiduciary relationship. See *id.*, at 227-235.

• • •

III

We were explicit in *Chiarella* in saying that there can be no duty to disclose where the person who has traded on inside information "was not [the corporation's] agent, ... was not a fiduciary, [or] was not a person in whom the sellers [of the securities] had placed their trust and confidence." 445 U.S., at 232. Not to require such a fiduciary relationship, we recognized, would "depar[t] radically from the established doctrine that duty arises from a specific relationship between two parties" and would amount to "recognizing a general duty between all participants in market transactions to forgo actions based on material, nonpublic information." *Id.*, at 232, 233. This requirement of a specific relationship between the shareholders and the individual trading on inside information has created analytical difficulties for the SEC and courts in policing tippees who trade on inside information. Unlike insiders who have independent fiduciary duties to both the corporation and its shareholders, the typical tippee has no such relationship.[14] In view of

---

14 Under certain circumstances, such as where corporate information is revealed legitimately to an underwriter, accountant, lawyer or consultant working for the corporation, these outsiders may become fiduciaries of the shareholders. The basis for recognizing this fiduciary duty is not simply that such persons acquired nonpublic corporate information, but rather that they have entered into a special confidential relationship in the conduct of the business of the enterprise and are given access to information solely for corporate purposes. When such a person breaches a fiduciary relationship, he may be treated more properly as a tipper than a tippee. See *Shapiro v. Merrill Lynch, Pierce, Fenner & Smith, Inc.*, 495 F.2d 228, 237 (CA2 1974) (investment banker had access to material information when working on a proposed public offering for the corporation). For such a duty to be imposed, however, the corporation must expect the outsider to keep the disclosed information confidential, and the relationship at least must imply such a duty.

this absence, it has been unclear how a tippee acquires the *Cady, Roberts* duty to refrain from trading on inside information.

A

The SEC's position, as stated in its opinion in this case, is that a tippee "inherits" the *Cady, Roberts* obligation to shareholders whenever he receives inside information from an insider: ...

This view differs little from the view that we rejected as inconsistent with congressional intent in *Chiarella*. In that case, the Court of Appeals agreed with the SEC and affirmed Chiarella's conviction, holding that " '[a]nyone—corporate insider or not—who regularly receives material nonpublic information may not use that information to trade in securities without incurring an affirmative duty to disclose.' " *United States v. Chiarella*, 588 F.2d 1358, 1365 (CA2 1978) (emphasis in original). Here, the SEC maintains that anyone who knowingly receives nonpublic material information from an insider has a fiduciary duty to disclose before trading.

In effect, the SEC's theory of tippee liability in both cases appears rooted in the idea that the antifraud provisions require equal information among all traders. This conflicts with the principle set forth in *Chiarella* that only some persons, under some circumstances, will be barred from trading while in possession of material nonpublic information. ...

Imposing a duty to disclose or abstain solely because a person knowingly receives material nonpublic information from an insider and trades on it could have an inhibiting influence on the role of market analysis, which the SEC itself recognizes is necessary to the preservation of a healthy market.[17] It is commonplace for analysts to "ferret out and analyze information." 21 S.E.C., at 1406,[18] and this often is done by meeting with and

---

17 The SEC expressly recognized that "[t]he value to the entire market of [analysts'] efforts cannot be gainsaid: market efficiency in pricing is significantly enhanced by [their] initiatives to ferret out and analyze information, and thus the analyst's work redounds to the benefit of all investors." 21 S.E.C., at 1406. The SEC asserts that analysts remain free to obtain from management corporate information for purposes of "filling in the 'interstices in analysis' ..." Brief for Respondent 42 (quoting *Investors Management Co.*, 44 S.E.C. at 646). But this rule is inherently imprecise, and imprecision prevents parties from ordering their actions in accord with legal requirements. Unless the parties have some guidance as to where the line is between permissible, and impermissible disclosures and uses, neither corporate insiders nor analysts can be sure when the line is crossed. ...

18 On its facts, this case is the unusual one. Dirks is an analyst in a broker-dealer firm, and he did interview management in the course of his investigation. He uncovered, however, startling information that required no analysis or exercise of judgment as to its market relevance. Nonetheless, the principle at issue here extends beyond these facts. The S.E.C.'s rule—applicable without regard to any breach by an insider—could have serious ramifications on reporting by analysts of investment views.

   Despite the unusualness of Dirks's "find," the central role that he played in uncovering the fraud at Equity Funding, and that analysts in general can play in revealing information that corporations may
   (The footnote is continued on the next page.)

questioning corporate officers and others who are insiders. And information that the analysts obtain normally may be the basis for judgments as to the market worth of a corporation's securities. The analyst's judgment in this respect is made available in market letters or otherwise to clients of the firm. It is the nature of this type of information, and indeed of the markets themselves, that such information cannot be made simultaneously available to all of the corporation's stockholders or the public generally.

B

The conclusion that recipients of inside information do not invariably acquire a duty to disclose or abstain does not mean that such tippees always are free to trade on the information. The need for a ban on some tippee trading is clear. Not only are insiders forbidden by their fiduciary relationship from personally using undisclosed corporation information to their advantage, but they may not give such information to an outsider for the same improper purpose of exploiting the information for their personal gain. ... Similarly, the transactions of those who knowingly participate with the fiduciary in such a breach are "as forbidden" as transactions "on behalf of the trustee himself." *Mosser v. Darrow*, 341 U.S. 267, 272 (1951). ... As the Court explained in *Mosser*, a contrary rule "would open up opportunities for devious dealings in the name of the others that the trustee could not conduct in his own." 341 U.S. at 271. See *SEC v. Texas Gulf Sulphur Co.*, 446 F.2d 1301, 1308 (CA2), cert. denied, 404 U.S. 1005 (1971). Thus the tippee's duty to disclose or abstain is derivative from that of the insider's duty. ... As we noted in *Chiarella*, "[t]he tippee's obligation has been viewed as arising from his role as a participant after the fact in the insider's breach of a fiduciary duty." 445 U.S. at 230, n. 12.

Thus, some tippees must assume an insider's duty to the shareholders not because they receive inside information, but rather because it has been made available to them *improperly*. And for Rule 10b-5 purposes, the insider's disclosure is improper only where it would violate his *Cady, Roberts* duty. Thus, a tippee assumes a fiduciary duty to the shareholders of a corporation not to trade on material nonpublic information only when the insider has breached his fiduciary duty to the shareholders by disclosing the information to the tippee and the tippee knows or should know that there has been a breach. As Commissioner Smith perceptively observed in *Investors Management Co.*: "[T]ippee responsibility must be related back to insider responsibility by a necessary finding that the tippee knew the information was given to him in breach of a duty by a person having a special relationship to the issuer not to disclose the information. ..." 44 S.E.C. at 651 (concurring in the result). Tipping thus properly is viewed only as a means of indirectly violating the *Cady, Roberts* disclose-or-abstain rule.

---

18   Continued ...

    have reason to withhold from the public, is an important one. Dirks's careful investigation brought to light a massive fraud at the corporation. And until the Equity Funding fraud was exposed, the information in the trading market was grossly inaccurate. But for Dirks's efforts, the fraud might well have gone undetected longer.

C

In determining whether a tippee is under an obligation to disclose or abstain, it thus is necessary to determine whether the insider's "tip" constituted a breach of the insider's fiduciary duty. All disclosures of confidential corporate information are not inconsistent with the duty insiders owe to shareholders. In contrast to the extraordinary facts of this case, the more typical situation in which there will be a question whether disclosure violates the insider's *Cady, Roberts* duty is when insiders disclose information to analysts. See n. 16, supra. In some situations, the insider will act consistently with his fiduciary duty to shareholders, and yet release of the information may affect the market. For example, it may not be clear—either to the corporate insider or to the recipient analyst—whether the information will be viewed as material nonpublic information. Corporate officials may mistakenly think the information already has been disclosed or that it is not material enough to affect the market. Whether disclosure is a breach of duty therefore depends in large part on the purpose of the disclosure. This standard was identified by the SEC itself in *Cady, Roberts*: a purpose of the securities laws was to eliminate "use of inside information for personal advantage." 40 S.E.C. at 912, n. 15. ... Thus, the test is whether the insider personally will benefit, directly or indirectly, from his disclosure. Absent some personal gain, there has been no breach of duty to stockholders. And absent a breach by the insider, there is no derivative breach. As Commissioner Smith stated in *Investors Management Co.*: "It is important in this type of case to focus on policing insiders and what they do ... rather than on policing information *per se* and its possession ..." 44 S.E.C. at 648 (concurring in the result).

The SEC argues that, if inside-trading liability does not exist when the information is transmitted for a proper purpose but is used for trading, it would be a rare situation when the parties could not fabricate some ostensibly legitimate business justification for transmitting the information. We think the SEC is unduly concerned. In determining whether the insider's purpose in making a particular disclosure is fraudulent, the SEC and the courts are not required to read the parties' minds. Scienter in some cases is relevant in determining whether the tipper has violated his *Cady, Roberts* duty.[23] But to determine whether the disclosure itself "deceive[s], manipulate[s], or defraud[s]" shareholders, *Aaron v. SEC*, 446 U.S. 680, 686 (1980), the initial inquiry is whether there has been a breach of duty by the insider. This requires courts to focus on objective criteria,

---

[23] *Scienter*—"a mental state embracing intent to device, manipulate or defraud," *Ernst & Ernst v. Hochfelder*, 425 U.S. 185, 193, n. 12 (1976)—is an independent element of a Rule 10b-5 violation. See *Aaron v. SEC*, 446 U.S. 680, 695 (1980). Contrary to the dissent's suggestion, ... motivation is not irrelevant to the issue of *scienter*. It is not enough that an insider's conduct results in harm to investors; rather, a violation may be found only when there is "intentional or willful conduct designed to deceive or defraud investors by controlling or artifically affecting the price of securities." *Ernst & Ernst v. Hochfelder*, supra, at 199. The issue in this case, however, is not whether Secrist or Dirks acted with *scienter*, but rather whether there was any deceptive or fraudulent conduct at all, i.e., whether Secrist's disclosure constituted a breach of his fiduciary duty and thereby caused injury to shareholders. ... Only if there was such a breach did Dirks, a tippee, acquire a fiduciary duty to disclose or abstain.

i.e., whether the insider receives a direct or indirect personal benefit from the disclosure, such as a pecuniary gain or reputational benefit that will translate into future earnings. Cf. 40 S.E.C., at 912, n. 15; Brudney, *Insiders, Outsiders, and Informational Advantages Under the Federal Securities Law*, 93 Harv. L. Rev. 324, 348 (1979) ("The theory ... is that the insider, by giving the information out selectively, is in effect selling the information to its recipient for cash, reciprocal information, or other things of value for himself ..."). There are objective facts and circumstances that often justify such an inference. For example, there may be a relationship between the insider and the recipient that suggests a *quid pro quo* from the latter, or an intention to benefit the particular recipient. The elements of fiduciary duty and exploitation of nonpublic information also exist when an insider makes a gift of confidential information to a trading relative or friend. The tip and trade resemble trading by the insider himself followed by a gift of the profits to the recipient.

Determining whether an insider personally benefits from a particular disclosure, a question of fact, will not always be easy for courts. But it is essential, we think, to have a guiding principle for those whose daily activities must be limited and instructed by the SEC's inside-trading rules, and we believe that there must be a breach of the insider's fiduciary duty before the tippee inherits the duty to disclose or abstain. In contrast, the rule adopted by the SEC in this case would have no limiting principle.

IV

Under the inside-trading and tipping rules set forth above, we find that there was no actionable violation by Dirks. It is undisputed that Dirks himself was a stranger to Equity Funding, with no pre-existing fiduciary duty to its shareholders.[26] He took no action, directly or indirectly, that induced the shareholders or officers of Equity Funding to repose trust or confidence in him. There was no expectation by Dirks's sources that he would keep their information in confidence. Nor did Dirks misappropriate or illegally obtain the information about Equity Funding. Unless the insiders breached their *Cady, Roberts* duty to shareholders in disclosing the non-public information to Dirks, he breached no duty when he passed it on to investors as well as to the *Wall Street Journal*.

It is clear that neither Secrist nor the other Equity Funding employees violated their *Cady, Roberts* duty to the corporation's shareholders by providing information to Dirks. The tippers received no monetary or personal benefit for revealing Equity Funding's secrets, nor was their purpose to make a gift of valuable information to Dirks. As the facts of this case clearly indicate, the tippers were motivated by a desire to expose the fraud. See supra, at 1-2. In the absence of a breach of duty to shareholders by the insiders, there was no derivative breach by Dirks. ... Dirks therefore could not have

---

26 Judge Wright found that Dirks acquired a fiduciary duty by virtue of his position as an employee of a broker-dealer. See 220 U.S. App. D.C., at 325-327, 681 F.2d, at 840-842. The S.E.C., however, did not consider Judge Wright's novel theory in its decision, nor did it present that theory to the Court of Appeals. The S.E.C. also has not argued Judge Wright's theory in this Court. The merits of such a duty are therefore not before the Court. See *SEC v. Chenery Corp.*, 332 U.S. 194, 196-197 (1947).

been "a participant after the fact in [an] insider's breach of a fiduciary duty." *Chiarella*, 445 U.S. at 230, n. 12.

V

We conclude that Dirks, in the circumstances of this case, had no duty to abstain from use of the inside information that he obtained. The judgment of the Court of Appeals therefore is reversed.

[The dissenting opinion of BLACKMUN J., in which BRENNAN and MARSHALL JJ. joined, has been omitted.]

Reversed.

Business Purposes. When a firm has a business interest in the confidentiality of a material change, it may find it advantageous to permit insider trading in order to move stock prices in the "right" direction. If, however, outsiders can learn through insider trading not only that good (or bad) news is imminent, but also what that news is, then the firm will seek to prevent insider trading so long as it has a business interest in confidentiality.

The principal example of this "strong" learning from insider trading arises in the context of a take-over bid. Offerors invariably seek to keep news of contested take-over bids as secret as possible prior to a public offer. Only a few senior executives of the offeror as well as a few lawyers and other members of the financial community are apprised of preliminary discussions. Code names are often used to describe the target corporation until the offer is made public. After disclosure, the price of the target's stock will likely increase, so that purchases prior to disclosure are generally profitable. However, the unusual activity in the target's shares prior to announcement of the offer may signal that a bid is impending, giving the target more time to consider defensive manoeuvres to defeat the bid.

Offerors will therefore wish to prevent insider trading in the target's stock prior to public disclosure of the bid. Paradoxically, however, the United States Supreme Court refused to impose liability for insider trading in *Chiarella v. United States*, 445 U.S. 222 (1980), a criminal action for violation of Rule 10b-5 brought against a typesetter employed by a financial printer. In the course of printing draft take-over circulars, the defendant cracked the code used by his employer's customers to conceal the identities of target corporations and purchased their stock. Since this presumably prejudiced his employer and its clients, Rule 10b-5 liability might have been thought a useful supplement to private fiduciary duties. Chiarella was convicted at trial and the conviction was upheld in the Court of Appeals. However, the Supreme Court reversed. A majority of the Court held that Chiarella did not violate Rule 10b-5 by purchasing the shares without disclosing what he knew of the impending take-over bids because he was under no fiduciary obligation to his vendors, being neither an insider nor even, since no one told him what he discovered, a tippee. Powell J. stated:

[T]he element required to make silence fraudulent—a duty to disclose—is absent in this case. No duty could arise from petitioner's relationship with the sellers of the target company's securities for petitioner had no prior dealings with them. He was not their agent, he was not a fiduciary, he was not a person in whom the sellers had placed their trust and confidence. He was, in fact, a complete stranger who dealt with the sellers only through impersonal market transactions.

• • •

Section 10(b) is aptly described as a catch-all provision, but what it catches must be fraud. When an allegation of fraud is based upon nondisclosure, there can be no fraud absent a duty to speak. We hold that a duty to disclose under s. 10(b) does not arise from the mere possession of nonpublic market information. [*Id.* at 232-33, 235]

Although the majority conceded that Chiarella could be said to have misappropriated the information and thereby to have breached a duty of silence owed to his employer or to its customers, according to the majority this theory had not been submitted to the jury in support of liability. It has, however, been submitted to and accepted in cases subsequent to *Chiarella*. See *United Sttaes v. Newman*, 664 F.2d 12 (2d Cir. 1981), cert. denied, 104 S. Ct. 193 (1983) (employee of investment banker used information entrusted to it by corporate clients); *S.E.C. v. Materia*, 745 F.2d 197 (2d Cir. 1984), cert. denied, 471 U.S. 1053, 105 S. Ct. 2112 (1985) (employees of financial printer). Misappropriation theories were also adopted by a unanimous Supreme Court as to liability under U.S. mail and wire fraud statutes. *Carpenter v. U.S.*, 108 S. Ct. 316 (1987).

After public disclosure of the offer, the offeror has an interest in seeing the market price of the target's shares rise, since this is evidence of the bid's likely success. Take-over bids are often made in the form of partial bids, in which the offer is conditional on a prescribed number of offeree shareholders (frequently 50%) tendering their shares. If less than that amount is tendered, the bid will fail. Tendering shareholders therefore take the risk that the bid will not succeed, in which case they will lose the benefit of the premium price offered by the bidder. To avoid this risk, they may sell the shares on the market rather than tender, for the target corporation's shares will rise in value if it is anticipated that the bid will succeed. The purchasers of these shares on the market will then tender their shares, pocketing the difference between offer and market price as an insurance premium if the bid succeeds. In the United States, the purchasers are often investment intermediaries called risk arbitrageurs, and sometimes come to own most of the target's shares during the course of the bid. Though the prosecution of Ivan Boesky has tarnished the popular image of risk arbitrageurs, shareholders of a target corporation are in fact benefitted by their activities, since they offer shareholders insurance against the risk of the bid's failure. Disclosure of confidential information to arbitrageurs will then facilitate take-over bids, dissipating uncertainty about their prospects.

3. Reputational Losses

A final efficiency argument against insider trading is that, whatever its other conse-quences may be, it imposes costs simply because investors dislike it. At its broadest, this argument claims that, were insider trading facilitated, investors would leave securities markets and invest in other kinds of property. In several respects, however, the argument may be thought less than persuasive. First, it would be difficult to see why investors would leave the securities market for other markets as a consequence of insider trading if the general rule in other industries is that antifraud standards do not extend to material omissions as opposed to actual misrepresentations. Second, such rough empirical evidence as is available does not suggest that this kind of externality is particularly troubling. When insider trading on public exchanges was permitted, in the 1920s, for example, shares were in fact widely held by investors.

A narrower version of this argument would focus on reputational losses suffered by the firm whose shares are traded. However, this argument suffers from the same difficulties as the first, and moreover does not provide a justification for a mandatory insider trading regime, as opposed to a presumptive rule. A further difficulty with the argument is that, in the absence of evidence of reputational injury (let alone a basis for measuring it), it looks tautological.

Diamond v. Oreamuno
New York Court of Appeals
248 N.E.2d 910 (1969)

FULD C.J.: Upon this appeal from an order denying a motion to dismiss the complaint as insufficient on its face, the question presented—one of first impression in this court— is whether officers and directors may be held accountable to their corporation for gains realized by them from transactions in the company's stock as a result of their use of material inside information.

The complaint was filed by a shareholder of Management Assistance, Inc. (MAI) asserting a derivative action against a number of its officers and directors to compel an accounting for profits allegedly acquired as a result of a breach of fiduciary duty. It charges that two of the defendants—Oreamuno, chairman of the board of directors, and Gonzalez, its president—had used inside information, acquired by them solely by virtue of their positions, in order to reap large personal profits from the sale of MAI shares and that these profits rightfully belong to the corporation. Other officers and directors were joined as defendants on the ground that they acquiesced in or ratified the assertedly wrongful transactions.

MAI is in the business of financing computer installations through sale and lease back arrangements with various commercial and industrial users. Under its lease provisions, MAI was required to maintain and repair the computers, but at the time of this suit, it lacked the capacity to perform this function itself and was forced to engage the manufacturer of the computers, International Business Machines (IBM), to service the machines. As a result of a sharp increase by IBM of its charges for such service, MAI's expenses for August of 1966 rose considerably and its net earnings declined from $262,253 in July to $66,233 in August, a decrease of about 75%. This information, although earlier known to the defendants, was not made public until October of 1966. Prior to the release of the information, however, Oreamuno and Gonzalez sold off a total of 56,500 shares of their MAI stock at the then current market price of $28 a share.

After the information concerning the drop in earnings was made available to the public, the value of a share of MAI stock immediately fell from the $28 realized by the defendants to $11. Thus, the plaintiff alleges, by taking advantage of their privileged position and their access to confidential information, Oreamuno and Gonzalez were able to realize $800,000 more for their securities than they would have had this inside information not been available to them. Stating that the defendants were "forbidden to use [such] information ... for their own personal profit or gain," the plaintiff brought this derivative action seeking to have the defendants account to the corporation for this difference. A motion by the defendants to dismiss the complaint—pursuant to CPLR 3211 (subd. [a], par. 7)—for failure to state a cause of action was granted by the court at Special Term. The Appellate Division, with one dissent, modified Special Term's order by reinstating the complaint as to the defendants Oreamuno and Gonzalez. The appeal is before us on a certified question.

In reaching a decision in this case, we are, of course, passing only upon the sufficiency of the complaint and we necessarily accept the charges contained in that pleading as true.

It is well established, as a general proposition, that a person who acquires special knowledge or information by virtue of a confidential or fiduciary relationship with another is not free to exploit that knowledge or information for his own personal benefit but must account to his principal for any profits derived therefrom. (See, e.g., *Byrne v. Barrett*, 268 N.Y. 199, 197 N.E. 217, 100 A.L.R. 680.) This, in turn is merely a corollary of the broader principle, inherent in the nature of the fiduciary relationship, that prohibits a trustee or agent from extracting secret profits from his position of trust.

In support of their claim that the complaint fails to state a cause of action, the defendants take the position that, although it is admittedly wrong for an officer or director to use his position to obtain trading profits for himself in the stock of his corporation, the action ascribed to them did not injure or damage MAI in any way. Accordingly, the defendants continue, the corporation should not be permitted to recover the proceeds. They acknowledge that, by virtue of the exclusive access which officers and directors have to inside information, they possess an unfair advantage over other shareholders and, particularly, the persons who had purchased the stock from them but, they contend, the corporation itself was unaffected and, for that reason, a derivative action is an inappropriate remedy.

It is true that the complaint before us does not contain any allegation of damages to the corporation but this has never been considered to be an essential requirement for a cause of action founded on a breach of fiduciary duty. ... This is because the function of such an action, unlike an ordinary tort or contract case, is not merely to compensate the plaintiff for wrongs committed by the defendant but, as this court declared many years ago (*Dutton v. Willner*, 52 N.Y. 312, 319, supra), "to *prevent* them, by removing from agents and trustees all inducement to attempt dealing for their own benefit in matters which they have undertaken for others, or to which their agency or trust relates." (Emphasis supplied.)

Just as a trustee has no right to retain for himself the profits yielded by property placed in his possession but must account to his beneficiaries, a corporate fiduciary, who is entrusted with potentially valuable information, may not appropriate that asset for his own use even though, in so doing, he causes no injury to the corporation. The primary concern, in a case such as this, is not to determine whether the corporation has been damaged but to decide, as between the corporation and the defendants, who has a higher claim to the proceeds derived from the exploitation of the information. In our opinion, there can be no justification for permitting officers and directors, such as the defendants, to retain for themselves profits which, it is alleged, they derived solely from exploiting information gained by virtue of their inside position as corporate officials.

In addition, it is pertinent to observe that, despite the lack of any specific allegation of damage, it may well be inferred that the defendants' actions might have caused some harm to the enterprise. Although the corporation may have little concern with the day-to-day transactions in its shares, it has a great interest in maintaining a reputation of integrity, an image of probity, for its management and in insuring the continued public acceptance and marketability of its stock. When officers and directors abuse their position in order to gain personal profits, the effect may be to cast a cloud on the corporation's name, injure stockholder relations and undermine public regard for the corporation's securities. As Presiding Justice Botein aptly put it, in the course of his opinion for the Appellate Division, "[t]he prestige and good will of a corporation, so vital to its prosperity, may be undermined by the revelation that its chief officers had been making personal profits out of corporate events which they had not disclosed to the community of stockholders." (29 A.D.2d at p. 287, 287 N.Y.S.2d at p. 303.)

The defendants maintain that extending the prohibition against personal exploitation of a fiduciary relationship to officers and directors of a corporation will discourage such officials from maintaining a stake in the success of the corporate venture through share ownership, which, they urge, is an important incentive to proper performance of their duties. There is, however, a considerable difference between corporate officers who assume the same risks and obtain the same benefits as other shareholders and those who use their privileged position to gain special advantages not available to others. The sale of shares by the defendants for the reasons charged was not merely a wise investment decision which any prudent investor might have made. Rather, they were assertedly able in this case to profit solely because they had information which was not available to any one else—including the other shareholders whose interests they, as corporate fiduciaries, were bound to protect.

* * *

In *Brophy v. Cities Serv. Co.* (31 Del.Ch.241, 70 A.2d 5, supra), for example, the Chancery Court of Delaware allowed a similar remedy in a situation not covered by the Federal legislation. One of the defendants in that case was an employee who had acquired inside information that the corporate plaintiff was about to enter the market and purchase its own shares. On the basis of this confidential information, the employee, who was not an officer and, hence, not liable under Federal law, bought a large block of shares and, after the corporation's purchases had caused the price to rise, resold them at a profit. The court sustained the complaint in a derivative action brought for an accounting, stating that "[p]ublic policy will not permit an employee occupying a position of trust and confidence toward his employer to abuse that relation to his own profit, regardless of whether his employer suffers a loss" (31 Del.Ch., at p. 246, 70 A.2d, at p. 8). And a similar view has been expressed in the Restatement, 2d, Agency (§ 388, comment c):

> c. *Use of confidential information.* An agent who acquires confidential information in the course of his employment or in violation of his duties has a duty ... to account for any profits made by the use of such information, although this does not harm the principal ... So, if [a corporate officer] has "inside" information that the corporation is about to purchase or sell securities, or to declare or to pass a dividend, profits made by him in stock transactions undertaken because of his knowledge are held in constructive trust for the principal.

• • •

The order appealed from should be affirmed, with costs, and the question certified answered in the affirmative.

BURKE, SCILEPPI, BERGAN, KEATING, BREITEL and JASEN JJ. concur.

Freeman v. Decio
United States Court of Appeals, Seventh Circuit
584 F.2d 186 (1978)

Before PELL and WOOD, Circuit Judges, and HARPER, Senior District Judge.

HARLINGTON WOOD, JR., Circuit Judge: The principal question presented by this case is whether under Indiana law the plaintiff may sustain a derivative action against certain officers and directors of the Skyline Corporation for allegedly trading in the stock of the corporation on the basis of material inside information. The district court granted summary judgment for the defendants on the ground that in light of the defendants' affidavits and documentary evidence, the plaintiff had failed to create a genuine dispute as to whether the defendants' sales of stock were based on material inside information. Alternatively, the court held that the plaintiff had failed to state a cause of action in that Indiana law has never recognized a right in a corporation to recover profits from insider trading and is not likely to follow the lead of the New York Court of Appeals in *Diamond v. Oreamuno*, 24 N.Y.2d 494, 301 N.Y.S.2d 78, 248 N.E.2d 910 (1969), in creating such a cause of action. We affirm. ...

Plaintiff-appellant Marcia Freeman is a stockholder of the Skyline Corporation, a major producer of mobile homes and recreational vehicles. Skyline is a publicly owned corporation whose stock is traded on the New York Stock Exchange (NYSE). Defendant Arthur J. Decio is the largest shareholder of Skyline, the chairman of its board of directors, and until September 25, 1972, was also the president of the company. Defendant Dale Swikert is a director of Skyline and prior to assuming the presidency from Decio in 1972 was Skyline's executive vice president and chief operating officer. Defendants Samuel P. Mandell and Ira J. Kaufman are outside directors of Skyline.

Throughout the 1960s and into 1972 Skyline experienced continual growth in sales and earnings. At the end of fiscal 1971 the company was able to report to its shareholders that over the previous five years sales had increased at a 40% average compound rate and that net income had grown at a 64% rate. This enormous success was reflected in increases in the price of Skyline stock. By April of 1972 Skyline common had reached a high of $72.00 per share, representing a price/earnings ratio of greater than 50 times earnings. Then, on December 22, 1972, Skyline reported that earnings for the quarter ending November 30, 1972, declined from $4,569,007 to $3,713,545 compared to the comparable period of the preceding year, rather than increasing substantially as they had done in the past. The NYSE immediately suspended trading in the stock. Trading was resumed on December 26 at $34.00 per share, down $13.50 from the preannouncement price. This represented a drop in value of almost 30%.

Plaintiff alleges that the defendants sold Skyline stock on the basis of material inside information during two distinct periods. Firstly, it is alleged that the financial results reported by Skyline for the quarters ending May 31 and August 31, 1972, significantly understated material costs and overstated earnings. It is further alleged that Decio, Kaufman and Mandell made various sales of Skyline stock totalling nearly $10 million during the quarters in question, knowing that earnings were overstated. Secondly, plaintiff asserts that during the quarter ending November 30 and up to December 22, 1972, Decio and Mandell made gifts and sales of Skyline stock totalling nearly $4 million while knowing that reported earnings for the November 30 quarter would decline.

• • •

Diamond v. Oreamuno and Indiana Law

Both parties agree that there is no Indiana precedent directly dealing with the question of whether a corporation may recover the profits of corporate officials who trade in the corporation's securities on the basis of inside information. However, the plaintiff suggests that were the question to be presented to the Indiana courts, they would adopt the holding of the New York Court of Appeals in *Diamond v. Oreamuno*, 24 N.Y.2d 493, 301 N.Y.S.2d 78, 248 N.E.2d 910 (1969). There, building on the Delaware case of *Brophy v. Cities Service Co.*, 31 Del.Ch. 241, 70 Ad.2d 5 (1949), the court held that the officers and directors of a corporation breached their fiduciary duties owned to the corporation by trading in its stock on the basis of material non-public information acquired by virtue of their official positions and that they should account to the corporation for their profits from those transactions. Since *Diamond* was decided, few courts have had an opportunity to consider the problem there presented.

• • •

It appears that from a policy point of view it is wisely accepted that insider trading should be deterred because it is unfair to other investors who do not enjoy the benefits of access to inside information. The goal is not one of equality of possession of information—since some traders will always be better "informed" than others by dint of greater expenditures of time and resources, greater experience, or greater anaytical abilities—but rather equality of access to information. Thus, in *Cady, Roberts & Co.*, 40 S.E.C. 907, 912 (1961), the SEC gave the following explanation of its view of the obligation of corporate insiders to disclose material inside information when trading in the corporation's stock:

Analytically, the obligation rests on two principal elements: first, the existence of a relationship giving access, directly or indirectly, to information intended to be available only for a corporate purpose and not for the personal benefit of anyone, and second, the inherent unfairness involved where a party takes advantage of such information knowing it is unavailable to those with whom he is dealing.

Yet, a growing body of commentary suggests that pursuit of this goal of "market egalitarianism"[11] may be costly. In addition to the costs associated with enforcement of the laws prohibiting insider trading, there may be a loss in the efficiency of the securities market in their capital allocation function.[12] The basic insight of economic analysis here is that securities prices act as signals helping to route capital to its most productive uses and that insider trading helps assure that those prices will reflect the best information available (i.e., inside information) as to where the best opportunities lie.[13] However, even when confronted with the possibility of a trade-off between fairness and economic efficiency, most authorities appear to find that the balance tips in favor of discouraging insider trading.[14]

Over 40 years ago Congress was stirred by examples of flagrant abuse of inside information unearthed during the hearings preceding the 1933 and 1934 Securities Acts to include in the latter a section aimed at inside trading. Section 16(b) provides for the automatic recovery by corporations of profits made by insiders in shortswing transactions within a six-month period. This automatic accountability makes the rule one of

---

11   This term comes from Loss, *The Fiduciary Concept as Applied to Trading by Corporate "Insiders" in the United States*, 33 Mod. L. Rev. 34, 35 (1970).

12   The efficiency implications of the regulation of insider trading were the subject of an early book by Professor Henry Manne—Insider Trading and the Stock Market (1966)—which has stimulated a deluge of commentary and criticism. See, e.g., W. Painter, Federal Regulation of Insider Trading (1968); Hetherington, supra note 9; Shotland, *Unsafe at any Price: A Reply to Manne, Insider Trading and the Stock Market*, 53 Va. L. Rev. 1425 (1967); Kripke, Book Review, 42 N.Y.U. L. Rev. 212 (1967); Loss, supra note 11; 5 Loss, Securities Regulation 2999-3000 (1969).

    For an analysis of the topic based more directly on general economic theory, see Wu, *An Economist Looks at Section 16 of the Securities Exchange Act of 1934*, 68 Colum. L. Rev. 260 (1968). See also R. Posner, An Economic Analysis of the Law 308 (2d ed. 1977); Note, *The Efficient Capital Market Hypothesis, Economic Theory and the Regulation of the Securities Industry*, 29 Stan. L. Rev. 1031, 1067-75 (1977).

13   See, e.g., Wu, supra note 12. However, it has been suggested that insider trading may harm the securities markets in indirect ways. See, e.g., Shotland, supra note 12; R. Posner, supra note 12. For one thing, outsiders might be less willing to invest in securities markets marked by the prevalence of a practice which they conside unfair. In addition an equal, if not greater degree of allocative efficiency can normally be achieved if the inside information is made public.

14   See, e.g., *Schein v. Chasen*, 478 F.2d 817, 825 (2d Cir. 1973) (Kaufman, J., dissenting); W. Painter, supra note 12; Hetherington, supra note 9; Shotland, supra note 12; 5 Loss, supra note 12; Loss, supra note 11.

relatively easy application and avoids very difficult problems concerning the measurement of damages, yet upon occasion leads to harsh results. The section has been characterized as a "crude rule of thumb." It is too narrow in that only short-swing trading
and short selling are covered, leaving untouched other ways of profiting from inside
information in the securities market. It is too broad in that short-swing trades not actually made on the basis of inside information are also caught in the Section's web of
liability.

The SEC has also used its full panoply of powers to police insider trading through
enforcement actions and civil actions. The agency has relied, *inter alia*, on Section 17(a)
of the 1933 Act, Section 15(c)(1) of the 1934 Act, and Rule 10b-5. The relief obtained
has included not only injunctions and suspension orders, but also disgorgement of profits earned in insider trading.

Lastly, the "victims"[20] of insider trading may recover damages from the insiders in
many instances. Absent fraud, the traditional common law approach has been to permit
officers and directors of corporations to trade in their corporation's securities free from
liability to other traders for failing to disclose inside information.[21] However, there has
been a movement towards the imposition of a common law duty to disclose in a number
of jurisdictions, at least where the insider is dealing with an existing stockholder. A few
jurisdictions now require disclosure where certain "special facts" exist,[22] and some even
impose a strict fiduciary duty on the insider *vis-à-vis* the selling shareholder.[23] But the

---

20   There is a good deal of ambiguity as to who should be considered a direct victim of insider trading.
     Those investors who actually bought from or sold securities to the insiders in face-to-face transactions
     may well feel cheated when they find out that the insiders were trading on the basis of material
     information unknown to the public. But what about traders involved in impersonal market transactions
     who were probably not even aware that insiders were trading in the market. These investors would have
     traded even if the insiders has stayed out of the market. However, if one instead asks the question of
     who might have acted differently if the insiders had made public their inside information at the time
     that they dealt with the market, these investors might be considered to have been injured by the inside
     trading, even if they were unaware of the insiders' activity. This latter class is capable of a variety of
     definitions, such as "all persons who traded at the same time as did the insiders" or, at the limit, "all
     persons who traded from the time that the insiders entered the market until the time that the insider
     information became public or was otherwise fully reflected in the stock price." See Fleischer, *Securities
     Trading and Corporate Information Practices: The Implications of the Texas Gulf Sulphur Proceedings*,
     51 Va. L. Rev. 1271, 1277-78 (1965); Note, *Damages to Uninformed Traders for Insider Trading on
     Impersonal Exchanges*, 74 Column. L. Rev. 299 (1974).

21   See, e.g., *Board of Comm'rs of Tippecanoe Co. v. Reynolds*, 44 Ind. 509 (1873); *Percival v. Wright*,
     [1902] 2 Ch. 421; see also Conant, *Duties of Disclosure of Corporate Insiders Who Purchase Shares*, 46
     Cornell L.Q. 53 (1960); Loss, supra note 11, at 40-41.

22   See, e.g., *Strong v. Repide*, 213 U.S. 419, 29 S. Ct. 521, 53 L.Ed. 853 (1909). See also Conant, supra
     note 21; 3 Loss, Securities Regulation 1446-47 (1961).

23   See, e.g., *Oliver v. Oliver*, 118 Ga. 362, 45 S.E. 232 (1903). See also Conant, supra note 21; 3 Loss,
     supra note 22.

most important remedies available to those injured by insider trading are found in the federal securities laws and in particular Rule 10b-5.* Judicial development of a private right of action under that rule has led to significant relaxation of many of the elements of common law fraud, including privity, reliance, and the distinction between misrepresentation and non-disclosure. The rule has proven a favorite vehicle for damage suits against insiders for failing to disclose material information while trading in their corporation's stock. ...

Yet, the New York Court of Appeals in *Diamond* found the existing remedies for controlling insider trading to be inadequate.

• • •

There are a number of difficulties with the *Diamond* court's ruling. Perhaps the thorniest problem was posed by the defendants' objection that whatever the ethical status of insider trading, there is no injury to the corporation which can serve as a basis for recognizing a right of recovery in favor of the latter. The Court of Appeals' response to this argument was two-fold, suggesting first that no harm to the corporation need be shown and second that it might well be inferred that the insiders' activities did in fact cause some harm to the corporation. ... Some might see the *Diamond* court's decision as resting on a broad, strict-trust notion of the fiduciary duty owed to the corporation: no director is to receive any profit, beyond what he receives from the corporation, solely because of his position. Although, once accepted, this basis for the *Diamond* rule would obviate the need for finding a potential for injury to the corporation, it is not at all clear that current corporation law contemplates such an extensive notion of fiduciary duty. It is customary to view the *Diamond* result as resting on a characterization of inside information as a corporate asset. The lack of necessity for looking for an injury to the corporation is then justified by the traditional "no inquiry" rule with respect to profits made by trustees from assets belonging to the trust *res*. However, to start from the premise that all inside information should be considered a corporate asset may presuppose an answer to the inquiry at hand. It might be better to ask whether there is any potential loss to the corporation from the use of such information in insider trading before deciding to characterize the inside information as an asset with respect to which the insider owes the corporation a duty of loyalty (as opposed to a duty of care). This approach would be in keeping with the modern view of another area of application of the duty of loyalty—the corporate opportunity doctrine. Thus, while courts will require a director or officer to automatically account to the corporation for diversion of a corporate opportunity to personal use, they will first inquire to see whether there was a possibility of a loss to the corporation—i.e., whether the corporation was in a position to potentially avail itself of the opportunity—before deciding that a corporate opportunity in fact existed. Similarly, when scrutinizing transactions between a director or officer and the corporation under the light of the duty of loyalty, most courts now inquire as to

---

*   The corporation here could not bring an action against its insiders under Rule 10b-5 because it was neither a purchaser nor a seller of securities. *Blue Chip Stamps v. Manor Drug Stores*, 421 U.S. 723 (1975).

whether there was any injury to the corporation, i.e., whether the transaction was fair and in good faith, before permitting the latter to avoid the transaction. An analogous question might be posed with respect to the *Diamond* court's unjust enrichment analysis: is it proper to conclude that an insider has been unjustly enriched *vis-à-vis* the corporation (as compared to other traders in the market) when there is no way that the corporation could have used the information to its own profit, just because the insider's trading was made possible by virtue of his corporate position?

Not all information generated in the course of carrying on a business fits snugly into the corporate asset mold. Information in the form of trade secrets, customer lists, etc., can easily be categorized as a valuable or potentially valuable corporate "possession," in that it can be directly used by the corporation to its own economic advantage. However, most information involved in insider trading is not of this ilk, e.g., knowledge of an impending merger, a decline in earnings, etc. If the corporation were to attempt to exploit such non-public information by dealing in its own securities, it would open itself up to potential liability under federal and state securities laws, just as do the insiders when they engage in insider trading. This is not to say that the corporation does not have any interests with regard to such information. It may have an interest in either preventing the information from becoming public or in regulating the timing of disclosure. However, insider trading does not entail the disclosure of inside information, but rather its use in a manner in which the corporation itself is prohibited from exploiting it.

· · ·

It must be conceded that the unfairness that is the basis of the widespread disapproval of insider trading is borne primarily by participants in the securities markets, rather than by the corporation itself. By comparison, the harm to corporate goodwill posited by the *Diamond* court pales in significance. At this point, the existence of such an indirect injury must be considered speculative, as there is no actual evidence of such a reaction. Furthermore, it is less than clear to us that the nature of this harm would form an adequate basis for an action for an accounting based on a breach of the insiders' duty of loyalty, as opposed to an action for damages based on a breach of the duty of care. The injury hypothesized by the *Diamond* court seems little different from the harm to the corporation that might be inferred whenever a responsible corporate official commits an illegal or unethical act using a corporate asset. Absent is the element of loss of opportunity or potential susceptibility to outside influence that generally is present when a corporate fiduciary is required to account to the corporation.

The *Brophy* case is capable of being distinguished on this basis. Although the court there did not openly rely on the existence of a potential harm to the corporation, such a harm was possible. Since the corporation was about to begin buying its own shares in the market, by purchasing stock for his own account the insider placed himself in direct competition with the corporation. To the degree that his purchases might have caused the stock price to rise, the corporation was directly injured in that it had to pay more for its purchases. The other cases cited by the *Diamond* court also tended to involve an agent's competition with his principal, harm to it, disregard for its instructions, or the like. The same is true of the situations covered in Comment c of the Restatement (Second) of Agency, with the exception of the case where the corporate agent undertakes stock transactions on the basis of knowledge that the corporation is about to declare or pass a dividend.

• • •

Since the *Diamond* court's action was motivated in large part by its perception of the inadequacy of existing remedies for insider trading, it is noteworthy that over the decade since *Diamond* was decided, the 10b-5 class action has made substantial advances toward becoming the kind of effective remedy for insider trading that the court of appeals hoped that it might become. Most importantly, recovery of damages from insiders has been allowed by, or on the behalf of, market investors even when the insiders dealt only through impersonal stock exchanges, although this is not yet a well-settled area of the law. In spite of other recent developments indicating that such class actions will not become as easy to maintain as some plaintiffs had perhaps hoped, it is clear the remedies for insider trading under the federal securities law now constitute a more effective deterrent that they did when *Diamond* was decided.

The judgment of the district court is Affirmed.

NOTES

1) In portions of the opinion omitted here, the Court of Appeals affirmed the trial Court's findings that the plaintiff had failed: (1) to make out a cause of action under s. 16(b) of the Securities Exchange Act since there was no instance of a purchase and a sale within a single six-month period; and (2) to create a genuine dispute as to whether the defendants' sales of stock had been made on the basis of material undisclosed information. The defendants sold the shares in the face of rising costs for lumber that Skyline could not recoup because of price controls. Both the rising lumber costs and the existence of price controls were public information, and the Court held that "[t]he fact that the defendants may have been in a position to better judge the impact of these factors on Skyline's earnings because of their greater familiarity with the corporation's affairs does not mean that they should be held liable for failing to educate the public."

2) In discussing the corporate opportunity doctrine, the Court stated that a manager will not be held liable to account unless the corporation might have availed itself of the opportunity. Where a public corporation makes use of inside information by repurchasing outstanding shares on undisclosed good news it is deemed an insider of itself. OSA s. 1(1) ("insider"), CBCA s. 127 ("insider"). The repurchase may also be an "issuer bid" under OSA s. 89(1), with take-over bid disclosure being mandated under OSA ss. 95-97. See Chapter Eleven, Section E. When the corporation seeks to profit from inside information by issuing new shares on undisclosed bad news, the transaction may contravene OSA prospectus requirements discussed in Chapter Five. The policies that animate these provisions seek to protect the market for firm claims. Do these policies also suggest a need for barriers to insider trading on share repurchases? On *any* public share repurchase, outsiders will know that the managers value the shares more highly than the market does, so that the concern for distributional effects is lessened. Indeed, share

repurchases have manifestly not destroyed the market for equity securities. In addition, they may be defended on signaling theories, since a firm's claims about hidden wealth become more creditable when it invests in its own shares. Repurchases are considered in Chapter Ten.

D. ELEMENTS OF INSIDER TRADING

Green v. Charterhouse Group Canada Ltd.
Ontario Court of Appeal
(1976), 12 O.R. (2d) 280, 68 D.L.R. (3d) 592

[Before ARNUP, McKINNON and HOWLAND JJ.A.]

ARNUP J.A. (by whom the judgment of the Court was delivered): In September, 1968, the plaintiff Arthur B. Green ("Green") issued a writ against five of his former associates in the defendant Imbrex Limited ("Imbrex"), plus D.L. Sinclair, and the five companies by which the personal defendants were employed or which they controlled. He claimed that the defendants had cheated him in acquiring his shares in Imbrex, and he alleged conspiracy and fraud against them. His claim, in money, was for $1,000,000.

His action was tried before Mr. Justice Grant in late 1972, and the early part of 1973, over a period totalling 47 days. It utterly failed. The trial Judge said that the accusations of fraud were unjustifiably made, and that the trial had lasted at least twice as long as it should have because of cross-examination "directed towards finding a conspiracy and fraud which did not exist." His judgment is reported: [1973] 2 O.R. 677, 35 D.L.R. (3d) 161.

All of the personal defendants who were still living went into the witness-box. In general their evidence was preferred to that of the plaintiff wherever there was a conflict.

In this Court Mr. Weir—who was not counsel at the trial—relied only upon the following two alternative grounds for recovery raised by the much amended statement of claim.

 (i) that the plaintiff was entitled to be compensated by the defendants under the "insider" provisions of s. 113(1) of The Securities Act (then S.O. 1966, chap. 142, now R.S.O. 1970, chap. 426);
(ii) that the defendants were under a fiduciary duty to the plaintiff, they had breached that duty, and were liable to the plaintiff for damages for such breach.

The trial Judge had found against the plaintiff on both of these grounds.

Mr. Weir did not attack any specific findings or credibility made by the trial Judge, although he suggested that this Court "would want to give very careful consideration" to one of the key letters in the case, when considering the findings of fact of the trial Judge. He also included as App. "E" to the appellant's statement a list of 20 alleged "additional major errors of the trial judge in his appreciation of the facts," and four "errors of the trial judge with reference to the market and market prices which influenced his decision." He made reference to a few paragraphs of this appendix in making certain specific submissions, but did not suggest that there was a cumulative effect flowing from this collection of alleged errors.

... While I will specifically comment later on certain findings of fact, my brothers and I were in agreement at the conclusion of the 10 days of argument before us that the findings of fact of the trial Judge should be accepted by us. There was ample evidence upon which to base them, and in many respects the case was one where findings of credibility were crucial. This careful and experienced trial Judge saw and heard all of the persons still living who had participated in the events in question. He did not misapprehend any oral or documentary evidence in any important respect. I will therefore recount the facts as he found them to be.

[Imbrex Ltd. was a public corporation with its shares listed for trading on various Canadian stock exchanges. it had been formed in the mid-1960s as an amalgam of firms selling floor coverings in various parts of Canada, and its largest shareholders had been the owners of the regional companies out of which Imbrex was formed. The plaintiff Green had been in the floor covering business in Ontario. He was a vice-president of Imbrex and at relevant times owned about 80,000 of its shares. Another vice-president was the defendant Lennox, whose business had been conducted in the Maritimes. The president and chief executive officer of Imbrex was the defendant Godbout, from Quebec. He held his Imbrex shares through a personal holding company, Tempo. Each of the named individuals was a director of Imbrex. Other directors were the defendants Alexander, a representative of Charterhouse Group Canada Ltd., a venture capital firm that had become a major Imbrex shareholder; Messrs. Cronyn and Ostiguy, both principals of the securities firm that had underwritten the public offering of Imbrex's shares; the brothers Charles and Trevor Jordon-Knox, who had been in the floor covering business in western Canada; and Pouliot, a Montreal lawyer. The defendant Sinclair, president of Charterhouse, became an Imbrex director upon Green's retirement from that position in February 1968.

Imbrex, as successor to the various regional firms out of which it was formed, was the exclusive distributor for Harding Carpets Ltd. everywhere in Canada outside Ontario. Harding Carpets accounted for about 60% of Imbrex's business, and by coincidence Imbrex accounted for about the same proportion of Harding's business—a fact which apparently caused some discomfort to Harding's controlling shareholder, Malim Harding.

In April 1967 the principal shareholders of Imbrex had entered into a buy-sell agreement under which any party wishing to sell shares of Imbrex had first to offer them to the other parties.]

Green Leaves Imbrex

Green's former company had a bad year in 1966 and the first half of 1967. Actual sales fell far below those estimated by Green and net profit after tax was less than half of that expected. A strike at the Armstrong Cork Company over a period of almost four months doubtless contributed partly to these poor results, but the other directors of Imbrex took a strong view that the primary responsibility was that of Green himself, and the trial Judge took the same view. In August, 1967, it was agreed that a general manager of Green's former company be appointed, with full authority to operate that company, and that its operations be reorganized. While Green expressed his willingness to co-operate to this end, it became apparent that relationships between himself and Godbout became strained at this time, and deteriorated steadily thereafter. There were protracted negotiations as to the terms on which Green would retire. Green's lawyers became involved with these, and eventually agreement was reached providing for a termination allowance. Green indicated he wanted to sell his shares to the others at $7 per share, which his associates thought was quite unreasonable. It was in fact far over the market price.

The trial Judge dealt at length with this period of negotiations but in view of the narrowing of the issues on this appeal, I do not need to comment further upon it other than to say that a new shareholders' agreement was negotiated and executed on December 7, 1967. The market price of Imbrex shares at that time was between $4.75 and $5 per share. The periods of time in the new agreement for acting upon offers, and other resulting steps, were greatly shortened. Since a good deal of the argument turned upon the precise terms of this agreement I propose to quote it in part, substituting the names of the appropriate party for the reference to "the Party of Second Part," etc.

After referring to the agreement of April 12, 1967, and to the fact that Green now owned 80,000 shares of Imbrex and not 100,144 as mentioned in the April agreement the December agreement continued:

AND WHEREAS THE PARTIES HERETO HAVE AGREED TO AMEND [the agreement of April 12, 1967] INSOFAR AS IT AFFECTS [Green] UPON THE TERMS AND CONDITIONS HEREAFTER SET FORTH:

WITNESSETH:

1. Notwithstanding any other term of the [April agreement] the parties, hereto agree that in the event [Green] is desirous of selling, assigning, transferring or otherwise disposing of all but not less than all of the said 80,000 shares he shall give notice to [Tempo] and to [Charterhouse] that he wishes to sell the said shares and the price, terms and conditions which he is willing to accept, the said notice being herein referred to as the "Notice of Offer." [Tempo and Charterhouse] shall have the right to purchase the said shares at the price, terms and conditions set out in the "Notice of Offer" and the "Notice of Offer" may be accepted by them or by either of them by notice to [Green] (herein called the "Notice of Acceptance") given within twenty four (24) hours from the time that the "Notice of Offer" is received. If the "Notice of Offer" is accepted by "Notice of Acceptance" as herein provided then the purchase and sale shall be closed within ten (10) days from the "Notice of Acceptance." If the "Notice of Offer" is not accepted as herein provided then [Green] may during a period of ten (10) days from the time of the receipt of the "Notice of Offer" sell the said shares to any other person, firm or corporation at price, terms and conditions per share not less favourable to [Green] than those per share set out in the "Notice of Offer"; if [Green] does not effect a sale of the said shares offered by the "Notice of Offer" during the said period of ten (10) days then the foregoing provisions hereof shall again apply thereto and so on from time to time.

2. The provisions of this agreement shall apply only if [Green] wishes to sell all but not less than all of the said 80,000 shares and if he wishes to sell less than 80,000 shares then the provi-

sions of the [April agreement] shall apply except that the words "ten (10) days" shall be substituted for "thirty (30) days" where referred to in paragraph 1 of the [April agreement] insofar as they are applicable to [Green].

3. Any notice given pursuant to this agreement may be given orally (personally or by telephone) to [Tempo] and/or to [Charterhouse] or sent by prepaid registered mail, cable or telegram to [Tempo] and [Charterhouse] to the address of the party concerned at the address of such party as given in this agreement. ...

4. The [April agreement] is also hereby amended in that [Green] hereby relieves all the other parties to the [April agreement] of any obligations which they may have towards [Green] with respect to the sale of their Imbrex shares and [Green] hereby waives any rights which he may have with respect to the same.

5. Notwithstanding paragraph 4 hereof the parties to this agreement other than [Green] hereby undertake for a period of six (6) months from the date hereof not to sell shares of Imbrex Limited during the period of thirty (30) days following the effective date of a "Notice of Offer" referred to in his agreement. This restriction to apply only as regards the first "Notice of Offer" to be given pursuant to this agreement and not to any other subsequent "Notice of Offer."

One important change from the previous arrangements was that Green no longer had a right to participate in a purchase of the shares of the others. This is understandable, since he had ceased to play any role in the management of the affairs of Imbrex.

Green's Desire to Sell his Shares

The ink was scarcely dry on the shareholders' agreement of December, 1967, when Green set about seeking a way to sell his shares. His son-in-law was a trainee in the Toronto office of Nesbitt, Thomson and Company Limited, a large brokerage firm. Green approached the firm and told them that he would be interested in disposing of his block of shares. He suggested that the firm approach Mr. Harding. Green indicated that he thought his shares, amounting to almost 10% of the outstanding stock of Imbrex, should command a premium price. He did not tell Nesbitt, Thomson of the buy-sell agreement with his former associates.

It appears that Green had in his mind that the Harding franchises were terminable on three months' notice, and since Harding was already displeased with the principals of Imbrex, Harding might teminate the Imbrex franchises, and in the end Green might be able to get back the distributing company he had started out with prior to the formation of Imbrex. To keep up the market price of Imbrex, Green purchased 1,300 shares about December 15, 1967, through another broker, without telling Nesbitt, Thomson.

Word of Green's activities soon got back first to Charterhouse and then to Godbout. In January and February, 1968, the market price gradually fell off to $3.75. Nesbitt, Thomson could find no purchaser for Green's block of shares, and while Green did not actually tell them to cease their efforts, he did not pursue the matter with them, and in addition, he was out of Canada from March 7th to March 29th. On March 30, 1968, the Toronto Globe & Mail carried a news item with respect to the annual meeting of Imbrex and quoted a prediction of Mr. Godbout that sales would go up 35% in the first two months of 1968, compared with the previous year. Cochran, Murray & Co. issued an encouraging analysis of Imbrex on April 23, 1968, and a brokerage firm in Vancouver did the same also in April. In the latter part of April there was unusual activity in the stock and the price rose to a range of $4.75 to $5. About April 23rd Green again asked his son-in-law to "see what interest could be developed in the block of stock."

First Quarter Earnings of Imbrex

The first quarter results of Imbrex were presented to a meeting of the executive committee of the board of directors on May 1, 1968, and immediately thereafter, on the same day, Godbout released to Canadian Dow Jones Limited certain figures, being the net profit and gross sales for the first quarter, representing a 27% increase in sales and 79% increase in net income. Most brokerage firms are subscribers to the Dow Jones service; Nesbitt, Thomson, James Richardson & Son Limited, Cochran, Murray & Co., and Morgan, Ostiguy were all clients of Dow Jones.

Dow Jones put the information on their telex system at 4:10 p.m. on May 1, 1968. The trial Judge was convinced that Green had the information contained in the Dow Jones release before May 6th, the date on which the transaction giving rise to this action was agreed upon.

• • •

Godbout's Discussion with Harding

For a long time Godbout had cherished the hope that some day a merger might be effected between the Harding company and Imbrex. In the light of hindsight it is clear that he had completely misjudged the situation and that such a merger was never an acceptable idea to Mr. Harding. The discussions, however, had relevance to some of the issues arising in this case, and must be noted.

In January, 1968, Godbout met Mr. Al Davidson, a senior officer of Harding, at Toronto and brought up the subject of some form of amalgamation between the two companies. Davidson later wrote to Godbout saying that he was coming to Montreal on February 8th and 9th and suggested a meeting, which was arranged. Godbout and one of his staff did a great deal of work in preparation for this meeting, which went on for most of a day. When Godbout followed this up with a letter to Davidson on February 9, 1968, Davidson replied that both he and Harding were going to be away a considerable part of the balance of February and March and said it would not be possible to review the matter prior to April. Godbout met Harding a few days before April 1st, and discussed a merger between the two companies. He sent a memorandum of the meeting of the two Jordan-Knoxes. A further meeting was arranged for early May, but Harding postponed it to May 21st.

Under date of May 1, 1968, Godbout sent a memorandum to all directors of Imbrex, marked "personal and confidential." Part of this memorandum relates to Neon, which I will deal with separately, but he reported on his discussions with Harding and with the senior management of the company's bank, at which latter meeting he had discussed with the bank the availability of funds if Imbrex were to acquire control of Harding. The significance of these events is related to what was called during argument "the warning letter" which was sent by Sinclair to Green when Green, at the end of April, raised with Sinclair the probability of his invoking the buy-sell provision with respect to his shares. I will come back to this subject.

What is important about the Godbout-Harding discussions is that at the end of April, 1968, Godbout believed that there was a real possibility of some form of permanent corporate association between Harding and Imbrex. It is not clear what views, if any, were held by the other directors on this topic, although they knew the discussions were taking place, and were perhaps more alive to the vulnerable position of Imbrex vis-à-vis Harding than Godbout was himself.

The Neon Negotiations

On February 29, 1968, Mr. John C. Chaston, vice-president of Pemberton Securities of Vancouver, brokers and investment dealers, wrote to Godbout, with copies to Ostiguy and Cronyn, inquiring as to the "circumstances under which all of the shares of your company might be for sale." He stated that the inquiry was a serious one and that there was no question about the financial capacity of their client to complete a deal. Godbout reported the receipt of the letter to the directors, and made inquiries of Chaston as to what price the interested party was considering offering. Without too much difficulty, Godbout had deduced that the interested company was Neon Products of Canada Limited ("Neon"). Neon was a public company whose shares were actively traded. Its guiding spirit was James Pattison of Vancouver, who had obtained control of the company by November of 1967. He had some American corporations as associates. He appears to have been virtually a compulsive "dealer," interested in constant expansion by acquisition of other companies.

Godbout was in Vancouver on April 16, 1968, and had previously written Chaston to see if an appointment could be arranged with Chaston's principal. Godbout arranged that the Jordan-Knox brothers would meet with him at Chaston's office. Some discussion with Pattison took place but no offer for the shares of Imbrex was made. An informal visit between Pattison and Godbout occurred later that same day but it was "general" in its terms.

There was no further communication between Godbout and Pattison until April 29th, when Pattison was in Montreal, called Godbout, found that Godbout was having a meeting with Alexander and invited Godbout and Alexander to have dinner with them. While no offer was made, Pattison appears to have indicated that he had in mind making an offer of around $10 per share for the control of Imbrex; Godbout (by what was apparently a virtually automatic reaction) indicated that he would not even communicate to his directors any figure less than $12.50. Godbout believed that Pattison was taking the matter seriously at that time. Alexander's impression was that there was only a slight possibility of Neon making any offer. (Imbrex stock was selling at under $5 at this time.)

Pattison asked permission to have his company's treasurer and one of his staff, who was both an accountant and a lawyer, come to the Imbrex offices to make a feasibility study. Pattison ended the discussions by saying that "if the arithmetic made sense, and he thought it would, he would be like to make an offer before the next meeting of Imbrex directors" (set for May 16th). Godbout gave the necessary permission.

Godbout was preparing to go to Europe on May 4th. In a memorandum which as typed bears date May 1, 1968, Godbout summarized for all of the directors of Imbrex his discussions in Vancouver and in Montreal with Pattison. This memorandum, ex. 38, is a key document in the case and is reproduced in full.

May 1, 1968

"PERSONAL & CONFIDENTIAL"
TO ALL DIRECTORS OF IMBREX LIMITED—

Gentlemen:

Monday, April the 29th, following a few hours in Ted Alexander's office, both Ted and I met Mr. Jim Pattison, a Director of Neon Products of Vancouver and effective this weekend the President of that company. As you know, Neon is a public company listed both on the Vancouver and Toronto Stock Exchange, whose stock is presently trading around $23.50.

Through Pemberton Securities as you know, we were approached to see at what price Imbrex would consider selling all of its stock. You have been kept informed by copy of correspondence re this matter. In my trips in Vancouver, both times I had the occasion to discuss with Mr. Pattison and showed no real interest in our part. Nevertheless, I told him that I would further consider our discussions, and when I left Vancouver that was the situation as it existed.

Mr. Pattison proceeded to Montreal and yesterday we had a meeting at which time he again asked at what price we would consider selling our stock for an exchange of Neon stock. Following a lengthy conversation I told Jim that it was up to him to quote a price and that if I felt that the price quoted was fair I would report it to the Directors and if I felt it was unfair I would not report it to the Directors. He then said that he was thinking of a price around $10.00 a share and I told him that I would not even report it to the Board; following further discussion I informed him that possibly the only price that I would think of reporting to the Board was $12.50 a share. He then said that if the arithmetic made sense, and he thought it very well could be, he would like to make an offer before our next Directors' Meeting of May the 16th. He informed me that his Mr. Harry Dunbar, Treasurer of Neon, would be down to visit us in Montreal the coming Monday. He is also employing a Mr. Don Sillman, Chartered Accountant and Barrister presently employed by [Peat] Marwick, but to join the Neon organization in the near future. These people want to have a talk with us to make a feasibility report to Jim Pattison. I should like to impress on everyone concerned that I made no commitment but said that at $12.50 if the other conditions were right, I would recommend same. Neon is building a conglomerate, it has substantial U.S. backing and a photostat of certain documentation will show you that its U.S. partners and Directors are indeed substantial people with substantial firms.

Following the visit of Harry Dunbar and Don Sillman, I would have a meeting with Him Pattison approximately the 13th of May and will then be able to carry the message back to the Board as to the extent of the proposition.

HARDING CARPETS—
I shall be meeting Malim Harding of Harding Carpets in Brantford on Tuesday, May the 21st. I propose at that time to show Malim Harding a tentative organization chart of what both our companies would look like if some fusion, merger or acquisition was made and the advantages that both firms could derive from a reorganization such as recommended. I will attempt not to talk dollars and cents, but should Mr. Harding ask questions in this direction I would say that we certainly would not be in a position to offer more than book value on the common stock. If he asks what part of the participating non-voting stock we would acquire, I would be prepared to tell him that we do not consider purchasing any of the participating non-voting.

I have had a session with the senior management of the Canadian Imperial Bank of Commerce telling them of our approach to Hardings and advising them of the possible fund requirements. To this I can report that Mr. Russ Harrison said that if the arithmetic made sense and that we undertook to make a public issue following the acquisition, he saw no reason why the bank would not give us the necessary finance for the interim period, that is from the time that we buy Hardings and pay for them until such a time as we make an issue. This again will be fully discussed at our next Directors' Meeting.

. . .

ART GREEN—

As you know, the block of Art Green has been offered quite widely with no takers. Art informed Mr. Sinclair that he felt he had an offer for a block of his stock at $4.92. I think we are morally compelled to inform Mr. Green that we have no objection to his selling the block, that he of course has to live with the buy-and-sell agreement, but on the other hand that there are negotiations at the Imbrex level which could put the Imbrex stock in a different price bracket which would be superior to the price he is considering selling now. I do not feel that we have any responsibility nor right to give further details but I do think that we are bound to tell Art that very possibly the stock could be worth considerably more than what he is selling due to negotiations presently going on.

FIRST QUARTER RESULTS—

By the time you receive this letter, I will have spoken verbally with every Director but I am pleased to confirm an increase of 27% in sales in the first quarter and an increase of 79% in net profit for the same period.

	1967	1968	$ Increase	% Increase
Sales	4,713,387	5,982,000	1,268,944	27%
Net Profit	48,188	86,322	38,134	79%
Net Profit Per Share	.06	.10		

In spite of these results, there are some weak spots that have to be corrected and if same can be corrected in the second half I feel that Imbrex would most probably surpass its budget or at least meet same.

NEW PRODUCTS—

We have practically completed a family group of products which will create quite a wall covering selection of products. We intend introducing the complete parcel to our management within 60 to 90 days maximum, and this should open a brand new field of endeavour for all subsidiaries.

Respectfully yours,
R.G. Godbout,
President

RGG/mm

There was a good deal of controversy at the trial, and before us, as to when this memorandum reached the various directors to whom it was sent, Mr. Godbout's secretary, who typed it, expressed the view that it would have been mailed not later than Thursday, May 2, 1968. In that event it might not have reached Toronto until late on May 3rd, and may not have been delivered to the various addresses in Toronto until Monday, May 6th.

The evidence of the addresses is important, since it was accepted by the trial Judge. Sinclair is "absolutely sure" that he did not read the memorandum until after the events of May 6th. The trial Judge accepted this testimony and found that Sinclair had no knowledge of the Neon discussions at the time of the purchase of Green's shares on the morning of May 6th. Trevor Jordan-Knox was away for the week-end, sailing, and does not believe he saw the memorandum until May 7th. Again, his evidence was accepted.

The subsequent events are that Neon, on June 10, 1968, did make an offer to buy all the Imbrex shares they could get, at $12 payable in Neon shares valued at the market price on June 10th. Those members of the control group of Imbrex who were sceptical of Neon, and who promptly sold their shares, turned out to have acted wisely, since Neon subsequently fell on evil days and its shares ended up at less than a tenth of their value at the time of the Imbrex acquisition. Those who acquired and held on to Neon shares—such as Pouliot and his partners—have come to regret it.

Green Sells his Shares

By April 29, 1968, the price of Imbrex shares was about $5. On the morning of Tuesday April 30th, Green telephoned Sinclair and told him he was thinking of selling his shares at $5 and sought Sinclair's advice. Sinclair suggested that Green wait awhile and that Green talk to Godbout. Green indicated he did not want to talk to Godbout, about anything, and Sinclair offered to do so, and did. Godbout was worried, in view of the discussions he was having with Harding, and called Sinclair back to suggest that Sinclair give Green information that some preliminary negotiations were on foot which might result in a higher price for Imbrex shares. Godbout felt that there was a moral obligation to inform Green, their old associate, of these negotiations.

As a result, Sinclair called Green and told him there was a discussion taking place which might be resolved in two weeks and which might affect the value of Green's shares. Whatever words were used, Green got the impression that the discussions involved a "takeover," because he used that term when he had a telephone conversation with Cronyn. Sinclair further wrote the "warning letter" (after first reading a draft to Cronyn by telephone) in these terms:

April 30, 1968

Private & Confidential
A.B. Green, Esq.,
930 Crozier Court,
Port Credit, Ontario

Dear Arthur:

After speaking to you this morning I discussed with Guy Godbout your desire to dispose of your holding of Imbrex common shares at the current market price or thereabouts.

Guy has asked me to tell you that preliminary discussions have taken place which conceivably might result in an offer being made for Imbrex shares at a price in excess of that at which the shares are now trading. It is expected that the matter will be resolved within the next two weeks and I will keep you informed to the extent my position permits.

Naturally, this information is given in strict confidence and I know you will treat it in this light.

Yours sincerely,
"Sandy"

D.L. Sinclair
/ag
Blind copies to: R.G. Godbout
                   J.B. Cronyn

There is no doubt that Green "got the message" that Sinclair was advising him against selling. Green's diary entry for that day reads: "spoke to Sinclair and he advises against selling."

• • •

The various persons within the Imbrex group who got copies of Sinclair's letter took different interpretations from it. Sinclair intended the letter to relate to the discussions between Godbout and Harding. Sinclair then knew nothing of the Pattison-Godbout meeting on April 29th. Alexander thought it related to the latter discussion, but of course he had been at those discussions. Cronyn and Godbout both thought the letter related to Neon but recognized that it fitted the Harding discussions also. In the view I take of the letter, as will appear, it does not matter *what* the subject was to which the letter from Sinclair was intended to relate.

On May 3rd, after his conversation(s) with Cronyn, Green called Nesbitt, Thomson who, according to Green, gave him the impression that interest in Green's block of shares was increasing at a price of $6. Green was watching the market closely. After these various calls on May 3rd, Green called Sinclair, as representative of Charterhouse, and stated that he was implementing the buy-sell agreement and offering his 80,000 shares under the agreement, at $6 per share. Sinclair asked if the offer could be left open until 10:00 a.m. on the following Monday (May 3rd was a Friday), to which Green agreed. Sinclair telephoned Godbout and told him of the offer.

Godbout arranged for 4:00 o'clock that afternoon a conference telephone call with all of the directors of Imbrex except Trevor Jordan-Knox, who had gone sailing. The participants thus included representatives of all parties to the buy-sell agreement (except Green) plus the underwriters. Godbout's purpose was to try to persuade the listeners on the conference call to take as many of the shares as they could be persuaded to take. Lennox would not take any, nor would the two brokers. Eventually Sinclair said Charterhouse would take 25,000 but would sell them on the market as soon as that could be done without depreciating the value of the shares. The Jordon-Knoxes originally agreed to take 20,000, and Godbout said he would be responsible for 15,000. This left them 20,000 short, and late that night Charles Jordon-Knox agreed to take another 20,000 making 40,000 in all. (When his brother returned from sailing, he was very upset about the commitment being doubled.) Godbout worked hard to persuade Pouliot to take

10,000 shares. Eventually Pouliot, on behalf of himself and his law firm, agreed to take 5,000, from Godbout's 15,000.

Since Godbout was about to leave for Europe, he instructed one Aubry, an officer of Imbrex, to pursue the matter on Monday morning, May 6th, and to ask Sinclair to see if Green would sell his block at \$5⅞, but to buy at \$6 if necessary.

On May 6th, Sinclair telephoned Green, told Green that the brokers would not take any shares because of the state of the market but that the group would take the entire block at \$5⅞. Green asked for an hour or so, telephoned Nesbitt, Thomson, who informed him they could not possibly come up to \$6 in the short time available, and he then called Sinclair back to accept the offer at \$5⅞.

In the end, Godbout and his wife took 10,000, Alexander took 500 from the block purchased by Charterhouse, Pouliot took 5,000 (from Godbout's 15,000), Jordans Rugs Limited took 40,000 and Charterhouse took the remaining 24,500. The purchase was actually closed on May 9, 1968. Green claimed he did not know, even then, who the individual purchasers were, but the trial Judge did not believe him, in view of the contradictory evidence of Mr. Rae of Charterhouse, who closed the transaction with Green on behalf of all of the purchasers.

What happened thereafter with respect to the shares is probably relevant only to the matter of damages, although it may explain Green's motivation in his lawsuit. The shares acquired by Charterhouse were sold in Vancouver at a slight profit of \$4,772.70. This was a fortunate sale, since it turned out that a firm of investment counsellors (Phillips, Hager & North) had decided Imbrex was a good company to buy, and were looking for shares for a trust they were managing. Jordans Rugs sold 5,000 shares at \$6 to the same trust but after the Neon offer had been made, they sold most of the rest of their 40,000 shares at a very substantial profit, amounting to \$253,762.50.

Alexander had already owned 500 shares of Imbrex. After the Neon offer he converted that 500 and the 500 he acquired from the Green transaction into shares of Neon (later Neonex), which he retained. He lost a large proportion of his investment.

The 10,000 shares Godbout acquired were placed in his wife's name. Some of these she sold on the market, others she converted to Neon, and then sold. She made a total profit of \$83,092.50 less brokerage.

Pouliot converted his firm's 5,000 Imbrex shares to 2,310 Neonex shares, which the firm still retains. They had lost approximately \$17,500 to the time of trial, and more since.

The Securities Act

As noted by the trial Judge, the important provisions of the Securities Act were enacted in 1966 by 1966 (Ont.), c. 142 (see now R.S.O. 1970, c. 426). Section 113 constitutes one of the two foundations of the appellant's claim as made in this Court, and much of the argument was devoted to its interpretation and to its application to the facts of this case. I reproduce the appropriate portions of the statute:

. . .

113. (1) Every insider of the corporation or associate or affiliate of such insider, who, in connection with a transaction relating to the capital securities of the corporation, makes use of

any specific confidential information for his own benefit or advantage that, if generally known, might reasonably be expected to affect materially the value of such securities, is liable to compensate any person or company for any direct loss suffered by such person or company as a result of such transaction, unless such information was known or ought reasonably to have been known to such person or company at the time of such transaction, and is also accountable to the corporation for any direct benefit or advantage received or receivable by such insider, associate or affiliate, as the case may be, as a result of such transaction.

I will deal in greater detail below with the arguments arising from s. 113. Broadly speaking Mr. Weir submitted that the defendants or some of them had made use of specific confidential information for their own benefit and advantage, that it was the kind of information to which the section relates, and that Green has suffered direct loss as a result of a transaction with the defendants. The specific confidential information was said to be related to two matters, the first quarter earnings of Imbrex, and discussions with Mr. Pattison on behalf of Neon with respect to an offer for Imbrex shares, culminating eventually in a firm offer. Mr. Weir did not rely upon the discussions by Godbout with Harding as a basis of relief under the section; on the contrary, he urged that the defendants were themselves putting forward in this action the Godbout-Harding discussions as a "cover" for the real information on which they were relying, namely, the probability of a take-over bid from Pattison on behalf of Neon.

[The Court ruled that the trial Judge had correctly received into evidence the Dow Jones release concerning Imbrex's first quarter earnings.]

Two comments should be made about our ruling. It should not be taken as laying down that information of the kind to which s. 113(1) relates is disclosed to all shareholders by having it put over the Dow Jones wire. I have in mind the discussions of the subject in *Securities & Exchange Com'n v. Texas Gulf Sulphur Co.* (1968), 401 F.2d 833, and the commentary upon the trial judgment in the instant case by Prof. David L. Johnston, 51 *Can. Bar Rev.* 676 at p. 687.

Secondly, it should be read in the light of what is said later herein as to s. 113(1) actions, and particularly as to each case requiring decision on its own facts.

All of the personal defendants gave evidence, including evidence that they did not in fact make use of what information they had, whatever its character. Evidence of this kind was given by Trevor Jordan-Knox as to the 40,000 shares purchased by himself and his brother. The plaintiff sought to lead evidence in reply with respect to "substantial purchases of Imbrex shares by one Baxter, the Cruises, and Phillips, Hager [the investment counsellors] early in May 1968." Apparently what was sought to be established was a connection between the Jordan-Knoxes and various of the purchasers in order to cast doubt upon the credibility of Trevor Jordan-Knox in asserting he and his brother had not made use of any confidential information. On this subject we ruled as follows:

(2) We do not accept the submission that the trial judge erred in rejecting the evidence tendered concerning purchase of Imbrex shares in Vancouver by persons allegedly connected with the Jordan-Knox's. While one or more of us may have additional reasons for reaching this conclusion, we are all agreed on two grounds for rejecting this argument:

(a) we are not satisfied that the trial judge erred in principle in refusing to admit this evidence in reply nor in exercising his discretion not to permit the plaintiff to re-open his case to adduce such evidence;

(b) the weight of this evidence was so tenuous, and the inferences sought to be drawn from it so unlikely, that neither the course of the trial nor its result were affected by the rejection of the evidence.

We similarly decline to exercise our discretion to permit this evidence to be now given.

• • •

Finally, we intimated that we did not require to hear argument from counsel for Alexander and Cronyn with respect to s. 113 of the Securities Act. Neither of those defendants acquired any shares from Green, directly or indirectly. It was suggested that Cronyn was an "insider" as a director of Imbrex and that s. 113 applied to him. However, the only basis on which it could be suggested that Green could recover from Cronyn was that the firm of which Cronyn was a director, Cochran, Murray & Co., had acted as a broker in the resale of some of the shares acquired from Green by Charterhouse and by Jordan Rugs Limited. However, there was no evidence whatever to indicate that this was of any personal benefit to Cronyn.

As to Alexander, he bought 500 shares from Charterhouse, from their block of 25,000 bought from Green, *after* the agreement between Green and the group was made on the morning of May 6th. He participated in no transaction with Green. No one in the group was his agent. He knew where the 500 shares came from, but that is far too tenuous a connection with Green to entitle Green to invoke s. 113 against Alexander.

• • •

The Claim under s. 113 of the Securities Act

As the trial Judge has pointed out, the Attorney-General of Ontario in October, 1963, appointed a committee on securities legislation to review and report on the provisions and working of securities legislation and particularly to consider certain problems, one of which was insider trading. That committee heard evidence and received representations from all sections of the community, and submitted its report (commonly called "the Kimber Report," after its chairman, Mr. J.R. Kimber, Q.C.) on March 11, 1966. In 1966 the Securities Act, in substantially the same form as it exists today, was enacted by the Legislature.

There can be no doubt that in enacting this legislation the Legislature of Ontario intended that the Victorian and Edwardian approach to the obligations of directors, as expressed in *Percival v. Wright*, [1902] 2 Ch. 421, should no longer be the policy of the law in the second half of the twentieth century. The case had been followed in Ontario and in other Canadian Provinces, albeit with a discernibly increasing degree of reluctance. No useful purpose would be served by tracing the history of this branch of the law before statutory intervention beyond saying that at common law directors of a corporation owed a duty to the corporation but not to its shareholders.

In considering the applicability of s. 113, nothing turns on the definition of "insider." It is true that Jordans Rugs Limited, which made the purchase of 40,000 shares from Green, did not prior to the purchase own equity shares of Imbrex carrying more than 10% of the voting rights attached to all equity shares of Imbrex for the time being outstanding, within the meaning of s. 109(1)(c)(ii) of the Act. It would appear, however, that Jordans Rugs Limited is an "associate" of the two Jordan-Knoxes, who were themselves insiders, as directors of Imbrex.

Leaving aside for the time being the phrase "make use of," did the defendants possess "specific confidential information ... that, if generally known, might reasonably be expected to affect materially the value of" Imbrex shares? The trial Judge was of the view that while the information was "confidential" (which was not disputed by anyone in this Court), it was not "specific." Taking the case of Godbout, who obviously had more information than anyone else, it is my view that the information he had on April 30, 1968, as to the first quarter earnings, and as to the state of the negotiations with Neon was in each case "specific." (Since Mr. West does not rely on Godbout's knowledge of the Harding discussions, it is not necessary to characterize that information.)

The facts Godbout had concerning Neon might have been unbelievable to other directors, or the proposals which were being made to him might have been totally unacceptable to them or some of them. The information may not have been worthy of credence or of sufficient weight to justify any positive action by the board of Imbrex. Nevertheless, in my view the information was "specific"; the word is used by the section in contradistinction to "general," or "not specific." A useful illustration of the difference between what is specific and what is not is the state of the information possessed by Godbout following the meetings with Pattison in Vancouver on April 16th. The two men met because Pattison had made an inquiry concerning the circumstances under which all of the Imbrex shares might be for sale. Pattison talked about Neon and its "goals and ambitions." When they talked later in the day, Pattison again talked to Neon, but made no offers or overtures concerning Imbrex shares. Without attaching undue significance to Godbout's evidence at trial describing their conversations as "general," the information Godbout had on April 16th was "general," and not "specific."

The heart of the s. 113 issue is whether the defendants or some of them "made use of" specific confidential information for his or their own benefit or advantage. The issue is illustrated by the opposing arguments. Mr. Weir submits that if an insider has the information, and makes a purchase of shares from a shareholder who does not have the information, s. 113 at once comes into play, without more. The argument of the defendants was that it is not enough to *have* the information. To "make use of" it, they submit, the information must be a "factor" in the insider's participation in the transaction which the insider carries out with the person alleged to be aggrieved, "either by inducing him to enter into it or by assisting him or otherwise influencing him in the manner in which he performs it" (the quotation is from Mr. Genest's factum).

The trial Judge accepted this argument but attached to it a proviso that once it is proven that an insider had specific confidential information, and had bought shares from a shareholder who did not have such information, an "onus of explanation" devolves upon the insider to establish that he did not make use of the information.

I would also accept the proposition that a plaintiff invoking s. 113 must show that there was specific confidential information, which the insider had, and that it was a factor (in the sense stated) in the action the insider took whereby the plaintiff suffered loss. The proviso or corollary I would link to this principle is that once it is shown that the insider had such information, and entered into a transaction involving the purchase of shares of a shareholder who did not have it, the burden of proof is thereafter upon the insider to show that in fact he did not make use of the information in the transaction, that is, that the information was not a factor in what he did. This is more than an "onus of explanation"; it is a burden of proof that rests on the insider to the end of the case. It is of course one that is satisfied by a preponderance of credible evidence, on a balance of probabilities—the standard burden of proof in civil cases.

This difference between my statement and that of the trial Judge does not affect the result in this case, because his findings of fact are clear and unequivocal, and amply satisfy the burden of proof which rested upon the defendants. We are therefore not involved in any semantic niceties concerning the difference between an "onus of explanation" and a "burden of proof," and in whether the trial Judge misdirected himself in using the former expression instead of the latter.

In my view it is a question of fact in each case, and with respect to each individual in a case, whether the individual made use of specific confidential information. In this case there are clear findings of fact with respect to each of the individuals that he or they did not "amek use of" the information. Particularly with respect to Godbout, this is a finding which we are all persuaded we must approach with caution. Godbout knew a greal deal; it was specific and confidential. The fact is that he gave evidence to show why it could not be said of him that he made use of the confidential information that he had. He was cross-examined at greath length. The trial Judge, approaching this evidence with a healthy scepticism, might well have disbelieved it. In fact he chose to accept it. On this particular issue, the trial Judge's disbelief of Green is not a correlative of his affirmation of the credibility of Godbout. That latter finding must stand by itself. It is one which it was quite open for the trial Judge to make, and after considering all of the important documents in the case, as well as all of the evidence at trial to which we were referred (and much more), we are not prepared to disturb his finding.

The case against the other defendants is considerably less strong than that against Godbout. Without recapitulating the evidence led against each one of them, there are specific findings that Sinclair (on behalf of Charterhouse) did not make use of the information that he had, which was considerably less than that possessed by Godbout, and similar findings were made with respect to the other insiders.

An experienced trial Judge such as Grant J. without doubt would approach with scepticism the evidence of Godbout that he did not tell the other listeners on the conference call of the discussions with Pattison which had taken place so recently. The fact that Godbout did not tell them is corroborated by the other parties to the call, and of course is sworn to by Godbout himself. Again, it was open to the trial Judge to disbelieve Godbout but he chose to accept his evidence. Similarly, the trial Judge found that Sinclair did not know of the Pattison-Godbout discussions of April 29th until after the contract with Green had been made. There is no reason to upset this finding. The same conclusion must be reached with regard to the findings concerning Pouliot and Charles Jordan-Knox.

I should comment upon Sinclair's so-called "warning letter" of April 30, 1968. Whatever may be said of this letter as being a discharge of the "moral obligations" which Godbout thought Green's former associates owed to Green, the letter was not the disclosure which may provide a defence to an action under s. 113(1) of the Securities Act. While the letter does not say so, the writer is really saying that "confidential information exists which might be of substantial significance to you but which I am not at liberty to disclose." Once the necessary ingredients of a cause of action against an insider under s. 113(1) are shown to exist, then the resulting obligation is discharged by disclosure of "such information." It is not discharged by disclosing it exists, without saying what it is.

Writing the letter to Green was a decent thing to do. The writing of it, and what it said, were of the greatest significance in a case involving allegations of conspiracy and fraud against its writer and those associated with him in the transaction which shortly followed its writing. Its legal effect in the action as presented on this appeal is minimal.

No doubt the Ontario legislation was influenced by the American provisions, particularly s. 10(b) of the Securities Exchange Act of 1934 and Rule 10b-5, which have been discussed in several cases involving *Texas Gulf Sulphur Co. Inc.* (as its name then was), and in *Re Cady, Roberts & Co.* (1961), 40 S.E.C. 907 at p. 912. While in very broad and general terms the underlying purpose of s. 10(b) and Rule 10b-5 and of the Ontario Act are the same, in trying to impose limitations upon insiders of corporations and in laying down standards of disclosure by the company and its directors, the plain fact is that the language of the Ontario Act is not the same as the American. The trial Judge was right in saying he did not need to look at American cases to interpret plain words in an Ontario statute. The American law prior to 1934 was not the same as our inherited principles of *Percival v. Wright*.

Nor have I found it necessary to resort to any canons of construction based on "enactments restrictive of common law rights." Like the trial Judge, I have taken the Legislature's words as I found them.

Some misgivings have been expressed as to the trial Judge's reference to information "acquired for corporate purposes": Prof. Johnston's commentary, supra, at p. 683. With respect, I would not so confine "confidential information" (assuming the trial Judge intended thus to qualify or limit the section). The probabilities doubtless are that the insider acquired his information through participation in the company's affairs, but that is not a *sine qua non* to the operation of the section. The insider may learn something that no one else knows, but which fulfils all the attributes of specific, confidential information found in s. 113(1).

[In the concluding portions of the judgment, the Court held that none of the defendants owed fiduciary duties to Green, and it made brief and inconclusive observations on the calculation of damages under s. 113.]

Appeal dismissed.

The "Make Use of" Requirement. The Court of Appeal reversed the trial Court's finding that Godbout's information concerning Neon's interest in a possible merger with Imbrex was not "specific" at the time that the insiders agreed to buy Green's shares.

That reversal did not change the result with respect to Godbout, however, because the Court of Appeal did not disturb (although it may have been disturbed by) the trial judge's critical finding that Godbout, who knew more than any other of the defendants, did not make use of his information in buying Green's shares. Why then did Godbout and the others agree to buy Green's shares? According to the trial judge, it was to prevent the price decline that would follow if Green had dumped his shares into the thin market for Imbrex shares. [1983] 2 O.R. at 736-38. Were the defendants' concerns about a price depression motivated by a desire to keep the price up for the purposes of whatever merger opportunity, whether with Harding Carpets or with Neon, might eventuate? If so, did the defendants make use of the information?

Despite the burden of proof in *Green*, insiders were also found not to have made use of inside information *In the Matter of Connor*, [1976] O.S.C.B. 149. Several senior officers of National Sea Products Ltd., who were privy to specific, confidential and material information about an indicated decrease in the corporation's sales, sold (either individually or through corporations they controlled) 100,000 National Sea shares to the Jodrey family. The market price of National Sea shares fell from $15-16 at the time of the sale to $9.25 bid one week after disclosure of the information, and continued to decline thereafter. The action was not, however, brought by the Jodreys, but took the form of an administrative hearing before the O.S.C. to determine whether it was in the public interest to deny trading exemptions under s. 19(5) of the 1966 Ontario Securities Act for insider trading and for failure to comply with Uniform Act Policy no. 2-12 (Timely Disclosure). (See now National Policy Statement No. 40.)

The negotiations for the sale of the securities were initiated by the Jodreys, who controlled a pulp and paper company whose largest customer was National Sea. The senior officers of National Sea were for their part quite ready to welcome the Jodrey's interest in their corporation. Several of the sellers who had retired and who no longer had active managing interests in the corporation wished to reduce their holdings in it. Others wished to repay burdensome bank loans that they had taken out to finance their holdings. Finally, the senior officers of National Sea had for some years feared that they might lose control of the corporation. The report does not indicate who the potential acquirer was, but the Commissioners "were satisfied. ... that there was good reason for the concern." *Id.* at 161. "The paramount wish of the sellers" was therefore "to place some of their holdings in safe hands while maintaining their existing control position. The interest of the Jodreys was uniquely suited to meet that wish." *Id.* at 168. In the circumstances the Commissioners held that the insiders' knowledge of the expected decline in business "was not in any way a motivating or even influencing factor in the sale." *Id.* at 169. "There was," moreover, "not a shred of direct evidence that they positively made use of the information." *Id.* at 170.

The O.S.C.'s search for further "direct evidence" of how use was made of the information, apart from the sale itself, may seem inconsistent with the burden of proof in *Green*. This is not an area of the law where smoking guns abound. In addition, had the Jodreys known of the losses they would likely have bargained for a lower price. When disclosure was publicly made the price dropped by almost 40%. Does this suggest that the insiders "made use of" the information in their decision not to disclose the losses? In addition to the 100,000 shares purchases by the Jodreys, the insiders sold a further

16,500 National Sea shares on the market. Presumably the O.S.C. found that the insiders did not make use of their information in this sale because their purpose was to retire personal bank loans. Is this consistent with *Green*?

The interpretation given to the "make use of" test in *Green* and *Connor* might perhaps be thought to amount to the judicial nullification of inefficient legislation. However, the two cases were severely criticized by supporters of insider trading legislation. The authors of 2 *Proposals for a Securities Market Law for Canada* (1979) suggested that the "make use of" prerequisite for insider trading liability "may not unreasonably be said to have led to an incorrect result in every case in which it has been considered," and proposed its elimination in their draft statute. *Id.* at 221. More recently, however, courts appear to have applied a stronger presumption that those who trade with knowledge of inside information make use of it, in finding the insider liable. See, e.g., *NIR Oil Ltd. v. Bodrug* (1985), 18 D.L.R. (4th) 608 (Alta. C.A.), leave to appeal refused, (1985), 39 Alta L. Rep. (2d) xlvi; *Tongue v. Vencap Equities Alberta Ltd.*, [1994] 5 W.W.R. 674.

The "make use of" test is still to be found in CBCA s. 131(4). In OSA ss. 76 and 134, however, it has been replaced with a knowledge test. In other words, the presumption in *Green* that one who trades with knowledge of inside information makes use of it has become irrebuttable under the OSA. This imposes its own problems, however. A knowledge test will appear overbroad when an insider is engaged in a program of regular periodic buying of his corporation's shares at the market price prevailing from time to time. Thus, in a dividend reinvestment plan, a shareholder may opt to receive dividends in the form of new shares rather than as a cash payout. If the insider continues to participate in the program for a long period of time, irrespective of the information he may have as to firm value at any one time, insider trading liability that attaches at those times when he is in possession of material, undisclosed information may be thought excessive. Denying the manager an exemption in these circumstances might prevent him from participating in a dividend reinvestment program, which may be undesirable if such programs reduce agency costs by aligning his incentives more closely with those of the firm. On the other hand, were an insider to terminate his participation in a dividend reinvestment plan at a time when he is aware of undisclosed bad news about the firm, the argument for an exemption would be weakened. An exemption for dividend reinvestment plans may now be found in OSA Regulation 175(2)(b).

Another problem with a knowledge test is that it might catch the broker who recommends a trade at a time when he is not aware of undisclosed material information, but someone else in his firm is. This difficulty is particularly troubling for brokers, who will seek to avoid liability by erecting a "Chinese Wall" between their brokerage and underwriting departments. This would likely insulate them from liability under a "make use of" standard, but not under a knowledge test if the knowledge of members of one department can be imputed to members of another. Imposing liability in such circumstances would be tantamount to requiring brokers to divest themselves of their underwriting departments. See Lipton & Mazur, *The Chinese Wall Solution to the Conflict Problems of Securities Firms*, 50 N.Y.U. L. Rev. 459 (1976). The Chinese Wall solution is adopted in OSA Regulation 175(1).

Quality of Information: Specificity and Materiality. The information must be "specific" as well as confidential under CBCA s. 131(4). In *Green v. Charterhouse*, "specific" was contrasted with "general" or "vague." Specificity may also relate to the event's probability of occurrence. On this view, specificity is closely allied to the concept of materiality, and some American insider trading decisions link materiality and specificity. See, e.g., *S.E.C. v. Geon Industries Inc.*, 531 F.2d 39 (2d Cir. 1976); *Harnett v. Ryan Homes Inc.*, 496 F.2d 832 (3d Cir. 1974).

A separate requirement of specificity may be puzzling if it means that some information, though material, is yet too general to support insider trading liability. However, the two concepts are so closely related that the class of general, material information may be empty. Information as to general possibilities, even if the existence of these possibilities has not been discussed outside the inner circle of corporate management, is often too uncertain or immature to have much effect on the value of the corporation's securities. At any moment, the price of securities will reflect a whole range of possible future scenarios. Information becomes specific only when these possibilities achieve a certain likelihood, though what this threshold is no doubt depends on the magnitude of the event.

"Material" is used in CBCA s. 131(4) to refer to the effect the information, if disclosed, would reasonably be expected to have upon the value of the securities in question. In the OSA a change or a fact is material if "it would reasonably be expected to have a significant effect upon the market price or value of ... the securities." OSA s. 1(1). An expansive test of materiality was adopted in *Royal Trust Co. Ltd. v. O.S.C.* (1983), 42 O.R. (2d) 147 (Div. Ct.), a case whose facts aroused considerable public controversy at the time in revealing alliances among a hierarchy of Toronto business leaders. White and Scholes were senior officers of Trustco who led a successful campaign to defeat a take-over bid for Trustco by Campeau Corp. In the course of this, they persuaded many Canadian financial institutions not to tender their shares to Campeau. Late in the campaign, White and Scholes approached the Toronto-Dominion Bank for this purpose. They told bank officers that the bid was likely to fail because by this time approximately 60% of the Trustco shares were in the hands of Trustco allies. The O.S.C. found this otherwise undisclosed information to be a material fact and suspended the securities trading privileges of White and Scholes. On appeal, the Court affirmed, also finding the information to be material:

In my opinion, the information disclosed fell easily within the category of material facts within the context of the legislation and in the prevailing circumstances. That the respondents could not guarantee that the known holders of Trustco's shares would not sell or deposit their shares does not reduce the disclosure to a level less than fact. It was made clearly to encourage the officers of the bank not to sell or deposit the 10% of the outstanding shares of Trustco that it had acquired after earlier representations to it by White and Scholes and it achieved that purpose. Having in mind the general object of [s. 76], which is to prevent improper or unfair disclosure, I do not think the term "fact" should be read super-critically. In my opinion, the information was sufficiently factual or a sufficient alteration of circumstances to be a material "change" and to fall within the section. In my opinion the Commission was justified in holding that the section had been breached. [*Id.* at 152]

Market Information. Discussions of insider trading often distinguish between information concerning the affairs of the corporation, usually bearing upon the earnings power of its assets, and information about the market for the corporation's securities, such as that a take-over bid is about to be made or a securities analyst is about to publish a report on the investment merits of the corporation's securities. See Fleischer, Mundheim & Murphy, *An Initial Inquiry into the Responsibility to Disclose Market Information*, 121 U. Pa. L. Rev. 798 (1973). If the rationale for the prohibition against insider trading is that corporate fiduciaries ought not be permitted to use for their private gain information that in some sense "belongs" to the corporation, then "market information," as the latter type is often called, should be excluded from the scope of the prohibition since usually it is generated outside the corporation. The CBCA, which speaks of "specific confidential information ... that, if generally known, might reasonably be expected to affect materially the value of the security" makes no distinction between corporate information and market information. Neither does the OSA. The distinction between internally generated and externally generated information was rejected by Berger J. of the British Columbia Supreme Court in *Pelling v. Pelling* (1981), 130 D.L.R. (3d) 761, 16 B.L.R. 150, and by the Ontario Court of Appeal in *Green v. Charterhouse*. However, one type of market information appears to fall outside of the CBCA's civil liability provision. That is information that a securities analyst is about to publish a report on the issuer. If the analyst has a following, the fact that he is about to issue a report—apart altogether from facts about the issuer appearing in the report—may itself be material. The analyst might trade securities of the issuer in anticipation of the publication of his report, a practice known as "scalping," but in so doing he would not appear to incur any civil liability because he is not an insider. An opposite result would apply, however, where the material fact is that a take-over bid is impending, because the officers and directors of the bidder are deemed to have been insiders of the target for six months before the bid. In addition, scalping has been held to violate Rule 10b-5 in one of the most publicized recent insider trading cases, involving former Wall Street Journal reporter R. Foster Winans, *U.S. v. Carpenter*, 791 F.2d 1024 (2d Cir. 1986). This decision was affirmed by an evenly divided Supreme Court, with a unanimous decision that Winans had also breached U.S. mail and wire fraud statutes by expropriating the business information that constituted the property of the Wall Street Journal. *Carpenter v. U.S.*, 108 S. Ct. 316 (1987).

Developments in S.E.C. Rule 10b-5. Throughout the 1960s and well into the 1970s, the courts and the S.E.C. seemed constantly to be expanding the reach of Rule 10b-5 as a private cause of action for defrauded or even disappointed securities market participants. Doubts as to the scope of the section were usually resolved in favour of its coverage, the Commission and the courts almost invariably citing a famous dictum of the United States Supreme Court to the effect that securities legislation was to be construed "not technically and restrictively, but flexibly to effectuate its remedial purposes" (*S.E.C. v. Capital Gains Research Bureau*, 375 U.S. 180, 195 (1963), quoted in *Superintendant of Insurance v. Bankers Life & Casualty Co.*, 404 U.S. 6, 12 (1971), and in *Affiliated Ute Citizens v. United States*, 406 U.S. 128, 151 (1972)). Beginning in about 1975, this expansionary trend was brought to a halt and indeed was reversed (although generally without overruling the cases from the earlier era) by the Supreme Court. Very likely, one reason for the shift was the potentially staggering liabilities suggested by the outcome of the private litigation arising out of the facts of *Texas Gulf Sulphur* and the *McDonnell Douglas* affair. See *Shapiro v. Merrill, Lynch, Pierce, Fenner & Smith Inc.*, 495 F.2d 228 (2nd Cir. 1974). In these cases the courts absolved Rule 10b-5 plaintiffs of the need to show any semblance of privity with defendants in insider trading. In addition, the extension of Rule 10b-5 liability had impinged on state corporate law. As noted in Chapter Three, Section A, state law experimentation in legal regimes can be seen as a race to the top, and such benefits are lost when corporate wrongdoing becomes a federal offence.

Six cases may be selected as representative of the Supreme Court's conservative trend over the last 20 years. In *Ernst & Ernst v. Hochfelder*, 425 U.S. 185 (1976), the Court held that Rule 10b-5 was not breached when the defendant was merely negligent. Rather, the defendant had to be shown to have acted with an intent to deceive or defraud. This intent (known in the United States as *scienter*) could be made out by a showing of knowing misconduct; the Court left open whether recklessness would suffice. While *Ernst & Ernst* was a private action, its requirements for the defendant's mental state were extended to injunctive actions initiated by the S.E.C. in *Aaron v. S.E.C.*, 446 U.S. 680 (1980). In *Blue Chip Stamps v. Manor Drug Stores*, 421 U.S. 723 (1975), the Court held that a private action for violation of Rule 10b-5 could be maintained only by a purchaser or seller of securities and not by a person injured in any other capacity, for example, by having refrained from trading as a result of the defendant's deceptive conduct. In *Santa Fe Industries Inc. v. Green*, 430 U.S. 462 (1977), the Court held, in the context of a corporate transaction designed to squeeze out the minority shareholders, that conduct, however unfair and oppressive, not involving deceit did not come within the terms of Rule 10b-5. Finally, in its decisions in *Chiarella* and *Dirks* the Court read a fiduciary requirement into Rule 10b-5 liability, with a duty to abstain or disclose restricted to those in a pre-existing duty to the firm or its shareholders.

Subsequent to the narrowing of the scope of Rule 10b-5, there has been a marked increase in the number of S.E.C. enforcement actions. In addition, the Insider Trading Sanctions Act of 1984, 15 U.S.C. 78a ss. 21(1)(d), 32, 15(c)(4), 20 (1984), permitted the S.E.C. to seek treble damages for inside trading. These developments are analyzed from the perspective of public choice theory in Haddock & Macey, *Regulation on Demand: A Private Interest Model, with an Application to Insider Trading Regulation*, 30 J.L. & Econ. 311 (1987). According to the two authors, a homogenous group of institutional investors will seek to curb insider trading, since it diminishes their opportunities for profitable trades.

Corporate Recovery. An insider is not only liable to those with whom he traded, but is also "accountable to the corporation for any direct benefit or advantage received or receivable by [him] as a result of the transaction" (CBCA s. 131(4)(b)). The corporation's action would presumably be brought as shareholder derivative litigation in most cases since it is unlikely that the corporation would sue its own director or officer. Under OSA s. 135 provision is also made for the O.S.C. to bring the action on behalf of the corporation. The authors of the Kimber Report, which recommended creation of statutory accountability to the corporation, stated that the legislation should be drafted so as not to create double liability. The Dickerson Report recommended against statutory provision of any liability to the corporation on the perhaps not totally consistent grounds that the common law of corporate opportunity was perfectly adequate to deal with the problem and that the corporation suffered no injury anyway. However, statutory civil liability to the corporation for insider trading was provided in the CBCA. It can be argued that, where a private plaintiff recovers first, no action will thereafter lie by or on behalf of the corporation because there is no "advantage received or receivable by the insider." It has already been taken away from him. Where, however, the corporation secures a judgment before the private plaintiff, the private plaintiff's action would not be foreclosed since he has still suffered damage. It would certainly be odd that the question of double liability should turn upon the happenstance of who sues first. If the purpose of the liability provisions is to deter the conduct, then potential double liability may perhaps be justified, the more so since a personal action may founder on the privity bar.

CHAPTER NINE

Senior Securities

A. DEBT SECURITIES

1. Priority Rights

Senior securities refer to both preferred shares and long-term securities such as bonds and debentures. While "bonds" and "debentures" are not terms of art, they generally refer to different kinds of debt securities. Bonds are typically secured by a specific or fixed charge over land or chattels. Debentures are unsecured or secured by a floating charge over the issuer's after-acquired assets. A security interest will give the debt holder a measure of protection in the event of the issuer's default of the terms of the loan agreement.

Debt securities evidence a promise to pay a debt in the same way that a promissory note does. But unlike notes, debt securities are normally issued to a large number of long-term creditors. Since a security interest over the issuer's collateral cannot be conveniently given to each security holder, the assignment is made to a trustee for bond-holders or debentureholders. The trust indenture between the issuer and the trustee often contains many protective provisions, and the trustee is given the power to enforce these rights on behalf of the security holders.

Senior debt securities are normally issued for a specified term, often between 5 and 20 years. Thereafter the issuer undertakes to repay the moneys borrowed by redeeming the securities. There is normally no such duty for an issuer to redeem preferred shares. In addition, debt securities contain a promise by the issuer to pay out interest, and a failure to perform this obligation may result in a petition in bankruptcy. By contrast, the decision by directors as to dividend payments on shares is ordinarily one of business judgment, and courts are reluctant to impeach it.

A. Dewing, The Financial Policy of Corporations
236-37 (5th ed. 1953), vol. 1

Attitude Toward Bonded Debt. The intent of bonds is that they should be paid. The difference between bonded debt and bank loans is merely the period during which the loan shall remain outstanding. The bank expects the loan to be paid when due; the investor expects the bond to be paid when due. Yet, in view of the longer life of the bond, there has developed, through the years, two distinctly different attitudes which a corporation management may take with reference to long-term debt. In the one case the management may look upon corporate debt, and the bonds issued to represent it, as the evidence of borrowed capital; and inherent in the nature of borrowed capital is the obvious fact that the equivalent in money, once borrowed, must be returned at a later time. Debt, however distant its due date, must be paid. The other point of view ignores the strict legal implication of debt. A corporate management regards the issue of bonds as a device to give investors a favored participation in the fortunes of the enterprise in return for the willingness, on the part of investors, to accept a low fixed return. The explicit implications of the debt can be ignored; in the continuing success of the corporation, new debt can be incurred to refund the old and if the corporation is not a success, the debt holders can be paid only out of the dying body of the corporation. In the event of failure, the debt holders must take their fortunes along with the stockholders, except that they will be paid first out of the proceeds of liquidation or be given prior rights in any attempt to rehabilitate the business. The one point of view looks upon the bondholders as creditors beyond the pale of the corporation—outsiders who have lent capital which must be returned; the other point of view looks upon bondholders as joint heirs in the corporate fortunes—participants in the success or failure who have been given preferential rights in the common hazard.

Prevalence of the Different Points of View. In the days before extensive railroad building in the United States, corporate debt of all forms was looked upon as an obligation to pay money at a distant time. Ordinarily debt arose as the result of a definite loan of capital in which the lender had no intention of acquiring an interest in the corporation— much as a commercial bank today lends money to a corporation with the expectation of its payment after a designated period of time. The bank neither desires nor anticipates becoming a partner in the customer's business. With the extensive railroad building in the period after 1840, bonds—outwardly the evidence of debt—were issued to defray a large part of the cost of construction. Gradually thereafter the financial world became aware that bondholders were participants in the success or the failure of the railroad— for under no circumstances could the property of the road be torn up and sold in order to pay the debt. Furthermore if, in the long-distant future, the debt is to be paid at all, it must be paid as a result of a high general corporate credit engendered by years of profitable operation. This point of view gradually extended from railroads to other large corporations—public utilities, for example—which secure a considerable proportion of their capital from bond issues. It was strengthened by the development of a reorganization technique in which the bondholder was looked upon by the courts as a joint owner rather than as a creditor; and it has been further strengthened by recent legislation, which has removed from the bondholder the last vestige of independent action following the failure and bankruptcy of his corporation.

Nevertheless, the fact remains that, in spite of much legislation intended to imperil the legal rights of the bondholder, the corporation manager must face the legal obligation that bonds should be paid at maturity unless the business is to become bankrupt or at best forced into a program of compulsory readjustments. Whether or not under recent ameliorative statutes, anything can be salvaged for the stockholder is an entirely different matter. This is true, whatever attitude a management may take toward its funded debt. The presence of funded debt implies, from the point of view of the corporation, either the finding of means to pay the maturing bonds or else a financial crisis with results inevitably inimcal to the stockholders.

Corporate Reorganizations. Corporate reorganization law is best understood from a corporate governance perspective. If managers are not expected to misbehave, creditors have no reason to replace them. Nor do they require bankruptcy code provisions as to the repayment of claims. Absent management misbehaviour, creditors may assume that firm debts will be paid in their order of priority, and that assets will be liquidated when it is value-increasing to do so.

The issue of debt claims will however introduce the adverse incentive costs described in Chapter One, Section C. Because their incentives are imperfectly correlated with each other, and because agent behaviour is not perfectly observable, agents will misbehave and thereby impose costs on their principals. The agency cost problem will be particularly severe where the firm approaches insolvency, and shareholders are gambling with the creditors' money. In these circumstances, it will usually be value-increasing to transfer control of the firm from equity to debt holders, through a bankruptcy petition or a private receivership.

Apart from the conflict of interest between shareholders and debt holders, management's interests will also conflict with debt holders on insolvency. In the same way that managers have an incentive to resist take-over bids, they might resist bankruptcy proceedings, where job losses are often permanent. Defensive tactics in the bankruptcy context might then be as costly to the firm as managerial resistance to tender offers. For example, managers might resist an efficient liquidation, which moves assets to more highly valued users but destroys managerial positions.

Debtor firms will reduce their cost of credit by conceding termination rights to monitoring creditors, under which incumbent managers can be expeditiously replaced on an event of default. Lender management rights of this kind have been observed to reduce agency costs in Germany and Japan (see Mark Roe, *Some Differences in Corporate Governance in Germany, Japan, and America*, 102 Yale L.J. 1927 (1993)) and informal, bank-led "kereitsus" in Canada might also serve useful monitoring efficiencies. In particular, the Canadian private receivership served to police misbehaviour by managers of insolvent firms. Under the private receivership, a debtor's major secured lenders bargained for the right to enforce their security on default by appointing a receiver to seize control of the debtor's assets and to manage them on behalf of the appointing creditor. In the United States, this remedy was not available, since the repossessory remedies of creditors are stayed by a Chapter 11 bankruptcy reorganization filing. In Canada, secured lender repossessory rights were not stayed under the former Bankruptcy Act, but now may be stayed through a proposal under the Canadian Bankruptcy and Insolvency Act (BIA). See Buckley, *The American Stay*, 3 S. Cal. Interdisciplinary L.J. 733 (1994).

On an agency cost analysis, the BIA stay might be regretted. Self-entrenched managers will resist value-increasing control challenges by shareholders or creditors. On a take-over bid, managers will employ defensive tactics such as poison pills to repel bidders. Similarly, a debtor's voluntary filing under the BIA closely resembles a poison pill. However, the Canadian statute is more pro-creditor than Chapter 11. A Chapter 11 reorganization lasts on average two to three years, and during that time incumbent managers remain in control. By contrast, the Canadian stay cannot last more than six months. In addition, Canadian secured lenders cannot be crammed down, or forced to accept a plan against their wishes, as might happen to American creditors.

Even before the new Act, the repossessory rights of a Canadian secured lender might have been stayed through a Companies' Creditors Arrangement Act filing. R.S.C. 1985, c. C-36 (CCAA). While the CCAA applies only to debtors that have issued bonds, debtors began to evade this requirement in the 1980s by issuing a trivial amount of bonds immediately prior to a filing. Surprisingly, this practice was generally upheld by Canadian courts. See Crozier, *Good Faith and the Companies' Creditors Arrangement Act*, 15 C.B.L.J. 89 (1990). Traditionally, Canadian courts have been reluctant to fetter statutory remedies with good faith duties. But at the same time as they refused to police strategic CCAA filings, Canadian courts imposed good faith duties on creditors who sent in a private receiver. See, e.g., *Mister Broadloom Corp. v. Bank of Montreal* (1983), 44 O.R. (2d) 368. Apart from the anti-creditor bias, these rules are inconsistent.

Scaling Back Senior Rights. Apart from the BIA and the CCAA, the rights of senior lenders might be scaled back through a private agreement among all lenders (called a "work-out"), or through a "majority clause" in a trust indenture. Majority clauses in trust indentures are simply provisions in the contract between trustee and issuer that permit the alteration of bondholder rights.* Since the trust deed is a binding agreement whose terms are incorporated in bond certificates, bondholders are deemed to have consented to changes so effected to their interests. Majority clauses typically permit a change in the debt holders' rights on two-thirds approval of those voting on the matter. The scheme of reorganization need not be submitted to court, though a dissenting debt holder might perhaps be permitted to apply to set it aside in a CBCA s. 241 oppression action.

Since the effect of a reorganization scheme is to alter rights for which the claimholders have bargained, it might be asked why they would ever purchase securities whose conditions may be altered without their consent. However, unanimity requirements would be rejected in a claimholders' bargain because they give rise to free rider problems. A reorganization usually requires debt claimants to scale down their rights in order to reduce the probability of default. Frequently, debt interests in the old firm are exchanged for equity interests in the reorganized firm. Suppose, for example, that a firm presently worth $100 has issued five debt claims with a face value of $40 each. Since debt value is $200, the firm is insolvent and would seek to reorganize through a debt-for-equity swap. One way in which this might be done is by cancelling all five debt interests in exchange for five equity claims worth $20 each. As long as there are any positive costs associated with the threat of bankruptcy,

---

*   In Canada, one generally refers to a trust "deed" on an issue of bonds, and to a trust "indenture" on an issue of debentures.

the firm will be worth more after the reorganization, such that the five claimants will collectively be better off by agreeing to the scheme. But now consider what happens when four debt holders agree to the scheme and one does not. If four of the old debt claims are cancelled, the reorganized firm will be quite solvent, and the hold-out might see his interest buoyed up to its face value of $40. The four claimholders who consent to the reorganization would then share the residual value of $60, for a claim of $15 each. This free rider problem will make the reorganization unstable, with the possibility that no claimholder would consent to it so long as one of the claimholders might seek the advantages of a hold-out strategy. The possibility of free riding is more than merely theoretical. For example, it was a constant concern in the proposed work-out of Dome Petroleum. See further, Roe, *The Voting Prohibition in Bond Work-Outs*, 97 Yale L.J. 232, 245 n. 40 (1987).

A further question concerns the desirability of judicial or administrative screening of the substantive fairness of the scheme. Judicial review of the scheme as mandated in BIA and CCAA reorganizations is a bare possibility in a majority clause reorganization, and is likely entirely unavailable in a work-out. This may affect the kind of schemes presented for approval. Suppose, for example, that the liquidation value of a firm is $90, while its going concern value under a BIA reorganization is $120, and its going concern value in a work-out is $110. (The work-out is assumed to be more costly than a BIA reorganization because of the need to secure the consent of all creditors.) Suppose further that the firm has issued secured claims in the face amount of $80 to a bank, and unsecured claims in the face amount of $50 to debentureholders. Since the value of the firm in reorganization is at most $120, while the face value of debt claims is $130, the firm is insolvent. With judicial scrutiny of the BIA scheme, assume that the rights of debentureholders to be paid in priority of equity holders are respected, such that the payout to the bank would be $80 and to debentureholders $40. On the other hand, without judicial scrutiny in a work-out, the managers of the firm might propose the following payments: bank—$85; debentureholders—$15; equity holders—$10. This scheme may seem unstable because the debentureholders will gain $25 more in a BIA reorganization. However, it may be possible for a coalition of equity holders and the bank to bring the debentureholders to accept the work-out scheme if there is a creditable threat of liquidation, under which the debentureholders will be paid $5 less than they would receive in the work-out.

As a consequence of these strategic considerations, the Trust Indenture Act of 1939 in the United States substantially restricted the scope of reorganizations pursuant to majority clauses. Since majority clauses offered little in the way of a fairness review, the statute provided that they were ineffective to alter the rights of bondholders to be paid principal and interest when due. This eliminated majority clauses as a reorganization technique in the United States, leaving insolvent firms to choose between bankruptcy reorganization and work-outs. This is not, however, what happened in Canada, where some portions of the 1939 Act were incorporated into CBCA ss. 82-93, but not the restrictions on majority clauses. The justification for their continued existence in Canadian trust deeds may then be sought in the reduced costs of a less formal and quicker reorganization technique, as well as in the limited nature of the fairness review in fact offered in BIA reorganizations.

Standards of fairness when judicial approval of a reorganization scheme is sought will depend on the nature of the proceedings. In a liquidation, the senior debt holders' absolute priority rights will be enforced. What this means is that junior claimants do not share in the proceeds of distribution if the senior creditor's bankruptcy claim, measured by principal and accrued interest, is not fully paid. In the United States, this absolute priority doctrine governs Bankruptcy Code Chapter 11 reorganizations of corporations with public equity or secured debt interest. See, e.g., *Consolidated Rock Prods. Co. v. Du Bois*, 312 U.S. 510, 529 (1941) ("If [creditors] receive less than ... full compensatory treatment, some of their property rights will be appropriated for the benefit of stockholders without compensation. That is not permissible.") By contrast, a less exacting relative priority standard, in which junior claimholders are permitted to participate even though seniors are not made whole, is applied in English reorganizations, and would likely govern Canadian ones as well. For example, in *Re Alabama, N.O., Tex. & P. Junction Ry*, [1891] 1 Ch. 213 (C.A.), junior claimholders were permitted to participate in the reorganization even though the corporation could not earn enough to pay the interest on senior securities.

The application of the relative priority doctrine has generated skepticism about the protective value of a trust indenture, as the following excerpt from N. Buchanan, *The Economics of Corporate Enterprise* 135 (1940) indicates:

The indenture is of little interest to the bondholders if the interest is paid regularly and the principal repaid at maturity. On the other hand, if default occurs, the course of events is typically not according to the solemnities of the indenture; usually the corporation is reorganized which means that the bondholders' claims are often abrogated and scaled down, or the bondholders seize the property only to discover to their sorrow that the property is worth no more than what it can be made to earn, and that on this showing their total claims will have to be scaled down likewise. In short, the indenture is of little moment if there is no default, and it does not determine the course of events or ensure full payment of bondholders' claims if default does occur. At the most, perhaps, it determines the order of priority among creditors; if there are several mortgages on the same assets, those holding a first mortgage will doubtless be in a stronger position than those holding junior mortgages. Thus, perhaps in the final analysis one ought not to regard the added rights of bondholders under an indenture as of any vital significance; they are of no importance prior to default, and after default they do little more than determine relative priorities. On the only occasion on which it might be of some relevance, the strict language of the bond indenture is but rarely honored in full.

The most common objection to the relative priority standard is that it effects a wealth transfer from seniors to juniors, because it fails to respect the priority rights for which the former bargained. From an *ex ante* perspective, however, we should not expect such wealth transfer effects to persist. Instead, senior claims will be discounted on issuance to reflect the possibility of subsequent distributional effects. The firm will then pay for the expropriation option on bankruptcy through a higher cost of credit. See Warner, *Bankruptcy, Absolute Priority, and the Pricing of Risky Debt Claims*, 4 J. Fin. Econ. 239 (1977). Moreover, there is evidence that efficient debt markets anticipate deviations from absolute priority in the pricing of debt claims. See Eberhart & Sweeney, *Does the Bond Market Predict Bankruptcy Settlements?* 47 J. Fin. 943 (1992). In addition, a secured lender may react to the possibility of deviations from absolute priority by accelerating the date of default, making it more likely that he will be fully secured and repaid in full. See Buckley, *The Termination Decision*, 61 U.M.K.C. L. Rev. 243 (1992). This would explain why secured lenders appear to be accorded absolute priority on default. See Weiss, *Bankruptcy Resolution: Direct Costs and Violation of Priority of Claims*, 27 J. Fin. Econ. 285 (1990) (finding that absolute priority was maintained in 92% of the sample). See Warner, *id.* In addition, fears that small investors will be euchred through a reorganization scheme are now largely dissipated, since most bonds and debentures are today held by institutional investors.

It has not yet been convincingly demonstrated which fairness standard is more efficient. The absolute priority doctrine requires a greater investment by the courts in the production of information, since it is based on an evaluation of the firm as a going concern. However, absent such valuation, it is difficult to make any estimate of the fairness of the payout. A more serious criticism of the absolute priority test is that it prolongs the length of time corporations spend in reorganization. Juniors who would be wiped out have an incentive to delay the implementation of the scheme in the hope that the corporation might become more valuable in the interim, permitting them to participate in it. In addition, the relative priority doctrine might reduce the adverse incentive costs of equity misbehaviour, since it gives shareholders a greater participation in downside returns. See Jackson & Scott, *On the Nature of Bankruptcy: An Essay on Bankruptcy Sharing and the Creditors' Bargain*, 75 Va. L. Rev. 155 (1989).

See further Bebchuk, *A New Approach to Corporate Reorganizations*, 101 Harv. L. Rev. 775 (1988); Billyou, *Corporate Mortgage Bonds and Majority Clauses*, 57 Yale L.J. 595 (1948); Blum, *Full Priority and Full Compensation in Corporate Reorganizations: A Reappraisal*, 25 U. Chi. L. Rev. 417 (1958); Bonbright & Bergerman, *Two Rival Theories of Priority Rights of Security Holders in a Corporate Reorganization*, 28 Colum. L. Rev. 127 (1928); Brudney, *The Investment-Value Doctrine in Corporate Readjustments*, 72 Harv. L. Rev. 645 (1959); Meckling, *Financial Markets, Default, and Bankruptcy: The Role of the State*, 41 Law & Contemp. Probs. 13 (1977); Roe, *Bankruptcy and Debt: A New Model for Corporate Reorganization*, 83 Colum. L. Rev. 527 (1983).

Varieties of Debt Securities. Debt securities are normally classified according to the nature of their security interest. A *mortgage bond* is secured by a mortgage over the issuer's fixed assets, particularly real estate, and is frequently the corporation's most senior security. On default, the trustee may apply the property in payment of the debt by foreclosing, in the same way that a conventional mortgagee would. But in most cases the scrap value of the property is much less than its going concern value, and the bondholders' rights in the collateral will merely establish their priority position on reorganization.

When an issuer in financial difficulties requires further moneys, bondholders may expressly agree to subordinate their claims to new lenders, who are issued *prior lien bonds*. The corporation's assets may also be mortgaged more than once, in which case one speaks of "First Mortgage Bonds" and "Second Mortgage Bonds." The latter security is deferred to the former, even as a second mortgage in a house is to a first mortgage. *Collateral trust bonds* are secured by an interest in the issuer's securities or accounts receivable.

Subordinated debentures are not merely unsecured, but also provide that other outstanding indebtedness has priority to repayment. These securities may be issued when the corporation has an excessive amount of debt and is unable to attract equity investors. Like conventional debentures, subordinated obligations are unconditional promises to pay interest and principal. But such payments are deferred until a distribution is made to the senior debt holders to whom the debentures are subordinated.

Bond provisions have achieved a considerable complexity as a reaction to the enormous shifts in interest rates. A purchase of a bond at a fixed interest rate represents a gamble on interest rates generally as well as on the solvency of the firm. For example, a purchaser of a high quality bond in 1970 might have been adequately compensated for the risk of default with a 10% rate of return. But with higher interest rates 10 years later, such securities would have traded at a discount. For example, if an investor had purchased an equivalent risk security promising a 20% rate of return in 1980, the first security would have traded at a 50% discount; if it had been issued at $100, promising yearly interest payments of $10, it would trade in 1980 at $50, promising a 20% return ($10). The rate of return on outstanding securities, based on current market values and expressed in a percentage figure, is called the securities' *yield*. In the example, the security's interest rate, based on face value, was 10%, while its yield in 1980 was 20%.

The increase in interest rates during the 1960s and 1970s resulted in a massive transfer of wealth from debt to equity holders. This is not of course to say that the initial issue of securities was distributionally troubling, any more than is the purchase of a lottery ticket that subsequently turns out to be a loser. The increase in interest rates did, however, lead to exotic debt provisions when such securities were issued in the 1980s. There was first a movement from long maturity terms (such as 20 years) to shorter periods (usually 5 to 10 years), since narrower fluctuations in interest rates will be anticipated in shorter time periods. Firms also issued "extendible" debt having a short maturity period, but giving its holders an option to convert to long-term debt in the event that interest rates fell. "Retractable" debt is usually long-term debt, but permits its holders to force redemption after a 5- or 10-year period as a hedge against any increase in interest rates. A further insurance against changes in interest rates is provided by variable interest rate debt. As an example of such securities, "floating rate" debt bears a rate of interest tied to the prime rate available to chartered banks, adjusted at specified intervals. See further Sullivan, *Methods of Long-Term Corporate Financing*, in *Income Tax Aspects of Corporate Financing* 1, 14-27 (1980).

More recently, low-grade bonds have come to be more popular than at any time in the recent past. Such bonds lack an investment-grade rating (Baa or better) from bond raters like Standard and Poor and have a non-trivial chance of default. For this reason they are referred to as *junk bonds*. On some estimates, junk bonds constituted one-quarter of new corporate public debt in the United States prior to the October 1987 stock market crash. Bus. Week, July 7, 1986 at 56, 61. Though junk bonds are unconventional, they are not in themselves objectionable, for if they are characterized by a relatively high degree of risk, they also promise a higher income. Moreover, junk bonds are overwhelmingly held by institutional intermediaries, who presumably can look after themselves. See Roe, *The Voting Prohibition in Bond Work-Outs*, 97 Yale L.J. 232, 258-60 (1987) (reportedly 95% of junk bond market held by institutional investors).

2. Protective Features of the Trust Indenture

Corporate statutes provide shareholders with a thick set of rights and remedies. By contrast, the rights of bondholders and of debentureholders depend to a much greater extent upon their contract or trust deed. CBCA ss. 82-93, which deal with debt security holders, give them more limited protection than the rights given to shareholders under the statute, with any further rights to be provided in the trust deed.

On a literal reading of "complainant" in CBCA s. 238, bondholders have the same status as shareholders to bring derivative and oppression actions under ss. 239 and 241. "Complainant" means a security holder, with "security" defined in s. 2 to include a debt obligation. However, this does not mean that, in the event of a particular management breach, bondholders' enforcement rights will be the same as those of shareholders. At common law, bondholders had severely restricted rights to litigate on behalf of their corporation, for reasons discussed by Eve J. in *Lawrence v. West Somerset Mineral Ry.*, [1918] 2 Ch. 250, 257:

[C]an a debenture stock holder who has no enforceable charge, who is not a creditor but an annuitant whose annuity is not in arrear, properly be held to be so directly interested in the administration of the affairs of the company liable to pay his annuity as to be a competent plaintiff in such an action as this? I do not think he can. If he can, I do not see why it should not be open to every creditor or potential creditor of the company to commence a similar action.

This passage was adopted in *Re MacRae* (1984), 10 D.L.R. (4th) 216 (B.C.), where a debentureholder sought leave to commence a derivative action against directors for payment of a dividend at a time when the corporation was allegedly insolvent. BCCA s. 225(1) provides that a "member" of the firm may bring a derivative action, with member defined in s. 225(8) to include:

(a) a beneficial owner of a share in the company; and

(b) any other person who, in the discretion of the court, is a proper person to make an application under this section.

The Court declined to exercise its discretion to find that the debentureholder was a "member" for the purposes of a derivative action, and stated that the term should be restricted to persons who have "a direct financial interest in how the company is being managed." *Id.* at 225. The Court did not consider whether the debentureholder had such an interest in the corporation by virtue of the fact that it was undergoing a CCAA reorganization, such that from a financial point of view the debentureholders might have been regarded as the residual claimants of the firm.

Bondholders and debentureholders will therefore rely for their protection primarily on the contractual provisions of the trust deed. Formally, the trust deed is a contract between the issuer and the trustee for bondholders, but its terms are incorporated by reference in bond certificates. The most important terms in the contract state the amount of money borrowed, the interest rate and the times for repaying interest and principal. The indenture will also state whether a security interest is given in the issuer's collateral, and what that interest is. Additional clauses detail the rights and obligations of the issuer to the mortgaged property, the powers and duties of the trustee and the means by which debt holders may vary their rights or enforce their security. Finally, restrictive covenants in the indenture seek to preserve the value of the underlying security by limiting the discretion of management in financing and investment decisions.

The Sinking Fund. When a debt security matures at the end of its term, moneys borrowed must be repaid. This usually entails a major expenditure that the issuer is unable to make out of current revenues. The redemption of the securities will then be financed by a further issue of securities, for example, by replacing old with new bond-holders at current interest rates. In addition, most indentures have a sinking fund to provide for the orderly repayment of a substantial portion of the debt prior to maturity. Sinking fund provisions typically require the issuer to provide the trustee with a speci-fied amount of money each year to purchase or "sink" the securities. The debentures to be purchased may be either chosen by lot for redemption or bought in the open market. Alternatively, the issuer itself may be permitted to purchase the debentures, depositing them with the trustee. Securities acquired by the trustee in any of these ways are can-celled and cannot be reissued.

The corporation's right to reacquire the debentures amounts to a "call" option, and may be very valuable to the firm as a hedge against decreases in interest rates. For example, if the firm has issued 10% debentures and interest rates fall so that the deben-tures trade at a premium above their face value, the firm will find it advantageous to reacquire them, financing the purchase if need be by an offer of lower yield senior securities to the public.

See further A. Dewing, *The Financial Policy of Corporations* vol. 1, 245-46, 250-51 (5th ed. 1953).

Restrictive Covenants. As a substitute for the governance structures offered to share-holders, bondholders may be offered a variety of protective devices to guard against the possibility of destruction of their claims. First, the agency cost problem may be tackled through a flat prohibition against certain kinds of financing strategies. One important financing restriction is a negative pledge, under which the issuer promises not to issue new debt ranking equal or prior to the negative pledge debentures. This is similar to the protection offered by a security interest in the issuer's assets, although if the issuer were to issue new debt in breach of the negative pledge, the clause would probably not bind subsequent lenders, at least if they had no actual notice of it. Negative pledges have been criticized as cumbersome where the corporation is in need of a new injection of cash and debt securities provide the best method of raising money. See McDaniel, *Are Negative Pledge Clauses in Public Debt Issues Obsolete?* 38 Bus. Law. 867 (1983).

In addition, trust deeds often restrict the discretion of directors to distribute funds to shareholders, whether by way of dividends or share repurchases. Such restrictions are frequently more exacting than those encountered in CBCA, as discussed in the next chapter. A typical restriction prohibits the payment of a dividend unless the amount of current assets less current liabilities is at least 25% of middle- or long-term debt. For examples of such provisions, see *Commentaries and Model Debenture Indenture Provisions* 402-17 (1971); Manning, *A Concise Textbook on Legal Capital* 96-106 (2d ed. 1981).

The trust indenture may also restrict management's discretion with respect to investment decisions. However, these restrictions, which parallel the *ultra vires* rule for shareholders, are generally inefficient for solvent issuers, since foreclosing investment opportunities is likely more costly than any benefits the debentureholders might derive therefrom. Some evidence of these costs is provided by their rarity in trust debentures, which suggests that most firms regard them as undesirable. See Smith & Warner, *On Financial Contracting: An Analysis of Bond Covenants*, 7 J. Fin. Econ. 117, 121-22, 125-31, 152-53 (1979) (under "costly contracting hypothesis," relative absence of investment restrictions is evidence of their cost). Exceptions to this arise in the case of certain major investment decisions, such as mergers and sales of substantially all of the corporation's assets, which frequently require the authorization of the trustee for debentureholders.

Equity value declines dramatically as a firm nears insolvency, and as a consequence the firm's residual value is transferred to senior claimants. And yet incumbent management may remain in control throughout a reorganization, unless displaced by a receiver appointed by secured creditors or a court. Since management is presumed allied to the equity holders who elect it, this may give rise to the adverse incentive costs discussed in Chapter One, Section C. To alleviate these costs, borne by the firm in efficient credit markets, the firm may seek to provide displacement techniques through which equity-elected boards are replaced by bondholders in near insolvency situations. One such technique is receivership itself, where senior claimants obtain the right to appoint as their agent a receiver to manage the firm.

Premature termination will, however, impose its own costs, so long as some value attaches to the equity claims. In addition to assigning termination rights to creditors on default, therefore, the firm may also wish to provide for less drastic displacement techniques. For example, bondholders might be given the right to elect a portion of the board when more generous financial solvency tests are not met. Voting rights will, however, impose the risk that bondholder claims in bankruptcy will be subordinated to the claims of other creditors under the equitable subordination doctrine, as seen in Chapter Two, Section B. See DeNatale & Abram, *The Doctrine of Equitable Subordination as Applied to Non-Management Creditors*, 40 Bus. Law. 417 (1985). Bondholders whose directors control the firm may also become "related persons" of the firm under BIA s. 4(2), so that moneys repaid them over the 12-month period prior to bankruptcy might be impeached as fraudulent preferences under ss. 3, 95-96. The limitation period for non-related parties is only 3 months. Finally, other creditors might seek to charge bondholder directors with mismanagement. See Douglas-Hamilton, *Creditor Liabilities Resulting from Improper Interference with the Management of a Financially Troubled Debtor*, 31 Bus. Law. 343 (1975); Lungdren, *Liability of a Creditor in a Control Relationship with Its Debtor*, 67 Marq. L. Rev. 523 (1984).

On protective features of trust deeds, see generally McDaniel, *Bondholders and Corporate Governance*, 41 Bus. Law. 413 (1986).

3. Trustees Under Trust Indentures

Lawrence Report
Report of the Ontario Select Committee on Company Law
99-103 (1967)

11.1.1. It is the invariable practice of companies issuing bonds, debentures, notes or other obligations for sale to the public to issue such obligations under a formal trust document known variously as a trust deed, a trust indenture, a note indenture or the like. The indenture contains the terms and conditions upon which the obligations are issued and sets out in elaborate detail not only the security, if any, for the obligations but also provisions as to issuance, certification and transfer of the obligations, requirements for sinking fund and for redemption or purchase of the obligations, specific covenants to which the issuer becomes subject with respect to the particular obligations and, in the case of secured issues, provisions as to insurance, possession, use and release of mortgaged property, etc. The indenture also contains extensive provisions as to the administration of the trust and for the protection of the trustee. The trustee is a party to the indenture and, by entering into the indenture, becomes a trustee for all the holders of the obligations pursuant to the terms and conditions of the indenture. Trustees under indentures are almost invariably one of the federally or provincially incorporated trust companies carrying on business in Canada.

11.1.2. While the Committee is conscious of the fact that the practices and abuses concerning trustees under trust indentures as they existed in the United States thirty years ago are not, either in degree or kind, necessarily duplicated in Ontario today, nevertheless it is useful as a background to this topic to set out at some length an extract from the Report of the Securities and Exchange Commission of the United States reporting to Congress in 1936. The report in question was directed by Congress to be made at the time the Securities Exchange Act of 1934 was passed.

Under modern trust indentures securing issues of corporate bonds, debentures and notes, important powers are vested in the trustee. The security holders themselves are generally widely scattered and their individual interest in the issue is likely to be small. The trustee, on the other hand, is usually a single [trust company]. By virtue of the broad discretionary powers vested in it under the typical trust indenture it is in a position to take immediate action in a variety of ways to protect or enforce the security underlying the bonds, debentures and notes. But the security holders are rarely given any voice in formulation of policies which the trustee pursues; the trust indenture ordinarily does not require that they be consulted before the trustee acts. Hence the trustee generally need not be delayed or embarrassed by the necessity of consulting the security holders or of reconciling their divergent opinions and policies. Theoretically, the result should be beneficial to all concerned: to the security holder because of increased efficiency, expedition and economy; to the issuer because a trustee is a convenient legal device for conveying title, and because the presence of the trustee relieves the issuer of possible suits and supervision by many individual security holders.

But, as a matter of fact, this arrangement has resulted in injury to thousands of investors. They have bought securities and have retained no effective control over the issuer's performance of its obligations in respect to them. Such control has been surrendered to or assumed by the trustee. It has been invested with power to certify securities; to supervise the deposit and the withdrawal of collateral and application of funds; to take action upon default; and, in short, to do everything upon which the protection and enforcement of the security of a bondholder depends.

Both in law and in practice, this reliance of the security holder upon the trustee for protection of his investment is complete. It is a matter of common knowledge that purchasers of securities seldom examine the terms of the trust indenture, although they are legally bound by its terms. Even if they did examine the indenture, the significance of its elaborate provisions would appear only to specialists. In some instances, indeed, it is so drafted that vital provisions apparently escape the notice of highly trained investment agencies. Reliance for adequacy of the security underlying the bonds, notes or debentures, is placed by the investor upon the reputation of the issuer, the underwriting bankers and the trustee. And for honest, faithful and efficient operation of the provisions of the indenture, reliance is placed upon the trustee as representative of the security holders under the terms of the indenture.

... [A]n examination of the provisions of modern trust indentures and their administration by trustees will show that this reliance is unfounded. It will show that typically the trustees do not exercise the elaborate powers which are the bondholders' only protection; that they have taken virtually all of the powers designed to protect the bondholders, but have rejected any duty to exercise them; and that they have shorn themselves of all responsibilities which normally trusteeship imports. The "so-called trustee" which is left is merely a clerical agency and a formal instrument which can be used by the bondholders when and if enough of them combine as specified in the indenture.

. . .

It is readily admitted by these trustees that they are a species different from the usual trustee of a testamentary or *inter vivos* estate. They say they have not intended in the indentures the assumption of a full quantum of trusteeship duties.

Nevertheless one basic, fundamental fact cannot be overlooked; the trustee is the only agency avowedly designed for the protection of security holders during the entire life of the security. Furthermore, under the modern trust indenture it alone is capable of effective action. The individual security holder is impotent when acting alone and can get together with his fellow security holders only at great labor and expense. It is likewise true that the common understanding of the lay investor is that the trustee is his *alter ego* in safeguarding his rights. On these facts the trustee should not be allowed, through indenture provisions never seen by the beneficiary, and which would not be understood if they were seen, to whittle away at the number of his express duties until they are practically non-existent, and to surround itself with exculpatory clauses which leave it harmless, despite inactivity or negligence.

11.1.3. The Securities and Exchange Commission concluded in its Report to Congress that it was necessary in the public interest and for the protection of investors (a) that trustees under indentures be disqualified from acting or serving if they have or acquire conflicts of interest incompatible or inconsistent with their fiduciary obligations, and (b) that they be transformed into active trustees with the obligation to exercise that degree of care and diligence which the law attaches to such a fiduciary position. Accordingly, Congress enacted the Trust Indenture Act of 1939 which is, in form, Title III to the Securities Act of 1933 and closely integrated with that Act. The three primary purposes of the Trust Indenture Act were:

1. To provide full and fair disclosure, not only at the time of original issue of bonds, notes, debentures, and similar securities, but throughout the life of such securities;
2. To provide machinery whereby such continuing disclosure may be made to the security holders, and whereby they may get together for the protection of their own interets; and
3. To assure that the security holders will have the services of a disinterested indenture trustee, and that such trustee will conform to the high standards of conduct now observed by the more conscientious trust institutions.

Each of these three primary purposes are, in the opinion of the Committee, of interest and concern to investors in Ontario. However, in view of the fact that the Legislature has recently enacted The Securities Act, 1966 which fundamentally revises the degree and quality of disclosure in connection with the primary distribution of securities to the public, the Committee is now concerned more directly with the third primary purpose of the Trust Indenture Act, namely, to ensure that the security holders will enjoy the services of a disinterested indenture trustee and that such trustee will conform to high standards of conduct. ...

[Paragraph 11.1.4 contains the recommendations subsequently enacted into OBCA ss. 46-52. Cf. CBCA ss. 82-93.]

11.1.5. The recommendations in paragraph 11.1.4 impose upon indenture trustees duties and responsibilities commensurate with their proper role as fiduciary for the security holders. The indenture trustee must be independent and must conform to a high standard of conduct in discharging its prescribed duties. There are, however, other problems arising under indentures securing obligations issued to the public. For example, what role should be played by the indenture trustee and, perhaps, by the security purchasers themselves, in seeing to the enforcement of special covenants in the indenture such as the maintenance of specified security for the benefit of the security holders? These other problems should attract the careful and fairminded attention of issuers, underwriters and fiscal agents so that, through the give and take of contract negotiations leading to the entering into of the indenture, the best interets of the investing public will be served. If the parties to indentures cannot or do not strengthen and upgrade indenture provisions designed to protect the investor, the Legislature will have no alternative but to do by law what could more flexibly be accomplished by strengthening the indenture provisions in the interests of the security holders.

The Role of the Trustee. The 1936 Securities and Exchange Commission Report contemplated that trustees would play a monitoring role for the protection of bondholders. See Levmore, *Monitors and Freeriders in Commercial and Corporate Settings*, 92 Yale L.J. 49, 72-73 (1982). Notwithstanding this, the extent of trustee responsibilities to bondholders under CBCA ss. 82-93 remains unclear. First, it has not yet been established in what circumstances, if at all, the trustee owes an affirmative duty prior to default. For example, would it suffice if he merely collects the yearly certificates of compliance from the issuer under ss. 86-88? Or does the trustee have a further obligation to investigate the issuer to determine if it has committed an event of default? In what circumstances should a trustee, exercising the care of a reasonably prudent trustee for debentureholders under s. 91(b), require further evidence of compliance under s. 86(1)? Would s. 92 provide a defence in all but the grossest cases of neglect? In fact, prior to receiving notice of an event of default under s. 90, trustees normally do not scrutinize the issuer's affairs. This is not, however, to say that such inactivity should amount to a breach of trust, since the argument that affirmative, pre-default monitoring is efficient remains speculative.

Prior to the statutory codification of their duties, trustees under a trust indenture were said to owe the same duties of loyalty and care as ordinary trustees. *Re Magadi Soda Co.* (1925), 41 T.L.T. 297. Applications could be brought under trustee legislation, and bondholders and debentureholders were said to be *cestuis que trust*. In the United States, on the other hand, it was never entirely clear whether trustees under an indenture were ordinary trustees or mere stakeholders, whose duties depended solely on the terms of the trust indenture. If these duties arose only from contract and not from status, they were slight indeed, since exemption clauses frequently relieved trustees from all liability save for fraud. Such clauses were also upheld in Canada and England. *Stothers v. Toronto Gen. Trusts Corp.* (1918), 44 O.L.R. 432 (C.A.); *Leeds City Brewery Ltd. v. Platts*, [1925] 1 Ch. 532 (C.A.).

Duties of trustees for debentureholders are now codified under the CBCA. Under s. 93, exemption clauses cannot negative s. 91 duties. Moreover, apart from the contract, s. 91 imposes general duties of loyalty and care on trustees. However, the s. 91 standard is based not upon an ordinary trustee, but rather a trustee for debentureholders. See CBCA s. 82(1) ("trustee").

Trust indentures normally state in great detail how rights may be enforced on default. An "event of default" is typically defined to include any default in the payment of principal or interest, as well as the breach of any other covenant. On an event of default the trustee may, in his discretion, accelerate all payments of principal and interest. This will almost invariably bankrupt the issuer and a strict insistence on compliance with all obligations will often be more harmful to the security holders than permitting the issuer to continue in default. Nothing in the CBCA requires the trustee to enforce the covenants apart from the general duty in s. 91, and he need not even give notice of default to the security holders under s. 90 if he "reasonably believes that it is in the best interests of the debt obligations to withhold such notice." Most trust indentures also provide that, basic covenants excepted, the issuer has a period of time to cure the breach. Cf. CBCA s. 82(1) ("event of default" does not arise until all provisions for notice or lapse of time are met).

No Action Clauses. While the trustee has a broad discretion to take action on an event of default, most trust deeds place enormous obstacles in the path of an individual security holder who seeks to enforce his claim. A typical "no action clause" prevents a debentureholder from exercising any remedy unless the trustee fails to act on receipt of a "debentureholders' request," signed by the holders of at least 25% of the principal amount of outstanding debentures. The trustee is obliged to take such action as the request directs, if provided with security for all expenses and liabilities by the debentureholders. If a trustee fails to commence proceedings thereafter, any debentureholder at his own expense may bring an individual action to enforce his claim. But a security holder will seldom be able to afford to do so. Where the securities are widely held, securing the consents of the other debentureholders will be very expensive, and to this must be added the indemnity the trustee will request for costs. Few debentureholders will have a sufficiently large stake in the issuer to make such expenses worthwhile. The practical effect of a no action clause is therefore to leave the question of when to enforce the indenture to the sole discretion of the trustee.

Aladdin Hotel Co. v. Bloom
United States Court of Appeals, Eighth Circuit
200 F.2d 627 (1953)

GARDNER C.J.: As originally brought this was in form a class action in which Josephine Loeb Bloom as plaintiff sought for herself and other minority bondholders of the Aladdin Hotel Company similarly situated equitable relief. She named as defendants Aladdin Hotel Company, a corporation, Charles O. Jones, Inez M. Jones, Charles R. Jones, Kathryn Dorothea Jones, Barbara Ann Jones and Mississippi Valley Trust Company, a corporation. She alleged that the class whom she purported to represent consisted of approximately 130 members who were the owners of a minority in value of certain bonds issued by the Aladdin Hotel Company, and that the object of the action was to obtain an adjudication of claims which affected specific property involved in the action and that common questions of law and fact affecting the rights of the parties constituting the class were involved; that on September 1, 1938, the Aladdin Hotel Company executed and delivered a series of 647 bonds aggregating in principal amount the sum of $250,000.00. The bonds on their face were made payable September 1, 1948, with interest to that date at 5 per cent per annum payable only out of net earnings and with interest at the rate of 8 per cent annum from maturity until paid; that the Hotel Company to secure payment of said bond issue executed its deed of trust by which it mortgaged certain real estate owned by it in Kansas City, Missouri; that the mortgage also covered furnishings and fixtures in the hotel property owned by the Aladdin Hotel Company; that the Mississippi Valley Trust Company was named as trustee in said deed of trust; that the bonds and deed of trust contained provision empowering the bondholders of not less than two-thirds principal amount of the bonds, by agreement with the Hotel Company to modify and extend the date of payment of said bonds provided such extension affected all bonds alike. She then alleged that she was the owner of some of said bonds of the total principal amount of $3500; that the defendants, other than the Hotel Company and the Mississippi Valley Trust Company, were all members of the so-called Jones family and during the period from May 1, 1948, to the time of the commencement of this action they were the owners of a majority of the stock of the Hotel Company and controlling members of its Board of Directors and dominated and controlled all acts and policies of the Hotel Company; that they were also the owners and holders of more than two-thirds of the principal amount of said bonds, being the owners of more than 72 per cent thereof; that they entered into an agreement with the Hotel Company June 1, 1948 to extend the maturity date of said bonds from September 1, 1948 to September 1, 1958. It was also alleged that other changes were similarly made, on various dates, in the provisions of the trust deed but as the trial court deemed them immaterial we pretermit reciting them here in detail. It was alleged that the defendant Mississippi Valley Trust Company certified the modification as provided in the trust deed; that the purported changes were made on application of the Hotel Company and with the consent of the holders of two-thirds in principal value of the outstanding bonds; that no notice of said application for change in the due date of the bonds was given to the mortgage bondholders and that plaintiff did not consent nor agree to the modification. She then alleged that the modifications were invalid because not made in good faith and were not for the equal benefit of all bondholders but were made corruptly for the benefit of the defendants and such modification deprived plaintiff and other mortgage bondholders of their rights and property; that said modification extended for ten additional years the powers and compensation of the Mississippi Valley Trust Company as trustee; that the Mississippi Valley Trust Company is made defendant because it is a party to the aforesaid modifications and waivers and participated in effecting them and because it benefitted by aforesaid modifications, waivers and certifications. Other allegations as to grounds of invalidity had reference to certain other modifications which the court held immaterial and they are therefore not here recited. Plaintiff prayed for a declaratory judgment declaring and holding that the purported modifications, waivers and certifications are illegal, inequitable and void; that she and all other bondholders of the defendant Aladdin Hotel Company have judgment against defendant Aladdin Hotel Company for the principal amount of the bonds held by each of them with interest thereon at 8 per cent per annum (allowing said defendant credit thereon, however, for the 5 per cent annum interest paid thereon) from September 1, 1948 until the payment of such principal and interest.

On trial the court dismissed as to all individual defendants, including the Mississippi Valley Trust Company, and made findings that the amendments benefitted the Hotel Company and the Joneses but did not benefit the bondholders; that all bondholders were entitled to notice of any proposed amendments; that the Joneses acting as the Hotel Company's officers and as majority bondholders, had a legal duty to exercise an honest discretion in extending the bonds; that the power to postpone the maturity date of the bonds could not be legally recognized in the majority bondholders under the facts of this case; that the decree, however, should be limited to a money judgment because that would grant plaintiff full relief. The court refused to enter a declaratory judgment which might affect the rights of others not parties to the action and it exonerated the Mississippi Valley Trust Company from all charges of conspiracy or bad faith. No judgment was entered against any of the defendants save and except the Hotel Company. The judgment was a money judgment for the amount due on plaintiff's bonds.

In seeking reversal the Hotel Company in substance contends: (1) that the modification of the provisions of the trust deed extending the time of maturity of the bonds was effected in strict compliance with the provisions of the contract of the parties and hence was binding on all the bondholders; (2) that whatever right of action resulted from the alleged unlawful acts of the parties to the contract vested in the plaintiff's grantors, and being an equitable right as alleged by plaintiff, was not transferred to her by assignment of the bonds which she owns; (3) that if the acts of the parties to the contract in effecting such modification were not in the first instance authorized they were subsequently ratified by the plaintiff and her assignors; (4) that if a cause of action resulted from the acts of the parties to the contract it could be prosecuted only by the Mississippi Valley Trust Company, named as trustee in the trust deed.

The trust deed contained provision that,

In the event the Company shall propose any change, modification, alteration or extension of the bonds issued hereunder or of this Indenture, such change, if approved by the holders of not less than two-thirds in face amount of the bonds at the time outstanding, shall be binding and effective upon all of the holders of the then outstanding bonds, provided, however, that such modification, change, alteration or extension shall affect all of the outstanding bonds similarly.

The bonds, including those held by plaintiff, contained the following:

The terms of this bond or of the Indenture securing the same may be modified, extended, changed or altered by agreement between the Company and the holders of two-thirds or more in face amount of bonds of this issue at the time outstanding. Any default under the Indenture may be waived by the holders of two-thirds or more in face amount of the bonds at the time outstanding.

The bonds also contained the following provision:

For a more particular description of the covenants of the Company as well as a description of the mortgaged property, of the nature and extent of the security, of the rights of the holders of the bonds and of the terms and conditions upon which the bonds are issued and secured, reference is made to said General Mortgage Deed of Trust.

It appears without dispute that the modification here under consideration was made in strict compliance with the provisions contained in the trust deed and by reference embodied in the bonds. The Hotel Company made the application to the trustee and it was approved by the holders of more than two-thirds in face amount of the bonds at the time outstanding. When this application for modification was made to the trustee he was guided in his action by the terms of the contract between the parties. That contract made no provision for notice. It required that such application have the approval of those holding two-thirds or more in face value of the bonds. The only other limitation contained in the contract with reference to the power to modify its terms was to the effect that "such modification, change, alteration or extension shall affect all of the outstanding bonds similarly." The modification did affect all outstanding *bonds* similarly and it is important, we think, to observe that the contract does not require that such modification affect all *bondholders* similarly. What effect this change might have on various bondholders might depend upon various circumstances and conditions with which the trustee was not re-quired to concern itself. The so-called Joneses were the controlling stockholders of the Hotel Company and were its officers and the court found that the alteration was advanta-geous to the Hotel Company. It was doubtless effected primarily to benefit the financial standing and operating efficiency of the hotel. It does not follow, however, that such modification was prejudicial to the bondholders. Their security was greatly improved in value by the management and it is inconceivable that the Joneses should deliberately act to the prejudice or detriment of the bondholders when they held and owned some 72 per cent of the entire outstanding bond issue. It is urged that because the Joneses were acting in a dual capacity they became trustees for the other bondholders and that as such it was incumbent upon them to do no act detrimental to the rights of the bondholders. The rights of the bondholders, however, are to be determined by their contract and courts will not make or remake a contract merely because one of the parties thereto may become dissatisfied with its provisions, but if legal will interpret and enforce it. ... There is no question that the provision in the trust deed and bonds was a legal provision which violated no principle of public policy nor private right. The sole ground for holding the modification extending the time for payment void is that no notice was given the minority bondholders. If the Joneses had not been acting in a dual capacity, then, we assume, the modification, effected as it was with the approval of the holders of two-thirds of the face value of the outstanding bonds, would have been held good. It is conceded that under such circumstances no notice would have been necessary. We think the situation must be viewed realistically. No notice was required so far as the parties to the contract were concerned. Their rights must be determined by their contract and not by any equitable doctrine, and notice to the other bondholders could have served no possible purpose. Litigants have no standing in a court of equity where a remedy at law is available. The holders of more than two-thirds of the face value of the bonds could not have been prevented from approving the proposed change even had notice been given and the acts of the parties must be determined in relation to the terms of their contract. It follows that no prejudice could have been suffered by plaintiff or her grantors by the fact that notice of the proposed change or modification was not given them.

We have searched the record with great care and find no substantial evidence warranting a finding of bad faith, fraud, corruption or conspiracy of the Joneses. When Charles O. Jones became manager of the hotel properties in 1944 no interest had been paid on the bonds prior to that date. The Hotel Company paid the interest to all bondholders in 1944 and the interest has been paid each year since. Numerous improvements were made in the hotel property at an expense of over $300,000. At the time the Joneses took over the management in 1944 the Company had a deficit of $70,000 and a balance due of $24,000 on the first mortgage of $50,000, all of which has been paid off, and the gross income of the hotel has increased from $219,000 in 1944 to $600,000 in 1951, and the book value of the stock has increased from $384,000 in 1944 to $916,000 in 1951. The properties covered by the trust deed were at the time of the trial of the proximate value of $1,000,000.

It appears without dispute that the changes made in the provisions of the trust deed were made before plaintiff acquired her bonds. The bonds on their face were past due when she purchased them. Her predecessors in title were given notice by the trustee that changes had been made in the provisions of the instrument and at its request the bonds were returned to it and it thereupon endorsed thereon the following legend:

The maturity of this bond has been extended to September 1, 1958, and the requirements of deposit of sinking fund payments and the filing of reports and audits with the trustee by the obligor have been cancelled by agreement dated June 1, 1948, between the obligor and the holders of more than two-thirds of the face value of the then outstanding bonds, as evidenced by a certificate of extention by the trustee on July 2, 1948, and duly reported as is required in the mortgage deed of trust.

They also knew that they had not had notice of the application to modify the provisions of the trust deed. If any equities in favor of the bondholders wee infringed by reason of the modifications of the provision of the trust deed relative to the due date of the bonds it occurred while these bonds were owned and in possession of plaintiff's grantors and if any equitable right of action accrued it accrued to them and not to plaintiff. It is, however, urged that plaintiff, by securing an assignment of the bonds, also acquired whatever equitable right of action had vested in her assignors.

• • •

Plaintiff by her suit sought equitable remedies for alleged acts affecting the rights of her assignors. We think she did not, by securing an assignment of these bonds, secure the right to maintain such a suit.

As has been previously observed, plaintiff's assignors were given notice of the change made in the deed of trust and they knew the method by which such change could be effected. They were charged with the knowledge of the provisions of the deed of trust and of the recitals in their bonds. They also knew that they had not had notice of the application made for such modification. They not only did not repudiate the action taken but they acquiesced therein by sending in their bonds so that the change might be noted thereon. After receiving the bonds with the legends stamped thereon, showing specifically what change had been made, they still did not repudiate the action taken nor protest with reference thereto. In addition to this they received interest payable only under the provisions of the bond and deed of trust as changed. The plaintiff likewise, with notice of the change made, and with knowledge that she had had no notice of the application for such change, made no effort to repudiate it until she brought this suit, but accepted interest payable under the provisions of the contract and bond as thus changed. She has retained the interest thus paid her.

If the Joneses as holders of the majority of the outstanding bonds became under the circumstances trustees for all bondholders, then in consenting to the change they were acting as agents for all bondholders. It is a well established principle of agency that ratification of an alleged unauthorized act by the agent may be expressed as spoken or written words, or it may be implied from any act, words or course of conduct on the part of the principal which reasonably tend to show an intention on his part to ratify the unauthorized acts or transactions of the alleged agent. Restatement, Agency, Sec. 93. The parties, effecting this change in the contract were agents of plaintiff's assignors and their actions and the actions of the plaintiff subsequent to knowledge of the acts of their agent, and with knowledge that they had not had notice of such proposed change, we think clearly established ratification. The court separated these acts instead of considering them all together, holding that plaintiff's acceptance of the bonds with the endorsement thereon "standing alone" did not effect a ratification, and the court overlooked the vital fact that plaintiff's grantors knew that they had not been given notice of the application to make the change complained of. The court also held that acceptance of the interest payments "standing alone" did not indicate a ratification. But the course of conduct of plaintiff and her assignors cannot thus be divided up into segments but must be considered in its entirety and when so considered is entirely inconsistent with the thought that either plaintiff's assignors or plaintiff repudiated the acts of their agents in effecting the change in the provisions of the deed of trust. It is clear that the altered contract was not void but voidable only, and plaintiff's assignors, with knowledge that the change was made without notice to them, made no protest but acquiesced therein, the unequivocal acts showing that they treated the altered contract as their own. The acts of plaintiff's assignors were such as to ratify the change complained of and plaintiff was bound by that ratification.

It remains to consider the contention that plaintiff in her individual capacity could not maintain this action. The deed of trust provides that,

No holder of any bond hereby secured shall have any right to institute any suit or other action hereunder unless the Trustee shall refuse to proceed within thirty (30) days after written request thereto of the holders of not less than twenty per cent (20%) in face value of the bonds then out-standing and after tender to it of indemnity satisfactory to the Trustee.

More than 20 per cent of the bonds were in the hands of the minority bondholders but no written request was made upon the trustee to bring this suit. The court has held that the trustee at all times acted in good faith and no reason appears why he was not requested to bring this suit. Plaintiff is the owner of only $3500 face value of a bond issue of $250,000. According to her complaint there are 130 other minority bondholders and if she can maintain this action individually then the defendant may be subjected to 130 other similar lawsuits. As stated by this court in *Central States Life Ins. Co. v. Koplar*, 80 F.2d 754, 758:

The reason for the rule is not far to seek. If in a mortgage securing thousands of bonds every holder of a bond or bonds were free to sue at will for himself and for others similarly situated, the resulting harassment and litigation would be not only burdensome but intolerable. ...

We think plaintiff could not maintain this action in her individual capacity without first having complied with the provisions of the deed of trust which vests in the trustee the right to maintain such an action. ...

Rabinowitz v. Kaiser-Frazer Corp.
New York Supreme Court, Special Term
111 N.Y.S.2d 539 (1952)

HART J.: Defendant Kaiser-Fraser Corporation (hereinafter referred to as Kaiser-Frazer) moves to dismiss the complaint on the grounds that: (1) there is a nonjoinder of indispensable parties, and (2) the plaintiff has no legal capacity to sue.

This action was instituted against the three named defendants, Kaiser-Frazer, Bank of America National Trust and Savings Association (hereinafter referred to as Bank of America) and Graham-Paige Motors Corporation (hereinafter referred to as Graham-Paige) by the service of summons and verified complaint upon each of them. Graham-Paige joined issue by interposing its answer. Kaiser-Frazer unsuccessfully moved to set aside the service of process upon it. ... Bank of America, appearing specially, successfully moved to vacate the service of process against it upon jurisdictional grounds. ... A notice of appeal from the order on that motion was served in April 1950 but up to the present time no further action has been taken to prosecute the appeal.

The plaintiff is the original owner and holder of $10,000 in principal amount of 4% Convertible Debentures of Graham-Paige which were issued under an indenture with the Bank of America as trustee and has brought this action on behalf of himself and all other owners of such debentures similarly situated.

The material facts, as alleged in the complaint, may be summarized as follows: Prior to World War II Graham-Paige was engaged primarily in the production, distribution and sale of automobiles and replacement parts therefor. During the war Graham-Paige was engaged almost entirely in the production of war materials. On August 9, 1945, Joseph W. Frazer, then Chairman of the Board of Directors and President of Graham-Paige, and one Henry J. Kaiser were instrumental in the formation of Kaiser-Frazer. On September 20, 1945, Graham-Paige purchased 250,000 shares of common stock of Kaiser-Frazer. On that same date Graham-Paige and Kaiser-Frazer entered into an agreement for joint use of the former bomber plant at Willow Run in Ypsilanti, Michigan, for the manufacture of automobiles and farm equipment. Under this agreement, Graham-Paige was entitled to use one-third of Willow Run's automotive production facilities; Kaiser-Frazer the other two-thirds.

In order to obtain its share of the needed capital to convert the Willow Run plant to automobile production and to obtain other working capital, Graham-Paige issued $11,500,00 of 4% Convertible Debentures due April 1, 1956, under an Indenture with Bank of America as trustee. Behind these debentures were pledged the Graham-Paige plant in Detroit, Michigan and the aforesaid 250,000 shares of Kaiser-Frazer common stock.

Graham-Paige convenanted in said Indenture (Article "Third" relating to "Sinking Fund and Redemption of Debenture") that on or before April 1 of each year to and including April 1, 1956, so long as any of the debentures are outstanding, it would pay to the trustee, as and for a Sinking Fund for the retirement of the debentures, an amount in cash equal to 25% of its net earnings for the preceding calendar year.

Article Thirteenth of the Indenture, in so far as applicable herein, also provided:

§ 13.01. Nothing in this Indenture shall prevent ... any sale or conveyance, subject to the lien of this Indenture on the mortgaged and pledged property, of all or substantially all of the property of the corporation (Graham-Paige) to any other corporation; ... provided, however, and the corporation covenants and agrees, that

(1) Any such ... sale or conveyance shall be upon such terms as fully to preserve and in no respect to impair the lien of security of this Indenture, ... and

(2) Upon any such ... sale or conveyance, ... the corporation to which all or substantially all the property of the Corporation shall be sold or conveyed shall execute with the trustee and record an indenture, satisfactory to the trustee, whereby the successor corporation shall expressly agree to pay duly and punctually the principal of and the interest and premium, if any, on the Debentures according to their tenure, and shall expressly assume the due and punctual performance and observance of all the covenants and conditions of this Indenture to be performed or observed by the Corporation.

§ 13.02. Upon any such ... sale or conveyance ... such successor corporation shall succeed to and be substituted for the Corporation with the same effect as if it had been named as the party of the first part (Graham-Paige). ...

By a contract dated December 12, 1946, effective February 1, 1947, Graham-Paige agreed to sell to Kaiser-Frazer all of its automotive assets (excluding only such assets as had been acquired for use in the manufacture of farm equipment) in consideration, among other things, the issue to Graham-Paige of 750,000 shares of common stock of Kaiser-Frazer, of an agreement by Graham-Paige to pay Kaiser-Frazer $3,000,000 and by a debenture payment agreement (subsequently executed on February 10, 1947) between Graham-Paige and Kaiser-Frazer whereunder the latter undertook to pay the interest on and the principal of the debentures of Graham-Paige then outstanding ($8,524,000).

The agreement of December 12, 1946 (Article XI), specifically provides that Kaiser-Frazer shall not be required to pay the principal of any or all said 4% Convertible Debentures of Graham-Paige prior to the maturity date thereof (except for default in the payment of interest) and the debenture payment agreement of February 10, 1947, specifically provided (Article V) that except as therein provided Kaiser-Frazer does not "assume or agree to perform any of the promises, covenants, terms or conditions of the Indenture to be performed by" Graham-Paige and that neither the trustee under the indenture nor any debenture holder shall have any rights by virtue of such agreement and that the undertakings of Kaiser-Frazer are solely for the benefit of Graham-Paige and that they are limited to the making to Graham-Paige of the payments Kaiser-Frazer therein agreed to make.

At this point it is significant to note that by virtue of the foregoing provisions Kaiser-Frazer specifically avoided any undertaking on its part to apply 25% of its annual net profits to the sinking fund of the debentures in accordance with the provisions of Article Third of the Debenture. It is this failure of Kaiser-Frazer to have assumed the obligations of the sinking fund and to have paid 25% of its annual profits into such fund which presents the crux of this case and which forms the basis for the recovery sought herein against Kaiser-Frazer.

The complaint then proceeds to allege that the sale in question to the knowledge of Bank of America and Kaiser-Frazer constituted a conveyance of "all or substantially all" of the property of Graham-Paige and thereby terminated Graham-Paige's manufacturing and other activities in the automotive field; that Bank of America and Kaiser-Frazer knew or should have known that the sale as consummated would have the effect of depriving Graham-Paige of an opportunity to earn any moneys in the immediate or foreseeable future and would result in rendering nugatory the provisions in the indenture requiring Graham-Paige to make deposits in the sinking fund.

It is further alleged that by reason of the said sale Bank of America was under a duty, as trustee, and within its powers under the terms of the indenture, to obtain from Kaiser-Frazer a supplemental indenture satisfactory in form to itself, whereby Kaiser-Frazer would expressly assume the performance of *all* the covenants and conditions of the indenture to be performed by Graham-Paige, particularly those provisions of the indenture (Article Third) relating to the "Sinking Fund and Redemption of Debentures"; that Bank of America failed or refused to perform its duties as trustee in this respect and thereby breached the trust indenture; that by reason of the negligent and wilful misconduct on the part of Bank of America, plaintiff and all other debenture holders similarly situated were deprived, and unless this Court interferes, will be deprived of the benefits of the Sinking Fund provisions of the Indenture to the extent of the automotive assets of Graham-Paige and the earnings of Kaiser-Frazer, to the damage of the debenture holders in the amounts hereinafter set forth, "for which Bank of America is liable." ...

It is also alleged that Kaiser-Frazer is bound by the terms of the trust indenture despite its failure to execute a supplemental indenture to assume expressly the provisions relating to the "Sinking Fund"; that Kaiser-Frazer should have deposited with the trustee each year an amount in cash equal to 25% of its net earnings for the next preceding year; to wit, for the year 1947 the sum of $4,753,889.25 and for the year 1948 the sum of $2,590,524.50, making a total of $7,344,413.75, no part of which has been paid, and that Kaiser-Frazer is further obligated to the trustee for future sinking fund payments as provided in Article "Third" of the Indenture.

As of the date of this complaint there was outstanding $8,524,000 principal amount of the said 4% Convertible Debentures of Graham-Paige.

It is also alleged that Graham-Paige made no deposit with the trustee of any part of its net earnings for the years 1947 and 1948; that there was a net income for the calendar year 1947 of $123,766.73 but for the calendar year 1948 Graham-Paige had a net loss of $3,391,113.36, and that Graham-Paige's manufacturing operations of the farm equipment business were closed early in 1949.

The complaint contains the following allegation: "Thirty-Third: This action and the relief herein sought are not for the remedies provided by the Indenture, this being an action invoking the inherent powers of this Court as a court of equity to declare, protect and preserve the rights of the debenture holders. No demand upon the Trustee to institute or prosecute this action is necessary, nor has such demand been made for the reason that the Trustee is a defendant herein and is liable to the plaintiff and other debenture holders similarly situated, for its own negligent and wilful misconduct with respect to the acts herein complained of, and would be demanding that the Trustee sue itself, and such demand would be entirely useless and futile."

After alleging that he has no adequate remedy at law the plaintiff demands judgment as follows:

1. Declaring and decreeing that Kaiser-Frazer has assumed the due and punctual performance and observance of all of the covenants and conditions of the Indenture, dated as of April 1, 1946, between Graham-Paige and Bank of America, with the same effect as if Kaiser-Frazer had been named in the Indenture in place and stead of Graham-Paige.

2. Adjudging and decreeing that Kaiser-Frazer is liable to Bank of America, as Trustee, and shall pay over to Bank of America, as Trustee, or any Successor Trustee, for the benefit of the plaintiff and all other debenture holders similarly situated, the sum of $7,344,413.75, to be held and disposed of by the Trustee, in accordance with Article "Third" of said Indenture relating to "Sinking Fund and Redemption of Debentures."

3. Declaring and decreeing that so long as any of the said debentures are outstanding, 25% of the net earnings of Kaiser-Frazer, as defined in said Indenture, for each of the calendar years

1949 through 1954 be paid by Kaiser-Frazer to Bank of America, as Trustee, or any Successor Trustee in accordance with said Article "Third" of said Indenture.

4. Adjudging and decreeing that Bank of America be directed to account to the plaintiff and all other debenture holders similarly situated for its acts and for its failure to act as Trustee under said Indenture and that it be surcharged and directed to pay to itself as Trustee or to any Successor Trustee any and all damages sustained by the Trust Estate by reason of such acts or failure to act.

5. Granting such other and further relief as to the Court may seem just and proper together with the costs and disbursements of this action, and reasonable and proper counsel fees to plaintiff's attorneys.

As stated above, plaintiff has instituted this action on behalf of himself and all other bondholders similarly situated. The plaintiff alleges ownership of less than one-eighth of 1% of the outstanding debentures. The obligation that plaintiff lacks the legal capacity to sue is predicated on the language of § 8.08 of the Indenture which provides in substance that "no holder of any Debenture ... shall have any right to institute any suit ... unless such holder previously shall have given to the Trustee written notice of default ... and unless also the holders of not less than 25% in aggregate principal amount of the Debentures then outstanding shall have made written request upon the Trustee to institute such action and the Trustee ... shall have neglected or refused to institute any such action. ..."

The opposing parties to this motion are in virtual accord as to the general proposition that ordinarily a request upon a trustee to take action must be made by the holders of the prescribed percentage of bonds before a class action may be instituted by a bondholder. ...

The plaintiff, however, urges that notwithstanding the presence of a "no action" clause, an individual bondholder has the right to bring a class action to protect his interests and the interests of all other bondholders of the same issue whenever the Indenture Trustee has acted in such a manner as to put itself in a position where it cannot faithfully and competently discharge its duty as a fiduciary. It seems to me that plaintiff's position is sound and is supported by such cases as *Ettlinger v. Persian Rug & Carpet Co.*, 142 N.Y. 189, 36 N.E. 1055; *Campbell v. Hudson & Manhattan R. Co.*, 277 App.Div. 731, 102 N.Y.S.2d 878, affirmed 302 N.Y. 902, 100 N.E.2d 183; *Birn v. Childs Co.*, Sup., 37 N.Y.S.2d 689; *Farmers Loan & Trust Co. v. Northern Pacific R. Co.*, C.C., 66 F. 169; *Buel v. Baltimore & O.S. Ry. Co.*, 24 Misc. 646, 53 N.Y.S. 749. In the *Ettlinger* case, supra, the incompetency of the trustee to act for the bondholders was predicated upon the trustee's absence from this country and his probable insanity. In the *Birn* case the trustee's incompetency was based on its unreasonable refusal to sue. In the *Buel* case the incompetency of the trustee was predicated upon its inconsistent position as trustee of conflicting trusts. In the *Campbell* case, 277 App.Div. 731, 102 N.Y.S.2d 878, where the trustee "renounced" or "abdicated" its function to sue, the Court made the following apposite statement 277 App.Div. at pages 734-737, 102 N.Y.S.2d at page 881: "All of those cases, and others like them, presuppose a trustee competent to act, and exercising its judgment in good faith respecting what is best for the bondholders as a whole concerning the matter in issue. If a trustee under such an indenture acts in bad faith, or, abdicating its function with respect to the point in question, declines to act at all, bondholders for themselves and others similarly situated may bring a derivative action in the right of the trustee, rather than in their own individual rights as bondholders. In that event they are not subject to the limitations of Article Seventh of the Indenture, which are not imposed on the trustee or on bondholders acting in the status of the trustee. This subject was considered lucidly, and the same result reached, by Justice Walter in *Birn v. Childs Co.*, Sup., 37 N.Y.S.2d 689, 696. He said: 'That the restrictive or non-action clause does not operate, under such circumstances, to prevent a court of equity from granting relief at the suit of a single holder was in effect held in *Ettlinger v. Persian Rug & Carpet Co.*, 142 N.Y. 189, 36 N.E. 1055, 40 Am. St. Rep. 587, and *O'Beirne v. Allegheny & Kinzua R. Co.*, 151 N.Y. 372, 383, 45 N.E. 873.' "

Plaintiff's affidavit in opposition to the instant motion sets forth that subsequent to the date of the Indenture, Bank of America made several loans to both Kaiser-Frazer and Graham-Paige which were enmeshed with the sale of the automotive assets of the latter to Kaiser-Frazer. The nature of these transactions was such as to create a conflict in the interests of Bank of America as trustee and Bank of America as a creditor of both Graham-Paige and Kaiser-Frazer. As trustee it was bound to protect the interests of the debenture holders and was charged with the duty of requiring Kaiser-Frazer to assume the sinking fund provisions when the latter company acquired the automotive assets of Graham-Paige. On the other hand, as a bank creditor and in its self-interest Bank of America gave its express written consent to the terms of the Sales Agreement whereby Kaiser-Frazer delimited its undertakings with respect to the debentures so that it did not assume the obligations of the Sinking Fund provision of the Indenture. At the same time, in order to protect its own interests, in making a loan of $12,000,000 to Kaiser-Frazer, Bank of America required Kaiser-Frazer to amortize that loan to the extent of 25% of its annual net profits in addition to securing a mortgage on all of Kaiser-Frazer's property as well as on the property of Graham-Paige, the sale of which to Kaiser-Frazer was being contemplated and in the course of negotiation.

It seems to me that when Bank of America consented to Kaiser-Frazer's declination of assuming any of the provisions of the Indenture, including the sinking fund provisions, it placed itself in a position which was antagonistic to and in conflict with the interests of the debenture holders.

As was stated in *Farmers' Loan & Trust Co. v. Northern Pacific R. Co.*, C.C., 66 F. 169, 176: "A trustee cannot be permitted to assume a position inconsistent with or in opposition to his trust. His duty is single, and he cannot serve two masters with antagonistic interests."

The movant urges that under the circumstances of this case plaintiff's proper remedy is to have a new or substitute trustee appointed but such argument is untenable for the same reasons that the Court in the *Ettlinger* case rejected a similar contention. There the Court stated at page 193 of 142 N.Y., at page 1056 of 36 N.E.: "But the special terms say that in such event a new trustee should have been appointed. That simply reproduces the same difficulty in another form, for a court would hardly remove a trustee without notice to him, and giving him an opportunity to be heard; and why should a new appointment be made, when any one of the bondholders can equally do the duty of pursuing the foreclosure? The court, in such an action, takes hold of the trust, dictates and controls its performance, distributes the assets as it deems just, and it is not vitally important which of the two possible plaintiffs sets the court in motion. The bondholders are the real parties in interest. It is their right which is to be redressed, and their loss which is to be prevented; and any emergency which makes a demand upon the trustee futile or impossible, and leaves the right of the bondholder without other reasonable means of redress, should justify his appearance as plaintiff in a court of equity for the purpose of a foreclosure."

In view of the foregoing it is my view that the "no action" clause involved in the case at bar is inoperative and inapplicable. ...

Accordingly, this motion is denied in all respects. ...

NOTES

1) Extending the maturity date of bonds does not in itself necessarily prejudice bondholders. If a market exists for the bonds, they may be sold on it before the maturity date. Bondholders might even be better off if a maturity date is extended if the interest rate on the bonds exceeds contemporary interest rates on equivalent risk securities. Is this what happened in *Aladdin Hotel*?

2) Is it necessarily correct to assume that the Joneses would not, because of their 72% holdings of the bonds, deliberately wish to prejudice bondholders?

3) Would Bloom have received a windfall had she recovered, given the absence of contemporaneous ownership? You will recall that contemporaneous ownership is not required in a CBCA s. 239 derivative action. Is it nonetheless a factor a court might consider in determining whether to exercise its discretion to grant an order for oppression under s. 241?

4) Did the failure of Kaiser-Frazer in the *Rabinowitz* case to undertake to honour the sinking fund provision in the indenture substantially prejudice Graham-Paige debentureholders?

5) Banks do not act as trustees for debentureholders in Canada. Would a debentureholder's s. 241 action for oppression invariably fail because of non-compliance with a "no action" letter?

No action clauses have generally been upheld in the United States. In one case, the indenture provided that no proceedings could be brought unless the holders of 85% of the debentures joined in the action. However, the Court found that this was not unreasonable and upheld the restriction. *Sass v. New Yorker Towers Ltd.*, 258 N.Y.S.2d 765 (App.Div. 1965).

In Canada, debt holders were said to have an absolute right to bring an action in cases where the indenture either clearly or apparently lacked a no action clause. *Perron v. L'Eclaireur* (1933), 57 B.R. 445; *Re Imperial Steel Corp.* (1925), 28 O.W.N. 242, aff'd, [1925] S.C.R. 703; *Shaugnessy v. Imperial Trusts Co.* (1904), 3 N.B. Eq. 5. But no action clauses have been found to bar individual actions. *Levis County Ry. v. Fontaine* (1904), 13 B.R. 523. Cf. *Pethybridge v. Unibifocal Co.*, [1918] W.N. 278.

B. CONVERTIBLE SECURITIES, RIGHTS AND WARRANTS

Hills, Convertible Securities—Legal Aspects and Draftsmanship
19 Calif. L. Rev. 1, 2-4 (1930)

Conversion may be broadly defined as the act of exchanging securities of one class for securities of a different class, the exchange being effected by a surrender of the original security and the issuance to the holder of a new security in its place. Convertible securities are corporate securities which may, pursuant to their terms, be changed into or exchanged for other securities, such as bonds or notes exchangeable for preferred or common stock, or preferred stock exchangeable for common stock. Except in isolated cases the privilege of conversion is optional with the holder of the security, and senior securities are convertible into junior securities of the same company. In each case the privilege of conversion is created or evidenced by a certificate of incorporation, trust indenture, deed of trust or other document setting forth in full the terms and conditions under which the privilege may be exercised. In this study all such documents are, for the sake of brevity, called the conversion instrument.

The conversion privilege is inherently the same whether attached to corporate obligations or to shares of stock. Bonds, notes and shares of stock retain their respective characteristics upon being made convertible into other securities, the conversion privilege being an optional and alternative right of the holder in addition to and separate from the right to be paid a sum of money or to exercise the usual rights of a stockholder. Although the privilege may not be divorced from the holder of the security to which it is attached, it is no part of the security itself and must be construed as if embodied in a separate instrument. Fundamentally, it is an independent optional right. The privilege is, however, inseparably connected with the security which evidences it and is available only to the holder. It may not be exercised by, or transferred to, one who is not the holder of the security itself. A transfer of the security acts also as a transfer of the privilege.

• • •

The holder of a convertible obligation is not a stockholder in equity or at law nor is he a subscriber to shares of stock of the issuing company. Being merely the holder of a contractual privilege pursuant to which he has the option of becoming a stockholder he can acquire none of the rights of a stockholder unless and until he complies with all of the terms and conditions of his contract. It has therefore been held that such holder has no right to question the declaration or payment of cash or stock dividends, the authorization or issuance of additional shares of the class issuable upon conversion, or the change in par value of existing shares issuable upon conversion.

Stock purchase warrants and convertible securities are closely related in that both are contractual options for the purchase of shares. A conversion instrument and a warrant instrument are substantially alike in principle and draftsmanship, and a warrant instrument will contain all the essential adjustments and other protective features later referred to as customary in conversion instruments. Taking them as a class the only essential difference is in the consideration payable. A warrant is exercised by the payment of cash, while a privilege of conversion is exercised by the surrender of a corporate obligation or a share of stock. In some cases, however, the obligation to which a warrant is attached upon original issue may be surrendered in lieu of cash, in which case the warrant is in effect a detachable conversion privilege as well as a true warrant. Practically all warrants are attached to corporate obligations or to shares of stock upon original issuance, and the company can select the type of security best suited to its corporate structure by determining whether it would prefer to receive cash upon the exercise of an option warrant or obtain the discharge of an obligation, or of stock carrying a fixed redemption and dissolution value, upon the exercise of a conversion privilege.

Rights and Warrants. Warrants are options to acquire shares for a cash consideration. They are often issued with debt securities, and are then very similar to conversion privileges, save for the consideration payable on exercise of the option. Securities issued with a conversion privilege may be exchanged for other kinds of securities of the issuer. When securities are issued with a warrant, the warrant permits its holder to subscribe for a different class of securities for cash. The underlying security is then retained. If "attached" to the bonds, the warrants cannot be sold separately from them. But warrants are generally "detachable," and can be transferred even if the bonds are retained.

Rights are options to purchase shares which are usually offered to existing shareholders at current market value on a *pro rata* basis. While warrants generally give their holders the right to purchase shares over a period of several years, rights are seldom exercisable more than a few months after issue.

See W. Grover & D. Ross, *Materials on Corporate Finance* 113-14 (1975); Sullivan, *Methods of Long-Term Corporate Financing*, in *Income Tax Aspects of Corporate Financing* 1, 40-43, 50-54 (1980).

Valuation of Conversion Privileges and Warrants. An option to acquire a security is a thing of value in itself, quite apart from the security it enables one to obtain. Thus an option, exercisable today, to purchase a share now trading at $100 at an exercise price of $80 is worth $20. By purchasing the option for $20 and exercising it for $80, its holder can acquire a $100 security. The valuation of a conversion privilege or warrant is, however, much more difficult, since the option may be exercisable at any time over the next few years at an exercise price that exceeds the share's current market value. An option, exercisable at any time over the next three years, to purchase for $110 a share of X Corp. now trading at $100 represents a bet that the value of the share will rise above $110 during that period. That possibility makes the option valuable today.

An option is a much more volatile security than the shares it entitles one to purchase. To illustrate, assume that the option in the above example is publicly traded, with a market value of $10. For $100, an investor can buy either one share or 10 options, each of which permits him to buy one share for $110 over the following three years. If the shares do not rise above $100 in value, the investor would still have a valuable security had he purchased the share, but would have lost his $100 investment had he bought the options. If the shares rise in value to $120, the investor would have made $20 had he chosen the share, and would not have made any profits had he purchased the options. In the latter case, he would have spent $100 to acquire the right to purchase $1,200 worth of shares for $1,100. Finally, if the shares rise to $200, he would have made $100 had he purchased the share and $800 had he bought the options. Options therefore magnify risks and returns, by comparison with shares.

Bratton, The Economics and Jurisprudence of Convertible Bonds
1984 Wisc. L. Rev. 667, 673-76

The issuer incorporating a conversion privilege into its bonds grants a future claim on its equity. For investors, this future claim gives convertible bonds the advantage of combining desirable features of straight bonds, such as fixed income payments and principal repayment, with the upside potential of common stock. In exchange for the future equity claim, bondholders customarily accept a coupon rate lower than that of an equivalent straight bond, less restrictive business covenants, and subordinated status. To issuers, these concessions give convertibles advantages over straight debt, such as cost savings, increased future capacity to incur senior debt, and great flexibility to advance the interests of the common stockholders. The value of the conversion privilege stems from these mutual perceptions of advantage.

The following Figure illustrates the upside and downside interrelations of the three constituent elements of value—debt value, conversion value and conversion premium—for a typical convertible bond at various possible values of the issuing corporation.[23]

Debt value[24] is the value of an equivalent straight bond with the same coupon rate. It is sensitive to the variables dominant in straight bond valuation, such as interest rate levels and the issuer's equity cushion. *Conversion value* is the value of the amount of common stock into which the bond can be converted. It depends on the market value of the underlying common stock and the price, the "conversion price," at which the bonds, taken at their face value, are convertible.[25] If the conversion price is a constant, conver-

---

23   Theoretical option valuation models have been applied to convertible bonds. Only the nature of the variables identified in this body of scholarship need be noted for purposes of this article.

    The seminal, theoretical article is Black & Scholes, *The Pricing of Options and Corporate Liabilities*, 81 J. Pol. Econ. 637 (1973), which sets forth an equilibrium pricing model for put and call options grounded in stochastic calculus. See also Cox, Ross & Rubinstein, *Option Pricing: A Simplified Approach*, 7 J. Fin. Econ. 229, 229-30 (1979); Smith, *Option Pricing*, 3 J. Fin. Econ. 3 (1976). ...

24   The term "debt value" is unique to this Article and is employed for reasons of clarity. "Bond value" is the customary term.

25   Commonly set 10 to 20% above the market price of the underlying common stock at the time of issue, conversion price may remain constant for the life of the conversion privilege ... or be stepped up at stated intervals.

    The "conversion ratio" expresses the number of shares of common stock the bondholder receives upon conversion:

(The footnote is continued on the next page.)

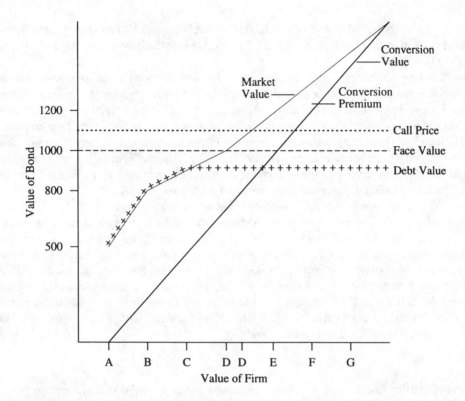

sion value is subject to the same determinants as the stock price, and goes up and down in lockstep with it. Although arbitrage possibilities prevent the bond from selling below the lower of debt or conversion value, nothing prevents it from selling above the higher of these two values. *Comversion premium* is the amount by which market value exceeds debt or conversion value. If we characterize the conversion privilege as a long term option[28] on the underlying common, the premium represents the option's value.

Assume that the bond illustrated in the Figure is priced, issued and sold for its $1000 face value with a conversion price of $50. Assume further that at the time of the bond's issue the issuer's stock is trading at $40 and the issuer's value is at D. Debt value at issue is $900, reflecting the convertible's lower coupon rate. Conversion value is $800, reflecting that the $50 conversion price exceeds the $40 market price of the underlying common. The premium at issue is $100, the difference between the higher of

---

25   Continued ...

$$\text{Conversion Ratio} = \frac{\text{Face Value}}{\text{Conversion Price}}$$

For example, a bond with a face value of $1000 and a conversion price of $50 has a conversion ratio of 20. See generally J. Van Horne, Financial Management and Policy 594 (4th ed. 1977). ...

28   Otherwise known as a "warrant." ... [A] warrant can be conceived of as a long term option on the common stock of a corporation granted for consideration by the corporation itself.

debt or conversion value and the initial $1000 market price. Valuation at issue reflects the expectation that the issuer's value will increase substantially during the early years of the bond's term.

Looking to the right of D in the Figure, we see the bond's conversion value and market value rising in tandem with higher issuer values, illustrating the convertible bond's upside potential. Debt value, in contrast, is limited by a fixed coupon rate and does not rise significantly. As issuer values increase, the market behavior of the convertible increasingly mirrors the market behavior of the underlying common stock and the premium accordingly becomes progressively smaller. Eventually, at G, the issuer's value and the dividend payout on the underlying common exceeds the expected return on the bonds. As a result, the premium disappears and the holders convert.

We see the bond's downside market behavior by looking to the left of D. Conversion value declines in tandem with the issuer's value and the premium disappears as the decline in value becomes extreme. Debt value, protected by the bond contract, shows more stability and resilience. At B, the bond's market value has fallen so far as to have become nearly contiguous with debt value; this is the "bond floor." As the issuer's value goes into extreme decline to the left of B, even the bond floor begins seriously to give away. With the issuer's value at A, we reach the end of the line—a hypothetical bankruptcy liquidation pursuant to which the holders of the convertible issue receive $500 per bond and the stockholders receive nothing.

Anti-Dilution Provisions. The value of a conversion privilege is based on the probability of the conversion price exceeding the market price of the share during the term of the option. Should the market price remain permanently below the conversion price because of the firm's business losses or a generalized market decline, the privilege will be worthless, and the purchaser must be taken to have accepted this risk. However, he will not have accepted the risk of a decline in the market price through a reorganization of outstanding shares such as occurs in a stock split. For example, shareholders may be called upon to exchange one old share with a market value of $100 for two new shares, with a market value of about $50 each. To preserve the exchange ratio, "anti-dilution" clauses in trust indentures will usually reduce the conversion price from $110 to $55.

Which other corporate transactions deserve anti-dilution protection may be a matter of some controversy. Conversion rights are protected in the case of an amalgamation, with the privilege extended to an equivalent number of shares in the new company. Stock dividends involve an issue of new shares to existing shareholders on a *pro rata* basis and, like stock splits, normally trigger an adjustment in conversion price.

These anti-dilution clauses are designed to treat the convertible holder as though he were a shareholder and protect his pro-rata position. But a problem is created when additional shares of common are issued for consideration which may be more or less than the conversion formula price. Ordinarily the existing common shareholder acquires no special rights when additional shares are issued for cash and modern corporate charters even permit waiver of pre-emptive rights in this situation. It has long been the practice, however, to protect the convertible holder against issuance of additional common shares at below the conversion price and to require some adjustment in the formula to take cognizance of it. Several approaches have evolved:

1. Adjust the conversion price to the lower price received for the common shares. This is a kind of "most favored nations clause" and is very beneficial to the convertible holder. It is little used today except in private placements where the investor can require this special type of protection.

2. Adjust the conversion price to the weighted average of the price of any securities sold below the conversion price and the conversion price then in effect. Identified as the "traditional" type of clause, it is in most common use. It does not provide for any adjustment upwards for sales above the conversion price. The formula is as follows:

$$\frac{\text{Number of shares previously outstanding times conversion price}}{\text{Plus consideration for additional shares}}$$
$$\frac{}{\text{Divided by}}$$
$$\text{Number of shares outstanding after original issue}$$

3. A third approach uses the above adjustment formula, but does not apply when the new shares are sold to other than the present shareholders. Called the "market" type of clause, it protects only against the shareholders issuing to themselves shares at lower than the conversion price for whatever reasons. This clause is said to give more flexibility to the company in its financing and to recognize that markets fluctuate and the holder of the convertible is entitled to no protection because his purchase occurred at a higher price than the company at a later date is able to get for its stock in the market.

There has been a good deal of discussion in the Journals on this subject[15] and some more knowledgeable investors, particularly among institutions, have been known to read the long and complicated text of these provisions, but one cannot see any market difference in the pricing of issues because of different provisions. [Katzin, *Financial and Legal Problems in the Use of Convertible Securities*, 24 Bus. Law. 359, 365-66 (1969)]

In addition to adjusting the conversion price, indentures may provide at least two other ways to prevent dilution.

1. Prohibit the Company from taking any acts that would cause dilution. Provisions of this type are rarely used, since they unduly restrict the Company such as making it impossible under certain circumstances for the Company to raise additional equity capital if needed.

2. Require the company to give advance notice to holders of convertible debentures of the taking of any acts that may cause dilution. This permits the holders to convert their debentures and as shareholders to receive the benefits of the proposed action. It does not protect the holder who does not wish to convert his debenture, especially when the market value of the common stock is substantially below the conversion price. [*Commentaries on Model Debenture Indenture Provisions* (American Bar Federation 1971)]

---

15 See Kaplan, Piercing the Corporate Boilerplate: Anti-Dilution Clauses in Convertible Securities, 33 Univ. Chicago Law Rev. 1 (1966); Ratner, Dilution and Anti-Dilution: A Reply to Professor Kaplan, 33 Univ. Chicago Law Rev. 494 (1966); Irvine, Some Comments Regarding "Anti-Dilution" Provisions Applicable to Convertible Securities, The Business Lawyer, July, 1958, P. 729.

Where the trust deed does not feature a call provision giving the issuer an option to redeem bonds, management may wish to propose a triggering transaction to force their conversion. This will be especially desired when bondholders do not wish to convert, even though shares are trading above the conversion price, because the corporation is not paying dividends. They will then delay conversion until just before the expiry date, so that they may receive interest in the interim. With a large number of convertible bonds overhanging, equity securities will be difficult to value and this will make a new issue of shares more costly. Management may then seek to induce conversion by providing bondholders with a notice of either a transaction to dilute the value of the convertible bonds or of a dividend payment on the shares. See Bierman, *Convertible Bonds as Investments*, 36 Fin. An. J. 59 (1980).

Implied Terms and Fiduciary Obligations. To say that the rights of bondholders depend essentially upon their contract with the issuer does not imply that the trust deed must be read literally, with no room for implied contractual terms. In a hypothetical contract, the parties might want some room for judicial manoeuvring through the application of implied terms of good faith or fiduciary responsibility. On this analysis, it is not helpful to think of good faith norms as resting upon abstract fiduciary duties, in the sense of obligations imposed without respect to the background contract.

Pittsburgh Terminal Corp. v. Baltimore and Ohio R.R.
United States Court of Appeals, Third Circuit
680 F.2d 933 (1982)

GIBBONS J.: Pittsburgh Terminal Corporation, Monroe Guttmann, Loretta Guttmann, Evelyn Bittner and Janet Rees (the Bondholders), holders, prior to December 13, 1977, of convertible debentures issued by The Baltimore and Ohio Railroad Company (B & O), appeal from a final judgment dismissing their complaint, which charged that a dividend by the B & O on that date of stock of Mid-Allegheny Corporation (MAC) to B & O stockholders of record on that date violated the federal securities laws and the laws of several states. The defendants are B & O, a Maryland corporation, The Chesapeake & Ohio Railway Company (C & O), a Virginia corporation which on December 13, 1977, owned more than 99% of B & O's common stock, Chessie System, Inc. (Chessie), a Virginia corporation which is a holding company for C & O and its subsidiaries, and fourteen present or former directors of B & O. The convertible debentures owned by the Bondholders are B & O Series A, dated January 1, 1956 and maturing January 1, 2010, paying interest at 4.5%, and convertible at any time before maturity into 10 shares of B & O common stock for each $1000 of face value. The action of which the Bondholders complain is the action of the defendants in fixing December 13, 1977, as both the date of declaration of, and the record date for participation in, the in kind dividend of MAC stock to B & O common stockholders. The action deprived debenture holders of the opportunity to convert before the record date and thereby participate in the dividend. The District Court held that it violated no legally protected rights of the debenture holders. We reverse.

I

B & O owns and operates a railroad regulated by the Interstate Commerce Commission (ICC). Prior to the transactions giving rise to this lawsuit, B & O also owned substantial non-rail assets such as real estate, timber and mineral reserves. At one time both its common stock and its debentures were traded on the New York Stock Exchange (NYSE). When C & O acquired 99.63% of B & O's common stock, trading in that security ceased and it was delisted, although 13 individuals still held some shares. The NYSE listing of B & O's convertible debentures continued. No dividends were paid on the B & O common stock after 1961. Thus the holders of convertible debentures had no particular incentive to exercise the conversion privilege unless the no dividend policy were to change.

Because the regulations of the ICC prohibited a railroad corporation from engaging in non-rail business, B & O's and C & O's assets not used in rail transportation remained undeveloped. Beginning in 1973 when Chessie was formed, C & O began segregating its non-rail assets in a separate corporation, Chessie Resources, Inc., so that they could be developed free of constraints imposed by the ICC. The Chessie management desired to accomplish the same result with respect to B & O's non-rail assets. To that end, in January of 1977, the Chessie Corporation Restructuring Committee settled on a plan whereby the B & O would transfer those assets to MAC, a wholly owned B & O subsidiary, and then distribute the MAC stock as a dividend to B & O's fourteen common stockholders.

If, prior to the dividend in MAC stock, the number of B & O common stockholders were to increase substantially, B & O might have had to file a registration statement for MAC with the Securities and Exchange Commission (SEC). 15 U.S.C. § 77f (1976). There were practical difficulties with the preparation of a registration statement, especially that of placing a value on B & O's non-rail assets. But if notice of the MAC transaction had been given to the convertible debenture holders prior to the record date of the in kind dividend, many of them might have elected to convert. Thus the Restructuring Committee concluded that the MAC transaction should be structured in such a way that the convertible debenture holders would not have such notice until after the record date. This, it was thought, would permit counsel for B & O to obtain from the SEC a no-action letter with respect to registration of the MAC stock.

At the time the MAC transaction was under consideration, B & O had outstanding bond obligations under three trust indentures. One of these, a Convertible Income Bond Debenture, contained a provision requiring B & O to pay into a surplus income sinking fund an amount equal to any dividend. A second, the Refunding and General Mortgage Indenture, required that arrearages in the sinking funds had to be made up before a dividend could be paid. It was these provisions which had prevented B & O from paying dividends since 1961. The third Indenture was that governing the convertible debentures held by the Bondholders. In order to facilitate the dividend in MAC stock, B & O called for redemption the Convertible Income Bonds, and discharged the sinking fund arrearages on the Refunding and General Mortgage Indenture by paying the sinking funds approximately $7,000,000. These steps were accomplished by the summer of 1977. The Restructuring Committee then turned to the Indenture for the convertible debentures.

The convertible debentures also contained a redemption feature which in 1977 called for payment of a premium of 2.5% of their face amount. B & O did not elect to redeem. Conversion privilege features of the indenture oblige B & O to reserve sufficient common stock and to adjust for changes in par value. Conversion rights to the bondholders are protected in the event of merger or sale. Article V, section 12 of the Indenture provides:

Section 12. The Company covenants and agrees that it will not declare and/or pay any dividend on its common stock payable in stock or create any rights to subscribe for stock or securities convertible into stock unless in any such case notice of the taking of a record date for the determination of the stockholders entitled to receive such dividend, distribution or right is given at least ten days prior thereto by at least one publication in an Authorized Newspaper. A copy of each such published notice shall promptly after such publication be filed with the Trustee.

When the convertible debentures were issued in 1956, B & O entered into a listing agreement with the NYSE relating to them, which incorporated by reference B & O's earlier listing agreements. Listing Agreement A-12653 for an earlier bond issue, incorporated by reference in that for the 1956 convertible debenture issue, provides:

4. The Corporation will give the Exchange at least ten days' notice in advance of the closing of the transfer books, or of the taking of a record of its stockholders for any purpose.

5. The Corporation will publish promptly to the holders of any of its securities listed on the Exchange any action taken by the Corporation with respect to dividends or to the allotment of rights to subscribe or to any rights or benefits pertaining to the ownership of its securities listed on the Exchange; and shall give prompt notice to the Exchange of any such action; and shall afford the holders of its securities listed on the Exchange a proper period within which to record their interests and to exercise their rights; and shall issue all such rights in form approved by the Exchange and will make the same transferable, payable and deliverable in the Borough of Manhattan, in the City of New York.

In addition to the Listing Agreements, the B & O is bound by the Rules of the NYSE. Section A-2 of its Manual, "Timely Disclosure," provides:

A corporation whose securities are listed on the New York Stock Exchange Inc., is expected to release to the public any news or information which might reasonably be expected to materially affect the market for those securities. This is one of the most important and fundamental purposes of the listing agreement which each corporation enters into with the exchange.

509 F.Supp. at 1008.

In November of 1977, by which time impediments to the payment of dividends on B & O stock in the Convertible Income Bond Debenture and the Refunding and General Mortgage Indenture had been removed, plaintiff Monroe Guttmann wrote to the Secretary of B & O:

As one of the very few public owners of B & O common stock, we are concerned that we may not be made aware of any dividend the directors declare on the common stock in sufficient time to convert any of our convertible debentures.

Although it may not be customary to do so in view of the fact that declaration of a dividend may not be widely publicized, if publicized at all, we ask that you notify us promptly of any such dividend declaration so that we will have an opportunity to convert debentures in time to receive such dividend if we choose to do so.

Will you please let me know what provisions there are in the bylaws of the company that govern the time which must elapse between the declaration of a dividend, the record date and the payable date.

To this pointed inquiry the Secretary, on November 17, 1977, replied:

Thank you for your letter of November 11. We appreciate your concern as a holder of B & O Convertible Debentures as to whether B & O would fail to disclose the declaration of a dividend in its common stock.

You may be assured that if B & O should have any information to announce regarding dividend action on B & O stock, such information will be disseminated promptly to the public at large. Because we cannot prefer you over the public at large advance advice cannot be sent to you, but I will make sure that you get a copy of such press release. We are not in a position to help you with respect to your decision whether or not to convert.

There is no by-law provision relating to the timing of the declaration, record, and payment dates.

By the time of Guttmann's inquiry and the Secretary's reply, the Restructuring Committee's plan to structure the MAC transaction so as to avoid timely notice to the convertible bondholders was well advanced.

Four in-house attorneys employed by B & O or C & O, one of whom was Chairman of the Restructuring Committee, examined the 1956 indenture and the New York Stock Exchange listing agreements. They concluded that the indenture required notice of stock dividends in B & O stock, but not of distributions of stock of subsidiaries. They concluded that that provision in the New York Stock Exchange listing agreement was inapplicable because it requires 10 days notice only with regard to dividends declared on listed stocks, and B & O common stock had been delisted. They concluded that under Maryland law, absent any action by the directors, the payment date of a dividend could be the same as the declaration date. The Restructuring Committee determined, before, to avoid giving notice to the convertible debenture holders. Their purpose in doing so was to prevent conversions which might require filing a registration statement for MAC stock.

The General Counsel of B & O retained the law firm of Hunton & Williams of Richmond, Virginia, to submit to the SEC a request for a no-action letter with respect to B & O's distribution of MAC shares. Prior to the time Hunton & Williams wrote to the SEC, the B & O Board of Directors met and adopted two resolutions. In the first resolution the Board authorized B & O's officers to convey a list of non-rail assets to MAC as a contribution to its capital. In the second, the Board resolved to distribute the MAC stock as a dividend to B & O shareholders. That resolution provides in part:

RESOLVED, that the dividend on the Common Stock as specified in the next preceding resolution be payable on this date to shareholders of record at the close of business on this date; provided, however, that such payment shall be made by depositing such stock of Mid Allegheny Corporation with Mercantile Safe Deposit and Trust Company of Baltimore, Maryland, in trust, to be delivered to such shareholders of this Company on the earlier of the following dates, viz.: two days following the receipt of a letter from the Securities and Exchange Commission that it will take no action if the stock of Mid Allegheny Corporation is distributed to this Company's shareholders without registration under the provisions of the Securities Act of 1933; or two days following the date of an effective registration statement with respect to the stock of Mid Allegheny Corporation.

Thus actual delivery of the MAC stock certificates to shareholders was made contingent upon the obtaining of a no-action letter or the filing of a registration statement. It seems clear from the wording of the resolution that B & O intended to file a registration statement if it could not obtain a no-action letter, for the dividend declaration is unconditional.

Three days after B & O's dividend action, Hunton & Williams sent a request for a no-action letter to the SEC. That firm's December 16 letter to the Commission requested a no-action letter only with respect to a distribution of MAC stock to C & O and 13 individual B & O stockholders. It made no mention of the rights of convertible debenture holders. In its request Hunton & Williams opined that the distribution of MAC shares by B & O was not a sale within the meaning of section 2(3) of the Securities Act of 1933, 15 U.S.C. § 77b(3). Alternatively the firm suggested that if a sale were involved, the transaction was exempt under 17 C.F.R. § 230.240 (1981). That SEC rule, issued pursuant to section 3(b), 15 U.S.C. § 77c(b), exempts from registration certain securities of an issuer to fewer than 100 persons, provided that restrictions on transferability are legended on the certificates. The no-action letter was not immediately forthcoming from the SEC, and on January 18, 1978, Hunton & Williams withdrew its reliance on 17 C.F.R. § 230.240. Another written request was filed on June 29, 1979, relying solely on the contention that the dividend in MAC stock was not a sale. In September of 1979, long after the commencement of this lawsuit, the SEC issued a no-action letter "provided that MAC shares distributed to persons other than C & O are restricted as to transfer." The SEC letter noted that the District Court had by then entered an order that the defendants must hold at least 940 shares of MAC for tender to the convertible debenture holders if they prevailed.

II

The first of these consolidated actions was commenced by Pittsburgh Terminal Corporation on December 28, 1977, and the others soon followed. On March 7, 1978 the District Court issued a preliminary injunction restraining the defendants from proceeding with the dividend in MAC stock. Defendants appealed from that order, and when they agreed to hold sufficient shares of B & O and MAC stock to satisfy the claims of the convertible debenture holders, should they prevail, this court reversed that injunction. The Bondholders sought class action certification, which was denied as a result of an agreement between C & O and the Trustee under the 1956 indenture that should plaintiffs prevail, all debenture holders similarly situated will be accorded the treatment required by any judgment in plaintiffs' favor. Motions for summary judgment in favor of the defendants were denied. Thus the consolidated cases went to trial on amended complaints challenging the December 13, 1977 actions of the B & O Board of Directors. The complaints alleged that those actions violated section 10(b) of the Securities and Exchange Act, 15 U.S.C. § 78j(b), the contractual rights of the convertible debenture holders under the provisions of the Indenture, their rights as third party beneficiaries of the NYSE listing agreements, the obligations of B & O under the rules of the NYSE, and the fiduciary duties of directors and of majority stockholders under Maryland law. The District Court, over defendants' objection, held that the convertible debenture holders had standing to make these claims, but rejected each of them. The court held that there was an insufficient showing of scienter for a section 10(b) violation; that section 6 of the Securities and Exchange Act of 1934, 15 U.S.C. § 78f, does not permit private enforcement of the NYSE rules; that the listing agreements confer no rights on any party other than the NYSE; that the indenture does not require notice of a dividend in a stock of a subsidiary; and that the December 13, 1977 MAC transactions were entirely legal under Maryland law. Without ruling definitively, the court also expressed doubts about what relief would be proper assuming liability had been established.

* * *

Duty to Speak

The Bondholders contend that by fixing the dividend date and the record date of the MAC dividend so as to prevent them from exercising their conversion option in time to participate in that dividend, the defendants violated section 10(b) and SEC Rule 10b-5(a) and (c), 17 C.F.R. 240.10b-5(a) and (c) (1981). It is undisputed that the defendants made a knowing decision to time the December 13, 1977 transactions so as to prevent the Bondholders from obtaining timely notice of them. Defendants contend that the decision was lawful because they made no affirmative misrepresentation and because they were under no affirmative obligation to speak.

In *Chiarella v. United States*, 445 U.S. 222, 228, 100 S.Ct. 1108, 1114, 63 L.Ed.2d 348 (1980), the Court observed that "one who fails to disclose material information prior to the consummation of a transaction commits fraud only when he is under a duty to do so." It held that a printer, who had no fiduciary obligation to a corporation or its shareholders, and who did not receive information as a result of the breach of any fiduciary relationship, could not be liable for a criminal violation of section 10(b). "He was not [the sellers'] agent, he was not a fiduciary, he was not a person in whom the sellers had placed their trust and confidence." 445 U.S. at 232, 100 S.Ct. at 1116. The defendants contend that *Chiarella* requires an affirmance, because like the printer who happened upon material market information, none of them had a duty to speak.

To put that contention in context, we note that the Bondholders were on December 13, 1977, holders of options to acquire B & O equity securities, while C & O was a majority holder of those securities having voting control of B & O. The convertible debentures were listed on the NYSE, and the listing agreement applicable to them imposed on B & O the affirmative duties (a) to give ten days notice to the Exchange of a record date for a dividend, and (b) to "afford the holders of its securities listed on the Exchange a proper period within which to record their interests and exercise their rights." These requirements of the listing agreement parallel those in SEC Rule 10b-17, which provides:

(a) It shall constitute a "manipulative or deceptive device or contrivance" as used in section 10(b) of the Act for any issuer of a class of securities ... to fail to give notice in accordance with paragraph (b) of this section of the following actions relating to such class of securities:

(1) A dividend or other distribution in cash or in kind, except an ordinary interest payment on a debt security, but including a dividend or distribution of any security of the same or another issuer; ...

17 C.F.R. § 240.10b-17 (1981). B & O is the issuer of the convertible debentures, the MAC distribution is a dividend of a security, and that dividend related to the convertible debentures since it was material to a decision about exercising the conversion option. The convertible debentures were not simple debt securities, for which the information about dividends ordinarily would not be material.

Whatever may be the fiduciary duty of majority stockholders and corporate directors under Maryland law to general unsecured creditors, we are here dealing with securities having an equity option feature. Maryland follows the settled rule that a control stockholder owes a fiduciary obligation not to exercise that control to the disadvantage of minority equity participants. ... Similarly, Maryland directors must act as fiduciaries to all equity participants. ... Although no Maryland case has been called to our attention presenting the precise issue of fiduciary obligations to holders of securities containing stock options, we would be very much surprised if Maryland or any other state would today hold that no such obligations were owed by an issuer of such securities and its directors. Moreover the scope of the obligation of the fiduciary depends upon the nature of the interest of the beneficiary. If the beneficiary of a fiduciary duty needs information in order intelligently to protect that interest, the withholding of it, especially when withholding it confers advantage upon others (in this case C & O and Chessie), is an obvious breach of duty.

The 1956 Indenture under which B & O borrowed the sums evidenced by the convertible debentures was made in New York and the loan transaction completed there. B & O's obligation, therefore, is a New York contract. The law of that state is "that in every contract there is an implied covenant that neither party shall do anything which will have the effect of destroying or injuring the right of the other party to receive the fruits of the contract. ..." *Kirke La Shelle Co. v. Paul Armstrong Co.*, 263 N.Y. 79, 87, 188 N.E. 163, 167 (1933). *See Van Gemert v. Boeing Co.*, 553 F.2d 812, 815 (2d Cir. 1977); Restatement (Second) of Contracts § 205 (1981). Defendants in this case took steps to prevent the Bondholders from receiving information which they needed in order to receive the fruits of their conversion option should they choose to exercise it. As a matter of New York contract law, B & O had a duty to speak.

In the present context we do not look to the listing agreement, Rule 10b-17, the Maryland law of fiduciary obligations, and the New York law of contracts, as sources of independent causes of action, though they well may be. Rather we look to them as sources of a duty to speak, breach of which under section 10(b) and Rule 10b-5(a) and (c) gives rise to a cause of action for fraud. Those four independent sources of duty to speak in the circumstances of this case amply serve, separately or collectively, to distinguish it from *Chiarella v. United States*, supra. We need not consider other sources of such duty relied on by the Bondholders.

Scienter

The defendants urge that even if they were under a duty to speak, their decision not to do so in this instance did not involve the scienter required by the Supreme Court's interpretation of section 10(b). The District Court, relying on *Ernst & Ernst v. Hochfelder*, 425 U.S. 185, 96 S.Ct. 1375, 47 L.Ed.2d 668 (1976), accepted this argument. It found that there was a legitimate business purpose in removing the non-rail assets from ownership and control of B & O. That finding is not relevant, however, for what is complained of is not the formation of MAC or the decision to spin it off, but the decision to do both while concealing those steps from the Bondholders until it was too late for them to participate by exercising conversion rights if they chose to do so.

In this record, and indeed in the court's findings of fact, it is plain that the Restructuring Committee and B & O's Directors knew (1) that the information about the dividend in MAC shares, or information about any other dividend action after a lapse of sixteen years, was material to the Bondholders; (2) that cutting off conversion options would inure to the benefit of C & O, the majority stockholder; and (3) that the decision not to announce the dividend was intended to prevent timely exercise of the conversion privilege. The decision to time the MAC transaction so as to prevent notice to the Bondholders until too late was both knowing and intentional. No more is required by the governing cases. ...

The defendants insist that despite their intention to prevent timely exercise of conversion rights prior to the MAC dividend, they lacked the necessary scienter as a matter of law for two reasons. First, they contend, they had a valid business purpose in cutting off conversion rights in that they desired to avoid having to file a registration statement for MAC stock. This is a business reason, certainly, but not a valid one. Of course, the removal of non-rail assets from the reach of the conversion privilege, and the avoidance of the expense of preparing and filing a registration statement, was good business for some of the interested parties. Clearly, however, it was bad business for the Bondholders. Any manipulative act or practice can be justified by focusing only on the business purpose of the side of the transaction which benefited from it.

● ● ●

On the facts as found, therefore, the District Court erred in ruling that the defendants lacked the scienter required for a section 10(b) violation.

We hold, therefore, that on the facts found by the District Court, the December 13, 1977 transaction, designed to deprive the Bondholders of timely notice in order to exercise their conversion option if they should so desire was a manipulative or deceptive device or contrivance in violation of section 10(b).

IV

Our holding in Part III requires a reversal. The Bondholders also contend that they proved a breach of the Indenture, a claim as a third party beneficiary for breach of the listing agreement and breaches of fiduciary duty under Maryland law. In the District Court they pleaded, as well, a cause of action under section 6 of the Securities and Exchange Act of 1934, 15 U.S.C. § 78f, for violation of the NYSE rules. They do not suggest, however, that the relief available under section 10(b) is less extensive than would be available under these alternative legal theories. Since it appears that no different remedies would be available were we to decide in the Bondholders' favor on those alternative legal theories, there is no reason to address them.

• • •

[The judgment of Garth J., who concurred in the finding of liability based on a breach of Rule 10b-17, is omitted.]

ADAMS J. (dissenting): The Supreme Court recently has made clear that liability for nondisclosure of material information under the federal securities laws cannot be imposed absent a duty to speak. *Chiarella v. United States*, 445 U.S. 222, 235, 100 S.Ct. 1108, 1118, 63 L.Ed.2d 348 (1980). Aware of this precept, Judge Gibbons has pointed to no fewer than four possible sources from which to derive a duty, on the part of The Baltimore and Ohio Railroad, to notify its convertible debenture holders prior to the declaration of the MAC dividend. Judge Garth, concurring, has limited the duty analysis solely to the provisions of Rule 10b-17; the holding of the Court, therefore, rests on that narrow ground. Unlike my two colleagues, I conclude that B & O was under no legal obligation—pursuant to Rule 10b-17 or otherwise—to provide plaintiffs with advance notice of the MAC dividend. I therefore respectfully dissent.

I

Convertible debentures frequently are characterized as "hybrids," embodying the attributes of both debt and equity securities. *See, e.g., Broad v. Rockwell International Corp.*, 642 F.2d 929, 940 (5th Cir.) (en banc), cert. denied, 454 U.S. 965, 102 S.Ct. 506, 72 L.Ed.2d 380 (1981); American Bar Foundation, *Commentaries on Indentures* 523 (1971); Note, Hoff & Harff: *Does the Convertible Debenture Holder Have Standing to Maintain a Shareholder Derivative Action?*, 26 Syracuse L.Rev. 730, 751 (1975). As such, they have proven to be an attractive and effective means of corporate financing. Like most debt securities, convertible debentures provide a fixed rate of return and assure the investor priority, over common shareholders, in claims on the issuer's assets. Should the market price of the common stock rise, however, the debentureholder may exercise an option to convert the debt security into shares of common stock. "Thus there is the opportunity to benefit from a rise in stock prices from the comparative safety of a debt … position." Katzin, *Financial and Legal Problems in the Use of Convertible Securities*, 24 Bus. Law. 359, 361 (1969).

From the corporation's standpoint the issuance of convertible debentures can be similarly advantageous. Primarily, the convertible securities provide a way to raise new capital indirectly—by permitting management "to raise funds today at tomorrow's higher common stock prices." Fleischer & Cary, *The Taxation of Convertible Bonds and Stock*, 74 Harv.L.Rev. 473, 474 (1961) (quoting Pilcher, *Raising Capital with Convertible Securities*, 61, 138 (1955)). In addition,

the new funds will be contributing to income by the time the debentures are converted. In the interim, while the company is putting the new money effectively to work, the charge takes the form of interest—deductible for tax purposes—rather than a reduction in income per share. Thus the dilution of earnings which traditionally accompanies an equity issue in deferred until the firm is making more money.

Id. (footnote omitted). Finally, because the conversion feature is so attractive to investors, the issuer can often offer the debentures at an interest rate lower than that required on other debt securities. Katzin, supra, at 362. *But see* Klein, *The Convertible Bond: A Peculiar Package*, 123 U.Pa.L.Rev. 547, 558-59 (1975) (referring to this rationale as "flimflam").

Whatever financial advantages attach to the issuance or purchase of convertible debentures, the legal status of these hybrid securities remains inherently complex. As debt securities, the debentures impose a specific set of obligations on the corporation— namely, the regular payment of interest and the repayment of principal upon maturity. As equity securities, in contrast, the debentures may require a broader range of duties from the issuer. The difficulty lies not in the characterization of the debenture as *either* debt or equity—for it is both—but in determining, in each case, the extent to which the investor is owed rights and remedies beyond those commonly accorded debt holders.

The traditional view is that the convertible debenture holder is a mere creditor until conversion, whose relationship with the issuing corporation is governed by contract and statute. In an early Massachusetts decision, for example, the court rejected a convertible note holder's claim that he had an equitable interest in newly-issued shares of stock. *Pratt v. American Bell Telephone Co.*, 141 Mass. 225, 5 N.E. 307 (1886). The plaintiff was "in no sense a stockholder," declared the court; his "rights and interest as a stockholder of the corporation were postponed to the time when he made his option and demanded his stock. Pending this time, the contract gave him the right to payment of the coupons attached to the notes, and nothing more." 5 N.E. at 311.

Several years later, Justice Holmes expanded upon this principle, holding for the Supreme Court of Massachusetts that the debenture holder had no right, apart from contract, to object to corporate actions that dilute or destroy the value of the conversion option:

[the option] imposes no restriction upon the obligor in regard to the issue of new stock, although the issue may be upon such terms as to diminish the value of the right. It leaves the management of the company in accordance with its other interests unhampered. It is simply an option to take stock as it may turn out to be when the time for choice arrives. The bondholder does not become a stockholder, by his contract, in equity any more than at law. ...

... [T]he contract does not prevent the corporation from consolidating with another in such a way as to make performance impossible, any more than it prevents the issue of new stock in such a way as to make performance valueless.

Parkinson v. West End St. Ry. Co., 173 Mass. 446, 53 N.E. 891, 892 (1899). See also *Gay v. Burgess Mills*, 30 R.I. 231, 74 A. 714 (1909). And in *Lisman v. Milwaukee, L.S. & W. Ry. Co.*, 161 F. 472 (E.D. Wis. 1908), aff'd. 170 F. 1020 (7th Cir. 1909), the court held that convertible debenture holders could not complain when the railroad company in which they had invested merged with another railroad. The fact that the parties "were bound to" have anticipated such a consolidation when they entered into the option contract was dispositive.

The rights and remedies of convertible debenture holders have expanded since the turn of the century. Most notably, the Securities Exchange Act of 1934 accords convertible debenture holders the federal statutory rights of "equity security holders,"[2] able, for example, to employ section 10(b) of the Act to protect against fraud or manipulative devices. 15 U.S.C. § 78j. Congress's explicit recognition of convertibles as equity, as well as debt, securities has had significant consequences. In *Kusner v. First Pennsylvania Corp.*, 531 F.2d 1234 (3d Cir. 1976), for instance, this Court held that a convertible debenture holder, who alleged that he had purchased the securities in reliance on a false and misleading prospectus, had standing to sue under section 10(b). *Kusner* depicts the precise sort of situation in which a section 10(b) remedy is appropriate for debenture holders in their role as equity investors. As the Court explained, in such a case, the debenture holder's need for accurate information about the corporation was as pressing as any shareholder's:

If during the conversion period the value of the common stock (a function of its market price and dividend position) greatly exceeds the value of the fixed payment and interest obligation, a holder probably will exercise the conversion privilege. The possibility that the value of common stock will increase to a point where it exceeds the value of the bond is the sales feature with which the issuer obtained a lower-than-market interest rate on the bond. Thus ... a misrepresentation in the prospectus that would be material to a stock purchaser would be material to a convertible bond purchaser. The convertible bond purchaser may well have been defrauded of the interest differential.

531 F.2d at 1238 (footnote omitted).

The mere availability of a securities act remedy for fraud, however, does not answer the question whether the common law rule of *Parkinson* remains the applicable standard by which to judge whether or not a corporation has, indeed, acted fraudulently. That question was addressed and analyzed perceptively in a recent en banc Fifth Circuit decision, *Broad v. Rockwell International Corp.*, 642 F.2d 929 (5th Cir.), cert. denied, 454 U.S. 965, 102 S.Ct. 506, 72 L.Ed.2d 380 (1981). There, the plaintiff debenture holders complained that when the company in which they had invested was acquired by another entity in a cash merger, they lost their right to convert into common stock. The Court concluded that the plaintiffs had "received ... all to which they were contractually entitled under the Indenture" and that, as a result, no violation of section 10(b) could have occurred:

There is no doubt but that there was concerted, intentional conduct by the defendants to bring about [the] result [about which plaintiffs complain]. But as a matter of law, there was no violation of section 10(b) or Rule 10b-5 because there was no fraud. "Section 10(b) is aptly described as a catch-all provision, but what it catches must be fraud." *Chiarella v. United States*, 445 U.S. 222, 234-35 [100 S.Ct. 1108, 1117-1118, 63 L.Ed.2d 348], ... (1980) (criminal prosecution under section 10(b) and Rule 10b-5). It is elementary that section 10(b) and Rule 10b-5 reach only conduct involving manipulation or deception. *E.g., Santa Fe Industries, Inc. v. Green*, 430 U.S. 462 [97 S.Ct. 1292, 51 L.Ed.2d 480], ... (1977); *Ernst & Ernst v. Hochfelder*, 425 U.S. 185 [96 S.Ct.

---

2   The Act defines the term "equity security" broadly to include "any stock or similar security; or any security convertible, with or without consideration, into such a security. ..." 15 U.S.C. § 78c(11).

1375, 47 L.Ed.2d 668], ... (1976). The defendants' conduct involved neither; they merely carried out their contractual obligations. As a conceptual matter, they could not have fraudulently schemed to deprive the holders of Debentures of a right that those holders did not in fact have.

642 F.2d at 963.

Virtually every modern commentator appears to agree with the *Broad* court that convertible debenture holders have no cause to complain about legal corporate conduct that adversely affects the value of the conversion option unless such conduct has been explicitly proscribed or otherwise addressed in the debenture indenture. As explained by the American Bar Foundation:

> Inasmuch as ownership of a convertible debenture does not give the holder the rights of a share-holder, the holder of a convertible debenture would have almost no protection against acts by the Company which would adversely affect the value of the common stock issuable on conversion, such as split-up of shares, stock dividends, distribution of assets, issuance or sale of other convertible securities, issuance of options, issuance or sale of common stock at prices below the current conversion or market price, merger, sale of assets, or dissolution and liquidation of the Company. Events of this type are customarily described as "diluting" the value of the conversion privilege, *and if protection is desired against such dilution, appropriate provisions must be included in the indenture.*

Commentaries, supra, at 527 (emphasis added) (footnote omitted). See also *Broad v. Rockwell International Corp.*, supra at 943; *Kessler v. General Cable Corp.*, 92 Cal. App.3d 531, 155 Cal. Rptr. 94, 99-100 (1979); 6A W. *Fletcher Cyclopedia of the Law of Private Corporations* §§ 2694-2694.1 (perm. ed. 1981). Such so-called "anti-dilution clauses" are thus among the most important of the various contract provisions that can be negotiated between the issuing corporation and the debenture holders or their representatives.[4] Commonly, they require the corporation to give the debenture holder advance notice of specific acts that may erode or destroy the conversion option, so that the investor can convert, if he so chooses, prior to the act in question. Alternatively, the anti-dilution clause can provide for the adjustment of the conversion price to reflect the change in value. See Irvine, *Some Comments Regarding "Anti-Dilution" Provisions Applicable to Convertible Securities*, 13 Bus.Law 729 (1958). Less frequently, the anti-dilution provision is drafted to prohibit the corporation from taking certain actions that may cause diminution in the value of the conversion option. See Commentaries, supra, at 527-28.

---

4 See Hills, *Convertible Securities—Legal Aspects and Draftsmanship*, 19 Calif.L.Rev. 1, 1-2 (1930) ("Poor draftsmanship and a disregard of possible corporate changes, rather than a general misunderstanding of the conversion privilege, may be set down as the principal causes of litigation on this subject. The decisions resulting from such litigation have acted as danger signals, attorneys have become more careful and litigation has been reduced to a minimum"); Kaplan, *Piercing the Corporate Boilerplate: Anti-Dilution Clauses in Convertible Securities*, 33 U.Chi. L.Rev. 1, 29 (1965) ("The anti-dilution clause is an integral and necessary part of any convertible security. The clause is a complex, difficult and intriguing exercise in corporate draftsmanship. It requires the draftsman to protect against the whole gamut of potential corporate rearrangement or manipulation which might adversely affect the rights of the holders of the convertible securities. So intricate and precise an instrument should be prepared with the greatest care and diligence.").

The conduct at issue in the present case—namely, the transfer of B & O's non-rail assets to MAC and the distribution of the MAC stock to B & O's common shareholders—is clearly of the sort that could have been addressed by the inclusion of an appropriate anti-dilution provision within the indenture. Such a provision could have taken any number of forms. In its Commentaries on the Model Debenture Indenture provisions, for instance, the American Bar Foundation noted that "[w]hen individuals are declared and paid other than in shares of common stock or as normal cash dividends," the debenture holder's conversion rights can be protected against dilution "by providing for a reduction of the conversion price to reflect the diminution of the corporate assets resulting from such dividends." Commentaries, supra, at 529. Moreover, the Bar Foundation continued, "[i]t is sometimes provided that, upon exercise of his conversion rights, the debentureholder shall receive, in addition to the shares to which he is entitled, the amount of assets (or a sum equal to the value thereof) which would have been distributed to him if he had exercised his right to convert immediately prior to the record date for such distribution." Id.[5] And at least one commentator has suggested that it is advisable to insert in the indenture a provision giving holders of convertible securities adequate notice in the event that "the Company shall propose ... to pay any dividend payable in stock of any class to the holders of its Common Stock *or to make any other distribution to the holders of its Common Stock (other than a cash dividend payable out of earnings or earned surplus legally available for the payment of dividends ...)*." Kaplan, supra note 4, at 13 n. 24 (emphasis added). Such a notice provision would clearly encompass the kind of arrangement against which Pittsburgh Terminal has complained in the case at bar.

Significantly, although the commentators have been careful to consider the situation in which a corporation distributes its assets in forms other than ordinary cash or stock dividends, the indenture at issue here contains no such provision. While the indenture

---

5   The model indenture discussed in the Commentaries includes at least two provisions that address this point. One stipulates, for example, that:

> In the event that the Company shall make *any distribution of its assets* upon or with respect to its Common Stock, as a liquidating or partial liquidating dividend, *or other than as a dividend payable out of earnings or any surplus legally available for dividends* under the laws of the state of incorporation of the Company, each Holder of any Debenture then Outstanding shall, upon the exercise of his right to convert after the record date for such distribution, receive, in addition to the shares subscribed for, the amount of such assets (or, at the option of the Company, a sum equal to the value thereof at the time of distribution as determined by the Board of Directors in its sole discretion) which would have been distributed to such Holder if he had exercised his right to convert immediately prior to the record date for such distribution, or, in the absence of a record date, immediately prior to the date of such distribution. [Commentaries, supra, at 547 (emphasis added) (footnote omitted).]

An alternate provision, addressing the situation in which the corporation distributes to its shareholders "evidence of its indebtedness or assets" excluding dividends paid out of earned surplus, declares that "in each such case the Conversion Price shall be adjusted" to compensate for the distribution of the corporation's assets to its shareholders. *Id.* at 553.

does address a variety of potentially diluting acts—including a change in the par value of the outstanding common stock; a change of outstanding common stock from par to no par; and a possible consolidation, merger, or sale of the company—we have been directed to no provision in the indenture here that addresses the situation in which the company spins off a portion of its assets to a subsidiary and distributes those assets, in the form of a stock dividend, to its common shareholders. Plaintiffs are able to point to only one section in the indenture that is even arguably apposite. That provision, entitled "Notice to be Given of Record Date for Stock Dividend, etc.," provides that:

The Company covenants and agrees that it will not declare and/or pay any dividend on its common stock *payable in stock* or create any rights to subscribe for stock or securities convertible into stock unless in any such case notice of the taking of a record date for the determination of the stockholders entitled to receive such dividend, distribution or right is given at least ten days prior thereto by at least one publication in an Authorized Newspaper.

Indenture Article 5, Section 12 (appendix at 357a) (emphasis added).

Plaintiffs assert that the term "stock dividend" in the table of contents, as well as the words "payable in stock," which are found in the body of the provision, suggest that the clause is "in no way limited to the common stock of the B & O," but, rather, applies to distributions of MAC stock as well. Brief of Appellant at 34. Plaintiffs also contend that, even assuming the phrase "payable in stock" refers only to B & O common stock, the provision violates the New York requirement of fair dealing. I find neither of these two arguments convincing.

It is a well-established principle of New York corporate law that a "stock dividend" is "any dividend payable in stock *of the corporation declaring or authorizing such dividend*." ... The declaration of such a dividend generally is conceived of as a capitalization of surplus, which neither depletes the assets of the corporation nor increases the holdings of the stockholder. See *Gibbons v. Mahon*, 136 U.S. 549, 559-60, 10 S.Ct. 1057, 1058-1059, 34 L.Ed. 525 (1890); *Equitable Trust Co. v. Prentice*, 250 N.Y. 1, 164 N.E. 723, 725 (1928) (Cardozo C.J.) ("When a dividend is paid in cash, the ownership of the corporate assets is changed; the company owns less, and the shareholder owns more, or something essentially different, though its value be no greater. Upon the distribution of a stock dividend, ownership of the assets is precisely as it was. 'A stock dividend does not distribute property, but simply dilutes the shares as they existed before.' "). Thus stock dividends traditionally have been distinguished "from [dividends] payable in the stock of a subsidiary" or another independent corporation. *Id.*; see also *Kellogg v. Kellogg*, 166 Misc. 791, 4 N.Y.S.2d 219, 221, aff'd., 254 App.Div. 812, 5 N.Y.S.2d 506 (1938). The latter sort of dividend—stock in subsidiaries or other corporations—is considered the equivalent of a cash dividend—"diminish[ing] the property of the corporation by exactly the amount paid out and correspondingly increas[ing] the property of the individual stockholders. ..." 11 *W. Fletcher Cyclopedia of the Law of Private Corporations* § 5355 (perm. ed. 1971) (footnote omitted).

Applying these precepts to the case at hand, it is clear that the distribution of the MAC stock was *not* a "stock dividend," as that term traditionally has been defined. B & O was not capitalizing surplus; it was divesting itself of a considerable portion of its assets. In practical terms, the effect of the MAC dividend was no different than if

B & O had sold its non-rail assets for cash and then distributed an extraordinary cash dividend to its shareholders. ... Had the B & O indenture contained a more broadly inclusive notice clause, B & O might have been required to inform the debenture holders prior to the declaration of the MAC dividend. The sample provision quoted above, for example, requires notice both for dividends "payable in stock of any class" and for "any other distribution," excluding normal cash dividends. Kaplan, supra note 4, at 13 n. 24. But the fact remains that the B & O indenture contains no such clause. Accordingly, the plaintiffs cannot rely upon the terms of the indenture as a source of B & O's purported duty to speak.

Apparently mindful of the limited protection afforded to them by the indenture, the plaintiffs maintain that, notwithstanding any lack of an adequate notice provision within the indenture, New York's law of fair dealing required that in any event notice be given prior to the declaration of the MAC dividend. Judge Gibbons credits this argument, concluding that, in failing to give notice, B & O violated the principle "that in every contract there is an implied covenant that neither party shall do anything which will have the effect of destroying or injuring the right of the other party to receive the fruits of the contract. ..." At 941 (quoting *Kirke La Shelle Co. v. Paul Armstrong Co.*, 263 N.Y. 79, 87, 188 N.E. 163, 167 (1933)).

Such an analysis is clearly inappropriate. By its terms, the principle of fair dealing expressed in *Kirke* and quoted by Judge Gibbons applies only when one party infringes the other's *rights* "to receive the fruit of the contract." Here, under the well-settled *Parkinson* doctrine, Pittsburgh Terminal *had no right*, under the contract, to receive advance notice of the MAC dividend because *no anti-dilution provision to that effect had been included in the indenture*. Thus, the risk of dilution was "inherent in the investment made by the holders of Debentures. ... [B & O] did nothing that could be described as 'destroying or injuring the right of the other party to receive the fruits of the contract,' because ... the benefits that the holders of Debentures received were all the rights to which they were contractually entitled." *Broad v. Rockwell International Corp.*, supra at 958.

Van Gemert v. Boeing Co., 520 F.2d 1373 (2d Cir.), cert. denied, 423 U.S. 947, 96 S.Ct. 364, 46 L.Ed.2d 282 (1975), appeal after remand, 553 F.2d 812 (2d Cir. 1977), a Second Circuit case relied upon by Judge Gibbons, does not support a contrary result. In *Van Gemert*, debenture holders complained that Boeing had provided inadequate notice of its intention to redeem the debentures, thereby depriving the investors of the opportunity to convert prior to redemption. The Second Circuit agreed. Observing that the newspaper notice that was provided "may have conformed to the requirements of the Indenture," the court nonetheless concluded that such notice "was simply insufficient" under New York's fair dealing law "to give fair and reasonable notice to the debenture holders." 520 F.2d at 1383. In its decision after remand, the court clarified its earlier decision:

We did find significant ... the fact that the debentures did not explicitly set forth the type of notice which appellants could expect if Boeing decided to call the bonds. Without such a declaration, we held as matter of law that appellants were entitled to expect that Boeing would employ a method of notification reasonably calculated to inform the debenture holders of the call.

553 F.2d at 815.

Van Gemert thus stands for the narrow proposition that, if the debenture holders are contractually entitled to notice, such notice must be "fair and reasonable." But *Van Gemert* in no way addresses the question posed to us today: namely, whether the B & O debenture holders were entitled to any notice at all. That question, as has already been suggested, can be answered only by reference to the language of the indenture itself.

[Adams J. also dissented on the issue of liability under Rule 10b-17, holding that that rule was not intended to override the common law and provide debentureholders with significant additional substantive rights.]

III

Had the debenture holders foreseen the possibility that B & O would spin off its non-rail assets, arguably they may have bargained for—and paid for—the right to advance notice of the event. Despite the well-settled precedent of *Pratt* and *Parkinson*, however, the B & O indenture did not require such notice to the debenture holders and the price of the debenture presumably reflected this fact. For this Court today—almost thirty years after the drafting of the indenture—to ignore what was set forth as the intent of the parties and fundamentally to alter the terms of the contract is, in my view, not only legally erroneous but improvident.

I therefore respectfully dissent.

NOTE

A justification for extending the scope of a trust deed through the technique of implying new terms may be sought in a hypothetical claimholders' bargain. The parties may very well wish to leave some terms to be implied by a court, since they can express their intent more economically when they bargain against the backdrop of established conventions. In the absence of any such conventions as to the interpretation of the trust deed, it would be a considerably longer document than it is today. In policing misbehaviour under good faith norms, a court enjoys the advantage of hindsight. It need not predict every kind of future misbehaviour, as the parties must when they seek to provide against misbehaviour *ex ante* in their bargain, but instead may concentrate on the misbehaviour that actually occurred. But the broadening of a contract through the device of implying terms imposes error costs, with the possibility that the court will fail to replicate the terms, which the parties would have bargained for had they in fact considered them. What then is at issue is whether the uncertainty concerning the proper interpretation of the contract may be resolved more cheaply by the courts or by the parties in drafting the express terms of the trust deed.

Apart from the individual bargain, a court must be sensitive to the need to preserve the general quality of its stock of implied terms. Goetz and Scott argue that such terms should not be seen as merely suppletive, since they constrain choice by virtue of (1) the limited set of implied terms which are available, and (2) the barriers to opting out of the implied terms by express terms. Once the implied terms are in place, the parties cannot costlessly bargain around them. New express terms are costly to draft, and the parties will run the risk that their new term will be interpreted as merely expressing policies animating existing implied terms. The content of the implied terms is, however, parasitic upon the observed behaviour of parties in other bargaining contexts, for the court will seek information as to how the parties would have bargained by reviewing how other parties bargained in similar circumstances. An excessive readiness to imply terms may then impede the evolutionary growth of new implied terms by erecting barriers against the experimentation with novel express terms. "Overprotection of implied terms threatens the integrity of express trumping provisions because the interpreter will be reluctant to give express terms meanings that conflict with the apparent factual and legal context." Goetz & Scott, *The Limits of Expanded Choice: An Analysis of the Interactions between Express and Implied Contract Terms*, 73 Calif. L. Rev. 261, 290 (1985).

Since convertible debentureholders are merely creditors prior to conversion, American courts have held that they may not sue derivatively. However, a personal action on grounds of actual or constructive fraud may be brought. *Harff v. Kerkorian*, 347 A.2d 133 (Del. 1975), rev'g, 324 A.2d 215 (1974). Would a Canadian court be more ready to find that a convertible bondholder is a "complainant" in CBCA s. 238 than a straight bondholder?

C. PREFERRED SHAREHOLDERS

P. Hunt, C. Williams & G. Donaldson, Basic Business Finance
358-61 (5th ed. 1974)

The preferred stock represents a type of corporate financing which is somewhat paradoxical as between its nominal characteristics and its practical application. On the surface, it appears to provide the corporation with a security coupling the limited obligation of the bond with the flexibility of the common stock—a combination that would be unusually attractive to the issuer. Unfortunately, general experience does not bear out such expectations.

From the purely legal point of view the preferred stock is a type of ownership and thus takes a classification similar to that of the common stock. Accounting practice recognizes this by placing preferred stock along with common stock in the net worth section of the balance sheet. ... Unlike the bond, the preferred stock does not contain any promise of repayment of the original investment; and as far as the shareholders are concerned, this must be considered as a permanent investment for the life of the company. Further, there is no legal obligation to pay a fixed rate of return on the investment.

The special character of the prferred stock lies in its relationship to the common stock. When a preferred stock is used as a part of the corporate capital structure, the rights and responsibilities of the owners as the residual claimants to the asset values and earning power of the business no longer apply equally to all shareholders. Two types of owners emerge, representing a voluntary subdivision of the overall ownership privileges. Specifically, the common shareholders agree that the preferred shareholder shall have "preference" or first claim in the event that the directors are able and willing to pay a dividend. In the case of what is termed a nonparticipating or *straight preferred stock*, which is the most frequent type, the extent of this priority is a fixed percentage of the par value of the stock or a fixed number of dollars per share in the case of stock without a nominal or par value.

• • •

In most cases the prior position of preferred stock also extends to the disposition of assets in the event of liquidation of the business. Again, the priority is only with reference to the common stock and does not affect the senior position of creditors in any way. It has meaning and value only if asset values remain after creditors have been fully satisfied—a condition which is by no means certain in the event of liquidation following bankruptcy. ...

So far, we have considered the preferred stock in terms of the formal rights and responsibilities inherent in this type of security. The impression created is that of a limited commitment on dividends coupled with considerable freedom in the timing of such payments. In reality, experience with preferred stocks indicates that the flexibility in dividend payments is more apparent than real. The management of a business which is experiencing normal profitability and growth desires to pay a regular dividend on both common and preferred stock because of a sense of responsibility to the corporate owners and/or because of the necessity of having to solicit further equity capital in the future. The pressure for a regular common dividend in many cases assures the holder of a preferred stock that his regular dividend will not be interrupted, even in years when profits are insufficient to give common shareholders a comparable return, for it is very damaging to the reputation of a common stock (and therefore its price) if preferred dividend arrearages stand before it. The fact that most preferred issues are substantially smaller in total amount than the related common issue means that the cash drain of a preferred dividend is often less significant than the preservation of the status of the common stock.

The result is that management comes to view the preferred issue much as it would a bond, establishing the policy that the full preferred dividend must be paid as a matter of course. The option of passing the dividend still exists, but it is seen as a step to be taken only in case of unusual financial difficulty. Under such a circumstance, the obvious question presents itself: Why, then, use preferred stock as a means of raising permanent capital? Why not use bonds instead? The primary advantage of the preferred stock becomes identical with that of a bond, namely, the opportunity to raise funds at a fixed return which is less than that realized when the funds are invested. On the other hand, the dividend rate on preferred stock is typically above the interest rate on a comparable bond and has the additional disadvantage of not developing a tax shield. Of course, the bond is more likely to have a sinking fund, so that the *burden* of bond and preferred stock may not be greatly different.

The differential in cost between a preferred stock and an alternative debt issue may be considered a premium paid for the option of postponing the fixed payments. If management is reluctant to exercise this option, it is likely that the premium will be considered excessive. However, the closer a company gets to its recognized debt limits, the more management is likely to appreciate the option to defer the dividend on a preferred stock issue and be willing to pay a premium for this potential defense against a tight cash position.

---

1. Rights to Dividends

The special rights attached to a preferred share must be stated in the corporate charter. CBCA s. 6(1)(c)(i). These rights usually include prior rights to dividends and to a return of moneys on dissolution. The contract may also contain restrictive covenants, such as sinking fund and anti-dilution provisions, similar to those found in a trust indenture.

Preferences as to dividends are generally expressed to be *cumulative*. Dividends not paid in one year must then be declared in a following year before they can be paid to junior shareholders. If the shares are *non-cumulative*, dividends not paid in one year are lost forever, and in a subsequent year the corporation need only declare that year's dividends to the preferred before paying dividends to the juniors. If the articles provide for special dividend rights, but do not state whether they are cumulative or non-cumulative, they are presumed to be the former. *Webb v. Earle* (1875), L.R. 20 Eq. 556. Indeed, there is little investor interest in non-cumulative shares, which are most frequently issued on a corporate reorganization, when rights are generally scaled down.

The articles may also provide that preferred shares are *participating* as to dividends. They are then entitled to share on a plane of equality when dividends are declared to junior shareholders, after preferred dividends are paid. This gives preferred shareholders an opportunity to share in the growth of the enterprise. If not clearly provided for, preferred shares are presumed to be non-participating. *Will v. United Lankat Plantations Co.*, [1914] A.C. 11 (H.L.). *Re Canadian Pacific Ltd.* (1990), 68 D.L.R. (4th) 9 (Ont.). Because of this, an oppression action to impeach a dividend payout to common shareholders was denied in *Westfair Foods Ltd. v. Watt* (1991), 79 D.L.R. (4th) 48 (Alta. C.A.). Westfair had had a long-standing policy of retaining a significant proportion of its earnings, while paying a regular dividend to its common shareholders. For tax reasons, it began in 1985 to pay out its entire net annual earnings as dividends. The preferred ("Class A") shareholders objected to this. They had no right to dividends beyond a $2 dividend to be paid them before the common shares received any dividend. In the event of liquidation, however, they ranked equally with the common shares on any surplus assets. In their action, therefore, the preferred shareholders sought to force a compulsory liquidation. The trial judge granted the remedy and the Court of Appeal reversed. Delivering the judgment of the Court, Kerans J. stated:

This case decides that, as between preference shares and common shares, it is fair that the common shareholders take all unneeded earnings as dividends after the preferred dividend is paid. ...

My disagreement with the learned Chief Justice, while of great significance, can be simply stated. In the passage quoted, he said that the right to share in distribution of the assets on liquidation created an expectation by class A shareholders that they would share in the "success or failure" of the company. In my view, any expectation that they would share in the future success (as opposed to failure) of the company in a measure beyond the dividend promised them was not a reasonable expectation.

Conflict always exists between common shareholders as a class and the classification of those shareholders who have a right to claim a dividend in priority to the common shareholders. ... The latter chose to purchase shares with a special form of access to earnings, the first claim on the dividend pool. Their advantage is to receive a dividend in lean years when there is nothing for the common shareholders. The price they pay is to give up any claim to share in larger profits in the years of plenty. From this point of view, undue emphasis on breakup rights gives the second class an indirect second dip in the dividend pool and an arguably unfair advantage over the common shareholders.

Unless dividend rights are participating, then, the dividend preference establishes a ceiling. If the preferred shareholders want greater rights to the earnings, they must bargain for participating shares or for a right to convert their shares into common shares.

When a dividend is declared, the corporation becomes the shareholder's debtor for the amount of the dividend. *Re Northern Ontario Power Co.*, [1954] 1 D.L.R. 627 (Ont.). But shareholders normally have no rights to a dividend prior to its declaration by the directors. Thus in *Bond v. Barrow Haematite Steel Co.*, [1902] 1 Ch. 353, the Court rejected arguments by cumulative preferred shareholders that the corporation should be required to pay out dividends. The directors had refused to do so because the corporation's assets were found to be overvalued on the balance sheet. Farwell J. stated that:

The necessity for the declaration of a dividend as a condition precedent to an action to recover is stated in general terms in Lindley on Companies, 5th ed. p. 437, and, where the reserve fund article applies, it is obvious that such a declaration is essential, for the shareholder has no right to any payment until the corporate body has determined that the money can properly be paid away. It is urged that this puts the preference shareholders at the mercy of the company, but the preference shareholders came in on these terms, and this argument does not carry much weight in an action such as this, where bona fides is conceded. The opposite conclusion might enable the preference shareholders to ruin the company, and would certainly lead to great inconvenience in enabling them to compel the payment out of the last penny without carrying forward any balance. Granted that it is a hardship to go without dividends for a time, this hardship presses more heavily on the ordinary shareholders who have to wait until the preference shareholders have received all arrears before they can get anything.

· · ·

The Courts have, no doubt, in many cases, overruled directors who proposed to pay dividends, but I am not aware of any case in which the Court has compelled them to pay when they have expressed their opinion that the state of the accounts did not admit of any such payment. In a matter depending on evidence and expert opinion, it would be a very strong measure for the Court to override the directors in such a manner. [*Id.* at 362, 368]

This reluctance to intrude on internal corporate affairs very nearly hardened into an absolute rule of law. In *Burland v. Earle*, [1902] A.C. 83 (P.C. from Ont. C.A.), Lord Davey stated that:

Their Lordships are not aware of any principle which compels a joint stock company while a going concern to divide the whole of its profits amongst its shareholders. Whether the whole or any part should be divided, or what portion should be divided and what portion retained, are entirely questions of internal management which the shareholders must decide for themselves, and the Court has no jurisdiction to control or review their decision, or to say what is a "fair" or "reasonable" sum to retain undivided, or what reserve fund may be "properly" required. And it makes no difference whether the undivided balance is retained to the credit of profit and loss account, or carried to the credit of a rest or reserve fund, or appropriated to any other use of the company. These are questions for the shareholders to decide subject to any restrictions or directions contained in the articles of association or by-laws of the company. [*Id.* at 95]

There are, however, two kinds of cases in which shareholders may impeach the directors' decision not to pay a dividend. The first of these is where the articles expressly require the directors to declare a dividend when sufficient returns are earned. See *Evling v. Israel & Oppenheimer Ltd.*, [1918] 1 Ch. 101. Such shares are called *mandatory dividend preferred*, and are quite uncommon. If that degree of security is desired, a corporation is more likely to issue bonds or debentures. Second, in exceptional circumstances shareholders may seek relief when the decision not to declare dividends is tainted with self-dealing. One example of this, seen in Chapter Seven, is where a close corporation does not pay dividends and a minority shareholder is fired as a director. Another circumstance where self-dealing may be feared is where the decision to cut dividends precedes an attempt by insiders to purchase minority shares.

Dodge v. Ford Motor Co.
Michigan Supreme Court
170 N.W. 668 (1919)
[See Chapter Six]

Ebrahimi v. Westbourne Galleries Ltd.
House of Lords
[1973] A.C. 360
[See Chapter Seven]

Berwald v. Mission Development Co.
Supreme Court of Delaware
185 A.2d 480 (1962)

[Before Southerland C.J. and Wolcott and Terry JJ.]

SOUTHERLAND C.J.: Plaintiffs, owners of 248 shares of the stock of Mission Development Corporation, brought suit to compel the liquidation of Mission and the distribution of its assets to its stockholders. Mission answered and filed a motion for summary judgment, based on affidavits and depositions. Plaintiffs tendered to contradictory proof. The Vice Chancellor granted the motion and the plaintiffs appeal.

The facts are as follows:

Defendant, Mission Development, is a holding company. Its sole significant asset is a block of nearly seven million shares of Tidewater Oil Company. Tidewater is a large integrated oil company, qualified to do business in all the States of the Union. It is controlled, through Mission Development and Getty Oil Company, by J. Paul Getty.

Mission Development was formed in 1948 for the purpose of acquiring a block of 1,416,693 shares of Tidewater common stock then owned by Mission Corporation, a Nevada corporation. Its avowed purpose was to invest only in Tidewater stock, and in furtherance of this purpose to acquire additional stock to fortify its position in Tidewater. Accordingly, Mission of Delaware issued to Mission of Nevada 2,833,386 shares of its common stock and received the block of Tidewater stock held by Mission. Appropriate orders under the Investment Company Act were obtained from the Securities and Exchange Commission. The shares of both Mission Development and Tidewater are listed on the New York Stock Exchange.

Mission of Delaware will be hereinafter referred to as "Mission."

From 1948 to 1951 Mission acquired an additional 1,050,420 shares of Tidewater. Thereafter, and by 1960, Mission's holdings of Tidewater, through a 100% stock dividend and annual stock dividends of five per cent, increased to 6,943,957 shares.

In 1954 Tidewater discontinued the payment of cash dividends, thus effecting a discontinuance of Mission's income. Mission, as above noted, received thereafter until 1960 an annual 5% stock dividend, but Mission's proportionate ownership of Tidewater was not thereby increased, and its management accordingly deemed it unwise to distribute the shares as a dividend, since to do so would have decreased its proportionate ownership of Tidewater.

As hereafter shown, Tidewater's discontinuance of cash dividends was prompted by the adoption in 1954 of a policy of corporate expansion and modernization. The use of its available cash for this purpose left it without funds for dividends.

Later in the same year, Tidewater proposed to its stockholders to exchange shares of its cumulative $1.20 preferred stock for shares of its common stock held by the stockholders. Getty Oil Company and Mission were excluded from this offer.

All of the foregoing facts were reported to Mission stockholders by letter of J. Paul Getty, President of the corporation, dated April 11, 1955.

We pause to note that some of the plaintiff's stock in Mission Development was bought in 1956 and 1959.

In 1960 Tidewater discontinued the practice of distributing stock dividends. In the same year it submitted to its stockholders an exchange offer similar to the one made in 1955, again excluding Getty Oil and Mission.

From September 1960 to and including August 1961 Getty Oil Company acquired 510,200 shares of Mission. Some of these were purchased off the market.

In November 1960 this suit was filed.

As above indicated, plaintiffs seek to compel a complete or partial liquidation of the defendant and the distribution of its assets, either through the medium of a winding-up receivership, or by means of a court order compelling the management to distribute, or to offer to distribute, at least part of the Tidewater shares in exchange for Mission shares.

The extreme relief of receivership to wind up a solvent going business is rarely granted. To obtain it there must be a showing of imminent danger of great loss resulting from fraud or mismanagement. ... Like caution is dictated in considering an application to compel a corporation to make a partial distribution.

Since no showing is made of fraud or mismanagement inflicting injury upon the corporation, what is the basis of plaintiff's case?

Plaintiff's argument proceeds as follows:

There is an inherent conflict of interest between the controlling stockholder of Mission, Mr. J. Paul Getty, and the minority stockholders. This arises out of the dividend policy of Tidewater. Because of high income taxes, Mr. Getty, it is said, is not interested in receiving dividends; he is interested in acquiring more shares of Tidewater. To achieve this end, it is charged, he has caused Tidewater to discontinue all dividends and to announce, in 1960, that no dividends could be expected for five years. The necessary effect of this policy, plaintiffs say, was to depress the market value of Mission shares, and enable Mr. Getty to buy more Mission shares at an artifically low price, at the expense of Mission's minority stockholders. This, plaintiffs charge, is just what he has done, as is proved by Getty Oil's purchases of stock in 1960 and 1961. Thus he and Mission have inflicted a serious wrong upon the minority stockholders.

It is quite true that in some cases the interests of a controlling stockholder and of the minority stockholders in respect of the receipt of dividends may conflict, because of the existence of very high income taxes. See Cases and Materials, Baker and Cary, p. 1375. And in some cases this may work hardship on the minority. But we find no such situation here.

It is plain that the whole argument based on a charge of conflict of interest rests upon the claim that Tidewater's dividend policy, and its public announcement of it, were designed to serve the selfish interest of Mr. Getty and not to further its own corporate interests. If the opposite is true—if Tidewater's policy was adopted in furtherance of its own corporate interest—then Mission's stockholders have not been subjected to an actionable wrong and have no complaint. The fact of Mr. Getty's purchase of Mission Development stock then becomes irrelevant.

What does the record show with respect to Tidewater's dividend policy?

In the ten years prior to 1953 Tidewater's expenditure for capital improvements did not exceed $41,100,000 in any one year. Shortly prior to 1954 Tidewater began to expand and modernize its facilities. In February 1955 it closed and subsequently sold its obsolete refinery at Bayonne, New Jersey, and built a new and modern refinery in New Castle County, Delaware at a cost in excess of $200,000,000. Also, it commenced and still continues the expansion and modernization of its refinery facilities at Avon, California, and the increase of its crude oil and natural gas resources. As of November 3, 1960, the budget for new capital projects to be begun in 1961 was $111,000,000.

It is unnecessary to elaborate the point. It is entirely clear from the facts set forth in the affidavits that Tidewater's cash has since 1960 been largely devoted to capital improvements and that, in the opinion of management, funds were not available for dividends. These facts are uncontradicted, and they constitute a refutation of the basic argument of plaintiffs that dividends were discontinued to enable J. Paul Getty to buy Mission stock at a depressed price.

Some point is sought to be made of the unusual action of the Tidewater management in announcing that dividends could not be expected for five years. As defendant's counsel says, this was done out of common fairness to its stockholders and to prospective purchasers of its stock.

It is earnestly argued that plaintiffs should be allowed to go to trial and adduce testimony on the issue of the selfish motives of the controlling stockholder. Plaintiffs say that they could show by expert testimony that the market price of Mission common was artifically depressed.

It is first to be noted that the record of market prices put in by the plaintiffs themselves fails to show any drop in prices coincident with or closely following the announcement of the cessation of dividends. Plaintiffs reply that this fact is meaningless because at that time the market was steadily going up, and say that expert testimony will establish this. The answer to this argument is that if plaintiffs had such proof they should have come forward with it. ...

There are other facts in this case that support the conclusion above indicated. The sole corporate purpose of Mission is and has been to hold Tidewater stock. Any investor in its shares could readily ascertain this fact. Because of this he knows, or should know, that he is buying for growth and not for income.

Some point is made of the exclusion of Mission from the exchange offers made by Tidewater to its stockholders in 1954 and 1960. Obviously, for Mission Development to have been included in the exchange would have defeated the very purpose of its corporate existence.

However the various arguments are put they come to this: Plaintiffs are in effect seeking to wind up the corporation, either wholly or partially, because it is doing exactly what it was lawfully organized to do.

We think the plaintiffs have failed to make a case.

The judgment below is affirmed.

NOTE

Was there sufficient evidence of self-dealing in *Berwald* to invoke the intrinsic fairness test, under which the onus would be placed on Getty Oil Co. to demonstrate the objective fairness of the transaction? For a statement of the rule and an application of it to a case of allegedly excessive dividends, see *Sinclair Oil Corp. v. Levien*, 280 A.2d 717 (Del. 1971) (Chapter Seven).

Can a holder of one class of shares allege that he has been unfairly treated because dividends are paid only to shareholders of another class? In *Winram v. M.N.R.* (1972), 27 D.L.R. (3d) 763 (Fed. Ct.), the deceased owned 9 of the 10 class "A" voting shares of a company. His wife owned the remaining class "A" share and all 990 class "B" non-voting shares. The husband and wife were the only directors of the company, and the husband was the President and Chairman of the board of directors. As Chairman, he had a second or casting vote at board meetings. The articles provided that dividends might be declared for one class of shares but not the other. On the husband's death, the 9 voting shares were transferred to the wife. While the executors valued them at $1,780, the Ministry of

National Revenue assessed them as being worth $178,000. This assessment was upheld on the basis that all the surplus of the company might have been paid by dividend to class "A" shareholders to the exclusion of class "B" shareholders. Gibson J. stated that "Such action would not be an abuse of [the husband's] power in respect of the rights of class "B" shareholders. The case authorities are not applicable which hold that the Court will interfere to protect the minority, where the majority of the company propose to benefit themselves at the expense of the minority. All such authorities are cases where the majority and minority held the same class of shares" (26 D.L.R. (3d) at 767).

See generally Brudney, *Dividends, Discretion, and Disclosure*, 66 Va. L. Rev. 85 (1980) (proposing disclosure of the reasons for, and import of, dividend decisions by management); Fischel, *The Law and Economics of Dividend Policy*, 67 Va. L. Rev. 699 (1981) (criticizing the imposition of restrictions on management's discretion in the dividend decision); Stewart, *Judicial Review of Dividend Policy in Suits by Minority Shareholders*, 12 Am. Bus. L.J. 43 (1974).

NOTE ON DIVIDEND THEORY

Valuation of Shares. The source of value for a security, like a firm, is its anticipated future earnings. The valuation formula for a security is therefore similar to that for the issuer itself, as discussed in Chapter One, Section A.

$$V \text{ SECURITY} = E/k = EM$$

where E is expected earnings per share, k the capitalization rate and M the multiplier. If the issuer has only one class of securities, their capitalization rate and multiplier will be the same as that of the issuer itself. But this will not happen if several classes of equity and debt securities are outstanding, since not all will bear the same degree of risk. In that case, the value of the firm will still be equal to the value of all outstanding securities of every class, even as the value of the separate earnings components are equal to the value of the whole.

On traditional financial analysis, the dividend decision is an important factor in valuing shares.

[D]ividends constitute the only cash flows produced by the firm for its shareholders and therefore represent the one observable return they receive on their investment. ... Such individuals cannot spend the firm's retained earnings on goods and services; they can spend only the dividends—the *cash* payments—they receive. Retained earnings are not necessarily relevant, but they are relevant only insofar as they generate higher *future* dividends. [W. Lewellen, *The Cost of Capital* 89 (1978)]

On a dividend capitalization model, a share would then be valued as follows:

$$V = D/k$$

where D is the anticipated future dividend payment for a share and k is the capitalization rate for that class of shares. This analysis is, however, incomplete insofar as it leaves out a factor for expected growth. To account for growth, a new term, g, is introduced in the valuation formula:

$$V = \frac{D}{k - g} = \frac{D}{k - br}$$

where b is the retention ratio (ratio of retained earnings to total earnings) and r is the rate of return on retained earnings. By reducing the capitalization rate, the growth factor increses the multiplier and the value of the share. Suppose that a firm earns $20 per share and pays out $10 as dividends. If the market capitalization rate is 20% and the internal rate of return (r) is 25%, the market value of the firm's shares is:

$$V = \$10/0.20 - (0.5)\ (0.25) = \$10/0.075 = \$133.33$$

This formula also permits an analysis of when investment opportunities should be taken up in order to maximize firm value. Briefly, the firm should do so whenever the investment opportunity's rate of return (r) exceeds the capitalization rate (k). To see how this works, observe that the investment will then increase the growth rate (br or g) and reduce $k - g$. This in turn will lead to a higher multiplier. If, on the other hand, $r < k$, taking up the opportunity will reduce the value of the shares and it should be declined. Where $r = k$, the firm will be indifferent to the opportunity unless it wishes to maximize something in addition to the market value of the shares, such as the size of the firm.

The Dividend Irrelevance Proposition. After deciding to take up an investment opportunity, the firm must determine how it is to be paid for. This might be done either from retained earnings with a reduction in dividend payments, or from an issue of new securities or debt obligations. While investment and financing decisions are logically distinct, traditional financial analysts regard them as related. In their view, some attractive investment opportunities whose $r > k$ may have to be rejected if they can be financed only by a reduction in dividends.

The traditional view was, however, rejected by Modigliani and Miller (hereinafter "M & M"). Miller & Modigliani, *Dividend Policy, Growth, and the Valuation of Shares*, 34 J. Bus. 411 (1961), reprinted in Posner & Scott 291. M & M set forth a dividend irrelevance proposition under which the value of a firm and its securities is not related to the dividend payment question. The only thing that gives value to the securities is the right to share in the firm's earnings, and since the earnings are independent of the firm's retention ratio, the investment decision is not related to the financing decision. To maximize earnings, the firm has merely to accept all investment opportunities whose $r > k$. Thereafter, the firm cannot bootstrap up the value of the shares by its dividend decision. The shareholders will not demand dividend payments, as suggested by Lewellen, since they may satisfy their cash needs by selling shares, in effect making "homemade dividends."

M & M offer a mathematical proof of their thesis, based on the usual perfect capital market assumptions, together with a new assumption that the firm has a stable dividend policy: it announces that "regular" dividends will be paid and adheres to this plan. Critics of the M & M position have not taken issue with the mathematical proof. Instead, they have argued that when the assumptions are removed, dividend policies will affect the value of the shares in real world conditions. Several of the consequences of removing these assumptions are discussed in the following excerpt.

J. Van Horne, C. Dipchand & J. Hanrahan, Financial Management and Policy
349-56 (Canadian 9th ed. 1993)

Taxes and Dividends

The irrelevance of dividend argument assumes an absence of market imperfections. To the extent imperfections exist, they may support the contrary position, namely, that dividends are relevant. We shall examine various imperfections bearing on the issue, beginning with taxes. After we consider the theory, we will look at various empirical evidence bearing on the topic.

Unimportance of Corporate Income Taxes. Unlike the capital structure decision, corporate income taxes have no bearing on dividend relevance. Under present law, earnings of the firm are taxed at the corporate level, regardless of whether or not a dividend is paid. In other words, it is the profit after corporate taxes that is divided between dividends and retained earnings. Corporate income taxes could affect dividend relevance if tax laws were changed, as would occur under various methods to eliminate the double taxation of dividends.

Taxes on the Investor. Taxes paid by the investor are another matter. To the extent that the personal tax rate on capital gains is less than that on dividend income, there may be an advantage to the retention of earnings. When we allow for taxes, there are a variety of effects. The most important of these is the special treatment of capital gains from any source and of dividends from Canadian companies. Individuals can accumulate up to $100,000 in capital gains tax free. Thereafter, 75 percent of capital gains are taxable. Dividends from Canadian companies are first multiplied by $5/4$; then this grossed-up amount is fully taxed at the marginal tax rate. The taxpayer is then allowed a dividend tax credit of about 13.7 percent of the grossed-up value of dividends. Provincial taxes are determined by applying a stated percentage of the federal tax payable. The dividend tax credit is merely a device to reduce, in some manner, the incidence of double taxation.

The $100,000 life-time exemption on capital gains is extremely attractive to individuals. Furthermore, any tax on capital gains is deferred until the actual sale of the stock. These two factors combined provide a valuable timing option to shareholders of a firm which retains earnings as opposed to paying dividends. The effective (present value) tax on capital gains will be less than that on dividends even if the marginal tax rates on the two types of income are about equal. This suggests that a dividend-paying stock will need to provide a higher expected before-tax return than will a non-dividend-paying stock of the same risk. According to this notion, the greater the dividend yield of a stock, the higher the before-tax return required, all other things being the same. Thus, security markets would equilibrate in terms of systematic risk, dividend yield, and, perhaps, other factors. ...

When we consider other investors, we note even wider divergences in tax provisions relating to capital gains and dividends. Institutional investors such as retirement and pension funds pay no tax on either dividends or capital gains. On the other hand, dividends and capital gains for brokers and dealers are taxed as ordinary income. Then we have the special case of most corporate investors: inter-corporate dividends are generally non-taxable. However, 75 percent of capital gains are taxable. These corporate investors will have a preference for dividend-paying stocks.

Investor Clientele Neutrality. With different tax situations, clienteles of investors may develop with distinct preferences for dividend- or non-dividend-paying stocks. Many corporate investors will prefer dividend-paying stocks, whereas wealthy individual investors may prefer stocks that pay no dividends. Tax-exempt investors will be indifferent, all other things the same. If dividend-paying stocks were priced in the marketplace to provide a higher return than non-dividend-paying stocks, however, they would not be indifferent. They would prefer dividend-paying stocks.

If various clienteles of investors have dividend preferences, corporations should adjust their dividend payout to take advantage of the situation. Expressed differently, corporations should tailor their dividend policies to the unfulfilled desires of investors and thereby take advantage of an incomplete market. ... Suppose two-fifths of all investors prefer a zero dividend payout, one-fifth prefer a 25 percent payout, and the remaining two-fifths prefer a 50 percent payout. If most companies pay out 25 percent of their earnings in dividends, there will be excess demand for the shares of companies paying zero dividends and for the shares of companies whose dividend-payout ratio is 50 percent. Presumably, a number of companies will recognize this excess demand and adjust their payout ratios in order to increase share price. The action of these companies eventually will eliminate the excess demand.

In equilibrium, the dividend payouts of corporations will match the desires of investor groups. At this point, no company would be able to affect its share price by altering its dividend. As a result, even with taxes, dividend payout would be irrelevant. Black and Scholes are principal proponents of the neutral position, based on corporations adjusting the supply of dividends to take advantage of any mispricing of stocks in the marketplace.[4]

Another argument against clientele effects is that investors can use combinations of put and call options to isolate movements in stock price. By so doing, the investor effectively strips the dividend from the capital gains component of the stock. If investors are able to separate dividends from capital gains to suit their needs, the tax-induced clientele argument for particular stocks is weakened.

Tax Effect. In Canada, there is very little difference between the effective tax rates for individuals in the highest tax bracket on dividends and capital gains. However, for capital gains there is a $100,000 exemption, and the payout of tax is deferred until realization. These factors tend to create a bias for the retention of earnings if shareholders are not tax-exempt investors. Before examing empirical evidence on the subject, we must look at other factors that may influence the payment of dividends.

---

4   Fischer Black and Myron Scholes, "The Effects of Dividend Yield and Dividend Policy on Common Stock Prices and Returns," *Journal of Financial Economics*, 1 (May 1974), 1-5. ...

Influence of Other Factors on Dividend

Flotation Costs. The irrelevance of dividend payout is based on the idea on the idea that in accordance with the investment policy of the firm, funds paid out by the firm must be replaced by funds acquired through external financing. The introduction of flotation costs favors the retention of earnings in the firm. For each dollar paid out in dividends, the firm nets less than a dollar after flotation costs per dollar of external financing. Moreover, the smaller the size of the issue, the greater in general the flotation costs as a percentage of the total amount of funds raised. In addition, stock financing is "lumpy" in the sense that small issues are difficult to sell even with high flotation costs.

Transaction Costs and Divisibility of Securities. Transaction costs involved in the sale of securities tend to restrict the arbitrage process in the same manner as that described for debt. Shareholders who desire current income must pay brokerage fees on the sale of portions of their stock if the dividend paid is not sufficient to satisfy their current desire for income. This fee varies inversely, per dollar of stock sold, with the size of the sale. For a small sale, the brokerage fee can be a rather significant percentage. Because of this fee, shareholders with consumption desires in excess of current dividends will prefer that the company pay additional dividends. Perfect capital markets also assume that securities are infinitely divisible. The fact that the smallest integer is one share may result in "lumpiness" with respect to selling shares for current income. This, too, acts as a deterrent to the sale of stock in lieu of dividends. On the other hand, shareholders not desiring dividends for current consumption purposes will need to reinvest their dividends. Here again, transaction costs and divisibility problems work to the disadvantage of the shareholder, although in the opposite direction. Thus, transactions costs and divisibility problems cut both ways, and one is not able to draw directional implications about dividends versus retained earnings.

Institutional Restrictions. Certain institutional investors are restricted in the types of common stock they can buy or in the portfolio percentages they can hold in these types. The prescribed list of eligible securities is determined in part by the duration over which dividends have been paid. If a company does not pay a dividend or has not paid dividends over a sufficiently long period of time, certain institutional investors are not permitted to invest in the stock.

Also, a number of trusts have a prohibition against the liquidation of principal. In the case of common stocks, the beneficiary is entitled to the dividend income, but not to the proceeds from the sale of stock. As a result of this stipulation, the trustee who manages the investments may feel constrained to pay particular attention to dividend yield and seek stocks paying reasonable dividends. Though the two influences described are small in aggregate, they work in the direction of a preference for dividends as opposed to retention and capital gains.

Preference for Dividends. Finally, we must allow for the possibility of a preference for dividends on the part of a sizable number of investors. The payment of dividends may resolve uncertainty in the minds of some. Also, such payments may be useful in diversification of investments in an uncertain world. If in fact investors can manufacture "homemade" dividends, such a preference is irrational. Nonetheless, sufficient statements from investors make it difficult to dismiss the argument. Perhaps, for either psychological or inconvenience reasons, investors are unwilling to manufacture "homemade" dividends.

• • •

Financial Signaling

Cash dividends may be viewed as a signal to investors. Presumably, firms with good news about their future profitability will want to tell investors. Rather than make a simple announcement, dividends may be increased to add conviction to the statement. When a firm has a target-payout ratio that is stable over time and it changes this ratio, investors may believe that management is announcing a change in the expected future profitability of the firm. The signal to investors is that management and the board of directors truly believe things are better than the stock price reflects. In this vein, Merton H. Miller and Kevin Rock suggest that investors draw inferences about the firm's internal operating cash flows from the dividend announcement. The notion is based on asymmetric information. Management knows more about the true state of the company's earnings than do outside investors.

Accordingly, the price of the stock may react to this change in dividends. To the extent dividends provide information on economic earnings not provided by reported accounting earnings and other information, share price will respond. Put another way, dividends speak louder than words under these circumstances.

• • •

Financial Signaling Studies. Testing for a financial signaling effect has involved a different methodology. Typically, an event study is employed where daily share price changes, relative to the market, are analyzed around the announcement of a dividend change. A number of studies report findings consistent with a dividend announcement effect: increases in dividend leading to positive excess returns and decreases to negative excess returns. The effect seems to be more pronounced for companies that previously overinvested free cash flow in projects with returns less than what the financial markets require. After all, those cash flows belong to the shareholders and should not be invested in negative NPV projects.

In a study of firms initiating dividends for the first time or after a long hiatus, Asquith and Mullins discover significant excess returns. They interpret this finding as supporting the view that dividends convey valuable information to investors over and above that available from other sources. As would be expected, companies that omit dividends because of poor present earnings and future prospects suffer a share price decline.

NOTE

Capital gains that accrue after 1994 are no longer eligible for the $100,000 capital gains exemption, as a consequence of the federal government's February 22, 1994 budget. As of early 1995, however, other exemptions of a similar nature were still in place: for example, a $500,000 lifetime capital gains exemption for investments in small businesses and farms.

The legal investment restrictions discussed by Van Horne, Dipchand and Hanrahan are imposed on insurance, trust and loan companies, as well as pension funds, which together account for a major portion of purchases of new issues of stock. A typical restriction provides that no more than 7% (called the "basket") of the firm's investment portfolio may include securities issued by firms that have not paid out dividends in four of the last five years. Securities acquired as non-basket investments may thereafter be retained by the institutional investor even if the issuer never pays another dividend, and for this reason the securities are called "legal for life." The amount of dividends a non-basket firm must pay out is calculated as a percentage of its issued capital, and generally does not represent a difficult hurdle for most widely held issuers. However, firms regard the need to comply with legal for life restrictions as enormously important, since basket clause securities are difficult to distribute on a public issue.

The protective value of investment restrictions is now under attack from portfolio theorists, who note that by diversifying investments over a broad range of securities an investor may diversify away the idiosyncratic risk specific to any one of the issuers. It is therefore argued that investment restrictions should focus not on any specific security in the portfolio but rather on the portfolio as a whole. Indeed, diversification goals may be served if some securities are high risk, high return, such as basket clause securities. See Langbein & Posner, *The Revolution in Trust Investment Law*, 62 Am. Bar Ass. J. 887 (1976).

Judge Frank Easterbrook has advanced a bonding explanation of dividend payouts. Berle and Means had earlier feared that managers had become indifferent to shareholder concerns because of the firm's ability to finance new projects out of retained earnings. Without the discipline of capital markets, managers would then have a lesser incentive to maximize firm wealth. The firm may address the agency cost problem through a bonding strategy, in which it commits to efficient behaviour. Bonding here may take the form of devices to prevent the firm from achieving any independence from capital markets, and a high dividend payout policy would assist in such goals by reducing the firm's retained earnings. See Easterbrook, *Two Agency-Cost Explanations of Dividends*, 74 Am. Econ. Rev. 650 (1984). In the same way, maintaining a high dividend policy is value-increasing where the shareholders can invest the moneys at a higher return than the firm can. Failing to pay dividends in these circumstances is a form of management misbehaviour, which Arthur Jensen called the agency cost of "free cash flow." See Jensen, *Agency Costs of Free Cash Flow, Corporate Finance, and Takeovers*, 76 Am. Econ. Rev. 323 (1986).

On dividend theory, see further Black, *The Dividend Puzzle*, 2 J. Portfolio Man. 5 (1976), reprinted in Posner & Scott 307.

2. Rights on Liquidation

International Power Co. v. McMaster University
Supreme Court of Canada
[1946] S.C.R. 178, aff'g, [1945] 2 D.L.R. 93 (Que. C.A.)

TASCHEREAU J.: The Porto Rico Power Co. Ltd. was incorporated under the Dominion Companies Act of 1902, by letters patent dated the 29th of August, 1906. Its original authorized capital was $3,000,000 divided into 30,000 common shares of $100 each, all of which were issued and fully paid. In 1909, the Company increased its capital by creating and issuing $500,000 of preference stock, divided into 5,000 shares of $100 each, and again in 1911, a further increase of $500,000 raised the amount of preference stock to $1,000,000 and, as a result of which, the total capitalization of the company was $4,000,000.

The provisions of both supplementary letters patent, dealing with the rights of preference shares are the following:

The said increased capital stock of five hundred thousand dollars shall be preference stock entitled out of any and all surplus net earnings whenever ascertained to cumulative dividends at the rate of seven per cent. per annum for each and every year in preference and priority to any payment of dividends on common stock, and further entitled to priority on any division of the assets of the company to the extent of its repayment in full at par together with any dividends thereon then accrued due and remaining unpaid.

The main holdings, if not the only, of the Porto Rico Power Company, Limited were the shares of a certain Porto Rican subsidiary, the assets of which were expropriated by the Porto Rico Water Resources Authority, of the Porto Rican Government. As a result of this transaction, the Montreal Trust Company, in its quality of liquidator of Porto Rico Power Company, Limited, now in voluntary liquidation, had in its treasury more than $6,000,000 available for distribution amongst both classes of shareholders. The present appellant owns 29,357 of the 30,000 common shares of the Porto Rico Power Company, Limited, and the respondents are the holders of a substantial number of preference shares.

The Montreal Trust Company of Montreal was appointed liquidator on the 26th of January, 1944, and was authorized by the Court to make a preliminary distribution of $100 per share to the preference shareholders and $150 per share to the holders of common stock, and it also prayed the Court to determine how the surplus money amounting to $500,000 should be distributed. The Montreal Trust Company submitted that the holders of common shares are alone entitled to share in any surplus assets available for distribution after payment by priority of $100 per share to the preference shareholders, plus dividends thereon accrued due and remaining unpaid, and that the holders of preference shares are entitled only to said payment by priority of $100 per preference share and dividends thereon accrued and remaining unpaid, and that they are not entitled to share *pro rata* with the holders of shares of common stock in any surplus assets. The contention is that the rights of the holders of the preference shares of stock of the Porto Rico Power Company Limited, in liquidation, are completely and exhaustively set out in the by-laws and supplementary letters patent and that, after having received cumulative dividends at the rate of 7 per cent. per annum, which in fact they have received, they are entitled to only $100 per share in the distribution of the assets of the company which is the repayment in full of their shares at par.

The respondents intervened to contest the petition of the liquidator claiming that the preference shareholders are entitled to equal treatment in all respect with the common shareholders, except to the extent to which the said preference shares are given a priority by the supplementary letters patent and the by-laws of the company. They further alleged that no limitation whatsoever is placed upon the rights of the preference shareholders, and all that the said by-laws and supplementary letters patent provide is the extent of the priority given to the preference shareholders.

The respondents further claimed that the company in liquidation has paid dividends to the common shareholders in excess of the 7 per cent. received by the preference shareholders, and that the said dividends paid to the common shareholders constitute an advance in respect of which the preference shareholders are entitled to be placed on an equal basis.

Mr. Justice Boyer dismissed the contention of the McMaster University and directed that the $500,000 and all further assets subject to distribution should be distributed to the common shareholders only, and to the exclusion of the preferred shareholders.

The Court of King's Bench allowed the appeal of the McMaster University, ordered that the judgment *a quo* be modified to the extent of ordering, and ordered, the liquidator to distribute amongst the holders of preference shares the sum of $500,000 in proportion to their holdings of said shares, with interest at the rate of 5 per cent. per annum from the 2nd day of February, 1944. The Court of King's Bench further ordered the liquidator to distribute amongst the holders of preference and common shares in proportion to their holdings of the said shares, without any distinction, any or all balance of surplus assets available for distribution, but dismissed the claim of preferred shareholders as regards dividends.

The decision of this case depends upon the true construction of the essential words of the supplementary letters patent and by-laws already cited. It is clear, I think, that under the Dominion Companies Act, a preferred shareholder has all the rights and liabilities of a common shareholder. This proposition is found in section 49 of the Companies Act, R.S.C. 1906, chap. 79, which reads as follows: "Holders of shares of such preference stock shall be shareholders within the meaning of this part, and shall in all respects possess the rights and be subject to the liabilities of shareholders within the meaning of this part."

The preferred shareholders are however entitled to additional preferences and rights which are authorized by section 47 of the Act, which is to the effect that the directors of the company may make by-laws for creating and issuing any part of the capital stock as preference stock, giving the same such preference and priority, as respects dividend and in any other respect, over ordinary stock as is by such by-laws declared, and this is confirmed by subsection 49, which, after stating that holders of shares of preference stock are shareholders within the meaning of the Act, says that they are, as against the ordinary shareholders, entitled to the preferences and rights given by the by-laws.

Many judgments have been cited by both parties. As it will be seen the consensus of opinion appears to be that preference shareholders have all the rights and liabilities of common shareholders, and that the additional preferences and priorities, to which they may be entitled, must be found in the by-laws, and supplementary letters patent of the company.

The oldest case is, I think, the case of *Birch v. Cropper* [(1889), 14 App. Cas. 525]. In that case, the articles of association of an English company incorporated under the Companies Act of 1862 provided that the net profits for each year should be divided *pro rata* upon the whole paid-up share capital, and that the directors might declare a dividend thereout on the shares in proportion to the amount paid up thereon. The articles contained no provisions as to the distribution of assets on the winding-up of the company. The original capital consisted of ordinary shares partly paid up. Afterwards, preference shares were issued entitling the holders to a dividend at a fixed rate with priority over all dividends and claims of the ordinary shareholders. The preference shares were fully paid up. The undertaking having been sold under an Act which made no provision for the distribution of the purchase money amongst the shareholders, the company was voluntarily wound up and assets remained for distribution. It was held by the House of Lords, reversing the decision of the Court of Appeal, that in distributing the assets "amongst the members according to their rights and interests in the company" and in adjusting "the rights of the contributors amongst themselves," the liability of the ordinary shareholders for the unpaid balance of their shares must not be disregarded; and that, after discharging all debts and liabilities and repaying to the ordinary and preference holders the capital paid on their shares, the assets ought to be divided amongst all the shareholders, not in proportion to the amounts paid on the shares, but in proportion to the shares held.

At page 531, Lord Herschell said:

To treat them as partners receiving only interest on their capital and not entitled to participate in the profits of the concern, or to regard them as mere creditors whose only claim is discharged when they have received back their loan, appears to me out of the question. They are members of the Company, and as such shareholders in it as the ordinary shareholders are; and it is in respect of their thus holding shares that they receive a part of the profits. I think, therefore, that the first contention of the appellant wholly fails.

• • •

And at page 546, Lord Macnaghten says also:

The ordinary shareholders say that the preference shareholders are entitled to a return of their capital, with 5 per cent. interest up to the day of payment, and to nothing more. That is treating them as if they were debenture-holders, liable to be paid off at a moment's notice. Then they say that at the utmost the preference shareholders are only entitled to the capital value of a perpetual annuity of 5 per cent. upon the amounts paid up by them. That is treating them as if they were holders of irredeemable debentures. But they are not debenture-holders at all. For some reason or other the company invited them to come in as shareholders, and they must be treated as having all the rights of shareholders, except so far as they renounced those rights on their admission to the company. There was an express bargain made as to their rights in respect of profits arising from the business of the company. But there was no bargain—no provision of any sort—affecting their rights as shareholders in the capital of the Company.

[Taschereau J. then approved several English decisions, including *Re William Metcalfe and Sons Ltd.*, [1933] Ch. 142 (C.A.). That company's memorandum had provided that the cumulative shareholders should "rank, as to capital as well as dividends, in priority to the other shares. ..." It was held that, after the repayment of paid-up capital to all shareholders, the preferred shareholders were entitled to participate *pari passu* with the common shareholders on the distribution of surplus assets.]

From all these numerous judicial pronouncements, and from a careful reading of the Companies Act, I believe that one may rightly gather that the rights of all classes of shareholders are on a basis of equality, unless they have been modified by the by-laws or the letters patent of the company, and, that the right to the return of invested capital, and the right to share in surplus assets are quite different and distinct matters.

Holders of preference stock are shareholders within the meaning of the Act, and they possess in all respects the rights, and are subject to the same liabilities as the other classes of shareholders. Section 49 on this point is quite clear and unambiguous. It is in virtue of this section that the ordinary rights of preference shareholders are created. These rights put them on an equal footing with the common shareholders as to the sharing in surplus assets.

It is in the letters patent and the by-laws of the company that have to be found the priorities that may be attached to preference shares, and which are clearly authorized by section 47. It may of course happen that these priorities are exhaustive of the rights of the preference shareholders, and therefore negative any additional rights, or it may be also that they create additional rights which coexist with the original rights inherent to all classes of shareholders. But in order to determine the true meaning and the legal effect of these preference and priority clauses, one must necessarily look at the creating clauses in order to find if there is or not an express or implied condition, which limits or adds to the ordinary rights of the shareholders. It is a mere question of construction of these clauses, which form part of the contract under which the shareholders hold their shares.

I entirely agree with the Court of King's Bench that the provisions of the by-laws of the company do not expressly or by necessary implication, limit the rights of the holders of preference shares. They do create priorities, but these priorities are in addition to the existing rights, and are not a declaration of all the rights of this class of shareholders. These priorities consist in a right for the preference shareholders to be repaid of the invested capital at par, together with any dividends accrued and remaining unpaid, but do not affect their right to share in the profits. For the sharing in the profits, which is the fundamental right to all shareholders, is a matter entirely different from the priority given to the preference shareholder which is the additional privilege given to him.

In the present case the priority to repayment "on any division of the assets of the company to the extent of its repayment in full at par together with any dividends thereon then accrued due and remaining unpaid" is a definition of the existing priority as to the sharing of assets, and cannot, I believe, be construed as a bar or a limitation to any further rights.

For these reasons, I come to the conclusion that the preference shareholders have a priority to be repaid at par, and that they are further entitled to share *pari passu* in the distribution of the assets of the company with the common shareholders, after the latter had received payment at par.

The main appeal should therefore be dismissed.

It is the contention of the cross-appellant that the stipulation for payment of cumulative dividends at the rate of 7 per cent. per annum for each and every year, in a preference and priority to any payment of dividends on common stock, was not limitative in its terms and that in the event of the common shareholders receiving, in any year, a dividend exceeding the said rate of 7 per cent. per annum, then, the preferred shareholders were entitled to be paid on a basis of equality.

The preference shareholders have received each year the stipulated dividends of 7 per cent. until the winding-up of the company, and the common shareholders until 1931 have received dividends lower than 7 per cent. per year. However, from 1931 to 1942, the directors have declared for the benefit of the common shareholders an annual dividend of 8 per cent. and in 1943 this dividend was 49½ per cent. The preference shareholders ask for equal treatment in the matters of dividends. I cannot agree with this proposition, and it seems that the cases cited by the respondents on the main appeal defeat this very contention.

The question, I think, has been settled by the case of *Will v. United Lanket Plantations Company, Limited* [[1914] A.C. 11]. In that case the Court of Appeal [[1912] 2 Ch. 571] decided that, in the distribution of profits, holders of the preference shares were not entitled to anything more than a 10 per cent. dividend, and in the House of Lords Viscount Haldane said:

Moreover, I think that when you find—as you do find here—the word "dividend" used in the way in which the expression is used in the resolution and defined to be a "cumulative preferential dividend" you have something so definitely pointed to as to suggest that it contains the whole of what the shareholder is to look to from the company.

The right to dividends, while the company is a going concern and the right to capital and surplus assets in the winding-up, are quite distinct. In the present case, the right of preference shareholders is to be paid an annual dividend of 7 per cent. and they have a priority for dividends accrued due and remaining unpaid. These dividends have been paid, and the preference shareholders, as to dividends, have therefore received all that they are legally entitled to.

The by-laws give priority to the preference shareholders to obtain reimbursement of their invested capital, in addition to their right to share in the division of assets, but a similar privilege as to dividends is not given. In the latter case, the privilege is only to assure the payment of a dividend of 7 per cent. which has been declared, and which at the time of the winding-up accrued and remained unpaid. I should dismiss the cross-appeal.

As agreed, all costs of the parties will be paid by the liquidator out of the mass of the estate.

[Estey J. concurred with Taschereau J. The concurring judgments of Rand and Kerwin JJ. and the dissenting judgment of Rinfret C.J.C. are omitted.]

Appeal and cross-appeal dismissed.

Participation on Liquidation. Problems of the kind posed in *International Power* may be easily prevented by proper draftsmanship. Difficulties only arise when the articles do not clearly state liquidation preferences.

In interpreting a similar provision, the House of Lords came to a different conclusion in *Scottish Insurance Corp. v. Wilsons & Clyde Coal Co.*, [1949] A.C. 462 (H.L. Sc.). In overruling the *Metcalfe* decision, Lord Simonds stated that "the last thing a preference stockholder would expect to get ... would be a share of surplus assets, and ... such a share would be a windfall beyond his reasonable expectations. ..." *Id.* at 487.

The Supreme Court held that preferred shares were presumed to be participating on a liquidation and, following *Will v. United Lankat Plantations, Co.*, non-participating as to dividends. Is this inconsistent? Lord Simonds stated in the *Scottish Insurance* case that "I do not find ... in [*Will*] any suggestion that a different result would have followed if the dispute had been in regard to capital" ([1949] A.C. at 489). Do you agree with Taschereau J. that "[t]he right to dividend, while the company is a going concern and the right to capital and surplus assets in the winding-up, are quite distinct"?

The Claim to Arrearages. What is the extent of a preferred shareholder's priority on liquidation if cumulative dividends have not been paid in past years? Had the corporation continued as a going concern, such arrears would have had to have been paid before juniors could receive dividends. But is the claim to arrears lost on dissolution?

Once again, this is a drafting problem, which can be cured by specific reference to arrears in the articles. In the absence of such a provision, clauses which stated that preferred shareholders should have "priority as to dividend and capital" on dissolution were interpreted as giving them arrears of dividends. *Re F. de Jong & Co.*, [1946] Ch. 211. On the other hand, a provision that shareholders had priority to a payment of capital was presumed to exclude further rights to arrears on liquidation. *Re Canada Tea Co.* (1959), 21 D.L.R. (2d) 90 (Ont.) (no cumulative dividends ever paid in 16-year life of the corporation).

CHAPTER TEN

Distributions to Shareholders

A. DIVIDEND REGULATION

The issue of excessive dividends, considered in this section, is very different from that of insufficient dividends, as seen in the last section. The problem in cases like *Berwald v. Mission Development* was to determine when shareholders may impeach the dividend decision because the directors lack a sufficient incentive to pay out dividends. The question posed in this section, however, is when excessive dividend payouts should be prohibited for the protection of creditors.

Barriers to excessive dividends are aimed at fraudulent preferences and assignments. Absent any restrictions on excessive dividends, management could transfer all firm value to equity holders when insolvency looms, destroying the value of senior claims. This would reduce firm value in two ways. First, management might seek to pay dividends even where valuable business opportunities (whose $r > k$) are available to the firm; and second, the market for senior claims might unwind if their value could so easily be destroyed. Because of these costs, the firm will covenant not to pay out excessive dividends.

Restrictions on excessive dividends were first set forth in English decisions on the "maintenance of capital," and are discussed in the following case.

Verner v. General and Commercial Investment Trust
English Court of Appeal
[1894] 2 Ch. 239

[The defendant company was a mutual fund, whose assets were composed primarily of securities of other companies. On the company's financial year end in 1894, its net income, after all expenses and interest payments, was £23,000. However, some of its investments had turned out to be quite worthless, and the market value of most of the others had fallen. In all, the investments had declined by at least £250,000 from the figure they were carried at in the firm's balance sheet.

A friendly action was begun by one of the company's directors to determine whether it could pay out a dividend in these circumstances.]

LINDLEY AND A.L. SMITH L.JJ.: ... The broad question raised by this appeal is, whether a limited company which has lost part of its capital can lawfully declare or pay a dividend without first making good the capital which has been lost. I have no doubt it can—that is to say, there is no law which prevents it in all cases and under all circumstances. Such a proceeding may sometimes be very imprudent; but a proceeding may be perfectly legal and may yet be opposed to sound commercial principles. We, however, have only to consider the legality or illegality of what is complained of.

As was pointed out in *Lee v. Neuchatel Asphalte Company* [41 Ch. D. 1], there are certain provisions in the Companies Act relating to the capital of limited companies; but no provisions whatever as to the payment of dividends or the division of profits. Each company is left to make its own regulations as to such payment or division. The statutes do not even expressly and in plain language prohibit a payment of dividend out of capital. But the provisions as to capital, when carefully studied, are wholly inconsistent with the return of capital to the shareholders, whether in the shape of dividends or otherwise, except, of course, on a winding-up, and there can, in my opinion, be no doubt that even if a memorandum of association contained a provision for paying dividends out of capital such provision would be invalid. The fact is that the main condition of limited liability is that the capital of a limited company shall be applied for the purposes for which the company is formed, and that to return the capital to the shareholders either in the shape of dividend or otherwise is not such a purpose as the Legislature contemplated.

But there is a vast difference between paying dividends out of capital and paying dividends out of other money belonging to the company, and which is not part of the capital mentioned in the company's memorandum of association. The capital of a company is intended for use in some trade or business, and is necessarily exposed to risk of loss. As explained in *Lee v. Neuchatel Asphalte Company*, the capital even of a limited company is not a debt owing by it to its shareholders, and if the capital is lost, the company is under no legal obligation either to make it good, or, on that ground, to wind up its affairs. If, therefore, the company has any assets which are not its capital within the meaning of the Companies Act, there is no law which prohibits the division of such assets amongst the shareholders. Further, it was decided in that case, and, in my opinion, rightly decided, that a limited company formed to purchase and work a wasting property, such as a leasehold quarry, might lawfully declare and pay dividends out of the money produced by working such wasting property, without setting aside part of that money to keep the capital up to its original amount.

There is no law which prevents a company from sinking its capital in the purchase or production of a money-making property or undertaking, and in dividing the money annually yielded by it, without preserving the capital sunk so as to be able to reproduce it intact either before or after the winding-up of the company.

A company may be formed upon the principle that no dividends shall be declared unless the capital is kept undiminished, or a company may contract with its creditors to keep its capital or assets up to a given value. But in the absence of some special article or contract, there is no law to this effect; and, in my opinion, for very good reasons. It would, in my judgment, be most inexpedient to lay down a hard and fast rule which would prevent a flourishing company, either not in debt or well able to pay its debts, from paying dividends so long as its capital sunk in creating the business was not represented by assets which would, if sold, reproduce in money the capital sunk. Even a sinking fund to replace lost capital by degrees is not required by law.

It is obvious that dividends cannot be paid out of capital which is lost; they can only be paid out of money which exists and can be divided. Moreover, when it is said, and said truly, that dividends are not to be paid out of capital, the word "capital" means the money subscribed pursuant to the memorandum of association, or what is represented by that money. Accretions to that capital may be realized and turned into money, which may be divided amongst the shareholders, as was decided in *Lubbock v. British Bank of South America* [[1892] 2 Ch. 198].

But, although there is nothing in the statutes requiring even a limited company to keep up its capital, and there is no prohibition against payment of dividends out of any other of the company's assets, it does not follow that dividends may be lawfully paid out of other assets regardless of the debts and liabilities of the company. A dividend presupposes a profit in some shape, and to divide as dividend the receipts, say, for a year, without deducting the expenses incurred in that year in producing the receipts, would be as unjustifiable in point of law as it would be reckless and blameworthy in the eyes of business men. The same observation applies to payment of dividends out of borrowed money. Further, if the income of any year arises from a consumption in that year of what may be called circulating capital, the division of such income as dividend without replacing the capital consumed in producing it will be a payment of a dividend out of capital within the meaning of the prohibition which I have endeavoured to explain.

It has been already said that dividends presuppose profits of some sort, and this is unquestionably true. But the word "profits" is by no means free from ambiguity. The law is much more accurately expressed by saying that dividends cannot be paid out of capital, than by saying that they can only be paid out of profits. The last expression leads to the inference that the capital must always be kept up and be represented by assets which, if sold, would produce it; and this is more than is required by law. Perhaps the shortest way of expressing the distinction which I am endeavouring to explain is to say that fixed capital may be sunk and lost, and yet that the excess of current receipts over current payments may be divided, but that floating or circulating capital must be kept up, as otherwise it will enter into and form part of such excess, in which case to divide such excess without deducting the capital which forms part of it will be contrary to law. ...

[The concurring judgment of Kay L.J. is omitted.]

Appeal dismissed.

Maintenance of Capital. The prohibition in *Verner* against paying dividends out of "capital" refers to something quite different from the corporations' stated capital. Instead, a firm's capital was the assets it received on an issue of shares "or what is represented by money." The test is discussed further in Gold, *Fixed and Circulating Capital and the English Law of Dividends*, 6 U. of Toronto L.J. 14, 35-41 (1945).

There are two fundamentally opposed theories of the nature of capital. One theory is that capital is a *res*, a particular thing or aggregate of things, the thing or things being the actual moneys subscribed by shareholders or the actual assets in which the contributions of shareholders are in-

vested. The other is that capital is a *quantum*, a sum of money. That sum may be fixed by reference to the *amount* of shareholders' contributions or the *value* at the time of receipt of assets received from shareholders, but the sum is an ideal one and is not identified with the contributions
or assets except for the purposes of measurement.

· · ·

If the *quantum* view of capital is adopted, the payment of dividends at a time when the *quantum*, whatever it may be, is impaired is a return of capital, or a reduction otherwise than in accordance with the statutory machinery. However, if capital is the aggregate of certain specific
assets, an impairment of their value does not prevent the payment of dividends so long as those
assets or the proceeds of their sale are not themselves divided. It cannot be said that the dividends
are paid from the assets, which constitute the capital of the company or are a reduction of them.
The company has the same capital assets after the dividend is paid as it had before.

The courts have chosen the *res* theory of capital.

· · ·

The rules for fixed and circulating assets follow naturally enough from the *res* view of capital. Capital must not be returned to shareholders as dividends. If fixed assets are not themselves
divided, a distribution of earnings which ignores a loss of fixed assets is not a return of capital.
Furthermore, no allowance need be made for depreciation since this phenomenon is the necessary
consequence of the retention of fixed assets. Circulating assets are turned over regularly, but the
total proceeds of sale may not be divided, because that would involve a return of circulating capital. The amount of capital invested in circulating assets must, therefore, be deducted from the
earnings, or, in other words, circulating capital must be preserved intact.

Moreover, the *res* view of capital explains why it is possible at all to distinguish between
fixed and circulating capital. Since capital consists of an aggregate of specific assets, the aggregate of fixed assets becomes fixed capital and the aggregate of circulating assets becomes circulating capital. Although fixed and circulating assets can be distinguished on some other theory of
capital, fixed and circulating capital can be distinguished only on the *res* theory. That theory
makes it possible to assume that certain entries on the assets side of a balance sheet are represented by particular entries on the liabilities side, so that it can be said that the loss of a particular
asset is a loss of fixed capital.

On the *quantum* view of capital there is no relation between individual entries on the two
sides of a balance sheet. Capital in this sense implies a relation between the two sides each taken
as a whole. It implies that the *net* assets, i.e., the total assets less liabilities (except to shareholders) and reserves, equal, at least, the *quantum* of capital. Loss of a particular asset is not loss of a
particular kind of capital. There will be a loss of capital, without any qualifying adjective, if, as a
result of the loss of a particular asset, the value of the remaining assets does not exceed liabilities
and reserves by the *quantum* of capital.

The courts have, however, adopted the *quantum* theory of capital in dealing with realized appreciation of fixed assets. One would expect, in accordance with the *res* theory, that the proceeds
of sale of a fixed asset would not be divisible, since this would be a return of capital. At the very
least, one would expect that the analogy of circulating capital would be followed, and that the excess of the proceeds of sale over the cost of the asset would be divisible without regard to the
quantum of capital, whatever it may have been fixed at, or the value of the remaining assets. Actually, the courts have decided that part or all of the proceeds of sale may be divided, and that the

amount divisible is the excess of the value of all the assets over all the liabilities including the *quantum* of paid-up capital.

The *quantum* view of capital, as illustrated by the court's attitude to realized appreciation, is the only usable one in practice. The resources of a company are manifold, and can be described, generally speaking, only in terms of a money value. "You cannot add a piece of real estate, a lot of machinery, a list of securities, valuable contracts, money, accounts receivable, and goodwill and write the sum at the end unless you have some measure of value." Money is the only common denominator. But the *quantum* concept of capital is based on something more compelling than convenience. A company's resources consist of money or assets subscribed by shareholders, advances by creditors, and earnings. There are not, however, distinct funds which the company keeps carefully segregated. It is unrealistic, and perhaps impossible, to pretend that any particular asset represents any one of the various resources of the company. If this is recognized, "capital" is not the assets received from shareholders, since those assets are commingled with the other resources of the company and may not be traceable, but the value of those assets at the time of receipt, whether it be their actual value or the value placed upon them.

. . .

The true reason for the later adoption of the *res* concept seems to have been not so much the influence of ideas derived from settlements of land as the desire, motivated by a laissez-faire outlook, to formulate a rule which would give directors maximum scope in their dividends policies, but which at the same time could be reconciled with the rules prohibiting the return of capital or its informal reduction.

These old decisions, with their antique notions of accounting, might well be ignored by a Canadian court today. First of all, the *res* test is unrelated to any protection that a creditor might reasonably desire. It was seen in Chapter Four that the amount of a firm's issued capital is often of no predictive power in determining the likelihood of the issuer's default. If the issued capital is frequently unimportant, then, how much less relevant is the distinction between fixed and circulating capital? Second, the cases offer few restrictions on management's discretion, looking to realized appreciation to permit increased dividends, but not to realized depreciation to require reduced dividends. In *Lubbock v. British Bank of South America*, [1892] 2 Ch. 198, for example, the defendant corporation was incorporated with a paid-up capital of £500,000. The assets of the corporation included a banking business in Brazil, which it sold in 1891 at a profit of £750,000. It set aside £500,000 as representing the paid-up capital and proposed to pay the balance of £250,000 as a dividend. Chitty J. held that the dividend might be paid since the paid-up capital was intact. However, if a dividend can be paid from a realized appreciation of fixed assets, as in *Lubbock*, it is somewhat artificial to permit an unrealized decline in fixed assets to be ignored, as in *Verner*. In addition, Scrutton L.J. stated that dividends might be paid without regard to depreciation (a realized decline in the value of fixed assets) in *Ammonia Soda Co. v. Chamberlain*, [1918] 1 Ch. 266 (C.A.). As a consequence, these cases are consistent only to the extent that they refuse to impeach the dividend decision. Like the Edsel, then, the *res-quantum* distinction was a false start, ultimately leading nowhere. Of course, this is no bad thing if creditors are adequately protected by CBCA solvency requirements and by the creditors' ability to bargain for better protection if they desire it.

See further Bryden, *The Law of Dividends*, in 1 Ziegel 270; Yamey, *Aspects of Law Relating to Company Dividends*, 4 Mod. L. Rev. 273 (1941).

Modern Restrictions. Modern restrictions on excessive dividends are found in (1) bankruptcy legislation, (2) corporations acts and (3) restrictive covenants in trust deeds. These are listed in ascending order of stringency, with BIA standards being easiest to comply with. Section 101 of that statute permits recovery against directors when a dividend is paid or shares repurchased when the corporation is insolvent. Insolvency arises under s. 2 when:

(1) the firm is unable to meet its obligations as they become due or ceases paying its current obligations in the ordinary course of business as they generally become due, or

(2) the firm's assets, if disposed of under legal process, would not be sufficient to permit payment of all the firm's accrued and unaccrued obligations.

Creditors may have a greater cushion under CBCA s. 42, which prohibits dividend payments if there are reasonable grounds for believing that the realizable value of the corporation's assets would be less than the sum of its liabilities and stated capital of all classes. What this might amount to was discussed in *Randall v. Bailey*, 23 N.Y.S.2d 173, 184-85 (Trial Div. 1980), aff'd on other grounds, 43 N.E.2d 43. Section 58 of the New York Stock Corporation Law prohibited dividend payouts unless the value of the firm's remaining assets exceeded liabilities plus capital, and a trustee in bankruptcy sought to recover against former directors of the corporation for breach of this provision. The action failed, but the Court pointed out that the statute did require directors to consider firm value in their dividend decisions:

I see no cause for alarm over the fact that this view requires directors to make a determination of the value of the assets at each dividend declaration. On the contrary, I think that is exactly what the law always has contemplated that directors should do. That does not mean that the books themselves necessarily must be altered by write-ups or write-downs at each dividend period, or that formal appraisals must be obtained from professional appraisers or even made by the directors themselves. That is obviously impossible in the case of corporations of any considerable size. But it is not impossible nor unfeasible for directors to consider whether the cost of assets continues over a long period of years to reflect their fair value, and the law does require that directors should really direct in the very important matter of really determining at each dividend declaration whether or not the value of the assets is such as to justify a dividend, rather than do what one director here testified that he did, viz. "accept the company's figures." The directors are the ones who should determine the figures by carefully considering values, and it was for the very purpose of compelling them to perform that duty that the statute imposes upon them a personal responsibility for declaring and paying dividends when the value of the assets is not sufficient to justify them. What directors must do is to exercise an informed judgment of their own, and the amount of information which they should obtain, and the sources from which they should obtain it, will of course depend upon the circumstances of each particular case. ...

If directors have blindly or compliantly accepted either cost or any other arbitrary figures as indicative of value, they have not exercised either discretion or judgment and no court is required to act as if they had. When directors have in fact exercised an informed judgment with respect to the value of the company's assets, the courts obviously will be exceedingly slow to override that judgment, and clear and convincing evidence will be required to justify a finding that such judgment was not in accordance with the facts.

Apart from such provisions, creditors who want a greater cushion must bargain for it. This is frequently done in trust deeds and bank loan agreements, whose dividend restrictions usually contain more stringent financial ratio tests than those found in CBCA s. 42. As a consequence, the issue of excessive dividends is now largely a matter of contract. If management of a near-insolvent firm seeks to pay out dividends, it will usually run afoul of restrictive covenants in trust deeds well before statutory limitations on the dividend decision.

Spin-Offs. CBCA s. 43(1) permits a firm to pay a dividend in kind—that is, not in cash but in assets. This might be in any kind of goods, provided that a *pro rata* payment is made to each shareholder. This is most often done through a distribution of securities of another firm. When the securities so distributed are those of wholly owned subsidiary, this is called a "spin-off," and amounts to a voluntary divestiture of the subsidiary. After the spin-off, the two firms are entirely separate, apart from the fact that initially their shareholders are identical.

This kind of negative merger assumes that the value of the separate divisions exceeds their value when combined, and existing evidence suggests that spin-offs do in fact increase shareholder wealth. See, e.g., Schipper & Smith, *Effects of Recontracting on Shareholder Wealth: The Case of Voluntary Spin-Offs*, 12 J. Fin. Econ. 437 (1983) (abnormal stock price increases after spin-offs announced); Cusatis, Miles & Woolridge, *Restructuring Through Spinoffs: The Stock Market Evidence*, 33 J. Fin. Econ. 293 (1993) (same). But if shareholders are better off, debt holders are not if there is any possibility of default, since anticipated firm value in bankruptcy will have decreased. See Galai & Masulis, *The Option Pricing Model and the Risk Factor of Stock*, 3 J. Fin. Econ. 53, 69 (1976). However, secured creditors and the parent corporation may bargain for successor corporation liability in these circumstances, with a portion of debt claims allocated to the subsidiary. Management of the parent will in fact wish to do so, since this will increase the parent's value. See further McDaniel, *Bondholders and Corporate Governance*, 41 Bus. Law. 413, 421-23 (1986).

Stock Dividends and Stock Splits. The mechanics of stock dividends and stock splits are easy enough to explain, but why a firm might choose to use either device is quite another matter. Both amount to paper transactions, or accounting changes, which do not in any way affect underlying economic realities. In efficient markets, such changes do not change the value of the firm's shares, for investors would see through the financial illusions. Since these transactions are not costless, the challenge is to explain why firms would adopt them.

A stock dividend is a *pro rata* issue of new share certificates to existing shareholders. When new shares are distributed as a stock dividend in perfect capital markets, the value of existing shares is diluted so that underlying values are not affected. Suppose, for example, that a corporation with 10,000 outstanding shares earns $500,000 a year, with earnings per share of $50, all of which are paid out as dividends. The market value of each share is $500 and the market capitalization rate is 10%. What will happen if stock dividends are paid out on the basis of 1 new share for 10 old shares? The corporation will then have 11,000 shares, with earnings per share of $45.45. If a capitalization rate of 10% is applied to these earnings, the shares will be valued at $454.50, and the stock dividend will not have increased firm value. The value of each share will be diluted to offset exactly the number of new shares.

Stock dividends may be declared by simple resolution of the board under CBCA s. 43(1). While legal restrictions on stock dividends are virtually non-existent, they must at least be accounted for with an adjustment to the stated capital account under s. 43(2). The directors must add to stated capital "the declared amount of the dividend." But what amount may that be? The market price of outstanding shares? The mean consideration received on issues of shares in the past, on the model of s. 39(1) in the case of share repurchases? The amount selected by directors, whatever it may be? If creditors are indifferent to an issue of stock dividends, should it matter what figure is chosen under s. 43(2)?

A stock split results in a change in the number of outstanding shares, but not in the stated capital account. Thus 1,000 old shares might be exchanged for 2,000 new ones, with a constant stated capital of $10,000. Since no transfer is made from surplus to capital, this is even more a paper transaction than a stock dividend. Paradoxically, however, stock splits require greater formalities than stock dividends. The articles must be amended under CBCA s. 173(1)(h), with separate class voting rights for shareholders under s. 176(1)(g).

Under perfect capital market assumptions, stock dividends and stock splits would not offer any advantages to a firm. An explanation for their use must therefore refer to ways in which such assumptions are violated. The leading imperfection might at first seem to be the existence of taxes, but on closer analysis this does not explain why firms declare stock dividends. Under the Income Tax Act, cash dividends are treated as income, while no taxes are paid on stock dividends until the shares are sold, at which time the investor may realize a capital gain. However, the tax consequences of stock dividends do not increase shareholder wealth, since the same tax advantages are available when no dividends of any kind are paid out, and existing shares appreciate. In addition, the firm will already have attracted a clientele of investors who favour the particular mix of capital gains and income in the firm's dividend policy, so that they will often not approve of changes in that policy.

A more promising, though limited, explanation of stock dividends and stock splits is that they economize on brokerage fees paid by the investors in secondary trades of their securities. For example, an investor who wishes for a cash return in a firm that has a low dividend policy may sell some of his existing shares in order to manufacture "homemade dividends," paying out fees to brokers on both trades. But if the firm provides a free conversion privilege as between two classes of its shares, one of which pays cash and the other stock dividends, investors may costlessly adjust their dividend payouts. These schemes, also called dividend reinvestment plans, are only feasible if shareholders who do not receive cash dividends are issued stock dividends, since their shares would otherwise be diluted when the other class receives cash dividends.

A further explanation of stock dividends and stock splits is that they provide a signal of hidden firm value. When a firm with earnings per share of $50 pays out a stock dividend on the basis of 1 new share for 10 old shares, earnings per share might be expected to decline to $45.45. However, given the information asymmetry between managers and the public, the stock dividend might be taken as a signal that earnings will increase, and that even with 10% more shares, each share will continue to have earnings per share of $50. This would explain why it is that investors greet announcements of stock dividends or stock splits favourably, with something less than full dilution in both cases. However, this does not mean that the stock dividend or stock split itself creates value. One study indicates that two-thirds of firms effecting a stock split subsequently paid out increased cash dividends. When these higher dividends were paid, share value did *not* increase. However, when the remaining firms did not increase their dividend payout, their share prices fell to the values that prevailed well before the split. From this, Brealey and Myers conclude that "the split was accompanied by an explicit or implicit promise of a subsequent dividend increase, and the rise in price at the time of the split has nothing to do with a predilection for splits as such but with the information that it was thought to convey." R. Brealey & S. Myers, *Principles of Corporate Finance* 305 (4th ed. 1991).

Divestiture efficiencies are most plausibly attributed to deconglomerization gains. Throughout the 1960s and early 1970s, corporate conglomerization, or the acquisition of new firms in unrelated lines of business, was thought to offer an easy method of advancing stock price. By the 1970s, however, conglomerates began to appear less valuable than their underlying assets, with the separate parts of the firm worth more than the whole. In the 1980s, conglomerate acquisitions of unrelated businesses were associated with significant negative returns. See Morck, Shleifer & Vishny, *Do Managerial Objectives Drive Bad Acquisitions?* 45 J. Fin. 31, 43 (1990). When inefficiently large firms were publicly held, the difference between conglomerate and break-up value offered enormous arbitrage gains to take-over bidders. As conglomerates became take-over targets, conglomerate managers adopted divestiture policies as a defensive tactic. The sharp increase in the level of voluntary divestitures in the 1980s may thus be attributed to the discipline of corporate control markets. See Buckley, *The Divestiture Decision*, 16 J. Corp. L. 805 (1991).

B. SHARE REPURCHASES

Share repurchases are similar to dividend payments, in that both transfer money from the corporation to shareholders. What distinguishes a share repurchase (also called a buyback) from a dividend is that the cash payment in a repurchase is made only to selling shareholders, while dividends are paid out *pro rata* to all shareholders. Buybacks give rise to many of the same issues of the creditor protection as do cash dividends. In addition, special concerns for shareholder protection are expressed on a buyback as a consequence of the formally different consequences for selling and non-selling shareholders.

1. Creditor Protection

The repurchase may be made on the open market or, in the case of redeemable preferred shares, pursuant to rights granted to the firm in the share conditions. Since repurchases and redemptions involve a return of assets to shareholders, barriers to such transactions are required where they might permit the firm to destroy the claims of creditors. Redemptions of preferred shares have always been permitted, so long as not made in contemplation of bankruptcy, but share purchases were formerly illegal.

Trevor v. Whitworth
House of Lords
(1887), 12 App.Cas. 409

[James Schofield & Sons Ltd. was incorporated in 1865 under the 1862 English Companies Act. Its articles provided that:

Article 179. Any share may be purchased by the company from any person willing to sell it, and at such price, not exceeding the then marketable value thereof, as the board think reasonable. ...

Article 181. Shares so purchased may at the discretion of the board be sold or disposed of by them or be absolutely extinguished, as they deem most advantageous for the company.

The plaintiffs, as executors of a deceased shareholder, brought an action against Trevor, the company's liquidator, for the balance of the price of shares repurchased by the company prior to liquidation and not wholly paid for.]

LORD HERSCHELL: ... I pass now to the main question in this case, which is one of great and general importance, whether the company had power to purchase the shares. The result of the judgment in the Court below is certainly somewhat startling. The creditors of the company which is being wound up, who have a right to look to the paid-up capital as the fund out of which their debts are to be discharged, find coming into competition with them persons who, in respect only of their having been, and having ceased to be, shareholders in the company, claim that the company shall pay to them a part of that capital. The memorandum of association, it is admitted, does not authorize the purchase by the company of its own shares. It states, as the objects for which the company is established, the acquiring certain manufacturing businesses and the undertaking and carrying on the businesses so acquired, and any other business and transaction which the company consider to be in any way auxiliary thereto, or proper to be carried on in connection therewith.

It cannot be questioned, since the case of *Ashbury Railway Carriage and Iron Company v. Riche* [Law Rep. 7 H.L. 653], that a company cannot employ its funds for the purpose of any transactions which do not come within the objects specified in the memorandum, and that a company cannot by its articles of association extend its power in this respect. These propositions are not and could not be impeached in the judgments of the Court of Appeal, but it is said to be settled by authority, that although a company could not under such a memorandum as the present, by articles authorize a trafficking in its own shares, it might authorize the board to buy its shares "whenever they thought it desirable for the purposes of the company," or "in cases where it was incidental to the legitimate objects of the company that it should do so." The former is Lord Justice Cotton's expression; the latter that of Lord Justice Bowen.

I will first consider the question apart from authority, and then examine the decisions relied on.

The Companies Act 1862 requires (sect. 8) that in the case of a company where the liability of the shareholders is limited, the memorandum shall contain the amount of the capital with which the company proposes to be registered, divided into shares of a certain fixed amount; and provides (sect. 12) that such a company may increase its capital and dividend it into shares of larger amount than the existing shares, or convert its paid-up shares into stock, but that "save as aforesaid, no alteration shall be made by any company in the conditions contained in its memorandum of association."

What is the meaning of the distinction thus drawn between a company without limit on the liability of its members and a company where the liability is limited, but, in the latter case, to assure to those dealing with the company that the whole of the subscribed capital, unless diminished by expenditure upon the objects defined by the memorandum, shall remain available for the discharge of its liabilities? The capital may, no doubt, be diminished by expenditure upon and reasonably incidental to all the objects specified. A part of it may be lost in carrying on the business operations authorized. Of this all persons trusting the company are aware, and take the risk. But I think they have a right to rely, and were intended by the Legislature to have a right to rely, on the capital remaining undiminished by any expenditure outside these limits, or by the return of any part of it to the shareholders.

Experience appears to have shewn that circumstances might occur in which a reduction of the capital would be expedient. Accordingly, by the Act of 1867 provision was made enabling a company under strictly defined conditions to reduce its capital. Nothing can be stronger than these carefully-worded provisions to shew how inconsistent with the very constitution of a joint stock company, with limited liability, the right to reduce its capital was considered to be.

Let me now invite your Lordships' attention to the facts of the present case. The company had purchased, prior to the date of the liquidation, no less than 4142 of its own shares; that is to say, considerably more than a fourth of the paid-up capital of the company had been either paid, or contracted to be paid, to shareholders, in consideration only of their ceasing to be so. I am quite unable to see how this expenditure was incurred in respect of or as incidental to any of the objects specified in the memorandum. And, if not, I have a difficulty in seeing how it can be justified. If the claim under consideration can be supported, the result would seem to be this, that the whole of the shareholders, with the exception of those holding seven individual shares, might not be claiming payment of the sums paid upon their share as against the creditors, who had a right to look to the moneys subscribed as the source out of which the company's liabilities to them were to be met. And the stringent precautions to prevent the reduction of the capital of a limited company, without due notice and judicial sanction, would be idle if the company might purchase its own shares wholesale, and so effect the desired result. I do not think it was disputed that a company could not enter upon such a transaction for the purpose of reducing its capital, but it was suggested that it might do so if that were not the object, but it was considered for some other reason desirable in the interest of the company to do so. To the creditor, whose interests, I think, sects. 8 and 12 of the Companies Act were intended to protect, it makes no difference what the object of the purchase is. The result to him is the same. The shareholders receive back the moneys subscribed, and there passes into their pockets what before existed in the form of cash in the coffers of the company, or of buildings, machinery, or stock available to meet the demands of the creditors.

What was the reason which induced the company in the present case to purchase its shares? If it was that they might sell them again, this would be a trafficking in the shares, and clearly unauthorized. If it was to retain them, this would be to my mind an indirect method of reducing the capital of the company. The only suggestion of another motive (and it seems to me to be a suggestion unsupported by proof) is that this was intended to be a family company, and that the directors wanted to keep the shares as much as possible in the hands of those who were partners, or who were interested in the old firm, or of those persons whom the directors thought they would like to be amongst this small number of shareholders. I cannot think that the employment of the company's money in the purchase of shares for any such purpose was legitimate. The business of the company was that of manufacturers of flannel. In what sense was the expenditure of the company's money in this way incidental to the carrying on of such a business, or how could it secure the end of enabling the business to be more profitably or satisfactorily carried on? I can quite understand that the directors of a company may sometimes desire that the shareholders should not be numerous, and that they should be persons likely to leave them with a free hand to carry on their operations. But I think it would be most dangerous to countenance the view that, for reasons such as these, they could legitimately expend the moneys of the company to any extent they please in the purchase of its shares. No doubt if certain shareholders are disposed to hamper the proceedings of the company, and are willing to sell their shares, they may be bought out; but this must be done by persons, existing shareholders or others, who can be induced to purchase the shares, and not out of the funds of the company. ...

[The concurring judgments of Lords Watson, Fitzgerald and Macnaghten are omitted.]

NOTE

Until the passage of modern corporations statutes such as the CBCA, the principal method by which a company could acquire non-redeemable shares was by reducing its capital under "carefully worded provisions" derived from the 1862 statute. See Canada Corporations Act, ss. 52-60, Ontario Corporations Act, ss. 35-38. This required the approval of a court, which would not be given unless all creditors consented, were paid off or had their claims secured. These provisions were interpreted strictly and all uncertainties resolved against the applicants. *Re Bunn-Munro Ltd.*, [1923] 3 W.W.R. 314 (Sask.).

Under the CBCA, a corporation may decide to reduce its stated capital in four ways. It may first redeem preferred shares under s. 36. Second, it may reduce the stated capital by special resolution under s. 38, by distributing cash, reducing liabilities or writing down overvalued assets. Third, s. 173(1)(f) permits a reduction of capital by amending the articles. Finally, shares may be repurchased under ss. 34 and 35, unless the corporation is prohibited from doing so by its articles. Apart from this, a firm may be required to reduce its stated capital under the appraisal remedy of s. 190 or an oppression action under s. 241.

Distributions to shareholders under these sections can only be made if the firm complies with insolvency restrictions. Note that these are differently worded. For example, s. 34(2) is more exacting than ss. 35(3), 36(2) and 38(3). Directors who authorize a distribution to shareholders that contravenes these restrictions are personally liable to reimburse the corporation under s. 118(2). As in the case of excessive dividends, they may apply to court under s. 118(4) for a s. 118(5) order rescinding the purchase. To the extent that moneys are recovered, the director's liability is reduced. Again, directors have a defence of good faith reliance on experts under s. 123(4).

When shares are reacquired by a corporation through any means, they must be either cancelled or, if the articles limit the number of authorized shares, restored to the status of authorized but unissued shares. CBCA s. 39(5). Repurchased shares that are not cancelled are known as "treasury stock" in the United States. However, such stock is not treated as an asset of the corporation. Under CBCA s. 39(1), for example, a deduction must be made from the stated capital account on a share repurchase. The figure deducted is not the purchase price, but the average stated capital per share prior to the repurchase. If the corporation in fact paid more than this, a further sum must be deducted from a surplus account.

Special problems of creditor protection have arisen when the repurchase is made by instalment, with the firm paying part of the purchase price immediately and the balance later. If bankruptcy intervenes, can the shareholder prove as an ordinary creditor for the unpaid purchase price? Most American cases have held that the shareholder's claim is deferred in such cases. See *Robinson v. Wangemann*, 75 F.2d 756, 757-58 (5th Cir. 1935) ("It is immaterial that the corporation was solvent and had a sufficient surplus to make payment when the agreement was entered into. It is necessary to a recovery that the corporation should be solvent and have sufficient surplus to prevent injury to creditors when the payment is actually made."). But in *Wolff v. Heidritter Lumber Co.*, 163 A. 140, 141 (N.J. Ch. 1932), the Court held "that the vendor ... becomes forthwith a creditor, instead of a stockholder, of the company and entitled to rank equally with other creditors in the event of a subsequent insolvency of the company, provided that at the time of the purchase the company has sufficient assets to pay its creditors in full. ..." CBCA s. 40 follows the majority American poisiton of subordinating shareholders in such cases. The instalment vendor becomes a creditor under s. 40(1) so long as the sale was not in violation of insolvency restrictions. However, under s. 40(3) he ranks ahead of shareholders but behind other creditors. This subordinated claim will usually be worthless on bankruptcy.

2. Shareholder Protection

While dividends are paid on a *pro rata* basis, shareholders are treated disparately on a repurchase, being divided into insiders who retain their shares and outsiders who sell out.

This has given rise to concerns that, as a consequence of the formally unequal treatment, one class of shareholders may be unduly favoured to the detriment of the other.

At first glance, a buyback may seem objectionable because of its distributional effects, with the fear that wealth will be transferred from selling shareholders to the firm and its non-selling shareholders. However, these concerns dissipate where the firm makes a pre-purchase announcement of the buyback, as it is required to do by s. 187(2) of the OSA Regulations. Empirical studies indicate that stock markets greet the announcement of a buyback with significant stock price increases, and that these increases are attributable to the information signalled from the repurchasing firm. See Buckley, *When the Medium is the Message: Corporate Buybacks as Signals*, 65 Ind. L.J. 493 (1990); Dann, Masulis & Mayers, *Repurchase Tender Offers and Earnings Information*, 14 J. Acc. & Econ. 217 (1991). The announcement of a buyback is taken by the market as a reliable signal that the firm perceives its shares to be undervalued. Stock price goes up, and selling shareholders will obtain more for their shares than they would have received had the buyback not been made. In addition, outsider shareholders will tender their shares with a knowledge of the higher value that management presumably attributes to the shares. Indeed, selling shareholders may expect that, however high the price may advance after the buyback announcement, management will always attribute a higher value to the shares.

There is a further reason why distributional concerns may not seem compelling. If the repurchase is profitable for the firm, all non-selling shareholders will share in this benefit. On the other hand, where managers believe that shares are undervalued by the market and do not repurchase the shares, wealth transfer effects will still arise. But here the class of beneficiaries will be restricted to the much smaller group of purchasing shareholders on the market, who buy at bargain prices. To complain that shareholders receive differential treatment on the buyback is thus meaningless, since full equality is not possible. Egalitarianism might in fact lead one to prefer share repurchases, which offer wider sharing among shareholders than when the gains accrue solely to outside purchasers.

Share repurchasers will give rise to the possibility of insider trading sanctions if the repurchase is made at a time when the firm possesses informational advantages. A reporting issuer that reacquires its securities is deemed to be an insider of itself under OSA s. 1(1) ("insider"), and the firm will then be subject to civil remedies under OSA s. 134. Even private firms may be liable to civil remedies under CBCA s. 131 when they make use of material undisclosed information on a buyback.

Share repurchases are often subject to special disclosure requirements under the OSA. These are similar to take-over bid requirements, although more disclosure is required on a share repurchase or "issuer bid." An issuer bid is defined under s. 89(1) as *any* offer by an issuer to buy, or an acceptance by it of an offer to sell, its equity securities. Unless the bid is exempted, it must then be made under s. 95, with an offer made to all holders of that class and kept open for 21 days. The bid must be accompanied by an issuer bid circular under OSA Form 33 containing prescribed information about the issuer. Misrepresentations in the circular can lead to liability under s. 131(3).

Exemptions from issuer bid requirements are found in s. 93(3). For example, private companies may reacquire shares without complying with the above provisions. For public companies, the primary exemption is for market purchases of up to 5% of the shares of a class every 12 months. Section 187 of the Regulations then requires that a Form 31 Notice of Intention be publicly released at least five days prior to the bid, with issuers disclosing any plans or proposals for material changes in their affairs. A "going private" issuer bid, in which public shareholders are to be eliminated, will also require a valuation of the firm under OSA Regulation 182(2) and Ontario Policy s. 9.1. If instead it is expected that public shareholders will continue to have a market for their shares, a valuation is not required. Going private transactions are discussed further in Chapter Eleven, Section D.

A share repurchase may be adopted as a defensive strategy in a take-over bid. When an insurgent seeks to acquire control of a target corporation, the target may seek to chill the take-over by competing with the insurgent in the purchase of its shares. Sometimes the target repurchases shares held by the insurgent in order to remove a pesky shareholder. Because this may be very profitable for the insurgent, such repurchases are called "greenmail." Defensive repurchases on a take-over bid and greenmail are considered in Chapter Eleven.

A special problem of unfairness arises when the corporation pays too much for the shares. For example, it may wish to bail out friendly shareholders when the possibility of insolvency looms. The former Ontario Business Corporations Act therefore required the repurchase be made at the lowest price at which, in the opinion of the directors, the shares were available. No such restriction is found in the OBCA or the CBCA, apart from the prohibition against repurchasing redeemable shares at a price exceeding the redemption price. CBCA s. 36(1). On the other hand, a "sweetheart" purchase from corporate insiders when the firm nears insolvency would likely be impeached under general fiduciary principles. See Brudney, *Fiduciary Ideology in Transactions Affecting Corporate Control*, 65 Mich. L. Rev. 259 (1966). Such distributions would also prejudice creditors, and if made by an insolvent firm that becomes bankrupt within 12 months thereafter, they may be impeached as fraudulent preferences under BIA s. 101.

Share repurchases may, however, be motivated by benign considerations. The repurchase may amount to a disinvestment strategy by a firm with surplus cash flow after all profitable opportunities have been taken up. The retention of surplus cash, without a repurchase program, will reduce claimholder wealth, since investors have better use for the cash than the firm if $k > r$. See Jensen, *Agency Costs of Free Cash Flow, Corporate Finance, and Takeovers*, 76 Am. Econ. Rev. 323 (1986). Of course, the firm could simply return the surplus cash to shareholders through a cash dividend. However, the firm's clientele of investors may prefer share repurchases to cash dividends because of tax considerations. Share repurchases will trigger capital gains tax for selling shareholders, while cash dividends are treated as income.

Share repurchase strategies may also be used as a technique of signalling hidden firm value to the market. Suppose that, with better information about underlying firm value, management believes that its shares are trading at bargain prices. Share repurchases will then have the effect of moving prices to a better informed level, through both the increase in demand for the shares and (more importantly) the signal provided to the market as to management's beliefs about stock value. Apart from the general advantages of more efficient stock markets in moving capital to its most highly valued users, this will also reduce deadweight losses associated with information production which would be incurred by market intermediaries were buybacks prohibited.

Signalling theories of share repurchases are, however, subject to several difficulties. First, the easiest method of eliminating informational disparities between a firm and outside public investors might seem to be through disclosing the information. Compared with the cost of mounting a share repurchase campaign, the cost of press release disclosure is trivial.

Disclosure strategies may not, however, be an adequate substitute for share repurchases. Bargain opportunities in the firm's stock may persist beyond disclosure of material information, since management's valuation may be based on "soft" information, or general impressions rather than hard material facts. In such cases, managers could presumably simply disclose that they feel that stock price is undervalued. But such disclosure may not be entirely creditable, such that buybacks may provide useful signals as to hidden firm wealth. Share repurchases may then serve the same efficiency purposes as tipping, as discussed in Chapter Eight, Section C.

A further objection to signalling theories of buybacks is that they may be adopted as part of a fraudulent scheme by management to inflate stock price. This possibility is discussed in the following case.

Davis v. Pennzoil Co.
Supreme Court of Pennsylvania
264 A.2d 597 (1970)

[Before Bell C.J. and Jones, Cohen, Eagen, O'Brien, Roberts and Pomeroy JJ. Opinion of the Court.]

COHEN J.: On April 16, 1965, appellant, Walter Davis, filed an action of assumpsit in the Court of Common Pleas of Allegheny County against the Pennzoil Company, appellee, on two causes of action. The first seeks recovery of $16,661,489, plus interest, for financial advice allegedly given to South Penn Oil Company (appellee's prior name) by appellant under an agreement to pay him at the prevailing rate in the custom of the trade if the recommendations were accepted and used in whole or part. ...

Taking the record in a light as favorable to appellant as possible, the factual background is as follows. James Breene, whose family had long been connected with the corporate affairs of appellee, and who was about to inherit stock in South Penn, met with appellant in Arizona in March, 1962. He explained to appellant that in his opinion South Penn "wasn't going any place" and that appellant with his extensive experience in corporate matters could be of great use to the company. He stated that John Selden, President, Chief Executive Officer, and Chairman of the Board of Directors of appellee, should want to know about any recommendations appellant might have. Over the next few months appellant studied South Penn's situation and formulated recommendations. He spoke with Breene several times about his ideas during this period. Towards the end of May, 1962, Breene contacted Selden and told him that Walter Davis would like to discuss with him some matters concerning South Penn. Breene told appellant that Selden had agreed to meet with him and had suggested that he have ready an outline of the plan. After an abortive attempt on June 11 in Pittsburgh, they met on June 24 in Toronto.

In the course of that meeting appellant outlined to Selden the plan he had developed. In essence that plan recommends that:

1. South Penn should advance continually the market price of its shares by purchase of its own shares on the open market on the American Stock Exchange.

2. South Penn should acquire Tidewater's holdings of its shares (amounting to 9-11% of outstanding shares) and thus eliminate a large bloc overhanging the market and eliminate a source of opposition to an expansion program.

3. South Penn should negotiate property-reserve acquisitions through shares of its stock which with South Penn leading the way will be increasing in value.

4. In addition South Penn should

    a. increase the number of authorized shares from 1,715,000 to 10,000,000.

    b. change its listing from the American to the New York Exchange.

    c. change its name to Pennzoil Company.

    d. strengthen the board of directors by replacing those who retire by experienced corporate executives of national prestige.

5. South Penn should expand earnings through acquisition of additional oil and gas production and reserves through merger and/or purchase with shares at advanced prices. Also, there should be substantial extension of product-distributorships, plants and marketing facilities under experienced personnel.

6. South Penn should

    a. issue quarterly reports to shareholders.

    b. split the shares as the market price advances.

    c. increase dividends.

    d. not make any purchases involving the issuance of any substantial amount of stock-conversion rights.

In his deposition appellant states that at that meeting Selden promised to compensate him to the extent of "10 per cent of the difference of the market price value of the outstanding shares of the company on use, adoption and completion or implementation of the plan as determined by me ... compensation related to the difference between the market price of the outstanding shares on completion of the plan as compared to the market value of the outstanding shares at the time of the agreement by Selden to compensate me."

• • •

The court below found that the "dominant theme" of the plan appellant relies on as the basis of the contract pleaded in Count 1 involved a violation of federal securities law. Relevant to this issue are sections 9(a)(2) and 10(b) of the Securities Exchange Act of 1934 (Exchange Act), 15 U.S.C. § 78i(a)(2), 15 U.S.C. § 78j(b), which state respectively:

It shall be unlawful for any person, directly or indirectly, by the use of the mails or any means or instrumentality of interstate commerce, or of any facility of any national securities exchange, or for any member of a national securities exchange—... to effect, alone or with one or more other persons, a series of transactions in any security registered on a national securities exchange creating actual or apparent active trading in such security or raising or depressing the price of such security, for the purpose of inducing the purchase or sale of such security by others.

It shall be unlawful for any person, directly or indirectly, by the use of any means or instrumentality of interstate commerce or of the mails, or of any facility of any national securities exchange—... to use or employ, in connection with the purchase or sale of any security registered on a national securities exchange or any security not so registered, any manipulative or deceptive device or contrivance in contravention of such rules and regulations as the Commission may prescribe as necessary or appropriate in the public interest or for the protection of investors.

The famous rule 10b-5 promulgated under § 10(b) states:

It shall be unlawful for any person, directly or indirectly, by the use of any means or instrumentality of interstate commerce, or of the mails, or of any facility of any national securities exchange,

(a) to employ any device, scheme, or artifice to defraud,

(b) to make any untrue statement of a material fact or to omit to state a material fact necessary in order to make the statements made, in the light of the circumstances under which they were made, not misleading, or

(c) to engage in any act, practice, or course of business which operates or would operate as a fraud or deceit upon any person, in connection with the purchase or sale of any security.

In order to determine how appellant's plan relates to these statutes, it is necessary to quote excerpts from that plan.

SP should advance continually the market price of its shares from the prolonged, rather static range in the low 30's commensurate with the carrying out of this program and general economic and market conditions. Such advance should be implemented by South Penn or one or more of its officials on its behalf, by purchasing shares of South Penn on the open market on the ASE. The relatively small floating supply of shares ... of this long, generous dividend-payer, should make a relatively easy job of continually advancing SP's market price and such advance will be assisted substantially (if not taken over in a major way from time to time by the investing public and brokerage fraternity) when it becomes apparent through publicity and market action that SP has entered on an accelerated *expansion program*. At the moment, on the basis of 1961 earnings of $2.40 per share, SP's shares at around $32.00 are selling at only about 13 times earnings whereas they could and should be selling at least 20 to say 23 times earnings or around $48.00 to $55.00 per share. This 20 times (plus) ratio will materialize without difficulty as soon as the investing public learn that SP has embarked on a constructive aggressive expansion program. ...

... The shares purchased in the open market as above mentioned as well as Tidewater's SP shares, if purchased, can, of course be used in negotiating future property acquisitions ... then SP shares market price could continually make new highs, with occasional market help of SP.

South Penn's leading the way, from time to time, in continually advancing the market price of its shares consistent with the circumstances as mentioned, will be beneficial to the company in many ways, especially in establishing a much higher and more favorable price-structure basis on which to negotiate thru shares, well selected property-reserve acquisitions in its expansion program. ...

Earnings-expansion through acquisition ... (of reserve) ... thru merger and/or purchase ... with payment for same being made by the company out of its treasury and increased shares at advanced stock market prices for SP shares as above mentioned. ...

There are two elements to the conduct proscribed by § 9(a)(2)—"(i) effecting the requisite series of transactions and (ii) doing so for the purpose of inducing the purchase or sale of such security by others." 3 Loss, Securities Regulation 1550 (2d ed. 1961). It would almost seem that in drafting his plan appellant was trying to model his words on those contained in the statute. What Davis was proposing was that South Penn expand by "purchasing" companies cheaply with stock that was valued at high levels as a result of South Penn's own market activity and the effect that activity would have on the "investing public and the brokerage community." "Of course, it is axiomatic that it is the ticker record of a stock that attracts customers, and here, by buying purchasing power and increasing activity, there was attention called to the stock and a marked advance was achieved by it." *SEC v. Torr*, 22 F. Supp. 602, 608 (S.D. N.Y. 1938). The plan clearly envisages a series of transactions by appellee for the purpose of creating public interest in the stock and thus raising its price.

Appellant acknowledges that market manipulation of the type described is unlawful but argues that the court below ignored portions of the exhibit from which inferences favorable to it could be drawn. He specifically refers to the language "... commensurate with the carrying out of this program and general economic and market conditions. ..." This language, however, is extremely general and cannot detract from the very specific references to proposed conduct clearly violated of § 9(a)(2). In addition, the following appears in appellant's deposition testimony:

Q. How would that be increased? How would you increase the price? A. By the company purchasing some of its shares in the open market.

Q. To recreate a demand for the stock and make it go up? Is that what you idea was?
A. By South Penn purchasing shares of its own stock in the open market at higher prices.

Appellant next argues that there is no prohibition against a corporation repurchasing its own shares on the open market. That is certainly true. See Note, Corporate Stock Repurchases Under the Federal Securities Laws, 66 Colum. L. Rev. 1292, 1293-95 (1966). The only question concerns the reason for the repurchase, and the wording of the plan plus appellant's own testimony graphically show that purpose to be violative of federal law.

Finally, appellant argues that the cases cited by the court below involved situations in which persons created an artificially high market in order to sell securities or exercise options and thus realize a profit. Regardless whether that is true or not, § 9(a)(2) prohibits the effecting of a series of transactions for the purpose of inducing others to buy or sell and does not inquire in any way into why the individual engaged in that conduct. Also, in its proceeding against Genesco, Inc., CCH Fed. Sec. L. Rep. para. 77354 (1966), the commission forced Genesco to admit that it may have violated § 9(a)(2) when it exchanged over 1,000,000 shares of its common stock for stock or assets of other companies at the same time that it was purchasing large numbers of its shares in the open market for its Employee Stock Purchase Plan and its Special Stock Purchase Plan. This is almost exactly what appellant proposed.

As to the application of § 10(b) and rule 10b-5, the Second Circuit Court of Appeals held in *SEC v. Texas Gulf Sulphur Co.*, 401 F.2d 833 (2d Cir. 1968), that an insider, which would include the corporation itself, could not purchase shares of that company without disclosing to the public material facts. The court said, 401 F.2d at 849, "'The basic test of materiality ... is whether a reasonable man would attach importance ... in determining his choice of action in the transaction in question. ...' This, of course, encompasses any fact '... which in reasonable and objective contemplation might affect the value of the corporation's stock or securities. ...'" Therefore, a corporation could not begin a program of purchasing its own stock in the open market for the purpose of creating investor interest in it and thereby driving up the price without disclosing that purpose to the public for such information would be material by any definition of that word.

As the Commission stated in *Halsey, Stuart & Co., Inc.*, 30 SEC 106, 112 (1949):

It is of utmost materiality to a buyer to know that he may not assume that the prices he pays were reached in a free market, and the manipulator cannot make sales not accompanied by disclosure of his activities without committing fraud.

... Certainly what the Commission said about sales would be valid for purchases also. It is just as important that sellers be able to assume that the prices they received were reached in a free market.

• • •

Therefore, appellant's plan called for violations of 10(b) and 10b-5 as to two time periods—(1) by not disclosing its manipulative intentions during the time it was buying shares to create public interest in the stock and (2) by not disclosing to prospective merger partners and recipients of its shares in exchange for stock or assets that the value of South Penn shares they would receive were inflated because of the company's manipulative activity.

Appellant argues that fraud cannot be presumed but must be proved by clear and precise evidence. The only way the plan would have been successful, however, would have been if the necessary disclosures had not been made. Certainly no prudent investor would deal in a stock if he knew the company was manipulating its price, and no company would consider a merger or sale of assets for stock if it knew the value of the stock it would receive had not been set in a free market. Complying with the requirements of 10(b) and 10b-5 would have rendered the plan valueless, and under those circumstances there is no need for a finder of fact to hear evidence on the question. Therefore, we conclude that the court properly found that an essential part of the plan violated federal securities law. ...

Judgment and orders affirmed.

Stock Manipulation. The Davis plan provides an example of how a market "bubble" might develop through rational speculation. Share repurchases at a price that exceeds management's estimate of value will ordinarily decrease firm value. But if management is presumed allied to its existing shareholders, and not to shareholders who are issued shares subsequently, it may propose a buyout at a price that exceeds its estimate of firm value. The buyback would represent a profitable opportunity to existing shareholders, who could be expected to tender at the premium price. In doing so, they would minimize wealth transfer effects among themselves since all would have an opportunity to participate in the buyback. However, if stock price increased because of the buyback and remained inflated thereafter, there would be a further distributional effect when the firm subsequently issued shares to new shareholders at the inflated price. The buyback would then effect a wealth transfer from subsequent to existing shareholders. Thus the share repurchases by South Penn would then have reduced the cost of its subsequent acquisition program, since it was to be financed through an exchange of inflated South Penn stock.

These distributional effects are, however, of lessened concern when outside investors are aware of the possibility of stock price manipulation on a buyback. The strength of the signal of undervaluation on a buyback announcement would then be weakened, unless there were some way of distinguishing "honest" from "dishonest" buybacks. But if distributional concerns are not compelling, an allocational case may yet be made for s. 9(a)(2) liability if it would assist in strengthening the signal to the market. Thus, with liability for stock manipulation, the announcement of a buyback would provide better information about management's honest belief in the undervaluation of the firm. The liability rule might then be justified as dissipating informational asymmetries between inside managers and outside public investors.

Whether antifraud techniques, such as s. 9(a)(2) of the 1934 Act, are desirable will, however, depend on whether the benefits of prohibiting stock manipulation are exceeded by the costs associated with chilling more benign buybacks. With liability for "fraudulent" buybacks, managers will be less willing to announce a share repurchase when they lack an honest belief that stock prices are undervalued. If, however, it is difficult to prove management's honest belief that the stock is undervalued, the possibility exists that the liability rule will deter managers from repurchasing shares even where they do have better information about firm value. The result would be a market that is less, not more, informed about firm value. Review the *Pennzoil* decision to see if you can be sure that management was in fact fraudulent in its belief about the undervalued market price for South Penn shares.

Share repurchases are also useful in stabilizing speculative markets during crashes. Corporate buyback announcements were an important reason for the revival of the market after its crash on October 19, 1987. Where the stock market seems to undervalue firm assets, the price differentials between stock and asset value provide profitable arbitrage opportunities for the firm itself in a share repurchase or for tender offerors in a take-over bid. In either case, the ability to move wealth from one market to the other reduces the likelihood of pathologies affecting one market only, and serves stabilization norms.

The OSA does not have a provision equivalent to s. 9(a)(2), but stock manipulation is prohibited by the Toronto Stock Exchange General By-law, 1 Can. Stock Exchange Manual (CCH) para. 802-548:

Sec. 11.26. *Manipulative or Deceptive Method of Trading.*—(1) no member or approved person shall use or knowingly participate in the use of any manipulative or deceptive method of trading in connection with the purchase or sale of any security which creates or may create a false or misleading appearance of trading activity or an artificial price for the said security.

(2) without in any way limiting the generality of the foregoing the following shall be deemed manipulative or deceptive methods of trading:

. . .

(d) making purchases of or offers to purchase any security at successively higher prices, or sales of or offers to sell any security at successively lower prices for the purpose of creating or inducing a false or misleading appearance of trading in such security or for the purpose of unduly or improperly influencing the market price of such security;

(e) effecting, alone or with one or more persons, a series of trades in any security, for the purpose of inducing the purchase or sale of such security, which creates actual or apparent trading in such security or raises or depresses the price of such security.

Article 380(2) of the Canadian Criminal Code provides that "[e]very one who, by deceit, falsehood or other fraudulent means, whether or not it is a false pretense within the meaning of this Act, with intent to defraud, affects the public market price of stocks, shares ... or anything that is offered for sale to the public, is guilty of an indictable offense and is liable to imprisonment for a term not exceeding 10 years." Would this section have prohibited the Davis plan?

See Getz, *Some Aspects of Corporate Share Repurchases*, 9 U.B.C.L. Rev. 9 (1974); Phillips, *The Concept of a Corporation's Purchase of Its Own Shares*, 15 Alta. L. Rev. 324 (1977).

CHAPTER ELEVEN

Mergers and Acquisitions

A. ECONOMIC CONSIDERATIONS

Corporate combinations or mergers had an enormous impact on the Canadian economy in the 1980s. In some cases, such as "short-form" amalgamations of parent corporations with their wholly owned subsidiaries under CBCA s. 184, a merger would not have significant economic effects. But when the combination represents the union of distinct businesses, substantial new value may be created.

Assets are purchased because they are worth more to their purchaser than to their seller. We might therefore presume that assets acquired in a merger will be worth more when held together than when held apart. That is, the combination will result in the synergistic gains of uniting firm-specific assets, where $2 + 2 = 5$. If V_{AB} is the value of the combined firm, and the separate firms are worth V_A and V_B, then

$$V_{AB} > V_A + V_B$$

The difference between the value of the firms in combination and their value when held separately is the *gain* from the merger.

$$\text{Gain} = V_{AB} - (V_A + V_B)$$

Opportunities for profitable mergers therefore exist so long as the gain from the merger exceeds its cost. If the merger is seen as an acquisition by firm A of firm B, the cost for firm A is the amount by which the purchase price of B exceeds its value when held separately.

$$\text{Cost} = \text{Price} - V_B$$

The gain from the merger can then be seen as the total amount of surplus value produced by the combination, with the cost equal to that portion of the surplus assigned to the seller of firm B. From the perspective of firm A, the merger will be attractive so long as it has a positive net present value (*NPV*), defined as

$$\begin{aligned} NPV &= \text{Gain} - \text{Cost} \\ &= V_{AB} - (V_A + V_B) - (\text{Price} - V_B) \\ &= V_{AB} - (V_A + \text{Price}) \end{aligned}$$

For example, suppose that firm A has a value of $1,000,000 and firm B a value of $500,000, but that the two firms have a value when combined of $1,700,000. The gain from the merger is then $200,000. If firm B is purchased for $650,000, the cost of the merger from the perspective of firm A is Price $- V_B = \$150,000$, and the *NPV* for firm A will be $50,000.

Corporate combinations do not always represent bargain opportunities. Some acquisitions may represent a value-decreasing conglomerization, as on the purchase of an unrelated business. Firm value may then be increased through deconglomerization, or the disposition by conglomerates of unprofitable divisions. One way in which this may be accomplished is through a spin-off dividend of shares in a subsidiary, as discussed in Chapter Ten, Section A. The firm might also sell off a division and pay the proceeds to shareholders as a cash dividend. If the firm does not reduce its size voluntarily, and asset value exceeds market value, it becomes a candidate for a break-up or bust-up merger, in which insurgents gain control of a firm and finance their acquisition expenses through a sale of a division of the firm. All of these transactions assume that the firm had grown too large, and that divesting itself of a division represents a bargain opportunity. These are cases of negative synergy, where $4 - 2 = 3$.

Arbitrage possibilities in a break-up merger will arise only if

$$V_A + V_B > V_{AB}$$

with a break-up gain equal to

$$\text{Gain} = (V_A + V_B) - V_{AB}$$

If the insurgents propose to sell off division B after the acquisition, the cost of the merger will equal its price less the value of the combined enterprise.

$$\text{Cost} = \text{Price} - V_{AB}$$

The acquisition of the firm will then represent an attractive opportunity so long as its *NPV* is positive.

$$\begin{aligned} NPV &= \text{Gain} - \text{Cost} \\ &= V_A + V_B - \text{Price} \end{aligned}$$

In other words, if V_A is $1,000,000 and V_B is $500,000 but V_{AB} is $1,300,000, the acquirer will pay any price up to $1,500,000 for the combined firm.

Efficiency Consequences of Mergers. There is a great deal of evidence that take-over bids are associated with significant gains for offeree shareholders, and that the defeat of a take-over bid results in offeree shareholder losses. The gains are permanent when the bid is successful, but are reversed when the bid is defeated by the defensive manoeuvres of offeree firm management. See Bradley, Desai & Kim, *The Rationale Behind Interfirm Tender Offers: Information or Synergy?* 11 J. Fin. Econ. 183 (1983); Bradley, Desai & Kim, *Synergistic Gains From Corporate Acquisitions and their Division between the Stockholders of Targets and Acquiring Firms*, 21 J. Fin. Econ. 3 (1988); Jarrell, Brickley & Netter, *The Market for Corporate Control: The Empirical Evidence Since 1980*, 2 J. Econ. Persp. 49 (1988). While this evidence comes from studies of American take-overs, the Canadian evidence is not dissimilar. See Eckbo, *Mergers and the Market for Corporate Control: The Canadian Evidence*, 19 Can. J. Econ. 236 (1986).

There is also evidence that acquiring firms share in the merger gains, though not as much as target shareholders. Jensen and Ruback found that successful tender offerors earned a 3.8% abnormal return in the two-month period surrounding announcement of the offer. In another study, Bradley found that offeree shareholders received an average 49% premium for their shares, but that the average appreciation of target stock through one month after the take-up of shares was 36%. Offerors therefore suffered a 13% loss on every share they purchased. Yet the same offerors saw their own shares appreciate by 9% as a result of the offer, likely as a consequence of anticipated merger gains. Bradley, *Interfirm Tender Offers and the Market for Corporate Control*, 53 J. Bus. 345 (1980). In his study of 1,500 Canadian offerors from 1964 to 1983, Eckbo reported positive abnormal returns of 4.3% for the 12-month period preceding a successful bid. Eckbo, *Mergers and the Market for Corporate Control: The Canadian Evidence*, 19 Can. J. Econ. 236, 251 (1986). However, while most studies indicate that both firms do better from a merger, a few studies have found that shareholders of acquiring firms are unaffected by mergers. See Asquith, *Merger Bids, Uncertainty, and Stockholder Returns*, 11 J. Fin. Econ. 51 (1983) (statistically insignificant loss of 0.46%); Asquith & Kim, *The Impact of Merger Bids on the Participating Firms' Securityholders*, 37 J. Fin. 1209 (1982).

Evidence that acquirers make smaller gains than target shareholders is not inconsistent with efficiency explanations of the move to merge, and may even reflect an equal split of the synergy if the target corporation is considerably smaller than the acquirer. For example, if the acquiring firm is worth $100 and the target $10, an equal division of merger gains of $2 would mean a 1% increase for the acquirer's shareholders and a 10% increase for the target's shareholders. In addition, a finding that most merger gains accrue to target shareholders may simply indicate that the market for corporate control is competitive. For example, if a rival bidder seeks control of the target, the auction for it ensures that target shareholders will be the principal beneficiaries of the merger.

There are several reasons why two firms may plausibly be worth more in combination than when held apart. First, the acquired corporation may be managed inefficiently such that new management could operate it more profitably. Under Henry Manne's market for corporate control (discussed in Chapter Six), a corporation with low share prices is a take-over bid target if the acquiring corporation believes that it can increase share prices by replacing inefficient with efficient management. The discipline provided by take-over bids would then provide an important incentive to reduce agency costs.

Mergers may also result in efficiency gains through synergistic benefits which arise when two firms are combined. One source of this synergy may be economies of scale, where larger firms achieve efficiencies in production and marketing that are unavailable to smaller firms. For example, economies of scale are available when $1,000,000 spent on research and development by a major firm will likely produce more results than $100,000 spent separately by each of 10 smaller firms. See F. Scherer, *Industrial Market Strategy and Economic Performance* 81-104 (2d ed. 1980). Another example of synergy arises through vertical integration, where a firm merges with a supplier of inputs or purchaser of outputs. Thus, a distributor might merge with its manufacturer, or a mining company with a steel manufacturer. Vertical integration will then reduce the transaction costs of bargaining between separate firms. Though the amalgamated entity will lose the information provided by price signals, internal organization within the firm may permit adaptive decision-making, which economizes on strategic planning. See O. Williamson, *Markets and Hierarchies: Analysis and Antitrust Implications* 20-40 (1975).

"Bad Bidders" and Bust-Up Gains. Other explanations for the modest gains reported for offeror shareholders focus on bidder pathologies. Even if most bids are value-increasing, bidder gains might be masked by a smaller group of "bad bidders." In particular, we might expect that bids made to acquire unrelated firms will be value-decreasing.

Throughout the 1960s and early 1970s, corporate conglomerization, or the acquisition of new firms in unrelated lines of business, was thought to offer an easy method of advancing stock prices. Where offeror and offeree firms operated in different industries, it was difficult to see how the combination would result in synergistic gains. However, a variety of explanations were offered for conglomerization gains. In particular, it was suggested that conglomerization gave shareholders an easy method to diversify risk. However, it was quickly realized that shareholders could diversify as easily as the firm, and that it might well be far more costly for the firm to do so if it had to pay a premium price to acquire large blocks of target stock. See Levy & Sarnat, *Diversification, Portfolio Analysis and the Uneasy Case for Conglomerate Mergers*, 25 J. Fin. 795 (1970).

Conglomerization was also thought to work a crude fraud upon financial markets. For example, it was thought that the market would attribute the offeror's low capitalization rate when it acquired a less valuable firm with a higher capitalization rate. Through an aggressive merger policy, then, the firm could cheaply boost up its earnings.

How this supposedly works may be illustrated through the following example. Assume that A Corp. proposes to acquire B Corp., the corporations having the following characteristics:

	A Corp.	B Corp.
Issued shares	100,000	100,000
Net income per year	$100,000	$100,000
Earnings per share	$1	$1
Market value per share	$25	$10
Multiplier	25	10
Market value of corporation	$2,500,000	$1,000,000

A Corp. and B Corp. amalgamate as AB Corp. on the basis that A Corp. shareholders are given one share in AB Corp. for each share held by them, and B Corp. shareholders are given one share in AB Corp. for each two shares held by them. This will presumably be acceptable to B Corp. shareholders, who contribute shares worth 40% of A Corp.'s value in return for a payout worth 50% of the payout to A Corp.'s shareholders. After the amalgamation, it is hoped that the value of the combined enterprise will be as follows:

	AB Corp.
Issued shares	150,000
Net income per year	$200,000
Earnings per share	$1.33
Multiplier	25
Value per share	$33.33
Value of corporation	$5,000,000

Does this make sense? The valuation of AB Corp. shares at $33.33 each depends on the assumption that a multiplier of 25 will be applied to the earnings of $1.33. In other words, the combined enterprise is seen to get the benefit of B Corp.'s cheap earnings without any change in the multiplier of A Corp. to compensate for the greater risk associated with B Corp. As a result, the combined value of the two corporations is increased by $1,500,000. However, unless economic realities are affected, any difference in the value of the combined enterprise from its separate components is inconsistent with the ECMH.

Another flimflam explanation of conglomerate mergers looked to the different techniques for accounting for the acquisition, with the merged firm reporting higher earnings under "pooling" as opposed to "purchase" accounting. These theories of merger gains are inconsistent with efficient stock markets, and there is no evidence that the choice of accounting technique "fooled" investors. See Hong, Kaplan & Mandelker, *Pooling vs. Purchase: The Effects of Accounting for Mergers on Stock Prices*, 53 Acct. Rev. 31 (1978) (finding that stock price was unaffected by the choice of pooling or purchase accounting); Nathan, *Do Firms Pay to Pool?: Some Empirical Evidence*, 7 J. Acc. & Pub. Pol. 185 (1988) (finding no evidence that acquirers paid for pooling through a higher purchase price, as might have been expected if pooling offered merger gains). Pooling accounting is in any event quite rare in Canada.

Thus the benefits of conglomerization were highly suspect. In addition, conglomerization began to be seen as a defensive strategy aimed at repelling bidders. At a time when bankers were loath to fund take-over bids, a firm might perhaps remove itself from corporate control markets by becoming too big for most bidders. In addition, conglomerization strategies might result from excessive managerial risk aversion. A manager who sought to keep his job might pass up a more valuable opportunity for a less promising but more secure investment.* In fact, manager-controlled firms are more heavily

---

* Managerial risk reduction explanations of the move to merge overlap with "hubris" theories, under which managers overestimate their ability to rescue ailing offeree firms, and thus overpay for them. See Roll, *The Hubris Hypothesis of Corporate Takeovers*, 59 J. Bus. 197 (1986), reprinted in Romano 242. Another explanation of bidder overpayment focuses on "winner's curse" problems. Suppose that several firms bid for an offeree, with similar synergies available to each. Each bidder must value the offeree and anticipated synergy gains, and the winner of the auction will be the firm that attributes the highest value to the merger—that is, the outlier, not the mean valuation, will win. The winner might thus find that it has overbid for the offeree. See Black, *Bidder Overpayment in Takeovers*, 41 Stan. L. Rev. 597 (1989).

diversified than firms controlled by a major shareholder. See Amihud & Lev, *Risk Reduction as a Managerial Motive for Conglomerate Mergers*, 12 Bell J. Econ. 605 (1981).

Management risk aversion offers a useful insight into "managerialist" theories of the firm. Such theories regard managers not as profit maximizers but as "satisfiers." In other words, they seek only that level of profits which will keep other claimholders satisfied, and beyond that level maximize firm size and not firm value. With greater firm size, the manager enjoys increased political leverage within the firm as well as greater security. The best known recent statements of managerialism are R. Cyert & J. March, *A Behavioral Theory of the Firm* (1963) and R. Marris, *The Economic Theory of "Managerial" Capitalism* (1964), though its ideas are also familiar to readers of John Kenneth Galbraith. Managerialism attracts considerably fewer adherents today than it did 20 years ago, since it likely overstates management's independence. Even if agency costs are not eliminated, such devices as the market for corporate control, internal monitoring strategies and compensation techniques can do much to realign management interests with those of the residual owners. But some residual managerial risk aversion will likely still arise, and managers might then propose inefficient conglomerate mergers.

Early studies failed to detect evidence of conglomerization gains, and even noted a conglomerate discount. See Mason & Goudzwaard, *Performance of Conglomerate Firms: A Portfolio Approach*, 31 J. Fin. 39 (1976) (finding that conglomerates earned average annual accounting returns of 7.46% from 1962 to 1967, while a matched portfolio of non-conglomerate holdings earned 13.99%). See also Melcher & Rush, *The Performance of Conglomerate Firms: Recent Risk and Return Experience*, 28 J. Fin. 381 (1973). Conglomerate acquisitions of unrelated businesses in the 1980s were associated with significant negative returns. See Morck, Shleifer & Vishny, *Do Managerial Objectives Drive Bad Acquisitions?* 45 J. Fin. 31, 43 (1990) (reporting excess returns of −4.09% for 115 1980-1987 unrelated acquisitions, and excess returns of 2.88% for related acquisitions). Firms whose acquisitions are value-reducing are also more likely to become take-over targets than efficient acquirers. See Mitchell & Lehn, *Do Bad Bidders Become Good Targets?* 98 J. Pol. Econ. 372 (1988). Other evidence of the "bad bidder" phenomenon was provided by findings that acquisitions by low-performing firms were on average value-decreasing. See Lang, Stultz & Walkling, *Managerial Performance, Tobin's Q, and the Gains from Successful Tender Offers*, 24 J. Fin. Econ. 137, 147 (1988) (finding that bidders with a high ratio of market to replacement value gain and low-ratio bidders lose value, with a significant 5.2% difference between their returns).

When inefficiently large firms are publicly held, the difference between conglomerate and break-up value offers enormous arbitrage gains to take-over bidders. Moreover, by the 1980's the sheer size of conglomerates no longer deterred bidders, because high-yield ("junk bond") financing enabled them to capture even the largest of corporate behemoths. Thus a smaller firm could bid for a much larger firm if it could persuade lenders that the offeree's break-up value exceeded its market value. With its new source of financing, the offeror would bid for the firm and eliminate the negative synergies through a divestiture or break-up. Many of the merger gains during the 1980s resulted from undoing the inefficient conglomerization of the 1960s and 1970s. See Morck, Shleifer & Veshny, *Do Managerial Objectives Drive Bad Acquisitions?* 45 J. Fin. 31, 43 (1990).

What emerged from the break-up was a smaller firm (or series of firms), frequently with more concentrated stock ownership. Instead of dispersed stock holdings, and a separation of management and control, a single blockholder might emerge with voting control of the firm. The blockholder was often a firm manager or the lender who financed the acquisition. Thus the transformation of the firm promoted monitoring efficiencies, and released negative synergies. Junk bonds also served monitoring goals, since they were issued to major lenders. With higher debt-equity ratios, a firm also bonded itself against the retention of free cash flow, or earnings inefficiently retained by the firm which can be put to better use when distributed to investors. Firm managers have the discretion to omit dividends to shareholders, but not principal and interest payments to debt holders. Even if the firms that emerged from a junk bond restructuring had a greater probability of default, then, most economists regard the break-up merger boom in the 1980s to have been a great success. See Jensen, *Agency Costs of Free Cash Flow, Corporate Finance, and Takeovers*, 76 Am. Econ. Rev. 323 (1986); Jensen, *Eclipse of the Public Corporation*, [1989] Harv. Bus. Rev. 61. During that period, American public firms began to resemble less the Berle-Means firm of independent managers and high agency costs, and to resemble more the typical Canadian public firm, with its less diversified assets, monitoring blockholders, and powerful bankers.

This view of break-up mergers is not without its critics. On human capital theories, a break-up might breach an implicit contract with managers. The possibility of dismissal might lead a manager to underinvest in firm-specific skills, whose value is lost when the manager leaves the firm. Promises of job tenure, in the form of anti-takeover barriers, might therefore promote human capital efficiencies. See Shleifer & Summers, *Breach of Trust in Hostile Takeovers*, in A. Auerbach (ed.), *Corporate Takeovers: Causes and Consequences* 33 (1988), reprinted in Romano 237; Coffee, *Shareholders Versus Managers: The Strain in the Corporate Web*, 85 Mich. L. Rev. 1 (1986).

Stakeholders. Shareholder wealth gains on a take-over would be suspect if they resulted from distributional rather than efficiency effects. Thus shareholder gains might be attributed to a wealth transfer from four kinds of stakeholders: the state, in the form of a lower tax burden; consumers, through monopolistic profits; creditors; and employees.

As noted in Chapter One, Section C, the U.S. Tax Code subsidizes debt financing by permitting firms to deduct interest but not dividend payments. A portion of the gains behind bust-up mergers financed by junk bonds might thus reflect the benefits of the higher debt shield. On the other hand, firms may increase their debt levels without a merger, and this account of merger gains requires an explanation why managers had forgone such benefits before the merger. A more plausible tax explanation of the merger movement focuses on the free "step-up" available before the 1986 Tax Code changes. Where the offeror paid more for the offeree's assets than they were valued in the hands of the offeree, the offeror could carry them at the higher acquisition cost without paying any tax on the appreciation. However, tax considerations appear unable to account for all, or even the major part of, pre-1986 U.S. merger gains. One study of 1968-1983 mergers reported that only 20% of them resulted in tax benefits, and that in such cases the value of the tax benefit was substantially lower than the take-over premium. See Auerbach & Reihus, *Taxation and the Dynamics of Corporate Control: The Uncertain Case for Tax*

Motivated Acquisitions, in J. Coffee, L. Lowenstein & S. Rose-Ackerman, *Knights, Raiders and Targets: The Impact of Hostile Takeovers* 271 (1988). See also Kaplan, *Management Buyouts: Evidence on Taxes as a Source of Value*, 44 J. Fin. 611 (1989).

In theory, merger gains might be attributed to increased market concentration and the prospect of monopolistic profits. However, there is no evidence that corporate acquisitions result in greater levels of industry concentration. See Eckbo, *Mergers and the Corporate Concentration Doctrine: Evidence from the Capital Markets*, 58 J. Bus. 325 (1985).

Mergers that result in increased debt levels increase the likelihood of default, and might effect a wealth transfer from existing creditors. Before the advent of junk bond financing, mergers did not appear to affect creditor wealth. See Kim & McConnell, *Corporate Mergers and the Co-Insurance of Corporate Debt*, 32 J. Fin. 349 (1977). However, in the leveraged buyouts (LBOs) of the 1980s, where the firm repurchased public stock interests and financed them with an issue of high-yield debt claims, debt levels increased dramatically and creditor losses were reported. For example, in one study of 15 LBOs, the outstanding debt of eight firms was downgraded while the debt of the remaining firms was put on a credit watch. Amihud, *Leverage Management Buyouts and Shareholders' Wealth*, in Y. Amihud, *Leveraged Management Buyouts: Causes and Consequences* 11 (1989). But even then, shareholder gains have been found greatly to exceed creditor losses. See Lehn & Poulsen, *The Economics of Event Risk: The Case of Bondholders in Leveraged Buyouts*, 15 J. Corp. L. 199, 209-10 (1990) (reviewing findings that bondholder losses account for less than 4% of shareholder gains). This suggests that problems of creditor expropriation should be left to the creditors themselves to cure, through veto or conversion rights on a take-over or LBO. For example, after the highly publicized RJR Nabisco LBO of 1988, where bond values declined by $1 billion, lenders insisted on stronger protective devices. See Kahan & Klausner, *Antitakeover Provisions in Bonds: Bondholder Protection or Management Entrenchment?* 40 U.C.L.A. L. Rev. 931 (1993).

Finally, break-up mergers might effect a wealth transfer from employees. Not merely might employees lose their jobs when firms downsize, but the job loss might constitute an expropriation of firm-specific skills. Where the firm has implicitly promised its employees tenure to promote investment in such skills, employee terminations will constitute a form of shareholder opportunism. Given the threat of job loss, employees will inefficiently underinvest in these skills. On such arguments, therefore, all parties may be made better off through the concession of job tenure to employees. See Shleifer & Summers, *Breach of Trust in Hostile Takeovers*, in A. Auerbach (ed.), *Corporate Takeovers: Causes and Consequences* 33 (1988). Before this amounts to a persuasive argument for take-over bid barriers or job tenure, however, certain assumptions must be made. First, it must be assumed that the employees were under a bargaining handicap that prevented them from negotiating for tenure. Otherwise employees could protect themselves as easily as lenders did after encountering the first LBOs. Thus the argument for paternalistic rules is weakest for unionized employees who delegate bargaining duties to skilled negotiators. Second, the skills must indeed be job-specific. That is, the argument for mandatory tenure is weakest for low-skill jobs, or for skills that are fungible. Third, even if job tenure is efficient for some employees who cannot bargain for themselves, this is not an argument for take-over bid barriers, but only for restrictions on termination rights under labour contracts. Finally, the stakeholder theorist should be able to show that take-overs result in job losses. Thus far, the evidence points in the other direction. See Brown & Medoff, *The Impact of Firm Acquisitions on Labor*, in A. Auerbach (ed.), *Corporate Takeovers: Causes and Consequences* 9 (1988); Blackwell, Marr & Spivey, *Plant-closing Decisions and the Market Value of the Firm*, 26 J. Fin. Econ. 277 (1990) (finding little evidence of a relationship between plant closings and take-over attempts); but see Bhagat, Shleifer & Vishny, *Hostile Takeovers in the 1980's: The Return to Corporate Specialization*, in M. Bailey & C. Winston (eds.), *Brookings Papers on Economic Activity: Micro-economics 1*, 55 (1990) (finding that layoffs are an important but not dominant source of tender offer gains).

The failure to detect strong evidence of employee terminations on a take-over bid is not surprising. Firms that are spun off after a break-up merger usually continue to operate as going concerns, and it is excessive to regard them as "dogs": in most cases they simply do not fit in the reorganized venture. The argument that links plant closings with mergers is also suspect insofar as it assumes that financing decisions dictate investment decisions. One would expect managers to decide upon plant closings by comparing going concern and liquidation values, which are unaffected by mergers. If, however, management refuses to close inefficient plants when liquidation value exceeds going concern value, the firm might indeed become a candidate for a break-up acquisition. But here the decision to keep an inefficient plant in operation, when closing it would permit the firm to open another profitable plant elsewhere, benefits employees in the first location at the expense of possible employees in the second. On distributional theories, then, arguments against closing inefficient plants are controversial.

See further Gillen 339-48; Daniels, *Stakeholders and Takeovers: Can Contractarianism Be Compassionate?* 43 U. of Toronto L.J. 315 (1993).

B. FORMAL ASPECTS OF MERGERS

"Merger" is not a term of art in Canada. While it is most often used to refer to a statutory amalgamation, it is also used to describe every form of business combination, whether effected by an amalgamation, a purchase or sale of shares or a purchase or sale of assets. The term may also be extended to other forms of combinations, as where one corporation transfers its business to another under a long-term lease. From a financial point of view, there may be little difference between these kinds of combinations. However, different legal problems may arise depending on which technique is selected.

One kind of problem concerns the procedural requirements necessary to accomplish the transaction. For example, some but not all mergers require shareholder approval. In addition, appraisal rights, under which dissenting shareholders may require the corporation to purchase their shares at fair value, are triggered in some but not all cases. Further issues arise when shareholders receive disparate treatment on the merger. One example of this is buyout transactions, described further in Section D, in which minority shareholders are frozen out of the amalgamated corporation, receiving cash for their shares, while majority shareholders are permitted to participate in the combined enterprise.

1. Sale of Shares

A sale of a controlling block of shares in one corporation to another corporation or to the latter's shareholders will vest control of the two enterprises in common hands. Selling shareholders may receive a purely monetary consideration for their shares, in which case they will have no interest in the merged corporation. However, they will continue to participate in the combined corporation if the consideration for their shares is shares of the purchaser. When all of the shareholders of one corporation sell their shares to another corporation in return for its shares, the combination is identical from a financial point of view to a statutory amalgamation under CBCA ss. 181-86.

The kinds of consideration received may give rise to different tax consequences, for capital gains tax liability might be triggered on a cash-out merger, while tax liability is deferred through a rollover on a share-for-share exchange. As a result, shareholders may be prepared to accept a lower price on a share exchange than a sale for cash.

Since shares are personal property, their sale does not require shareholder approval by special resolution. The sale may, however, trigger duties of compliance with take-over bid legislation. An offer to purchase shares which, when aggregated with the offeror's existing shares in the target corporation, exceeds 20% of the target's outstanding voting securities is a take-over bid under OSA s. 89(1). (The corresponding figure in CBCA s. 194 is 10%.) The offeror is then required to make the same offer to all shareholders of the class of securities sought, with special duties of disclosure in a take-over bid circular. Take-over bid legislation is discussed further in Section E. A further concern arises when a control block of shares is sold at a premium above market price. Since the control premium is not offered to non-controlling shareholders, the two classes of shareholders are not accorded equal treatment. Corporate egalitarians have therefore complained of these transactions, and they are discussed in Section F.

Mergers accomplished through a sale of shares do not directly affect the value of debt claims. For example, if all of the shareholders of A Corp. sell their shares to B Corp., creditors of A Corp. may continue to assert rights against that firm, whose value is unchanged. A Corp. will have outside debt claims but no outside equity claims, and will become a wholly owned subsidiary of B Corp.

2. Sale of Assets

Two corporations may combine if one sells to the other all or substantially all of its assets. The same transaction may be structured as a lease of assets if the term of the lease is so long that the lessor obtains substantially all of the economic value of the leased business. As in a sale of shares, the selling or leasing corporation may receive either shares of the purchasing corporation or cash. If the sale is paid for with a share consideration and the selling corporation distributes all of the shares it receives to its shareholders, the transaction is equivalent to a share-for-share amalgamation. Even if no distribution of shares is made by the selling corporation, a sale of assets for shares is financially identical to an amalgamation, for the selling firm will become a holding corporation whose only asset is shares in the purchasing corporation.

A sale or lease of all or substantially all of the corporation's assets requires approval by two-thirds of the votes cast by shareholders under CBCA s. 189(3), with even non-voting shares endowed with voting rights under s. 189(6). In a widely held corporation, this will require compliance with proxy regulation requirements, including the mailing of an information circular to all shareholders. If a shareholder dissents from the special resolution, he may subsequently require the corporation to repurchase his shares by asserting appraisal rights under CBCA s. 190(1)(e), as discussed in Section C.

Shareholder wealth gains on a sell-off are well-documented. In their study of 1963-1981 sell-offs, Hite, Owers and Rogers reported two-day shareholder gains of 1.7%, while Jain reported five-day returns of 0.7% for 1976-1978 sell-offs. With a 100-day window, an 8.0% increase was reported for sellers who completed the sell-off, and a 13.4% decrease for terminating sellers. Shareholder gains are substantially larger on a total divestiture of all the firm's assets than on a partial divestiture. Hite, Owers and Rogers reported two-day returns of 12.24% on the announcement of a voluntary total liquidation, with two-day returns of 18.3% in cases where the firm had not been involved in a control contest in the prior two years. Buyer gains on a sell-off are more modest than seller gains, though still significant. See Hite, Owers & Rogers, *The Market for Interfirm Asset Sales: Partial Sell-offs and Total Liquidations*, 18 J. Fin. Econ. 229 (1987); Jain, *The Effect of Voluntary Sell-off Announcements on Shareholder Wealth*, 40 J. Fin. 209 (1985).

Whether a sale is of substantially all of a firm's assets is not always clear, as the following case illustrates.

Gimbel v. Signal Co.
Delaware Court of Chancery
316 A.2d 599, aff'd, 316 A.2d 619 (1974)

QUILLEN C.: This action was commenced on December 24, 1973 by plaintiff, a stockholder of the Signal Companies, Inc. ("Signal"). The complaint seeks, among other things, injunctive relief to prevent the consummation of the pending sale by Signal to Burmah Oil Incorporated ("Burmah") of all of the outstanding capital stock of Signal Oil and Gas Company ("Signal Oil"), a wholly-owned subsidiary of Signal. The effective sale price exceeds 480 million dollars.[1] The sale was approved at a special meeting of the Board of Directors of Signal held on December 21, 1973.

The agreement provides that the transaction will be consummated on January 15, 1974 or upon the obtaining of the necessary governmental consents, whichever occurs later, but, in no event, after February 15, 1974 unless mutually agreed. The consents evidently have been obtained. On Monday, December 24, 1973, on the occasion of the plaintiff's application for a temporary restraining order, counsel for Signal and Signal

---

[1] The purchase price consists of 420 million dollars cash to be paid by Burmah at the closing, the cancellation of approximately 60 million dollars in indebtedness of Signal to Signal Oil, and the transfer by Signal Oil to Signal of a 4¾% net profits interest in the unexplored portion of Block 211/18 in the North Sea. Compare *Baron v. Pressed Metals of America, Inc.*, 35 Del.Ch. 581, 123 A.2d 848 (Supr.Ct. 1956).

Oil reported to this Court that the parties would not consummate this transaction prior to this Court's decision on the plaintiff's application for a preliminary injunction or January 15, 1974, whichever should occur first.

• • •

Thus, in my judgment, the factual and legal issues are basically reduced to two. First, does the sale require authorization by a majority of the outstanding stock of Signal pursuant to 8 Del.C. § 271(a)?[3] Second, was the action by Signal's Board in approving the 480 million dollar sale price reckless as to justify the entry of a preliminary injunction prohibiting the consummation of the sale?

• • •

I turn first to the question of 8 Del.C. § 271(a) which requires majority stockholder approval for the sale of "all or substantially all" of the assets of a Delaware corporation. A sale of less than all or substantially all assets is not covered by negative implication from the statute. Folk, The Delaware General Corporation Law, Section 271, p. 400, ftnt. 3; 8 Del.C. § 141(a).

It is important to note in the first instance that the statute does not speak of a requirement of shareholder approval simply because an independent, important branch of a corporate business is being sold. The plaintiff cites several non-Delaware cases for the proposition that shareholder approval of such a sale is required. But that is not the language of our statute. Similarly, it is not our law that shareholder approval is required upon every "major" resturcturing of the corporation. Again, it is not necessary to go beyond the statute. The statute requires shareholder approval upon the sale of "all or substantially all" of the corporation's assets. That is the sole test to be applied. While it is true that test does not lend itself to a strict mathematical standard to be applied in every case, the qualitative factor can be defined to some degree notwithstanding the limited Delaware authority. But the definition must begin with and ultimately necessarily relate to our statutory language.

---

3   "Every corporation may at any meeting of its board of directors sell, lease, or exchange all or substantially all of its property and assets, including its good will and its corporate franchises, upon such terms and conditions and for such consideration, which may consist in whole or in part of money or other property, including shares or stock in, and/or other securities of, any other corporation or corporations, as its board of directors deems expedient and for the best interests of the corporation, when and as authorized by a resolution adopted by a majority of the outstanding stock of the corporation entitled to vote thereon at a meeting duly called upon at least 20 days notice. The notice of the meeting shall state that such a resolution will be considered."

The predecessor statute was evidently originally enacted in 1916 in response to Chancellor Curtis' statement of the common law rule in *Butler v. New Keystone Copper Co.*, 10 Del. Ch. 371, 377, 93 A. 380, 383 (Ch. 1915): "The general rule as to commercial corporations seems to be settled that neither the directors nor the stockholders of a prosperous, going concern have the power to sell all or substantially all, the property of the company if the holder of a single share dissent."

In interpreting the statute the plaintiff relies on *Philadelphia National Bank v. B.S.F. Co.*, 41 Del.Ch. 509, 199 A.2d 557 (Ch. 1964), rev'd on other grounds, 42 Del.Ch. 106, 204 A.2d 746 (Supr.Ct. 1964). In that case, B.S.F. Company owned stock in two corporations. It sold its stock in one of the corporations, and retained the stock in the other corporation. The Court found that the stock sold was the principal asset B.S.F. Company had available for sale and that the value of the stock retained was declining. The Court rejected the defendant's contention that the stock sold represented only 47.4% of consolidated assets, and looked to the actual value of the stock sold. On this basis, the Court held that the stock constituted at least 75% of the total assets and the sale of the stock was a sale of substantially all assets.

But two things must be noted about the *Philadelphia National Bank* case. First, even though shareholder approval was obtained under § 271, the case did not arise under § 271 but under an Indenture limiting the activities of B.S.F. for creditor financial security purposes. On appeal, Chief Justice Wolcott was careful to state the following:

We are of the opinion that this question is not necessarily to be answered by references to the general law concerning the sale of assets by a corporation. The question before us is the narrow one of what particular language of a contract means and is to be answered in terms of what the parties were intending to guard against or to insure.

42 Del.Ch. at 111-112, 204 A.2d at 750.

Secondly, the *Philadelphia National Bank* case dealt with the sale of the company's only substantial income producing asset.

The key language in the Court of Chancery opinion in *Philadelphia National Bank* is the suggestion that "the critical factor in determining the character of a sale of assets is generally considered not the amount of property sold but whether the sale is in fact an unusual transaction or one made in the regular course of business of the seller." (41 Del.Ch. at 515, 199 A.2d at 561). Professor Folk suggests from the opinion that "the statute would be inapplicable if the assets sale is 'one made in furtherance of express corporate objects in the ordinary and regular course of the business' " (referring to language in 41 Del.Ch. at 516, 199 A.2d at 561). Folk, supra, Section 271, p. 401.

But any "ordinary and regular course of the business" test in this context obviously is not intended to limit the directors to customary daily business activities. Indeed, a question concerning the statute would not arise unless the transaction was somewhat out of the ordinary. While it is true that a transaction in the ordinary course of business does not require shareholder approval, the converse is not true. Every transaction out of normal routine does not necessarily require shareholder approval. The unusual nature of the transaction must strike at the heart of the corporate existence and purpose. As it is written at 6A Fletcher, Cyclopedia Corporations (Perm. Ed. 1968 Rev.) § 2949.2, p. 648:

The purpose of the consent statutes is to protect the shareholders from fundamental change, or more specifically to protect the shareholder from the destruction of the means to accomplish the purposes or objects for which the corporation was incorporated and actually performs.

It is in this sense that the "unusual transaction" judgment is to be made and the statute's applicability determined. If the sale is of assets quantitatively vital to the operation of the corporation and is out of the ordinary and substantially affects the existence and purpose of the corporation, then it is beyond the power of the Board of Directors. With these guidelines, I turn to Signal and the transaction in this case.

Signal or its predecessor was incorporated in the oil business in 1922. But, beginning in 1952, Signal diversified its interests. In 1952, Signal acquired a substantial stock interest in American President lines. From 1957 to 1962 Signal was the sole owner of Laura Scudders, a nationwide snack food business. In 1964, Signal acquired Garrett Corporation which is engaged in the aircraft, aerospace, and uranium enrichment business. In 1967, Signal acquired Mack Trucks, Inc., which is engaged in the manufacture and sale of trucks and related equipment. Also in 1968, the oil and gas business was transferred to a separate division and later in 1970 to the Signal Oil subsidiary. Since 1967, Signal has made acquisition of or formed substantial companies none of which are involved or related with the oil and gas industry. See Walkup affidavit, docket number 34. As indicated previously, the oil and gas production development of Signal's business is now carried on by Signal Oil, the sale of the stock of which is an issue in this lawsuit.

According to figures published in Signal's last annual report (1972) and the latest quarterly report (September 30, 1973) and certain other internal financial information, the following tables can be constructed.

SIGNAL'S REVENUES (in millions)

	9 Mos. Ended September 30, 1973	December 31, 1972	December 31, 1971
Truck manufacturing	$655.9	$712.7	$552.5
Aerospace and industrial	407.1	478.2	448.0
Oil and gas	185.8	267.2	314.1
Other	16.4	14.4	14.0

SIGNAL'S PRETAX EARNINGS (in millions)

	9 Mos. Ended September 30, 1973	December 31, 1972	December 31, 1971
Truck manufacturing	$55.8	$65.5	$36.4
Aerospace and industrial	20.0	21.5	19.5
Oil and gas	10.1	12.8	9.9

SIGNAL'S ASSETS (in millions)

	9 Mos. Ended September 30, 1973	December 31, 1972	December 31, 1971
Truck manufacturing	$581.4	$506.5	$450.4
Aerospace and industrial	365.2	351.1	331.5
Oil and gas	376.2	368.3	369.9
Other	113.1	102.0	121.6

SIGNAL'S NET WORTH (in millions)

	9 Mos. Ended September 30, 1973	December 31, 1972	1971
Truck manufacturing	$295.0	$269.7	$234.6
Aerospace and industrial	163.5	152.2	139.6
Oil and gas	280.5	273.2	254.4
Other	(55.7)	(42.1)	(2.0)

Based on the company's figures, Signal Oil represents only about 26% of the total assets of Signal. While Signal Oil represents 41% of Signal's total net worth, it produces only about 15% of Signal's revenues and earnings. Moreover, the additional tables shown in Signal's brief from the Chitiea affidavit are also interesting in demonstrating the low rate of return which has been realized recently from the oil and gas operation.

PRE-TAX DOLLAR RETURN ON VALUE OF ASSETS

	9 Mos. Ended September 30, 1973	[December 31,] 1972	1971
Truck manufacturing	12.8%	12.9%	8.1%
Aerospace and industrial	7.5	6.1	5.9
Oil and gas	3.6	3.5	2.7

PRE-TAX DOLLAR RETURN ON NET WORTH

	9 Mos. Ended September 30, 1973	[December 31,] 1972	1971
Truck manufacturing	25.1%	24.2%	15.5%
Aerospace and industrial	16.8	14.1	14.0
Oil and gas	4.8	4.7	3.9

While it is true, based on the experience of the Signal-Burmah transaction and the record in this lawsuit, that Signal Oil is more valuable than shown by the company's books, even if, as plaintiff suggests in his brief, the $761,000,000 value attached to Signal Oil's properties by the plaintiff's expert Paul V. Keyser, Jr., were substituted as the asset figure, the oil and gas properties would still [constitute] less than half the value of Signal's total assets. Thus, from a straight quantative approach, I agree with Signal's position that the sale to Burmah does not constitute a sale of "all or substantially all" of Signal's assets.

In addition, if the character of the transaction is examined, the plaintiff's position is also weak. While it is true that Signal's original purpose was oil and gas and while oil and gas is still listed first in the certificate of incorporation, the simple fact is that Signal is now a conglomerate engaged in the aircraft and aerospace business, the manufacture and sale of trucks and related equipment, and other businesses besides oil and gas. The very nature of its business, as it now in fact exists, contemplates the acquisition and disposal of independent branches of its corporate business. Indeed, given the operations since 1952, it can be said that such acquisitions and disposition have become part of the ordinary course of business. The facts that the oil and gas business was historically first and that authorization for such operations are listed first in the certificate do not prohibit disposal of such interest. As Director Harold M. Williams testified, business history is not "compelling" and "many companies go down the drain because they try to be historic." Williams' deposition, docket number 301 p. 28.

It is perhaps true, as plaintiff has argued, that the advent of multi-business corporations has in one sense emasculated § 271 since one business may be sold without shareholder approval when other substantial businesses are retained. But it is one thing for a corporation to evolve over a period of years into a multi-business corporation, the operations of which include the purchase and sale of whole businesses, and another for a single business corporation by a one transaction revolution to sell the entire means of operating its business in exchange for money or a separate business. In the former situation, the processes of corporate democracy customarily have had the opportunity to restrain or otherwise control over a period of years. Thus, there is a chance for some shareholder participation. The Signal development illustrates the difference. For example, when Signal, itself formerly called Signal Oil and Gas Company, changed its name in 1968, it was for the announced "need for a new name appropriate to the broadly diversified activities of Signal's multi-industry complex." Walkup affidavit, docket number 34.

The situation is also dramatically illustrated financially in this very case. Independent of the contract with Burmah, the affidavit of Signal's Board Chairman shows that over $200,000,000 of Signal Oil's refining and marketing assets have been sold in the past five years. Walkup affidavit, docket number 34. This activity, prior to the sale at issue here, in itself constitutes a major restructuring of the corporate structure.

I conclude that measured quantitatively and qualitatively, the sale of the stock of Signal Oil by Signal to Burmah does not constitute a sale of "all or substantially all" of Signal's assets. This conclusion is supported by the closest case involving Delaware law which has been cited to the Court. *Wingate v. Bercut*, 146 F.2d 725 (9th Cir. 1944). Accordingly, insofar as the complaint rests on 8 Del.C. § 271(a), in my judgment, it has no reasonable probability of ultimate success. ...

The Qualitative Test. When should managers be required to submit a transaction to shareholders for their approval? Where a class of transactions is invariably value-increasing, shareholder consent might be thought a wheel that turns nothing. Equally, shareholder approval is unnecessary where the transactions are always value-decreasing. There the transaction should simply be banned. Ratification requirements should thus be reserved for transactions that are not always efficient or inefficient, and where shareholder approval might usefully serve to distinguish the sheep from the goats.

Is there then any reason for shareholder ratification for transactions that appear wholly benign, such as the sell-off of unrelated firm assets? Such divestitures reverse inefficient acquisitions, and are associated with significant positive shareholder returns. Should the qualitative test be applied to exempt such sales, even if they amount to a quantitatively large portion of the firm's assets? While Signal had begun in the oil business, for example, the firm had become a conglomerate, whose ordinary course of business included acquisitions and divestitures. The relaxation of ratification requirements facilitated what appeared to be an efficient deconglomerization.

Contrariwise, the qualitative standard might reasonably be applied to require ratification when the firm proposes to sell its historical core assets for the purpose of thwarting a take-over bid. The sale will not release negative synergies, and may amount to a "scorched earth" policy whose sole purpose is to reduce the firm's attractiveness as a target. Even when not made in the face of a control contest, a core asset sale might be value-reducing. Sell-offs of core assets made to resist take-over bids are associated with significant declines in the price of offeree stock. See Dann & DeAngelo, *Corporate Financial Policy and Corporate Control: A Study of Defensive Adjustment in Asset and Ownership Structure*, 20 J. Fin. Econ. 87 (1988) (reporting a decline of 2.33%).

A sell-off is more likely to require shareholder consent where the division represents core assets. In *Katz v. Bregman*, 431 A.2d 1274 (Del. Ch. 1981), for example, a plan to sell 51% of Plant Industries' assets generating 45% of its net sales had to be put to the shareholders for approval. The assets in question had been the only ones to produce income in the previous four years, and their sale "represented a radical departure from [the seller's] historically successful line of business."

However, shareholder ratification was waived on a defensive sell-off of core assets in *Re Olympia & York Enterprises Ltd.* (1986), 37 D.L.R. (4th) 193; 59 O.R. (2d) 254 (Div. Ct.). The sell-off was one of the devices used by Hiram-Walker to resist an Olympia & York take-over. Hiram-Walker sold its liquor division to Allied-Lyons, a British food and drink manufacturer, who with Hiram-Walker funded a third corporation, which made a rival bid for the Hiram-Walker stock at a higher offer price than the O & Y bid. The liquor interest represented 43% of total assets of Hiram-Walker at market value, 29% of total assets at book value, and accounted for 40% of earnings and 30% of annual sales. Following *Gimbel*, the Court held that this was "not even close to all the assets. ... It is fallacious to suggest that when a holding company that has three distinct divisions and sells one of three divisions for 2.6 billion dollars out of a total worth of six billion dollars, it could possibly fall within [s. 189(3)]." Can this result be defended on the basis that the sell-off usefully brought a second bidder into an auction contest for Hiram-Walker? The decision that the sell-off did not require ratification might have benefitted Hiram-Walker shareholders. Through its existing stock interest in the target and its superior knowledge of Canadian business conditions, O & Y had important first mover advantages over the British bidder, and Allied-Lyons might have refused to take the risk that the O & Y offer would fail had the asset sale required ratification. Hiram-Walker shareholders might then have accepted the low premium offer from O & Y. See further Buckley, *The Divestiture Decision*, 16 J. Corp. L. 805 (1991).

When the question of whether a sale of substantially all of the corporation's assets arises under restrictive covenants in trust indentures, courts are generally reluctant to find that a covenant is breached if the transaction does not seriously impair the creditors' security. See, e.g., *Sharon Steel Corp. v. Chase Manhattan Bank N.A.*, 691 F.2d 1039 (2d Cir. 1982), cert. denied, 103 S. Ct. 1253 (1983).

3. Amalgamation

The third way in which the business combination may be effected is by filing articles of amalgamation under CBCA s. 181 *et seq.* If one corporation is wholly owned by another, or if both are wholly owned by the same person, they may amalgamated without formal shareholder consent under s. 184 as a "short-form" amalgamation. In other cases, the amalgamation agreement under s. 182 must be approved by special resolutions of the shareholders of both corporations. In widely held corporations, this will require full disclosure of the details of the amalgamation and prospectus-level financial disclosure in the information circular. See CBCA Reg. s. 35(gg). Amalgamations also give rise to appraisal rights under s. 190(1)(c).

Upon the date set forth in the certificate of amalgamation, the two corporations continue as one corporation possessing all the rights and property and subject to all the liabilities of each of the two amalgamating corporations. CBCA s. 186. Questions have nevertheless arisen about whether an amalgamation continues or extinguishes the predecessor corporations. In *R. v. Black and Decker Mfg. Co.*, [1975] 1 S.C.R. 411, the accused corporation was charged with offences under the Combines Investigation Act alleged to have occurred between 1966 and 1970. Black & Decker Manufacturing Co. was incorporated in 1922 under the federal Companies Act and in 1971 amalgamated with two other corporations under the Canada Corporations Act. The charges in question were laid in 1972 and the question arose whether the amalgamated corporation was liable for them. Section 137(13)(b) of the Canada Corporations Act provided that "the amalgamated company possesses all the property, rights, assets, privileges and franchises, and is subject to all the contracts, liabilities, debts and obligations of each of the amalgamated companies," while s. 137(14) stated that "all debts, contracts, liabilities and duties of [a predecessor] company ... attach to the amalgamated company and may be enforced against it." While these provisions might have seemed to have provided an answer to the question, the Ontario Court of Appeal held that they did not extend to criminal liability under the Combines Investigation Act. The Supreme Court nevertheless held that criminal liability for offences committed prior to 1971 survived the amalgamation. Mr. Justice Dickson, who delivered the judgment of the Court, found the successor corporation guilty of the offence.

The word "amalgamation" is not a legal term and is not susceptible of exact definition: *In re South African Supply and Cold Storage Company* [[1904] 2 Ch. 268]. The word is derived from mercantile usage and denotes, one might say, a legal means of achieving an economic end. The juridical nature of an amalgamation need not be determined by juridical criteria alone, to the exclusion of consideration or the purposes of amalgamation. Provision is made under the *Canada Corporations Act* and under the Acts of various provinces whereby two or more companies incorporated under the governing Act may amalgamate and form one corporation. The purpose is economic: to build, to consolidate, perhaps to diversify, existing businesses; so that through union there will be enhanced strength. It is a joining of forces and resources in order to perform better in the economic field. If that be so, it would surely be paradoxical if that process were to involve death by suicide or the mysterious disappearance of those who sought security, strength and, above all, survival in that union. Also, one must recall that the amalgamating companies *physically* continue to exist in the sense that offices, warehouses, factories, corporate records and correspondence and documents are still there, and business goes on. In a physical sense an amalgamating business or company does not disappear although it may become part of a greater enterprise.

There are various ways in which companies can be put together. The *assets* of one or more existing companies may be sold to another existing company or to a company newly-incorporated, in exchange for cash or shares or other consideration. The consideration received may then be distributed to the shareholders of the companies whose assets have been sold, and these companies wound up and their charters surrendered. In this type of transaction a new company may be incorporated or an old company may be wound up but the legal position is clear. There is no fusion of corporate entities. Another form of merger occurs when an existing company or a newly-incorporated company acquires the *shares* of one or more existing companies which latter companies may then be retained as subsidiaries or wound up after their assets have been passed up to the parent company. Again there is no fusion. But in an amalgamation a different result is sought and different legal mechanics are adopted, usually for the express purpose of ensuring the continued existence of the constituent companies. The motivating factor may be the Income Tax Act or difficulties likely to arise in conveying assets if the merger were by asset or share purchase. But whatever the motive, the end result is to coalesce to create a homogeneous whole. The analogies of a river formed by the confluence of two streams, or the creation of a single rope through the interwining of strands have been suggested by others.

Counsel for the accused argued that an amalgamation agreement provides for so many changes (s. 137(3)) and the transformation of the amalgamating companies is so complete as to amount to extinction of life. I do not agree. A company can, by supplementary Letters Patent, make equally drastic changes without affecting, in the slightest, corporate longevity.

It was also submitted that if the amalgamating companies continue in amalgamation, in all their plenitude, then ss. 137(13)(b) and 137(14) are mere surplusage. I would not so regard them. These sections spell out in broad language amplification of a general principle, a not uncommon practice of legislative draftsmen. If ss. 137(3)(b) and 137(14) are to be read, however, as other than merely supportive of a general principle and other than all-embracing, then some corporate incidents, such as criminal responsibility, must be regarded as severed from the amalgamating companies and outside the amalgamated company. What happens to these vestigial remnants? Are they extinguished and if so, by what authority? Do they continue in a state of ethereal suspension? Such metaphysical abstractions are not, in my view, a necessary concomitant of the legislation. The effect of the statute, on a proper construction, is to have the amalgamating companies continue without subtraction in the amalgamated company, with all their strengths and their weaknesses, their perfections and imperfections, and their sins, if sinners they be. Letters patent of amalgamation do not give absolution. [*Id.* at 420-22]

In a case decided on the same day, the Supreme Court came to similar conclusions with respect to an amalgamation under the Ontario statute. *Witco Chemical Co. v. Oakville*, [1975] 1 S.C.R. 273, 43 D.L.R. (3d) 413. Spence J., who delivered the judgment of the Court, stated that the Ontario Act was even more clear on the effect of an amalgamation than the Canadian Act, since s. 197(4)(d) of that statute provided that the articles of each of the amalgamated corporations are amended to the extent necessary to give effect to the amalgamation agreement. The plaintiffs were therefore permitted to amend their writ after the limitation period had lapsed to change the name of the defendant, which had been amended in an amalgamation. Any remaining questions on the continuing status of an amalgamated corporation would appear to have been answered by CBCA s. 186.

Successor corporation liability replicates the agreement that creditors would have reached with the predecessor corporations in a hypothetical claimholders' bargain. After the certificate of amalgamation, the identities of the predecessor firms are merged into the successor corporation, so that claim value would be destroyed without successor corporation liability. But for CBCA s. 186, then, creditors would likely require amalgamating corporations to covenant not to enter into an amalgamation agreement that did not provide for an assumption of liability by the amalgamated firm. Even this, however, might not suffice if the successor corporation was not bound by the agreement. CBCA s. 186 therefore seems justified as a device to prevent the destruction of claim values.

Successor corporation liability can be avoided through a bankruptcy discharge. A bankruptcy reorganization resembles a sell-off of assets to the reorganized firm, with old claimholders paid off with claims in the new, purchasing firm. Where the whole point is to scale down debt claims in order to reduce equity adverse incentive costs, successor corporation liability would render a reorganization futile. The firm would emerge from the reorganization with the same debt levels, and the same adverse incentive costs. This leaves open the question, best left for a bankruptcy course, whether a firm should be permitted to bargain out of bankruptcy law by issuing non-dischargeable debt claims.

As in a share or asset transaction, the CBCA contemplates that the acquisition may be paid for through either a share or a cash consideration. Thus CBCA s. 182(1)(d) states that the amalgamation agreement must set out whether shareholders of an amalgamating corporation are to receive shares in the amalgamated firm or cash. This appears to permit amalgamations to be structured as cash-out mergers, with shareholders of one predecessor firm receiving shares in the successor firm and shareholders in the other predecessor firm paid off in cash. Buyouts are discussed in Section D.

4. Other Merger Techniques

In addition to the above, there are a variety of other methods that may be used to effect a corporate combination. On a purchase of assets, a large corporation (Bigco) normally purchases a business operated by a smaller company (Litco). Litco shareholders must then approve the transaction under s. 189(3) and may, if they choose, dissent under CBCA s. 190, requiring the corporation to purchase their shares. If this presents a problem, it may perhaps be avoided by reversing the roles and selling Bigco's business to Litco. So long as the consideration is Litco shares and the entire Bigco business and assets are acquired, it makes relatively little difference who purchases whom. The requirement of shareholder ratification and the appraisal remedy will then arise in the case of Bigco, but possibly not Litco. If Bigco shares are not widely held or if Bigco is incorporated in a jurisdiction that lacks an appraisal remedy, this may be a very real advantage. But see "The De Facto Merger Doctrine" in Section C.

A *triangular merger* is one that involves a subsidiary of one of the merging corporations. For example, Bigco may prefer to amalgamate Litco with one of Bigco's subsidiaries. This would offer several advantages. Bigco would be insulated from Litco's liabilities, which would be assumed by the amalgamated corporation. The transaction would not have to be approved by a shareholder meeting of Bigco, and Bigco's shareholders could not assert the appraisal remedy. Thus Bigco may form a subsidiary and issue the subsidiary's shares to Litco shareholders in the amalgamation. Alternatively, in order to make the amalgamation more palatable to them, Litco shareholders may be issued shares of Bigco itself and not of the new subsidiary. This is sometimes done in the United States by having Bigco create a subsidiary and then transferring Bigco's stock to the subsidiary. However, this device is prohibited by CBCA s. 30(1), which prohibits a subsidiary from holding a parent's shares. A triangular merger may perhaps be accomplished under s. 182(1)(d), which expressly contemplates that shareholders of an amalgamating corporation may receive securities of a corporation other than the amalgamated corporation. This might then permit Litco shareholders to receive Bigco shares on the amalgamation, without a prohibited issue of the parent's shares to the subsidiary. Since the Bigco shares are not held by its subsidiary prior to the amalgamation, they must be issued by Bigco in return for further Litco shares.

C. THE APPRAISAL REMEDY

In the circumstances referred to in CBCA s. 190, dissenting shareholders have the right to require the corporation to repurchase their shares. What triggers these appraisal rights are "fundamental" corporate transactions, such as amalgamations and sales of substantially all of the firm's assets. Appraisal rights may therefore be seen as a trade-off for the loss of individual veto rights, which shareholders had when these transactions required unanimous approval. Thus a firm may now amalgamate over the wishes of dissenting shareholders, but the amalgamation is only effective if approved by special resolution, with appraisal rights for dissenters. The exit option provided by appraisal rights therefore supplements the requirement of super-majoritarian ratification through a special resolution.

On a claimholders' bargain model, however, appraisal rights cannot be justified as a political trade-off. Individual veto rights were lost because the delegation of authority to managers was efficient and because of the possibility of opportunistic holdout strategies by individual shareholders. The substitution of liability for property rules when the appraisal remedy replaced veto rights mitigates the holdout problem, but creates its own costs. The principal one is the corporation's need to stay liquid to meet appraisal claims. In some cases, the firm may be quite prepared to buy back shares, even if valuation uncertainties in what is likely already an exceedingly complicated transaction will impose their own costs. But the possibility of large appraisal claims may deter some firms from entering into a triggering transaction. Evidence of this is provided by frequent conditions in amalgamation agreements that the transaction may be abandoned if a specified number of shareholders (often 5%) decide to appraise out.

The remedy is also of limited benefit to a shareholder. If he does not appraise out on a share-for-share amalgamation, the issue of shares to him by the amalgamated corporation will not be taxable. But moneys paid on an exercise of the appraisal remedy may give rise to taxable dividend or taxable capital gains treatment. In addition, without a lawyer he will find it very difficult to understand how to assert appraisal rights. The procedure is highly technical, with several distinct steps to be completed in limited time periods. Appraisal rights do not arise unless the shareholder dissents or abstains at the meeting and sends a written objection under s. 190(5) to the corporation at or before the shareholder meeting. The appraisal remedy is not triggered by this written objection and the shareholder must still send a demand for payment to the corporation within the 20-day period of s. 190(7) before it has a duty to repurchase the shares. Dissenting shareholders must also return the share certificates under s. 190(8) within 30 days there-after. If an offer is made by the corporation, the shareholder has 30 days to accept it under s. 190(14). If no offer is made, or if the offer is rejected, the corporation can bring the matter to court, failing which the shareholder has a 20-day period to do so under s. 190(16). Failure to perform one step in the allotted time may mean that appraisal rights are lost, although courts sometimes do not interpret these requirements strictly. See *Re Domglas Inc.* (1980), 13 B.L.R. 135, 157-58 (Que.). A further cost arises through the time all this will take, during which the investment is frozen. After the demand for payment is sent in, the dissenting shareholder loses any rights to participate in the corporation under s. 190(11). A shareholder may also be called upon to pay expert witness fees in any dispute as to the true value of the shares. Given these costs, the shareholder may simply prefer to sell his shares on the market, rather than assert appraisal rights. See Manning, *The Shareholder's Appraisal Remedy: An Essay for Frank Coker*, 72 Yale L.J. 223 (1962) (costs of the appraisal remedy outweigh its benefits).

However, even with these costs, the appraisal remedy still finds its defenders. The following extract from Eisenberg, *The Legal Roles of Shareholders and Management in Modern Corporate Decision Making*, 57 Calif. L. Rev. 1, 85-86 (1969), summarizes the conclusions of one of the leading advocates of appraisal rights:

It has already been seen that the appraisal right presents many difficulties from the shareholder's perspective: It is always technical; it may be expensive; it is uncertain in result, and, in the case of a publicly held corporation, is unlikely to produce a better result than could have been obtained on the market; and the ultimate award is taxable. It is, in short, a remedy of desperation—gener-ally speaking, no shareholder in a publicly held corporation who is in his right mind will invoke the appraisal right unless he feels that the change from which he dissents is shockingly improvi-dent and that the fair value of his shares before the change will far exceed the value of his shares after the change. But may not the existence of just such a right—a switch which will be pulled only in case of emergency—be desirable in connection with transactions of the utmost gravity, in which self-interest and lack of investment skills may seriously obscure management's vision?

Eisenberg regards the appraisal remedy as a no-fault buyout right, where a share-holder who suspects oppression may exercise a "put" option by requiring the corpora-tion to repurchase his shares without demonstrating unfairness. On this analysis, the appraisal remedy can be justified only if the list of triggering transactions corresponds to those circumstances where oppression is most to be feared, and a prophylactic remedy is preferred to one that requires proof of oppression. However, the list of triggering trans-actions in s. 190 seems imperfectly correlated with real shareholder concerns. For exam-ple, is an amendment to the firm's objects clause really of such fundamental importance that shareholders should be permitted to assert appraisal rights? If the true fear is of self-dealing, should appraisal rights instead be offered whenever the firm enters into an interested director's contract? If instead it is thought that the transaction must be economically significant, compare the s. 190 list with Bayless Manning's list of the following business events:

- the corporation loses a major client;
- it is audited by the taxing authority;
- new technology makes its products obsolete;
- its president dies in an airplane crash; and
- management announces that dividends are to be cut for the indefinite future.

In the United States, the statutory list of triggering transactions has been extended to analogous cases under the "*de facto* merger doctrine."

Farris v. Glen Alden Corp.
Supreme Court of Pennsylvania
143 A.2d 25 (1958)

COHEN, Justice: We are required to determine on this appeal whether, as a result of a "Reorganization Agreement" executed by the officers of Glen Alden Corporation and List Industries Corporation, and approved by the shareholders of the former company, the rights and remedies of a dissenting shareholder accrue to the plaintiff.

Glen Alden is a Pennsylvania corporation engaged principally in the mining of anthracite coal and lately in the manufacture of air conditioning units and firefighting equipment. In recent years the company's operating revenue had declined substantially, and in fact, its coal operations have resulted in tax loss carryovers of approximately $14,000,000. In October 1957, List, a Delaware holding company owning interests in motion picture theatres, textile companies and real estate, and to a lesser extent, in oil and gas operations, warehouses and aluminum piston manufacturing, purchased through a wholly owned subsidiary 38.5% of Glen Alden's outstanding stock.[1] This acquisition enabled List to place three of its directors on the Glen Alden board.

On March 20, 1958, the two corporations entered into a "reorganization agreement," subject to stockholder approval, which contemplated the following actions:

1. Glen Alden is to acquire all of the assets of List, excepting a small amount of cash reserved for the payment of List's expenses in connection with the transaction. These assets include over $8,000,000 in cash held chiefly in the treasuries of List's wholly owned subsidiaries.

2. In consideration of the transfer, Glen Alden is to issue 3,621,703 shares of stock to List. List in turn is to distribute the stock to its shareholders at a ratio of five shares of Glen Alden stock for each six shares of List stock. In order to accomplish the necessary distribution, Glen Alden is to increase the authorized number of its share of capital stock from 2,500,000 shares to 7,500,000 shares without according pre-emptive rights to the present shareholders upon the issuance of any such shares.

---

1   Of the purchase price of $8,719,109, $5,000,000 was borrowed.

3. Further, Glen Alden is to assume all of List's liabilities including a $5,000,000 note incurred by List in order to purchase Glen Alden stock in 1957, outstanding stock options, incentive stock options plans, and pension obligations.

4. Glen Alden is to change its corporate name from Glen Alden Corporation to List Alden Corporation.

5. The present directors of both corporations are to become directors of List Alden.

6. List is to be dissolved and List Alden is to then carry on the operations of both former corporations.

Two days after the agreement was executed notice of the annual meeting of Glen Alden to be held on April 11, 1958, was mailed to the shareholders together with a proxy statement analyzing the reorganization agreement and recommending its approval as well as approval of certain amendments to Glen Alden's articles of incorporation and bylaws necessary to implement the agreement. At this meeting the holders of a majority of the outstanding shares, (not including those owned by List), voted in favor of a resolution approving the reorganization agreement.

On the day of the shareholders' meeting, plaintiff, a shareholder of Glen Alden, filed a complaint in equity against the corporation and its officers seeking to enjoin them temporarily until final hearing, and perpetually thereafter, from executing and carrying out the agreement.

The gravamen of the complaint was that the notice of the annual shareholders' meeting did not conform to the requirements of the Business Corporation Law, 15 P.S. § 2852-1 et seq., in three respects: (1) It did not give notice to the shareholders that the true intent and purpose of the meeting was to effect a merger or consolidation of Glen Alden and List; (2) It failed to give notice to the shareholders of their right to dissent to the plan of merger or consolidation and claim fair value for their shares, and (3) It did not contain copies of the text of certain sections of the Business Corporation Law as required.[3]

By reason of these omissions, plaintiff contended that the approval of the reorganization agreement by the shareholders at the annual meeting was invalid and unless the carrying out of the plan were enjoined, he would suffer irreparable loss by being deprived of substantial property rights.[4]

The defendants answered admitting the material allegations of fact in the complaint but denying that they gave rise to a cause of action because the transaction complained of

---

3   The proxy statement included the following declaration: "Appraisal Rights."

    "In the opinion of counsel, the shareholders of neither Glen Alden nor List Industries will have
    any rights of appraisal or similar rights of dissenters with respect to any matter to be acted upon at
    their respective meetings."

4   The complaint also set forth that the exchange of shares of Glen Alden's stock for those of List would
    constitute a violation of the pre-emptive rights of Glen Alden shareholders as established by the law of
    Pennsylvania at the time of Glen Alden's incorporation in 1917. The defendants answered that under
    both statute and prior common law no pre-emptive rights existed with respect to stock issued in
    exchange for property.

was a purchase of corporate assets as to which shareholders had no rights of dissent or appraisal. For these reasons the defendants then moved for judgment on the pleadings.[5]

The court below concluded that the reorganization agreement entered into between the two corporations was a plan for a *de facto* merger, and that therefore the failure of the notice of the annual meeting to conform to the pertinent requirements of the merger provisions of the Business Corporation Law rendered the notice defective and all proceedings in furtherance of the agreement void. Wherefore, the court entered a final decree denying defendants' motion for judgment on the pleadings, entering judgment upon plaintiff's complaint and granting the injunctive relief therein sought. This appeal followed.

When use of the corporate form of business organization first became widespread, it was relatively easy for courts to define a "merger" or a "sale of assets" and to label a particular transaction as one or the other. See, *e.g.*, 15 Fletcher, Corporations §§ 7040-7045 (rev. vol. 1938); *In re Buist's Estate*, 1929, 297 Pa. 537, 541, 147 A. 606; *Koehler v. St. Mary's Brewing Co.*, 1910, 228 Pa. 648, 653-654, 77 A. 1016. But prompted by the desire to avoid the impact of adverse, and to obtain the benefits of favorable, government regulations, particularly federal tax laws, new accounting and legal techniques were developed by lawyers and accountants which interwove the elements characteristic of each, thereby creating hybrid forms of corporate amalgamation. Thus, it is no longer helpful to consider an individual transaction in the abstract and solely by reference to the various elements therein determine whether it is a "merger" or a "sale." Instead, to determine properly the nature of a corporate transaction, we must refer not only to all the provisions of the agreement, but also to the consequences of the transaction and to the purposes of the provisions of the corporation law said to be applicable. We shall apply this principle to the instant case.

Section 908, subd. A of the Pennsylvania Business Corporation Law provides: "If any shareholder of a domestic corporation which becomes a party to a plan of merger or consolidation shall object to such plan of merger or consolidation ... such shareholder shall be entitled to ... [the fair value of his shares upon surrender of the share certificate or certificates representing his shares]." ...

This provision had its origin in the early decision of this Court in *Lauman v. Lebanon Valley R.R. Co.*, 1858, 30 Pa. 42. There a shareholder who objected to the consolidation of his company with another was held to have a right in the absence of statute to treat the consolidation as a dissolution of his company and to receive the value of his shares upon their surrender.

The rationale of the *Lauman* case, and of the present section of the Business Corporation Law based thereon, is that when a corporation combines with another so as to lose its essential nature and alter the original fundamental relationships of the shareholders

---

5 Counsel for the defendants concedes that if the corporation is required to pay the dissenting shareholders the appraised fair value of their shares, the resultant drain of cash would prevent Glen Alden from carrying out the agreement. On the other hand, plaintiff contends that if the shareholders had been told of their rights as dissenters, rather than specifically advised that they had no such rights, the resolution approving the reorganization agreement would have been defeated.

among themselves and to the corporation, a shareholder who does not wish to continue his membership therein may treat his membership in the original corporation as terminated and have the value of his shares paid to him. ...

Does the combination outlined in the present "reorganization" agreement so fundamentally change the corporate character of Glen Alden and the interest of the plaintiff as a shareholder therein, that to refuse him the rights and remedies of a dissenting shareholder would in reality force him to give up his stock in one corporation and against his will accept shares in another? If so, the combination is a merger within the meaning of section 908, subd. A of the corporation law. ...

If the reorganization agreement were consummated plaintiff would find that the "List Alden" resulting from the amalgamation would be quite a different corporation than the "Glen Alden" in which he is now a shareholder. Instead of continuing primarily as a coal mining company, Glen Alden would be transformed, after amendment of its articles of incorporation, into a diversified holding company whose interests would range from motion picture theaters to textile companies. Plaintiff would find himself a member of a company with assets of $169,000,000 and a long-term debt of $38,000,000 in lieu of a company one-half that size and with but one-seventh the long-term debt.

While the administration of the operations and properties of Glen Alden as well as List would be in the hands of management common to both companies, since all executives of List would be retained in List Alden, the control of Glen Alden would pass to the directors of List; for List would hold eleven of the seventeen directorships on the new board of directors.

As an aftermath of the transaction plaintiff's proportionate interest in Glen Alden would have been reduced to only two-fifths of what it presently is because of the issuance of an additional 3,621,703 shares to List which would not be subject to pre-emptive rights. In fact, ownership of Glen Alden would pass to the stockholders of List who would hold 76.5% of the outstanding shares as compared with but 23.5% retained by the present Glen Alden shareholders.

Perhaps the most important consequence to the plaintiff, if he were denied the right to have his shares redeemed at their fair value, would be the serious financial loss suffered upon consummation of the agreement. While the present book value of his stock is $38 a share after combination it would be worth only $21 a share. In contrast, the shareholders of List who presently hold stock with a total book value of $33,000,000 or $7.50 a share, would receive stock with a book value of $76,000,000 or $21 a share.

Under these circumstances it may well be said that if the proposed combination is allowed to take place without right of dissent, plaintiff would have his stock in Glen Alden taken away from him and the stock of a new company thrust upon him in its place. He would be projected against his will into a new enterprise under terms not of his own choosing. It was to protect dissident shareholders against just such a result that this Court one hundred years ago in the *Lauman* case, and the legislature thereafter in section 908, subd. A, granted the right of dissent. And it is to accord that protection to the plaintiff that we conclude that the combination proposed in the case at hand is a merger within the intendment of section 908, subd. A.

Nevertheless, defendants contend that the 1957 amendments to sections 311 and 908 of the corporation law preclude us from reaching this result and require the entry of judgment in their favor. Subsection F of section 311 dealing with the voluntary transfer of corporate assets provides: "The shareholders of a business corporation which acquires by sale, lease or exchange all or substantially all of the property of another corporation by the issuance of stock, securities or otherwise shall not be entitled to the rights and remedies of dissenting shareholders." ...

And the amendment to section 908 reads as follows: "The right of dissenting shareholders ... shall not apply to the purchase by a corporation of assets whether or not the consideration therefor be money or property, real or personal, including shares or bonds or other evidences of indebtedness of such corporation. The shareholders of such corporation shall have no right to dissent from any such purchase." ...

Defendants view these amendments as abridging the right of shareholders to dissent to a transaction between two corporations which involves a transfer of assets for a consideration even though the transfer has all the legal incidents of a merger. They claim that only if the merger is accomplished in accordance with the prescribed statutory procedure does the right of dissent accrue. In support of this position they cite to us the comment on the amendments by the Committee on Corporation Law of the Pennsylvania Bar Association, the committee which originally drafted these provisions. The comment states that the provisions were intended to overrule cases which granted shareholders the right to dissent to a sale of assets when accompanied by the legal incidents of a merger. See 61 Ann.Rep.Pa.Bar Ass'n 277, 284 (1957).[7] Whatever may have been the intent of the *committee*, there is no evidence to indicate that the *legislature* intended the 1957 amendments to have the effect contended for. But furthermore, the language of these two provisions does not support the opinion of the committee and is inapt to achieve any such purpose. The amendments of 1957 do not provide that a transaction between two corporations which has the effect of a merger but which includes a transfer of assets for consideration is to be exempt from the protective provisions of sections 908, subd. A and 515. They provide only that the shareholders of a corporation which acquires the property or purchases the assets of another corporation, *without more*, are not entitled to the right to dissent from the transaction. So, as in the present case, when as part of a transaction

---

7 "The amendment to Section 311 expressly provides that a sale, lease or exchange of substantially all corporate assets in connection with its liquidation or dissolution is subject to the provisions of Article XI of this Act, and that no consent or authorization of shareholders other than what is required by Article XI is necessary. The recent decision in *Marks v. Autocar Co.*, D.C.E.D.Pa., Civil Action No. 16075 [153 F.Supp. 768] is to the contrary. This amendment, together with the proposed amendment to Section 1104 expressly permitting the directors in liquidating the corporation to sell only such assets as may be required to pay its debts and distribute any assets remaining among shareholders (Section 1108, [subd.] B now so provides in the case of receivers) have the effect of overruling *Marks v. Autocar Co.*, ... which permits a shareholder dissenting from such a sale to obtain the fair value of his shares. The *Marks* case relies substantially on *Bloch v. Baldwin Locomotive Works*, 75 [Pa.] Dist. & Co. R. 24, also believed to be an undesirable decision. That case permitted a holder of stock in a corporation which *purchased* for stock all the assets of another corporation to obtain the fair value of his shares. That case is also in effect overruled by the new Sections 311 [subd.] F and 908 [subd.] C." 61 Ann.Rep. Pa. Bar Ass'n, 277, 284 (1957).

between two corporations, one corporation dissolves, its liabilities are assumed by the survivor, its executives and directors take over the management and control of the survivor, and, as consideration for the transfer, its stockholders acquire a majority of the shares of stock of the survivor, then the transaction is no longer simply a purchase of assets or acquisition of property to which sections 311, subd. F and 908, subd. C apply, but a merger governed by section 908, subd. A of the corporation law. To divest shareholders of their right of dissent under such circumstances would require express language which is absent from the 1957 amendments.

Even were we to assume that the combination provided for in the reorganization agreement is a "sale of assets" to which section 908, subd. A does not apply, it would avail the defendants nothing; we will not blind our eyes to the realities of the transaction. Despite the designation of the parties and the form employed, Glen Alden does not in fact acquire List, rather, List acquires Glen Alden, cf. *Metropolitan Edison Co. v. Commissioner*, 3 Cir., 1938, 98 F.2d 807, affirmed sub nom., *Helvering v. Metropolitan Edison Co.*, 1939, 306 U.S. 522, 59 S.Ct. 634, 83 L.Ed. 957, and under section 311, subd. D[8] the right of dissent would remain with the shareholders of Glen Alden.

We hold that the combination contemplated by the reorganization agreement, although consummated by contract rather than in accordance with the statutory procedure, is a merger within the protective purview of sections 908, subd. A and 515 of the corporation law. The shareholders of Glen Alden should have been notified accordingly and advised of their statutory rights of dissent and appraisal. The failure of the corporate officers to take these steps renders the stockholder approval of the agreement at the 1958 shareholders' meeting invalid. The lower court did not err in enjoining the officers and directors of Glen Alden from carrying out this agreement.

Decree affirmed at appellants' cost.

NOTES

1) The *de facto* merger doctrine did not meet with uniform acceptance in the United States. In particular, Delaware courts held that it was a general principle of the corporate law of that state that action may be validly taken pursuant to one section of a statute which would not be permitted under another section. As a consequence, implied appraisal rights did not arise in an asset sale when Del. s. 271 did not expressly grant such rights. *Hariton v. Arco Electronics Inc.*, 188 A.2d 123 (Del. 1963). However, there was no conflict of interest in *Hariton*, while in *Glen Alden* the boards of List and Glen Alden

---

8   "If any shareholder of a business corporation which sells, leases or exchanges all or substantially all of its property and assets otherwise than (1) in the usual and regular course of its business, (2) for the purpose of relocating its business, or (3) in connection with its dissolution and liquidation, shall object to such sale, lease or exchange and comply with the provisions of section 515 of this act, such shareholder shall be entitled to the rights and remedies of dissenting shareholders as therein provided. ..."

were closely interwined. See Kanda & Levmore, *The Appraisal Remedy and the Goals of Corporate Law*, 32 U.C.L.A. L. Rev. 429, 464 n. 114 (1985).

2) Given Canadian approaches to statutory interpretation and the more inclusive list of triggering transactions under CBCA s. 190 than in Pennsylvania, would a Canadian court apply the *de facto* merger doctrine? If not, dissenting shareholders would be left in non-triggering transactions to fault-based remedies such as CBCA s. 241. However, a transaction is more likely to be impeached if it amounts to a buyout of minority interests, as discussed in the next section.

The Market Exception. Appraisal rights may be most useful to shareholders in close corporations, where no market exists for the shares. In a widely held firm, shareholders may prefer to sell their shares on the market rather than absorb the costs associated with appraising out. The Ontario Business Corporations Act formerly restricted the appraisal remedy to non-public offering corporations, and in the last 20 years approximately 20 states, including Delaware, have abolished appraisal rights for firms whose shares are listed on a stock exchange or are widely traded. The market exception was, however, deleted in the OBCA and never appeared in the CBCA.

Report on Mergers, Amalgamations and Certain Related Matters
52 (Ontario Select Committee on Company Law 1973)

Most of the corporation statutes in the United States provide that the dissenting shareholder is entitled to receive the "value" or the "fair value" of his shares. In the case of the shares of corporations listed on a stock exchange or actively traded in the over the counter market, what is such value? The experience in the United States would seem to indicate that the courts, in most instances, have refused to go beyond an enquiry as to the market price of the stock on the date determined to be relevant. Where the shares of a corporation are not actively traded, or there is no market at all, the determination of value or fair value is more difficult and a court must then come up with its own estimate of value using whatever techniques for value it deems appropriate. If, in the case of a corporation whose shares are actively traded, the criterion of value or fair value is the price put on the shares by the market, one may question the value of an appraisal remedy except perhaps in the situation where the market has taken a sudden drop in reaction to the proposed transaction. While in theory the appraisal remedy may, in the case of shares which are actively traded, seem to give dissenting shareholders the benefit of an independent valuation, it is extremely doubtful that courts in Canada would do more than seems to have been the case in the United States, i.e., accept the value placed on the stock by the investing public.

* * *

The Committee has decided that, on balance, it should not recommend the extension of the appraisal remedy to shareholders of a corporation whose shares are being offered to the public. In the view of the Committee the determining factor on which an appraisal remedy, if it should be granted at all, should rest is the presence or absence of a market.

In the case of the shares of a corporation which are actively traded, the remedy would not appear to be any more effective than if the shareholder were to sell his stock in the face of a triggering transaction and certainly not persuasive enough to compensate for the cash drain which may be caused a corporation, to the possible detriment of the corporation, its creditors and the majority or the possibility that a transaction might have to be called off, because of the cash drain in meeting appraisal rights, to the detriment of the majority of shareholders who had voted in its favour. The Committee agrees with the conclusion reached by Bayless Manning in his article on the subject where he concluded "Appraisal should be considered an economic substitute for the stock exchange and its use should be limited to situations in which the exchange, or some kind of a reasonable market, is not available." The Committee has, accordingly, concluded that the rights granted by section 100 of the Act should not be extended to a corporation whose shares are being offered to the public.

Re Wall & Redekop Corp.
British Columbia Supreme Court
(1974), 50 D.L.R. (3d) 733, [1975] 1 W.W.R. 621

MACFARLANE J.: This is an application for an order, pursuant to s. 228(4) of the Companies Act, 1973 (B.C.), c. 18:

(a) requiring B.W. Estlin, a dissenting member who has given notice of dissent to a resolution of Wall & Redekop Corporation to amalgamate with certain of its subsidiaries, and who has been given by Wall & Redekop Corporation notice of its intention to act upon the authority of the said special resolution, to sell, and Wall & Redekop Corporation to purchase, the shares of which the said notice of dissent has been given namely 5,700 common shares of Wall & Redekop Corporation,

(b) fixing the price and terms of the purchase and sale, or ordering that such price and terms be established by arbitration,

(c) making such consequential orders and giving such directions as the Court consider appropriate.

The applicable statutory provisions are contained in Division (2) entitled "Dissent Proceedings" of the new Companies Act and they read as follows:

228.(4) A dissenting member who has complied with subsection (3), the company, or, if there has been an amalgamation, the amalgamated company, may apply to the Court, which may

(a) require the dissenting member to sell, and the company or the amalgamated company to purchase, the shares in respect of which the notice of dissent has been given,

(b) fix the price and terms of the purchase and sale, or order that such price and terms be established by arbitration, in either case having due regard for the rights of creditors;

(c) join in the application any other dissenting member who has complied with subsection (3); and

(d) make such consequential orders and give such directions as it considers appropriate.

(5) The price to be paid to a dissenting member for his shares be the fair value thereof as of the day before the date on which the resolution referred to in subsection (1) was passed, including any appreciation or depreciation in anticipation of the vote upon the resolution, and every dissenting member who has complied with subsection (3) shall be paid the same price.

Both counsel for the applicant and Mr. Estlin agreed at the hearing that I should make the order called for under cl. (a) of s-s. (4) and I have done so. I then reserved the question of what price should be paid for the shares, and how that price should be determined.

Counsel for the applicant contends that the price to be paid for the shares should be the stock-market value of the same just before the passage of the resolution to amalgamate. The special resolution was passed on May 29, 1974, and on that day 100 shares traded for $2.40. The affidavit filed on behalf of the applicant shows in para. 8 the following particulars with regard to the price of the common shares of the company in 1974:

8. THAT I have ascertained from the Vancouver Stock Exchange Review that the price for the common shares of the Company in the months of March, April and May 1974 were:

	High	Low	Shares Traded
March	$2.60	$2.50	7,200
April	$2.55	$2.40	3,300
May	$2.50	$2.40	4,500

The "High" for 1974 is $3.00 and the "Low" for 1974 is $2.40

Mr. Estlin, the only dissenting member of the company, appearing on his own behalf, asserted that the shares traded were few in number of the total of 1,831,340 shares issued and outstanding. He also contended, on the basis of an information circular issued by Wall & Redekop Corporation Ltd. dated April 30, 1974, that a few persons and companies controlled the majority of the shares of the company in question. The following appears on p. 2 of that circular:

Name	Number of Shares Owned	Percentage of Outstanding Shares
Peter Wall	501,465	27.38
Peter Redekop	145,860	7.96
John Redekop	99,160	5.41
* Peter Redekop Holdings Ltd.	243,777	13.31
* John Redekop Holdings Ltd.	231,888	12.66

* Peter Redekop is the controlling member of Peter Redekop Holdings Ltd. and John Redekop is the controlling member of John Redekop Holdings Ltd.

The position of Mr. Estlin as indicated by his affidavit sworn July 24, 1974, is that the shares in question have a book value of between $7 and $8 per share.

It is not possible for me to determine the fair value of these shares on the limited material presently before me. I am not persuaded at this point that the fair value of the shares is necessarily to be ascertained by reference to the stock-market quotations which have been put before me. Counsel for the applicant, in asking me to fix a price based on the stock exchange quotations, relied on *Untermeyer v. A.-G. B.C.*, [1929] 1 D.L.R. 315, [1929] S.C.R. 84, a decision of the Supreme Court of Canada, in which it was held that, for succession duty purposes, the market price for shares is a safe guide to their market value. That case is of limited value to me here. What was under consideration in that case was "fair market value" whereas the Companies Act speaks of "fair value." Secondly, there appears to have been an active market in the shares in question in the *Untermeyer* case and of course the purpose for determining the value was completely different than it is here.

The legislation with which I have to deal is unique in Canada, except perhaps for Ontario's Business Corporations Act, R.S.O. 1970, c. 53, which is dissimilar because it does not apply in the case of a corporation which sells its shares to the public. Several American cases have considered the problem of the valuation of shares held by dissenting minority members. In *American General Corp. v. Camp et al.* (1937), 190 A. 225, the Maryland Court of Appeals in 1937 considered the appraisal of the fair value of the stock of minority shareholders in subsidiary corporations which had been consolidated into the American General Corporation. The statutory provision under consideration was that the "consolidated corporation or the corporation surviving the merger, as the case may be, shall pay such stockholder the value of his stock. ..." The Court had this to say at p. 228:

The problem of finding *the fair value* of stock is a special problem in every particular instance. ... The owner of shares of stock in a corporation whose legal existence is at an end would be entitled to receive the aliquot proportion which the number of shares held would be entitled to receive in the distribution of the net amount of the corporate funds in which his particular kind of stock would be entitled to share. Thus, by an ascertainment of all the assets and liabilities of the corporation, the intrinsic value of the stock, and not merely its market value, when traded by the public, would be determined. If the dissenting owner receive this amount, so ascertained, he would receive *the fair value* of his stock. (My italics.)

Although the Court would appear to be saying that the corporation's assets should be valued on a liquidation basis, it should be kept in mind that in the *American General* case the assets of the corporation were primarily bonds and other marketable securities so that a hypothetical liquidation was an appropriate method to apply. The limitation imposed by the particular circumstances of that case was recognized by the same Court in 1959 in *Warren v. Baltimore Transit Co.* (1959), 154 A.2d 796 at pp. 799-800. Even in the earlier case the Court recognized that one method was not necessarily appropriate in all cases. At p. 229 the Court had this to say:

The general problem, therefore, would be, in every instance of an appraisal pursuant to the statute, to ascertain the fair value. Every appraisal would as a rule be a particular problem which would vary with the kind of corporation, the nature, extent, and methods of its operations, the state of its assets, the form and incidence of its liabilities, and with many other circumstances too numerous to admit of a general classification. These general remarks are to direct attention to the manifold possibilities and difficulties of the problem, and the impracticability of the statement of any rule of uniform application as to the factors of fair value.

... In the conversion of assets into money, the value of every item should be investigated and determined with respect to market price, actual worth, and yield in liquidation. After the deduction of the approximated expense of winding up the corporate affairs and of paying the corporate obligations, the net result of these estimates would be the net asset value, which could be tested and rectified, if need be, by the market value of the stock of the consolidated or merged corporation, where there was a market at the time of the merger or consolidation of sufficient volume and activity to afford a basis for comparison. A further check on the accuracy of the total net assets would be, in proper cases, a capitalization of the estimated future income. Another concurrent test of doubtful utility, which should be cautiously used, are book values.

Although the Maryland Court in the *American General* case chose the net asset value or hypothetical liquidation method, it is clear from the decision that there are at least three ways of determining the fair value of shares in any given corporation. That value may be determined by reference to the market value of the shares on the stock exchange, by calculating the net asset value or the amount to be obtained upon a hypothetical liquidation, or the investment value of the shares based on a capitalization of the earnings of the company. This becomes more clear as one continues to examine the American authorities.

In 1947 the Supreme Court of Ohio interpreted the term "fair cash value" in a statutory provision providing for compulsory acquisition of the shares of stockholders who dissent in a merger. In *Roessler et al. v. Security Savings & Loan Co.* (1947), 72 N.E. 2d 259, the Court said this at pp. 260-1:

We believe that to be the correct interpretation of this phrase. Intrinsic value is the true interest and essential value; it is not synonymous with market value. Market value may be considered in proper cases in determining intrinsic value, but market value is not the sole or basic test, unless it is provided as such by statute. Certainly it would not be just to allow the shareholder the market value when such value is less than the intrinsic worth.

The full rule may be stated thus: "Fair cash value" of the shares of a dissenting shareholder in a corporation means the intrinsic value of such shares determined from the assets and liabilities of such corporation, considered in the light of every factor bearing on value.

... It is not possible for the court to enumerate all of the possible factors to be considered in determining said fair cash value of said shares, but as illustrative of the factors that may be considered, the court mentions the following factors to which consideration may be given as they were as of June 23, 1943, to wit: the business of the defendant and the prospects of its business for the future; the nature of its property; its financial condition; the value of its assets; the amount and nature of its fixed and contingent liabilities; its earnings in the past and its prospects of earnings in the future; the dividends paid by it in the past and its prospects for paying dividends in the future; its management and reputation; the value of its good will; the market value of its shares; and its future prospects in a financial way.

• • •

It is to be noted that in most of the cases to which I have referred the question of appraisal of the shares was referred by the Court to experts for report. I think that would be an appropriate course to follow here. The material before me at this time does not enable the Court to fix the price of the shares, nor, indeed, to decide which method should be applied in determining that price. Whatever method is employed the dissenting shareholder is to be paid for his proportionate interest in the company as a going concern on the day before the resolution was passed *including* any appreciation or depreciation in anticipation of the vote upon the resolution. It is to be observed that the latter consideration was excluded in the *Roessler* case, supra.

I will hear counsel for the applicant and Mr. Estlin at some time convenient to both of them on the question of who should be appointed as a referee and what instructions should be given to the person so appointed. I will also entertain submissions with regard to the question of costs. The reference which I intend to make will be pursuant to s. 16 of the *Arbitration Act*, R.S.B.C. 1960, c. 14, and to s. 63 ... of the Supreme Court Act, R.S.B.C. 1960, c. 374.

Valuation of Dissenters' Shares. While the Merger Report suggested that courts would not second guess market value in valuing dissenters' shares, such cases are in fact the exception and *Wall & Redekop* the norm. For example, until recently courts in Delaware applied a weighted average method of valuation, under which various elements of value, including dividends, earnings, market and asset values, were each assigned a particular weight. There were often little satisfactory explanation of how a figure was chosen for any one component of value, though a consistently high weight was placed on asset or book value, which ordinarily was higher than market or earnings values. See Note, *Valuation of Dissenters' Stock Under Appraisal Statutes*, 79 Harv. L. Rev. 1453, 1468-71 (1966). As a result, the Delaware "block," as the weighted average test came to be called, gave dissenting shareholders a greater return than they would have received had they sold their shares on the market.

Canadian courts also place a heavy emphasis on asset and earnings value, in effect awarding the dissenter a premium over market value. There are exceptions to this. Where there were no allegations of unfairness and the shares were widely traded, the market value for Shell Canada Ltd. of $16.50 was accepted in place of an alleged asset value of $28.50 in *Re Montgomery* (1980), 111 D.L.R. (3d) 116 (Sask.). The plaintiff held 550 of the 63,840,000 class A common shares of the corporation, and dissented from an innocuous resolution authorizing the creation of a new class of preferred shares. Estey J. stated that asset value should be discounted when a corporation is a going concern and its shares are actively traded.

The identification in *Montgomery* of fair value with market value has much to commend it. If an appraisal premium were systematically offered to dissenting share-holders, they would be given an incentive to appraise out in triggering transactions, which might then be abandoned by the firm even if wealth-maximizing. This suggests that strategic assertions of the appraisal remedy may be feared unless market price is taken to reflect the value of widely held shares. In addition, the market price of widely traded shares may ordinarily be presumed better informed than the mythic "intrinsic" value discovered by a court.

Several arguments have, however, been made for second-guessing market value, and these must now be considered. First, market value may be discounted as a measure of firm worth if the shares are thinly traded, as in *Wall & Redekop*. A stock market listing does not always entail a broad market for the shares, with investment intermedi-aries absorbing substantial screening costs to determine firm value. The judgment of insiders concerning firm value is then more likely to diverge from the market's judgment than in the case of a widely traded firm. In addition, the information presented to court about firm value in such cases is largely in management's hands, so that assigning a relatively high weight to asset value (where it exceeds market value) may be thought a reasonable response to business realities. After all, management is unlikely to argue that the firm is undervalued on the market when the appraisal remedy is asserted.

The second argument for second-guessing market value is that it may be depressed simply because the dissenters wish to sell their shares. For this to happen, the block of shares would have to be very large, since the demand for widely traded shares is generally very elastic. In other words, a change in the number of demanders will ordinarily not affect market value significantly.* Even if sales by some large shareholders (usually institutional investors) might in fact alter market price, they will no doubt have taken this into account when purchasing the securities in the first instance. The empirical evidence indicates that the magnitude of the price depression on a sale of a large block of securities is typically no more than a few percentage points of stock price, and on average is less than 1%. See MacIntosh, *The Shareholders' Appraisal Right in Canada: A Critical Reappraisal*, 24 Osgoode Hall L.J. 201, 218-19 (1987). Block trades made at prices lower than those that prevailed prior to the trade may be attributed to the signalling effect of the trade. The fact that a major investor wants out may reveal information about the firm's declining prospects.

It may also be argued that market value should be discounted because the market will already have reacted to the transactions that triggered the appraisal rights. Prior to 1979, shareholders were entitled to sell out at pre-adjustment prices, since the CBCA specifically excluded "any change in value reasonably attributable to the anticipated adoption of the resolution" from the court's determination of value. See *Neonex Int. Ltd. v. Kolasa* (1978), 84 D.L.R. (3d) 446, 452 (B.C.). Since the dissenting shareholder has objected to the particular transaction, this may at first glance seem reasonable. However, disagreements about corporate policy are unlikely in the case of widely held firms whose shareholders are passive investors. Even if policy differences are observed, moreover, this may not justify granting appraisal rights unless management's investment policies are so improvident as to diminish market price. In the absence of management misbehaviour, then, an investor who disagrees with management might be left to his exit option of selling out on the market. On the other hand, where the triggering transaction might appear to give rise to fairness concerns, there may be a stronger reason to discount market value as at the date of the resolution.

Under Canadian statutes, the valuation of dissenters' stock is generally made as of the date of the resolution, and not as of a time prior to the announcement of the transaction. BCCA s. 228(5), as seen in *Wall & Redekop*, provides that fair value is to include "any appreciation or depreciation in anticipation of the vote upon the resolution." As presently worded, CBCA s. 190(3) appears to echo the British Columbia provision, since fair value is to be determined "as of the close of business on the day before

---

* See, e.g., Scholes, *The Market for Securities: Substitution Versus Price Pressure and the Effects of Information on Share Prices*, 45 J. Bus. 179 (1972).

the resolution was adopted or the order was made." By that time, market price would have reacted to news of the change. But see *Canadian Gas & Energy Fund Ltd. v. Sceptre Resources Ltd.*, [1985] 5 W.W.R. 43, 57 (Alta.) (market value not adopted on a CBCA appraisal because the market had reacted to the triggering transaction).

Courts have, however, circumvented these provisions in buyout transactions. A large number of appraisal cases in fact arise in cash-out mergers, where all that is at issue is the adequacy of the payout. If one motive for the buyout is an insider's desire to acquire shares on the cheap in what amounts to insider trading, this might be thought to justify second-guessing market price. In such cases, management has also an incentive to depress market price—for example, through non-disclosure of good news concerning the firm, since this will decrease the purchase price of the shares to be acquired. These considerations suggest an explanation of why Canadian and American courts have in recent years granted dissenting shareholders a special premium in cash-out mergers.

The first such case was *Re Domglas Inc.* (1980), 13 B.L.R. 135, 228-29 (Que.), aff'd, 138 D.L.R. (3d) 521, where Greenberg J. awarded dissenting shareholders a 20% premium. He stated at pp. 222-23:

In legislating the term "*a* fair value," Parliament conveyed upon the Court the equitable jurisdiction and the obligation to fix a value which is fair, just and equitable, having regard to all of the circumstances; including, in particular, a situation which is tantamount to an expropriation of the shares held by the minority shareholders.

. . .

In cases of the "squeeze-out" of the dissenting shareholders, which is equivalent to an expropriation, "fair value" goes beyond the concept of "intrinsic value," in that the former must include a premium for forcible taking, and is not subject to a minority discount.

In this Court's opinion, in a "squeeze-out" situation, as exists in the case at Bar, the absence of a discount in valuing a minority holding and the increment or premium for forcible taking are the essence of the distinction between "fair market value" and "fair value."

The Court will, therefore, first calculate and establish the "fair market value" of the dissenting shareholders' shares; and from there go on to fix "*a* fair value" for those shares.

. . .

The payment by the petitioner of "*a* fair value," even if more than the "intrinsic value" of the shares, is the price that must be paid by it for the privilege of effecting the amalgamation over the protest of the dissenting shareholders, who in effect are being ousted from the corporation.

See also *Les Investissements Mont-Soleil Inc. v. National Drug Ltd.*, [1982] C.S. 716.

A buyout premium would also have been awarded in *Weinberger v. UOP, Inc.*, 457 A.2d 701 (Del. 1983), where the defendant's majority shareholder sought to eliminate minority shareholders in a cash-out merger. Though the plaintiff had not sought an appraisal but rather rescissionary damages, the Chancellor held that the weighted average method of valuation should be employed. On appeal, the Delaware Supreme Court rejected the "mechanistic procedure" of the Delaware block, preferring instead "a more liberal approach [that] must include proof of value by any techniques or methods which are generally considered acceptable in the financial community and otherwise admissible in court ... ." *Id.* at 713. One of the factors that a court might then take into account is the nature of the triggering transaction, for when a dissenter objects to a cash-out merger he may be entitled to a premium for his shares.

Whether this means that shareholders in Delaware firms will obtain more when they appraise out on a cash-out merger is by no means clear. The Delaware block already gave shareholders a premium through heavy weighting of asset value. If asset value is discounted and a premium granted, the end result may be to leave shareholders no better off. The same may not be true in Canada, however, if a premium over an already inflated asset price is granted. If the Delaware block was prompted by a fear of cash-out mergers, a further *Domglas* premium might chill efficient buy-outs of minority shareholders. Moreover, the premium would be reflected in a higher issue price of shares, so that shareholders would pay for the premium on purchase of their shares.

Two-Tier Buyouts. A further defence of appraisal premiums is based on "whipsaw" or *distorted choice* problems on take-over bids. In a partial take-over bid, the offeror seeks something less than 100% of the target corporation's shares. The offeror will then retain the right not to take up any shares if less than the stipulated amount is tendered, while shares will be purchased on a *pro rata* basis if more than that amount is tendered. For example, if current market price is $100 and the offer price is $120, all shareholders might be expected to tender on a 50% bid, absent transaction costs and taxes. A shareholder with 10 shares will then be prorated, selling only 5 of them to the offeror.

When making the bid, the offeror will disclose any plans he may have to acquire shares that are not purchased in the take-over bid. These remaining shares may be eliminated in a second step buyout, the mechanisms of which are discussed in the next section. The buyout price may be the same as the offer price, but in the United States more typically is less. In this case the offer is described as "two-tiered."

In a two-tier partial offer, the payoff to offeree shareholders is a blended price, composed of the offer price for those shares that are tendered and taken up and the buyout price for the balance. Suppose, for example, that the offer price is $120 and the buyout price $60. If all shareholders tender in a 50% partial bid, then each shareholder will receive an average per share consideration of $90. The offer would then be identical in its effect to one with a first and second tier price of $90.

Several authors have, however, argued that there is an important game theoretic distinction between these two bids, inasmuch as the tender decision in a two-tier bid may be coloured by the fear of receiving the lower buyout price. Suppose, for example, that market value is $100 and that this is taken by all offerees as an accurate measure of share value. The shareholders can then be expected to reject an offer with a price of $90 on both steps. However, when the offer price is $120 and the buyout price $60 on a 50% partial bid (for a blended price of $90), it may be feared that shareholders will tender on the first step in order to avoid the $60 buyout price. While all offerees would be better off if none of them tendered, each offeree will individually be better off if he tenders.

How a decision that is collectively irrational may be individually rational can be seen when the tender decision is analyzed as a prisoner's dilemma game.* In the follow-

---

* For a discussion of the characteristics of prisoner's dilemma games, see R. Axelrod, *The Evolution of Corporation* 7-11 (1984).

ing matrix, the first figure in each box refers to the payoff to Shareholder 1 and the
second to the payoff of Shareholder 2.

Shareholder 2

		Tender	Do not tender
Shareholder 1	Tender	90, 90	120, 60
	Do not tender	60, 120	100, 100

For the purpose of simplicity, it is assumed that there are only two shareholders,
each of whom holds one share. Any communication between them is prohibited, and
each will make his tender decision in ignorance of what the other has decided. The
payoff to each party is, however, a function of how the other party chooses. Shareholder 1 will know that if he tenders, he will receive $90 if shareholder 2 also tenders
and $120 if shareholder 2 does not. If shareholder 1 does not tender, he will receive $60
if shareholder 2 tenders and $100 if shareholder 2 does not. Whatever shareholder 2
does, shareholder 1 will always be better off if he tenders (making $30 more if share-
holder 2 tenders and $20 more if he does not).* Unfortunately, the same is true as well
of shareholder 2, who will also tender. The two shareholders will then consent to an
acquisition of their shares for $180, where total share value without tendering is $200.
See Bebchuk, *Toward Undistorted Choice and Equal Treatment in Corporate Takeovers*,
98 Harv. L. Rev. 1693, 1720-29 (1985); Carney, *Shareholder Coordination Costs, Shark
Repellents, and Takeout Mergers: The Case Against Fiduciary Duties*, [1983] Am. Bar
Found. Res. J. 341.

This analysis assumes that shareholders would not face the same distorted choice
problem if the offer and buyout prices are both $90. In that case, a no-tender strategy
will dominate the alternative of tendering. For this reason, a legal response might be
sought to the game theoretic problem, either by flatly prohibiting two-tier buyouts or
(what amounts to the same thing) by offering a *Domglas* premium on appraisal.

Distorted choice theories assume that an offeror might acquire a firm whose shares
are trading at $100 by making a partial bid at $105, with a buyout price at $20. However,
there is no evidence that shareholders tender in value-decreasing two-tier bids. In one
study, buyout price was 44.8% higher than market price, and offer price was 15.7%
higher than buyout price. See Office of the Chief Economist of the S.E.C., *The Economics of Any-or-All, Partial, and Two-Tier Tender Offers* 19 (April 19, 1985). While offer
price will exceed buyout price, then, both will be higher than pre-bid market price.

---

*   When one strategy always outperforms another in this way, game theorists say that it "dominates" the
other strategy.

Presumably, offeree shareholders realize not only that a value-decreasing bid is unattractive, but that other shareholders will know this as well, and will moreover know that all other shareholders realize this. When this happens, the pressure to tender is wholly removed. The question is therefore whether shareholders will see through every offer, accepting only those whose blended price exceeds market price (taken as a proxy for shareholders' valuations of the shares). In other words, when market value is $100, would shareholders tender on a 50% partial bid with an offer price of $120 and a buyout price of $90, but refuse to tender if the buyout price is lowered to $70? Once again, the evidence that on average even the buyout price exceeds market price suggests that distorted choice issues may not be particularly troublesome. See also Schwartz, *The Fairness of Tender Offer Prices in Utilitarian Theory*, 17 J. Legal Stud. 165, 170-86 (1988).

In addition, as a consequence of other pathologies, two-tier offers may actually be desirable. For example, if an offeree shareholder could count on an appraisal premium that equalled offer price, his incentive to tender would be weakened. Good bids might then fail through shareholder inertia. Moreover, if buyout price exceeded offer price, offeree shareholders might even reject a bid whose blended price represented a substantial premium over market price. While it would be collectively rational to accept the tender offer, holdout strategies would be individually rational, with shareholders refusing to tender in the hope of getting the higher buyout price. But this strategy will work only if other shareholders tender; if they too seek the higher buyout price and do not tender, the bid will fail. The result is a prisoner's dilemma game in which the Pareto-inferior outcome of mutual defection dominates wealth-maximizing cooperative strategies. One response to this problem might be two-tiered pricing, in order to prompt shareholders to accept at least good bids. See Grossman & Hart, *Takeover Bids, the Free-Rider Problem and the Theory of the Corporation*, 11 Bell J. Econ. 42 (1980); Easterbrook & Fischel, *Corporate Control Transactions*, 91 Yale L.J. 698, 708-11, 727-28 (1982) (free rider problem arises if no buyout is planned and shareholders believe that firm value will increase after take-over).

This would explain why offer prices exceed the post-offer prices of target stock. See Bradley, *Interfirm Tender Offers and the Market for Corporate Control*, 53 J. Bus. 345 (1980).

See further Fischel, *The Appraisal Remedy in Corporate Law*, 1983 Am. B. Found. Research J. 875.

D. BUYOUTS

The techniques by which a firm acquires all or substantially all of its outside shareholder interests are described as *buyouts*. To the extent that a firm is permitted to acquire shares in this way, buyout rights represent call options similar to those which the firm has for redeemable preferred shares or bonds. Buyout rights are therefore to be distinguished from rights that shareholders may have to require the firm to repurchase their shares, such as those available under the appraisal remedy. These rights are similar to put options in the hands of shareholders, and do not give the firm any right to require the securities to be resold to it.

Buyout techniques are also described by a variety of other terms. *Freezeouts* are transactions in which insiders require outside shareholders to resell their shares to the corporation. The net result of the freezeout is then to leave inside shareholders as sole residual owners of the firm. In Canada, the term *squeezeout* is used synonymously with freezeout. While buyouts refer generally to all transactions in which outside shareholders are eliminated, freezeout is the more specific term, describing compulsory acquisition techniques.

Buyouts are also frequently referred to as *going private* transactions, though that term more narrowly describes the transformation of the corporation from a widely to a closely held firm. When this happens, the corporation will delist from stock exchanges on which its securities are traded and seek exemptions from disclosure requirements under securities and corporations statutes. Freezeouts are then going private transactions, though not all going private transactions are freezeouts. For example, a firm may delist after shares are repurchased on an issuer bid, with all but a few shareholders tendering their shares. However, if the shares of the remaining outside shareholders are not compulsorily reacquired, they will not have been frozen out.

When shares are acquired in a *management buyout*, residual value is transferred from outsiders to an insider team of managers. This kind of transaction is therefore to be distinguished from one in which the shares come to rest in the hands of a major shareholder. The shareholders whose shares are so acquired may be either widely dispersed or else concentrated in a major shareholder. In the latter case, the management buyout sometimes occurs when a parent shareholder seeks to dispose of one of its divisions. If, as is usually the case, the transaction is financed by large loans from a bank, it is also called a *leveraged buyout*. This refers to a buyout that leaves the firm with a high ratio of debt to equity, frequently after the issue of junk bonds. Prior to the 1987 stock market crash, management buyouts were sometimes followed a few years later by a public issue of shares at a price that represented a substantial profit for management. At a time when this seemed a foolproof method of making large sums of money, it attracted severe academic criticism, which perhaps is now somewhat muted as a consequence of the crash.

Management may seek to freeze out minority shareholders through a variety of methods, some of which have been seen already. The following is a non-exclusive list of such methods:

- *Pursuant to a statutory power of expropriation.* See CBCA s. 206, discussed below in *Neonex International Ltd. v. Kolasa* (note that at the time that *Neonex* was decided, the relevant provision was numbered s. 199 of the CBCA). As a matter of procedure, this is the most difficult method of going private, since it requires the concurrence of 90% of the minority shareholders.
- *Amalgamation.* This involves a statutory amalgamation of the corporation with a shell corporation that is wholly owned by the principal shareholder. In the amalgamation, the minority shareholders are given redeemable preference shares and the majority shareholders are given common shares. The preference shares are redeemed immediately thereafter. See, for example, the strategy used in *Neonex International Ltd. v. Kolasa* and in *Alexander v. Westeel-Rosco Ltd.*, both of which are reproduced below.

- *Arrangement.* A cash-out amalgamation may also be effected pursuant to CBCA s. 192 or similar arrangement provisions in other statutes. Instead of an amalgamation, the arrangement may involve a stock split under which 1,000 existing shares are reclassified as 1 new share, with fractional shares eliminated. This is referred to as a reverse stock split. Arrangements under CBCA s. 192 differ from s. 181 amalgamations in that, in the former case, judicial approval is expressly required.
- *Amendment to the articles.* CBCA s. 173(1)(g) specifically provides for reclassification of shares. The shares may then be changed into redeemable shares, which are convertible into a new class of shares. The principal shareholder (and some minority shareholders) will convert their shares, while the other shareholders will be redeemed out for an attractive redemption price. A reverse stock split may also be accomplished by amending the articles.
- *Sale of assets.* A corporation may sell its assets to an affiliate for cash or redeemable preference shares. The vendor corporation would then go into dissolution and distribute the consideration to its shareholders. A sale of substantially all of the assets triggers the appraisal remedy, but a dissolution does not.

For a further discussion of buyout techniques, see Glover & Schwartz, *Going Private in Canada*, 3 C.B.L.J. 3 (1978).

Neonex International Ltd. v. Kolasa
British Columbia Supreme Court
(1978), 84 D.L.R. (3d) 446, [1978] 2 W.W.R. 593, 3 B.L.R. 1

BOUCK J.: Neonex International Ltd. is applying by way of petition pursuant to s. 184(15) of the Canada Business Corporations Act, 1974-75-76 (Can.), c. 33 (the "C.B.C.A."), for an order:

1. Fixing the fair value of certain shares for those respondents who dissented to a scheme of amalgamation, and
2. For directions regarding entitlement if any of the remaining respondents to be paid for the value of the shares formerly held by them.

The respondents McCartney and Sladden are two of the dissenting shareholders. They ask for an adjournment of the petition for the purpose of obtaining further information from the petitioner as to the fair value of the shares.

Because it was impossible to know whether the respondents were entitled to an adjournment without knowing the nature of the claim, the whole of the facts and the law giving the rights of the petitioner to apply and the rights of the respondents were fully argued before me by counsel.

I am grateful to them for their thorough and thoughtful presentations.

Facts

There are or have been two separate corporations called Neonex International Ltd. Prior to November 1, 1977, it carried on a variety of enterprises across Canada. On that latter date it amalgamated with Jim Pattison (British Columbia) Ltd. ("J.P.L.") and out of this merger arose a new company bearing the identical name—Neonex International Ltd.

For convenience it will be appropriate to refer to them as "Old Neonex" and "New Neonex." Old Neonex existed prior to November 1, 1977, and New Neonex came into existence after that date.

On September 8, 1977, Old Neonex sent a 67-page management proxy circular to its members. Its purpose was to inform the shareholders of the reason for a special meeting set for September 30, 1977, in Winnipeg.

In this circular was a copy of an unsigned amalgamation agreement made as of October 3, 1977. The parties to the contract were J.P.L. and Old Neonex. By its terms the two companies agreed to amalgamate upon the approval of their respective shareholders.

J.P.L. was wholly owned by a Mr. James A. Pattison through a company called Jim Pattison Holdings Ltd. ("Holdings"). At the time of the proposed amalgamation Pattison alone, or through associated companies which he controlled, also held 46.5% of the shares of Old Neonex.

Each shareholder of Old Neonex other than Pattison could elect to receive either $3 in cash for one share or a non-voting preference share in New Neonex with a stated capital of $3. Pattison agreed to exchange the 46.5% interest he held in Old Neonex for preference shares in New Neonex. The two companies who were parties to the amalgamation agreement also contracted to exchange the 3,866,667 common shares of J.P.L. held by Holdings for 3,866,667 common shares of New Neonex. Through these manoeuvres Pattison then became the direct owner of 100% of the equity capital of New Neonex.

The meeting of the shareholders of Old Neonex took place in Winnipeg on September 30, 1977. At that time the company had an authorized capital of 14,000,000 common shares. Of these 7,214,748 were issued. Only 5,381,660 votes were cast; 302,588 (5.6%) voted or were deemed to have been voted against the special resolution. Pattison's 46.5% controlling interest represented approximately 3,354,857 shares or 62.3% of the votes cast in favour of amalgamation.

All that was required to complete the transaction was a special resolution of the shareholders of Old Neonex and J.P.L. Section 2 of the C.B.C.A. defines a special resolution as a resolution passed by a majority of not less than two-thirds of the votes cast by the shareholders. Since Pattison held 62.3% of the shares present at the meeting and since all that was required was a vote by 66⅔%, it was not difficult to achieve this percentage. And so on November 1, 1977, a certificate of amalgamation was issued.

Old Neonex had retained earnings of $23,649,000. After amalgamation the retained earnings of New Neonex were stated to be $7,943,000. A number of unexplained accounting entries in the *pro forma* balance sheet of the consolidated companies left me with the impression that these retained earnings were used by Pattison to purchase the other 53.5% of the shares of Old Neonex. In other words the shareholders' own money in the form of retained earnings was spent to buy their shares. It looks as if it cost Pattison nothing.

The respondents objected to the resolution of amalgamation and this triggered the dissent provisions of the C.B.C.A.

Prior to amalgamation and after, Old Neonex and New Neonex carried on many kinds of enterprises either directly or through associated or affiliated companies. In the jargon of the trade it could be called a conglomerate. One segment referred to as the Consumer Products Division operated 42 self-serve supermarkets and five discount food markets in British Columbia. Another division manufactured and distributed mobile homes, travel trailers and the like in Western Canada and New Brunswick. The Service Industry Division manufactured, sold and leased electric signs throughout Canada and outdoor advertising displays in British Columbia.

In 1976 and 1977 Old Neonex acquired a total of 41% of the common shares of Crush International Ltd. of Toronto for about $22,000,000. Crush produces and distributes soft drink concentrates to over 60 countries around the world. As well, Old Neonex owned real estate in Canada and the United States of America.

The book value of Old Neonex as at December 31, 1976, was $4.21 and as at June 30, 1977, $4.10. The common shares of the company were traded on the Toronto and Vancouver stock exchanges. From the first quarter of 1975 until the end of the second quarter in 1977 they had a high of $2.40 per share and a low of $1.04 per share. There was conflicting affidavit evidence filed by both parties as to whether or not the market was controlled by the insiders during 1977. The inference I was asked to draw was that the market price was therefore artificial. Since it is impossible to decide this issue on conflicting affidavits I cannot reach such a conclusion. However, on the petitioner's own material for the period January, 1975 to July, 1977, 2,155,373 shares were traded on the Toronto Stock Exchange and of these 494,223 were sales or purchases by insiders.

Following the issuance of the certificate of amalgamation on November 1, 1977, the board of directors of New Neonex decided the fair value of the common shares to be purchased from the dissenting shareholders was not $3 per share but only $2.50. Accordingly, on November 8, 1977, New Neonex caused to be sent to the shareholders who had not accepted the offer of $3 and who had dissented in accordance with the provisions of the C.B.C.A. another offer, of $2.50 per share. This was not acted upon. At the hearing before me counsel for the petitioner stated the offer had now been amended and the original one of $3 per share restored.The respondents McCartney and Sladden oppose the petition. They ask for further information so they might decide whether $3 does in fact represent the fair value of their shares. They also move for the appointment of an appraiser pursuant to s. 184(21) of the C.B.C.A.

Law

The C.B.C.A. is a relatively new statute which was enacted in 1975. It replaced the Canada Corporations Act, R.S.C. 1970, c. C-32. A comparison between the previous legislation and the new Act in relation to the so-called forcing-out provisions and amalgamation may be helpful. I have collected the relevant sections of both statutes in the Appendix.

First of all, the forcing-out sections: By s. 136 of the 1970 legislation, 90% of the shareholders could approve a contract to transfer their shares to a purchasing corporation. Should any of the shareholders representing not more than 10% of the issued shares dissent to the proposal, they could then apply to the Court to stop the sale. It is important to remember the 90% majority meant just that and not 90% of the votes counted at a meeting of the shareholders. In the latter instance only a minority of shareholders might attend the meeting and so Parliament decided, meeting or no meeting, the approval must be based on 90% of the issued shares.

When a minority applied to the Court to stop the sale the ground rule was to place the onus of proof on them to establish the terms of the sale were unfair. Discovery was not allowed. The theory was that since 90% had accepted the offer this gave considerable weight to its fairness. Furthermore, the takeover could not be completed until the dissenters either settled or were ordered to transfer their shares by the direction of the Court.

The Supreme Court of Canada in *Esso Standard (Inter-America) Inc. v. J.W. Enterprises Inc. et al.* (1963), 37 D.L.R. (2d) 598, [1963] S.C.R. 144, commented upon these provisions. They held the 90% required must be made up of shares independently held. It could not include shares held by the offering company.

The same idea has been carried forward into the C.B.C.A., Part 16, s. 199. Parliament also adopted the common law interpretation set out in the *Esso Standard* case. When proceedings are taken under Part 16 to fix the fair value of a dissenting shareholder a Court is given very wide powers. In fact it may "make any order it thinks fit" during the course of the litigation.

Now to amalgamation: Section 137 of the Canada Corporations Act also had a code of procedure which two companies were required to follow if they proposed to amalgamate. Generally speaking, the arrangement required the approval of 75% of the votes cast at a meeting called for the purpose of approving an amalgamation agreement. A dissenter holding at least 10% of the shares could apply to a Court to set aside the agreement of amalgamation which had been approved by the majority. If no such action were taken the two companies could then ask the Minister to issue new letters patent in the name of the amalgamated company.

If a dissenter succeeded in his opposition to the amalgamation it was annulled. If he failed he had no right to anything more than what the amalgamation agreement provided.

The 1970 Act did not allow a company to purchase its own shares. An amalgamation such as this one could not have taken place because the statute would have prevented Neonex from buying out its own shareholders.

Besides these changes, significant alterations have been made to the law on amalgamation by other sections of the C.B.C.A. First of all, a shareholder may now dissent to an amalgamation and be paid the fair value of his shares (s. 184). Before, a successful action by a dissenting shareholder resulted in the annulment of the amalgamation agreement but he was not entitled to be bought out. Secondly, an amalgamation agreement may now be approved by 66⅔% of the shareholders and not 75% as was the previous requirement (s. 176(5)). Thirdly, once the amalgamation agreement is approved by the shareholders and new articles of association filed with the Director of the Act, the amalgamation is achieved upon his issuance of a certificate (ss. 179, 180). Before, a certificate of amalgamation might be held up when there were proceedings before the Court. Now, the fact that some of the shareholders have dissented and applied to the Court for relief does not by itself prevent the amalgamation from going ahead.

Since the Director has issued his certificate of amalgamation no complaints can now be raised so as to prevent the amalgamation from proceeding. The matter is closed. There is no way it can be undone. Parliament decided to grant a controlling shareholder an easier way to force out the minority than was previously the case. Pattison accepted the offer. The legality of the amalgamation is not in question. Its morality is for others to assess.

William Kolasa appeared in person. He had no law books nor any particular legal point to make but what he had to say goes to the heart of the matter. I can only paraphrase his comments since no court reporter was present. Nor can I reproduce on paper the deep sense of hurt which was evident in his remarks. He said:

The leaders of this country have asked us all to invest in Canada as good citizens. My wife and I took our savings and bought shares in Neonex for over $5.00 each. Now we are told we must sell them for $3.00. We seem to have little choice. Why is this so?

Why indeed.

The reason for these new provisions is not clear because it would seem the 90% forcing-out method (s. 199) is redundant.

A majority shareholder need not bother using that process when the same result can be achieved with only a vote of 66⅔% of those present at a meeting. What is more the instigator of the takeover can even count his own shares in arriving at the 66⅔%.

If Pattison had been compelled to follow the normal forcing-out provisions enunciated in s. 199, a variety of protective mechanisms would have been available to the minority which are not available on amalgamation. In particular there is no definition of fair value in the s. 199 procedure. It is at least arguable that the fair value should reflect any benefit the majority might receive by reason of the takeover. However, where a Court is called upon to assess the fair value of a dissenter's shares on an amalgamation such as this, the calculation must be determined at the close of business on the day before the amalgamation resolution was adopted (s. 184(3)). Any change in value reasonably attributable to the anticipated adoption of the resolution must be excluded. This seems to mean that any benefits Pattison gained by the amalgamation cannot be taken into consideration when valuing the dissenter's shares.

Such a result is in direct contradiction to the earlier legislation because where two companies amalgamated under that statute the minority shared any benefits given the majority in the amalgamated company. It was a pro rata distribution of shares amongst all the shareholders and not a confiscation of their shares at a fixed price.

I have outlined the facts in the very barest of detail. Eventually witnesses will be called and all of the evidence presented for analysis. There are several reasons for pursuing such a course. They are not necessarily based on previous case law because this is an entirely new statute which requires a somewhat different approach.

Counsel for the petitioner submitted the material was adequate enough to determine summarily the fair value of the shares without further evidence or argument. In support of his position a number of cases were cited to me which were decided under the earlier 90% forcing-out sections. They included such authorities as *Esso Standard (Inter-America) Inc. v. J.W. Enterprises Inc.*, supra; *Re Hoare & Co., Ltd.*, [1933] All E.R. Rep. 105; *Re Press Caps Ltd.*, [1949] Ch. 434. Because of the unique and different nature of the new legislation it is my respectful opinion these decisions do not apply. New ground must be plowed and new principles enunciated.

If a shareholder wants to acquire all the other shares in the company by using the amalgamation sections rather than the forcing-out provisions then the law will be particularly concerned over the rights of the dissenters. Their property is being expropriated. It has always been the policy of the common law to protect the rights of the minority as against the abuse of an unreasonable majority. This is more so where an individual's property is being taken by the majority and it is claimed there has not been adequate compensation.

If Parliament intended to deprive the minority of these common law rights then the law demands the statute say so in the most clear and unequivocal language. Otherwise, the common law will blossom through the cracks and crevices of the legislation and try to ensure that justice is done.

Because of these principles and because of the facts which I have enunciated, a heavy burden rests upon Neonex to show that it has offered the dissenters a fair value for their shares. Any reasonable argument the dissenters may present calls for an inquiry. Unlike the earlier forcing-out legislation it should not be assumed the majority is entitled to its way simply because of a 66²/₃% approval.

The respondents' submissions which have persuaded me they must be given a hearing are as follows:

1. At the time of the meeting the book value of Neonex shares was $4.10. No convincing explanation was set out in the information circular as to why the fair value should be $1.10 less than the book value.
2. There are at least four ways of valuing shares in a company:

   (a) Market Value: this method uses quotes from the stock exchange.
   (b) Net Asset Value: this takes into account the current value of the company's assets and not just the book value.
   (c) Investment Value: this method relates to the earning capacity of the company.
   (d) A combination of the preceding three.

The information circular did not specify in any detail under these separate headings an assessment of the fair value using each method. The material attempted to support the offer of $3 mainly on a comparison with the market price, which was something less. That is insufficient, particularly where a large block of controlling shares amounting to 46.5% is lurking in the background. Such a block must have had some depressing effect upon the true or fair value of the stock.

3. Pattison controlled Neonex. He derived substantial benefits because of the amalgamation. It would be naive to think that he detailed all the facts in the information circular which illustrated the highest fair value for the shares. His interests were to offer as little as was reasonably possible. $3.00 may represent the fair value of the shares, but the dissenters should not be compelled to accept Pattison's assurances on blind faith and untested evidence.

What is the next step? The petitioner has asked the court to fix a fair value. The respondents want an adjournment so they can get further information. They also ask for the appointment of an appraiser.

Where an amalgamated company has only one easily appraised piece of property, the appointment of an independent appraiser might be appropriate. It is not suitable for this kind of a complaint due to the complex nature of the operations of New Neonex. Many practical problems come to mind if the respondents' suggestion is followed. For example, who would pay the cost of the appraiser during the course of such an inquiry? Costs are a creature of statute and not the common law. An appraiser could take months or years conducting an investigation. Generally speaking, the rules and procedure of this Court only allow an award of costs at the conclusion of a proceeding. They cannot be advanced part way through to help finance the other side's claim or defence.

From whom would the appraiser take his instructions? Not from the Court, because it must remain impartial if it is to perform its proper function. If the Court did appoint an appraiser where does the onus of proof lie? Whose witness is the appraiser? What happens if his evidence is shown to be erroneous? What other evidence would the Court then have to reach a decision?

Our procedure, our rules of evidence and our adversary system cannot adjust to the kind of inquiry as recommended by the respondents. Although it may be tempting to embark upon a hearing of this nature and see if it can be done, I believe the wisest course is to stick to what has been tried and tested in the past. In the long run it will be less expensive.

There are seriously contested issues of fact to be resolved. A petition is not an appropriate vehicle to handle this kind of a dispute. Issues are not crystallized as in an action because pleadings are not exchanged. Consequently discovery, if allowed, is unwieldy and the advantages of testing the admissibility of evidence on the basis of the issues as raised in the pleadings is lost. Trials drag on. More time is spent in argument than in resolution.

Therefore I intend to order the petition be converted into an action. One side will be the plaintiff and the other the defendant.

At first I was inclined to think the respondents should be the plaintiffs because it was in their interest to move the matter along. But on reflection it seems this would place the burden of proof upon them. They would have to show the fair value was not $3 but something more. All the petitioner would have to do is to defend the allegation. That would be unfair.

The better, but not the perfect answer is to put the petitioner in the position of the plaintiff and require that it prove the fair value of each share is in fact $3. Through discovery of documents and examination for discovery the respondents will be able to inquire into the basis of the petitioner's evaluation.

I quite appreciate the financial burden this may place upon the respondents. Also, I am not overlooking the obvious. It will be in the petitioner's interest to try and prove the fair value was something less than $3. There is no particular answer to this dilemma which has been created by the legislation. Since the Act does not shut out the dissenters' right to a trial it seems to be the only common law remedy left available to them. ...

NOTES

1) Ignoring votes cast by Pattison or corporations controlled by him, what percentage of minority shareholders of Old Neonex voted in favour of the special resolution? To what extent does this provide evidence of the fairness of the amalgamation?

2) If 90% approval by minority shareholders is required under CBCA s. 206 (s. 199 at the time *Neonex* was decided), does this suggest that courts should be less ready to question the fairness of the transaction and impeach the take-over bid price? It has been said that the offering price should be presumed to establish the fair value of the remaining shares under s. 206(3)(c)(ii). *Esso Standard (Inter-America) Inc. v. J.W. Enterprises Inc.*, [1963] S.C.R. 144, 149; *Re Shoppers City Ltd.*, [1969] 1 O.R. 449, 3 D.L.R. (3d) 35; *Re Whitehorse Copper Mines Ltd.* (1980), 10 B.L.R. 113 (B.C.) However, dissenting shareholders were said not to have the onus of proving the offering price to be unfair in *Cyprus Anvil Mining Corp. v. Dickson* (1982), 40 B.C.L.R. 180, 196-97, 20 B.L.R. 21, 42-43. In determining whether an onus of proof arises, should a court consider other factors, such as whether the transaction was an arm's length one, or whether adequate disclosure was made in the information circular?

3) Was it in fact the case that the transaction "cost Pattison nothing"?

4) The theme that a certificate of incorporation from the relevant government department, however procured, will not be impeached occurs frequently in Canadian cases. Thus the legality, if not the morality, of the amalgamation in *Neonex* was not open to question. This is often desirable, since a contrary result may introduce an intolerable uncertainty in business affairs. In an amalgamation of two operating corporations, it might indeed be extremely difficult thereafter to redivide the combined enterprise. But do these considerations apply in an amalgamation of the kind in *Neonex*?

5) If Kolasa had such a deep sense of hurt about being frozen out, why did he assert dissenting shareholders' rights under s. 190 (s. 184 at the time *Neonex* was decided) instead of petitioning under s. 241 (the statutory oppression remedy)? Do you think that the statutory oppression remedy (seen in Chapter Seven, Part II) ought to enable a minority shareholder to obtain an order blocking or unwinding the kind of transaction seen in *Neonex*? Presumably Old Neonex's board of directors, which was subject to its fiduciary duty to act in the best interests of Old Neonex, thought that the amalgamation was in the best interests of Old Neonex. In your view, what consideration should have the upper hand: the need for a company to have the flexibility to rearrange its capital structure to suit its objectives or a shareholder's desire to remain as a shareholder of that company? In the light of the material on the nature of the share seen in Chapter Four, do you agree with Bouck J.'s view that *Neonex* involves a situation in which the dissenters' "property is being expropriated"? What basis is there for suggesting that a shareholder has a right to remain a shareholder of a corporation until such time as she decides to stop being a shareholder?

As noted in Part II of Chapter Seven, questions concerning majority-minority shareholder relations in a corporation have been addressed under several different branches of Canadian corporate and securities law. But it is not always clear that these different branches reflect a common understanding of the best way to balance a company's need for flexibility with respect to its capital structure and the interests of shareholders. While revisions to the CBCA introduced in the 1970s were designed to ensure that corporations had some room to manoeuvre when seeking to alter their capital structure (with shareholders typically being given the option to seek fair value for their shares), since that time securities regulators have imposed fairness standards on transactions that are designed to squeeze out shareholders. For example, OSC Policy 9.1 (discussed in greater detail later in this section) imposes a requirement that a majority of shareholders other than the one(s) seeking to effect the squeeze out approve a so-called going private transaction. OSC Policy 9.1 defines a going private transaction as one pursuant to which "the interest of a holder of a participating security of the issuer in that security may be terminated without the consent of that holder and without substitution therefor of an interest of equivalent value in a participating security of the issuer or of a successor to the business of that issuer or of another issuer than controls the issuer or the successor to the business of the issuer." OSC Policy 9.1 does not, however, require minority approval with respect to going private transactions effected pursuant to a statutory provision that allows the holder of 90% or more of a class of participating securities to buy out the remaining shareholders: e.g., CBCA s. 206.

OSC Policy 9.1's injection of distinctive fairness principles into the picture obviously limits a company's ability to effect the kind of transaction seen in *Neonex*. Is the introduction of this kind of veto power for minority shareholders a step forward or a step backward in the development of Canadian corporate law? Are the fairness principles that underlie OSC Policy 9.1's call for majority of the minority approval consistent with the fairness or equality principles found in the corporate law on the nature of the share (see Chapter Four)? With the corporate law's treatment of the oppression remedy (see Chapter Seven, Part II)?

Following on the heels of the securities regulators, the Director appointed under the CBCA has struggled with questions concerning the fairness principles that should govern going private transactions and how best to balance the corporation's need for flexibility with shareholder interests. In particular, the Director has had to consider whether compulsory acquisitions may only be accomplished under the CBCA by way of section 206 (the only section in the CBCA that specifically authorizes squeezing out minority shareholders) or whether tactics of the kind seen in *Neonex* and *Westeel-Rosco* (seen below) are permissible. Initially, the Director took the position that the elimination of shareholders could only be effected pursuant to s. 206: see "Policy Statement-November 9, 1989," reproduced at (1994), 17 OSCB 1749. The case law has, however, been less than consistent on this point and the advent of OSC Policy 9.1 has led the Director to consider whether going private transactions may be accomplished using techniques other than the one provided for in section 206 (relying on OSC Policy 9.1 and the oppression remedy as tools to protect the interests of minority shareholders): see "Going Private Transactions under the CBCA-Discussion Paper" (April 1994), reproduced at (1994), 17 OSCB 1745. In your view, what accounts for the failure of the Director and the securities regulators to develop a unified approach to these issues? How would you balance a corporation's need for flexibility with shareholder interests in this context?

Alexander v. Westeel-Rosco Ltd.
Ontario High Court
(1978), 22 O.R. (2d) 211, 93 D.L.R. (3d) 116, 4 B.L.R. 313

MONTGOMERY J.: Both applications are for an order restraining the defendants from convening any meeting of shareholders to consider or take any steps in furtherance of an amalgamation by the defendant Westeel-Rosco Limited ("Westeel") which has the effect of eliminating the plaintiffs' participation through the ownership of common shares in Westeel or in any company resulting from the amalgamation.

In the alternative, the plaintiffs seek to be allowed to vote on the proposed amalgamation as a class of shareholders for the purposes of approval of the amalgamation under s. 177(1) and (5) ... of the Canada Business Corporations Act, 1974-75-76 (Can.), c. 33.

At the time of the commencement of these actions Westeel was a corporation incorporated under the Canada Corporations Act, R.S.C. 1970, c. C-32.

On September 1, 1978, Westeel sent to its shareholders a notice of meeting and management proxy circular calling a meeting for September 25, 1978, to consider the continuation of Westeel under the Canada Business Corporations Act ("CBCA") as well as an amalgamation with three other companies which would eliminate the plaintiffs' position as common shareholders in Westeel or its successor company.

The Canada Corporations Act is being phased out. All new federal companies must now be incorporated under the CBCA. Companies incorporated under the old Act may vote to continue the company and then they become subject to the provisions of the CBCA. Westeel so voted on September 25, 1978. The balance of the matters to be considered by that meeting were adjourned pending the disposition of these applications.

The CBCA was enacted in 1975. There is only one reported decision to date under the Act and it does not purport to deal with the same sections I am called upon to consider herein.

These applications were brought under s. 234 ... of the CBCA for the injunctive relief sought in the two actions.

Westeel is a steel fabricator and a public corporation trading on the Canadian exchanges.

Jannock Limited ("Jannock") on April 25, 1978, in an arm's length transaction, acquired a block of 469,180 shares of Westeel at $21.75 per share. On April 27, 1978, Jannock made a take-over bid for the remaining shares at the same price and thus obtained a further 1,015,688 shares.

Jannock thus owned	1,484,868	for	76.5%
Plaintiffs in Rossmere action	240,170	for	12.4%
Plaintiffs in Alexander action	124,768	for	6.7%
Other public shareholders	88,610	for	4.4%
	1,938,416		100%

Westeel has proposed an amalgamation under the CBCA which would have the result of eliminating as shareholders the plaintiffs and other public shareholders.

The individual defendants are all directors of Westeel who favour the proposed amalgamation.

On August 2, 1978, Jannock incorporated Glamorgan Investments Limited ("Glamorgan") and on August 21, 1978, transferred to Glamorgan its 76.5% of the shares of Westeel. Glamorgan has not carried on any business other than the above transaction since its incorporation.

Jannock in its take-over bid stated its intention to acquire all of the shares of Westeel by availing itself of the provisions of s. 199(2) of the CBCA if it were successful in acquiring 90% of the shares. That section provides that if 90% of the shares of the company are acquired through a take-over bid the remaining 10% may be purchased by the offeror *without the consent* of the owners thereof provided certain formalities are met.

Jannock also stated in its take-over bid that if it were not successful in acquiring all shares of Westeel, Jannock might in the future make some alternative proposal to the holders of such shares to enable Jannock to end up owning all of the shares of Westeel or a successor corporation.

Jannock only held 76.5% after the take-over bid. It now seeks by amalgamation to squeeze out the 23.5% minority against their will.

The proposed amalgamation is with three subsidiaries of Jannock, namely, the defendant Glamorgan, Jannock Tube Limited ("Tube") and Sonco Steel Tube Limited ("Sonco"). The proposed amalgamation was first introduced to some of the directors on July 13, 1978, which was prior to the date of incorporation of Glamorgan.

All of the issued and outstanding shares of Glamorgan, Tube and Sonco are beneficially owned by Jannock.

What then are the reasons for the proposed amalgamation? The management proxy circular deals with it in three lines:

The Company, Tube and Sonco are all engaged in the steel business. It is anticipated that the proposed amalgamation will result in economic and administrative advantages through combining all steel operations of the above companies and will also result in a more efficient use of the combined assets.

No one can quarrel with this statement as far as it goes. It does not, however, in my view, represent full, frank disclosure. If these companies were the only ones to be amalgamated there would be no application before me. What then is the purpose for including Glamorgan in the amalgamation? The applicant says the reason is so that Jannock may try to avail itself of the provisions of s. 176(2) of the CBCA and oust minority shareholders.

• • •

The proposed terms of the amalgamation will result in the involuntary elimination of the shares of the plaintiff and other minority shareholders in Westeel and will result in Jannock owning a 100% interest in the shares of the amalgamated company. This may be clearly seen from para. 3, p. 3, of the management proxy circular.

None of the material sent to shareholders makes reference to any reason justifying the elimination of minority interests.

It is contended by the respondent's counsel that there were tax reasons for including Glamorgan. Indeed a favourable tax ruling was obtained which would give the minority, if ousted, a reasonable tax treatment. That, however, is not a "reason" to include Gla-morgan. It is the tax result if Glamorgan is included.

The irresistible inference is that Glamorgan is being included in the amalgamation in an attempt to use s. 176(2) of the CBCA to oust a minority who could not be ousted under s. 199(2) when Jannock failed on its take-over bid.

The applicants pose a number of issues to be determined.

1. Does the proposed amalgamation effect an improper expropriation of the plaintiff's property?
2. Does the scheme advanced unfairly and improperly discriminate against minority shareholders?
3. Are the majority shareholders in promoting and approving the scheme breaching their duty to the minority?
4. Are the defendant directors breaching their duty to the company by proposing the amalgamation?
5. Is the conduct of the majority and of the directors oppressive, discriminating and prejudicial within the meaning of s. 234 of the CBCA?
6. Are the minority shareholders entitled to vote on the amalgamation proposal as a separate class?
7. Have the defendants breached statutory procedures in respect of the notice and the proposed meeting?
8. Will irreparable harm result to the applicants if the respondents are not enjoined?
9. Does the balance of convenience favour granting the injunction?

Issue #1

In considering whether the proposed amalgamation effects an improper expropriation of the plaintiffs' property, it is helpful to look at the Canada Corporations Act, s. 136(1), and the Canada Business Corporations Act, s. 199(2).

• • •

Both sections provide a scheme which permits the majority to expropriate the shares of the minority but only if the majority acquires at least 90% of the shares and if it complies strictly with the terms of the statute.

Having failed in its take-over bid to get 90%, Jannock seeks an amalgamation of a nature that would squeeze out the 23.5% minority.

The CBCA was enacted in December of 1975. The only reported decision under the new Act is *Neonex Int'l Ltd. v. Kolasa et al.* (1978), 84 D.L.R. (3d) 446, [1978] 2 W.W.R. 593. The application before Bouck J. was by petition under s. 184(15) of the CBCA to fix fair value for certain shares for those respondents who dissented in the scheme of amalga-mation. It also asked the Court for directions regarding entitlement, if any, of the remain-ing respondents to be paid for the value of the shares formerly held by them.

Two significant facts distinguish *Neonex* from the case before me. In *Neonex* the amalgamation was an accomplished fact before the action came before the Court. Sec-ondly, no application was made by the respondents for relief under s. 234.

• • •

This brings me directly to an examination of s. 176(2) of the CBCA. Mr. Pepper has urged me to deal directly with this section and I shall do so.

Glamorgan does nothing but hold shares of Westeel. The corporate efficiencies described in the information circular could have been achieved by a lateral amalgamation and there would have been no ouster of shareholders. The introduction of Glamorgan creates a vertical amalgamation. It provided a vehicle for a tax ruling favourable to an ousted minority. It also provided the only manner of doing an end run around s. 199 of the CBCA. If there was a valid reason for the inclusion of Glamorgan, why was it not set forth in layman's language in the information circular? If the Legislature intended this section to encompass expropriatory powers, they should have said so in clear, unambiguous words. In my view the section should not be construed to import such powers. They now purport to do indirectly what they failed to accomplish directly on a take-over bid.

At common law the majority could not expropriate the minority.

The essence of *Esso Standard (Inter-America) Inc. v. J.W. Enterprises Inc. et al. and M. A. Morrisroe*, [1963] S.C.R. 144, 37 D.L.R. (2d) 598, is now enshrined in s. 199 of the CBCA. In referring to the case of *Re Bugle Press Ltd.*, [1961] 1 Ch. 270 (C.A.) in the *Esso Standard* case, Judson J., at p. 150 S.C.R., pp. 602-3 D.L.R. stated:

Buckley J. made the order sought by the minority shareholder. He held that in the circumstances of this particular case the onus was on the transferee company to show that the scheme was one which the minority shareholder ought to be compelled to accept. This was a reversal of the onus placed on the dissenting shareholder in the ordinary case to show unfairness. He also held that when the 90 per cent majority shareholders are themselves in substance the transferee company, the Court ought to "order otherwise" when compulsory acquisition is sought.

The Court of Appeal, in affirming Buckley J., founded its judgment upon his second ground—substantial identity of interest between the majority shareholders and the transferee company. With this identity of interest the whole proceeding, as Laidlaw J.A. stated it, is a sham with a foregone conclusion, for the purpose of expropriating a minority interest on terms set by the majority.

Issue #2

Does the scheme unfairly and improperly discriminate against minority shareholders? It is clear from the respondents' documents that the minority shareholders will receive non-voting preference shares which will be redeemed for cash, while the majority will receive common shares in the new company.

In *Greenhalgh v. Arderne Cinemas, Ltd.*, [1951] Ch. 286 at p. 291, [1950] 2 All E.R. 1120 at p. 1126 (C.A.), Lord Evershed M.R. said:

... it is now plain that "bona fide for the company as a whole" means not two things but one thing. It means that the shareholder must proceed on what, in his honest opinion, is for the benefit of the company as a whole. The second thing is that the phrase, "the company as a whole," does not (at any rate in such a case as the present) mean the company as a commercial entity, distinct from the corporators: it means the corporators as a general body. That is to say, the case may be taken of an individual hypothetical member and it may be asked whether what is proposed is, in the honest opinion of those who voted in its favour, for that person's benefit.

I think that the matter can, in practice, be more accurately and precisely stated by looking at the converse and by saying that a special resolution of this kind would be liable to be impeached if the effect of it were to discriminate between the majority shareholders and the minority shareholders so as to give to the former an advantage of which the latter were deprived.

It appears on the facts before me that the minority are being treated as second-class citizens.

Issue #3

Are the majority shareholders in promoting and approving the scheme breaching their duty to the minority? In *Brown v. British Abrasive Wheel Co., Ltd.*, [1919] 1 Ch. 290, a majority of 98% sought to buy out the remaining 2% of the shares. At pp. 295-6, Astbury J. said:

The question therefore is whether the enforcement of the proposed alteration on the minority is within the ordinary principles of justice and whether it is for the benefit of the company as a whole. I find it very difficult to follow how it can be just and equitable that a majority, on failing to purchase the shares of a minority by agreement, can take power to do so compulsorily.

Issue #4

Are the defendant directors breaching their duty to the company by proposing the amalgamation? The applicants argue that a duty is breached by the directors when they propose and take steps in furtherance of an amalgamation for the purpose of excluding particular shareholders.

The proponents of the scheme say an amalgamation will result in economies of scale. This should increase profits. Why then should they cut out the minority shareholders from these future profits?

In *Canadian Aero Service Ltd. v. O'Malley*, [1974] 1 S.C.R. 592 at pp. 606-7, 40 D.L.R. (3d) 371 at pp. 381-2, 11 C.P.R. (2d) 206, Laskin C.J.C. said:

It follows that O'Malley and Zarzycki stood in a fiduciary relationship to Canaero, which in its generality betokens loyalty, good faith and avoidance of a conflict of duty and self-interest. Descending from the generality, the fiduciary relationship goes at least this far: a director or a senior officer like O'Malley or Zarzycki is precluded from obtaining for himself, either secretly or without approval of the company (which would have to be properly manifested upon full disclosure of the facts), any property or business advantage either belonging to the company or for which it has been negotiating: and especially is this so where the director or officer is a participant in the negotiations on behalf of the company.

An examination of the case law in this Court and in the Courts of other like jurisdictions on the fiduciary duties of directors and senior officers shows the pervasiveness of a strict ethic in this area of the law. In my opinion, this ethic disqualifies a director or senior officer from usurping for himself or diverting to another person or company with whom or with which he is associated a maturing business opportunity which his company is actively pursuing; he is also precluded from so acting even after his resignation where the resignation may fairly be said to have been prompted or influenced by a wish to acquire for himself the opportunity sought by the company, or where it was his position with the company rather than a fresh initiative that led him to the opportunity which he later acquired.

And at p. 610 S.C.R., p. 384 D.L.R.:

What these decisions indicate is an updating of the equitable principle whose roots lie in the general standards that I have already mentioned, namely, loyalty, good faith and avoidance of a conflict of duty and self-interest. Strict application against directors and senior management officials is simply recognition of the degree of control which their positions give them in corporate operations, a control which rises above day-to-day accountability to owning shareholders and which comes under some scrutiny only at annual general or at special meetings. It is a necessary supplement, in the public interest, of statutory regulation and accountability which themselves are, at one and the same time, an acknowledgment of the importance of the corporation in the life of the community and of the need to compel obedience by it and by its promoters, directors and managers to norms of exemplary behaviour.

Issue #5

Is the conduct of the majority and of the directors oppressive, discriminating and prejudicial within the meaning of s. 234 of the CBCA? Section 234 of the CBCA gives the Court broad powers of discretion to preclude prejudicial conduct of a majority against its minority.

It is my view that the conduct of the directors is discriminatory. This swings the balance further in favour of the applicants in weighting the issues before me. I comment no further under this section as it is better left to the trial Judge after hearing evidence to do so.

Issue #6

Are the minority shareholders entitled to vote on the amalgamation proposal as a separate class? It is argued by the applicants that they ought to be allowed to vote as a separate class as they will be treated differently in the amalgamated company.

Section 177(1) and (5) of the CBCA reads:

177.(1) The directors of each amalgamating corporation shall submit the amalgamation agreement for approval to a meeting of the holders of shares of the amalgamating corporation of which they are directors and, subject to subsection (4), to the holders of each class or series of such shares.

    ...

(5) An amalgamation agreement is adopted when the shareholders of each amalgamating corporation have approved of the amalgamation by special resolutions of each class or series of such shareholders entitled to vote thereon.

In essence, Jannock wants to vote on both sides—as a vendor and as a purchaser.

Issue #7

Have the defendants breached statutory procedures in respect of the notice and the proposed meeting?

Section 176 of the CBCA provides that each company proposing to amalgamate shall enter into an amalgamating agreement. No agreement has been entered into.

The information circular states that Martin ... will be a director of the amalgamated company. Martin had never agreed. This can only be viewed as an attempt to gain support from the minority group. Jannock knew that Martin was opposed as a director and as president of Rossmere.

Issue #8

Will irreparable harm result to the applicants if the respondents are not enjoined? ...

I am satisfied that damages are not an adequate remedy in this case. If the future of the company is as predicted by Jannock, the future profits may be sizeable. How are they to be calculated? Mr. Pepper says any harm can be undone after a trial and after amalgamation if the Court sees fit under s. 234 of the CBCA. But how could one sort out the probable multiplicity of intercorporate financial transactions? How do you unscramble an egg?

I am of the view that irreparable harm would result if the respondents are not enjoined. Argument advanced by the respondents is that it is costly to set up corporate meetings and send out information to shareholders. They are to be reminded that the plaintiffs bear almost one-quarter of this cost. I do not think it a strong argument.

Issue #9

Does the balance of convenience favour granting the injunction? Since the applicants have satisfied me that there are substantial issues to be tried and that irreparable harm will, in my view, occur if no injunction is issued, relief ought to be granted to preserve the *status quo* pending trial.

On the preponderance of convenience, having in mind the effect on both parties, I am of the view that an interim injunction should be granted in the terms set forth in the notice of motion.

Costs to the applicants.

Injunction accordingly.

NOTES

1) Note that Jannock had acquired 76% of the shares of Westeel five months before in an arm's length transaction at $21.75. Montgomery J. does not state the price at which the minority shares were to be redeemed. Had it been $21.75, would it have been unfair? Note that take-over bids are usually made at a substantial premium (often 20%-30%) above market value. Did the amalgamation discriminate between the dissenting shareholders and those shareholders who had sold or tendered their shares six months previously?

2) CBCA s. 182(1)(d) (s. 176(1)(d) at the time *Westeel* was decided) specifically contemplates that shareholders of one of the amalgamating corporations may be paid out

in cash. Does this provide the "clear, unambiguous" power to freeze out minority share-holders that Montgomery J. was unable to find in the Act?

3) An interim injunction in cases such as *Alexander* is in effect very like a final disposition. Few corporations pursue the matter further because of the costs associated with remaining liquid and because the result is uncertain.

Exclusivity of CBCA Section 206. Do you agree with Montgomery J. that s. 206 is the exclusive method for CBCA corporations to go private? If so, all going private amalga-mations under s. 181 would be prohibited, even if substantially fair. If 90% shareholder approval is a sufficient badge of fairness, does 89% approval suggest unfairness? It does not in fact logically follow that s. 206 is redundant if a going private amalgamation with less than 90% approval is permitted. Section 206 establishes a code for eliminating minority shareholders, and courts may be more prepared to accept the take-over bid price as the fair value of the shares under s. 206(14) than a redemption price after an amalgamation. Could a going private s. 181 amalgamation then be upheld, upon proof of its fairness?

As mentioned above, while the Director under the CBCA issued a policy in 1989 suggesting that s. 206 was the only avenue open to a company wishing to eliminate minority shareholders, there are signs that this view is softening and that the Director is prepared to allow for other buyout techniques, provided that certain procedural protec-tions are honoured. It would seem, then, that the Director has recognized that exclusivity can be a double-edged sword. Are you sympathetic with the argument, still accepted in some American courts, that the appraisal remedy is a dissenting shareholder's exclusive remedy on a going private amalgamation? See *Ferguson v. Imax Systems Corp.* (1980), 12 B.L.R. 209, 220-22, rev'd, (1983), 43 O.R. (2d) 128 (C.A.). Or do you favour instead the Ontario Securities Commission's view as expressed in OSC Policy 9.1 that minority shareholders should be able to veto a going private transaction?

While an analogy to the short-form merger provision of the Delaware General Corporation Law exists, CBCA s. 206 was derived from s. 209 of the U.K. Companies Act. A going private arrangement under s. 206 of the British statute was nevertheless upheld in *Re National Bank Ltd.*, [1966] 1 W.L.R. 819 (Ch.). Plowman J. stated that:

the two sections, sections 206 and 209, involve quite different considerations and different ap-proaches. Under section 206 an arrangement can only be sanctioned if the question of its fairness has first of all been submitted to the court. Under section 209, on the other hand, the matter may never come to the court at all. If it does come to the court, then the onus is cast on the dissenting minority to demonstrate the unfairness of the scheme. There are, therefore, good reasons for re-quiring a smaller majority in favour of this scheme under section 206 than the majority which is required under section 209 if the minority is to be expropriated. [*Id.* at 829-30]

This decision was approved by Templeman J. in *Re Hellenic & General Trust Ltd.*, [1976] 1 W.L.R. 123 (Ch.), although it was said that a very high standard of proof of the fairness of the transaction is placed on the majority shareholder in a going private arrangement as opposed to a s. 209 transaction. In contrast to s. 206 of the English statute, CBCA ss. 181-186 do not require submission of the proposed amalgamation to a court.

Securing 90% shareholder approval under s. 206 does not in fact guarantee the fairness of the proposal. The shareholders may simply wish to accept the price in order to cut their losses in a losing venture. Moreover, if the offeror is already in control of the corporation, an absence of full disclosure may give rise to insider trading liability and misrepresentations in an issuer bid circular. In such cases, a presumption that the offering price is fair, such as was said to arise in the *Esso Standard* decision, would not seem warranted. Might it be possible for dissenting shareholders to prevent the freezeout from proceeding with a s. 241 application? If so, do we still need OSC Policy 9.1's rules on going private transactions? Does the power to freeze out minority shareholders under s. 206 mean that the corporation invariably has the right to do so?

The *Alexander* decision was followed in *Carlton Realty Co. v. Maple Leaf Mills Ltd.* (1978), 22 O.R. (2d) 198 and *Burdon v. Zeller's Ltd.* (1981), 16 B.L.R. 59 (Que.). However, *Alexander* was distinguished in *Stevens v. Home Oil Co.* (1980), 123 D.L.R. (3d) 297 (Alta.), since the amalgamation in that case had to be submitted to court for approval under s. 156 of the Alberta Companies Act. With greater judicial screening, there was a lesser need for prophylactic rules.

Class Voting Rights. Holders of a separate class of shares, such as preferred shareholders, have the right to vote separately as a class in the circumstances listed in s. 176(1). Class voting rights may also arise on a long-form amalgamation (s. 183(4)), a sale of assets (s. 189(6)) and a dissolution (s. 211(3)). In this way, a proposal which unduly favours one class at the expense of a less numerous one is unlikely to secure approval.

This will protect public preferred shareholders from elimination by a majority common shareholder. But what of minority common shareholders? The primary meaning of a "class" of shares is a group of shares with special rights, privileges or restrictions listed in the articles under s. 6(1)(c). However, in *Re Hellenic & General Trust Ltd.*, [1976] 1 W.L.R. 123 (Ch.), the minority shareholders of the Hellenic company who faced elimination under a going private arrangement were held to constitute a separate class. A company referred to as M.I.T. held 53% of Hellenic's common shares, while the objector, National Bank of Greece S.A., held 14%. M.I.T.'s shares were all held by Hambros Ltd. Under the arrangement, all common shares would be cancelled for cash, and new common shares would be issued to Hambros, which would become Hellenic's sole shareholder. The arrangement required three-quarters class approval and would have failed had not M.I.T. voted in favour of it. On these facts, Templeman J. held that the minority common shareholders constituted a separate class.

Hambros are purchasers making an offer. When the vendors meet to discuss and vote whether or not to accept the offer, it is incongruous that the loudest voice in theory and the most significant vote in practice should come from the wholly owned subsidiary of the purchaser. No one can be both a vendor and a purchaser and in my judgment, for purpose of the class meetings in the present case, M.I.T. were in the camp of the purchaser. [*Id.* at 126]

It will be recalled that Montgomery J. also suggested that minority shareholders were entitled to vote as a separate class in *Alexander*. In addition, the absence of the approval of a buyout by a majority of minority shareholders was held to be "significant, although not determinative" in *Re Universal Explorations Ltd.*, [1983] 1 W.W.R. 542,

545 (Alta.). "This is especially so in the case of an amalgamation where one amalgamating company owns a controlling interest in the other company." *Id.* Class voting rights for minority shareholders in a buyout were specifically rejected in *Stevens v. Home Oil Co.* (1980), 123 D.L.R. (3d) 297 (Alta.). In that case, however, management had voluntarily undertaken to secure approval by a majority of minority shareholders.

O.S.C. Buyout Requirements: OSC Policy 9.1. As noted earlier in this section, the O.S.C. has imposed special procedural duties under Ontario Policy 9.1 (formerly Ontario Policy 3-37) on a "going private transaction." The Quebec Securities Commission has adopted an analogous policy statement, Policy Q-27. Although the British Columbia Securities Commission was considering whether to adopt a similar policy statement, as of the end of 1994 no Canadian securities commission other than the O.S.C. and the Q.S.C. had adopted the policy statement.

OSC Policy 9.1 was first adopted in 1977, but was subsequently revised and expanded in 1991. The adoption of the revised Policy 9.1 was the source of considerable controversy due to what many observers felt was inadequate public consultation. In essence, the O.S.C. was accused by some of having unilaterally imposed a detailed, complex and expensive panoply of requirements on a wide range of transactions (i.e., insider bids, issuer bids, going private transactions and related party transactions) without having adequately considered either how the policy statement was to interact with business corporations acts or the views of those who have to live with OSC Policy 9.1. For a discussion of OSC Policy 9.1 and related party transactions, see Chapter Seven, Part I, Section D.

The policy was amended and expanded in 1991 in order to deal with problems that the O.S.C. felt were particular to the Canadian business community, notably the fact that (unlike the United States) Canada has a significant number of companies with a controlling or majority shareholder. The O.S.C. was therefore concerned that considerable potential exists in Canada for the unfair treatment of minority shareholders. Accordingly, the O.S.C. decided that certain kinds of transactions should comply with procedural requirements designed to protect the interests of minority shareholders. The O.S.C. did not, however, explain why it felt that the oppression remedy was not up to the job. In view of the decision in *KeepRite* (seen in Chapter Seven, Part II), do you think that there was a need for a detailed code of conduct to protect minority shareholders or was the common law up to the task?

Insofar as "going private transactions" are concerned, the policy extends to any transaction in which a security holder's interest in a participating security is terminated without that person's consent and without the substitution of an interest of equivalent value in a participating security of the issuer or successor to that issuer. A participating security includes a security that carries the right to participate in earnings to an unlimited degree (including a security that is convertible into a participating share). This would exclude, for example, preferred shares whose interest in residual value is limited to a stipulated dividend payout.

On a going private transaction, a corporation must first prepare a formal valuation in accordance with detailed rules, set out in part VI of the policy. The formal valuation must be prepared by a qualified and independent valuer. The valuation must value the securities in which the interests of the holder will be terminated. A formal valuation report must be prepared in accordance with guidelines set out in the policy statement and it must be filed with the O.S.C. A summary of the formal valuation must then be included in the proxy circular. The summary of the valuation "must disclose the credentials of the valuer, the date the valuer was retained, the financial terms of the retainer, the subject matter of the formal valuation, the date of the formal valuation, the scope, including limitations on the scope of the formal valuation, the meaning of the word "value" in the circumstances, a description of the type of any information the valuer requested but was denied, the purpose of the formal valuation, the valuation approaches relied on, the key assumptions made and the valuation conclusion."

Upon an application under s. 182(6) of the Regulations, the Director under the OSA may waive disclosure if it would cause a detriment to the corporation or its security holders that would outweigh the benefits of disclosure. The firm is exempt from valuation requirements if the price was arrived at within the 12 months immediately preceding the date of the announcement of the transaction through an arm's-length transaction or negotiation with a selling security holder of a control block of securities. Here management must certify that no material changes have occurred since the control transaction.

Policy 9.1 also requires that the firm consider whether it should set up a special committee of the board of directors consisting of directors who are not officers of the company or insiders of the shareholder who is driving the transaction. The special committee should review the fairness of the transaction and may need to retain its own advisors to assist it with that process. A recommendation will then be made to shareholders regarding the fairness of the transaction.

The corporation must also comply with a *majority of the minority* test, securing the approval of a majority of outside shareholders. This requirement is waived if the controllers hold 90% of the shares and statutory appraisal rights are available. In addition, on a two step acquisition those shares tendered to the corporation in the first step take-over bid may be included for the purposes of computing the majority of the minority in the second step freezeout transaction if the intent to eliminate minority shareholders was disclosed when the offer was made. In some circumstances, the O.S.C. will require a two-thirds majority, for example, where the consideration is less than the value indicated in the valuation.

Because of these restrictions, Ontario buyouts are seldom two tiered. A further reason why Ontario offerors usually set the freezeout price at the first tier offer price is the fear that two tier bids will be impeached in an oppression action. But a partial bid that is formally single tiered (with freezeout price equalling offer price) may yet offer shareholders strong inducements to tender in the first step take-over bid. If the freezeout is not scheduled to occur until some time after the first step acquisition, the offerees will have lost the time value of their money in the gap. In addition, the firm's choice as to effecting a subsequent freezeout has a "heads I win, tails you lose" quality: if the value of the firm declines after the offer, the freezeout will not be made; however, it will be made if share value increases. Finally, even where no freezeout is planned, offerees may still wish to avoid the loss of a market for their shares. See Bebchuk, *Toward Undistorted Choice and Equal Treatment in Corporate Takeovers*, 98 Harv. L. Rev.

1693, 1709-13 (1985). As noted in the previous section, however, this lack of substantive equivalence may be defended on the basis that, without it, offerees would have
imperfect incentives to accept valuable bids. If the second tier price exceeded that of a
first tier partial bid, holdouts would be tempted to reject the bid to obtain the higher
premium in the second tier freezeout. When enough shareholders defect in this manner,
the bid may be defeated even if its blended price exceeds market value.

It is clear that if a firm cannot bring itself within an exemption from the requirements of OSC Policy 9.1, it will have to comply with a time consuming and expensive
set of requirements. In your view, is the cost waranted? Would it have been enough
simply to rely on the oppression remedy and to allow a board of directors to decide for
itself what procedures should be followed? The oppression remedy would have left
companies greater flexibility than OSC Policy 9.1 with respect to the measures to be
taken to ensure that the interests of minority shareholders were not unfairly disregarded.
But it would not necessarily have provided the degree of protection offered in OSC
Policy 9.1. Whether or not one is an advocate of measures like OSC Policy 9.1 will in
part depend on just where one stands on the debate about the importance of providing a
corporation with flexibility with respect to its affairs versus the protection of shareholder
interests, an issue that surfaces again and again in Canadian business law.

Buyouts in Delaware. Many of the recent buyouts in the United States have been
accomplished through mergers under the Delaware Statute. Del. s. 251, though worded
in much the same way as CBCA s. 182(1)(d), has even been thought to invite cash-out
mergers, in providing that the agreement of merger must state:

the manner of converting the shares of each of the constituent corporations into shares or other
securities of the corporation surviving or resulting from the merger or consolidation, and, if any
shares of any of the constituent corporations are not to be converted solely into shares or other securities of the surviving or resulting corporation, the cash, property, rights or securities of any
other corporation which the holders of such shares are to receive in exchange for, or upon conversion of such share ..., which cash, property, rights or securities of any other corporation may be
in addition to or in lieu of shares or other securities of the surviving or resulting corporation. ...

In addition, s. 253 of the Delaware statue permits short-form mergers under which
shareholder ratification is not required on parent-subsidiary amalgamations when the
parent holds 90% of the subsidiary's outstanding shares of each class. Section 253 also
contemplates the possibility of a cash consideration.

Delaware courts upheld parent-subsidiary mergers only on proof by the parent of
the entire fairness of the transaction. *Sterling v. Mayflower Hotel Corp.*, 93 A.2d 107
(Del. 1952). However, the fairness test was not perceived as imposing a heavy burden
on parent corporations or restricting going private transactions in any substantial way.
As a response to this, the United States Second Circuit Court of Appeals held that a
short-form going private merger was prohibited by Rule 10b-5. *Green v. Santa Fe
Industries Inc.*, 533 F.2d 1283 (1976). The plaintiff had argued that the cash-out price
was unfair, but his principal objection was an alleged lack of a business purpose for the
merger other than to purchase the shares at an unfair price. This, he said, constituted a
fraudulent device or practice under Rule 10b-5. On appeal, the United States Supreme

Court held that Rule 10b-5 is an antifraud provision and does not prohibit substantively unfair transactions where full disclosure has been made. 430 U.S. 462 (1977). The Supreme Court also stated that such questions of corporate wrongdoing are more properly to be litigated in state than in federal American courts.

The *Santa Fe* decision set the stage for a series of recent Delaware cases in which going private mergers were subjected to a business purpose standard. The first of these cases was *Singer v. Magnovox Co.*, 380 A.2d 969 (Del. 1977), where it was held that a merger entered into solely to eliminate minority shareholders was a violation of the duty owed to such shareholders. This test, related to the proper purposes doctrine under Anglo-Canadian law, gave rise to numerous difficulties. It was not clear, for example, what constituted a "business" purpose, or how substantial such purpose had to be if the simple desire to eliminate minority shareholders was also present.

The business purpose test was, however, rejected by the Delaware Supreme Court in *Weinberger v. UOP, Inc.*, 457 A.2d 701 (1983). The Court reaffirmed the entire fairness test of *Sterling v. Mayflower Hotel*, and stated that a parent corporation and its directors owe fiduciary duties to outside shareholders of a subsidiary in a buyout. As a preliminary matter, the plaintiff must allege specific acts of fraud, misrepresentations or misconduct that show unfairness to the minority, and must demonstrate some basis for invoking the fairness test. Thereafter, the insiders have the ultimate burden of proof. They must satisfy the court that full disclosure was made to shareholders and that there was both fair dealing and a fair price. However, if the buyout secures the approval of a majority of minority shareholders, the burden of proof is shifted back to dissenters. For successful plaintiffs, the primary monetary remedy is ordinarily confined to appraisal, though this may now include a freezeout premium.

Benefits and Costs of Buyouts. Though buyouts are regarded with suspicion by courts, it is important to recognize that they offer potential gains to shareholders. One such benefit is the cost savings associated with the favourable tax treatment under the Canadian Income Tax Act granted to Canadian-controlled private corporations. In addition, public corporations must make costly disclosure under corporations and securities statutes. If the firm is willing to absorb these costs when it requires an injection of capital, it may find them entirely wasteful when it has sufficient surplus cash to contemplate a buyout. Retention of "free cash flow" (i.e., cash flow exceeding the firm's investment needs) in these circumstances would in fact give rise to the agency costs described in Chapter Six, Section A since it would prove an inefficient way to maximize the wealth of the firm and its participants. In addition, agency costs are eliminated when outside principals are bought out. For example, the firm would not have to concern itself with the costs of requisitions, proposals, shareholder meetings, auditors, internal monitoring devices, as well as of annoying shareholder litigation. The impact of the myriad securities laws, regulations and policies that apply to public companies (and that are both time consuming and expensive to comply with) would be significantly reduced. Beyond this, the firm will not bear the residual agency costs of outside equity which resist governance and liability strategies. Because of all of these costs, a close corporation may decide not to go public, and once public may wish to go private.

In fact, minority shareholders appear to do well from buyouts. One study reports that outside shareholders earned positive abnormal returns* of 30.4% from a period 40 days prior to the announcement of the buyout to the announcement date. DeAngelo, DeAngelo & Rice, *Going Private: Minority Freezeouts and Stockholder Wealth,* 27 J.L. & Econ. 367 (1984). This suggests that, even if the transactions do occasion some costs, they may be swamped by buyout efficiencies.

If these buyout efficiencies are available only if all shareholders cash in their shares, then one might expect each of them to do so even without the compulsion of a freezeout. A further justification for the expropriation of dissenters' shares may, however, be provided by the game theoretic problems that would ensue without such compulsory "takings." Consider the analogy to the real estate developer seeking to acquire a block of 10 homes to erect an office building. If the homes are each worth $100,000 on a resale market, the total value of the block for present residential purposes is $1,000,000. However, the developer may believe the land to be worth $5,000,000 as a site for an office building. If he can acquire all 10 sites without any homeowner becoming aware of his plans, he will have made a profit of $4,000,000 (nor is he obliged to disclose his plans). But now suppose that he has purchased 9 homes at $100,000, and the last homeowner learns of his plans and of the anticipated profit of $4,000,000. The last homeowner might then seek a large chunk of this profit for himself. Similarly, the last few shareholders in a buyout might demand a large amount of money for their stock. A holdout problem may then ensue, with each shareholder seeking to become the last person to deal with the firm. Though it is collectively rational for all shareholders to agree to the buyout, then, it may be individually rational for each shareholder to dissent from the scheme. Compulsory freezeout techniques are a response to this free rider problem.

Apart from the evidence of its benefits, some of the costs that critics of buyouts have identified do not seem particularly troubling on closer scrutiny. One obvious cost arises through the transactions and tax-related expenses associated with a buyout. If outside shareholders are cashed out and wish to reinvest in another firm, they may do so only on payment of brokerage fees. While in an individual case such costs may not be great, in the aggregate they may in fact be significant. In addition, outside shareholders may be subjected to capital gains tax in a cash-out merger, without a rollover available as on a share-for-share amalgamation. These concerns were discounted in *Re Hellenic & General Trust Ltd.,* [1976] 1 W.L.R. 123 (Ch.). The shares had been trading at 36p. and the offer price was 48p. Templeman J. stated at pp. 129-30 that:

I am satisfied that [the arrangement] is more than fair. The shares of the company are listed on the Stock Exchange and in common with other investment trust companies normally stand between 20% and 25% below the net asset value of the company's assets. Thus the offer price of 48 p, if it represents the true net asset value of the shares, is 20% to 25% more than the shareholders can

---

*   Abnormal returns for any period of time are stock price movements that are either higher (positive) or lower (negative) than those of securities of the same risk characteristics, as measured by the firm's dispersion of outcomes in the past. Under this method of measuring stock price performance (called the capital asset pricing model by finance economists), abnormal returns are the residuals that remain after the stock's anticipated value (according to its risk characteristics) is subtracted from its actual value.

now obtain elsewhere. The assets of the company consist largely of cash and Stock Exchange investments, so that the ordinary shareholders, if they receive 48 p, instead of their existing shares, can follow the same outline of investment and will have roughly 48 p to invest instead of the share worth on the Stock Exchange 36 p. ...

... It was said that the scheme would involve the ordinary shareholders in a disposal for the purposes of United Kingdom capital gains tax and that would not apply to [the majority shareholder]. On the other hand, I was told that in fact the effect will be disadvantageous to [the majority shareholder] and that losses will not be allowed to be carried forward. The imposition of capital gains tax is a fate which we must all suffer. ...

... Accordingly I am quite satisfied that the scheme is fair or more than fair to the ordinary shareholders as a class.

While these arguments may not seem particularly compelling, it is at least possible to compensate outside shareholders for such costs through a premium in the buyout. Formally this may be done through an explicit recognition of a right of the shareholders to share in the firm's buyout gains, as in *Re Ripley Int. Ltd.* (1977), 1 B.L.R. 269 (Ont.). This may even be thought unnecessary, since buyout prices systematically far exceed market prices that obtain prior to the buyout announcement. Apart from this, legal rights to a buyout premium would likely be reflected in the price of widely held shares on issuance, so that shareholders would pay for the better protection.

A second arguable harm concerns the inframarginal shareholder, or the shareholder who ascribes a greater value to his shares than the market does. Inframarginality presumes that the demand curve for the shares is sloping, or less than perfectly elastic. In that case, not every shareholder will agree on what constitutes a fair buyout price. However, most economists believe that the demand for shares in widely held firms is very elastic, with investors generally unwilling to pay more than market price for them.

In some cases, however, shareholders have argued that they have a special interest in owning shares in a particular firm, so that buyouts should be impeached. This raises the question seen both in Chapter Four and earlier in this section regarding whether shareholders are properly speaking "owners" of the corporation who are entitled to veto a decision to "expropriate" their interest in the corporation. The O.S.C., with its shareholder oriented mandate, has on more than one occasion suggested that shareholders should be able to resist attempts to squeeze them out. For example, in *In the Matter of Loeb, Ltd.*, [1978] O.S.C.B. 333, Provigo Inc. sought to eliminate minority Loeb shareholders through an amalgamation between it and a wholly owned Provigo subsidiary. Provigo had acquired 80% of Loeb's common shares in 1977, and both firms carried on business in central Canada as food wholesalers. One of the minority Loeb shareholders, Empire Co., also carried on business as a food retailer in the Maritimes. Empire's argument that the buyout would contravene OSC Policy 3-37 was accepted by the Commission, which refused to grant an exemption from the Policy. The O.S.C. listed several reasons why Empire had a special interest in owning Loeb shares.

- Empire wished to participate in the food business on a nationwide basis and the investment in Loeb and Provigo was its only opportunity to do so. Empire would

therefore have been willing to take Provigo shares in exchange for Loeb shares. It was not, however, willing to take cash for the Loeb shares, since there was not an equivalent type of investment in the food business available in Canada.
- Other minority shareholders, apart from Empire, had purchased their shares for long-term investment purposes, and did not wish to be deprived of them for cash compensation.
- Some of these latter shareholders were members of the Loeb family who attached a sentimental and historic value to their shares.

Even here, however, inframarginality arguments may not seem persuasive. From a distributional perspective, the cashout was attacked because it failed to give Empire the premium value over market price (called consumers' surplus by economists) that Empire had attached to the shares when it purchased them. But since Empire had not paid for this premium on purchase, it is not clear why it should have received it on the freezeout. In addition, the failure to compensate the inframarginal shareholder would likely not have efficiency effects. By definition, the inframarginal purchaser does not set market price, which therefore would be unaffected by his departure as a demander of the shares. In addition, Empire's special interest in Loeb shares would have been lost had Provigo not been a food retailer itself and had it proposed a share-for-share merger. In that case, Empire's rights would have been restricted to the appraisal remedy, which suggests that the shares might reasonably be treated as fungible with cash.

Could the minority shareholders who were members of the Loeb family have prevented Provigo from changing the name of the corporation? How difficult would it be for *any* dissenting shareholder, on reading *Loeb*, to come up with an inframarginality argument against a freezeout. In other contexts, it has been presumed (no doubt correctly) that investors do not attach great sentimental value to their portfolio of securities. See *Asamera Oil Corp. v. Sea Oil & General Corp.*, [1979] 1 S.C.R. 633, 644.

The last argument against buyouts is that market price may discount true firm value. This may happen through the market's mistaken perception of firm worth because insiders choose not to disclose good news about the firm in order to minimize the cost of the buyout. On the other hand, the market may recognize firm value all too clearly, discounting it as a consequence of perceived managerial inefficiency. It may then be thought that, in fairness, market price should be second-guessed, particularly if what is proposed is a management buyout.

Brudney & Chirelstein, A Restatement of Corporate Freezeouts
87 Yale L.J. 1354, 1356-74 (1978)

[T]he recent Delaware decisions, though plainly intended to increase the protection of public investors, seems ambiguous in critical ways and possibly erroneous. In particular, the *Singer* decision, however laudable in spirit, contains two potential errors that ought to be avoided or corrected before they become fixed and general. One such error may be a failure to perceive that all freezeout transactions are not alike—that there are important contextual distinctions among freezeouts that need to be observed. As others have pointed out, freezeouts fall into three analytically distinct categories: (a) two-step, or integrated, mergers; (b) pure going-private transactions; and (c) mergers of long-held affiliates. The corollary, overlooked in *Singer*, is that different fairness criteria and different protections for minority stockholders are appropriate to each. In addition, and relatedly, the Delaware court's effort to distinguish "good" from "bad" freezeouts by use of a business purpose test was misdirected. Such a test has no role whatever to play in this field. Instead, the presence or absence of a business purpose should be treated as *inherent* in the categories mentioned above.

The time thus seems quite appropriate for a restatement of corporate freezeouts in clearer terms. By way of limitation, we should note that our discussion is directed solely at freezeouts involving public stockholders—roughly, stockholders who have no active role in management and whose percentage interest in the company is small. Freezeouts involving closely held firms raise issues, essentially deadlock problems, that are very different from those addressed here.

• • •

Our own view is that mergers representing merely a second step in the takeover of a target firm by a previously unrelated company present the least need for protective regulation and can be dealt with largely through the familiar medium of advance disclosure. At the other extreme, pure going-private transactions are of small value and high risk and hence should be prohibited. Mergers between affiliated operating companies, though also susceptible to abuse, at the same time promise social benefits in varying degree, and in our opinion are best regulated by rules relating to fairness of price. A strong tradition of fiduciary obligation is present in the last two situations; little or none in the first (when properly viewed). In each case the context itself defines the appropriate regulatory reaction; in none is there a need to engage in a hectic search for independent business reasons to justify the transaction.

A. *Two-Step Mergers*

Majority rule in cases of mergers or sales of assets between unrelated companies is an unobjectionable and universal feature of the corporate law. The stockholders of the acquired company will hold heterogeneous views on the intrinsic value of its shares, but once the acquiring company offers a price per share for the target company's assets that equals or exceeds the value assigned to those shares by a statutory majority, the case for majority rule becomes overwhelming. The alternative—to permit a single nay-voter to bar the merger—is well-nigh unthinkable, for, by compelling or encouraging stockholders to engage in hold-up behaviour, it would, in effect, make mergers and sales of assets a practical impossibility. No one, presumably, would view that consequence as desirable. In conventional theory, the takeover of one company by another offers major social and private benefits in the form of improved management, and the threat of takeover is thought to operate as an essential element of market discipline upon incumbent managers. One may have reservations about how aptly the theory applies in a given case, but surely no sensible legal system would impose a rule of stockholder unanimity on the sale of a business. Some, indeed, have doubted whether even so mild a right of individual dissent as appraisal can be justified in this context.

Straightforward asset purchase is not, of course, the only form of business acquisition. Especially when the target company's management opposes the sale of the firm, the acquiring company may seek to effect the acquisition by cash tender offer for the target's shares. Such an offer, again at a premium over the current sale price, may be for all of the target's stock and is rarely for an amount less than that which would assure control to the acquiring company. Assuming the tender offer succeeds, there will always remain some untendered shares outstanding, whether through inertia or because the tender price is thought too low by a minority of the stockholders. Often in these circumstances the acquiring company will act promptly to eliminate the untendered shares by merging the target company with itself or with a wholly owned subsidiary created for that purpose. Since the acquiring company now controls the target, it can unilaterally set the terms of the merger and vote through its approval.

Quite obviously, however, the two steps in the acquisition—tender offer plus merger—are integrated and represent a "plan." The analogy to a unitary purchase of assets is close and compelling; the only major difference is the absence of initial approval of the takeover by the target company's board, a factor that may increase, rather than reduce, the total price paid by the acquirer. Although the tag-end merger appears to be an example of self-dealing by the majority stockholders, it is only superficially of that class. Realistically, the tender-plus-merger procedure is merely a way of bypassing the target company's proxy machinery, which is controlled by the incumbent board, and submitting the acquisition proposal to direct referendum of the stockholders. Those who accept the tender offer are properly to be regarded as aye-voters, those who do not, as nay- or non-voters. Tender by a majority is the equivalent of a conventional majority vote; the subsequent merger merely gives effect to the majority's decision to accept the terms of the acquisition. The requisite "vote" has already been cast by the time the tender offer is completed, and the acquiring company is not really a voter in the original constituency at all.

In these circumstances, there really is no transaction between related parties and no self-dealing whatever. The acquiring company should be seen as an unrelated outsider throughout the takeover—from the time the tender offer is made to the time the merger is concluded. It has, or should be held to have, no fiduciary obligation as such, since as an outsider offering cash for the target's assets, it owes no duty to the stockholders of the sort that normally attaches to those who manage a firm or who own the controlling interest. It has no obligation to set a "fair" price for the target's property and should have no duty to disclose its management plans or to reveal any other values that it has discovered as an outsider. The heart of the takeover process is the exploitation of opportunities through the purchase of ownership and the substitution of new management. Seen as a takeover, the context is plainly *not* one in which fiduciary duty has any plausible or customary application. It is, literally, and despite the forced merger, an instance of arm's-length dealing.

The authors have suggested elsewhere that two-step takeovers, though not affected by fiduciary concepts, do require a modicum of regulation in view of the fact that public market transactions are involved and in view of the dangers of deception and "whipsaw."[14] Thus we have proposed that tender offerors who contemplate a second-step merger be required to announce their intention at the time the tender offer is made. In addition, we think it appropriate that the price paid in the merger for the shares then outstanding be the same as the price offered on the initial tender. ...

Somewhat ironically from our standpoint, *Singer v. Magnovox Co.* not only involved a two-step acquisition, but even appears to have met the procedural requirements stressed in the preceding paragraph. A less promising case for the assertion of the need for business purpose is therefore difficult to imagine.

•   •   •

B. *Going Private*

Going-private transactions of the sort that have made financial headlines in recent years exhibit a factual pattern quite distinct from that of the two-step merger. Here, controlling stockholders who are responsible for the company's management, having determined that its shares are undervalued by the market relative to its prospects and expectations, seek to terminate the public stockownership and return the firm to the status of a closely held entity. Typically, the insiders create a holding company, to which they transfer their controlling shares, and then propose a merger of the operating company into the holding company. The plan is that public stockholders of the operating company receive cash (borrowed by the operating company or drawn from its working capital) equal to the current market value of their shares plus a premium, while the insiders emerge as sole owners of the equity. Quite obviously, the insiders are not engaged in a takeover as North American was in *Singer*, because by definition they controlled the firm to start with. They aim simply to increase their investment interest from a controlling fraction of the company's stock to one hundred percent.

The "fiduciary" status of the controlling shareholders in these circumstances is presumably beyond question, and it is here, no doubt, that *Singer's* close scrutiny of the insiders' motives is best applied. Indeed, it has been argued that the impact of "fiduciary duty" should be even stricter than *Singer* suggests, and that insiders simply ought not to be permitted to use corporate processes to eliminate the public interest in the firm. Although insiders may of course purchase shares in their individual capacities by bidding for them in the market, the exploitation of the corporate proxy machinery, to which they alone have access, for the purpose of forcing public stockholders to give up their shares is regarded as a significant "abuse" in all but "exceptional" situations. In this view, the element of sheer coercion is fatally objectionable. Others find unfairness in the circumstance that the firm, having gone public when the market was buoyant and high, now elects to go private when the same market is depressed, and will presumably go public again when market averages recover. Taking advantage of market swings—first sucking in the public's money, and then squeezing out the public's participation—is

---

14   "Whipsaw" refers to shareholders' rushing to accept the tender offer because they fear that, if the bid for control succeeds, they will be frozen out at a lower price.

deemed a misappropriation of a corporate asset. Still other critics have urged that existing standards on disclosure of inside information, though adequate to regulate individual
market purchases, simply never can be stringent enough to prevent abuse when the
entire minority interest is *forced* out through a merger. Timing, as well as price, is within
the discretion of the majority, and even if all relevant financial information has been
disclosed, it is argued, insiders ought not to be allowed to act on their own interpretation
of the data by *compelling* other stockholders to accept a more pessimistic view of the
company's outlook than the one they hold themselves.

From the standpoint of the corporation, the justification commonly offered for going private is that the elimination of public investors will enable the company to save the
legal and accounting costs of complying with SEC and stock-exchange disclosure requirements as well as the expense of carrying on stockholder relations in one form or
another. This, however, is an inadequate justification, and in many instances we would
doubt its sincerity. The costs of monitoring management's conduct are incurred for the
benefit of the public stockholders, and it hardly rests with the fiduciary to cite the saving
of those costs as a reason for terminating the beneficiaries' interest without their consent. Moreover, the amount of that saving, measured per share of stock outstanding, is
too small in most cases to explain the company's action—itself costly—in retiring a
major fraction of its stock. The *Singer* decision strongly implies that a *corporate* purpose is necessary to sustain the legal validity of going private. To meet that condition,
the proponents should be required to show that public stockownership is actually inconsistent with the company's continued viability, not merely that public ownership entails
a cost that can be avoided by eliminating the public's interest. But we are not aware that
such a showing has ever been made in a going-private case, and we doubt it ever could
be. As suggested above, takeovers by *outsiders,* which may include merger as a second
step, must be assumed to involve at least the possibility of an improvement in the target
company's management. And as suggested below, mergers between affiliated corporations may entail economic and related benefits in the form of "synergy" or the like. By
contrast, going private simply shifts publicly owned stock into the hands of the insiders
and promises no economic gains *to the enterprise* that can be regarded as significant.

With so little to justify dilution of its strictest mandate, the fiduciary principle
suggests that going private transactions should in all cases be prohibited.

• • •

C. Mergers of Affiliates

Yet a third, and a different, regulatory problem is presented by a proposed merger
between a parent company and subsidiary corporation that the parent has controlled for a
more or less extended period of time. Here, as in the going-private context, the aspect of
fiduciary duty is clear. ...

Mergers between affiliates are thus distinguishable from two-step takeovers, which
are essentially arm's-length deals between unrelated parties. But though obviously not at
arm's length, affiliated mergers offer private and social benefits of sufficient importance
to distinguish them from pure going-private transactions as well. Moreover, they can
feasibly be tested for "fairness."

In many instances, the merger of a partly held subsidiary into its parent is designed to achieve operating economies or other gains that are unavailable, or less readily available, when the two firms are maintained as separate entities. Elimination of duplicated functions, tax savings, and financial and stock market gains are among the benefits commonly cited as potentially realizable through unification of parent and subsidiary. These may or may not be substantial factors in a particular case, but the possibility that joint ownership can result in a larger overall value for the two firms than the sum of their values as separate companies makes it impossible to deny that a business purpose may exist, and exceedingly difficult, in any given case, to prove that a commercial goal for the merger is wholly lacking. If the elimination of the separate subsidiary does or even can produce a larger aggregate, then presumably that step should not be discouraged and must not be prohibited.

Even if "synergistic" gains of the sort just described were minimal in a particular instance, there is a sound and creditable reason for management to want to reduce to *one* the number of stockholder constituencies to which it is legally responsible. The difficulty of placing inter-company dealings on a fair basis, of allocating overhead costs and (where relevant) tax benefits between the companies, and in particular the nearly impossible task of attributing opportunities for growth and diversification to the "appropriate" unit— these and related fiduciary problems present issues of practical day-to-day administration that are notoriously hard to solve. Corporate law spends much of its time policing fiduciary conflicts, and all the sanctified literature in the field is directed *against* the danger of serving two masters. It is not easy, therefore, to take the position that a legal mechanism, even such a mechanism as contrived merger, that aims to dissolve an existing conflict by bringing one such relationship to an end should be unavailable. ...

To conclude that mergers between publicly held parents and subsidiaries serve ends sufficiently desirable to preclude categorical prohibition of such transactions does not end the inquiry. As the authors have suggested elsewhere, that conclusion underscores the need for a rigorous "fairness" test. Such a test should assure that the subsidiary's stockholders are enabled to maintain their participation in the combined enterprise if they so desire. Although ideally this goal should be carried out by requiring that the subsidiary's stockholders be offered common stock in the parent, state laws frequently depart from this ideal by permitting debt or cash as well as stock to be paid out in a merger. Even so, the standard of fairness should dictate that the recipients receive enough in value to enable them to reacquire the same proportionate interest in the parent that they would have possessed had the consideration received been common stock alone. Under this standard, the use of cash in an affiliated merger is to be seen as involving an exchange of the parent's common shares for those of the subsidiary, followed by the parent's repurchase of a portion of its "outstanding" stock. The direct use of cash in the merger collapses these two steps into one, but the use of a shortcut (if permitted) should not be allowed to disadvantage the minority stockholders.

This approach, we think, implies a "proportionate sharing" rule of the kind applied by the Seventh Circuit in *Mills v. Electric Auto-Lite Co.* In *Auto-Lite* the court found that the *pre*merger value of the subsidiary's publicly owned shares was about $28 million, that of the parent $67 million—a total of $95 million. The *post*merger value of the securities of the combined enterprise was $99 million. Hence the increment in value resulting from the merger was roughly $4 million. Since the minority shares of the subsidiary constituted twenty-nine percent (28/95ths) of the total premerger value of the stock of both companies, the court held that the transaction would be treated as "fair" if—and, indeed, found it to be "fair" because—the minority stockholders received consideration worth not less than the premerger value of their *shares plus* twenty-nine percent of the "merger increment."

Under *Auto-Lite* therefore, if the value of a merged entity exceeds the summed values of the parent and subsidiary taken separately, the increment must be divided between both sets of stockholders in proportion to the premerger values of their respective shares. Once again, the simplest and least costly method for assuring "fairness" under this formula is for the parent to issue its own common shares to the subsidiary's stockholders in a ratio reflecting the values of each set of shares just prior to the announcement date. But the benchmark is the same for payments in cash or debt: after the merger the former stockholders of the subsidiary must be in a position to participate in the combined enterprise as fully as if payment had been in stock. By requiring that any merger increment be shared proportionately, *Auto-Lite* helps to assure that this objective will be met. Its virtue is that it *prevents* freezeout by putting minority stockholders in a position to reacquire their investment in the enterprise without dilution. ...

NOTE

Under the Brudney and Chirelstein analysis, how many of the above Canadian buyout cases were correctly decided?

A proportionate sharing rule was adopted in *Re Ripley Int. Ltd.* (1977), 1 B.L.R. 269 (Ont.). In dismissing an application by the corporation for an order approving a buyout under the arrangement provisions of the old Ontario Business Corporations Act, the Court stated:

The small shareholders, who would not be permitted to continue under the proposed arrangement, were invited originally to invest in a public corporation. If their shareholders are now to be eliminated, against their wishes, in order to permit the applicant—and that means the few continuing shareholders of the applicant—to enjoy tax savings as a private corporation, then the price to be paid for their shareholdings would not be fair and reasonable, in my judgment, unless it reflected a pro rata participation in the anticipated tax savings. In other words, their shareholding should be valued as if they would have been able to remain as shareholders in the newly constituted private corporation. [*Id.* at 273-74]

Brudney and Chirelstein's suggestions on how to allocate synergy on a merger were first made in *Fair Shares in Corporate Mergers and Takeovers*, 88 Harv. L. Rev. 297 (1977). In calculating the value of the minority's interest on a parent-subsidiary merger, one compares the value of the parent corporation with the value of the minority interests in the subsidiary. The parent's shares in the subsidiary are entirely disregarded, since taking them into account would result in doublecounting. The allocation of synergy is made more easily on a share-for-share exchange, where all that is necessary is to compute the value of the parent and of the minority interest in the subsidiary. Since all parties continue to participate in the enterprise, it is unnecessary to measure the synergy. However, on a cash-out merger, the synergy must be valued before it is allocated.

The Brudney and Chirelstein proposal has been said to be impracticable because of the difficulty in determining the value of the synergy as at the time of a cash-out merger. See Lorne, *A Reappraisal of Fair Shares in Controlled Mergers*, 126 U. Pa. L. Rev. 955, 964 n. 29, 970-87 (1978). As Brudney has noted, a sharing rule has received something less than wholehearted judicial support. Brudney, *Equal Treatment of Shareholders in Corporate Distributions and Reorganizations*, 71 Calif. L. Rev. 1072, 1104 (1983). In addition, the proportionate sharing rule is criticized as inefficient in Easterbrook & Fischel, *Corporate Control Transactions*, 91 Yale L.J. 698, 728 (1982). Buyouts result in efficiency gains, and a sharing rule will result in fewer buyouts, since the incentive to eliminate minority shareholders will have been reduced. Easterbrook and Fischel also criticize the Brudney and Chirelstein requirement that the freezeout be accomplished at the same price as the take-over bid in a two-step merger. Arguments for and against these two tiered mergers were considered in Section C. Finally, distributional effects are discounted, since the absence of a sharing rule will be reflected *ex ante* in the issuance price of the securities.

E. TAKE-OVER BIDS

1. Control Transactions

Control transactions refer to the techniques by which incumbent management is displaced by a new set of managers. Such transactions include, therefore, the debt holder's termination decision, where a default is declared and a receiver or trustee in bankruptcy sent in to manage the firm. However, our focus in this section is on control transactions, which occur not when the firm is on the verge of insolvency but when shareholders seek a change in control. Since control transactions are costly, some advantage must be held out to insurgents, in the form of the gains discussed in Section A of this chapter.

Selecting the Target Corporation. An acquisition-minded corporation will typically look for reasonably successful, relatively debt-free target corporations. It helps if management does not hold much stock of the target, and if shareholders have no great attachment to management. When institutional investors own large blocks of shares, the offeror should have some idea of how closely allied they are to management. While it may be difficult to gauge how management of the target will react to a control transaction, the offeror will wish to know how likely it is that the offer will be rejected or countered with defensive manoeuvres.

In some cases, the acquisition of a target may prove difficult because of regulatory statutes in, for example, the broadcasting, natural resource and transportation industries. In sensitive industries the target may seek political support through the review techniques provided for in these statutes (for example, early in 1995 a bid launched by Canfor Corporation ("Canfor") for Slocan Forest Products Ltd. ("Slocan") came to a grinding halt when it became clear that the Minister responsible for the administration of the Forest Act in British Columbia was not comfortable with allowing Canfor to seize control of Slocan). The Investment Canada Act, which replaced the more burdensome Foreign Investment Review Act will also be relevant in cases where the bidder is a non-Canadian (although since early 1995 Investment Canada has allowed members of World Trade Organization nations to invest up to $160 million without review). The Competition Act, S.C. 1986, c. 26 may pose less of a barrier than American anti-trust statutes, though mandatory prenotification requirements, inspired by the U.S. Hart-Scott-Rodino Premerger Notification Act, require parties to a merger to notify the competition bureau in advance of completing a merger if (1) both parties with their affiliates have total assets or Canadian sales of $400 million, and (2) the acquired firm has assets or sales of $35 million. The competition bureau will then have a limited period to decide whether it will challenge the merger.

Information about the target corporation may be gleaned from business publications, such as the Financial Post Survey of Industrials. The target's articles, proxy circulars and prospectuses are publicly filed and readily available. The articles will in particular be examined for provisions designed to make it difficult for the insurgent to acquire control of the target. Consideration will be given to whether the target has adopted a shareholder rights plan (discussed below) and, if so, how to deal with that rights plan. In addition, insider trading reports will reveal the target's major shareholders. Finally, the insurgent may perhaps obtain inside information about the target through a variety of sources. See further Troubh, *Characteristics of Target Companies*, 32 Bus. Law. 1301 (1977).

Though the extent of the search activities by insurgents is not undisputed, it seems reasonably clear that some costs arise in identifying potential targets. If they could be spotted without cost, their price would rise well in advance of the control transaction to reflect the probability of merger gains. However, all of the available evidence suggests that the price of the target's shares is constant or declining until very shortly before the control transaction is announced. See, e.g., Bradley, *Interfirm Tender Offers and the Market for Corporate Control*, 53 J. Bus. 345, 370-71 (1980). This implies that even sophisticated investors cannot easily identify potential targets, for if they could the bargain opportunity would have been eliminated well in advance of the take-over bid. In your view, does the fact that bidders clearly believe that bargain opportunities exist with respect to publicly traded companies suggest that the capital markets are less than completely efficient at incorporating all available information about a target's value into its share price?

Techniques of Acquiring Control. Control transactions may take the form of either a proxy battle or a take-over bid. Proxy battles have already been discussed in Chapter Six, Section E, and are considerably less popular than take-over bids as a technique for displacing management. One reason for this may be shareholder apathy, since it may not be worth the time of investors to determine which side is best able to manage the firm. In addition, if the control transaction is motivated by anticipated merger gains, insurgents will not share in them directly unless they acquire an equity interest in the firm.

However, some offerors have used proxy battles to supplement a take-over bid. For example, where target directors have responded to the threat of a take-over bid with strong defensive tactics, offerors have sought to impeach these tactics by placing their own slate of directors on the board, or by requesting in a precatory resolution that the tactics be abandoned. See Cowan, *The Trench Warriors*, N.Y. Times, May 29, 1988, at F1, col. 2.

Take-over bids (or tender offers) are launched through a public offer for the shares mailed to all of the shareholders. Even before this, however, the offeror may buy up to 20% of the target's voting stock without triggering the O.S.A. take-over bid requirements of s. 95. (This figure is 10% in CBCA s. 194 for offeree firms incorporated under that Act.) However, the offeror must disclose when he has acquired 10% of the target's voting stock under OSA s. 101. Pre-bid purchases are frequently made at a lower price than the offering price, and therefore economize on the cost of acquiring control. They also make it more likely that the offeror will acquire voting control in the bid (in part because other bidders may be deterred by the prospect of having to live with a shareholder who already holds a significant stake in the company). Pre-bid notification under s. 101 therefore increases the cost of the bid for the offeror because it alerts other shareholders to the potential for a take-over bid and may lead to an increase in the market price of the target company's shares.

Take-over bids may be classified as "friendly" or "unfriendly," depending on the reaction of the target's management. A friendly take-over bid is uncontested by the target, which will issue a directors' circular indicating its support for the offer. The offeror will then be far more likely to succeed than a contested bid, where the target's management attempts to defeat the take-over bid through defensive manoeuvres.

A further advantage of an uncontested offer is that the offeror will have a far better idea of firm value than in a contested offer. During the course of the negotiations, the offeror will be privy to a substantial amount of confidential information about the target, and with this may more accurately determine the offering price. The disclosure of information will also give the offeror a considerable advantage over rival offerors who may make an offer for the target's shares in competition with the first offeror. From the perspective of target management, a cooperative attitude in the negotiations may make the offeror better disposed to incumbent management, but at the same time this will increase the likelihood of the bid's success. Once confidential information is disclosed, it becomes difficult for target management to break off negotiations, since the offeror may then follow up with a contested offer, with a substantial informational advantage over rival bidders. For this reason, the target will seldom open up all of its books to the offeror prior to the offer.

The offeror may commence preliminary negotiations with a "casual pass." This involves a vague indication that a tender offer is contemplated or some other form of business union desired. Price is not specified, and if the target does not wish to pursue the matter further, no public disclosure is necessary. On a casual pass, there may be no pressure on the target corporation to react immediately.

As an alternative to protracted negotiations with a target, the offeror may adopt a "bear hug" approach. Here, target management is notified of a proposed take-over bid at a stated price, but without an immediate public announcement by the purchaser. For example, the target may have the weekend to consider it if the initial contact is made on a Friday, after trading has ceased. Negotiations during such a period have occasionally resulted in an uncontested offer.

A less friendly alternative is a "strong bear hug," where the offeror notifies the target corporation of the bid at the same time as publicly announcing it. The target is placed under the same pressure to react quickly as on an unfriendly bid. However, the blow may be considerably softened if the offeror informs the target that its management team will not be dismissed if the bid succeeds.

An unfriendly offer is commenced without any communication to target management apart from a copy of the offer and accompanying circular on the same day they are mailed out to offeree shareholders. Such bids might formerly have been open for acceptance for a few days, though longer periods are now prescribed by take-over bid legislation (e.g., 21 days under the Ontario Securities Act).

A decision will also have to be made about the price to be offered to the target company's shareholders. This will involve some very careful strategic thinking when making an unfriendly bid. A bidder might wish to make a "blowout bid," in which case it will seek to offer a sizeable premium over the current trading price of the target company's shares. The bidder will thereby seek both to make clear to third parties that if they enter the fray they will likely overpay for the company and to put pressure on the target's board of directors to acknowledge that the bid will provide shareholders with fair value for their shares. Alternatively, the bidder may wish to see whether other bidders are likely to come out of the woodwork. The bid may then be designed with the knowledge that the offer price will likely have to be increased if another bidder enters the picture.

Take-over bids may be classified as "partial," "any-or-all" or "two tiered." A *partial offer* is made subject to the condition that a specified number of shares are tendered to the bid (say 50%). If the condition is not met, the offeror is not obligated to take up the shares. If more than that number are tendered, the offeror must take them up on a *pro rata* basis under OSA s. 95.7. Sometimes a partial offer also gives the offeror the option of taking up all shares tendered at the offer price if more than the stimulated amount is tendered. An *any-or-all offer* is made for all of the shares that are tendered, so that the offeror must purchase all such shares even if they are not sufficient to amount to a control block. A *two tier offer*, as discussed in the last section, is a partial bid where the offeror announces that if he obtains control, he will freeze out non-tendering shareholders at a price that is less than the offer price. Even if not formally two tiered, however, a partial offer might give rise to similar distorted choice problems if offer price exceeds anticipated post-expiration stock price.

All such bids on average offer shareholders a premium over the pre-offer market price. The Office of the Chief Economist of the S.E.C. studied 148 tender offers from 1981 to 1983, and reported that the average premium for any-or-all bids was 63.4%, for partial offers was 31.3% and for two tier offers was 55.1%. *The Economics of Any-or-All, Partial, and Two-Tier Tender Offers* (April 19, 1985).

2. Defensive Tactics

In order to defeat a take-over bid, management of a target corporation may adopt a variety of strategies to make acquisition of control by an offeror more difficult. These may be either pre-offer tactics adopted prior to a take-over bid or post-offer measures made in response to a bid.

Pre-offer tactics include "shark repellent" provisions in the corporate charter whose purpose is to deflect hostile bids. Post-offer strategies also require some kind of advance planning. Though OSA take-over bids are kept open for acceptance at least 21 days under s. 95.2, target management must still be in a position to react very quickly and coherently to the offer. This generally entails the assembly of a take-over team to take charge of formulating and executing a response. A senior officer is frequently designated to head the team, which is also composed of in-house and outside lawyers, bankers and investment counsel. The transfer agent will be instructed to report immediately to the corporation when a request is made for the shareholders' list. At times a "black book," containing drafts of shareholder letters, newspaper ads and board resolutions, is prepared. This is usually of limited utility, since most take-over bids require something more than stock answers. In addition, the existence of a black book may become embarrassing to the target corporation should litigation ensue, since disclosure of its existence might suggest that management did not adequately consider the merits of the bid.

Making the Target Seem Attractive. The first tactic that the target may adopt is one aimed at making it look more attractive to its shareholders. If this strategy is successful, the firm will not appear to be a suitable candidate for a take-over bid which is motivated by the offeror's belief that he can manage the firm more efficiently. These strategies may include, for example, the reduction of agency costs by dividend payouts or share repurchases which eliminate free cash flow. The possibility of a take-over bid may then increase firm value, in the manner suggested by Henry Manne's market for corporate control.

The target may also seek to defeat a take-over bid by appealing to the loyalty of existing shareholders through newspaper ads or letters to the effect that the shares are worth more than the offer price. Propaganda campaigns are likely to be of limited utility, however, since the target's claims will not seem entirely creditable when control is on the line. More tangibly, after a bid is made, target management may declare a dividend or effect a buyback in the expectation that this will be taken as a signal that the firm's market price is undervalued.

Making the Target Seem Unattractive. The target may also seek to repel offerors by making itself seem more unattractive to them. If the offeror seeks to acquire control of a particularly attractive division (called a "crown jewel"), the target may agree to sell it off to a third firm. Another method is a shareholder rights plan (also known as a "poison pill"), which might be adopted either before or after a take-over bid is commenced. This is a device (discussed in greater detail later in this section) in which the acquisition of control in a take-over triggers contractual rights that may decrease firm value. For example, the target might issue new kinds of securities which are convertible into voting shares on a change of control by all holders other than the bidder, and which would then dilute the voting power of the bidder should it proceed with its bid. The target may also arrange for provisions in its relational contracts, such as bank loan agreements, pursuant to which those contracts would terminate on a change of control. It has also been suggested that golden parachutes, considered in Chapter Seven, Part I, Section B, amount to a form of poison pill. These are contractual arrangements in which management may treat a change of control as constructive dismissal, with relatively large amounts of money to be paid by the target as compensation to managers who leave the firm. In "tin parachutes," similar rights are given to non-management employees, whose claims in the aggregate may turn out to be relatively large as well.

Offensive Tactics. Another strategy might be to take the fight to the offeror. Sometimes this is the point of a propaganda campaign, which attacks the capacity of the offeror to increase firm value. The offeror may be described as a "raider," though this pejorative term has been defined as "somebody else's client." More dramatically, the target corporation may adopt a "Pac-Man" defence of making a reverse offer to purchase shares of the offeror. The target may also bring defensive law suits. If a misrepresentation is apparent in the take-over bid circular (and even if one is not), the target corporation might seek an injunction to prevent the bid from continuing. The target might also request securities commissions across Canada to issue cease trading orders on the basis of alleged misrepresentations in the circular.

Share Transactions. Finally, the target may embark on a series of share transactions designed to make acquisition of control more difficult for the offeror. One device might be a new issue of securities to an inside group or to one of its allies (called a "white knight") better disposed to incumbent management. Unless impeached, such tactics might easily defeat the bid, preventing offeree shareholders from participating in the premium.

The least troubling defensive manoeuvre is the solicitation of a rival take-over bid, since the auction of the firm as between the initial offeror and the rival bidder has been seen to serve efficiency goals. Evidence of the value of an auction to offeree shareholders is provided by a study which found that (1) target firms that vigorously resisted an offer by bringing defensive law suits earned higher returns than passive targets, but that (2) when these same firms actually defeated the initial bidder, they did significantly worse than passive targets. Jarrell, *The Wealth Effects of Litigation by Targets: Do Interests Diverge in a Merger?* 28 J.L. & Econ. 151 (1985). The key to the puzzle is apparently that litigious targets are much more likely to be the subject of an auction among competing bidders. If an auction develops, and a competing bidder succeeds, he will do so only at a higher price than that offered by the initial bidder. But if the target defeats all bids, its shares will be worth less than the initial offer price.

The value of an auction to offeree shareholders provides an answer to a similar puzzle, uncovered by Bradley, Desai & Kim, *The Rationale Behind Interfirm Tender Offers: Information or Synergy?* 11 J. Fin. Econ. 183 (1983). The three authors found that target firms that successfully resisted take-overs experienced negative abnormal returns when the defeat of the bid was apparent, but still ended up with a positive abnormal return of 20.16% from pre-offer prices. But this increase was likely in anticipation of further offers, for when the same firms were not the subject of successful take-overs in the following two years, their decline in value more than offset the earlier gains.

Auction theories may perhaps explain a third puzzle—the findings that "greenmail" may be beneficial to the shareholders of the firm that pays it. Greenmail usually refers to the purchase by a firm of a block its own shares at a premium over market price, though it may also describe a lump sum payment to a shareholder in return for a promise not to make a take-over bid. Under the managerial passivity thesis, such payments would appear to increase agency costs by eliminating a threat of a tender offer. In addition, it may be feared that the premium paid to a greenmailer for his shares will transfer wealth from other shareholders. On the other hand, while stock prices decline at the time of the greenmail payment, several empirical studies have found net gains when these declines are aggregated with increases that occurred when the greenmailer purchased his shares. See Macey & McChesney, *A Theoretical Analysis of Corporate Greenmail*, 95 Yale L.J. 13 (1985), where the evidence is reviewed. The two authors suggest that these net gains may result from the signal provided by the greenmailer that the firm is a suitable take-over target, with the benefit of an increased probability of a take-over bid swamping the costs to shareholders of the dilution of stock value through the payment to the greenmailer. On reviewing the evidence, Macey and McChesney conclude that greenmail may not in every case increase shareholder wealth, but in the theoretical vacuum argue against a flat prohibition.*

Greenmail was upheld by the Delaware Chancery Court in *Cheff v. Mathes*, 199 A.2d 548, 555 (1964) under the business judgment rule, the defendants having satisfied the burden of proof by showing "reasonable grounds to believe a danger to corporate policy and effectiveness" had resulted from the greenmailer's stock ownership. The *Cheff* decision was adopted by Berger J. in *Teck Corp. v. Millar* (1972), 33 D.L.R. (3d) 288 (B.C.S.C.) (reproduced below).

Take-Overs and Stakeholders. As discussed in Section A of this chapter, much of the literature in North America concerning take-overs has focused on the impact of take-overs on the share price of the target company and, to a lesser extent, on the share price of the company making the bid. Much of this literature suggests that take-overs are good for share price and profitability. But other studies are a good deal more ambivalent: see, for example, Tarasofsky & Corvari, *Corporate Mergers and Acquisitions: Evidence on Profitability* (1991), which looked at the performance of more than 100 Canadian companies acquired from 1963 to 1983 and concluded that although some 42% became more profitable after they were acquired, 43% showed a decrease in profit (with the balance (15%) remaining essentially unchanged). In your view, are share price and profitability all that are at stake in a take-over? You might here review the discussion of stakeholder theory in Chapter Six.

If a bidder has concluded that the target would be more efficient if it got out of certain businesses, then the bidder may intend to "bust up" the target company by selling off particular units, which may lead to significant dislocation for employees of the target corporation. The question therefore arises whether directors should take into account the interests of constituencies other than shareholders when evaluating one or more bids for the company and, if so, what weight should be given to those interests relative to those

---

* Greenmail has significantly abated in the United States as a consequence of December 1987 changes to the Internal Revenue Code, with a 50% penalty imposed on any gains derived from a premium stock repurchase if the seller has threatened to make a public tender offer for the firm. As will be seen, greenmail is effectively prohibited in Ontario through OSA s. 93(3) (no exemption available from issuer bid requirements).

of shareholders. The answer to this question will turn in part on the vision of the firm that one favours. If one thinks that shareholders are "owners" of the corporation, then one may well favour the argument that directors should concentrate on how best to "maximize shareholder value." If one sees the firm as a "nexus of contracts," then one may feel that it is appropriate for the board of directors to consider the impact of a bid on constituencies such as creditors and employees. The question would then be what weight should be given to the interests of those constituencies relative to the weight given to the interests of shareholders. Similarly, thought would have to be given to the extent to which promoting the interests of target company shareholders (who may well be bought out as part of, or subsequent to, the take-over bid) in this equation will result in a more efficient, productive and successful company.

Where one lands in this debate will have considerable influence on how one thinks liability strategies concerned with directors' duties and the oppression remedy should be structured (see Chapter Seven). Moreover, one's conclusions may well affect the view that one takes of the role that securities regulators and courts should play with respect to take-over bids. One might, for example, be concerned that because securities regulators are concerned first and foremost with shareholder interests, securities commissions provide a less than ideal setting in which to assess the merits of a board of directors' response to a take-over bid. Depending on the view that one takes with respect to the constituencies that the liability strategies explored in Chapter Seven should be sensitive to, one may feel that courts are better placed to weigh the competing factors that directors must consider than securities commissions and that the law on directors' duties and the oppression remedy provides a better avenue for regulating take-over bids than securities law.

These issues are particularly germane in Canada because in recent years securities regulators have assumed an increasingly prominent role with respect to the regulation of take-over bids. For example, tactics seen in some U.S. bids have simply been outlawed in Canada. Companies seeking to challenge defensive tactics adopted by Canadian companies have also shown an inclination to bring challenges to those defensive tactics before securities commissions. The heightened presence of securities commissions in the take-over bid process has not, however, been accompanied by much in the way of public debate about the proper balance between shareholder interests, the interests of creditors and/or employees and other groups with an interest in the take-over bid process. As you review the decision in *Teck* (set out below) and subsequent take-over cases, ask yourself what vision of the firm underlies the analysis set out in the case and whether you share that vision of the firm.

Teck Corp. v. Millar
British Columbia Supreme Court
(1972), 33 D.L.R. (3d) 288, [1973] 2 W.W.R. 385

[At issue in this case was an attempt by the plaintiff, Teck Corp., to take over Afton Mines Ltd., and the alleged manoeuvres of Afton's directors to prevent such a takeover. From Afton's inception in 1965, it had lacked sufficient capital to carry out its plans.

Since several past underwritings had yielded unsatisfactory returns, it directors (Millar, Price and Haramboure) sought to interest wealthier companies to participate in developing its mines. In the normal course of event, such companies (called majors) would provide capital for exploration and development, personnel, technical assistance and managerial and marketing experience in return for an equity interest in the mining company. This arrangement is known in mining circles as an "ultimate deal."

Teck was anxious to obtain an ultimate deal with Afton, but Afton preferred to deal with Placer Development Ltd., which, while it had made a less generous offer than Teck, had nevertheless a much better reputation. On March 22, 1972, Afton reached a preliminary agreement with Canadian Exploration Ltd. (Canex), a Placer subsidiary. The contract provided for the sale of 100,000 Afton shares to Canex and gave it a right of first refusal on any future ultimate deals submitted to Afton. The final details of the contract were left open.

When it learned of this, Teck indicated that it would offer terms twice as advantageous as any made by Canex. After being rebuffed by Afton, Teck began purchasing Afton shares on the open market on May 8. By May 31 it owned 1,312,011 of Afton's 2,600,000 outstanding shares.

The defendant Afton directors reached an oral agreement with Canex officers on May 30. While Canex initially wanted 60% of Afton's equity, it finally agreed to take only 30%. However, the agreement was conditional upon a favourable feasibility study, to be carried out by Canex. If Canex determined that the Afton property should not be put into production, then no shares would be issued to Canex. If Canex decided to place the property into production, it would receive sufficient shares to equal 30% of the issued shares. Teck would then no longer be Afton's majority shareholder.

On May 30, Teck directors requisitioned a shareholders' meeting. Afton's agreement with Canex was made public on June 2. On that date, Teck launched the present action.]

BERGER J.: ... The claim for declaratory relief is based on the allegations that the directors were actuated by an improper purpose. It is said that their purpose in signing the contract was to defeat Teck's majority share position, and that Canex knew it. If that allegation is made out then the means adopted to effectuate that purpose cannot be allowed to stand. The contract of May 30th would have to be declared null and void. That is the whole basis of Teck's action. So if the plaintiff establishes that the contract was simply a colourable device to further the directors' improper purpose, the plaintiff ought to have its declaration.

· · ·

Teck had the right, however, like any other shareholder, to challenge the exercise of any power by the directors on the ground that such power was being exercised for an improper purpose. This is not an allegation that the directors acted *ultra vires*, it is rather an allegation of abuse of power: Gower, *Principles of Modern Company Law*, 3rd ed. (1969), at p. 524.

The cases decided in the United Kingdom make it plain that directors, in the exercise of their powers, must act in what they *bona fide* consider to be the best interests of the company. If they issue shares to retain control for themselves, that is an improper purpose: *Fraser v. Whalley* (1864), 2 H. & M. 10, 71 E.R. 361; *Punt v. Symons & Co., Ltd.*, [1903] 2 Ch. 506; *Piercy v. S. Mills & Co. Ltd.*, [1920] 1 Ch. 77. The cases decided in Canada proceed on the same footing: *Madden et al. v. Dimond* (1905), 12 B.C.R. 80 (Full Court); *Bonisteel v. Collis Leather Co. Ltd.* (1919), 45 O.L.R. 195 (Ont. High Court); *Smith et al. v. Hanson Tire & Supply Co., Ltd.*, [1927] 3 D.L.R. 786, 21 S.L.R. 621, [1927] 2 W.W.R. 529 (Sask. C.A.).

Now counsel for Teck does not accuse the defendant directors of a crass desire merely to retain their directorships and their control of the company. Teck acknowledges that the directors may well have considered it to be the best interests of the company that Teck's majority should be defeated. Even so, Teck says, the purpose was not one countenanced by the law. Teck relies upon *Hogg v. Cramphorn Ltd.*, [1967] Ch. 254, [1966] 3 W.L.R. 995, [1966] 3 All E.R. 420. In that case the directors of Cramphorn Ltd. established a trust for the benefit of the company's employees and allotted shares to the trust, nominating themselves as trustees to enable them to purchase the shares. Buckley J. (as he then was) found that the directors had done so to ensure that a Mr. Baxter, who was seeking to acquire control of the company, could not achieve a majority. Buckley J. was persuaded that the directors had acted in good faith, believing they were serving the best interests of the company. He said at pp. 265-6:

It is common ground that the scheme of which this allotment formed part was formulated to meet the threat, as the directors regarded it, of Mr. Baxter's offer. The trust deed would not have come into existence, nor would the 5,707 shares have been issued as they were, but for Mr. Baxter's bid and the threat that it constituted to the established management of the company. It is also common ground that the directors were not actuated by any unworthy motives of personal advantage, but acted as they did in an honest belief that they were doing what was for the good of the company. Their honour is not in the least impugned, but it is said that the means which they adopted to attain their end were such as they could not properly adopt.

I am satisfied that Mr. Baxter's offer, when it became known to the company's staff, had an unsettling effect upon them. I am also satisfied that the directors and the trustees of the trust deed genuinely considered that to give the staff through the trustees a sizeable, though indirect, voice in the affairs of the company would benefit both the staff and the company. I am sure that Colonel Cramphorn and also probably his fellow directors firmly believed that to keep the management of the company's affairs in the hands of the existing board would be more advantageous to the shareholders, the company's staff and its customers than if it were committed to a board selected by Mr. Baxter. The steps which the board took were intended not only to ensure that if Mr. Baxter succeeded in obtaining a shareholding which, as matters stood, would have been a controlling shareholding, he should not secure control of the company, but also, and perhaps primarily, to discourage Mr. Baxter from proceeding with his bid at all.

Buckley J. found the primary purpose was to retain control. He said at p. 266:

Accepting as I do that the board acted in good faith and that they believed that the establishment of a trust would benefit the company, and that avoidance of the acquisition of control by Mr. Baxter would also benefit the company, I must still remember that an essential element of the scheme, and indeed its primary purpose, was to ensure control of the company by the directors and those whom they could confidently regard as their supporters. Was such a manipulation of the voting position a legitimate act on the part of the directors?

Buckley J. then said at pp. 268-9:

It is not, in my judgment, open to the directors in such a case to say, "We genuinely believe that what we seek to prevent the majority from doing will harm the company and therefore our act in arming ourselves or our party with sufficient shares to outvote the majority is a conscientious exercise of our powers under the articles, which should not be interfered with."

Such a belief, even if well founded, would be irrelevant. A majority of shareholders in general meeting is entitled to pursue what course it chooses within the company's powers, however wrongheaded it may appear to others, provided the majority do not unfairly oppress other members of the company. These considerations lead me to the conclusion that the issue of the 5,707 shares, with the special voting rights which the directors purported to attach to them could not be justified by the view that the directors genuinely believed that it would benefit the company if they could command a majority of the votes in general meetings. ... The power to issue shares was a fiduciary power and if, as I think, it was exercised for an improper motive, the issue of these shares is liable to be set aside.

Buckley J. then turned to the loan made to the trustees. He said at p. 270:

I am led, therefore, to the conclusion that the loan of £28,293 to the trustees was tainted with the same vice as the rest of the scheme, that is to say, it was an integral part of a scheme for securing for the directors the support of a controlling body of votes. The loan was not made with the single-minded purpose, or even with the primary purpose, of benefiting the company otherwise than by securing that control for the directors or facilitating their securing that control. Accordingly, although I do not question that the loan was made with honourable intentions, the making of it was not, in my judgment, a conscientious exercise by the directors of their powers to make loans of the company's funds for the purpose of the company's business or purposes reasonably incidental thereto.

Thus Buckley J. takes the view that the directors have no right to exercise their power to issue shares, in order to defeat an attempt to secure control of the company, even if they consider that in doing so they are acting in the company's best interests.

Counsel for Teck says the reasoning in *Hogg v. Cramphorn Ltd.*, supra, is applicable in the case at bar. He says the defendant directors believed Teck would use its dominant position to compel Afton to give Teck the ultimate deal. They believed that under Teck's management the property would not be developed as profitably as it would under Placer's management. They also believed that the value of Afton's shares, including their own, would decline, under Teck's management. Therefore, the argument goes, the defendant directors entered into the contract with Canex so that shares would be allotted under the contract to defeat Teck's majority. The case then is on all fours with *Hogg v. Cramphorn Ltd.*

Counsel for Teck says that *Hogg v. Cramphorn Ltd.* offers an elaboration of the rule that directors may not issue shares for an improper purpose. If their purpose is merely to retain control, that is improper. So much may be taken for granted. Counsel then goes on to say that *Hogg v. Cramphorn Ltd.* lays down that an allotment of shares, and any transaction connected with it, made for the purpose of defeating an attempt to secure a majority is improper, even if the directors genuinely consider that it would be deleterious to the company if those seeking a majority were to obtain control.

This, it seems to me, raises an issue of profound importance in company law. Lord Greene M.R. expressed the general rule in this way in *Re Smith & Fawcett Ltd.*, [1942] Ch. 304 at p. 306, [1942] 1 All E.R. 542: "They [the directors] must exercise their decision bona fide in what they consider—not what a court may consider—is in the interests of the company, and not for any collateral purpose." Yet, if *Hogg v. Cramphorn Ltd.*, supra, is right, directors may not allot shares to frustrate an attempt to obtain control of the company, even if they believe that it is in the best interests of the company to do so. This is inconsistent with the law as laid down in *Re Smith & Fawcett Ltd.* How can it be said that directors have the right to consider the interests of the company, and to exercise their powers accordingly, but that there is an exception when it comes to the power to issue shares, and that in the exercise of such power the directors cannot in any circumstances issue shares to defeat an attempt to gain control of the company? It seems to me this is what *Hogg v. Cramphorn Ltd.* says. If the general rule is to be infringed here, will it not be infringed elsewhere? If the directors, even when they believe they are serving the best interests of the company, cannot issue shares to defeat an attempt to obtain control, then presumably they cannot exercise any other of their powers to defeat the claims of the majority or, for that matter, to deprive the majority of the advantages of control. I do not think the power to issue shares can be segregated, on the basis that the rule in *Hogg v. Cramphorn Ltd.* applies only in a case of an allotment of shares.

Neither can it be distinguished on the footing that the power to issue shares affects the rights of the shareholders in some way that the exercise of other powers does not. The Court's jurisdiction to intervene is founded on the theory that if the directors' purpose is not to serve the interest of the company, but to serve their own interest or that of their friends or of a particular group of shareholders, they can be said to have abused their power. The impropriety lies in the directors' purpose. If their purpose is not to serve the company's interest, then it is an improper purpose. Impropriety depends upon proof that the directors were actuated by a collateral purpose, it does not depend upon the nature of any shareholders' rights that may be affected by the exercise of the directors' powers.

Should *Hogg v. Cramphorn Ltd.* be followed? ...

In Canada there is authority on both sides of the question: in *Bonisteel v. Collis Leather Co. Ltd.* (1919), 45 O.L.R. 195, Rose J. anticipated *Hogg v. Cramphorn Ltd.* He said at p. 199:

Upon the evidence there is no doubt at all that the purpose of the defendant directors in all that they did was to deprive the plaintiff of the controlling position which he had acquired. No doubt they thought it was not in the best interest of the company that he should control its affairs, and, in that sense, they acted in good faith and in what they believed to be the best interest of the company; but, nevertheless, I think that what they attempted to do was exactly what *Martin v. Gibson* (1907), 15 O.L.R. 623, shows that directors have no right to do: they were making a one-sided allotment of stock with a view to the control of the voting power ...

On the other hand, Harvey C.J.A., in *Spooner v. Spooner Oils Ltd.*, [1936] 2 D.L.R. 634 at pp. 635-6, [1936] 1 W.W.R. 561, said quite the opposite:

The cases cited and relied on by the plaintiff on this branch of the case merely establish that when an issue of shares by the directors for the purpose of giving control cannot be deemed to be intended to be in the interest of the shareholders generally but on the contrary appears to be intended to accomplish some other purpose, then it constitutes a breach of trust on the part of the directors who occupy a fiduciary position in which they must act *bona fide* for the interests of the general body of shareholders. It is simply an instance of the acts of the directors being at variance with this duty. There is nothing in the authorities cited that would stand in the way of ... giving someone control of the company if the directors honestly believed on reasonable grounds that it was for the interest of the company that that should be done.

The classical theory is that the directors' duty is to the company. The company's shareholders are the company: Boyd C., in *Martin v. Bigson* (1907), 15 O.L.R. 623, and therefore no interests outside those of the shareholders can legitimately be considered by the directors. But even accepting that, what comes within the definition of the interests of the shareholders? By what standards are the shareholders' interests to be measured?

In defining the fiduciary duties of directors, the law ought to take into account the fact that the corporation provides the legal framework for the development of resources and the generation of wealth in the private sector of the Canadian economy: Bull J.A., in *Peso Silver Mines Ltd. (N.P.L.) v. Cropper* (1966), 56 D.L.R. (2d) 177 at pp. 154-5, 54 W.W.R. 329 (B.C.C.A.); affirmed 58 D.L.R. (2d) 1, [1966] S.C.R. 673, 56 W.W.R. 641.

... the corporation has become almost the unit of organization of our economic life. Whether for good or ill, the stubborn fact is that in our present system the corporation carries on the bulk of production and transportation, is the chief employer of both labor and capital, pays a large part of our taxes, and is an economic institution of such magnitude and importance that there is no present substitute for it except the State itself.

Jackson J., in *State Tax Commission v. Aldrich et al.* (1942), 316 U.S. 174 at p. 192.

A classical theory that once was unchallengeable must yield to the facts of modern life. In fact, of course, it has. If today the directors of a company were to consider the interests of its employees no one would argue that in doing so they were not acting *bona fide* in the interests of the company itself. Similarly, if the directors were to consider the consequences to the community of any policy that the company intended to pursue, and were deflected in their commitment to that policy as a result, it could not be said that they had not considered *bona fide* the interests of the shareholders.

I appreciate that it would be a breach of their duty for directors to disregard entirely the interests of a company's shareholders in order to confer a benefit on its employees: *Parke v. Daily News*, [1962] Ch. 927. But if they observe a decent respect for other interests lying beyond those of the company's shareholders in the strict sense, that will not, in my view, leave directors open to the charge that they have failed in their fiduciary duty to the company. In this regard, I cannot accept the view expressed by Professor E.E. Palmer in *Studies in Canadian Company Law*, c. 12, "Directors Power and Duties," pp. 371-2.

So how wide a latitude ought the directors to have? If a group is seeking to obtain control, must the directors ignore them? Or are they entitled to consider the consequences of such a group taking over? In *Savoy Corp. Ltd. v. Development Underwriting Ltd.* (1963), N.S.W.R. 138 at p. 147, Jacobs J. said:

It would seem to me to be unreal in the light of the structure of modern companies and of modern business life to take the view that directors should in no way concern themselves with the infiltration of the company by persons or groups which they bona fide consider not to be seeking the best interests of the company.

My own view is that the directors ought to be allowed to consider who is seeking control and why. If they believe that there will be substantial damage to the company's interest if the company is taken over, then the exercise of their powers to defeat those seeking a majority will not necessarily be categorized as improper.

I do not think it is sound to limit the directors' exercise of their powers to the extent required by *Hogg v. Cramphorn Ltd.*, [1967] Ch. 254, [1966] 3 W.L.R. 995, [1966] 3 All E.R. 420. But the limits of their authority must be clearly defined. It would be altogether a mistake if the law, in seeking to adapt itself to the reality of corporate struggles, were to allow the directors any opportunity of achieving an advantage for themselves at the expense of the shareholders. The thrust of companies legislation has brought us a long way since *Percival v. Wright*, [1902] 2 Ch. 421.

If the directors have the right to consider the consequences of a take-over, and to exercise their powers to meet it, if they do so *bona fide* in the interests of the company, how is the Court to determine their purpose? In every case the directors will insist their whole purpose was to serve the company's interest. And no doubt in most cases it will not be difficult for the directors to persuade themselves that it is in the company's best interests that they should remain in office. Something more than a mere assertion of good faith is required.

How can the Court go about determining whether the directors have abused their powers in a given case? How are the Courts to know, in an appropriate case, that the directors were genuinely concerned about the company and not merely pursuing their own selfish interests? Well, a similar task has been admitted in cases of conspiracy to injure. There the question is whether the primary object of those alleged to have acted in combination is to promote their own interests or to damage the interests of others: *Crofter Hand Woven Harris Tweed Co. v. Veitch*, [1942] A.C. 435.

I think the Courts should apply the general rule in this way: The directors must act in good faith. Then there must be reasonable grounds for their belief. If they say that they believe there will be substantial damage to the company's interest, then there must be reasonable grounds for that belief. If there are not, that will justify a finding that the directors were actuated by an improper purpose.

A similar test has been adopted in English law in another context. In *Shuttleworth v. Cox Brothers & Co.*, [1927] 2 K.B. 9, a decision of the English Court of Appeal, the question was whether a company's articles were being changed *bona fide* for the benefit of the company. Scrutton L.J. at p. 23 laid down the test that ought to apply. He said that it was necessary to contrast:

... the acts of those, who honestly endeavour to decide and to act for the benefit of the company as a whole, with the conduct of others who act with a view to the interest of some of the shareholders and against that of others. Now when persons, honestly endeavouring to decide what will be for the benefit of the company and to act accordingly, decide upon a particular course, then, provided there are grounds on which reasonable men could come to the same decision, it does not matter whether the Court would or would not come to the same decision or a different decision. It is not the business of the Court to manage the affairs of the company. That is for the shareholders and directors. The absence of any reasonable ground for deciding that a certain course of action is conducive to the benefit of the company may be ground for finding lack of good faith or for finding that the shareholders, with the best motives, have not considered the matters which they ought to have considered.

In the United States the whole question of directors' exercise of their powers to defeat an attempt to take over a company has been considered in the State of Delaware. In the United States the law allows a company to purchase its own shares, and the cases have usually arisen where directors have sought to deal in the company's shares. Of course, directors in the exercise of such a power must *bona fide* consider the best interests of the company. The Delaware Courts have held that they cannot exercise their power merely for the purpose of retaining control: *Bennet v. Propp* (1962), 187 A.2d 405 (Supreme Court of Delaware). But in *Kors v. Carey* (1960), 39 Del. Ch. 47, 158 A.2d 136 (Court of Chancery of Delaware), it was held that directors were entitled to exercise their power to deal in the company's shares for the purpose of defeating an attempt to take over the company that they believed would not be in the best interests of the company. The Delaware Courts regard the presence of reasonable grounds for the directors' exercise of their powers as the test of good faith. The directors must have considered the consequences of a transfer of control, and must have acted upon reasonable grounds: *Cheff v. Mathes* (1964), [199] A.2d 548 (Supreme Court of Delaware).

If there are no reasonable grounds for the directors' alleged belief, but their purpose is merely to freeze out a group of shareholders, the transaction will be set aside: *Condec Corp. v. Lukenheimer Co.* (1967), 230 A.2d 769 (Court of Chancery of Delaware). What extent of damage must the directors anticipate to justify the exercise of powers to defeat those seeking a majority? In both *Kors v. Carey* and *Cheff v. Mathes* the directors anticipated a change in policy, though in each case a fundamental change. That change was in each case one that would have had profound consequences to the company's whole way of doing business, and one that the directors believed would damage the company's interests. It was held that constituted reasonable grounds for the exercise of the directors' powers.

I am not prepared therefore to follow *Hogg v. Cramphorn Ltd.*, supra. I think that directors are entitled to consider the reputation, experience and policies of anyone seeking to take over the company. If they decide, on reasonable grounds, a take-over will cause substantial damage to the company's interests, they are entitled to use their powers to protect the company. That is the test that ought to be applied in this case.

8. *The directors' purpose in the case at bar*

The whole case, in my view, turns on the question of Millar's motivation. His was the dominant mind on the board, his purpose was the board's purpose. Teck, in support of its contention that Millar was primarily concerned to defeat Teck's majority, relies upon the evidence that I have already outlined in this judgment. Then Teck goes further, and says that the terms of the contract of June 1st itself show that the defendant directors could only have signed it to frustrate Teck's attempt to obtain control.

Teck says that Millar was inconsistent. He said one thing and did another. He maintained throughout in his discussions with Teck that Afton intended to complete a feasibility study before entering into any contract. He indicated from time to time that he was considering the possibility of bringing the mine into production without the assistance of a major. He conceded on discovery that Teck's argument that, as a major shareholder, it could offer Afton a deal on better terms than any other developer, made "a lot of sense." Despite all of this, Millar then entered into a contract with a major, before feasibility, and without going back to Teck to see if Teck could in fact offer a deal twice as good.

The plaintiff relies on the statements made by Millar, even as late as May 29th, that he intended to go it alone. There is the evidence of Mr. Halle, an investment analyst, who says Millar told him then that he expected he would not have to give up more than a 20% bonus to a major. The plaintiff says that shows Millar made a desperate bargain with Canex, giving up a larger share of equity than he intended, because he had to in order to defeat Teck's attempt to obtain control.

I do not think the evidence supports such a conclusion. Millar made a lot of statements. Some were expressions of half-formed thoughts. Others were a reflection of deliberate policies. Others were made for bargaining purposes. He told Halle he intended to go it alone. He said he thought he would not have to give up more than 20% bonus. Those statements are themselves inconsistent. It was Millar's testimony, and I accept it, that he felt throughout that, though Afton might possibly be able to finance the project itself, it would inevitably need technical, managerial and marketing assistance from a major, indeed that without it, the banks would not lend Afton the money for the project anyway. The Bank of Montreal extended a $300,000 line of credit to Afton early in May, but that was simply to enable Afton to carry on with its drilling programme. The capital required to develop the mine itself was estimated by Mr. Hallbauer of Teck at 23 million dollars, and by Mr. Triggs, an engineer at Placer, at 39 million dollars. Millar indicated he found it hard to conceive the bank lending sums of that magnitude to himself and his friends without the participation of a major. When he spoke to Halle he was considering financing the project alone. He had some reasonable possibility, he thought, of achieving that objective. Ultimately, he did not. That is as far as it goes.

Then it is said that Millar stated many times that he was going to complete a feasibility study before making an ultimate deal. Yet he made a deal before his own exploratory drilling programme had even been completed.

I think that Millar's position is one that can be understood. He was considering bringing the project through to the completion of feasibility, and he told all of the majors that approached him that he intended to. But, he says, and I accept it, that he was prepared throughout to enter into an ultimate deal with Placer, or even with another major for that matter, before feasibility, if a deal were offered that he found acceptable.

What about Teck's claim that it could make a deal twice as good as anybody else? Why did not Millar go back to Teck to see if they could better Canex' last offer? Millar explained it in this way, and I accept his explanation. He was wary of Teck. He had misgivings regarding Teck's financial capacity, its technical expertise, its managerial strength, and its marketing experience. He did not put Canex's 70-30 offer to Teck, because he felt that it was not likely that Teck would make a specific offer—after all,

Teck had not done so to that point, confining itself to asserting that it would make an offer twice as good as any other major. Furthermore, Adie [Placer's exploration manager] had indicated that he did not want the 70-30 offer shopped around. So when Mr. Adie made the 70-30 offer, I do not think it is surprising that Mr. Millar should have accepted it at once, without going back to Teck to see if Teck could better it.

Teck was, I think, conducting a holding operation. They did not want to make a deal with Afton once their attempt to acquire control was under way. That is why they did not make any specific offer at the meetings held on May 29th and May 30th. No criticism can be made of Teck on that account. They were entitled to seek control, and once they got it, to take every reasonable advantage of it. But at the same time it was an attitude that in my view led to their unwillingness to put forward a specific proposal, once they had achieved a large share position, and it was an important factor in Millar's decision to conclude his deal with Canex without going back to Teck.

In any event Millar did not regard Teck's boast that it could do twice as good a deal as anyone else as quite believable. He felt that, from Afton's point of view, it was necessary, to off-set what he considered to be Placer's great experience, that Teck offer a deal 10 to 15% better than Placer, before similar offers from the two companies could be compared. He considered it unlikely that Teck could meet such terms on any satisfactory footing.

The plaintiff relies on Millar's statement, made at Kamloops on May 27th, that Price was running around trying to dilute Teck down. I accept the evidence that Millar made the statement. It reveals he was aware that Teck was concerned that if Afton signed a contract providing for the issuance of shares, Teck's position would be jeopardized. It shows that Millar was well aware that Teck's whole purpose would be frustrated if further shares were issued pursuant to a contract. But does that mean that was Millar's purpose, to dilute Teck's share interest? Or was his purpose to sign a contract that he considered to be in the best interests of the company? Millar, after all, said he did not think he approved of what Price was doing, and then he laughed. I do not think this establishes any Machiavellian intent on Millar's part. He knew that what he had said would consternate the Keevils [directors and officers of Teck]. It was, I think, to some extent an expression of his personality, and to some extent a matter of deliberate calculation. Does it show that Millar was primarily actuated by a desire to frustrate Teck's attempt to gain control? Millar gave evidence that he was by that time resigned to Teck obtaining control. He did not think he could prevent that. Indeed he could not. Teck did obtain its majority. It now controls the company. I do not think the evidence shows that Millar was willing to make any deal so long as it would lead to the issuance of shares in sufficient numbers to frustrate Teck.

· · ·

Then the plaintiff turns to the contract of June 1st and says it is patently improvident from Afton's point of view.

It is no part of this Court's function to decide what contract Afton should have made or whom it should have made it with. Evidence relating to the question whether Afton's directors sold the mine at an egregious undervalue, was admitted because it was argued that the contract of June 1st was on the face of it so improvident that Millar, Price and

Haramboure must have been impelled to make it by an overriding purpose—to defeat Teck's rights, not to make the best deal they could for the company and its shareholders.

To start with, it is said that Afton could have financed the development of the property by itself, so the surrender of 30% equity to Canex can only be explained on the basis that the defendant directors' purpose was to ensure the issuance of shares to defeat Teck's majority. Mr. Sullivan, a distinguished geological engineer, and Mr. Godin, the retired president of McIntyre Porcupine, were called by Teck to prove that there was no need at all to surrender any equity, that Afton could have gone ahead on its own. Both of them conceded, however, that since the exploratory drilling programme had not been completed, there was still some "downside" risk, that is, a risk that there would not in fact turn out to be a mineable reserve when the property had been drilled off. They both conceded that the property was certainly not yet ready for senior financing. But the vital weakness in their evidence, and in Teck's whole argument on this point, is that no one could say that Millar and his group could have raised the millions needed to develop the property, even if the property itself were, all other things being equal, acceptable as collateral. I am satisfied that to obtain financing, it would have been necessary to line up the personnel required to manage the mine and firm marketing arrangements for their copper concentrates. It was quite unlikely that Millar and his group, unaided, could have obtained the management people and the markets. So the involvement of a major, at the very least in management and marketing, was virtually inevitable. Millar realized this. It meant that there had to be a surrender of some equity to a major.

Mr. Sullivan and Mr. Godin claimed that it was quite unnecessary for Afton to give up 30% of equity. But neither of them knew of any other deal ever made between a major and a junior mining company where the major had agreed to accept less than 50% of equity, let alone 30%. Mr. Cannon, a geologist, who gave evidence for the defendants, said that majors almost invariably insist upon 50% of equity, and the evidence of Mr. Sullivan and Mr. Godin bears him out on this point. If the division of equity found in this agreement is thrown into the scales, as Teck urges, the only conclusion I can draw is that the contract of June 1st has not been shown to be an improvident one, rather if anything it is a good contract from Afton's point of view.

Counsel for Teck's argument was elaborated on the basis of certain clauses found in the drafts of the contract and in the contract itself. It is said that many of them are patently disadvantageous to Afton, so they must have been agreed upon because the Afton directors were prepared to sign any agreement that would enable them to issue shares to Canex to frustrate Teck's ambition. And, of course, it is said that Canex and its officers and executives knew this and forced a hard bargain upon them.

Counsel argued that the contract does not provide any minimum expenditure that Canex must make on feasibility. Mr. Bruk said that such a provision was not necessary, that if Canex was going to enter into such a contract it would be for the purpose of carrying out a proper feasibility study; that it would be pointless for Canex to enter into the contract simply in order to tie up the property. They would not receive their shares, Teck would then be in a position to obtain the development contract itself, and nothing would have been gained. I think Mr. Bruk's position is convincing on this point.

Then it is said the contract provides that if Canex elects to bring the property into production, it does not have to do so within a time certain, but only "as soon as reasonably and economically feasible." That provision, it is said, would enable Canex to make its election and then to sit tight on the property. I think it may well be that, from Afton's point of view, this clause would be difficult to enforce. But again, Mr. Bruk defended this clause from a practical point of view. He said that a feasibility study would likely cost a million dollars at least (the witnesses representing Canex agreed) and that, having spent such an amount, Canex would want to bring the property into production as soon as possible. Canex would have nothing to gain by delay. I do not think Teck can make anything out of the wording of this clause.

Then it is said that the contract does not say that Canex must guarantee financing. Now obviously Canex wanted to avoid going on a guarantee. According to Mr. Little, executive vice-president of Placer, they would not have agreed to a 30% bonus, but would have insisted on a larger bonus if the contract had provided that Canex had to guarantee financing. Mr. Millar understood that one way or the other, under the contract, Canex had to arrange financing. Indeed, that is what the contract says. Bruk felt that once Canex were committed to bring the mine into production, and turned to the banks for financing, it would likely have to provide a guarantee anyway. I do not think anything can be made of this.

Then the plaintiff turns to the changes in the clause relating to the issuance of shares to Canex. The first draft, prepared by Zink [Placer's corporate solicitor], provided that Canex was to receive its shares upon giving notice that it intended to place the property into production. But in the second draft, at Bruk's suggestion, it was provided that the shares should issue to Canex immediately upon the signing of the agreement. I am satisfied that one of the reasons Bruk made this suggestion was because he felt it would strengthen the position of the defendant directors by depriving Teck of its majority. But he did not insist upon it. And Zink would not agree to it, because Canex would have found itself in a disadvantageous tax position. So it went out.

Now it seems to me that the removal of the clause relating to the immediate issuance of shares, when it is put in the scales, is weighty evidence against a finding of any improper purpose. If the directors of Afton had been motivated solely or primarily to defeat Teck's majority interest, it seems to me they would have given Bruk instructions to insist upon this clause remaining. Yet there is no evidence they gave him instructions at all on the point, or that they were even aware the matter was being discussed.

But the whole argument regarding these provisions overlooks the fact that, once agreement had been reached between Millar and Adie, the whole transaction was turned over to the lawyers, Bruk and Zink. It was Bruk and Zink who discussed the clauses that were to be included in the contract, and their wording. They were both of them, in my view, seeking to serve the interests of their clients. There is no footing upon which it can be said that Bruk was under instructions from Millar and the other directors of Afton to agree to anything Canex wanted so long as swift agreement was reached and provision made for immediate issuance of shares to Canex.

The point is that it was Bruk and Zink who haggled over the terms of the contract. There is no evidence that the directors of Afton had anything at all to do with the negotiation of these particular clauses of the agreement. So I do not think there is any basis for saying that the defendant directors were deliberately making an agreement they themselves felt was not in Afton's best interest, in order to defeat Teck.

I do not think the terms of the contract afford any ground for saying that the defendant directors made this contract with one overriding purpose, to frustrate Teck's attempt to obtain control. I do not think the terms are such that the defendant directors must be taken to have entered into it without considering the best interests of Afton's shareholders or deliberately putting the shareholders' interests to one side.

So what conclusions ought to be drawn? Now I think Millar was to a great extent acting intuitively. He did not weigh the alternatives and consider the implications on a finely balanced scale. People usually do not make decisions in that way. Most important decisions in life contain an intuitive element. That is why it is quite mistaken to think that Millar's thinking can be entirely reconstructed. I am not convinced that he himself—or anyone else in the like position—would be capable of that.

This question of motive has been canvassed exhaustively with the defendant directors since these proceedings were begun. When Teck brought its application for an injunction back in June, the directors made affidavits and they were cross-examined before Mr. Justice Anderson. Then examinations for discovery of all concerned, including all the directors, were held. The directors have given evidence in this trial and have been cross-examined at length, and what they said in their affidavits and on discovery has been canvassed with them. It would not be surprising if inconsistencies emerged, and some have. Despite this, I think their evidence regarding their motives and purposes ought to be accepted.

The difficulty of determining a man's state of mind has sometimes been discounted by the Courts. Bowen L.J. once said that a man's state of mind is as much a matter of fact as the state of his digestion. But like most aphorisms it does not take us very far. I suppose you could determine the state of a man's digestion today, but it is not so easy to determine what the state of a man's digestion was six months ago.

So how ought the Court go about unravelling the motives of the directors? The whole problem was, in my view, articulated in the most illuminating way in *Mills et al. v. Mills et al.* (1938), 60 C.L.R. 150 (High Court of Australia).

* * *

Dixon J. (as he then was) said at pp. 185-6:

When the law makes the object, view or purpose of a man, or of a body of men, the test of the validity of their acts, it necessarily opens up the possibility of an almost infinite analysis of the fears and desires, proximate and remote, which, in turn, form the compound motives usually animating human conduct. But logically possible as such an analysis may seem, it would be impracticable to adopt it as a means of determining the validity of the resolutions arrived at by a body of directors, resolutions which otherwise are ostensibly within their powers. The application of the general equitable principle to the acts of directors managing the affairs of a company cannot be as nice as it is in the case of a trustee exercising a special power of appointment. It must, as it seems to me, take the substantial object the accomplishment of which formed the real ground of the board's action. If this is within the scope of the power, then the power has been validly exercised. But if, except for some ulterior and illegitimate object, the power would not have been exercised, that which has been attempted as an ostensible exercise power will be void, notwithstanding that the directors may incidentally bring about a result which is within the purpose of the power and which they consider desirable.

So it is necessary, then, to disentangle the directors' primary motive or purpose from subsidiary ones. I do not think it is necessary to distinguish motive, purpose or object. The question is, what was it the directors had uppermost in their minds?

• • •

I find their object was to obtain the best agreement they could while they were still in control. Their purpose in that sense was to defeat Teck. But, not to defeat Teck's attempt to obtain control, rather it was to foreclose Teck's opportunity of obtaining for itself the ultimate deal. That was, as I view the law, no improper purpose. In seeking to prevent Teck obtaining the contract, the defendant directors were honestly pursuing what they thought was the best policy for the company.

The judgment of the High Court of Australia in *Harlowe's Nominees Pty. Ltd. v. Woodside (Lakes Entrance) Oil Co. et al.* (1968), 42 A.L.J.R. 123, is applicable here. There it was alleged that the directors of a company had allotted additional shares to a company called Burmah for the purpose, to Burmah's knowledge, of frustrating an attempt by the plaintiff to obtain control of the company. The Court, consisting of Barwick C.J., McTiernan and Kitto JJ., delivered a joint judgment. The Court said at p. 125:

Directors in whom are vested the right and the duty of deciding where the company's interests lie and how they are to be served may be concerned with a wide range of practical considerations, and their judgment, if exercised in good faith and not for irrelevant purposes, is not open to review in the Courts. Thus in the present case it is not a matter for judicial concern if it be the fact, that the allotment to Burmah would frustrate the ambitions of someone who was buying up shares as opportunity offered with a view to obtaining increased influence in the control of the company, or even that the directors realized that the allotment would have that result and found it agreeable to their personal wishes: *Mills v. Mills* (1938), 60 C.L.R. 150. But if, in making the allotment, the directors had an actual purpose of thereby creating an advantage for themselves otherwise than as members of the general body of shareholders, as for instance by buttressing their directorships against an apprehended attack from such as Harlowe, the allotment would plainly be voidable as an abuse of the fiduciary powers, unless Burmah had no notice of the facts.

I subscribe to this definition of the proper limits of directors' lawful purposes.

I have put the defendants' purpose in a negative way, that is, I have said they wanted to foreclose to Teck's opportunity of obtaining the development contract. But in a larger sense their purpose was a positive one. They wanted to make a contract with Placer while they still had the power to do so. But not at any price. Millar stood firm in his rejection of Placer's 60-40 offer of May 19th, even when he knew that Teck's share position was eroding his control of the company. He was not prepared to concede 40% equity simply in order to sign a contract providing for the issuance of shares to Placer. He held out for a better contract, and he got it. Now I suppose it is possible that if Millar had held out even longer, if he had carried on with his drilling programme he would have been able to negotiate a contract even more favourable to Afton than the contract of June 1st, but I do not think there was any reasonable basis for him to think he could have. The odds were against it. Teck would soon be in a position to compel Afton to sign a contract with them, and Millar did not believe that Canex's first right of refusal offered

Afton any real protection against such an eventuality. He knew that time was short. At the same time, Placer knew that if it was going to obtain the contract, it would have to reach agreement with Millar before Teck had an opportunity of replacing the directors. So all things conspired to bring about the signing of the contract. Teck was the catalyst. Millar, Price and Haramboure were, in my view, acting in the best interests of the company. And the evidence shows that they had reasonable grounds for that belief.

Now Teck, of course, was a shareholder. And it is said that it was no part of Millar's purpose to protect Teck's interests. I think it is fair to say that Millar's primary purpose was to make the most advantageous deal he could for Afton. That is as far as the Court ought to go in seeking to analyze his motivation. And, in my view, in trying to make the best deal he could for Afton, Millar was acting in the best interests of the general body of shareholders, including Teck, because Teck's interest in acquiring control is put to one side, its interest, like that of the other shareholders, was in seeing Afton make the best deal available. I find Millar's purpose was to serve that interest.

The defendant directors were elected to exercise their best judgment. They were not agents bound to accede to the directions of the majority of the shareholders. Their mandate continued so long as they remained in office. They were in no sense a lame duck board. So they acted in what they conceived to be the best interests of the share-holders, and signed a contract which they knew the largest shareholder, holding a major-ity of the shares, did not want them to sign. They had the right in law to do that. When a company elects its board of directors and entrusts them with the power to manage the company, the directors are entitled to manage it. But they must not exercise their powers for an extraneous purpose. That is a breach of their duty. At the same time, the share-holders have no right to alter the terms of the directors' mandate except by amendment of the articles or by replacing the directors themselves.

• • •

If I am wrong in rejecting *Hogg v. Cramphorn Ltd.*, [1967] Ch. 254, [1966] 3 W.L.R. 955, [1966] 3 All E.R. 420, it is not applicable here in any event. In *Hogg v. Cramphorn Ltd.* the primary purpose of the directors was to frustrate an attempt to obtain control of the company. In the case at bar the primary purpose of the directors was to make the best contract that they could for Afton. I find that the primary purpose of the directors was to serve the best interests of the company. Their primary purpose was to see that the ultimate deal the company made was a deal with Placer, not Teck. They were not motivated by a desire to retain control of the company. They may have thought the issuance of shares under the contract with Canex would enable them, if they had Canex' support, to regain control from Teck. If they did, that was a subsidiary purpose. On any view of the law, therefore, no allegation of improper purpose can be sustained against the defendant directors.

• • •

The plaintiff's action is dismissed with costs.

Action dismissed.

NOTE

Do you agree with Berger J. that the classical theory of the firm must "yield to the facts of modern life"? Securities regulators in Canada have suggested in National Policy 38 that the "primary objectives of take-over bid legislation is the protection of the interests of the shareholders of the target company" (see below). In your view, does this statement reflect what Berger J. calls a classical theory of the firm? Is it compatible with Berger J.'s view that it should be open to a board of directors to "observe a decent respect for other interests lying beyond those of the company's shareholders in the strict sense"?

Managerial Passivity. Berger J.'s proper purposes test closely resembles Delaware decisions that apply a business judgment standard to control transactions. The leading such case, approved by Berger J. in *Teck*, is *Cheff v. Mathes*, 199 A.2d 548 (Del. 1964). In that case, the paramount question was said to be the motives of the target directors in making a greenmail payment:

[T]he allegation is that the true motives behind such purchases were improperly centered upon perpetuation of control ... . [I]f the actions of the board were motivated by a sincere belief that the buying out of the dissident stockholder was necessary to maintain what the board believed to be proper business practices, the board will not be held liable for such decision. ... On the other hand, if the board has acted solely or primarily because of the desire to perpetuate themselves in office, the use of corporate funds for such purposes is improper. [*Id.* at 554]

On this standard, where management demonstrates that its motives were based on a difference of policy between it and the offeror, then the conflict of interest is treated as resolved and a business judgment rule is applied. Since management can ordinarily find a policy difference between itself and the offeror without too much difficulty, the test may then be thought to collapse into the business judgment standard. See Gilson, *A Structural Approach to Corporations: The Case Against Defensive Tactics in Tender Offers*, 33 Stan. L. Rev. 819, 821-31 (1981).

Though *Hogg v. Cramphorn* and *Teck* represent variants of the proper purposes doctrine, the two tests are strikingly different. The proper purposes doctrine in *Hogg* is an objective one: any issue of shares to retain control is improper, even if management is actuated by an honest belief that firm value is maximized if it remains in control. Mr. Justice Berger's test is more subjective: shares may be issued to defeat a take-over bid if the board, on reasonable grounds, *bona fide* believes it to be in the best interests of the corporation that the bid not succeed. But though the board's belief must be reasonable, it may be doubted whether this amounts to a substantial qualification of the test. It would likely not, for example, require a court to investigate the rival merits of both parties to manage the target corporation, since that clearly is beyond judicial competence. Thus the difference between the *Teck* and *Hogg* tests does not appear to go to a review of managerial motives. Under *Teck*, the target has a considerable discretion to adopt defensive manoeuvres, while in *Hogg* the rule collapses into a flat prohibition of certain defensive tactics. The issue, then, is not what management feels but what it does.

Which test one prefers will depend on one's attitude to take-over bids. A target's resistance to a take-over bid increases the probability that the bid will fail, and thus increases its cost. Passivity duties, such as those of *Hogg*, therefore encourage take-over bids, which are made more costly under *Teck* standards. Since take-over bids are broadly viewed as serving efficiency goals, many recent writers have preferred strong barriers to defensive manoeuvres, like those of *Hogg*. See, e.g., Easterbrook & Fischel, *The Proper Role of a Target's Management in Responding to a Tender Offer*, 94 Harv. L. Rev. 1161 (1981); Easterbrook & Jarrell, *Do Targets Gain from Defeating Tender Offers?* 59 N.Y.U.L. Rev. 277 (1984); Office of the Chief Economist, Securities and Exchange Commission, *A Study on the Economics of Poison Pills*, Fed. Sec. L. Rep. (CCH) para. 83,971 [1985-86 Transfer Binder].

Other writers adopt a more benign view of defensive manoeuvres. Even if merger gains result from a successful take-over bid, a target's resistance may increase the price the offeror will pay to acquire control. The first way this may happen is by shifting a greater portion of the merger gains to target shareholders. With a stronger bargaining position, target shareholders can anticipate a larger share of the bargaining surplus. In addition, defensive tactics may draw out a rival bidder to participate in an auction for control of the target. This will result in a further increase in the offer price if the rival is prepared to pay more than the first bidder was. These distributional concerns do not, however, provide an allocational justification of auctions. In addition, the probability of a higher offer price must be balanced against the reduced probability that a bid will be made in the first instance, since the first bidder's incentives to make the offer will have been reduced. Auction theorists have therefore argued that this incentive cost is not great, and that an auction will move a target to its most highly valued user. These arguments are considered below.

A second argument for defensive manoeuvres focuses upon target management's human capital investment in the firm. As noted in Chapter Seven, Part I, Section B, management may be led to make an inefficient investment in managerial services if its anticipated returns through long-term compensation may be cut off in a take-over bid. A successful take-over bid can then be seen as shareholder opportunism, and reducing its likelihood through defensive tactics may encourage managers to make a more efficient investment in firm-specific personal services. See Coffee, *Shareholders Versus Managers: The Strain in the Corporate Web*, 85 Mich. L. Rev. 1 (1986); Haddock, Macey & McChesney, *Property Rights in Assets and Resistance to Tender Offers*, 73 Va. L. Rev. 701, 712-17 (1987). This argument will not, however, be persuasive unless it is shown that management's human capital investment cannot adequately be protected by golden parachutes.

Haddock, Macey and McChesney suggest another argument against barriers to defensive tactics: if such prohibitions were efficient, firms could be expected to commit to them voluntarily—for example, by charter provisions in which the firm forswears their use. The promise to abstain from defensive manoeuvres in the charter of a widely traded firm, if efficient, would lead the firm to promise managerial passivity on a take-over bid in order to reduce its cost of capital. There must, however, be some limit to the inferences one can draw from silence in a firm's articles on liability rules, so long as legal rules are justified on gap-filling theories. A firm could not, in other words, be expected to replicate all of corporate law in its charter documents. On the other hand, when a firm seeks to bargain out of strict legal rules in its articles, the change may in some circumstances be regarded as justified. In particular, where the articles are amended prior to the firm going public, they may reasonably be upheld even if they depart from long-accepted legal norms, at least if the ostensible beneficiaries of these norms are the public shareholders. A charter amendment to relax barriers to defensive manoeuvres on a take-over bid that is adopted after the firm has gone public will, however, offer considerably weaker evidence of efficiency, and may well be regarded as an attempt by management to transfer wealth from public shareholders to itself.

Though *Teck* is the best-known recent Canadian decision on the proper purposes doctrine, other courts have taken a very different approach to defensive tactics. The objective English test was adopted in *Bonisteel v. Collis Leather Co.* (1919), 45 O.L.R. 195 and *Bernard v. Valentini* (1978), 18 O.R. (2d) 656. *Teck* was, however, adopted by the Manitoba Court of Appeal in *Olson v. Phoenix Ind. Supply Ltd.* (1984), 9 D.L.R. (4th) 451, and in *Olympia & York Enterprises Ltd. v. Hiram Walker Resources Ltd.* (unreported judgment 10465/86, April 9, 1986 Ont.), aff'd on other grounds, [1986] O.J. No. 679 (Div. Ct.) (competing bid by subsidiary of target). *Teck* was also approved in *First City Financial Corp. v. Genstar Corp.* (1982), 33 O.R. (2d) 631, 646; *Northern & Central Gas Corp. v. Hillcrest Colliers Ltd.* (1976), 59 D.L.R. (3d) 533 (Alta.); *Shield Development Co. v. Snider*, [1976] 3 W.W.R. 44 (B.C.).

The Privy Council reaffirmed the objective English test in *Howard Smith Ltd. v. Ampol Petroleum Ltd.*, [1974] 1 All. E.R. 1126, an appeal from New South Wales. Howard Smith and Ampol both sought to acquire control of a third corporation, which issued a large block of shares to Ampol to defeat Howard Smith's tender offer. In finding that the issue was improper, the Court noted that "an issue of shares purely for the purpose of creating voting power has repeatedly been condemned." *Id.* at 1135. The *Teck* decision was distinguished on the basis that the issue of shares in Afton was made to give Canex the "ultimate deal," and not simply to defeat a control transaction.

The English test is, however, considerably eroded by the relative ease with which breaches of the proper purposes doctrine may be ratified. In *Hogg v. Cramphorn* itself, Buckley J. obligingly stood the action over to permit shareholders to approve the allotment of shares. In that case, Cramphorn Ltd. was a corn and seed distributor, with 60 retail branches. Earnings were not high, and there was some suggestion that the corporation would be worth more were it to sell off its retail outlets. The shares were relatively widely held, but were not listed on a stock exchange. Of the 126,000 issued shares, management controlled 37,000. When approached with an offer to buy all of Cramphorn's issued shares, its directors issued further shares to its employees' pension fund, of which they were trustees, loaning the fund the money to purchase shares on interest-free terms. It was conceded that the purpose of the issue of shares was to prevent the take-over bid from succeeding, though management's *bona fide* belief that the issue was in the best interests of the corporation and its shareholders was not contested. The take-over bid had, not unexpectedly, an "unsettling" effect on the employees in the 60 retail outlets. While the issue of shares was found to be improper, the breach was held ratifiable and the directors permitted "to convene a general meeting to consider such resolutions as may be submitted to it." [1967] 1 Ch. at 272. The editor of the Chancery Reports noted in a footnote that the shareholders "ratified and adopted every act and deed done by the directors of the company ... in connection with these matters." *Id.* See also *Bamford v. Bamford*, [1970] 1 Ch. 212 (C.A.)*

Canadian securities commissions have indicated in National Policy No. 38 that they may impeach defensive manoeuvres that would likely result in offerees being deprived of the ability to respond to a take-over or competing bid. The Policy, however, distinguishes defensive tactics aimed at entrenching an incumbent board in power from those adopted as part of a genuine search by the target for a competing offer at a better price from a third party. The securities administrators stated that they did not seek to favour either party in a contested bid, and that unrestricted auctions produce the most desirable results in a tender offer. For further discussion of National Policy 38, see the decision in *Producers Pipelines* (reproduced below) and the notes thereafter.

3. Take-Over Bid Regulation and Auction Theories

Take-Over Bid Regulation. The 1966 Ontario Securities Act pioneered comprehensive take-over bid requirements extending to both cash offers (shares for cash) as well as exchange offers (shares for shares). The OSA,† like its 1966 ancestor, regulates the techniques of acquisition with the goals of equality of treatment of offerees and an open environment for competing offers. The offer must be mailed to all Ontario shareholders of the same class along with a take-over bid circular. This must contain prescribed disclosure, but need not be pre-cleared with securities administrators. The offer must then remain open for acceptance for at least 21 days. Where a bid is made for less than all of a class of shares, the statute requires the offeror to take up the shares on a *pro rata* basis.

Before these provisions are triggered, the offer must come within the definition of a take-over bid under OSA s. 89(1). First, an offer to purchase shares of a class which, when aggregated with the offeror's existing shares of the same class in the target corporation, do not exceed 20% of the target's outstanding voting securities of that class is not a take-over bid. The corresponding figure in CBCA s. 194 is 10%. The 20% figure is an absolute criterion of an OSA take-over bid, and an accumulation of shares in a target corporation up to that threshold will not trigger the other tender offer requirements. At 20%, an offer to purchase one more share is a take-over bid, subject to the exemptions provided by OSA s. 93. Even before the 20% figure is reached, however, the offeror may find that the target's stock price has increased as a response to the anticipated take-over bid. One way this might happen is through a slippage of inside information. In

---

* Recall that in *Foss v. Harbottle* (Chapter Seven, Part I, Section D), Wigram V.C. stated that it would be futile to permit a shareholder to sue derivatively when ratification was possible. Yet the action in Hogg was derivative rather than corporate. Why did Buckley J. not dismiss the action rather than permit ratification? If a ratifiable breach is capable of supporting a derivative action, it constitutes a "true" exception to the rule in *Foss v. Harbottle*.

† Take-over bid provisions are found in both the CBCA and in provincial securities legislation. The focus in this section is, however, on the OSA. That statute deals with take-over bids in a more comprehensive fashion than the CBCA, and the class of bidders who must comply with the OSA is greater than that which must comply with the CBCA.

addition, OSA s. 101, added in 1987, requires offerors to disclose publicly forthwith upon acquiring 10% of the target's voting shares, and thereafter each time an additional 2% of the voting shares is purchased up to a total of 20% of the stock. This means that an offeror cannot expect that bargain prices for the target's stock will persist after the first disclosure reveals that the target is "in play," which will significantly reduce the profits available to an offeror, since the merger gains on a public tender offer appear to accrue largely to target shareholders. See Bradley, *Interfirm Tender Offers and the Market for Corporate Control*, 53 J. Bus. 345 (1980). Pre-bid purchasers then represent an important source of profit to offerors, and OSA s. 101 can be expected to increase the cost of acquiring non-CBCA corporations.

Prior to 1979, the exemption for private agreements under s. 93(1)(c) was relied upon when the offeror sought to purchase a controlling block of shares at a premium. However, the availability of the exemption is conditioned on a control share premium that does not exceed the market price for the relevant securities by more than 15%. Sale of control issues are considered in Section F. A further exemption is provided for private issuers under s. 93(1)(d). A *de minimis* exemption is available under s. 93(1)(b) on the acquisition of 5% of the target's voting securities during a 12-month period, provided that the purchase is not effected above market price plus reasonable brokerage fees. Finally, an exemption is created under s. 93(1)(a) for bids made on recognized stock exchanges. At one time this permitted offerors to avoid all of the restrictions of the OSA. Thus bids were made in the early 1970s through the T.S.E., at a substantial premium on a non-*pro rata* basis, with the bid kept for only a few days. As a method of avoiding compliance with OSA take-over bid legislation, however, the stock exchange exemption is now subject to substantial restrictions imposed by the T.S.E., so that it no longer provides offerors with the same advantage over an OSA bid. See T.S.E. By-laws, Part XXIII, TSE Policy Statement on Stock Exchange Take-Over Bids and Issuer Bids. As a "formal bid" under s. 89(1), exchange bids are also subject to s. 94, which prohibits collateral purchases of shares subject to the bid during its course.

Take-over bids must be made to Ontario shareholders of the same class and kept open for a minimum period of 21 days under OSA ss. 95.1-2. Shareholders who tender their shares on a take-over bid assume the risk that the bid will fail through the offeror's reliance on one of the terms or conditions of the offer, as permitted by s. 95.9. For example, partial offers are frequently contingent on at least 50% of the offeree shareholders tending their shares. Shares tendered by an offeree shareholder my be withdrawn by an offeree at any time during the first 21 days of the bid under s. 95.4, but whenever he tenders, the offeree will have to consider whether he should retain his share in the hope of attracting a competing bid at a higher price.*

From the perspective of the offeree shareholders, the tender decision involves a comparison of an existing offer with those which might come from competing bidders. At the moment when it is made, the value of the initial offer is V_i, defined as

$$V_i = P_i \ (\text{Price}_i - M)$$

---

*   If the offeror subsequently increases his price in response to a rival bid, the increased consideration must be offered to shareholders who have already tendered their shares. OSA s. 97(3).

where P_i is the probability of the initial offeror's success, Price$_i$ is the blended price of the initial offer (representing a weighted average of offer price and freezeout price in a two tier acquisition), and M is the pre-bid market price for the firm's shares. The offeree shareholder will then tender if V_i exceeds V_c, the value of anticipated competing bids.

$$V_c = P_c \ (Price_c - M)$$

where P_c is the probability that a competing bid will succeed and Price$_c$ is its blended price. The value of a share of the target is then $(M + V_i + V_c)$. After the initial bid is made, market price will increase to reflect the market's estimate of the likelihood of the success of one of the bids. Indeed, much of the increase often takes place in the month or two prior to public announcement of the bid, likely as a consequence of trading by insiders or tippees in anticipation of a bid.

Auction Theories. The desirability of take-over bid legislation has been the subject of a lively debate. First of all, Easterbrook and Fischel have argued that the best take-over bid regulation is no regulation at all, since the 21-day waiting period of OSA s. 95 makes tender offers less likely to be successful. The target is given more time to react with defensive manoeuvres, and competing offerors may also free ride on the first offeror's identification of a suitable target. With less chance of ultimate success, the offeror will be less ready to absorb these search costs.

Unless either a legal regimen or some system of self-help creates informal property rights, firms will produce too little information, just as farmers will grow too few apples unless there is a rule against theft. So, for example, when Exxon searches for oil, its ability to realize the value of its information depends on contracts backed up by (or implied in) legal rules that prevent its employees from selling geophysical data to rivals, and on its legal privilege to buy land through nominees who need not disclose what they know. If, after finding oil, Exxon had to announce its discovery and wait for an auction on the tract in question, it would undertake a suboptimal amount of searching.

Easterbrook & Fischel, *Auctions and Sunk Costs in Tender Offers*, 35 Stan. L. Rev. 1, 4 (1982). See also Easterbrook & Fischel, *The Proper Role of a Target's Management in Responding to a Tender Offer*, 94 Harv. L. Rev. 1161 (1981); Schwartz, *Search Theory and the Tender Offer Auction*, 2 J.L. Econ. & Org. 229 (1986); Schwartz, *Bebchuk on Minimum Offer Periods*, 2 J.L. Econ. & Org. 271 (1986).

Take-over bid regulation has, however, been defended in a series of articles by Lucian Bebchuk and Ronald Gilson. See Bebchuk, *The Case for Facilitating Competing Tender Offers*, 95 Harv. L. Rev. 1028 (1982); Bebchuk, *The Case for Facilitating Competing Tender Offers: A Reply and Extension*, 35 Stan. L. Rev. 23 (1982); Bebchuk, *The Case for Facilitating Competing Tender Offers: A Last (?) Reply*, 2 J.L. Econ. & Org. 253 (1986); Gilson, *A Structural Approach to Corporations: The Case Against Defensive Tactics and Tender Offers*, 33 Stan. L. Rev. 819 (1981); Gilson, *Seeking Competitive Bids Versus Pure Passivity in Tender Offer Defense*, 35 Stan. L. Rev. 51 (1982). See also Lowenstein, *Pruning Deadwood in Hostile Takeovers: A Proposal for Legislation*, 83 Colum. L. Rev. 249 (1983) (proposing that bids remain open for acceptance for six months to facilitate an auction).

First, Bebchuk argues that the abolition of take-over bid regulation would give rise to fairness concerns, since an offeror might otherwise keep the offer open for only a day or two in a "Saturday night special." This will violate egalitarian norms, since geographically remote shareholders will have a lessened ability to participate in the offer. These concerns are, however, mitigated (though not eliminated) by an offeree's ability to diversify his investments, purchasing shares of possible offerors as well as of possible targets. The argument may also overestimate the effect of the relative remoteness of Moose Jaw as compared with Mississauga. In addition, even if there is an observable difference (left uncompensated by government transfer payments!), the argument assumes that the offeror should not be permitted to direct the offer to one group of shareholders—for example, those with easy access to their brokers.

The strongest arguments by the two authors for take-over bid regulation may therefore seem those based on efficiency concerns. By requiring the offeror to keep the take-over bid open for at least 21 days, OSA s. 95 permits competing bids to come forward from other offerors. In the auction between rival bidders, the winner will be the firm that values the target most, with the auction moving assets to their highest-valued user. As against this, Easterbrook and Fischel argue that the first offeror could still resell the target to a higher-valued user in a second transaction, and that the costs of a drawn-out auction might exceed the transactions costs of a subsequent sale of the target. Since the likelihood of the offeror's success is reduced when auctions are permitted, offerors will also be less ready to incur search costs in identifying potential targets, and the number of take-over bids will decline. On the other hand, auction theorists argue that Easterbrook and Fischel overemphasize the costs of identifying potential targets, and that they may be sufficiently compensated for such costs by pre-bid purchases of stock up to the disclosure threshold (5% in the United States and 10% under the OSA), even if the major portion of take-over bid gains still accrues to offeree shareholders. Moreover, fears that the 21-day period will permit the target to defeat the first take-over bid would be somewhat dissipated if, as most auction theorists propose, defensive manoeuvres were restricted. As such, they argue, auctioneering will permit the bidder who values the target most to acquire the target.*

Do auction theories justify an issue of shares by a target to a white knight, in addition to a solicitation of rival bids? The difference between the two strategies is that (1) the share issuance may lock up control in the white knight, rather than opening up the possibility of a bidding war; (2) offeree shareholders will not be able to sell out at a premium price; and (3) the issue price may not be higher than the offer price. On auction theories, assistance from white knights should therefore be restricted to competing offers

---

*   Auction theorists also argue that no-auction regimes may give rise to excessive searches, if they are motivated by a demand for undervalued shares as opposed to efficiency gains. If all that a take-over does is to provide "foreknowledge" of undervaluation when this information would come to the market eventually, the search costs may represent a deadweight loss. However, Alan Schwartz has argued that excessive search is unlikely since the target will have sought to reveal its hidden value in order to make it a less attractive candidate for a tender offer. Schwartz, *Search Theory and the Tender Offer Auction*, 2 J.L. Econ. & Org. 229, 240-42 (1986).

to offeree shareholders. Similarly "lock-up" options, which assure the white knight of control, may be viewed more unfavourably than other defensive manoeuvres whose effects are less dramatic. Lock-ups are discussed below.

Lucian Bebchuk argues for refinements to take-over bid regulation in order to resolve the distorted choice problem discussed in the last section. It is feared that offerees in a two tier bid will tender their shares even if they believe that the blended price is less than the value of the shares, since failure to tender will leave them with even less than the offer price in the second tier freezeout if the bid succeeds. Bebchuk therefore proposes that, instead of simply tendering their shares, offerees be permitted to express their preferences on (1) whether they would like to sell their shares in the event that the bid succeeds; (2) whether they would like to sell their shares in the event that the bid fails; and (3) whether they would like the bid to succeed or fail. Bebchuk, *Toward Undistorted Choice and Equal Treatment in Corporate Takeovers*, 98 Harv. L. Rev. 1693, 1748 (1985). When the blended price is less than the value ascribed by shareholders to their shares, they may then avoid any distorted choice problems by voting "yes" for the first question and "no" for the other two.

4. Defensive Share Repurchases

When a take-over bid is made, target managers may seek to compete with the offeror through an issuer bid, in which the target offers to repurchase its shares. Though such buybacks may at first appear a potent defensive tactic, stock repurchases may perhaps be unobjectionable when either (1) the target's shares are undervalued because material good news about it is withheld from the market, or (2) incumbent management and its allies do not begin the auction with a large block of shares already under their control.

Offerors who are aware that a target's shares are undervalued on the market may seek to acquire the target as a bargain opportunity. Since the tender offer will lead to a more "correct" stock price (in the sense of one that would obtain if all inside information were disclosed), the take-over bid may serve efficiency goals. However, the under-valuation may more quickly be eliminated if the target is permitted to repurchase its shares, thereby making more creditable its disclosures about itself. See Dann & DeAngelo, *Standstill Agreements, Privately Negotiated Stock Repurchases and the Market for Corporate Control*, 11 J. Fin. Econ. 27 (1983). In addition, buybacks may reduce deadweight search costs borne by offerors in seeking out undervalued targets. On the other hand, if buybacks are motivated by the threat of a take-over, anything that reduces the offeror's likelihood of success can be expected to reduce the probability of his making a tender offer.

When tender offers are motivated not by foreknowledge as to undervaluation but by perceived efficiency gains, defensive share repurchases are not troubling when both offeror and insiders start with the same number of shares. Repurchased shares do not have voting rights, so that buybacks may simply make the offeror's task easier. If the target has 100 shares, repurchasing 21 of them will reduce the number of shares the offeror will have to acquire to gain control from 51 to 40. Moreover, when the offeror is the highest-valued user of target assets, he can always outbid the target in any auction for the target's shares. See Bradley & Rosenzweig, *Defensive Stock Repurchases*, 99

Harv. L. Rev. 1378, 1387-99 (1986). Finally, when the efficiency gain arises through the elimination of what Michael Jensen calls "free cash flow," or cash flows exceeding the firm's investment needs, the buyback itself will reduce such costs. Jensen, *Agency Costs of Free Cash Flow, Corporate Finance, and Takeovers*, 76 Am. Econ. Rev. 323 (1986).

Share repurchases, may, however, advantage a target's management if it begins the auction contest with a substantial block of shares already committed to it. Suppose, for example, that target insiders in a 100 share firm start out with 40 shares, such that a repurchase of 21 shares will prevent an offeror from acquiring control. Each share has a market value of $10 for a firm value of $1,000, and the target's management loots the firm (in the form of some kind of overcompensation) in the amount of $200. The looting is discovered by the offeror, which makes a take-over bid for 50% of the shares at a price of $11 per share. The target's management might then either tender its shares or attempt to defeat the bid. Tendering its shares will give it (20 × $11 =) $220 if all other shareholders tender, with its remaining 20 shares worth (1/5 × $1,200 =) $240, assuming new management does not loot. Total value of incumbent management's shares will then be $460. However, if the target repurchases 21 shares for $12 each (the highest price the offeror will be willing to go)* so as to immunize itself from the take-over threat, target management will be better off. Firm value will fall from $1,000 to $748 (with $252 paid out to tendering shareholders on the repurchase). The value of management's 40 shares will be $379, which together with the $200 looting privilege equals $579, or $119 more than is available if target management tenders its shares to the outside offeror.

On a share repurchase, a firm must comply with OSA issuer bid requirements, which parallel the statute's take-over bid provisions. Unless exempted by OSA s. 93(3), any repurchase is an issuer bid under s. 89(1). One of the exemptions permits market purchases of up to 5% of the issuer's securities over a 12-month period, though here a pre-purchase notice of the repurchase must be given. Issuer bid circulars under OSA Form 33 also contemplate full disclosure of material information by offerors.

Unocal Corp. v. Mesa Petroleum Co.
Delaware Supreme Court
493 A.2d 946 (1985)

MOORE, Justice. We confront an issue of first impression in Delaware—the validity of a corporation's self-tender for its own shares which excludes from participation a stock-holder making a hostile tender offer for the company's stock.

The Court of Chancery granted a preliminary injunction to the plaintiffs, Mesa Petroleum Co., Mesa Asset Co., Mesa Partners II, and Mesa Eastern, Inc. (collectively

---

*   This assumes that the offeror sees his gain arising through displacing inefficient management, rather than through synergistic gains. However, the offeror may be prepared to pay as much as $14 a share for 50% of the target's stock if it plans to use the $200 looting privilege. Though this prospect in part dissipates fears of distributional consequences for minority shareholders, stock value may be destroyed in a competition for a looting privilege exceeding $200.

"Mesa"),[1] enjoining an exchange offer of the defendant, Unocal Corporation (Unocal) for its own stock. The trial court concluded that a selective exchange offer, excluding Mesa, was legally impermissible. We cannot agree with such a blanket rule. The factual findings of the Vice Chancellor, fully supported by the record, establish that Unocal's board, consisting of a majority of independent directors, acted in good faith, and after reasonable investigation found that Mesa's tender offer was both inadequate and coercive. Under the circumstances the board had both the power and duty to oppose a bid it perceived to be harmful to the corporate enterprise. On this record we are satisfied that the device Unocal adopted is reasonable in relation to the threat posed, and that the board acted in the proper exercise of sound business judgment. We will not substitute our views for those of the board if the latter's decision can be "attributed to any rational business purpose." *Sinclair Oil Corp. v. Levien*, Del.Supr., 280 A.2d 717, 720 (1971). Accordingly, we reverse the decision of the Court of Chancery and order the preliminary injunction vacated.

I.

The factual background of this matter bears a significant relationship to its ultimate outcome.

On April 8, 1985, Mesa, the owner of approximately 13% of Unocal's stock, commenced a two tier "front loaded" cash tender offer for 64 million shares, or approximately 37%, of Unocal's outstanding stock at a price of $54 per share. The "backend" was designed to eliminate the remaining publicly held shares by an exchange of securities purportedly worth $54 per share. However, pursuant to an order entered by the United States District Court for the Central District of California on April 26, 1985, Mesa issued a supplemental proxy statement to Unocal's stockholders disclosing that the securities offered in the second-step merger would be highly subordinated, and that Unocal's capitalization would differ significantly from its present structure. Unocal has rather aptly termed such securities "junk bonds."[3]

---

[1]   T. Boone Pickens, Jr., is President and Chairman of the Board of Mesa Petroleum and President of Mesa Asset and controls the related Mesa entities.

[3]   Mesa's May 3, 1985 supplement to its proxy statement states:

> (i) following the Offer, the Purchasers would seek to effect a merger of Unocal and Mesa Eastern or an affiliate of Mesa Eastern (the "Merger") in which the remaining Shares would be acquired for a combination of subordinated debt securities and preferred stock; (ii) the securities to be received by Unocal shareholders in the Merger would be subordinated to $2,400 million of debt securities of Mesa Eastern, indebtedness incurred to refinance up to $1,000 million of bank debt which was incurred by affiliates of Mesa Partners II to purchase Shares and to pay related interest and expenses and all then-existing debt of Unocal; (iii) the corporation surviving the Merger would be responsible for the payment of all securities of Mesa Eastern (including any such securities issued pursuant to the Merger) and the indebtedness referred to in item (ii) above, and such securities and indebtedness would be repaid out of funds generated by operations of Unocal;

(The footnote is continued on the next page.)

Unocal's board consists of eight independent outside directors and six insiders. It met on April 13, 1985, to consider the Mesa tender offer. Thirteen directors were present, and the meeting lasted nine and one-half hours. The directors were given no agenda or written materials prior to the session. However, detailed presentations were made by legal counsel regarding the board's obligations under both Delaware corporate law and the federal securities laws. The board then received a presentation from Peter Sachs on behalf of Goldman Sachs & Co. (Goldman Sachs) and Dillon, Read & Co. (Dillon Read) discussing the bases for their opinions that the Mesa proposal was wholly inadequate. Mr. Sachs opined that the minimum cash value that could be expected from a sale or orderly liquidation for 100% of Unocal's stock was in excess of $60 per share. In making his presentation, Mr. Sachs showed slides outlining the valuation techniques used by the financial advisors, and others, depicting recent business combinations in the oil and gas industry. The Court of Chancery found that the Sachs presentation was designed to apprise the directors of the scope of the analysis performed rather than the facts and numbers used in reaching the conclusion that Mesa's tender offer price was inadequate.

Mr. Sachs also presented various defensive strategies available to the board if it concluded that Mesa's two-step tender offer was inadequate and should be opposed. One of the devices outlined was a self-tender by Unocal for its own stock with a reasonable price range of $70 to $75 per share. The cost of such a proposal would cause the company to incur $6.1-6.5 billion of additional debt, and a presentation was made informing the board of Unocal's ability to handle it. The directors were told that the primary effect of this obligation would be to reduce exploratory drilling, but that the company would nonetheless remain a viable entity.

The eight outside directors, comprising a clear majority of the thirteen members present, then met separately with Unocal's financial advisors and attorneys. Thereafter, they unanimously agreed to advise the board that it should reject Mesa's tender offer as inadequate, and that Unocal should pursue a self-tender to provide the stockholders with a fairly priced alternative to the Mesa proposal. The board then reconvened and unanimously adopted a resolution rejecting as grossly inadequate Mesa's tender offer. Despite the nine and one-half hour length of the meeting, no formal decision was made on the proposed defensive self-tender.

On April 15, the board met again with four of the directors present by telephone and one member still absent. This session lasted two hours. Unocal's Vice-President of Finance and its Assistant General Counsel made a detailed presentation of the proposed terms of the exchange offer. A price range between $70 and $80 per share was considered, and ultimately the directors agreed upon $72. The board was also advised about

---

3   Continued ...

   (iv) the indebtedness incurred in the Offer and the Merger would result in Unocal being much
   more highly leveraged, and the capitalization of the corporation surviving the Merger would differ
   significantly from that of Unocal at present; and (v) in their analyses of cash flows provided by
   operations of Unocal which would be available to service and repay securities and other obligations of the corporation surviving the Merger, the Purchasers assumed that the capital expenditures
   and expenditures for exploration of such corporation would be significantly reduced.

the debt securities that would be issued, and the necessity of placing restrictive covenants upon certain corporate activities until the obligations were paid. The board's decisions were made in reliance on the advice of its investment bankers, including the terms and conditions upon which the securities were to be issued. Based upon this advice, and the board's own deliberations, the directors unanimously approved the exchange offer. Their resolution provided that if Mesa acquired 64 million shares of Unocal stock through its own offer (the Mesa Purchase Condition), Unocal would buy the remaining 49% outstanding for an exchange of debt securities having an aggregate par value of $72 per share. The board resolution also stated that the offer would be subject to other conditions that had been described to the board at the meeting, or which were deemed necessary by Unocal's officers, including the exclusion of Mesa from the proposal (the Mesa exclusion). Any such conditions were required to be in accordance with the "purport and intent" of the offer.

Unocal's exchange offer was commenced on April 17, 1985, and Mesa promptly challenged it by filing this suit in the Court of Chancery. On April 22, the Unocal board met again and was advised by Goldman Sachs and Dillon Read to waive the Mesa Purchase Condition as to 50 million shares. This recommendation was in response to a perceived condition of the shareholders that, if shares were tendered to Unocal, no shares would be purchased by either offeror. The directors were also advised that they should tender their own Unocal stock into the exchange offer as a mark of their confidence in it.

Another focus of the board was the Mesa exclusion. Legal counsel advised that under Delaware law Mesa could only be excluded for what the directors reasonably believed to be a valid corporate purpose. The directors' discussion centered on the objective of adequately compensating shareholders at the "back-end" of Mesa's proposal, which the latter would finance with "junk bonds." To include Mesa would defeat that goal, because under the proration aspect of the exchange offer (49%) every Mesa share accepted by Unocal would displace one held by another stockholder. Further, if Mesa were permitted to tender to Unocal, the latter would in effect be financing Mesa's own inadequate proposal.

On April 24, 1985 Unocal issued a supplement to the exchange offer describing the partial waiver of the Mesa Purchase Condition. On May 1, 1985, in another supplement, Unocal extended the withdrawal, proration and expiration dates of its exchange offer to May 17, 1985.

Meanwhile, on April 22, 1985, Mesa amended its complaint in this action to challenge the Mesa exclusion. A preliminary injunction hearing was scheduled for May 8, 1985. However, on April 23, 1985, Mesa moved for a temporary restraining order in response to Unocal's announcement that it was partially waiving the Mesa Purchase Condition. After expedited briefing, the Court of Chancery heard Mesa's motion on April 26.

On April 29, 1985, the Vice Chancellor temporarily restrained Unocal from proceeding with the exchange offer unless it included Mesa. The trial court recognized that directors could oppose, and attempt to defeat, a hostile takeover which they considered adverse to the best interests of the corporation. However, the Vice Chancellor decided that in a selective purchase of the company's stock, the corporation bears the burden of showing: (1) a valid corporate purpose, and (2) that the transaction was fair to all of the stockholders, including those excluded.

Unocal immediately sought certification of an interlocutory appeal to this Court pursuant to Supreme Court Rule 42(b). On May 1, 1985, the Vice Chancellor declined to certify the appeal on the grounds that the decision granting a temporary restraining order did not decide a legal issue of first impression, and was not a matter to which the decisions of the Court of Chancery were in conflict.

However, in an Order dated May 2, 1985, this Court ruled that the Chancery decision was clearly determinative of substantive rights of the parties, and in fact decided the main question of law before the Vice Chancellor, which was indeed a question of first impression. We therefore concluded that the temporary restraining order was an appealable decision. However, because the Court of Chancery was scheduled to hold a preliminary injunction hearing on May 8 at which there would be an enlarged record on the various issues, action on the interlocutory appeal was deferred pending an outcome of those proceedings.

In deferring action on the interlocutory appeal, we noted that on the record before us we could not determine whether the parties had articulated certain issues which the Vice Chancellor should have an opportunity to consider in the first instance. These included the following:

a) Does the directors' duty of care to the corporation extend to protecting the corporate enterprise in good faith from perceived depredations of others, including persons who may own stock in the company?

b) Have one or more of the plaintiffs, their affiliates, or persons acting in concert with them, either in dealing with Unocal or others, demonstrated a pattern of conduct sufficient to justify a reasonable inference by defendants that a principle objective of the plaintiffs is to achieve selective treatment for themselves by the repurchase of their Unocal shares at a substantial premium?

c) If so, may the directors of Unocal in the proper exercise of business judgment employ the exchange offer to protect the corporation and its shareholders from such tactics? *See Pogostin v. Rice*, Del. Supr., 480 A.2d 619 (1984).

d) If it is determined that the purpose of the exchange offer was not illegal as a matter of law, have the directors of Unocal carried their burden of showing that they acted in good faith? *See Martin v. American Potash & Chemical Corp.*, 33 Del.Ch. 234, 92 A.2d 295 at 302.

After the May 8 hearing the Vice Chancellor issued an unreported opinion on May 13, 1985 granting Mesa a preliminary injunction. Specifically, the trial court noted that "[t]he parties basically agree that the directors' duty of care extends to protecting the corporation from perceived harm whether it be from third parties or shareholders." The trial court also concluded in response to the second inquiry in the Supreme Court's May 2 order, that "[although the facts, ... do not appear to be sufficient to prove that Mesa's principle objective is to be bought off at a substantial premium, they do justify a reasonable inference to the same effect."

As to the third and fourth questions posed by this Court, the Vice Chancellor stated that they "appear to raise the more fundamental issue of whether directors owe fiduciary duties to shareholders who they perceive to be acting contrary to the best interests of the corporation as a whole." While determining that the directors' decision to oppose

Mesa's tender offer was made in a good faith belief that the Mesa proposal was inadequate, the court stated that the business judgment rule does not apply to a selective exchange offer such as this.

On May 13, 1985 the Court of Chancery certified this interlocutory appeal to us as a question of first impression, and we accepted it on May 14. The entire matter was scheduled on an expedited basis.

II.

The issues we address involve these fundamental questions: Did the Unocal board have the power and duty to oppose a takeover threat it reasonably perceived to be harmful to the corporate enterprise, and if so, is its action here entitled to the protection of the business judgment rule?

Mesa contends that the discriminatory exchange offer violates the fiduciary duties Unocal owes it. Mesa argues that because of the Mesa exclusion the business judgment rule is inapplicable, because the directors by tendering their shares will derive a financial benefit that is not available to *all* Unocal stockholders. Thus, it is Mesa's ultimate contention that Unocal cannot establish that the exchange offer is fair to *all* shareholders, and argues that the Court of Chancery was correct in concluding that Unocal was unable to meet this burden.

Unocal answers that it does not owe a duty of "fairness" to Mesa, given the facts here. Specifically, Unocal contends that its board of directors reasonably and in good faith concluded that Mesa's $54 two tier tender offer was coercive and inadequate, and that Mesa sought selective treatment for itself. Furthermore, Unocal argues that the board's approval of the exchange offer was made in good faith, on an informed basis, and in the exercise of due care. Under these circumstances, Unocal contends that its directors properly employed this device to protect the company and its stockholders from Mesa's harmful tactics.

III.

We begin with the basic issue of the power of a board of directors of a Delaware corporation to adopt a defensive measure of this type. Absent such authority, all other questions are moot. Neither issues of fairness nor business judgment are pertinent without the basic underpinning of a board's legal power to act.

The board has a large reservoir of authority upon which to draw. Its duties and responsibilities proceed from the inherent powers conferred by 8 *Del.C.* § 141(a), respecting management of the corporation's "business and affairs."[6] Additionally, the

---

6   The general grant of power to a board of directors is conferred by 8 *Del.C.* § 141(a), which provides:

> (a) The business *and affairs* of every corporation organized under this chapter shall be managed by or under the direction of a board of directors, except as may be otherwise provided in this chapter or in its certificate of incorporation. If any such provision is made in the certificate of incorporation, the powers and duties conferred or imposed upon the board of directors by this chapter shall be exercised or performed to such extent and by such person or persons as shall be provided in the certificate of incorporation. (Emphasis added)

powers here being exercised derive from 8 *Del.C.* § 160(a), conferring broad authority upon a corporation to deal in its own stock.[7] From this it is now well established that in the acquisition of its shares a Delaware corporation may deal selectively with its stockholders, provided the directors have not acted out of a sole or primary purpose to entrench themselves in office. *Chefs v. Mathes*, Del.Supr., 199 A.2d 548, 554 (1964); *Brennett v. Propp*, Del.Supr., 187 A.2d 405, 408 (1962); *Martin v. American Potash & Chemical Corporation*, Del.Supr., 92 A.2d 295, 302 (1952); *Kaplan v. Goldsamt*, Del.Ch., 380 A.2d 556, 568-569 (1977); *Kors v. Carey*, Del.Ch., 158 A.2d 136, 140 141 (1960).

Finally, the board's power to act derives from its fundamental duty and obligation to protect the corporate enterprise, which includes stockholders, from harm reasonably perceived, irrespective of its source. See e.g. *Marshall Field & Co.*, 646 F.2d 271, 297 (7th Cir. 1981); *Crouse-Hinds Co. v. Internorth, Inc.*, 634 F.2d 690, 704 (2d Cir. 1980); *Heit v. Baird*, 567 F.2d 1157, 1161 (1st Cir. 1977); *Cheff v. Mathes*, 199 A.2d at 556; *Martin v. American Potash & Chemical Corp.*, 92 A.2d at 302; *Kaplan v. Goldsamt*, 380 A.2d at 568-69; *Kors v. Carey*, 158 A.2d at 141; *Northwest Industries, Inc. v. B.F. Goodrich Co.*, 301 F.Supp. 706, 712 (M.D.Ill. 1969). Thus, we are satisfied that in the broad context of corporate governance, including issues of fundamental corporate change, a board of directors is not a passive instrumentality.[8]

Given the foregoing principles, we turn to the standards by which director action is to be measured. In *Pogostin v. Rice*, Del.Supr., 480 A.2d 619 (1984), we held that the business judgment rule, including the standards by which director conduct is judged, is applicable in the context of a takeover. *Id.* at 627. The business judgment rule is a "presumption that in making a business decision the directors of a corporation acted on an informed basis, in good faith and in the honest belief that the action taken was in the best interests of the company." *Aronson v. Lewis*, Del.Supr., 473 A.2d 805, 812 (1984) (citations omitted). A hallmark of the business judgment rule is that a court will not substitute its judgment for that of the board if the latter's decision can be "attributed to any rational business purpose." *Sinclair Oil Corp. v. Levien*, Del.Supr., 280 A.2d 717, 720 (1971).

When a board addresses a pending takeover bid it has an obligation to determine whether the offer is in the best interests of the corporation and its shareholders. In that respect a board's duty is no different from any other responsibility it shoulders, and its decisions should be no less entitled to the respect they otherwise would be accorded in

---

7   This power under 8 *Del.C.* § 160(a), with certain exceptions not pertinent here, is as follows:

    (a) Every corporation may purchase, redeem, receive, take or otherwise acquire, own and hold, sell, lend, exchange, transfer or otherwise dispose of, pledge, use and otherwise deal in and with its own shares; ...

8   Even in the traditional areas of fundamental corporate change, i.e., charter, amendments [8 *Del.C.* § 242(b)], mergers [8 *Del.C.* §§ 251(b), 252(c), 253(a), and 254(d)], sale of assets [8 *Del.C.* § 271(a)], and dissolution [8 *Del.C.* § 275(a)], director action is a prerequisite to the ultimate disposition of such matters. See also, *Smith v. Van Gorkom*, Del.Supr., 488 A.2d 858, 888 (1985).

the realm of business judgment.[9] See also *Johnson v. Trueblood*, 629 F.2d 287, 292-293 (3d Cir. 1980). There are, however, certain caveats to a proper exercise of this function. Because of the omnipresent specter that a board may be acting primarily in its own interests, rather than those of the corporation and its shareholders, there is an enhanced duty which calls for judicial examination at the threshold before the protection of the business judgment rule may be conferred.

This Court has long recognized that:

> We must bear in mind the inherent danger in the purchase of shares with corporate funds to re-move a threat to corporate policy when a threat to control is involved. The directors are of neces-sity confronted with a conflict of interest, and an objective decision is difficult.

Bennett v. Propp, Del.Supr., 187 A.2d 405, 409 (1962). In the face of this inherent conflict directors must show that they had reasonable grounds for believing that a danger to corporate policy and effectiveness existed because of another person's stock ownership. *Cheff v. Mathes*, 199 A.2d at 554-55. However, they satisfy that burden "by showing good faith and reasonable investigation ..." *Id.* at 555. Furthermore, such proof is materially enhanced, as here, by the approval of a board comprised of a majority of outside independent directors who have acted in accordance with the foregoing stand-ards. *See Aronson v. Lewis*, 473 A.2d at 812, 815; *Puma v. Marriott*, Del.Ch., 283 A.2d 693, 695 (1971); *Panter v. Marshall Field & Co.*, 646 F.2d 271, 295 (7th Cir. 1981).

IV.

A.

In the board's exercise of corporate power to forestall a takeover bid our analysis begins with the basic principle that corporate directors have a fiduciary duty to act in the best interests of the corporation's stockholders. *Guth v. Loft, Inc.*, Del.Supr., 5 A.2d 503, 510 (1939). As we have noted, their duty of care extends to protecting the corporation and its owners from perceived harm whether a threat originates from third parties or other shareholders.[10] But such powers are not absolute. A corporation does not have unbridled discretion to defeat any perceived threat by any Draconian means available.

---

9   This is a subject of intense debate among practicing members of the bar and legal scholars. Excellent examples of these contending views are: Block & Miller, *The Responsibilities and Obligations of Corporate Directors in Takeover Contests*, 11 Sec.Reg.L.J.44 (1983); Easterbrook & Fischel, *Takeover Bids, Defensive Tactics, and Shareholders' Welfare*, 36 Bus.Law. 1733 (1981); Easterbrook & Fischel, *The Proper Role of a Target's Management In Responding to a Tender Offer*, 94 Harv.L.Rev. 1161 (1981); Herzel, Schmidt & Davis, *Why Corporate Directors Have a Right To Resist Tender Offers*, 3 Corp.L.Rev. 107 (1980); Lipton, *Takeover Bids in the Target's Boardroom*, 35 Bus.Law. 101 (1979).

10   It has been suggested that a board's response to a takeover threat should be a passive one. Easterbrook & Fischel, supra, 36 Bus.Law. at 1750. However, that clearly is not the law of Delaware, and as the proponents of this rule of passivity readily concede, it has not been adopted either by courts or state legislatures. Easterbrook & Fischel, supra, 94 Harv.L.Rev. at 1194.

The restriction placed in a selective stock repurchase is that the directors may not have acted solely or primarily out of a desire to perpetuate themselves in office. See *Cheff v. Mathes*, 199 A.2d at 556; *Kors v. Carey*, 158 A.2d at 140. Of course, to this is added the further caveat that inequitable action may not be taken under the guise of law. *Schnell v. Chris-Craft Industries, Inc.*, Del.Supr., 285 A.2d 437, 439 (1971). The standard of proof established in *Cheff v. Mathes* and discussed supra at page 16, is designed to ensure that a defensive measure to thwart or impede a takeover is indeed motivated by a good faith concern for the welfare of the corporation and its stockholders, which in all circumstances must be free of any fraud or other misconduct. *Cheff v. Mathes*, 199 A.2d at 554-55. However, this does not end the inquiry.

B.

A further aspect is the element of balance. If a defensive measure is to come within the ambit of the business judgment rule, it must be reasonable in relation to the threat posed. This entails an analysis by the directors of the nature of the takeover bid and its effect on the corporate enterprise. Examples of such concerns may include: inadequacy of the price offered, nature and timing of the offer, questions of illegality, the impact of "constituencies" other than shareholders (i.e., creditors, customers, employees, and perhaps even the community generally), the risk of non-consummation, and the quality of securities being offered in the exchange. See Lipton and Brownstein, *Takeover Responses and Directors' Responsibilities: An Update*, p. 7, ABA National Institute on the Dynamics of Corporate Control (December 8, 1983). While not a controlling factor, it also seems to us that a board may reasonably consider the basic stockholder interests at stake, including those of short term speculators, whose actions may have fuelled the coercive aspect of the offer at the expense of the long term investor.[11] Here, the threat posed was viewed by the Unocal board as a grossly inadequate two tier coercive tender offer coupled with the threat of greenmail.

Specifically, the Unocal directors had concluded that the value of Unocal was substantially above the $54 per share offered in cash at the front end. Furthermore, they determined that the subordinated securities to be exchanged in Mesa's announced squeeze out of the remaining shareholders in the "back-end" merger were "junk bonds"

---

11   There has been much debate respecting such stockholder interests. One rather impressive study indicates that the stock of over 50 percent of target companies, who resisted hostile takeovers, later traded at higher market prices than the rejected offer price, or were acquired after the tender offer was defeated by another company at a price higher than the offer price. See Lipton, supra 35 Bus.Law. at 106-109, 132-133. Moreover, an update by Kidder Peabody & Company of this study, involving the stock prices of target companies that have defeated hostile tender offers during the period from 1973 to 1982 demonstrates that in a majority of cases the target's shareholders benefited from the defeat. The stock of 81% of the targets studied has, since the tender offer, sold at prices higher than the tender offer price. When adjusted for the time value of money, the figure is 64%. See Lipton & Brownstein, supra ABA Institute at 10. The thesis being that this strongly supports application of the business judgment rule in response to takeover threats. There is, however, a rather vehement contrary view. See Easterbrook & Fischel, supra 36 Bus.Law. at 1739-1745.

worth far less than \$54. It is now well recognized that such offers are a classic coercive measure designed to stampede shareholders into tendering at the first tier, even if the price is inadequate, out of fear of what they will receive at the back end of the transaction.[12] Wholly beyond the coercive aspect of an inadequate two tier tender offer, the threat was posed by a corporate raider with a national reputation as a "greenmailer."[13]

In adopting the selective exchange offer, the board stated that its objective was either to defeat the inadequate Mesa offer or, should the offer still succeed, provide the 49% of its stockholders, who would otherwise be forced to accept "junk bonds," with \$72 worth of senior debt. We find that both purposes are valid.

However, such efforts would have been thwarted by Mesa's participation in the exchange offer. First, if Mesa could tender its shares, Unocal would effectively be subsidizing the former's continuing effort to buy Unocal stock at \$54 per share. Second, Mesa could not, by definition, fit within the class of shareholders being protected from its own coercive and inadequate tender offer.

Thus, we are satisfied that the selective exchange offer is reasonably related to the threats posed. It is consistent with the principle that "the minority stockholder shall receive the substantial equivalent in value of what he had before." *Sterling v. Mayflower Hotel Corp.*, Del.Supr., 93 A.2d 107, 114 (1952). See also *Rosenblatt v. Getty Oil Co.*, Del.Supr., 493 A.2d 929, 940 (1985). This concept of fairness, while stated in the merger context, is also relevant in the area of tender offer law. Thus, the board decision to offer what determined to be the fair value of the corporation to the 49% of its shareholders, who would otherwise be forced to accept highly subordinated "junk bonds," is reasonable and consistent with the directors' duty to ensure that the minority stockholders receive equal value for their shares.

V.

Mesa contends that it is unlawful, and the trial court agreed, for a corporation to discriminate in this fashion against one shareholder. It argues correctly that no case has ever sanctioned a device that precludes a raider from sharing in a benefit available to all other stockholders. However, as we have noted earlier, the principle of selective stock repur-

---

12   For a discussion of the coercive nature of a two tier tender offer see e.g. Brudney & Chirelstein, *Fair Shares in Corporate Mergers and Takeovers*, 88 Harv.L.Rev. 297, 337 (1974); Finkelstein, *Antitakeover Protection Against Two Tier and Partial Tender Offers: The Validity of Fair Price, Mandatory Bid, and Flip-Over Provisions Under Delaware Law*, 11 Sec.Reg. L.J. 291, 293 (1984); Lipton, supra, 35 Bus.Law at 113-14; Note, *Protecting Shareholders Against Partial and Two-Tiered Takeovers: The Poison Pill Preferred*, 97 Harv.L.Rev. 1964, 1966 (1984).

13   The term "greenmail" refers to the practice of buying out a takeover bidder's stock at a premium that is not available to other shareholders in order to prevent the takeover. The Chancery Court noted that "Mesa has made tremendous profits from its takeover activities although in the past few years it has not been successful in acquiring any of the target companies on an unfriendly basis." Moreover, the trial court specifically found that the actions of the Unocal board were taken in good faith to eliminate both the inadequacies of the tender offer and to forestall the payment of "greenmail."

chases by a Delaware corporation is neither unknown nor unauthorized. *Cheff v. Mathes*, 199 A.2d at 554; *Bennett v. Propp*, 187 A.2d at 408; *Martin v. American Potash & Chemical Corporation*, 92 A.2d at 302; *Kaplan v. Goldsamt*, 380 A.2d at 568-569; *Kors v. Carey*, 158 A.2d at 140-141; 8 *Del.C.* § 160. The only difference is that heretofore the approval transaction was the payment of "greenmail" to a raider or dissident posing a threat to the corporate enterprise. All other stockholders were denied such favored treatment, and given Mesa's past history of greenmail, its claims here are rather ironic.

However, our corporate law is not static. It must grow and develop in response to, indeed in anticipation of, evolving concepts and needs. Merely because the General Corporation Law is silent as to a specific matter does not mean that it is prohibited. See *Providence and Worcester Co. v. Baker*, Del.Supr., 378 A.2d 121, 123-124 (1977). In the days when *Cheff, Bennett, Martin* and *Kors* were decided, the tender offer, while not an unknown device, was virtually unused, and little was known of such methods as two tier "front-end" loaded offers with their coercive effects. Then, the favored attack of a raider was stock acquisition followed by a proxy contest. Various defensive tactics, which provided no benefit whatever to the raider, evolved. Thus, the use of corporate funds by management to counter a proxy battle was approved. *Hall v. Trans-Lux Daylight Picture Screen Corp.*, Del.Supr., 171 A. 226 (1934); *Hibbert v. Hollywood Park, Inc.*, Del.Supr., 457 A.2d 339 (1983). Litigation, supported by corporate funds, aimed at the raider has long been a popular device.

More recently, as the sophistication of both raiders and targets has developed, a host of other defensive measures to counter such ever mounting threats has evolved and received judicial sanction. These include defensive charter amendments and other devices bearing some rather exotic, but apt, names: Crown Jewel, White Knight, Pac Man, and Golden Parachute. Each has highly selective features, the object of which is to deter or defeat the raider.

Thus, while the exchange offer is a form of selective treatment, given the nature of the threat posed here the response is neither unlawful nor unreasonable. If the board of directors is disinterested, has acted in good faith and with due care, its decision in the absence of an abuse of discretion will be upheld as a proper exercise of business judgment.

To this Mesa responds that the board is not disinterested, because the directors are receiving a benefit from the tender of their own shares, which because of the Mesa exclusion, does not devolve upon *all* stockholders equally. See *Aronson v. Lewis*, Del.Supr., 473 A.2d 805, 812 (1984). However, Mesa concedes that if the exclusion is valid, then the directors and all other stockholders share the same benefit. The answer of course is that the exclusion is valid, and the directors' participation in the exchange offer does not rise to the level of a disqualifying interest. The excellent discussion in *Johnson v. Trueblood*, 629 F.2d at 292-293, of the use of the business judgment rule in takeover contests also seems pertinent here.

Nor does this become an "interested" director transaction merely because certain board members are large stockholders. As this Court has previously noted, that fact alone does not create a disqualifying "personal pecuniary interest" to defeat the operation of the business judgment rule. *Cheff v. Mathes*, 199 A.2d at 554.

Mesa also argues that the exclusion permits the directors to abdicate the fiduciary duties they owe it. However, that is not so. The board continues to owe Mesa the duties of due care and loyalty. But in the face of the destructive threat Mesa's tender offer was perceived to pose, the board had a supervening duty to protect the corporate enterprise, which includes the other shareholders, from threatened harm.

Mesa contends that the basis of this action is punitive, and solely in response to the exercise of its rights of corporate democracy.[14] Nothing precludes Mesa, as a stockholder, from acting in its own self-interest. See, e.g., *DuPont v. DuPont*, 251 Fed. 937 (D.Del. 1918), aff'd 256 Fed. 129 (3d Cir. 1918); *Ringling Bros.-Barnum & Bailey Combined Shows, Inc. v. Ringling*, Del.Supr., 53 A.2d 441, 447 (1947); *Heil v. Standard Gas & Electric Co.*, Del.Ch., 151 A. 303, 304 (1930). But see, *Allied Chemical & Dye Corp. v. Steel & Tube Co. of America*, Del.Ch., 120 A. 486, 491 (1923) (majority shareholder owes a fiduciary duty to the minority shareholders). However, Mesa, while pursuing its own interests, has acted in a manner which a board consisting of a majority of independent directors has reasonably determined to be contrary to the best interests of Unocal and its other shareholders. In this situation, there is no support in Delaware law for the proposition that, when responding to a perceived harm, a corporation must guarantee a benefit to a stockholder who is deliberately provoking the danger being addressed. There is no obligation of selfsacrifice by a corporation and its shareholders in the face of such a challenge.

Here, the Court of Chancery specifically found that the "directors' decision [to oppose the Mesa tender offer] was made in the good faith belief that the Mesa tender offer is inadequate." Given our standard of review under *Levitt v. Bouvier*, Del.Supr., 287 A.2d 671, 673 (1972), and *Application of Delaware Racing Association*, Del.Supr., 213 A.2d 203, 207 (1965), we are satisfied that Unocal's board has met its burden of proof. *Cheff v. Mathes*, 199 A.2d at 555.

VI.

In conclusion, there was directorial power to oppose the Mesa tender offer, and to undertake a selective stock exchange made in good faith and upon a reasonable investigation pursuant to a clear duty to protect the corporate enterprise. Further, the selective stock repurchase plan chosen by Unocal is reasonable in relation to the threat that the board rationally and reasonably believed was posed by Mesa's inadequate and coercive two tier tender offer. Under those circumstances the board's action is entitled to be measured by the standards of the business judgment rule. Thus, unless it is shown by a preponderance of the evidence that the directors' decisions were primarily based on perpetuating themselves in office, or some other breach of fiduciary duty such as fraud, overreaching, lack of good faith, or being uninformed, a Court will not substitute its judgment for that of the board.

---

14   This seems to be the underlying basis of the trial court's principal reliance on the unreported Chancery decision of *Fisher v. Moltz*, Del.Ch. No. 6068 (1979), published in 5 Del.J.Corp.L. 530 (1980). However, the facts in *Fisher* are thoroughly distinguishable. There, a corporation offered to repurchase the shares of its former employees, except those of the plaintiffs, merely because the latter were then engaged in lawful competition with the company. No threat to the enterprise was posed, and at best it can be said that the exclusion was motivated by pique instead of rational corporate purpose.

In this case that protection is not lost merely because Unocal's directors have tendered their shares in the exchange offer. Given the validity of the Mesa exclusion, they are receiving a benefit shared generally by all other stockholders except Mesa. In this circumstance the test of *Aronson v. Lewis*, 473 A.2d at 812, is satisfied. See also *Cheff v. Mathes*, 199 A.2d at 554. If the stockholders are displeased with the action of their elected representatives, the powers of corporate democracy are at their disposal to turn the board out. *Aronson v. Lewis*, Del.Supr., 473 A.2d 805, 811 (1984). See also 8 *Del.C.* §§ 141(k) and 211(b).

With the Court of Chancery's findings that the exchange offer was based on the board's good faith belief that the Mesa offer was inadequate, that the board's action was informed and taken with due care, that Mesa's prior activities justify a reasonable inference that its principle objective was greenmail, and implicitly, that the substance of the offer itself was reasonable and fair to the corporation and its stockholders if Mesa were included, we cannot say that the Unocal directors have acted in such a manner as to have passed an "unintelligent and unadvised judgment." *Mitchell v. Highland-Western Glass Co.*, Del.Ch., 167 A. 831, 833 (1933). The decision of the Court of Chancery is therefore REVERSED, and the preliminary injunction is VACATED.

NOTES

1) The decision in *Unocal* accepts that provided that a board of directors lives up to its fiduciary duties, it may deal selectively with its shareholders. Thus, it was open to Unocal's board to exclude Mesa from Unocal's exchange offer. This clearly involves treating shareholders of the same class differently. In view of the analysis of the nature of a share set out in Chapter Four, would such discriminatory tactics be allowed in Canada? Did Berger J. effectively allow the use of similar discriminatory tactics in *Teck*? What are the implications of these decisions from the debate seen in Chapter Four concerning the concept of equality that should govern the treatment of shareholders?

2) Mesa's two tier bid for Unocal was designed to place pressure on shareholders to tender to the bid. Moreover, if successful, it would have resulted in Unocal having to carry a more substantial debt load than it had prior to the bid. In assessing the "threat posed" by Mesa's bid, the Court stated that a board of directors in the exercise of its fiduciary duties was entitled to consider the impact of the bid on constituencies other than shareholders. Is this a matter that directors *should* bear in mind? Is *Unocal's* approach to this issue consistent with the approach Berger J. favoured in *Teck*? Do *Teck* and *Unocal* share a common vision of the firm?

3) It is worth noting that in *Unocal* the Court relied extensively on the 1964 decision of the Delaware Chancery Court in *Cheff v. Mathes*, a decision that Berger J. also looked to for inspiration in *Teck*. In view of the shared reliance on *Cheff v. Mathes*, do you think that Canadian courts looking to build on the decision in *Teck* should be willing to look for guidance to *Unocal* and other Delaware decisions that build on *Cheff v. Mathes*?

4) One of the reasons why Unocal's self-tender was upheld was because the Mesa bid was two tiered. However, a self-tender was itself impeached as two tiered in *AC Acquisitions Corp. v. Anderson, Clayton & Co.*, 519 A.2d 103 (Del. Ch. 1986), a deci-

sion which allayed fears that defensive self-tenders would uniformly be upheld after *Unocal*. The target corporation had sought to resist a tender offer at $56 per share through a buyback offer to acquire 65% of its outstanding stock at $60 per share. But while the tender offeror proposed a cashout merger at $56 per share, the target did not seek to acquire more than 60% of its stock and the Court accepted evidence that shareholders who failed to tender in the share repurchase were very likely on its success to experience a substantial loss in the market value of their shares. In these circumstances, the Court held that the self-tender could not be characterized as opening up an auction for the stock. A rational shareholder would have no effective choice as between the two offers, but would have to accept the selftender. In the result, though target management had demonstrated a "reasonable ground for believing that [the tender offer constituted] a danger to corporate policy," it failed to satisfy the second leg of the *Unocal* test, that the defensive measure was "reasonable in relation to the threat posed." *Id.* at 112, 113.

A share repurchase effected through the target's subsidiary was upheld in *Olympia & York Enterprises Ltd. v. Hiram Walker Resources Ltd.* (1986), 59 O.R. (2d) 254 (Div. Ct.). An Olympia & York affiliate made a take-over bid for 39% of Hiram Walker's 103,000,000 shares at $32 a share, which apparently represented a premium of only 11.3% over immediately preceding trading highs for the shares. See Simmonds, *Note*, 66 Can. Bar Rev. 626, 627 (1987). Hiram Walker responded with (1) a sale of a liquor division to Allied-Lyons PLC for $2.6 billion, and (2) a competing offer for 48% of Hiram Walker shares at $40 a share by a Hiram Walker subsidiary. The sale of the liquor division would then finance Hiram Walker's competing offer. These transactions were approved by the Hiram Walker board, two-thirds of whose members were independent directors (with the offer made by the subsidiary rather than by Hiram Walker itself for tax reasons). Olympia & York raised its bid to $35, and succeeded in acquiring control of Hiram Walker. Olympia & York then sought to reacquire the liquor division, which had been sold to Allied-Lyons, arguing that the sale and the self-tender offer breached the proper purpose doctrine. Montgomery J. rejected this argument. Adopting the *Teck* decision, he stated:

I am satisfied on the basis of the affidavits that the sole purpose of the conduct of the directors of Hiram Walker was to maximize the position of all their shareholders after Gulf's take-over bid. It is idle speculation and complete hearsay ... to attempt to attribute motives to the directors of Hiram Walker. As a question of fact I am satisfied that the directors acted prudently, properly, reasonably and fairly upon the advice of their legal and financial advisers and resorting to the opinions of management and their collective store of business acumen. [Counsel for Olympia & York] argued that while the board of Hiram Walker has a discretion to carry on a certain type of conduct, there is a line beyond which it may not go. He contended that the board had gone too far. I am satisfied that the board did not cross that line. It was a legitimate objective for the directors to insure that as much as possible of all economic value go to *all* shareholders and not just to *these* shareholders. I also find as a fact that that was the sole and primary objective of the directors. [*Id.* at 35-36]

On appeal, the Divisional Court affirmed the decision of Montgomery J. in rejecting the application for interlocutory relief. Some doubt was expressed about the use by Hiram Walker of a subsidiary to make the offer in view of OBCA s. 28(1)(b), under which a subsidiary may not hold shares of its parent. See CBCA s. 30(1)(b). However, the Court declined to hold that the offer was illegal, leaving open the possibility that the transaction might have been upheld as an indirect repurchase by Hiram Walker of its own shares under OBCA s. 30(1) (CBCA s. 34).

5. Poison Pills and Other Defensive Tactics

Poison Pills. One of the most popular defensive tactics seen in Canada and the United States is the so-called poison pill or shareholder rights plan. Typically, a shareholder rights plan grants to shareholders certain contractual rights ("Rights") to purchase additional securities of the company that has adopted the plan (with one Right issued for each voting share). Initially, these Rights are not exercisable and simply trade with the voting shares. When a bidder announces a bid, the Rights detach from the voting shares and become freely tradeable, although at this stage they are usually only exercisable at a price that is significantly higher than the market price of the voting shares. However, upon the bidder acquiring a certain percentage of the target company's shares (e.g., 20%)—an event known as a "flip-in event"—the Rights suddenly entitle their holders to purchase voting shares at what is effectively half price. In addition, the bidder is not entitled to exercise the Rights: the shareholder rights plan will provide that that person's Rights become null and void once it has crossed the designated threshold.

Poison pills therefore threaten a bidder who has not convinced the target company's board of directors to terminate the pill with the prospect of a massive dilution of the bidder's stake in the company. The purpose of a shareholder rights plan is to make it extremely unattractive for a bidder to proceed with a bid without having convinced the target company's board of directors to do away with the rights plan.

By the start of 1995, poison pills had been adopted by well over a thousand companies in the United States and by approximately 100 Canadian companies. In the United States, poison pills come in many different forms. Originally, they involved a so-called flip-over provision, which entitled the Rights holder (other than the bidder) to acquire securities in the successor corporation on a merger. While flip-over provisions are still found in U.S. pills, they are no longer common in Canadian pills. Instead, Canadian pills rely almost exclusively on the so-called flip-in provision, one that is also common in U.S. pills.

A "lollipop" is an issue of retractable preferred shares in a stock dividend, with the holders given the right to resell the shares to the corporation on specified control transactions. A "back-end" pill is similar to a lollipop, except that the preferred shares are not retractable, but instead convertible to common shares. In "poison debt," the shareholders are issued shares which, on control transactions, are convertible into debt securities or notes (for a variant of poison debt, see the *Revlon* decision below). In all of these cases, the pill features rights or privileges that permit their holders to acquire new interests at an attractive price.

All of these pills are accomplished by board action, without the need for shareholder approval. In Canada, however, in response to the presence of National Policy 38 and the rules of stock exchanges governing the issuance and listing of new securities, companies have frequently sought to have their shareholders ratify the adoption of a shareholder rights plan. Boards have nonetheless been known to put a pill in place quickly without shareholder approval, something that may be very useful where management seeks to respond to a hostile take-over bid (see, for example, the decision in *Producers Pipeline* below).

In Canada, poison pills have evolved rather differently in recent years than in the United States. The first Canadian company to adopt a poison pill (Inco Limited in 1988) embraced a U.S. style pill. Since then Canadian companies have adopted rights plans that contain a so-called permitted bid provision. These provisions state that a bidder may acquire more than the percentage of shares that would otherwise trigger the shareholder rights plan in the event that the bid satisfies a number of conditions. Initially, Canadian permitted bid provisions contained a detailed list of conditions. However, institutional investors in Canada have placed considerable pressure on companies to shorten the list of conditions. Because Canadian companies (responding to the concerns of securities regulators and stock exchanges) have typically sought shareholder ratification of rights plans, institutional investors have come to have a good deal more influence on the structure of rights plans in Canada than in the United States. As a result, rights plans being adopted in early 1995 in Canada contained permitted bid provisions that required little more than that the bid be kept open for a fixed period (e.g. 60 days) and that, in the event that more than 50% of the shares of the class subject to the bid were tendered to that bid, the bid be extended for a further 10 days (to allow remaining shareholders to participate in the bid, thereby eliminating the possibiliity that shareholders might feel obliged to tender to an inadequate bid, but ensuring that they may tender if it becomes clear that others have accepted the bid).

Canadian companies adopting rights plans have continued to insist that the 21 day period that Canadian securities legislation requires a bid be kept open does not provide sufficient time to a board to prepare an effective response, one designed to get maximum value for target company shareholders. Critics of Canadian rights plans have not necessarily disagreed with this point, but do contend that 60 days is too much time and that rights plans give management too much of a say in the take-over bid process. Obviously, one's views about the usefulness of rights plans will be intimately linked to one's views about the nature of a shareholder's interests in a corporation and the appropriate balance of power between a board of directors and shareholders.

As of early 1995, only one bid for a Canadian target with a shareholder rights plan in place had been made by way of a permitted bid (i.e. Amoco Canada Petroleum's June 1995 bid for Home Oil Co. Ltd.). Hostile bids launched in 1994 continued to be conditioned on the target company's rights plan being found invalid or being otherwise terminated. Nonetheless, in those instances where the target's board has refused to terminate the shareholder rights plan, the process of challenging the plan before the courts or securties commissions has taken time and has given the target company more than the statutory 21 days in which to respond to an unsolicited bid. See, for example, *Producers Pipelines* (reproduced below), as well as *Lac Minerals Ltd.* and *Regal Greetings & Gifts Inc.* (both of which are discussed in the Notes following *Producers Pipelines*). For a lively exchange concerning the value of shareholder rights plans in Canada, see J. MacIntosh, *The Poison Pill: A Noxious Nostrum for Canadian Shareholders*, 15 Can. Bus. L.J. 276 (1989); P. Dey & R. Yalden *Keeping the Playing Field Level: Poison Pills and Directors' Fiduciary Duties in Canadian Take-Over Law*, Can Bus. L.J. 252 (1990); J. MacIntosh, *Poison Pills in Canada: A Reply to Dey and Yalden*, 17 Can. Bus. L.J. 323

(1991); R. Yalden, *Controlling the Use and Abuse of Poison Pills in Canada: 347883 Alberta Ltd. v. Producers Pipelines Inc.*, 37 McGill L.J. 887 (1992).

Shark Repellents. Charter provisions that place obstacles in the path of potential acquirers are called shark repellents. One example of such restrictions are the barriers found in poison pills, as incorporated in the firm's articles. In addition, the charter might provide for supermajoritarian voting barriers to second step transactions, such as freezeouts. For example, a merger or sale of substantially all the assets might require as much as 95% shareholder approval, instead of the two-thirds approval for a special resolution. Another voting restriction prevents shareholders who have acquired stock in the firm after a certain date from voting the shares until three years after their purchase. An acquiring firm might then have to wait years to assume control. These voting provisions are of course ineffective unless their amendment requires supermajoritarian ratification as well. Otherwise, the new owners of the firm could simply remove a 95% ratification requirement through a two-thirds vote of shareholders in a special resolution.

Defensive Weapons and the Unocal Test. In *Moran v. Household International, Inc.*, 500 A.2d 1346 (1985), the Delaware Supreme Court upheld a board's adoption of a poison pill that involved a flip-over provision. The Court found that Household's board had adopted its shareholder rights plan as a preventive mechanism to ward off advances rather than as a response to a particular raider. The Court was of the view that under Delaware law a board was entitled to adopt a shareholder rights plan, provided that in doing so it lived up to its fiduciary duties. But when faced with a tender offer, that board's use of the shareholder rights plan would be evaluated in the light of the proportionality test set out in *Unocal*. In commenting on the board's use of the shareholder rights plan, the Court made the following observations:

The business judgment rule is a "presumption that in making a business decision the directors of a corporation acted on an informed basis, in good faith and in the honest belief that the action taken was in the best interests of the company." *Aronson v. Lewis*, Del.Supr., 473 A.2d 805, 812 (1984) (citations omitted). Notwithstanding, in *Unocal* we held that when the business judgment rule applies to adoption of a defensive mechanism, the initial burden will lie with the directors. The "directors must show that they had reasonable grounds for believing that a danger to corporate policy and effectiveness existed. ... [T]hey satisfy that burden 'by showing good faith and reasonable investigation. ...' " *Unocal*, 493 A.2d at 955 (citing *Cheff v. Mathes*, 199 A.2d at 554-55). In addition, the directors must show that the defensive mechanism was "reasonable in relation to the threat posed." *Unocal*, 493 A.2d at 955. Moreover, that proof is materially enhanced, as we noted in *Unocal*, where, as here, a majority of the board favoring the proposal consisted of outside independent directors who have acted in accordance with the foregoing standards. *Unocal*, 493 A.2d at 955; *Aronson*, 473 A.2d at 815. Then, the burden shifts back to the plaintiffs who have the ultimate burden of persuasion to show a breach of the directors' fiduciary duties. *Unocal*, 493 A.2d at 958.

There are no allegations here of any bad faith on the part of the Directors' action in the adoption of the Rights Plan. There is no allegation that the Directors' action was taken for entrenchment purposes. Household had adequately demonstrated, as explained above, that the adoption of the Rights Plan was in reaction to what it perceived to be the threat in the market place of coercive two tier tender offers. Appellants do contend, however, that the Board did not exercise informed business judgment in its adoption of the Plan.

Appellants contend that the Household Board was uninformed since they were, *inter alia*, told the Plan would not inhibit a proxy contest, were not told the plan would preclude all hostile acquisitions of Household, and were told that Delaware counsel opined that the plan was within the business judgment of the Board.

As to the first two contentions, as we explained above, the Rights Plan will not have a severe impact upon proxy contests and it will not preclude all hostile acquisitions of Household. Therefore, the Directors were not misinformed or uninformed on these facts.

Appellants contend the Delaware counsel did not express an opinion on the flipover provision of the Rights, rather only that the Rights would constitute validly issued and outstanding rights to subscribe to the preferred stock of the company.

To determine whether a business judgment reached by a board of directors was an informed one, we determine whether the directors were grossly negligent. *Smith v. Van Corkom*, Del.Supr., 488 A.2d 858, 873 (1985). Upon a review of this record, we conclude the Directors were not grossly negligent. The information supplied to the Board on August 14 provided the essentials of the Plan. The Directors were given beforehand a notebook which included a three-page summary of the Plan along with articles on the current takeover environment. The extended discussion between the Board and representatives of Wachtell, Lipton and Goldman, Sachs before approval of the Plan reflected a full and candid evaluation of the Plan. Moran's expression of his views at the meeting served to place before the Board a knowledgeable critique of the Plan. The factual happenings here are clearly distinguishable from the actions of the directors of Trans Union Corporation who displayed gross negligence in approving a cash-out merger. *Id.*

In addition, to meet their burden, the Directors must show that the defensive mechanism was "reasonable in relation to the threat posed." The record reflects a concern on the part of the Directors over the increasing frequency in the financial services industry of "boot-strap" and "bust-up" takeovers. The Directors were also concerned that such takeovers may take the form of two tier offers. In addition, on August 14, the Household Board was aware of Moran's overture on behalf of D-K-M. In sum, the Directors reasonably believed Household was vulnerable to coercive acquisition techniques and adopted a reasonable defensive mechanism to protect itself.

In contrast with *Moran*, a back-end and flip-over pill was impeached in *Dynamics Corp. v. CTS Corp.*, 794 F.2d 250 (7th Cir. 1986), rev'd on other grounds, 107 S. Ct. 1637 (1987). According to Judge Richard Posner, the poison pill would have effectively insulated the board from a take-over. The poison pill was also triggered at a low ownership level (15%), and was adopted in the heat of an ongoing control contest. Judge Posner also stated that a pill should give shareholders "the same price per share [as the offer price]—not a higher price calculated to kill off the tender, indeed to kill off any tender." *Id.* at 259. Though some protective devices will be upheld, distinguishing valid from invalid devices will not be easy.

New S.E.C. rules would negate the *Unocal* decision with respect to discriminatory tender offers. Rules 13e-4(f)(8)(i) and 14d-10(a)(i), adopted in 1986, require bidders to extend the offer to all securities holders of the class of securities subject to the offer. A similar "all-holder" requirement is featured in OSA s. 95.1, though this is restricted to

Ontario holders. The *Unocal* decision is, however, still of considerable interest as to the validity of poison pills in general.

Supporters of poison pills and shark repellents argue that, like OSA requirements that bids be kept open for 21 days, they facilitate auctions for the target's voting shares because they provide a target's board with much needed time to explore all available options designed to maximize shareholder value. To date, the results of empirical studies of poison pills have, however, been somewhat ambiguous. In March 1986, Gregg Jarrell and the S.E.C. staff released a study which found that the announcement of a new poison pill appeared to have no significant statistical effect on the price of a firm's stock. Office of the Chief Economist, Securities and Exchange Commission, *A Study on the Economics of Poison Pills*, Fed. Sec. L. Rep. (CCH) para. 83,971 [1985-86 Transfer Binder]. One possible explanation for this is that the announcement of a pill is taken as a signal that the firm is a suitable candidate for a tender offer, with the disadvantages of the pill (lower probability of a successful take-over) cancelled out by its advantages (higher probability that a take-over will be made). Such a theory would explain an exception which the S.E.C. staff noted to its findings: when the announcement was made during a take-over, average negative returns of 2.4% indicated that the pills were not beneficial. Here, the beneficial effects of the announcement of a pill would be absent, since the market would already have reacted to the fact that the firm was a suitable take-over bid candidate. The decline was not so significant, however, to suggest that the pills guaranteed control for incumbents. See also DeAngelo & Rice, *Antitakeover Charter Amendments and Stockholder Wealth*, 11 J. Fin. Econ. 329, 349-55 (1983) (negative result but not statistically significant); Linn & McConnell, *An Empirical Investigation of the Impact of "Antitakeover" Amendments of Common Stock Prices*, 11 J. Fin. Econ. 329, 249-55 (1983) (shareholders experience small but statistically significant positive returns); but see Office of the Chief Economist, Securities and Exchange Commission, *Shareholder Wealth Effects of Ohio Legislation Affecting Takeovers* (May 1987) (passage of Ohio legislation under which a majority of disinterested shareholders must approve an acquisition of control had a large negative effect on the share prices of Ohio corporations that lobbied for the statute, and a smaller, but still statistically significant, negative effect on those Ohio corporations that did not do so).

Whether pills are benign may depend crucially upon their special features. In particular, pills and shark repellents that aim at extracting a "fair price" from offerors have not been shown to harm target shareholders. A typical provision of this kind would prevent a transfer of a control block of shares unless (1) the transfer is approved by the old board or by a supermajority vote of the minority shareholders, or (2) the purchaser has paid a fair price for the shares. Fair price is usually identified as the higher of market price at the time of the merger or the highest price the offeror paid to acquire the shares around the time of the offer. The "board-out" provision permits an easy transfer of control in the case of a friendly bid, while the "fair price" requirement makes it difficult for an offeror to acquire large blocks of shares in private transactions prior to announcing a hostile bid. Fair price charter amendments are increasingly common in the United States, and were seen in a recent study to have a statistically insignificant negative effect on the value of target stock. Jarrell & Poulsen, *Shark Repellents and Stock Prices: The*

Effects of Antitakeover Amendments Since 1980, 19 J. Fin. Econ. 127 (1987). Certain shark repellents that did not feature fair price rights were, however, found to have a statistically significant negative effect. Similarly, Roberto Romano has noted that recent state take-over legislation providing for presumptive fair price rights did not appear to have had a statistically significant effect on target shareholder wealth. Romano, *The Political Economy of Takeover Statutes*, 73 Va. L. Rev. 111, 180-87 (1987). One explanation of these findings is that the costs to target shareholders of fair price rights are equalled by their benefits. The costs, then, would be the reduced likelihood that a bid would be made because of the pill. The benefits would be (1) a greater share of the merger surplus, and (2) a signal that the firm is a suitable target as a consequence of its very adoption of the pill. But even if fair price rights do not harm target shareholders, an analysis of their effects must also take into account the forgone merger gains lost by the offeror's shareholders, through either (1) a lessened share of merger gains, or (2) deadweight losses when tender offers are not made or are withdrawn because of the pill. If these losses are significant, an apparently neutral (for the target) pill may yet on balance be inefficient.

Anti-Takeover Legislation. State legislatures in the United States responded to increased take-over bids in the last 10 years with anti-takeover statutes. The first series of such laws were passed in at least 35 states, and typically required pre-tender notification by the bidder and a review by state officials of the fairness of the bid. The constitutional validity of these statutes was impeached in *Edgar v. MITE Corp.*, 457 U.S. 624 (1982), where the Illinois statute was held to trench on the broad interstate commerce power of the federal government. A second generation series of statutes then ensued, with less burdensome restrictions on offerors. These statutes apply only to domestically incorporated firms, and require shareholder (and not state agency) approval. The constitutionality of these statutes was upheld by the Supreme Court in *CTS Corp. v. Dynamics Corp.*, 107 S. Ct. 1637 (1987), and they have now been adopted in many U.S. states. Even Delaware has now enacted an anti-takeover law. New Del. s. 203 provides that unwanted buyers who acquire more than 15% of a target's stock will not be permitted to complete the take-over for three years unless (1) the buyer acquires, all at once, 85% of the target's stock, excluding management shares, (2) two-thirds of the shares voting in a special election, excluding the bidder's shares, approve the acquisition, or (3) the target has exempted itself from the statutory provision. See *Debate Over a New Takeover Law*, *N.Y. Times*, Feb. 1, 1988, at D1, col. 3.

The popularity of anti-takeover legislation is troubling for managerial passivity theorists, particularly if in other contexts they would argue that competition in the provision of state corporations legislation is efficient. See Chapter Three, Section A. It would seem difficult to resist the conclusion that either (1) the pure managerial passivity thesis is overstated, or (2) the competition for the provision of corporations law may at times produce pathological results.

Assuming first that, contrary to the managerial passivity thesis, some kinds of shark repellents are efficient, then state legislation adopting such provisions may be defended on gapfilling theories. This is particularly true of presumptive rules, which firms may opt out of through charter amendments. If, however, these provisions are inefficient, their popularity in state legislatures might be explained in at least two ways. First, a state may wish to adopt inefficient legislation when its costs are exported to another state. For example, a state may propose restrictions on plant closings within its borders even if the gains from a closing to non-state shareholders and employees exceed losses to plant employees within the state. If a state anticipated plant closings on the acquisition of a local firm by a non-state offeror, then, it might ignore the external costs and adopt anti-takeover legislation. See Levmore, *Interstate Exploitation and Judicial Intervention*, 69 Va. L. Rev. 563, 622-24 (1983). This explanation of anti-takeover laws is, however, speculative, since the relation between control changes and plant closings is unproven. The second explanation of legislative pathologies looks to possible wealth transfers from shareholders to managers. Thus a firm might issue shares when incorporated in a state without anti-takeover legislation, and where the corporation's charter does not contain shark repellents. The firm's cost of capital will then reflect the possibility of take-over bid premiums. If the firm subsequently persuades the legislature to pass an anti-takeover statute (which may in fact be cheaper for the firm to do than to amend its charter), the shareholders may be deprived of the value of anticipated take-over gains. In this way the firm will have immunized itself from a tender offer, while issuing shares at a higher price than it would have received had the anti-takeover devices been in place prior to the public share issue. Unlike cost-exporting theories of anti-takeover legislation, this interest-group explanation focuses on the greater political clout (in the form of political contributions) that centralized target management will possess as compared to diffuse shareholder interests. See Fischel, *From MITE to CTS: State Anti-takeover Statutes, The Williams Act, The Commerce Clause and Insider Trading*, 1987 Sup. Ct. Rev. 47.

Due Care Requirements. The decision of the Delaware Supreme Court in *Smith v. Van Gorkom* (Chapter Seven, Part I, Section C) introduces a further constraint on rapid responses by target management to a take-over bid. In the same way that a quick decision to accede to a cashout merger proposal led to liability under the due care standard, a snap rejection of a tender offer might also be impeached. In *Hanson Trust PLC v. ML SCM Acquisition, Inc.*, 781 F.2d 264 (2d Cir. 1986), the Court enjoined a proposed asset option given to Merrill Lynch by SCM to acquire a valuable part of SCM's business at a bargain price. The option would be triggered by a third party acquiring more than one-third of SCM's common stock, and was designed to persuade a competing offeror, Hanson Trust, to abandon a tender offer for SCM stock. The winner of the contest would then be Merrill Lynch, which proposed a leveraged buyout of SCM. The SCM board had gone some way to comply with *Van Gorkom* due care standards, having solicited the advice of an investment banker and secured the formal consent of independent SCM board members. However, the SCM directors were held to have breached their duty of care. The board had no notice of the asset option agreement before the meeting to consider it, and gave little or no thought to whether the triggering event for the asset option had already occurred. In addition, they did not consider whether Hanson Trust's bid was better than that of Merrill Lynch, they did not review the Hanson Trust offer carefully, and they accepted a fairness option from the investment banker without inquiring into the range of fair values.

A want of due care by directors in adopting a poison pill in response to a take-over bid was also criticized by Judge Posner in *Dynamics Corp. v. CTS Corp.*, 794 F.2d 250 (7th Cir. 1986), rev'd on other grounds, 107 S. Ct. 1637 (1987). The board did not evaluate the offer "in a cool, dispassionate, and thorough fashion," but proceeded by way of "judgment first, trial later, as the [Queen of Hearts said in *Alice in Wonderland*]." *Id.* at 257. However, the Court also observed that it had "no desire to judicialize board of directors meetings." *Id.* It will be recalled that some of the most trenchant criticisms of *Van Gorkom* focused on the costs associated with the increased procedural requirements imposed on directors. Due care issues are discussed in the following case.

Revlon, Inc. v. MacAndrews & Forbes Holdings, Inc.
Delaware Supreme Court
506 A.2d 173 (1986)

Before McNEILLY and MOORE JJ., and BALICK, Judge.

MOORE, Justice: In this battle for corporate control of Revlon, Inc. (Revlon), the Court of Chancery enjoined certain transactions designed to thwart the efforts of Pantry Pride, Inc. (Pantry Pride) to acquire Revlon.[1] The defendants are Revlon, its board of directors, and Forstmann Little & Co. and the latter's affiliated limited partnership (collectively, Forstmann). The injunction barred consummation of an option granted Forstmann to purchase certain Revlon assets (the lock-up option), a promise to Revlon to deal exclusively with Forstmann in the face of a takeover (the no-shop provision), and the payment of $25 million cancellation fee to Forstmann if the transaction was aborted. The Court of Chancery found that the Revlon directors had breached their duty of care by entering into the foregoing transactions and effectively ending an active auction for the company. The trial court ruled that such arrangements are not illegal *per se* under Delaware law, but that their use under the circumstances here was impermissible. We agree. *See MacAndrews & Forbes Holdings, Inc. v. Revlon, Inc.*, Del.Ch., 501 A.2d 1239 (1985). Thus, we granted this expedited interlocutory appeal to consider for the first time the validity of such defensive measures in the face of an active bidding contest for corporate control. Additionally, we address for the first time the extent to which a corporation may consider the impact of a takeover threat on constituencies other than shareholders. *See Unocal Corp. v. Mesa Petroleum Co.*, Del.Supr., 493 A.2d 946, 955 (1985).

In our view, lock-ups and related agreements are permitted under Delaware law where their adoption is untainted by director interest or other breaches of fiduciary duty. The actions taken by the Revlon directors, however, did not meet this standard. Moreover, while concern for various corporate constituencies is proper when addressing a takeover threat, that principle is limited by the requirement that there be some rationally related benefit accruing to the stockholders. We find no such benefit here.

---

[1]   The nominal plaintiff, MacAndrews & Forbes Holdings, Inc., is the controlling stockholder of Pantry Pride. For all practical purposes their interests in this litigation are virtually identical, and we hereafter will refer to Pantry Pride as the plaintiff.

Thus, under all the circumstances we must agree with the Court of Chancery that the enjoined Revlon defensive measures were inconsistent with the directors' duties to the stockholders. Accordingly, we affirm.

I.

The somewhat complex manoeuvres of the parties necessitate a rather detailed examination of the facts. The prelude to this controversy began in June 1985, when Ronald O. Perelman, chairman of the board and chief executive officer of Pantry Pride, met with his counterpart at Revlon, Michel C. Bergerac, to discuss a friendly acquisition of Revlon by Pantry Pride. Perelman suggested a price in the range of $40-50 per share, but the meeting ended with Bergerac dismissing those figures as considerably below Revlon's intrinsic value. All subsequent Pantry Pride overtures were rebuffed, perhaps in part based on Mr. Bergerac's strong personal antipathy to Mr. Perelman.

Thus, on August 14, Pantry Pride's board authorized Perelman to acquire Revlon, either through negotiation in the $42-$43 per share range, or by making a hostile tender offer at $45. Perelman then met with Bergerac and outlined Pantry Pride's alternate approaches. Bergerac remained adamantly opposed to such schemes and conditioned any further discussions of the matter on Pantry Pride executing a standstill agreement prohibiting it from acquiring Revlon without the latter's prior approval.

On August 19, the Revlon board met specially to consider the impending threat of a hostile bid by Pantry Pride.[3] At the meeting, Lazard Freres, Revlon's investment banker, advised the directors that $45 per share was a grossly inadequate price for the company. Felix Rohatyn and William Loomis of Lazard Freres explained to the board that Pantry Pride's financial strategy for acquiring Revlon would be through "junk bond" financing followed by a break-up of Revlon and the disposition of its assets. With proper timing, according to the experts, such transactions could produce a return to Pantry Pride of $60 to $70 per share, while a sale of the company as a whole would be in the "mid 50" dollar range. Martin Lipton, special counsel for Revlon, recommended two defensive measures: first, that the company repurchase up to 5 million of its nearly 30 million outstanding shares; and second, that it adopt a Note Purchase Rights Plan. Under this plan, each Revlon shareholder would receive as a dividend one Note Purchase Right (the Rights) for each share of common stock, with the Rights entitling the holder to exchange one common share for a $65 principal Revlon note at 12% interest with one-year maturity.

---

3   There were 14 directors on the Revlon board. Six of them held senior management positions with the company, and two others held significant blocks of its stock. Four of the remaining six directors were associated at some point with entities that had various business relationships with Revlon. On the basis of this limited record, however, we cannot conclude that this board is entitled to certain presumptions that generally attach to the decisions of a board whose majority consists of truly outside independent directors. See *Polk v. Good & Texaco*, Del.Supr., — A.2d —, — (1986); *Moran v. Household International, Inc.*, Del.Supr., 500 A.2d 1346, 1356 (1985); *Unocal Corp. v. Mesa Petroleum Co.*, Del.Supr., 493 A.2d 946, 955 (1985); *Aronson v. Lewis*, Del.Supr., 473 A.2d 805, 812, 815 (1984); *Puma v. Marriott*, Del.Ch., 283 A.2d 693, 695 (1971).

The Rights would become effective whenever anyone acquired beneficial ownership of 20% or more of Revlon's shares, unless the purchaser acquired all the company's stock for cash at $65 or more per share. In addition, the Rights would not be available to the acquiror, and prior to the 20% triggering event the Revlon board could redeem the rights for 10 cents each. Both proposals were unanimously adopted.

Pantry Pride made its first hostile move on August 23 with a cash tender offer for any and all shares of Revlon at $47.50 per common share and $26.67 per preferred share, subject to (1) Pantry Pride's obtaining financing for the purchase, and (2) the Rights being redeemed, rescinded or voided.

The Revlon board met again on August 26. The directors advised the stockholders to reject the offer. Further defensive measures also were planned. On August 29, Revlon commenced its own offer for up to 10 million shares, exchanging for each share of common stock tendered one Senior Subordinated Note (the Notes) of $47.50 principal at 11.75% interest, due 1995, and one-tenth of a share of $9.00 Cumulative Convertible Exchangeable Preferred Stock valued at $100 per share. Lazard Freres opined that the notes would trade at their face value on a fully distributed basis.[4] Revlon stockholders tendered 87 percent of the outstanding shares (approximately 33 million), and the company accepted the 110 million shares on a pro rata basis. The new Notes contained covenants which limited Revlon's ability to incur additional debt, sell assets, or pay dividends unless otherwise approved by the "independent" (non-management) members of the board.

At this point, both the Rights and the Note covenants stymied Pantry Pride's attempted takeover. The next move came on September 16, when Pantry Pride announced a new tender offer at $42 per share, conditioned upon receiving at least 90% of the outstanding stock. Pantry Pride also indicated that it would consider buying less than 90%, and at an increased price, if Revlon removed the impeding Rights. While this offer was lower on its face than the earlier $47.50 proposal, Revlon's investment banker, Lazard Freres, described the two bids as essentially equal in view of the completed exchange offer.

The Revlon board held a regularly scheduled meeting on September 24. The directors rejected the latest Pantry Pride offer and authorized management to negotiate with other parties interested in acquiring Revlon. Pantry Pride remained determined in its efforts and continued to make cash bids for the company, offering $50 per share on September 27, and raising its bid to $53 on October 1, and then to $56.25 on October 7.

In the meantime, Revlon's negotiations with Forstmann and the investment group Adler & Shaykin had produced results. The Revlon directors met on October 3 to consider Pantry Pride's $53 bid and to examine possible alternatives to the offer. Both Forstmann and Adler & Shaykin made certain proposals to the board. As a result, the directors unanimously agreed to a leveraged buyout by Forstmann. The terms of this

---

4   Like bonds, the Notes actually were issued in denominations of $1,000 and integral multiples thereof. A separate certificate was issued in a total principal amount equal to the remaining sum to which a stockholder was entitled. Likewise, in the esoteric parlance of bond dealers, a Note trading at par ($1,000) would be quoted on the market at 100.

accord were as follows: each stockholder would get $56 cash per share; management would purchase stock in the new company by the exercise of their Revlon "golden parachutes";[5] Forstmann would assume Revlon's $475 million debt incurred by the issuance of the Notes; and Revlon would redeem the Rights and waive the Notes covenants for Forstmann or in connection with any other offer superior to Forstmann's. The board did not actually remove the covenants at the October 3 meeting, because Forstmann then lacked a firm commitment on its financing, but accepted the Forstmann capital structure, and indicated that the outside directors would waive the covenants in due course. Part of Forstmann's plan was to sell Revlon's Norcliff Thayer and Reheis divisions to American Home Products for $335 million. Before the merger, Revlon was to sell its cosmetics and fragrance division to Adler & Shaykin for $905 million. These transactions would facilitate the purchase by Forstmann or any other acquiror of Revlon.

When the merger, and thus the waiver of the Notes covenants, was announced, the market value of these securities began to fall. The Notes, which originally traded near par, around 100, dropped to 87.50 by October 8. One director later reported (at the October 12 meeting) a "deluge" of telephone calls from irate noteholders, and on October 10 the Wall Street Journal reported threats of litigation by these creditors.

Pantry Pride countered with a new proposal on October 7, raising its $53 offer to $56.25, subject to nullification of the Rights, a waiver of the Notes covenants, and the election of three Pantry Pride directors to the Revlon board. On October 9, representatives of Pantry Pride, Forstmann and Revlon conferred in an attempt to negotiate the fate of Revlon, but could not reach agreement. At this meeting Pantry Pride announced that it would engage in fractional bidding and top any Forstmann offer by a slightly higher one. It is also significant that Forstmann, to Pantry Pride's exclusion, had been made privy to certain Revlon financial data. Thus, the parties were not negotiating on equal terms.

Again privately armed with Revlon data, Forstmann met on October 11 with Revlon's special counsel and investment banker. On October 12, Forstmann made a new $57.25 per share offer, based on several conditions.[6] The principal demand was a lock-up option to purchase Revlon's Vision Care and National Health Laboratories divisions for $525 million, some $100-$175 million below the value ascribed to them by Lazard Freres, if another acquiror got 40% of Revlon's shares. Revlon also was required to accept a no-shop provision. The Rights and Notes covenants have to be removed as in the October 3 agreement. There would be a $25 million cancellation fee to be placed in escrow, and released to Forstmann if the new agreement terminated or if another acquiror got more than 19.9% of Revlon's stock. Finally, there would be no participation by Revlon management in the merger. In return, Forstmann

---

5   In the takeover context "golden parachutes" generally are understood to be termination agreements providing substantial bonuses and other benefits for managers and certain directors upon a change in control of a company.

6   Forstmann's $57.25 offer ostensibly is worth $1 more than Pantry Pride's $56.25 bid. However, the Pantry Pride offer was immediate, while the Forstmann proposal must be discounted for the time value of money because of the delay in approving the merger and consummating the transaction. The exact difference between the two bids was an unsettled point of contention even at oral agreement.

agreed to support the par value of the Notes, which had faltered in the market, by an exchange of new notes. Forstmann also demanded immediate acceptance of its offer, or it would be withdrawn. The board unanimously approved Forstmann's proposal because: (1) it was for a higher price than the Pantry Pride bid, (2) it protected the noteholders, and (3) Forstmann's financing was firmly in place.[7] The board further agreed to redeem the rights and waive the covenants on the preferred stock in response to any offer above $57 cash per share. The covenants were waived, contingent upon receipt of an investment banking opinion that the Notes would trade near par value once the offer was consummated.

Pantry Pride, which had initially sought injunctive relief from the Rights plan on August 22, filed an amended complaint on October 14 challenging the lock-up, the cancellation fee, and the exercise of the Rights and the Notes covenants. Pantry Pride also sought a temporary restraining order to prevent Revlon from placing any assets in escrow or transferring them to Forstmann. Moreover, on October 22, Pantry Pride again raised its bid, with a cash offer of $58 per share conditioned upon nullification of the Rights, waiver of the covenants, and an injunction of the Forstmann lock-up.

On October 15, the Court of Chancery prohibited the further transfer of assets, and eight days later enjoined the lock-up, no-shop, and cancellation fee provisions of the agreement. The trial court concluded that the Revlon directors had breached their duty of loyalty by making concessions to Forstmann, out of concern for their liability to the noteholders, rather than maximizing the sale price of the company for the stockholders' benefit. *MacAndrews & Forbes Holdings, Inc. v. Revlon, Inc.*, 501 A.2d at 1249-50.

II.

To obtain a preliminary injunction, a plaintiff must demonstrate both a reasonable probability of success on the merits and some irreparable harm which will occur absent the injunction. *Gimbel v. Signal Companies*, Del.Ch., 316 A.2d 599, 602 (1974), aff'd, Del.Supr., 316 A.2d 619 (1974). Additionally, the Court shall balance the conveniences of and possible injuries to the parties. *Id.*

A.

We turn first to Pantry Pride's probability of success on the merits. The ultimate responsibility for managing the business and affairs of a corporation falls on its board of directors. 8 *Del.C.* § 141(a). In discharging this function the directors owe fiduciary duties of care and loyalty to the corporation and its shareholders. *Guth v. Loft, Inc.*, 23 Del.Supr. 255, 5 A.2d 503, 510 (1939); *Aronson v. Lewis*, Del.Supr., 473 A.2d 805, 811

---

7   Actually, at this time about $400 million of Forstmann's funding was still subject to two investment banks using their "best efforts" to organize a syndicate to provide the balance. Pantry Pride's entire financing was not firmly committed at this point either, although Pantry Pride represented in an October 11 letter to Lazard Freres that its investment banker, Drexel Burnham Lambert, was highly confident of its ability to raise the balance of $350 million. Drexel Burnham had a firm commitment for this sum by October 18.

(1984). These principles apply with equal force when a board approves a corporate merger pursuant to 8 *Del.C.* § 251(b); *Smith v. Van Gorkom*, Del.Supr., 488 A.2d 858, 873 (1985); and of course they are the bedrock of our law regarding corporate takeover issues. *Pogostin v. Rice*, Del.Supr., 480 A.2d 619, 624 (1984); *Unocal Corp. v. Mesa Petroleum Co.*, Del.Supr., 493 A.2d 946, 953, 955 (1985); *Moran v. Household International, Inc.*, Del.Supr., 500 A.2d 1346, 1350 (1985). While the business judgment rule may be applicable to the actions of corporate directors responding to takeover threats, the principles upon which it is founded—care, loyalty and independence—must first be satisfied.[10] *Aronson v. Lewis*, 473 A.2d at 812.

If the business judgment rule applies, there is a "presumption that in making a business decision the directors of a corporation acted on an informed basis, in good faith and in the honest belief that the action taken was in the best interests of the company." *Aronson v. Lewis*, 473 A.2d at 812. However, when a board implements anti-takeover measures there arises "the omnipresent specter that a board may be acting primarily in its own interests, rather than those of the corporation and its shareholders ..." *Unocal Corp. v. Mesa Petroleum Co.*, 493 A.2d at 954. This potential for conflict places upon the directors the burden of proving that they had reasonable grounds for believing there was a danger to corporate policy and effectiveness, a burden satisfied by a showing of good faith and reasonable investigation. *Id.* at 955. In addition, the directors must analyze the nature of the takeover and its effect on the corporation in order to ensure balance—that the responsive action taken is reasonable in relation to the threat posed. *Id.*

B.

The first relevant defensive measure adopted by the Revlon board was the Rights Plan, which would be considered a "poison pill" in the current language of corporate takeovers—a plan by which shareholders receive the right to be bought out by the corporation at a substantial premium on the occurrence of a stated triggering event. See generally *Moran v. Household International, Inc.*, Del.Supr., 500 A.2d 1346 (1985). By

---

10   One eminent corporate commentator has drawn a distinction between the business judgment rule, which insulates directors and management from personal liability for their business decisions, and the business judgment doctrine, which protects the decision itself from attack. The principles upon which the rule and doctrine operate are identical, while the objects of their protection are different. See Hinsey, *Business Judgment and the American Law Institute's Corporate Governance Project: The Rule, the Doctrine and the Reality*, 52 Geo. Wash. L.Rev. 609, 611-13 (1984). In the transactional justification cases, where the doctrine is said to apply, our decisions have not observed the distinction in such terminology. See *Polk v. Good & Texaco*, Del.Supr., — A.2d —, — (1986); *Moran v. Household International, Inc.*, Del.Supr., 500 A.2d 1346, 1356 (1985); *Unocal Corp. v. Mesa Petroleum Co.*, Del.Supr., 493 A.2d 946, 953-55 (1985); *Rosenblatt v. Getty Oil Co.*, Del.Supr., 493 A.2d 929, 943 (1985). Under the circumstances we do not alter our earlier practice of referring only to the business judgment rule, although in transactional justification matters such reference may be understood to embrace the concept of the doctrine.

8 *Del.C.* §§ 141 and 122(13)[11] the board clearly had the power to adopt the measure. See *Moran v. Household International, Inc.*, 500 A.2d at 1351. Thus, the focus becomes one of reasonableness and purpose.

The Revlon board approved the Rights Plan in the face of an impending hostile takeover bid by Pantry Pride at $45 per share, a price which Revlon reasonably concluded was grossly inadequate. Lazard Freres had so advised the directors, and had also informed them that Pantry Pride was a small, highly leveraged company bent on a "bust-up" takeover by using "junk bond" financing to buy Revlon cheaply sell the acquired assets to pay the debts incurred, and retain the profit for itself.[12] In adopting the Plan, the board protected the shareholders from a hostile takeover at a price below the company's interest value, while retaining sufficient flexibility to address any proposal deemed to be in the stockholders' best interests.

To that extent the board acted in good faith and upon reasonable investigation. Under the circumstances it cannot be said that the Rights Plan as employed was unreasonable, considering the threat posed. Indeed, the Plan was a factor in causing Pantry Pride to raise its bids from a low of $42 to an eventual high of $58. At the time of its adoption the Rights Plan afforded a measure of protection consistent with the directors' fiduciary duty in facing a takeover threat perceived as detrimental to corporate interests. *Unocal*, 493 A.2d at 954-55. Far from being a "show-stopper," as the plaintiffs had contended in *Moran*, the measure spurred the bidding to new heights, a proper result of its implementation. See *Moran*, 500 A.2d at 1354, 1356-67.

Although we consider adoption of the Plan to have been valid under the circumstances, its contained usefulness was rendered moot by the directors' actions on October 3 and October 12. At the October 3 meeting the board redeemed the Rights conditioned upon consummation of a merger with Forstmann, but further acknowledged that they would also be redeemed to facilitate any more favorable offer. On October 12, the board unanimously passed a resolution redeeming the Rights in connection with any cash proposal of $57.25 or more per share. Because all the pertinent offers eventually equalled or surpassed that amount, the Rights clearly were no longer any impediment in the contest for Revlon. This mooted any question of their propriety under *Moran* or *Unocal*.

---

11   The relevant provision of Section 122 is:

Every corporation created under this chapter shall have power to:

(13) Make contracts, including contracts of guaranty and suretyship, incur liabilities, borrow money at such rates of interest as the corporation may determine, issue its notes, bonds and other obligations, and secure any of its obligations by mortgage, pledge or other encumbrance of all or any of its property, franchises and income, ..." 8 *Del.C.* § 122(13).

See Section 141(a) in n. 8, supra. See also Section 160(a), n. 13, infra.

12   As we noted in *Moran*, a "bust-up" takeover generally refers to a situation in which one seeks to finance an acquisition by selling off pieces of the acquired company, presumably at a substantial profit. See *Moran*, 500 A.2d at 1349, n. 4.

C.

The second defensive measure adopted by Revlon to thwart a Pantry Pride takeover was the company's own exchange offer for 10 million of its shares. The directors' general broad powers to manage the business and affairs of the corporation are augmented by the specific authority conferred under 8 *Del.C.* § 160(a), permitting the company to deal in its own stock. *Unocal*, 493 A.2d at 953-54; *Cheff v. Mathes*, 41 Del.Supr. 494, 199 A.2d 548, 554 (1914); *Kors v. Carey*, 39 Del.Ch. 47, 158 A.2d 136, 140 (1960). However, when exercising that power in an effort to forestall a hostile takeover, the board's actions are strictly held to the fiduciary standards outlined in *Unocal*. These standards require the directors to determine the best interests of the corporation and its stockholders, and impose an enhanced duty to adjure any action that is motivated by considerations other than a good faith concern for such interest. *Unocal*, 493 A.2d at 954-55; see *Bennett v. Propp*, 41 Del.Supr. 14, 187 A.2d 405, 409 (1962).

The Revlon directors concluded that Pantry Pride's $47.50 offer was grossly inadequate. In that regard the board acted in good faith, and on an informed basis, with reasonable grounds to believe that there existed a harmful threat to the corporate enterprise. The adoption of a defensive measure, reasonable in relation to the threat posed, was proper and fully accorded with the powers, duties, and responsibilities conferred upon directors under our law. *Unocal*, 493 A.2d at 954; *Pogostin v. Rice*, 480 A.2d at 627.

D.

However, when Pantry Pride increased its offer to $50 per share, and then to $53, it became apparent to all that the break-up of the company was inevitable. The Revlon's board's authorization permitting management to negotiate a merger or buyout with a third party was a recognition that the company was for sale. The duty of the board had thus changed from the preservation of Revlon as a corporate entity to the maximization of the company's value at a sale for the stockholders' benefit. This significantly altered the board's responsibilities under the *Unocal* standards. It no longer faced threats to corporate policy and effectiveness, or to the stockholders' interests, from a grossly inadequate bid. The whole question of defensive measures became moot. The directors' role changed from defenders of the corporate bastion to auctioneers charged with getting the best price for the stockholders at a sale of the company.

III.

This brings us to the lock-up with Forstmann and its emphasis on shoring up the sagging market value of the Notes in the face of threatened litigation by their holders. Such a focus was inconsistent with the changed concept of the directors' responsibilities at this stage of the developments. The impending waiver of the Notes covenants had caused the value of the Notes to fall, and the board was aware of the noteholders' ire as well as their subsequent threats of suit. The directors thus made support of the Notes an integral part of the company's dealings with Forstmann, even though their primary responsibility at this stage was to the equity owners.

The original threat posed by Pantry Pride—the break-up of the company—had become a reality which even the directors embraced. Selective dealing to fend off a hostile but determined bidder was no longer a proper objective. Instead, obtaining the highest price for the benefit of the stockholders should have been the central theme guiding director action. Thus, the Revlon board could not make the requisite showing of good faith by preferring the noteholders and ignoring its duty of loyalty to the shareholders. The rights of the former already were fixed by contract. *Wolfensohn v. Madison Fund, Inc.*, Del.Supr., 253 A.2d 72, 75 (1969); *Harff v. Kerkorian*, Del.Ch., 324 A.2d 215 (1974). The noteholders required no further protection, and when the Revlon board entered into an auction-ending lock-up agreement with Forstmann on the basis of impermissible considerations at the expense of the shareholders, the directors breached their primary duty of loyalty.

The Revlon board argued that it acted in good faith in protecting the noteholders because *Unocal* permits consideration of other corporate constituencies. Although such considerations may be permissable, there are fundamental limitations upon that prerogative. A board may have regard for various constituencies in discharging its responsibilities, provided there are rationally related benefits accruing to the stockholders. *Unocal*, 493 A.2d at 955. However, such concern for non-stockholder interests is inappropriate when an auction among active bidders is in progress, and the object no longer is to protect or maintain the corporate enterprise but to sell it to the highest bidder.

Revlon also contended that by *Gilbert v. El Paso Co.*, Del.Ch., 490 A.2d 1050, 1054-55 (1984), it had contractual and good faith obligations to consider the noteholders. However, any such duties are limited to the principle that one may not interfere with contractual relationships by improper actions. Here, the rights of the noteholders were fixed by agreement, and there is nothing of substance to suggest that any of those terms were violated. The Notes covenants specifically contemplated a waiver to permit sale of the company at a fair price. The Notes were accepted by the holders on that basis, including the risk of an adverse market effect stemming from a waiver. Thus, nothing remained for Revlon to legitimately protect, and no rationally related benefit thereby accrued to the stockholders. Under such circumstances we must conclude that the merger agreement with Forstmann was unreasonable in relation to the threat posed.

A lockup is not *per se* illegal under Delaware law. Its use has been approved in an earlier case. *Thompson v. Enstar Corp.*, Del.Ch., — A.2d — (1984). Such options can entice other bidders to enter a contest for control of the corporation, creating an auction for the company and maximizing shareholder profit. Current economic conditions in the takeover market are such that a "white knight" like Forstmann might only enter the bidding for the target company if it receives some form of compensation to cover the risks and costs involved. Note, *Corporations-Mergers—"Lock-up" Enjoined Under Section 14(e) of Securities Exchange Act—Mobil Corp. v. Marathon Oil Co., 669 F.2d 366 (6th Cir. 1981)*, 12 Seton Hall L.Rev. 881, 892 (1982). However, while those lock-ups which draw bidders into the battle benefit shareholders, similar measures which end an active auction and foreclose further bidding operate to the shareholders' detriment. Note, *Lock-up Options: Toward a State Law Standard*, 96 Harv. L. Rev. 1068, 1081 (1983).[14]

---

14   For further discussion of the benefits and detriments of lock-up options, also see: Nelson, *Mobil Corp. v. Marathon Oil Co.—The Decision and Its Implications for Future Tender Offers*, 7 Corp.L.Rev 233,

(The footnote is continued on the next page.)

Recently, the United States Court of Appeals for the Second Circuit invalidated a lock-up on fiduciary duty grounds similar to those here.[15] *Hanson Trust PLC, et al. v. ML SCM Acquisition Inc. et al.*, 781 F.2d 264 (2nd Cir. 1986). Citing *Thompson v. Enstar Corp.*, supra, with approval, the court stated:

In this regard, we are especially mindful that some lock-up options may be beneficial to the shareholders, such as those that induce a bidder to compete for control of a corporation, while others may be harmful, such as those that effectively preclude bidders from competing with the optionee bidder. 781 F.2d at 274.

In *Hanson Trust*, the bidder, Hanson, sought control of SCM by a hostile cash tender offer. SCM management joined with Merrill Lynch to propose a leveraged buy-out of the company at a higher price, and Hanson in turn increased its offer. Then, despite very little improvement in its subsequent bid, the management group sought a lock-up option to purchase SCM's two main assets at a substantial discount. The SCM directors granted the lock-up without adequate information as to the size of the discount or the effect the transaction would have on the company. Their action effectively ended a competitive bidding situation. The Hanson Court invalidated the lock-up because the directors failed to fully inform themselves about the value of a transaction in which management had a strong self-interest. "In short, the Board appears to have failed to ensure that negotiations for alternative bids were conducted by those whose only loyalty was to the shareholders." *Id.* at 277.

The Forstmann option had a similar destructive effect on the auction process. Forstmann had already been drawn into the contest on a preferred basis, so the reasons for approving the transactions were: (1) better financing, (2) noteholder protection, and (3) higher price. As the Court of Chancery found, and we agree, any distinctions between the rival bidders' methods of financing the proposal were nominal at best, and such a consideration has little or no significance in a cash offer for any and all shares. The principal object, contrary to the board's duty of care, appears to have been protection of the noteholders over the shareholders' interests. While Forstmann's $57.25 offer was objectively higher than Pantry Pride's $56.25 bid, the margin of superiority is less when the Forstmann price is adjusted for the time value of money. In reality, the Revlon board ended the auction in return for very little actual improvement in the final bid. The principal benefit went to the directors, who avoided personal liability to a class of

---

14   Continued ...

    265-68 (1984); Note, *Swallowing the Key to Lock-up Options: Mobil Corp v. Marathon Oil Co.*, 14 U.Tol.L.Rev. 1055, 1081-83 (1983).

15   The federal courts generally have declined to enjoin lock-up options despite arguments that lock-ups constitute impermissible "manipulative" conduct forbidden by Section 14(e) of the Williams Act [15 U.S.C. § 78n(e)]. See *Buffalo Forge Co. v. Ogden Corp.*, 717 F.2d 757 (2nd Cir. 1983), cert. denied, 464 U.S. 1018, 104 S.Ct. 550, 78 L.Ed.2d 724 (1983); *Data Probe Acquisition Corp. v. Datatab, Inc.*, 722 F.2d 1 (2nd Cir. 1983); cert. denied 465 U.S. 1052, 104 S.Ct. 1326, 79 L.Ed.2d 722 (1984); but see *Mobil Corp. v. Marathon Oil Co.*, 669 F.2d 366 (6th Cir. 1981) The cases are all federal in nature and were not decided on state law grounds.

creditors to whom the board owed no further duty under the circumstances. Thus, when a board ends an intense bidding contest on an insubstantial basis, and where a significant by-product of that action is to protect the directors against a perceived threat of personal liability for consequences stemming from the adoption of previous defensive measures, the action cannot withstand the enhanced scrutiny which *Unocal* requires of director conduct. See *Unocal*, 493 A.2d at 954-55.

In addition to the lock-up option, the Court of Chancery enjoined the no-shop provision as part of the attempt to foreclose further bidding by Pantry Pride. *MacAndrews & Forbes Holdings, Inc. v. Revlon, Inc.*, 501 A.2d at 1251. The no-shop provision, like the lock-up option, while not *per se* illegal, is impermissible under the *Unocal* standards when a board's primary duty becomes that of an auctioneer responsible for selling the company to the highest bidder. The agreement to negotiate only with Forstmann ended rather than intensified the board's involvement in the bidding contest.

It is ironic that the parties even considered a no-shop agreement when Revlon had dealt preferentially, and almost exclusively, with Forstmann throughout the contest. After the directors authorized management to negotiate with other parties, Forstmann was given every negotiating advantage that Pantry Pride had been denied: cooperation from management, access to financial data, and the exclusive opportunity to present merger proposals directly to the board of directors. Favoritism for a white knight to the total exclusion of a hostile bidder might be justifiable when the latter's offer adversely affects shareholder interests, but when bidders make relatively similar offers, or dissolution of the company becomes inevitable, the directors cannot fulfil their enhanced *Unocal* duties by playing favorites with the contending factions. Market forces must be allowed to operate freely to bring the target's shareholders the best price available for their equity.[16] Thus, as the trial court ruled, the shareholders' interests necessitated that the board remain free to negotiate in the fulfilment of that duty.

The court below similarly enjoined the payment of the cancellation fee, pending a resolution of the merits, because the fee was part of the overall plan to thwart Pantry Pride's efforts. We find no abuse of discretion in that ruling.

IV.

Having concluded that Pantry Pride has shown a reasonable probability of success on the merits, we address the issue of irreparable harm. The Court of Chancery ruled that unless the lock-up and other aspects of the agreement were enjoined, Pantry Pride's opportunity to bid for Revlon was lost. The court also held that the need for both bidders to compete in the marketplace outweighed any injury to Forstmann. Given the complexity of the proposed transaction between Revlon and Forstmann, the obstacles to Pantry Pride obtaining a meaningful legal remedy are immense. We are satisfied that the plaintiff has shown the need for an injunction to protect it from irreparable harm, which need outweighs any harm to the defendants.

---

16 By this we do not embrace the "passivity" thesis rejected in *Unocal*. See 493 A.2d at 954-55, nn. 8-10. The directors' role remains an active one, changed only in the respect that they are charged with the duty of selling the company at the highest price attainable for the stockholders' benefit.

V.

In conclusion, the Revlon board was confronted with a situation not uncommon in the current wave of corporate takeovers. A hostile and determined bidder sought the company at a price the board was convinced was inadequate. The initial defensive tactics worked to the benefit of the shareholders, and thus the board was able to sustain its *Unocal* burdens in justifying those measures. However, in granting an asset option lock-up to Forstmann, we must conclude that under all the circumstances the directors allowed considerations other than the maximization of shareholder profit to affect their judgment, and followed a course that ended the auction for Revlon, absent court intervention, to the ultimate detriment of its shareholders. No such defensive measure can be sustained when it represents a breach of the directors' fundamental duty of care. See *Smith v. Van Gorkom*, Del.Supr., 488 A.2d 858, 874 (1985). In that context the board's action is not entitled to the deference accorded it by the business judgment rule. The measures were properly enjoined. The decision of the Court of Chancery, therefore, is

Affirmed.

NOTES

1) In *Unocal*, the Court suggested that it was open to a board of directors seeking to abide by the proportionality test to consider the interests of constituencies other than shareholders. However, in *Revlon* the Court suggests that such consideration must end once it becomes clear that the break-up of the company is inevitable. Do you think that this is a necessary conclusion? Why should a board not be entitled to consider which among several offers for a company will most likely ensure that the company is able to look after the interests of creditors and employees in addition to those of shareholders? While target company shareholders will naturally wish to accept whatever bid offers them the most money for their shares, once in the *Revlon* auction mode should a target's board be entitled to consider whether that bid may lead to the demise of the corporation?

2) In your view, do the *Unocal* and *Revlon* decisions rely on the same vision of the firm? Is the decision in *Revlon* internally consistent in its vision of the corporation?

3) How would you advise a Canadian board of directors faced with the issues seen in *Revlon*? What impact would the presence of the oppression remedy, with its explicit reference to the interests of creditors, have on your application of *Revlon* to a Canadian company?

4) A lockup is an option given by a target to one of its allies to purchase part of the target's assets at a bargain price. Lockups may also refer to options to purchase shares from the target at a price that is usually equal to the price offered by the take-over bidder. Asset lockups as in *Revlon* and *Hanson Trust* are, however, regarded as more effective than stock lockups.

Four devices adopted by Revlon management were thought objectionable by the Court. First, Forstmann received an option to purchase Revlon's Vision Care and National Health Laboratories divisions for $525 million, about $100-175 million below the value ascribed to them by Revlon's investment bankers, Lazard Freres. Second, the Court thought it "significant" that Revlon disclosed confidential information to Forstmann. Third, Revlon agreed not to solicit further competing bidders through a "no shop" undertaking. Finally, the Court objected to the cancellation fee to Forstmann. If the first tactic was a "show-stopper," might the other three have been upheld under *Thompson v. Enstar Corp.* as necessary to draw a competing bidder into the auction?

The Court found that management's assertion of policy differences was no longer creditable after it contemplated a break-up merger in a management buyout. In fact, a break-up of Revlon would appear to have served efficiency goals, since all parties believed that firm value would be increased through divestiture. Was management's initial claim that it opposed that Pantry Pride offer in order to keep assets intact one which contemplated a "rationally related benefit accruing to the stockholders"?

Revlon appears to provide some content to the *Unocal* requirement that the defensive tactics be reasonable in relation to the threat posed, tilting the playing field back toward the offeror. Are these reinforced duties, however, restricted to cases where target management competes with the offeror through a proposed break-up merger? More broadly, if defensive tactics are justified on auction theories, should managerial passivity be mandated whenever an auction has commenced?

The *Revlon* case was distinguished by the Delaware Court of Chancery where a lockup was given not to vest control in the purchaser but to keep the target independent. *Ivanhoe Partners v. Newmont Mining Corp.*, Fed. Sec. L. Rep. para. 93, 503 (1987) [Current Binder]. Ivanhoe commenced a hostile tender offer against Newmont, which responded with (1) a $33 dividend, and (2) a proposed "street sweep," or private or open market purchases of stock, which are not within the scope of the definition of a tender offer under U.S. take-over bid legislation. The street sweep was to be accomplished not by Newmont but by its largest shareholder, Gold Fields, whose holdings in the target would then increase from 26 to 49.9%. Gold Fields did not seek control of Newmont, and in fact entered into a "standstill" agreement the day before the street sweep in which it promised not to increase its Newmont holdings beyond 49.9%. The Court found that it could not say that Newmont management "were motivated by an overriding subjective intent to entrench themselves." Moreover, the *Revlon* decision was inapposite, since its duties arose only "when circumstances make it inevitable that the company will be sold to one of the bidders competing to acquire it." That was not the case in *Newmont Mining*, since its directors sought instead to keep it independent through the standstill agreement. Newmont was also found to have satisfied the two-part *Unocal* test. First, the Newmont board reasonably believed that Ivanhoe's offer represented a threat to corporate policy and effectiveness, since (1) the offer was two-tiered, and (2) Newmont's strategy was planned by an independent directors' committee with independent legal and financial advice. As for the second part of the *Unocal* test, the Newmont tactics were reasonable in relation to the threat posed, since (1) minority shareholders were given a benefit in the form of the dividend and possibly better management, and (2) the street sweep was in part a response to Gold Fields' independent desire to ensure the defeat of the Ivanhoe offer.

"Just Say No." One of the most difficult issues that a board of directors and its advisers may have to consider in the face of a hostile take-over bid is when, if ever, it will be open to that board to refuse altogether to entertain the bid. While many targets will initially respond to a hostile bid by asserting that the bid is inadequate and that in any event the target is not for sale, as *Revlon* makes clear the critical question is whether there comes a point past which a board is no longer entitled to adopt this position. The following case has generated considerable debate with respect to this very issue.

Paramount Communications, Inc. v. Time, Inc.
Court of Chancery, Delaware
1989 Federal Securities Law Reporter 94, 514

Opinion of ALLEN, Chancellor: Pending are motions in several related lawsuits seeking, principally, a preliminary injunction restraining Time Incorporated from buying stock under a June 16, 1989, offer to purchase 100 million shares of common stock (comprising 51% of the outstanding common stock) of Warner Communications Inc. at $70 per share cash. That offer may close no earlier than July 17, 1989. The only condition to that closing is the submission of tenders of at least 100 million of Warner's outstanding shares. The offer contains no financing condition and in all events the $10.4 billion necessary to finance the purchase and related re-financings has been obtained. See Britt Aff., ¶¶ 2, 3. The motion does not seek to require Time to dismantle its "poison pill" takeover defense or to take other action sought in the complaints.[1]

Plaintiffs in these lawsuits include Paramount Communications Inc. and its KDS Acquisition Corp. subsidiary, which is itself currently extending an offer to purchase up to all shares of Time at $200 per share; various holders of modest amounts of Time common stock, who purport to represent Time shareholders as a class; and several very substantial Time shareholders who sue on their own behalf. Defendants are Time Incorporated, all 12 of its current and three recently resigned directors, as well as Warner Communications Inc.

On this motion, the court is required to express an opinion on the question whether the directors of Time, who plainly have been granted the legal power to complete a public tender offer transaction that would be the first stage in accomplishing a thoughtfully planned consolidation of the business of Time with that of Warner Communications, have a supervening fiduciary obligation to desist from doing so in order that it be made more likely that the shareholders of Time will be afforded an opportunity to accept the public tender offer for all shares extended by Paramount's KDS subsidiary. The record in this case indicates—and the information before the

---

[1]   In their complaints, plaintiffs seek, among other relief, to require the board to excuse a follow-up merger between Time and any Paramount affiliate from certain voting requirements of the Time certificate of incorporation and of Section 203 of the Delaware General Corporation Law; to require the board to redeem the company's preferred stock purchase rights that impede the closing of any offer; and to rescind a certain Share Exchange Agreement between Time and Warner, which is touched upon below.

Time board on June 16 when it made the critical decision to reject the transaction offered by Paramount indicated as well—that it is very unlikely that the market price of Time stock immediately following consummation of the now planned two-stage Warner transaction will equal the initial $175 price offered by Paramount.

It is the gist of plaintiff's position in the various lawsuits now before this court that Time's board of directors does have such a supervening fiduciary duty and has failed to understand or, more accurately, has chosen to ignore that fact, in order to force the Warner transaction upon the corporation and its shareholders—a transaction that, plaintiffs assert, the shareholders would not approve, if given the opportunity to vote on the matter. The board of Time is doing this, it is urged, not for any legitimate reason, but because it prefers that transaction which secures and entrenches the power of those in whose hands management of the corporation has been placed.

It is the gist of the position of the directors of Time that they have no fiduciary duty to desist from accomplishing the transaction in question in these circumstances. They contend, quite broadly speaking, that their duty is to exercise their judgment prudently (i.e., deliberately, in an informed manner) in the good faith pursuit of legitimate corporate goals. This, they say, the record shows they have done. Moreover, they assert that the result of that judgment is a proposed transaction of extraordinary benefit and promise to Time and its shareholders. It is quite reasonable, they contend, for the board to prefer it, on behalf of the corporation and its shareholders, to the sale of the company presently for $200 per share cash, which sale is plainly inconsistent with accomplishment of the proposed Warner transaction. In short, the directors say the question whether the Warner transaction in its current form should be pursued or not in the corporation's interest is for them to decide, not the shareholders; that they have addressed it deliberately and in good faith; and that while some shareholders, even a majority of shareholders, may disagree with the wisdom of their choice, that fact provides no reason for this court to force them, under the guise of a fiduciary obligation, to take another, more popular course of action.

These same points are made by Warner, which is also a defendant. In addition, Warner asserts its own rights under the contracts in question. It said there is no evidence that it has acted other than as an arm's-length negotiator; that it has now changed its position (in part by the public announcement of the merger agreement and in part in entering into contracts with others in reliance upon the merger agreement); and entry of any injunctive relief at this point would disregard its rights and cause it irreparable injury.

Before attempting to define the legal issues raised by these motions, it is appropriate to turn to a statement of the facts as they appear at this time. While these actions have been actively litigated for only a matter of weeks, the record developed through discovery and by affidavit is very extensive. The following facts, from my review of that record, appear to be in many respects uncontested (even if the legal consequence of those facts is ardently contested), and in other respects the subject of dispute. Insofar as there is dispute with respect to a relevant fact, I will assume the fact in favour of the moving party if it appears after evaluating all of the evidence in the record that there is a reasonable likelihood that on final hearing that fact will be so established by a preponderance of the evidence.

I.

A. *Time Incorporated and the composition of its board of directors*

Time Incorporated is a Delaware corporation with its principal offices in New York City. Time's businesses will fall into four broad segments: its traditional business of the publication of magazines, most notably *Time* magazine but also including *People, Fortune, Sports Illustrated* and numerous others; the publication of books, including The-Book-of-the-Month Club, Little, Brown & Co., Time Life Books and others; the production of pay television programming through its Home Box Office, Inc. and Cinemax subsidiaries; and the ownership and operation of cable television franchises through its American Television and Communication Corporation subsidiary. For the year ending December 31, 1988, Time had gross revenues of $4.5 billion and reported net income of approximately $289 million.

Time's capital stock consists of 200 million authorized shares of common stock and 25 million shares of preferred stock. As of May 1, 1989, 56,977,150 shares of common stock were issued and outstanding and no preferred stock was issued and outstanding.

• • •

B. *The genesis of the March 3, 1989 Time-Warner merger agreement*

1. Strategic planning and management's commitment to maintaining Time as an independent enterprise

Over the years, Time's business appears to have evolved from one completely dominated by its publishing activities to one in which to an increasingly important degree, video supplies the medium in which its products reach consumers. Simultaneously, the firm has tended to reinterpret its mission from one of supplying information to a relatively educated market segment to one in which entertainment of a mass audience plays an important role.[3] Time was, of course, founded as a journalistic enterprise. That meant most importantly that its writers created the material that it offered for sale. Publishing continues to be vitally important to it.[4] As Time has in this decade become importantly dependent upon video media for its income and growth, however, it has recognized a need to create for itself and thus own the video or film products that it delivers through its cable network (HBO) and cable franchises. To fail to develop this capacity would, it was apparently feared, leave the firm at the mercy of others (both as to quality and to price) with respect to the element most critical to success in the video entertainment business. Thus, for some time, management of the corporation has reviewed ways in which the firm might address this need. See, e.g., Bere Aff., ¶ 7.

Another large-scale consideration that has played a role in the strategic thinking of Time's management and its outside directors (see, e.g., Perkins Dep., ¶ 6; Horner Aff.,

---

3   It was this evolution that disheartened director Temple. ...

4   Time's magazines earn about 20% of the revenues generated in the United States magazine industry and more than a third of the profits. McManus Aff., ¶¶ 14, 21; Munro Dept. at 201; Nicholas Dep. at 148-49.

¶¶ 6, 10-11) is the emergence of a deeply interrelated global economy. Recognition of this fact coupled with the objective of creating a stronger, more dominant company led management and the company's outside directors to perceive the expansion of Time into international markets in a more substantial way, as an important long-term goal for the company. See, e.g., Levin Dep. at 36, 99; Finkelstein Dep. at 155; Munro Dep. at 220; Opel Dep. at 65.

Neither the goal of establishing a vertically integrated entertainment organization, nor the goal of becoming a more global enterprise, was a transcendent aim of Time management or its board. More important to both, apparently, has been a desire to maintain an independent Time Incorporated that reflected a continuation of what management and the board regarded as distinctive and important "Time culture." This culture appears in part to be pride in the history of the firm—notably *Time* Magazine and its role in American life—and in part a managerial philosophy and distinctive structure that is intended to protect journalistic integrity from pressures from the business side of the enterprise. See, e.g., Perkins Aff., ¶¶ 13-17; Temple Dep. at 116; Nicholas Dep. at 149; Dingman Dep. at 16-18; Hill Dep. at 24-25.

I note parenthetically that plaintiffs in this suit dismiss this claim of "culture" as being nothing more than a desire to perpetuate or entrench existing management disguised in a pompous, highfalutin claim. I understand the argument and recognize the risk of cheap deception that would be entailed in a broad and indiscriminate recognition of "corporate culture" as a valid interest that would justify a board in taking steps to defeat a non-coercive tender offer. Every reconfiguration of assets, every fundamental threat to the status quo, represents a threat to an existing corporate culture. But I am not persuaded that there may not be instances in which the law might recognize as valid a perceived threat to a "corporate culture" that is shown to be palpable (for lack of a better word), distinctive and advantageous. In any event, for now it is enough to note that the management and the outside board members of Time from early in this process did, in any transaction that might satisfy the perceived need to acquire better access to video production and to global markets, seek to maintain a distinctive Time organization, in part at least in order to maintain a distinctive Time corporate culture. There has never been the slightest subjective interest in selling to or submerging Time into another entity.

2. Anti-takeover protections

Management and the outside board of Time have been concerned for some while that the company have in place certain of the protections against uninvited acquisition attempts. In fact, Time seems to have equipped itself with a full armory of defenses including, among other things, a staggered board, restriction on shareholder action by consent or to call a meeting, rather long (50-day) notice of shareholder motions at meetings, and a poison pill preferred stock rights plan, which was recently (1988) amended to reduce its trigger to acquisition of a 15% stake in the company.

3. Exploration of possible opportunities to meet strategic goals

Time's management appears to have been alert to opportunities to meet the goal of providing the corporation with a video production capacity. In the spring of 1987, senior management (i.e., Messrs. Munro, Nicholas and Levin) advised members of the board (e.g., Perkins Aff., ¶ 7; Horner Aff., ¶¶ 5, 6; Grum Aff., ¶ 5) that, upon the initiative of Steven Ross, chief executive officer of Warner (Ross Dep. at 8-9), management was pursuing conversations with Warner in order to explore the mutual advantages of a joint venture involving at least each company's cable television franchises and perhaps HBO and Warner Brothers Studios. The outside directors were encouraging, with the exception of Mr. Temple. Warner was seen as a firm that might provide both an outstanding video or film production capacity and talent, and a substantial and effective international marketing relationship and organization. E.g., Perkins Aff., ¶¶ 7-8; Horner Aff., ¶ 6.

•   •   •

[After reviewing events from July 1988 to March, 1989 (which included lengthy and detailed negotiations between Time and Warner) Chancellor Allen continued with a description of the original Time-Warner merger agreement.]

D. The initial Time-Warner merger agreement

On March 3, 1989, the boards of both companies authorized entering into the merger agreement, which was done also on that day. Both corporations have a majority of outside directors. Both approved the transaction after receiving investment banking and legal advice. There were no dissenting votes. There is nothing in the large record that has been created, of which I am aware, that would support a charge that the March 3 agreement was other than an arm's-length negotiated agreement between two parties seeking individual advantage through mutual action.

As a technical matter, the merger agreement contemplated the merger of Warner into a wholly-owned Time subsidiary (TW Sub Inc.) with Warner as the surviving corporation. The common stock of Warner would be converted into common stock of Time Incorporated at the agreed upon ratio. The name of Time would then be changed to Time-Warner. In such circumstances, the Delaware General Corporation Law requires for the effectuation of a merger an affirmative vote of a majority of the shareholders of Warner (since its stock is being converted into something else in the merger), but does not require a vote of the shareholders of Time (since its stock will remain unaffected by the merger and the issuance of additional shares did not require amendment of Time's certificate of incorporation). See 8 Del. C. § 251. The merger agreement, however, contemplated a stockholder vote by both corporations since under New York Stock Exchange rules, issuance of the number of Time shares contemplated required such a vote.

E. Steps to protect the merger

1. The Share Exchange Agreement

At the same time that they authorized entering into the merger agreement, each board authorized execution of a Share Exchange Agreement. This agreement gave each party the option to trigger an exchange of shares in which event, if triggered, Warner would acquire 7,080,016 shares (11.1%) of Time, and Time would acquire 17,292,747 shares (9.4%) of Warner's outstanding stock. These blocks of stock would have had approximately equal value if calculated on average closing prices of Time and Warner stock for the five business days preceding the announcement of the merger. Aboodi Dep. at 210-11. This agreement is said to have served several purposes including giving each party an investment in the other should the merger fail to be completed for any reason. For present purposes, I assume its principal purpose was to discourage any effort to upset the transaction. See Munro Exh. 19 at A001649, A001676; Temple Dep. at 45-46; Finkelstein Dep. at 92, 141-42.

Parenthetically, I note that earlier in this litigation and promptly upon announcing its initial $175 offer, Paramount sought a restraining order with respect to the Share Exchange Agreement on the theory that it was an impermissible impediment to achieving the best available transaction for the shareholders. The premise of the motion—that the signing of the merger agreement put the corporation in a "Revlon mode" in which there was an obligation to justify transactions that might impede effectuation of an offer to acquire control of the corporation—was contested. Without addressing that question, the application was denied on the basis that, as both parties to the agreement were before the court, effective relief could be fashioned at a later stage if that appeared warranted.

Thereafter, Warner did trigger the Share Exchange Agreement and that exchange has now occurred.

2. Restriction on information and "dry-up" agreements

Everyone involved in this negotiation realized that the transaction contemplated might be perceived as putting Time and Warner "in play." Realizing that the corporation might be deemed "in play," management sought and paid for commitments from various banks that they would not finance an attempt to take over Time. See, e.g., Munro Exh. 19 at A001676-77. In this litigation they are cited by plaintiffs as wrongful attempts by the "target" corporation to interfere with the ability of an offeror to present the shareholders with the best available price. In all events, these "dry up" fees appear to be a dubious, futile innovation at this point when the global economy seems awash in cash available to finance takeovers.

An additional attempt to secure the closing of the merger may be reflected in a provision of the merger agreement that severely limits the ability of Time to enter into any takeover negotiations prior to the closing of the merger. "Time may not solicit or encourage or take any other action to facilitate any inquiries on the making of any proposal which constitutes or may ... lead to, any takeover proposal." Ross Exh. 10 at 16-17. The only exception to such provision would occur if a hostile tender offer for 25% or more of Time's stock is announced (or 10% of its stock is purchased), at which time Time may, after consultation with Warner, communicate with the offeror (or stockholder). In all events, such an occurrence would not excuse Time's performance under the merger agreement, but would give Warner an out.

F. Paramount announces a $175 cash offer on June 7

The Time board had fixed June 23 as the date for the annual shareholders meeting of the company at which the Time-Warner merger was to be presented for shareholder approval. On June 7, Paramount announced that it was extending an offer to purchase all of the outstanding common stock of Time at $175 per share cash. While the step had been under consideration from mid-March, the announcement was timed to await the distribution of proxy materials for the June 23 meeting so that Time would be publicly committed to a shareholder vote on the merger agreement. Hope Dep. at 202; Pattison Dep. at 93.

Paramount's offer was subject to a number of conditions, the most pertinent of which were the following:

1. termination of the Time-Warner merger agreement (or the agreement being left subject to a vote in which Paramount controlled 51% of the vote);
2. termination or invalidation of the Share Exchange Agreement under circumstances in which there would be no liability to Time;
3. Paramount to be satisfied in its sole discretion that all material approvals, consents and franchise transfers relating to Time's programming and cable television business had been obtained on terms satisfactory to Paramount;
4. removal of a number of Time-created or Time-controlled impediments to closing of the offer (e.g., redemption of a "poison pill" preferred rights purchase plan) or effectuation of a second-stage merger (e.g., supermajority voting requirements of 8 Del. C. § 203 and supermajority voting provisions of Time's certificate of incorporation); and
5. financing and majority acceptance of the offer.

G. Market reaction to the Paramount offer

The Time-Warner merger had been warmly received. The stock for both companies rose on the market, although perhaps that only reflected that both began to receive attention from arbitrageurs. In any event, Time stock which had been traded in a $103 5/8–$113 3/4 range in February, rose to $105–$122 5/8 in March and April; Warner stock, which had been trading in a range of $38 7/8–$43 3/4 in February, prior to the announcement of the merger agreement, traded in a $42 7/8–$50 1/2 range in March and April.

The prospect of immediate $175 cash payment, however, excited the market even more. Following the announcement of the Paramount offer, Time stock jumped 44 points in one day to $170; it hit a high of $182 3/4 on June 13 whence it relaxed to close at $146 1/4 on the day of presentation of this motion.

A lot of stock changed hands after the Paramount offer. Average daily trading volume for Time over recent months has been as follows: 139,953 in February; 490,109 in March; 317,660 in April; 24,600 in May; and 1,679,977 in June.

H. Time and Warner react to the demand to terminate their negotiated contract

Time's management immediately responded to Paramount's announcement, aggressively sending to Mr. Davis of Paramount a biting letter attacking his "integrity and motives" and calling the offer "smoke and mirrors." Munro Exh. 21 at 2. Mr. Munro, who never considered exploring what Paramount might be willing to do on a negotiated basis, stated "[w]e had made a deal with Warner that we were planning to conclude and … we were not for sale." Munro Dep. at 126. Management also appears to have sought to cause delay in the process that Paramount would engage in to secure necessary governmental approvals for the transfer of cable franchises.

Time's board met on June 7, June 11, June 15 and June 16 to consider the $175 offer. No one suggested talking to Paramount. Nicholas Dep. at 160-61; Opel Dep. at 215-18 ("[t]here was no purpose to meet with Mr. Davis to discuss anything"); Dingman Dep. at 140-41 ("[w]e were under a commitment to do a deal with Warner"). Director Finkelstein reports that as a result of the June 8 board meeting:

... the board members had each individually thought that one, the Paramount deal was so insufficient and that the Warner deal, if it could be put on track, was so much more attractive, that it made no sense to deal with Paramount at all.

Finkelstein Dep. at 131-32. See also id. at 133.

The board resolved on June 16 after further negotiations with Warner to reject the implicit demands of Paramount and to recast the Warner transaction in a form (a cash acquisition of a majority stake in Warner to be followed by a merger for cash or securities, or a combination of both) that would not require shareholder approval, which now, of course, was problematic.

While plaintiffs in these lawsuits interpret these actions as those of directors determined to ignore shareholder rights and interests in the pursuit of a transaction that assures them continued access to the salaries and prerequisites of a powerful corporation, the Time board purports to have been motivated on June 16 chiefly by two considerations: (1) a reasonable belief that the $175 per share offer was inadequate if Time were to be sold, and (2) a reasonable belief that if Time were not to be sold, which was the board's determination, then Warner was a far more appealing partner with whom to have ongoing business consolidation than was Paramount.

• • •

With the determination to decline Paramount's invitation to negotiate the sale of Time and to continue to pursue the Warner transactions, the directors faced the fact that it was problematic whether the Time shareholders would share the board's express view that $175 cash now should be rejected in order to afford the company's management some additional years to manage the trading value of Time shares to levels materially higher than the future value of $175 now. The annual meeting had been set for June 23. Time's shares are held largely by institutional investors. While some of these investors could be expected to continue, despite the emergence of a cash option, to support what had been widely supported as a fine transaction,[9] it is reasonable to suppose that most

---

9   For example a money manager who serves as a senior vice president of a firm in a fiduciary capacity owns approximately 7% of Time's common stock, 7% of Warner's common stock and just under 5% of Paramount's common stock, and who himself specializes in research in the entertainment and media industries, has submitted the expert opinion (his own, not as a representative of his firm) that for an investor with a long-term investment horizon (undefined by him) "the proposed Time-Warner combination is superior for Time shareholders ... to the currently outstanding Paramount [$200 per share cash] offer." See Crawford Aff., ¶¶ 1-3.

such money managers would be tempted by the cash now. While the record here contains testimony about a possible concern about confusion or deception of shareholders as part of the reason that the board elected to abandon the merger form of transaction and pursue a cash offer, I will decide this motion not on the understanding that the board was reacting to a threat of confusion (arising, for example, from alleged misperception about how quickly a Paramount offer could or would close), but on the understanding that it sought to avoid the risk that the merger would not get an affirmative vote even if there were not confusion.

Thus, the "return" to a cash acquisition format must be seen as a reaction of the effect that emergence of the Paramount offer could be expected to have on the shareholder vote. While in this litigation Time seeks to avoid or obscure that point, the point seems evident and, in fact, has been admitted by Time in its Schedule 14D-9 filing:

In response to the serious threat posed by the PCI Offer to Time's effectiveness in furthering such strategic objectives and corporate policies, including its ability to consummate the Original Merger, the Board of Directors determined to modify the terms of the Original Merger as described in Item 7 below.

There had been sentiment on Time's part for a cash acquisition originally, even though the stock for stock deal was trumpeted by Time management as outstanding because it did not follow the trend towards greater leverage. The higher leverage that a cash acquisition implied might be expected to boost the value of Time's equity, so long as the debt could be effectively managed. With respect to an appropriate price for Warner in a cash deal, the investment bankers advised that a $70 cash price would be fair from Time's point of view. Warner had been trading at around $45 prior to the announcement of the merger so the price represented about a 56% premium. Because of the increased leverage that would be involved, Shearson-Lehman advised the board that immediately following completion of the tender offer merger transaction, Time's stock could be expected to trade at a price higher than that expected if the original merger transaction were to be completed. See Rossoff Aff., ¶ 12.

The revamped transaction was negotiated at arm's-length. Warner sought a control premium, of course. It sought assurances that certain of the "governance" provisions, principally those dealing with the co-CEO concept and evenly divided board representation that had made the original merger agreement acceptable to its board would remain. It negotiated tight commitments that would assure that if it were to in effect announce it was for sale by accepting the restructured deal, the deal would close unless enjoined. See Greenough Aff., ¶¶ 10, 11; Ross Dep. at 179; Nicholas Dep. at 213. Specifically, the agreement provided no condition to Time's obligation to buy Warner stock under the offer if the minimum number of shares were tendered.

Effectuation of the reformatted transaction would accomplish the basic purposes of the initial merger transaction, from Time's point of view. It would afford the company a video production capacity of recognized talent, it would extend the company into global markets in a substantial way, and it would continue the Time identity and the Time "corporate culture" (i.e., in this instance, it would assure that Mr. Nicholas ultimately will serve as the CEO of the enterprise). The revised transaction will be significantly different in some respects, however. Now, at the conclusion of the transaction, Time's balance sheet will have at least $7 billion of new debt and may have $10 billion or more of new debt,[10] and will have reduced ability to support substantial additional borrowing.[11] Secondly, under the revised merger reported earnings of the new entity are expected to be essentially eliminated by the necessity to amortize approximately $9 million of goodwill as a result of the purchase method of accounting for the revised merger. Thirdly, the revised deal pays a large control premium to Warner shareholders whereas the earlier transaction paid them a premium of approximately 12%.

At meetings on June 15 and 16, Warner's board approved the restructured proposal. That same day, Warner caused the exchange of shares contemplated by the Share Exchange Agreement to be triggered.

I. Paramount's $200 offer and Time's rejection of it on June 26

On June 23, Paramount, not having been able to induce Time to engage in negotiations, unilaterally increased the cash price of its offer to $200. That subject was addressed at a June 26 meeting of the Time board. The factors that had earlier led to the decision not to pursue a sale transaction with Paramount apparently continued to dominate the board's thinking. The increase in price did not overcome the factors earlier relied upon: the continued possibility of delay, the presence of possible Paramount outs in the cable franchise approval process and the comparison of the new price with the ranges of sale values earlier discussed. In addition, Time had, as of June 16, entered into an agreement that the board felt was legally binding to complete the Warner transaction. Abandonment of that transaction was a condition of the $200 offer and the Time board had not negotiated a contract right to abandon its offer in the event that Paramount or another potential acquiror might condition an all cash, all shares offer on such abandonment. The record is uncontradicted at this stage that Warner would not have agreed to such a provision. It is equally plain that Time did not seek it.[12]

. . .

---

10 Consideration in the second-stage merger, it now seems, will be half equity. See Waters Aff., ¶ 3.

11 Compare Waters Aff., ¶ 5 (company "tapped out") with Saegal Aff., ¶¶ 2, 3 (not so). In all events, the balance sheet of an ongoing enterprise is never in a final condition. If the merged entity is the success that is proponents believe it will be, Time-Warner could replace this debt with equity through a new offering and move towards the balance sheet originally envisioned—without, however, the income statement advantages of pooling of interest accounting treatment.

12 Time airily (Answering Brief, p. 114) dismisses Paramount's complaint that the board ought to have tried—its duty in these circumstances required it to try—to maintain flexibility. "What offeror has included a fiduciary out?" Time's counsel asks. It is, of course, the case that circumstances have rarely if ever arisen in which an offeror need concern itself with likely changes in circumstances affecting its shareholders prior to the proposed closing of its offer. But that general condition provides no answer to the specifics here, which may be answered more substantively by reference to Warner's negotiation position.

II.

The legal test for the issuance of a preliminary injunction has essentially three parts. First, those seeking the relief must establish a reasonable likelihood of success on the merits of their claims. Second, it must be established that failure to grant the relief sought will result in injury to plaintiffs that will not be remediable by later injunctive relief or compensable by an award of damages. Lastly, the court must evaluate the chance that the defendants (or other persons) will be injured by the granting of the improvident relief sought and whether any injury of that kind could itself be remedied later. Thus, the court must weigh and balance all of the equities. See, e.g., *Ivanhoe Partners v. Newmont Mining*, Del. Supr. 535 A.2d 1334 (1987); *Shields v. Shields*, Del. Ch., 498 A.2d 161 (1985).

Before turning to an analysis of the merits of plaintiff's complaint, I pause to make one observation that should be apparent. It is not part of the function of the court to evaluate whether the Time-Warner deal is a good deal for Time shareholders or a poor one. The Time shareholders complain, feeling that under the revised merger Warner shareholders get all of the premium and they get little—except a promise that Mr. Nicholas will someday guide their company, and knowledge that they may be foreclosed from a comparable premium from Paramount. Plaintiffs find this to be cold comfort. Determination of the legal issues, however, does not require this court to try to evaluate, in light of the evidence, whether Mr. Ross and his negotiator, Mr. Aboodi, out-negotiated Time's Mr. Levin and Mr. Nicholas in this transaction.

III.

On June 16, the board of directors of Time, upon what would appear competent advice, resolved that it would commit the corporation to the revised Warner transaction. It then implemented its decision in a way intended to assure that no future event would upset achievement of the goal embraced. I am convinced that in doing so, the board understood that it was foreclosing for the present, as a practical matter, the option for Time shareholders to realize $175 cash for their shares—indeed it understood that $175 could be realized from Mr. Davis and perhaps substantially more from him or others—and, more significantly, the board understood that immediately following the effectuation of a Warner merger, the stock market price of Time stock was likely to be materially lower than the $175 then "on the table," perhaps $150, but more likely, within the wide range of $106-$188 (see p. 32, supra).

The board explains its choice—for despite the long negotiations and the agreements with Warner, it was free to let the Warner transaction go to the shareholders, and thus on June 16 it was free to choose—by reference to the view that the long-term value of a Time-Warner combination would be superior not only to the premium $175 presently available to the shareholders, but to any current sale price in the ranges it had been told could be achieved. See, e.g., Finkelstein Dep., supra at 182-84. This is the heart of the matter: the board chose less current value in the hope (assuming that good faith existed, and the record contains no evidence to support a supposition that it does not) that greater value would make that implicit sacrifice beneficial in the future.

That decision raises many subsidiary, but two overarching questions: First, does it make any sense, given what we understand or think we understand about markets, to posit the existence of a distinction between managing for current value maximization and managing for longer-term value creation—a distinction which implies, unless I am wrong, that current stock market values fail to reflect "accurately" achievable future value? The second overarching question raised by the decision of June 16 is this: who, under the evolving law of fiduciary obligations is, or should be, the agency for making such a choice in circumstances of the sort presented here—the board or the shareholders? The legal analysis that follows addresses this second overarching question in terms of two related sets of doctrines.

A.

The legal analysis that follows treats the distinction that the Time board implicitly drew between current share value maximization and long-term share value maximization. For some, this is a false distinction. "The lawyers may talk about a premium for control. But to a true believer of efficient markets, there cannot be a premium for control."[13] Therefore, before turning to the legal analysis that does employ that distinction, I pause to address in some brief way the notion that the distinction between any long-term and short-term stock value, at least where there is a large, active, informed market for the shares of the company, is an error; that the nature of such markets is precisely to discount to a current value the future financial prospects of the firm; and that markets with their numberless participants seeking information and making judgments do this correctly (at least in the limited sense that no one without inside information can regularly do it better).[14]

This view may be correct. It may be that in a well-developed stock market, there is no discount for long-term profit maximizing behaviour except that reflected in the discount for the time value of money. It may be the case that when the market valued the stock of Time at about $125 per share following the announcement of the merger, an observer blessed with perfect foresight would have concurred in that value now of the future stream of all returns foreseen into eternity. Perhaps wise social policy and sound business decisions ought to be premised upon the assumptions that underlie that view.

---

13 The statement is Professor Martin Shubik's, the Seymour H. Knox Professor of Mathematical Institutional Economics at Yale. Professor Shubik apparently is not a true believer in efficient markets. He goes on to suggest:

> If, in contradistinction to the adherents of the single, efficient market, we suggest that there are several more or less imperfect markets involving the market for a few shares, the market for control, the market for going-business assets, and the market for assets in liquidation, then we have a structure for interpreting what is going on in terms of arbitage among these different markets.

Shubik, "Corporate Control, Efficient Markets, and the Public Good," Knights, Raiders & Targets: The Impact of the Hostile Takeover (Coffee, Lowenstein and Rose-Ackerman eds 1988).

14 See e.g., Gordon & Kornhauser, "Efficient Markets, Costly Information and Securities Research." 60 N.Y.U.L. Rev. 761 (1985).

But just as the Constitution does not enshrine Mr. Herbert Spencer's social statics, neither does the common law of directors' duties elevate the theory of a single, efficient capital market to the dignity of a sacred text.

Directors may operate on the theory that the stock market valuation is "wrong" in some sense, without breaching faith with shareholders. No one, after all, has access to more information concerning the corporation's present and future condition. It is far from irrational and certainly not suspect for directors to believe that a likely immediate market valuation of the Time-Warner merger will undervalue the stock. The record in this case refers to instances in which directors did function on a theory that they understood better than the public market for the firm's shares what the value of their firm was, and were shown by events to be correct:

> The Walt Disney Company case is an example of an entertainment company that rejected a $72.50 hostile offer in June 1984 and is now trading at the equivalent of $380 per 1984 share. Another example of an entertainment company that achieved better results by remaining independent and growing than by cashing in when it was undervalued in the market is Warner itself. In early 1984, Warner was the subject of unsolicited interest on the part of Rupert Murdoch. At that time Warner was selling for $10 to $12 a share, adjusted for a subsequent two-for-one split. Today, of course—five and a half years later—Warner is the subject of a $70 per share merger agreement with Time and was selling at $45 (or about four times its early 1984 price) before its merger with Time was announced.

Crawford Aff., ¶ 4.

On the level of legal doctrine, it is clear that under Delaware law, directors are under no obligation to act so as to maximize the immediate value of the corporation or its shares, except in the special case in which the corporation is in a "Revlon mode." *Mills Acquisition Co. v. Macmillan, Inc.*, Del. Supr. Nos. 415 & 416 (May 3, 1989); *Ivanhoe Partners v. Newmont Mining*, Del. Supr., 535 A.2d 1334 (1987); *Revlon v. MacAndrews & Forbes Holdings, Inc.*, Del. Supr. 506 A.2d 173 (1986). See generally *TW Services Inc. v. SWT Acquisition Corp.*, Del. Ch., C.A. No. 10427 (March 2, 1989). Thus, Delaware law does recognize that directors, when acting deliberately, in an informed way, and in the good faith pursuit of corporate interests, may follow a course designed to achieve long-term value even at the cost of immediate value maximization.[15]

The legally critical question this case presents then involves when must a board shift from its ordinary long-term profit maximizing mode to the radically altered state recognized by the Revlon case in which its duty, broadly stated, is to exercise its power in the good faith pursuit of immediate maximization of share value. Surely, when as in Revlon itself and other cases construing its command, most notably *Macmillan*,[16] the

---

15   It is this recognition that, in part, permits a corporation to make reasonable charitable contributions, to grant scholarships or take other action that will have a direct or immediate positive impact upon the financial performance of the firm.

16   See also *In Re J.P. Stevens & Co., Inc. Shareholders Litigation*, Del. Ch., 542 A.2d 770 (1988); *In Re RJR Nabisco, Inc. Shareholders Litigation*, Del. Ch., Cons., C.A. No. 10389 (January 31, 1989); *In Re*

(The footnote is continued on the next page.)

board decides to enter a change in control transaction, it has elected to enter the Revlon zone. But it now appears resolved that a subjective disinclination to sell the company will not prevent that duty from arising where an extraordinary transaction including, at a minimum, a change in corporate control is involved:

[Revlon's requirements pertain] whether the "sale" takes the form of an active auction, a management buyout, or a "restructuring" such as that which the Court of Chancery enjoined in *Macmillan I.*

Mills Acquisition Co. v. Macmillan, Inc., slip op. at 56.

Thus, more specifically, the first overarching question presented by these facts reduces legally to the inquiry whether the board was, on June 16, involuntarily in that special state—what one can call, as a shorthand, the "Revlon mode"—in which it was required to maximize immediate share value. This question is treated at pp. 54-63 below. If the board was itself under no duty to choose to maximize current value, then the second overarching question must be addressed in terms of the legal questions presented.

B.

The second overarching question is where legally (an easy question) and equitably (more subtle problem) the locus of decision-making power does or should reside in circumstances of this kind. The argument of plaintiffs is that the directors' duty of loyalty to shareholders requires them at such a time to afford to the shareholders the power and opportunity to designate whether the company should now be sold. This position is supported with two distinct legal arguments. First, certain of the plaintiffs argue that the commitment of the original Warner transaction to a shareholder vote gave rise to a fiduciary obligation to permit the shareholders to decide the matter. The reformatting of the deal in order to avoid the risks of shareholder non-approval is thus seen as a breach of duty of loyalty. Principally involved in this analysis are cases dealing with the exercise of the franchise. E.g. *Schnell v. Chris-Craft Industries,* Del. Supr., 285 A.2d (1971); *Frantz Manufacturing Company v. EAC Industries,* Del. Supr., 501 A.2d 401 (1985); *Condec Corporation v. Lunkenheimer Company,* Del. Ch., 230 A.2d 769 (1967); *Aprahamian v. HBO & Co.,* Del. Ch., 531 A.2d 1204 (1987); *Blasius Industries, Inc. v. Atlas Corp.,* Del. Ch., C.A. No. 9720 (July 25, 1988). This argument is treated at pp. 64-68 below.

The second and more difficult doctrinal setting for the question of whose choice is it, is presented by *Unocal Corp. v. Mesa Petroleum Co.,* Del. Supr. 493 A.2d 946 (1985) and a string of Chancery opinions construing its test to require, in certain circumstances, the taking of action—typically the redemption of a so-called poison pill—to permit shareholders to choose between two functionally equivalent alternative transactions. *Grand Metropolitan PLC v. The Pillsbury Company,* Del. Ch., C.A. No. 10319 (Decem-

---

16 Continued ...

Fort Howard Corp. Shareholders Litigation, Del. Ch., Cons. C.A. No. 9991 (August 8, 1988); *In Re Holly Farms Corporation Shareholders Litigation,* Del. Ch., C.A. No. 10350 (December 30, 1988), slip op. at 12.

ber 16, 1988); *City Capital Associates Limited v. Interco, Inc.*, Del. Ch., 551 A.2d 787 (1988); *Robert M. Bass Group, Inc. v. Edward P. Evans*, Del. Ch., 552 A.2d 1227 (1988); *AC Acquisition Corp. v. Anderson, Clayton & Co.*, Del. Ch., 519 A.2d 103 (1986). This question is discussed at p. 68-70 below.

IV.

Were the Time Directors Under an Obligation to Seek, in Good Faith, Only to Maximize Current Share Value on June 16?: Plaintiffs' Revlon Argument

A.

Plaintiffs' first argument,[17] restated most simply, is that the original merger agreement constituted an implicit decision by the board of Time to transfer control of the company to Warner, or more correctly its shareholders, and when the board decided to consider doing that, its duties changed from long-term management of the corporation for the benefit of the company's shareholders to the narrow and specific goal of present maximization of share value. That is, it entered a "Revlon mode." See *Revlon v. MacAndrews & Forbes Holdings, Inc.*, Del. Supr., 506 A.2d 173, 182 (1986). The class action plaintiffs assert that any change in corporate control triggers this special duty. The individual shareholder plaintiffs urge a different theory as triggering the special Revlon duty. They contend that the original merger, if effectuated, would have precluded the Time shareholders from ever (that is, in the foreseeable future) realizing a control premium transaction, and thus, in its impact upon Time shareholders, the merger contemplated by the March 3 agreement would have implicitly represented the same loss of a control premium as would a change in control transaction with no premium. Thus, these plaintiffs assert that even if the stock for stock merger did not represent a change in control, the same duty to maximize current value should attach to it as to a "sale."

Plaintiffs, having purportedly shown that the board really was in a Revlon mode, then go on to argue that the board violated its Revlon duty by not seeking a current value maximizing transaction and by entering into a number of agreements that were intended to preclude or impede the emergence of current value maximizing alternatives. These agreements include the "dry up" fee payments, the Share Exchange Agreement and the restrictions on supply information to or entering into discussions with anyone seeking to acquire control of Time.

Defendants respond first that the board did not consider that it was appropriate in March or thereafter to "sell" the company; the purpose of the original merger was quite the opposite in that it sought to preserve and improve the company's long-term performance. Second, defendants say that if something other than their subjective intention is relevant, it simply is not the case that the stock for stock merger they authorized represented a change in control. It is irrelevant in their view that some 62% of the equity of Time would be owned by former Warner shareholders after the merger, that Mr. Ross would serve as co-CEO or that half of the members of the enlarged board would be

---

17   This argument is advanced principally by the shareholder plaintiffs.

former Warner directors. There was no control block of Time shares before the agreement and there would be none after it, they point out. Before the merger agreement was signed, control of the corporation existed in a fluid aggregation of unaffiliated shareholders representing a voting majority—in other words, in the market. After the effectuation of the merger it contemplated, control would have remained in the market, so to speak.

As to the individual plaintiffs' theory, defendants say it is flawed in law and in fact. Legally, they contend that a transaction that is otherwise proper cannot be deemed to trigger the radical "Revlon mode" obligations simply because it has the effect of making an attempted hostile takeover of the corporation less likely. All manner of transactions might have that effect and our cases, it is said, have explicitly rejected the notion that a would-be acquiror can compel a target to maintain itself in status quo while its offer proceeds. See, e.g., *USI, Inc. v. Walbro Corp.*, Del. Ch., C.A. No. 9323 (October 6, 1987); *City Capital Associates Limited v. Interco Inc.*, Del. Ch., 551 A.2d 787 (1988) at 800-01.

Factually, defendants claim that this record does not establish a reasonable probability that the initial merger, if it had been consummated, would have precluded a future change in control transaction. The merged Time-Warner company would be large, it is true (a "private market" value approaching $30 billion, it is said), but recent history has shown that huge transactions can be done. While such a transaction would be rare, if a leveraged acquisition of both participants was feasible before the merger, one cannot say that a stock for stock consolidation of such firms would necessarily preclude an acquisition of it thereafter, or so defendants contend.

In *Mills Acquisition Co. v. Macmillan, Inc.*, Del. Supr. Nos. 415 & 416 (May 3, 1989), the Supreme Court, while noting that there was no need for it to address in detail the question when Revlon duties arose, did note that:

Clearly not every offer or transaction affecting the corporate structure invokes the Revlon duties. A refusal to entertain offers may comport with a valid exercise of business judgment. See *Bershad*; *Ivanhoe* at 1341-42; *Pogostin*, 480 A.2d at 627; *Aronson*, 473 A.2d at 812-16. Circumstances may dictate that an offer be rebuffed, given the nature and timing of the offer; its legality, feasibility and effect on the corporation and the stockholders; the alternatives available and their effect on the various constituencies, particularly the stockholders, the company's long-term strategic plans; and any special factors bearing on stockholder and public interests. *Unocal*, 493 A.2d 954-56. See also *Smith*, 488 A.2d 872-78. In *Ivanhoe* we recognized that a change in corporate structure under the special facts and circumstances of that case did not invoke *Revlon*. 535 A.2d at 1345.

Mills Acquisition Co. v. Macmillan, Inc., supra, at p. 44, n. 35.

Elsewhere in *Macmillan* our Supreme Court did indicate that a board may find itself in a Revlon mode without reaching an express resolve to "sell" the company:

At a minimum, *Revlon* requires that there be the most scrupulous adherence to ordinary principles of fairness in the sense that stockholder interests are enhanced, rather than diminished, in the conduct of an auction for the sale of corporate control. *This is so whether the "sale" takes the form or an active auction, a management buyout, or a "restructuring" such as that which the Court of Chancery enjoined in Macmillan I.* Revlon, 506 A.2d at 181-82.

Id. at p. 56 (emphasis added).

Thus, I do not find it dispositive of anything that the Time board did not expressly resolve to sell the company. I take from *Macmillan*, however, and its citation of the earlier *Macmillan I* opinion in this court, that a corporate transaction that does represent a change in corporate control does place the board in a situation in which it is charged with the single duty to maximize current share value. I cannot conclude, however, that the initial merger agreement contemplates a change in control of Time. I am entirely persuaded of the soundness of the view that it is irrelevant for purposes of making such determination that 62% of Time-Warner stock would have been held by former Warner shareholders.

If the appropriate inquiry is whether a change in control is contemplated, the answer must be sought in the specific circumstances surrounding the transaction. Surely under some circumstances a stock for stock merger could reflect a transfer of corporate control. That would, for example, plainly be the case here if Warner were a private company. But where, as here, the shares of both constituent corporations are widely held, corporate control can be expected to remain unaffected by a stock for stock merger. This in my judgment was the situation with respect to the original merger agreement. When the specifics of that situation are reviewed, it is seen that, aside from legal technicalities and aside from arrangements thought to enhance the prospect for the ultimate succession of Mr. Nicholas, neither corporation could be said to be acquiring the other. Control of both remained in a large, fluid, changeable and changing market.

The existence of a block of stock in the hands of a single shareholder or a group with loyalty to each other does have real consequences to the financial value of "minority" stock. The law offers some protection to such shares through the imposition of a fiduciary duty upon controlling shareholders. But here, effectuation of the merger would not have subjected Time shareholders to the risks and consequences of holders of minority shares. This is a reflection of the fact that no control passed to anyone in the transaction contemplated. The shareholders of Time would have "suffered" dilution, of course, but they would suffer the same type of dilution upon the public distribution of new stock.

B.

More subtle is Literary Partners' argument that the preclusion of a future change in control transaction ought to be deemed to trigger Revlon duties, to which I now turn.

The argument, as I understand it, is that the original Time-Warner merger, even if it represented no change in control, precluded a future control premium or private market transaction and that as a consequence of that fact, the directors' fiduciary duties required them to capture a control premium now—to sell the company. This brief restatement lacks much of the subtlety of the individual plaintiffs' moderate and skilful advocacy, but is, I think, essentially the argument.

It is plain that the original transaction did not legally preclude or impede a later sale or change in control transaction. It does seem reasonable to assume, however, that effectuation of the merger would, as a practical consequence, reduce the likelihood of such a transaction substantially. Our cases, however, have stated the obvious: a would-be acquiror (or the target company's shareholders) has no right to stay the exercise of director power under Section 141 pending the resolution of an attempt to acquire control. So long as the board acts in good faith and deliberately, its acts during such period will be undisturbed unless they are found to be defensive, in which event they must be shown to be reasonable in relation to a threat posed by the offer under *Unocal*. Thus, for example, in *USI v. Walbro*, supra, it was said at pp. 8–9:

... [I]t is well established that a tender offeror has no right to freeze the business he seeks to ac-quire while his offer goes forward. Not only has a board the responsibility to continue to manage the enterprise generally, but a board, if it acts in good faith and with due care, may also take steps to defeat a tender offer that it finds to be unfair to some shareholders. In taking such action, a board necessarily acts under the suspicion that it seeks to protect its personal interests. Thus, those actions must pass later judicial review as being reasonable in relation to a threat to corpo-rate or shareholder welfare. But action designed to defeat a tender offer that the board finds to be at an unfair price—particularly an offer that is for less than all of the stock and has no announced second step at all—is not *ipso facto* invalid simply because it is effective and thus does deprive some shareholders of an option they might have taken. With these generalities in mind, it seems a stretch to seek to enjoin as yet unproposed transactions that may have the effect of making the Company a less desirable or less practically achievable target to a particular tender offeror.

In *Interco*, among the propositions addressed was the question whether the sale of a division should be enjoined pending completion of the contest for control that was going forward. A number of circumstances indicated that the transaction could be expected to have only modest impact upon the prospects of the pending offer. That fact compelled the conclusion that the asset sale there involved was reasonable under *Unocal*. The general formulation, however, has some bearing on the present argument:

The question of reasonableness in this setting seems rather easy. Of course, a board acts reason-ably in relation to an offer, albeit a noncoercive offer, it believes to be inadequate when it seeks to realize the full market value of an important asset.

· · ·

I do understand that this step [the sale of a substantial division] complicates [the bidder's] life and indeed might imperil CCA's ability to complete its transaction. CCA, however, has no right to demand that its chosen target remain in status quo while its offer is formulated, gradually increased and, perhaps, accepted.

Interco, 551 A.2d at 801.

The individual plaintiff's argument is an argument for extension of the *Revlon* case beyond sales or other change in control transactions. I have earlier expressed the view that *Revlon* was not a radical departure from existing Delaware, or other, law (*i.e.*, it has "always" been the case that when a trustee or other fiduciary sells an asset for cash, his duty is to seek the single goal of getting the best available price), as well as the view that to be in a Revlon mode is for a director to be in a radically altered state. The suggested rule, however, would constitute an expansion of *Revlon* beyond the traditional principle alluded to above which underlies that case. Plaintiffs can cite no authority compelling or commanding this expansion, which would dramatically restrict the functioning of the board whenever an offer was made. Under our law, the validity of "defensive" measures is addressed under a *Unocal* analysis, not under the narrower *Revlon* case.

V.

*Did the Combination of Circumstances Existing on June 16 Impose Upon the Time
Board a Fiduciary Obligation to Afford to Shareholders a Choice With Respect to
Whether the Corporation Should Be "Sold" or Managed for the Long-Term?*

This is the second overarching question referred to above. Two legal theories are advanced by plaintiffs in support of their position that the board was under a duty to provide, or at least not practically preclude, a choice to accept the Paramount offer or another, higher offer for sale of the entire company now. The first, simpler, theory relates to the franchise; the second to the analysis of "defensive" corporate acts envisioned by the important *Unocal* case. *Unocal Corp. v. Mesa Petroleum Co.*, Del. Supr., 493 A.2d 946 (1985).

A. The recasting of the transaction in a form that avoided a shareholder vote when the vote seemed destined to go against management

The principle is well established in Delaware law that manipulation of the corporate machinery for the accomplishment of inequitable purposes will not be countenanced. *E.g. Schnell v. Chris-Craft Industries*, Del Supr., 285 A.2d 437 (1971); *Frantz Manufacturing Company v. EAC Industries*, Del. Supr., 501 A.2d 401 (1985); *Canada Southern Oils, Ltd. v. Manabi Exploration Co., Inc.*, Del. Ch., 96 A.2d 810 (1953); *Aprahamian v. HBO & Co.*, Del. Ch., 531 A.2d 1204 (1987); *Blasius Industries, Inc. v. Atlas Corp.*, Del. Ch., C.A. No. 9720 (July 25, 1988).

Primary reliance is placed upon the recent decision in *Blasius v. Atlas*. There, a board acted in apparent good faith to prevent an already commenced consent solicitation from having the effect that it was intended to have by the consenting shareholders. Specifically, the board used its legal power to fill vacancies on the board so that the holders of a (presumed) majority of shares could not appoint the number of directors, through the consent "vote," necessary to confer effective control upon the consent-designated directors.

It was there held that such action, even if taken in the good faith belief that it was necessary to protect the corporate enterprise from likely harm from the untenable business plan espoused by the shareholders initiating the consent, involved the basic allocation of power between shareholders and directors; and that action, designed and effectuated to thwart the election of directors by consent, was not the sort of question that was entitled to the presumption of validity of the business judgment rule (see slip op. at 21-24), but required the board to demonstrate a compelling justification for such action. See *Blasius* at 25-31; *Aprahamian*, 531 A.2d at 1206-07; *Phillips v. Insituform of North American, Inc.*, Del. Ch., C.A. No. 9173 (August 27, 1987) at 23-24. But see *American Rent-A-Car Inc. v. Cross*, Del. Ch., C.A. No. 7583 (May 9, 1984). In *Blasius*, defendants were found to have offered no compelling justification for their action that in effect disenfranchised shareholders in the process of exercising the consent power.

Plaintiffs' reliance upon *Blasius* is misplaced here. There are critical distinctions between the facts of that case and this one. There, the shareholders were in the process of exercising statutorily conferred rights to elect directors through the consent process.

See 8 Del. C. § 228. In contrast, Delaware law created no right in these circumstances to vote upon the original Warner merger.[18] Indeed, a merger transaction requires board determination approving an agreement of merger. See 8 Del. C. § 251(b). I am aware of no principle, statute or rule of corporation law that would hold that once a board approves an agreement of merger, it loses power to reconsider that action prior to a shareholder vote. Equally fundamentally, Delaware law creates no power in shareholders to authorize a merger without the prior affirmative action of the board of directors. Thus, a board resolution rescinding approval of an agreement of merger and removing the matter from the agenda of an annual meeting is altogether different from a resolution designed to interfere with the statutory shareholder power to act through consent.

This case is closer to (indeed a fortiori of) *American Rent-A-Car, Inc.*, supra, in which this court declined to enjoin action authorized by a bylaw which was amended by the board at a time when it seemed quite likely to fail of stockholder approval.[19] See also *Lowenschuss v. The Option Clearing Corporation*, Del. Ch., C.A. No. 7972 (March 26, 1985) (failure to achieve shareholder approval of recapitalization of Phillips Petroleum Company did not provide basis to enjoin board authorized self-tender and buyback of shares that had similar financial effect).

I therefore conclude that plaintiffs have not shown that the June 16 decision to recast the transaction entailed any intrusion upon the effective exercise of a right possessed by the shareholders, either under our statutes or under the corporation's charter. The June 16 decision can therefore not be seen as implicating the policy of protection of the corporate franchise, which our law has studiously sought to protect.

B. The claim that the Warner tender offer is a disproportionate response to a noncoercive Paramount offer that threatens no cognizable injury to Time or its shareholders

1. Does Unocal apply?

Powerful circumstances in this case include the fact that the original Time-Warner merger agreement was, or appears at this stage to have been, chiefly motivated by strategic business concerns; that it was an arm's-length transaction; and, that while its likely effect on reducing vulnerability to unsolicited takeovers may not have been an altogether collateral fact, such effect does not appear to be predominating.[20] Time urges

---

18 Recall that it was only NYSE rules that prompted the proposed submission of that transaction to the Time annual meeting.

19 In *Blasius*, I noted my own view that judicial review of franchise issues does not fall into a business judgment format and noted that *American Rent-A-Car* indicated a contrary approach. That observation on form of review did not extend to the substantive holding of the case. See *Blasius*, slip op. at 5.

20 This fact distinguishes in a material way the case of *AC Acquisition Corp. v. Anderson, Clayton & Co.*, Del. Ch. 519 A.2d 103 (1986) which originated from a threat to the existing control arrangement. Other material distinctions are that the two transactions there involved were competing versions of a "bust up" plan for the corporation as it had existed and the board could not determine that either was inadequate.

that judicial review of the propriety of the Warner tender offer should involve the same business judgment form of review as would have been utilized in a challenge to the authorization of the original merger agreement. It cites the case of *Crouse-Hinds Co. v. InterNorth, Inc.*, 634 F. 2d 690 (2d Cir. 1980) as its authority for this position, and contends that the inclusion of that authority in a string of citations in the *Unocal* opinion supports the notion that the rearrangement of a preexisting transaction in reaction to a hostile takeover qualifies for "unenhanced" (by Unocal) business judgment review. Even the quickest review of *Unocal* demonstrates that in citing that case in the place that it did, our Supreme Court was not intending to implicitly, indeed silently, create an exception to the innovative and important rule that it there announced.

Moreover, a rather lengthy list of cases from this court has construed *Unocal* to mean that its form of review applies, at the least, to all actions taken after a hostile takeover attempt has emerged that are found to be defensive in character.[21] See, e.g., *AC Acquisition Corp. v. Anderson, Clayton & Co.*, Del. Ch., 519 A.2d 103, Allen, C. (1986); *Robert M. Bass Group, Inc. v. Edward P. Evans*, Del. Ch., 552 A.2d 1227 (1988); *The Henley Group, Inc. v. Santa Fe Southern Pacific Corp.*, Del. Ch., C.A. No. 9569, Jacobs, V.C. (March 11, 1988); *Doskocil Companies Inc. v. Griggy*, Del. Ch., C.A. Nos. 10095, 10106, 10107, 10108, 10116, Berger, V.C. (August 18, 1988), slip op. at 18-19. Thus, while the preexistence of a potential transaction may have pertinence in evaluating whether implementing it or a modified version of it after the board is under attack is a reasonable step in the circumstances, that fact has not been thought in this court to authorize dispensing with the *Unocal* form of analysis. The risks that *Unocal* was shaped to protect against are equally present in such instances.

Factually it is plain, indeed Time's Schedule 14D-9 filing admits, that the reformatting of the stock for stock merger into a leveraged purchase transaction was in reaction to the emergence of the Paramount offer and its likely effect on the proposed Warner transaction. See pp. 36-37, supra.

2. Does the Paramount all cash, all shares offer represent a threat to an interest the board has an obligation or a right to protect by defensive action?

Unocal involved a partial offer for cash; consideration in the second-step merger was to be highly subordinated securities. Equally significant, the facts there justified "a reasonable inference" that the "principal objective [of the offeror was] to be bought off." Thus, the case presented dramatically and plainly a threat to both the shareholders and the corporation.

In two cases decided during the last year, this court has held under similar circumstances that an all cash, all shares offer falling within a range of value that a shareholder might reasonably prefer, to be followed by a prompt second-step merger for cash, could not, so long as it involved no deception, be construed as a sufficient threat to share-

---

21   When I say at the least, I refer to fact that the *Unocal* form of analysis will also be utilized when a preemptive defensive measure is deployed, where the principal purpose of the action (and not simply a collateral, practical effect) is defensive in a change of control sense. E.g., *Moran v. Household International, Inc.*, Del. Supr., 500 A.2d 1346 (1985).

holder interests to justify as reasonable board action that would permanently foreclose shareholder choice to accept that offer. See *Grand Metropolitan PLC v. The Pillsbury Company*, Del. Ch., C.A. No. 10319, Duffy, J. (December 16, 1988); *City Capital Associates v. Interco Incorporated*, Del. Ch., 551 A.2d 787 (1988). Cf. *Shamrock Holding, Inc. v. Polaroid Corp.*, Del. Ch., C.A. Nos. 10075, 10079, 10582 and 10585, Berger, V.C. (March 17, 1989), slip op. at 29-32. Those cases held that in the circumstances presented, "whatever danger there is relates to shareholders and that concerns price only." *Pillsbury*, supra, slip op. at 17-18, or that "in the special case of a tender offer for all shares, the threat posed, if any, is not importantly to corporate policies ... but rather ... is most directly to shareholder interests." *Interco*, 551 A.2d at 796.

Plaintiffs argue from these cases that since the Paramount offer is also for all shares and for cash, with a promised second-step merger offering the same consideration, the only interests the board may legitimately seek to protect are the interests of shareholders in having the option to accept the best available price in a sale of their stock. Plaintiffs admit that this interest would justify defensive action at this stage. The board may leave its stock rights plan in place to provide it time to conduct an auction or to arrange any other alternative that might be thought preferable to the shareholders. But, they say, this stockholder interest cannot justify defensive action (the revised merger) that is totally unrelated to a threat to shareholders.

In my opinion, the authorities relied upon do not establish that Time has no legally cognizable interest that the Paramount offer endangers. In each of those cases, the board sought to assure continued control by compelling a transaction that itself would have involved the sale of substantial assets, an enormous increase in debt and a large cash distribution to shareholders. In other words, in those cases, management was presenting and seeking to "cram down" a transaction that was the functional equivalent of the very leveraged "bust up" transaction that management was claiming presented a threat to the corporation.

Here, in stark contrast, the revised transaction, even though "reactive" in important respects, has its origin and central purpose in bona fide strategic business planning, and not in questions of corporate control. Compare *AC Acquisition Corp.*, supra (recapitalization had its genesis in a threat to corporate control posed by the imminent termination of trusts that had exercised effective control for years); *Robert M. Bass Group v. Evans*, supra (recapitalization under consideration prior to acquisition proposal would have shifted control to management group of a substantial portion of corporation's assets). To be sure, Time's management and its board had, at all times, one eye on the takeover market, considered that market in all they did, and took steps to afford themselves the conventional defenses. But I do not regard that fact as darkly as do plaintiffs. It is inevitable today for businessmen to be mindful of this factor. At this stage, I do not regard the record as establishing, as was done in *AC Acquisitions, Bass, Interco* or *Pillsbury*, that there is a reasonable likelihood that such concern provided the primary motivation for the corporate transaction. Nor is this transaction an alternative to the sale Paramount proposes (i.e., the functional equivalent) in the way the enjoined transactions in the cited cases can be said to be equivalents of sales.

The more apt parallel than the cited cases is provided by the recent decision in *Shamrock Holdings, Inc. v. Polaroid Corp.*, Del. Ch., C.A. Nos. 10075 and 10079,

Berger, V.C. (January 6, 1989). There, this court found "entirely fair" a transaction (the establishment of an Employee Stock Ownership Plan) that had a significant anti-takeover effect, largely because it was a transaction that had been planned prior to the emergence of the acquisition attempt, plainly could be thought to serve long-term profit maximizing goals, and did not appear motivated primarily as a device to affect or secure control.

Similarly here, I conclude that the achievement of the long-term strategic plan of the Time-Warner consolidation is plainly a most important corporate policy; while the transaction effectuating that policy is reactive in important respects (and thus must withstand a *Unocal* analysis), the policy itself has, in a most concrete way, its origin in non-defensive, bona fide business considerations. In this respect, the Second Circuit's opinion in *Crouse-Hinds* is instructive if not directly applicable. Moreover, the Paramount offer and the Warner merger are not, conceptually, alternative transactions; they are alternatives at the moment only because Paramount has conditioned its offer as it has.

In my opinion, where the board has not elected explicitly to assume the special burdens recognized by *Revlon*, but continues to manage the corporation for long-term profit pursuant to a preexisting business plan that itself is not primarily a control device or scheme, the corporation has a legally cognizable interest in achieving that plan. Whether steps taken to protect transactions contemplated by such plan are reasonable in all of the circumstances is another matter, to which I now turn.

3. Is the Warner tender offer a reasonable step in the circumstances?

This step requires evaluation of the importance of the corporate objective threatened; alternative methods for protecting that objective; impacts of the "defensive" action and other relevant factors. In this effort it is prudent to keep in mind that the innovative and constructive rule of *Unocal* must be cautiously applied lest the important benefits of the business judgment rule (including designation of authority to make business and financial decisions to agencies, i.e. board of directors, with substantive expertise) be eroded or lost by slow degress. See *Interco*, 551 A.2d at 796.

In this instance, the objective—realization of the company's major strategic plan—is reasonably seen as of unquestionably great importance by the board. Moreover, the reactive step taken was effective but not overly broad. The board did only what was necessary to carry forward a preexisting transaction in an altered form. That "defensive" step does not legally preclude the successful prosecution of a hostile tender offer. And while effectuation of the Warner merger may practically impact the likelihood of a successful takeover of the merged company, it is not established in this record that that is foreclosed as a practical matter. Recent experience suggests it may be otherwise. *In Re RJR Nabisco, Inc. Shareholders Litigation*, Del. Ch., C.A. No. 10389 (January 31, 1989).

I therefore conclude that the revised merger agreement and the Warner tender offer do represent actions that are reasonable in relation to the specific threat posed to the Warner merger by the Paramount offer.

●   ●   ●

Reasonable persons can and do disagree as to whether it is the better course from the shareholders' point of view collectively to cash out their stake in the company now at this (or a higher) premium cash price. However, there is no persuasive evidence that the board of Time has a corrupt or venal motivation in electing to continue with its long-term plan even in the face of the cost that course will no doubt entail for the company's shareholders in the short run. In doing so, it is exercising perfectly conventional powers to cause the corporation to buy assets for use in its business. Because of the timing involved, the board has no need here to rely upon a self-created power designed to assure a veto on all changes in control.[22]

The value of a shareholder's investment, over time, rises or falls chiefly because of the skill, judgment and perhaps luck—for it is present in all human affairs—of the management and directors of the enterprise. When they exercise sound or brilliant judgment, shareholders are likely to profit; when they fail to do so, share values likely will fail to appreciate. In either event, the financial vitality of the corporation and the value of the company's shares is in the hands of the directors and managers of the firm. The corporation law does not operate on the theory that directors, in exercising their powers to manage the firm, are obligated to follow the wishes of a majority of shares. In fact, directors, not shareholders, are charged with the duty to manage the firm. See *Smith v. Van Gorkom*, Del. Supr. 488 A.2d 858 (1985); *Sealy Mattress Co. of New Jersey, Inc. v. Sealy, Inc.*, 532 A.2d 1324 (1987).

In the decision they have reached here, the Time board may be proven in time to have been brilliantly prescient or dismayingly wrong. In this decision, as in other decisions affecting the financial value of their investment, the shareholders will bear the effects for good or ill. That many, presumably most, shareholders would prefer the board to do otherwise than it has done does not, in the circumstances of a challenge to this type of transaction, in my opinion, afford a basis to interfere with the effectuation of the board's business judgment.

• • •

Having therefore concluded that plaintiffs have not shown a reasonable probability that they possess a right in these circumstances to require the board to abandon or delay the long-planned Warner transaction so that the stockholders might enhance their prospects of a control premium or private market transaction now, I need not discuss the issue raised by Warner concerning its rights as an intensely interested third party. The application shall be denied.

It is so ordered.

NOTES

1) On appeal, the Delaware Supreme Court agreed that Time's board of directors had satisfied the *Unocal* test and that *Revlon* auction duties had not been triggered. See

---

22 Thus, in my view, a decision not to redeem a poison pill, which by definition is a control mechanism and not a device with independent business purposes, may present distinctive considerations than those presented in this case.

Paramount Communications, Inc. v Time, Inc., 571 A.2d 1140; 1990 Federal Securities Law Reporter, para. 94,938. The Supreme Court also stated that it thought it unwise to place undue emphasis on questions of long-term value versus short-term value. In its view, directors "are obliged to charter a course for a corporation which is in its best interests without regard to a fixed investment horizon ... [A]bsent a limited set of circumstances as defined under *Revlon,* a board of directors, while always required to act in an informed manner, is not under any *per se* duty to maximize shareholder value in the short term, even in the context of a takeover" (at paras. 95,207-95,208). Finally, the Supreme Court stressed that the "fiduciary duty to manage a corporate enterprise includes the selection of a time frame for achievement of corporate goals. That duty may not be delegated to the stockholders. *Van Gorkom,* 488 A.2d at 873. Directors are not obliged to abandon a deliberately conceived corporate plan for a short-term shareholder profit unless there is clearly no basis to sustain the corporate strategy."

In your view, should a shareholder's natural desire to see a healthy return on an investment be the board of directors' primary consideration in the face of a take-over bid? What role *should* a consideration of the interests of other constituencies play in the board's decision about the selection of a time frame for achievement of corporate goals?

2) The decision in *Time* has not always proven easy to digest. In particular, there has been some question as to whether it stands for the proposition that a board may simply refuse to negotiate with a bidder on the basis that in the board's view (as supported by the advice of its investment bankers) the target company will be better able to generate long-term value on its own than under the control of the bidder. In this respect, the more recent *Paramount* decision discussed below provides some insight into the Delaware courts' views on the limits of a so-called "just say no" defence. Should it be open to a board of directors to "say no" to a bid on the basis that the company's existing strategy is in its view more likely to produce healthy returns for shareholders? Is a board ever likely to conclude that its strategy on the direction the company should take is less likely to be right than the one that a hostile bidder is proposing? Does the fact that in early 1995 Time-Warner's stock was trading at approximately U.S.$40 (as opposed to the significantly more substantial amount management thought the merger might generate) have any impact on your answer? For an analysis of the implications of the decision in *Time* for the status of *Unocal* and *Revlon,* see L. Johnson & D. Miller, *The Case Beyond Time,* 45 The Business Lawyer 2105 (1990).

In turn, the question has arisen at what point a company can be said to have decided to put itself up for sale, such that its board of directors is subject to a *Revlon* duty to seek the best price possible for the company's shares. Must the decision be a conscious one on the part of the board of directors or is it enough that they have chosen to execute a transaction that will effectively give rise to a change of control?

3) After three to four years of relative calm in the take-over markets in North America, activity picked up in one of its cyclical bursts in 1994. Ironically, Paramount once again found itself in the middle of the action, although this time as the unreceptive target of a hostile bid. After agreeing with Viacom Inc. in late 1993 to enter into a merger agreement pursuant to which Viacom was to acquire control of Paramount, the latter suddenly found itself subject to an unsolicited take-over bid launched by QVC Network Inc. As with *Time,* Paramount had looked long and hard for a suitable partner

in the entertainment industry before agreeing to enter into detailed discussions with Viacom. The critical difference, as it turned out, was that unlike Time it agreed to let Viacom acquire control of its shares through a tender offer to be followed up with a second-step merger (rather than following in Time's footsteps and acquiring Viacom). In the Delaware Supreme Court's view Paramount's decision to proceed in this fashion amounted to a decision to effect a change of control transaction. Paramount's board of directors was therefore subject to a *Revlon* duty to obtain the best value reasonably available for its stockholders. Assuming that Paramount's board of directors was sincere about wishing to secure the long-term viability of the company, why should it matter that rather than acquiring Viacom it decided to let itself be acquired by Viacom?

The Delaware Supreme Court felt that there was a fundamental distinction, noting that:

In the case before us, the public stockholders in the aggregate currently own a majority of Paramount's voting stock. Control of the corporation is not vested in a single person, entity, or group, but vested in the fluid aggregation of unaffiliated stockholders. In the event the Paramount-Viacom transaction is consummated, the public stockholders will receive cash and a minority equity voting position in the surviving corporation. Following such consummation, there will be a controlling stockholder who will have the voting power to: (a) elect directors; (b) cause a break-up of the corporation; (c) merge it with another company; (d) cash-out the public stockholders; (e) amend the certificate of incorporation; (f) sell all or substantially all of the corporate assets; or (g) otherwise alter materially the nature of the corporation and the public stockholders' interests. Irrespective of the present Paramount board's vision of a long-term strategic alliance with Viacom, the proposed sale of control would provide the new controlling stockholder with the power to alter that vision. Because of the intended sale of control, the Paramount-Viacom transaction has economic consequences of considerable significance to the Paramount stockholders. Once control has shifted, the current Paramount stockholders will have no leverage in the future to demand another control premium. As a result, the Paramount stockholders are entitled to receive, and should receive, a control premium and/or protective devices of significant value. There being no such protective provisions in the Viacom-Paramount transaction, the Paramount directors had an obligation to take the maximum advantage of the current opportunity to realize for the stockholders the best value reasonably available.

In your view, is this a convincing basis upon which to distinguish the decision in *Time*?

The Court went on to observe that a board of directors in these circumstances is not limited to considering only the amount of cash involved and "is not required to ignore totally its view of the future value of a strategic alliance." Nonetheless, the Court made clear that the focus had to be which alternative is most likely to offer the best value to stockholders. And as in *Revlon* there was no suggestion that it was open to a board of directors to balance the interests of stockholders against those of other constituencies.

In the end, the Court found that Paramount's board of directors had breached its fiduciary duties when it engaged in a series of defensive manoeuvres designed to frustrate the QVC bid, including accepting a "No-Shop Provision" in its merger agreement with Viacom that prohibited it from negotiating with parties other than Viacom. The Court found that a contract purporting to require a board of directors to act in a manner that is not consistent with its fiduciary duties is invalid and unenforceable. The end result was that Viacom and QVC engaged in an open fight for control of Paramount, with Viacom ultimately securing control of Paramount.

Paramount is but one more in what promises to be an ongoing series of cases before the Delaware courts that consider a board's fiduciary duties in the context of an unsolicited take-over bid. As you review the next case, ask yourself whether a similar body of law could not be developed in Canada in the light of the decision in *Teck* (which you will recall looked to the decision of the Delaware courts in *Cheff v. Mathes* for inspiration) or whether it is necessary to look to the views of Canadian securities regulators to provide the appropriate framework within which take-over bids should unfold.

347883 Alberta Ltd. v. Producers Pipelines Inc.
Saskatchewan Court of Appeal
[1991] 4 W.W.R. 577

SHERSTOBITOFF J.A. (TALLIS J.A. concurring):—The issue in this appeal [from [1991] 4 W.W.R. 151] is the validity of a poison pill defence strategy undertaken by the directors of the respondent public corporation, Producers Pipelines Inc. ("P.P.I."), to stave off an apprehended take-over bid by Saskatchewan Oil & Gas Corporation, ("Saskoil") through its wholly owned subsidiary, 347883 Alberta Ltd., the appellant.

The appellant, as a shareholder in P.P.I., applied for an order under s. 234 of the Business Corporations Act, R.S.S. 1978, c. B-10, setting aside a shareholder rights agreement ("S.R.A.") and an issuer bid, the mechanisms used to implement the defence strategy, as being oppressive, or unfairly prejudicial to, or as unfairly disregarding the interests of the appellant and other shareholders in P.P.I. The application was dismissed and this appeal is against that dismissal.

The facts

The judge below outlined the facts as follows [pp. 153-58 W.W.R.]:

Background

Producers is a Saskatchewan incorporated public corporation with approximately 170 shareholders. The shares are not listed on any stock exchange, but are traded in the over-the-counter market. Because of the limited number of shareholders, it appears that there has never been any significant trading in the shares.

In August 1990 there were 1,433,945 common shares of Producers outstanding and 230,000 preferred shares. Penfund Capital (No. 1) Limited ("Penfund") owned all of the preferred shares and 280,000 common shares. It also controls an additional 170,800 common shares. It, therefore, owned or controlled approximately 31.4 per cent of the common shares.

On February 15, 1991 Penfund converted all of its preferred shares into common shares. Consequently, there are now 1,663,945 common shares outstanding. The percentage of voting shares owned or controlled by Penfund is now 40.9 per cent.

A nominee of Penfund is a director of Producers. Penfund, together with the other directors of Producers and their associates, controlled more than 50 per cent of the voting shares prior to December 1990. On December 3, 1990 Saskatchewan Oil and Gas Corporation ("Saskoil") purchased, through a wholly owned subsidiary—the applicant—all of the shares of one of the directors. The applicant now owns 143,200 shares, acquired at a price of $18.25 per share.

Saskoil had written to the president of Producers on August 27, 1990, stating that it was "able, willing and wishes to make an offer for all of the shares of Producers." It was further stated that "On the basis of the somewhat limited information received to date an offer would likely be in the range of $16.00–18.00 per share." The letter prompted the implementation of the "poison pill"—the shareholder rights agreement.

Poison Pill

The shareholder rights agreement, dated as of August 27, 1990, is between Producers and the Royal Trust Company, as rights agent. It is a lengthy and detailed agreement. The initial article in the agreement, entitled "Certain Definitions," comprises, in itself, over 12 pages.

The principal purpose of the agreement was to grant rights to each shareholder as of August 27, 1990 to purchase 10 additional common shares of Producers for a price equivalent to $7.50 per share upon the occurrence of certain events. If no "triggering" event occurred, the agreement, and the rights granted, would expire on December 27, 1990.

The agreement was unquestionably designed as a defensive tactic to a hostile take-over bid. Although there is a lengthy definition in the agreement of a "permitted bid," which specifies the types of take-over bids which are permissable, the definition excludes a take-over bid by a person, not "grandfathered" by the agreement, beneficially owning more than 5 per cent, and not more than 10 per cent, of the outstanding common shares of the Producers. The acquisition by the applicant on December 3, 1990 of 143,200 common shares made Saskoil the beneficial owner of approximately 9.9 per cent of the outstanding common shares of Producers.

A "triggering" event, permitting exercise of the rights to purchase additional common shares, includes, of course, a non-permitted take-over bid. If the bid should emanate from a person who beneficially owned more than 5 per cent of the common shares of Producers, such as Saskoil, that person would not be entitled to exercise any rights which might be annexed to his or its common shares.

The principal complaints of the applicant, however, involve two other aspects of the shareholder rights agreement. The first is an amendment to the agreement, by resolution of the directors of Producers on December 15, 1990, that even before a "permitted" take-over bid, as defined in the agreement, can be so categorized, it must receive the unanimous approval of the board of directors of Producers. The second complaint is that the agreement, although expressed to be valid only until December 27, 1990, was extended, by resolution of the board of directors of Producers, to February 26, 1991 and further extended to April 15, 1991, without shareholder approval. Although the annual meeting of shareholders was held on October 26, 1990, and a special meeting was held on February 25, 1991, the agreement was not presented to the shareholders for their approval at either meeting.

Saskoil was fully aware of the existence of the agreement when it acquired its shares on December 3, 1990, but it had anticipated that the agreement would expire, by its own terms, when it was not presented to the shareholders at the annual meeting for their approval.

A special general meeting of the shareholders on February 25, 1991 was convened for the purpose of passing a resolution authorizing Producers to make the issuer bid to purchase a maximum of 560,000 of its shares at a price of $21.50. 88 per cent of the outstanding shares were represented in person or by proxy at the meeting. 88.2 per cent of the shares represented at the meeting voted in favour of the resolution. 11.8 per cent voted against the resolution, including Saskoil.

The last date upon which shareholders may tender their shares, pursuant to the issuer bid, is March 28, 1991. Producers may take up and pay for any tendered shares immediately after March 28, but must do so, in any event, within ten days thereafter.

The circular annexed to the issuer bid includes a rather lengthy summary of the evaluation report of Meyer Corporate Valuations Ltd., requisitioned by the directors, wherein it expressed the opinion that, as of October 31, 1990, the fair market value of the shares of Producers was in the range of $19 to $21.50 per share.

The circular also stated that the "board group members," comprising the directors of Producers and their affiliates and associates, but not including the nominee of Penfund, would not be tendering their shares, comprising 314,435 shares. It was also stated that Penfund, owning or controlling 680,800 shares, would tender some but not all of its shares. The shareholders were informed at the special general meeting that Penfund would tender 196,000 shares.

If all of Penfund's tendered shares are taken up by Producers, the number of shares which it will then own and control would be reduced to 484,800. That number of shares, when added to the shares owned or controlled by the "board group members," total 799,235. If 560,000 shares should be tendered and taken up by Producers, the number of outstanding shares will then be reduced to 1,103,945.

The applicant does not object to the issuer bid per se, but complains that the existence of the issuer bid, while the shareholder rights agreement remains in force, has the practical effect of precluding a take-over bid by Saskoil. The only complaint expressed with respect to the issuer bid itself is that if 560,000 shares, or even a significant portion of that number, are acquired by Producers, the board of directors will be "entrenched."

Producers Since 1985

In 1985 Producers became a public company. Its principal business at that time consisted of a crude oil gathering system in southern Saskatchewan. However, in 1988-89, it acquired a significant interest in a gas field, and a 100 per cent interest in a gas gathering network and processing plant in western Saskatchewan. An asphalt plant in Moose Jaw was purchased in 1989 ...

The initial issue price of the shares of Producers has not been revealed in the material filed. However, share options and warrants were exercised from 1987 to 1990, in one instance at $5.50, and in all other cases at $7 per share.

The over-the-counter price of the shares apparently was approximately $5.25 until at least the spring of 1990. But in a letter dated August 23, 1990, ScotiaMcLeod Inc. informed an officer of Producers that the market price in the last trade of Producers shares was at $10 per share.

On August 31, 1990 Producers informed R.B. Richards, the President and Chief Executive Officer of Producers, and a director, that his employment was terminated as of that date for cause. Mr. Richards was not re-elected as a director of Producers at the annual meeting on October 26, 1990, and he sold the 143,200 common shares owned or controlled by him to Saskoil on December 3, 1990.

There are some other pertinent facts not mentioned by the chambers judge in his summary of the facts. The management information circular, which accompanied the notice of special meeting of shareholders to be held on February 25, 1991, indicated that a shareholders agreement was in the process of being concluded between board group members and the Penfund group members whereby they agreed not to tender their shares into a take-over bid unless the bid satisfied a number of conditions. One of the conditions was that the take-over bid be an all cash bid for all the shares of the corporation at some minimum price per share. In the circular accompanying the issuer bid it is indicated that on February 20, 1991, the minimum price per share was established at $25.

One other pertinent fact not mentioned by the chambers judge is that the shareholders were not advised that the S.R.A. would be extended from February 28, 1991, to April 15, 1991, until a news release dated February 25, 1991. This information was not conveyed to shareholders in the material which accompanied the notice of meeting.

The issues

The appellant's grounds of appeal are that the directors of P.P.I. acted unlawfully (1) in failing to obtain shareholder approval of the S.R.A., although two shareholders' meetings were held after its implementation, (2) in amending the S.R.A. to provide that the directors must unanimously approve any take-over bid before it could be put to the shareholders as a permitted bid under the amended S.R.A., (3) in entering into the S.R.A. when it discriminated against the appellant shareholder, and (4) in failing to act in the best interests of the corporation because it could not be demonstrated that there was any valid business purpose for the issuer bid and that the effect of it would be to entrench the board of directors and give them control of a majority of the shares in the corporation.

For its part, aside from the above issues, the respondent questioned the right of this appellant to relief under s. 234 for two reasons: (1) it purchased its shares in P.P.I. after S.R.A. was in place and thus voluntarily "bought in to any oppression" that might exist, and (2) its purpose in bringing the application was to permit it to make a take-over bid, something unrelated to the rights conferred by ownership of the shares.

Poison pills in Canada

The poison pill was developed in the United States as a defence to coercive take-over bids. It has begun to appear more frequently in Canada and has been subjected to critical analysis in Coleman, "Poison Pills in Canada" (1988), 15 Can. Bus. L.J. 1, and Jeffrey

G. MacIntosh, "The Poison Pill: A Noxious Nostrum for Canadian Shareholders" (1988-89), 15 Can. Bus. L.J. 276. The poison pill in this case conforms with the typical poison pill described by Mr. Coleman at pp. 1 and 2:

How Pills Work

A typical poison pill plan works as follows: A corporation distributes rights to acquire common shares. The rights trade with the common shares and have a life of 10 years but their "strike price" is sufficiently high (say, $100 compared to a $25 market price) to make them worthless. The rights carry no vote and are redeemable at a nominal amount by the board of directors before the poison pill provision is triggered and, in some cases, for a short period after the poison pill is triggered (to allow the board to negotiate an acceptable deal).

A first generation poison pill, such as that considered by the Delaware Supreme Court in *Moran v. Household International Inc.*, is triggered upon the acquisition by a third party of 20% or more of the corporation's common shares or upon a take-over bid being made for 30% or more of the common shares. At that point, the rights separate from the common shares to which they were formerly attached, trade separately from them and become exercisable.

Upon the further occurrence of a defined "merger event," the rights "flip-over" allowing the rights holders to purchase shares of the acquiror or the merged entity at half price. This is achievable only where a contract is entered into between the target and the acquiring company (such as a merger or sale of assets).

Should the acquiring company attempt to avoid the "flip-over," for instance by engaging in defined "self-dealing" transactions which do not require a contract between the acquiring company and the target, then the rights holders, other than the acquiring company, are entitled to purchase stock of the target at half price (the "flip-in").

In transactions where there is no merger event or self-dealing, there is no flip-over or flip-in. Accordingly, what has evolved is a second generation Pill in which a percentage-based flip-in feature is added. This provision allows the rights holders, other than the acquiror of a specified percentage (say, 20%), of the target's stock, to purchase shares in the target at a 50% discount upon the accumulation by the acquiror of the specified percentage (*i.e.*, no self-dealing is required). Poison pill plans which include the percentage-based flip-in feature are now common because they give the Board an opportunity to negotiate an acceptable acquisition with a hostile acquiror which treats shareholders fairly and equally (*i.e.*, the Board can redeem the Pill if a deal meeting these criteria is struck).

The two competing overall views of the function and purpose of poison pills are best summarized in Mr. MacIntosh's article at pp. 278-81:

(1) Shareholder Interest Hypothesis

The germ of this explanation is that a hostile acquiror is able to employ coercive tactics that effectively force target shareholders to tender into a low bid, even though shareholders as a group would prefer to hold out for more. The poison pill is the antidote to this coercion. By making an acquisition prohibitively expensive without the co-operation of management, the pill enables management to, in effect, act as a bargaining agent for shareholders. So empowered, management may either defeat a bid that is too low, force the acquiror to make a more generous offer, or shop the company around for a better bid. Alternatively, management may use the breathing space accorded them by the pill to put together a competing proposal, like a "self-tender" (issuer bid), recapitalization, divestiture of assets or the like resulting in greater value for the target shareholders. In this way, shareholders will receive "full and fair value" of their shares.

(2) The Management Entrenchment Hypothesis

When a successful hostile takeover bid occurs, the end result may be, and often is, loss of employment for the incumbent managers. This creates a potent conflict of interest for target managers, who may be more tempted to preserve their jobs at all costs than to act in the best interests of shareholders. Thus, the power given target management by the pill may be used abusively, rather than beneficially, to deter or thwart hostile bids and preserve managerial tenure. Because takeover bids usually result in the payment of large premiums to target shareholders, foreclosing a bid will result in a loss of potential takeover premiums with a corresponding diminution in share values. Moreover, incumbent managers will be insulated from the market for corporate control; shareholders may therefore find themselves stuck with inefficient managers, resulting in further losses in share value. [footnotes omitted]

The coercive tactics which the poison pill was intended to counteract are two tier bids, street sweeps and greenmail. They are described by Mr. Coleman at p. 3 and Mr. MacIntosh at pp. 279-80. However, in Canada, these tactics are limited by securities laws designed to protect shareholders in cases of take-over bids. Such legislation was first enacted in Ontario and in Saskatchewan is Pt. XVI of the Securities Act, 1988, S.S. 1988-89, c. S-42.2. This Part includes rules:

(i) requiring that identical consideration be paid to all shareholders in connection with the bid (s. 106);

(ii) integrating prebid purchases made within 90 days prior to a formal offer by requiring that the subsequent offer be made at a consideration at least equal to the consideration paid in connection with the prebid purchases (s. 103(6));

(iii) restricting market acquisitions during the course of a bid (s. 103(2));

(iv) prohibiting postbid acquisitions for a period of 20 days following the expiration of a bid (s. 103(7));

(v) restricting private agreement acquisitions at a premium to the market price (ss. 103(2), (6), (7), 104 and 106);

(vi) regulating certain private transactions (ss. 110, 111).

The effect of these provisions is to prohibit, or at least render less effective, coercive tactics available to corporate raiders in the United States. As a result, Canadian securities regulators have generally taken the position that poison pills are unnecessary in Canada.

This is reflected in National Policy No. 38, published by the Canadian Securities Administrators, which says, in part, as follows:

2. The primary objective of take-over bid legislation is the protection of the bona fide interests of the shareholders of the target company. A secondary objective is to provide a regulatory framework within which take-over bids may proceed in an open and even-handed environment. The rules should favour neither the offeror nor the management of the target company, but should leave the shareholders of the offeree company free to make a fully informed decision. The administrators are concerned that certain defensive measures taken by management may have the effect

of denying to shareholders the ability to make such a decision and of frustrating an open take-over bid process.

5. The administrators consider that unrestricted auctions produce the most desirable results in take-over bids and is reluctant to intervene in contested bids. However, the administrators will take appropriate action where they become aware of defensive tactics that will likely result in shareholders being deprived of the ability to respond to a take-over bid or to a competing bid.

6. The administrators appreciate that defensive tactics, including those that may consist of some of the actions listed in paragraph 4, may be taken by a board of directors in genuine search of a better offer. It is only those tactics that are likely to deny or severely limit the ability of the shareholders to respond to a take-over bid or a competing bid, that may result in action by the administrators.

The National Policy also makes the point that prior shareholder approval of corporate action against apprehended or actual take-over bids would, in appropriate cases, allay concerns over shareholders' rights.

F. Iacobucci, then Dean, Faculty of Law, University of Toronto, in an article, "Planning and Implementing Defences to Take-over Bids: The Directors' Role" (1980-81), 5 Can. Bus. L.J. 131, said at p. 160:

The takeover bid provisions of the Ontario Securities Act were the first of their kind adopted in North America. It is interesting to recall what the Kimber Committee stated was the primary objective of the take-over bid laws:

"The Committee has concluded that the primary objective of any recommendations for legislation with respect to the take-over bid transaction should be the protection of the bona fide interests of the shareholders of the offeree company. Shareholders should have made available to them, as a matter of law, sufficient up-to-date relevant information to permit them to come to a reasoned decision as to the desirability of accepting a bid for their shares. In arriving at its conclusions, however, the Committee attempted to ensure that its recommendations would not unduly impede potential bidders or put them in a commercially disadvantageous position vis-à-vis an entrenched and possibly hostile board of directors of an offeree company."

In furtherance of these aims, the Securities Act recognizes that the acceptance or rejection of the offer is still the prerogative of the offeree shareholders.

He also said at p. 165:

Shareholders should enjoy the fundamental rights of disposing of their shares and of deciding who shall run the affairs of the corporation, free from director interference.

Part XVI of the Securities Act, 1988, also places certain duties on the directors of a corporation in respect of which a takeover bid has been made. Section 108 provides as follows:

108(1) Where a take-over bid has been made, a directors' circular shall be prepared and delivered, not later than 10 days after the date of the bid, by the board of directors of an offeree issuer to every person and company to whom a take-over bid must be delivered pursuant to subsection 104(2).

(2) The board of directors shall include in a directors' circular either:

(a) a recommendation to accept or to reject a take-over bid and the reasons for their recommendation; or

(b) a statement that they are unable to make or are not making a recommendation and if no recommendation is made, the reasons for not making a recommendation.

(3) An individual director or officer may recommend acceptance or rejection of a take-over bid if the director or officer delivers with the recommendation a circular prepared in accordance with the regulations.

(4) Where a board of directors is considering recommending acceptance or rejection of a take-over bid, it shall, at the time of sending or delivering a directors' circular, advise the security holders of this fact and may advise them not to tender their securities until further communication is received from the directors.

(5) Where subsection (4) applies, the board of directors shall deliver the recommendation or the decision not to make a recommendation at least seven days before the scheduled expiry of the period during which securities may be deposited under the bid.

(6) Where, before the expiry of a take-over bid or after the expiry of the bid but before the expiry of all rights to withdraw the securities that have been deposited under the bid:

(a) a change has occurred in the information contained in a directors' circular or in any notice of change to a directors' circular that would reasonably be expected to affect the decision of the holders of the securities to accept or reject the bid, the board of directors of the offeree issuer shall immediately deliver a notice of the change to every person or company to whom the circular was required to be sent disclosing the nature and substance of the change; or

(b) a change has occurred in the information contained in an individual director's or officer's circular or any notice of change to that directors' or officers' circular that would reasonably be expected to affect the decision of the holders of the securities to accept or reject the bid, other than a change that is not within the control of the individual director or officer, as the case may be, the individual director or officer, as the case may be, shall immediately deliver a notice of change to the board of directors.

(7) Where an individual director or officer submits a circular pursuant to subsection (3) or a notice of change pursuant to clause (6)(b) to the board of directors, the board, at the offeree issuer's expense, shall deliver a copy of the circular or notice to the persons and companies mentioned in subsection (1).

(8) A directors' circular, director's or officer's circular and a notice of change shall be in the form and contain the information required by this Part and the regulations.

This background as to adoption of poison pills, as created in the United States, and imported into Canada, and the policy behind the take-over bid provisions in the provincial Securities Acts in Canada is important to this case. One of the fundamental issues in this case is the extent to which the policy considerations behind the securities legislation should influence the court's interpretation of (a) the powers of directors to act, in respect of actual or apprehended take-over bids, with or without the approval of shareholders, (b) the duties of the directors to act in the best interests of the corporation, including the shareholders, and (c) the right of shareholders to decide the disposition of their shares and the terms of disposition.

Powers and duties of directors in respect of issue of shares: the proper purpose test

The effectiveness of the poison pill generally, and the S.R.A. in this case, is based on the power of the directors to issue new shares and rights to purchase new shares at a discount to real value (ss. 25 and 29, the Business Corporations Act). The appellant's argument is that this power was used for an improper purpose.

The powers and duties of the directors are set out in ss. 97(1) and 117(1) of the Business Corporations Act:

97.—(1) Subject to any unanimous shareholder agreement, the directors of a corporation shall:

(a) exercise the powers of the corporation directly or indirectly through the employees and agents of the corporation; and

(b) direct the management of the business and affairs of the corporation.

117.—(1) Every director and officer of a corporation in exercising his powers and discharging his duties shall:

(a) act honestly and in good faith with a view to the best interests of the corporation; and

(b) exercise the care, diligence and skill that a reasonably prudent person would exercise in comparable circumstances.

Although the duties of the directors are stated to be to the corporation, the authorities say that the corporation cannot be considered as an entity separate from its shareholders. The directors must act in the best interests of the corporation and all of its shareholders. In *Martin v. Gibson* (1907), 15 O.L.R. 623, Boyd C. said [p. 632]:

Now, the persons to be considered and to be benefitted are the whole body of shareholders—not the majority, who may for ordinary purposes control affairs—but the majority plus the minority—all in fact who, being shareholders, constitute the very substance (so to speak) of the incorporated body.

Evershed M.R. said in *Greenhalgh v. Arderne Cinemas*, [1951] Ch. 286 at 291, [1950] 2 All E.R. 1120 (C.A.):

... the phrase, "the company as a whole" does not (at any rate in such a case as the present) mean the company as a commercial entity, distinct from the corporators: it means the corporators as a general body.

There are limits to the powers of directors to issue shares to defeat a take-over bid. *Howard Smith Ltd. v. Ampol Petroleum Ltd.*, [1974] A.C. 821, [1974] 2 W.L.R. 689, [1974] 1 All E.R. 1126 (P.C.), is the leading case cited by those who attack the validity of the poison pill. Lord Wilberforce said at pp. 1135-36:

Just as it is established that directors, within their management powers, may take decisions against the wishes of the majority of shareholders, and indeed that the majority of shareholders cannot control them in the exercise of these powers while they remain in office ... so it must be unconstitutional for directors to use their fiduciary powers over the shares in the company purely for the purpose of destroying an existing majority, or creating a new majority which did not previously exist. To do so is to interfere with that element of the company's constitution which is separate from and set against their power ... The right to dispose of shares at a given price is essentially an individual right to be exercised on individual decision and on which a majority, in the absence of oppression or similar impropriety, is entitled to prevail. Directors are of course entitled to offer advice, and bound to supply information, relevant to the making of such a decision, but to use their fiduciary power solely for the purpose of shifting the power to decide to whom and at what price shares are to be sold cannot be related to any purpose for which the power over the share capital was conferred on them.

See also *Hogg v. Cramphorn Ltd.*, [1967] Ch. 254, [1966] 3 W.L.R. 995, [1966] 3 All E.R. 420.

On the surface, *Teck Corp. Ltd. v. Millar* (1972), [1973] 2 W.W.R. 385, 33 D.L.R. (3d) 288 (B.C.S.C.), presents a different point of view on this issue. Berger J. held that it was within the proper purposes of the directors to consider who is attempting to take over the company, and whether this would be in the interest of the company as a whole. If it was not, then it would be appropriate for the directors to take action with the purpose of defeating such a take-over notwithstanding that they acted contrary to the wishes of the majority shareholders. He said at p. 315:

My own view is that the directors ought to be allowed to consider who is seeking control and why. If they believe that there will be substantial damage to the company's interests if the company is taken over, then the exercise of their powers to defeat those seeking a majority will not necessarily be categorized as improper.

However, as Richard J. points out in *Exco Corp. v. Nova Scotia Savings & Loan Co.* (1987), 35 B.L.R. 149 at 259, 78 N.S.R. (2d) 91, 193 A.P.R. 91 (T.D.), *Teck* could have been decided on a much narrower footing. In *Teck*, the company over which control was sought was a small company with a mining interest it wished to develop. The normal practice in the industry was for such a small company to find a major mining company to participate in the development. It was customary in such a venture for the major mining partner to acquire a significant shareholding in the minor company. Thus, the question of the allotment of shares in *Teck* was inextricably bound up in a question of business judgment concerning the ordinary course of the affairs of the business. This factor placed the decision properly within the purview of the directors. Indeed, Lord Wilberforce spoke of *Teck* with approval in *Howard Smith* (at p. 1135) on this basis.

In *Teck*, the following test was formulated for determining whether or not the directors acted with a proper purpose at pp. 315-16:

I think the Courts should apply the general rule in this way: The directors must act in good faith. Then there must be reasonable grounds for their belief. If they say that they believe there will be substantial damage to the company's interests, then there must be reasonable grounds for that belief. If there are not, that will justify a finding that the directors were actuated by an improper purpose.

In *Exco*, Richard J. said this at p. 261:

Even the test laid out by Berger J., in the *Teck* case requires further refinement if it is to be applied generally. When exercising their power to issue shares from treasury the directors must be able to show that the considerations upon which the decision to issue was based are consistent only with the best interests of the company and inconsistent with any other interests. This burden ought to be on the directors once a treasury share issue has been challenged. I am of the view that such a test is consistent with the fiduciary nature of the director's duty, in fact, it may be just another way of stating that duty.

At p. 262 he stated:

In relating the facts of this case to the law respecting the duty of directors in issuing treasury shares I find that NSS&L directors made a one-sided allotment of shares for the purpose of "watering down" the commanding share equity position of the so-called EXCO group. The NSS&L directors used their rather substantial power for a wrong purpose, i.e., a purpose which was not demonstrably in the best interests of the company. They used their power to support one group in a take-over, a group which the directors had sought out and which was "not unfriendly" to those directors. What the directors did in this case is more consistent with a finding of self-interest than with bona fide company interest. Or, to put it more in the context of the test which I previously set out, what the directors did was not inconsistent with self-interest. In so doing they breached their fiduciary duty to the general body of the shareholders.

In *Olympia & York Enterprises Ltd. v. Hiram Walker Resources Ltd.* (1986), 37 D.L.R. (4th) 193, 59 O.R. (2d) 254 (Div. Ct.), Montgomery J., whose judgment was approved by the Divisional Court [59 O.R. (2d) at 255, 37 D.L.R. (4th) at 194], approved certain defensive tactics undertaken by the directors on the ground that he was satisfied that the directors' actions were taken bona fide for the purpose of maximizing the value of the shares for all shareholders. He cited the *Teck* judgment with approval. The underlying fact situation bore some resemblance to this case. The company which was a target for a take-over bid was trading in the market for considerably less than it was really worth. The take-over bid offer was made for a price above the market, but below the true value. Montgomery J. outlined this situation at p. 210:

Hiram Walker's board found the intrinsic value of the company was not being recognized by those people who trade in the stock exchange. They found that while the market was trading at $28 a share and Gulf was offering $32, the real value of the shares was between $40 and $43 a share. What options did the directors have? If they did nothing, it would be a breach of duty to shareholders. It would be apparent to them that because of the premium over market, sufficient shares might be acquired for Gulf to buy control of the company at an unreasonably low price. Then the vast majority of shareholders would be denied the right to benefit from the real value of the company in which they held shares. No one can assail their advice to shareholders to reject the Gulf bid.

However, Montgomery J. found that not only were the directors justified in advising the shareholders to reject the take-over bid, the directors were also justified in taking other action, in this case, selling certain assets, to ensure that the shareholders received a fair price for their shares [pp. 210-11]:

As Mr. Thompson argued, this is a battle over money. Gulf and I.P.L. want the company and its assets at the cheapest possible price. The board wants the shareholders to get more. How then could they achieve that single purpose? They decided to sell the distilled-spirits business at a price over premium—indeed, at the true value for the benefit of all shareholders. If, as Mr. Laskin wanted, an issuer bid had been the vehicle, control would pass to Gulf at no cost. This is so because shares that are acquired on an issuer bid are cancelled by the company. If the Fingas offer is foreclosed by this court, all shareholders will be denied the opportunity to sell their shares for $40 a share.

Mr. Sexton's complaint is that it is not fair when the company's money is used to better the offer of an outsider. What is not fair is for all shareholders to be compelled to take less than proper value for their shares. I.P.L. would be happy with $40 a share if it were here in its capacity as a shareholder. I.P.L. feels prejudiced because I.P.L. wants the bargain that is in sight and does not want the directors to keep it from I.P.L. and provide it to all shareholders. The same may be said of Olympia & York. There is no obligation, as the applicants would like, to force the directors to use an issuer bid as opposed to a third-part bid. It is clear from Mr. Fatt's affidavit that the third-party approach will save $300 million in tax to Hiram Walker.

The tests adopted by Berger J. in *Teck* and by Richard J. in *Exco*, while stated in a different way, do not conflict with the business judgment rule developed in the United States. Although different states have developed different rules, some of the more notable jurisdictions in corporate law have developed a business judgment rule. It recognizes that, in a take-over situation, the directors will often be in a conflict of interest situation, and, in implementing a poison pill defence strategy, the directors must be able to establish that (a) in good faith they perceived a threat to the corporation, (b) they acted after proper investigation, and (c) the means adopted to oppose the take-over were reasonable in relationship to the threat posed: *Unocal Corp. v. Mesa Petroleum Co.*, 493 A.2d 946 (Del. S.C., 1985) and *Desert Partners Ltd. Partnership v. USG Corp.*, 686 F.Supp. 1289 (N.D. Ill., 1988).

The tests developed in *Teck* and *Exco*, and in the American authorities above referred to, contain relevant considerations. They also extend considerable deference to bona fide business judgments of the directors. However, they do not go far enough to determine this case. They give no principles for determining whether or not the defensive strategy was reasonable in relationship to the threat posed. They do not deal with the principle that shareholders have the right to determine to whom and at what price they will sell their shares as stated in *Howard Smith Ltd.* They fail to consider the effect of the take-over provisions in the provincial securities legislation.

In respect of the latter, National Policy No. 38 of the Canadian Securities Administrators referred to earlier in this judgment accurately reflects the policy considerations behind that legislation and must have a substantial impact in any review of defensive tactics against take-overs. Just as the provisions were intended to prevent abusive, coercive or unfair tactics by persons making take-over bids, they were equally intended to limit the powers of directors to use defensive tactics which might also be abusive, coercive or unfair to shareholders, or tactics which unnecessarily deprive the shareholders of the right to decide to whom and at what price they will sell their shares. Section 108 of the Securities Act, 1988, indicates that the primary role of the directors in respect of a take-over bid is to advise the shareholders, rather than to decide the issue for them. As noted in the policy statement, the primary objective of the legislation is to protect the bona fide interests of the shareholders of the target company and to permit take-over bids to proceed in an open and even-handed environment. Unrestricted auctions produce the most desirable results in take-over bids. Accordingly defensive measures should not deny to the shareholders the ability to make a decision, and it follows that, whenever possible, prior shareholder approval of defensive tactics should be obtained. There may be circumstances where it is impractical or impossible to obtain prior shareholder approval, such as lack of time, but in such instances, delaying measures will usually suffice to give the directors time to find alternatives. The ultimate decision must be left with the shareholders, whether by subsequent ratification of the poison pill, or by presentation to them of the competing offers or other alternatives to the take-over bid, together with the take-over bid itself.

In summary, when a corporation is faced with susceptibility to a take-over bid or an actual take-over bid, the directors must exercise their powers in accordance with their overriding duty to act bona fide and in the best interests of the corporation even though they may find themselves, through no fault of their own, in a conflict of interest situation. If, after investigation, they determine that action is necessary to advance the best interests of the company, they may act, but the onus will be on them to show that their acts were reasonable in relation to the threat posed and were directed to the benefit of the corporation and its shareholders as a whole, and not for an improper purpose such as entrenchment of the directors.

Since the shareholders have the right to decide to whom and at what price they will sell their shares, defensive action must interfere as little as possible with that right. Accordingly, any defensive action should be put to the shareholders for prior approval where possible, or for subsequent ratification if not possible. There may be circumstances where neither is possible, but that was not so in this case. Defensive tactics that result in shareholders being deprived of the ability to respond to a take-over bid or to a competing bid are unacceptable.

Conclusion as to proper purpose

In applying the above criteria to the facts of this case, the most important issue is whether the directors, in adopting the defensive tactics culminating in the issuer bid, met the onus upon them to show that they acted in the best interests of the corporation as a whole, and whether their actions were reasonable in relation to the threat posed. There was no direct evidence from the directors as to their purpose in implementing their defensive strategy. The evidence from which the court must draw its inferences may be summarized as follows.

From the point of view of the directors, the stated purpose of the S.R.A. in documents circulated to the shareholders was to give the directors time to assess any take-over offer and to consider alternatives. Later, after amendment of the S.R.A., the purpose was stated to be "to protect shareholders from an unfair, abusive, or coercive take-over bid." The circular accompanying the issuer bid to shareholders stated as follows:

2. Purpose of the Offer

The directors believe that the Corporation's prospects in the medium to long term are excellent. The Corporation is not, however, widely known in the capital markets nor are its Shares listed for trading on any stock exchange. Although the Shares trade in the over-the-counter market, because of the small number of shareholders and the nature of the shareholdings, trading in the Shares is extremely limited and the trading value of the Shares is not reasonably ascertainable. Accordingly, the opportunity for shareholders to realize on their investment is limited and the directors believe that the price available to shareholders for their Shares does not adequately reflect their value. The directors believe that the purchase by the Corporation of up to 560,000 Shares at a price of $21.50 a Share represents a worthwhile investment and is an appropriate use of the Corporation's funds while providing the Corporation's shareholders with an opportunity to sell a portion of their Shares at a favourable price.

From the point of view of the appellant, as a minority shareholder, the affidavit of Ron Ludke stated as follows:

3. In June, 1985, I was employed as a registered representative of Pemberton Houston Willoughby, the sole securities broker responsible for distributing shares in Producers Pipelines Inc. (hereinafter referred to as "PPI") pursuant to the initial offering of shares in PPI and in such capacity sold shares of PPI to my clients.

4. Since the initial offering of shares in PPI, I have been the most active registered representative trading shares in PPI in Saskatchewan.

5. That I currently have approximately 40 clients who collectively beneficially own in excess of 200,000 shares in PPI.

6. The market for PPI's shares has historically been limited due to the fact that the shares are not traded on any recognized stock exchange and due to the limited number of shares outstanding.

7. A significant number of my clients are interested in disposing of all of their shares in PPI. Under these circumstances, any option for liquidity in the form of a take-over bid by a third party would be beneficial to my clients. It is my understanding, based on Press Releases made by PPI that PPI has adopted a Shareholders Rights Plan (hereinafter referred to as the "SRP") which effectively prevents any interested party from making a take-over bid to acquire the shares of the corporation without first obtaining the approval of the Board of Directors.

8. On October 26, 1990, I attended the annual shareholders meeting of PPI. At that meeting, one of my clients, Thomas Pavlosky, attempted to introduce a resolution in the form attached as Exhibit "A" hereto, however, his request was ruled out of order by the Chairman. [The resolution was that the SRA be rescinded as being against the interests of the shareholders.]

9. In my opinion, my clients are capable of making their own investment decisions with respect to whether any offer to purchase their shares is in their best interests and the SRP is effectively denying them the opportunity to make such decisions and vests such authority with the Board of Directors of PPI.

10. In my opinion, by effectively preventing potential bidders from making an offer to acquire shares in PPI directly to shareholders, the directors have acted in a manner which unfairly disregards the interests of my clients. I have advised my clients who wish to dispose of all of their shares in PPI that at the present they have no alternative but to tender their shares to the issuer bid and then sell any shares not taken up by PPI in the over-the-counter market after the issuer bid. I have also advised my clients that the opportunities for investors to dispose of their shares in PPI in the over-the-counter market after the issuer bid will be even more limited by virtue of the fact that there will be fewer shares outstanding and fewer shareholders, and accordingly, shares can be expected to trade at a substantial discount from $21.50.

11. I have reviewed the issuer bid by PPI to purchase 560,000 of its shares at a price of $21.50 per share and am of the opinion that it is highly unlikely that any third parties will make a take-over bid for the shares of PPI after the completion of the issuer bid since the parties to the Shareholders Agreement between Penfund and the directors of PPI (discussed on Page 21 of the

Offer and Circular sent to all shareholders by PPI) will effectively control PPI after the completion of the issuer bid.

It is fair to infer that the board of directors saw the proposed bid of Saskoil in August to be too low and that, in response, it implemented the S.R.A. to give it until December 27, 1990, when the agreement would expire, to consider alternatives. In view of the subsequent valuation of the shares at $19 to $21.50 per share, the concern of the directors was clearly justified and their actions to this point were reasonable, except in one respect. They did not put the S.R.A. to the shareholders for ratification at the meeting in October 1990. It was said that this was done because the S.R.A. would lapse, by its own terms, on December 27. However, that proved not to be the case.

It was the extension and amendment of the S.R.A., which was outlined in a management information circular accompanying the notice of special general meeting of the shareholders scheduled for February 25, 1991, which was the real cause for complaint. The circular stated as follows:

In order to protect shareholders from an unfair, abusive or coercive takeover bid, on December 15, 1990, the Board of Directors amended the Rights plan to extend its operation until February 28, 1991. The Rights plan was also amended to provide that a permitted bid can now only be made with the prior approval with the Board of Directors even if it is an all cash bid for all the common shares of the Corporation. The Rights plan will terminate on February 28, 1991.

Later, the S.R.A. was again extended to April 15, 1991, a date after which the issuer bid would be completed.

The purpose of the extended and amended S.R.A., in conjunction with the issuer bid, was, at this point, unequivocal. The terms of a permitted take-over bid were, all cash, for all shares, and only with the unanimous approval of the board of directors. There was agreement among the directors that approval would not be given at a price less than $25 a share, a price 25 per cent above the appraised value. These terms were so onerous that any take-over bid was effectively prohibited.

At the same time as the shareholders were deprived of the right to consider any take-over bid, they were forced to consider authorization of the issuer bid. The effect of these tactics was coercion of the shareholders for the reasons stated in Mr. Ludke's affidavit. In view of the lack of liquidity, due to lack of market for the shares, those shareholders who wanted to realize anything approaching the appraised value of a portion of their shares had no choice but to tender to the issuer bid. While the result would be liquidation of an uncertain number of their shares at appraised value, they would be left with a substantial number of the shares which, if saleable at all, would be saleable at a substantially less value. A shareholder seeking some liquidity, with the knowledge that take-over bids were effectively prohibited, would have no choice but to authorize the issuer bid and to tender to it. For these reasons, no weight can be given to the shareholder vote authorizing the issuer bid.

The purpose of the defensive action is apparent: effective prohibition of the appellant's proposed take-over bid or any other take-over bid, until after the shareholders were forced to consider authorization of and tender to the issuer bid. The result was to deprive the shareholders of any alternative to the issuer bid except to hold their shares which, if marketable, would no doubt continue to trade at a value substantially less than appraised value. The fact that the S.R.A. was not put to the shareholders for ratification either prior to, or simultaneous with, the issuer bid confirms the view that the purpose of the directors was to force the issuer bid on the shareholders without the choice of any possible alternative such as the appellant's proposed take-over bid or any other take-over bid.

These actions were in interference with the shareholders' rights to determine the disposition of their shares. That raises the question of whether acting without shareholder approval of the S.R.A. was necessary in the circumstances. No reason was advanced by the directors for failure to put the matter to the shareholders. The only inference which can be drawn from that is that the directors wished to make the decision themselves in order to ensure their continued control of the company. They thus acted for an improper purpose.

There are a number of other reasons which support a conclusion that the defensive action was neither reasonable in proportion to the threat posed, nor taken in the best interests of the company, but was taken with a view to further entrenching the directors group: (a) the board of directors made no effort to show that a take-over by Saskoil would be harmful to the corporation except that the proposed offer at $16 to $18 per share was below the appraised value of the shares; (b) they made no effort to negotiate with Saskoil to increase the amount offered per share; (c) they did not seek any competitive bids (except their own issuer bid) although the material indicated that a couple of other parties had indicated an interest in making a take-over offer; (d) they made no effort to establish, through evidence, that tender of shares to the issuer bid would ultimately result in a better value to the shareholders for all of their shares than a take-over bid, even at a price of $16 to $18 per share; (e) they agreed among themselves that they would not permit a bid under the S.R.A. at less than $25 per share, some 25 per cent above appraised value; (f) they offered no valid business reason, from the point of view of the company, for the issuer bid, the completion of which would further entrench the directors at the expense of a substantial increase in the indebtedness of the company.

None of these things point to any effort to increase or maximize the value of the shares, or to obtain the best possible offer for them. They point to one objective, and one objective only: the prohibition of any take-over bid until after completion of the issuer bid, the result of which would be that the directors group would control a majority of the shares, thus making the company impregnable to any take-over bid unacceptable to the board.

In fairness to the directors, it was assumed by all parties, and accepted by the court, that the board of directors acted bona fide and in the belief that the future of the company was such that the shareholders would be better off maintaining the corporation as it was, rather than letting it be taken over by Saskoil.

However, as noted above, the directors did not meet the onus upon them to show that their actions were necessarily in the best interests of the company. Furthermore, a decision of that nature was one to be taken by the shareholders, and the directors were not, in the circumstances, entitled to deprive them of the right to make that decision.

The chambers judge found that the purpose of the S.R.A. could not be to entrench the directors because they were already entrenched. The evidence is unclear as to the exact percentage of the shares that the directors group controlled at the time Saskoil purchased its shares. It was certainly over 40 per cent. Whatever percentage was control-led by the directors at all relevant times, the effect of the S.R.A. and completed issuer bid would be to increase it and thus increase the control of the directors. If that was to be the effect, the inference must be that that was the purpose. And that was an improper purpose unless the board could show that it was for the benefit of the corporation as a whole, including the shareholders. It did not do so.

The actions taken by the directors in this case amounted to telling Saskoil that it would not, under any circumstances, permit itself to be taken over. We agree with the following comment by Mr. Coleman in his article at p. 6:

Some U.S. securities lawyers have suggested that so long as they act in good faith and on reason-able grounds, boards of directors can just say no to a potential acquiror whose price the board be-lieves to be inadequate. In such a case, it is argued, directors should be able to resist pressure to withdraw poison pill defences and they do not have to seek higher bidders or recapitalize to boost short term value. Because it is reminiscent of the "just say no" anti-drug campaign, this approach has been termed the "Nancy Reagan defence."

Does a Board breach its fiduciary duty by refusing to negotiate with a potential acquiror to remove the coercive and inadequate aspects of an offer? A Board may decide not to bargain over the terms of an offer because doing so conveys a message to the market that (a) the company is for sale when, in fact, it is not; and (b) the initial offer by the bidder is "in the ballpark" when, again, it is not. However, it can be expected that the courts will conclude that a "just say no" re-sponse to a cash take-over bid for all shares does not justify keeping a Pill in place indefinitely if shareholders are prevented from responding to the bid.

The S.R.A. is objectionable in three other respects. First, as found by the trial judge, it may, in certain circumstances, require the directors to act contrary to the rule that the directors cannot, without the consent of the shareholders, fetter their future discretion: Gower, Principles of Modern Company Law, 4th ed. (1979), p. 582; *Ringuet v. Bergeron*, [1960] S.C.R. 672, 24 D.L.R. (2d) 449 [Que.]. Second, it may, in certain circumstances, require the directors to act contrary to s. 108 of the Securities Act, 1988, quoted above, which imposes certain duties upon the directors when a take-over bid is made, including the duty to send a directors' circular to every person affected within ten days of a take-over bid. Third, its extension beyond December 27, 1990, violated the terms of the S.R.A. itself, which provided that it would expire on December 27, 1990, if not previously ratified by the shareholders of the corporation.

The appellant made an argument that the S.R.A. was illegal to the extent that it discriminated against the appellant, as a shareholder, by making it ineligible, in the event of a take-over bid by it, to exercise the rights granted by the S.R.A. to other shareholders. The appellant would thus suffer punitive dilution. The substance of this argument is summarized by Mr. Coleman in his article at p. 9. In view of our conclu-sions above, we need not consider this aspect of the matter.

Section 234, Business Corporations Act

This application is brought under s. 234 of the Business Corporations Act, which pro-vides as follows:

234.—(1) A complainant may apply to a court for an order under this section.

(2) If, upon an application under subsection (1), the court is satisfied that in respect of a corporation or any of its affiliates:

(a) any act or omission of the corporation or any of its affiliates effects a result;

(b) the business or affairs of the corporation or any of its affiliates are or have been carried on or conducted in a manner; or

(c) the powers of the directors of the corporation or any of its affiliates are or have been exercised in a manner;

that is oppressive or unfairly prejudicial to or that unfairly disregards the interests of any security holders, creditor, director or officer, the court may make an order to rectify the matters complained of.

For convenience, the remedy under s. 234 will be referred to in this judgment as the oppression remedy whether based on a finding that the actions were "oppressive," "unfairly prejudicial" or that "unfairly disregard." The meaning of these terms was considered by this court in *Eiserman v. Ara Farms*, [1988] 5 W.W.R. 97, 52 D.L.R. (4th) 498, 67 Sask. R. 1. The legislation is remedial and is to be given a broad interpretation. Each case turns on its own facts: what may be oppressive or unfairly prejudicial in one case may not necessarily be so in a different setting: *Eiserman*, supra; *Ferguson v. Imax Systems Corp.* (1983), 43 O.R. (2d) 128, 150 D.L.R. (3d) 718 (C.A.).

The respondent argued that since the appellant acquired its shares in the respondent for the purpose of a take-over bid, and that its purpose in making this application was to permit it to proceed with a take-over bid, a remedy under s. 234 was inappropriate since the right to make a take-over bid had nothing to do with rights accruing from ownership of shares. That overlooks the fact that when the appellant acquired its shares, for whatever purpose, it acquired the same rights as any other shareholder. And those included the right to determine to whom and at what price to sell its shares in the event of a take-over bid. While its own proposed offer was the only one in evidence, and it could not sell to itself, the poison pill was effective against any possible take-over bid. There was some evidence that others were interested in a take-over. Thus, the appellant, as a shareholder, was deprived of the right to consider possible take-over bids and thus had status to claim relief under s. 234. In any event, any shareholder has status to object to an illegal poison pill whether any offer is in prospect or not. This judgment has determined that the appellant's right to determine disposition of its shares was violated by the directors acting beyond their powers. Such action was unfairly prejudicial to the appellant and entitles the court to grant relief under s. 234.

The respondent argued that, since the appellant purchased its shares when it knew the S.R.A. was in place, it knowingly bought into any oppression and should be denied relief. However, the actions found to be beyond the powers of the directors occurred later. In any event, we agree with the reasoning of Southey J. in *Palmer v. Carling O'Keefe Breweries of Canada Ltd.* (1989), 41 B.L.R. 128, 56 D.L.R. (4th) 128 at 136-37, 67 O.R. (2d) 161, 32 O.A.C. 113 (Div. Ct.):

I am unimpressed with the argument that no relief should be given in respect of shares purchased after the intention to amalgamate became known. The submission was that, in respect of those shares, the purchasers "bought into the oppression." If relief is given to anyone in these proceedings, it will mean that the applicant correctly appreciated the legal rights of the preference share-holders. If the applicant and others could not take advantage of those rights with respect to the shares they were bold enough to purchase while those rights were still in dispute, it would mean that less sanguine owners would be deprived of the advantage of selling their shares during the pending litigation at prices reflecting the purchasers' estimate of the chances of success. Any such rule would place a new and, in my view, unwarranted restriction on the price of shares that are traded on a stock exchange.

The conduct of the applicant and those associated in the same interest will either turn out to have provided an effective check on unlawful acts by the directors, or it will prove to have been a very expensive exercise in tilting at windmills. The owners of small numbers of shares probably could not afford to run the risks involved in providing such check.

Remedy

P.P.I. suggested that an appropriate remedy, if oppression were found, would be to require the respondent to buy the appellant's shares. It further argued that any order setting aside the issuer bid might be unfairly prejudicial to those shareholders who had tendered to it and had expected to receive the proceeds of the sale.

We are fully aware of the breadth of s. 234 and the problem of balancing the rights of an individual shareholder in conflict with the rights of the company as a whole, or with the rights of all of the other shareholders.

This case poses no such problem in that a remedy is available which will give the shareholders, as a whole, the right to determine the issue themselves. The remedy is to set aside the S.R.A. and to extend the closing date of the issuer bid from March 28, 1991, to 45 days after the date of this judgment. All other dates under the issuer bid are extended accordingly. Otherwise, all terms remain the same. This will permit the appellant, or any person interested, to make a take-over bid and will give all shareholders a choice between the issuer bid (if the respondent chooses not to with-draw it) and any take-over bid. The parties are to agree on the form of the formal judgment before it is issued and, failing agreement, application may be made to the court for further directions.

The appellant will have its costs of this application under double col. V.

NOTES

1) The Court of Appeal makes reference to the decision in *Unocal* in passing, only to conclude that the U.S. case law does not provide enough guidance with respect to the standards that should govern the use of defensive tactics. In the light of the Delaware jurisprudence reviewed earlier in this section, do you think that this is a valid observa-tion? Was it necessary to turn to National Policy 38 for guidance? Is it appropriate for a court to rely on the pronouncements of securities regulators regarding their approach to take-over regulations when interpreting sections of a Business Corporations Act? For one perspective on these questions, see Yalden, *Controlling the Use and Abuse of Poison Pills in Canada: 347883 Alberta Ltd. v Producers Pipelines Inc.*, 37 McGill L.J. 887 (1992).

2) In the same way that Canadian securities regulators have imposed their own vision of fairness in the context of buyout transactions through OSC Policy 9.1, so too they have introduced distinctive standards in the take-over context through the adoption of National Policy 38. Once again, one needs to consider whether this is in fact necessary and whether the desire to impose a particular vision of fairness on the take-over process comes at the cost of restricting a target company's flexibility in pursuing corporate objectives. We have already seen that the decision in *Teck* relied on *Cheff v. Mathes* for guidance, the very same decision of the Delaware courts that underlies cases stretching from *Unocal* through *Revlon* to *Time* and *Paramount*. Could take-overs in Canada not be regulated through a similar body of law that builds on the decision in *Teck*?

In reaching to National Policy 38, the Court of Appeal relied on a policy statement that is influenced by a particular vision of the corporation. For example, Stanley Beck, the chairman of the Ontario Securities Commission at the time that the statement was adopted, has written that "National Policy 38 reflects an attempt to ensure that the owners of the company have the ability to sell their ownership rights; hence a restriction on target management intervention": S. Beck & R. Wildeboer, *National Policy 38 as a Regulator of Defensive Tactics, Meredith Memorial Lectures*, 119-39 (1987). Do you share this vision of the shareholder's relation to the corporation? Is it consistent with the vision of the firm set out in *Teck*? In view of the material seen in Chapter Four, is it accurate to refer to shareholders as the owners of the corporation?

3) While *Producers Pipeline* was brought by way of a claim under the oppression remedy, in fact little time is spent analyzing the oppression remedy. Do you think that the court should have spent more time looking at the role of the oppression remedy in connection with take-overs instead of focusing on National Policy 38? What conclusions might it have reached? Does the oppression remedy offer a framework for considering the impact of take-overs on the interests of constituencies other than shareholders?

4) In late 1994, the Ontario Securities Commission was twice called upon to consider poison pills that *had* been ratified by shareholders: *Lac Minerals Ltd. and Royal Oak Mines Inc.* (1994), 17 O.S.C.B. 4963 and *MDC Corporation and Royal Greetings & Gifts* (1994), 17 O.S.C.B. 4971. In both cases the O.S.C. acknowledged that boards of directors must abide by their fiduciary duties when assessing the merits of an unsolicited take-over bid and that this process involves decisions about whether it is appropriate to terminate a rights plan. But the O.S.C. went on to state that its responsibility was not to assess whether directors were acting for a proper purpose and reasonably in using the rights plan. Rather, its job was "to focus on whether it is in the public interest, more particularly the interest of target company shareholders, that the shareholder rights plan be allowed to continue to operate" (*Lac*, at 4968). In both cases the O.S.C. allowed a shareholder rights plan to stay in place for a limited period, but made clear that after that period it would issue a cease trade order in respect of the Rights issued under the shareholder rights plan in order to allow the target company's shareholders to decide on the merits of the bid. The O.S.C. referred to National Policy 38 as a touchstone for its analysis. It also placed considerable weight on the views of shareholders regarding the merits of keeping the shareholder rights plan in place.

The O.S.C. has therefore set about assessing the merits of rights plans on a basis that does not treat questions concerning a board's fiduciary duties as the focal point for analysis. At the same time, *Producers Pipeline* suggests that courts that focus on fiduciary duties are prepared to look to National Policy 38 to provide content to an analysis of those duties (even though that policy statement is not an expression of the will of the legislature). As for the oppression remedy, it has received very little attention indeed.

Does the way in which this picture is unfolding (including the weight being placed on National Policy 38) trouble you? Does it leave any room for a consideration of the interests of constituencies other than shareholders? Is the decision in *Teck* now irrelevant to an analysis of rights plans?

5) In the first case to come before the O.S.C. in which a rights plan was challenged (*In the Matter of Canadian Jorex Limited and Mannville Oil & Gas Ltd.* (1992), 15 O.S.C.B. 257), the O.S.C. found that the time had come for a rights plan that had not been ratified by shareholders "to go." Commenting on this decision, the O.S.C. stated:

Underlying our conclusion was our view of the public interest in matters such as this. As is amply reflected in National Policy 38, the primary concern of the Commission in contested take-over bids is not whether it is appropriate for a target board to adopt defensive tactics, but whether those tactics "are likely to deny or severely limit the ability of the shareholders to respond to a take-over bid or a competing bid" (paragraph 6) or "may have the effect of denying to shareholders the ability to make a [fully informed] decision and of frustrating an open take-over bid process" (paragraph 2). If so, then as National Policy 38 clearly indicates, the Commission will be quite prepared to intervene to protect the public interest as we see it. For us, the public interest lies in allowing shareholders of a target company to exercise one of the fundamental rights of share ownership—the ability to dispose of shares as one wishes—without undue influence from, among other things, defensive tactics that may have been adopted by the target board with the best of intentions, but that are either misguided from the outset or, as here, have outlived their usefulness.

If the facts seen in *Time* had occurred in Ontario and had come before the O.S.C., would the result have been the same or would the O.S.C. have forced *Time* to bring its rights plan to end? What would the result have been if the facts in *Time* had come before the Saskatchewan Court of Appeal?

6. Disclosure and Defensive Suits

Despite the occasional decision decided by the courts (e.g., *Re Calgary Power Ltd.* (1980), 115 D.L.R. (3d) 625, 12 B.L.R. 16 (Alta. Q.B.)), securities decisions in Canada, unlike the United States, are generally rendered not by the courts but by securities commissions, most often the O.S.C. One reason for this reluctance to decide securities cases is a belief that such decisions should be left to the O.S.C. This is particularly the case when the contest is between rival bidders, as in *Forefront Consol. Explorations Ltd. v. Lumsden Bldg. Corp.*, 3 Can. Sec. L. Rep. (CCH) para. 70-117. Thus in *First City Financial Corp. v. Genstar Corp.* (1981), 33 O.R. (2d) 631, 642-43, Reid J. stated that:

The issue, therefore, is simply whether there has been wrongful non-disclosure. I see no real difference between the requirements of the common law in relation to directors and the requirements of the Securities Act in relation to directors. ... If I am right in that conclusion it follows that resort to the Ontario Securities Commission for intervention in this contest for an alleged failure by defendants to make disclosure would amount to an equally effective alternative to an interlocutory injunction.

Indeed, it seems to me that the alternative is more than simply equal; it is preferable. Broadly speaking, the Ontario Securities Commission has a mandate to regulate trading in securities. Trading is defined to include an offer. It has a broad mandate to represent the interests of the public. In that way shareholders in a contest such as this are represented. It has extensive means to ensure that the provisions of the Act in relation to disclosure are complied with. In the circumstances of this case that means that Canada Permanent shareholders may be required to be given information material to their consideration of the competing bids.

Thus, my concern that shareholders are not represented here would be set at rest. It appears to me that the Commission has adequate jurisdiction and power to deal with the issue of non-disclosure in the circumstances of this case. If that is not found under s. 123 of the Act, then other sections may well be available, both to create jurisdiction and to authorize action.

See also *Royal Trustco Ltd. v. Campeau Ltd.* (1980), 31 O.R. (2d) 75, aff'd, 31 O.R. (2d) 130 (C.A.). Apart from the O.S.C., the Director under the CBCA may also commence proceedings on breach of CBCA take-over bid requirements. See *Sparling v. Royal Trustco Ltd.* (1984), 45 O.R. (2d) 484 (C.A.).

For an eye-opening discussion of litigation tactics to advance or defeat a take-over bid, see Wachtell, *Special Tender Offer Litigation Tactics*, 32 Bus. Law. 1433 (1977).

Disclosure by Target Corporations. Unlike tender offer legislation in the United States, the OSA imposes special disclosure duties on target corporations. One of the purposes of mandating such disclosure is to ensure that the target corrects any material misrepresentations made in the take-over bid circular. See Form 35, Item 10. Will Canadian courts therefore be more tolerant of such misrepresentations? In *Forefront Consol. Explorations Ltd. v. Lumsden Bldg. Corp.* (1978) (unreported judgment, Ontario Supreme Court, December 1, 1978), the target's motion for injunctive relief for misrepresentations in a take-over bid circular failed because, among other reasons, the target had itself advised its shareholders of the misrepresentations. See the note of the case in 3 Can. Sec. L. Rep. (CCH) para. 70-117.

Canadian securities legislation places significant obstacles in the path of a tender offeror and, to the extent that standing is granted, useful tactical defences in the hands of a target. By contrast, notwithstanding the requirement of a directors' circular, restrictions on the response of the target have generally been left to the common law and the proper purposes doctrine. Does this tip the scales excessively in favour of the target? If so, decisions such as *Lumsden* may be welcomed.

A further response is to suggest that directors of a target corporation have a duty to disclose defensive manoeuvres they undertake to defeat a take-over bid. The issue arose in *In the Matter of Royal Trustco Ltd.*, [1981] 2 O.S.C.B. 322C, where a significant portion of the Canadian financial community joined forces to help Royal Trustco Ltd. defeat a take-over bid by Campeau Corp. The take-over bid circular was mailed on August 29, 1980 and a directors' circular on September 8. The directors' circular stated that management had been advised "by a large number of persons ... that they intend to purchase shares of Royal Trustco in the market during the Offer Period. While all of the purposes of such purchases are not known to the directors and officers, many have stated that their purposes include maintaining Royal Trustco as a public company not under control of a single individual or corporation ... ." *Id.* at 338C. On September 19, the Campeau bid was extended and the price increased. On September 22, White, the President of Royal Trustco, responded with a letter that affirmed the earlier recommendation to reject the Campeau bid. It was alleged that the directors' circular and the September 22 letter did not adequately disclose the indications of support that Royal Trustco had received from its allies in its attempts to defeat the bid. The evidence also suggested that White and Scholes, another senior officer of Royal Trustco, had tipped off institutional investors that the bid was likely to fail.

It appears clear that the officers and directors of a target company may properly take steps to oppose a take-over bid where they believe honestly and in good faith that the defeat of the bid would be in the best interest of the corporation and its shareholders. It is not suggested that it is improper to request existing shareholders not to tender to the bid (as the Trustco directors did through the September 8 and 22 communications), to solicit friends to purchase shares for the purpose of denying them to the bidder, or to seek white knights. Having embarked on such an active defence, apart from telling the shareholders the negative features of the offer and recommending against it, what positive obligation do the directors have to communicate details of the defence activity to the shareholders together with a report on its perceived success?

The decision in *Chris-Craft Industries Inc. v. Piper Aircraft Corp.*, 480 F.2d 341 (2d Cir., 1973) describes the responsibility of officers and directors in the context of a contested take-over bid at pages 364-65 as follows,

> Corporate officers and directors in their relationship with shareholders owe a high fiduciary duty of honesty and fair dealing ... By reasons of the special relationship between them, shareholders are likely to rely heavily upon the representations of corporate insiders when the shareholders find themselves in the midst of a battle for control. Corporate insiders therefore have the special responsibility to be meticulous and precise in their representations to shareholders.

The Notice of Hearing alleges that the September 8 Directors' Circular was deficient, to the knowledge of White and Scholes, in that it failed to disclose the nature, and the extent of the defensive action being taken by Trustco's managers. The circular in fact misdirects the reader from the success they actually were having in mounting this defence in stating,

> ... The directors and officers of Royal Trustco have been advised by a large number of persons acting independently that they intend to purchase shares of Royal Trustco in the market during the Offer Period. While all of the purposes of such purchases are not known to the directors and officers, many have stated that their purposes include maintaining Royal Trustco as a public company not under the control of a single individual or corporation.

As noted previously under sections 96 and 97 of the Act the directors were obliged to send a directors' circular to each shareholder within ten days of the offer. Section 165 of the Regulation to the Act provides that the directors' circular shall provide the information contained in Form 32. Item 12 of Form 32 requires the directors to,

State the particulars of any other information not disclosed in the foregoing but known to the directors which would reasonably be expected to affect the decision of the security holders of the offeree company to accept or reject the offer.

. . .

Any attempt to characterize the September 22 White letter as a Directors' Circular ... and to determine whether it is required to be sent under the existing legislation is not helpful. It was at the least a communication in the nature of a Directors' Circular issued with the authority of the directors. It refers to the September 8 Directors' Circular and, in effect, purports to update the information referring to subsequent events. It fails to make even the simplest of statements concerning the efforts that had been made, the alternative plans considered, all of which had resulted in the purchases recorded above. Indeed it would have been possible to state that in excess of 50% of the shares were held by persons or corporations who had indicated they were purchasing for investment and not for the purpose of tendering to the bid. This would be more accurate than stating, as we noted above, that "many (purchasers) have stated their purpose including maintaining Royal Trustco as a public company not under the control of a single person or corporation." This latter statement is subject to criticism for what it omits to say.

Duty to Update

Some members of the panel are of the view that, while White and Scholes might not have had enough reliable information on September 5-8 to include a status report on the success of the defence in the Directors' Circular that was not the case on September 11 or 16 when White reported to the directors and on September 17 when White and Scholes felt obliged to report to the T.D. officers. In this case, in the face of the extended Campeau bid, the Trustco directors through the September 22 letter purported to update the original Directors' Circular. The deficiencies perceived in the original circular were compounded by the additional information in the possession of White and Scholes and through them the other Trustco directors by September 22.

There appears to be little case law dealing with a duty to update. Section 52(1) of the Act requires that, during the period of distribution, where a material change occurs an amendment must be filed to the prospectus within ten days of the change. There is no parallel requirement for take-over documents. But in a case like the present one there should be an obligation on the issuer of a document to update previously disclosed information if, as in this case, it would be reasonable to assume the shareholders continued to rely on it in reaching a decision as to whether to tender the shares, hold them or sell them into the market.

In *S.E.C. v. Shattuck Denn Mining Corp.*, 297 F. Supp 470, 476 (S.D.N.Y. 1968) the corporation's press release, although accurate when issued, became materially misleading shortly thereafter. The court held that the president of the corporation, who sold stock with knowledge of the new information, violated Rule 10b-5 by trading without correcting the release. The corporation was not held liable because it had not benefitted from the failure to correct. The president, today in Ontario, would have violated section 75 of the Act.

The Commission is of the view that there is in Ontario today a duty to update information previously communicated when that information in the light of subsequent events and absent further explanation, becomes misleading.

"Tipping": Disclosure by Person in "Special Relationship" of Material Facts

All members of the panel, excepting Commissioner Miles, are of the opinion that Messrs. White and Scholes, being persons in a special relationship with Trustco, a reporting issuer, in the terms of section 75(1)(b) of the Act,

> informed, other than in the ordinary course of business, the senior officers of T.D. about facts which they knew (believed) were material facts before the material facts had been generally disclosed.

These were the disclosures of September 17, discussed previously.

Section 75, while not mandating an update, provides sanctions for those who fail to provide material facts to investors generally while informing only some investors. This conduct was contrary to the public interest representing an attempt to confer a benefit upon T.D., by communicating undisclosed information, in order to assist T.D. in reaching its decision not to tender to the Campeau bid.

Sanction

It is the conclusion of the majority of the Commission that Messrs. White and Scholes, being in possession of material facts obtained as a result of the defences undertaken, were able to determine and did determine in reasonably accurate terms the percentage of outstanding Trustco shares being held from time to time by persons or corporations who had no present intention of tendering them to the Campeau bid. This information was volunteered by concerned shareholders and gathered through the initiatives taken by Trustco's management. This information could have been published without the necessity of naming the known holders of shares and in the absence of any commitment not to tender. The shareholders generally were entitled to the material facts communicated on September 17 to the T.D. officers and others. Through the failure to communicate these material facts White and Scholes deprived the remainder of their shareholders of the opportunity to make the same kind of informed investment decisions as to whether to hold, tender to the Campeau bid, or sell into the market. This conduct was not in the best interests of all of their shareholders no matter what moral gloss is placed on their motives in attempting to defeat the Campeau bid. Accordingly some sanction is indicated. [*Id.* at 343C-347C]

Remedies. OSA s. 131 gives offerees remedies for misrepresentations in a circular, and OSA s. 133 provides further rights to shareholders when a circular is not mailed to them. Beyond that, the scope of any implied civil remedies with respect to a circular is not clear. For example, can an offeror sue for misrepresentations in a directors' circular? Can rival bidders sue for misrepresentations in their take-over bid circulars? When a statutory civil remedy is not provided, it is difficult to predict when civil remedies will be implied by a court. Leigh, *Securities Regulation: Problems in Relation to Sanctions*, in 3 *Proposals for a Securities Market Law for Canada* 509, 561 (1979).

Broader statutory rights are available if the corporation is incorporated under the CBCA. Special remedies are provided under s. 205(3) to all of the "interested persons" listed in s. 205(4) when a take-over bid does not comply with the statute or the regulations.

As under OSA s. 130 actions for misrepresentations in a prospectus, offeree share-holders are deemed to have relied on misrepresentations in a take-over or issuer bid circular under OSA s. 131.

F. SALE OF CONTROL

Perlman v. Feldmann
United States Court of Appeals, Second Circuit
219 F.2d 173, cert. denied, 349 U.S. 952 (1955)

CLARK, Chief Judge: This is a derivative action brought by minority stockholders of Newport Steel Corporation to compel accounting for, and restitution of, allegedly illegal gains which accrued to defendants as a result of the sale in August, 1950, of their controlling interest in the corporation. The principal defendant, C. Russell Feldmann, who represented and acted for the others, members of his family,[1] was at that time not only the dominant stockholder, but also the chairman of the board of directors and the president of the corporation. Newport, an Indiana corporation, operated mills for the production of steel sheets for sale to manufacturers of steel products, first at Newport, Kentucky, and later also at other places in Kentucky and Ohio. The buyers, a syndicate organized as Wilport Company, a Delaware corporation, consisted of end-users of steel who were interested in securing a source of supply in a market becoming ever tighter in the Korean War. Plaintiffs contend that the consideration paid for the stock included compensation for the sale of a corporate asset, a power held in trust for the corporation by Feldmann as its fiduciary. This power was the ability to control the allocation of the corporate product in a time of short supply, through control of the board of directors; and it was effectively transferred in this sale by having Feldmann procure the resignation of his own board and the election of Wilport's nominees immediately upon consummation of the sale.

The present action represents the consolidation of three pending stockholders' actions in which yet another stockholder has been permitted to intervene. Jurisdiction below was based upon the diverse citizenship of the parties. Plaintiffs argue here, as they did in the court below, that in the situation here disclosed the vendors must account to the non-participating minority stockholders for that share of their profit which is attributable to the sale of the corporate power. Judge Hincks denied the validity of the premise, holding that the rights involved in the sale were only those normally incident to the possession of a controlling block of shares, with which a dominant stockholder, in the absence of fraud or foreseeable looting, was entitled to deal according to his own

---

[1]   The stock was not held personally by Feldmann in his own name, but was held by the members of his family and by personal corporations. The aggregate of stock thus had amounted to 33% of the outstanding Newport stock and gave working control to the holder. The actual sale included 55,552 additional shares held by friends and associates of Feldmann, so that a total of 37% of the Newport stock was transferred.

best interests. Furthermore, he held that plaintiffs had failed to satisfy their burden of proving that the sales price was not a fair price for the stock per se. Plaintiffs appeal from these rulings of law which resulted in the dismissal of their complaint.

The essential facts found by the trial judge are not in dispute. Newport was a relative newcomer in the steel industry with predominantly old installations which were in the process of being supplemented by more modern facilities. Except in times of extreme shortage Newport was not in a position to compete profitably with other steel mills for customers not in its immediate geographical area. Wilport, the purchasing syndicate, consisted of geographically remote end-users of steel who were interested in buying more steel from Newport than they had been able to obtain during recent periods of tight supply. The price of $20 per share was found by Judge Hincks to be a fair one for a control block of stock, although the over-the-counter market price had not exceeded $12 and the book value per share was $17.03. But this finding was limited by Judge Hincks' statement that "[w]hat value the block would have had if shorn of its appurtenant power to control distribution of the corporate product, the evidence does not show." It was also conditioned by his earlier ruling that the burden was on plaintiffs to prove a lesser value for the stock.

Both as director and as dominant stockholder, Feldmann stood in a fiduciary relationship to the corporation and to the minority stockholders as beneficiaries thereof. *Pepper v. Litton*, 308 U.S. 295, 60 S.Ct 238, 84 L.Ed. 281; *Southern Pac. Co. v. Bogert*, 250 U.S. 483, 39 S.Ct. 533, 63 L.Ed. 1099. His fiduciary obligation must in the first instance be measured by the law of Indiana, the state of incorporation of Newport. ... Although there is no Indiana case directly in point, the most closely analogous one emphasizes the close scrutiny to which Indiana subjects the conduct of fiduciaries when personal benefit may stand in the way of fulfilment of trust obligations. In *Schemmel v. Hill*, 91 Ind.App. 373, 169 N.E. 678, 682, 683, McMahan J. said: "Directors of a business corporation act in a strictly fiduciary capacity. Their office is a trust. ... When a director deals with his corporation, his acts will be closely scrutinized. ... Directors of a corporation are its agents, and they are governed by the rules of law applicable to other agents, and, as between themselves and their principal, the rules relating to honesty and fair dealing in the management of the affairs of their principal are applicable. They must not, in any degree, allow their official conduct to be swayed by their private interest, which must yield to official duty. ... In a transaction between a director and his corporation, where he acts for himself and his principal at the same time in a matter connected with the relation between them, it is presumed, where he is thus potentially on both sides of the contract, that self-interest will overcome his fidelity to his principal, to his own benefit and to his principal's hurt." And the judge added: "Absolute and most scrupulous good faith is the very essence of a director's obligation to his corporation. The first principal duty arising from his official relation is to act in all things of trust wholly for the benefit of his corporation."

In Indiana, then, as elsewhere, the responsibility of the fiduciary is not limited to a proper regard for the tangible balance sheet assets of the corporation, but includes the dedication of his uncorrupted business judgment for the sole benefit of the corporation, in any dealings which may adversely affect it. *Young v. Higbee Co.*, 324 U.S. 204, 65 S.Ct. 594, 89 L.Ed. 890; *Irving Trust Co. v. Deutsch*, 2 Cir., 73 F.2d 121, certiorari denied 294 U.S. 708, 55 S.Ct. 405, 79 L.Ed. 1243; *Seagrave Corp. v. Mount*, 6 Cir., 212 F.2d 389; *Meinhard v. Salmon*, 249 N.Y. 458, 164 N.E. 545, 62 A.L.R. 1; *Commonwealth Title Ins. & Trust Co. v. Seltzer*, 227 Pa. 410, 76 A. 77. Although the Indiana case is particularly relevant to Feldmann as a director, the same rule should apply to his fiduciary duties as majority stockholder, for in that capacity he chooses and controls the directors, and thus is held to have assumed their liability. *Pepper v. Litton*, supra, 308 U.S. 295, 60 S.Ct. 238. This, therefore, is the standard to which Feldmann was by law required to conform in his activities here under scrutiny.

It is true, as defendants have been at pains to point out, that this is not the ordinary case of breach of fiduciary duty. We have here no fraud, no misuse of confidential information, no outright looting of a helpless corporation. But on the other hand, we do not find compliance with that high standard which we have just stated and which we and other courts have come to expect and demand of corporate fiduciaries. In the often-quoted words of Judge Cardozo: "Many forms of conduct permissable in a workaday world for those acting at arm's length, are forbidden to those bound by fiduciary ties. A trustee is held to something stricter than the morals of the market place. Not honesty alone, but the punctilio of an honor the most sensitive, is then the standard of behavior. As to this there has developed a tradition that is unbending and inveterate. Uncompromising rigidity has been the attitude of courts of equity when petitioned to undermine the rule of undivided loyalty by the 'disintegrating erosion' of particular exceptions." *Meinhard v. Salmon*, supra, 249 N.Y. 458, 464, 164 N.E. 545, 546, 62 A.L.R. 1. The actions of defendants in siphoning off for personal gain corporate advantages to be derived from a favorable market situation do not betoken the necessary undivided loyalty owed by the fiduciary to his principal.

The corporate opportunities of whose misappropriation the minority stockholders complain need not have been an absolute certainty in order to support this action against Feldmann. If there was possibility of corporate gain, they are entitled to recover. In *Young v. Higbee Co.*, supra, 324 U.S. 204, 65 S.Ct. 594, two stockholders appealing the confirmation of a plan of bankruptcy reorganization were held liable for profits received for the sale of their stock pending determination of the validity of the appeal. They were held accountable for the excess of the price of their stock over its normal price, even though there was no indication that the appeal could have succeeded on substantive grounds. And in *Irving Trust Co. v. Deutsch*, supra, 2 Cir., 73 F.2d 121, 124, an accounting was required of corporate directors who bought stock for themselves for corporate use, even though there was an affirmative showing that the corporation did not have the finances itself to acquire the stock. Judge Swan speaking for the court pointed out that "The defendants' argument, contrary to *Wing v. Dillingham* [5 Cir., 239 F. 54], that the equitable rule that fiduciaries should not be permitted to assume a position in which their individual interests might be in conflict with those of the corporation can have no application where the corporation is unable to undertake the venture, is not convincing. If directors are permitted to justify their conduct on such a theory, there will be a temptation to refrain from exerting their strongest efforts on behalf of the corporation since, if it does not meet the obligations, an opportunity of profit will be open to them personally."

This rationale is equally appropriate to a consideration of the benefits which Newport might have derived from the steel shortage. In the past Newport had used and profited by its market leverage by operation of what the industry had come to call the "Feldmann Plan." This consisted of securing interest-free advances from prospective purchasers of steel in return for firm commitments to them for future production. The funds thus acquired were used to finance improvements in existing plants and to acquire new installations. In the summer of 1950 Newport had been negotiating for cold-rolling facilities which it needed for a more fully integrated operation and a more marketable product, and Feldmann plan funds might well have been used toward this end.

Further, as plaintiffs alternatively suggest, Newport might have used the period of short supply to build up patronage in the geographical area in which it could compete profitably even when steel was more abundant. Either of these opportunities was Newport's, to be used to its advantage only. Only if defendants had been able to negate completely any possibility of gain by Newport could they have prevailed. It is true that a trial court finding states: "Whether or not, in August, 1950, Newport's position was such that it could have entered into 'Feldmann Plan' type transactions to procure funds and financing for the further expansion and integration of its steel facilities and whether such expansion would have been desirable for Newport, the evidence does not show." This, however, cannot avail the defendants, who—contrary to the ruling below—had the burden of proof on this issue, since fiduciaries always have the burden of proof in establishing the fairness of their dealings with trust property. *Pepper v. Litton*, supra, 308 U.S. 295, 60 S.Ct. 238; *Geddes v. Anaconda Copper Mining Co.*, 254 U.S. 590, 41 S.Ct. 209, 65 L.Ed. 425; *Mayflower Hotel Stockholders Protective Committee v. Mayflower Hotel Corp.*, 84 U.S.App. D.C. 275, 173 F.2d 416.

Defendants seek to categorize the corporate opportunities which might have accrued to Newport as too unethical to warrant further consideration. It is true that reputable steel producers were not participating in the gray market brought about by the Korean War and were refraining from advancing their prices, although to do so would not have been illegal. But Feldmann plan transactions were not considered within this self-imposed interdiction; the trial court found that around the time of the Feldmann sale Jones & Laughlin Steel Corporation, Republic Steel Company, and Pittsburgh Steel Corporation were all participating in such arrangements. In any event, it ill becomes the defendants to disparage as unethical the market advantage from which they themselves reaped rich benefits.

We do not mean to suggest that a majority stockholder cannot dispose of his controlling block of stock to outsiders without having to account to his corporation for profits or even never do this with impunity when the buyer is an interested customer, actual or potential, for the corporation's product. But when the sale necessarily results in a sacrifice of this element of corporate good will and consequent unusual profit to the fiduciary who has caused the sacrifice, he should account for his gains. So in a time of market shortage, where a call on a corporation's product commands an unusually large premium, in one form or another, we think it sound law that a fiduciary may not appropriate to himself the value of this premium. Such personal gain at the expense of his co-venturers seems particularly reprehensible when made by the trusted president and director of his company. In this case the violation of duty seems to be all the clearer because of this triple role in which Feldmann appears, though we are unwilling to say, and are not to be understood as saying, that we should accept a lesser obligation for any one of his roles alone.

Hence to the extent that the price received by Feldmann and his co-defendants included such a bonus, he is accountable to the minority stockholders who sue here. Restatement, Restitution §§ 190, 197 (1937); *Seagrave Corp. v. Mount*, supra, 6 Cir., 212 F.2d 389. And plaintiffs, as they contend, are entitled to a recovery in their own right, instead of in right of the corporation (as in the usual derivative actions), since neither Wilport nor their successors in interest should share in any judgment which may be rendered. See *Southern Pacific Co. v. Bogert*, 250 U.S. 483, 39 S.Ct. 533, 63 L.Ed. 1099. Defendants cannot well object to this form of recovery, since the only alternative, recovery for the corporation as a whole, would subject them to a greater total liability.

The case will therefore be remanded to the district court for a determination of the question expressly left open below, namely, the value of defendants' stock, without the appurtenant control over the corporation's output of steel. We reiterate that on this issue, as on all others relating to a breach of fiduciary duty, the burden of proof must rest on the defendants. ... Judgment should go to these plaintiffs and those whom they represent for any premium value so shown to the extent of their respective stock interests.

The judgment is therefore reversed and the action remanded for further proceedings pursuant to this opinion.

SWAN, Circuit Judge (dissenting): With the general principles enunciated in the majority opinion as to the duties of fiduciaries I am, of course, in thorough accord. But, as Mr. Justice Frankfurter stated in *Securities and Exchange Comm. v. Chenery Corp.*, 318 U.S. 80, 85, 63 S.Ct. 454, 458, 87 L.Ed. 626, "to say that a man is a fiduciary only begins analysis; it gives direction to further inquiry. To whom is he a fiduciary? What obligations does he owe as a fiduciary? In what respect has he failed to discharge these obligations?" My brothers' opinion does not specify precisely what fiduciary duty Feldmann is held to have violated or whether it was a duty imposed upon him as the dominant stockholder or as a director of Newport. Without such specification I think that both the legal profession and the business world will find the decision confusing and will be unable to foretell the extent of its impact upon customary practices in the sale of stock.

The power to control the management of a corporation, that is, to elect directors to manage its affairs, is an inseparable incident to the ownership of a majority of its stock, or sometimes, as in the present instance, to the ownership of enough shares, less than a majority, to control an election. Concededly a majority or dominant shareholder is ordinarily privileged to sell his stock at the best price obtainable from the purchaser. In so doing he acts on his own behalf, not as an agent of the corporation. If he knows or has reason to believe that the purchaser intends to exercise to the detriment of the corporation the power of management acquired by the purchase, such knowledge or reasonable suspicion will terminate the dominant shareholder's privilege to sell and will create a duty not to transfer the power of management to such purchaser. The duty seems to me to resemble the obligation which everyone is under not to assist another to commit a tort rather than the obligation of a fiduciary. But whatever the nature of the duty, a violation of it will subject the violator to liability for damages sustained by the corporation. Judge

Hincks found that Feldmann had no reason to think that Wilport would use the power of management it would acquire by the purchase to injure Newport, and that there was no proof that it ever was so used. Feldmann did know, it is true, that the reason Wilport wanted the stock was to put in a board of directors who would be likely to permit Wilport's members to purchase more of Newport's steel than they might otherwise be able to get. But there is nothing illegal in a dominant shareholder purchasing from his own corporation at the same prices it offers to other customers. This is what the members of Wilport did, and there is no proof that Newport suffered any detriment therefrom.

My brothers say that "the consideration paid for the stock included compensation for the sale of a corporate asset," which they describe as "the ability to control the allocation of the corporate product in a time of short supply, through control of the board of directors; and it was effectively transferred in this sale by having Feldmann procure the resignation of his own board and the election of Wilport's nominees immediately upon consummation of the sale." The implications of this are not clear to me. If it means that when market conditions are such as to induce users of a corporation's product to wish to buy a controlling block of stock in order to be able to purchase part of the corporation's output at the same mill list prices as are offered to other customers, the dominant stockholder is under a fiduciary duty not to sell his stock, I cannot agree. For reasons already stated, in my opinion Feldmann was not proved to be under any fiduciary duty as a stockholder not to sell the stock he controlled.

Feldmann was also a director of Newport. Perhaps the quoted statement means that as a director he violated his fiduciary duty in voting to elect Wilport's nominees to fill the vacancies created by the resignations of the former directors of Newport. As a director Feldmann was under a fiduciary duty to use an honest judgment in acting on the corporation's behalf. A director is privileged to resign, but so long as he remains a director he must be faithful to his fiduciary duties and must not make a personal gain from performing them. Consequently, if the price paid for Feldmann's stock included a payment for voting to elect the new directors, he must account to the corporation for such payment, even though he honestly believed that the men he voted to elect were well qualified to serve as directors. He can not take pay for performing his fiduciary duty. There is no suggestion that he did do so, unless the price paid for his stock was more than its value. So it seems to me that decision must turn on whether finding 120 and conclusion 5 of the district judge are supportable on the evidence. They are set out in the margin.[1]

Judge Hincks went into the matter of valuation of the stock with his customary care and thoroughness. He made no error of law in applying the principles relating to valua-

---

1   "120. The 398,927 shares of Newport stock sold to Wilport as of August 31, 1950, had a fair value as a control block of $20 per share. What value the block would have had if shorn of its appurtenant power to control distribution of the corporate product, the evidence does not show."

"5. Even if Feldmann's conduct in cooperating to accomplish a transfer of control to Wilport immediately upon the sale constituted a breach of a fiduciary duty to Newport, no part of the moneys received by the defendants in connection with the sale constituted profits for which they were accountable to Newport."

tion of stock. Concededly a controlling block of stock has greater sale value than a small lot. While the spread between $10 per share for small lots and $20 per share for the controlling block seems rather extraordinarily wide, the $20 valuation was supported by the expert testimony of Dr. Badger, whom the district judge said he could not find to be wrong. I see no justification for upsetting the valuation as clearly erroneous. Nor can I agree with my brothers that the $20 valuation "was limited" by the last sentence in finding 120. The controlling block could not by any possibility be shorn of its appurtenant power to elect directors and through them to control distribution of the corporate product. It is this "appurtenant power" which gives a controlling block its value as such block. What evidence could be adduced to show the value of the block "if shorn" of such appurtenant power, I cannot conceive, for it cannot be shorn of it.

The opinion also asserts that the burden of proving a lesser value than $20 per share was not upon the plaintiffs but the burden was upon the defendants to prove that the stock was worth that value. Assuming that this might be true as to the defendants who were directors of Newport, they did show it, unless finding 120 to be set aside. Furthermore, not all the defendants were directors; upon what theory the plaintiffs should be relieved from the burden of proof as to defendants who were not directors, the opinion does not explain.

The final conclusion of my brothers is that the plaintiffs are entitled to recover in their own right instead of in the right of the corporation. This appears to be completely inconsistent with the theory advanced at the outset of the opinion, namely, that the price of the stock "included compensation for the sale of a corporate asset." If a corporate asset was sold, surely the corporation should recover the compensation received for it by the defendants. Moreover, if the plaintiffs were suing in their own right, Newport was not a proper party. The case of *Southern Pacific Co. v. Bogert*, 250 U.S. 483, 39 S.Ct. 533, 63 L.Ed. 1099, relied upon as authority for the conclusion that the plaintiffs are entitled to recover in their own right, relates to a situation so different that the decision appears to me to be inapposite.

I would affirm the judgment on appeal.

NOTE

To what extent does *Feldmann* require all controlling shareholders who sell their shares at a premium to share the premium with minority shareholders? The case has generally been interpreted narrowly, and analogized to such looting cases as *Gerdes v. Reynolds*, 28 N.Y.S.2d 622 (Sup.Ct. 1941). In *Gerdes* the defendants sold their majority shares in Reynolds Investing Co. for $2 a share at a time when, according to the Court, they could not have been worth more than 75 cents each. The defendants had made only a superficial check of the buyer, and, on the sale, resigned from their positions in Reynolds so that nominees of the purchaser could be elected. The purchaser then proceeded to loot the corporation of its assets. The Court imposed liability on two grounds. First, the defendants were in effect selling their offices in Reynolds to the purchaser in breach of their fiduciary duties. Second, the defendants were liable as controlling shareholders for selling their shares without taking adequate care to ensure that the purchaser would not loot the corporation. The defendants were required to pay the Reynolds company both the total amount of the premium as well as the amount taken from the company by the purchaser.

Would the defendants still have been liable in the *Feldmann* case if the purchaser had been Twentieth Century Fox Ltd.? In *Essex Universal Corp. v. Yates*, 305 F.2d 572 (1962), the Second Circuit Court of Appeals characterized its earlier decision in *Feldmann* as a corporate opportunity case. "Our theory was basically that the controlling shareholders in selling control to a potential customer had appropriated to their personal benefit a corporate asset: the premium which the company's product could command in a time of market shortage." (*Id.* at 576)

An alternative explanation of *Feldmann* is that control is a corporate asset, and can never be sold for private gain. See Berle, *"Control" in Corporate Law*, 58 Colum L. Rev. 1212 (1958). The right to control a corporation is of course not an asset of the corporation itself. However, in Berle's view, a controlling shareholder may not sell the element of control by demanding a premium over market for the shares.

A third rationale for a prohibition against selling controlling shares at a premium is provided in the following article.

Andrews, The Stockholder's Right to Equal Opportunity in the Sale of Shares
78 Harv. L. Rev. 505, 515-32 (1965)

The rule to be considered can be stated thus: whenever a controlling stockholder sells his shares, every other holder of shares (of the same class) is entitled to have an equal opportunity to sell his shares, or a prorata part of them, on substantially the same terms. Or in terms of the correlative duty: before a controlling stockholder may sell his shares to an outsider he must assure his fellow stockholders an equal opportunity to sell their shares, or as high a proportion of theirs as he ultimately sells of his own. There are qualifications in the application of the rule, to which I will return; but for purposes of argument we can begin with this broad statement of it.

Now let us look briefly at what the rule means. First, it neither compels nor prohibits a sale of stock at any particular price; it leaves a controlling stockholder wholly free to decide for himself the price above which he will sell and below which he will hold his shares. The rule only says that in executing his decision to sell, a controlling stockholder cannot sell pursuant to a purchase offer more favorable than any available to other stockholders. Second, the rule does not compel a prospective purchaser to make an open offer for all shares on the same terms. He can offer to purchase shares on the condition that he gets a certain proportion of the total. Or he can make an offer to purchase 51 per cent of the shares, no more and no less. The only requirement is that the offer, whatever it may be, be made equally or proportionately available to all stockholders.

Obviously if a purchaser offers to buy only 51 per cent of the shares, and the offer must be made equally available to all stockholders, no stockholder accepting the offer can count on selling all his shares. There are established mechanics for dealing with this situation. The purchaser makes a so-called tender offer, indicating the price at which he wants to buy and how many shares, and inviting all stockholders to tender their stock if they wish to sell at that price. If more shares are tendered than the purchaser is willing to take, then he purchases pro rata from each tendering stockholder. The device of a tender offer has been widely used when a purchaser wants to buy from the public; indeed the *New York Stock Exchange Company Manual* contains provisions dealing with tender offers, designed to ensure that such offers are made equally accessible to all stockholders.

The asserted right would prevent just what happened in *Feldmann*: a private sale by a controlling stockholder at a price not available to other stockholders. But there are two modes of compliance with the rule: either the purchaser can extend his offer to all stockholders, or the seller can offer participation in the sale to his fellow stockholders. A sale is prevented from taking place only when the purchaser is unwilling to buy more than a specified percentage of the shares, and the seller will sell only if he can sell out completely. Indeed, even under these circumstances it is an overstatement to say the rule would prevent a sale taking place, since the minority stockholders may consent to the sale. They may even sell to the purchaser at a lower price than what he pays the controlling stockholder, provided they are adequately informed of what is going on. Thus the rule only operates to prevent a sale when (1) the purchaser is unwilling to purchase more shares, (2) the seller insists on disposing of all his shares, and (3) the minority stockholders are unwilling to stay in the enterprise under the purchaser's control.

●   ●   ●

There is a substantial danger that following a transfer of controlling shares corporate affairs may be conducted in a manner detrimental to the interests of the stockholders who have not had an opportunity to sell their shares. The corporation may be looted; it may just be badly run. Or the sale of controlling shares may operate to destroy a favorable opportunity for corporate action. Recent events confirm that gross mismanagement may follow a sale of controlling shares.

The equal opportunity rule does not deal directly with the problem of mismanagement which may occur even after a transfer of control complying with the rule; but enforcement of the rule will remove much of the incentive a purchaser can offer a controlling stockholder to sell on profitable terms. Indeed, in the case of a purchasing looter there is nothing in it for the purchaser unless he can buy less than all the shares; there is no profit in stealing from a solvent corporation if the thief owns all the stock. But the controlling stockholder will be loath to sell only part of his shares (except at a price that compensates him for all of his shares) if he expects the purchaser to destroy the value of what he keeps. The rule forces the controlling stockholder to share equally with his fellow stockholders both the benefits of the price he receives for the shares he sells and the business risks incident to the shares he retains. This will tend strongly to discourage a sale of controlling shares when the risk of looting, or other harm to the corporation, is apparent; and it will provide the seller with a direct incentive to investigate and evaluate with care when the risks are not apparent, since his own financial interest continues to be at stake.

●   ●   ●

Of course a transfer of control may have advantageous effects for a corporation and its stockholders—and these may be just as subtle as any adverse effects. Many sales of controlling shares come about because the selling stockholders are not doing as well with a business as a purchaser believes he can do; and the belief is often right. Often the sellers are members of a family that has simply run out of managerial talent or interest.

If the rule of equal opportunity would prevent sales in this sort of situation, that would be a high price to pay for the prevention of harm in other cases. Some writers have rejected on this ground any interpretation or extension of *Feldmann* that would eliminate the issue of harm to the corporation. For my own part I do not believe the rule of equal opportunity would have much tendency to discourage beneficial transactions. After all, if the purchaser is optimistic—and can convince his bankers to share his optimism—he should be willing to buy out everyone. If the seller is optimistic about the consequences of the transfer, he should be willing to retain some of his shares. If minority shareholders are optimistic, they should be willing to hold their shares. If the financial community is optimistic (in the case of a publicly held corporation), the market itself should offer the minority stockholders a chance to sell at a price that satisfies the rule. Thus, on the face of it the rule would only operate to prevent a sale when all four of these—the seller, the purchaser, the minority stockholders, and the financial community—take a pessimistic view of the transfer.

• • •

The most important reason a purchaser might pay a premium for controlling shares, and one that has to be met squarely, is that an investment in controlling shares is a more promising, or at least a safer, investment than one in noncontrolling shares for the simple reason that it will enable the investor to implement what he believes to be the best policies in the management of his investment. Even though the minority stockholder receives exactly the same return per share as does the controlling stockholder, the controlling stockholder has the advantage of knowing that his judgment will prevail whenever there is a difference of view as to how the corporate business should be run. To be more concrete, a prospective purchaser may rationally take the position that he would be willing to pay a substantial price for stock in a corporation if he achieved control, but not a nickel otherwise, because he believes that his management of the corporation would turn it from a poor investment into a profitable one. The premium paid for control under these circumstances reflects an honest difference of investment appraisal, not an intention to realize on the investment through any relationship other than that of stockholder.

• • •

The rule of equal opportunity does not, however, prevent a purchaser from offering more per share if he acquires control, than if he does not. The rule tends to operate automatically to distinguish between a premium paid for the opportunity of entering into extra-stockholder relations, and one that reflects a change in investment appraisal resulting from a shift in control. This is one of the greatest advantages of the rule of equal opportunity over any corporate asset theory of control, and it needs to be set out and explored in some detail.

• • •

The argument can be made first in relatively abstract terms. Assume that the only factors that would cause a particular purchaser to pay more for his shares than for others are the two so far discussed: (a) that he wants to enter into some advantageous extra-stockholder relationship with the corporation, which he can only achieve by gaining control; and (b) that he views the corporate stock as a better (safer or more profitable or both) investment if he is in control than if he is not. Assume further that the purchaser can be made to state the top price he would pay for any particular portion of the company's outstanding shares.

On these assumptions, if in a particular case the purchaser is only actuated by the second factor—by a difference in investment appraisal associated with his acquisition of control—then the only differential that will appear in his schedule of prices will be a differential between what he will pay per share if he does not achieve control, and what he will pay per share if he does achieve control. There will be no difference between his price per share for a bare controlling block, and his price per share for any larger amount. The return on his investment will be proportionate to the number of shares he owns; therefore he will be willing to pay in proportion to the number of shares he acquires; and his marginal price for supercontrol shares will be equal to what he would pay per share for a controlling block. For this purchaser, in this case, the rule of equal opportunity imposes no burden. The rule permits him to condition an offer to purchase at a particular price, on his achieving control. If he purchases a controlling block the rule only requires him to offer the same price per share for more shares, something he should be willing to do in any event.

On the other hand, if a purchaser is willing to pay more per share for a barely controlling block of shares than for a larger block—still making the assumptions stated above—this would show that he is actuated in part at least by the first factor, by the intention or expectation of enjoying some profit or advantage from entering into some extra-stockholder relationship with his newly acquired corporation. The measure of his investment appraisal with himself in control is the marginal price per share he would pay for shares in excess of those required to achieve control. If he is willing to pay more than that marginal price, for any number of shares, he must be paying for something other than the investment value of the shares. On the assumptions stated above, it must be an intention to derive a profit from some sort of extra stockholder relationship. And that explanation fits the fact because the profit to be derived from an extra-stockholder relationship will be no greater on account of the purchase of supercontrol shares; therefore if a purchaser were motivated by an intention to derive that sort of profit, one would expect him to offer more per share for a controlling block than for supercontrol shares.

To put it in figures, suppose a purchaser is willing to pay $3 a share for a small lot of stock, $10 a share for 50 + per cent of the corporation's stock, and only $9 a share for all the stock. The offer of $9 a share for all the stock represents only a marginal price of $8 a share for the last 50 − per cent, since the purchaser is willing to pay $10 for the first 50 + per cent. This pattern tends to indicate that the return that the purchaser expects the corporation to produce for its stockholders as such, once he has taken control, justifies a price of $8 a share—while under present control the stock is only worth $3. The purchaser's willingness to pay $10 for 50 + per cent, or $9 for all the stock, on the other hand, tends to show that he expects some other return on his investment than the normal return of a stockholder—some element of return that will not be increased through the purchase of more shares. The price he will pay for this element of return is represented by the excess of his offer over $8 a share. In this case the amount is $2 ($10 − $8) times 50 per cent of the number of shares outstanding, or $1 ($9 − $8) times 100 per cent of the number of shares outstanding. The fact that this is a fixed dollar amount independent of the number of shares purchased is consistent with the assertion that it reflects an expectation of return through some extra-stockholder relationship, since the element of return does not increase with an increase in shareholders beyond 50 + per cent.

The rule of equal opportunity does of course impose a burden with respect to the sort of differential that reflects an intention to profit from some extra-stockholder relationship. The rule would tend to prevent the purchaser in the last paragraph from buying out the 50 + per cent stockholder at $10 a share, something he would otherwise be willing to do, because if he did he would be required to offer to buy all the stock at that price, which by hypothesis he is unwilling to do. The rule does not, however, prohibit a purchaser from paying something in anticipation to extra-stockholder advantages. The purchaser in the last paragraph is in no way limited to $8 a share; he can offer $9 to everyone and the rule is satisfied even though $1 of his purchase price is clearly payment for the expectation of extra-stockholder advantages. Or he can offer $10 for 50 + per cent of the shares if the offer is made proportionately to everyone. The effect of the rule is not to prohibit a purchaser from paying for extra-stockholder advantages but only to require that, if he does, the payment be offered proportionately to all stockholders alike. This is exactly in accord with the outcome in *Feldmann*. The court here did not seek to bar Wilport from purchasing Newport steel; nor did it seek to make Feldmann return any part of the premium to Wilport; it only required that the premium be divided equally among stockholders.

• • •

What else, besides the hope of exploiting some extra-stockholder relationship, might account for a purchaser's willingness to pay more per share for controlling shares than for super-control shares? One answer is lack of funds; the purchaser just may not have the wherewithal to pay what he views as a fair price, or indeed, perhaps, any price, for additional shares, after he has paid for the controlling block.

Of course lack of funds, in the simplest sense, is the common plight of businessmen; many forms of financial organization exist just to answer the promoter's need for other people's funds to carry out his business ideas. The purchaser of a controlling interest in a corporation, if he pays any premium for his shares, is in a way a promoter, speculating on the profitability of a new combination between his talents and the purchased company's property and business. If he has not sufficient funds of his own to meet a requirement that he bid for all the shares, the requirement does not exclude him from the market; it only requires him to arrange financing.

The financing, of course, may take any of a variety of forms. If the purchaser can convince others to share his optimistic view of the corporation's future under his control, then it can take the form of a simple participation by those others in the purchase. One potential source of financing, in effect, is from the present minority stockholders themselves. If the purchaser can convince them that their stock will soon be worth the price he is paying for the controlling stockholder's shares, once the purchaser is in control, then they will turn down his offer to buy their shares at that price and the effect will be the same as if he found someone else to make the purchase. In a sense the question is whether the minority stockholders should be given a choice whether or not to invest, at the same price as the purchaser, in the new enterprise resulting from the shift in control.

• • •

People who argue against any extension of *Feldmann* point out that sometimes minority stockholders will benefit from a change in control to which they are not parties—perhaps by as much as the premium paid to the sellers of the controlling block. The rule of equal opportunity puts it up to the principals to demonstrate that this is a reasonable expectation. The purchaser can prove that he thinks so by offering to buy everyone out at the same price.

NOTE

A conflicting view of costs that would arise if controlling shareholders were required to share the premium is found in the following excerpt from Javaras, *Equal Opportunity in the Sale of Controlling Shares: A Reply to Professor Andrews*, 32 U. Chi. L. Rev. 420, 425-26 (1965):

I believe that the gravest defect in Professor Andrews' theory is a grievous underassessment of the costs of a preventive rule in restraining beneficial transactions. Such restraint would operate on the purchaser by imposing higher required investment—the price of all the shares of the corporation rather than only those owned by the controlling shareholder. Professor Andrews minimizes the effects of this factor on two grounds. First, the controlling shareholder under the rule of equal opportunity, when confronted with a purchaser who wants the controlling shares and no more, may be induced to retain some of his shares and share the sale ratably with the non-controlling shareholders. Admittedly, this requires faith in the management of the purchaser. Second, a beneficial purchaser should be willing to buy all the shares because, after all, the noncontrolling shares have the same investment value as the controlling shares. All the purchaser would have to do, therefore, if he did not have the capital is to borrow it. If he could not, that would be a reflection either of superior knowledge in the financial community or dislocations in the capital market.

It is doubtful whether sufficient controlling sellers can be induced to retain their shares so as to eliminate the higher capital requirement. First, as pointed out by Professor Stigler in his recent assessment of the work of the Securities and Exchange Commission, sales of securities are not dictated merely by an appraisal of investment value. Many sellers simply want immediate cash. Second, a controlling seller may not wish to hold, say twenty-five per cent as compared to his prior fifty per cent, because of the possibility of his views differing from those of the controlling purchaser in the future. This reticence would partly stem from the politics of large shareholdings for which judicial intervention is not only ineffective but undesirable. But it would also arise from the controlling seller's assessment of the change in risks when he is deprived of control. The loss of control would subject him to the risk of poor management, which might dictate a lesser investment in this corporation on the principle of risk diversification.

Likewise the purchaser himself might be unwilling that the seller retain some of his shares, particularly where working control (less than fifty per cent) is the subject of the offer. He might well be reluctant to have a large block of stock outstanding whose owners, under conditions of dissension, could mobilize the other shareholders and displace his control of the board of directors.

In effect then, the rule of equal treatment would impose higher capital requirements on beneficial purchasers in a substantial number of transactions. Professor Andrews inappropriately assumes, however, that the purchasers should be willing to meet these higher costs because the investment value of the additional shares is the same. He errs in that his reasoning is incomplete. It is true that the investment value is the same. But even if the capital market did function perfectly and the purchaser could arrange the financing, a rational businessman might not want to buy all the shares at a premium price justified by the investment potential. It might be sensible to decline to buy more than the bare amount necessary for control on the principles of diversification of risk and of opportunity. This might render the equal treatment rule ineffectual as a means of automatically distinguishing "good" and "bad" purchasers. I would think that the number of prospective beneficial purchasers prevented because of a desire to diversify will be much larger than those simply unable to raise the capital. Until empirical evidence is adduced to the contrary, I am predisposed to consider this cost of restraining beneficial transactions substantial when compared with the cases of detriment with which the present law is incompetent to deal.

If a prohibition of control premiums will substantially restrict sales of control, will minority shareholders in the end be better off? Suppose, for example, that on the facts of *Hogg* (Section E), the majority shareholders had sold their shares at a premium to real estate developers, who redeveloped the properties of the corporation. Presumably all the shareholders, the minority included, would then have been better off. So long as efficiency gains are anticipated, a change of control will benefit minority shareholders, whether or not they share in the premium.

Though Andrews' arguments for a prohibition of control share premiums are based on perceived efficiency gains, the distributional consequences of a sale of control may also seem troubling. However, it is difficult to see how, on distributional theories, a minority shareholder has a right to participate in a control premium where the control block had been in existence when he acquired his shares. The right to share in a sale of control would then amount to a windfall for minority shareholders. Moreover, even when the control block was assembled after a public issue of shares, the absence of a right to participate in a control premium would have been reflected in stock price on issuance.

An *ex ante* perspective suggests a further criticism of prohibitions of control share premiums. If the right to participate on a sale of control serves efficiency norms, as Andrews suggests, then why should firms not be left to self-help remedies? A firm may after all provide for restrictions on control share transactions in its articles. If the benefits of such provisions exceeded their costs, one would predict that firms would adopt them without the need for mandatory rules. The failure by widely held firms to do so at a time when legal rules did not clearly prohibit control share premiums may then perhaps indicate that such mandatory rules are inefficient.

Jones v. H.F. Ahmanson & Co.
Supreme Court of California
460 P.2d 464 (1969)

[See Chapter 7, Part I, Section F]

NOTE

In *Brown v. Halbert*, 76 Cal. Rptr. 781 (Ct. App. 1969), majority shareholders were required to share a premium paid to them on a sale of control with the minority. The purchaser had wished to acquire complete control of the corporation. However, he was rebuffed by the majority shareholders, who insisted on a sale of their 53% interest in the corporation for $1,550 per share. Thereafter, they assisted the purchaser in his offer to purchase the remaining 47% of the shares at $300 per share, recommending that the shares be sold for about that price. The Court held that the majority shareholder had a duty in these circumstances to obtain for the minority the same terms as were available on the sale of controlling shares.

The existence of a general prohibition of sales of controlling shares at a premium has been specifically denied in several American cases. Thus in *Honigman v. Green Giant Co.*, 309 F.2d 667 (8th Cir. 1962), cert. denied, 372 U.S. 941 (1963), the Court refused to upset a reorganization in which 44 shares of old Class A voting stock were exchanged for 44,000 new voting shares, and 428,998 shares of Class B non-voting stock were exchanged for the same number of new voting shares. The plaintiff relied heavily on Berle's theory that control is a corporate asset. However, the Eighth Circuit Court of Appeals, applying Minnesota law, rejected this theory and upheld the reorganization. See also *Zetlin v. Hanson Holdings Inc.*, 421 N.Y.S.2d 877, 397 N.E.2d 387 (1979); *Clagett v. Hutchinson*, 583 F.2d 1259 (4th Cir. 1978); *Yerke v. Batman*, 376 N.E.2d 1211 (Ind. Ct. App. 1978); *Ritchie v. McGrath*, 571 P.2d 17 (Kan. Ct. App. 1977); *McDaniel v. Painter*, 418 F.2d 545 (both Cir. 1969); *Short v. Treasury Commissioners*, [1948] A.C. 534, 546 (H.L.).

See further R. Gilson, *The Law and Finance of Corporate Acquisitions*, 617-21 (1986); Easterbrook & Fischel, *Corporate Control Transactions*, 91 Yale L.J. 698 (1982); E. Elhauge, *The Triggering Function of Sale of Control Doctrine*, 59 U. Chi. L. Rev. 1465 (1992).

OSA Requirements. A private sale of a control block of shares is a take-over bid under OSA s. 89(1) unless exempted by s. 93(1)(c). The consideration for shares purchased under the exemption may not, however, include a premium exceeding 15% of the market price of the securities. If the purchase price is more than 115% of market value, or if more than five vendors sell their shares, the sales will fall without the exemption, such that the purchaser will be in breach of the OSA requirements that the offer be made on the same terms to all other Ontario shareholders.

Though imposed on different parties, similar issues of policy animate both the purchaser's duties under the OSA and any duties that might be imposed on the seller at common law to account for a premium received on a sale of controlling shares. In one respect, however, OSA s. 93(1)(c) is considerably broader than common law fiduciary standards. It has not been suggested that non-controlling shareholders might be liable to account for a premium on a sale of their shares under decisions like *Jones v. Ahmanson*. Nevertheless, a sale by non-controlling shareholders at a premium of 15% or more above market price will trigger OSA take-over bid requirements. Attempts to obtain control of a target by negotiating with holders of blocks of shares, no one of whom controls the target, are then restricted. Moreover, even if the purchases are not made at a 15% premium, purchases from more than five shareholders are not within the s. 93(1)(c) exemption.

The effect of these restrictions is to prevent an acquiring firm from obtaining control of a target by "sweeping the street," or purchasing large blocks of shares at a premium, often from non-controlling financial institutions or major investors. This acquisition technique, seen above in *Newmont Mining*, was popular in the United States in the mid 1980s as a result of decisions that such purchases are beyond the scope of tender offer legislation in that country. Street sweeps are, however, illegal in Ontario if either the number of sellers is more than five or the price exceeds market price by more than 15%. The result is to make it more difficult to acquire control of targets when major blocks of their shares are held by noncontrolling shareholders. In this respect, the effect of OSA s. 93(1)(c) is similar to that of fair price shark repellents.

A purchaser of a control block of shares may seek an exemption from follow-up duties under OSA s. 104(2). The Commission's early thoughts on when exemptions should be granted were indicated in OSC Policies 3-41. The O.S.C. stated that it would be favourably disposed to grant an exemption unless the sale fell into one of the following three categories:

(1) A sale of control where the result is clearly unfair or abusive to the remaining shareholders;
(2) The sale of control follows a public distribution of equity securities of the same corporation (whether newly issued or derived from the control block) in which it may reasonably be assumed that investors relied on continued involvement of the controlling shareholder in the corporation's affairs, and the sale of control occurs within, say, 10 years after the public distribution; or
(3) The offeror proposes obtaining effective control at a premium through purchases from fewer than 15 shareholders, none of whom individually has effective control, at a premium unavailable to the remaining shareholders.

Even if the sale did fall into one of these categories, an exemption might still be granted in various special cases listed in this Policy, as where control is repatriated in Canada.

OSC Policy 3-41 was, however, brought into question in the first decision under it, where an exemption was not granted even though the case did not easily fall within one of the three criteria listed above. *In the Matter of Ronalds-Federated Ltd.*, [1980] O.S.C.B. 304. On the other hand, the Commission shortly thereafter granted an exemption in *In the Matter of Atco Ltd.*, [1980] O.S.C.B. 412, in circumstances which did not seem materially more fair than those of *Ronalds Federated*. OSC Policy 3-41 is now repealed. Whether an exemption will be granted today is largely a matter of guesswork.

Index